DOCUMENTS IN
MYCENAEAN GREEK
SECOND EDITION

PLATE I

46=Au102, Mycenaean tablet of 'page' shape

DOCUMENTS IN MYCENAEAN GREEK

FIRST EDITION BY

MICHAEL VENTRIS

AND

JOHN CHADWICK

WITH A FOREWORD BY THE LATE
ALAN J. B. WACE

SECOND EDITION BY

JOHN CHADWICK

CAMBRIDGE
AT THE UNIVERSITY PRESS
1973

Published by the Syndics of the Cambridge University Press
Bentley House, 200 Euston Road, London NW1 2DB
American Branch: 32 East 57th Street, New York, N.Y. 10022

© Cambridge University Press 1973

Library of Congress Catalogue Card Number: 72–89804

ISBN: 0 521 08558 6

First published 1956
Reprinted with corrections 1959
Second edition 1973

Printed in Great Britain
at the University Printing House, Cambridge
(Brooke Crutchley, University Printer)

To the memory of

HEINRICH SCHLIEMANN

1822–1890

FATHER OF MYCENAEAN ARCHAEOLOGY

I had always passionately longed to learn Greek; but up to the time of the Crimean War it appeared to me inadvisable to abandon myself to this study, since I feared that the powerful fascination of this wonderful language would take too great a hold on me and would alienate me from my commercial interests. But when the first news of peace arrived at St Petersburg in January 1856, I could no longer contain my desire, and without delay I applied myself with great diligence to the new study. Again I faithfully followed my old methods. In order to master the vocabulary in a short time (even more difficult for me than in the case of Russian), I obtained a modern Greek translation of Paul et Virginie; *and read this from cover to cover, all the time carefully comparing each word with its counterpart in the French original. After a single reading I had absorbed at least half of the words in the book, and after a repetition of this process I had learnt practically all of them—without having wasted a single moment in looking a word up in a dictionary. In this way I succeeded, within the short space of six weeks, in mastering the difficulties of modern Greek. Then I embarked on the study of the ancient language, of which I gained a sufficient knowledge in three months to enable me to understand some of the ancient authors—especially Homer, whom I read again and again with the greatest enthusiasm....*

(SELBSTBIOGRAPHIE, *pp. 21–2.*)

This second edition is dedicated also to the memory of

MICHAEL VENTRIS

1922–1956

whose name can stand alongside Schliemann's
as the founder of a new branch of study

CONTENTS

Illustrations . . . . *page* xi
Preface to the Second Edition xiii
Preface to the First Edition xvii
Foreword by A. J. B. Wace xxi

PART I. SCRIPT, LANGUAGE AND CULTURE

CHAPTER I. DISCOVERY AND DECIPHERMENT 3

1 The Homeric Age as myth 3
2 Mycenae and Knossos: the pioneers 6
3 The years of stagnation 10
4 The American contribution: preludes to decipherment . . . 14
5 June 1952: the language is Greek 21
6 The widening of the ranks 24

CHAPTER II. THE MYCENAEAN WRITING SYSTEM 28

1 Chronological table 28
2 Origins: the Cretan 'hieroglyphic' script 28
3 Linear Script A 31
4 The derivation of Linear Script B 37
5 The spelling rules 42
6 The Mycenaean ideograms 48
7 Numerals and methods of measurement 53
8 The absolute values of the symbols for weight . . . 57
9 The absolute values of the symbols for volume . . . 58
10 Possible survivals: the Cypriot scripts 60

CHAPTER III. THE MYCENAEAN LANGUAGE 67

1 Script and language 67
2 Foreign elements in Mycenaean 70
3 The relation of Mycenaean to the historical dialects . . . 73
4 Dialect differences in Mycenaean 75
5 Phonology 76
6 Morphology 83
7 Syntax 89
8 Vocabulary 90

CHAPTER IV. THE PERSONAL NAMES   *page* 92

1   Men's names   93
2   Women's names   101
3   Names recurring at different places   102
4   Homeric parallels   103
5   The names given to oxen   105

CHAPTER V. THE EVIDENCE OF THE TABLETS   106

1   The extent of Mycenaean literacy   109
2   Bureaucratic methods   110
3   Mycenaean arithmetic   117
4   Social organization   119
5   Mycenaean religion   125
6   Agriculture and land tenure   129
7   Industry and trade   133
8   Historical evidence   137
9   Geographical names   139
10 List of places named at Knossos and Pylos   146

PART II. SELECTED TABLETS

Explanatory notes on the presentation   153

CHAPTER VI. LISTS OF PERSONNEL   155

1   Women and children at Pylos (Aa, Ab, Ad)   155
2   Women and children at Knossos (Ai, Ak)   162
3   Men, women and children at Knossos (Ag, Ai)   .   .   .   165
4   Women workers at Knossos   165
5   Women workers at Pylos   166
6   Individual men at Knossos (As)   168
7   Individual men at Pylos (Ac)   169
8   Work groups of men at Knossos (Am, As, B)   .   .   .   170
9   Work groups of men at Pylos (An)   172
10 Work groups of men at Mycenae   179
11 Lists of mixed tradesmen at Knossos   179
12 Lists of mixed tradesmen at Pylos   180
13 Rowers and troops at Pylos   183

CONTENTS

CHAPTER VII. LIVESTOCK AND AGRICULTURAL PRODUCE   *page* 195

1   Flocks of sheep and goats at Pylos (Cc, Cn) 199
2   Flocks of sheep at Knossos (Da, Dg) 201
3   Flocks of sheep and consignments of wool at Knossos (Dk, Dl) . . 203
4   Miscellaneous livestock at Pylos (Cn) 205
5   Miscellaneous livestock at Knossos (C, Ca, Ch, Co, Dm, Dn) . . 208
6   Grain consignments and rations at Knossos (E, F) . . . 213
7   Grain rations at Pylos (Fn) 215
8   Oil consignments or rations at Knossos and Mycenae (Fh, Fo) . . 217
9   Mixed rations and consignments at Knossos (F) 218
10 Mixed rations and consignments at Pylos (Un) 219
11 Spices at Knossos (Ga, Og) 221
12 Spices at Pylos (Un) 223
13 Spices at Mycenae (Ge) 225

CHAPTER VIII. LAND OWNERSHIP AND LAND USE   232

1   Typical formulae on short Pylos tablets 239
2   The first Pylos set 240
3   The second Pylos set 250
4   The third Pylos set 252
5   The fourth Pylos set 258
6   The estates of the king 264
7   Knossos land-tenure tablets 269
8   Knossos orchards 272

CHAPTER IX. PROPORTIONAL TRIBUTE AND RITUAL OFFERINGS   275

1   The Pylos 'dosmos' tablets 275
2   Proportional tribute from Pylos villages 289
3   The Knossos *Mc*-series 301
4   Offerings to divinities at Knossos 303

CHAPTER X. TEXTILES, VESSELS AND FURNITURE   313

1   Textiles at Knossos 313
2   Textiles at Mycenae 322
3   Textiles at Pylos 323
4   Mycenaean vessel names 323
5   Inventories of vessels at Knossos 329
6   Vessels at Mycenae 331
7   Inventories of vessels and furniture at Pylos 332
8   Pylos lists of miscellaneous content 348

CHAPTER XI. METALS AND MILITARY EQUIPMENT *page* 351

1	Metals at Pylos	352
2	Metals at Knossos	359
3	Swords, spears and arrows at Knossos	360
4	Chariots without wheels at Knossos	361
5	Chariot wheels at Knossos	369
6	Chariot wheels at Pylos	373
7	Corslets and helmets at Pylos	375
8	Chariots and corslets at Knossos	379

PART III. ADDITIONAL COMMENTARY

CHAPTER I	*page* 385
CHAPTER II	387
CHAPTER III	395
CHAPTER IV	404
CHAPTER V	405
CHAPTER VI	418
CHAPTER VII	432
CHAPTER VIII	443
CHAPTER IX	456
CHAPTER X	486
CHAPTER XI	508

PART IV

Glossary	527
Bibliography	595
General Index	606
Concordances	616

ILLUSTRATIONS

PLATES

I   **46** = Au102, Mycenaean tablet of 'page' shape . . . . *frontispiece*

II (*a*) **82** = Ca895 from the Northern Entrance Passage at Knossos . *facing p.* 110

    (*b*) **31** = Ae04 from the Archive Room at Pylos

    (*c*) **270** = Sd0402 from the 'Arsenal' at Knossos

III (*a*) **140** = Eb35 from Pylos, recording tenure of land by a priestess *facing p.* 111

    (*b*) **236** = Ta641, found at Pylos in 1952

FIGURES

1   Three-sided cornelian seal-stone from eastern Crete (P. 49* in Evans, *Scripta Minoa I*, p. 159) . . . . *page* 9

2   Linear B 'chariot' tablet found in the Knossos 'Armoury', 1904 (for a translation, see **265** = Sd0403, p. 365) 12

3   The state of the 'grid' prior to decipherment (February 1952) . . 20

4   Proposed values of the Mycenaean syllabary 23

5   'Hieroglyphic' tablet from Phaistos 30

6   The Linear A syllabary in use at Agia Triada (after Carratelli), with possible cognates in the 'hieroglyphs' (**H**) and in Linear B (**B**) . . 33

7   The commonest Agia Triada ideograms 34

8   Agia Triada tablet HT 14 35

9   The Mycenaean syllabary (after Bennett). **K** = Knossos, **P** = Pylos, **M** = Mycenae, **T** = Thebes 41

10 The Mycenaean ideograms (after Bennett), with their most usual tablet contexts and suggested meanings 50–1

11 The Cypriot linear script, as used on the 1953 tablets from Enkomi and Ugarit 62

12 The classical Cypriot syllabary (after Mitford) 64

13 Diagrammatic plan of the palace at Knossos 115

14 Key plan of the palace at Pylos (based on the survey by Theocharis, 1954) 116

15 The Agia Triada sarcophagus 282

16 Mycenaean vessel ideograms and their names 324

17 Knossos tablet K 93 325

18 Contents of the Tomb of the Tripod Hearth, Zafer Papoura (Evans, *Palace of Minos*, II, p. 634, fig. 398) . . . . *page* 326

19 Late Helladic drinking cups 327

20 Pedestalled bowl from the Fourth Shaft Grave, Mycenae . . . 328

21 The gold signet ring from Tiryns 333

22 MM IIIb (or LM Ia?) bathtub from the S.E. Bathroom, Knossos . . 338

23 Ivories from Mycenae and Dendra 346

24 Typical LM II sword hilt 347

25 The Mycenaean chariot, and Egyptian yoke arrangements . . . 362

26 Late Minoan and Mycenaean helmets 377

27 New table of the values of Mycenaean syllabic signs 385

28 Linear B and Cypriot syllabic signs compared 388

PREFACE TO THE SECOND EDITION

Had Michael Ventris not been killed at the very moment of publication of the first edition of this book, we should doubtless have brought out long since a completely new edition. In the circumstances, however, I have been very reluctant to move even one stone of the structure we planned and built together; for our collaboration was not the sort where the work of two authors is collected between the covers of one book, but was jointly planned, and even if one of the authors was responsible for the first draft of a section, it was not printed until the other had discussed, amended and added to it, so that it was truly a joint enterprise. In a few cases where we did not reach agreement, our differing views were recorded. Only Chapter I was essentially Ventris's.

But with the passage of time it has become clear that much more needed to be said about these texts, though I am convinced that most of the commentary is still valid: and new discoveries demand that additions be made to the selection of texts. Yet to write a new book would have been impossible without drawing heavily on the old; and it has always seemed like impiety to tamper with the text now Michael Ventris is no longer here to be consulted about the change. I have therefore adopted a compromise, which is forced upon me by the tragic end of our collaboration. I have reprinted unchanged the whole of Parts I and II, apart from the correction of a very few minor slips. But in the margins I have inserted references to a new Part III, which is a collection of notes on the texts, bringing up to date the information about them and stating my present views.

I must warn the reader that I have made no attempt to present and discuss all the suggestions that have been put forward between the completion of the first edition in 1955 and now; had I done so, Part III would have been far larger than the original book, and its usefulness as a basic introduction to the subject would have been lost. Thus I have simply ignored a great many ideas which I do not myself accept, and I have only cited what seem to me the more important books and articles. Scholars who wish to pursue any subject further have now the admirable indexes published under the title *Studies in Mycenaean Inscriptions and Dialect* (Baumbach, 1968, covering the period 1953–64, and annual volumes from 1965 onwards edited by L. J. D. Richardson and published by the London University Institute of Classical Studies). There is therefore little point in trying to duplicate such lists of references. Similarly I have often had to content myself with a brief statement of opinion where the question really merits a long discussion; but I hope I have said enough on the major problems to show the reasons for my opinions, and to serve as an introduction to further research. I am glad that this method has enabled me to refrain from overmuch polemic, and I have tried to avoid naming authors merely in order to attack their views; though I have of course in many cases had to argue against views which I consider ill-founded or wrong.

Part III of the first edition consisted of a Vocabulary, an Index of Personal Names, Bibliography, General Index and Concordances. It was evident that here major changes were needed, and I have, not without reluctance, suppressed the whole of this Part and replaced it with what is now Part IV. This has given me the opportunity to correct what I now think was a wrong decision though understandable in the circumstances, to split up the total Mycenaean word-list into separate sections, so that a given word must be sought in as many as three different places, if one does not know how to classify it. Thus I have compiled a new Glossary, which includes in one alphabet every Mycenaean word known at the beginning of 1972, unless it is too incomplete to be usable. No word has been excluded, even if I am unable to decide to which category it belongs. The general principles of the Vocabulary have been followed, and some entries are copied from the first edition; but every item has been closely scrutinized and checked, and a great many are modified or new. The considerable expansion of the number of entries has in turn produced pressure on space, and a few of the less important items have been omitted, such as the Modern Greek descendants of Mycenaean words, not because I regard them as without interest, but because the relevant information is easily available elsewhere. It should be emphasized that the Glossary is in no way a substitute for the invaluable *Mycenaeae Graecitatis Lexicon* (Morpurgo, 1963), for it omits line references and frequently gives only a selection of tablet references.

The Bibliography has been much expanded, but it should be noted that it contains only books and articles referred to in the text, and it is not a complete index to the now vast literature; omissions from it are not to be taken as evidence that I am either unaware of any item or have not found it profitable. Here too pressure of space must be blamed.

When the first edition was already at a late stage of proof, we received a copy of Bennett's second edition of *The Pylos Tablets* (Bennett, 1955), from which we learned to our horror that the system of numeration for these tablets was to be changed. We were able to insert the new numbers, in [ ], where the texts were cited, and to include a new concordance (C); but many references had to stand uncorrected. These consequently remain in Parts I and II, but in Parts III and IV the new numbers are used exclusively, and there is now a concordance (C) for converting the old numbers still in the text to the new system. I regret this inconvenience, but it was impracticable to alter all these figures in Parts I and II. Users of this book are reminded that the old system has been superseded, and before quoting a tablet reference the number should be checked in the Glossary or Concordance.

In preparing this edition I have had the benefit of an advance draft of the new edition of *The Pylos Tablets in Transcription* (Bennett and Olivier), as well as repeated consultation with its editors. Thus the texts quoted have been adapted to the new edition, and any significant changes recorded. In the texts I have not troubled to give new readings, if they concern only the degree of certainty attaching to a particular sign. The texts and numbering of the Knossos tablets have been revised in accordance with the *The Knossos Tablets*, fourth edition (Chadwick, Killen and Olivier, 1971); numbers beginning 04– are now 44–. The Glossary incorporates a few minor improvements due to subsequent work.

The access of new material since 1955 has not been large, though welcome as confirmation of our interpretations and enlarging our understanding of the archives. I have selected twenty-five new documents to supplement the original three hundred, and of these two (**304** and **313**) were earlier known but then excluded, one (**322**) has been much enlarged by joins, and one (**305**) only became available when the first edition was well advanced, so that it could not be properly discussed and numbered as a document. The new documents are scattered through Part III so that they fall into the appropriate chapters; their numbers run from **301** to **325**, and their page numbers can be found from Concordance A on p. 619.

The adoption of international standards of transcription, which did not exist in 1955, has set new problems. Since it was impossible to change the English names of the ideograms to the current Latin ones in Parts I and II, the English ones have been retained in the text throughout; but this is merely a necessary expedient, and does not imply any retraction of the international agreement on this subject. In the transcription of syllabic signs the modifications at present agreed have been introduced throughout Parts III and IV, even though discrepancies may cause some difficulty to the uninitiated. A note listing these will be found at the beginning of the Glossary (p. 527). The typography adopted for transcriptions follows the pattern established for the first edition, and is not to be construed as a rejection of the current international convention.

The task of thanking those who have, in one way or another, contributed to the production of this second edition is one which I cannot adequately discharge: any list of names would inevitably omit some from whose work I have profited. I hope my colleagues will be prepared to accept this statement as an acknowledgement of my debt. I must particularly thank my colleague, Dr J. T. Killen, who has patiently listened to many of my attempts to think through the problems, and by his criticism has much improved the text of Parts III and IV. I should also like to take this opportunity of expressing my gratitude to all the Directors of Greek Museums and others who have continued to make it possible for us to work on the original tablets.

My thanks are also due to the Syndics and staff of the Cambridge University Press, Mrs B. Black and others who have assisted in the production and checking of a very involved book. Nor can I forget the Classical Faculty of the University of Cambridge, which has consistently fostered Mycenaean studies and has done much to make the production of this book possible.

No book on a subject still only twenty years old is likely to be perfect, and this will doubtless prove to have its share of imperfections. But the progress made by many hands in interpreting the texts justifies a new look at the problems, and I hope that this new edition will not only give the experts some fresh ideas, but will serve as an introduction to those who are approaching the subject for the first time.

J. C.

CAMBRIDGE
July 1972

PREFACE TO THE FIRST EDITION

During the months following the appearance of our first article 'Evidence for Greek dialect in the Mycenaean archives' (*JHS*, **73**, 1953, pp. 84–103) we received several invitations to discuss the results of our decipherment at book length. Our first reaction was to regard the writing of such a book as premature, in view of the uncertainty and incompleteness of much of the interpretation; but since 1953 there have been a number of changes in the situation:

1. A large number of new Mycenaean tablets, found at Pylos and Mycenae in the seasons 1952–4, have been added to the known material and must now be taken into account. Through the kindness of Prof. C. W. Blegen, Prof. A. J. B. Wace, Dr Emmett L. Bennett Jr. and Dr Ch. Karouzos (director of the National Museum in Athens), we have been able to study many of these documents in advance of publication; our thanks are also due to Dr N. Platon (director of the Iraklion Museum) and to his assistant S. Alexiou for making available to us the originals of the Knossos tablets, many of which are not to be found in Evans and Myres' *Scripta Minoa II*. We are indebted to them for the photographs of tablets which appear in the Plates. While this book contains a selection of all the Mycenaean tablets known at the time of writing (Easter, 1955), it is uncertain whether the next few seasons' excavation will provide any material addition to their numbers, and this may therefore be an opportune moment to review the evidence.

2. The 1952–4 tablets have enabled us to improve many of our earlier interpretations of signs, vocabulary and grammar, and have provided new and conclusive evidence that the language of the Mycenaean script really is a form of Greek. The documents here published are thus of great importance in forming almost the earliest record of Indo-European speech (of the family to which our own language belongs), and in providing the present-day speakers of Greek with a language history which may now be traced back more than 3350 years. A complete and detailed Mycenaean Vocabulary is becoming a necessity for comparative purposes.

3. A large number of classical scholars, philologists and archaeologists have begun to join in the interpretation of the documents. A general survey of the evidence will, we hope, be useful as a background against which to appreciate this new research discipline, already embodied in numerous articles dealing with points of detail. It may also provide a useful summary of its first results for those who have not the time for the cryptographic technicalities, but who

nevertheless wish to know more about the subject-matter that the tablets record and of the language in which they are written. While we would be the first to admit that our translations of the tablets are necessarily very tentative and imperfect, we hope that this book will have the advantage over previous articles in offering the remaining sceptics an overwhelming mass of evidence to show that the widespread support for the principle of the decipherment is justified.

The book has been planned in three sections. Part I contains a retrospective account of the half-century of research which has culminated in decipherment; a detailed discussion of the Mycenaean script, language and proper names; and a summary of the cultural evidence which can be extracted from the tablets. Part II, the core of the book, is devoted to the printing of 300 selected texts from Knossos, Pylos and Mycenae in transliteration, together with translation and commentary. We have tried to include all the tablets which provide useful material for a discussion of language, life and institutions, and have divided these into six chapters according to their different subject-matter. Part III comprises a complete Mycenaean Vocabulary, a selective list of personal names and a bibliography, together with concordances to the tablet numbering and a general index.

Our views on the detailed relationship of this Greek dialect are given in ch. III; but until a satisfactory terminology is agreed we have preferred to refer to it non-committally as 'Mycenaean Greek', which is intended to mean no more than 'that form of Greek which has so far been proved to occur in a Mycenaean context'. It may be objected that this would leave us without a distinguishing label for the speech of Mycenae itself, should further evidence reveal dialect differences between it and those of Pylos or Knossos; but similar considerations have not prevented the term 'Mycenaean' from coming into general use to describe the culture of the same wide area. Some apology is, however, due to the archaeologists for the necessity of referring to 'Mycenaean' dialect, script or institutions at Knossos in the period whose culture is properly known as Late Minoan II.

For the convenience of the printer and of those unfamiliar with the Mycenaean script, texts and words have generally been printed in the syllabic transliteration shown in fig. 4 (p. 23). Since in several respects the phonology of our dialect does not necessarily coincide with that of the later classical Greek, we have reluctantly decided to print the reconstructed Mycenaean forms in Roman letters (as in the transcription of other ancient Near Eastern scripts) rather than by an anachronistic use of the Greek alphabet. This has been replaced by the conventions *a b g d e w z h ē th i k l m n x o p r s t u ph kh ps ō*. The labio-velar series is represented by q^u g^u q^uh; *ê* and *ô* indicate vowels in which compensatory lengthening might be expected (Attic 'spurious' diphthongs ει and ου). This transcription is to be regarded as no more than a conventional approximation; the exact pronunciation of these phonemes may be subject to considerable uncertainty (particularly in the case of z, h, q^u and s).

We have wherever possible taken account of the interpretations of individual words, signs and contexts which have been proposed by other scholars during the period from 1953 up to the completion of this manuscript at Easter, 1955, and have tried to give them due credit in the commentaries and Vocabulary. Bennett's edition of the 1939–54 Pylos tablets unfortunately appeared too late (February 1956) for full conformity to be ensured, particularly with regard to his new numbering of the 1939 tablets (see p. 153). We have preferred to leave many details of the interpretation as uncertain, where the solutions so far advanced appear to be premature or unsatisfactory. There will inevitably be cases where we withhold credit to others for solutions at which we had in fact already arrived independently, and for any such apparent injustice we apologize in advance. Books and articles have been referred to in the text merely by their author and year of publication (or other abbreviation), for which the key will be found in the bibliography on pages 428–33.

In preparing the first draft of this book, we divided its contents between us in alternating sections; but these were subsequently amended, and where necessary rewritten, to take account of the other's criticisms, so that it is hardly possible to apportion responsibility. Continuous discussion and correspondence have resolved most of our differences; where we still hold strongly to opposing views this is indicated.

We are greatly indebted to Prof. Alan J. B. Wace for writing the Foreword to this book, which enables us to leave in his competent hands the discussion of the historical background to the Knossos and Mainland records; to Prof. C. W. Blegen for the encouragement and generous facilities given to our studies in connexion with his successive finds at Pylos; to Dr Emmett L. Bennett, Jr. for his indispensable published reference works, for a prolonged and fruitful private exchange of views, and for assistance with the tables of phonetic signs and ideograms; to Mr T. B. Mitford for the tables of Cypriot syllabary signs shown in fig. 12; and to Monsieur O. Masson for help with the table of Cypriot linear signs (fig. 11).

We must also acknowledge with thanks the benefit which many different parts of our book have derived from discussion and correspondence with Professors E. G. Turner, T. B. L. Webster and L. R. Palmer, Col. P. B. S. Andrews and other members of the seminar of the Institute of Classical Studies in London; with Professors G. Björck ✠, P. Chantraine, A. Furumark, M. S. Ruipérez and E. Sittig ✠, Dr F. Stubbings, Mr T. J. Dunbabin ✠, Herr Hugo Mühlestein; and with many others.

Our thanks are due to the Trustees of the Leverhulme Research Fellowships for a grant which enabled John Chadwick to make a special journey to Greece in the spring of 1955 to examine the original documents; and to the British School of Archaeology at Athens for the hospitality and facilities extended to us on this and other occasions.

We are indebted to the Oxford University Press for permission to reproduce the illustration from *Scripta Minoa I* shown as fig. 1, and to Messrs Macmillan for fig. 18, taken from *The Palace of Minos*.

We must express our gratitude, finally, to the Cambridge University Press for the speed, accuracy and co-operativeness with which it has undertaken the printing of our far from straightforward manuscript.

M. G. F. VENTRIS
J. CHADWICK

LONDON
CAMBRIDGE
May 1955

FOREWORD

CHRONOLOGICAL NOTE

The Aegean area divides geographically into three main regions, the Greek Mainland, the Archipelago, and Crete. The archaeological finds from these three regions are dated archaeologically by what are called 'sequence dates'. From the successive strata of the sites that have been excavated, such as Knossos, Phylakopi, Korakou, Lianokladi, Eutresis, the succession of the different styles is known although their absolute dating is by no means certain. For the sake of convenience the whole Aegean Bronze Age is divided into three main periods, Early, Middle and Late. Each period can be sub-divided into three sub-periods. The finds from the three main regions are thus described as Early, Middle and Late Helladic for the Mainland, Cycladic for the Archipelago, and Minoan for Crete. The three main periods are roughly parallel with the three great periods of Egypt, the Old Kingdom, the Middle Kingdom, and the Late Empire. This gives an approximate dating, which although not exactly accurate is not so far out as to make much difference. The Late Bronze Age begins with the establishment of the XVIIIth Egyptian Dynasty about 1580 B.C. and comes to an end in the days of the XXth Dynasty towards the end of the twelfth century. The sub-periods of the Late Bronze Age which most concern us, Late Helladic I, Late Helladic II and Late Helladic III, can be dated approximately as 1580–1500, 1500–1400, and 1400–1100 B.C. Many points are still under discussion, but new discoveries and future study are not very likely to change these approximate dates seriously. The sequence dates are of course fixed, unless there is an archaeological revolution, which is hardly possible.

In 1874 Schliemann made a series of trial pits on the Acropolis of Mycenae in order to select the most promising area for future excavations on a larger scale. In these tests Mycenaean pottery and Mycenaean terracotta figurines were found.[1] In 1876 Schliemann carried out his really epoch-making excavation at Mycenae when he discovered the Grave Circle and the royal graves with all their astonishing treasures. This, as he said, opened out a new world for archaeology: this was the beginning of Aegean Archaeology and the first landmark in the revelation of the prehistoric civilization of Greece. The second landmark came with the opening of Evans' excavations at Knossos in 1900, when he first discovered the clay tablets inscribed in Linear Script B, as he called it. The third landmark came in 1952 when Michael Ventris announced

---

[1] Actually in 1809 Thomas Burgon picked up at Mycenae 'south of the southernmost angle of the wall of the Acropolis' some fragments of Mycenaean pottery. These he published in 1847 in a coloured plate in his paper 'An Attempt to point out the Vases of Greece Proper which belong to the Heroic and Homeric Age' (*Transactions of the R. Society of Literature*, Vol. II, New Series, pp. 258 ff., pl. IV, A, B, C) which in some respects foreshadows the results of modern research.

that he had succeeded in deciphering the Linear B script as Greek. These are the three main stages in the unveiling of the earliest ages of Greece.

In the years between these landmarks much patient archaeological work was carried out, especially by Tsountas, but the results of this were not immediately seen in their correct perspective. In 1884 Schliemann and Dörpfeld excavated the fortress of Tiryns and discovered the Mycenaean palace there. Unfortunately the interest of the architectural remains was allowed to overshadow the purely archaeological side of stratigraphy, and the ruins of the palace itself were interpreted in the light of the assumptions of Homeric critics about the plan and appearance of a Homeric house. In the years 1896 to 1899 the British School at Athens excavated a prehistoric island site at Phylakopi in Melos which gave the successive phases of the Bronze Age culture in the Cyclades. In 1901 the excavations at Dimini in Thessaly brought the first knowledge of the Neolithic Age of Greece, and subsequent research began to find a place in the series for various finds from many sites which had not been properly evaluated before.

The point which archaeologists were slow in recognizing was the all-important one of stratification. Furtwängler and Loeschcke, publishing in 1879 and 1886 the pottery from Schliemann's excavations at Mycenae and pottery of similar types which had been found elsewhere, had recognized that the matt-painted pottery was probably older than the pottery with lustrous paint, but practically no excavator up to 1900 in southern Greece at least had endeavoured to disentangle the order of the strata that had preceded the Mycenaean Age, as it was called. It was customary to label everything as pre-Mycenaean, and though much of interest had come to light at important sites like Eleusis and Thorikos, no stratigraphic study was attempted; even the sequence of burials in the chamber tombs which were found at many sites was not noted. Moreover, the pottery from the chamber tombs excavated by Tsountas at Mycenae itself was not studied or even mended. Much valuable evidence was thus lost.

Gradually, with the beginning of the new century and after Evans' discoveries at Knossos, a fresher spirit entered into Greek prehistoric archaeology. The stratification of the Thessalian sites provided a guide, and the Bavarian work at Orchomenos and the Greek work in Boeotia and Phokis showed something of the earlier periods of the Bronze Age before the greatness of Mycenae.[1] The stratigraphic sequence was at last provided by Blegen's excavations at Korakou near Lechaeum in 1915 and 1916, where the sequence of what we

---

[1] Fimmen's *Kretisch-mykenische Kultur*, published in 1920, is a good conspectus of our knowledge down to 1915.

now call Early Helladic, Middle Helladic and Late Helladic was clearly revealed.[1] Four years later came the new excavations at Mycenae, which at last began to reveal the true history of the site, and other evidence accumulated from new excavations at sites like Asine, Eutresis and Eleusis, where the sequences illustrated by Korakou proved of invaluable assistance. In 1939 Blegen discovered in the Palace of Nestor at Pylos several hundred clay tablets inscribed in the Linear B script, which when analysed by Bennett proved of inestimable value in the decipherment studies of Ventris.

By 1930 the archaeologists had, by studying the successive strata, come to accept generally the thesis that the Greeks must have first entered Greece with the beginning of the Middle Bronze Age, deducing this from the following archaeological facts. The first stage of civilization in Greece is represented by the prehistoric mounds of Thessaly and contemporary sites in Central and Southern Greece. The earliest layers are Neolithic, and though we cannot as yet suggest even an approximate date, they probably are not later than the fourth millennium B.C. Their earliest inhabitants had reached a pottery stage of development and (to judge by the presence of Melian obsidian) were able to cross the narrow seas. We know nothing of their origin, which is still a matter of archaeological debate. They were succeeded at the beginning of the Bronze Age by a new people who, to judge from their artefacts, were racially dissimilar.[2] This new people used copper and later bronze and made pottery of a more sophisticated type, but had not yet learnt the potter's wheel. It would appear that this people introduced into Greece many words, mostly place and plant names, ending in -*nthos*, -*assos*, -*ttos* and -*ene* which are recognized as non-Indo-European: such words are Korinthos, *terebinthos*, *asaminthos*, Parnassos, Hymettos, Mykene. The original home of the Early Helladic people is usually placed in south-western Asia Minor, where similar place-names occur, but there is as yet no proof for this. This folk was akin to the contemporary Bronze Age peoples of the Cyclades and of Crete, and thus we can recognize that the cultures of the Early Bronze Age in these areas were not only contemporary but closely related. These cultures may not have been actually sisters, but were probably at least first cousins.

The Early Helladic people overran the Mainland, and presumably did not extirpate the Neolithic folk but coalesced with the survivors. In any case, as far as we can tell, they were not Indo-European. Some German

[1] Wace and Blegen, *BSA*, XXII, pp. 175 ff.

[2] Some writers (Matz, *Historia*, 1, p. 173) believe that the early stage of the Early Helladic period overlapped with the later stage of the Neolithic period. There is, however, so far no stratigraphic evidence in favour of this, and the stratification at Lianokladi, Hagia Marina, Tsani, Prosymna and Orchomenos is against it.

scholars,[1] however, wish to see in the Early Helladic period two strains, one Indo-European and one non-Indo-European, basing their ideas on the tectonic and syntactic character of some of the ornament on the patterned pottery. To extract ethnological conclusions from psychological speculations of this type is, to say the least, unwise: archaeology, especially prehistoric archaeology, should be as factual as possible and not imaginative to this extent.

With the beginning of the Middle Bronze Age on the Mainland of Greece in the nineteenth century B.C. a new element appears. In the stratification of excavated sites such as Korakou, Eutresis and Lianokladi it is obvious that there is no transition or evolution from the Early Bronze Age culture to that of the Middle Bronze Age. It is clear that a new factor at this time came into Greece; and since the material signs of its culture, pottery (which was made on the wheel), house plans, tombs, and in general all artefacts, differ markedly from those of the preceding Early Bronze Age, we assume that these differences mean a difference of race. This new racial element presumably in its turn also overran and amalgamated with the survivors of the Early Helladic inhabitants. From this time onwards there is no similar sign of any cultural break: the Middle Bronze Age develops slowly and naturally into the Late Bronze Age. This can be seen clearly in the pottery from the late Middle Helladic grave circle at Mycenae recently excavated by Dr Papademetriou and Professor George Mylonas.[2] Likewise at the end of the Late Bronze Age there can be observed, in spite of the more or less general destruction of the principal sites like Mycenae and Tiryns, a similar *gradual* change in culture (visible most of all in the pottery) from the end of the Bronze Age into the Early Iron Age. From the Early Iron Age henceforward there is no break in the development of culture in Greece: the Early Iron Age evolves naturally into the Orientalizing and Archaic periods and so into the great Classical Age of Greece. Thus by a process of elimination we deduce that since neither the Neolithic nor the Early Helladic people were Indo-Europeans, that is Greeks, then the Middle Helladic people who introduced into Greece the mysterious pottery called Minyan Ware (the characteristic pottery of the Middle Bronze Age) were probably the first Greeks to enter Hellas. So far no sign of their presence in the north of the Balkan peninsula can be found, and apart from Troy we have no indications of their presence in Asia Minor. The original home of the Greeks still remains a problem awaiting solution.

The Middle Helladic people apparently did not immediately come into contact with Crete and the Minoan culture; they met however in Melos,

---

[1] E.g. Matz, *Handbuch der Archäologie*, II, p. 203. He develops similar ideas in his *Torsion*.

[2] *Archaeology*, v, pp. 194 ff.

where at Phylakopi Kamares ware and Minyan ware are found side by side in the same Middle Cycladic strata. Towards the end of the Middle Bronze Age some of the painted Middle Helladic pottery shows signs of Cretan (Kamares) influence, but actual imports from Crete are rare. During the transition from the Middle to the Late Bronze Age the Mainland people became at last fully aware of the Minoan culture, which influenced the Mainland in much the same way as that in which classical Greek culture influenced Etruria. Just as in Crete the latest Middle Minoan products almost abruptly change into the new style of Late Minoan I, so on the Mainland the last style of Middle Helladic gives way rather suddenly to the bloom of Late Helladic I. The oversea connexions of the Mainland in this and the following period are to be seen in the fact that the 'Aegean' pottery found in Egypt at this date is Late Helladic and not Late Minoan.[1] Little or no Middle Helladic pottery has been observed in Crete;[2] but Melian vases of Middle Cycladic III date were found in the Knossian temple repositories of Middle Minoan III, and a small vase of Knossian faience of the same period in Shaft Grave A of the new Middle Helladic grave circle at Mycenae.[3] At all events from Late Minoan I/Late Helladic I onwards the contacts between Crete, Knossos in particular, and the Mainland (as exemplified at Mycenae) were frequent and intimate. The trained eye can, however, nearly always distinguish between Cretan and Mainland vases. The Zakro cups, for instance, are quite different in fabric from their contemporaries on the Mainland. In the succeeding Late Minoan II or Palace Period, actual Mainland vases are found at Knossos[4] and imitations of them are common, for instance the Ephyraean goblets of Knossos.[5]

As pointed out below, it was the fashion down to the beginning of Evans' excavations at Knossos to call the remains of the prehistoric age of Greece Mycenaean or pre-Mycenaean; and thus the Late Bronze Age remains of Crete were designated as Mycenaean, the Middle Bronze Age in Crete was called the Kamares period, and so on. Gradually Evans by 1905 evolved the Minoan system of sequence dating, and so thenceforward he and others working in Crete began to speak of Early, Middle and Late Minoan for their three phases of the Cretan Bronze Age. As Evans developed his theory that the Late Bronze culture of the Greek Mainland was due to a Cretan or Minoan

---

[1] Wace and Blegen, *Klio*, XXXII (1939), pp. 145 ff. Even the famous Marseilles ewer is Late Helladic II. We re-examined it in 1952. It was in the collection of Clot Bey which was formed in Egypt.

[2] Evans notes only one sherd of Minyan ware as found at Knossos (*PM*, II, p. 309).

[3] Excavated by Dr Papademetriou and Professor Mylonas.

[4] E.g. Evans, *PM*, II, p. 484, fig. 291 *d* and *e*.

[5] Evans, *PM*, IV, p. 360, figs. 301, 302, 306.

conquest and colonization, he began to call the Late Bronze Age remains of the Mainland Late Minoan; this nomenclature has persisted in some cases, such as in the writings of Myres, down to the present time. After the resumed excavations at Mycenae in 1920, it became clear to archaeologists such as Karo working on the Greek Mainland that the culture of the Mainland, though undoubtedly influenced by Crete, was largely independent of it; thus the system of Early, Middle and Late Helladic was proposed as a parallel series for the development of the culture of the Greek Mainland. Evans naturally was opposed to this because he refused to the last to modify his views about the relationship of Crete and the Mainland. He called those who refused to accept his views preposterous and perverse. His pan-Minoan theories are everywhere prominent in his *Palace of Minos*.[1]

With the impulse of excavations such as Korakou and the new work at Mycenae, students of prehistoric Greek archaeology began to recognize certain facts which emphasize the differences and likenesses of Knossos and the Greek Mainland in the second phase of the Late Bronze Age (Late Minoan II and Late Helladic II).

In Crete at this time, which Evans called the Palace Period at Knossos, it must be observed that Knossos differed much from the rest of Crete. The Palace Style, as such, is practically non-existent in the rest of Crete outside Knossos, and if examples of it are found they are generally considered as imports from Knossos. It has long been recognized that in East Crete, for instance, the Late Minoan II Palace Style period does not exist, but that there is instead a prolongation of the Late Minoan I style which gradually evolves into the Late Minoan III style. It should also be remarked that the Linear B script is so far known in Crete only at Knossos, whereas the Linear A script is known both at Knossos and in the rest of Crete. The Linear B script is the only script so far found on the Mainland, and it is far more widespread there than in Crete, where it occurs only at one site, for it is known at Orchomenos, Thebes, Eleusis, Tiryns, Mycenae and Pylos.

In the excavations at Korakou a type of pottery was first noticed to which the name of Ephyraean was applied. This belongs to the Late Helladic II period and is characterized by a class of well designed and proportioned goblets of fine, smooth, buff fabric painted with floral and marine patterns. They are easily distinguished by their patterns and fabric and are remarkable for their simplicity and dignity. In 1920 it was observed that a class of vases similar to

---

[1] Evans always refused to recognize any distinction between the Late Bronze Age pottery of the Mainland and that of Crete. He called it all Late Minoan and thus obscured much of the historical value of his discoveries.

the Ephyraean vases of the Mainland was found at Knossos belonging to the same general date, the second phase of the Late Bronze Age. The Knossian examples, however, are less well made and less well designed; they also lack the simplicity of the Mainland examples and the patterns on them are too large in proportion. Further, it became apparent that the type of vase called by Evans an *alabastron*, which occurs throughout the Late Bronze Age, is far more common on the Mainland of Greece than in Crete. Because vases of this shape in actual alabaster were found in the ruins of the throne room at Knossos[1] it was assumed that it must be a Cretan shape; there are, however, from chamber tombs at Mycenae excavated by Tsountas, two vases[2] of this shape in gypsum which may well be of Mainland manufacture. The tombs[3] in Crete in which clay alabastra are found are of this Late Minoan II period, the period which is characterized by the so-called Palace Style of decoration for pottery.

Vases of the Palace Style, large amphorae, are on the Mainland a notable feature of the Late Helladic II period, especially in the beehive tombs. Kurt Müller long ago pointed out that those found at Kakovatos were of local and not of Cretan fabric, in opposition to the then current belief that all Palace Style vases were Cretan imports, a view which some apparently still hold.[4] All the large Palace Style jars found on the Mainland are definitely of local manufacture: those found at Vaphio, for instance, are of the same pinkish clay as the later Laconian vases of the Orientalizing period. Careful study of these three classes of vases indicates that in all probability their occurrence in Crete is due to influence from the Mainland.

Other Mainland influences can be discerned. The beehive tombs so characteristic of the Mainland, especially in Late Helladic II, are represented by a few examples at Knossos; and at Knossos alone in the whole of Crete at this time, so far as our present knowledge goes. On the other hand, on the Mainland between forty and fifty beehive tombs are known: thus if number is the principal test beehive tombs seem to be a feature of the Mainland, where their structural development can be followed, rather than of Knossos.

The three palaces so far exacavated on the Mainland at Tiryns, Mycenae and Pylos have throne rooms. Knossos has a throne room which belongs to the latest part of the palace and seems to be a later insertion into an earlier plan;[5] the other Cretan palaces have not so far revealed throne rooms. At

---

[1] *BSA*, VI, p. 41.

[2] National Museum at Athens, No. 2769, from a chamber tomb at Mycenae 1887–88, and No. 3163 from Tomb 88 at Mycenae.

[3] See below, p. xxv.

[4] Picard, *Religions Préhelléniques*, p. 282.

[5] According to Evans (*PM*, IV, pp. 901 f.) it is a 'revolutionary intrusion' of the early part of LM II.

Knossos several fragmentary examples of friezes carved with rosettes or with the Mycenaean triglyph pattern have been found. Evans wished to attribute these to Middle Minoan III and to regard them as the models for similar friezes from Mycenae and Tiryns, which are of Late Helladic III date. The stratification of the fragments from Knossos is by no means secure: they belong to the upper strata of the palace, and are probably due to Mainland influence. There are fluted columns at Knossos, but these again belong to the Late Minoan II period and we know now that fluted columns were used at Mycenae and also at Pylos; fluted columns are not known at Phaestus and other Cretan sites outside Knossos.

Two other points call for mention. It has been observed that the style of the frescoes[1] of the last palace at Knossos is much more akin to that of the frescoes of Mycenae, Thebes, Tiryns and other Mainland sites than to the style of the frescoes found at Phaestus and other Cretan sites. The Cretan frescoes are naturalistic in character; those of Knossos and the Mainland are more interested in the human figure and in warlike scenes. Evans noted the military spirit of Knossos in this time, Late Minoan II.

In the palace at Knossos Evans found a store of blocks of green porphyry, *lapis Lacedaemonius*, the only source of which is Krokeai in Laconia, half-way between Sparta and the sea. This stone was popular at Mycenae and other Late Helladic centres for making stone vases, and the raw material seems to have been brought from Laconia to Mycenae to be worked. This porphyry is then yet another hint of Mainland influence on Knossos in Late Minoan II.

It was from a study of such points that several archaeologists had come to the conclusion that Knossos at this time, the Palace Period, stood apart from the rest of Crete and had more kinship with the Mainland. They suggested that the factors which Evans had interpreted as proofs of a Minoan colonization and conquest of the Mainland really pointed in the opposite direction, and that they indicated strong Mainland influence on Knossos as opposed to the rest of Crete. They at the same time emphasized the necessity for distinguishing between Late Minoan and Late Helladic pottery, especially at such sites as Phylakopi in Melos and Ialysos in Rhodes. At Phylakopi Cretan influence is first to be observed in the Middle Bronze Age, when Middle Minoan pottery (Kamares ware) was freely imported at the same time as Minyan ware from the Mainland makes its appearance in the island. With the Late Cycladic period both Late Minoan I and Late Helladic I pottery are found at Phylakopi, by Late Cycladic II the quantity of Mainland Late Helladic II pottery outstrips the Late Minoan II, and by Late Cycladic III

---

[1] Banti in Γέρας ᾽Αντωνίου Κεραμοπούλλου, pp. 119 ff.

Mainland Late Helladic pottery is dominant and there is little if anything from Crete. In the early days before Aegean archaeologists recognized that it was possible to distinguish between Late Minoan I and Late Helladic I pottery (and the importance of doing so), practically all imported Late Bronze Age vases at Phylakopi were called Minoan, even some which we now know are obviously of Late Helladic II fabric.[1] This gradual displacement of Cretan influence by Mainland influence is a point to which too little attention has been paid.

At Ialysos[2] the earliest Aegean settlement seems to have taken place at the end of the Middle Bronze Age, for late Middle Minoan pottery has been found there. With the opening of the Late Bronze Age both Late Minoan and Late Helladic vases are present, with perhaps the Cretan in the lead. By the second phase of the Late Bronze Age the story of Phylakopi is repeated and Late Helladic II influence becomes dominant, and by that time the occupation or perhaps colonization of Rhodes from the Mainland was so strong that 'Mycenaean' pottery was by then being made on the island.

At Knossos actual Late Helladic II vases have been found,[3] and the recently discovered tombs also show Mainland influence. The new warrior graves, apart from weapons, contain Palace Style vases, alabastra and Knossian imitations of Ephyraean ware;[4] the other graves of the same date recently discovered at Katsamba near Knossos show the same characteristics.[5] Thus Aegean archaeologists had deduced that the relations between Mycenae and Knossos were not as believed by Evans, but rather the reverse, that the Mainland had strongly influenced or dominated Knossos. Evans had pointed out[6] that in his Palace Period (when he suggested that a new dynasty with strong military tendencies was in power at Knossos) other Cretan centres were overthrown; he attributed this to the dominance of Knossos over the rest of Crete, and at the same time he believed that this strong military Knossos had extended its power to the Mainland and had established a colonial empire there. The inherent natural strength of the Middle Helladic tradition, which persisted all through Late Helladic in spite of any influences absorbed from Crete or else-

[1] *BSA*, xvii, Pl. XI.

[2] Monaco, *Clara Rhodos*, x, pp. 41 ff. Furumark's paper (*Acta Inst. Rom. R. Sueciae*, xv, pp. 150 ff.) on the Ialysos discoveries was written without his ever seeing the actual pottery, which my wife and I have been allowed to study in the Rhodes Museum by the kindness of Dr Kontes.

[3] Evans, *PM*, ii, p. 485, fig. 291 *d* and *e*. The Palaikastro ogival canopy jug (*ibid.* p. 490, fig. 296 *a*) is of Cretan fabric.

[4] *BSA*, xlvii, pp. 246 ff.

[5] *BCH*, 1954, pp. 150 f., figs. 50, 51. The vases include Knossian Ephyraean goblets, Palace Style vases and alabastra. Compare *Antiquity*, xxviii, pp. 183 f.

[6] *PM*, iv, pp. 884 f., 944 f.

where, shows clearly to those who have eyes to see that the Mainland and Crete during the Late Bronze Age are basically and essentially different.[1]

Thus the general belief was spreading among those who had devoted serious study to the problem and knew the actual objects (in short, the excavators and field archaeologists) and who had already deduced that the Mycenaeans must be Greeks, that at this time Knossos must have been at least under strong Mainland influence, perhaps even under the rule of a Mainland prince.[2] It was consequently suggested that the destruction of Knossos at the close of the fifteenth century (at the end of Late Minoan II) was not due to an invasion from overseas or an earthquake, but to a revolt of the native Cretans, the 'Minoans', against the intruding Greek dynasty or overlords. The deductions about Mainland influence at Knossos[3] were based on facts, archaeological facts, the value of which far outweighs all theories and hypotheses about Minoan empires and colonies.

The Aegean archaeologists naturally believed that the 'Mycenaeans' of the Mainland were Greeks, and that they would have spoken and written Greek. Thus the discovery of the Pylos tablets in 1939 and their obvious similarity in script and probably in language with the Linear B tablets from Knossos posed an entirely new problem, which could only be solved by the decipherment of the script. The 'Minoans' naturally held that the Pylos tablets proved the Minoan conquest of the Mainland. One scholar even suggested that the tablets were loot from Knossos! The 'Mainlanders' believed that the Pylos tablets ought to be written in Greek, and toyed with the idea that the Knossos tablets might be Greek also, though even they did not then see the wider implications of the result of all this. 'Whether the language of the Mainland, probably then Greek, was the same as that of Crete we cannot yet determine.'[4]

In 1952, as explained below, Mr Ventris announced his decipherment of the Linear B script as Greek,[5] and many things thereupon became clear and the archaeological deductions received linguistic confirmation, a great triumph for both methods. Working independently, the archaeologists and the linguists had come to the same conclusions. It is not often that learned researches support one another so decisively or so neatly.

Thus at one stroke what is practically a revolution has taken place in Greek

[1] Compare Furumark, *op. cit.* pp. 186 ff.

[2] Pendlebury, *Archaeology of Crete*, p. 229. This suggestion was rejected by Matz, *Handbuch der Archäologie*, II, p. 271.

[3] Compare Kantor, *The Aegean and the Orient in the Second Millennium B.C.*

[4] Wace, *Mycenae* (1949), p. 117.

[5] If the Linear B script which is that of the Mainland represents Greek, then the Linear A script, known so far only in Crete, probably represents the Minoan language.

studies. The prehistoric period of the Middle and Late Bronze Ages on the Mainland (Middle and Late Helladic) must now be recognized as Hellenic; we cannot include Crete, because we cannot yet read the Minoan Linear A script, which represents a different language from the Linear B script, and thus the Minoan culture cannot be called Hellenic. We must in future differentiate between the Linear A *Minoan* script and the Linear B *Mycenaean* script; for the latter is far commoner on the Mainland, where it is found from Orchomenos in the north to Pylos in the south, than it is in Crete.

We must in future speak of pre-Classical and Classical Greek art and culture. From the beginning of Schliemann's discoveries at Mycenae the conservatism of classical archaeologists has obstructed progress in the study of Greek civilization as a whole. Because the pre-Classical Mycenaean culture was in many ways naturally unlike the culture of Classical Greece of the sixth, fifth and fourth centuries B.C., archaeologists refused to believe that it could possibly be Greek. They could hardly have expected that the culture of Mycenae, one thousand years older, and that of Periclean Athens would be the same. The more, however, we study Mycenaean art and culture, the more we find in it elements that anticipate Classical Greek art.

From the first, because Mycenaean art was unlike Classical Greek art, it was dismissed as oriental. Even when it was admitted that the Greeks might have arrived in Greece at the beginning of the Middle Bronze Age, it was stated that Greek art did not develop until one thousand years later, after an interregnum of chaos. One writer for example says: 'When the sun of Homer rose out of the darkness of this wild time, it shone over the ruins of Creto-Mycenaean culture; but the new life of pure Hellenism grew up out of its ruins.'[1] We are told that the first creation of Greek art was the Geometric style, as though it had suddenly descended from Olympus about 1000 B.C. These 'orthodox' archaeologists never reflected for one moment on the growth and evolution of the Geometric style. We now know that it evolved gradually from the pre-Classical culture of the Late Bronze Age, just as that in its turn evolved from the culture of the Middle Bronze Age. Nature does not work *per saltus* but by slow and sometimes painful processes of growth and change and development. In any study of Greek art to concentrate on the Classical period alone is a fatal mistake. The true student of Greek art must begin his studies with the Middle Bronze Age at least; also, he must not end his studies with the death of Alexander, as so many do, and refuse even to look at Hellenistic art.

Schliemann in the enthusiasm of his first discoveries was overawed by the

---

[1] Pfuhl, *Masterpieces of Greek Drawing and Painting*, pp. 10f.

'experts', who insisted that his finds could not be Greek but must be Phoenician, Asiatic and so on. When he found frescoes at Mycenae, the 'experts' insisted that they could not possibly be prehistoric and deterred him from publishing them. Other 'experts' have held that there is a great chasm between pre-Classical and Classical Greece. An Oxford professor wrote[1] as late as 1911: 'The chasm dividing prehistoric and historic Greece is growing wider and deeper; and those who were at first disposed to leap over it now recognize such feats are impossible.' It is this spirit which has impeded progress in our studies of pre-Classical Greece. Now, with the revelation of a pre-Homeric Greek going back to the fifteenth century B.C., we have before us a great opportunity to discard old assumptions and the shibboleths once regarded almost as sacred dogma.

The history of Greece and of Greek culture will have to be rewritten from the outlook of our present knowledge, and as more pre-Classical texts are found and deciphered, so our knowledge will grow. Greek art is one and indivisible, and has a continuous history from the first arrival of the Greeks. A fresh examination of the legends of early Greece must also be undertaken to estimate their archaeological and historical value.

There are three points, at least, which future discoveries and study will undoubtedly make clearer. The orthodox view of classical archaeologists is that there was a 'Dark Age', when all culture in Greece declined to barbarism, at the close of the Bronze Age and in the early period of the ensuing Iron Age. Even now, when it is admitted that the Greeks of the Late Bronze Age could read and write with the Linear B script, it is still believed by some that in the transition from the Age of Bronze to that of Iron the Greeks forgot how to read and write, until about the eighth century when they adopted the Phoenician alphabet. It is incredible that a people as intelligent as the Greeks should have forgotten how to read and write once they had learned how to do so. It is more probable that the Linear B script continued in use, and perhaps even overlapped the first appearance of the Greek adaptation of the Phoenician alphabet. This would have taken place in much the same manner as that in which the native Cypriot syllabary continued in use until the third century B.C. and overlapped the Greek alphabet in the island. The Cypriot syllabary seems to be a development of the local so-called Cypro-Minoan script, examples of which have been found at Enkomi and Ras Shamra. Future discoveries may well reveal to us that the Linear B script continued into the Early Iron Age and was then gradually replaced by the Phoenician alphabet, which the Greeks found more convenient for writing their language.

[1] P. Gardner, *JHS*, 1911, p. lix.

The clay tablets with the Linear B Mycenaean script so far found at Pylos, Knossos or Mycenae are all inventories of one kind or another. No documents such as letters or anything of a literary character have yet been found. We can hardly doubt that such existed, though they were probably written on materials less able to survive disaster than clay: the inventories of clay were baked and so preserved by the violent fires which destroyed so much. Letters or literary texts may well have been on wooden tablets or some form of parchment or even papyrus; some fortunate discovery will possibly one day reveal them to us. So elaborate a system of writing cannot have been employed only for recording inventories of goods or payments of taxes, things in themselves ephemeral; the Linear B script was probably also used for letters, treaties and even literary texts.

Evans[1] long ago suggested that perhaps the earliest Greek epics had been written in 'Minoan' and then translated into Greek. There is now no longer any need to imagine this, since we know that the Linear B tablets are in Greek and an early epic poet, had he been so minded, could have recorded his masterpieces on clay. Homer is the earliest existing monument of Greek literature and the *Iliad* can hardly have been the first Greek poem ever composed: its very perfection in language, composition, style and metre shows that it is not the work of a mere prentice hand, but that of a master who must have learned his art from a long succession of predecessors. We need not therefore be surprised if excavation or some casual find in Greece gives us an early document—a letter, or a literary text, a history or a poem—from some long-forgotten forerunner of Homer.

As we have said, historians and archaeologists are accustomed to speak of the period of transition from the Bronze Age to that of Iron, and of the early years of the Iron Age, as a 'Dark Age' and to assume that culture in Greece then underwent a severe recession; thus they assert that literacy was forgotten, civilization declined, all was turmoil and barbarism. Actually the principal reason why this is called a 'Dark Age' is that we have little or no evidence for it in archaeology, in history or in literature. No inhabited site of this period or of the Geometric period has been excavated. Our earliest sites are sanctuaries like the Orthia site at Sparta and like Perachora. The evidence of the cemeteries which have been excavated (as at the Kerameikos) shows that from

---

[1] See Evans' paper in *JHS*, 1912, pp. 277 ff., especially p. 288. In this paper he rightly says (p. 277): 'The scientific study of Greek civilization is becoming less and less possible without taking into constant account that of the Minoan and Mycenaean world that went before it.' He throughout emphasizes the pre-Classical survivals in Classical Greek art, which in the light of the decipherment of Linear B as Greek is almost prophetic. The reader should, however, remember that Evans makes no distinction between Minoan and Mycenaean.

the close of the Bronze Age to the Early Iron Age there was no violent archaeo-logical break, only a gradual transition or evolution from one age to the next. Likewise in Dorian Argolis, as in non-Dorian Attica, evidence is slowly accumu-lating to show that a similar process of evolution took place. As exploration proceeds, evidence of the same kind will no doubt come to light from the other areas of Greece. Tombs do not usually, even at the height of the Classical period, yield much if any epigraphical material.

But what of the Dorians and the so-called Dorian Invasion? The effects of the Dorian migration into the Peloponnese have been exaggerated by his-torians. To the Greeks of the Classical period there was no great Dorian Invasion. They called it the 'Return of the Herakleidai', and we know from Homer that even at the time of the Trojan war Herakleidai were in power in Greece: Tlepolemus,[1] the son of Herakles, the great Dorian hero, led the contingents from Rhodes and the southern Sporades. The Dorians, according to Thucydides, came into the Peloponnese with the returning Herakleidai. There is nowhere in the Greek tradition any hint that the Dorians were different except in dialect from any other Greek tribe. The Dorians were Greeks and found Greeks already thoroughly established in Hellas. There is no suggestion that they introduced any new or foreign culture: all efforts to find in the archaeological remains things specifically Dorian have failed completely. There are undoubtedly changes and developments in the artefacts from the close of the Bronze Age down into the Iron Age and the Geometric period, but these are natural developments and not revolutionary changes: we must not deny to the intelligence of the Greeks any touch of inventiveness or originality. Matz[2] who says 'Das wirklich Neue beginnt erst mit dem Protogeometrischen' overlooks the clear evidence of the evolution of proto-Geometric from the latest Mycenaean wares. The Dorian migration brought about not a cultural but only a political change in Greece. The return of the Alkmaionidai and their clients is a parallel event and we need not imagine that the Dorians altered in Laconia, for instance, anything but the political structure of the country. The Dorians on the Return of the Herakleidai to the Peloponnese obtained political control of Corinth, Argos, Laconia and Messenia. Pausanias' notes on the gradual occupation of Laconia by the Dorians suggest no more than the slow winning of political control. In Argolis Mycenae remained independent until some time after her co-operation in the victory of Plataea.

[1] Some Homeric critics call him a Dorian interpolation, e.g. Lorimer, *Homer and the Monuments*, p. 47. He occurs, however, in the Homeric Catalogue inscription of the late third century B.C. from Chios (*JHS*, 1954, p. 162).

[2] *Handbuch der Archäologie*, II, p. 305. Compare Furumark, *Acta Inst. Rom. R. Sueciae*, X (*Op. Arch.* III), p. 195 n. 1.

At Tiryns the palace was destroyed some time in the third phase of the Late Bronze Age (Late Helladic III), but the megaron was rebuilt on a smaller scale;[1] it presumably continued in use for some time thereafter. Unluckily, owing to the circumstances of the excavation of the palace at Tiryns, we have no archaeological evidence to tell us when the megaron was destroyed or when it was reoccupied.

The importance of Mr Ventris' decipherment can hardly be over-estimated, for it inaugurates a new phase in our study of the beginnings of classical Hellas. We must recognize the Mycenaean culture as Greek, and as one of the first stages in the advance of the Hellenes towards the brilliance of their later amazing achievements. We must guard against the facile assumptions of the past and look at everything afresh from the new point of view. In culture, in history and in language we must regard prehistoric and historic Greece as one indivisible whole. The way has been prepared for us by the pioneer archaeological work of Schliemann, Tsountas and Evans, and we must follow boldly in their footsteps under the guiding light now provided for us by Mr Ventris and Mr Chadwick.[2]

[1] Blegen's suggestions (*Korakou*, pp. 130 ff.) are undoubtedly right. The German ideas that the reconstructed megaron was a classical temple are untenable.

[2] This Introduction was written in the winter of 1954–5 while I was a member of the Institute for Advanced Study at Princeton. It owes much to the collaboration of my wife and to the criticism of several friends in America who read it in first draft.

A. J. B. W.

PART I

SCRIPT, LANGUAGE AND CULTURE

CHAPTER I

DISCOVERY AND DECIPHERMENT

1. THE HOMERIC AGE AS MYTH

THE Hellenes of the classical period preserved no clear memory either of a system of writing earlier than the Greek alphabet, or of a time when they and their language were not firmly rooted on the Greek mainland.

The source of the alphabet is clearly acknowledged by Herodotus (v, 58–9, in Rawlinson's translation):

Now the Phoenicians who came with Cadmus, and to whom the Gephyraei belonged, introduced into Greece upon their arrival a great variety of arts, among the rest that of writing, whereof the Greeks till then had, as I think, been ignorant. And originally they shaped their letters exactly like all the other Phoenicians, but afterwards, in course of time, they changed by degrees their language, and together with it the form likewise of their characters. Now the Greeks who dwelt about those parts at that time were chiefly the Ionians. The Phoenician letters were accordingly adopted by them, but with some variation in the shape of a few, and so they arrived at the present use, still calling the letters Phoenician, as justice required, after the name of those who were the first to introduce them into Greece. Paper rolls also were called from old διφθέραι by the Ionians, because formerly when paper was scarce they used, instead, the skins of sheep and goats—on which many of the barbarians are even now wont to write. I myself saw Cadmeian characters engraved upon some tripods in the temple of Apollo Ismenias in Boeotian Thebes, most of them shaped like the Ionian. One of the tripods has the inscription following:

Me did Amphitryon place, from the far Teleboans coming.

This would be about the age of Laius, the son of Labdacus, the son of Polydorus, the son of Cadmus.

The ease with which Herodotus was able to read this and two other inscriptions in the same temple, allegedly written some four generations or so before the Trojan war, may have left him with some suspicion that their great antiquity was only a pious fraud; and a more general feeling that writing was wholly out of place in the heroic age is reflected in Homer, whose only reference to a visual message is couched in such vague terms as to leave doubt whether true writing is intended at all (*Il.* VI, 155–70):

Now Glaukos was the father of blameless Bellerophon, whom the gods had endowed with beauty and manly grace, but whom Proitos, his overlord, expelled from Argos in

3

murderous anger. Proitos' wife Anteia had conceived a passionate desire to go to bed with him secretly, but was unable to prevail on the prudent and high-minded Bellerophon. So she went with a lying story to King Proitos: 'May death be yours if you do not kill Bellerophon: he has tried to rape me.' The king was seized with fury when he heard this; taboo restrained him from killing him on the spot, but he dispatched him to Lycia with a folded board, scratched with many malevolent symbols designed to bring him ruin: he had only to show them to the king's father-in-law for his doom to be sealed.

But although Agamemnon, Odysseus and Nestor might have been illiterate, and although their ancient palaces and cities had long since crumbled into dust, it was in ancient times accepted without question that the Homeric heroes had been Greeks in language, religion and every other distinguishing feature, and that among their subjects were to be numbered the ancestors of most, if not all, of the classical population. Homer possessed no term which could be used without anachronism to refer to this linguistic unity (though the Carians are called βαρβαρόφωνοι in *Il.* II, 867); but for Herodotus the Trojan war was a clear-cut struggle between Ἕλληνες and Asiatics, and a direct antecedent of the rivalry which was to culminate in the Persian invasions (I, 3–5).

Both Homer and Herodotus agreed, however, that among the segmented and constantly-shifting population of the early Aegean there had also been elements which did not speak Greek. This is clear from the description of Crete in *Od.* XIX, 172–7: 'There is a land called Crete, in the middle of the wine-dark sea, beautiful and rich, with water on all sides; on her are innumerable men and ninety cities, and one language jostles another: there are Achaeans, and great-hearted True-Cretans, Cydonians, Dorians divided into their three tribes(?), and excellent Pelasgians.'

In a significant passage (I, 57–8) evidently based on personal investigation, Herodotus concludes from the speech of the 'Pelasgians' living in his time on the Hellespont, on Lemnos and in the problematical city of 'Creston' (who in earlier times had inhabited Thessaliotis and Attica, where they had built the wall round the Acropolis) that this widespread people had spoken a barbarous tongue. In order to reconcile Pelasgian and Athenian claims to autochthony, he argues that the Athenians must have been Pelasgians who at some time adopted the Greek language; and goes on, with a disregard for his own previous argument and for our own more careful discrimination between 'race' and 'language', to describe the Hellenic race as one which had never changed its language, but had been 'severed' (ἀποσχισθέν) from the Pelasgians and had increased its numbers at their expense. The same ambiguities are

4

present in his description of the Ionians (VII, 94): 'When they dwelt in the Peloponnese and inhabited the land now called Achaea (which was before the arrival of Danaus and Xuthus in the Peloponnese) they were called, according to the Greek account, "Pelasgians of the sea-shore", but afterwards, from Ion the son of Xuthus, they were called Ionians.' Both Sophocles (in his *Inachus*) and Thucydides (IV, 109, 4) use 'Tyrrhenian' as a synonym for 'Pelasgian', in allusion to the widespread belief in a Pelasgian migration from Thessaly and the North Aegean to Italy, associated or identical with the Etruscan migration derived from Lydia by Herodotus. This theory, found in Hellanicus of Lesbos (fifth century B.C.), Andron of Halicarnassus, Varro, Diodorus Siculus, Strabo and others, has been subjected to detailed but inconclusive criticism both by Dionysius of Halicarnassus in antiquity ('Ρωμ. 'Αρχ. I, xxv–xxx) and recently by Pallottino (1947). A germ of historical truth is indicated by the discovery at Kaminia on Lemnos in 1885 of a sixth-century stele inscribed in what is almost certainly a language closely related to Etruscan.

The classical picture of a Greece inhabited since the birth of mankind by a number of Greek-speaking tribes, living side-by-side with Pelasgians, Eteocretans, Leleges and other obscure peoples, was to be undermined by the Jewish-Christian cosmogony which, while retaining a finite date for the Creation, dismissed the possibility of local autochthony in favour of a diffusion of all languages and peoples from a common centre in Asia. A long period of unprofitable speculation on the mutual relationship of languages, in which Hebrew played a pernicious role, continued until 1796, when Sir William Jones gave first public expression to the view that Sanskrit, Latin and Greek had 'sprung from some common source, which perhaps no longer exists'.

In the next twenty years Franz Bopp and Rasmus Rask were able to show conclusively that the Greek language, like its relatives, was in fact the result of a continuous evolution from a common 'Indo-European' ancestor, and that it must therefore at one time have been brought into Greece from some more central location somewhere on the great plains which stretch from Poland to Turkestan. The age in which the hypothetical parent language had begun to differentiate into separate dialects, and the date at which the first Greek-speakers had entered the Balkan peninsula, could not however be determined by any existing historical evidence; and the obvious unhistoricity of the greater part of Greek legend made any classical testimony to the language situation before the eighth century B.C. appear entirely untrustworthy.

The same uncertainties veiled the process by which the classical Greek dialects, whose study was stimulated by progress in linguistic theory and in the search for inscriptions, had reached their geographical distribution. It was clear that a large and definite movement of population was necessary to explain the occupation of the Peloponnese by the Dorian-speakers, keeping in subjection a helot class, and cutting off the Arcadians entirely from the sea-coasts from which their nearest relatives the Cypriots had evidently emigrated. But it would have been rash to accept as historical fact Thucydides' account of the 'Return of the Herakleidai' (I, 12), or Eratosthenes' precise dating of it to 1104 B.C., eighty years after the fall of Troy.

2. MYCENAE AND KNOSSOS: THE PIONEERS

In the brilliantly perceptive first twelve paragraphs of his history Thucydides sketched the early development of Hellas, from a conglomeration of migrating tribes without cities, commerce or security of communication, down to the rallying of the Greek forces under Agamemnon for the Trojan war.

Mycenae was certainly a small place, and many of the towns of that period do not seem to us today to be particularly imposing; yet that is not good evidence for rejecting what the poets and the general tradition have to say about the size of the expedition. Suppose, for example, that the city of Sparta were to become deserted, and that only the temples and foundations of buildings remained, I think that future generations would, as time passed, find it very difficult to believe that the place had really been as powerful as it was represented to be. We have no right, therefore, to judge cities by their appearances rather than by their actual power, and there is no reason why we should not believe that the Trojan expedition was the greatest that had ever taken place.

But most nineteenth-century historians (particularly in Germany) were inclined to dismiss Troy and Mycenae as mere figments of poetic imagination; preferring to telescope Thucydides' narrative, by the omission of the Heroic Age, to read as if the development of the classical city-states had been the first interruption of that primitive state of barbarism that he so vividly described.

The first proof that a golden age of Mycenae had really existed was due to the vision and persistence of one man, Heinrich Schliemann. Born in 1822, the son of a poor North German pastor, he was fascinated in boyhood by the story of Troy (which in daydreams he already saw himself excavating) and enthralled by the cadences of Homer's Greek, first heard on the lips of a drunken miller. At the age of forty-six, having amassed a fortune in Russia and having learnt fifteen languages, he retired from business, married a sixteen-year-old Greek girl and devoted himself to archaeology—for which, even in those early days of the science, he began with few technical qualifications apart from great enthusiasm and a common-sense appreciation of stratification. After three seasons at Troy, where the ancient settlement was triumphantly laid

6

bare, he began in August 1876 to excavate the citadel of Mycenae, whose great Gate of the Lions had ever since prehistoric times been clearly visible above ground.

Rich hoards of gold, massive architecture and sophisticated art forms soon proved that the 'Mycenaeans' had reached a level of civilization which was indeed far removed from primitive barbarism, and which fully justified Homer's reminiscence of it. The chronology of his finds was not at first exactly appreciated, but the Mycenaean age appeared to be approximately contemporary with the Egyptian New Kingdom (c. 1580–1100 B.C.). Schliemann was equally vague about the race to which his 'Mycenaeans' had belonged. At the time of his excavations he was confident that he was indeed recovering the burials of Agamemnon and of the other Achaeans of his dynasty; but in a letter to Virchow nine years later (18 June 1885) he says:

> I have been at pains to demonstrate that Tiryns and Mycenae must necessarily have been built and inhabited by the *Phoenicians,* who in a remote prehistoric age flooded Greece and the islands of the Ionian and Aegean seas with colonies, and who were only finally expelled, around 1100 B.C., by the so-called Dorian Invasion.

This view, perhaps pressed on Schliemann by the 'experts', was still being held by Dörpfeld in 1936. Reconsidering Schliemann's discoveries, Tsountas (1897) insisted that, although the Mycenaeans were illiterate (since no sign of indigenous writing had apparently been found on the Mainland), they were nevertheless Greeks; so too did Leaf in his introduction to Schuchhardt's *Schliemann* (1891):

> Now we should rather suppose that the original dialect (of the Homeric poems) was that of the ancestors of these Asiatic Aeolians, the Achaians of the eleventh century. What the form of their speech was we cannot now pretend to say. It must have differed greatly from Fick's 'Aeolic'; it was the common parent of Thessalian, Arcadian and Cyprian, in all of which we see various points of connexion with the Epic language. These affinities do not allow of an even approximate reconstruction of the parent speech; but they do allow us to assume that there was once a *common Achaian language* spoken by the dwellers in Mycenae and Tiryns, and over the greater part of the Greek mainland.

In a letter (1 January 1889) written two years before his death, Schliemann confided that 'I would like to end my life's labours with one great work—the prehistoric palace of the kings of Knossos in Crete'. Since its description by Buondelmonti in the fifteenth century, this ancient site had been known to lie at the village of Makrotikho or Makritikhos, six kilometres south of Candia (now Iraklion) in a sheltered valley leading into the interior, and out of sight

7

of the sea. In 1877 the Spanish consul Minos Kalokairinos, a native of Candia, had made a small dig on the top of the Κεφάλα Τσελεμπῆ, 'Squire's Knoll', during which he had uncovered some of the magazines with their large *pithoi* and had recovered an inscribed tablet, now Ga34 (Evans later found others in Kalokairinos' spoil-heaps); one of the *pithoi* then found is in the National Museum at Athens. Three years later the American W. J. Stillman, who had noticed the double axe signs on the masonry, applied in the name of the newly-founded Archaeological Institute of America to the Imperial Ottoman Government for a *firman* to excavate at Knossos. He was allowed to anticipate the arrival of permission and began to dig; but the *firman* never materialized and he was forced to stop. Schliemann in 1886 confirmed the 'Mycenaean' character of the remains; in 1889 he tried to buy the knoll from its multiple owners, but found their price too high for a site which 'I had satisfied myself I would easily be able to excavate in a week with a hundred workmen'. In addition to the rapacity of the proprietors Schliemann met with the usual obstruction from the Ottoman authorities, as always highly suspicious of archaeologists whom they suspected of subversive designs, and discouragement from the native Syllogos that administered the Candia Museum, who were afraid of what might happen to any treasures unearthed in the prevailing state of political unrest. His plan to excavate Knossos was postponed in favour of another season at Troy and cut short by his death: for this narrow escape Evans was lastingly thankful.

In 1886 Evans, then keeper of the Ashmolean Museum in Oxford, was presented by Greville Chester with a seal-stone from Crete of a type recently publicized by Milchhoefer, engraved with unfamiliar 'hieroglyphs'. His intuition that Crete held the clue not only to a widespread system of writing among the 'Mycenaeans', but also to the origins of their civilization, brought Evans to Athens in 1893. He was there able to buy further specimens of Cretan seal-stones, and also to show that among the Mycenae finds there were in fact two vessels bearing writing. His travels to Crete in the following spring brought sufficient new evidence of writing (largely in the form of seal-stones similar to that shown in fig. 1, worn as γαλόπετρες or milk-charms by the women of the villages) to decide him to buy a part share of the Kephala site, thereby forestalling Joubin of the French School; and to publish his preliminary conclusions (1894). He argued that the 'Mycenaeans' must, in view of their advanced civilization, have been literate; and distinguished two phases, an earlier 'pictographic' script and a later linear or 'quasi-alphabetic'.

There is the strongest presumption for believing that in Crete at least the race among whom the earlier Aegean characters were originally rife was of non-Hellenic stock.

But if, at any rate towards the close of the Mycenaean period, there was already a Greek population in Crete, it becomes probable that the mysterious characters with which we are dealing may also have been used by men of Greek speech.

Further travels through Crete in 1895 and 1896, partly in company with the young Myres, gave material for a further article (1897) which included the inscribed libation table from Psykhro (Linear A). In November 1899 the Turks finally evacuated Crete; at the New Year Evans was able to buy the whole Kephala site; and permission was given for a Knossos excavation, under the auspices of the British School, to be partly financed by the new Cretan Exploration Fund.

Fig. 1. Three-sided cornelian seal-stone from eastern Crete (P. 49* in Evans, *Scripta Minoa I*, p. 159).

The first of six seasons, in which Evans was assisted by Mackenzie with Fyfe as architect, began on 23 March 1900. Within a week the first of a very large number of inscribed tablets (Linear B) were found: some of these depicted vessels similar to those illustrated among foreign offerings in an Egyptian tomb of the reign of Queen Hatshepsut (1516–1481 B.C.), which gave an approximate indication of their date. Later evidence showed that the tablets had been written just before the final destruction of the palace, which further Egyptian parallels proved to have occurred early in the reign of Amenhotep III (1414–1378 B.C.).

Evans also found, under a staircase adjoining the magazines, a deposit of clay documents inscribed with 'hieroglyphs' and bearing the impressions of seal-stones of the γαλόπετρα type. In the excavation report for 1900 he recorded the 'hieroglyphic' and linear tablets as being contemporary; explaining the first as the product of the native Eteocretans who had been responsible for the 'Kamares' pottery of the earlier period, the second as evidence of 'the intrusion of a new element' which had brought with it the Mycenaean civilization from the Mainland.

In the 1902 report the sequence *Kamares—Palace Style* was amended to *Middle Minoan—Proto-Mycenaean—Mycenaean*, with an indiscriminate use of the terms 'Mycenaean' and 'Minoan' as a general label for the palace and its

9

treasures. From 1903 onwards the term 'Mycenaean' was dropped by Evans, to be replaced in due course by the now canonical division into the nine periods from *Early Minoan* I to *Late Minoan* III. The civilization of Crete had proved to be both more ancient and more autonomous than had been realized when the earlier terminology was evolved, as he emphasized in his presidential address to the Hellenic Society (1912):

When we come to regard the Minoan remains themselves as stratified by the various catastrophes, it becomes evident that they are the results of a gradual evolution. There is no break. The unity of the whole civilization is such as almost to impose the conclusion that there was a continuity of race. If the inhabitants of the latest Palace structures are to be regarded as 'Achaeans', the Greek occupation of Crete must, on this showing, be carried back to Neolithic times—a very improbable conclusion.

How Evans' Knossocentric view had come to affect his perspective on the Mycenaean civilization itself is shown a page later, where he describes it as no more than 'a Minoan plantation' and as 'a Mainland branch of the Minoan culture':

We must clearly recognize that down to at least the twelfth century B.C. the dominant factor both in Mainland Greece and in the Aegean world was still non-Hellenic, and must still unquestionably be identified with one or other branch of the old Minoan race. But this is far from saying that even at the time of the first Minoan conquerors in the Peloponnese, or approximately speaking the sixteenth century B.C., they may not have found settlers of Hellenic stock already in the land.

Simultaneously with Evans' discoveries at Knossos, tablets in a somewhat different script (Linear A) were found at Agia Triada in the south of Crete by Halbherr (not published till 1945) and also in smaller numbers at other Cretan sites. In 1908 Pernier found the unique Phaistos disk, stamped in clay from movable pictographic 'type': its Cretan origin is still disputed. Keramopoullos in 1921 discovered twenty-eight stirrup-jars in a storeroom of the Mycenaean palace at Thebes, lettered in a script which proved to be identical with the Linear B of Knossos: these greatly extended the evidence for the character of Mainland writing, previously confined to a few uncertain inscriptions with variable forms on pots from Mycenae, Tiryns, Eleusis and Orchomenos.

3. THE YEARS OF STAGNATION

Evans' *Scripta Minoa I* (1909) contained his collection of inscribed seal-stones, the hieroglyphic and Linear A material from Knossos, and fourteen of the Linear B tablets (five had already appeared in the 1900 dig report). No further publication of the Linear B tablets, of which well over 3000 pieces are known to have been excavated, was made until the fourth volume of his *Palace of Minos* (1935), where a total of 120 were illustrated in line drawings with a short commentary and sign-lists. At the same time (1932, 1936) Sundwall added thirty-eight more which he had copied himself in Iraklion at the cost of Evans' displeasure. At the time of Evans' death in 1941 his notes for *Scripta Minoa II*, which was to contain the Knossos Linear B archives, were still in disorder; and the originals in the museum at Iraklion, which had never been properly examined for joins and which had in some cases disappeared, were no longer available for study and were exposed to destruction by war. The task of completing their publication from Evans' drawings and photographs, fifty years after their discovery, was then heroically undertaken by Myres.

Two generations of scholars had been cheated of the opportunity to work constructively on the problem. Though it is difficult to forgive Evans for his failure to complete or to delegate publication, we are now in a position to appreciate that, even if he had made known all the tablets in an orderly way at the time of their discovery, they would probably not by themselves have provided sufficient material for a successful decipherment. Evans himself realized that the chances of reading them without a bilingual were almost non-existent, since he thought that they were written in an unknown 'Eteocretan' or 'Anatolian' language where the words, even if one knew how they were to be pronounced, would remain meaningless.

The only certain facts were established by Evans at the outset: the tablets were all inventories of persons, animals and commodities; these were indicated by pictorial 'ideograms' and counted by a decimal system of numbers, while the introductory wording of the tablets consisted of sign-groups of two to seven letters which were evidently words of the 'Minoan' language. Since there were about ninety of these phonetic signs, far too numerous for an alphabet, they in all probability represented syllables (*ta te ti to tu*, etc.). This arrangement is clearly seen on a typical tablet from the 'Armoury' (fig. 2) which lists 'three CHARIOTS' after a descriptive specification of twelve words written syllabically.

The problem of decipherment posed by this new writing was too fascinating to be resisted, in spite of the fact that the published material was too small either for the breaking of the code or for the proof of a successful solution. During the half-century 1901–51 continual attempts were made by reputable scholars, by talented amateurs and by cranks of all kinds from the lunatic fringe of archaeology. Most of these followed Evans' lead in treating the 'hieroglyphs', Linear A and Linear B (and even the Phaistos disk) together as varying expressions of the same language; most of them took as their starting-point apparent similarities between 'Minoan' signs and those of the classical syllabary used for writing Cypriot Greek (whose values had been known since the seventies); and all attempted to read into the tablets a form of some language which was already known. The search for possible candidates spread over an absurdly wide area, and included Hittite, Egyptian, Basque, Albanian, Slavonic, Finnish, Hebrew and Sumerian. Apart from Evans' own work, nearly every attempt to discuss the script prior to 1944 may safely and decently be consigned to oblivion (critical bibliography by Deroy, 1948 and 1953).

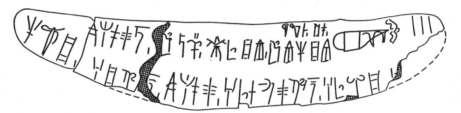

Fig. 2. Linear B 'chariot' tablet found in the Knossos 'Armoury', 1904
(for a translation, see 265 = Sd0403, p. 366).

Notable exceptions are an article by Cowley (1927) in which he showed that Knossos totals are introduced by either 𐀴𐀖 or 𐀲𐀴, and that 𐀠𐀖 and 𐀠𐀚 mean 'boy' and 'girl', conceivably a phonetic indication 'as if for κοῦ-ρος and κού-ρη' (which we now know to be correct); and the long series of articles by Sundwall, stretching from 1914 to the present. In these he has recognized the need to examine the context of the tablets by purely internal comparisons, to identify the objects represented by the ideograms, and to explore the system of numbers, fractions and measures. His suggestions for interpretation have, however, followed a somewhat lonely path due to his belief in the predominantly religious context of the tablets.

The Greek readings of the script prematurely made by Persson (1930), Hempl and Stawell (1931) appeared doubtful enough for Linear B at Knossos, in view of Evans' prevailing theories of 'Minoan supremacy'; but they were doubly suspect (as they would still be today) for the earlier Linear A and for the 'hieroglyphic' seal-stones.

Towards the end of his life the Czech orientalist Hrozný, who in 1915 had brilliantly established cuneiform Hittite as an Indo-European language and had later played a less responsible part in the reading of hieroglyphic Hittite, began to lose his critical faculties and embarked on a wholesale attack on the remaining undeciphered scripts of the world. His readings of the then-published Linear B tablets (1940–9) are a painful hotch-potch of Hittite and Babylonian words, which has proved only too easy to discredit. From this occupational disease of decoders we may all wish to be preserved.

More scholarly work was done by Fick (1905), Meillet (1909), Cuny (1910), Kannengiesser (1911), Huber (1921), Hammarström (1921) and others in trying to determine, from sources other than the Minoan-Mycenaean inscriptions, what the early languages of the Aegean might be expected to be like. They drew up lists of Greek vocabulary which seemed to have no Indo-European etymology (at least according to the evolutionary rules normal to Greek), and catalogued the many indigenous place-names of the area. Both these series are characterized by the endings *-nthos* and *-ssos* and show certain controversial analogies, not only with early names in Anatolia, but also with Etruscan; suggesting, together with the evidence of the stele from Kaminia on Lemnos, that a language in some way related to Etruscan may have been among those spoken in the Aegean before the arrival of the Greeks.

Ventris' interest in the problem dates from the 1936 exhibition arranged for the jubilee of the British School at Athens, when Evans lectured on his Minoan section of the exhibits; he tested the theory of an Etruscan relationship on the Knossos tablets in an adolescent article (1940), and did not entirely abandon it until 1952.

Kretschmer (1925) suggested that other Indo-European speakers had probably inhabited Greece before the arrival of the Greeks themselves. The Bulgar Georgiev reconstructed a 'pre-Hellenic language' (1941, 1945) similar to van Windekens' 'Pélasgique' (1952), in which the aberrant Greek words which had previously been taken as 'Aegean' borrowings are explained as Indo-European forms which have followed different evolutionary rules. In his later attempts to read the Linear B tablets in terms of this language (1949, 1950, 1953) Georgiev describes it as an 'Aegean-Asianic dialect related to Hittite', but in fact many of his readings are explained by Greek forms. In view of his recent (1954) switch to the view that the tablets contain a specifically Greek dialect identical with that described in the present book, it is as well to emphasize that his earlier quasi-Greek readings nowhere coincide with ours, and that they appear to have been arrived at by quite arbitrary and unscientific procedures.

Defying both Evans (for whom the Mycenaeans were merely Minoan invaders from Crete) and the linguists (who wished to turn them into Pelasgians, Etruscans, Illyrians or Hittites), a number of archaeologists had arrived independently at the same conclusion as Tsountas and Leaf—that the Mycenaeans had spoken (and possibly written) Greek, and that they had not been subject to any foreign domination. Disagreement with Evans contributed to Wace's retirement from the direction of the British School at Athens in 1923 and to his temporary exclusion from archaeology in the field. The articles by Buck (1926) and by Blegen and Haley (1928) emphasized the historical evidence for placing the arrival of the Greeks about 1900 B.C., and regarded the pre-Hellenic place-names in -*nthos* and -*ssos* as a legacy not of the Mycenaeans but of the Early Bronze Age pattern of settlement in the third millennium B.C. Nilsson (1927, 1932, 1933) argued that Greek religion and myth, and not only the Greek language, had firm roots in the Mycenaean age; and Blegen and Wace (1939) marshalled the archaeological evidence against a domination of Mycenae by Knossos in the Late Minoan period, with arguments further reinforced by Kantor (1947) and discussed by Wace in the Foreword to the present book.

4. THE AMERICAN CONTRIBUTION: PRELUDES TO DECIPHERMENT

In 1939, during the course of a joint Greek and American reconnaissance of western Messenia, Blegen discovered the site of a large Mycenaean palace at Ano Englianos, ten kilometres north of the classical Pylos (Koryphasion). The immediate indications were that this palace, set on an olive-covered ridge with a panoramic view over the bay of Navarino to the south and of mount Aigaleon in the east, was to be identified with the Pylos described in the third book of the *Odyssey* as the seat of the aged Nestor. By good fortune Blegen's trial trenches passed through one half of the archive room, from which over six hundred pieces of clay tablet were carefully extracted (later reduced by joins to 566). These were cleaned and mended in Athens, and admirably photographed by Alison Frantz before being buried away at the approach of war. These photographs were taken to America in June 1940 by Mrs Wace on the Italian declaration of war by the last American ship to leave the Mediterranean. The eventual editing of the tablets was entrusted to Emmett L. Bennett Jr. (without whose contributions to Mycenaean epigraphical studies this book could not have been written), but preliminary work in Cincinnati was interrupted by his cryptographic duties in the U.S. armed forces.

The seven photographs published by Blegen (1939) showed clearly, however, that the Pylos tablets were identical in script, layout and language with the Linear B documents which Evans had found at Knossos, even though the associated pottery dated them to *c.* 1200 B.C., towards the very close of the Mycenaean age. This could perhaps be explained as the survival of a Minoan scribal language or *lingua franca* (similar to the use of Latin in the Middle Ages) and as confirmation of Evans' views of Cretan influence on the Mainland: Nilsson consequently refused to believe that the tablets had been written at Pylos at all. The alternative possibility, that both the Pylos tablets *and the Knossos tablets* might be written in Greek, was not generally considered, least of all by Ventris.

'In attempting to decipher documents written in an unknown language with an unknown script, the first step is to establish the facts that are obvious from an inspection of the available documents. The second step in the decipherment is to find, by careful analysis and logical deduction, what conclusions can be drawn from these fundamental facts.' This prim but necessary programme, purposely stopping short of the third and crucial step (the attempt to substitute actual sounds and words), was undertaken by Alice Kober of Brooklyn in a series of fundamental articles on Linear B published between 1943 and her premature death in 1950.

The first necessity was an accurate list of the phonetic signs, arranged in a convenient and generally-accepted order for indexing. Though she pointed out some of Evans' errors, neither Kober nor the editors of the Pylos tablets were able to influence the awkward and unreliable signary later published by Myres (1946) and included in *Scripta Minoa II*.

She did, however, undertake for Myres a systematic classification of the Knossos tablets according to their commodity ideograms (included in *SM II*, pp. 77–89, but now superseded by Bennett's classification); and she rightly emphasized the danger of studying words or tablets in isolation without reference to these wider contexts with which they are associated.

Her chief contribution was to show that the tablets contained, as might reasonably be expected, a language with grammatical inflexions; this conclusion was unaccountably resisted by Myres (*SM II*, p. 50). Her first example was the varying description of CHARIOTS on some tablets from the 'Armoury' (now known to be a difference between dual and plural):

Sd0401: 𐀸𐀺𐀪 , 𐀸𐀪𐀨𐀸 , 𐀀𐀴𐀹 , 𐀼𐀃� 𐀠𐀤 𐀸

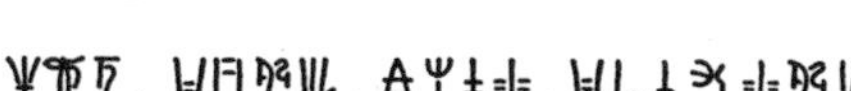

Sd0403: 𐀸𐀺𐀸 , 𐀸𐀪𐀨𐀪 , 𐀀𐀴𐀹 , 𐀼𐀃� 𐀠𐀤 𐀪

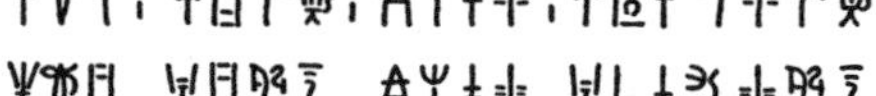

and she suggested that 'it is highly likely that the forms in –𐀨𐀸 and –𐀨𐀪 are verbal' (they are in fact passive participles). From a number of published tablets she gathered a series of words which significantly appear in three alternative forms (that the basic word is really the same in each case is proved by the fact that they recur in lists together, or in identical positions on the same class of tablets):

	Type A		Type B			C	D	E
Case I:	𐀀𐀀𐀀𐀀	𐀀𐀀𐀀𐀀	𐀀𐀀𐀀𐀀	𐀀𐀀𐀀𐀀	𐀀𐀀𐀀𐀀𐀀	𐀀𐀀𐀀𐀀	𐀀𐀀𐀀𐀀	𐀀𐀀𐀀
Case II:	𐀀𐀀𐀀𐀀	𐀀𐀀𐀀𐀀	𐀀𐀀𐀀𐀀	𐀀𐀀𐀀𐀀	𐀀𐀀𐀀𐀀𐀀	𐀀𐀀𐀀𐀀	𐀀𐀀𐀀𐀀	𐀀𐀀𐀀
Case III:	𐀀𐀀𐀀	𐀀𐀀𐀀	𐀀𐀀𐀀	𐀀𐀀𐀀	𐀀𐀀𐀀𐀀	𐀀𐀀𐀀	𐀀𐀀	𐀀𐀀

Of these triplets Case III is the shortest form, whereas Case I and Case II regularly add the signs -𐀀 and -𐀀 respectively; in this process the -𐀀 of all the Type A words is changed to -𐀀-, and the -𐀀 of Type B to -𐀀-; similar changes are seen in Types C, D and E. Kober pointed out the interesting implications of this phenomenon by the analogy of another inflected language, Latin (not necessarily related, of course), where words of the second declension would appear in syllabic spelling as:

ser-vu-s	*a-mi-cu-s*	*bo-nu-s*
ser-vu-m	*a-mi-cu-m*	*bo-nu-m*
ser-vi	*a-mi-ci*	*bo-ni*
ser-vo	*a-mi-co*	*bo-no*

Like the ablative endings -*vo* -*co* -*no* so too the series of parallel endings 𐀀 𐀀 𐀀 𐀀 𐀀 might be expected to share the same vowel but different consonants; whereas 𐀀/𐀀 𐀀/𐀀 etc. are probably pairs sharing the same consonant but different vowels, like *vo*/*vu*, *co*/*cu* and *no*/*nu*. This result can be tabulated in a diagrammatic form labelled by Kober 'the beginning of a tentative phonetic pattern', and known familiarly as 'the grid' among the team of decoders. This diagram has been of fundamental importance throughout the process of decipherment. Other examples of inflexion, as well as other variations and errors in spelling, give evidence of further pairs of signs which evidently share either the same vowel or the same consonant; and with these the 'grid' can be extended in both directions as far as the number of possible vowels or consonants will allow (in our case five vowels and thirteen consonants, as it turned

	VOWEL	
	1	2
CONSONANT 1	𐀀	𐀀
CONSONANT 2	𐀀	𐀀
CONSONANT 3	𐀀	𐀀
CONSONANT 4	𐀀	𐀀
CONSONANT 5	𐀀	𐀀

out). During this process, the grid conveniently takes the form of a wooden board covered with a regular pattern of nails, on which square labels bearing the signs of the syllabary can be hung and frequently rearranged to suit the developing evidence. In the end we are left with a well-covered chequerboard

of some sixty-five squares, from which all that is lacking is the actual pronunciation of the vowels and consonants themselves (fig. 3). This method of
attack precludes random attempts to give a premature vocalization to isolated
words (since every assumed syllabic value automatically leads to a 'chain-
reaction' among the signs which are grouped with it on the same vertical and
horizontal columns), and makes it easy to disprove any such arbitrary attempts
by others.

Also of great importance was Kober's demonstration (1949) that the words
for 'total' 𐀴 𐀴, like those for 'child' identified by Cowley 𐀀 𐀀, are
masculine and feminine variants of the same words. Of the surviving languages
with which that of Linear B might be compared, the Indo-European are almost
alone in forming feminines by a change of vowel in the ending rather than by
the addition of an extra syllable: some I.-E. languages, such as Hittite and its
relatives, anticipate the evolution of English and Danish in having no feminine
forms at all, while the Semitic dialects add -(a)tu, Egyptian -(e)t.

Kober recognized that -𐀁 was a frequent ending in the descriptions of
WOMEN, but did not see the feminine function of her Case I; it was left to
Sundwall (1948) to recognize in the -𐀁/-𐀶 endings of Case I and Case II
an adjectival formation meaning 'belonging to'.

A parallel analysis of the Pylos material was summarized by Bennett in his
unpublished doctoral dissertation at Cincinnati (1947), which we have not
seen. The publication of the *The Pylos Tablets* (spring 1951) contained a detailed
grouping of the texts according to their ideogram context by means of prefixes
Aa- Ab-, etc., and the first reliable sign-lists (whose order is preserved in
figs. 9 and 10). Both these advances were later extended to the Knossos
material in his *Minoan Linear B Index* (1953). In his first published article
(1950) Bennett brilliantly explained and codified the Linear B system of
written weights and measures (see below, pp. 53–5), and added them to the
evidence for believing with Kober (1948) that Linear B at Knossos represents
a new language introduced from without.

The seven further Pylos tablets which thereby received advance publication
in 1950 encouraged Ventris to begin a new series of analytical studies of his
own, for which the material had previously seemed too small. These were
continued in twenty mimeographed *Work Notes* (of which no spare copies
remain) circulated for discussion among two dozen colleagues between January
1951 and June 1952. Several of these were taken up with the unproductive
testing of 'Aegean' and Etruscan parallels (Greek readings still being regarded
as out of the question, in spite of a hint by Bennett); but other Notes which
now seem to have been on the main line of progress may perhaps be mentioned

here. They no doubt re-trod much of the ground covered in his dissertation by Bennett, with whom a fruitful exchange of views on decipherment technique was maintained over the period.

Notes 2 and 10 showed that the ending -⊕ found linking groups of Linear B words is an enclitic conjunction 'and', and that ᴎ ꜰ ⊕ (now 'and *not*') has a similar function.

Note 8 gave statistics for the frequency of each phonetic sign at Pylos, broken down by position into initial, medial and final; this necessary calculation was repeated independently by Bennett (1951 *b*) and later extended to Knossos by Ktistopoulos (1954). The great frequency of ᶣ- ᴎ- ᴀ- as initials suggested, on the analogy of the statistics resulting from other known syllabaries, that they were the signs for simple vowels by themselves; and for the first two the values *a*- (already guessed privately by Kober, Chadwick and Ktistopoulos) and *i*- were considered.

Note 11 drew attention to two alternating phrases ⧧ᴮʳ, ꜰᴀᵻ and ⧧ᴮʳ, ꜰᴀ ᴸₑ on the long series of Pylos *E*- tablets (see nos. **108–154** below) and showed them to be male and female variants of a title meaning something like 'manservant' and 'maidservant of the ⧧ᴮ-'. A possible *do-we-lo* (cf. δοῦλος) for ꜰᴀᵻ was thrown in as a wild guess, always of course on the assumption that the 'Minoan' word had been later borrowed by Greek. The personal names which were qualified by ꜰᴀᵻ and ꜰᴀ ᴸₑ clearly had distinct endings (as on the Knossos lists of personnel accompanied by the MAN or WOMAN sign, pointed out by Evans, *PM*, IV, pp. 714–15), the males characteristically in -ᵺ -ꞙ -ᵻ -ꜰᶠ, the females in -ᴮ (cf. Kober's Case I). That ꝙᴎᵎ meant 'boy, son' and not 'girl, daughter' was shown by such Pylos tablets as Ad03:

$$\text{ᵞꜰꝙꞙᵻ} \quad \text{ᴤᵞᴮʳ, ᵸᴮᴮʳ, ꝙᴎᵎ} \quad \text{ᴤ ''' ꝙᴎᵎ '''}$$

where three MEN and nine 'boys' are all described as 'sons of the Such-and-such women'; the words used to describe the women, which on the *Aa*- and *Ab*- tablets with a WOMAN ideogram are spelt ᴤᵞᴮ, ᵸᴮᴮ, here have a -ᴮʳ (-*i*??) added, which is evidently the mark of the genitive plural for feminines.

Note 12 attempted a functional classification of the Pylos sign-groups, purely on the basis of an exhaustive comparison of their contexts, into:

(*a*) Apparent personal names of men and women.
(*b*) Apparent names of departments, institutions or places.
(*c*) Names of trades and titles applied to men and women.
(*d*) General vocabulary, including adjectives, verbs, etc.

As typical of category (*b*) were quoted the nine names which are repeatedly listed at Pylos (e.g. on **75** = Cn02, **257** = Jn09, **250** = Vn01), and which, as we afterwards discovered, Blegen and Bennett had already tentatively compared either with the nine towns tributary to Nestor in the Catalogue of Ships or with the nine ἕδραι in which the men of Pylos sacrificed on the seashore (*Od.* III, 7).

It was pointed out that the characteristic 'inflexion' in -ΛΗ, -ΛР of Kober's triplets seemed to be confined to words of category (*b*), and might therefore be an adjective formation of a departmental or geographical kind.

Notes 1, 13, 14 reviewed the now much fuller evidence for inflexion, and showed that men's names are declined in at least six different 'declensions', generally predictable from the last syllable of the nominative:

NOMINATIVE:	𐄁	𐄁	𐄁	𐄁	𐄁	𐄁
GENITIVE:						
'PREPOSITIONAL':						

The same rules of declension evidently applied to sign-groups of categories (*c*) and (*d*), names of trades and other vocabulary; and where there were numerals on the tablets it was possible to distinguish between singular and plural forms:

SINGULAR:								
PLURAL:								

The four examples on the right show an added syllable in the spelling, conceivably the written indication of an inflexion such as the Greek

SINGULAR:	τέκτων	= *te-ko-to-ne*	or	*tek-ton?*
PLURAL:	τέκτονες	= *te-ko-to-ne-se*	or	*tek-ton-es?*

But the lack of change shown by the first four plurals was surprising. If 𐄁 really was κοῦρος (*κόρϝος) as Cowley had guessed, then the spellings could only be justified by assuming that *kor-wos* and *kor-woi* were written with exactly the same letters, and not distinguished as they would be by the fuller Cypriot spelling *ko-ro-vo-se* and *ko-ro-vo-i*. The lack of a regular written sign to indicate the expected nominative ending -*s* in men's names and vocabulary nouns seemed in fact to militate against Greek or a related Indo-European language.

Note 9 listed scribal variations in spelling such as 𐄁/𐄁, 𐄁/𐄁, etc., which enabled the alternating letters to be given adjacent positions on the grid. This note also considered how the inflexions could be explained in terms of Etruscan declension, which began to appear more and more unsuited.

Notes 1, 15, 17 illustrated successive stages in the build-up of the grid, and gave the criteria by which the different columns were arranged. A detailed summary of evidence for grid equations was printed in *JHS*, 1953, pp. 87–8, and may now be supplemented from the new Pylos material published by Bennett (1955). Fig. 3 shows the state of the grid in February 1952. There was still uncertainty about the number of vowel columns to be allowed, and some signs were put into two alternative squares; but in spite of its incomplete nature the grid had the virtue of being founded entirely on internal evidence dispassionately sifted, and not on any biased attempt to identify the language or give values to the signs.

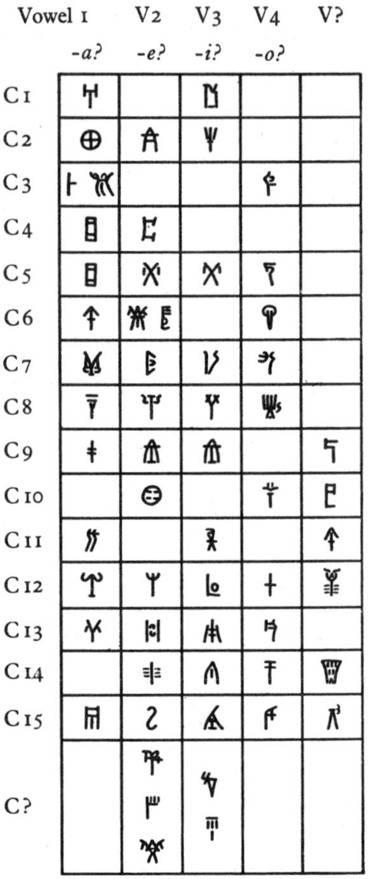

But almost inevitably certain 'hunches' about possible phonetic values lurked at the back of Ventris' mind. ⊬ and ⫚ were simple vowels, and initial ⊬– was almost certainly *a*-. The ending of the feminine adjectives in Kober's Case I in –⋀⊟, etc., might well be *-i-ja* (since derivative women's names in *-ia* occur in Greek, Lycian and Etruscan): in this case Vowel 3 (in ⋀, ⋔, etc.) was *-i*, and Vowel 1 was *-a*. Vowel 2 might be *-e*, if the very numerous men's names in –⦀ƒ –⫚ƒ –⋎ƒ, etc., were ancestral to Greek -εύς (Note 16); and Vowel 4 might then be left with the value *-o*.

The value of the consonants was much more difficult to guess. It was tempting to compare Cypriot values (see fig. 12), but clearly unrealistic: ⧻ might be taken at its Cypriot value of *pa*, but then it was impossible to read ⫞, in quite another line of the grid, as *pe* by the same analogy. Consonants 11–12 might, however, be *l-* or *r-*, since they seemed to enter into inflexional variations of spelling involving two successive syllables, possibly of the type *-tro-/-tri-*, etc., which Cypriot would have to spell *-to-ro-/-ti-ri-*, etc.

	Vowel 1	V2	V3	V4	V?
	-a?	*-e?*	*-i?*	*-o?*	
C1	⊬		◻		
C2	⊕	⋀	⫚		
C3	⊢ ⫶⫶			⫯	
C4	⊟	⫞			
C5	⊟	⋊	⋊	⋎	
C6	⬆	⫶⫶ ⫞		⬤	
C7	⋈	⫞	⫶	⋇	
C8	⋎	⫝	⫝	⫶⫶	
C9	⧻	⬆	⬆		⫰
C10		⊖		⫟	⫞
C11	⫶		⫟		⬆
C12	⫝	⫝	⫞	⫯	⫶
C13	⋊	⫞	⋔	⫞	
C14		⫶⫶	⋀	⫯	⫟
C15	⫝	⫞	⋀	ƒ	⋊
C?		⫝⫝ ⫟ ⋊	⫶ ⫰		

Fig. 3. The state of the 'grid' prior to decipherment (February 1952).

5. JUNE 1952: THE LANGUAGE IS GREEK

Myres' edition of the Knossos tablets appeared in February 1952, two years before his death. That *Scripta Minoa II* is incomplete, unwieldy and in many respects inaccurate is not due to any lowering of his own high standard of scholarship, but results from the enormous difficulty of interpreting and reconciling Evans' notes after his death, from the inaccessibility of the Cretan originals during the war years, and from his own failing eyesight. Although a few corrections provided by the first of Bennett's two long visits to Iraklion in 1950 and 1954 were included in *SM II*, the edition cannot safely be used without taking into account Bennett's privately-distributed *Corrections of Scripta Minoa II* (1952) dealing with errors in page, tablet and sign numbering; his revised Knossos vocabulary incorporated in the *Index* (1953), which also references a thousand more fragmentary tablets not recorded by Evans; some three hundred joins made by Bennett between Knossos tablets in 1954; and the discovery of some further fragments at Iraklion by Chadwick in 1955. The latter have now been incorporated in *The Knossos Tablets* (1956).

Though relatively little new evidence for inflexion could be found on the Knossos tablets now added to the material, nearly all of it tended to confirm the arrangement of the grid shown in fig. 3. There was one puzzling feature: while some vocabulary words (like ⟨Linear B⟩/⟨Linear B⟩) showed a reasonable spelling variation in their ending between –⟨sign⟩ (*-ja* ?) and –⟨sign⟩ (*-a* ?), there were also others of the same type (like ⟨Linear B⟩/⟨Linear B⟩ on the CHARIOT tablets) which showed an apparently indifferent variation between –⟨sign⟩ (*-šo* ??) and –⟨sign⟩ (*-i* ?). In an effort to introduce a more satisfactory symmetry into this corner of the grid Ventris took up again the value *jo* for ⟨sign⟩, which had been summarily rejected in Note 9, and assumed the following pattern:

$$⟨sign⟩ \quad a \qquad ⟨sign⟩ \quad ja \qquad\qquad ⟨sign⟩ \quad o \qquad ⟨sign⟩ \quad jo$$

This would have three important consequences. The frequent -⟨sign⟩ or -⟨sign⟩⟨sign⟩ in the ending of men's names in the genitive (Note 14) would become -(*o*)*jo* and -(*i*)*jojo* and recall Homeric forms like Αὐτολύκοιο and Ἰκαρίοιο; the feminine genitive plural ending –⟨sign⟩⟨sign⟩ (Note 11) would become -(*i*)-*ja-o* and suggest the archaic γαιάων, θεάων, etc.; and it would be possible to transcribe the first five of Kober's triplets quoted on p. 16 (using numbers 'algebraically' for the unknown consonants) as:

$L.-^6i-^{14}i\text{-}ja$	$^9a-^2i-^{14}i\text{-}ja$	$..-li-^{13}i\text{-}ja$	$^6o-^8o-^{13}i\text{-}ja$	$A-^7i-^8i-^{13}i\text{-}ja$
$L.-^6i-^{14}i\text{-}jo$	$^9a-^2i-^{14}i\text{-}jo$	$..-li-^{13}i\text{-}jo$	$^6o-^8o-^{13}i\text{-}jo$	$A-^7i-^8i-^{13}i\text{-}jo$
$L.-^6i-^{14}o$	$^9a-^2i-^{14}o$	$..-li-^{13}o$	$^6o-^8o-^{13}o$	$A-^7i-^8i-^{13}o$

It did not require very great imagination to realize that if one substituted the values $6=k$, $7=m$, $8=n$, $9=p$, $13=s$, and $14=t$, one would be left with the names of five of the most important Cretan towns (including the capital) in the bottom line, and above these the feminine and masculine adjectives derived from them:

Λύκτιαι	Φαίστιαι	Τυλίσιαι	Κνώσιαι	’Αμνίσιαι
Λύκτιοι	Φαίστιοι	Τυλίσιοι	Κνώσιοι	’Αμνίσιοι
Λύκτος	Φαιστός	Τυλισός	Κνωσός	’Αμνισός

By the inevitable 'chain-reaction' thirty-one of the signs on the grid would thereby receive fixed phonetic values. Note 20 (June 1952, the last of the series) discussed this new line of attack and suggested a small number of vocabulary identifications: ⟨signs⟩ = κόρϝος, ⟨signs⟩ = κόρϝα, ⟨signs⟩ = κορίαννον 'coriander', ⟨signs⟩ = κορίαννα, ⟨signs⟩ = τόσσοι 'so many', ⟨signs⟩ = τόσσαι, and ⟨signs⟩, ⟨signs⟩ on the CHARIOT tablets = ἀραρυῖαι ἁνίαφι 'fitted with reins'. It ended, however, with the admission that these Greek words were probably a mirage, and that the proposed spelling rules, according to which final -s -n -r were not indicated at all, seemed contrary to reasonable expectation.

But while Note 20 was still in the post Ventris realized, from the application of the new phonetic values to a larger number of tablets, that the unexpected Greek solution was inescapable. Not only could vocabulary words be identified (like the trades *po-me*, gen. *po-me-no*, 'shepherd', *ka-ke-u* 'smith', *ke-ra-me-u* 'potter', *ka-na-pe-u* 'fuller', *i-e-re-u* 'priest', *i-je-re-ja* 'priestess') which exactly tallied with their functions as predicted in Note 12 (see p. 18); but the inflexions codified over the past eighteen months could immediately be explained in terms of archaic Greek declension; and some sense could already be made of complete sentences, notably on Pylos **31** = Ae04, **28** = An42, **253** = Jn01 and **252** = Vn06. It was at this stage that Myres put Ventris in touch with John Chadwick, who had been working independently on Linear B in Oxford for six years and whose cryptographic flair and specialist knowledge of the Greek dialects have been invaluable in all our subsequent collaboration.

Largely through the good offices of T. J. Dunbabin (whose tragic early death has occurred since this chapter was drafted) space was found in *JHS* for a detailed article (*Evidence*, etc.), completed in November 1952. In this we identified the Linear B language as a Greek dialect ancestral to Arcado-Cyprian, proposed a large number of interpretations, and published a table of sign values which, apart from a few additions, is identical with that here printed in fig. 4.

As we wrote then (p. 90), 'with no bilingual or other external aids to decipherment available, the reality of a proposed transliteration can only be tested by applying it to the material as a whole. If consistent series of vocabulary and grammatical forms result, which are in agreement with the probable context of the tablets, then we may be justified in believing that even those features which remain intractable will eventually be accounted for.'

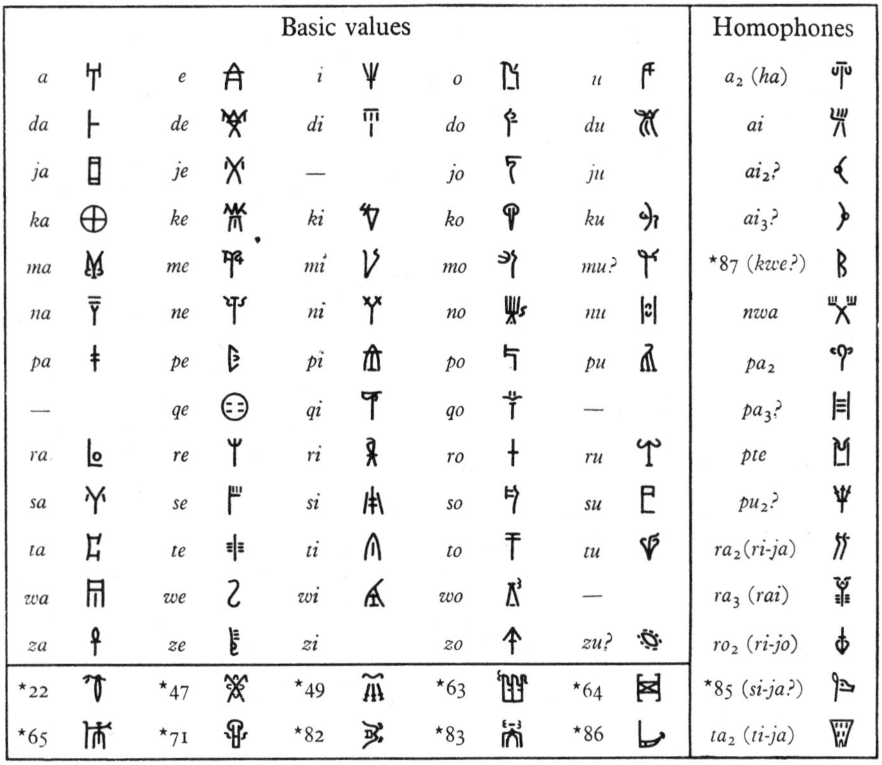

Basic values					Homophones	
a	e	i	o	u	a_2 (ha)	
da	de	di	do	du	ai	
ja	je	— jo		ju	ai_2?	
ka	ke	ki	ko	ku	ai_3?	
ma	me	mi	mo	mu?	*87 (kwe?)	
na	ne	ni	no	nu	nwa	
pa	pe	pi	po	pu	pa_2	
—	qe	qi	qo	—	pa_3?	
ra	re	ri	ro	ru	pte	
sa	se	si	so	su	pu_2?	
ta	te	ti	to	tu	ra_2 (ri-ja)	
wa	we	wi	wo	—	ra_3 (rai)	
za	ze	zi	zo	zu?	ro_2 (ri-jo)	
*22	*47	*49	*63	*64	*85 (si-ja?)	
*65	*71	*82	*83	*86	ta_2 (ti-ja)	

Fig. 4. Proposed values of the Mycenaean syllabary.

Similar reservations must be made today, for the much larger number of texts discussed in the present book. It may be difficult to assess the point at which ultimate scientific proof can be conceded, but a relative degree of certainty must be granted to the theory when we try to estimate the odds against its results having been obtained by chance, and when we consider the success with which it has been used by independent researchers to interpret new texts, unknown when it was first formulated.

6. THE WIDENING OF THE RANKS

The reception of our proposed Greek decipherment by our fellow linguists and archaeologists was immeasurably more favourable than might have been expected, considering the enormous number of ill-considered attempts which had been prematurely publicized over the past fifty years. Already before the publication of *Evidence*, lectures and an advanced summary had secured the allegiance of Björck and Furumark at Uppsala and of Palmer at Oxford: their many valuable contributions to the readings of the signs and to the interpretation of the tablets (together with those put forward by other scholars mentioned below) are fully referenced in our bibliography for the period up to May 1955, and are as far as possible evaluated and acknowledged in the commentary and vocabulary of the present book. Welcome encouragement was also given at this stage by Barnett, Düring, Gelb, Myres, Page, Säflund and others.

Three other works, already in manuscript or proof when *Evidence* appeared, independently came to a similar conclusion from a different approach to the evidence. Dow (1954) in a long survey of *Minoan Writing*, devoted largely to delimiting the extent of Linear A and Linear B literacy, described 'the reasonings which in spring 1953 forced themselves upon me as decisive in favor of the then (otherwise) unproved hypothesis that Linear B was Greek'. Miss Henle's dissertation (1953) argued on historical grounds that 'the language of Class B is probably Greek', and supplied a comparative analysis of syllabic frequencies in Linear B and in Homeric Greek. It did not arrive at any useful phonetic values, due to her failure to undertake any detailed study of inflexion and context, or to recognize the usefulness of the grid procedure. Wace (1953, written 1951) hinted that the Pylos and Knossos tablets might both be written in Greek and that 'perhaps in Late Minoan II a Mainland Dynasty had gained power in Crete'—a suggestion already made by him in 1938 (Pendlebury (1939), p. 229). He was therefore particularly ready to accept the conclusions published in *Evidence*; so too were Stubbings, to whom a similar view of Knossos had occurred, and Marinatos (1953). Criticism from a 'Minoan' partisan was levelled in a review by Platon (1954), director of the Iraklion Museum.

Although Ventris' first 1952 proposals had received encouragement from Blegen as fitting his own view of the Mainland language and of the probable contexts of the tablets, he was cautious about accepting them in detail. Bennett too reserved judgment: 'I think there is not yet enough material available to make a deciphering of these tablets certain one way or the other. Michael

Ventris' theory that the language of the Minoan tablets is very early Greek is a tempting possibility; that is all I would say at this stage' (interview 20 November 1952).

Their caution was justified by a new factor which now had to be taken into consideration. That summer Blegen had resumed excavation at Pylos, and the material had been extended by a large number of new tablets (eventually 333 when mends and joins had been made); these had not yet been cleaned sufficiently for study. Smaller finds of tablets were repeated at Pylos in 1953, 1954 and 1955. At Mycenae, too, a tablet had been found on the surface by Petsas in 1950. In 1952 Wace unearthed thirty-eight more in the 'House of the Oil Merchant' (significantly the first series to be found apparently outside of the royal palaces), later edited by Bennett (1953). These were followed in 1953 by one tablet from the 'House of Shields' and inscribed seal-impressions from the 'House of Sphinxes'; the latter in 1954 yielded ten more tablets, edited by Bennett (1956) with vocabulary notes by Chadwick.

On his return to Athens in the spring of 1953 Blegen examined the new Pylos tablets in detail, and was able to send us (16 May 1953) exciting news of tablet **236** = Ta641 which 'evidently deals with pots, some on three legs, some with four handles, some with three, and others without handles. The first word ⚟ by your system seems to be *ti-ri-po-de*, and it recurs twice as *ti-ri-po* (singular?). The four-handled pot ⚏ is preceded by *qe-to-ro-we*, the three-handled ⚏ by *ti-ri-o-we-e* or *ti-ri-jo-we*, the handleless pot ♀ by *a-no-we*. All this seems too good to be true. Is coincidence excluded?'

Almost simultaneously (22 May 1953) and without knowledge of Blegen's discovery, Sittig announced to us the generous abandonment of his own previous attempt to decipher Linear B (1951), and by a remarkable coincidence drew attention to the ideogram ⚐ on Knossos **232** = K 875: this is there described as *di-pa a-no-wo-to*, which he rightly suggested reading as δέπας ἀνούατον 'goblet without a handle'. ἀνούατον and the Pylos *a-no-we* = ἀνῶϝες could easily be explained as variants of the same compound adjective, and gave additional force to Blegen's identifications.

Blegen gave **236** = Ta641 advance publication (1953) and it was further discussed by Ventris (1954 *a*). This striking new evidence reinforced the arguments of *Evidence*, and brought agreement in principle from Bennett, Carratelli, Chantraine, Daux, Dumézil, Friedrich, Georgiev, Lejeune, Meriggi, Peruzzi, Sundwall and others. In January 1954 London University's new Institute of Classical Studies followed Uppsala's example in beginning (under Turner and Webster) a useful seminar on Linear B studies, which among other subjects has debated the phonological theories advanced by Andrews (see p. 46), and has produced duplicated editions of the Pylos and Knossos tablets in transcription. Later in the year a similar seminar was instituted in Paris by Lejeune and Chantraine, who with Gelb had given generous support at the international congress for classical studies in Copenhagen in August 1954; and similar interest was taken in Switzerland. In Russia Tiumenev (1954) invoked the new decipherment in an attack on Georgiev's earlier theory of the Mycenaean language situation.

Bennett's edition of the 1952, 1953 and 1954 Pylos tablets (*PT II*, 1955) provided much new material for study, special interest being aroused by the other tablets of the *Ta* group to which the 'tripods' belong (see **235–247**, ch. x); this series, with its vivid descriptions of Mycenaean furniture, was discussed in an article by Ventris (1955). Meanwhile Evans and Myres' edition of the Knossos tablets was corrected from the originals in Iraklion Museum in successive visits by Bennett, Chadwick and Ventris, during which a large number of joins were made, and over two thousand unpublished fragments were cleaned and catalogued (nos. 5000–6068 and 7000–8075).

The welcome co-operation of so many specialists will inevitably take the interpretation of the Mycenaean documents far beyond the tentative translations printed in Part II of this book. But in case too optimistic a picture may seem to have been painted of the prospects of 'total decipherment', it may be as well to end this historical survey with a summary of the limitations to our understanding which are likely to remain in force unless a much larger number (and preferably a different kind) of texts can be unearthed in the future.

1. Since the tablets are without exception administrative records of a summary and abbreviated kind (inventories, catalogues, accounts and nominal rolls, consisting largely of proper names), we must resign ourselves to the complete absence of literary or historical matter; to a very one-sided vocabulary deficient in verbs, adverbs, prepositions and pronouns; and to only the simplest patterns of syntax.

2. For a sign to be allotted a fixed syllabic value it must occur in a vocabulary word (not merely in a personal name!) whose Greek identification is absolutely certain from the context; or be found in a larger number of words whose identification is at least probable; or else be shown to alternate regularly with a sign whose value is already known. There are obviously a number of syllabic signs, especially those confined to proper names, to which we may never be in a position to assign a value; these are shown in the bottom section of fig. 4.

3. Even when we can transliterate our text mechanically into syllables, we are still a long way from reading it. Owing to the latitude allowed by the spelling rules (see pp. 42–8) the same sign-groups may often with equal justification be read as quite different Greek words: thus *pa-te* as either πατήρ or πάντες, *pa-si* as φᾱσί or πᾶνσι, and so on.

4. Though we will probably not be justified in invoking the presence of many 'Minoan' or 'Aegean' loan-words on the tablets (*-inthos* and *-ssos* do not seem to be any commoner than in later times), their vocabulary inevitably contains many word-stems, derivatives and compounds which are very much further removed from 'normal' classical Greek than the unfamiliar glosses recorded by Hesychius as late as the fifth century A.D. To have to interpret them is rather like trying to read Chaucer with only a knowledge of twentieth-century English. Comparative philology is of great use in helping us to infer the probable Mycenaean forms of known classical words, but is notoriously misleading (as has been proved in the study of Hittite, Phrygian and Messapian) in suggesting meanings for unfamiliar words on the basis of analogies in other Indo-European languages.

5. Except where they are clearly pictorial (like MEN, WOMEN, CHARIOTS and TRIPODS) the meanings of the ideograms and other abbreviations are impossible to guess unless there are generous clues in the context.

6. Even where the dictionary meaning of the words on the tablets can be established with certainty (for example in a phrase like 'the smiths do not give' on **176** = Ma12), this is no guarantee that we can understand the full significance of such a remark; and the actual situation or transaction which the scribe is recording can sometimes only be guessed at with the aid of very distant analogies.

7. The inherent difficulty of reading these ancient syllabic texts can be appreciated by comparing the results achieved on the classical Cypriot inscriptions (see Mitford, 1952). Though written in a known Greek dialect and in a syllabary whose values have been established since the 1870's, many of them are still as full of uncertainties as, for instance, the notorious Golgi inscription (Schwyzer, *Dial.* 685[1]):

> *ka-i-re-te   ka-ra-si-ti   va-na-xe   ka-po-ti   ve-po-me-ka   me-po-te-ve-i-se-se*
> *te-o-i-se   po-ro-a-ta-na-to-i-se   e-re-ra-me-na   pa-ta-ko-ra-i-to-se*
> *o-vo-ka-re-ti   e-pi-si-ta-i-se   a-to-ro-po   te-o-i   a-le-tu-ka-ke-re*
> *te-o-i   ku-me-re-na-i   pa-ta   ta-a-to-ro-po-i   po-ro-ne-o-i   ka-i-re-te*

CHAPTER II

THE MYCENAEAN WRITING SYSTEM

1. CHRONOLOGICAL TABLE

HIEROGLYPHS	*c.* 2000 B.C.	Foundation of palaces at Knossos and Mallia.
	c. 2000–1925	MIDDLE MINOAN I a.
	c. 1925–1850	MIDDLE MINOAN I b.
	c. 1850–1700	MIDDLE MINOAN II (Knossos and Phaistos only).
	c. 1700	1st destruction level at Knossos (Evans).
	c. 1700–1660	MIDDLE MINOAN III a.
	c. 1660	1st destruction level at Mallia (Chapouthier), Phaistos (Banti). Minor earthquake at Knossos (Evans).
LINEAR A	*c.* 1660–1580	MIDDLE MINOAN III b.
	c. 1600	2nd destruction level at Knossos only.
	c. 1580–1510	LATE MINOAN I a. Minor earthquake at Knossos (Evans).
	c. 1510–1450	LATE MINOAN I b.
		2nd destruction level at Phaistos, Agia Triada, Mallia?
LINEAR B	*c.* 1450–1405	LATE MINOAN II (Knossos only). 3rd destruction level at Knossos.
	MAINLAND:	
	c. 1405–1340	LATE HELLADIC III a.
	c. 1340–1200	LATE HELLADIC III b.
		Destruction of Pylos, and Mycenae sites outside citadel.
?	*c.* 1200–1100	LATE HELLADIC III c. Destruction level at Mycenae (citadel).

2. ORIGINS: THE CRETAN 'HIEROGLYPHIC' SCRIPT

It is not easy to arrive at a detailed understanding of the way in which the earlier Minoan scripts originated and developed. The 'hieroglyphic' and Linear A inscriptions are few and undeciphered, and archaeologists are not in full agreement on the relative dating of objects and events in different Cretan palaces. In the absence of historical records, the Minoan 'periods' are primarily intended to differentiate pottery styles: one of the styles in the sequence may be lacking at a particular site, or several may be found in use together.

It is certain, however, that the Minoan 'hieroglyphic' seal-stones—the first

28

evidence found by Evans in the nineties—represent the beginnings of writing in Crete. Since most of these signets are surface finds from various parts of the island, their dating cannot be exact; but the earliest 'hieroglyphic' seal-impressions from the pre-Palatial 'Vat Room deposit' are assigned by Evans to MM Ia (*PM*, I, p. 171). Seal-stones engraved with groups of one to six signs of a more advanced 'hieroglyphic' script ('Class B') came into general use in MM II; and a cursive form of this script began to be incised on clay, mostly in the form of circular labels or rectangular bars, both of these being pierced for attachment by strings.

In its early use the script thus served mainly as a means of identification, discharging more efficiently the function of the owners', potters', bronze-founders' and masons' marks of an earlier period; such marks, like those in use down to the classical period, must be clearly distinguished from writing in the true sense of the word, and their forms generally have only a fortuitous resemblance to alphabetic or linear writing signs. In their shapes the Cretan 'hieroglyphs' probably show some influence from Egyptian models, either by way of imported scarabs and other small objects, or resulting from the actual observations of merchants travelling in the wake of the Kamares pottery now being exported in quantity (Kantor, 1947, p. 18). There are few specific identities, however, and we need not suppose that the actual principles of Egyptian writing were uncritically adopted—that unwieldy combination of ideographic, phonetic and determinative signs within the same word, common to those writing systems which remained in the 'word-syllabic' stage (Gelb, 1952, p. 194), e.g.

EGYPTIAN: $\cancel{}$ *wśr-ś-r-*^{activity} = *waśr* 'strong'.

HITTITE: $\cancel{}$ ^{god}-STORMGOD-*ḫu-ta-s* = 'Storm god Tarḫuntas'.

From *c.* 2200 B.C. onwards Syria and Palestine were the scene of successive experiments in the design of a writing system which was eventually to oust all its competitors. From the beginning this West Semitic model was entirely phonetic, without ideograms; and from the quasi-syllabic stage of the Byblos script (Dhorme, 1948) it rapidly passed, influenced by the structure of the Semitic languages, to the stage of the Phoenician and Ugaritic 'consonantal alphabets' or, as Gelb prefers it, 'syllabaries without vowels'. Evans is probably right in deducing from the small number of signs that the Cretan 'hieroglyphs' were also predominantly phonetic in value (*SM I*, p. 247). The earliest Minoan script may have been deliberately designed as a syllabary; but it is useless to argue, as many have done, a direct Minoan influence on the Phoenician scripts, which are earlier in origins and more sophisticated in principle.

From the small number of 'hieroglyphic' inscriptions found, Dow (1954) argues that 'there is no ground for imagining that literacy existed in any developed sense'. Though the absence of durable and monumental records, so strikingly in contrast with most of the contemporary cultures, is a characteristic of all periods of Minoan-Mycenaean life, his conclusion may well be valid for this early period.

An incomplete list of 'hieroglyphic' signs was printed by Evans in *SM I*, p. 232 and *PM*, I, p. 282. To the use of an embryonic syllabary for spelling out names and titles, the requirements of the palace administration added two mechanisms which were to remain characteristic of all later Aegean inscriptions:

1. The development of a list of standard *ideograms* as abbreviations for the commodities being counted, and as a more graphic indication of the tablets'

Fig. 5. 'Hieroglyphic' tablet from Phaistos.

contents to the non-literate members of the household. With doubtful exceptions, ideograms (in the sense of symbols which stand for a definite word-meaning rather than for a conventional sound-value) *only occur with numerals* in all three Aegean scripts, never in the spelling of ordinary words or sentences. Evans and Myres were often deluded by the more naturalistic signs into giving them a symbolic value, which their frequency and use in different positions render most unlikely.

2. A written system of numerals and fractions. In this respect the 'hieroglyphic' script differs in its conventions from those of the Linear Scripts.

1,234 is written ◊ \\:))))

and the fractional quantities appear in the forms *ℓ ƭ ƫ* (or ſ ſ), which may represent $\frac{1}{2}$ $\frac{1}{4}$ $\frac{1}{8}$ (*ƭ* and ſ are ideograms).

The tablet illustrated in fig. 5 was an unstratified find at Phaistos (Pernier, 1935, p. 425). After a word of two signs, the top line records quantities of

$20\frac{1}{2}$(?) units of each of the commodities 𝌆 𐊹 𐊺 𐊻. These four staples, which there is reason to believe represent WHEAT, OIL, OLIVES and FIGS, recur with similar symbols in both Linear A and Linear B (see p. 35). The second may be a simplification of Evans' 'jug and olive-spray' sign.

The Knossos 'hieroglyphic archives' consist of nineteen lumps of clay sealed with inscribed signets, and of sixty-three clay sealings tablets, bars or labels, found in the earth fill of a chamber under the staircase at the north end of the long corridor to the magazines (R on fig. 13, p. 115). First assigned by Evans to 'within the limits of MM III' (SM I, p. 21, dating the fill of the chamber to the second destruction), the documents were later placed entirely within MM II, the use of the 'hieroglyphs' ceasing abruptly with the end of this period (PM, I, p. 612). This conclusion is doubted by Chapouthier (1930), and is based on no very certain stratigraphic evidence.

3. LINEAR SCRIPT A

Both the cause and date of the introduction of Linear A are uncertain. A desire to simplify the naturalistic forms of the 'hieroglyphs' for hurried writing on clay is hardly sufficient reason, since even Linear B still contains a fair proportion of complex signs, of a dozen strokes or more, which perhaps reflect a calligraphic use of the script on other more perishable materials.

The earliest Linear A inscriptions were believed by Evans (PM, I, p. 612) to be those written in ink on two Knossos cups, which he dated by their shape to MM III a. The archives deposit from Mallia, discovered by Renaudin and Charbonneaux in 1923, apparently dates from the reoccupation of the palace at the beginning of MM III b, and is significant in showing a late use of the 'hieroglyphs' side by side with incipient Linear A, in one case on two sides of the same tablet. The numeration of both Mallia scripts still uses dots for the tens (a peculiarity recurring on some Agia Triada tablets) but circles for the hundreds. It is difficult to reconcile the Knossos and Mallia evidence with the discovery of two dozen tablets at Phaistos in 1953 and 1955, in a level of the First Palace dated by the excavators to MM I a, which allegedly show a transition from the 'hieroglyphic' to the linear script; for an illustration, see *Annuario della scuola archeologica italiana di Atene*, 30–32 (n.s. 14–16), p. 418.

The latest and largest group of surviving Linear A documents comprises 150 rectangular clay tablets and a number of sealings (*cretule*) found in the 'Royal Villa' at Agia Triada associated with remains of LM I a frescoes and stone jars. They cannot at any rate be later than the destruction of the villa, ascribed by Evans (PM, IV, p. 786) to 'the new and aggressive dynasty' which he believed took power at Knossos at the beginning of LM II. Carratelli similarly dates the Agia Triada tablets to before 1450 B.C.; but Pendlebury (1939, p. 228) and the Italian excavators regard the destruction of Agia Triada as contemporary with that of Knossos itself in *c.* 1405 B.C.

With very minor exceptions, all other Linear A inscriptions appear to be of MM IIIb date. They include tablets and sealings from Knossos, Phaistos, Tylissos, Zafer Papoura, Zakro and Palaikastro, and libation tables and ritual objects from these and a number of other sites (see Carratelli, pp. 590–602 and Dow, 1954, p. 113). Their total number is very small compared to the Linear B material, but the language appears to be identical throughout. Carratelli points to the word 𐘇𐘇𐘇𐘇𐘇 which occurs both on a steatite libation table from Palaikastro and on the stone ladle from near Arkhanes (Dow, p. 100), and to the word 𐘇𐘇𐘇 or 𐘇𐘇𐘇 which occurs on no less than five religious objects from different parts of the island. But of the words written entirely in signs paralleled in Linear B, there are only one or two which recur on a Knossos Linear B or Mycenaean mainland inscription. A solitary example of a possible grammatical variation may be seen by comparing]𐘇𐘇𐘇𐘇𐘇[on the fragment of a steatite libation-bowl found by Marinatos at Apodoulou (Carratelli, *Ap 1*) with]𐘇𐘇𐘇𐘇𐘇 on the piece of a steatite libation-table perhaps from Petsofá (*Pc 10*): if mechanically transcribed with their apparent Linear B values, these words would read *no-pi-na-ma-*[and *no-pi-na-mi-na*.

In spite of considerable disagreement, we are probably justified in inferring that the standardized form of Linear A came into general use at the beginning of MM IIIb, and that it did not survive the introduction of Linear B at Knossos. It is difficult to visualize the *Pa-i-to* = Phaistos of our Linear B tablets as conducting its records and its correspondence with the capital in Linear A; Dow's statement (1954, p. 120) that to the end of LM II 'the rest of the island continued to use Linear A' can, perhaps, only be true of unattested writing in the native 'Minoan' language outside the offices of the royal administration.

The Agia Triada tablets, being latest and most numerous, probably show Linear A in its most representative form: they have been used as the basis for the list of seventy-five syllabic signs published here (fig. 6), from which a few † rare Agia Triada signs of doubtful form and function have been omitted. The possible similarities which have been shown with 'Hieroglyphs' (H) or with Linear B signs (B) should not be taken to argue an identical sound-value; such an identity could only be proved by a cogent decipherment, which in view of our complete ignorance of the 'Minoan' language is probably impossible. The signs are numbered *L 1*, etc., in accordance with Carratelli (pp. 467–74); to which is added Myres' inconvenient numeration, whereby *AB 1*, etc., represent

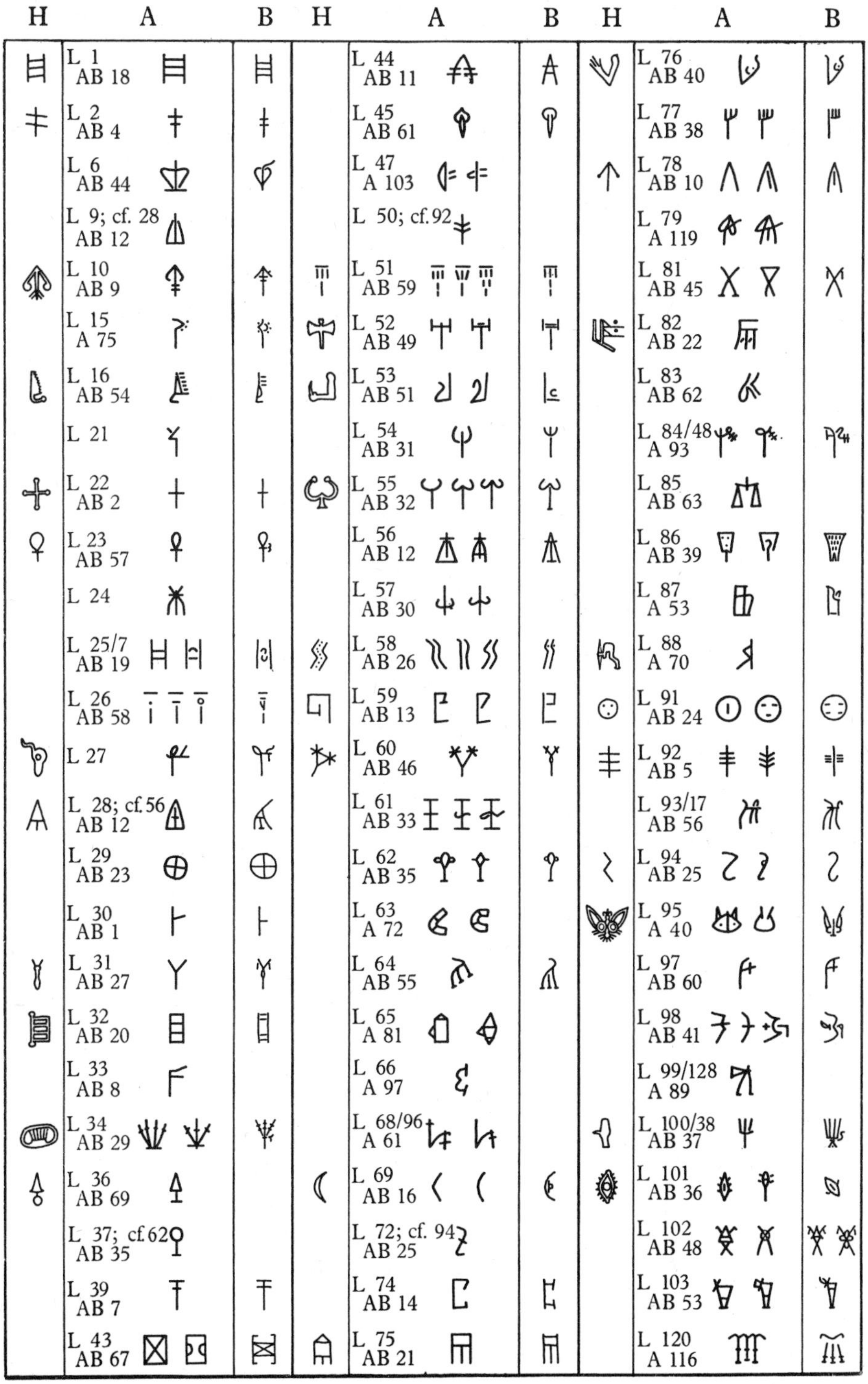

H	A	B	H	A	B	H	A	B
	L 1 / AB 18			L 44 / AB 11			L 76 / AB 40	
	L 2 / AB 4			L 45 / AB 61			L 77 / AB 38	
	L 6 / AB 44			L 47 / A 103			L 78 / AB 10	
	L 9; cf. 28 / AB 12			L 50; cf. 92			L 79 / A 119	
	L 10 / AB 9			L 51 / AB 59			L 81 / AB 45	
	L 15 / A 75			L 52 / AB 49			L 82 / AB 22	
	L 16 / AB 54			L 53 / AB 51			L 83 / AB 62	
	L 21			L 54 / AB 31			L 84/48 / A 93	
	L 22 / AB 2			L 55 / AB 32			L 85 / AB 63	
	L 23 / AB 57			L 56 / AB 12			L 86 / AB 39	
	L 24			L 57 / AB 30			L 87 / A 53	
	L 25/7 / AB 19			L 58 / AB 26			L 88 / A 70	
	L 26 / AB 58			L 59 / AB 13			L 91 / AB 24	
	L 27			L 60 / AB 46			L 92 / AB 5	
	L 28; cf. 56 / AB 12			L 61 / AB 33			L 93/17 / AB 56	
	L 29 / AB 23			L 62 / AB 35			L 94 / AB 25	
	L 30 / AB 1			L 63 / A 72			L 95 / A 40	
	L 31 / AB 27			L 64 / AB 55			L 97 / AB 60	
	L 32 / AB 20			L 65 / A 81			L 98 / AB 41	
	L 33 / AB 8			L 66 / A 97			L 99/128 / A 89	
	L 34 / AB 29			L 68/96 / A 61			L 100/38 / AB 37	
	L 36 / AB 69			L 69 / AB 16			L 101 / AB 36	
	L 37; cf. 62 / AB 35			L 72; cf. 94 / AB 25			L 102 / AB 48	
	L 39 / AB 7			L 74 / AB 14			L 103 / AB 53	
	L 43 / AB 67			L 75 / AB 21			L 120 / A 116	

Fig. 6. The Linear A syllabary in use at Agia Triada (after Carratelli), with possible cognates in the 'hieroglyphs' (H) and in Linear B (B).

signs he imagined to be identical in A and B, while *A 40*, etc., refer to signs peculiar to A. The same syllabary, with the addition of a few local variants, underlies all the other inscriptions in Linear A. Since the signs are purely phonetic, and since the language from which any acrophonic principle might be derived is unknown, no useful purpose is served by discussing the objects which the signs may originally have represented; in so far as the Mycenaean signs are derived from Linear A, the same is true of them.

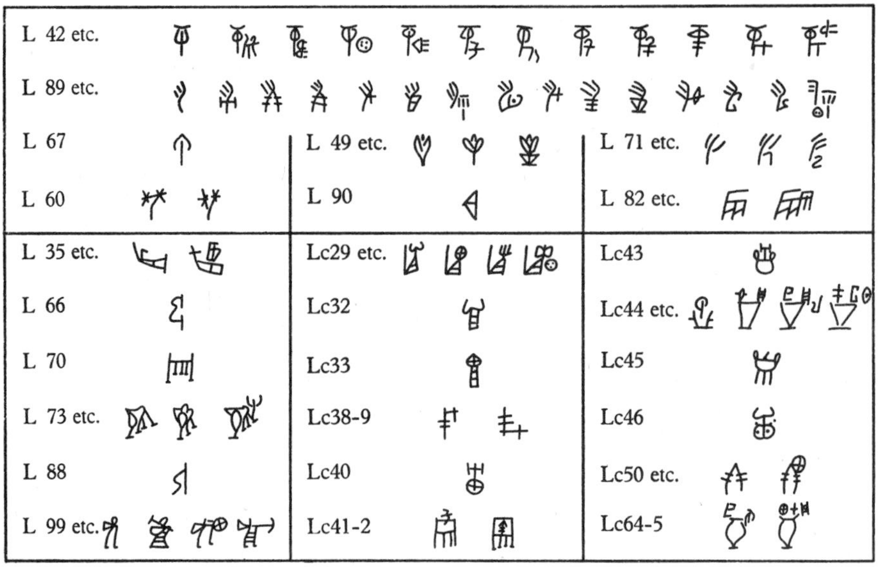

Fig. 7. The commonest Agia Triada ideograms.

The Agia Triada tablets are all of the 'page' shape, with space for four to nine short lines, rather than of the frequent Mycenaean 'palm-leaf' shape enclosing one or two long lines. The layout is consequently cramped, with entries and even individual words often divided from one line to another. The word-divider is written as a single dot in the middle of the line-height; the direction of writing, which had been variable in the 'hieroglyphs', is now uniformly left-to-right. The different mechanisms for indicating the commodities by means of ideograms already show considerable conformity with Mycenaean practice (see fig. 10):

1. The use of pictorial and conventional symbols restricted to an ideographic function.

2. The employment of single phonetic signs as ideograms, presumably starting from an acrophonic principle.

3. The telescoping of two or more phonetic signs into a 'monogram'.

4. The attachment of single phonetic signs in and around an existing ideogram in order to differentiate its meaning ('ligatures').

On some tablets whole words appear in small letters as 'adjuncts' over or after ideograms (e.g. with the tripods and cups of HT 31), whereas these qualifications would normally be written out before the ideogram in Linear B.

A single syllabic sign, most often ⚹ or ⚹, frequently stands alone after the first word on the tablet. Myres regards these occurrences as 'transaction signs' (i.e. abbreviations for some such words as 'has received', etc.), and they come near to forming an exception to the general rule 'no ideograms unless followed by numerals'. Proper names may occasionally be subject to a similar abbreviation or telescoping.

Most of the tablets from Agia Triada appear to record rations of various agricultural products issued to named individuals: there are no visible equivalents to the Linear B ideograms denoting persons or animals. Five of the most frequently recorded commodities are generally listed in the order ⚹ ⚹ ⚹ ⚹ ⚹ (compare HT 14, reproduced in fig. 8): four of these are the descendants of the 'hieroglyphic' ⚹ ⚹ ⚹ ⚹ (see fig. 5), whose Mycenaean equivalents ⚹ ⚹ ⚹.⚹ also tend to appear in the same order. Note the progressive deformation in the shape of the signs, which in Linear B has reached a purely graphic symbolism—a warning against trying to translate ideograms entirely on the basis of their external appearance. The identification of ⚹, the product which bulks largest on both the Linear A and Mycenaean household accounts, as 'poppy-

Fig. 8. Agia Triada tablet HT 14.

seed' (Sundwall, accepted by Myres), appears to be poppycock; the same objection to large amounts of a laboriously-harvested substance applies in the case of Evans' identification of ⚹ as 'saffron' (*PM*, IV, p. 718; this identification may yet hold good for the Linear B ideogram ⚹). The ideogram ⚹, apparently derived from the Knossos 'hieroglyph' ⚹, Mallia ⚹, occurs on the rim of a two-handled vase and on a pithos from the ninth magazine at Knossos, and has been shown to represent a liquid in Linear B (Bennett, 1950). Sundwall's suggestion 'wine', comparing the corresponding Egyptian ⚹ *irp*, is very plausible.

The greatest number of 'ligatures' are added to the ideograms ⚹ and ⚹, as can be seen from fig. 7. How they in fact differentiate the 'grain' and 'oil' is obscure, but the distinction cannot be very fundamental, since the various ligatured amounts are totalled under the simple commodity sign (e.g. on HT 116b).

Two of the Agia Triada ligatures, in 喬 and 圓 on HT 38, recur with the same ideogram at Knossos, and the 'monogram' 器 becomes the Mycenaean 𝖶. Since these Mycenaean ideograms were evidently taken over from Linear A as they stood, it is useless to look for a Greek word to round out the component syllables; and the same possibility must be faced in the case of other composite signs.

Totals are introduced at Agia Triada by the word ⅄⼗ (*ku-ro* ??), cumulative totals by ⼁Ŧ⼂⼗ (HT 122b); Georgiev's (1954) reading as *u-lo* = οὖλον ignores the fact that the Common Greek form should be *holwon. Subsidiary amounts, totalled separately, are sometimes introduced by ⼁⼗ (*ki-ro* ??); this may have a function analogous to the Mycenaean *o-pe-ro* 'owing, missing'.

Except for the possible use of 𝕸 to mean 'by weight' or to indicate a unit weight, all Agia Triada ideograms are directly followed by whole numbers and fractions, without the metrical symbols characteristic of Mycenaean accounts.

1,234 is written ⟡𐄡꞊⁻‖ or ⟡𐄡꞉⁻‖

The signs for the fractions comprise the following, singly or in combination:

ㄥ⼍⼊⼐ Τ⼇⼈ ⼋⼌⼍ ⼎⼏

Attempts to assign absolute values have been made by Sundwall (1942), Carratelli (1946), Bennett (1950) and Stoltenberg (1955); but the summations on HT 8, HT 9a, HT 13 and HT 123+124 do no more than make it likely that ㄥ $=\frac{1}{2}$, ⼍ $=\frac{1}{4}$ and ⼐ $=\frac{3}{4}$. As for the other symbols, it appears probable that they represent a series of aliquot parts decreasing in size from $\frac{1}{2}$ to $\frac{1}{32}$ or less; that smaller terms are combined with larger in order to express fractions like $\frac{3}{8}$ and those larger than $\frac{1}{2}$; and that their descending order of size corresponds very approximately to the order in which they have been printed above. There is probably a direct connexion between ⼈ Τ ⼎ ⼋ ⼌ and some of the Mycenaean signs for weights and measures (see pp. 54–60). If we assume that the fractional signs have been adapted to units with similar ratios, we may guess for instance that ⼌ may have represented something like $\frac{1}{30}$ in Linear A.

4. THE DERIVATION OF LINEAR SCRIPT B

Before it was recognized that the Linear B tablets are written in Greek, the usual view of their script was that expressed by Evans (*PM*, IV, p. 683) in 1935:

> Although Class B covers a somewhat later period and illustrates in many of its features a more developed stage in the Art of Writing, it cannot be regarded as simply a later outgrowth of A. It is on the whole of independent growth, though both systems largely go back to a common prototype (namely, the 'hieroglyphs').... Apart from the absence of ligatures, however, the general arrangement of the script remains the same, except that in the B system it is clearer.... Moreover, the language itself is identical.... We have not here the indications of a violent intrusion at the hands of some foreign Power. Equally with the other, the new system is rooted in the soil of Crete itself and is part and parcel of its history. Rather the evidence may be thought to point to a change of dynasty.

The discovery of tablets at Pylos (1939) and Mycenae (1950 and 1952), Wace, Blegen and Kantor's discussions of the relation of LM II Knossos to the Mainland, and his own work on Mycenaean weights and measures (1950) enabled Bennett to state positively in 1953, even before the publication of a decipherment:

> It is becoming increasingly apparent that the difference between the Linear A and the Linear B scripts is a serious one; not a matter of gradual development, nor of an elegant variation, but of a radical adaptation of the old to the new; or perhaps even a new construction following roughly an older model. The language also, and the names appearing on the accounts, are clearly different, and where the same sign is used in both Linear A and B there is no guarantee that the same value is assigned to it. At the same time the affinity of Knossos in LM II in script and in methods of book-keeping is clearly shown to be with the Mycenaean mainland rather than with the rest of Crete. Is it possible that we should speak of the *Minoan Linear Script* and the *Mycenaean Linear Script* rather than of Minoan Linear A and B? We cannot be sure where Linear B was created, or when, but it need not have been at Knossos. Yet it was clearly longer and more widely known in the Mycenaean than in the Minoan civilization, and so might well deserve a new and distinctive name.

Dow (1954), in an article written at the same time, devoted five pages to a discussion of this problem and arrived at a similar conclusion.

Knossos tablet **231** = K 872 was believed by Evans (*PM*, IV, p. 729) to have been oven-baked and was assigned, from the similar fabric of the Linear A tablets and from the style of its cups and bulls' heads, to LM Ia. With this doubtful exception, the Linear B tablets are merely sun-dried, if dried at all, and owe their survival to the fact that they were baked hard in the conflagrations which destroyed their storage rooms. Since such tablets must have been periodically thrown away or pulped, Myres (*SM II*, p. 40) is no doubt correct in assuming that 'they belong to the very latest days of the Palace occupation, and probably represent little more than the last year's vouchers before the catastrophe'. This is equally true of the archive room at Pylos, destroyed at the beginning of Late Helladic IIIc, and of the tablets found in the row of private houses ('Shields, Oil Merchant, and Sphinxes') at Mycenae, consigned to the flames at the end of Late Helladic IIIb. Unless the destruction of Knossos is to be set later than 1405 B.C. (a possibility suspected by Blegen), these accidentally-preserved tablets thus bracket a period of a full 200 years, from which no intermediate examples of writing survive except a few short inscriptions on Mainland vases, notably on the twenty-eight paint-inscribed stirrup jars of Late Helladic IIIa date (*c.* 1360 B.C.?) found by Keramopoullos in the Kadmeion at Thebes (*PM*, IV, p. 740; Björck, 1954). If it were possible to extend the area of excavation at Thebes, tablets might well come to light † there too, and possibly from this intermediate period. Myres' view (*SM III*, in MS.) that the inscribed jars from Tiryns are considerably earlier than the Knossos tablets is probably based on a misunderstanding.

The initial stimulus to devise a writing system for the Greek language may well go back to the events of *c.* 1580 B.C., which initiated the specifically Mycenaean culture of the Mainland and the rise of Mycenae and its satellites at the expense of Knossos—however these events are to be interpreted historically (both Karo and Schachermeyr assume a Greek invasion of Crete, not followed by an occupation). Linear B could have been devised at Mycenae itself at any time after 1580, but Dow (1954, p. 117) suggests Knossos as the most plausible place of origin, since the script is first attested there and a native bureaucracy would have been at hand to furnish the model.

The most likely period for the occupation of Knossos by a Greek-speaking ruling class is the beginning of LM II, which sees the appearance of Evans' 'New Dynasty of Aggressive Character' (*PM*, IV, pp. 884ff.), the introduction of the 'Palace Style' and of other features with Mainland connexions (see Professor Wace's foreword to this book, p. xxiv), and the drastic remodelling of part of the western section of the palace into a Throne Room suite. Evans' dating of the beginning of LM II is confirmed by the recent discovery that one panel in the Theban tomb of the vizir Rekhmara, that which depicts 'the peaceful embassy of the princes of the land of *Kftjw* (Crete) and of the Islands which are in the middle of the sea', was deliberately repainted between 1470 and 1450 B.C., apparently with the intention of replacing the traditional 'Minoan' dress of the Cretan envoys by costumes showing a more specifically Mainland character. That this final period was not very long is shown by the fact that a renovation of the Domestic Quarter, regarded by Evans (*PM*, IV, p. 889) as springing from the same impulse as the construction of the Throne Room, was actually in process at the moment of final destruction. But though the Knossos tablets may prove only to date from within one or two years of that catastrophe, a reasonable period of experiment and experience must be assumed for the script before its recorded appearance, in order to account for the astonishing uniformity which the Knossos tablets show with those of Pylos and Mycenae, in script, spelling and arrangement.

The signs of the Mycenaean syllabary which show an unmistakable similarity to Linear A phonetic signs in use at Agia Triada are shown in the third columns of fig. 6 above. These identifications do not entirely agree with the AB list proposed by Myres (*SM II*, Table I), whose intended function as a standard signary order is further vitiated by not distinguishing phonetic signs from ideograms. Of the eighty-seven known syllabic signs on Mycenaean tablets (eighty-four if we exclude possible variants) forty-five have close equivalents in Linear A, while ten have more doubtful parallels; leaving twenty-nine Mycenaean signs (or exactly a third) as apparent innovations. The last category includes many of the rarer signs, and in a comparison of running texts the proportion of divergent signs may be as little as 15 per cent.

What is the reason for these apparent innovations in the Mycenaean syllabary? One might assume that its inventors, like St Cyril adapting the Greek alphabet to the needs of a Bulgarian gospel, devised new symbols for the Greek syllables whose vowel or consonant sounds had no equivalent in 'Minoan'; but this does not fit the values of the signs as deciphered (or indeed as arranged dispassionately on the grid, fig. 3). Thus for the syllables expressing the Greek labio-velar sounds q^u and g^u, which we might expect to be foreign to 'Minoan', we admittedly have innovations in 𐀣 *qi* and 𐀦 *qo*, but 𐀤 *qe* is a frequent sign at Agia Triada; 𐀗 *mo* and possibly 𐀕 *me* are new, but 𐀔 *ma* and 𐀖 *mi* are not; and so on. Such an explanation of the need for innovation might presuppose that the value of the existing Linear A signs had suffered a wholesale reshuffling in the process; although from its great frequency as an initial it is likely that 𐀀, at any rate, already had its later value (*a*) at Agia Triada, and 𐀊 (Mycenaean *ja*) probably represented a closely-related syllable.

A feature of the system of Mycenaean syllabic values as revealed by decipherment is the presence of a considerable number of 'homophones' (pa_2, etc.), which are listed in the right-hand column of fig. 4, p. 23. Palmer suggests that these are a relic of a series of symbols for 'Minoan' sounds foreign to Greek, probably of a palatalized nature, which have been adopted for various special uses (see also p. 46). †

There is no trace in our syllabary of the practice occasionally seen in Hittite and regularly in Japanese and the Indian scripts, whereby two related syllables may be formed from a single basic sign by the addition of diacritical marks.

Evans' and Myres' theory that the modifications and innovations of Linear B represent 'a re-selection from the same older repertory' is difficult to control. Though a few seal-stones or libation-tables inscribed with 'hieroglyphs' may have survived into Late Minoan times, it is unlikely that the scribes retained any real familiarity or facility with their script. The forms of many of the Mycenaean signs are undoubtedly more ornate and curvilinear than their Agia Triada counterparts, the sign ꝛ *ku* showing, for example, some re-elaboration as the naturalistic 'flying bird' which the Linear A ꝛ may once have represented. But there are a greater number of examples where, far from harking back to a 'hieroglyphic' prototype, the Mycenaean form has made the naturalistic pattern quite unrecognizable. Thus the Linear A 𐄘, in which Evans and Carratelli recognize the 'cat's head' hieroglyph, becomes 𐀔 (*ma*) in Linear B, and is taken by Myres as a flower. Only one Mycenaean syllable, 𐁆 *nwa*, has a close parallel in the 'hieroglyphs' (P 117a, *SM I*, p. 177) but none in Linear A, and even here the omission from A may be due to the accidents of discovery.

The alternative source of innovations suggested by Evans, the repertory of masons' and potters' marks in use in Crete and neighbouring areas, is even more uncontrollable: attempts to bring these marks into systematic connexion with regular scripts are very uncertain, since their common denominator is generally no more than the fact that they are the patterns most easily made by a limited number of straight strokes. We may have to conclude that some of the Mycenaean signs may have had no external 'derivation' at all, other than in the calligraphic fantasy of their inventors. An attempt to explain the innovations by the initial syllables of specific Greek words is not likely to be any more fruitful.

The Mycenaean syllabic signs are printed in fig. 9 in the order of Bennett's numeration (see fig. 4, p. 23, for an alphabetic arrangement according to their phonetic values); this indicates the main variations in their shape which have been found at Knossos, Pylos and Mycenae, and on the Theban vases. These variations give little evidence for a chronological development of the script, and discoveries of new tablets have tended to show that forms we had believed characteristic of a particular time and place are in fact only permissible variations of style, which may be shown at any period by the graduates from the evidently conservative scribal schools. The signs painted on vases show few features that can be attributed to their different writing materials, but some

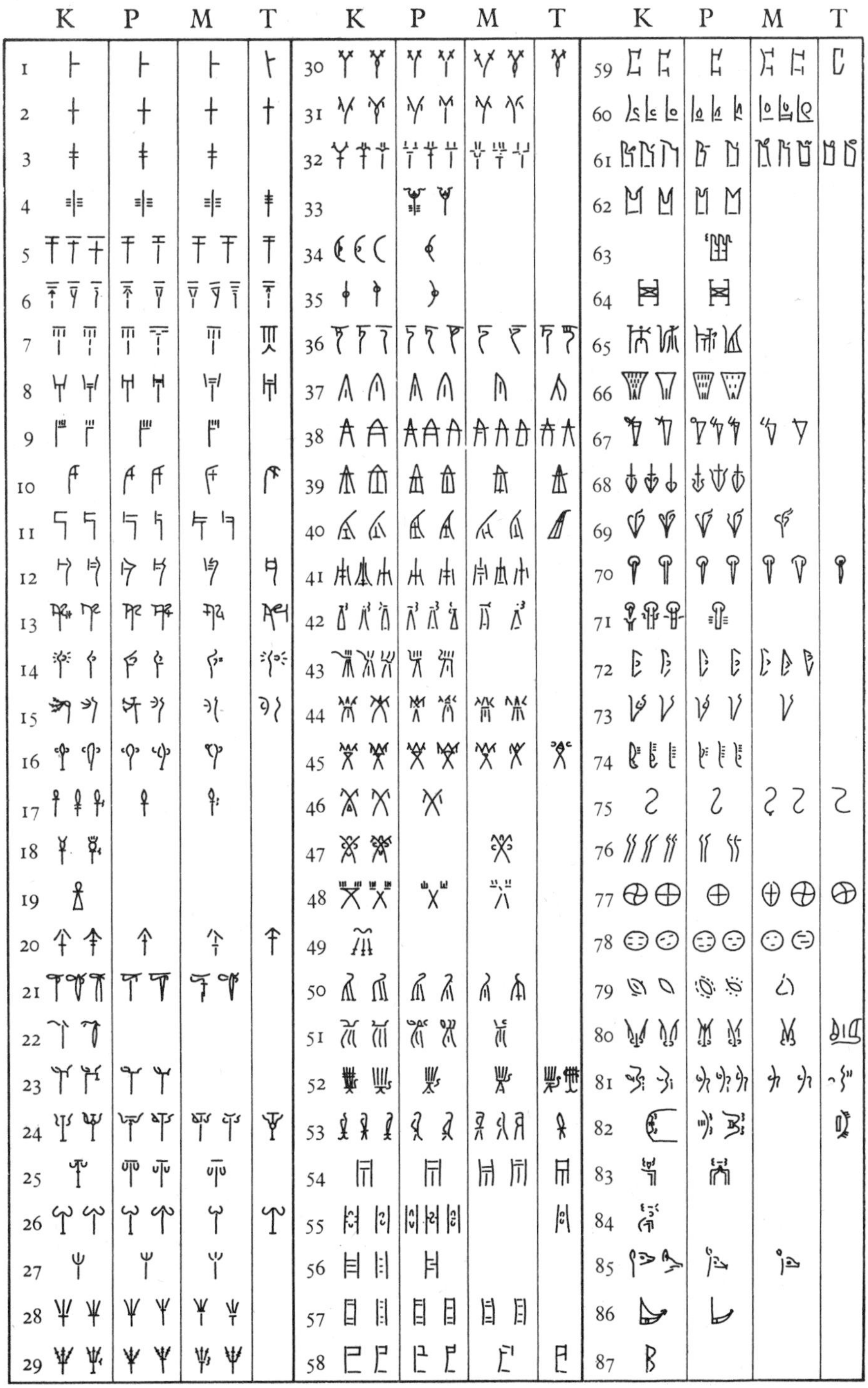

Fig. 9. The Mycenaean syllabary (after Bennett). K = Knossos, P = Pylos, M = Mycenae, T = Thebes.

of them are evidently careless or semi-literate. The incised design on the rim of a jar from Asine, interpreted by Persson (1930) as a Greek invocation to Poseidon in a form of the Linear Script, is probably not to be regarded as intelligible writing at all, though some of the shapes may have been suggested by Mycenaean signs. The complete omission of a rarer Mycenaean sign from one or another site is not significant, and is continually being corrected as new material is unearthed.

Except where they can be shown to derive from the initial sounds of a Greek word, the bulk of the Mycenaean ideograms or 'commodity signs' (see fig. 10, p. 50) were probably adapted directly from their Linear A prototypes as used by the earlier Knossos bureaucracy. The omission of the symbols for men, women and animals from the surviving Linear A tablets is evidently accidental; the survival of the ideograms for some of the main agricultural staples has been noted above (p. 35); even though their shapes, like those of some of the syllabic signs, have been subjected to a graphic distortion which removes them still further from their prototypes in the 'hieroglyphs' and in nature. Some commodities which are themselves innovations in LM II, such as horses, chariots, body-armour and specific vessel types, naturally require new symbols: these, unlike the inherited ideograms, are markedly naturalistic and are often accompanied by their Greek descriptions in long-hand.

The system of numbers was taken over from Linear A without modification, but fractions as such have not been found on any Mycenaean tablet. The new symbols for weights and measures ('fractional quantities') are discussed below, pp. 54–60.

5. THE SPELLING RULES

The Ionic alphabetic inscriptions of the fifth century B.C. show a more faithful and economical adaptation to the contemporary pronunciation than any other form of written Greek before or since. At the same period, Cypriot Greek was still being written in an archaic syllabary (see fig. 12, p. 64) whose conventions do violence to Greek in several important respects:

1. There are single series of syllabic signs for κγχ, πβφ, τδθ, so that *e-ko* may represent either ἐγώ or ἔχω.

2. μ and ν are omitted before a following consonant, so that πάντα is spelt *pa-ta*; final -ς shows several instances of omission.

3. Extra vowels have to be written to round out clusters of consonants: πτόλιν becomes *po-to-li-ne*.

As might be expected, the earlier Mycenaean syllabary is even more imprecise and incomplete in its rendering of Greek: this is due largely to a closer adherence to what appears to have been the initial principle in the development of syllabaries, that of writing *only one sign for each syllable of the pronunciation*.

The following notes summarize the conventions which we believe the Mycenaean scribe to have followed in reducing spoken Greek to a syllabic spelling. They will indicate the limits within which equivalents may be found for words in the texts transcribed in Part II of this book, and for the proper names and vocabulary listed in the appendices. More than one equivalent may often be possible within these rules, and the full range of possibilities may sometimes have escaped us; some details of the spelling rules may themselves still require modification.

We will postpone to pp. 67–75 the discussion of what conclusions may legitimately be drawn from these orthographical peculiarities as to the structure of the earlier 'Minoan' language, as to the precise relationships of the Mycenaean dialect, and as to the racial character of the scribes who were employed to record it. The following notes are based on the general assumption that the pronunciation behind the spelling is a normal though archaic form of East Greek, such as had already been inferred for the period by philologists.

§ 1. *Vowels*

The syllabary differentiates five vowels -*a* -*e* -*i* -*o* -*u* (for a possible sixth vowel, see §13). Long vowels are not specially indicated, nor are syllables beginning with an aspirate: *a-ni-ja=hāniai* ἡνίαι.

§ 2. *Diphthongs*

au, eu, ou (both long and short) are regularly indicated with the aid of the †
sign *u*: *na-u-si=nausi, ka-ke-u-si=khalkeusi, a-ro-u-ra=aroura*. This does not of course apply to classical -ου- where it is merely the graphic indication of a lengthened close *o*: 'they have' (Att. ἔχουσι, Arc. ἔχονσι) is written *e-ko-si*, and Att. τρίπους (Hom. τρίπος) appears as *ti-ri-po*.

The second element of *ai, ei, oi* (both long and short) is invariably omitted in the dat. sing. and nom. plur. of nouns and adjectives, and generally elsewhere too (except for the regular use of the sign *ai* initially). A fuller spelling with the aid of the sign *i* is found in the Knossos *ko-to-i-na* compared with Pylos *ko-to-na=ktoina*, and sometimes alternates on tablets of the same set: *a-na-ta/ a-na-i-ta* on the Knossos 'chariot' tablets, *ko-no/ko-i-no* on the Mycenae 'spice' tablets. Dative singulars in -*e-i* are disyllabic from names in -*ēs*: *E-u-me-de-i=Eumēdeï*. The spellings *mi-to-we-sa-e* (**269**=Sd0404, nom. plur. fem.), *e-qe-ta-e* (**29**=As821), *to-e* (Eb842, τῷ?) are exceptional and probably erroneous.

From the example of *Pa-i-to* = Phaistos we had concluded that the dative plurals in *-a-i* and *-o-i* were to be read *-ais*, *-ois*. The *-ois* of the instr. plur. masc. is, however, spelt simply *-o* on the Pylos 'furniture' tablets (see below, p. 334): Merlingen and Andrews suggest that the datives should be vocalized *-āhi*, *-oihi*, with loss of intervocalic *-s-*.

§ 3. 'Glides'

Vowels following *-i-* are generally spelt with a *j-* syllable: *i-ja-te* = *iātēr*, *i-je-ro* = *hieros*, *i-jo* = *iōn*; those following *-u-* with a *w-* syllable: *ku-wa-no* = *kuanos*. This rule is invariable in the endings of adjectives in *-ios*: *ko-no-si-ja* = *Knōsia*, *ku-wa-ni-jo* = *kuanios*. In the middle of a word a_2 may replace *ja*: *a-pi-a$_2$-ro* = *Amphialos*, *pi-a$_2$-ra* = *phialai*; sometimes even on the same tablet: *ko-ri-ja-da-na*/ *ko-ri-a$_2$-da-na* on Mycenae Ge605 (cf. *ti-ri-o-we-e*/*ti-ri-jo-we* on **236** = Ta641).

A diphthong followed by a vowel may be written with the glide syllable alone: *a-ra-ru-ja* = *araruiai*, *i-je-re-ja* = *hiereia*, *e-wa-ko-ro* = *Euag(o)ros* (but also *e-u-wa-ko-ro*, *e-u-we-to* = *Euētōr*), unless an etymological **s>h* intervenes: *E-u-o-mo* = *Eu-hormos*.

§ 4. *P, K, T and D*

†   *p-* can represent *p-* or *ph-*: *pa-te* = *patēr*, *pa-ka-na* = *phasgana*. The only words so far identified with *b* are *pa$_2$-si-re-u* = *basileus*, *po-pa$_2$* = *phorbā*?, *te-pa$_2$-de* = *Thēbans-de*?; for *pa$_2$* see § 13.

k- can represent *k-*, *g-*, *kh-*: *ka-ko* = *khalkos*, *ka-ra-we* = *grāwes*. *t-* can represent *t-* or *th-*: *te-ko-to* = *tektōn*, *te-o* = *theos*; *d-* is invariably indicated by its own syllabic series: *ti-ri-po-de* = *tripode*, *di-do-si* = *didonsi*, *e-pi-de-da-to* = *epi-dedastoi*.

§ 5. *L and R*

l- and *r-* are written with a single syllabic series, here transliterated *r-*: *ti-ri-po* = *tripos*, *tu-ri-so* = *Tulisos*; *tu-ro$_2$* = *turoi*, *pi-ti-ro$_2$-we-sa* = *ptilowessa*; *ku-ru-so* = *khrusos*, *ku-ru-me-no* = *Klumenos*. Attempts to apportion the numerous homophones exclusively to either *l* or *r* have not met with success.

‡ § 6. *Z*

z- spells a Greek ʒ from **gj* in *me-zo* = *mezōn* μέζων, *wo-zo* = *worzōn* ῥέζων; from **dj* in *to-pe-za* = *torpeza* τράπεζα; from **j* in *ze-u-ke-u-si*; but there are puzzling alternations with the *k-* series: Knossos *a-ze-ti-ri-ja*/*a-ke-ti-ri-ja*, Pylos *ze-i-ja-ka-ra-na*/*ke-i-ja-ka-ra-na*. Palmer regards the *z-* series as inherited from a Minoan palatalized *ǩ*, and used for a variety of Greek affricates and spirants, including on occasion *l* (*me-za-ne* = *melanes* 'black'?).

44

§ 7. *Labio-velars*

q- may represent q^u (>Attic τ or π) or g^u (>Attic δ or β): *qe*=*q*^{u}*e* τε, †
a-pi-qo-ro=*amphiq*^{u}*oloi* ἀμφίπολοι, *qo-u-ko-ro*=*g*^{u}*oukoloi* βουκόλοι. The only apparent instances of an aspirated *q*^{u}*h* (>Attic θ or φ) are a few names in *-qo-ta*/
-qo-i-ta which may represent -φόντης or -φοίτης; and the word *qe-te-a*, which
may be related to θέσσασθαι.

*q^u*u* has probably become *ku*: *pe-re-ku-wa-na-ka*=Πρεσβύ-αναξ. No sign is
known for *q*^{u}*a*, which may already have become *pa*: cf. the spelling *pa-ra-jo*
'old' (probably from **q*^{u}*ala*-, cf. τῆλε) and *pa-te* 'all' (from **k̑wantes*, cf.
ἅπας/Skt. *çáçvant-*). The name of the horse *i-qo*=*iqq*^{u}*os* (from **ek̑wos*) already
shows transference to a labio-velar; the ending of the perfect participle (e.g.
te-tu-ko-wo-a=*tetukhwoa*) is preserved from this development, as in the classical
dialects. The classical -βάτης, -βατος has a different vocalism in Mycenaean:
-qo-ta, *-qo-to* (from **g*^{u}*m̥t*-).

Bennett has pointed out some irregularities at Pylos: the spelling *qi-si-pe-e*
for *xiphee*; the variations *ra-qi-ti-ra₂*/*ra-pi-ti-ra₂* and *qe-re-qo-ta-o*/*pe-re-qo-ta*
(**116**=En659); and the names *e-ri-ko-wo* (masc.)/*e-ri-qi-ja* (fem.), possibly
compounded with 'horse'.

§ 8. *Final -L, -M, -N, -R, -S*
‡

At the end of a syllable these sounds are omitted from the spelling: *ka-ko*=
khal-kos, *a-pi*=*am-phi*, *pa-ka-na*=*phas-gana*, *a-to-ro-qo*=*an-thrōq*^{u}*os*, *pa-te*=*pa-tēr*
or *pan-tes*, *a-ku-ro*=*ar-guros*. The clusters *-rg-*, *-rm-*, *-sm-* seem to receive fuller
treatment on occasion: *we-re-ke*=εἴργει?, *we-re-ka-ra-ta*=*wergal-*?, *wo-ro-ki-jo-
ne-jo*=*worgioneios*, *a-ra-ro-mo-te-me-na*=*ararmo-*, *de-so-mo*, *do-so-mo*.

§ 9. *Initial S and W*
¶

Before a consonant initial *s*- is generally omitted: *ta-to-mo*=*stathmos*, *pe-ma*=
sperma, etc. A possible exception is *sa-pa-ka-te-ri-ja* (KN Dv941), which recalls
Sphakteria.

On the basis of the place-name *ri-jo* 'Ρίον (**wrison*?) and the trade *ra-pte*
'tailor' (**wrap-*?) we had assumed that initial *w*- before a consonant is also
omitted. Palmer (1954) denies this, adducing *wi-ri-ne-jo*=*wrineios* 'of leather'
(Ϝρινός), *wi-ri-za*=*wriza*. The passive participle *e-ra-pe-me-na*=*errapmena*
'stitched' revealed by the join of **221**=L 647 shows no trace of a digamma.

§ 10. *Consonant clusters*

Doubled consonants are not distinguished. Where a plosive consonant precedes another consonant, it is written with the vowel of the succeeding syllable:

ka-na-pe-u=*knapheus*, *ki-ti-me-na*=*ktimenā*, *ko-no-so*=*Knōsos*, *ku-ru-so*=*khrusos*. A few irregularities are found with -*kt*-: *wa-na-ka-te-ro*=*wanakteros* 'royal', *ru-ki-to*=*Luktos* (*ru-ki-ti-jo*=*Luktios* is regular). Otherwise the rule is preserved in declension (e.g. *ko-ri-ja-do-no* sing./*ko-ri-ja-da-na* plur.), and is extended to clusters of three consonants: *re-u-ko-to-ro*=*Leuktron*, *a-re-ku-tu-ru-wo*=*Alektruōn*.

x (ξ), *ps* (ψ) and *q^{u}s* are treated as *k-s-*, *p-s-*, *q-s-*: *ka-sa-to*=*Xanthos*, *ke-se-nu-wo* =*xenwos*, *ko-so-u-to*=*Xouthos*. When final, they shed the -*s* and take the vowel of the preceding syllable: *wa-na-ka*=*wanax*, *ai-ti-jo-qo*=Αἰθίοψ. An exception † is the Knossos ox name *wo-no-qo-so*=Οἶνοψ.

m is preserved in *mn*-: *de-mi-ni-ja*, *a-mi-ni-so*, etc. *r* in -*rw*- is usually omitted: *ko-wo*=*korwos*, *pa-we-a*=*pharwea*; but it is retained in *a-ra-ru-wo-a*=*ararwoa* ‡ (cf. the feminine *a-ra-ru-ja*). The group -*nw*- is usually written -*nu-w*-: *ke-se-nu-wi-ja*=*xenwia*, *pe-ru-si-nu-wo*=*perusinwon*; the sign *nwa* sometimes replaces -*nu-wa*-: *pe-ru-si-nwa*, *pa₂-nu-wa-so*/*pa₂-nwa-so*, *a-mi-nu-wa-ta*/*a-mi-nwa*-, *e-nu-wa-ri-jo*/*e-n̬w̬a̬-ri-jo*.

¶ § 11. *Polysyllabic signs*

Nearly all the Mycenaean signs indicate a simple vowel (*a*, *e*, etc.) or a consonant-plus-vowel open syllable (*ta*, *ka*, etc.); there is no evidence for syllables of the types common in cuneiform, *at*, *ak*, etc., and *tar*, *kar*, etc.

But in addition to the special sign for *nwa*, *62 appears to represent *pte*: *pe-te-re-wa*/*pte-re-wa* on the Knossos 'chariot wheel' tablets. Two other complex syllables are each confined to a single word on the same 'wheel' tablets, and are probably abbreviations resulting from long repetition: *o-da*-*87-*ta* replaces *o-da-ku-we-ta* (also *o-da-ke-we-ta* and even *o-da-tu-we-ta*) and seems to represent *kwe*; *te-mi*-*71-*ta* contains a sign which looks like a 'monogram' of *ne*+*ko* at Knossos (but *te*+*ko* in the later Pylos version), though this interpretation is contested.

§ 12. *Polyphones*

We have not so far been forced to assume any cases of a sign carrying two or more quite different phonetic values, a complication present to a high degree in cuneiform.

†† § 13. *Homophones*

There are a number of signs which appear to duplicate values already covered, e.g. *a₂* *ai₂* *pa₂* *pu₂*? *ra₂* *ra₃* *ro₂* *ta₂* on the right-hand column of fig. 4. Andrews assumes that there is in fact a sixth vowel *schwa* (ə), and also allots signs for palatalized and labialized consonants; Palmer suggests that Linear A had a series of palatalized consonants whose syllables were taken over by the Greeks for various abbreviating uses. A consistent pattern in the function of these supernumerary signs is not yet discernible.

-i-a₂- alternates with *-i-ja-* in the middle of words (see § 3), especially where an *-h-* may be suspected of intervening: *a-pi-a₂-ro* = *Amphihalos*. *a₂* may also represent initial *ha-* in *a₂-te-ro* = *hateron*. But its most frequent use at Pylos and Mycenae is to represent the final *-a* of neuter *-s-* stems in the nominative plural: *pa-we-a₂* = *pharweʰa*, *ke-re-a₂* = *skeleʰa*, *me-zo-a₂* = *mezoʰa* 'larger', *te-tu-ko-wo-a₂* = *tetukhwoʰa*. Such words are spelt with *-a* at Knossos, with the exception of *]-a₂* on Le786–788 and Ld1009, which is perhaps to be restored as *pa-we-a₂* (as on the newly transcribed Knossos fragment L 7378). The usage may vary within the same set of tablets: *we-a-re-ja/we-a₂-re-jo* on the Pylos tablets.

pa₂ sometimes represents *ba* (see § 4), but note *pa₂-ra-to-ro* = *spalathron*, *ku-su-to-ro-pa₂* = *xunstrophā*.

ra₂ probably represents *-ria* in the ending of female agent nouns such as *a-ke-ti-ra₂/a-ke-ti-ri-ja*, etc., but not necessarily in the Pylos man's name spelt indifferently *Ta-ra₂-to* and *Ta-ra-to*.

ra₃ seems to represent *rai/lai* in *pi-je-ra₃* = *phielai* (plur.), *e-ra₃-wo* = *elaiwon*, *ku-te-ra₃* and *ze-pu₂?-ra₃* (plur.), *pe-ra₃-ko-ra-i-ja*.

ro₂ appears to show no differentiation in *tu-ro₂* = *turoi*, *ku-pa-ro₂/ku-pa-ro*, *pi-ti-ro₂-we-sa* = *ptilowessa*, but to represent *rio* in *po-pu-ro₂* cf. *po-pu-re-ja*.

ta₂ represents *tia* in Pylos *ra-wa-ra-ta₂* cf. *ra-wa-ra-ti-jo*, *a-*85-ta₂/a-si-ja-ti-ja*, probably not in the adjective *ko-ro-ta₂* cf. *ko-ro-to*. The vocalization of the Pylos man's name (gen.) *o-ta₂-we-o/o-to-wo-o* is quite uncertain.

§ 14. *Incomplete spellings*

In repeated writing of long words in standard formulae, a middle or final sign may be omitted: this is probably to be regarded as a scribal error rather than as a valid part of the spelling rules.

It is common in the ending *-me-na*: *a-ja-me-⟨na⟩*, *ki-ti-me-⟨na⟩*, *ke-ke-me-⟨na⟩*. Note also *A-⟨re⟩-ku-tu-ru-wo*, *e-pi-⟨de⟩-da-to*, *Te-qi-⟨ri⟩-jo-ne*, *to-⟨so⟩-pe-mo*, *a-⟨ra⟩-ro-mo-te-me-na*.

§ 15. *The use of the divider*

Word-division follows the classical pattern, with a few exceptions. The enclitic conjunctions *-qᵘe* 'and', *-de* 'but', are always joined to the preceding word; the adverbs *ou-, ouki-* 'not' and *hō-* or *hōs-* 'thus' (or 'how'?) to the word that follows. A few word-pairs recurring together in standard formulae may be written without division: *a-ta-na-po-ti-ni-ja* = *Athānā potnia*, *a-ne-mo-i-*

je-re-ja=*anemōn hiereia*, *to-so-pe-ma*=*tosson sperma*. Conversely compounds are occasionally split: *a-pu* | *ke-ka-u-me-no*=*apukekaumenos*, *e-ne-wo* | *pe-za*=*ennewopeza*. The divider will be indicated by the absence of a hyphen in transcription.

Risch has suggested that the syllabary has an antipathy to words of only one sign, liable to be taken as ideograms: hence such spellings as *to-so-pa*=*tossos pans* (but *to-so* | *pa-te*=*tossoi pantes*), *qo-o* (for monosyllabic *g^{u}ōns* ?).

6. THE MYCENAEAN IDEOGRAMS

†

The objects and commodities being counted may sometimes only be written out long-hand, as on the Pylos 'furniture' tablets or on some of those from Mycenae which list condiments; but more often the numbers are preceded by an ideogram, either a purely visual symbol or a syllabic sign used in abbreviation. This is invariably the case with cereals, wine, oil and livestock; and where groups of tradespeople are being counted, the sign for MAN or WOMAN is always inserted. 'Thirty shepherds' will appear as '*poimenes* MAN 30', a visual parallel to the 'classifiers' obligatory in Chinese counting, e.g. *san ko jên*='three *piece* man', *i p'i lü*='one *single-animal* donkey', etc.

The Mycenaean ideograms known at Easter 1955 are listed on fig. 10 in the numbered order agreed with Bennett, which follows in principle, but not in detail, the referencing system proposed by Dow (1954, p. 88). These of course represent only a fraction of the ideograms which may have been in daily use in the palaces and merchants' houses; the syllabary evidently forms a virtually closed system, but new ideograms could at any time be extemporized to describe new objects. The Knossos, Pylos and Mycenae tablets show, however, that the signs for the staple commodities of Mycenaean life were completely standardized.

Evidence for the meanings of the ideograms will be discussed in the sections of Part II dealing with the tablets on which they mainly occur; let us concentrate here on the general principles of their use and derivation. The following classification into six types does not materially affect their status (and may have been differently appreciated by the scribes themselves), but merely indicates the basis on which they appear to us to have been devised:

1. *Naturalistic and self-explanatory pictorial signs*

The indication of 'foal' (*po-ro*) by omitting the mane from the HORSE ideogram finds an exact counterpart on the proto-Elamite tablets. CHARIOTS are differentiated to show the presence or absence of bodywork and wheels, and the various types of vessels, implements and weapons are specified by detailed drawings. In all such cases a verbal description in long-hand generally precedes the ideogram. It has been thought odd that the words 'a small three-handled goblet' should require further illustration by the symbol ♉, but no other explanation is possible where, as often, the same description occurs with the same ideogram on tablets from different sites. In the specification of such manufactured articles, the verbal description is probably the primary one, the ideogram being added partly as a habitual 'classifier', partly to aid the non-literate members of the household (which may have included the highest as well as the lowest) in seeing the contents of the tablets at a glance. The ideograms of this first type have of course given invaluable help to the decipherment by indicating the general context of the tablets and specific vocabulary equations.

2. *Conventionalized and abstract pictorial symbols*

The possible meaning of these ideograms may be guessed from the vocabulary context of the tablets, or from more naturalistic counterparts in Linear A and in the 'hieroglyphs', like the agricultural staples discussed on p. 35. But it is only proved certain where the Greek long-hand spelling is itself added, e.g. *pa-we-a* 'cloths' to ⊟ on **214**=Ld571, *ka-ko* 'bronze' to ⊨ on **253**=Jn01, or *e-ra₃-wo* 'olive oil' to ⋟ on a new Pylos tablet (Gn1184). Though schematic, the MAN and WOMAN signs are unmistakable from their more detailed variants; but the difference of meaning intended by the more naturalistic MAN [B] and MAN [C] is unknown.

3. *Ideograms ligatured with a syllabic sign*

Where we find a pictorial symbol differentiated by a syllabic sign 'surcharged' above or inside it, it is a reasonable assumption that we have to do with the abbreviation of a Greek noun or adjective; this is confirmed by cases where the same ideogram may also be described by words in long-hand. The A written within the AMPHORA symbol clearly stands for the *amphiphorēwes* of **233**=Uc160; the KO within the HIDE sign differentiates it as a *kōwos*, 'sheepskin' (**171**=Un718) from the HIDE+WI (*wrinos*, 'oxhide'); PIGS+SI evidently represents *sialoi*, 'fattened pigs' (**75**=Cn02); and SHEEP+TA may be connected with the word *ta-to-mo* on Cn09.

But the ligatures CLOTH+ZO and CLOTH+KU already occur in the same form at Agia Triada (HT 38), and warn us against pressing the argument too far. The frequent division of CATTLE, PIGS, SHEEP, GOATS, HORSES

K	P	M		K	P	M

People and animals

No.	Code	K	P	M	Meaning
100	A-				MAN
101	A-				MAN^C
102	A-				WOMAN
103	B				MAN^B
104	Cn				DEER
105	Ca S-				HORSE
105^a	Ca				HE-ASS
105^c	Ca				FOAL
106^a	C- D-				RAM
106^b	C- D-				EWE
	Cn				SHEEP+TA
*21					SHEEP
*75					Kind of sheep
107^a	C-				HE-GOAT
107^b	C- Mc				SHE-GOAT
*22					GOAT
108^a	C-				BOAR
108^b	C-				SOW
					PIG+SI
					PIG+KA
*85	C-				PIG
109^a	C-				OX/BULL
109^b	C-				COW
	C-				OX+SI
*23	C-				OX

No.	K	P	M	Meaning
118				TALENT
*72	G-			Bunch?
*74	S-			Pair
*15	S-			Single
*61				Deficit

By dry measure

No.	Code	K	P	M	Meaning
120	E- F-				WHEAT
121	F-				BARLEY
122	F- U-				OLIVES
	F				OLIVES+A
	F				OLIVES+TI
*30	F-				FIGS
*65	F-				FLOUR
123	G- Un				CONDIMENT
	G-				Coriander
*70	G-				Coriander
*31	G-				Sesame
*81	G-				Cumin
*9	G-				Celery
*80	G-				Fennel
124	G-				Cyperus
125	F-				Cyperus?
126	F-				Cyperus?
*34					Month's ration?
127	Un				Fruit?
128	G-				Safflower

Units of measurement

No.	Code	K	P	M	Meaning
110					Volume
111					Volume
112					Dry
113					Liquid
114					Weight
*21					Weight
*2					Weight
115					Weight
116					Weight
117					Weight

By liquid measure

No.	Code	K	P	M	Meaning
130	F- G				OLIVE OIL
	G				OIL+A
131	Fs U-				WINE
132	Un				?
133	Un				Unguent?
134	Un				?
135	Fs Gg				HONEY
	Gg				Amphora of honey
*13	Un				Honey?

50

No.	Code	K	P	M	Meaning
		By weight			
140	J-	[ideogram]	[ideogram]	[ideogram]	BRONZE
141	Kn		[ideogram]		GOLD
142	Mc	[ideogram]			Beeswax?
*53	Ma		[ideogram]		?
*44	Ma		[ideogram]		Beeswax?
*61	Ma		[ideogram]		?
*33	Np		[ideogram]		SAFFRON
143	La	[ideogram]	[ideogram]		Silver?
		By weight or in units			
*31	N-	[ideogram]	[ideogram]		Linen
145	L- O-	[ideogram]	[ideogram]	[ideogram]	WOOL
146	M-	[ideogram]	[ideogram]	[ideogram]	A textile?
		Counted in units			
150	Mc	[ideogram]			Agrimi goat?
151	Mc	[ideogram]			Agrimi horn
152	M-	[ideogram]	[ideogram]		OXHIDE
153	Un	[ideogram]			SHEEPSKIN
154	On	[ideogram]			?
155	G-		[ideogram]		A container
156	Un	[ideogram]			CHEESE
157	Un	[ideogram]			?
158	Ld	[ideogram]			Bundle
159	L-	[ideogram]			CLOTH
	L-	[ideogram]	[ideogram]	[ideogram]	CLOTH+PA
	L-	[ideogram]			CLOTH+TE
	L	[ideogram]			CLOTH+ZO
	L	[ideogram]			CLOTH+PU
	L	[ideogram]			CLOTH+KU
160	La		[ideogram]		A kind of cloth?
161	L-	[ideogram]	[ideogram]		?
162	Sc	[ideogram]			CORSLET
	Sc	[ideogram]			TUNIC+QE
	L	[ideogram]			TUNIC+KI
	L	[ideogram]			TUNIC+RI
163	Sh	[ideogram]			CORSLET (set)
164	L	[ideogram]	[ideogram]		A kind of cloth?
165	Sc	[ideogram]			INGOT

No.	Code	K	P	M	Meaning
166	Oa	[ideogram]			Silver ingot?
167	Oa	[ideogram]	[ideogram]		INGOT
168	Pp	[ideogram]			Adze?
169	Pa		[ideogram]	[ideogram]	?
170	Ch	[ideogram]			?
171	G Sn	[ideogram]	[ideogram]		?
172	U	[ideogram]	[ideogram]		Beeswax?
173	Mn U	[ideogram]	[ideogram]	[ideogram]	?
174	Gv	[ideogram]	[ideogram]		Seedling?
175	Gv	[ideogram]			FIG TREE
176	Gv	[ideogram]			OLIVE TREE
177	U	[ideogram]			?
178	U	[ideogram]			?
179	U	[ideogram]			?
180	U	[ideogram]			?
181	U	[ideogram]			Thong?
182	U	[ideogram]			?
183	U	[ideogram]			?
184	U	[ideogram]			?
185	Ws	[ideogram]			?
186	Wa		[ideogram]		?
187	Xa		[ideogram]		cf. 130?
188			[ideogram]		?
		Vessels			
200–213		See Chapter 10, fig. 16			
		Furniture			
220	Ta		[ideogram]		FOOTSTOOL
		Weapons			
230	R	[ideogram]			SPEAR
231	R	[ideogram]			ARROW
232	Ta		[ideogram]		?
233	Ra	[ideogram]			SWORD
		Chariots			
240	Sc	[ideogram]			WHEELED CHARIOT
241	Sd Se	[ideogram]			WHEEL-LESS CHARIOT
242	Sf Sg	[ideogram]			CHARIOT FRAME
243	Sa So	[ideogram]	[ideogram]		WHEEL
	Sa		[ideogram]		WHEEL+TE

Fig. 10. The Mycenaean ideograms (after Bennett), with their most usual
tablet contexts and suggested meanings.

and ASSES into two categories by a variation in the form of the upright (generally taken to be a sex distinction) is likely to have been inherited from Linear A, and even there it may not necessarily have been based on a ligature with phonetic signs.

4. *Single syllabic signs used as ideograms*

Here, too, the derivation of the sign use from the initials of Greek words is proved by a number of examples. o and *o-pa-wo-ta* 'plates?' are equated on such Pylos tablets as **292** = Sh740; similarly PA with *parawaiō* 'pair of cheek-pieces', and KO with *koruthos* (gen.) 'helmet'. On the Mycenae 'condiment' tablets (**105–107**) the commodities may be written long-hand as *koriandna*, *sāsama*, *kuminon*, etc., or counted by the abbreviations KO, SA, KU, etc.; 'coriander' is in addition found as KO either before or inside ideogram no. 123.

Where the syllabic and ideographic uses of the sign have evidently developed side by side from Linear A and the 'hieroglyphs', the search for a Greek derivation is of course pointless: the syllable ¥ *ni* is also used as the ideogram for 'figs', but the pronunciation of the latter is probably indicated by the quite unrelated *su-za* (=*sūka* ?). In some cases the 'syllabic' ideograms stand not for the commodity itself but for an *adjective* describing some subdivision of it which is being counted: they are in fact 'adjuncts' (see § 6) being counted apart from the ideograms to which they refer. This is the case with the secondary numbers associated with the symbol o, frequent on all classes of

† Mycenaean tablets and sometimes expanded to *o-pe-ro*, which probably stands for *ophêlontes*, *ophêlomena*, etc., 'things which ought to have been there but aren't'. It will be seen that the same syllabic abbreviations may stand for quite different meanings in different contexts.

5. *Two or three syllabic signs telescoped into a 'monogram'*

The frequent 'monogram' ₩ (probably WOOL) is apparently inherited from Linear A, and may originally have represented a 'Minoan' MA+RU; but the process of forming such abbreviations from Greek words is clearly seen in the alternative spellings *ka-na-ko*/KA+NA+KO 'safflower' on the Mycenae 'condiment' tablets, and in *me-ri*/ME+RI 'honey' on Knossos **206** = Gg705, etc. 'Honey' is still spelt in full *me-ri-to* (gen. *melitos*) on Pylos **171** = Un718, and this variability suggests that most of the 'monograms' are only optional abbreviations, which may be used at the scribe's discretion where time or space is short.

Pylos **171** = Un718 provides the surprising examples TU+RO$_2$ 'cheeses' and A+RE+RO (or A+RE+PA 'fat' ?), which are actually introduced by the full spelling of the words on their first occurrence—as if to say 'in what follows, TU+RO₂ is to be taken as an abbreviation for *tu-ro₂*'. After being used for over 200 years one might have expected such abbreviations to be self-explanatory.

6. *'Adjuncts', small syllabic signs written before ideograms*   †

Apart from the ubiquitous *o.-* (=*ophêlomenon*, etc.), the 'adjuncts' are most frequently found categorizing WOMEN, children, SHEEP and CLOTHS; they are not included in fig. 10. They probably all stand for the initial syllables of Greek adjectives or nouns, intended to differentiate the meaning of the ideograms, but their identification is largely guesswork except where they can clearly be seen to replace a word spelt out in full. Thus *mi.* CLOTHS (distinguished from *pe.* CLOTHS) is proved by Knossos L 1568 to represent *mi-ja-ro* ('dirty'?); and *di.* WOMEN and *di.* *children* are probably connected with the words *de-di-ku-ja* = *dedi⟨da⟩khuiai* or *di-da-ka-re* = *didaskal-* and refer in some way to training or education. In a number of situations *ne.-*, *pe.-* and *pa.-* may be suspected of standing for *newos* 'young, new', **presgus/presguteros* 'senior' (or *perusinwos* 'last year's'?) and *palaios* 'aged, old'; but proof is difficult. The adjuncts *e.-* and *ma.-* added to the enigmatic ideogram no. 177 on Knossos U 0478 may suggest some such contrast as *elakhus* 'short'/*makros* 'long'.

Ideograms indicating material or contents are occasionally added in a manner equivalent to adjuncts or monograms, e.g.: GOLD (?) joined to CUPS, etc., on **172** = Kn02 and **238** = Tn996, BRONZE linked with a *dipas* vessel on **230** = K 740, and HONEY with AMPHORA on Gg706.

7. NUMERALS AND METHODS OF MEASUREMENT

Such items as MEN, WOMEN, SHEEP, JUGS or CHARIOTS are naturally counted in units, their numbers being expressed by a simple decimal notation, by which

$$12{,}345 \text{ is written } ◊\text{𝟐 }\text{𝟖°}{=}{=}\text{⫶⫶}$$

This system is identical with that of Linear A, though the sign for 10,000 is not yet attested there. Dow (1954, p. 124) has described the most usual patterns for the strokes making up the tens and units. The sign for the numeral 1 is usually distinguishable from the word-divider by being lifted to the top of the line (ˈ), and where a list of names is so divided, for example Jn725 or Knossos V 831 (Evans' 'contract or official pronouncement', *PM*, IV, p. 698), we must in fact read aloud 'one' after each item. No signs for fractions have been found following numerals on the Mycenaean tablets, but this does not prove their non-existence; if we happened to have a record of such things as '$1\frac{1}{2}$ loaves' or '$3\frac{1}{4}$ days' we might well see fractional symbols used, possibly identical with those of Linear A (see p. 36).

When the scribe counts CHARIOT-HORSES, DRAUGHT-OXEN, WHEELS and sometimes CORSLETS, the numerals are preceded by the signs ZE or MO. The numbers occurring with ZE vary from 1 to 462, but only 1 is found after MO, and this item always comes last if at all. Furumark (1954, p. 28) independently recognized that ZE represents *zeugos* 'a pair' and that MO stands for *monwos* (Att. μόνος) 'a single one'. With 'one pair' and 'two pairs' the nouns and adjectives describing the commodity are written in the dual form (see p. 370). 'Five wheels' are written ⊕ɟ" ʔı, or 'two pairs and a single one'. The typical entry for the complement of a chariot on the Knossos *Sc*-tablets (see pp. 379–81) is:

Man's name: 𐃺 " 𐃺➤ı 𐃺 ɟı

Evans (*PM*, IV, pp. 797, 807) proposed to interpret ZE and MO symbolically, the 'saw' denoting carpentry-work and the 'whip' the function of the charioteer.

For the larger number of agricultural and industrial commodities measured by weight and by bulk, the Mycenaean scribe possessed a series of signs for *fractional quantities*, whose function and ratios have been brilliantly explained by Bennett (1950). A given weight of metal is expressed in the form

$$\text{𐃺 } 1 \quad \text{𐃺 } 22 \quad \text{♯ } 2 \quad \text{𐃺 } 6,$$

where the successively smaller measures are parallel to our '1 cwt., 3 qr., 20 lb., 10 oz.', and we may assume that the Mycenaean symbols stood, like ours, for the actual names of units. The Mycenaean practice is in striking † contrast to that of Linear A, where no such subsidiary measures are found. The odd amounts are there expressed as fractions of the primary units, e.g. $1+\frac{1}{2}+\frac{1}{8}+\frac{1}{16}=1\frac{11}{16}$; and of these units only that for weight appears to have a distinguishing symbol. Bennett saw here a fundamental difference in methods of measurement. The Linear A fractions imply that odd amounts of, let us say, grain were estimated by pouring the residue once only into a number of smaller vessels scaled successively $\frac{1}{2}$, $\frac{1}{4}$, $\frac{1}{8}$, etc., of the primary unit; the Mycenaean stewards measured grain in vessels representing $\frac{1}{10}$ and $\frac{1}{60}$ of the unit, each of which was filled as many times as the residue allowed. He recognized in the Linear B weights and measures a system introduced, together with the new language, from outside Crete, probably from the Greek mainland or from its trading dependencies. It should be noted, however, that several of the

Mycenaean symbols are clearly derived from Linear A fractions (see p. 36), and possibly express analogous ratios.

The ratios of Mycenaean weights and measures established by Bennett (1950), and revised from more recent material, are as follows:

	DRY MEASURE				LIQUID MEASURE			
Unit:	1st	2nd	3rd	4th	1st	2nd	3rd	4th
Symbol:	None	T	◁,ᗡ,Ϝ	▽	None	ዋ,ዣ	◁,ᗡ,Ϝ	▽
Fraction of the preceding:		$\frac{1}{10}$	$\frac{1}{6}$	$\frac{1}{4}$		$\frac{1}{3}$	$\frac{1}{6}$	$\frac{1}{4}$
Fraction of the whole:	1	$\frac{1}{10}$	$\frac{1}{60}$	$\frac{1}{240}$	1	$\frac{1}{3}$	$\frac{1}{18}$	$\frac{1}{72}$

It will be seen that the third and fourth terms have the same ratios and symbols in both series, and probably represent identical names and quantities: compare our own two series, which share *pint* and *quart* but diverge to *bushel* and *gallon*. T and ዋ both represent six times ◁, and must also be equivalent, though probably with different names. The primary dry unit is $3\frac{1}{3}$ times the size of the liquid unit; neither of these has a distinguishing symbol, so that numbers directly following WHEAT or WINE apply to the appropriate largest unit.

	WEIGHT				
Unit:	1st	2nd	3rd	4th	5th
Symbol:	⚖	ᗱ,ᗰ	╫ (†)	ᗱ,ᗱ,ᗱ	ዋ(ϯ)
Fraction of the preceding:		$\frac{1}{30}$	$\frac{1}{4}$	Probably $\frac{1}{12}$	$\frac{1}{6}$ or less
Fraction of the whole:	1	$\frac{1}{30}$	$\frac{1}{120}$	$\frac{1}{1440}$	$\frac{1}{8640}$ or less

The status of the rare symbols enclosed in brackets is uncertain. The com- †
modity 𝕍 is generally measured in whole numbers, but on several Knossos tablets (e.g. **71** = Dk1072) it is evidently weighed in units which are $\frac{1}{10}$ of ⚖ and are divided fractionally into 3 ᗱ. Some commodities, like RI on Pylos Ma03, occasionally occur in quantities like ᗱ 63, not reduced to the primary unit.

Bennett's ratios are confirmed by the summations which occur on a number of tablets: the weight series especially by Pylos Jn845; the liquid series by **200** = Fpl and **93** = Fo101; and the dry series by F 51 (Bennett, *MT I*, pp. 446–8).

In order not to distort the transcriptions of the tablets in Part II, quotations of weights and measures will be printed with the original Mycenaean symbols; but for a fuller understanding of the texts in translation it is desirable to arrive at approximate conversion factors which will enable us to assess the actual quantities involved.. Four types of evidence must here be reconciled:

1. The analogy of contemporary and classical systems of weights and measures, especially where they show parallel ratios.

2. Minoan-Mycenaean objects believed to be standards of weight or volume, or to show serial gradation of size. Logarithmic graph paper will be found useful in all these comparisons.

3. The use of contemporary and classical records to suggest 'reasonable' amounts of the commodities listed, especially where they appear to be rations for a fixed period.

4. Cases where the scribe himself appears to record a conversion factor, either of weight in terms of volume, or of weight or volume in terms of some standard object.

The following comparative data for weights and measures are subject to controversy and should be used with caution, as should those printed in works of reference, many of which perpetuate the confusion expertly introduced into the subject by Lehmann-Haupt and Sir Flinders Petrie. It is clear, too, that beside the official standards a great variety of local measures probably existed side by side for various special purposes.

Babylonia and other areas using cuneiform script (c. 1400 B.C.).
>WEIGHT: 1 *biltu* (light talent of 30·1 kg.) = 60 *manû* = 3600 *šiqlu* (8·5 g.); but a *kakkaru* at Alalakh has only 1800 shekels.
>VOLUME: 1 *qurru*/GUR (c. 300 litres) = 3 *imêru* ('donkey-load' of c. 100 l.) or 5 *massiktu*/PI = 30 *sûtu*/BAN = 300 *qa*/*sila* (c. 1·0 l.). Thureau-Dangin first suggested *qa* = 0·4 l., later concluded *qa* = c. 1·0 l., accepted by Lacheman (1939) and Goetze. Lewy (1944) argues that *qa* = 1·34 l.

Egypt (c. 1400 B.C.).
>WEIGHT: 1 *dbn* (90·95 g.) = 10 *qdt* ('kit' of 9·09 g.).
>VOLUME: 1 *ḥr* (80 l.) = 4 *oipě* (20 l.) = 16 *ḥḳt* (5 l.) = 160 *hin* (0·5 l.).

Biblical measures, with traces of a similar system at Ugarit (capitals).
>WEIGHT: 1 *kikkâr*/KKR (34·3 kg.) = 50 *mâneh*/MN = 3000 *šeqel*/ṬKL (11·42 g.).
>DRY: 1 *ḥômer* or *kor* (230–400 l.) = 2 *letek*/LTḤ = 10 *'efâ* = 30 *še'a*.
>LIQUID: 1 *baṭ* (= '*efâ* of 23–40 l.) = 6 *hîn* = 18 *qab* = 72 *lôg*/LG (0·31–0·54 l.). The higher figures are based on traditional Roman equations, the lower are estimated from restored measuring vessels of the early period (Barrois, 1953) and confirmed by Lewy (1944).

Classical Athens.
>WEIGHT: 1 *talanton* (c. 25·8 kg.) = 60 *mnai* = 3000 *stateres* (8·6 g.) = 6000 *drakhmai* (4·3 g.). Aeginetan standards heavier by $\frac{3}{7}$.
>DRY: 1 *medimnos* (43·5 l.) = 6 *hekteis* = 48 *khoinikes* (0·906 l.) = 192 *kotylai* (0·227 l.). Spartan ('Pheidonian') *medimnos* perhaps larger by $\frac{3}{7}$.
>LIQUID: 1 *metretes* (21·75 l. ?) = 8? *khoes* = 96? *kotylai* (0·227 l.).

8. THE ABSOLUTE VALUES OF THE SYMBOLS FOR WEIGHT

Evans (*PM*, IV, p. 651) and Sundwall (1932) very plausibly identified the 'Palace Standard' of weight as a talent (cf. Greek τάλαντα 'pair of scales'), equal in value to the gypsum octopus weight of 29,000 grams found in Magazine 15 at Knossos, or to the average weight of the nineteen copper ingots from Agia Triada (29,132 grams). The latter may admittedly not be LM II in date, but such a talent tends to remain constant, due to its limiting value as the largest ingot which can conveniently be shouldered by one man (compare the *Kftjw* tribute-bearers on the Egyptian wall-paintings), and as the largest unit weight which can be lifted on to the scales (which may explain the etymology of τάλαντον). Two Knossos tablets in fact record the weight of ingots: Oa730 lists sixty ingots at a total of ៙ $52\frac{2}{30}$, Oa733 lists ten ingots at a figure which may be completed as 6 or 8 ៙. If the talent ៙ has a value of exactly 29 kg., the absolute values will be as in the first column of the following table; but at the cost of a possible slight error, the more even figures of the last column will be used in the translations in Part II of this book.

៙ 1 =	29 kg.	(64 lb.)	≈ 30 kg.
៙ 1 =	967 g.	(2 lb., $2\frac{1}{2}$ oz.)	1 kg.
♯ 1 =	242 g.	($8\frac{5}{8}$ oz.)	250 g.
៙ 1 =	20·2 g.	(312 grains)	20·8 g.
ᛃ 1 =	3·36 g. or less		3·4 g. or less

The commodity ᛃ is consequently measured in units of just under 3 kg. † (6·4 lb.). As it appears frequently both on Knossos SHEEP and textile tablets, it probably represents WOOL (as suggested by Evans, *SM II*, p. 28) and 'woollen cloth'. On Alalakh tablet no. 361 (Wiseman, 1952, p. 100) 308 sheep yield ninety shekels weight (or 760 g.) of usable wool each: the measure ᛃ therefore represents approximately the wool from four sheep. Why such a unit should be chosen is not clear, but it is perhaps significant that the units of WOOL stipulated on the Knossos *Dk*- tablets are regularly $\frac{1}{4}$ the number of sheep (e.g. **71** = Dk1072).

Little correspondence can be traced between our suggested weight values and the miscellaneous metrical objects, of varied place and date, listed by Evans (*PM*, IV, pp. 653–6) and Glotz (1925): these do not indeed form any consistent series among themselves. A striking exception is the gold coils and rings from the Mycenae Acropolis Treasure (see p. 359).

The Mycenaean talent is similar in value to the contemporary Babylonian light talent, and its subdivision into thirty may distantly reflect the sexagesimal division of the latter; but note that the biblical and Ugaritic talent is divided into fifty minas, not sixty. Any similarity to the classical standards of weight is evidently due to the persistence of the 'talent' in the East Mediterranean under Phoenician trade domination, and not to the preservation of Mycenaean standards on Greek soil through the 'Dark Ages': the absence of any central authority capable of enforcing such standards makes a direct survival of weights or measures unlikely.

9. THE ABSOLUTE VALUES OF THE SYMBOLS FOR VOLUME

The smallest unit of volume is indicated by ▽, clearly the measure of a 'cup', paralleled by the Greek *kotyle*, Egyptian '*hin*', Israelite *lôg* and Akkadian *qa*. If we assume that its value lies, like these, between 0·227 and 1·0 litre (roughly between ½ pint and 2 pints), then the primary dry unit will be 240 times larger, or between 54½ and 240 litres.

Bennett (1950, p. 219) pointed out a parallel between the relative sizes of the Mycenaean dry and liquid units and the classical *medimnos* and *metretes*, but the proportion he quotes for the smallest unit of all, the *kyathos*, is incorrect. Sundwall (1953) identified ▽ as a *kotyle* of 0·227 litre, giving a dry unit of 320 *kotylai* = 1 'Aeginetan' *medimnos* of 72·48 (?) litres, and a liquid unit of 96 *kotylai* = 1 Attic *metretes* of 21·75 litres; but his number of ▽ is based on a divergent and probably erroneous scheme of ratios. He suggests a direct link between the Mycenaean and classical systems.

On the 'condiment' tablets from Mycenae (ch. VII, pp. 225–31) the commodity *knākos eruthrā* (the red florets of *Carthamus tinctorius*) is measured by weight, in some cases paired with dry measures of *knākos leukā* (the seeds of the same plant).

The weights of *eruthrā* vary from ⩰ 1 to ⩰ 3 (967–2900 g.), the volumes of *leukā* are regularly ◁ 1. If we assume for the sake of argument that *eruthrā* has a density of about 15 lb. per cubic foot (= 240 g. per litre), and *leukā* of about 40 lb. (= 800 g. per litre), and that the recorded amounts of both substances fall approximately within the same range, then two possible sets of limiting values for the primary dry unit are suggested:

1. If ◁ 1 of *leukā* is equal *in bulk* to ⩰ 1–3 of *eruthrā*, then the dry unit has a value of $\dfrac{967 \text{ to } 2900}{240} \times 60 = 240$–725 litres.

2. If ◁ 1 of *leukā* is equal *in weight* to ⩰ 1–3 of *eruthrā*, then the dry unit has a value of $\dfrac{967 \text{ to } 2900}{800} \times 60 = 72$–216 litres.

These wide limits, which are compatible with those deduced from the parallels of *kotyle*, etc., can be narrowed somewhat by considering the evidence for rations, in the light of the following parallels:

Mesopotamia (2100–1400 B.C.): The tablets from Ur (Legrain, 1947, nos. 894–1189) and Lagaš (Genouillac, 1909, p. xxxv) agree with the later Nuzi texts (Lacheman, 1939, p. 6) in fixing the monthly grain ration of women slaves and menial workers at 30 *qa* (40 l. on Lewy's equation, with a daily value of *c.* 2845 calories, 30 l. on Thureau-Dangin's), of their children at 20 or sometimes 10 *qa*, and of artisans at 40–120 *qa* according to skill and status. Lewy suggests that the 30 *qa* workers ate their grain roasted, while the higher social groups received a larger amount to allow for milling and baking; but the latter may equally have been designed for the support of families and for the privilege of bartering the surplus.

Estimate for the Persian army (Herodotus VII, 187): at least 1 *khoinix* of wheat a day = 27½ l. per month. This same figure is assumed as the Athenian daily ration, and implicit in the Homeric use of the term.

Spartan army at Sphakteria (Thuc. IV, 16): 2 *khoinikes* of barley a day, or 55 l. per month.

There are three Mycenaean contexts where groups of people, not individually named, have rations listed after them:

1. The Pylos *Ab-* tablets, where numbers of women and children are credited with equal amounts of WHEAT and FIGS. No exact ratio per person is observed, but though some groups receive up to 50 per cent more, the basic or minimum allowance seems to be T 2 per woman and T 1 per child (see p. 157). If this T 2 is equated with the Mesopotamian women's ration of 30 or 40 l., the primary † dry unit will have a value of 150–200 l., within the range of our 'cup' and *knākos* analogies above; but a somewhat lower value may be suggested by the fact that most of the women actually get more than T 2, and a ration of figs as well.

2. Knossos **35** = Am819, where eighteen men and eight boys receive '*sitos* CRESCENT 1 BARLEY 9¾'. As hinted by Myres (*SM II*, p. 9) the CRESCENT may mean 'one month's work', for which each person receives an average of exactly T 3¾, perhaps between 56 and 75 l. on the equation just proposed. ‡

3. Pylos An31, where fifty-two men apparently receive 2⅔ units of WHEAT, 2⅔ of FIGS and 5⅓ of BARLEY; the combined cereal ration would be only T 1½ per man (perhaps between 22½ and 30 l.), which is on the low side and perhaps not the scale for a full month.

The most frequent size of Mycenaean stirrup-jar, such as have been found in quantity in the basements of the Mycenae houses excavated by Wace since 1952, and at many other sites both in Greece and in the Near East, has

† a capacity of approximately 12–14 l. Like our own quart and pint bottles, it is likely that this stirrup-jar represents a unitary quantity in the system of liquid measure, and the most probable value seems to be one liquid ⋎ (equivalent to one dry T, which we have seen to have a possible value of 15 l. or less). In the translations of Part II, the value of ⋎ will be taken at the convenient figure of 12 l.:

Dry Measure	Liquid Measure
1 unit = 120 litres	1 unit = 36 l.
T 1 = 12 l.	⋎ 1 = 12 l.

$$\triangleleft\ 1 = 2\ \text{l.}$$
$$\triangledown\ 1 = \tfrac{1}{2}\ \text{l. (approx. 1 pint)}$$

A more accurate determination must await further evidence; the 1954 Pylos tablet Gn1184 may conceivably be taken to show that the normal volume of the stirrup-jar in fact contains ⋎ $1\tfrac{1}{2}$ (see p. 217), in which case all the above figures must be reduced somewhat. The difficulty which results from these conversion factors in interpreting *pe-mo* on the Pylos land tablets as 'seed corn' will be discussed below (pp. 237–8).

Evans (*PM*, IV, p. 648) states that the later *pithoi* in the Knossos magazines normally contain about 185 litres, or the contents of about fourteen stirrup-jars; but their recorded dimensions and illustrations suggest that their volume is in fact about 50 per cent larger than this, and nearer to that of the *pithoi* from the basement of the House of the Oil Merchant at Mycenae.

It will be noted that the ratios and volumes of the biblical system for liquids show some analogy with the Mycenaean: there are reasons for regarding the former as survivals of a general Canaanite system, traces of which can be seen in use at Ugarit, but a direct influence on Mycenae is perhaps doubtful. The primary dry unit also corresponds, perhaps accidentally, with the Babylonian *imêru* or 'donkey-load', which is similarly subdivided into ten.

‡ ## 10. POSSIBLE SURVIVALS: THE CYPRIOT SCRIPTS

No evidence has been found for writing in Greece between the Pylos tablets of *c*. 1200 B.C. and the introduction of an alphabetic system based on the Phoenician in about 850 B.C. Wace (1954) is unwilling to accept this *argumentum e silentio* for a break in Greek literacy, but this is not the only field in which sub-Mycenaean culture appears to show a retrogression. Though recent excavations have tended to show that the break caused by the 'Dorian invasion' is less fundamental than had been thought, the great palaces which had fostered (and perhaps monopolized) the art of writing certainly ceased to exist.

A possible descendant of Minoan-Mycenaean writing is, however, to be found in Cyprus, where a linear syllabary was in use during the Late Bronze Age. First identified on three clay balls from Enkomi found by Murray in 1896, it was named the 'Cypro-Minoan script' by Evans (*SM I*, p. 69): this term begs the question of a possible relationship, and it would be safer for the present to refer to it simply as the 'Cypriot linear script'. The material admirably reviewed by Daniel (1941) has been considerably increased by excavation (see Masson, 1954) and falls into six groups:

1. Signs incised on the handles, or painted on the bottoms, of Cypriot pottery in both the Mycenaean and local styles (from many sites in Cyprus and the Near East).

2. Signs incised on copper ingots.

3. Signs written with a blunt stylus on clay balls, afterwards baked (twenty-seven from Enkomi, one from Hala Sultan Tekke), or engraved on seals.

4. Three baked clay tablets found at Enkomi in 1952–3, and dated to 1225 B.C. or earlier (Dikaios, 1953, p. 237). Two are much damaged, but the third preserves twenty-two continuous lines of text, representing the surviving quarter of an opisthographic tablet of two columns, which must have contained some two hundred lines, probably of a literary nature. The very small characters are written left-to-right with jabbing strokes of a sharp stylus, and are separated by word-dividers but not by guide-lines. Masson is probably right in considering that they represent a more advanced stage in the use of the script than (3).

5. A fragmentary tablet, with seven lines on each face, found by Schaeffer in a private house at Ras Shamra (Ugarit), together with records in Ugaritic and Akkadian (to be published in *Ugaritica*, III).

6. Three lines of a baked tablet, found at Enkomi in 1955 and kindly communicated to us by Dr Dikaios. The signs are more than twice as large as those of (4), and are freer, more continuous and more 'linear' in outline; there are guide-lines but not, apparently, word-dividers. It is dated by its Late Cypriot I context to *c.* 1500 B.C.

Our signary (fig. 11) is restricted to the fifty-seven syllabic signs so far clearly differentiated on the later Enkomi tablets (4) which constitute the most extensive examples of the script; appended to these are the twenty-five signs which can be isolated on the Ugarit tablet (5), kindly supplied by Masson. It will be noted that there are divergences as well as identities between the two series; the scripts of the other categories of Cypriot inscriptions also show a general, rather than a detailed, relationship with each other, and more examples of each are required before we can judge whether they in fact represent successive stages of a single development.

The bulk of the Cypriot material comes from Enkomi, a site which Schaeffer regards as the seat of a Mycenaean king. The theory of an 'Achaean' settlement of part of Cyprus between 1400 and 1350 B.C., contemporary with the sudden preponderance of Mycenaean pottery, is also accepted by Myres, Gjerstad, Furumark and Stubbings, and finds some support in Hittite references to the activities of *Aḫḫijawā*. Sittig (1955*b*) has already attempted to read the 1953 tablet in Greek, but the material will hardly be sufficient to offer hope

No.	Sign	Count	No.	Sign	Count	No.	Sign	Count	No.	Sign	Count	No.	Sign	Count	No.	Sign	Count
Enkomi			15	⟨sign⟩	×2	29	⟨sign⟩	×6	43	⟨sign⟩	×5	57	⟨sign⟩	×7	12	⟨sign⟩	×1
1	⟨sign⟩	×2	16	⟨sign⟩	6	30	⟨sign⟩	12	44	⟨sign⟩	10	58	⟨sign⟩	9	13	⟨sign⟩	1
2	⟨sign⟩	13	17	⟨sign⟩	5	31	⟨sign⟩	3	45	⟨sign⟩	11	Ugarit			14	⟨sign⟩	1
3	⟨sign⟩	7	18	⟨sign⟩	3	32	⟨sign⟩	21	46	⟨sign⟩	1	1	⟨sign⟩	2	15	⟨sign⟩	1
4	⟨sign⟩	7	19	⟨sign⟩	13	33	⟨sign⟩	5	47	⟨sign⟩	8	2	⟨sign⟩	3	16	⟨sign⟩	1
5	⟨sign⟩	9	20	⟨sign⟩	11	34	⟨sign⟩	1	48	⟨sign⟩	2	3	⟨sign⟩	5	17	⟨sign⟩	3
6	⟨sign⟩	9	21	⟨sign⟩	5	35	⟨sign⟩	1	49	⟨sign⟩	10	4	⟨sign⟩	1	18	⟨sign⟩	2
7	⟨sign⟩	1	22	⟨sign⟩	10	36	⟨sign⟩	9	50	⟨sign⟩	5	5	⟨sign⟩	1	19	⟨sign⟩	3
8	⟨sign⟩	2	23	⟨sign⟩	2	37	⟨sign⟩	6	51	⟨sign⟩	7	6	⟨sign⟩	3	20	⟨sign⟩	2
9	⟨sign⟩	4	24	⟨sign⟩	5	38	⟨sign⟩	4	52	⟨sign⟩	12	7	⟨sign⟩	3	21	⟨sign⟩	1
10	⟨sign⟩	2	25	⟨sign⟩	14	39	⟨sign⟩	3	53	⟨sign⟩	10	8	⟨sign⟩	1	22	⟨sign⟩	1
11	⟨sign⟩	3	26	⟨sign⟩	6	40	⟨sign⟩	2	54	⟨sign⟩	4	9	⟨sign⟩	1	23	⟨sign⟩	1
12	⟨sign⟩	14	27	⟨sign⟩	4	41	⟨sign⟩	2	55	⟨sign⟩	21	10	⟨sign⟩	3	24	⟨sign⟩	1
14	⟨sign⟩	13	28	⟨sign⟩	12	42	⟨sign⟩	1	56	⟨sign⟩	9	11	⟨sign⟩	2	25	⟨sign⟩	2?

Fig. 11. The Cypriot linear script, as used on the 1953 tablets from Enkomi and Ugarit. The smaller figures show the number of recognizable occurrences.

of decipherment until the discovery of the main Enkomi archives confidently predicted by Schaeffer. It is clear, at any rate, that the Cypriot linear script is far from being merely a local variety of Linear B. Though analogous in its general layout, word-division and predominantly left-to-right direction, it shows few exact resemblances in the forms of the signs; and if the Enkomi tablets really contain an 'Achaean' dialect brought from the Greek mainland, it is surprising that they are not written in Linear B, which at all other Mycenaean sites shows such complete uniformity. At best one might suppose that the Achaeans arrived in Cyprus at a time when Linear B had not yet come into general use in Greece, and that they adapted an indigenous script already in use in the island.

Writing does in fact seem to have been known in Cyprus before the proposed date of the Mycenaean influx. The American excavations at Bamboula (Kourion) were said to reveal a use of the Cypriot linear script extending from Late Cypriot Ia:2 (c. 1500 B.C.) down to about 1150 B.C. (Daniel, 1941, pp. 251, 270); the bulk of this material consists of single potters' marks (notoriously untrustworthy as evidence for a developed script), and the vessels earlier than 1400 B.C. merely carry the elementary patterns +, X or ∌. But Dikaios' 1955 tablet (6) may provide conclusive proof that the Cypriot linear script was already in use before the evolution of the Mycenaean syllabary, and may lend support to Evans' view that it was derived directly from the Linear A of Crete.

The latest use of writing at Enkomi is found on bronze ingots of the twelfth–eleventh centuries (Cypriot Iron I), i.e. from after Schaeffer's suggested occupation of the city by the 'Sea Peoples' prior to its final destruction about 1050 B.C. There are no certain examples of non-Semitic writing in Cyprus between this date and the first occurrence of the classical Cypriot syllabary on pottery of the seventh or eighth century. We are thus faced with a problem of interrupted literacy similar to that in Greece itself, and aggravated by the fact that the eleventh century is precisely the date generally assumed for the larger influx of population which gave classical Cyprus its predominantly Greek character.

The Cypriot syllabary, first detected by the Duc de Luynes in 1852 and partially deciphered by George Smith in 1871, has fifty-five signs. More than 500 inscriptions are known, extending in date down to the end of the third century B.C. The majority contain the local Arcado-Cyprian dialect of Greek (whose affinities with the dialect of our Mycenaean tablets will be stressed in ch. III), but never the *koinē*; the syllabary is also used for an indigenous language which has been called 'Eteocyprian' (*corpus* in Friedrich, 1932) and which remains incomprehensible in spite of a bilingual from Amathus. It is often a matter of dispute whether a particular inscription is written in Greek or in 'Eteocyprian' (as pointed out in the good general review of Cypriot epigraphy by Mitford, 1952). It is a surprising fact that Cyprus, part of which was occupied by the Phoenicians from at least the ninth century, was the area in which a non-alphabetic writing of Greek survived longest.

The published signaries of the syllabary uncritically lump together forms of widely differing place and date, and are misleading as a basis for comparison

4-2

TABLE A: the non-Paphian signary

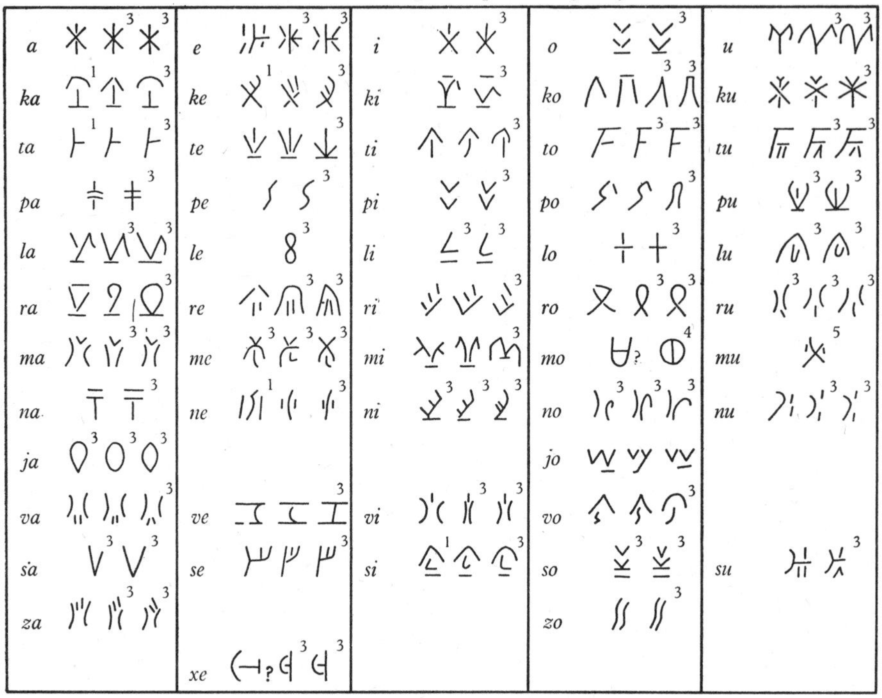

a	e	i	o	u
ka	ke	ki	ko	ku
ta	te	ti	to	tu
pa	pe	pi	po	pu
la	le	li	lo	lu
ra	re	ri	ro	ru
ma	me	mi	mo	mu
na	ne	ni	no	nu
ja			jo	
va	ve	vi	vo	
sà	se	si	so	su
za			zo	
	xe			

TABLE B: the Paphian signary

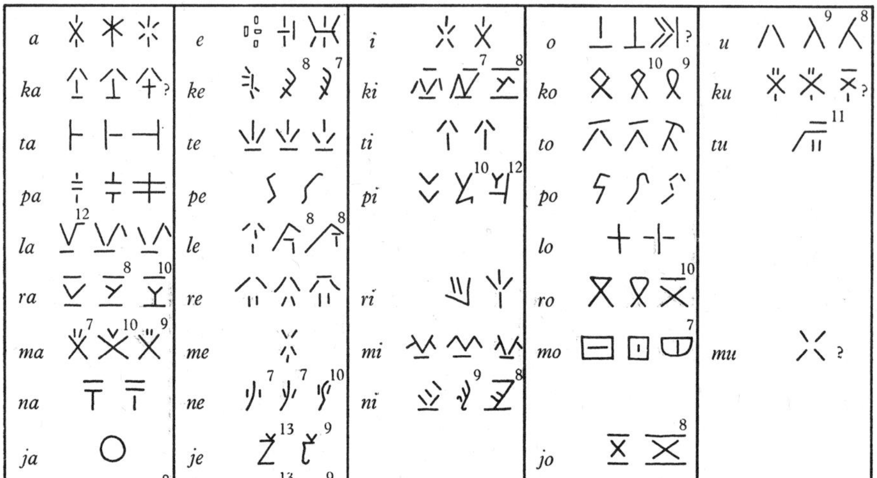

a	e	i	o	u
ka	ke	ki	ko	ku
ta	te	ti	to	tu
pa	pe	pi	po	
la	le		lo	
ra	re	ri	ro	
ma	me	mi	mo	mu
na	ne	ni		
ja	je		jo	
va	ve		vo	
sa	se	si	so	
za			zo	

Fig. 12. The classical Cypriot syllabary (after Mitford).

with earlier scripts. T. B. Mitford has kindly supplied us with the material for fig. 12, and with the following explanatory notes:

(i) These two tables are composed at first-hand from the following inscriptions:

TABLE A:

1. An unpublished epitaph from Marium of the mid-sixth century.
2. The 'Bulwer Tablet' from the Western Karpas (*Sitzb. Berl.* 1910, pp. 148 ff.). This is thought by Meister to be of sixth-century date, and is probably early.
3. The Bronze Tablet of Idalium (*SGDI*, 60), dated either to the time of the Ionic Revolt (so E. Meyer, Oberhummer, Gjerstad) or to the mid-fifth century (so Hill). Cf. G. F. Hill, *A History of Cyprus*, 1, pp. 153 ff.
4. An unpublished epitaph from Marium which is probably early.
5. The Bilingual of Idalium (*SGDI*, 59), dated to 389/8 B.C.

TABLE B:

6. Unpublished inscriptions from the Kouklia siege-mound constructed during the Persian investment of Old Paphos in 499/8 B.C.
7. *JHS*, **9** (1888), p. 256, no. 2 (Hoffmann, *Gr. Dialekte*, 59, no. 109), from the Aphrodite temple at Old Paphos and probably of fourth- or fifth-century date.
8. The First Stele of Agia Moni (Meister, *Gr. Dialekte*, 2, no. 36a), of the late fourth century.
9. The Second Stele of Agia Moni (Meister, *Gr. Dialekte*, 2, no. 36b), of the late fourth century.
10. An unpublished inscription of New Paphos of the late fourth century.
11. The First Inscription from the Grotto of Apollo Hylates at New Paphos (*SGDI*, 31), of fourth(?)-century date.
12. The Second Inscription from the Grotto of Apollo Hylates (*SGDI*, 32), of fourth(?)-century date.
13. The Khapotami Stele (*Anatolian Studies presented to W. H. Buckler*, pp. 197 ff.), of the late fourth century.
14. An unpublished inscription of Lapithiou, of the fifth or sixth century.

(ii) In these tables signs taken from (2) and (6) are not specially numbered.

(iii) There is no significance in the order in which the variants of each sign are presented.

In spite of the missing historical links, the small number of signs which correspond exactly, and its generally *right-to-left* direction, Masson (1954, p. 444) is probably correct in assuming that this Cypriot syllabary represents a direct descendant of the linear script of the Enkomi tablets. We may well expect a few changes and substitutions in the intervening 700 years, even if both systems contain Greek; and we must also reckon with the influence of varying writing materials. Myres thought that the Cypriot syllabary forms were determined, like those of the Northern runes and oghams, by being cut on wood; the same influences might account for the divergence of the 'Cypro-Minoan' forms from the more flowing lines of the supposed 'Minoan' prototypes; and the script of the Enkomi tablets is clearly somewhat specialized in being minutely written on clay (less than half the normal size of Linear B), its outlines being dissolved into patterns of small jabbing incisions.

It will be clear, then, that the attempt to trace a continuous and detailed descent 'Hieroglyphic'—Linear A—Linear B—Cypriot linear script—Cypriot syllabary is fraught with obstacles which are likely to remain insuperable so long as evidence for the successive links is missing, and until more of the successive phases have been deciphered. One can have little confidence in an apparent similarity between a Linear B sign and a sign of the Cypriot syllabary if no plausible intermediate form can be recognized among the Enkomi signary of fig. 11. The most ambitious tabulation has so far been Daniel's (1941, figs. 1, 2, 3, 9). He believed with Evans that the Cypriot scripts were derived from Minoan Linear A rather than from Mycenaean Linear B; Casson (1937) on equally slender grounds derived the Cypriot linear script from Greek mainland forms.

But it is only fair to admit that Daniel, in tracing what may appear rather superficial similarities, did succeed in deducing correct Linear B values from the Cypriot signs for *da/ta, lo, na, pa, po, se* and *ti*. These are in fact among the simplest patterns (common to both Linear A and B) which might occur spontaneously in any 'linear' script; but the fact that the phonetic values also agree does indicate some fundamental connexion; further explanation must await the decipherment of the Enkomi tablets. The more complex Cypriot signs *a, e, ka, ke, ku, la, me, pe, pu, ra, si, su, te, tu, zo* led Daniel to erroneous equations, as might be expected.

The known syllabic values for the half-dozen or so simplest Cypriot syllabary signs played no deliberate part in our decipherment of Linear B, which on principle excluded evidence from outside scripts. That is not to say that suggestions like Evans' *po-lo* = πῶλος 'foal' (*PM*, IV, p. 799) may not have been an unconscious influence in our choice of sound-values for testing.

CHAPTER III

THE MYCENAEAN LANGUAGE

1. SCRIPT AND LANGUAGE

THE account of the decipherment has shown how the idea that the language underlying the script was Greek first gained credence. It seemed obvious that a solution which yielded immediately recognizable Greek words could not be totally wrong, and this was confirmed by two other factors: the possibility of explaining the pattern of declension by archaic Greek models, and the subsequent discovery that many at first sight aberrant forms agreed with the hypothetical reconstructions of the comparativists.

On the other hand the inadequacy of the script led to considerable uncertainty about the exact form of many words, which could only be given an intelligible shape by the assumption of certain rules of orthography. The suspicion therefore arose whether the attempt to force Mycenaean spellings to fit classical forms might not be a Procrustean operation which would arbitrarily produce far greater similarity than in fact existed. Mycenaean might be a non-Greek, but closely related Indo-European language; or it could be an aberrant dialect of Greek, showing, like the dubious remains of Macedonian, a general resemblance but considerable difference in its specific forms.

If there were reason to believe that the script was evolved originally for the recording of Greek, we might argue that its inadequacy for classical Greek proved that Mycenaean was radically different. But in view of the certainly Minoan origin of the Linear Scripts, this argument is unfounded. Any script is better than none, and the Mycenaeans cannot be criticized for having failed to adopt the refinements which made syllabic writing a more serviceable instrument for the later Cypriots. The suggestion that documents of the type so far found require a less accurate notation than continuous prose is true, but dangerous in view of our restricted knowledge of the extent of literacy; we have already one sentence running to twenty-three words, and another of complicated construction has seventeen.

We may first examine the claim of Mycenaean to be a dialect of Greek. This will be justified if we can demonstrate enough features which are known to be typical of Greek. The material, though scanty, is none the less sufficient to show some of the principal phonetic changes: loss of initial and intervocalic

*-s-; loss of initial *j- or its replacement in some words by z-; devoicing of
I.-E. voiced aspirates (concealed by the script except in the case of the dentals);
the development of *kj, *tj before vowel to s, of *gj, *dj to z; the vocalism a
(in some cases o) from syllabic liquids or nasals. Typically Greek features of
morphology are: the wide extension of stems in -εύς; the 3rd sing. of the present
indicative of the thematic verb in -e (=-ει); and the form of the infinitive in
-(e)en. It is, however, the vocabulary that is most strikingly Greek. It contains
a considerable number of words which are known in Greek, but have no certain
cognates in other languages: e.g. ἄναξ, βασιλεύς, δέπας, ἔλαιον, μάραθον,
σέλινον, σῖτος. It could be argued that these are pre-Greek and therefore
without significance. But a much larger number, although belonging to well-
known I.-E. families, appear in forms which are specifically Greek. A few
examples must suffice: ἀμφιφορεύς, ἀνίαι, γραῦς, θεός, θρᾶνυς, κᾶρυξ, μέζων,
πᾶς, τρίπος, φάσγανον, χαλκός.

This evidence taken together proves beyond reasonable doubt that Mycenaean
is a form of Greek. It remains therefore to establish its affinities within that
language. Study of the historical dialects had long since led to the conclusion
that Arcadian and Cypriot were the relics of a dialect once widely spoken over
Southern Greece. Since this was largely replaced by Doric dialects, and the
end of the Mycenaean age was identified with the legend of the Dorian
invasions, it was a natural conclusion that the dialect of Mycenaean Greece
would be an ancestor of Arcadian. This view, however, has been challenged
by Merlingen (1954, 1955) and by P. B. S. Andrews in discussions at the London
Seminar and elsewhere.

†   Before we turn to the positive evidence we must therefore discuss certain
objections. While a few modifications of the traditional view of the prehistory
of the Greek language seem possible, the main outlines are well established.
The historical distribution, with dialects as widely separated linguistically as
Attic and Megarian in close geographical contact, could not have arisen without considerable movements of population. The position of the West Greek
dialects strongly suggests that they were newcomers displacing other dialects
or compressing them into small areas such as Arcadia and Attica, where the
local traditions agree in representing the inhabitants as 'autochthonous'. But
at the time of this Dorian migration, East and West Greek must already have
been differentiated; therefore the period when all Greeks spoke a common
dialect (*Urgriechisch*) must have been considerably earlier, and it has been
generally supposed that it preceded the arrival of the first Greeks in Greece,
but the theory of Risch (1955) makes this unnecessary. Merlingen (1954, p. 4)
assumes from the mutual intelligibility of the historical dialects that their

break-up could not go back as much as 1000 years; but this is to ignore the effects of convergence, which was certainly at work long before the influence of Attic became dominant. Another factor bearing on the chronology of the dialect distribution is the close agreement between Arcadian and Cypriot. This implies not only that Arcadian was once spoken on the coast of the Peloponnese, but, since the colonization of Cyprus took place in Mycenaean times (Schaeffer, 1952, I, p. 343), that it was the dialect spoken at that period. Any attempt to displace Mycenaean from its assumed position of ancestor to Arcadian and Cypriot must demonstrate circumstances in which the ancestral dialect could have occupied Southern Greece. Such a dialect must have existed in that area in the Mycenaean period, and the tablets give clear evidence of the language in use at three of the principal sites; the conclusion of their identity seems inescapable.

If the script represents accurately the phonetics of Mycenaean Greek, then it follows that this dialect had no descendants recorded in classical times. If the Mycenaeans confused the *sounds* of *l* and *r*, then their descendants could never have separated them again correctly. We have therefore to reconcile our suggestion that Mycenaean is likely to be the ancestor of Arcadian with the admitted difficulties of the script.

It is certain that Linear B is derived from an earlier Minoan script, probably represented by Linear A. It is therefore a reasonable assumption that the form of the syllabary reflects not Greek but another language, which we may for convenience designate 'Minoan'. This may perhaps have resembled the Polynesian type, consisting mainly of open syllables, final consonants being either absent or at least not significant, after the pattern of *hula hula* or *kia ora*, rather than that of κνώψ or Σφίγξ. Likewise the oppositions of the stops—voiced/unvoiced, aspirated/unaspirated—seem to have had no place in the system. But examples from other scripts warn us against explaining as linguistic evidence features that may only be economy measures. Many cuneiform signs are used with a lack of discrimination between *b/p*, *d/t*, etc., which (except in the case of Hittite) does not necessarily reflect on the language being written; and the lack of written vowels in Phoenician does not imply the previous existence of a language without them. On the other hand 'Minoan' may have contained oppositions of a different kind, which would make little impression on ears accustomed to the phonemic distinctions of Greek. Two signs have been identified of a second series for *r* (=*l*), and it seems almost certain that these represented in 'Minoan' some sort of palatalized liquid (see p. 47). Similarly Palmer (1955 b, p. 42) has suggested that the syllabary contains a whole series of doublets based on an original opposition between palatalized and non-palatalized consonants. On the value of pa_2 see below (p. 81). The opposition of $d/t(h)$ is probably not to be referred to 'Minoan'; rather we may suppose that language to have had two dental sounds distinguished by their place of articulation, and this distinction being useless in Greek, the signs were adopted to represent an opposition which was important for Greek. This is the more probable in view of a precisely similar development in the adaptation to Greek of the Phoenician alphabet. The opposition of $t/ṭ$ being unknown in Greek, the sign for $ṭ$ was superfluous; but it was seized upon to represent the distinction of t/th, which was important for Greek. This value of θ is common to all the earliest Greek alphabets, and the corresponding sounds ph and kh are either not distinguished from the unaspirated or are noted by the digraphs ΠΗ, ΚΗ.

2. FOREIGN ELEMENTS IN MYCENAEAN

It has been suggested that Mycenaean is a mixed language, containing both Greek and other elements. It is hardly necessary to point out that a completely 'pure' language is virtually unknown; and that Greek itself contains a large number of vocabulary elements which cannot be certainly traced in the other I.-E. languages. It is possible that the proportion of non-Greek words was higher in Mycenaean than in Attic, or even Homeric Greek; but it would be rash to assume that all the words that so far defy interpretation were of foreign origin. Experience has shown that they often prove to be unfamiliar forms or derivatives of known Greek roots; or to be explicable with the aid of dialect words preserved in Glossaries. The final classification of a language depends ultimately on its grammar and syntax, and it will be shown in what follows that in this respect Mycenaean displays undeniably Greek features. Even without the supposition of extensive borrowing, a considerable alteration in the vocabulary may be expected in the period intervening between the Mycenaean tablets and classical texts and inscriptions. The links would be even fewer if the epic dialect did not constitute a bridge between the two, enshrining as it undoubtedly does many relics of the Mycenaean vocabulary which would otherwise be quite unknown to us. Nor must we forget that the dialects most likely to be descended from Mycenaean are among the worst known.

It cannot be denied that there are Mycenaean words which appear to have no relatives in Greek; but this cannot be asserted unless we can determine independently the meaning of the Mycenaean word in question. One example may suffice: the word *a-ja-me-no* (fem. *a-ja-me-na*) occurs in contexts which allow us to deduce the meaning. It is frequently, though not always, constructed with a dative (instrumental), e.g. *e-re-pa-te*=*elephantei*; and it must mean 'decorated', or possibly decorated in some special way, perhaps by inlay. No one so far has been able to suggest a Greek word with which it can be associated; nevertheless it has the appearance of a passive participle of the ordinary Greek type; the spelling *a-ja-* may conceal a reduplicated form (*aiai-*); and it appears to have as its opposite *a-na-i-ta*, which shows the familiar privative *a(n)-* combined with an unreduplicated base and a *-to-* suffix. In such cases it is tempting to scour the I.-E. languages for a possible etymology (Georgiev has in fact found a possible parallel in Hieroglyphic Hittite); but the etymological method as a means of interpretation in the absence of contextual confirmation is rightly out of favour, and has recently been strongly condemned by Friedrich (1954, pp. 123–8). There are many factors which can have con- † tributed to the loss of Mycenaean words from the later Greek vocabulary.

Some speculation has centred round the question of the native language of the scribes. If more than one language were in use in Mycenaean Greece, this would lead to interesting historical conclusions. It may be deduced from the areas of non-Greek speech in historical times that such communities also existed at the earlier period. There is, however, nothing in the tablets to confirm this except the undoubted presence of non-Greek names. There are no tablets of reasonable extent which do not give some sign of being written in Greek, though of course lists of names may well have a foreign look. Merlingen (1955, p. 45) supposes the Greeks to have been a subject class, who kept all the accounts, under the rule of non-Greek 'Achaean' masters; Andrews prefers to make the rulers Greek, but the scribes foreigners obliged to write in their masters' language. There is not a scrap of real evidence to support the former hypothesis; only some rather questionable deductions from a group of words in Greek alleged to be borrowings from a hypothetical I.-E. language. Even if this language really existed, there is no reason to assign it to the rulers of Mycenaean Greece. Nor does this theory account satisfactorily for the clearly Greek names borne by some of the leading citizens of Pylos; *E-ke-ra₂-wo* is ‡ a man of great importance and may even be the king (see p. 265), but it is hard to believe that he has not a Greek name, *Ekhelāwōn*. It does not seem possible to correlate the Greek names of the tablets with any social class.

The contention of Andrews is based upon rather more solid evidence, namely the apparent blunders in spelling and grammar which mar the texts. It is of course true that in the early years of Greek rule foreign scribes may have been employed. But even if such a situation is conceivable at Knossos at the end of the fifteenth century, it can hardly have been true of Pylos also two centuries later. There is of course a serious objection to the acceptance of the theory that

71

the scribes were not fully conversant with Greek. It will allow every inconvenient form to be set aside, and great liberties can be taken with the interpretation. At one stroke Andrews would thus destroy the discipline that we have imposed on the solution: that the forms should be consistent and explicable in terms of comparative or historical parallels. Any new form which does not fit into the accepted pattern has been rigorously tested before being admitted, or is regarded merely as tentative and provisional. Whereas, if Andrews be right, it is unnecessary to frame any theory to explain these forms, as each can be explained away separately as an incorrect form due to the ignorance of the scribes. This is not to say that scribes make no errors; they are as frequent as in any other group of documents not intended for publication—the non-literary papyri would afford a close parallel. Such erroneous forms have frequently caused us much trouble. The curious *wo-zo-e*, obviously connected with the finite verb *wo-ze* and the participle *wo-zo*, was at first thought to be an optative; but the discovery of further similar texts has revealed that it should be an infinitive, and the expected *wo-ze-e* has now been found. Similar errors may underlie some of the other isolated forms which still cause difficulty.

Certain writers have shown a cavalier attitude to the strict linguistic tests which we have tried to apply. Admittedly no promising interpretation should be abandoned merely because it conflicts with a suggested but not well grounded etymology. But equally no interpretation can afford to ignore hard facts, such as the digamma in ἔλαιον (Carratelli, 1955, p. 3) or the original long $\bar{e}$ of ἀνέθηκε (Meriggi, 1954a, p. 69). Where the interpretation conflicts with an accepted but not certainly proved view, this should be noted and some explanation attempted; contrast Furumark's casual omission to mention the difficulty of finding the suffix -τέος (believed to be from *-τέϝος) in the word *qe-te-a* (1954, p. 42).

†   A further point which may be debated is the language of the inventor of Linear B. Here all evidence fails us and we can only argue from general probability. Since the script is derived from a Minoan source, the adapter must have been to some extent bilingual; whether Greeks would have learned Minoan or Minoans Greek depends upon the circumstances in which they came into contact. Furumark (1954, p. 107) attributes the formation of Linear B to the mainland at the time when Cretan influence was strong in the shaft-grave era; this view is supported by Carratelli (1954, p. 116), who adduces as further evidence the mature style of writing on the mainland vases, which he dates early. If this assumption is correct it is perhaps more likely that a Minoan craftsman should have taught his Greek employers the secret of writing; but in making deductions about speech habits from writing habits we

must not lose sight of the fact that the codifiers of the ancient scripts were experts in neither phonetics, comparative philology nor time-and-motion study, and their solutions are not always those which a UNESCO sub-committee might have proposed.

3. THE RELATION OF MYCENAEAN TO THE HISTORICAL DIALECTS

It cannot be denied that during the Mycenaean period the differences of the Greek dialects then in existence must have been much less strongly marked. The digamma has left traces in every branch of the language; only in Attic-Ionic is it never found, but its presence at no very remote date may be deduced. The form κόρη implies that Attic preserved ϝ after ρ until the change of ᾱ to η was completed, a change which in central Ionic was not complete at the end of the seventh century. The Ionic form of the same word with compensatory lengthening shows that the loss of ϝ took place after the separation of Attic from Ionic, which is almost certainly post-Mycenaean. Thus many of the distinctive dialect features will vanish as we approach the period of Common Greek. The preservation of an archaic form, which is often distinctive in the historical period, ceases to have any significance at such an early date. The only criteria for this purpose are those in which the dialect has made an innovation or a choice between two available forms. It need scarcely be added that the material is still too scanty to answer many of the questions we should like to ask.

Most significant is the change in certain circumstances of -*ti* to -*si*. This is † characteristic of the fundamental division of the dialects into East and West Greek. It is certainly present in Mycenaean, though it must be stressed that since the interpretation of the script is empirical, the sibilant may represent not the σ of classical Greek, but some intermediate stage such as *ts*. Examples are: 3rd plur. of pres. indic. act. *e-ko-si*, *di-do-si*, etc.; verbal nouns *a-pu-do-si* (Latin and Sanskrit -*ti*-); the preposition *po-si* = ποτί (Arcad., etc., πός); derivatives of stems ending in *t*: *ra-wa-ke-si-jo* (*ra-wa-ke-ta*), *e-qe-si-jo* (*e-qe-ta*), *pa-qo-si-jo* (*pa-qo-ta*), *u-wa-si-jo* (*u-wa-ta*), *e-pi-ko-ru-si-jo* (cf. κόρυς, -υθος), *ke-ro-si-ja* (= γερουσία < *geront-iā), *ko-ri-si-jo* (*ko-ri-to* = Κόρινθος), *za-ku-si-jo* (cf. Ζάκυνθος). The classical forms in -νθιος are analogical or borrowed from West Greek; cf. Att. Προβαλίσιος from Προβάλινθος (Schwyzer, *Gram.* 1, p. 272). Parallel to this is the change in the divine name *po-se-da-o* = *Poseidāōn* (W.Gk. Ποτ-, E.Gk. Ποσ-); perhaps influenced by the adjective *po-si-da-i-jo* = Epic Ποσιδήϊος. There are, however, some signs that the development was not complete in the

Mycenaean period. -*ti*- followed by a vowel survives in some proper names: e.g. *pa-i-ti-jo* (from *pa-i-to*=Φαιστός) as in classical Φαίστιος, as regularly following *s*, *ti-ri-ti-ja* (*ti-ri-to*), *ra-ti-jo* (*ra-to*=Λατώ) classical Λάτιος; *mi-ra-ti-ja*= *Milātiai* (Μίλητος); men's names *o-ti-na-wo* perhaps='Ορσι-, *ta-ti-qo-we-u*= Στᾶσι- (Στησι-)? In two cases the word shows both forms: the man's name *tu-si-je-u* is also written *tu-ti-je-u*, and the feminine ethnic adjective *ti-nwa-si-ja* has its genitive plural written *ti-nwa-ti-ja-o*.

Other evidence for Mycenaean's affinities with East Greek is to be found in the form of certain words: *i-je-ro* (and derivatives) reflects E.Gk. ἱερός not W.Gk. ἱαρός; and *a-te-mi-to*=*Artemitos* E.Gk. Ἄρτεμις, not W.Gk. Ἄρταμις.

Proceeding by elimination we can next point to several differences between Mycenaean and Attic-Ionic, although, as indicated above, the proto-Ionic which presumably existed in the Mycenaean period would not be strongly differentiated from other forms of East Greek. The preposition *a-pu* is the most striking instance, agreeing with Arc., Cypr., Lesb. and Thess. ἀπύ against Att.-Ion. ἀπό. This is surely not to be explained as due to the Arc.-Cypr. change of final -o to -υ, since it is shared with the Aeolic dialects. The development of the vocalism *o* instead of *a* from a syllabic liquid or nasal is a feature † of both Arc.-Cypr. and Aeolic. The circumstances of this are not yet fully explained, but it is unnecessary to adopt the suggestion of Merlingen (1954, p. 3) that the spellings reflect the presence of the unmodified sounds. *qe-to-ro-q^uetro*- is exactly paralleled by Thess. πετρο-, and if the other examples are not directly attested this is only due to the lack of adequate dialect records. The ‡ treatment of the contract verbs is still too obscure to use in evidence; but the form *te-re-ja*, if rightly interpreted as 3rd sing. pres. indic., seems to suggest an athematic conjugation (see Vocabulary, p. 409). The infinitive, however, is in -*en*, as probably in Attic where *-αεν>-ᾶν (Schwyzer, *Gram.* 1, p. 807). The athematic conjugation of these verbs is found in Arc., Cypr., Lesb. and Thess. The form *i-ja-te iātēr* agrees with Cypr. against Att. ἰατρός, Ion. ἰητρός; but since agent nouns in -*tēr* are common in Mycenaean and the type in -τρος is an innovation, this may not be conclusive.

We are left then with a probable connexion with two dialect groups: Arcado-Cyprian and Aeolic. On historical grounds we might expect the affinities of Mycenaean to lie rather with the former, and Palmer has expressed his support for that view. But although there is some positive evidence, there seems as yet to be little certain indication which dissociates Mycenaean from the Aeolic group. This may be partly due to the difficulty of reconstructing a common Aeolic from dialects which have been strongly influenced by West Greek. We can, however, point to a few features of Mycenaean which are especially typical of Aeolic: adjectives of material in -ειος and -ιος (see p. 89); and the use of patronymic adjectives in place of the genitive of the father's name, which is not found in Arc. or Cypr. On the other hand the evidence of vocabulary seems to emphasize rather the connexion with Arc.-Cypr. Such words as δέπας and φάσγανον are said to be Cypr. The form of the temporal adverb *o-te*=*hote* agrees with Arc.-Cypr. (and also Att.-Ion.) ὅτε against Lesb. ὅτα. The probable presence of primary medio-passive endings of the 3rd person in -*toi* rather than -*tai* is not significant now that Ruipérez (1952) has demonstrated that these are not innovations of Arc.-Cypr. but inherited.

The traditional view of the Aeolic dialects has been surprisingly changed by Porzig (1954) and Risch (1955), who have demonstrated that East Thessalian preserves a purer form of the dialect than Lesbian. On this theory the Aeolic dialects belong to the group which retain -τι (e.g. in ποτί, against Lesbian πρός, which may be borrowed from Ionic). The effect of this change is to emphasize the affinity of Mycenaean to Arcado-Cyprian, and to suggest that Ionic may in fact be no more than a subsequently differentiated branch of Arcado-Cyprian. Certainly the Mycenaean vases from Boeotia and Attica, which † might be assumed to be Ionic at this period (cf. Herodotus v, 58, 2), show no traces of significant variation in the dialect, though their evidence is too meagre to afford any satisfactory proof.

4. DIALECT DIFFERENCES IN MYCENAEAN

It would not be surprising if Knossos and Pylos, in view of their separation in time rather than space, showed differences of dialect. In fact the dialect appears to be extremely uniform, and the differences which have been found are more likely matters of orthography than phonetics. Pylos makes much greater use of a_2 than Knossos (e.g. in the plural of neuter *s*-stems), and Knossos often prefers the fuller spelling of an *i*-diphthong (KN *ko-to-i-na* PY *ko-to-na*, KN *a-pi-qo-i-ta* PY *a-pi-qo-ta*—if this is the same name). But some differences have been shown by new finds to be merely a matter of personal choice: the Knossos spelling *ko-ri-ja-do-no* with *ja* but Pylos *ko-ri-a_2-da-na* with a_2 has been shown to be without significance by a tablet from Mycenae (Ge605) which exhibits both forms.

Since the bulk of the material so far comes from Pylos it is not always possible to confirm particular features at Knossos. But nothing has emerged so far which seems likely to be significant. The material from Mycenae is much more scanty, and hardly allows the drawing of any conclusions about the dialect in use there; but with one exception the forms found there agree very closely with those at Pylos. The exception is the distinct preference shown by Mycenae texts for the third declension dative singular in -*i* instead of -*e* (see p. 86). But datives in -*i* are not unknown at Pylos (e.g. *ko-re-te-ri* On01), and Mycenae also has examples of -*e*, so there is no consistent differentiation. Fresh finds may lead us to revise our views on this point; but at present the dialect presents an extraordinary degree of homogeneity compared with classical inscriptions as widely scattered in time and space. Not until Hellenistic times was Greece to recapture such linguistic unity.

It is possible that this is a false appearance due to the conservatism of the scribal schools; thus the texts may represent not the actual state of Greek at 1200 B.C., but that at some earlier date—perhaps the sixteenth–fifteenth centuries—when the spelling was fixed. Aberrations from the standard would then be explicable as due to the influence of the actual speech of the period. Certainly such a theory will help to explain the problems of *z* and *pa₂*. On the other hand a strong central influence has a stabilizing effect on a language, and spoken Greek too may have remained at an archaic stage throughout the Mycenaean period, only giving way to innovative change in the chaos following the dissolution of the Achaean empire.

5. PHONOLOGY

This section collects representative examples from the vocabulary to illustrate the relationship of the Mycenaean spelling to the historical development of the sounds as far as known. Only the most restricted use has been made of proper names. References for all the words quoted will be found in the Vocabulary, or in the case of proper names in the Index of Personal Names, or the lists of place-names at the end of ch. v (pp. 146–50).

VOWELS

a, a₂ = ă, ā: *a-ke* = *agei*, *ma-te* = *mātēr*;
  = ə: *pa-te* = *patēr*;
  = m̥, n̥: *a₂-te-ro* = *hateron*, acc. *pe-re-u-ro-na* = *Pleurona*, *a-ki-ti-to* = *aktiton*;
   a+*r* = r̥, l̥: *ta-ra-si-ja* = *talasiā*, *pa-we-a₂* = *pharwea*, cf. *a-re-pa* (in ligature, see p. 284) = *aleiphar*.

e = ĕ, ē: *e-ke* = *ekhei*, *pa-te* = *patēr*;
  = ĭ: *ku-te-so* = *kutisos*; = 'prothetic' *e*: *e-ru-ta-ra* = *eruthrā*.

¶ *Note.* Most of the certain examples of *e* = Gk. ι are in proper names or non-Greek words: *i-pe-me-de-ja* = Ἰφιμέδεια (not from ἴφι, contrast *wi-pi-no-o* = Ἰφίνοος), *me-nu-wa* = Μινύας, *ai-ke-wa-to* = *ai-ki-wa-to*, *pa₂-me-si-jo* = *pa₂-mi-si-jo* (cf. Πάμισος), *de-ko-to*

= *di-ko-to* (?), *e-pa-sa-na-ti* = *i-pa-sa-na-ti* (where an error is excluded by the deliberate correction of *e-* to *i-*). Examples in apparent diphthongs are not easily explained: *mi-to-we-sa-e*, *e-qe-ta-e*, *to-e* (*wo-zo-e* is erroneous). On the question of datives in -*e* see p. 85. Cf. *i* = *ĕ*.

i = *ĭ*, *ī*: *e-pi* = *epi*, *si-to* = *sītos*;

= *ĕ*: *di-pa* = *depas*.

Note 1. *i* = Gk. ε is less frequent than the reverse, see above. Also perhaps in *i-mi-ri-jo* = *Hīmerios*. It is a possible explanation of *i-qo* = ἵππος < *eĥwos*, but this is Common Greek. For a possible dissimilation of *e-e* > *e-i*, cf. KN *a-pe-i-si* ? = PY *a-pe-e-si* = *apeensi*, and the dative singular of stems in -*s* (see p. 86).

Note 2. Confusion of *ĭ* and *ŭ* is not only found in the κοινή, but also in pre-Greek words and names: e.g. Ἐλευσύνιος (Olus, Thera), Ἐλευhύνια (Sparta) = Ἐλευσίνιος (Att., etc.); Lacon. Τινδαριδᾶν for more usual Τυνδ-; μόλιβ(δ)ος = μόλυβδος, βίβλος = βύβλος. There seem to be rare examples of this in Myc.: man's name *ta-ni-ko* = *ta-nu-ko*, place-name *u-ta-no* = Ἴτανος; cf. *mo-ri-wo-do* = *moliwdos* (?) = μόλυβδος.

o = *ŏ*, *ō*: *po-de* = *podei*, *do-se* = *dōsei*.

= *ă*: < *ṛ*, *ḷ*: *qe-to-ro* = Thess. πετρο- Att. τετρα-, *to-pe-za* = *torpeza* (τράπεζα), *wo-ze* = *worzei* < *wṛgj-*, *o-ka* = *orkhā* (ἀρχή; but perhaps from *ṃ*); < *ṃ*, *ṇ*: *a-no-wo-to* = *anouoton* (< *ṇ-ousṇ-to-*, cf. gen. οὔατος), *a-pi-qo-to* = *amphigʷotos* † (< *-gʷṃ-to-*), *e-ne-wo-* = *ennewo-* (< *(e)newṇ-*); of uncertain origin: *pa-ro* = παρά, *ko-wo* = κῶας (< *ə*?), *ko-no-ni-pi* (κανών?), place-name *u-pa-ra-ki-ri-ja* = *u-po-ra-ki-ri-ja*. Similar alternations occur in Arc., Cypr., Lesb., Thess. and Boeot.; also in words of uncertain etymology: e.g. ἀστακός/ὀστακός, ἀσταφίς/ὀσταφίς.

= *ŭ*: *e-wi-su-zo-ko* = *e-wi-su-zu?-ko* = *-zugo-*; possible in *po-ro-du-ma-te*, *po-ru-da-* ‡ *ma-te*, see Vocabulary *s.v.* *du-ma*.

u = *ŭ*, *ū*: *e-ru-ta-ra* = *eruthrā*, *tu-ro₂* = *tūroi*;

as silent vowel: before *w*: *ke-se-nu-wi-ja* = *xenwia*; before *m*?: see *du-ma* in Vocabulary; cf. anaptyctic *u* in Lat. *dracuma*, etc.

= *ĭ*: see above.

= *o*: *u-ru-pi-ja-jo* = Ὀλυμπιαῖοι. ¶

DIPHTHONGS

a-i: almost certainly not two syllables in *pa-i-to* = Φαιστός. Alternates with *a*: *a-na-i-ta* = *a-na-ta*. On the dat. plur. of *a*-stems see p. 84.

a-j = *ai*: in adjectives from feminines in -*a* (e.g. *a-ko-ra-jo* = *agoraios*).

ai: *ai-ka-sa-ma* = *aixmans*. Very rare except as initial. The identification of *34 †† as *ai₂* depends on the equation of **34*-ke-u* in PY **237** = Ta709 with *ai-ke-u* in **236** = Ta641, and is otherwise very dubious.

a-u: *pu-ra-u-to-ro*=*puraustrō*, *ka-ra-u-ko*=*Glaukos*.

† **e-i**: usually to be interpreted as two syllables. *pe-i* may represent Arc. σφεις. Final *-ei* in verbs is always written *-e*.

e-u: *e-u-da-mo*=*Eudāmos*, *re-u-ko*=*leukō*.

e-w: probably for *eu* in *e-we-pe-se-so-me-na*=*eu hepsēsomena*, *e-wa-ko-ro*=*e-u-wa-ko-ro*=*Euag(o)ros*, but this may be phonetic.

o-i: *ko-to-i-na*=*ko-to-na*=*ktoinā*; *ko-i-no*=*ko-no*=*skhoinos*. For *-o-i* in the dat. plur. of *o*-stems see p. 84.

o-j: *te-o-jo*=*theoio*.

o-u: negative *o-u-*, *a-ro-u-ra*=*aroura(ns)*.

u-j: fem. perf. part. *a-ra-ru-ja*=*araruia*.

VOWEL CONTRACTION

Elision of short final vowels is sometimes found in the compounded forms of the prepositions: e.g. *a-pe-e-si* (*ap-*=*apu-*), *pa-ra-wa-jo*=*par-āwaiō*, *me-ta-no*=*Met-ānōr*, *e-pe-ke-u*=*Ep-eigeus*; but in many cases the vowel is maintained, not only when an etymological *-h-* intervenes: *po-si-e-e-si*=*posi-eensi*, *o-pi-a₂-ra*=*opi-hala*, *e-pi-ja-ta*=*Epi-haltās*.

Vowel contraction of the types found in Classical Greek seems to be unknown; cases like *ko-to-na-no-no*=*ktoinā anōnos*, *ko-to-no-ko*=*ktoino-okhos* are isolated and probably faulty. Even like vowels are regularly retained in contact, though this would be explained if, as is not unlikely, intervocalic *-h-* survived: e.g. *ko-to-no-o-ko*=*ktoino-(h)okhos*, *e-ma-a₂*=*Herma(h?)āi*, *e-ke-e*=*ekhe(h)en*. The pre-Greek contractions are exemplified by *no-pe-re-a₂*=*nōphelea* from **ne-ophel-*.

SPURIOUS DIPHTHONGS

The 'spurious' diphthongs are of course represented in Mycenaean by the pure vowels, and where there is no contraction it is impossible to tell whether lengthening had taken place. *-o-sa* in the fem. participle probably represents *-onsa* (as in Arcadian); in other doubtful cases such vowels have been transcribed with a circumflex accent: e.g. *a-ke-re*=*agêrei*, *wo-ra-we-sa*=*wôlāwessa*.

SEMIVOWELS

j: used to indicate diphthongal *i* (see above) or as a glide: e.g. *i-je-re-u*=*hiereus*. This is sometimes omitted and we find *i-e-re-u* as an alternative spelling, just as in Cypr. ἱερεύς as well as ἰjερêος.

The loss of I.-E. *-j-* in intervocalic position is proved by the first component of a man's name *a-e-ri-qo-ta*=*Āeri-* (cf. Hom. ἦρι, ἠέριος, Avest. *ayarᵊ*).

-*sj*- appears usually to yield -*j*- as in the gen. of the *o*-stems: -*o-jo* < *-*osjo*. Although we have transcribed this form as -*oio* on the Homeric model, it may be questioned whether -*j*- has not here a consonantal value, thus accounting for the metrically recoverable Homeric forms in -oo. A similar wavering between the two values may explain the alternation of -*e-jo* and -*e-o* in the formation of adjectives of material (see p. 89). Similar alternations in spelling are not infrequent in names: e.g. *a-ti-ke-ne-ja* but *a-pi-ke-ne-a* = -*geneia*, *re-wa-jo*/*re-wa-o*. Advantage has been taken of this to put forward some interpretations: e.g. *ke-ra-ja-pi* = *keraiāphi*, Hom. κεραός, *a-ta-o* = *Antaios*.

The existence of medial -*wj*- seems likely in two words which have alternative spellings: *me-wi-jo*/*me-u-jo* = μείων, *di-wi-ja*/*di-u-ja* probably = Διϝία. Cf. [*pa*₂]-*si-re-wi-jo-te* = *basilewjontes* (βασιλεύω). †

Initial *j*- occurs in the adverb *jo*- (also *o*-), probably = *hō* < *jōd*. Other cases where it appears optional are: *ja-ke-te-re* = *a-ke-te-re*, man's name *ja-sa-ro* = *a-sa-ro*.

w: initial: *wa-na-ka* = *wanax*, *we-to* = *wetos*, *wi-pi-no-o* = *Wiphinoos*, *wo-ze* = *worzei*, *wo-i-ko* = *woikon*. From **sw-*, perhaps to be interpreted *hw*-: *wo-jo* = *hwoio* (?), *we-pe-za* = *hweppeza* (ἐκ + πεδ-). Before *r*: *wa-ra-wi-ta* = *wrāwista* 'damaged', *wi-ri-ni-jo* = *wrīniō*; cf. *o-u-ru-to* = *hō wruntoi*, *u* being written as there is no sign for *wu*. After *d*: *du-wo-u-pi* = *dwouphi* (?), *du-wo-jo* = *Dwoios*.

Intervocalic: *ka-ra-wi-po-ro* = *Klawiphoros*, *ka-ke-we* = *khalkēwes*.

With consonants: -*dw*-: *wi-do-wo-i-jo* = *Widwoios*; -*wd*-: *mo-ri-wo-do* = *moliwdos* (?) = μόλιβδος; -*nw*-: *ke-se-nu-wi-ja* = *xenwia*, *pe-ru-si-nu-wo* = *perusinwon*; -*rw*-: *do-we-jo* = *dorweios*, *ko-wa* = *korwā*, *pu-wo* = *Purwos* (< **purswos*); -*wr*-: *e-wi-ri-po* = *Ewrīpos* (or = *Eu-wripos*?); -*sw*-: *wi-so-wo-pa-na* = *wiswo-* (ἰσο-) but also *e-wi-su*-; -*thw*-: *ma-ra-tu-wo* = *marathwon* (in a loan-word, but *te-o* = *theon* if from **dhwes-* shows loss of *w* in an inherited word).

As a glide after *u*: *tu-we-a* = *thuea*, *ta-ra-nu-we* = *thrānues*, *ku-wa-no* = *kuanōi*, *a-re-ku-tu-ru-wo* = *Alektruōn*.

Note. In several words we have 'intrusive' *w*, where not expected from the etymology ‡ or dialect forms; e.g. *pe-ru-si-nu-wo*, *me-wi-jo*. In others the expected *w* is absent: *e-ne-ka* = *heneka* (not **henweka*), *o-ro-me-no* = *oromenos*, *i-je-re-ja* = *hiereia*, *po-se-da-o* = *Poseidāōn* (Corinth. -αϝων). On these see Chadwick (1954*b*, pp. 6–7) and p. 89.

w used to represent *u* before a vowel seems probable in *e-we-pe-se-so-me-na* = *eu* ¶ *hepsēsomena*, *e-wa-ko-ro* = *Euag(o)ros*, *a-no-wo-to* = *anouoton*. Cf. the alternations in proper names: *ru-ko-wo-ro*/*ru-ko-u-ro* = *Lukouros*, *ra-wa-ra-ta*/*ra-u-ra-ta* = *Laurantha* ?, adj. *ra-wa-ra-ti-jo*, *ra-wa-ra-ta*₂/*ra-u-ra-ti-jo*, -*ja*.

r $=r$, l: *re-wo-to-ro-ko-wo* $=lewotrokhowoi$. See p. 44.

m $=m$: *ma-te* $=m\bar{a}t\bar{e}r$.

n $=n$: *ne-wo* $=newos$.

Spirants

s: initial only in words of foreign origin or due to development from other sounds: *si-to* $=sitos$, *sa-sa-ma* $=s\bar{a}sama$, *se-ri-no* $=selinon$, *si-a₂-ro* $=sialons$, *su-za* $=$ *suka* (?). *su-qo-ta-o* $=sug^{u}ot\bar{a}\bar{o}n$ (συβώτης) is a familiar if inexplicable form. Preceding a consonant it is sometimes apparently dropped: *pa-ka-na* $=$ *phasgana*; written in *do-so-mo* $=dosmos$. In *ai-ka-sa-ma* $=aixmans$ it is preserved where classical Greek only retains its trace as an aspirate (αἰχμή). Intervocalic -*s*- $<t$ before j or in some cases i (see p. 73): *to-so* $=tossos$, *e-ko-si* $=$

† *ekhonsi*; $<kj$: *pa-sa-ro* $=passal\bar{o}$, *wa-na-se-wi-ja* from ϝάνασσα.

‡ **h**: There is no sign for the aspirate, nor are any aspirated consonants distinguished. In the absence therefore of any notation, interpreted forms have been given the form which agrees most closely with classical Greek: initial *h*- and aspirated consonants are written where expected on later or comparative evidence, intervocalic -*h*- is omitted, except in a few cases of compounds. This is not intended to express an opinion on the extent of psilosis in Mycenaean, but merely to accommodate the reconstructions to a familiar pattern. The absence of contraction (see p. 78) is a slight indication in favour of retention of intervocalic -*h*-; but where the etymology is uncertain or disputed the choice is not easy; should we for instance be justified in writing *dohelos*? (Cf. Chadwick, 1954, p. 14.)

The use of a_2 where we expect *ha* does not involve any departure from the principle laid down. It is reasonable to suppose that 'Minoan' distinguished no aspirates, and the opposition of a/a_2 may have corresponded to something like the Hebrew א/ע. It is noticeable that a_2 sometimes alternates with *ja* (see p. 47). Andrews' theory of a sixth (*schwa*) vowel is not yet supported by convincing examples, and the variations in spelling are better explained as due to uncertainty in the use of signs having an original value without phonemic significance in Greek.

¶ **z**: *z* has been used to transliterate the consonant which has obvious affinities with the Greek ζ (see p. 44). This is not to say that its sound was identical, but it serves as a useful symbol. The cases of alternation with *k* suggest a palatalized *k'*, *g'*; but the fact that it also represents **dj* in -*pe-za* $<$ **-pedja* seems to prove that it was already some sort of sibilant. A theory which would account for its behaviour as observed so far is that in 'Minoan' it had the value *k′*, which was occasionally substituted for *k* by Greeks, the distinction of velars and palatals having been lost in Common Greek; it was correctly used for **gj* but with assibilation of this sound it was extended to similar sounds with a different history. So far it seems to be restricted to voiced stops, which, like *d*, conflicts with the theoretical basis of the syllabary. This is, however, the natural result of the development of **kj* to *ss* in Greek (cf. p. 80), which is a further proof that *z* was a sibilant in Mycenaean.

z is also used in those words which show ʒ- initially from I.-E. **j-*: *ze-u-ke-u-si=zeugeusi*, *ze* abbreviation of *zeugos*, *e-wi-su-zu?-ko* (also *-zo-ko*) = *-zugo-*; *ze-so-me-no*, *a-re-pa-zo-o*, *zo-a* from the root of ʒέω.

The use of *za*=γα in Cypriot may be connected, but Lejeune rejects the transliteration *za* in favour of *ka²*.

Stops

p, k, t, d: the use of these is shown on p. 44, §4. A theory to account for the separation of *d/t(h)* is suggested above (p. 70). The question of *pa₂* is discussed in the next section.

Labio-velars: **q**. The presence of labio-velars in *Urgriechisch* has long been †
accepted. The date at which they were lost no doubt differed in the dialects, Aeolic confusing them with the labials, while Arcadian maintains a distinction before ε and ι in the early inscription from Mantinea (Schwyzer, *Dial.* 661). In Cypriot the labio-velar is confused with *s*: *si-se*=τις. Their sound in Mycenaean can only be conjectured; the interpretation assumes that they remained at that date more or less unchanged (hence written *qᵘ*, *gᵘ* or *qᵘh*, as devoicing of mediae aspiratae is assumed, see p. 68). Palmer (1954*b*, p. 53), however, suggests that they were already assibilated, hence his identification of the man's name *a-i-qe-u* as *Aïsseus* and the verbal form *e-ke-qe* as future=*hexei*. Against this it may be observed that *q-s-* is once used to write *x* (*qi-si-pe-e*=*xiphee*), though this does not necessarily exclude a sound such as *kš*. The identification of *mo-qo-so*=Μόψος=Hitt. *Mukšaš* was discussed by Chadwick (1954*b*, p. 5).

The same signs evidently do duty for **kw* as for the labio-velar: *i-qo*=ἵππος; hence we may legitimately expect to find them used also for **ghw* in compounds of θήρ; see entries beginning *qe-r-* in Index of Personal Names, p. 424.

As stated above (p. 45) there is no sign for *qa*, but *pa* is regularly used to denote the initial syllable of πᾶς, if this is correctly derived from **kwānt-*. It is possible that before *a* the loss of the velar element had already begun, though the distinction remained elsewhere. Thus if *pa₂* were originally *qa*, phonetic change would have made it a homophone of *pa*. *pa₂* occurs in a number of words in which we postulate a labio-velar: e.g. *o-pa₂-wo-ni* *Opāwoni* (but *o-pa*); but in most cases the etymology is too obscure: e.g. *pa₂-si-re-u*=βασιλεύς, *ti-ri-jo-pa₂*=Τριόπας, *pa₂-ra₂*=Πάλλας. In *pa₂-ra-to-ro* the variants σπάλαθρον, σκάλαυθρον, etc., point to *sqᵘa-*. But *ku-su-to-ro-pa₂*= *xunstrophā* is derived from **strebh-*.

In other positions too there are some signs of an alternation of *p* and *q*. In PY **116**=En659 the man's name *Qe-re-qo-ta-o* (gen.) is apparently repeated in the dative as *Pe-re-qo-ta*, though their identity is not certain (see p. 245). If this name represents classical **Τηλεφόντης* or the like, the development of the labio-velar before *e* to *p* would be surprising as this is found in Aeolic but not Arcadian. Easier to accept is the alternative spelling *ra-qi-ti-ra₂* for *ra-pi-ti-ra₂*=*raptriai*, since the development to *p* before a consonant is universal. As the traditional etymology of ῥάπτω is disproved by the lack of the initial digamma, there is no external evidence to prove which spelling is the original one; but the masculine *raptēr* is spelt with *pte*, and the participle *e-ra-pe-me-na* also shows *p* instead of the expected assimilation. Thus the use of *q* here seems to be the abnormality, whereas in the former case it is the use of *p*. These examples are perhaps to be explained by a theory of traditional spelling (see p. 76); this would imply that the pronunciation was at least in a transitional phase. If this is really so, it is remarkable that there is so little inconsistency in the spelling.

Although the decipherment has confirmed the etymology of many words containing labio-velars (note especially *a-to-ro-qo* ἄνθρωπος) there are a few surprises. *to-ro-qo* is plausibly identified with τρόπος, cf. *to-ro-qe-jo-me-no* and the man's name *e-u-to-ro-qo*, which conflicts with Skt. *trápate*, Lat. *trepit*; if correct we must accept Meillet's connexion with Lat. *torqueo*: see *to-ro-qo* in Vocabulary. If the equation of *qe-to* with πίθος be right, this destroys another accepted etymology; but it should be noticed that the spelling with *e* for *i* may indicate a foreign origin.

† ASSIMILATION

Evidence of assimilation of another consonant before *p* is fairly extensive, though the nature of the resultant group can only be conjectured from the notation. A stop+*p* appears to yield *-pp-* (cf. Hom. κάππεσε, etc.): *po-pi*<*pod-phi*, *e-ka-ma-pi*<*ekhmat-phi* (or *egma-* ?), *ko-ru-pi*<*koruth-phi*; *we-pe-za*<(*h*)*wek-pedja*. We may assume partial assimilation of *n*>*m*: *ki-to-pi*<*khitōn-phi*; and of *nt*>*m*: *re-wo-pi*<*lewont-phi* (cf. *re-wo-te-jo*=*lewonteios*), *a-di-ri-ja-pi*<*andriant-phi*. It is hardly without significance that Homer has no examples of the -φι termination with stems in stops or liquids (ἐσχαρόφι and κοτυληδονόφι are plainly

82

secondary); was *λέομφι too far removed from λεόντων and too easily replaced by λέουσι?

Assimilation before the -si of the dative plural can sometimes be assumed: *pi-we-ri-si* is probably from *piwerid-si*, cf. dat. sing. *pi-we-ri-di*; *pa-si*<*pant-si* (presumably=*pansi*), *de-ma-si*<*dermat-si*; *pi-ri-e-te-si* (cf. nom. plur. *pi-ri-je-te-re*) is ambiguous.

On the other hand 'etymological' spellings are found where we should expect assimilation; possibly merely as a convention to avoid confusion. *po-ni-ki-pi*<*phoinik-phi* may be an exception in a foreign word. More surprising are *e-ra-pe-me-na*<*errap-mena* (perf. pass. of ῥάπτω); *a-ra-ro-mo-te-me-na* where the variant *a-ra-ro-mo-to-me-na* points to -*tm*-.

INITIAL *pt*-

Initial *pt*- for classical π- seems to occur in two personal names: *po-to-re-ma-ta* =*Ptolemātās*, [*e-u*]-*ru-po-to-re-mo-jo*=*Euruptolemoio*. Another apparent instance is *po-to-ri-jo*=*Ptoliōn*? KN **39**=As1517, but until the context is clear this must remain tentative. This feature cannot be used to determine dialect affinities, since its use in proper names is much more widespread than in vocabulary words.

6. MORPHOLOGY

NOUNS

The case system is remarkably close to that of Homer. Four cases can be †
distinguished in the singular, five in the plural, the instrumental being marked by the suffix -*pi* in the first and third declensions. In the sing. the instr. coalesces with the dat. in all declensions.

Feminine a-stems

	Sing.		Dual		Plur.	
Nom.	{ *i-je-re-j* { *po-ti-ni-j*	*a* *a*	*to-pe-z*	*o*	*a-ni-j*	*a*
Acc.	*ta-ra-si-j*	*a*			*ko-to-n*	*a*
Gen.	*i-je-re-j*	*a*	*ko-to-n*	*o* ?	*ko-to-n*	*a-o*
Dat.	*po-ti-ni-j*	*a*			*a-ke-ti-ri-j*	*a-i*
Instr.					*a-ni-j*	*a-pi*

‡

This may be interpreted according to the spelling rules as: sing. -ă, -ăn, -ās, -āi; plur. -ai, -ans, -āōn, -ā'i, -āphi.

†   Dual: the extension of *-ai* as the nom. plur. termination led to its replacement as the inherited dual ending. This gap was filled by Attic with -ᾱ on the analogy of the *o*-stems. Mycenaean appears to have borrowed the ending of the *o*-stems *-ō*; cf. fem. dual καλυψαμένω (Hes. *Op.* 198), and the use of τώ as feminine even in Attic. The restoration of the genitive is less certain; *-oin* is possible under the spelling rules. Other examples of the dual are *i-qi-jo*, *pte-no*, and adjectives agreeing with these substantives.

    Acc. plur.: *ko-to-na* seems to be acc. plur. in PY **43** = Sn01; other examples are *a-ro-u-ra* PY **154** = Eq01, *o-pi-ke-re-mi-ni-ja* (acc. of respect) PY **243** = Ta708, *ai-ka-sa-ma* PY **257** = Jn09.

    Dat. plur.: on the interpretation of this form see below.

Masculine a-stems

    These follow exactly the pattern of the feminines except that the gen. sing. is in *-a-o* = *-āo*; there is no example of an instrumental plural. Two obscure forms in *-a-e* may be duals: *e-qe-ta-e* KN **29** = As821, *we-ka-ta-e* KN X 1044; possibly to be explained as an extension of the dual ending of the consonant stems. This might account for the Homeric dual of masculine stems in -ᾱ (not -η); and it may be significant that Homer never uses the dual of a feminine

‡ *a*-stem. The presence or absence of final *-s* in the nom. sing. cannot be tested; in view of Homeric and dialect forms without *-s*, it may well have been absent. In interpreted forms, however, this *-s* has been restored to mark the distinction from the feminines.

O-stems

	Sing.		Dual		Plur.	
Nom.	*ko-w*	o	*pa-sa-r*	o	*ko-w*	o
Acc.	*te-*	o			*si-a₂-r*	o
Gen.	*te-*	o-jo			*a-ne-m*	o
Dat.	*da-m*	o			*te-*	o-i
Instr.					*e-re-pa-te-j*	o

Neuters:	Sing.		Plur.	
Nom.	*ko-ri-ja-do-n*	o	*ko-ri-ja-da-n*	a
Acc.	*a₂-te-r*	o	*do-r*	a

    These may be interpreted: sing. *-os*, *-on* (neut. *-on*), *-oio*, *-ōi*; dual *-ō*; plur. *-oi*, *-ons* (neut. *-a*), *-ōn*, *-oi'i* (?), *-ois* (?).

¶   Dat. plur.: the spelling *-o-i* is clearly parallel to *-a-i* in the *a*-stems and must represent a similar form. We originally interpreted these as *-ois*, *-ais* (*-ōis*, *-āis*?), the I.-E. instrumental ending (Skt. *-ais*). But the new Pylos furniture tablets have shown that the 'instrumental' of *o*-stems is in *-o*, not *-o-i* or *-o-pi* (e.g. *e-re-pa-te-jo a-di-ri-ja-pi re-wo-pi-qe* **243** = Ta708). Since this case is distinguished in the spelling from the dative (e.g. *pa-si-te-o-i*) it is probably different in form, though we cannot exclude the possibility that *-o* and *-o-i* are merely alternative spellings of *-ois* (cf. p. 44). Theoretical considerations have led to the postulation of a dative (originally locative): *-oihi* < *-oisi*, which was later restored by analogy. Merlingen and Andrews have therefore suggested that this is what the spelling implies. A definite decision is hardly possible on the evidence so far, but *-oi'i* has been adopted as the interpretation in order to maintain the distinction. In any case the *a*-stems must here be copying the *o*-stems, and we have written *-ā'i* to match.

Instrumental: a very few cases of the termination *-o-pi* have been found, † only at Knossos, so that this may be a dialect difference. At least it is clear that this termination was not restricted to consonant stems, as proposed by Shipp (1953, p. 9). KN Se1042 (joined with 1006) contains the words: *e-re-pa-te-jo-pi o-mo-pi*, where the latter word may be *hormophi*; *e-re-pa-te-jo-pi* is repeated in line 2, but here unfortunately we have lost the noun in agreement. *i-ku-wo-i-pi* KN **207** = V 280 is an isolated form of uncertain meaning; Ventris proposes an instrumental dual.

Locative: Ventris suggests that *di-da-ka-re* (see p. 162) is a locative *didaskalei* of the type of οἴκει. A termination *-οι* would be indistinguishable from the dative.

Note. Compound adjectives in *-os* (often used as substantives) have two terminations: e.g. *a-ka-ra-no* agreeing with *to-pe-za* PY **241** = Ta715; *a-pi-qo-ro ko-wo* = *amphiqʷolōn* (fem. gen. plur.) *korwoi* PY **11** = Ad690.

Consonant stems

		Sing.		Dual		Plur.	
Nom.	{	*po-me*		*ti-ri-po-d* | *e*		*po-me-n*	*e*
	{	*wa-na-ka*					
Acc.		*pe-re-u-ro-n*	*a*			*pa-ki-ja-n*	*a* (?)
Gen.		*po-me-n*	*o*			*ka-ra-ma-t*	*o* (?)
Dat.	{	*po-me-n*	*e*			*pa-*	*si*
	{	*ko-re-te-r*	*i*				
Instr.						*po-*	*pi*

‡

Interpretation: sing. zero or *-s*, *-a*, *-os*, *-ei* or *-i*; dual *-e*; plur. *-es*, *-as*, *-ōn*, *-si*, *-phi*.

Dat. sing.: two explanations of *-e* are possible. It may be part of the general ¶ confusion of *ĕ* and *ĭ* (see p. 76), and stand for the original *-i* of the locative.

This seems to be certain in those cases where the script has -*i*. This is much less frequent than -*e* at Pylos and Knossos, except in the *s*-stems (see below). Mycenae, however, shows a marked preference for -*i* (e.g. *ka-ke-wi*, *ke-ra-me-wi*, *pi-we-ri-di*), though -*e* does also occur (*o-pe-ra-no-re*). Alternatively we may interpret -*e* as -*ei*, the old I.-E. dative termination preserved in Old Latin and other languages, and in traces in Greek. The latter has been adopted in this book, but again without any desire to prejudge the issue.

Stems in *s*: the type in -*ēs* shows the declension: nom. -*e* (neut. -*e*), gen. -*e-o*, dat. -*e-i*; dual -*e-e* (all genders); plur. neut. -*e-a* or -*e-a$_2$*, dat. -*e-si* (=-*essi*), instr. -*e-pi* (=-*esphi*). The neuter *di-pa*=*dipas* has dual *di-pa-e*. Comparative
† adjectives do not show -*n*- in the declension: *me-zo*, *me-wi-jo* (=*mezōn* or *mezōs*? etc.) have dual -*o-e*, plur. -*o-e*, neut. -*o-a$_2$* (=-*oes*, -*oa*, Att. -*ους*, -*ω*). Perfect participles in the masculine and neuter show the same declension: neut. plur. *a-ra-ru-wo-a*, *te-tu-ko-wo-a$_2$*.

Stems in *i*: some examples are found in the nom. sing., e.g. *a-pu-do-si*=*apudosis*; but there is no evidence of the declension except instr. plur. *po-ti-pi*=*portiphi*.

Stems in *u*: evidence is very scanty. Nom. sing. *ta-ra-nu* has plur. *ta-ra-nu-we*, -*ues*, like στάχυς; gen. sing. in man's name *e-te-wa-tu-o*=*Etewastuos*. The dative *ka-ru-we* (instr. plur. *ka-ru-pi*) presumably also belongs to this type; cf. Pylos place-name *a-pu$_2$?-we*. There is no evidence of the ablaut declension: -*υς*, -ε[ϝ]ος, except perhaps *te-re-te-we* and *pa-ke-we*=*pakhewes*.

Stems in *āu*: nom. plur. *ka-ra-we*=*grāwes*.

Stems in *ēu*: sing. nom. -*e-u*, gen. -*e-wo*, dat. -*e-we* (MY -*e-wi*); dual -*e-we*; plur. nom. -*e-we*, dat. -*e-u-si*, instr. -*e-u-pi*. To be interpreted: -*eus*, -*ēwos*, -*ēwei* or -*ēwi*; -*ēwe*; -*ēwes*, -*eusi*, -*euphi*.

Note 1. Adjectives of the type in -*went*- have feminine -*we-sa*=-*wessa* with analogical *e* for *a* < *-wṇtja*. The masculine is typified by the man's name *ko-ma-we*=*Komāwens*, gen. *ko-ma-we-to*=*Komāwentos*. Examples of the feminine are: *pi-ti-ro$_2$-we-sa*, *ko-ro-no-we-sa*, *mi-to-we-sa*. The perf. participle has fem. *a-ra-ru-ja*=*araruia* (<*-usja*); pres. part. of verb 'to be': *a-pe-a-sa*=*apeassai* (<*-esṇtja*), masc. *a-pe-o-te*=*apeontes*.

Note 2. The case and number of the termination -*pi*=-φι. It will be observed that the term 'instrumental' has been applied to the case formed by this suffix. This follows the generally accepted view that it is a relic of an I.-E. instrumental (cf. Skt. -*bhis*), and is supported by its use after passive or intransitive verbs such as 'equipped with', 'inlaid with'. Its frequent use with place-names seems equally to prove that it also has the value of locative.

Its number is proved to be plural (or dual) by the opposition of *ka-ru-we*/*ka-ru-pi*, *a-di-ri-ja-te*/*a-di-ri-ja-pi*, *e-ka-ma-te*/*e-ka-ma-pi*, *po-ni-ke*/*po-ni-ki-pi*, *po-de*/*po-pi* in parallel contexts on the furniture tablets. Cf. also *du-wo-u-pi te-re-ja-e* PY **148** = Ep04 with *e-me-de te-*[*re*]*-ja* Eb40.

This conclusion agrees as regards case, but not number, with that reached on the †
Homeric evidence by Shipp (1953, p. 15).

PRONOUNS

These are very rare and mostly doubtful.

mi = *min*: *da-mo-de-mi pa-si* = *dāmos de min phāsi* (?) PY **135** = Ep704; cf.
e-ke-de-mi PY **196** = Na70.

pe-i = *spheis, sphe'i* ? Dat. plur., cf. Arc. σφεις, Att. σφίσι.   ‡

to-e PY Eb842 = *to-me* PY **148** = Ep04 in identical context (see p. 263). The ¶
phrase is obscure, but *to-e/to-me* may represent the dative of a demonstrative.
If not erroneous *to-e* may be *tōi* or *tōi-e* = *τῷί (cf. Elean τοῖ, Boeot. τοιῖ, etc.).
to-me may be explained as *to-(s)me* with the suffix -(σ)μι found in Cret. ὅτιμι =
ᾧτινι, cf. Skt. loc. *tásmin.*

to-jo: possibly genitive of the demonstrative.

to-i-qe: dat. plur. *toi'i-qᵘe* ?

to-to: 'this' = τοῦτο; see Vocabulary, p. 410.   ††

wo-jo: = (*h*)*woio* = οἷο, gen. of pron. adj. 'his own' ?

Note. It seems most unlikely that any forms are to be explained as a definite article, since this is clearly absent from many contexts where its presence would be demanded by classical usage.

NUMERALS

These are poorly represented, mostly in compounds.   ‡‡

1: dat. *e-me* = *hemei* shows preservation of the original -*m*- replaced by -*n*- in all dialects.

2: instr. *du-wo-u-pi*; see Vocabulary, p. 391.

3: in compounds *ti-ri-* = *tri-*.

4: in compounds *qe-to-ro-* = *qᵘetro-* (-*ro-* < *ŗ*).

6: in compounds *we-* = (*h*)*wek-* (Cret., etc., ϝέξ).

9: in compounds *e-ne-wo-* = *ennewo-* (*o* < *ņ*).

THE VERB

Terminations

The theory of Ruipérez (1952) that the Arcadian medio-passive primary terminations in -τοι were original and not, as had been supposed, secondary is supported by the new evidence. As the final -*i* is not written and there is ordinarily no augment (see below), it is impossible to distinguish a present from an imperfect. But two considerations seem to indicate that we are right in taking these forms as present. (1) *e-ke-qe e-u-ke-to-qe . . . e-ke-e* PY **140** = Eb35; if both verbs are imperfect, then the *e-ke* of the common formula must be so too; but present is much more likely in such a formula. (2) *to-sa-de o-u-di-do-to* PY **198** = Ng02 is plainly parallel with *to-sa-de na-u-do-mo o-u-di-do-si* PY **189** = Na65, etc.; since *di-do-si* cannot be anything but present, so presumably is *di-do-to*. In many other passages a present is preferable, and *e-pi-de-da-to* is more likely to be perfect than pluperfect.

† *Augment*

The syllabic augment is normally absent, such forms as *a-pu-do-ke* = *apu-dōke* being regular in the secondary tenses. An apparent exception is *a-pe-do-ke* in a new Pylos tablet (Gn1184), which at present remains isolated. The temporal augment would of course be concealed by the notation.

Reduplication

Reduplication in the perfect follows the regular pattern; *a-ra-ru-ja* and *a-ra-ro-mo-te-me-na* show the special 'Attic' reduplication of verbs beginning with a vowel plus sonant. *e-ra-pe-me-na* has the ordinary form of reduplication = ἐρρ-.

Verbal forms

No finite forms other than third persons occur.

Active: thematic present: sing. *e-ke* = *ekhei*, plur. *e-ko-si* = *ekhonsi*; infin. *e-ke-e* = *ekheen*, *a-na-ke-e* = *anageen*, *wo-ze-e* = *worzeen*; part. *wo-zo* = *worzōn*, *e-ko-te* = *ekhontes*.

Athematic present: sing. *pa-si* = *phāsi* (?), plur. *di-do-si* = *dido*(*n*)*si*, *ki-ti-je-si* = *ktiensi*; part. *i-jo*, *i-jo-te* = *iōn*, *iontes*.

Future: sing. *do-se* = *dōsei*, plur. *do-so-si* = *dōsonsi*; part. *de-me-o-te* = *demeontes*.

Aorist: *a-ke-re-se* = *agrēse* (?), *wi-de* = *wide* (= εἶδε), *o-po-ro* = *ophlon*; part. *a-ke-ra₂-te* = *agêrantes*?

Perfect: part. *a-ra-ru-ja* = *araruia*, *te-tu-ko-wo-a₂* = *tetukhwoa*.

Middle: thematic present: *e-u-ke-to* = *eukhetoi*, *e-ke-jo-to* = *en-keiontoi* (?); part. *wo-zo-me-no*.

Athematic present: plur. *di-do-to* = *dido*(*n*)*toi*, *-u-ru-to* = *wruntoi*; part. *ki-ti-me-na* = *ktimenā*.

Future: part. *e-pe-se-so-me-na* = *hepsēsomena*, *ze-so-me-no* = *zesomeno-*.

‡ Aorist: *de-ka-sa-to* = *dexato*, *pa-ro-ke-ne-[to]* = *paro-geneto*, *de-ko-to* = *dekto*, *ze-to* = *gento*; infin. *wi-de-ta-i* = *widesthai* (?).

Perfect: *e-pi-de-da-to* = *epidedastoi*; part. *de-de-me-no* = *dedemenō*.

The contract verbs are barely represented, but we may detect one in *te-re-ja*, which seems to be 3rd sing. pres. indic. (=*teleiā*, like the proposed reading δάμνα for δαμνᾷ in Homer, cf. Schwyzer, *Gram.* I, p. 659); infin. *te-re-ja-e*= *teleiaen* (as Att. τιμᾶν<*τιμάεν, cf. Schwyzer, *Gram.* I, p. 807).

The verb 'to be':

Present: plur. *e-e-si*=*eensi* (also *ap-*, *en-*, *posi-*); dual *e-to*=*eston* (?).

Imperative: 3rd plur. *e-e-to*=*eentō* (? or imperfect?).

Part.: *e-o*, *e-o-te*=*eōn*, *eontes* (also *ap-*); fem. *a-pe-a-sa*=*apeassai*.

Imperfect: sing. *a-pe*=*ap-ēs* (?).

Future: *e-so-to*=*essontoi* (?).

WORD-FORMATION

Only a few points deserve special comment.

(1) Feminines in *-eia* from masculines in *-eus*. These forms have been discussed by Chadwick (1954 *b*, p. 7). The clearest is *i-je-re-ja*=*hiereia*, and it is now evident that contrary to all supposition the feminines do not contain the *-w-* of the masculine. Other examples are: the names *i-do-me-ne-ja*=*Idomeneia* ('Ιδομενεύς), *ke-ra-me-ja*=*Kerameia* (κεραμεύς), *e-ro-pa-ke-ja* (*e-ro-pa-ke-u*). Other occupational names are *do-qe-ja* (cf. man's name *do-qe-u*), *ri-ne-ja-o*, *i-te-ja-o*, *pa-ke-te-ja*, *ka-ru-ti-je-ja-o*, *a-ra-ka-te-ja*, *e-ne-re-ja*, *ko-u-re-ja*, *o-nu-ke-ja*, *te-pe-ja-o*. Contrast the adjectival formations *pa₂-si-re-wi-ja*, *i-je-re-wi-jo*, where the termination is *-ēwios*; cf. Cypr. *i-e-re-vi-ja-ne* 'sanctuary'.

(2) Adjectives of Material. These show an alternation between *-e-jo*, *-e-o*, and *-i-jo*, which recalls the similar variation between -εος and -ειος in Homer. Forms in -ιος are also found in Lesb. and Thess. One word exemplifies all three forms: *wi-ri-ne-jo*, *wi-ri-ne-o*, *wi-ri-ni-jo*=*wrīneos*.

(3) Adjectives in *-teros*. *wa-na-ka-te-ro* appears to be *wanakteros* 'royal'. The † objection of Meriggi (1954, p. 34) that in PY **130**=Eo371 (Ea24) *ke-ra-me-wo* *wa-na-ka-te-ro* shows lack of concord is hardly sufficient to outweigh the neuter *wa-na-ka-te-ra*. Such cases of grammatical oversight are not uncommon (see p. 72); and cf. PY **108**=Ea817, where we have *po-me* qualifying genitive *mo-ro-qo-ro-jo* instead of the correct *po-me-no* found on **109**=Ea782. Less certain is *po-ku-te-ro*, which appears to be formed from *po-ku-ta* of unknown meaning.

7. SYNTAX

There are several examples of perfect participles active used in the intransitive sense familiar in Homer: *a-ra-ru-ja*, *a-ra-ru-wo-a* 'fitted (with)', cf. σκολόπεσσιν ἀρηρότα (*Od.* VII, 45); *te-tu-ku-wo-a* 'well made' (of garments and wheels), cf. βοὸς ῥινοῖο τετευχώς (*Od.* XII, 423); possibly *de-di-⟨da⟩-ku-ja* 'taught'.

An idiom familiar in Sanskrit, the use of a reduplicated locative such as *pade-pade* 'at every step', *varṣe-varṣe* 'every year', is found for the first time in Greek: *we-te-i-we-te-i* 'annually' (see p. 279).

pa-ro governs the dative, where Attic παρά would demand the genitive; cf. the use of the dative with ἀπύ in Arcadian. *me-ta* also appears to govern the dative in the phrase *me-ta pe-i*, where the dative is Homeric. The accusative and infinitive construction appears to be proved by PY **140** = Eb35, cf. **135** = Ep704. One other subordinate clause has so far been identified, a relative temporal clause introduced by *o-te* = *hote* PY **235** = Ta711.

† The development of prepositions is already complete, as might be expected from comparative evidence. The instrumental -φι, however, often stands alone, and where accompanied by a preposition we may detect a relic of the earlier independence: *o-pi*...*qe-to-ro-po-pi o-ro-me-no* PY **31** = Ae04 suggests the 'tmesis' of the Homeric ἐπὶ...ὄρονται (*Od.* XIV, 104) where there is no noun expressed.

Word order would seem to be of importance where the inflexions are so largely hidden by the script. There seems to be some consistency in the formulas, though divergent orders are not to be excluded. The order: subject, verb, object, is regular. But the common introductory word *o-* (*jo-*) seems usually to have a verb following; possible exceptions are KN **260** = Og0467, **213** = L 641. The order then may be either subject, object (e.g. PY **257** = Jn09) or object, subject (e.g. PY **75** = Cn02) depending which is being listed. The clauses beginning *o-da-a$_2$* show more freedom; the subject usually follows immediately, the verb, if expressed, being postponed; but in PY **151** = Eb36 we have object, verb, subject. Adjectives tend to precede the noun, but this is often obscured by the fact that when items are being listed the noun naturally takes precedence. Two or more adjectives applied to one noun show asyndeton (e.g. PY **241** = Ta715. 2); but a series of attributive nouns are coupled with -*qe* (e.g. PY **242** = Ta707, **246** = Ta722). On occasion two instrumentals may be balanced on either side of a participle: *se-re-mo-ka-ra-a-pi qe-qi-no-me-na a-di-ri-ja-pi-qe* PY **243** = Ta708.

The definite article as such is clearly absent. Where forms of ὁ, ἡ, τό appear to occur they are probably demonstratives and are listed under Pronouns.

8. VOCABULARY

It was shown above (p. 68) that the vocabulary was essentially Greek. It remains here to discuss its affinities inside Greek. Of the words identified a remarkable number are rare and poetic, while some are known only from sources as late as Hellenistic times. It is most revealing to find that words we had thought to be post-classical are of such venerable antiquity; it should never be assumed that absence from the literary record implies absence from the vocabulary. A good example is the word *pu-ra-u-to-ro* in a list of vessels and implements; it can hardly be anything but *puraustrō* 'a pair of fire-tongs', found in Herodas (third century) and an inscription of the fourth century B.C. Such a humble item of furniture might well escape mention in literature altogether, and its late appearance can now be seen to be without significance.

The words which we know only in Homer and in poetry are archaic survivals †
of an earlier period, and there is nothing surprising in finding them in ordinary use in Mycenaean documents. The words for 'swords' and 'spears' (*phasgana*, *enkhea*) both belong to this category. The names of vessels are numerous and some of them cannot be identified with classical words; *a-pi-po-re-we* is especially notable as showing the Homeric form without haplology (*amphiphorēwes*), and its replacement by *a-po-re-we = amphorēwe* at Mycenae, and perhaps at Pylos, shows that the classical form is also of great antiquity. A few words are recorded by glossaries as Cypriot: *di-pa* δέπας, *pa-ka-na* φάσγανον. The name of the 'king' *wa-na-ka = wanax* was by classical times obsolete (except in special uses) in the whole of Greece but Cyprus.

Of special interest are the Semitic loan-words, which prove that Phoenician influence had begun in the Mycenaean period. The Greeks had already borrowed from them the names of two luxury articles: *ku-ru-so = khrusos*, and *ki-to = khitōn*; and of at least two spices: *ku-mi-no = kuminon* and *sa-sa-ma = sāsama*; probably also *ku-pa-ro = kupairos*. The word *po-ni-ke = phoinikei* 'griffin' (?) and *po-ni-ki-ja = phoinikia* 'red' also probably imply contact with Phoenicia.

The following particles are found:

-de = de 'but', 'and'. ‡

o-, *jo- = hō* (= ὡς) attested as Doric by grammarians, and found in the compounds Attic ὧ-δε, Alcman ὧ-τ'.

o-da-a₂: probably a strengthened form of the preceding; see Vocabulary, ¶
p. 400.

o-te = hote 'when'.

o-u- = ou 'not'.

o-u-ki = oukhi?

-qe = qᵘe (τε) 'and'. For usages where the meaning is obscure see p. 246.

Suffixes of motion:

-de = -de 'towards'.

-te = -then 'from': *a-po-te = apōthen?*, *a-po-te-ro-te = amphoterōthen*, *e-te = enthen?* A number of place-names ending in *-te* are more likely datives (locatives) of consonant stems.

CHAPTER IV

THE PERSONAL NAMES

† AT least 65 per cent of the recorded Mycenaean words are proper names, the interpretation of which is beset by even greater difficulties than those encountered in the interpretation of the vocabulary. The place-names are discussed elsewhere (see ch. V, pp. 139–50). The personal names, which occur on almost every tablet and often comprise the greater part of the text, are extremely numerous; well over a thousand have so far been recorded. A comparison with known Greek names, both legendary and historical, leads to many tempting identifications; but whereas the identification of a vocabulary word can be checked by its meaning as determined by context, that of a personal name must always depend entirely on the superficial resemblance. All the parallels proposed in this chapter must be regarded as subject to this qualification, and thus in a different class from the vocabulary words.

The degree of probability increases with the length of the word, for the longer the word, the less chance there is of a different word resulting in the same spelling. Thus the interpretation of *e-te-wo-ke-re-we-i-jo* as the patronymic adjective from Ἐτεοκλῆς can be regarded as certain; but shorter words often admit of several identifications, and when, as is frequently the case, only the nominative is recorded the range may be wide.

The methods adopted to distinguish personal names require description. The most obvious is the association of single words with the ideogram for MAN or WOMAN and the numeral 1, a feature of the long lists such as KN **38** = As1516, MY **46** = Au102. In other cases the context clearly demands a name, as in the lists of persons in the Pylos *Eo-* series (**118–130**), or the names of smiths in the Pylos *Jn-* tablets (**253–257**). Similarly some tablets appear to have a consistent formula, such as the Knossos *D* (sheep) series (**64–70**), all of which begin with a personal name. If names thus proved are found in other lists, there is a strong presumption that the remaining words in the same list are also names; though cases do occur of composite lists containing also places or trade-names (e.g. PY **258** = Kn01). In a few cases the identification of a name depends chiefly on its resemblance to a known Greek name.

In the present state of our knowledge there are many doubtful cases, and the catalogue has been compiled so as to err on the side of exclusion rather than inclusion. Many more words, especially on small fragments, are probably names, but evidence that might justify their inclusion is lacking. On the other hand it may be hoped that few words have been wrongly admitted, though in some cases doubt exists whether the name is that of a person, or is that of a place, an ethnic adjective, or a title.

One important question which we might expect to answer from a study of the names is the extent of foreign admixture among the Mycenaean Greek population. Unfortunately the problem admits no easy solution. If the Greek language were imposed on a foreign population, the subsequent generations would doubtless show progressively higher proportions of Greek names. But even in classical times there are large numbers which do not seem to be significant in Greek. Thus no exact correlation between names and origins can be expected. There is too a further problem: where do we draw the line between Greek and foreign? There must inevitably be disagreement about the degree of resemblance necessary to establish a Greek origin for a name; and when the effects of 'popular etymology' are taken into account, it is obvious that the basis for a statistical survey is lacking. Similar considerations apply to the Mycenaean names with even greater force; for we can only conjecture the form that underlies the spelling. The longer names are mostly explicable as Greek; the shorter ones offer such a range of possibilities that there must be few which the exercise of sufficient ingenuity will not allow us to derive from a known Greek base. The negative evidence is therefore lacking to permit a proportional calculation; we can only point to names which are clearly Greek and to others which have an unfamiliar aspect. Certainly the names cannot be used to support a theory that any language other than Greek was in actual use in the Mycenaean kingdoms.

It should be pointed out that the list of names given in the Index of Personal Names (pp. 414–27) is biased and must not be used for statistical purposes. It does not represent the complete catalogue from which this chapter has been compiled, but only the names occurring in the texts printed in Part II, and a selection of the more interesting ones from other tablets.

1. MEN'S NAMES

NAMES ENDING IN -*a*

Some of these names may in fact be unidentified feminines, owing to the impossibility of distinguishing the gender in the nominative (see Women's Names, p. 101). Otherwise these are mainly names corresponding to the Greek masculines of the first declension (-α(ς), gen. -ᾱο). In view of the existence of

† masculines in -α in Homer, Boeotian and Elean, it seems very doubtful if we are justified in restoring a final -ς in the nom. sing. The -s has been restored here in the forms quoted in interpretation merely as a convenient means of distinguishing masculines and feminines; it is not intended to imply any judgment as to the probable form (see p. 84). The other main type represented is that in -αυς (gen. -αντος); there are also a few anomalous types such as *pe-re-ku-wa-na-ka*, where the final -a is only a device of the spelling to suggest the double consonant of the ending -ϝάναξ.

Compared with later Greek names the most notable absence is that of names ending with the patronymic suffix -δᾱς (classical -άδης, -ίδης). The few names ending -a-da, -i-da do not appear to be of this type except possibly *da-i-ta-ra-da* (cf. Homeric Δαίτωρ). The same is, however, true of the Homeric names, where these patronymics are either epithets or used as substitutes for the real name.

There is a large group (50) ending in -a-ta, some of which seem to be the representatives of the classical suffix -ήτης: *a-ra-ta* = *Alātās* (Ἀλάτας Pindar), *ko-ma-ta* = *Komātās* (Κομήτης), *ko-ne-wa-ta* = *Skhoinewātās*? (cf. Σχοινάτας), *ma-ka-ta* = *Makhātās*?, *po-to-re-ma-ta* = *Ptolemātās* (Boeot. Πολεμάτας); *po-to-ri-ka-ta* = *Ptolikhātās*?, *ra-u-ra-ta* = *Laurātās*?, *re-u-ka-ta* = *Leukātās*, *se-ri-na-ta* = *Selinātās*, *ta-ra-ma-ta* = *Thalamātās* (ethnic of Θαλάμαι).

A smaller group in -e-ta contains probable representatives of the classical types in -έτης, -ήτης: *a₂-e-ta* = *Aetās*, *i-ke-ta* = *Hiketās*; *a-ke-ta* = *Agetās*?, *e-u-me-ta* = *Eumētās*. Other interesting names of this class are: *o-pe-ta* (cf. *o-pe-re-ta*, which may not, however, be the same word) = *Opheltās* (Thess. and Boeot.), *o-re-ta* = *Orestās*; *ko-ma-we-ta* = *Komawentās*?.

Finally there is an important group (15) in -qo-ta, one of which has at Knossos the variant -qo-i-ta. (See p. 43 on the possible significance of this as a spelling variant.) Owing to the ambiguity of the spelling and the peculiarity of the ‡ dialect this can correspond to four Greek suffixes: -$g^u otās$ = -βάτης (for change of *a* and *o* see p. 77, and cf. *a-pi-qo-to* in Vocabulary) or -βώτης, -$q^u hontās$ = -φόντης, or -$q^u hoitās$ = -φοίτης. The variant -qo-i-ta can only represent the last possibility. The following is the list of names with this suffix, together with some suggestions for the identification of the first part of the compound:

a-e-ri-qo-ta = Ἀερι- (Ἡρι-).
a-na-qo-ta = Ἀνα-.
a-no-qo-ta = Ἀνω-?
a-pi-qo-ta = Ἀμφι-, variant *a-pi-qo-i-ta*.
a-tu-qo-ta
da-i-qo-ta = Δηϊ- (Δηιφόντης).

94

> *do-qo-ta*
> *e-u-ru-qo-ta* = Εὐρυ- (Εὐρυβάτης Hom.).
> *pa-qo-ta*
> *pe-ri-qo-ta-o* (gen.) = Περι-.
> *po-ru-qo-ta* = Πολυ- (Πολυφόντης Hom.).
> *qe-re-qo-ta-o* (gen.) = Τηλε-.
> *qo-ta*
> *ra-wo-qo-ta* = Λαο- (cf. Λαοφόντη fem.).
> *ro-qo-ta*
> *wi-jo-qo-ta* = 'Ιο- (ἰός 'poison'; cf. 'Ιοβάτης).

NAMES ENDING IN -*e*

Of the several possible Greek types which this spelling may represent only two seem to be directly attested in the personal names: -ης, gen. -εος, and -ευς, gen. -εντος. Any others occurring are not attested in an oblique case which would reveal the declension. The most common type is that in -*e*, gen. -*e-o*, dat. -*e-i* (not apparently -*e-e*).

There is a group of names in -*me-de* corresponding to the Greek -μήδης:

> *a-no-me-de* = *Ana-*?
> *a-pi-me-de* = *Amphimēdēs* (possibly not a name but a title).
> *e-ke-me-de* = *Ekhemēdēs* (cf. 'Εχεμήδα fem.).
> *e-ti-me-de-i* (dat.).
> *e-u-me-de* = Εὐμήδης (Hom.).
> *pe-ri-me-de* = Περιμήδης (Hom.).

There is one certain name in -*me-ne*: *e-u-me-ne* = *Eumenēs*. The other names †
with this ending may represent different formations: *ri-me-ne* = *Limnes*?;
a-re-me-ne (with an apparent variant *a-re-zo-me-ne*) on the jars from Thebes.
The suffix -*ke-re-we* = Greek -κλέης, -κλῆς is found in: *e-ri-ke-re-we* = *Eriklewēs*?,
[*da*?]-*mo-ke-re-we-i* (dat.) = *Damoklewēs* (Δαμοκλῆς), *ke-ro-ke-re-we-o* (gen.) =
Khêroklewēs?, *na-u-si-ke-re*-[*we*] = *Nausiklewēs*; and the patronymic *e-te-wo-ke-re-we-i-jo* presupposes the name *Etewoklewēs* (= 'Ετεοκλῆς).

The other type of declension seems only to occur in names which are etymologically adjectives in -*went*- (-ήεις, -όεις): *ko-ma-we* (gen. *ko-ma-we-to*, dat. *ko-ma-we-te*) = *Komawens* (κομήεις), *ai-ta-ro-we* = *Aithalowens* (αἰθαλόεις).

NAMES ENDING IN -*i*

Hardly any of these names reveal their declension by oblique cases, and in many instances the gender is obscure; it is likely that a number of these are in fact feminine. Some are clearly shown to be masculine by association with the

5-2

ideogram MAN, or by their trade: *ke-ki* and *to-ro-wi* in lists of smiths (Κερκίς is attested only as a woman's name), *ka-ra-pi* an *e-te-do-mo*.

It seems likely that *to-ro-wi-ko* PY **62** = Cn655. 2 is the genitive of *to-ro-wi*; if so this is presumably a stem in -ιξ. We might expect a spelling **to-ro-wi-ki* on the analogy of *wa-na-ka*; but the latter is more likely a deliberate anomaly due to the ambiguity of **wa-na*.

NAMES ENDING IN -*o*

As might be expected this is by far the largest class of masculine names. On the basis of the inflected forms they may be subdivided into six groups:

	Nom.	Gen.	Dat.		Greek
(*a*)	-*o*	-*o-jo*	-*o*	-ος	-οιο
(*b*)	-*o*	-*o-o*		-ως	-οος
(*c*)	-*o*	-*o-no*	-*o-ne*	-ων	-ονος or -ωνος
(*d*)	-*o*	-*o-ro*	-*o-re*	-ωρ	-ορος
(*e*)	-*o*	-*o-to*	-*o-te*	-ων	-οντος
(*f*)	-*qo*	-*qo*	-*qe*	-οψ	-οπος

(*a*) *o-stems.* The great bulk of names fall certainly or probably into this class. For convenience of treatment these will be further subdivided. Owing to their great numbers only a small selection of the more interesting names is here analysed.

There is a large class which are known in Greek as common nouns (both substantives and adjectives), some at least being also attested as personal names. In the latter case the Greek word is given a capital letter.

Titles: *pu-ra-ko* Φύλακος (Hom.), *wi-do-wo-i-jo* Widwoios (cf. ἰδυῖοι, βίδυιοι, etc.).

Animals: *e-ki-no* ἐχῖνος, *ru-ko* Λύκος (or Λύκων?), *ta-u-ro* Ταῦρος.

Other objects: *ai-ta-ro* Αἴθαλος, *ku-pe-se-ro* Κύψελος, *ma-ma-ro* Μάρμαρος, *pe-po-ro* Πέπλος, *ru-ro* Λύρος, *ti-ri-po-di-ko* τριποδίσκος (also as common noun MY **234** = Ue611), *ze-pu₂-ro* Ζέφυρος.

Adjectives of colour: *e-ru-to-ro* Ἔρυθρος, *ka-ra-u-ko* Γλαῦκος (Hom.), *ka-sa-to* Ξάνθος (Hom.), *ko-so-u-to* Ξοῦθος, *pu-wo* Corinthian Πύρϝος (=Πύρρος), *re-u-ko-jo* (gen.) Λεῦκος (Hom.).

Other adjectives: *de-ki-si-wo* = Dexiwos (Δεξιός), *de-ko-to* δεκτός or δέκοτος (=δέκατος), *di-so* δισσός, *du-wo-jo* = Dwoios (δοιός), *mo-ro-qo-ro* = *Molog^uros* (μολοβρός), *na-pu-ti-jo* = *Nāputios* (νηπύτιος), *pe-se-ro* Ψελλός, *pi-ri-to-jo* (gen.) Φίλιστος, *po-ti-jo* Πόντιος, *si-mo* (cf. woman's name *si-ma*) Σῖμος.

Derivatives in -ιος (excluding those from place-names, see below): *a-ka-ta-jo*

Ἀκταῖος, a-ko-mo-ni-jo = Akmonios (Ἄκμων), a-ko-ra-jo ἀγοραῖος, a-pa-i-ti-jo = Hāphaistios (Ἥφαιστος), a-wo-i-jo = Āwōios (Ἠῶος?), ai-ki-jo Αἴγιος, ai-so-ni-jo = Aisonios (Αἴσων), e-ko-to-ri-jo = Hektorios (e-ko-to Ἕκτωρ; Hom. Ἑκτόρεος as adj.), e-ni-ja-u-si-jo Ἐνιαύσιος, ka-ri-si-jo Χαρίσιος, me-de-i-jo Μήδειος, o-pi-si-jo Ὄψιος, pa-na-re-jo = Panareios (Πανάρης), pa-ra-ti-jo (variant pa₂-ra₂-ti-jo) Παλλάντιος, pa-qo-si-jo = Pangᵘōsios? (cf. pa-qo-ta), qe-ra-di-ri-jo = Qᵘēlandrios (Τήλανδρος), sa-u-ri-jo = Saurios (Σαῦρος), wa-du-ri-jo = Wādulios (Ἥδυλος), we-we-si-jo = Werwesios (εἶρος, cf. εἰρεσιώνη), wi-tu-ri-jo = Witulios (Ἴτυλος).

A group of names in -me-no appear to be medio-passive participles: a-me-no †
Ἄρμενος?, a₂-nu-me-no = Arnumenos (ἄρνυμαι)?, ai-nu-me-no = Ainumenos (αἴνυμαι)?, e-u-ko-me-no = Eukhomenos (εὔχομαι), ku-ru-me-no Κλύμενος, o-po-ro-me-no = Hoplomenos (ὅπλομαι)?, wa-do-me-no = Wādomenos (ἥδομαι). Others less easy to explain are: ka-e-sa-me-no, ke-sa-me-no (possibly variants of the same name; cf. Κασσαμενός), pi-ra-me-no, and *ku-sa-me-no to be deduced from the patronymic ku-sa-me-ni-jo (κυνέω?).

Compound names of the typical Greek form and with obvious meaning are frequent; but both here and in other sections compounds occur one member of which seems obvious, while the other remains obscure. Some of these are here listed exempli gratia:

a-ke-ra-wo   Agelāwos   Ἀγέλαος
a-ko-ro-qo-ro   Agroqᵘolos?   (cf. Latin Agricola)
a-pi-a₂-ro   Ἀμφίαλος
a-pi-do-ro   Ἀμφίδωρος   (cf. woman's name a-pi-do-ra)
a-pi-ja-ko-ro-jo   (gen.)   Amphiagros or Amphiāgoros
a-pi-ja-re-wo   Amphiarēwos   Ἀμφιάρηος
a-pi-ra-wo   Amphilāwos
a-pi-wa-to   Amphiwastos?
a-ti-pa-mo   Antiphāmos   Ἀντίφημος
a-tu-ko   Atukhos?
a-u-po-no   Aupnos
a-wi-to-do-to   Awistodotos?
[de]-ke-se-ra-wo   Dexelāwos   Δεξίλαος
e-ke-da-mo   Ἐχέδαμος
e-ri-we-ro   Eriwēros   (= Hom. ἐρίηρος)?
e-ti-ra-wo   ? -lāwos   (cf. e-ti-me-de)
e-u-da-mo   Εὔδαμος
e-u-ka-ro   Eukālos   (εὔκηλος)
e-u-ko-ro   Εὔκολος, Εὔχορος, Εὔκλος?
e-u-na-wo   Eunāwos   Εὔνηος
e-u-po-ro   Εὔφορος, Εὔπορος
e-u-po-ro-wo   Euplowos   Εὔπλους

97

e-u-ru-da-mo   Εὐρύδαμος

[e-u]-ru-po-to-re-mo-jo   (gen.)   Εὐρυπτόλεμος

e-u-to-ro-qo   *Eutroqᵘos*   Εὔτροπος

e-u-wa-ko-ro   Εὐάγορος, Εὔαγρος

i-su-ku-wo-do-to   *Iskhuodotos*?

ma-na-si-we-ko   *Mnāsiwergos*   Μνησίεργος

ne-wo-ki-to   *Newo-*?

o-ku-na-wo   *Ōkunāwos*

o-pi-ri-mi-ni-jo   *Opilimnios*   (cf. Ἐπιλίμνιος)

o-ti-na-wo   *Ortināwos*?

pe-ri-to-wo   *Perithowos*   Πειρίθοος

pi-ro-we-ko   *Philowergos*   Φιλοῦργος

po-ru-ka-to   *Polukastos*?   (cf. Πολυκάστη)

ra-wo-do-ko   *Lāwodokos*   Λαόδοκος

ra-wo-po-qo   *Lāwopoqᵘos*?   (cf. Δημο-κόπος)

ra-wo-qo-no   *Lāwogᵘhonos*   (cf. Λεωφόντης)

ru-ko-wo-ro   (variant *ru-ko-u-ro*)   *Lukoworos*   (cf. Λυκουρία)

ti-ri-da-ro   *Tridālos*   (cf. Ἀρί-δηλος, etc.)

wa-du-ka-sa-ro   *Wādu-*?

wa-du-na-ro   *Wādu-*?

wa-tu-o-ko   *Wastuokhos*   Ἀστύοχος

wi-pi-no-o   *Wiphinoos*   Ἰφίνοος

The following names are identical with or are derived from place-names:

ai-ku-pi-ti-jo   Αἰγύπτιος

ai-ta-jo   *Aithaios*   (Αἴθαια)

i-wa-so   *Iwasos*   (cf. Ἴασον Ἄργος Hom.)

ka-so   Κάσος

ko-ru-da-ro-jo   (gen.)   Κορυδαλλός

ku-pi-ri-jo   Κύπριος

ku-ra-no   *Kullānos*   (Κυλλήνη)

ku-ta-i-jo   *Kutaios*   (Κύταιον)

ku-te-ro   *Kuthēros*   (Κυθήρα)

ma-ra-ni-jo   Μαλάνιος

o-ka-ri-jo   *Oikhalios*   (Οἰχαλίη Hom.)

pa₂-me-si-jo   (variant *pa₂-mi-si-jo*)   *Pamisios*   (Πάμισος)

pa₂-ra-jo   Φαραῖος

po-i-ti-jo   *Phoitios*   (Φοιτίαι)

ra-pa-sa-ko   Λάμψακος

re-pi-ri-jo   *Leprios*   (Λέπρεον)

re-u-ka-so   *Leukasos*   (Λευκασία)

ru-ki-jo   Λύκιος

ru-na-so   *Lurnassos*   (Λυρνησσός)

tu-ri-jo Τύριος?
tu-ri-si-jo-jo (gen.) Τυλίσιος

Names attested in Greek, but not otherwise classified: *a-nu-to* Ἄνυτος, *ko-do-ro* Κόδρος, *ko-ka-ro* Κώκαλος, *mo-qo-so* = *Moqᵘsos* (Μόψος; cf. Hittite *Mukšaš*), *pi-ra-jo* Φιλαῖος, *pi-ri-no* Φιλῖνος, *pu-wi-no* = *Purwinos* (Πύρρινος), *si-ra-no* Σιλᾱνός, *wi-ri-ja-no* = *Wrianos* (= Ῥιανός?).

(*b*) -ως, -ὄος. These are very rare; perhaps genitives *to-ro-o* (Τρώς, Τρωός?), *a-pi-qo-o*.

(*c*) -ων, -ονος or -ωνος. Most prominent is a class of names in *-a-wo*, though the identification is often uncertain in default of evidence of declension. Among those plausibly identified or certified by inflexion are: *a-ka-wo* (dat. *-ne*) = *Alkāwōn?*, *a-mu-ta-wo* (gen. *-no*) = Ἀμυθάων (Hom.), *a-re-ta-wo* = Ἀρετάων (Hom.), *a-ri-ja-wo* (dat. *-ne*), *a-ti-ja-wo* = *Antiāwōn* (= Ἀντίων)?, *e-ke-ra₂-wo* (gen. *-no*, dat. *-ne*) = *Ekhelāwōn* (cf. Ἐχέλαος), *ma-ka-wo* = Μαχάων, *me-za-wo* (dat. *-ni*) = *Mezāwōn?*, *o-pa₂-wo-ni* (dat.) = *Opāwōn?*, *pi-ri-ta-wo-no* (gen.) = *Brithāwōn?*, *pi-ro-pa₂-wo* = *Philoppāwōn* (cf. Φιλοκτήμων)?. The type with genitive -ωνος is represented by the divine name *po-se-da-o* (dat. *-ne* or *-ni*) Ποσειδάων; and is to be inferred from identifications such as *de-u-ka-ri-jo* Δευκαλίων.

(*d*) -ωρ, -ορος. There are two probable uncompounded names in this class: *a-ko-to* = Ἄκτωρ, *e-ko-to* = Ἕκτωρ (cf. *e-ko-to-ri-jo*); and a compound of uncertain identity: *e-u-we-to* (gen. *-ro*) *Euētōr?*. Apart from these most names belonging to this group are compounds ending in *-a-no* (= -ήνωρ):

a-ka-sa-no *Alxānōr* (Naxian Ἀλχσήνορ)
a-ta-no (gen. *-ro*, dat. *-re*) = Ἀντήνωρ
do-ri-ka-no *Dolikhānōr?*
e-ka-no *Ekhānōr* (cf. Ἐχάνδρα)
me-ta-no (dat. *-re*) *Metānōr* (cf. Μετάνειρα)
ne-ti-ja-no (dat. *-re*) *Nestiānōr?*
o-pe-ra-no (dat. *-re*) *Ophelānōr* (cf. Ὀφέλανδρος)
ra-ke-da-no (dat. *-re*) ? *-ānōr*

(*e*) -ων, -οντος. The only proven examples are *i-na-o* (dat. *i-na-o-te*), and *a-pi-(j)o-to* (gen.) perhaps *Amphiontos* (classical Ἀμφίονος).

(*f*) -οψ, -οπος. The presence of *-o* in the spelling of the nominative is purely formal; cf. the final *-a* of *wa-na-ka* = ϝάναξ: *ai-ti-jo-qo* (gen. *ai-ti-jo-qo*, dat. *ai-ti-jo-qe*) = Αἰθίοψ; *po-ki-ro-qo* probably *Poikiloqᵘs*.

NAMES ENDING IN -*u*

These are comparatively rare except for the stems in -*e-u* (see below). It is possible in default of inflexional evidence that some conceal consonantal terminations; e.g. *ko-ku* might be κόκκυξ used as a name. Others have a foreign look: e.g. *o-tu* which is perhaps the name Ὄτυς attested as Paphlagonian. Apparently Greek are: *e-te-wa-tu-o* (gen.) = *Etewastus*?, *o-ku* = *Ōkus*?, *re-u-ko-o-*
† *pu₂-ru* (read as *Leuk{r}ophrus* by Palmer), *wa-de-o* (gen.) = *Wādus* (ἡδύς).

There are over 100 names in -*e-u*, corresponding to the archaic Greek type in -εύς. Some have clear etymologies (e.g. *do-ro-me-u* = *Dromeus* from δρόμος); others, as in the historical names, are apparently foreign. An interesting group is formed by those derived from verbal stems with a -*s*- suffix: *a-re-ke-se-u* (ἀλεκ-), *a-we-ke-se-u* (ἀέξω), *de-ke-se-u* (δέκομαι), *e-ne-ke-se-u* (ἐνεγκ-), *ka-ri-se-u* (χαρίζομαι?), *o-na-se-u* (ὀνίνημι), *pa-ra-ke-se-we* (dat.) (πράσσω), *pi-re-se-[u]*
‡ (φιλέω), *qo-wa-ke-se-u* = *Gᵘow-axeus* (ἄγω), *te-se-u* (τίθημι).

A full list of these names in -*e-u* follows:

a-i-qe-u	*e-ta-je-u*
a-ka-re-u	*e-ta-wo-ne-u*
a-ke-u	*e-te-we* (dat.)
a-ki-re-u	*e-wi-te-u*
a-na-te-u	*i-mo-ro-ne-u*
a-pa-je-u	*i-ne-u*
a-pe-te-u	*i-te-u*
a-re-ke-se-u	*ka-e-se-u*
a-ri-ke-u	*ka-ke-u*
a-ro-je-u	*ka-nu-se-u*
a-ta-ma-ne-u	*ka-ri-se-u*
a-ta-ze-u	*ka-te-u*
a-to-re-u	*ke-me-u*
a-we-ke-se-u	*ke-re-te-u*
ai-ke-u	*ke-re-u*
ai-ki-e-we (dat.)	*ke-ro-u-te-u*
ai-re-u	*ki-e-u (ki-je-u)*
da-to-re-u	*ko-pe-re-u*
de-ke-se-u	*ko-te-u*
do-qe-u	*ku-ke-re-u*
do-ro-me-u	*ku-ne-u*
e-do-mo-ne-u	*ma-re-u*
e-ne-ke-se-u	*me-re-u*
e-ni-pa-te-we (dat.)	*me-te-we* (dat.)
e-o-te-u	*me-to-qe-u*
e-pe-ke-u	*mo-re-u*
e-po-me-ne-u	*ne-qe-u*
e-re-u (?)	*no-e-u*
e-ro-pa-ke-u	*o-ke-te-u*

o-ke-u
o-ko-me-ne-u
o-na-se-u
o-ne-u
o-pe-te-re-u (o-pe-to-re-u)
pa-da-je-u
pa-de-we-u
pa-ra-ke-se-we (dat.)
pa-sa-re-wo (gen.) (?)
pe-ke-u
pe-qe-u
pe-ri-te-u
pe-te-u
pi-ke-re-u
pi-re-se-[u?]
pi-ta-ke-u
po-i-te-u
po-ke-we (dat.)
po-ro-qe-re-je-wo (gen.)
po-ro-u-te-u
po-ru-we-wo (gen.)
po-te-u
pu-te-u
qe-re-me-ne-u

qe-ta-ra-je-u
qe-ta-se-u (= qe-te-se-u?)
qo-wa-ke-se-u
sa-ke-re-u
ta-mi-je-u
ta-re-u
ta-ta-ke-u
ta-ti-qo-we-u
te-pe-u
te-po-se-u
te-se-u
te-te-re-u
te-te-u
to-ke-u
tu-ke-ne-u
tu-ru-we-u
tu-si-je-u
tu-ti-je-u
u-re-u
wa-di-re-we (dat.?)
we-da-ne-wo (gen.)
we-te-re-u
wi-ja-te-wo (gen.)
wi-*65-te-u

2. WOMEN'S NAMES

In a number of cases it is possible to identify a name as belonging to a woman by the presence of an ideogram or the gender of an attribute. No distinction is possible on grammatical grounds, since the masculine and feminine a-stems cannot be distinguished unless the name occurs in the genitive. There are therefore a number of names which are ambiguous; and these are treated as masculine in default of evidence; where there is good reason to suspect they might be feminine this is indicated in the Index.

The great majority of proven women's names end in -a. The exceptions are a group of 10 ending in -i which presumably correspond to Greek stems in -ις: e-pa-sa-na-ti (variant i-pa-sa-na-ti), ko-pi, mu-ti Μύρτις, mu-ti-ri Μυρτιλίς, qo-ja-ni, sa-mi, tu-*49-mi, tu-ri-ja-ti (cf. Θυρεᾶτις fem. adj.), tu-ri-ti, wa-ra-ti; six ending in -o, presumably Greek -ώ: ka-na-to-po, ku-tu-pa$_2$-no, ru-ta$_2$-no, † ta-ka-to, tu-zo, *18-to-no; four in -u (Greek -υς, -υξ? perhaps foreign): a-zu?, ke-pu, ma-zu?, wi-ja-na-tu; and one in -e: si-nu-ke.

Other known or recognizable names include: a-pi-do-ra = Amphidora (cf. ᾿Αμφίδωρος), a-ti-ke-ne-ja = Antigeneia, Arti-? (for termination cf. ke-pu-ke-ne-ja), ai-wa-ja = Αἰαίη, i-do-me-ne-ja = Idomeneia (cf. ᾿Ιδομενεύς), ke-ra-me-ja (fem. of κεραμεύς), *mu-ka-ra* = Μυκάλη, *pi-ra-ka-ra* = *Philagrā* (cf. Φίλαγρος), *pi-ro-na* = *Philōnā*, *pu-wa* = Πύρρα (cf. *pu-wo*), *si-ma* = Σίμη, *ta-ra-mi-ka* = *Thalamikā*, *-iskā*?, *te-pa₂-ja* = Θηβαία, *u-wa-mi-ja* = *Huamiā* (cf. town Ὑάμεια in Messenia).

3. NAMES RECURRING AT DIFFERENT PLACES

A fair number of the personal names are attested at more than one place. There can be no question, at least as far as Knossos and Pylos are concerned, of these referring to the same persons. It is also probable that different people are intended when the same name recurs in the same place but in a different context; for instance *ti-pa₂-jo* who is called a shepherd (*po-me*) on PY **128** = Eo278 (Eb01) can hardly be the same man as *ti-pa₂-jo* who is a smith at *A-ke-re-wa* on **253** = Jn01.

†   The following lists show all the certain or probable personal names which occur at two or more places; where one source has only a different inflexional form or a variant spelling this is shown in brackets. Names which are certainly feminine are so shown.

KNOSSOS AND PYLOS

ai-ko-ta
ai-ta-ro-we
a-ka-sa-no
a-ka-ta-jo
a-ka-wo
a-ke-ra-wo
a-ke-ta
a-ki-re-u (PY *a-ki-re-we*)
a-no-ke-we
a-pi-me-de
a-pi-qo-ta
a-re-ki-si-to
a-si-wi-jo
a-ta-no (PY *a-ta-no-ro*)
a-ta-o
a-ta-wo
a-ti-pa-mo
a-ti-ro (?)
a-tu-ko
a-*64-jo
de-ki-si-wo (PY *de-ki-si-wo-jo*)
di-wo
do-ri-ka-o
du-ni-jo
e-ke-da-mo
e-ke-me-de

e-ki-no (PY *e-ki-no-jo*)
e-ta-wo-ne-u (KN *e-ta-wo-ne-we*)
e-te-wa (KN *e-te-wa-o*?)
e-u-ko-me-no
e-u-po-ro-wo
i-da-i-jo
i-ra-ta
i-wa-ka
ka-ro-qo
ka-so
ka-ta-no
ke-sa-do-ro
ke-ti-ro (?)
ke-to
ki-je-u (PY *ki-e-u*)
ki-ri-ja-i-jo (KN *ki-ra₂-i-jo*)
ko-do
ko-ma-we (PY KN *ko-ma-we-te*)
ko-pe-re-u
ko-ro
ko-sa-ma-to
ku-ri-sa-to
ku-ro₂ (KN *ku-ro₂-jo*)
ku-ru-me-no
ma-ri-ti-wi-jo
me-nu-wa

me-ta-no (KN me-ta-no-re)
me-za-wo (PY me-za-wo-ni)
mo-da
mo-go-so (PY mo-go-so-jo)
na-e-si-jo
na-pu-ti-jo
o-na-se-u
pa-na-re-jo
pa-pa-ro
pa-ra-ko
pa-wa-wo
pe-po-ro
pe-qe-u
pe-re-wa-ta
pe-ri-te-u
pi-ra-me-no
po-ro-ko
po-ro-u-te-u
po-ru-da-si-jo (?)

qo-te-ro
ra-u-ra-ta (PY ra-wa-ra-ta)
re-u-ka-ta
re-wa-jo (PY re-wa-o)
ri-so-wa
ri-zo
ru-ro
sa-mu-ta-jo
ta-we-si-jo (PY ta-we-si-jo-jo)
te-pa₂-ja (fem.)
te-u-to
te-wa-jo
ti-pa₂-jo
wa-na-ta-jo
we-we-si-jo
wo-di-je-ja (fem.)
wo-di-jo
zo-wi-jo

Pylos and Mycenae

i-na-o
ka-sa-to
ke-re-no

o-pe-ra-no (MY o-pe-ra-no-re)
te-ra-wo (PY te-ra-wo-ne)

Knossos and Mycenae

pe-se-ro (KN pe-se-ro-jo)

pu-wo

Knossos, Pylos and Mycenae

ka-ri-se-u

Knossos and Thebes

a-nu-to
e-u-da-mo

ta-de-so

Knossos, Pylos and Thebes

e-wa-ko-ro (PY e-u-wa-ko-ro)

Knossos and Eleusis

du-pu₂?-ra-zo (EL da-pu₂?-ra-zo)

4. HOMERIC PARALLELS

Among the personal names are a fair number which recall names familiar from Homer. The list appended enumerates fifty-eight, which, making due allowance for the spelling conventions and difference of dialect, may be equated with Homeric names. Not all of these may be correctly identified; but at least the majority are likely to be right. And to these may be added a further list of similar but not identical names. The root of the name may be the same but with a different suffix: e.g. *a-pi-jo-to* (gen.), cf. Ἀμφίων, Ἀμφίονος; *o-wi-ro*, cf. Ὀϊλεύς; *i-ke-ta=Hiketās*, cf. Ἱκετάων. There may be a difference of gender: e.g. *i-do-me-ne-ja*, feminine of Ἰδομενεύς (see p. 89). Or the word may occur in Homer, but not as a personal name: e.g. *na-pu-ti-jo=Nāputios* (νηπύτιος); *i-wa-so* (also a place-name), cf. Ἴασον Ἄργος (*Od.* xviii, 246).

None of the names can be plausibly identified with any historical character named by Homer; the name of Nestor is absent as well as that of Minos. Kretheus and Amythaon are figures in Pylian history, but the owners of these names on the tablets are hardly of sufficient importance to allow identification, even if the chronology were acceptable. The duplication of names (see p. 102) suggests that there was a comparatively limited range of names in use in Mycenaean times, and when Homer gives the same name to more than one character, his invention is not necessarily to be judged barren. The evidence that famous names such as Hector and Achilles (the latter found at both Knossos and Pylos) might be borne by a number of men—some of humble rank, for the former is *theoio doelos*—throws a new light on the attempts at identifying Achaean names in the Hittite documents. Our suggestion (*Evidence*, p. 95) that these names confirmed the view that the myths were already current has been rightly criticized by Banti (1954, p. 310) and others.

It is remarkable that this list includes twenty men who are named by Homer as Trojans or fighting on the Trojan side: Agelaos, Antenor, Aretaon, Deukalion Eumedes, Glaukos, Hektor, Ilos, Laodokos, Lykon, Pandaros, Pedaios, Pedasos, Perimos, Phegeus, Phylakos, Pyrasos, Pyris, Tros, Xanthos. Two of these names are also given to Greeks. A discussion of the conclusions to be drawn from this fact lies beyond the scope of this book; but twenty out of fifty-eight is a significant proportion. There is also a group of names which may be termed mythical, i.e. not given to real persons in the story of the poems: Aiaie, Aloeus, Ephialtes, Iphimedeia, Kastor, Tantalos. Two names, if the second is correctly interpreted, are those of Phaiakians: Amphialos, Ponteus.

Names which can be exactly paralleled in Homer

ai-ku-pi-ti-jo Αἰγύπτιος	*a-pa-re-u* Ἀφαρεύς
ai-ti-jo-qo Αἰθίοψ (only as ethnic)	*a-pi-a₂-ro* Ἀμφίαλος
ai-to Αἴθων	*a-pi-ja-re-wo* Ἀμφιάραος (Ἀμφιάρηος
ai-wa Αἴας	Pindar)
ai-wa-ja Αἰαίη	*a-re-ku-tu-ru-wo* Ἀλεκτρύων
a-ke-ra-wo Ἀγέλαος, Ἀγέλεως	*a-re-ta-wo* Ἀρετάων
a-ki-re-u Ἀχιλλεύς	*a-ro-je-u* Ἀλωεύς
a-ko-to Ἄκτωρ	*a-ta-no* Ἀντήνωρ
a-mu-ta-wo Ἀμυθάων	*de-u-ka-ri-jo* Δευκαλίων

e-ko-to	Ἕκτωρ	pe-da-i-o	Πήδαιος
e-pe-ke-u	Ἐπειγεύς	pe-ke-u	Φηγεύς
e-pi-ja-ta	Ἐφιάλτης	pe-ri-me-de	Περιμήδης
e-ta-wo-ne-u	Ἐτεωνεύς	pe-ri-mo	Πέριμος
e-u-me-de	Εὐμήδης	pe-ri-to-wo	Πειρίθοος
e-u-na-wo	Εὔνηος	po-ru-qo-ta	Πολυφόντης
e-u-ru-qo-ta	Εὐρυβάτης	po-te-u	Ποντεύς
i-pe-me-de-ja	Ἰφιμέδεια	pu-ra-ko	Φύλακος
ka-ra-u-ko	Γλαῦκος	pu-ra-so	Πύρασος
ka-ro-qo	Χάροπος, Χάροψ	pu-ri	Πῦρις
ka-sa-to	Ξάνθος	ra-wo-do-ko	Λαόδοκος
ka-to (gen. ka-to-ro)	Κάστωρ	re-u-ko-jo (gen.)	Λεῦκος
ke-re-te-u	Κρηθεύς	ru-ki-jo	Λύκιος (only as ethnic)
ko-pe-re-u	Κοπρεύς	ru-ko	Λύκων
ku-ru-me-no	Κλύμενος	ta-ta-ro	Τάνταλος
ma-ka-wo	Μαχάων	te-se-u	Θησεύς
ne-ri-to	Νήριτος	to-ro-o (gen.)	Τρώς
o-re-ta	Ὀρέστης	tu-we-ta	Θυέστης
pa-di-jo	Πανδίων	wi-pi-no-o	Ἰφίνοος
pa₂-da-ro	Πάνδαρος	wi-ro	Ἶλος, Ἶρος
pa₂-da-so	Πήδασος		

5. THE NAMES GIVEN TO OXEN

Furumark (1954, pp. 28–9) drew attention to a group of Knossos *Ch* tablets on which pairs of animals are given names (see p. 213). The ideogram which Furumark took to be HORSE is now identified as OX (see p. 195), and we have therefore the names given by the Greeks of Mycenaean Crete to several yokes of their oxen. Only horses have names in Homer; but we need not doubt that the Mycenaean ploughman had names for his oxen. Significantly all the names appear to be Greek: *ai-wo-ro* = *Aiwolos* (αἰόλος), *ke-ra-no* (κελαινός), [*ko*]-*so-u-to* (ξουθός, also as a man's name), *po-da-ko* (Πόδαργος, a name given to two horses in Homer), *to-ma-ko* (στόμαργος), *wo-no-qo-so* = *Woinoqᵘs* (οἶνοψ, an epithet of oxen as well as the sea in Homer).

CHAPTER V

THE EVIDENCE OF THE TABLETS

† T H I S chapter is intended to summarize the information which can be derived both from the circumstances in which the tablets were written and from the subject-matter that decipherment has revealed; and to supplement the picture of Mycenaean life which had been drawn from the purely archaeological evidence (see especially Wace, 1949, pp. 102–18). It inevitably repeats, though in a more synoptic form, many of the observations and conclusions in the commentary to Part II of this book, where the text of the key tablets quoted in evidence will be found.

Even before decipherment, a study of the more pictorial ideograms enabled a summary of the apparent contents of the Knossos tablets to be included in *PM*, iv (pp. 666–872) and *SM II* (pp. 50–62). Following our *JHS* 1953 article, valuable surveys of the picture resulting from the then published Mycenaean tablets were made by Furumark (1954), Carratelli (1954*a*) and others.

Similar summaries, based on more complex but more certainly interpreted material, have been published for the Akkadian tablets from the Hurrian palaces at Nuzi ('Epigraphical evidences of the material culture of the Nuzians', Lacheman, 1939) and at Alalakh (Wiseman, 1953, pp. 1–17). Together with the alphabetic and cuneiform tablets from Ugarit (published piecemeal by Virolleaud in *Syria*, and to be re-edited in the forthcoming definitive volumes on Ugarit), these contemporary records present the most useful and significant analogies with the Mycenaean tablets, and will often be found quoted in our commentary. In spite of some differences in climate and culture, the similarities in the size and organization of the royal palaces and in the purposes for which the tablets were written ensure close parallels, not only in the listed commodities and their amounts, but even on occasion in details of phraseology and layout. Some direct knowledge of each other's scribal methods, through the medium of Mycenaean traders, cannot be entirely ruled out. Some earlier cuneiform sets may also provide useful material for comparison, particularly the Akkadian tablets from Ur of the third dynasty (Legrain, 1947) and of the Old Babylonian period (Figulla & Martin, 1953). Conspicuously absent from the Mycenaean records are the contracts of sale, loan, exchange and marriage common in the other sets: this may argue a difference either in the judicial function of the king or in the materials on which such things were recorded.

No apology is needed for quoting Homeric parallels to the *linguistic* forms on the Mycenaean tablets: in spite of the relatively late date of our written texts, the *Iliad* and *Odyssey* may for the most part be safely taken as our earliest evidence for the classical language, and some of the features of our Mycenaean dialect are preserved by them alone.

But how far may we be justified in quoting from Homer *material* parallels to the subject-matter of our tablets? A full answer would require a discussion of the sources, composition and transmission of the epics for which we have neither space nor qualifications; but the reasonable view exemplified by Lorimer (1950) would impose a considerable degree of restraint. Although the substance of the *Iliad* and *Odyssey* is derived from a real historical setting in the Mycenaean age by a continuous tradition of retelling, the detail and simile in their final elaboration are for the most part taken from the material culture and institutions of the eighth century B.C.—except where anachronism would clearly offend a generally-remembered tradition (e.g. of bronze weapons, of the absence of Dorians or cavalry, and of the geographical extent of Greek settlement as reflected in the Catalogue of Ships). Some allusions to Mycenaean articles or institutions may be preserved in set phrases which the metre makes difficult to modify; and a very few more detailed memories may have been preserved embedded 'in the amber of traditional poetry', such as the descriptions of the boar's tusk helmet, of the metal inlay on Achilles' shield, and of Nestor's cup (though the last is denied by Furumark).

But even if we can find few specifically Mycenaean things in Homer, there are inevitably broad similarities between the activities of the Greeks for whom our tablets were written and the life which he and his audience, looking at the world around them, thought it reasonable that their ancestors should have led. The fact that this testimony is linked by an identity of climate and geography, and by continuity of history and race, to some extent annuls the priority which the Ugarit, Alalakh and Nuzi evidence might claim on account of its closeness of date.

It is extremely improbable that any distinctive passage of the *Iliad* or *Odyssey*, in the form in which we now know them, should already have been composed in Mycenaean times: in fact a large proportion of their lines will no longer fit the metre when retrospective allowance has been made for the intervening linguistic changes (though this is no argument against the intrinsic suitability of the hexameter as a vehicle for the earlier dialect). But both epics clearly derive from an earlier and wider repertoire, in which familiar themes were elaborated by extemporization, plagiarism or deliberate innovation, and with the aid of stock formulae and stereotyped devices for articulating the narrative; and they preserve some evidence of an earlier stage in which the native dialect of the rhapsodes was not Ionic but Aeolic or 'Achaean'. It is reasonable to suppose with Lorimer (1950, pp. 453–8) that similar poems in Greek, and probably in hexameters, were already being recited at Knossos, Pylos and Mycenae. Some of Homer's connective formulae may already have been indispensable in their Mycenaean forms, e.g. *ὣ φάτο, τῷ δὲ ... or *τὸν δ' ἀπαμειγʷόμενος ποσίφᾱ, etc.; we should perhaps not be surprised to find that some repetitive lines already existed in their entirety, let us say:

*δύσετό κʷ' ἀϝέλιος σκιϳάοντό κʷε πᾶνσαι ἀγυιαί.

Resistance to the idea of a developed Mycenaean poetry may well spring from a feeling that a form of Greek of such antiquity would not, like Homer, possess adequate resources of vocabulary compounds, connective particles, syntax patterns and inflexional forms. There is little basis for this prejudice, easy though it is to understand. In the language of everyday life, on which every literary style must ultimately be based, there is no reason to suppose that the men of Pylos and Mycenae were less articulate than their descendants of Socrates' time or our own; and the example of Anglo-Saxon poetry reminds us that the Indo-European languages have, with the passage of time and in areas of higher culture, tended to a progressive simplification of their formal resources rather than to their elaboration.

We tread on more dangerous ground when we speculate with Wace whether such Mycenaean epics may not already have been committed to writing, and have survived part at least of the 'dark age' in a Linear B edition; or with Webster (1955, p. 11) on the possibility that the scribes of the tablets were themselves the *aoidoi* of our period. He draws attention to the dactylic rhythm of the preambles to **41 = An14** and **53 = An12**; and finds an echo of the catalogue style of the 'furniture' and 'chariot' tablets (**235–246, 265–277**) in such passages as *Od.* vi, 69–70:

ἀπήνην
ὑψηλὴν ἐύκυκλον, ὑπερτερίῃ ἀραρυῖαν,

and *Od.* v, 234–5:

πέλεκυν μέγαν, ἄρμενον ἐν παλάμῃσι,
χάλκεον, ἀμφοτέρωθεν ἀκαχμένον.

Apart from such aberrant examples of literary description, it is difficult to find close parallels in alphabetic Greek to the context and phraseology of the

Mycenaean accounts except in some of the Attic temple inventories and in the papyri of the Ptolemaic and Roman periods. But in the effort to form a more precise picture of the transactions and administrative problems which give rise to the different groups of tablets and their formulae, there may well be other sets of records, further removed geographically but still in some respects closer to the tempo of Mycenaean civilization than to that of our own, which we should not neglect in the search for helpful analogies.

1. THE EXTENT OF MYCENAEAN LITERACY   †

Apart from some fifty inscriptions on jars (nearly all from Thebes and Tiryns) and one indistinct wall-graffito at Knossos, since destroyed (*SM I*, p. 51, fig. 27), all the surviving examples of Mycenaean writing are on clay tablets and sealings, and consist exclusively of lists of commodities and personnel. The clay documents were not baked by the scribes, but have been preserved by the fires which destroyed the various buildings in which they were kept. Though it is evident that very many more clay tablets must have been written than have been accidentally preserved, opinion is divided on the possible use of more perishable materials for literary purposes, and on the extent of Mycenaean literacy outside a narrow class of scribes serving the royal palaces. The following points have been cited in favour of an extensive knowledge of writing:

1. The tablets found in the three adjoining houses below the citadel at Mycenae appear to be the records of private citizens, probably merchants (Wace, 1953 *b*).

2. 'The inscriptions on stirrup-jars presumably mean that more persons than the upper and middle classes could read and write: it would obviously be no use to inscribe stirrup-jars if only a few persons could read what was written on them' (*ibid.* p. 426).

3. From an analysis of handwriting, perhaps still questionable in some details but unassailable in principle, Bennett has shown that at least six scribes wrote the tablets in the Mycenae 'House of the Oil Merchant'; and that more than thirty were responsible for each of the Pylos and Knossos sets, in some cases a particular scribe being associated with a single kind of record (*MT I*, 1953, p. 438).

4. The shapes of the Linear A and B signs suggest that they were not designed primarily for scratching on clay but for writing in ink on skins or papyrus (compare, too, Pliny's note that the Cretans had originally written on palm-leaves, *NH*, XIII, 69). The use of clay for store-room inventories was probably a protection against mice. Many of the Minoan clay sealings have

the impression of thin strings, perhaps securing papyrus, on one face; and clay sealings from the 1948 excavation at Sklavokampos near Knossos show impressions from identical seal-stones as sealings found at Agia Triada, Gournia and Zakro, proving an exchange of correspondence between these sites (Marinatos, 1951). The same function is assigned by Evans (*SM I*, p. 50) to the very numerous LM II sealings from the 'Room of the Archives' at Knossos (*N* on fig. 13, p. 115).

Linear B is not intrinsically unsuited to a literary use (at least by comparison with some of the contemporary scripts), and it is plausible that letters and merchants' accounts should have been written in it; but there are a number of points in favour of Dow's view of a restricted or 'special' literacy (1954, pp. 108–13, 120–2):

1. There is so far a more or less complete absence of styluses, pens and ink-pots from the archaeological record.

2. The script is never used publicly (like the Egyptian hieroglyphs and most ancient scripts) for descriptive texts to wall paintings or for monumental inscriptions of any kind. The number of inscribed stirrup-jars is very small compared with the vast numbers which have no trace of writing, and which include all those found as exports. Written inventories are a necessary precaution against theft, but poetry, liturgies and laws can be preserved orally.

3. It cannot yet be shown conclusively that the three Mycenae buildings really are the houses of private citizens, rather than appendages of the royal administration like the 'Armoury' and 'Little Palace' at Knossos. The mention of 'seventeen bakers' on **46** = Au102 arouses some suspicion.

4. If the break caused by the 'Dorian invasion' is as gentle as Wace argues, then the art of writing, which then to all intents and purposes disappears, cannot have been at all deeply rooted.

5. The almost identical sign-forms, spelling, phraseology and tablet shape and arrangement shown at Knossos, Pylos and Mycenae (despite considerable differences in date and place) may themselves show that writing was the preserve of specialists trained in a rigidly conservative scribal school.

2. BUREAUCRATIC METHODS

Many of the details of this fixed scribal routine have already been discussed by Evans and Bennett. The tablets were made from a plastic grey clay, which now appears dark grey, brown or red according to the temperature and oxygen supply of the fire which baked them; sometimes a body of coarser stuff was surfaced all over with a finer clay, now particularly liable to flake off. The

PLATE II

(a) **82** = Ca895 from the Northern Entrance Passage at Knossos

(b) **31** = Ae04 from the Archive Room at Pylos

(c) **270** = Sd0402 from the 'Arsenal' at Knossos

PLATE III

(a) **140** = Eb35 from Pylos, recording tenure of land by a priestess

(b) **236** = Ta641, found at Pylos in 1952

writing was done from left to right with a *drawing* motion (not jabbing or pressing) with the fine point of a stylus; its passage raises an edge and enables the order of making the strokes in each sign to be determined. The scribe or his assistant shaped the tablets on a flat surface, shortly before use, to the size and proportion to suit the expected length and nature of the record. The variety of sizes shows that a template was not used. The front of the tablet is generally a true flat surface, while the back is more domed and often bears traces of hand- and fingerprints. There are two basic shapes of tablet (see the † frontispiece):

1. The more frequent '*palm-leaf*' type, of the approximate proportions of a modern cheque-book, with rounded, pointed or square-cut ends; at Knossos often reinforced by a string down the middle. This was used to record a single transaction, particularly of the kind which was afterwards intended to be re-copied on to a larger summary tablet (e.g. Pylos **132** = Eb818 which reappears as the first line of **131** = Ep01). Many of the 'palm-leaves' have only a single line of writing. Others, after an introductory proper name in large letters, are divided by a longitudinal cross-line to allow for a more complex entry (e.g. Knossos **66** = Dc1129). A small number of tablets, where a single trans-action requires a long description or includes different sub-headings, are divided by one or more horizontal cross-lines from end to end, and the writing is all of the same size (e.g. Pylos **236** = Ta641): these can be regarded as inter-mediate in shape between the 'palm-leaf' and the second basic shape:

2. The rectangular '*page*' type, longer than wide and divided over its entire surface by horizontal cross-lines, drawn free-hand approximately 10 mm. apart. This shape was used particularly for long lists of personnel and rations, for transactions involving a number of different commodities, and for summaries of a number of separate 'palm-leaves'. The second letter of Bennett's prefix (at Pylos and Mycenae only) indicates the shape of the tablet: *a–m* are 'palm-leaves', *n–z* are 'pages'.

The writing on the tablets is generally punctuated into a number of suffi-ciently distinct sections by the commodity ideograms and numbers, which mostly occur at the end of a line; but on the few tablets which have no written ideograms and are written entirely in a continuous 'literary' form (e.g. **244** = Ta714) there is no indication whatever of commas and full stops. Frequently a secondary annotation immediately before the ideogram is written in smaller script than the rest of the tablet, and this change of letter-size, indicated as / in transcription, can generally be expressed as punctuation in translation. Where the entry is too long for the space allowed by the scribe on a 'palm-leaf' or between two cross-lines of a 'page', he continues the text *above* the first part:

consequently the mechanical transcription of a Mycenaean text does not always indicate the correct order of reading (e.g. on the Knossos 'chariot' tablets, see fig. 2).

Between 'paragraphs' and before totals, but not after the frequently introductory sentence of the first line, the text is generally spaced by leaving one line vacant. Where several lines are left vacant (as on **172** = Kn02 or **207** = V 280) some special reason must be sought. The use of *o-da-a₂*... (probably 'and in the following way') to introduce a new paragraph is so far confined to Pylos.

Sometimes, as on the Pylos *Jn-* tablets (**253–257**), two paragraphs have been separated before or after writing by cutting the tablet along one of the horizontal cross-lines. On two Mycenae tablets, Oe117 and Oe120, Wace suggests that the top line may have been deliberately broken off when the clay was dry as a kind of counterfoil, but this is uncertain in view of a possible tendency of the tablets to fracture accidentally along the cross-lines.

†   Where necessary the writing is continued on the back, the tablet being turned over in our own sideways fashion, not top-to-bottom as at Enkomi and in Mesopotamia. The front and back must have been written within a few hours of each other, before the clay became too dry to take writing cleanly: the same applies to erasures, corrections, additions and the use of × as an apparent check-mark to additions and subtractions (though on PY Cn04 this is stated to have been scratched on when the clay was dry, like line 8 of An24). Nevertheless, the connexion between the front and back of some tablets is obscure, as for example on Mycenae **234** = Ue611 and particularly Mycenae Oe106, whose reverse has the drawing of a standing man. Wace (1953 *b*, p. 425) explains this, perhaps not quite conclusively, as the trial sketch of a fresco-painter; and suggests that not only artists but also architects may have used clay tablets in designing. Knossos 1720 (*SM II*, pl. xviii) certainly looks like a 'seal-engraver's sketch'.

The comparatively rare examples of writing on the *edge* of a tablet were explained by Evans (*SM I*, p. 45) as a ready indication of its contents when 'stacked like books on a modern shelf'. In most cases, however, it contains a total or afterthought which could not be accommodated elsewhere on the tablet, and does not appear to be of any possible help in picking out a particular document from the files.

From the analogy of other contemporary tablets, we may expect that the scribe was called upon both to catalogue commodities and personnel arriving at the palace, and to record those sent out or assigned to particular purposes; and in addition, perhaps, to inventory the state of a particular store-room or labour group at a given time. In some cases we are helped by an explicit description, as in introductory sentences like 'Olive oil which Kokalos delivered to Eumedes' (Pylos Gn1184), 'Contributions by the wood-cutters to the workshops' (**252** = Vn06), 'Contributions of bronze for arrows and spears' (**257** = Jn09), 'Oarsmen to go to Pleuron' (**53** = An12), or 'Smiths receiving an allocation of bronze' (**253** = Jn01). In other cases, where the tablet merely contains lists of proper names and ideograms, it may be a matter of guesswork for us to determine whether the tablet records receipt or dispatch.

Where place-names occur with large amounts of agricultural staples, we may suspect that these represent actual or expected tribute *to* the palace; but when men's names are listed in the dative with small amounts of the same commodities, they are probably the recipients of rations *from* the palace. The lists of chariots, tripods, furniture and garments (see chs. X–XI) can be interpreted in different ways.

On some tablets listing miscellaneous persons and commodities (e.g. **41** = An14, **234** = Ue611) the relationship between the items and the order in which they are presented are now very difficult to explain. With these may be compared such Ugarit tablets as RŠ 11.799: 'The merchandise to Ybnn: 4200 measures of oil, 600 of perfumed oil, 2 talents of iron, 100 *teśrm* trees, 30 *almuggîm* trees, 50 talents of reeds, 2 talents of *brr*, 2 talents of perfume, 20 olive trees, 40 shekels of oil of myrrh.' Virolleaud comments (1940, p. 274): 'L'ordre suivant lequel sont énumérés ces différents produits paraît assez surprenant, et surtout l'alternance des objets volumineux ou nombreux avec des parfums subtils ne pesant que quelques grammes. S'il apparaît difficile aujourd'hui de se rendre compte de la suite des idées et des faits, quand on est en présence d'un document aussi concret que celui-là, on ne saurait s'étonner d'éprouver tant de peine à relier les unes aux autres les idées ou les images qui se trouvent notées—indiquées plutôt qu'exprimées ou décrites—dans les compositions poétiques de Ras Shamra.' This admission may warn us against the assumption that a Mycenaean literary text, if we were lucky enough to unearth one, might necessarily prove easier to interpret than the present tablets.

Since the palace revenue is presumably derived largely from feudal dues and † from foreign conquest, monetary or other media of exchange do not play any significant part in the records. We have not yet been able to identify any payments in silver or gold for services rendered, such as occur at Alalakh (Wiseman, 1953, pp. 101–3); and the Mycenae tablets, if they really are merchants' accounts, do not give any clear indication of the medium of exchange by which business was transacted (see **105** = Ge602).

A few of the tablets are introduced by the formula 'In the month of So-and- ‡

so' (e.g. **200** = Fp1 and **207** = V 280 at Knossos, and perhaps **167** = Es650 and **172** = Kn02 at Pylos): this exceptional dating is probably intended as a check on the fulfilment of a prescribed ritual rather than as a normal aid to the economic administration of the palace. The known Knossos month names, which include one striking correspondence with the classical Arcadian calendar, are listed on p. 304. No other dating, either by month, by year or by eponym, can be discerned: its absence is probably due to the seasonal nature of the tablets, which were pulped at intervals of a year or less (possibly after summarizing on papyrus or some other material). A characteristic feature, recurring on all types of Mycenaean tablet, is the secondary entry introduced by *o* or *o-pe-ro*, representing the amount which is *missing* from the consignment or nominal roll compared with the numbers expected. On the Pylos *Ma-* tablets (e.g. **179**) figures are given for the *pe-ru-si-nu-wo o-pe-ro*, 'amount owing last year' or 'from last year', which again suggests the annual nature of the records. There is a reference to *tōto wetos* 'this year' on **43** = Sn01, and to *hateron wetos* 'next year' on **178** = Ma13.

After writing, the tablets were dried (not baked) and then generally filed away in boxes of gypsum or wood, or in wicker baskets, and stacked on shelves in rooms set aside for the purpose. The boxes and baskets were secured with cord and sealed with prismatic lumps of clay impressed with seal-stones and † inscribed with personal names or with a reference to the itemized commodities. The name of the responsible scribe, which never seems to occur on the tablets themselves, may sometimes have been recorded here. Similar sealings were used to secure actual stores, like the wooden boxes of arrows found in the Knossos 'Armoury' (*PM*, IV, p. 617, see **264** = Ws1704).

‡ The Knossos tablets were found scattered over a wide area. The main find-spots are indicated on the key plan of the palace (fig. 13) by the letters *A* to *Q*, which will be added to the tablet headings in Part II:

A. Clay 'bath' in room near the south-west corner of the Central Court.
B. 'Deposit of the chariot tablets', in a closet under the small staircase north-east of the South Propylaea.
C. Room of the Column-bases = Lobby of the Stone Seat.
D. Magazine of the Vase Tablets, and further side of wall to south.
E. Third and fourth West Magazines, and the south end of the Long Corridor.
F. Eighth to twelfth Magazines, and the middle of the Long Corridor.
G. Fifteenth Magazine, and the north end of the Long Corridor.
H. Near the Corridor of the Stone Basin.
I. Room of the Saffron-gatherer Fresco.
J. Room of the Ceiling Spirals.
K. Northern Entrance Passage, adjoining the Bull Relief.

L. Upper East-west Corridor, in the Domestic Quarter.
M. Corridor of the Sword Tablets.
N. From above the Room of the Plaster Couch and the Queen's Bathroom.
O. West Court, outside the west wall of the Magazines.
P. Basement of the 'Arsenal' building, north-west of the palace.
Q. The Little Palace, on the other side of the modern road.
R. 'Hieroglyphic' deposit under staircase at the north end of the Long Corridor.

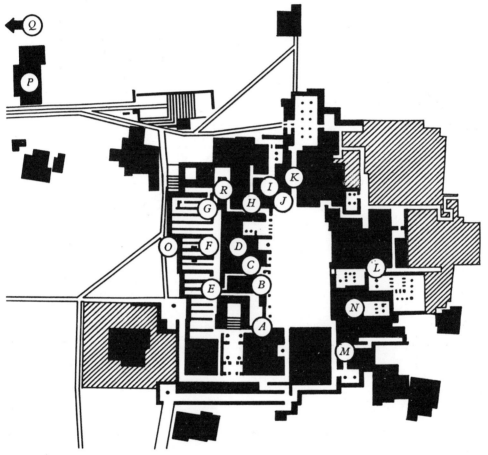

Fig. 13. Diagrammatic plan of the palace at Knossos.

No great reliance should be placed on the detailed attributions: it is clear that Evans' noting of find-spots, never entirely complete or consistent, has become further confused in the editing and printing of *SM II*. For example **231** = K 872, which is stated by Evans to be part of the 'Deposit of Vase Tablets' at *D* (*PM*, IV, p. 729), is assigned in *SM II* to *K*. This tablet was believed by Evans to have been specially baked, and was attributed, apparently from the style of the vessels represented, to the 'earlier stages of the Last Palace Period', or LM I b. The 'sword' tablets from *M* were first assigned to the LM III a period of reoccupation *after* the destruction, from the shape of the weapons (*SM I*, p. 55, corrected in *PM*, IV, p. 854). But Myres is probably right in regarding the tablets as the record of little more than the last year before the destruction.

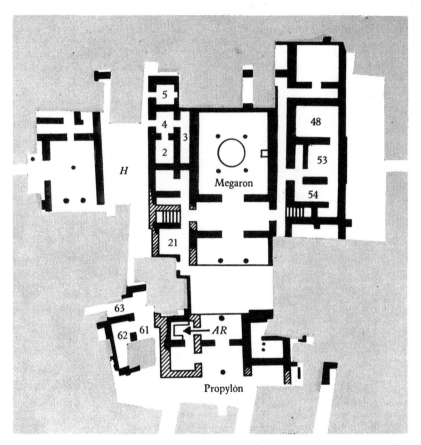

Fig. 14. Key plan of the palace at Pylos (based on the survey by Theocharis, 1954).

The only tablets found *in situ* were at *B*, a small ground floor chamber with the appearance of a bureau or office: the rectangular space at the back of which the shelves for the tablets had probably stood was cut off from the entrance by a bench. In all other cases Evans considered that the tablets had fallen into their present positions from an upper storey during the collapse and decay of the palace, as shown by the stratification of the floor structures: this also applies to the tablets found in the bath-shaped receptable at *A*

(*PM*, IV, p. 668). Considerable lateral drift may also have to be taken into account. Evans suggests that some tablets may even have fallen from a roof-terrace, where they were being dried at the time of the catastrophe (*ibid.* p. 669).

Many of the find-spots show mixed groups of different contexts, but there are consistent series dealing with ritual offerings of oil at *A*, with chariots and horses at *B*, with vases and honey offerings at *D*, with condiments at *E*, with women and children at *F*, with textiles at *F* and *G*, with livestock and wool at *K* and *L*, with swords at *M*, and with chariots, wheels and arrows at *P*. Remains of gypsum chests were found at *D*, *F* and *K*, and of wooden boxes at *A* and *N*.

With few exceptions the Pylos tablets probably represent the contents of the Archive Room at the time of its destruction. This small chamber (*AR* on fig. 14) has a raised bench running round three sides, and was probably linked by a doorway to the main gate of the palace (Blegen, 1955, p. 34). This location, very convenient for the supervision of incoming and outgoing goods and personnel, recalls the introduction to some of the Nuzi tablets: 'Written at the door of the palace gate' (Lacheman, 1939, p. 530). A considerable number of the tablets had found their way from the Archive Room into its annex and other adjoining spaces during the sack and disintegration of the palace and as the result of more recent stone-robbing. Tablets evidently derived from other offices, probably on an upper floor, include **238** = Tn996 (found in Pantry 4 in 1953) and fifteen red pieces recovered in the Megaron in 1952. The tablets found in the three Mycenae houses had all fallen into the basements from an upper floor, possibly two storeys higher (Wace, 1953*b*, p. 423).

3. MYCENAEAN ARITHMETIC   †

It is difficult to gauge the limits of the Mycenaean Greeks' mathematical ability from the tablets, since we do not possess (as we do from Egypt and Babylonia) any texts of a deliberately scientific or didactic nature; but there are no grounds for supposing that they lagged far behind their neighbours in the ability to use reasonably effective techniques of arithmetic and mensuration for the everyday purposes of palace economy, trade and building operations. It is unreasonable of Dow (1954, p. 123) to criticize them for not adopting a duodecimal or sexagesimal system of numeration, which is naturally alien to speakers of an Indo-European language (and to most men with ten fingers and toes): its ponderous, and by no means exclusive, use in Mesopotamia appears to be due to various accidents in the evolution of local weights and measures rather than to any theoretical advantages in operation (Lewy, 1949).

And it is absurd to expect them to anticipate the binary system used in modern electronic calculating machines (Dow, 1954, p. 124). He goes on to say: 'The Minoan system is so cumbrous that multiplication or division in it would be as difficult as in the Roman, or more so. We may reasonably conclude that the Minoans had no "mathematics" much beyond the sort preserved to us.' But it is dangerous to deduce from a certain clumsiness in expressing numbers on paper that more complex mathematical operations were in fact impossible; it is sufficient to recall the very elaborate mathematical reference tables used in Babylonia, with which the inherent difficulties of sexagesimal mental arithmetic were circumvented.

Many of the Mycenaean tablets contain a total derived by simple addition from the separate items of the list, or a subtraction to show the amount 'missing' by comparison with the expected contribution. These operations may be either in units, as in lists of men and women (e.g. **38** = As1516, **39** = As1517), or in weights and measures which, as described on pp. 53–5, are subdivided in heterogeneous ratios like our £. *s. d.* and *tons cwt. lb. oz.* Pylos tablet Jn845, for example, lists eight smiths each of whom receives 𒀸 1 ⧺ 2 of bronze, which is totalled in line 8 as 'so much bronze: 𒀸 12'. Similar summations of liquid measure are found on **200** = Fp1 and **93** = Fo101, and of dry measure on F 51. That the items and totals sometimes do not agree (as on **255** = Jn658) must be attributed to lapses or uncorrected afterthoughts by the scribe, rather than to any theoretical inability to carry out the operation.

Similar afterthought or incomplete erasure is generally responsible for anomalies in the order of writing the tens and digits; for cases where the tens or digits exceed 9 (e.g. Knossos Gg711 rev.); and for entries where the scribe quotes an excessive number of units of a weight or measure which should properly have been reduced to the higher unit (e.g. ¶ 3 on F 452). Bennett (*Index*, p. 117) quotes six examples of 'tallying', i.e. the use of a tablet or part of a tablet for a rough totting-up of units prior to the final writing-in of the total. Pylos Eq03 rev. shows a tallying by groups of 5 digits, eventually reduced to a total of 137. Knossos C 162, which totals sheep and pigs, contains surprising number groups in which hundreds, tens and digits are all in excess of 9, and appears to have been used several times over as rough working in carrying out the addition.

A more advanced calculation is shown by the Pylos *Ma-* tablets (see pp. 289–95), where a number of townships are put down for a contribution of six different commodities, mostly so far unidentified. The scale of the total contribution varies for each town, but the mutual proportions of the six commodities remain constant at 7:7:2:3:1½:150. The variation from the ideal values seldom exceeds 1·0, and it is generally due to the levelling of resulting fractions: it is clear that the Mycenaean administrator was quite capable of determining the correct answers to such an exercise in proportion. The *Ma*-tablets are of further interest in the operation of addition and subtraction by which the actual amounts delivered of these six commodities are compared with the stipulated contribution. Three other tablets (**75** = Cn02, **250** = Vn01 and Vn05) list contributions of a single commodity against nine of the same series of townships, and while not exactly proportional they conform to the same order of size as in the *Ma*- tablets. We may suppose that these townships were arranged, for the purposes of taxation, in a conventional order of size and importance.

A similar parallelism in the relative sizes of the entries, not governed by exact ratios, is shown by the Pylos *Es*- series (see pp. 275–80). The Knossos *Mc*- tablets (see p. 301), of which all but 11 are very fragmentary, contain lists of four commodities, one of which Evans identified as the horns of *agrimi* goats for making composite bows. Their amounts conform, with rather wider variations than on the Pylos *Ma*- tablets, to a ratio of 5:3:2:4.

A large number of the Knossos 'sheep' tablets list flocks whose totals are exactly 50, 100, 150, 200 or 300. These animals are subdivided into various categories, the main distinction being that of sex; where their irregular numbers do not add up to the exact 'hecatomb' total, the appropriate deficit is stated to be 'missing'. A further complication is shown by the Knossos *Dl*- series (**73–74**), where in addition a quantity of wool is recorded, whose stipulated weight in $\check{\imath}$ units is equal to $\frac{1}{10}$ of the number of sheep. On the *Dk*- series, however (**71–72**), which record RAMS alone, the proportion of wool is always $\frac{1}{4}$ of the number of sheep.

The Pylos *Ab*- series of tablets contain a long list of varying groups of women, girls and boys, together with their monthly (?) ration in grain and figs. Their minimum rate seems to be T 2 per woman and T 1 per child (see p. 157), but in most cases their total allocation is in excess of this figure. The lack of an exact and constant proportion is evidently due, not to the mathematical incompetence of the scribe, but to various unknown factors in the ages and circumstances of the different groups.

4. SOCIAL ORGANIZATION

The frequent qualification of people by occupational names makes it possible to draw some general deductions about the structure of society in a Mycenaean kingdom; further work will no doubt extend and correct the picture offered here. Most of the evidence comes from Pylos, but many of the important words recur at Knossos, and there is no indication that the social structure was significantly different. The absence of any palace records from Mycenae excludes any deductions about that kingdom, though there seems no reason to assume that Pylos was exceptional. The apparent differences between the Mycenaean and Homeric patterns are explicable in terms of the Homeric question (see p. 107).

† A monarchical system of government is proved for both Knossos and Pylos by references to the king (*wanax*); the absence of any further qualification shows that the state knew one king only. The suggestion of Palmer (1954 *b*, p. 37) that he was a priest-king is likely enough on archaeological as well as comparative grounds; but that his power was temporal as well as spiritual is guaranteed by the elaborate records of his civil service. A number of trades-men—a potter, a fuller and an armourer (?)—are referred to as 'royal' (*wanakteros*), and the same word in a doubtful context on a jar from Thebes seems at least to prove the existence of another kingdom there. The king is never referred to by name and title at once, though he may be mentioned by name alone: Ekhelawon at Pylos is clearly a man of supreme importance, and the precedence accorded him in **171** = Un718 makes it almost certain that we have here the first contemporarily attested Mycenaean monarch.

‡ The Pylos distribution of τεμένη (**152** = Er01) ranks next to the king's the allocation of the *lāwāgetās*. His name is a known Greek compound, surviving in verse in the form λαγέτας, though apparently meaning only 'leader', 'prince', without the technical sense it must bear in Mycenaean. There is no direct clue in the tablets to his peculiar function, but both the etymology and the Teutonic parallels adduced by Palmer (1954 *b*, pp. 35–6) suggest that he was the military commander whose duty it was to lead the host in war. If the Germanic parallel were exact (cf. Tacitus, *Germania*, 7), we might expect him to be elected only in time of war; and we may be sure from the military tablets (ch. VI) that Pylos was at this time on a war footing. But he is also found at Knossos, where so far there is no indication of preparations against an attack. Compare §§ 1, 22–4 of the autobiography of the Hittite king Hattusilis III: 'But when my father Mursilis became a god, my brother Muwatallis seated himself on the throne of his father; and before the face of my brother I became *chief of the armed forces* (EN KI.KAL.BAD).' Occupational names are also qualified by the adjective *lāwāgesios* (e.g. PY **195** = Na67).

¶ The *temenos* list enumerates next some officials called *te-re-ta*, τελεσταί, an official title which survived in Elis down to the classical period. They are assigned jointly the same amount of grain (land?) as the king, but it is divided among three holders, so that the individual holdings are the same as that of the *lāwāgetās*. Palmer (1954 *b*, p. 39) equates the *telestai* with the Hittite LÚ *ILKI* 'fief-holders' owing a special duty to the king, and contrasts them with the 'artisans', whom he equates with the Homeric δημιοεργοί, a word not found yet in the tablets, though *dāmos* is very common. Some sort of feudal system of land tenure is certain (see p. 234); but Palmer's view is open to objection, especially because of the newly published Pylos text **171** = Un718, where the *telestai* seem to be equated with the *dāmos*. Considerable numbers of *telestai* seem to be proved by the instance of **114** = En02, where the district *Pa-ki-ja-* alone contains fourteen, and at Knossos by **47** = Am826 where no less than forty-five *telestai* of Aptara are mentioned. It is likely that the verb *te-re-ja-e* (*teleiaen*?) expresses the function of the *telestās*, and since it is replaced in other cases by *wo-ze-e* (*worzeen*) which seems to be the function of the *ka-ma-e-u*, it probably indicates some kind of feudal service.

The *ka-ma-e-u* is plainly the holder of the land called *ka-ma*. The most †natural explanation of this is that it is the obsolete noun *χαμά from which the locative χαμαί was formed, a conclusion supported by a Cretan gloss in Hesychius. Its meaning, however, is more specialized and it denotes a particular kind of feudal holding (see p. 261). The men distinguished by this title seem to be of humble status; they include a baker (?) and a 'slave of the god'.

A more important title is the *e-qe-ta*, *heqʷetās* = ἐπέτης. It is a rare word in ‡classical Greek and seems to mean no more than 'companion, follower'. But Palmer (1954 *b*, p. 51) is probably right in seeing in this word the equivalent of the Homeric ἑταῖρος, and understanding it to mean 'companion of the king' like the late Latin *comes* and similar words in Celtic and Germanic. The proof of their position emerges from the military tablets, where they are regularly dignified by a patronymic, a rare distinction elsewhere. They seem to be attached to bodies of troops in the capacity of staff officers; possibly as liaison officers representing the central authority, the command being in the hands of the local lords. On the other hand they are occasionally mentioned in contexts relating to land tenure (e.g. PY **55** = An724, and **142** = Eb32 where one (or more) is coupled with the priestess, the key-bearers and a man called *We-te-re-u*). They may have slaves (p. 258), and they have a distinctive kind of garment (p. 317).

In addition to these we find also a number of officials who appear to be ¶confined to outlying regions. We do not find them associated with Pylos or Knossos, but with subordinate towns. The title *pa₂-si-re-u* is clearly to be connected with the Homeric βασιλεύς, who is not a king, but a kind of feudal lord, master of his own territory but owning allegiance to the king. Carratelli (1954, p. 217) disagrees with this view (also expressed by Furumark, 1954, p. 19) and would see in these βασιλεῖς religious functionaries like the φυλοβασιλεῖς. But their association with the outlying towns is significant. They have a *pa₂-si-re-wi-ja*, probably 'retinue', less likely 'palace', and in KN **38** = As1516 it is noteworthy that this term follows the place-name *Se-to-i-ja* and another name (*Phaistos?*) lost in a lacuna, while the first section contains the heading *Knōsiā lāwāge⟨si⟩ā*, implying a parallel between the *lāwāgetās* at Knossos and the *basileus* elsewhere.

The *ke-ro-si-ja*, *geronsia* = γερουσία is perhaps the council of a *basileus* since on PY **40** = An22 this word is associated with a man who is elsewhere called *pa₂-si-re-u*. It is less certain whether the erased *ke-ro-te* in KN B 800 is *gerontes*, and if so whether it should be connected as proposed by Carratelli (1954, p. 217).

Another title which seems likewise to be provincial is *mo-ro-pa₂*, probably to be interpreted *moroppās* (Palmer: μοιρόπᾱς) 'possessor of a portion, shareholder'. His importance is vouched for by the fact that Klumenos who is *moroppās* in PY **43** = Sn01 is on **58** = An654 commander of a regiment. Their regional location is to be inferred from a variety of indications: their presence in the tribute list **258** = Kn01; the fact that *Ka-do-wo moroppas* of **43** = Sn01 is elsewhere associated with the place-name *Ma-ro-*; the entry on the same tablet which shows that Klumenos was *ko-re-te* of the place *I-te-re-wa*.

Finally we hear of a local official called the *ko-re-te*, who seems to be a kind of mayor (Furumark: Dorfschulze). The word is an agent noun in *-tēr*, not yet satisfactorily interpreted, but his status emerges clearly enough from PY **257** = Jn09, where we have sixteen places named and contributions of bronze from the *ko-re-te* and *po-ro-ko-re-te* of each. The prefix *pro-* must mean in this case 'vice-' or 'sub-', a sense not preserved in any classical compound. The heading to this tablet enumerates not only these two, but also a variety of other titles which are not mentioned again below. Is the explanation that the heading gives all the possible alternative titles which are equivalent to the two general terms *ko-re-te* and *po-ro-ko-re-te*? Against this it may be argued that the *klawiphoroi* are elsewhere feminine, though it is less likely that the same is true of *du-ma-te*. The *da-mo-ko-ro* who is mentioned a few times may perhaps be another title or another local official appointed by the king. There are occasional references to *ki-ti-ta* 'settlers' and *me-ta-ki-ti-ta* 'colonists (?)', but it would not seem safe to draw any conclusions from these words yet.

†   Of the humbler members of the population we can say less. The variety of trades followed shows a highly developed division of labour, but it is not clear

how far the craftsmen were royal servants, or even slaves, or what other status they enjoyed. There is one very obvious omission from the list of trades, the absence of any word implying that the raising of crops was a specific occupation. On the contrary land tenure documents mention craftsmen such as fullers and agricultural workers such as shepherds. This suggests that everyone in addition to his special occupation also farmed a portion of land.

Among the occupational names there are many still not satisfactorily interpreted, and in some other cases the precise significance of the word is lost; etymology is often a poor guide to meaning. Thus the list of trades must be regarded as incomplete. For an explanation of the words quoted here see the Vocabulary.

Among the public servants we hear of a messenger and a herald (*a-ke-ro*, *ka-ru-ke*); but the name of the scribe still eludes us. The agricultural workers named include shepherds (*po-me*), goat-herds (*ai-ki-pa-ta*), huntsmen (*ku-na-ke-ta-i*), and wood-cutters (*du-ru-to-mo*). The building trades are represented by masons (*to-ko-do-mo*) and carpenters (*te-ko-to*); ship construction is a separate trade (*na-u-do-mo*). Metal-workers include bronzesmiths (*ka-ke-u*) and cutlers (?, *pi-ri-je-te*), and other manufacturers are bow-makers (*to-ko-so-wo-ko*), chair(?)-makers (*to-ro-no-wo-ko*) and potters (*ke-ra-me-we*). The making of cloth was a women's occupation; we hear of carders, spinners and weavers (*pe-ki-ti-ra$_2$*, *a-ra-ka-te-ja*, *i-te-ja-o*), and there are separate designations for flax-workers (*ri-ne-ja*), and perhaps for the makers of some of the other special kinds of garment (*a-pu-ko-wo-ko*, *e-ne-re-ja*, *o-nu-ke-ja*). The fulling of cloth was a man's trade (*ka-na-pe-u*) and the king had his own fuller. The making of garments was shared by men and women (*ra-pte*, *ra-pi-ti-ra$_2$*). Luxury trades are attested by unguent-boilers (*a-re-pa-zo-o*) and goldsmiths (*ku-ru-so-wo-ko*). We have one reference to a physician (*i-ja-te*). The grinding and measuring out of grain were done by women (*me-re-ti-ri-ja*, *si-to-ko-wo*), but the making of bread by men (*a-to-po-qo*); Blegen (1950) seems unjustified in his assumption that the Mycenaean figurine of a bread-maker is female. More menial occupations seem to be indicated by stokers (*pu-ka-wo*), ox-drivers (?, *ze-u-ke-u-si*) and, among the women, bath-attendants (*re-wo-to-ro-ko-wo*) and serving women (*a-pi-qo-ro*).

The existence of slavery in some form is certain. Some slaves (*do-e-ro*, *do-e-ra*) are plainly stated to be the property of individuals: e.g. the women of *Amphiq^{u}hoitās* (KN **20**=Ak824), or those belonging to the smiths and following their masters' trade (PY **253**=Jn01). The slave of *We-da-ne-u* is even in the position of having to contribute to his master's revenue and is not distinguished in his treatment from the rest of the group who appear to be free men (see

123

p. 276). The Pylos tablet **28** = An42 suggests that a single slave parent of either sex made the child a slave, contrary to the rule of classical Greece; but this
† deduction is not inevitable. The Pylos tablets of the classes *Aa* and *Ab* (see p. 155) imply that the labour force was recruited by raids in which captive women and children were brought home and taught trades, and this conclusion seems to be confirmed by the word 'captives' (*ra-wi-ja-ja*) applied to some of these women: others are referred to by ethnic adjectives. The *Ad* series suggests that the children of slaves were an important element in the manpower available. On the other hand there is some evidence that women of this class also worked for wages (*e-ke-ro-qo-no*); but possibly these were not wage-earners on their own account, but were hired out to augment the palace revenues.

But by far the greater number of slaves named at Pylos are 'slaves of the god (or goddess)'. Two explanations of this phrase are possible: we may either suppose that a number of slaves became the property of a deity instead of a man, or that the title really conceals some quite different status from that of ordinary slaves. In the former case we need not think exclusively of the ἱερόδουλοι or temple-slaves of later times; dedication to a deity could be a method of holding public property, as we see to be the case with the lands of Dionysus and Athena recorded in the famous tables of Heraclea. The other alternative is made attractive by the fact that slaves of the god have leases of land and seem in fact to live on much the same terms as free men. The translation 'slave' is probably here leading us to a false conception of social status, and it might be preferable to adopt feudal terminology, such as 'serf' or 'villein'. The parallel of Near Eastern societies in which similar titles are actually honorific probably does not hold good for Mycenaean Greece; for there are a few isolated cases in which the slave of a man seems to enjoy the same status as a slave of the god; and the slaves of the priestess raise an awkward point in social precedence.

At Knossos we learn almost nothing of the military organization apart from the existence of the *lāwāgetās*; but at Pylos preparations were being made against an attack, and a series of tablets are concerned with naval and military matters (see pp. 183–94). From these it appears that the command of the bodies of men detailed to watch the coast was in the hands of local lords, each of whom was assisted by a small group of officers; while each sector had allocated as well a *heqᵘetās*, who may have been a liaison officer representing the king. The details of the troops are obscure, since the words applied to them, *ke-ki-de* and *ku-re-we*, are not satisfactorily explained; Palmer (1954*b*, p. 52 n. 4) suggests that the latter word means elsewhere 'men-at-arms', but insists that it is here a place-name. Other groups of men are merely referred to by ethnic adjectives. The total number of troops recorded on the surviving tablets of the military series is 740.

Rowers to man warships seem to have been drawn as necessary from the coastal towns; it is probable that they were conscripts rather than professionals, at least if our interpretation of **55** = An724 is correct. Rowers are also mentioned as the fathers of the sons of some slave women at Pylos (**15** = Ad684). At Knossos rowers surprisingly figure in a list of local officials who are supplying or receiving cattle (**83** = Ch902).

5. MYCENAEAN RELIGION

The evidence of the tablets for the religious practices and beliefs of the † Mycenaean Greeks has naturally aroused much interest; the principal religious texts have been discussed by almost all writers, and Carratelli (1955*a*) has devoted a special article to this subject. It has also been discussed at the London Seminar, and Palmer has made many interesting suggestions in addition to those in his published articles. While much is still in dispute or obscure, this section can lay no claim to finality; it may be useful, however, to collect together the scattered evidence for further study.

The gods are mentioned on the tablets only in one capacity: as the recipients of various offerings. If we could be sure that the presence of one divine name in such a list guaranteed the divinity of the remainder, it would be easy to list the Mycenaean pantheon. But it is quite clear that the offering lists may contain—for what reason we can only guess—human beings as well; the clearest case is that of the Pylos *Es* tablets (see p. 279); and since the 'priestess of the winds' figures frequently at Knossos, some of the other entries too may be the names or titles of human representatives of a deity.

ZEUS is clearly intended in PY **172** = Kn02, where we have the dative *di-we* = *Diwei*, and (if the amended reading is accepted) the genitive in the next line: *Drimiōi Diwos hie⟨rē⟩wei*. The word *di-u-jo* = *Diwjo-* on the same tablet is plainly a derivative, though its gender and case can only be guessed (= the shrine of Zeus?). *di-u-ja* in the same text must therefore be the feminine, and this is proved to be the name of a goddess by the fact that she receives the offering of a gold cup and a woman. *di-wi-ja* in PY **28** = An42 is probably a variant spelling (*Diwja/Diwia*, cf. *me-u-jo/me-wi-jo*) of the genitive (*Diwias doela*); also without context on KN X 97. Cf. the goddess Διϝία in a Pamphylian inscription (Schwyzer, *Dial.* 686, 1), said to be the Magna Mater. One fact is clear, that this female counterpart to Zeus is not to be identified with Hera, who is mentioned on the same tablet and paired with Zeus in a quite classical manner. *di-we* is also found in obscure contexts (with offerings of barley?) on KN F 51 rev. and PY **44** = An29 rev.; *di-wo* on KN E 842 may be a divine name as the text includes the word *te-o-i*, but on Dx1503 it is a man's name in the nominative. The month name *Diwioio* (gen.) occurs once (KN Fp5).

† HERA is coupled with Zeus on PY **172** = Kn02. The spelling *e-ra* refutes the suspicious etymology from *"Ηρϝα (see p. 289). Her name is perhaps to be restored also in PY Un11. 8. The same spelling at Knossos is undoubtedly a place-name, the adjective from which is *e-ra-jo*, *-ja*, except perhaps **29** = As821.

POSEIDON is securely attested at both Knossos and Pylos. The spelling is consistently *po-se-da-o-*, thus proving that the Corinthian forms in -δάϝων are secondary (Chadwick, 1954 *b*, p. 7). He is the recipient of *dosmoi* in the Pylos *Es* tablets (p. 279) and of a wide range of offerings on **171** = Un718. As in classical Greek, derivatives show *i* for *ei* in the second syllable: *po-si-da-i-jo* (PY **172** = Kn02+) is *Posidāion* 'the shrine (or the like) of Poseidon'; *po-si-da-i-je-u-si* (PY Fn01) = *Posidāieusi* appears to be a dative plural, but its meaning is uncertain; and *po-si-da-e-ja* (**172** = Kn02) is another female counterpart, as Diwia is to Zeus. There is also a divinity called *e-ne-si-da-o-ne* (dat.; KN M 719, to be restored on **204** = Gg704, Gg707), probably = *Ennesidaōnei*; cf. the names of Poseidon Ἐννοσίδας, Ἐννοσίγαιος, etc. (see p. 309).

‡ ARES is not clearly named. The word *a-re* appears without context on a Knossos fragment (X 5816). *A-re-jo* KN Vc208, *A-re-i-jo* KN **213** = L 641, and *A-re-me-ne* Thebes III are all proper names which may be derived, though the Aeolic forms of Ἄρης (Ἄρευς, Ἀρεύιος) make this questionable. On *a-re-ja*, apparently an epithet of Hermes, see p. 288. The name *e-nu-wa-ri-jo* = Ἐνυάλιος figures in the list of gods KN **208** = V 52; whether on PY **55** = An724 the spelling *e-nwa-ri-jo* is the divine name is controversial.

¶ APOLLO does not appear, but we have *pa-ja-wo-* = Παιαϝων- (Homeric Παιήων), KN **208** = V 52. *pa-ja-ni-jo* KN Fp354, read by Furumark as *Paianiōi* (perhaps a month name?), is probably not connected, as the contraction of -*āwōn-* to -*ān-* cannot be Mycenaean.

†† HERMES has the form *e-ma-a₂* (dat.) = *Hermāāi* PY **172** = Kn02, Un11. On the form and etymology see p. 288.

ATHENA is clearly named once: *a-ta-na po-ti-ni-ja* (apparently without a divider) = *Athanāi Potniāi* KN **208** = V 52. Ventris also proposes to restore her name [*a*]-*ta-na* in MY X 1. It seems clear that at Knossos πότνια is used as the epithet of Athena, exactly as in the Homeric πότνι' Ἀθηναίη. But in other tablets from both Knossos and Pylos *Potnia* appears as a divine name standing by itself (e.g. KN **205** = Gg702, M 729, PY Fn01, **172** = Kn02, Vn07).

No evidence which would identify this deity has so far appeared, and thus none of the guesses can be tested; she seems to be of some importance, but is not necessarily the protectress of Pylos. There is also a derived adjective with the surprising form *po-ti-ni-ja-we-jo*, as if formed from Ποτνιεύς; cf. the adjective *wa-na-se-wi-ja* which stands in a similar relation to ϝάνασσα. This epithet appears chiefly on sheep tablets at Knossos; at Pylos it designates groups of smiths and is occasionally used of individuals; it may of course have no religious associations here.

ARTEMIS is the owner of the slave *Ai-ki-wa-ro* on PY **167** = Es650. Her name has the East Greek form *a-te-mi-to Artemitos*, with declension in τ not δ. PY Un11 lists along with other divine names *a-ti-mi-te* which may be the dative *Artimitei* with *i* for *e*. There is no evidence yet to support the suggestion that Artemis is the goddess meant in the common formula *theoio doelos*.

DIONYSUS is a surprising name to find, and there is no evidence to prove † that it is divine. It occurs only once in the genitive case on a Pylos fragment Xa06: *di-wo-nu-so-jo* [.

HEPHAESTUS is not directly mentioned, but may be assumed if the man's name *a-pa-i-ti-jo* (KN L 588) is correctly interpreted as *Hāphaistios* or *Hāphaistiōn*.

Of the minor deities known from Greek sources, EILEITHYIA is known at Knossos in the spelling *e-re-u-ti-ja* Ἐλευθία (recorded at Messene and elsewhere). KN **206** = Gg705 shows her as the recipient of a jar of honey at Amnisos, which recalls at once the famous cave mentioned in the *Odyssey* and by Strabo (see p. 310). She also seems to receive wool (KN Od714, Od715). ERINYS has been proposed by Furumark as the interpretation of *e-ri-nu* ‡ (apparently dative) in the offering list KN **200** = Fp1 (cf. Fs390). DEMETER ¶ may be the right interpretation of *da-ma-te* PY **114** = En02, but in use at least this is not a divine name; see the discussion on p. 242. A cult of the WINDS is attested by the Knossos offerings to *Anemōn hiereiāi*, the priestess of the Winds. A DOVE-GODDESS *pe-re-*82* = *Peleia* (Palmer) seems likely on PY **172** = Kn02; the name recurs on a new tablet found in 1954 (Un1189), with offerings of cows, sheep and pigs (cf. *suouetaurilia*).

Dedications to ALL THE GODS (*pansi theoi'i*) are a frequent feature of the †† Knossos offering lists, but do not appear at Pylos. This may suggest that it is a particularly Minoan feature which though adopted by the Greek rulers of Crete did not spread to the mainland; but arguments from silence can hardly be admitted until we have more material. Although not unknown in classical Greece, such dedications are commonest in Hellenistic times. It has been suggested that it implies a connexion with the Vedic hymns to the *Viśve Devāḥ*

(All-gods); but these are said to be a later accretion to the Veda, not an original inheritance.

A number of other deities or sacred places emerge from tablets such as KN **200**=Fp1 and PY **172**=Kn02, where a fuller discussion will be found. The Daidaleion seems an appropriate name for a shrine at Knossos. At Pylos we find Iphimedeia, a semi-mythical figure in Homer, apparently receiving divine honours. The identity of the other deities is unknown or conjectural.

The offerings recorded at Knossos differ from those at Pylos in that livestock are rarely mentioned. None of the tablets dealing with livestock can be proved to have any religious significance, though this is not always impossible; † Sundwall's theory of hecatombs must be abandoned (see p. 198). KN Fh347 is exceptional in showing both oil and cattle; but its religious context is not certain as it contains no demonstrably divine name. The usual offerings are grain (both wheat and barley) and flour, oil, wine, figs and honey; occasionally wool (e.g. G 866), and some of the vessels recorded in the K series may be intended as offerings though not so specified. At Pylos we have records of quantities of wheat contributed annually to Poseidon; these are presumably payments in kind for the upkeep of his shrine and ceremonial. A number of texts list miscellaneous commodities (*Un* series), but not all of these are offerings; the only one clearly identifiable as such is **171**=Un718. Here the contributions promised to Poseidon take the form of one ox, two rams; a considerable amount of wheat, flour and wine; some cheeses, honey, two sheepskins and a quantity of unguent. This may be provision for a sacrificial meal. ‡ **172**=Kn02 records offerings of gold vessels and human beings; what becomes of the latter is not clear, but they are more likely to be cup-bearers than victims for sacrifice. Some of the spice tablets at both Knossos and Pylos may be religious in motive.

Whatever the religious functions of the king may have been, he was assisted by a considerable priesthood. A priest called *We-te-re-u* figures prominently on the land tenure documents at Pylos, and two more are mentioned on **44**=An29. There is a priestess of the Winds at Knossos (see above). At Pylos we have frequent references to 'the priestess' without further qualification, just as we have one deity referred to as *theos* without a name. This can only refer to the principal deity of the town, who is therefore presumably female. There is also a priestess at *Pa-ki-ja-*, who may be in the service of Potnia. We have one reference to a *hieroworgos*; how this title is distinguished from *hiereus* is not clear. The *klawiphoroi* or 'key-bearers' appear in company with the priestess and are female; the title (in various forms) is well known in antiquity. ¶ The male occupational name *da-ko-ro* seems to be the same word as ζακόρος, but there is no proof that 'temple attendant' is here the right sense, and the etymological sense of 'floor-sweeper' is more probable. Other titles may well be religious, such as the women called *ki-ri-te-wi-ja*; but we can at present say nothing about their status or function.

6. AGRICULTURE AND LAND TENURE

The surviving tablets probably would not give anything like a complete picture of the domesticated and wild animals and plants which were important in the Mycenaean economy, even if their interpretation was certain. Many of the provisions are recorded by conventional symbols, rather than by recognizable pictures or by words spelt out in Greek. We can generally tell whether these provisions are counted in units, or measured by dry bulk or liquid volume, or weighed; but for a closer guess we must take into account the animal and plant remains which occur archaeologically at Minoan and Mycenaean sites, or which are represented in the art of the period. We may also use, more cautiously, the lists of foodstuffs found on the cuneiform tablets and mentioned in later Greek literature.

A full survey of the archaeological remains was made in Vickery's *Food in Early Greece* (1936), and this can be amplified by more recent finds. In the following list the asterisked items (*) have been found both at important Cretan sites (in Middle and Late Minoan) and at the chief Mycenaean centres of the Mainland; the rest are so far restricted to finds from one or other group.

Cereals: *wheat, *barley. These were certainly the most important Aegean grains: emmer wheat and barley appear predominantly on the cuneiform tablets, and are the only cereals listed in the Hittite laws. A single oat grain was found at Orchomenos; the supposed rye on Thera is very doubtful. Millet was restricted to Macedonia by Vickery, though Evans claims a find at Knossos (*PM*, IV, pp. 622, 630).

Leguminous plants: *broad beans (*Vicia faba*), *peas (*Pisum sativum*), *chick peas (*Cicer arietinum*), *grass peas (*Lathyrus sativus*), *bitter vetches (*Ervum ervilia*), *lentils (*Lens esculenta*). The same leguminous plants are found in contemporary cuneiform records, where they are often milled and used in bread-making, or else eaten as a kind of porridge (as in classical Greece).

Seasonings: aniseed (*Pimpinella anisum*, Thera), coriander (*Coriandrum sativum*, Thera); the latter is also common in cuneiform records.

Fruits: *olives and *olive oil, *grapes; dried figs (Phaistos), almonds (Phaistos); pears (only Sesklo and Dimini, Early Helladic).

Animals: *ox (mostly *Bos brachyceros*, also *Bos primigenius* and some hybrids), *sheep (*Ovis aries palustris*), *goat (*Capra hircus*), agrimi goat (*Capra aegagrus creticus*, Tylissos),

*pig (*Sus domesticus indicus*), wild boar (*Sus scrofa ferus*, Tylissos), ass (Tylissos), horse (Tylissos, LM I), dog (Tylissos). Remains of cheese were found on Thera.
Sea food: *shell-fish; fish-bones, oysters and mussels (Mycenae).

The shapes and meanings of the Mycenaean commodity ideograms will be discussed in greater detail in the appropriate chapters of Part II. The following summary is intended to show the extent to which the tablets conform to the archaeological picture, and to correct a few misleading identifications made in the surveys of the Knossos economy by Evans and Myres (*PM*, IV; *SM II*, pp. 59–61).

† The conventionalized symbols ⵕ and ⵆ represent the two main cereals. They form the first and more important component in rations, and are only once issued together (PY An31). ⵕ is the more frequent, and is alone used in calculating the acreages of fields. We have taken ⵕ to be wheat, and ⵆ to represent barley (the latter already suggested by Evans, *PM*, IV, p. 625); but it is conceivable that these identifications should be reversed.

The absence of recognizable bread-ovens from Mycenaean sites has led to some doubt whether bread was baked (as it certainly was by the Hittites and Semites), but this is resolved by the mention of the trade *arto-poqᵘoi* 'bakers' (cf. ἄρτοι in the *Odyssey*). *Meleuron* 'flour' was also issued as rations and for cult offerings (**171** = Un718).

Sundwall's identification of ⵕ as 'poppy-seed' is very improbable, especially in view of the large quantities involved. Of the two other supposed cereals listed by Myres (*SM II*, p. 32), ⵆ is a liquid measure, and ⵅ ('millet or beer') is proved by Pylos Gn1184 to represent *e-ra₃-wo* = *elaiwon* 'olive oil', as already suggested by Furumark (1954, p. 116) and Bennett (*MT I*, p. 448).

Olive oil is also very common both as a ration (e.g. MY **93** = Fo101) and as a cult offering (KN **200** = Fp1, etc.). The fruit of the olive seems to be represented by ⵙ, Pylos ⵚ (if the reading *e-ra-wa* in the last line of KN **94** = F 841 is in fact intended as a description of it). The ideogram cannot be saffron, as Evans thought (*PM*, IV, p. 718); but that plant may be represented by ⵛ, of which very small quantities, measured by weight in the units used for gold, are found at Knossos on Np267, etc. Issues of fruit generally accompany wheat or barley rations; equal to or smaller than the latter in the case of figs (**9** = Ab27, etc.), larger in the case of olives (Fn06). No other ideograms for fruit can yet be identified, but apples, pears and pomegranates were presumably cultivated in addition to the authenticated grapes and almonds.

‡ The ideogram ⵜ (**171** = Un718, etc., and cf. the Linear A version, p. 35) has plausibly been identified by Sundwall as wine, the existence of which is confirmed by the ox name *Wo-no-qo-so* = Οἶνοψ (Knossos Ch897, Ch1015),

parallelled by the Homeric βόε οἴνοπε. Evans (*PM*, I, p. 415) argued that beer was the main Minoan drink, but not only is there a lack of characteristic beer-straining vessels (such as were used for instance by the Philistines) but any memory of beer is totally absent from Homer. Though beer was commoner than grape-wine or date-wine in Mesopotamia, wine was the usual drink among the Hittites.

No signs for the leguminous plants can yet be identified; but Knossos, Pylos and Mycenae share a considerable list of condiments, of which coriander is the most frequent and which also mentions by name celery, cumin, cyperus, fennel, mint, pennyroyal, safflower (both flowers and seeds) and sesame (see pp. 221–31). Several of these have Semitic names and were probably derived from Syria, though they may have begun to be cultivated in Greece in Mycenaean times. Honey occurs in a number of ritual offerings (KN **206** = Gg705, PY **171** = Un718). Salt, included in some of the cuneiform ration lists, has not yet been identified. Flax was apparently grown locally (**184** = Nn01, etc.) and used for linen garments, and presumably also for making sails, thread, string and nets (cf. Homeric λίνον). Beetroots are apparently indicated by † the title *teutl-agoros* (?, **120** = Eo03), which may imply that they grew wild along the coastal areas. We might also expect to find cucumbers, onions, garlic, leeks and other vegetables included in the Mycenaean diet.

Seven kinds of livestock occur on the tablets, in the following descending order of numbers: sheep, goat, pig (*su-*), ox (*gᵘou-*), horse (*hiqqᵘos*), ass (*onos*) and deer (*eloph-*?); specific reference to asses has been provided by Chadwick's ‡ 1955 join to **82** = Ca895, where their ideograms are virtually indistinguishable from those of the horses. The livestock ideograms are differentiated in a number of ways (see p. 196), but of these distinctions only that between males and females, also regularly shown in cuneiform lists, is certain; and it is not clear whether different breeds are represented (on a possible sign for the wild goat, see p. 302). Evans, Myres and Furumark wrongly identified the 'ox' sign (no. 109) as a horse, and the 'goat' (no. 107) as an ox.

Numerous flocks of sheep and goats (perhaps belonging to the king) are ¶ recorded as pasturing on the lands of neighbouring towns under their shepherds, each of whom is responsible to one of a small group of overseers who *agêrei*, 'collects', the specified quotas of animals and wool (**63** = Cc660). The wool, whose consignments are measured by weight, is spun and woven by the palace women, and the finished cloths are measured in the same units (see p. 316); the sheep also provide sheepskins, *kōwea*, presumably for use as rugs, bedspreads and ceremonial skirts (cf. fig. 15). A special category of sheep is recorded as being kept in sheep-pens, *stathmoi* (Cn09, Cn10).

Among the swine a valuable category of *sialoi* 'fat pigs' is mentioned (**75** = Cn02), distinct from the larger herds listed with the sheep and goats (Cn11–Cn13), which were presumably left to forage in the woods. Among the relatively small numbers of cattle, teams of working oxen (*g^{u}owes*) *wergatai*, are mentioned on Knossos **84** = C 59; and these include a number of pairs whose actual names are given (e.g. **85** = Ch896). Horses are rare (only two are listed on the surviving Pylos tablets), and were probably intended primarily for chariot work, although some riding must certainly have been done (Hood, 1953).

Deer occur on two Pylos tablets (Cn01, Cn868): their ideograms are not differentiated for sex, etc., and they probably represent carcases of venison. The dog is implicit in the term *kun-āgetai* 'huntsmen' and occurs, of course, in Mycenaean hunting scenes.

† The cattle provide ox-hides, from which various leather (*wrineios*) articles are made. Of dairy produce, only cheeses (*turoi*, **171** = Un718) are mentioned by name; milk, cream and butter, which figure in the Babylonian and Hittite records, do not have any certain Mycenaean ideograms, and do not seem to have been much used in later Greece. The composition of the *aleiphar* used in preparing aromatic unguent (**103** = Un08), is uncertain, though the evidence of Pylos Gn1184 suggests that it may have been olive oil.

No birds or fish can be identified with certainty, though it is probable that the Mycenaeans kept or caught ducks, geese and pigeons. The man's name Ἀλεκτρυών (which also occurs in the *Iliad*) does nothing to solve the vexed question of when the cock was introduced into Greece, since the word probably simply means 'the pugnacious one'. The octopus (*polupos*) occurs as a decorative feature in ivory on **246** = Ta722, but it may well have been eaten, as it is today.

A large number of tablets from Pylos (**108–154**) apparently list the varying amounts of wheat which are to be sown on various fields. The practice of recording acreages by their amounts of seed (according to a fixed ratio which it is difficult to determine exactly) is also found at Nuzi and underlies the Sumerian methods of measuring area (Lewy, 1949). These tablets can thus be interpreted as a cadastral survey of land tenure, although the legal basis of such tenure and the exact purposes of the survey remain largely a matter of conjecture. The references to different types and sizes of holding (*temenos*, *ktoina*, *khama*, etc.), and to the different classes of individuals who occupy these, enable some deductions to be made as to the structure of society at Pylos (see above, pp. 120–4).

Discounting tablets whose entries are repetitious, the total amount of seed grain recorded on the surviving Pylos *E-* tablets appears to be about 720 dry units of wheat, possibly about 86,400 litres, perhaps sufficient for an arable area of 1730 *ha* (4270 acres): with a fivefold yield, this might feed 1500 slaves for a year. But it is dangerous to deduce much from these figures, since the tablets are only a fragmentary set and the scope of the survey is unknown.

There are only a few Knossos tablets of a similar class recording holdings of wheat land (**155–162**), and they add little to our picture of Mycenaean land tenure, which is discussed in detail at the beginning of ch. VIII. Also listed on a few tablets are orchards (*phutaliai*, KN E 849), whose olive and fig trees, numbered in hundreds, are illustrated ideographically (**165** = Gv862, etc.).

7. INDUSTRY AND TRADE

The long list of trades and occupations which can be identified on the tablets † (see p. 123) implies a specialization of labour which goes far beyond that seen in Homer, where King Odysseus knows how to build his own boat or bed, and boasts of his skill with the scythe and plough. The Homeric picture may be due in part to a lower standard of living in the eighth century B.C., but more, perhaps, to the fact that the poet's interest in institutions and economic life is not that of the modern sociologist, and introduces no more detail than is necessary to provide a consistent background for epic narrative. A more complex organization of production in Mycenaean times might in any case have been inferred from the high level of craftsmanship in many industries, from the size of the palace and settlements, and from the number of trades which can be identified on the similar tablets from Nuzi, Alalakh and Ugarit (see especially Virolleaud, 1940). This specialization is confirmed by nominal rolls (particularly the Pylos *E-* tablets, **108–151**) where the individual names are regularly identified by their occupations: 'Eumedes the unguent-boiler', 'Brithawon the potter', 'Thisbaios the shepherd', etc.

It is more difficult to determine the precise status of these different tradesmen, to guess where in the topography of the excavated sites their places of work are likely to have been, and to assess how far the products of their labour may have been available in a free market.

In the Mesopotamian temple-state economy of the third millennium B.C. the craftsmen were bondmen controlled and fed by the palace, and this relationship is still reflected in the low status of the smith as a *muškenu* in the Code of Ḥammurabi (§ 274). The Ur tablets (Legrain, 1947) list the activities of eight palace workshops, those of the sculptors, goldsmiths, lapidaries, carpenters, smiths, fullers and tanners, tailors, and caulkers (bitumen workers). A large proportion of the remaining production (textiles, food, pottery, etc.) was carried out by the large and varied female labour force attached to the palace. Imports from outside were the responsibility of the palace treasurer.

The later and more nearly contemporary records from Ugarit and Alalakh and from the Hittite country show the majority of the craftsmen constituting a more or less free 'middle class', organized in trade guilds and having their places of work in bazaars in the towns. Some craftsmen might be permanently employed by the palace, but a considerable proportion of its needs were fulfilled by outside hire and purchase (through the medium of silver), both of local production and of the imports made by more or less independent merchants.

It will be the task of the continuing analysis of the Mycenaean tablets to determine which of these two sets of conditions they more nearly fit. It is probable, at any rate, that the large numbers of women recorded on the Knossos and Pylos ration lists (see **1–28**), whose occupational names are largely connected with textile production, had a servile status and were recruited by pillage and barter abroad. Such tablets as **50 = An18**, with their enumeration of men pursuing fairly menial occupations, read like lists of palace servants; but others, like **52 = An26**, with their record of tailors, potters and goldsmiths in different places, might more reasonably be taken to refer to trades whose products were not the exclusive monopoly of the palace. If so, the absence of payment in metal or in kind (except for occasional rations in cereals and fruit as on Fn02, An31) may suggest census and records of seasonal forced labour (like the *luzzi* to which the Hittite 'men of the tool' were subject). References to the 'estate of the cowherds' (Ea12) and 'of the swineherds' (Ea08) and 'of the beekeepers?' (Ea820) possibly indicate that these formed some kind of collective associations (cf. the classical Ποιμενίδαι, etc.). Many craftsmen are described as holding land at Pylos; and Palmer (1955, p. 13) suggests that δημιοεργοί (which in the *Odyssey* is applied to seers, physicians, carpenters, bards and heralds) originally meant 'the class that tills the land of the village commune' rather than 'those who work for the common people', though this modification of the etymology does not seem essential to explain the apparent facts. Some of the craftsmen are expressly described as *wanakteros* 'belonging to the king' or as *lāwāgesios* 'belonging to the leader', which would certainly suggest that others of their profession were free to work on their own account. The occupations to which this applies are those of the *knapheus* 'fuller', *e-te-do-mo* 'artificer?', *poimēn* 'shepherd', *kerameus* 'potter' and *a-mo-te-u* 'chariot-builder and wheelwright?'; and it seems that groups of these, at any rate, must have formed part of the palace machine. The work of the potters was evidently decentralized to sites convenient for kilns, of which several Mycenaean remains have been found (Wace, 1949, p. 106); the workshop of the chariot-builders is probably to be identified in the *a-mo-te-jo-na-de* of Pylos **252** = Vn06, the only place of work to be named specifically on the tablets.

Decentralization is also shown by the Pylos *Jn-* tablets (**253–256**), which record the issue (or absence of issue) of weights of bronze to the smiths of a number of localities, similar to the distribution of piece-work from the palace store-houses recorded on the Sumerian inventories and on Alalakh tablets (**396–408**). Some of their headings look more like clan names than place-names, possibly suggesting small closed communities of tinkers. The smiths are the most frequent subject of an annotation in tribute lists which reads 'The So-and-so do not contribute' (e.g. on **176** = Ma12 and **192** = Na50), and this has generally been taken as a record of the preferential treatment which this trade receives on account of its full-time operations and its indispensability to the war effort: this status is paralleled in other primitive or early societies. The Pylos smiths are also distinguished by the possession of *doeloi* 'slaves'. In addition to bronze (*ka-ko*), other sets of tablets also mention gold (*ku-ru-so*, **231** = K 872, etc.), silver (*a-ku-ro*, **290** = Sa03) and lead (*mo-ri-wo-do*, **259** = Og1527); but there are no details of their working.

The inventories of pottery, metalware, furniture, weapons and chariots (see chs. x and xi) do not unfortunately record who made them or how they were acquired, and only seldom contain clues to a possible importation from outside. Among the latter, note the mention of Kydonia, Phaistos and *Se-to-i-ja* on the Knossos 'chariot' tablets (**265–277**), and the description *ke-re-si-jo we-ke*, 'of Cretan style or workmanship?', applied to tripod cauldrons on Pylos **236** = Ta641, etc. The Knossos tablets listing 'cloths' are, however, frequently introduced by adjectives derived from different Cretan place-names (e.g. **213** = L 641); but there is some uncertainty whether the textiles themselves always come directly from these towns, or are merely woven by women supplied to the palace by them.

Timbers specified on the 'chariot' and 'furniture' tablets include *pe-te-re-wa* (elm), *e-ri-ka* (willow), *ki-da-pa* (?), *ku-te-so* (ebony?), *mi-ra₂* (yew?), *pu-ko-so* (boxwood) and *ku-pa-ri-se-ja* (adj., cypress). Other materials used in their details and decoration are *kyanos* (see **239** = Ta642), horn (adj. **ke-ra-i-jo*) and, as we should expect from Homer and from Egyptian and Syrian parallels, extensive areas of ivory inlay (*e-re-pa*, adj. *e-re-pa-te-jo*). Wace (1949, p. 108) agrees with Barnett in suggesting that the raw material was imported from Syria (whose carved ivories show affinities with the Mycenaean, and where the elephant existed in early times) rather than through Egypt.

Evidence of contact with Syria (e.g. Ugarit, Byblos, Beirut, Tyre) is shown by the Semitic names of the three condiments *sa-sa-ma* = σήσαμα, *ku-mi-no* =

κύμινον and *ku-pa-ro* = κύπαιρος (e.g. on **102** = Ga517, **103** = Un08, **105** = Ge602, etc.); it is uncertain whether these reflect continuing imports, or earlier loan-words (perhaps through a 'Minoan' intermediary) for things now obtained from other more local sources. The latter is almost certainly the case with the other two Semitic borrowings *ku-ru-so* = χρυσός (see p. 343) and *ki-to* = χιτών (p. 319). These five words are shown to have already been absorbed by Greek in the Bronze Age, and not to be borrowings from the time of Phoenician initiative in the eleventh–eighth centuries B.C.

On the other hand the Greek use of the word Φοίνικες for the Canaanites was probably already current at the time of our tablets, even though the detailed development of the various meanings of this probably non-Indo-European word is obscure: it is significant that the Semitic 'Canaan' (*Kinaḫḫi*) itself appears to be related to a word for a dyestuff (cf. φοῖνιξ 'crimson'). *Po-ni-ki-ja* on the 'chariot' tablets (**267** = Sd0409, etc.) is probably 'painted crimson'; while *po-ni-ke* (instr. sing. of φοῖνιξ) possibly means 'griffin' on **246** = Ta722. *Po-ni-ki-jo* as the name of an unidentified substance on **99** = Ga418, etc., may refer to its colour, but it may equally well describe it as 'the condiment from Canaan'. The spelling of the initial in these words disproves any connexion with φόνος 'murder' (*$q^u honos$*).

Though the word *ku-pi-ri-jo* is probably Κύπριος, and implies that Cyprus was already known by its classical name (which bears no relation to its Hittite, Semitic and Egyptian names), in the three Pylos occurrences it is a man's name; but on Knossos Ga517 and Ga676, where it occurs with κύπαιρος and coriander, it may well indicate an import from the east. The word *ai-ku-pi-ti-jo* (revealed by Bennett's join of Db1105 with X 1446) is also only a man's name, but it presupposes that Αἴγυπτος was already the Greek name for 'Egypt'. At the same period the name at Ugarit for both 'Egypt' and 'Memphis' was *Ḥikupta* (Virolleaud, 1953, p. 192), corresponding to the *Ḥikuptaḥ* of the Amarna letters and to *Ḥt-k'-ptḥ* in Egyptian; and from these the Mycenaean name was evidently borrowed.

The hierarchy of officials needed to supervise the many craftsmen and the volume of imports and exports can only be guessed; but it is possible that *A-ko-so-ta*, who appears with various functions in the preamble to a number of Pylos tablets (**154** = Eq01, **103** = Un08, Pn01, Wa917), had a function similar to that of the *šatammum* or chief steward at Alalakh and at other places.

8. HISTORICAL EVIDENCE

In the absence of any Mycenaean monumental inscriptions, or of any tablets other than palace or household accounts, the documentary evidence for historical situations and events is extremely fragmentary and indirect.

The mere fact that Greek can now be shown to have been written at Knossos in LM II does, of course, supply new and conclusive proof of the theory that Crete had begun to be occupied by the 'Achaeans' during the fifteenth century B.C. or earlier (see Foreword, pp. xxii ff.); and the close relationship apparent between their dialect and those of the later Arcadians and Cypriots provides some confirmatory evidence for the sequence in which the Greek tribes settled in the Aegean.

The place-names which appear on the Knossos and Pylos tablets, where they can be identified with known sites, provide some evidence for the areas effectively controlled by these kingdoms at the time (see pp. 139 ff.); and a few possible references to foreign lands have been discussed under 'Industry and trade'.

Although many of the men's names on the tablets are identical with those of heroes recorded in Homer and other epic writers, there are (as might be expected) no cases where an actual historical personage can be identified. The possibility is discussed on p. 265 that the name of the last king of Pylos in fact occurs in the spelling *E-ke-ra$_2$-wo*, dat. *E-ke-ra$_2$-wo-ne* (also *E-ke-ra-ne*?), gen. *E-ke-ra$_2$-wo-no*. This does not fit the name of any Neleid king of Pylos preserved in the traditional genealogy, whose usual form reads:

Kretheus (Poseidon)

Neleus   Amythaon, etc. (migrate from Iolkos to Pylos)

Nestor   Periklymenos and ten other brothers

Thrasymedes   Antilokhos   Peisistratos   Stratios   Aretos   Perseus

Sillos

Alkmaion (expelled from Pylos, takes refuge in Athens)

Some similarity is shown by the name of Ekhelaos, son of Penthilos, colonizer of Lesbos; and by that of one of Nestor's brothers, which appears in different transmissions as Epilaos or Epileon.

Blegen's excavations show that the palace at Pylos was of comparatively short duration, 'wholly within the not very long stage called Late Helladic III B' (1955, p. 37); its foundation fairly late in the Mycenaean age may, as has been suggested, be connected with the traditional arrival of Neleus, and with the transfer of 'Pylos' from another site recorded by Pausanias (IV, 36, 1). It has been proposed that the name *ma-to-ro-pu-ro* (Cn10.5) should be interpreted *Mātro-pulos*, i.e. 'the original Pylos'.

Though the tablets record local kings and chieftains, there is no surviving evidence for the organization and foreign relations of 'Achaea' as a centralized power (which the Hittite references to *Aḥḥijawā* lead one to expect), beyond the spelling *a-ka-wi-ja-de* on Knossos **78** = C 914: this may conceivably represent *Akhaiwiān-de*, but even so it may be the name of a town rather than of a state. The two occurrences of the patronymic *Etewokleweïos* at Pylos confirm the Mycenaean connexions of the name Eteokles, and make it more probable that Forrer was right in identifying with it the name of the chieftain *Tawakalawas* who appears in Hittite correspondence with 'Achaea' concerning the port of *Milawata* (Miletos?).

†   Since the Knossos, Pylos and Mycenae tablets all appear to have been written shortly before the final destruction of their sites (probably by human agency), it is natural to speculate whether their subject-matter contains any anticipation of the impending catastrophe; but with few exceptions it would seem that their contents are no different from what one would expect from a routine year; the mere listing of swords, chariots and armour does not necessarily imply a desperate preparation against attack.

A definite historical value may, however, be given to the preamble of Pylos **53** = An12: *eretai Pleurōnade iontes* 'oarsmen to go to Pleuron'. Thirty men are listed in all, probably the complement of a single ship. If their destination is in fact the important Aetolian city of that name (cf. *Il.* II, 639), their journey may have some connexion with the disturbances constituting the 'Dorian invasion': this is traditionally regarded as having crossed towards Elis from the nearby town of Naupaktos (cf. Pausanias, X, 38, 10), and its first victims may well have been the inhabitants of the Mycenaean enclave on the north shores of the Gulf of Corinth.

The same historical situation may lie behind several of the Pylos *An-* tablets listing officers and men (**56-60**, pp. 188-94), if their function is correctly interpreted as that of a kind of Home Guard detailed to watch sectors of the coast for the approach of enemy ships. The masons listed on **41** = An14 may possibly be effecting repairs to the defences of Pylos, though *toikho-* might imply the walls of individual buildings rather than city-walls (for which there is no archaeological evidence).

9. GEOGRAPHICAL NAMES

Ἔστι Πύλος πρὸ Πύλοιο, Πύλος γε μὲν ἔστι καὶ ἄλλη.   (Proverbial)

The Cretan place-names played an important part in the process of decipherment (see p. 22). The characteristic feature of place-names thus revealed is the presence alongside the simple name of the ethnic adjective in -ios, and this provides a useful test by which the more frequently occurring names can be detected. A similar test is offered by names which recur with and without the suffix of 'motion towards' -de. With these criteria we can then establish the presence of a place-name in a set place in a formula, and deduce that all other words found in that position are likewise places. Similarly the presence of several place-names in a list may lead to the conclusion that the rest are also places.

Other formal considerations have been proposed, but these are somewhat dangerous. Turner (1954) in a very useful study of the Pylos place-names works also with the ending -te, which he interprets as the ablatival suffix -then. There is no reason to doubt the existence of this suffix in Mycenaean, and it is probably to be found in a-po-te-ro-te = amphoterōthen; nor is it disputed that most of the words listed by Turner are place-names. But it is noticeable that the names ending in -te belong almost exclusively to a class in -wo-te. In a few cases other forms are found which reveal a declension: nom. e-ri-no-wo, gen. e-ri-no-wo-to, dat.-loc. e-ri-no-wo-te. Thus we may regard all these names as locative datives in -tei, and the ending cannot therefore be used as a test. The dative and instrumental plurals in -si and -pi can also be used as locatives; but this too is not helpful as a criterion.

The remarks made in ch. IV (p. 92) on the risks of translating Mycenaean spellings into classical names apply with almost equal force to the identification of place-names. Certainly when the Knossos tablets present spellings which resemble the names of prominent Cretan towns we can feel confidence in the equation. But the presence at Pylos of names which could be places as far distant as Orkhomenos in Arcadia or even Corinth raises quite a different question. A glance at a classical dictionary is sufficient to disclose that in ancient Greece, as in every country, a number of places bear the same name. Thus even if we correctly interpret the spelling as a name, there is no guarantee, apart from the probability engendered by geographical proximity, that the name can be safely attached to any site. The case of the common Pylos name Re-u-ko-to-ro is instructive: there can be little doubt that this represents a name known in classical Greek as Λεῦκτρον. But unfortunately there are three such places known in the Peloponnese, two of them within reasonable distance of Pylos. And who is to say that there were not others, of which we have no record in our ancient sources? Mühlestein (1955a) in a suggestive pamphlet has spread the limits of the Pylian kingdom over half the Peloponnese; we beg to suggest that it is a sounder policy to expect the names to be confined to Messenia, or at least the south-western quarter of the Peloponnese. Names which seem to be located outside this area should be regarded with grave suspicion and not identified without strong reason.

Another difficulty that must be faced is the habit of migrants taking the name of their towns with them. Many of the duplicated names in Greece are said to be due to this process; but equally many may be common nouns in some pre-Greek language, and in default of clear historical tradition these two cases cannot now be distinguished. Old names may have been replaced for other reasons, and the decay of ancient towns and the rise of their neighbours is another factor leading to profound changes on a political map. If an expected name—for instance Gortys in Crete—is apparently absent from the tablets, we must not jump to hasty conclusions; it may be represented under a different name. Equally if an obviously important town on the tablets has no apparent equivalent in classical geography, no deductions are safe. The Messenian Pylos would appear to have moved twice: from its Mycenaean site at Ano Englianos to the classical one at Coryphasion (Paleókastro); and from there to its present position at the southern end of the bay of Navarino. Extreme caution must therefore guide our tentative discussion of the political geography of Mycenaean Crete and Messenia.

The analysis of the types of names found does not at Knossos lead to any † striking conclusions. The absence of names beginning with *n*, *o* or *q* may be purely accidental. At Pylos there are two distinctive types, neither of which is represented in the Knossos list. One is the type ending in -*e-wa*: *A-ke-re-wa*, *A-pi-te-wa*, *E-ra-te-wa* (plural), *I-te-re-wa*, *Si-re-wa*, *Wo-no-qe-wa*. These may correspond to the type of Τεγέα, Μαλέα, Κροκεαί, etc.; but the loss of the distinctive digamma makes this uncertain. The other has the dative ending -*wo-te* referred to above: A_2-*pa-tu-wo-te*, A_2-*ru-wo-te*, *Do-ro-qo-so-wo-te*, *E-ri-no-wo-te* (nom. *E-ri-no-wo*), acc. *Ne-do-wo-ta*, *Pe-re-wo-te*, *Sa-ri-nu-wo-te*, *Si-jo-wo-te*. With one exception the preceding vowel is *o* or *u*, which suggests that the termination is added directly to a stem ending in a consonant. We may have here the origin of the type in -οῦς, -οῦντος as in Σκιλλοῦς, Φλιοῦς, etc., though some may represent rather -ων, -οντος. There are also a number ending in -*eus*, but these are hard to separate from the ordinary ethnics of this form. The rarity of names with clear Greek meanings is obvious both at Knossos and Pylos.

The words which can plausibly be identified as place-names in the Knossos †
tablets are listed below. They amount to fifty-two separate places, excluding
the reference to Cyprus. Of these twelve can with varying degrees of certainty
be located on a map: Amnisos, Aptara, Dikte, Inatos, Itanos, Knossos, Kydonia,
Lato, Lyktos (Lyttos), Phaistos, Setaia, Tylissos. The doubtful cases are Itanos,
spelt *U-ta-no* (for other cases of variation between *i* and *u* see p. 77) and
Setaia, spelt *Se-to-i-ja*; *a* and *o* are confused elsewhere (see p. 77), but not in
a diphthong. To these we may perhaps add *Pa₂-ra-i-so* = Praisos and *Su-ki-ri-ta* =
Sybrita.

Two facts emerge clearly from these names: that the area in contact with,
and probably subject to, Knossos covers virtually the whole of Crete; and that
no names can be located outside the island. The isolated case of *Kuprios* applied
to spices implies no more than trade. Thus there is so far no evidence to
support the theory of a thalassocracy, at least at the time of the fall of Knossos.

The list of towns subject to Idomeneus in the Catalogue (*Il.* II, 645–9) is
restricted to the central area: Knossos, Gortys, Lyktos, Miletos, Lykastos,
Phaistos and Rhytion. Four of these do not appear (in a recognizable form)
on the tablets. Elsewhere in Homer we meet the Κύδωνες (*Od.* III, 292; XIX, 176);
their town Kydonia, which is mentioned on the tablets, is excluded from Homer
by its metrical shape. The same applies to Akhaiwia, which may be connected
with the Cretan Ἀχαιοί of *Od.* XIX, 175.

There does not seem to be sufficient evidence on which to found any attempt
at locating the place-names which cannot be identified. Most of them occur
singly on separate tablets, and there is nothing to show that lists such as
83 = Ch902 follow any regular geographical order.

Even more difficult to place on the map are the names on the Pylos tablets,
though this is perhaps not altogether surprising in view of the scanty information about Messenia given by the ancient authorities. The first problem concerns the site of Pylos itself, a hotly disputed subject even in antiquity. One
new fact which the decipherment has contributed to this problem is that the
tablets refer repeatedly to a place called *Pu-ro*; and that this is of supreme
importance appears from its prominence on a tablet such as **172** = Kn02, or
from the numbers of women assigned to it on the *Ab* tablets; and not less from
its omission from all documents which can be regarded as tribute lists. It is
a reasonable conjecture that it is the name of the site where the tablets were
found. The next step, that of identifying the Palace at Ano Englianos with ‡
the Pylos of Nestor, was taken in advance of the decipherment by Blegen and
Kourouniotis (1939*b*), and although their view has been challenged it obviously

now receives very strong support. The absence from the tablets of the names of Nestor and his family is no objection if the fall of Pylos took place a generation or more after the Trojan War, which is the conclusion of the most recent chronological surveys . The suggestion of Turner (1954, p. 20) that Pylos is the name of the aggregate of towns forming the kingdom is worth considering, though it appears to be used as an ordinary place-name, and can serve as an adequate definition of the whereabouts of two masons (**41** = An14). The name *Ke-re-za* appears to be a part of Pylos.

†   Two lists (**75** = Cn02, **250** = Vn01) enumerate nine towns in the same order; and a third example of this list can be restored in Vn05 owing to the joining of a new fragment. The same names form the first nine entries on the tablet dealing with contributions of bronze **257** = Jn09, except that *Ro-u-so* replaces *E-ra-to*. It is clear that these are the principal towns of the kingdom, and their occurrence in a fixed order has given rise to some speculation. The order cannot be one of relative importance, for *Pe-to-no*, the third, makes the largest contribution of fat hogs and receives the largest share of the wine (?) and probably also of the *sa-pi-de*; Jn09 is useless for this purpose as the contribution of all nine is the same. The figures are as follows:

	Cn02	Vn01	Vn05
*Pi-*82*	3	50	—
Me-ta-pa	3	50	—
Pe-to-no	6	100	200
Pa-ki-ja-	2	35	80
A-pu₂?-	2	35	60
A-ke-re-wa	2	30	40
E-ra-to	3	50	—
Ka-ra-do-ro	2	40	—
Ri-jo	2	20	—

The suggestion that the order is based on a standard (quasi-alphabetical) order of the syllabary—the two names which begin with the same sign come together —is ingenious but unverifiable. It is more plausible to assume a geographical order (north to south?), though this too cannot be demonstrated with certainty; and the parallel of the Athenian tribute lists shows that purely arbitrary orders may be adopted in such cases; it would be impossible to reconstruct the map of the Aegean merely from the Athenian documents. Only one of the places can be fixed with much probability: *Ri-jo* must be Rhion, a name associated with the promontory on which stands the modern Koróni (the ancient Asine); even this is not certain, for it is a name applicable to any promontory. *Ka-ra-do-ro* = *Kharadros* is likewise the name of a common geographical feature.

We were at first inclined to associate *Pa-ki-ja-* with Σφαγία, a known name of the island of Sphakteria. Two considerations, however, have caused us to question this: the Mycenaean name appears to be alternatively *Pa-ki-ja-na*, *Pa-ki-ja-ni-ja* (fem. *a*-stem?) or *Pa-ki-ja-ne* (=*-ānes*, plural), neither of which corresponds closely with any classical form of the name; and Webster has pointed out that it is an important place and that the amount of land it possesses seems too large for that available on Sphakteria; Chadwick was told in Pylos that the island is not now cultivable. It is possible that the name refers to the whole area of the mainland bordering the bay of Navarino, but this is only a guess. Metapa is known as the name of a town in Acarnania, but there were no doubt several of the same name. The most significant evidence here is that of an inscription in the Elean dialect found at Olympia (Schwyzer, *Dial.* 414) which mentions the Μετάπιοι. Perhaps therefore the town is to be located in the direction of Elis, somewhere in Triphylia. If Palmer's value for *$*82=ja_2$* is right, *Pi-ja$_2$* may be equated with Φειά in Pisatis, the modern Katákolo; but this is to stretch rather far the northern limits of the kingdom. Homer (*Od.* xv, 297) apparently mentions Φεαί as a place passed by Telemachos between Pylos and Elis.

It has not passed unnoticed that Homer assigns nine towns to Nestor's kingdom:

οἳ δὲ Πύλον τ' ἐνέμοντο καὶ Ἀρήνην ἐρατεινὴν
καὶ Θρύον, Ἀλφειοῖο πόρον, καὶ ἐΰκτιτον Αἰπὺ
καὶ Κυπαρισσήεντα καὶ Ἀμφιγένειαν ἔναιον
καὶ Πτελεὸν καὶ Ἕλος καὶ Δώριον.   (*Il.* II, 591–4)

Similarly in the *Odyssey* (III, 7) Telemachus arriving at Pylos finds the citizens sacrificing at nine altars. The coincidence is remarkable and may well be historical; it should, however, be noted that Homer's list includes Pylos in the nine, the tablets exclude it. Only one pair in the two sets of nine can be equated; *A-pu$_2$?-* is perhaps Αἰπύ, a name appropriate to any town on a height. It is not securely identified but is said to be in Elis. Of the other Homeric names Κυπαρισσήεις is represented on the tablets by the ethnic *Kuparissioi* and still bears a similar name, Kyparissía; the name [*Ku*]-*pa-ri-so* is a likely restoration on **187**=Na49. The word *A-pi-ke-ne-a* on a fragment could be Ἀμφιγένεια. Ἕλος is no doubt the correct interpretation of the dative *E-re-e* or *E-re-i*, but its location is uncertain. The meaning suggests that we should look for a site on marshy ground, and the obvious place is the seaward end of the Messenian plain.

This brings us to the remaining seven names of **257**=Jn09: *Ti-mi-to a-ke-e*, *Ra-wa-ra-ta$_2$*, *Sa-ma-ra*, *A-si-ja-ti-ja*, *E-ra-te-re-wa-pi*, *Za-ma-e-wi-ja*, *E-re-i*. These seem to form another group; they recur (except for the last) on the *Ma* tablets, so are certainly also tributary. On **257** = Jn09 they contribute no less bronze, and in some cases more, than the first nine, so they cannot be dismissed as less important towns. This is confirmed by their assessments on the *Ma* tablets (p. 291) where *Ra-wa-ra-ta₂* has a larger assessment than *Pe-to-no*. Their grouping is therefore probably geographical. Now the two *Ng* tablets (**198** and **199**) record the totals for two districts which are called *De-we-ro-ai-ko-ra-i-ja* and *Pe-ra₃-ko-ra-i-ja*, i.e. on this side and on that of some feature called *Ai-ko-ra-*. The most prominent natural feature visible from the site of the Palace is the wall of hills (Ayá, Antiláris, etc.) which runs parallel with the sea from Kyparissía in the north to a little south of Khora (Ligoudista). This is identified by Kiepert, by Blegen, by educated locals and by most modern maps with the Αἰγαλέον mentioned by Strabo (VIII, 4, 2) as the mountain under which the first city of Pylos had stood; it is tempting to regard this as the name contained in the compounds, for the substitution of *o* for *a* is not unusual. Marinatos once suggested Αἰγαλέον was the smaller hill of Manglavá, between Antiláris and Likódimo, and above the Mycenaean settlement at Íklina. On some maps the name Αἰγαλέον is attributed to the conical hill of Áyos Nikólaos (above the present town of Pylos/Navarino), for no good reason. The damaged tablet On01 seems to show that these two districts correspond to the groups of nine and seven. The heading is lost, but may be conjectured to have contained *De-we-ro-ai-ko-ra-i-jo*. The names preserved in the first paragraph are *E-ra-to* (in the adjectival form *E-ra-te-i-jo*) and *Pa-ki-ja-ni-ja* on a new fragment; both these belong to the nine. The second paragraph is headed *Pe-ra-a-ko-ra-i-jo*, and contains the names of five out of the seven (some differently spelt) together with *E-sa-re-wi-ja*, perhaps in place of *Za-ma-e-wi-ja* with which it is coupled in Vn03.

Ti-mi-to a-ke-e is interpreted by Palmer (1954*b*, p. 49) as *Themi(s)tos ageei* (ἄγος being given the sense 'sacred land'). This ingenious idea does not help us to locate it, for whatever its meaning it is undoubtedly the name of a locality like the others in this list. It has the variant form *Ti-mi-ti-ja* or *Te-mi-ti-ja*, where the preservation of *-ti-* goes to confirm the interpretation *Themistia*.

How far to the east the kingdom extends is not easy to determine. If *Ne-do-wo-ta* (acc.) on the military tablets is the river Νέδων flowing into the Messenian gulf, this might be a clue; but the interpretation comes into conflict with *U-ru-pi-ja-jo* = *Olumpiaioi* in the same line. *Re-u-ko-to-ro* might be the town usually called Λεῦκτρα on the Laconian border; but there is nothing to connect it with the coast, and it could equally well be Λεῦκτρον in southern Arcadia, if either of the two. The seven πτολίεθρα offered by Agamemnon to Achilles

(*Il.* ix, 149–52) are described as νέαται Πύλου ἠμαθόεντος, and seem to lie round the shores of the Messenian gulf; they must at that time have been an independent area belonging neither to Menelaos nor to Nestor, or some protest would have been made. This would limit the eastward extension of the kingdom, but there is nothing in the tablets to prove that this was also the situation at the time of the fall of Pylos.

To the north-east too the limits are undefined. A number of names can be equated with places in Arcadia, but how many of these should be accepted is doubtful. *Ro-u-so* = Λουσοί, *Ru-ko-a₂-* = Λυκόα, *A-si-ja-ti-ja* = Ἀσέα are plausible guesses; *E-ko-me-no*, however, is hardly likely to be the Arcadian Ὀρχομενός, nor *I-wa-so* Ἴασος on the eastern border of Arcadia.

The names of the places from which rowers come are presumably on the coast. *Ro-o-wa* may be the port of Pylos (see p. 187); *Ri-jo* and *A-ke-re-wa* are among the nine. *E-wi-ri-po* offers hope of identification, for Euripos implies the existence of a strait with an appreciable current. There are only two straits off the Messenian coast: that between the island of Próti and the mainland, which is relatively wide and affords a safe anchorage; and the Methóni strait formed by the island of Sapientsa. This is restricted by rocks and shoals to a narrow navigable channel, and according to the Admiralty Mediterranean Pilot Book (iii, p. 61) 'the current sets westward through the Methóni strait at the rate of about one knot during moderate weather'. This strongly suggests a location near this channel.

The military tablets (**56–60**) are prefaced by a reference to the coast which implies that the places where troops are stationed are coastal towns. This confirms the placing of *Ro-o-wa* and *A-ke-re-wa*, and adds *O-wi-to-no* and *Ti-mi-to a-ke-i*. The mention in these tablets of *U-ru-pi-ja-jo* and *O-ru-ma-si-ja-jo* strongly suggests Ὀλυμπία and Ἐρύμανθος, which would imply contacts far to the north; but these names are not found in the tribute lists, and they may well lie outside the limits of the kingdom of Pylos, though perhaps allied to it for defence. The same applies to the two references to Pleuron, if this is the famous city in Aetolia.

Other ethnic groups mentioned are the *Ko-ro-ku-ra-i-jo* who may be from Corcyra or Krokyleia; and the Zakynthians whose name is also associated with chariot wheels. The ethnic adjectives used to describe slave-women (see † p. 156) seem to belong to Asia Minor: Lemnos, Knidos and Miletos (though this might be the Cretan town) and possibly Khios. There are also women from Kythera, and perhaps even a colony of men from that island in the territory of Pylos.

† ## 10. LIST OF PLACES NAMED AT KNOSSOS AND PYLOS

The following two lists index the words which can be plausibly identified as place-names at Knossos and Pylos respectively. Only one reference is usually given for each form quoted, additional examples being indicated by the plus sign (+). Names which can with reasonable certainty be located on a map are printed in bold type.

KNOSSOS

a-ka, Da1350+.

  a-ka-i-jo, Vd62+. Ethnic.

a-ka-wi-ja-de, 78 = C 914. *Akhaiwiān-de*. [Cf. Hitt. *Aḫḫijawā*.]

a-mi-ni-so, 200 = Fp1+. *Amnisos* (on the site see p. 310). ['Αμνισός *Od.* XIX, 188.]

  a-mi-ni-so-de, 201 = Fp14+. *Amnison-de*.

  a-mi-ni-si-jo/-ja, 34 = Am601+. Ethnic: *Amnisios*.

a-pa-ta-wa, 83 = Ch902+. *Aptarwa*. ["Απταρα; the form "Απτερα is due to popular etymology.]

  a-pa-ta-wa-jo, 47 = Am826+. Ethnic: *Aptarwaios*.

da-da-re-jo-de, 200 = Fp1+. *Daidaleion-de*. [Cf. Δαίδαλος *Il.* XVIII, 592; Δαιδαλίδαι Attic deme.]

da-mi-ni-jo, V 337+. Ethnic? [Cf. 'Επίδαμνος; also PY *da-mi-ni-jo*.] See p. 161.

da-ra-ko, Dd1579+.

da-wo, 84 = C 59+. Ventris: *Dālwos* = Δῆλος?

  da-wi-jo/-ja, Am568+. Ethnic.

da-*22-to, As40+. (also ELEUSIS I). Georgiev: *Dakunthos* = Ζάκυνθος.

  da-*22-ti-jo/-ja, F 669+. Ethnic.

da-*83-ja, Dv1086.

  da-*83-ja-de, Fp363+. Acc. +-*de*.

  da-*83-ja-i, F 670. Loc. plur.: -*ā'i*.

di-ka-ta-de, Fp7+. *Diktan-de*. [Δίκτη.]

  di-ka-ta-jo, 200 = Fp1. Ethnic: *Diktaios*.

di-ro, Da1167+.

do-ti-ja, Ce139+. (In some cases possibly fem. or neut. ethnic.) [Cf. Δώτιον πεδίον in Thessaly.]

e-ko-so, Dx46+. *Exos*? [Not "Αξος = Fάξος.]

  e-ki-si-jo/-ja, As821+.

e-ra, Dc1298+.

  e-ra-de, Fh357. Acc. +-*de*.

  e-ra-jo/-ja, V 431+. Ethnic.

e-ti-wa, Fs19.

  e-ti-wa-ja, X 681. Ethnic; cf. woman's name Ap639.

ko-no-so, 213 = L 641+. *Knōsos*. [Κνωσός *Il.* II, 646+.]

  ko-no-si-jo/-ja, V 56+. Ethnic: *Knōsios*.

ku-do-ni-ja, 84 = C 59+. *Kudōnia*. [Κυδωνία; cf. Κύδωνες *Od.* III, 292.]

  ku-do-ni-ja-de, L 588. *Kudōniān-de*.

ku-pi-ri-jo, Fh347+. Ethnic: *Kuprios*. (Applied to spices; cf. man's name at Pylos.) [Κύπριος; cf. Κύπρος *Od.* IV, 83.]

ku-ta-to, X 80+. *Kutaistos*? [Cf. Κύταιον.]

  ku-ta-i-to, 83 = Ch902. Alternative spelling of the preceding?

  ku-ta-ti-jo/-ja, Ga419+. Ethnic.

ma-ri, Dl 947+.

ma-sa, Dw42+.

  ma-sa-de, X 744. Acc. +-*de*.

pa-i-to, E 36+. *Phaistos*. [Φαιστός *Il.* II, 648.]

  pa-i-ti-jo/-ja, X 681+. Ethnic: *Phaistios*.

pa₃-ko-we, Ap618+ (also TIRYNS II). The tempting identification *Phāgowens* (cf. Attic deme Φηγοῦς) is belied by the declension and derivatives.

  pa₃-ko-we-e, *pa₃-ko-we-i*, Dx794, Dn1093+. Loc.

  pa₃-ko-we-i-jo/-ja, 100 = Og424+. Ethnic.

pa₂-mo, Ga417+.

  pa₂-mi-jo/-ja, 88 = E 749+. Ethnic.

pa-na-so, E 843+. *Parnassos*?

pa₂-ra, L 473+. Furumark: *Pharai*. [Φαραί in various parts of the mainland, none in Crete.]

  pa₂-ra-jo, Ga423+. Ethnic: *Pharaios*.

  pa₂-ra-i-so, V 466, [X 5285.] Georgiev: *Paraisos* or *Praisos* (possibly a man's name). [Πραισός.]

  pa₂-sa-ro-we, Db1329. Ventris: *Psallowens*. [Cf. ψάλλος· ὕλη Hesych.]

pu-na-so, X 967+.

  pu-na-si-jo, Ga34+. Ethnic.

pu-so, As604+.

  pu-si-jo/-ja, 88 = E 749+. Ethnic.

ra-ja, Da1202+. *Laia*? [Cf. Λαιαῖοι people in Macedonia; Pylos place-name *ra-i-pi*.]

ra-ma-na-de, Fh353. Acc. +-*de*. [Cf. 'Ραμνοῦς, Λῆμνος?; Pylos *ra-mi-ni-jo*.]

ra-su-to, As606+. *Lasunthos*? [Cf. Λᾶσος, Λασαία.]

  ra-su-ti-jo, Lc761. Ethnic.

ra-to, J 58+. *Lātō*. [Λατώ.]

  ra-ti-jo, 87 = E 668. Ethnic: *Lātios*.

re-ko-no, C 918.

  re-ko-no-jo, C 912+. Gen.

ri-jo-no, Dm1174+. [Cf. 'Ριανός Cretan poet.]

  ri-u-no, X 149. Alternative spelling of the preceding?

  ri-*65-no, U 49. Perhaps alternative spelling.

  ri-jo-ni-jo/-ja, Od563+. Ethnic.

ru-ki-to, V 159+. *Luktos.* [Λύκτος *Il.* II, 647.]
   ru-ki-ti-jo/-ja, X 37+. Ethnic: *Luktios.*
sa-na-to-de, Fs2+. Acc.+-*de.*
sa-pa-ka-te-ri-ja, D1941. Sittig: *Sphaktēria.*
se-to-i-ja, As40+. *Sētoia.* [=Σηταία.]
si-ja-du-we, D1930+.
si-ra-ro, 83=Ch902+.
   si-ra-ri-ja, Lc512. Ethnic.
su-ki-ri-ta, Dn1092+. *Sugrita?* [=Σύβριτα?]
   su-ki-ri-ta-jo, C 911+. Ethnic: *Sugritaios.*
su-ri-mo, 29=As821+.
   su-ri-mi-jo, 99=Ga418. Ethnic.
te-re-no, Fp363. [Cf. Θήρην river near Knossos.]
ti-ri-to, Uf120+. [Cf. Τρίτα old name for Knossos (Hesych.).]

ti-ri-ti-jo/-ja, 88=E 749+. Ethnic.
tu-ni-ja, Db1606+. Place or ethnic? [Cf. 'Ελτυνία (now Kunári) south of Knossos.]
tu-ri-so, 84=C 59+. *Tulisos.* [Τυλισός *Inscr. Cret.* I, 30, 1; now Týlissos.]
   tu-ri-si-jo / -ja, 87=E 668+. Ethnic: *Tulisios.*
u-ta-no, 202=Fp13+. *Utanos.* [='Ίτανος.]
   u-ta-ni-jo, 88=E 749+. Ethnic: *Utanios.*
wi-na-to, As604+. *Winatos.* ['Ίνατος; probably on the present bay of Tsútsuro.]
Place-names with untranscribed initials.
**47-da-de*, 200=Fp1.
**47-ku-to-de*, 202=Fp13. Acc.+-*de.*
**47-so-de*, Fh351+. Acc.+-*de.*
**85-ri-mo-de*, 202=Fp13. Acc.+-*de.* [Cf. *su-ri-mo.*]

PYLOS

a-da-ra-te-ja, Aa785 [44=An29]. Place or description of women? *Adrasteia(i)?* [Cf. 'Αδρήστεια *Il.* II, 828.]
ai-wi-jo, Na25.
a₂-ka-a₂-ki-ṛi-jo, 60=An661. ----*akrion?*
   a₂-ka-a₂-ki-ri-ja-jo, 76=Cn22. Ethnic?
a-ka-si-jo-ne, 254=Jn04. Loc.?
a-ke-re-wa, 54=An19+. (One of the nine towns.)
   a-ke-re-wa-de, 250=Vn01. Acc.+-*de.*
a₂-ki-ja, 45=An830.
a₂-ki-ra, Na856.
a₂-ma-i-wa, Na39. [Cf. 'Αμαία title of Demeter.]
a-ne-u-te, Cn14. Loc.?
   a₂-ne-u-te, Cn12. Alternative spelling of the preceding.
a-nu-wa, 52=An26.
a-pa-re-u-pi, Cn643+. Loc. plur. Mühlestein: cf. 'Αφαρεύς.
a-pa-ri-ka-na-we-ja, Na16.
a-pa-ta, Na27.
a₂-pa-tu-wo-te, Cn12. Loc. [Cf. 'Απατούρια?]
a-pe-ke-e, Jn03. Loc.
   a-pe-ke-i-jo, Jn03. Ethnic.
a-pi-ke-ne-a, Xa12. *Amphigenea?* [Cf. 'Αμφιγένεια *Il.* II, 593.]
a-pi-no-e-wi-jo, 184=Nn01+. Place or ethnic?
a-pi-te-wa, 57=An43+.
a-po-ne-we, 53=An12+. Loc.
   a-pu-ne-we, 15=Ad684. Alternative spelling of the preceding.
a-pu-ka, 44=An29. Ethnic: -*ān?*
   a-pu₂?-ka-ne, 59=An656+. Nom. plur. of the preceding?
a-pu₂?-we, 49=An07+. Loc. *Aipuei?* (One of the nine towns.) [Αἰπύ *Il.* II, 592.]
   a-pu₂?-de, 250=Vn01. *Aipu-de.*
   a-pu₂?-ja, 258=Kn01. Ethnic: *Aipuia?*
a₂-ra-tu-a, 76=Cn22. Mühlestein: cf. 'Αραιθυρέα, 'Αραντία, old names of Phlius.
   a₂-ra-tu-wa, 57=An43. Alternative spelling of the preceding.

a₂-ru-wo-te, 56=An657. Loc.: *Halwontei?* ['Αλοῦς Arcadia, Paus. VIII, 25, 2.]
a-ro-wo, 251=Vn02. Possibly nom. of the preceding; or a common noun; see Vocabulary, p. 389.
a-sa-pi, Na33. Loc. plur.
a-si-ja-ti-ja, 31=Ae04+. [Cf. 'Ασέα Arcadia, (founded by 'Ασεάτας)?]
   a-sa-ti-ja, Mn02. Alternative spelling of the preceding.
   a-*85-ta₂, Ma17. Alternative spelling of the preceding.
a-te-re-wi-ja, Cn14+. [Cf. 'Ατρεύς?]
da-mi-ni-jo/-ja, 54=An19+. Ethnic or place? [Cf. 'Επίδαμνος; KN *da-mi-ni-jo.*]
da-we-u-pi, Cn03 [925]. Loc. plur.
de-we-ro-ai-ko-ra-i-ja, 198=Ng02. Name of a district; see p. 144. *Deuro-aigolaia?*
di-wi-ja-ta, 184=Nn01.
do-ro-qo-so-wo-te, Na07. Loc. (Divider after *qo* doubtful.)
e-ko-me-no, Cn12+. *Erkhomenos.* ['Ερχομενός= 'Ορχομενός, but hardly that in Arcadia.]
e-ko-me-ne-u, 183=Nn831 (=02). Ethnic or man's name?: *Erkhomeneus.* [Cf. man's name *O-ko-me-ne-u.*]
e-ko-me-na-ta-o, 44=An29+. Gen. plur. of ethnic: *Erkhomenātāōn.*
e-ko-so-no, Na31.
e-na-po-ro, 76=Cn22+. *Enarsphoros?* [Spartan hero 'Εναρσφόρος Alcm. *Parth.* 3; not a common noun (Debrunner, Von der Mühll).]
e-ni-pa-te-we, 255=Jn658+. Loc. [Cf. river-god 'Ενιπεύς *Od.* XI, 238?]
e-pi-qo-ra₂, Mn01. Place or common noun; see Vocabulary, p. 392. *Epiqʷolai?* ['Επιπολαί.]
e-ra-te-re-wa-o, 258=Kn01+. Gen. plur.: *Elatrewāōn.* [Cf. 'Ελάτρ(ε)ια='Ελάτεια Thesprotia; man's name 'Ελατρεύς *Od.* VIII, 11.]
e-ra-te-re-wa-pi, Cn01. Loc. plur.: *Elatrewāphi.*
e-ra-te-re-we, Ma07. Loc. sing.: *Elatrēwei.* (Possibly a different place.)

147

e-ra-to-de, 250 = Vn01. *Elatos-de*? (One of the nine towns.) [Cf. man's name Ἔλατος *Il.* VI, 33.]
e-ra-te-i, 75 = Cn02. Loc.: *Elateï*.
e-ra-te-i-jo, On01. Ethnic: *Elateïos*.
e-re-e, 258 = Kn01 +. Loc.: *Heleei*. [Ἕλος *Il.* II, 594.]
e-re-i, 257 = Jn09. Alternative spelling of the preceding.
e-re-e-u, 183 = Nn831 (= 02). Ethnic of preceding or separate name; not a place?
e-re-e-wo, Na60. Gen.: *-ēwos*.
e-re-e-we, An723 +. Loc.: *-ēwei*.
e-ri-no-wo, Na51.
e-ri-no-wo-to, 154 = Eq01. Gen.: *-wontos*?
e-ri-no-wo-te, Cn09 +. Loc.: *-wontei*?
e-ro-ma-to, An25. [Cf. *o-ru-ma-to*?]
e-ro₂-ne, Na34. Loc. Palmer: cf. Ἐλεών *Il.* II, 500.
e-sa-re-wi-ja, Ma15 +. Derivative of the title *e-sa-re-u* (cf. *pa₂-si-re-wi-ja*, *za-ma-e-wi-ja*); = 'estate of the *e*.'?
e-u-de-we-ro, 6 = Ab02 +. *Eudeiwelos*? [Cf. Εὐδείελος name of Aspledon, Strabo.]
e-u-ta-re-[, Na1085.
e-wi-ku-wo-te, Na10. Loc.: *-wontei*?
e-wi-ri-po, 54 = An19. *Ewripos*. [Εὔριπος; probably Methóni, see p. 145.]
e-wi-ri-pi-ja, Aa06. Ethnic: *Ewripiai*.
e-wi-te-u, Cn17.
e-wi-te-wi-jo, Mn01 +. Ethnic.
i-na-ne, 51 = An20. Nom. plur.?
i-na-pi, An24. Loc. plur.
i-na-ni-ja, Ae01 +. Ethnic or place?; cf. *pa-ki-ja-ni-ja*.
i-te-re-wa, 258 = Kn01 +.
i-wa-so, 57 = An43 +. *Iwasos*. [Cf. Ἴασον Ἄργος *Od.* XVIII, 246; Mühlestein identifies with Ἴασος on Arcadian-Laconian border.]
i-wa-si-jo-ta, 76 = Cn22. Ethnic: *Iwasiōtai*.
ka-pa-ra₂-de, 26 = An02 +. Fem. ethnic? (nom. plur.).
ka-pa-ra₂-do, Ad679. Gen. plur.
ka-ra-do-ro, 257 = Jn09 +. *Kharadros*. (One of the nine towns.) [Χάραδρος river near Messene, Paus. IV, 23, 5; cf. Χαλάδριοι in Elean inscr. Schwyzer, *Dial.* 415.]
ka-ra-do-ro-de, 250 = Vn01. *Kharadron-de*.
ka-ra-u-jo, An09.
ka-ro-ke-e, 52 = An26.
ke-e, Aa10 +. Loc.?
ke-i-jo, Na29. Ethnic or place? Georgiev: *Keios*.
ke-i-ja-ka-ra-na, 184 = Nn01. ----*krānā*?
ze-i-ja-ka-ra-na, Xa07. Alternative spelling of the preceding.
ke-ra-ti-jo-jo, An09. Gen.: *Geraistioio*. [Γεραίστιον Arcadia.]
ke-re-te, An31. Nom. plur.: *Krētes*? [Κρής.]
ke-re-ti-wo, Na09.
ke-re-za, Ab25 +. A place at Pylos. [Not = Κρῆσσαι.]
ki-ka-ne-wi-jo-de, Vn07. Acc. + *-de*.

ki-ni-di-ja, Ab12 +. Fem. ethnic: *Knidiai*. [Κνίδος.]
ki-ni-di-ja-o, Ad683. Gen. plur.: *Knidiāōn*.
ki-si-wi-ja, Aa770. Fem. ethnic: *Xiwiai*. [= Χῖαι? (Χῖος < Χίιος).]
ki-si-wi-ja-o, Ad675. Gen. plur.: *Xiwiāōn*.
ko-ri-to, Ad07. *Korinthos*. [Not the known Κόρινθος.]
ko-ri-si-jo, 52 = An26 +. Ethnic: *Korinsios*. [Cf. woman's name *ko-ri-si-ja*.]
ko-ro-du-wo, Na1041.
ko-ro-jo-wo-wi-ja, Mn01. *Khōroio worwia*?
ko-ro-ki-ja, 26 = An02 +. Fem. ethnic?
ko-ro-ki-ja-o, Ad680. Gen. plur.
ko-ro-ku-ra-i-jo, Na45 +. Ethnic; Ventris, Furumark: *Krokulaioi* (cf. Κροκύλεια); Sittig: *Korkuraioi*.
ko-tu-wo, 131 = Eq01. Gen.
ko-tu-we, Na908. Loc.
[ku]-pa-ri-so, 187 = Na49. *Kuparissos*. [Κυπάρισσος, Hom. Κυπαρισσήεις *Il.* II, 593, now Kyparissía.]
ku-pa-ri-si-jo, 56 = An657. Ethnic: *Kuparissioi*.
ku-te-ra₃, Aa14. Fem. ethnic?: *Kuthērai*. [Κύθηρα.]
ku-te-ra-o, Ad696. Gen. plur.: *Kuthērāōn*.
ku-te-re-u-pi, 28 = An42 +. Loc. plur. of ethnic or place: *Kuthēreuphi*?
ma-ra-ne-nu-we, 54 = An19. Loc.
ma-ra-ne-ni-jo, 175 = Ma10. Ethnic.
ma-ro, Cn05 +. [Cf. Μῆλος.]
ma-ro-pi, 61 = Cn04 +. Loc. plur.?
ma-to-ro-pu-ro, Cn10. Mühlestein: *Mātro-pulos* (i.e. the city from which Pylos was founded).
me-ka-o, Na12. Gen.: *Megāo*? [Cf. men's names Μέγης, Μεγάδης.]
me-sa-po, Na28. *Messapos*? [Cf. Μεσσαπέαι Laconia.]
me-ta-pa, 44 = An29 +. *Metapa*. (One of the nine towns.) [Μέταπα; cf. τὸς Μεταπίος in Elean inscr. Schwyzer, *Dial.* 414.]
me-ta-pa-de, 250 = Vn01. *Metapan-de*.
me-ta-pi-jo, 58 = An654. Ethnic: *Metapios*.
me-te-to, Na04 +.
me-te-to-de, 41 = An14. Acc. + *-de*.
mi-ra-ti-ja, Aa17 +. Fem. ethnic: *Milātiai*. [Μίλητος in Ionia or Μίλατος in Crete?]
mi-ra-ti-ja-o, Ad09, Ad689. Gen. plur.: *Milātiāōn*.
na-i-se-wi-jo, Jn692 +. Ethnic?
ne-do-wo-ta-de, 60 = An661. *Nedwonta-de*? [Νέδων river of E. Messenia.]
ne-we-u, Ad02. Masc. ethnic?
ne-we-wi-ja, Ab20 +. Fem. ethnic.
ne-we-wi-ja-o, Ad01. Gen. plur.
o-pi-ke-ri-jo, An35. Perhaps not a place: *Opiskherion*?
o-pi-ke-ri-jo-de, 55 = An724 (= 32). Acc. + *-de*?
o-re-e-wo, Cn11. Gen.: *Oreēwos*? [Cf. Ὠρεός Euboea.]
o-re-mo a-ke-re-u, Jn06.

o-ru-ma-to, 76 = Cn22. *Orumanthos?* [= 'Ερύμανθος.]
   o-ru-ma-si-ja-jo, 57 = An43. Ethnic.
o-wi-to-no, 44 = An29 +.
   o-wi-ti-ni-jo, 56 = An657. Ethnic.
pa-ka-a-ka-ri, 196 = Na70. *Pāgā Akharis?*
pa-ki-ja-na, 114 = En02, Na11 +. Apparently gen. and loc. (One of the nine towns.) [Possibly *Sphagian-*, cf. Σφαγία = Σφακτηρία: see p. 143.]
   pa-ki-ja-ni-ja, 114 = En02. Ethnic or alternative spelling?
   pa-ki-ja-ne, Xc01. Ethnic (masc. plur.) used as place-name?
   pa-ki-ja-pi, 257 = Jn09. Instr.-loc. plur.
   pa-ki-ja-si, 51 = An20 +. Dat.-loc. plur.
pa-ko, 49 = An07. *Phāgos?* [Cf. Φηγός Thessaly, Φήγεια Arcadia.]
pa-na-pi, Cn13. Loc. plur.: *Phanāphi?* [Cf. Φανά Aetolia.]
pa₂-wo-na-de, Vn07. Acc. + -*de*.
pe-ra₃-ko-ra-i-ja, 199 = Ng01 +. *Pera-aigolaia?* See p. 144.
   pe-ra-a-ko-ra-i-ja, On01. Alternative spelling of the preceding.
   pe-ra-ko-ra-i-ja, Ad15. Alternative (defective?) spelling.
pe-re-u-ro-na-de, 53 = An12. *Pleurōna-de*. [Πλευρών Aetolia, *Il.* II, 639 +.]
   pe-re-u-ro-ni-jo, 59 = An656. Ethnic: *Pleurōnios*.
pe-re-wo-te, Na08 +. Loc.
pe-to-no, 75 = Cn02 +. (One of the nine towns.)
   pe-to-no-de, 250 = Vn01. Acc. + -*de*.
pi-ka-na, 194 = Na58.
pi-pu-te, 49 = An07. Loc.
pi-*82, 75 = Cn02 +. (One of the nine towns.) *Phia?* [Φειά Triphylia? Cf. Φεαί, dubious reading in *Od.* xv, 297.]
   pi-*82-de, 250 = Vn01. *Phian-de*.
po-ra-i, 59 = An656. Dat.-loc. plur. = *po-ra-pi?*
po-ra-pi, 53 = An12 +. Loc. plur.: *Phorāphi?* [Φαραί Messenia?]
po-ti-ja-ke-e, 54 = An19 +. Loc. [Cf. *ti-mi-to a-ke-e*.]
po-to-ro-wa-pi, Aa11 +. Loc. plur.
po-wi-te-ja, Jn02 +.
pu₂?-ra₂-a-ke-re-u, 184 = Nn01. Ethnic? Palmer: *Puragreus*.
   pu₂?-ra₂-a-ki-ri-jo, Na52. Alternative spelling of the preceding?
pu-ro, Aa15 +. *Pulos*. [Πύλος *Il.* xi, 671 +.]
   pu-ro-jo, An15. Gen.: *Puloio*.
qe-re-me-e, Na10. Loc.
qo-pi-ja, Na30. [Cf. Βοίβη Thessaly, *Il.* II, 712; or Φοιβία Sicyon.]
qo-ro-mu-ro, Na841. *Bromulos?* [Cf. Βρόμος, Βρομίσκος against etymology.]
qo-ta, Na23.
qo-ta-wo, 50 = An18 rev. +.
ra-i-pi, Na17.
ra-mi-ni-jo/-ja, An13 +. Ethnic. *Lāmnios* or *Rhamnios?* [Λῆμνος, 'Ραμνοῦς.]
ra-ni-jo-ne, 52 = An26.

ra-u-ra-ti-ja, On01. *Lauranthia?*
   ra-wa-ra-ta₂, 257 = Jn09 +. Alternative spelling of the preceding.
   ra-u-ra-ti-jo, Ad664. Ethnic.
   ra-wa-ra-ti-jo/-ja, Cn13, 45 = An830. Alternative spelling of the preceding.
re-ka-ta-ne, 52 = An26. Loc. or ethnic?
re-pa₂-se-wo, Cn11. Gen.: -*ēwos*.
re-pe-u-ri-jo, Cn14. *Lepeurion?* [Cf. Λέπρεον Triphylia.]
re-si-we-i, 51 = An20. Loc.
re-u-ko-to-ro, 41 = An14 +. *Leuktron*. [Λεῦκτρον Laconia, Arcadia, Achaea.]
ri-jo, 53 = An12 +. (One of the nine towns.) *Rhion*. ['Ρίον Messenia (Strabo, VIII, 360); modern Koróni.]
ri-sa-pi, Na71. Loc. plur.: *Lissāphi?* [Cf. Λίσσα Crete, Λίσσαι Thrace.]
ri-so-we-ja, Na26.
ro-o-wa, 53 = An12 +. (Possibly the port of Pylos; see p. 187.)
ro-u-so, 7 = Aa717 +. *Lousoi*. [Λουσοί Arcadia.]
   ro-u-si-jo, 252 = Vn06 +. Ethnic: *Lousios*.
ru-ke-wo-wo-wi-ja, Na35. *Lu(n)kēwos worwia?*
ru-ko-a₂-[ke]-re-u-te, Jn08. *Lukoagreuthen?* [Cf. Λυκόα Arcadia.]
sa-ma-ra, 181 = Ma14 +.
sa-ma-ra-de, 41 = An14. Acc. + -*de*.
sa-ma-ri-wa, Na73.
sa-ri-nu-wo-te, An09 +. Loc.: *Salinwontei?* [Σελινοῦς stream in Triphylia.]
   sa-ri-no-te, Vn04. Alternative spelling of the preceding.
si-jo-wo-te, Cn09. Loc.
si-re-wa, 182 = Ma18 +.
so-ro-pe-o, 52 = An26.
so-wo-te, see *do-ro-qo-so-wo-te*.
ta-mi-ta-na, 191 = Na26.
ta-ra-ke-wi-[, An25. *Trakhewi[a]?* [Τραχεῖα.]
te-mi-ti-ja, On01. = *ti-mi-ti-ja*.
te-re-ne-we, 51 = An20. Loc. sing. or nom. plur.?
   te-re-ne-wi-ja, An38. Ethnic.
te-se-e, Na15. Loc.
te-ta-ra-ne, 53 = An12 +. Loc. or nom. plur. [Carratelli Τετράνη.]
te-tu-ru-we, 184 = Nn01 +. Loc. (Same place as the preceding?)
ti-mi-to a-ke-e, 176 = Ma12 +. Palmer: *Themi(s)tos ageei*.
   ti-mi-to a-ke-i, 60 = An661. Alternative spelling of the preceding.
   ti-mi-ti-ja, 258 = Kn01 +. Apparently not ethnic, but an alternative form of the place-name: *Themistia*. [Cf. *te-mi-ti-ja*.]
ti-nwa-si-jo/-ja, 258 = Kn01 +. Ethnic. [Cf. Τρινασός?]
   ti-nwa-ti-ja-o, 15 = Ad684, cf. Xa633. Alternative spelling of the gen. plur. fem. of the preceding.
to-ro-wa-so, Na47.
u-ka-jo, 184 = Nn01.

u-pa-ra-ki-ri-ja, An08. *Huparakria?* [= Ὑπερ-άκρια.]

u-po-ra-ki-ri-ja, Cn13. Alternative spelling of the preceding.

u-pi-ja-ki-ri-jo, 58 = An654. Alternative spelling?

u-po-di-jo-no, Na18. Gen.

u̜-ra̜-*86, Na37.

u-ru-pi-ja-jo, 57 = An43 +. Ethnic: *Ulumpiaios.* Cf. *u-ru-pi-ja-*[KN X 392. [Cf. Ὕλυμπος = Ὄλυμπος.]

u-ru-pi-ja-jo-jo, 76 = Cn22. Gen.: *Ulumpiaioio.*

u-wa-si, 59 = An656. Dat.-loc. plur.

wa-a₂-te-pi, Na19. Loc. plur.?

wa-a₂-te-we, 52 = An26. Ethnic?

wa-re-u-ka-ra, Na576.

wa-wo-u-de, 58 = An654, cf. Xb02.

wi-ja-da-ra, Ad02.

wi-ja-we-ra₂, Jn05 +.

wi-nu-ri-jo, 54 = An19.

wo-no-qe-wa̜, Na45, cf. 258 = Kn01.

wo-qe-we, 54 = An19 +. (Same place as the preceding?)

wo-tu-wa-ne, Cn09.

za-ku-si-jo/-ja, [54 = An19] 286 = Sa787 +. Ethnic: *Zakunsios.* [Ζάκυνθος; cf. man's name *za-ku-si-jo.*]

za-ma-e-wi-ja, 257 = Jn09 [Ma10 Vn03]. [Cf. *ka-ma-e-u* in Vocabulary.]

ze-i-ja-ka-ra-na, see after *ke-i-ja-ka-ra-na.*

[.]*-ka-si-da,* 52 = An26.

PART II

SELECTED TABLETS

TRANSCRIPTION, TRANSLATION, COMMENTARY

EXPLANATORY NOTES ON THE PRESENTATION

NUMBERING

We have chosen 300 of the most interesting Mycenaean tablets for discussion here; they include 122 from the Knossos excavations of 1900–4, 105 from Pylos 1939, sixty-three from Pylos 1952, one from Pylos 1953, five from Mycenae 1952 and four from Mycenae 1954. They have been arranged in groups according to their context and given consecutive numbers from **1** to **300**. These numbers are intended to help the user of this book, but Bennett's classification is everywhere added (e.g. **1** = Aa01), and should continue to be used alone in future references to the tablets. The new numbers adopted in *PT II* for the 1939 tablets were received too late for general use in this book, but have been added in square brackets where such tablets are transcribed.

A concordance of these tablets in the order of their original publication will be found on pp. 445–8; for the Knossos tablets Bennett's references consist of Evans' numeration (*SM II*) with the addition of a two-letter prefix indicating the context. A further concordance (pp. 449–52) lists all the 1939 Pylos tablets in serial order of their new numbers, irrespective of prefix, together with their old numbers. The Pylos tablets found in 1952 and later are referenced by their inventory numbers (as in *PT II*), which run upwards from 622.

The bracketed letters added by us to the Knossos tablet headings refer to the alleged find-spot (see fig. 13, p. 115), the Roman figures to the plate in *SM II* on which a legible photograph may be found; e.g. **29** = As821 (K lix).

TRANSCRIPTION

The transcription of the Mycenaean phonetic signs follows the values given in fig. 4, p. 23; where the value is unknown, Bennett's signary numbers are used with an asterisk, e.g. **85-de-we-sa*. Ideograms are transcribed in small capitals with the meanings suggested in fig. 10, pp. 50–1, and in the 'boxes' at the head of each section; evidence for these identifications will be given in the commentary. Unidentified ideograms are referred to by asterisked numbers **100–*243* as in fig. 10. Such spellings as *o.ki.* SHEEP refer to small syllabic signs used as 'adjuncts' (i.e. abbreviated descriptive notes): their function is discussed on p. 53 and in the commentary to the relevant groups of tablets. Weights and measures are printed with the original Mycenaean symbols, but in the translation are converted into their suggested metric equivalents with the ratios proposed on pp. 57–60.

The tablet readings published by Evans and Bennett have been independently checked by one or both of us from the originals in Greece. The state of the text is shown by the following conventions:

to-so   Faint, damaged or careless signs, whose traces are compatible with the restoration proposed, though not necessarily to the exclusion of other possible readings.

[End of the line broken off, or too abraded to be read.

153

[?	Uncertain whether part of the text has been lost or not.
to-so [	The evidence of the tablet, or reliable analogy, indicates that the word is complete before the lacuna.
to-so-[	The evidence indicates that the word is not complete.
to-so[	The evidence is insufficient to decide the question.
[*to*]-*so*	Editors' restoration of sign completely lost.
[..]	Two signs lost.
[±15]	Space for approximately fifteen lost or illegible signs.
[*X*]	A missing ideogram, whose identity cannot be inferred.
[*nn*]	Missing numerals and weights and measures.
25 [	Numerals probably complete.
+]25	Tens probably incomplete.
25[+	Digits probably incomplete.
25[	Uncertain whether numerals are complete or not.
{*to*}	Superfluous sign added in error by the scribe.
⟨*to*⟩	Sign accidentally or deliberately omitted by the scribe.
⟦*to*⟧	Sign erased by the scribe.
'*to*'	Scribe's corrected reading over erasure, or sign squeezed in above the line.
/	Change by the scribe to a different size of writing.

Translation

An attempted English rendering of each tablet is added, except where it consists entirely of repetitive phrases. Doubtful and controversial translations of words and ideograms are printed in italics, without which a number of the tablets would appear as an impenetrable forest of question-marks.

Proper names which do not have a possible Greek explanation are printed in the transcription form; otherwise they are 'translated' into an approximation to the contemporary Greek form. Where the assumed classical parallel is obscured by phonetic changes (e.g. *po-ru-qo-ta* = *Poluqᵘhontās* = Πολυφόντης), the reading can be checked in the index of personal names (pp. 414–27) and of place-names (pp. 146–50). Where necessary, place-names are distinguished by ᵖ, men's names by ᵐ and women's by ᶠ.

Notes

It was felt that a complete Greek version of each tablet would demand both excessive space and a premature finality in the interpretation. Where the equivalent Greek vocabulary and syntax are not obvious from the transcription and translation, they will be discussed in the Notes on the first appearance of the formula. The suggested Greek pronunciation and etymology of every word appearing on the published tablets can in any case be checked against the comprehensive Vocabulary (pp. 385–413).

Greek type will only be used for classical forms and quotations, the approximate Mycenaean pronunciation being indicated in Roman letters on the lines discussed in the Preface. We have adopted a conventional spelling of datives singular in *-ei* (e.g. *poimenei*, *wanaktei*) and of datives plural in *-a'i* (fem.) and *-oi'i* (masc.); the actual pronunciation of these forms is disputed (see p. 85).

CHAPTER VI

LISTS OF PERSONNEL

1. WOMEN AND CHILDREN AT PYLOS (Aa, Ab, Ad) †

THE Pylos tablets of these three series form a connected group. *Aa* and *Ab* tablets both enumerate women and children, the latter adding a reference to two commodities, wheat and figs. The *Ad* tablets list men and boys who are specifically stated to be the sons of various groups of women largely identifiable with those mentioned in *Aa* and *Ab*.

100	𓀀 𓀀	MAN
103	𓀀	MAN[b]
101	𓀀	MAN[c]
102	𓀀	WOMAN

The relation between the *Aa* and *Ab* series seems to be unique, for the headings in at least twenty-one cases are repeated in each series; and there is a general resemblance in the figures given which suggests that these record the numerical strength of the same groups at different times. Contrary to what appears to have been the usual custom, the first set were not destroyed on being replaced; possibly the second census was not complete when the records came to an end. There does not seem to be any means of gauging the interval between the two counts, though we may conjecture an annual revision of the lists to be likely. In one case the numbers remain constant (Aa795: Ab19; probably also Aa05: Ab11+35); elsewhere the increases and decreases seem to be about equal. The total of the numbers preserved on the *Aa* tablets is 631 women, 376 girls and 261 boys, or 1268 souls in all. Those on the *Ab* series are smaller (370+190+149=709). In estimating the actual numbers of this class allowance must be made for lost or damaged tablets; but the *Aa* group may contain a few duplicates.

Since some of these tablets contain nothing but an enumeration of the women and children, it follows that the record is primarily a census and the other entries are subsidiary. The same applies to the *Ad* tablets, where the only entry is the number of men and boys, except for three cases in which there is a further note of a deficit (*o-pe-ro*).

The groups of women are described in three ways, which may be variously combined. The description usually begins with a place-name, though this may be omitted (see below). Then the group is normally described by its trade or occupation: e.g. *lewotrokhowoi* 'bath-attendants', *meletriai* 'corn-grinders', *ampukoworgoi* 'headband-makers', *ālakateiai* 'spinners', *pektriai* 'carders'. In some cases an ethnic adjective appears to be substituted for the trade: *Knidiai* (Knidos), *Milātiai* (Miletus), *Kuther(i)ai* (Kythera), *Lāmniai* (?) (Lemnos). Others not identifiable but probably ethnic are *ti-nwa-si-ja, a-da-ra-te-ja* (cf. Ἀδρήστεια, *Il.* II, 828), *ze-pu₂?-ra, ki-si-wi-ja* (from an early form of Khios?). In the *Ad* tablets both trade and ethnic may be coupled: e.g. *ti-nwa-ti-ja-o i-te-ja-o* 'of the weavers of T.' (15 = Ad684). Here too there may in some cases be an indication of the fathers of the children; as in this same tablet where they are also called: *a-pu-ne-we e-re-ta-o ko-wo* 'the sons of rowers at A.'

It is tempting to speculate about the status and origin of these women. The menial tasks that they perform suggest that they were slaves: possibly the labour force for the industry on which the wealth of the Mycenaean kingdoms must at least in part have been built. The casual references to the fathers of the children also seem to indicate that they are not the product of any regular union. The absence of men listed in their own right is surprising; women appear to predominate, and where the men are listed it is as the sons of the women. The deficiency of men is to some extent compensated by certain of the lists in the *An* series, though these may not be strictly parallel; some at least seem to be allocations of labour for special purposes. It may be suggested that the labour force is in part the product of piratical raids on the non-Greek areas of the Aegean. If the defeated inhabitants were carried off into slavery this would account for the preponderance of women and children, most of the men being killed in the fighting or subsequently slaughtered. The interpretation of *ra-wi-ja-ja* as 'captives' (see 16 = Ad686) supports this view; though it might be supposed that these women are distinguished from the other categories. They would, however, only be called 'captives' for a short time, before being assigned to an occupation. Virolleaud (1953, p. 193) quotes an Ugaritic text which refers to *bn amht kt* 'the sons of the slave-women of *Kt*' (= Kition in Cyprus?)—an almost exact parallel for the *Ad* tablets. The ethnic names may then be a clue to the places raided by the ships of Pylos. It is plain from numerous references in Homer that 'Viking' raids of this sort were everyday occurrences in Mycenaean Greece; and the incursion of sea-peoples repelled by Ramses III was probably a major expedition of this type. Indeed the Trojan War may have begun as a similar operation. The insecurity of early Greece as described by Thucydides (1, 5, 6) is likely enough; and the *raison d'être* of the hegemony of Mycenae was probably the comparative security it afforded to the subordinate powers.

A notable characteristic of the *Ab* tablets, apart from the added formula, is a difference in the form of the heading. In *Aa* the location is ordinarily omitted if it is Pylos; Aa15 is exceptional, Aa16 is now reclassified as Ab564. The writer of the *Ab* series begins each entry with a place-name, though once or twice he seems to have forgotten it (e.g. Ab03) or to have inserted it as an afterthought (Ab23, Ab31+789). The hypothesis of at least two writers is supported by differences in spelling: *Aa* spells the feminine agent suffix *-ti-ri-ja*, *Ab -ti-ra$_2$*. A study of the handwriting confirms this conclusion.

Tablets of both groups end with a formula which has the usual form: DA I TA I (*Aa*) or DA TA (*Ab*); the distinction is not, however, absolute, and within each group either part or the whole formula may be omitted; the order may also be reversed. No numbers other than one ever appear, and it is therefore certain that the formula does not express any ration or allocation, which should show some variation according to the numbers of women concerned. This disproves Webster's suggestion (1954, p. 11) that DA is a measure of land, as in PY **114** = En02, where DA 40 is glossed *to-sa da-ma-te*. The same abbreviation may have different meanings in different contexts. For a possible correlation of this formula with the rations on the *Ab* tablets see below. The same formula appears on some Knossos tablets dealing with women and children (e.g. **18** = Ak611), and there the numeral following TA may be 2.

Where a ration of wheat and figs is specified (*Ab* tablets only), the amounts are roughly proportional to the numbers of women and children. The amounts of the two commodities are always identical. The basis of the calculation would appear to be a ration of T 2 for each woman, with half that amount for each child irrespective of sex. This is further proof that the calculation of rations is not the sole purpose of the census. In Ab15+899 eight women, three girls and three boys receive T 22 (=8×2+6); Ab31+789 six women, six girls ('boys' is here a scribal error) and three boys receive T 21 (=6×2+9); Ab41+745 two women and one girl receive T 5 (=2×2+1). The same scale is suggested by Ab06 where there are no children, but the number of women is damaged; the ration, however, is T 4, i.e. that presumed for two women.

Although the figures never fall below this basic level, in most cases the ration † is supplemented by a factor varying up to more than one-half (Ab19), and not infrequently one-third or more (Ab01, **6** = Ab02, Ab09, Ab17, Ab30). There appears to be no principle by which the amount of this supplement can be derived from the details recorded; it is perhaps an allowance for the skilled or heavy nature of the work performed. Of the three clear cases of the basic ration it is noticeable that in two the DA TA formula is absent, while in the third the right-hand edge of the tablet is missing; Ab06 has only TA. Wherever the full formula DA TA (or TA DA) is found, there is an improvement on the basic ration; TA alone is accompanied by a very small supplement (one-twelfth) on Ab16. This correlation may, however, be accidental, for the presence of the formula will not explain the variations in the proportion of the increase.

It was suggested in ch. II (p. 60) that T 2 represents an absolute value of approximately 24 litres. This was based partly on a possible equation between weight and bulk in the case of *knakos* 'safflower', and on a reasonable range of values for the smallest unit ᗉ 1; but also on the specific assumption that these *Ab* rations are monthly ones. Such a ration of 24 litres is little less than the *khoinix* (27 litres) regarded as the classical monthly ration for a fighting man; it is often supplemented and is in any case accompanied by an equal quantity of another commodity which is almost certainly figs. The identification is to some extent guesswork, but a monthly ration seems to fit better than a daily or yearly one.

Rations of figs are not unknown in antiquity. Two Cretan inscriptions (*Inscr. Cret.* IV, 79 and 144) give yearly rations (possibly for a group) which include 100 *medimni* of figs and 200 *medimni* of barley; cf. also IV, 77. Cato (*Agr.* 56) recommends a reduction in the ration of bread for slaves 'when they start eating figs'.

1 = Aa01 [62]

me-re-ti-ri-ja WOMEN 7   *ko-wa* 10   *ko-wo* 6

Seven corn-grinding women, ten girls, six boys.

me-re-ti-ri-ja: the identification of this word depends upon the interpretation of *me-re-u-ro* as 'flour' in PY **171** = Un718 (see Vocabulary, p. 399). Corn grinding is one of the tasks commonly undertaken by women; cf. γυνή...ἀλετρίς (*Od.* xx, 105).

† 2 = Aa815

a-ke-ti-ra₂ WOMEN 38   *ko-wa* 33   *ko-wo* 16   DA 1   TA 1

Thirty-eight nurses, thirty-three girls, sixteen boys; one *da-*, one *ta-*.

a-ke-ti-ra₂: not satisfactorily identified; for other suggestions see Vocabulary (p. 387). It is plainly a common occupation among women. The translation 'nurses' is based on the gloss of Hesychius ἀγέτρια· μαῖα; McKenzie's suggestion (*Cl. Quart.* xv, 48) that this word is a dissimilation of *ἀγρέτρια is only a guess, and the dissimilation might even be of Mycenaean date. On DA TA see above (p. 157).

3 = Ad694

pe-ki-ti-ra₂-o *ko-wo* MEN 4   *ko-wo* 3

Four sons of the carders, three boys.

pe-ki-ti-ra₂-o: *pektriāōn*, from πέκω

ko-wo: this word is used on these tablets in two senses: (*a*) 'son (of)', (*b*) 'boy' (as opposed to grown man).

4 = Aa04 [240]   †

a-ra-ka-te-ja WOMEN 21   *ko-wa* 25   *ko-wo* 4   TA 1

Twenty-one spinning-women, twenty-five girls, four boys; one *ta-*.

a-ra-ka-te-ja: a derivative of ἠλακάτη. This tablet and Aa03 appear to break the rule that there are not two tablets in the same series with identical headings; possibly the broken portion contained the statement of rations, which would assign it to the Ab class; but in these TA DA usually follows the rations.

5 = Aa792

ki-ni-di-ja WOMEN 21   *ko-wa* 12   *ko-wo* 10   DA 1   TA 1

Twenty-one Cnidian women, twelve girls, ten boys; one *da-*, one *ta-*.

ki-ni-di-ja: *Knidiai*, ethnic of Κνίδος.

6 = Ab02 [379]

| *e-u-de-we-ro* WOMEN 8   *ko-wa* 2   *ko-wo* 3 | WHEAT 2 T 8 | TA DA |
| | FIGS   2 T 8 | |

At Eudeiwelos: eight women, two girls, three boys; 336 l. of wheat, 336 l. of figs; *ta-*, *da-*.

e-u-de-we-ro: an unidentified place-name, which recalls the Homeric epithet, of uncertain meaning and etymology, εὐδείελος; if this is correct the spelling will help to resolve some of the difficulties of the Homeric word.

7 = Aa717   ‡

ro-u-so *a-ke-ti-ri-ja* WOMEN 32   *ko-wa* 18   *ko-wo* 8   DA 1   TA 1

At Lousoi: thirty-two nurses, eighteen girls, eight boys; one *da-*, one *ta-*.

ro-u-so: a place under the control of Pylos, cf. **178** = Ma13, **252** = Vn06, probably Λουσοί in Arcadia. The addition of the place-name distinguishes this entry from the nurses at Pylos (**2** = Aa815).

8 = Ad670

e-u-de-we-ro *ri-ne-ja-o* *ko-wo* MEN 4

At Eudeiwelos: four sons of the flax-workers.

The women are here given a trade-name, but may be the same group as those meant in **6** = Ab02 above.

ri-ne-ja-jo: a common occupation among women, probably *lineiāōn*, a derivative of λίνον.

9 = Ab27 [553]

				WHEAT 11	T 1
pu-ro *re-wo-to-ro-ko-wo* ⟨WOMEN⟩ 37 *ko-wa* 13 *ko-wo* 15				FIGS 11	T 1
				TA	DA

At Pylos: thirty-seven ⟨women⟩ bath-attendants, thirteen girls, fifteen boys;
   1332 l. of wheat, 1332 l. of figs; *ta-*, *da-*.

This tablet is remarkable for the omission of the ideogram for WOMEN before the
   numeral thirty-seven, clearly an oversight in view of the extreme regularity of this
   class. Bennett in *Index* read *re-wo-to-ro ko-wo* as two words, though there is no
   sign of a word-divider. That the bath-attendants are women is proved by the ideogram in Aa783, and the expression *re-wo-to-ro-ko-wo ko-wo* in **10** = Ad676.

re-wo-to-ro-ko-wo: lewotrokhowoi, Hom. λοετροχόος (*Od.* xx, 297). Their number is not
   excessive if their duties included the carrying of all the water required in the household. The apparent metathesis of the first two vowels is unexpected but not inexplicable. Ruipérez (1950) explains the disyllabic aorists of the type στορέσαι as
   arising from a metathesis of *στερόσαι. On this basis he is prepared to accept
   *λεϝόσαι > λοέσαι; thus the original base may have been λεϝο-. The same vowel order
   is shown by the adjective *re-wo-te-re-jo* **238** = Tn996.

10 = Ad676

pu-ro   *re-wo-to-ro-ko-wo*   *ko-wo*   MEN 22   *ko-wo* 11

At Pylos: twenty-two sons of the bath-attendants, eleven boys.

11 = Ad690

pu-ro   *a-pi-qo-ro*   *ko-wo*   MEN ⟦4⟧ 10   *ko-wo* 4 ⟦*o.* MEN 3⟧

At Pylos: ten sons of the waiting-women, four boys.

a-pi-qo-ro: amphiqʰolōn = ἀμφιπόλων.

† **12** = Ad671

        ka-ru-ti-je-ja-o-qe   *o.* MEN 5

pu-ro   *a-pu-ko-wo-ko*   *pa-ke-te-ja-o-qe*   MEN 6 ⟦9⟧   *ko-wo* 6

At Pylos: six ⟨sons⟩ of the headband-makers and the *musicians* and the
   sweepers, six boys; deficit five men.

The second line is to be read first, the words being written in above owing to lack of
   space. The sons of the women of three trades are recorded jointly; cf. the next tablet.

a-pu-ko-wo-ko: ampuko-worgōn; ἄμπυξ is Homeric (*Il.* xxii, 469).

pa-ke-te-ja-o-qe: no satisfactory explanation; if from the root of παίζω it should probably
   begin *pa-wi-*; possibly a derivative of πηκτίς.

ka-ru-ti-je-ja-o-qe: the form suggests a feminine from a masculine in -εύς. Perhaps from
   καλλύνω, cf. κάλλυνθρον, καλλυντής.

o.: as an abbreviation appears to stand for *o-pe-ro*, i.e. deficit (see Vocabulary, p. 401).

13 = Ad691   †

        e-ke-ro-qo-no-qe   *pa-wo-ko-qe*

pu-ro   *o-pi-ro-qo*   *ko-wo*   MEN 9

At Pylos: nine sons of the supernumerary women, and of the wage-earners and casual workers.

o-pi-ro-qo: opiloiq^{u}ōn, = ἐπιλοίπων; i.e. the women not yet allocated to particular duties.

e-ke-ro-qo-no-qe: Palmer (1954*b*, p. 23) proposes enkhêroq^{u}oinōn, from *ἐγχειρό-ποινος. For ἔγχειρα = μισθός cf. Schwyzer, *Dial.* 325[4], and Cypr. ὑχἕρōν Schwyzer, *Dial.* 679A[5].

pa-wo-ko-qe: the nominative *pa-wo-ke* occurs in Aa795. Palmer proposes *par-worges*, a compound of παρ- with the base **worg-*. The apocope of a preposition cannot yet be paralleled.

14 = Ad697 + 698   ‡

             e-ṛe-[.]*-qe-ṛo-me-no*

da-mi-ni-ja   [*ri*]*-ne-ja-o*   *ko-wo*   MẸṆ[

At Damnia: *x* sons of the flax-workers; . . .

da-mi-ni-ja: presumably a place-name since it is not a genitive plural. Cf. Ἐπί-δαμνος? *da-mi-ni-jo* MEN 40 occurs on **54** = PY An19 and is common on the Knossos tablets, chiefly those dealing with sheep (see p. 203). The top line gives further information about this group. Possibly restore *e-re-*[*e*] *qe-ro-me-no* = ereen g^{u}élomenoi 'willing to row', or *e-re-*[*ta*] *qe-ro-me-no* = eretai q^{u}elomenoi 'becoming rowers' (cf. Hom. πέλομαι).

15 = Ad684

        a-pu-ne-we   *e-re-ta-o*   *ko-wo*

pu-ro   *ti-nwa-ti-ja-o*   *i-te-ja-o*   *ko-wo*   MEN 5   *ko-wo* 2

At Pylos: five sons of the *Ti-nwa*-sian *weavers* (sons of rowers at *A-pu-ne-we*), two boys.

ti-nwa-ti-ja-o: the same as the *ti-nwa-si-ja* (nom.) PY Ab14. It is probably an ethnic adjective from an unrecorded place-name *ti-nwa-to (-ανθος?). Nouns in *-t-* usually form adjectives in *-si-jo* = -σιος (see p. 73); but there is some wavering, e.g. *mi-ra-ti-ja* from Μίλᾱτος. It is possible that the sound was at this stage intermediate, perhaps *-ts-* as suggested by Andrews.

i-te-ja-o: histeiāōn, a derivative with the suffix *-eia* from ἱστός (cf. ἱστουργός)?

a-pu-ne-we: a place-name, elsewhere spelt *a-po-ne-we* **53** = An12, **54** = An19, probably in the dative case. The top line is to be read together with the lower; i.e. the parentage is recorded on both sides, cf. **28** = An42.

16 = Ad686

        o-u-pa-ro-ke-ne-[*to ?a*]*-ka-ẉọ-ta-ra-kọ-po-ro*

pu-ro   *ke-re-za*   *ra-wi-ja-ja-o*   *ko-wo*   MEN 15

At *Ke-re-za*, Pylos: fifteen sons of the captives; *Alkawon* the. . .did not present himself.

ke-re-za: this word was taken by Furumark in Ab25 and Ab26 (reading *ke-re-ta₃*) as Κρῆτται; but although this interpretation might still be possible owing to the ambiguity of *za*, it seems to be disproved by this tablet, which shows that it is not part of the description of the women since it is not a genitive plural. It occurs as first word, followed by *ra-wi-ja-ja* on Aa807; and on Ab25 and Ab26 it is preceded by *pu-ro*, apparently without a divider. It seems more likely therefore that it is a place at Pylos.

ra-wi-ja-ja-jo: *lāwiaiāōn*, derivative of Dor. λαῖα, Ion. λητη 'booty'; cf. ληϊάδας. . . γυναῖκας (*Il.* xx, 193). This has also been proposed by Georgiev.

ou parogeneto Alkāwōn. . .-phoros: the name *a-ka-wo* occurs in other tablets at Pylos, though not qualified.

ta-ra-ko-po-ro: hardly *tragophoros* 'wearing a goat-skin' (cf. τραγηφόρος, *di-pte-ra-po-ro*). The reading *-ko-* is very uncertain.

2. WOMEN AND CHILDREN AT KNOSSOS (Ai, Ak)

This is a much less homogeneous group than the corresponding tablets at Pylos. The introductory word may be a Cretan place-name or the feminine of the ethnic adjective derived from one. In some cases there is added or substituted a man's name, which may be in the genitive (e.g. Ai63, Ak622), though in other cases the syntactic relationship is unexpressed and the name stands in the nominative as a mere heading (e.g. Ag91, **20**=Ak824; in this tablet Furumark is unjustified in presuming *a-pi-qo-i-ta* to be an adjective in agreement with *do-e-ra*, since a compound adjective should normally have only two terminations). This tablet specifically refers to the women as slaves, and it is likely that the same applies to the whole group. The children are further subdivided into 'older' (*me-zo*) and 'younger' (*me-wi-jo*, *me-u-jo*).

There are a number of other annotations, mostly abbreviations at which we can only guess (e.g. *pa. di.-*, *pe. di.-*, *ne. di.-*, *di. za.-*, *zo. di.-*, *de.-*, *tu.-*, **85.-*). The frequent *di.-* is fairly certainly a contraction of a word spelt more fully *di-da-ka-re ne.* **22**=Ak781, *di-da-ka-re*[Ak783, Ak784, *di-da-ka-*[Ak828. The form of this word is obscure; the final *ne.-* is probably an independent abbreviation (see below). The recurrent *di-da-ka-re* may then be for *didaskale(ion)*, but the dropping of the extra sign needed is surprising though not impossible; in the other cases the end of the word is lost and *di-da-ka* might stand for *didakhā(i)*. But the *-re* appears to be part of the word. Ventris suggests *didaskalei*, a locative of the type of οἴκει. Whatever the exact form it seems plausible to conjecture a meaning 'under instruction' or the like, and to compare it with *de-di-ku-ja* **18** = Ak611 (abbreviated to *de.*- Ak620?). This word too appears to be incorrectly spelt if intended for *dedidakhuiai*, perfect participle of διδάσκω; the meaning is clearly intransitive (see p. 89) 'having completed their training'. It is hardly likely that this has reference to general education; much more probably these are women newly enslaved who have to be taught a trade; cf. the Homeric custom by which slave-women are regularly described by such phrases as ἀμύμονα ἔργα ἰδυίας (*Il.* ιx, 270); cf. τὰς. . .ἔργα διδάξαμεν ἐργάζεσθαι *Od.* xxii, 422.

Of the other abbreviations *ne.*- and *pe.*- may be *newōterai* (or simply *newai*) † and *presguterai*; *pa.*- possibly *palaiai*. The same suggestions were made by Furumark (1954).

The expression DA I TA I already noted at Pylos recurs at Knossos, and here we have also TA 2. The relation of these entries to the rest of the text remains obscure.

17 = Ai739 (H li)
¹ *ra-su-to | a-ke-ti-ri-ja* WOMEN 2
² *ko-wa* I *ko-wo* I
At *Lasunthos*: two nurses, one girl, one boy.

ra-su-to: a place-name; the adjective *ra-su-ti-jo* occurs on Lc761; cf. Λᾶσος, Λασαία.

18 = Ak611 (? xliv) †
      DA I †
¹ *to-te-ja* TA 2 WOMEN 10[+   ] *dẹ-di-ku-ja* WOMAN I [
² *ko-wa me-zo-e* 4 *ko-wo me-wi-jo* I[
————: two *ta-*, one *da-*; 10+ women; one *trained* woman; four older girls, one younger boy.

to-te-ja: not found elsewhere.
de-di-ku-ja: see above.
me-zo-e: *mezoes*; on the form of the declension of *me-zo* and *me-wi-jo* see p. 86.

19 = Ak627 (F? lii) ¶
        DA I
¹   ]-*to a-no-zo-jo* TA I [WOMEN] 9 *pe. di.* 2
² *ko-wa me*]-*zo-e* 7 *ko-wa me-wi-jo-e* [9] '10'
³ *ko-wo me-zo*]-*e* 2 *ko-wo me-wi-jo-e* [9] '10'
At ————*to*: nine [female] (slaves) of *A-no-zo*; one *da-*, one *ta-*; two *older women under instruction*; seven older girls, ten younger girls, two older boys, ten younger boys.

a-no-zo-jo: presumably a man's name in the genitive.

pe.di-: see above, p. 162.

me-zo-e (line 3): here dual *mezoe*.

Compare the women and children of two sizes listed on the Sumerian palace ration-lists from Lagaš (e.g. Genouillac 1909, *TSA*, xii):

    40 l. of emmer-wheat to the woman Idlulaḫlaḫ,

    20 l. to a boy (*dumu-nita*),

    two girls (*dumu-sal*) at 20 l.,

    six serving-women at 40 l.,

    one small boy (*šag-dug-nita*) at 20 l.,

    two small girls (*šag-dug-sal*) at 20 l., etc.

20 = Ak824   (K   lviii)

¹ *a-pi-qo-i-ta* / *do-e-ra*   WOMEN 32   *ko-wa*   *me-zo-e* 5   *ko-wa*   *me-wi-jo-e* 15

²   *ko-wo*   *me-wi-jo-e* 4

Amphiq^{u}hoitas: thirty-two female slaves, five older girls, fifteen younger girls, four younger boys.

a-pi-qo-i-ta: only here in this spelling, which can hardly be anything but *Amphiq^{u}hoitās* = Ἀμφιφοίτης. Elsewhere we find *a-pi-qo-ta* (see index of personal names). Furumark understands as adjective ἀμφίφοιται (no meaning given), see p. 162.

21 = Ak624   (F?   xlvi)

                   DA[

¹ *ri-jo-ni-ja*   TA[

² *ne.* / *di.* 3   *ko-wa*   *me-zo-e* [nn

³ *ko-wo*   *di.* 3   *ko-wo*   *me-zo-e* [nn

Ri-jo-nian women: *x* da-, *x* ta-...; three *young women under instruction*, *x* older girls..., three boys *under instruction*, *x* older boys....

ri-jo-ni-ja: feminine ethnic of the place-name *ri-jo-no* (Ap639, etc.).

The annotation *di.-* applied to boys is unusual; in view of the order it may distinguish a class of boys older than those called *me-zo-e*.

22 = Ak781   (J   liii)

¹   ] WOMEN 17 [

²   ] *ko-wa* [

³] *di-da-ka-re*   *ne.* 1   *ko-wo* [

...seventeen women...*x* girls...one *young woman under instruction*, *x* boys....

di-da-ka-re: see commentary, p. 162 above.

3. MEN, WOMEN AND CHILDREN AT KNOSSOS (Ag, Ai)

Some tablets record only small numbers of women (and in one case men); they may be records of families, but the introductory name is ambiguous and may refer to the owner of a group of slaves as elsewhere.

23 = Ag1654 (?) †

qe-ri-jo MAN^c I WOMAN I *ko-wa* [
Qe-ri-jo (man), one woman (wife?), *one* girl (daughter?)....

qe-ri-jo: probably a personal name. But it may be genitive, i.e. slaves of *Q.*; cf. the next tablet.

24 = Ai63 (O xxiv)

pe-se-ro-jo e-e-si
WOMAN I *ko-wa* I *ko-wo* I
(The slaves? family?) of Psellos are: one woman (wife?), one girl (daughter?), one boy (son?).

pe-se-ro-jo: *Pselloio*; the name recurs in the nominative or dative on MY **105** = Ge602.
e-e-si: *eensi*, 3rd pers. plur. of pres. ind. of εἰμί (see p. 89).
ko-wa: the numeral is quite clear on the original.

4. WOMEN WORKERS AT KNOSSOS

At Knossos women are not so often referred to by trade-names as at Pylos; this sample shows a classification of women containing one of the words found at Pylos.

25 = Ap694 (G xlvi)

1]-*ja ko-u-re-ja* WOMEN [
2] *ka-ra-we* WOMEN [
3] *a-ze-ti-ri-ja* WOMEN [

ko-u-re-ja: here apparently a feminine trade-name, also found on textile tablets (Lc581) where it must be connected with the annotation *ko-u-ra* often associated with *pa-we-a* (*pharwea*). Georgiev notes '= κούρεια' without comment; presumably as feminine of κουρεύς; but this root has a spurious diphthong arising from *κορσ-. A connexion with κούρειον does not seem more satisfactory.
ka-ra-we: *grāwes*, 'old women'.
a-ze-ti-ri-ja: the same word as *a-ke-ti-ra₂* PY **2** = Aa815.

5. WOMEN WORKERS AT PYLOS

Some similar lists from Pylos record large groups of women classified according to occupation or origin.

† **26** = An02 [292]

<pre>
1   si-to-ko-wo
2   ka-pa-ra₂-de   WOMEN 24   ko-wo 10[+?
3   ko-ro-ki-ja   WOMEN 8   ko-wo [nn
4   ki-ni-di-[ja   WOMEN] 21   ko-[wo   nn
</pre>

Measurers of grain: twenty-four *Ka-pa-ra₂-de* women, 10+ boys, eight *Ko-ro-ki-ja* women, *x* boys, twenty-one Cnidian women, *x* boys.

si-to-ko-wo: *sitokhowoi*, presumably women responsible for measuring out the correct amounts of σῖτος. Bennett takes this as an abstract of Aa788, Aa02, and **5** = Aa792, and restores the numerals accordingly. In this case *ko-wo* will mean 'children'.

ka-pa-ra₂-de: the reading of the second sign has been corrected by Bennett to *pa*. Probably a feminine ethnic in -άδες. It reappears on Aa788 and the genitive *ka-pa-ra₂-do* on Ad679.

ko-ro-ki-ja: probably another feminine ethnic. Hardly from κρόκος or κρόκη (acc. κρόκα Hesych.). The word reappears on Pylos Aa02, Ab07, its genitive *ko-ro-ki-ja-o* on Ad680.

27 = Ae08 [303]

<pre>
        i-je-ro-jo   [[ku-ru-so-jo   i-je-ro-jo]].
</pre>

pu-ro i-je-re-ja do-e-ra e-ne-ka ku-ru-so-jo WOMEN 14[+

At Pylos: 14+ female slaves of the priestess on account of sacred gold.

i-je-re-ja: *hiereiās*. We find a woman named *e-ra-ta-ra* described as 'slave of the priestess' on **119** = Eo02.

e-ne-ka: *heneka*, despite the presumed *ἕνϝεκα of the etymologists.

ku-ru-so-jo i-je-ro-jo: *khrusoio hieroio*. The nature of the transaction is obscure; were the slaves given to the priestess in return for some gold which had been offered? Or are they allocated to look after the gold ritual objects?

28 = An42 [607]

<pre>
1 me-ta-pa ke-ri-mi-ja do-qe-ja ki-ri-te-wi-ja
2 do-qe-ja do-e-ro pa-te ma-te-de ku-te-re-u-pi
3   WOMEN 6 do-qe-ja do-e-ra e-qe-ta-i e-e-to
4 te-re-te-we WOMEN [[6]] '13'
5 do-qe-ja do-e-ro pa-te ma-te-de di-wi-ja do-e-ra
6 WOMEN 3 do-qe-ja do-e-ra ma-te pa-te-de ka-ke-u
7 WOMAN 1 do-qe-ja do-e-ra ma-te pa-te-de ka-ke-u
</pre>

⁸ WOMEN 3

vacant 2

11   *ka*

At Metapa: ——— women *barley-reapers*. Six women *reapers*, their father
a slave and their mother *among the Kytherans*; thirteen women *reapers*,
————————; three women *reapers*, their father a slave and their mother
a slave *of Diwia*; one woman *reaper*, her mother a slave and her father a smith;
three women *reapers*, their mother a slave and their father a smith.

The arrangement of this tablet is unusual since the phrases regularly run on from one
line to the next (2–3, 3–4, 5–6, 6–7, 7–8). It is therefore difficult to know how to
punctuate lines 1–2. Possibly *ki-ri-te-wi-ja* is part of the phrase *ma-te-de ku-te-re-u-pi*
inserted above for lack of space or as an afterthought.

Metapa: a well-known place-name, but hardly that in Acarnania; possibly on the
Elean border, see list of place-names (p. 148).

ke-ri-mi-ja: the only other instance of this word is on Knossos Lc535, a fragment
mentioning also *talasia* '*pensum*' and introduced by the totalling formula *to-sa*.
Possibly a derivative of χείρ, but the meaning is obscure; cf. also κελμίς glossed as
παῖς ἢ λύκιθον (*sic*) by Hesychius.

do-qe-ja: this is clearly a key-word on this tablet, but unfortunately it occurs nowhere †
else; a man's name *do-qe-u* KN B 804 looks like the corresponding masculine (cf.
i-je-re-u/i-je-re-ja; see p. 89). In this case, however, it must be a description of the
women. Various attempts at interpretation have been made; our original idea was to
connect it with δόρπον, but the sense is unsatisfactory. The analogy of other words
such as *to-no* = θρόνος leads one to suspect *dorqᵘeia* = *δρόπεια, cf. masc. μαλο-δρόπηες
(Sappho). The etymology of δρέπω is not certain; but there is no objection to a
labio-velar in the word, the π being generalized as frequently. The word will perhaps
mean 'picker', possibly 'reaper' or 'gleaner'.

ki-ri-te-wi-ja: elsewhere this word stands alone as a description of women (*ki-ri-te-wi-ja
e-ko-si* **131** = Eb21, **135** = Ep704, but is here probably an adjective qualifying *do-qe-ja*,
if the order is sound. If this means 'reaper', it may perhaps be connected with
κριθαί 'barley'; the form of the adjective is not without parallel, cf. *wa-na-se-wi-ja*
235 = Ta711 from ϝάνασσα.

doelos patēr, mātēr de . . . .

ku-te-re-u-pi: Georgiev and Andrews suggest *khutreuphi* 'potters'; but the ordinary word ‡
for 'potter' is *kerameus* (**52** = An26), and its recurrence as first word on Na01 seems
to prove that it is a place-name (see p. 297). It is presumably the instrumental plural
of an ethnic in *-eus*, used to designate the area. The *-phi* suffix must here have locative
functions. It is natural to connect this with *ku-te-ra₃* Aa14, Ab22, gen. plur. *ku-te-ra-o*
Ad696; some derivative of the island *Kuthēra*? *ku-te-re-u-pi* refers perhaps to a colony
of Kytherans settled within the Pylian territory.

e-qe-ta-i: *heqᵘetā'i* = ἑπέταις. The added *-i* is the mark of the dative plural, whatever the form intended (see p. 84). Palmer is right in supposing the *heq^{u}etās* to be an important person (see on **57**=An43 below), probably a companion of the king.

† *e-e-to*: the initial *e-e-* recalls *e-e-si* and suggests that this too is some part of εἰμί; possibly the 3rd plural present imperative, to be read *eestō(n)* or *eentō(n)*. But an imperative seems out of place here. Andrews has called attention to the gloss ἔαντο· ἦσαν (Hesych.), and suggested that this is some sort of 3rd plural imperfect (= *ēhent). Perhaps the middle conjugation is not impossible; cf. Hom., Aeol. ἔσσο, Delph. ἦται, Mess. ἦνται (dubious Hom. εἴατο *Od*. xx, 106).

te-re-te-we: apparently dative singular, or nominative plural or dual of a stem in *-us* or *-eus*. The difficulty is that if from *-eus*, it must be masculine and so cannot apply to the women. The analogy of the other entries leads us to expect that this too has something to do with parentage, but so far it has proved impossible to extract any convincing meaning from it. The figure 6 may have been changed to 13 to include the 7 recorded below.

di-wi-ja: possibly nominative feminine singular of an adjective *diwios* = Hom. δῖος; perhaps in the meaning 'of Zeus' not found in Homer; cf. the month name *di-wi-jo-jo* KN Fp5 (see p. 305). More likely to be equated with *di-u-ja* (cf. *me-wi-jo/me-u-jo*), both representing a pronunciation *diwja*, which is certainly a divine name in **172**=Kn02; cf. Διϝι[α] (=Magna Mater according to Meister) in a Pamphylian inscription (Schwyzer, *Dial*. 686, 1). If so, to be read here as genitive, another of the slaves belonging to deities.

6. INDIVIDUAL MEN AT KNOSSOS (As)

In some cases persons are recorded singly; in such cases the name is usually given, followed by the trade or duties to which he is assigned. The purpose of these records is probably to keep a note of the numbers for whose feeding or payment the palace is responsible, as in the case of the groups of women.

‡ **29**=As821　(K　lix)

1]-*ra-jo e-qe-ta-e̞ e-ne-ka ti-mi-to* MEN 2　*ki-ta-ne-to* / *su-ri-mo e-ne-ka o-pa* MAN 1
2]-*ṇẹ-we e̞-ṛạ i-je-*[*re*]-*u po-me e-ne-ka* / *o-pa* MAN 1　*ko-pe-re-u* / *e-qe-ta e-ki-si-jo*
　　　　　　　　　　　　　　　　　　　　　　　　　　　　　　　　　MAN 1

　…two followers on account of *tribute*; *Ki-ta-ne-to* at *Su-ri-mo^p* on account of *dues*; …priest at *E-ra*, shepherd on account of *dues*; *Kopreus*, follower, of *Exos^p*.

For the readings see *KT II*. The tablet is badly preserved and many signs are doubtful.
e-qe-ta-e: a strange form, but in view of the numeral 2 possibly intended as a dual. Perhaps the termination of the consonant stems extended to the masculine *a*-stems.
ti-mi-to: read by Palmer (1954*b*, p. 49) as *Themi(s)tos* in the Pylos place-name *ti-mi-to a-ke-e*. Here possibly as a common noun = 'dues, tribute', cf. λιπαρὰς τελέουσι θέμιστας *Il.* ix, 156 (if rightly so taken).

ki-ta-ne-to: a man's name which reappears in connexion with the place *Su-ri-mo* on Da1108.

o-pa: a word which recurs several times at Knossos and once at Pylos, usually following a man's name in the genitive. Perhaps *hopā* < **soqᵘā*, postulated as the base of ὀπάων. But a sense 'retinue, following' seems absurd here, in particular of a shepherd. It may be a feudal term and like *ti-mi-to* mean some form of service or goods due to the lord. This would give a satisfactory semantic development for ὀπάων, ὀπηδός, but the etymology is obscure.

e̦-ṛa i-je-[re]-u: Bennett read *ta-ra-pu₂?-je-[*. If correct *e-ra* may be either genitive of the goddess Hera, or more likely locative of the place-name. Is the same man both priest and shepherd?

ko-pe-re-u: a man's name also found at Pylos; = Κοπρεύς *Il.* xv, 639.

e-ki-si-jo: the word has been split to leave room for the ideogram and numeral. Ethnic adjective from the common place-name *e-ko-so*, thus showing that the vowel after *k* is 'dead'; cannot be Ἄξος (= Ϝάξος).

7.   INDIVIDUAL MEN AT PYLOS (Ae)

30 = Ae03 [264]   †

pi-ra-jo | ai-ki-pa-ta   su-ra-te   du-ni-jo-⟨jo⟩   me-tu-ra   su-ra-se   MAN [1]
Philaios the goat-herd (who is acting as?) *seizer has seized* the *cattle* of Dunios.

ai-ki-pa-ta: *aigipa(s)tās*? The first part of the compound is obvious; Palmer (1954*b*, p. 24) derives the second from the verbal root **pat-* 'see', found in Cypr. glosses, and in the reduplicated form παπταίνω.

su-ra-te: apparently the agent noun from the verb to which *su-ra-se* belongs. The identification with συλάω seems hard to avoid, but the sense is unsatisfactory. Cattle-raiding is not to be excluded, but the use of a formal agent noun added to the trade-name is puzzling. The phrase *du-ni-jo-jo me-tu-ra su-ra-se* recurs on two other tablets of this group (Ae01, Ae02).

du-ni-jo: a common name at Knossos as well as Pylos, where he is called 'servant of the god' (**143** = Ep705).

me-tu-ra: presumably the object of *su-ra-se*; = μίτυλα 'hornless cattle'?

su-ra-se: aor. *sulāse* or fut. *sulāsei*?

31 = Ae04 [134]   (see plate II (*b*), facing p. 110)

ke-ro-wo po-me a-si-ja-ti-ja o-pi ta-ra-ma-⟨ta⟩-o qe-to-ro-po-pi o-ro-me-no MAN I
Ke-ro-wo the shepherd at *A-si-ja-ti-ja*ᵇ watching over the cattle of Thalamatas.

ke-ro-wo: nom. of an *o*-stem, as the gen. *ke-ro-wo-jo* is found **62** = Cn655. Not therefore gen. to *ke-ro-we* Cn09, as proposed by Carratelli (1954, p. 90).

a-si-ja-ti-ja: it is impossible to determine the case, but a locative-dative is preferable to genitive on grounds of syntax.

ta-ra-ma-⟨ta⟩-o: restored from the following tablet.
qe-to-ro-po-pi: *qᵘetropo(d)phi* = τετράποσι.

32 = Ae05 [108]

qo-te-ro   ai-ki-pa-ta   o-pi   ta-ra-ma-ta-o   qe-[to-ro-po-pi]   o-ro-me-[no   MAN 1]
Qo-te-ro the goat-herd watching over the cattle of Thalamatas.

† **33 = Ae07 [26]**

ko-ru-da-ro-jo   do-e-ro   o-pi   pe-mọ   MEN 4[
Four (or more) slaves of Korudallos *in charge of seed-corn.*

pe-mo: *spermōi*: a more likely reading than *pe-mẹ*. The numeral must be between 4 and
  8 if written normally (cf. Dow, 1954, p. 124).

8. WORK GROUPS OF MEN AT KNOSSOS (Am, As, B)

‡ **34 = Am601   (? xciv)**

		e-te *e-so-to* *a-mo-ra-ma*
to-so	*a-mi-ni-si-jo*	MEN 9

Total men of Amnisos: nine; the *rations* are to be from there.

e-te: *enthen?*
e-so-to: either a full spelling of *estō* 'let there be', or a 3rd plur. future *essontoi.*
a-mo-ra-ma: *harmolāma* 'food-levy'? (cf. ἁρμαλιά and see Vocabulary, p. 387). The note
  presumably implies that Amnisos, not Knossos, is responsible for providing their rations.

¶ **35 = Am819   (K)**

	we-ke-i-ja	MEN 18 *ko-wo* 8
pa₂-ra	/ *si-to*	MONTH? 1 BARLEY 9 T 7 ◁ 3

At Pharai^P: wages for eighteen men and eight boys: grain *per month* 1170 l.
  of barley.

we-ke-i-ja: possibly a derivative of ἔργον. Furumark (1954, p. 22) = 'Tagewerk'.
  Ventris has suggested that the crescent-shaped ideogram **34* may be the moon,
  used ideographically for month, as frequently in other languages, though Greek uses
  different words. The quantity of the rations works out at 45 l. per person if the boys
  are reckoned on the same scale as the men. This is high in comparison with the
  issues to women at Pylos (p. 158). But this is an issue of barley, and is perhaps the
  wages of free men, not a ration for slaves.

†† **36 = B 817   (K   lx)**

to-so / ku-su-to-ro-pa₂   MEN^b [
So many men in aggregate....
ku-su-to-ro-pa₂: *xunstrophā.*
The significance of the alternative forms of the ideogram for man is still unknown.

37 = B 823

MEN[b] 10

tu-wi-jo | ta-pa-e-o-te   *a-pe-o-te*   MEN[b] 4

...men, ten *present*, four absent.

ta-pa-e-o-te: plainly the opposite of *apeontes* 'absent'; perhaps *tarpha eontes*, with an adverbial formation in *-ă* (cf. θαμά) from ταρφέες.

38 = As1516   (?   lxxxvii)   †

This, the longest Knossos tablet, consists of an enumeration by name of at least sixty-seven men, under headings which suggest, as seen by Furumark (1954, p. 19) administrative areas. There are a number, though not a large proportion, of convincingly Greek names: Philinos, Agoraios, Purwos, [De]xelawos, Khariseus, Opsios, Amphiwastos, Amphilawos. But many others are equally certainly non-Greek: e.g. *pa₂-me-si-jo, mi-ja-ra-ro, si-ja-pu₂?-ro, pi-ja-si-ro, pi-ja-se-me*.

¹ [illegible introduction in large letters]
² *ko-no-si-ja*   *ra-wa-ke-⟨si⟩-ja*   *a̯-nu-wi-ko*   MAN 1 [
³ *a-ra-da-jo*   MAN 1   *pi-ja-si-ro*   MAN 1   *da̯-me-*[   ]   MAN 1
⁴   ]-*ro*   MAN 1   *po-to*   MAN 1   *si-pu₂?*   MAN 1   *pu-te*   MAN 1   *ja-sa-no*
                                                    MAN 1
⁵ *pa₂-me-si-jo*   MAN 1   *mi-ja-ra-ro*   MAN 1   *mi-ru-ro*   MAN 1
⁶ [*a*]-*ki-wa-ta*   MAN 1   *u-ra-mo-no*   MAN 1   *pi-ri-no*   MAN 1
⁷ *qa-to-no-ro*   MAN 1   *pe-te-ki-ja*   MAN 1   *ko-ni-da-jo*   MAN 1
⁸ *a-ko-ra-jo*   MAN 1   *wa-du-na-to*   MAN 1   *qo-te-ro*   MAN 1
⁹ *i-te-u*   MAN 1   *pu-to-ro*   MAN 1   *ka-ri-se-u*   MAN 1   *ai-ko-ta*   MAN 1
¹⁰ *ka-ke*   MAN 1   *ru-na*   MAN 1   *pu-wo*   MAN 1   *a-ta-ze-u*   MAN 1
¹¹ *a-ra-na-ro*   MAN 1   *si-ja-pu₂?-ro*   MAN 1   *to-so* × MEN 31
¹² [*?pa-i*]-*ti--jo*   *a-nu-to*   *pa₂-si-re-wi-ja*   MAN 1   *su-ki-ri-to*   MAN 1,
                etc., etc.
¹⁹ *pi-ja-se-me*   MAN 1   *to-so* × MEN 23
²⁰ *se-to-i-ja | su-ke-re-o*   *pa₂-si-re-wi-ja*   MAN 1   *ku-to*   MAN 1,   etc.

This tablet divides into three sections, listing men under three place-names, Knossos, Setoia and a third which is lost in a lacuna. The first two sections end with a totalling formula and a check-mark; the end of the last section is lost. The heading is illegible.

ra-wa-ke-⟨si⟩-ja: almost certainly to be corrected as the corresponding term in sections 2 and 3 is *pa₂-si-re-wi-ja* (*basilēwia*); presumably a feminine or neuter noun has to be understood. The use of these terms suggests that the *basilēwes* of subordinate districts were in some sense analogous to the *lāwāgetās* at Knossos.

The first MAN ideogram in each paragraph does not seem to be included in the totals; possibly *a-nu-wi-ko* is an adverbial phase (see Vocabulary, p. 388).

† **39** = As1517   (?   lxxxviii)

1   ]-*no   re-qo-me-no*
2 ? *pa₂*]-*si-re-u* I   *a-di-nwa-ta* I
3 .]-*sa-ta* I   *ti-pa₂-jo* I
4 *da-wa-no* I   [   ]-*wo* I
5 *qi-qe-ro* I   *wi-du-*[   ] I
6 *ku-ra-no* I   *da̭-wi̭-*[.] I
7 *e-ru-to-ro* I   *ku-ta-i-jo* I
8 *ku-r̭o-nu-we-to* I   *pa₂-ra-jo* I
9 *ri-zo* I   *pa-na-re-jo* I
10 *ke-ka-to* I   *to-so*   MENᵇ 17
            vacat
12 *o-pi   e-sa-re-we   to-ro-no-wo-ko*
13 *po-to-ri-jo* I   *pe-we-ri-io* I
14   *dṷ-ni-jo* I

REVERSE: vacat
        za-mi-jo   MEN 9
                vacat

leiqᵘomenoi: 'being left'?

basileus: the local chieftain? Or a personal name? He is counted in the total. Note the omission of the MAN ideogram.

to-so: Bennett's reading *to-sa* seems to be unjustified when compared with the form of *sa* written in line 3. The sign was originally intended for something else, and has been corrected. Furumark (1954, p. 19) also reads *to-so*.

o-pi e-sa-re-we: *opi ---ēwei thronoworgoi*: *Ptoliōn, Pe-we-ri-jo, Dunios*. *e-sa-re-u* seems to be the title of an official, but the meaning of the whole phrase is obscure. *Thronoworgoi* may be makers of chairs or garlands, but notice that the form of θρόνος at Pylos is *to-no*. *Po-to-ri-jo* is more likely a man's name than the genitive of *ptolis*.

9.   WORK GROUPS OF MEN AT PYLOS (An)

The key to the following tablet lies in the word *ke-ro-si-ja*, which is found again only on An23. It appears to describe both individuals and groups of men, and is most likely *geronsia* (=γερουσία) 'council of elders'. Each entry is introduced by a name in the genitive. Of these four names, *A-pi-qo-ta* and *Ta-we-si-jo* are found as men's names at Knossos. The only one to recur at Pylos is *A-pi-qo-ta* who seems to be called *basileus* at *A-pe-ke-e* on Jn03; the entry is marred by a lacuna. It would therefore seem likely that these four are *basilēwes* or local chieftains, and the list records some of their counsellors. On the reverse the numbers seem to be much larger than the totals of the individual entries.

40 = An22 [261] (joined with 857) †

1   ]-*ẉẹ*   *ke-ʽke-tu-wo-e'*

2 *o-ta₂-we-o*   *ke-ro-si-ja*   *ai-nu-me-no*   MAN [1]

3 *o-ta₂-we-o*   *ke-ro-si-ja*   *qo-te-ro*   MAN [1]

4 *o-ta₂-we-o*   *ke-ro-si-ja*   *a₂-e-ta*   [MAN 1]

5 *o-ta₂-we-o*   *ke-ro-si-ja*   *o-du-pa₃-ro*   [MAN 1]

6 *a-pi-jo-to*   *ke-ro-si-ja*   *ku-[ne?]-u*   MAN [1]

7 *a-pi-jo-to*   *ke-ro-si-ja*   *o-wo-to*   MAN 1

8 *a-pi-jo-to*   *ke-ro-si-ja*   *a-ra-i-jo*   MAN 1

9 *a-pi-jo-[to]*   *ke-ro-si-ja*   *ri-zo*   MAN 1

10 *ta-we-[si-jo-jo]*   *ke-ro-si-ja*   [   ]   MAN 1

11 *ta-we-si-[jo]-jo*   *ke-ro-si-ja*   [   ]   MAN 1

12 *ta-we-si-[jo]-jo*   *ke-ro-si-ja*   [.]-*wa-ne-u*   MAN 1

13 *a-pi-qo-[ta-o]*   *ke-ro-si-ja*   *ai-so-ni-jo*   MAN 1

14 *a-[pi-qo-ta-o]*   *ke-ro-si-ja*   *a-[.]-te*   MAN [1]

15 [   ]   *ke-ro-si-ja*   *a-*[   ]   MAN 1

16 [   ]   MAN 1

17 [*ke-ro*]-*si-ja*   *o-*[.]-*ka-*[

18 *a-*[*pi-qo-ta-o*   *ke-ro-si*]-*ja*   *o-ro-*[

REVERSE:

1 *ta-we-si-jo-jo*   *ke-ro-si-ja*   *te-*[MAN 1]

2 [*ta-we*]-*si-jo-jo*   *ke-ro-si-ja*   *tu-ru-we-u*   MAN 1

               vacat

4 [*ta*]-*we-si-jo-jo*   *ke-ro-si*   (sic)   MEN 20

5 *a-pi-qo-ta-o*   *ke-ro-si-ja*   MEN 17

6 *a-pi-o-to*   *ke-ro-si-ja*   MEN [18]

7 *o-ṭo-ẉọ-*[*o*   *ke*]-*ro-si-ja*   MEN [14]

               vacat

9 *ka-ma-e-*[*we*]   MEN 10[+?]

It is singularly unfortunate that the first line is fragmentary. *ke-ke-tu-wo-e* is conceivably a perfect participle. At line 5 of the reverse the hand changes.

o-ta₂-we-o: it seems clear that this is the same name as that spelt *o-to-wo-o* in line 8 of the reverse and in An23, despite the phonetic difficulties. It is less certain if it is the same name as *o-tu-wo-we* who is a smith at *E-ni-pa-te-we* (**255** = Jn658, Jn725); the dative of which *o-to-wo-we-i* recurs on Vn851.

Lines 5–8 of the reverse are apparently repeated by An23 lines 1–4, thus allowing the restorations shown in the text.

ka-ma-e-we: this is the name given to holders of land called *ka-ma* who represent a special feudal class: see p. 261.

† **41** = An14 [35]

¹ *to-ko-do-mo   de-me-o-te*
² *pu-ro*   MEN 2   *me-te-to-de*   MEN 3
³ *sa-ma-ra-de*   MEN 3   *re-u-ko-to-ro*   MEN 4
            vacat
⁵ *a-ta-ro   tu-ru-pte-ri-ja   o-no*
⁶ WOOL 2   SHE-GOATS 4   Ⓜ 3   WINE 10   FIGS 4

Masons who are to build: Pylos two, to *Me-te-to*ᵖ three, to *Sa-ma-ra*ᵖ three,
Leuktron four.

A-ta-ro . . . : 6 kg. of wool, four she-goats, three . . . , 360 l. of wine, 480 l. of figs.

toikhodomoi demeontes. The classical distinction between τοῖχος and τεῖχος is not necessarily to be read into this compound. It is not impossible that this is an attempt to
put the defences in order, though it may relate merely to normal building operations.
The distinction between the places which have the suffix of motion *-de* and those
which have not may imply that the masons are already at Pylos and Leuktron (to be
read as locatives) and are being sent to the other towns.

a-ta-ro: the relation of this entry to the preceding is obscure; perhaps we should not
look for a connexion between them. The phrase *tu-ru-pte-ri-ja o-no* recurs on Un01,
preceded by *ku-pi-ri-jo* which is probably there a man's name, *Kuprios*; hence *a-ta-ro*
here may be one too.

tu-ru-pte-ri-ja: a connexion with θρύπτω seems obvious, though it is hard to interpret
if the meaning is 'crushing'.

o-no: Furumark (1954, p. 33) proposes to interpret as ὦνος despite the absence of
digamma (< *Ϝοσνος) 'Einkaufspreis'. Carratelli (1954, p. 94) similarly 'cost of
demolition'? Palmer (1954 *b*, p. 22) prefers ὄνος in the sense of 'mill-stone'. In the
latter case the significance of the commodities enumerated is obscure.

On the ideogram **146*, perhaps some sort of textile, see p. 290.

42 = An17 [37]

¹ *o-za-mi-*[   ] *e-ne-ka*
² *pa-ra-we-wo* [. .]-*jo*
³ *a-pi-no-e̦-*[   ] MEN 2
⁴ *e-na-*[*po-ro*   ] ɪ
⁵ [   ]

This tablet is clearly related to **250** = Vn01 (p. 348), which is an account of a distribution
of wine. The sense of the heading here is puzzling and no translation seems safe
enough to print.

o-za-mi-[: Ventris connects with ζημιόω 'thus they are penalized'. The occupational
name *za-mi-jo* (of uncertain meaning) might be better as this is a list of men; but
o- at Pylos is normally followed by a verb.

pa-ra-we-wo: cf. **250** = Vn01. Possibly a man's name. The next word is not [*wo-no*]-*jo*
   as the parallel might suggest. The list appears to consist of place-names in the locative.

An29 is unique among the Pylos 'man' tablets in that its second paragraph †
lists not MEN but the symbols 'ZE I' which normally indicate 'one pair'.
Webster has drawn our attention to the close parallel shown by Sn01, in which
the entries also count 'one pair'; where the paragraphs are similarly introduced by *o-da-a₂*; and where the *ktoinans ekhontes* of line 12 can be taken as
a direct antithesis to the *aktoinoi* of An29.9 (cf. *talasian ekhontes/atalasioi* on
253 = Jn01, etc.). The two tablets have here been printed together on the
assumption that they belong to a single set; they are similar in size and are in
the same hand.

The first paragraph of Sn01 would appear to introduce the set, since its
individuals are important enough to be described as *?ba]silēwjonte* and classified as *mo-ro-pa₂* and *ko-re-te* ('mayor of a village'?). This paragraph evidently
covers much the same territory as **258** = Kn01, a list of contributions of gold,
where the men's names Luros, Poikiloqᵘs, Psolion and the place-names *I-te-re-wa*
and *Ti-mi-ti-ja* recur (also *a-to-mo*).

The second paragraph of Sn01 and the two sections of An29 (here lettered
as § 3 and § 4, admittedly without any certain justification) then seem to
record members of successively lower classes in the hierarchy. § 2 embraces
the class of '*ktoina*-holders' or *telestai*; § 3 lists a class of men who are evidently
particularly involved in the 'military tablets', since the names *Ne-wo-ki-to*,
Ro-u-ko, *A-e-ri-qo-ta* and *Ai-ko-ta* recur there (**59** = An656, **57** = An43, **56** =
An657, **56** = An657); and finally § 4 refers to the men 'without a *ktoina*'. Other
names common both to this set and to the 'military tablets' are Klumenos
(§ 1 and **58** = An654), *Ke-ki-jo* (§ 4 and **56** = An657) and possibly Eruthras
(§ 1 and **58** = An654).

The identity of the object which is counted in pairs is not hinted at, and is
hard to guess (horses?). More puzzling still is the ideogram **Ï**, of which Sn01
shows a subsidiary accounting and which has earned Sn01 its isolated position
in Bennett's classification. This is found twice at Knossos, but not in helpful
contexts: G 464 records the *o-pe-ro* of two places, which is not less than **Ï** 4
and 3156 litres of barley in one case, and not less than **Ï** 4 and 1800 litres
of barley in the other. The other Knossos tablet, G 519, is only a fragment,
but mentions *kupairos* and *apudosis*. All that can be deduced from the Pylos
tablet is that it is counted in multiples of three, and is the object or product
of the verb *a-ke-re-se*; it does not occur where this verb is absent or negatived,
although the item 'one pair' is common to all the entries except two. The
enigmatic ideogram will be shown as x in transcription and translation.

† **43 = Sn01 [64]**

¹ [±5   ]-*ṣị-re-wi-jo-te*
² [   ]-*ja   mo-ro-pa₂   to-to   we-to   o-a-ke-re-se*   ZE I   X 3
³ *ka-do-wo   mo-ro-pa₂   o-u-qe   a-ke-re-se*   ZE I
⁴ *ru-ro   mo-ro-pa₂   o-u-qe   a-ke-re-se*   ZE I
⁵ *ku-ru-me-no   mo-ro-pa₂   i-te-re-wa   ko-re-te   to-to   we-to   [o]-a-ke-re-se*   X 6
⁶ *pẹ-ri-mo   ti-mi-ti-ja   ko-re-te   to-to   we-to   [o]-a-ke-re-se*   ZE I   X 3
⁷ *pe-ri-me-de-o   i-*65   po-so-ri-jo-no   te-ra-ni-ja   a-ke-re-se   to-to   we-to   'o-a-ke-re-se'*
                                                                           X 12

⁸ *po-ki-ro-qo   e-qe-o   a-to-mo*   ZE I
         vacant 3
¹² *o-da-a₂   ko-to-na   e-ko-te*
¹³ *e-ta-wo-ne-u   to-to-we-to   o-a-ke-re-se*   ZE I   X 6
¹⁴ *a-qi-zo-we   {to-to}   to-to-we-to   o-a-ke-re-se*   ZE I   [x nn]
¹⁵ *ne-qe-u   e-te-wo-ke-re-we-i-jo   to-to   we-to   o-a-ke-re-se*   ZE I   [x nn]
¹⁶ *me-ẉị   e-ru-ta-ra   me-ta-pa   ki-e-wo   to-to-we-to   o-a-ke-re-se*   ZE I   [x nn]

§ 1   Those functioning as *basilēwes* [contribute as follows?]:
[So-and-so] the share-holder this year *took* as follows: one pair, three x.
Ka-do-wo the share-holder did not *take*: one pair.
Luros the share-holder did not *take*: one pair.
Klumenos the share-holder, *mayor* of *I-te-re-wa*, this year *took* as follows: six x.
Perimos the *mayor* of *Thimistia* this year *took* as follows: one pair, three x.
The *son* of Perimedes *took*. . .of Psolion, this year he *took* as follows: twelve x.
Poikiloqᵘs the. . . : one pair.

§ 2   And the holders of land as follows:
Etawoneus this year *took* as follows: one pair, six x.
A-qi-zo-we this year *took* as follows: one pair, x x.
Ne-qe-u son of Etewoklewes this year *took* as follows: one pair, x x.
Me-wi Eruthras at Metapa *of Ki-e-u* this year *took* as follows: one pair, x x.

In line 1, Bennett suggests the restoration [*pa₂*]-*si-re-wi-jo-te* = *basilēwjontes*. It is in any
case likely that this fragmentary word is the nom. masc. plur. of a present participle
of a verb in -εύω (Elean -είω), thereby confirming Brugmann's proposed derivation
from *-ήϝjω (Schwyzer, *Gram.* I, p. 728 n. 1).
mo-ro-pa₂: *mo(i)ro-ppās* 'possessor of a share or portion'; evidently a high ranking title.
to-to we-to: despite the phonological difficulties this must be *tōto* (=τοῦτο) *wetos*;
contrast *hateron wetos* on PY **178** = Ma13.
o-a-ke-re-se: that this contains a separable *o-* is proved by lines 3, 4 and 7: *hō agrēse*.
The sense in which the verb is used cannot be guessed without a knowledge of the
meaning of the ideograms. A future *agrēsei* is also possible.

i-*65: Ventris suggests a comparison with Ἶνις; but it is not yet possible to give a certain value to this sign.

te-ra-ni-ja: is this perhaps the word represented by the ideogram x? 'Thus he took the *te-ra-ni-ja* of Psolion'? Or a place-name?

e-qe-o a-to-mo: cf. *e-qe-a-o a-to-mo* KN V 56. Mühlestein has suggested that *i-ẓạ a-to-mo-i* on **91** = Fn02 is an alternative spelling (though the trades there seem to be much more humble), and reads *eqⁿeaōn/iqⁿjās arthmos*, 'chariot joiner' (cf. *i-qi-ja* on **266** = Sd0401, etc.): this appears extremely doubtful.

o-da-a₂ ko-to-na e-ko-te: Andrews understands the word *o-da-a₂* as a verb, Furumark (1954, p. 38) as a substantive 'Anteil': he translates the heading to § 3 as 'Leute, die schuldig sind, Anteile zu liefern', and to § 4 as 'Folgende landlose Leute... Anteile'. But its position as first word in its clause, and the fact that it often parallels a verbal prefix *o-* elsewhere on the same tablet, make it virtually certain that it is an introductory particle, probably an expanded form of *o-*.

to-to to-to-we-to: dittography.

e-ru-ta-ra: to understand a feminine name here ('*Me-wi* the red'?) conflicts with the exclusively masculine character of the rest of the list. 'Eruthras the younger' (for *me-wi-jo*?).

ki-e-wo: gen. of *Ki-e-u* **55** = An724? His position in the syntax is obscure, but perhaps parallel to *Psolionos* in line 7.

44 = An29 [218]   †

1 *o-da-a₂   a-na-ke-e   o-pe-ro-ṭẹ   [?   ]*
2 *ri-so-wa   i-je-re-u   [   ]*   MAN I
3 *ne-wo-ki-to   i-je-[re]-u   da-i-ja-ke-re-u*   MAN I
4 *[ro]-u-ko   ku-sa-me-ni-jo   me-ta-pa*   MAN I
5 *a-e-ri-qo-ta   [   ]   o-wi-to-no*   MAN I
6 *ai-ko-ta   a-da-ra-[ti-jo?]*   MAN I

         vacant 2

9 *o-da-a₂   e-ke-jo-to   a-ko-to-no*
10 *pa-ku-ro₂   de-wi-jo*   ZE I
11 *[? a]-ka-re-u   e-ko-me-na-ta-o   ai₂?-te*   ZE I
12 *[   ]   ke-ki-jo*   ZE I
13 *[? pi]-me-ta   po-ru-da-si-jo*   ZE I
14 *[   ]   me-nu-a₂*   ZE I
15 *ma-ra-te-u   a-pu-ka*   ZE I
16 *[.]-qo-te-wo   i-*65*   ZE I

REVERSE:

di-we-si-p̣ọ-ụ-ti-mi-to-qo-[   ]

§ 3   And those who are obliged to bring (men?), as follows:
    Ri-so-wa the priest...: one man.

Ne-wo-ki-to the priest, the *divider of lands*: one man.
Ro-u-ko the son of Kusamenos at Metapa: one man.
Aeriq^{u}hoitas...at *O-wi-to-no^p*: one man.
Ai-ko-ta son of Adrastos: one man.

§ 4　And those without land *are included* as follows:

　Pa-ku-ro$_2$...: one pair,
　　　　　　etc.

a-na-ke-e: *anageen* 'bring, contribute'. There does not seem to be room in the damaged portion at the end of the line for an explicit object to the verb, but ἄγω demands that it should be a person or an animal. It is not clear whether the MAN ideograms in lines 2–6 refer to Aeriq^{u}hoitas, etc., or merely to unnamed men that they have supplied. The analogy of the other paragraphs favours the latter.
o-pe-ro-te: *ophélontes*.
da-i-ja-ke-re-u: this may also be a place-name (like *Me-ta-pa*, etc. in succeeding lines. Cf. *O-re-mo-a-ke-re-u*, *Pu$_2$?-ra$_2$-a-ke-re-u*.
e-ke-jo-to: possibly the 3rd plural present of ἔγκειμαι; see Vocabulary, p. 392.
ai$_2$?-te: cf. *ai-te-re*, name of an occupation on KN **48** = B 101.
ma-ra-te-u: perhaps a title rather than a name; cf. **56** = An657, **195** = Na67.
a-pu-ka: cf. *a-pu$_2$?-ka* **59** = An656, *a-pu$_2$?-ka-ne* **56** = An657. Apparently a place-name.
i-*65 with a name in the genitive: cf. **43** = Sn01.7.

The following badly damaged tablet is interesting for its reference to large numbers of men in various occupations, and to areas of land expressed by the abbreviation DA (see p. 242).

† **45** = An830

　　　　　　　3 lines illegible
　　^{4} *ma-ra-ti-sa*　[　　　　　　　　　　]
　　　　　　vacat
　　^{6} *a-te-re-wi-ja*　*e-o*　*ko-re-te-ri-jo*　*ke-ke-me-no*　DA 30[
　　　　　　vacat
　　^{8} *e-sa-re-wi-ja*　*pa-ro-ni-ja*　*te-u-po-ro-*[?]　⟦DA nn⟧
　　^{9} [　　　]*-no*　DA 50
　^{10} [　　　　　　　　　　　　] MEN 18
　^{11} [　　　*qo*]*-u-ko-ro*　*ra-wa-ra-ti-ja*　MEN 66
　^{12} *o-pi-da-mi-jo*　*pi-*82*　*qo-*[*u-ko*]*-ro*　MEN 60
　^{13} *a$_2$-ki-ja*　*qo-u-ko-ro*　MEN 60[

A-te-re-wi-ja: a place-name; derivative of Ἀτρεύς?
e-o: the masc. or neut. participle *eŏn* is surprising unless *A-te-re-wi-ja* is a masculine *a*-stem: 'which is common land belonging to the *ko-re-te*'? Bennett reads *e-so*.

178

DA: in view of **114** = En02 probably a unit of superficial area.

e-sa-re-wi-ja: a derivative of the title *e-sa-re-u*, apparently functioning as a place-name: 'the settlement of the *e*.'? Bennett reads *ro-ro-ni-ja* for *pa-ro-ni-ja*.

Lines 11–13 record *gʷoukoloi* 'cowherds' at three places; those at *Pi-*82 are described as *opidāmioi* 'local inhabitants'? *a₂-ki-ja* is not mentioned elsewhere. †

10. WORK GROUPS OF MEN AT MYCENAE ‡

One of the few tablets found at Mycenae seems to fall into this class of tablets dealing with occupational groups. It is a mere list of names, with the trade-name as a separate entry at the bottom.

46 = Au102 (see frontispiece) ¶

1 *wa-ra-pi-si-ro i-jo-qe*	MEN	2
2 *na-su-to*	MAN	1
3 *te-ra-wo ka-ri-ṣe-u-qe*	MEN	2
4 *e-ke-ne e-u-po-ro-qe*	MEN	2
5 **85-ja-to ko-no-pu₂?-du-ro-qe*	MEN	2
6 *ke-re-no*	MEN	2
7 *wa-a₂-ta de-u-ki-jo-qe*	MEN	2
8 *mo-i-da*	MAN	1
9 *o-ri-ko*	MEN	3
vacant 4		
14 *a-to-po-qo*	[ ]	

Where there are two names the second is linked with -*qᵘe*. The numerals in lines 6 and 9 are puzzling if these are men's names.

ke-re-no: *Gerēnos*? recurs in PY Cn12.

a-to-po-qo: *artopoqᵘoi* = ἀρτοκόποι: the lacuna may have contained the summation MEN 17. If so seventeen bakers seems a large number to figure in a tablet from a private house. ††

11. LISTS OF MIXED TRADESMEN AT KNOSSOS

These usually record a place-name followed by numbers of men analysed by trades.

47 = Am826 (K   lix) ‡‡

a-pa-ta-wa-jo / *te-re-ta*   MEN 45[
   te-ko-to-ne   MEN 5

Men of Aptara: forty-five (or more) fief-holders, five carpenters.

179

a-pa-ta-wa-jo: *Aptarwaioi*, cf. *a-pa-ta-wa Aptarwa* KN **83** = Ch902, = Ἄπταρα in Western Crete (so also Furumark, 1954, p. 22). The etymology of this name is unknown; the form Ἄπτερα is clearly due to popular etymology.

te-re-ta: *telestai*, officers of the feudal hierarchy: see Palmer, 1955, p. 11.

te-ko-to-ne: *tektones*.

† **48** = B 101 (? xxiv)

ko-wi-ro-wo-ko MEN[b] [nn] *ai-te-re* MEN[b] 8 [

ko-wi-ro-wo-ko: *kowiloworgoi* 'makers of hollow-ware'? Cf. κοῖλος ἄργυρος καὶ χρυσός Theopomp. *Hist.* 283a, 'silver and gold plate' (Liddell and Scott[9]).

ai-te-re: possibly the agent noun from the verb the participle of which appears as *a-ja-me-na* 'inlaid'. Cf. *ai₂?-te* PY **44** = An29. Chadwick suggests that the correct reading may be *du-*.

‡

12. LISTS OF MIXED TRADESMEN AT PYLOS

These are similar to the parallel group at Knossos though longer and more detailed. The documentation of the workers was obviously more highly organized at Pylos. The full significance of many of the occupational terms cannot now be grasped, even when they are etymologically clear.

¶ **49** = An07 [427]

```
¹ a-pu₂?-we   da-ko-ro   MEN 5   e-ri-no-wo-[te          ]
² pa-ko   me-ri-du-ma-te   MEN 5 [[a]]   a-ke-re-[wa          ]
³ a-to-po-qo   MEN 2 · pi-pu-te   pu-ka-wo   MEN 3   [   ]
```

At *Aipu* five *temple-servants*; at *E-ri-no-wo* . . . ; at *Pa-ko* five . . . ; at *A-ke-re-wa* . . . two bakers; at *Pi-pu* three fire-kindlers. . . .

a-pu₂?-we: a place-name in the dative; perhaps = Αἰπύ (*Il.* II, 592)?

da-ko-ro: *dakoroi* = ζακόροι?

e-ri-no-wo-[te]: cf. PY Na51, Cn09, etc.

me-ri-du-ma-te: one of the compounds of *du-ma*: see Vocabulary.

pu-ka-wo: *purkawoi*, cf. πυρκαεύς, etc.

†† **50** = An18 [39]

¹ *pu-ka-wo* +	MEN 16	
² *me-ri-du-ma-te*	MEN 10 +	
³ *mi-ka-ta* +	MEN 3	
⁴ *o-pi-te-u-ke-e-we*	MEN 4 +	
⁵ *e-to-wo-ko* +	MEN 5	
⁶ *ka-sa-to* +	MAN	

⁷ *pu-ka-wo* +   MEN 23
⁸ *me-ri-da-ma-te*   MEN 6
⁹ [*o-pi*]*-te-u-ke-e-we* MEN 5 +
¹⁰ [*mi-ka*]*-ta*   MEN 6 +
¹¹ [*e-to*]*-wo-ko*   MEN 3   *a-to-po-qo*   MEN 3

REVERSE:

¹ *po̭-ru-da-ma-te*   MEN 4
                    vacat
³ *pa₂-ra₂-te* MAN
⁴ *pu-ko-ro* MAN
⁵ *a̭-ko-so-ṭa̭* MAN
⁶ *pi-ri-ja-me-ja* MAN
⁷ *e-ni-ja-u-si-jo* MAN
⁸ *pte-jo-ṛị* MAN   *qo-ta-wo* [   ]
⁹ *a-ta* MAN   *te-o-po-*[   ]
                    vacant 2

Sixteen fire-kindlers, ten *me-ri-du-ma-te*, three *mi-ka-ta*, four *riggers*, five *armourers*; Xanthos.

Twenty-three fire-kindlers, six *me-ri-da-ma-te*, five *riggers*, six *mi-ka-ta*, three *armourers*, three bakers.

Four *po-ru-da-ma-te*.

For Pallas, Purkolos, Axotas, Priameias, Eniausios, *Pte-jo-ri*, *Qo-ta-wo* (?), Anthas, Theopo(mpos ?).

The obverse falls into two sections (1–6, 7–11) which are in different hands; the second writer also wrote the reverse. Almost all the entries are accompanied by a check-mark (+). The reverse consists, after the first line, of a list of individuals entered by name in the dative case.

me-ri-du-ma-te: see Vocabulary s.v. *du-ma*; in line 8 spelt with *-da-* for *-du-*.

mi-ka-ta: *miktai* 'mixers'?

o-pi-te-u-ke-e-we: *opiteukheēwes*, derivative of τεῦχος, but in what sense?

e-to-wo-ko: from ἔντεα? Cf. *e-te-do-mo*.

ka-sa-to: the attempt of Meriggi (1954, p. 33) and Carratelli (1954, p. 92) to read this as a common noun **xantos* = ξάντης is rendered unlikely by the absence of a numeral with the ideogram; cf. the list of names on the reverse. The mixing of names and occupations in a single list can be paralleled, e.g. An15.

a-ko-so-ta: *Axotas* or *Arxotas* is an important man at Pylos; cf. **154** = Eq01, **103** = Un08, **249** = Va02.

qo-ta-wo: only elsewhere on Na24, where it is probably a place-name; as the ideogram is missing this cannot be excluded here.

† **51** = An20 [18]

¹ e̯-re-u-te-ṛi-[
² te-ko-to-na-pe   MAN [I
³ i-na-ṇi-ja   MAN I [   ]   MAN [   ]
⁴ ṛe-si-we-i   [MAN] I   a-se-e   MAN I
          vacat
⁶ te-re-ne-we   to-ḳo-do-mo-a-pe-o   MAN I
⁷ i̯-na-ne   MAN I   te-ko-to-na-pe   I
          vacat
⁹ qo-u-ko-ro / ti-no   MEN 90
          vacat
¹¹ pa-ki-ja-si   to-so   te-ḳo-ṭo-ne / [ti]-ṇo
¹²   MEN 254[

The heading is again fragmentary and little is clear except that we are told of some missing carpenters and cowherds. The numbers are surprisingly large. Reference to men and women who are 'missing' is also made on **37** = B 823, **55** = An724, Ap633, An33; similar annotation to miscellaneous lists of craftsmen is seen in the Ur tablets (e.g. Legrain, 1947, no. 1486): 'Sculptor, goldsmiths (one missing, two at the smithy),...Ibni-Adad the bow-maker, two smiths (one missing): those of the scale-control. Goldsmiths, fullers, hired tailor, caulkers, two rope-makers (one ill): those in the workshop.'

e-re-u-te-ri-[: dat. of *e-re-u-te-re* PY **76** = Cn22? or *eleutheri(os)*?

te-ko-to-na-pe: the comparison of *te-ko-to a-pe* PY An24 shows convincingly that this is a rare case of sandhi, the final *-n* of *tektōn* coalescing with the initial vowel of the following word. This confirms our supposition that the final consonants were not lost in speech. The meaning of the second word is not plain, but in view of *a-pe-o* in line 6 is probably *apēs* imperfect of ἄπειμι 'was absent'.

i-na-ni-ja: a place-name, cf. PY Ae01, Ae02; the simpler form *i-na-ne* in line 7.

te-re-ne-we: possibly a place-name in the dative; cf. *te-re-ne-wi-ja* An852, a fragment which is clearly similar to this tablet.

to-ko-do-mo-a-pe-o: the word-divider is dropped, but there is no sandhi; *toikhodomos apeōn*.

ti-no: perhaps *thinos* 'of the coast'. Not to be compared with Cret. θῖνα (cf. Carratelli, 1954, p. 216) < θεῖνα. The reading is very uncertain.

pa-ki-ja-si: dat. *-ansi* (cf. *pa-ki-ja-ne* Xc01) of a variant form of the place-name *pa-ki-ja-na*.

‡ **52** = An26 [207]

          about 3 lines missing

⁴ [   ]   MEN 10
⁵ [   ] pi-ri-je-te-re   MEN 2
⁶ [?re-ka-ta]-ne   a-de-te-re   MEN 2
⁷ re-ka-[ta]-ne   ke-ra-me-we   MEN 2

8	*re-ka-ta-ne*	*da-ko-ro*	MEN 12
9	*wa-a₂-te-we*	*po-ku-ta*	MEN 10
10	*a-nu-wa*	*ku-ru-so-wo-ko*	MEN 4
11	[ ]	*me-ri-da-ma-te*	MEN 2
12	[ ]*-jo*	*to-ko-so-wo-ko*	MEN 5
13	*a-pi-no-*[*e-wi-jo*?]		MEN [nn]
14	*so-ro-pe-o*	*ra-pte-re*	[MEN nn]
15	*ko-ri-si-jo*	*ra-pte-re*	[MEN nn]
16	*ka-ro-ke-e*	*ra-pte-re*	[MEN nn]
17	*ra-ni-jo-ne*	*ra-pte-re*	MEN [nn]
18	[ ]*-ka-si-da*	*ra-pte-re*	MEN 20[

A list of tradesmen prefixed by what appear to be ethnic adjectives; very few of these are recorded elsewhere. Some seem to be place-names rather than adjectives. *a-pi-no-e-wi-jo* are mentioned in PY **184** = Nn01, etc.; *ko-ri-si-jo* is probably *Korinsioi* from *ko-ri-to Korinthos*, PY Ad07; *wa-a₂-te-we* is to be connected with *wa-a₂-te-pi* PY Na19.

pi-ri-je-te-re: the singular *pi-ri-je-te* is found on the Knossos sword tablets, which suggests a connexion with πρίω: *prietēre* 'cutlers'?

a-de-te-re: singular PY Eq887. Perhaps *an-detēre* 'binders'.

keramēwe: 'potters'.

da-ko-ro: see on **49** = An07.

po-ku-ta: *pos-khutai* 'wine-pourers'?

ku-ru-so-wo-ko: *khrusoworgoi* 'goldsmiths'.

to-ko-so-wo-ko: *toxoworgoi* 'bow-makers'.

ra-pte-re: *raptēres* 'tailors'; the word has no digamma, see Vocabulary, p. 407.

13. ROWERS AND TROOPS AT PYLOS

The following group of tablets falls into two parts: one naval, one military. The subject-matter of the naval tablets is indicated by the word 'rowers' which appears in the first line of all three. The first is a list of the numbers of rowers to be provided by various towns for an expedition to Pleuron. The second is probably somewhat similar, but the heading is almost all lost, and the numerals are much larger; in all 443 men are recorded, and some numbers are obviously missing in the lacuna at the right-hand edge. These numbers make it certain that we are not here concerned with a peaceful mercantile venture, but a naval operation; and it would be unlikely that the business of trade would be thus organized by a central authority. It is possible that the thirty men specified in **53** = An12 is the complement of a Mycenaean ship; but the evidence of Homer suggests a figure of fifty oarsmen per ship (G. Thomson,

1949, p. 423), so thirty may be only part of the complement or for a smaller ship. The second tablet then appears to allow for at least nine ships. Even so this is a small figure compared with the ninety which Nestor took to Troy. The third tablet is more enigmatic, for despite Bennett's join with a new fragment there are irritating lacunae; the heading speaks clearly of 'rowers who are absent' (without leave?). Until more of the linguistic problems are solved we must be cautious in theorizing about the significance of this document.

† The second group of tablets are distinguished by the word *o-ka*. Only one of these (**57**=An43) was known from the 1939 finds; even so several people, including Palmer (1955, p. 20) and Mühlestein (1954), had suggested that this was a military document, since it associated large numbers of men with place-names. Mühlestein's suggestion that a variant form of the MAN ideogram on these tablets meant 'armed man' is unfounded; it can be shown to be due merely to a difference of handwriting. Palmer interpreted the tablet as a record of troop movements to guard against a threatened invasion from the north— a threat which the destruction of Pylos shows to have been unsuccessfully countered. Mühlestein goes further in identifying some of the places mentioned with historical place-names scattered over the west, north and centre of the Peloponnese; if right this would imply a vast dominion stretching almost to the gates of Mycenae. But would such a kingdom have been controlled from a remote spot in the far south-west? There is no evidence in tradition for such a large kingdom, and it is at variance with the Catalogue of Ships, not that we can expect a close coincidence. More serious is the objection raised by one of the new tablets (**56**=An657), which has a heading preceding the recurrent formula and may therefore have introduced the whole series. This heading informs us that these are dispositions to guard the coastal regions. We must therefore reject any interpretations which involve places far distant from the sea.

Tradition and dialect evidence suggest that the Mycenaean kingdoms fell before invaders coming from the north-west; and there are reasons for thinking that Pylos was especially concerned with the coastal area to the north. The identification of *U-ru-pi-ja-jo* with Ὀλυμπία and of *O-ru-ma-si-jo* with Ἐρύμανθος has independently suggested to several minds that we have a reference to the general area of Elis. The two references to Pleuron are interesting as suggesting, not that Pleuron was in the orbit of Pylos, but that there was an alliance with an Aetolian kingdom; which would be natural enough if the danger came from the north-west. But *O-ka-ra₃* can hardly be the Aetolian Οἰχαλίη; it is very dangerous to press the evidence of place-names (see p. 139). Pylos may have been desperately engaged in an attempt to organize the defence of the whole west coast—an impossible task without immense resources, and the resultant splitting of forces may have been responsible for her defeat.

A curious fact which Palmer and Mühlestein have both emphasized is the connexion between **57**=An43 and **76**=Cn22. Several of the place-names recur, including the pair *o-ka-ra₃ a₂-ra-tu-(w)a*, and the phrase *pi-ru-te ku-re-we* (another pair of place-names according to Palmer). **76**=Cn22 is a list of oxen, and will be discussed in the next chapter. Palmer has attempted to bring the two into close connexion by supposing a religious motive for the distribution of cattle—sacrificial animals to ensure divine favour in the threatened sectors. The clue to this puzzle is the heading of the cattle tablet, on which there is unfortunately still no agreement.

The repeating pattern of the military tablets is plain, though the meaning of some of the key words is not. It begins with a man's name in the genitive followed by *o-ka*. This is most satisfactorily explained as *orkhā*=ἀρχή, presumably in the sense of 'command'; cf. ὄρχαμος. P. von der Mühll suggests *órkhā*=ὄρχος 'Reihe, Zug' (Mühlestein, 1955a, Nachtrag). Then we have a list of from three to seven names in the nominative, presumably the subordinate commanders. The pattern continues with varied phrases including two trade-names *ke-ki-de* and *ku-re-we* (some kind of troops?) accompanied by place-names or ethnics, and followed by MEN and a numeral. Palmer appositely quotes:

ἕπτ᾽ ἔσαν ἡγεμόνες φυλάκων, ἑκατὸν δὲ ἑκάστῳ
κοῦροι ἅμα στεῖχον.... (*Il.* ix, 85–6)

The final item is the formula *me-ta-qe pe-i e-qe-ta* followed by a name. The last word was at first thought to be a verb, but it now appears likely that the middle termination is *-toi* not *-tai* (see p. 87); it must therefore be the noun *heqᵘetās* (=ἑπέτης) used as a title. The name is usually accompanied by a patronymic adjective, a rare distinction which Palmer is probably right in supposing to prove the high rank of the *heqᵘetās*.

53=An12 [1] †

¹ *e-re-ta   pe-re-u-ro-na-de | i-jo-te*
² *ro-o-wa*   MEN 8
³ *ri-jo*   MEN 5
⁴ *po-ra-pi*   MEN 4
⁵ *te-ta-ra-ne* MEN 6
⁶ *a-po-ne-we*   MEN 7
            vacant 2

185

Rowers to go to Pleuron: eight from *Ro-o-wa*, five from Rhion, four from *Po-ra-*, six from *Te-ta-ra-ne*, seven from *A-po-ne-we*.

eretai Pleurōnade iontes: possibly the Homeric Pleuron in Aetolia (*Il.* ii, 639+), but there is no evidence to support a positive identification. All the towns from which the rowers come are mentioned elsewhere, but none are satisfactorily interpreted except *Ri-jo = Rhion*, a common place-name, which is associated with Asine in Messenia.

Po-ra-pi: presumably an instrumental plural serving as locative: *Phorāphi* (Φαραί)? Carratelli (1954, p. 226) = Σπορά(δ)φι.

Te-ta-ra-ne: hardly Τετράνη as suggested by Carratelli as it must be dative.

† **54 = An19 [610]**

1 [ ]-*ne* *e-re-ta*					
2 [ ]-*e* *ki-ti-ta*	MEN 46	[ ]			
3 [ ]-*ta*	MEN 19	[ ]			
4 [ ]-*ḳị-ti-ta*	MEN 36	[ ]			
5 *mẹ-ṭạ-ki-ti-ta*	MEN 3	[ ]			
6 *e-wi-ri-po*	MEN 9	*po-si-ke-te-re* [ ]			
7 *a-ke-re-wa*	MEN 25	*wo-qe-we* [ ]			
8 *ri-jo*	MEN 24	*wi-nu-ri-jo* [ ]			
9 *te-ta-ra-ne*	MEN 31	*me-ta-*[ ]			
10 *a-po-ne-we*	MEN 37	*me-ta-*[ ]			
11 *ma-ra-ne-nu-we*	MEN 40	*po-ti-ja-ke-e*			MẸṆ 6
12 [*za*]-*ku-si-jo*	MEN 8	*za-e-to-ro*			MEN 3
13 *da-mi-ni-jo*	MEN 40	*e-ke-ra₂-wo-no*			MEN 40
14 *we-da-ne-wo*	MEN 20	*ko-ni-jo* 126	*me-ta-ki-ti-ta*	MEN 26	
15 *pọ-ku-ta*	MEN 10	*we-re-ka-ra-⟨ta⟩*	*te-pa₂-ta-qe*	MEN 20	

vacant 5

ki-ti-ta: *ktitai* 'settlers', *metaktitai* 'new residents, metics'? In view of the association with *ktimena* the terms probably have a special feudal meaning.

E-wi-ri-po: place-name, *Euripos*; *A-ke-re-wa*, *Ri-jo*, *Te-ta-ra-ne*, *A-po-ne-we*, and *Ma-ra-ne-nu-we* are all also place-names; cf. **53 = An12**.

po-si-ke-te-re: *pos-ik(e)tēres* 'suppliants, refugees'?

wo-qe-we: cf. **55 = An724**; perhaps a place-name.

wi-nu-ri-jo: place-name or ethnic?

me-ta-[: *metaktitai* or *Metapa*?

po-ti-ja-ke-e: place-name; cf. *Ti-mi-to a-ke-e*.

[*za*]-*ku-si-jo*: cf. *za-ku-si-ja* PY **286** = Sa787 and man's name *Ƶa-ku-si-jo* MY Oe122; = *Ƶakunsioi* (of Zakunthos).

da-mi-ni-jo: a place-name, common on the *D* tablets from Knossos, but only found elsewhere at Pylos in the form *da-mi-ni-ja* **14** = Ad697.

E-ke-ra₂-wo-no, *We-da-ne-wo*: the entries so far have been either place-names, ethnic adjectives or descriptive titles; here we pass abruptly to the genitive of men's names. *Ekhelāwōn* and *We-da-ne-u* are obviously men of importance if they can produce forty and twenty men respectively; Bennett reads the latter figure too as forty; see further pp. 265 and 279.

ko-ni-jo: in view of the absence of the ideogram Ventris proposes *skhoinioi* 'ropes' (see Vocabulary); but the dropping of the ideogram may be due to lack of space.

we-re-ka-ra-⟨ta⟩: cf. PY An08.

55 = An724 (= An32 joined)   †

¹ *ro-o-wa   e-re-ta   a-pe-o-te*
² *me-nu-wa   a-pe-e-ke   a-re-sa-ni-e*
³ *o-pi-ke-ri-jo-de   ki-ti-ta   o-pe-ro-ta* 〚*e*〛
⁴ *e-re-e*   MAN I
⁵ *e-ke-ra₂-wo-ne   a-pe-e-ke   a₂-ri-e* 〚MAN I〛
⁶ *o-pe-ro-te   e-re-e*   MEN 5
⁷ *ra-wa-ke-ta   a-pe-e-[ke   ]-e̯*   MAN [nn]
⁸ *ta-ti-qo-we-u   o-[   ]-qe-[..]*   MAN I
⁹ *a-ke-re-wa   ki-e-u   o-pe-[   ]-e̯   a-ri-ja-to*
¹⁰ *ki-ti-ta*   MAN I   *o-ro-ti-jo   di-qo   a-[..]*
¹¹ *o-pe-r̯o̯ [...]   e-ko-si-qe   e-qe-ta   ka-ma*
¹² *e-to-ni-jo   e-n̯w̯a̯-ri-jo*   MAN I
¹³ *wo-qe-we   [e]-qo-te   ru-ki-ja   a-ko-wo*   M̯A̯N̯ [nn]
¹⁴ *ri-jo   o-no   e-qo-te*   MEN 10[

No translation is attempted in view of the numerous problems. The general sense is plain: there are rowers missing, and certain places and lords are responsible; but it does not seem possible to offer an easy solution to the question why they are missing —absent without leave?—or what is being done about it.

Ro-o-wa: obviously an important coastal town; it provides eight of the thirty men for Pleuron (**53** = An12); it is the seat of a coastal command (**57** = An43). As the Lawagetas and other important people such as Ekhelawon are associated with it here, it may well be the port of Pylos itself.

Me-nu-wa: a man's name found in the form *Me-nu-a₂* **44** = An29; = Μινύας? In view of *E-ke-ra₂-wo-ne* all the three nouns preceding *a-pe-e-ke* are presumably datives. This suggests that *a-pe-e-ke* is an impersonal verb and *a-re-sa-ni-e* and *a₂-ri-e* are infinitives following it. Satisfactory interpretations are lacking. *a-pe-e-ke* fits well as *apheēke* (ἀφίημι), though this is not used impersonally. But there are other possibilities: *ap-eekhe* (ἀπέχω) or *amphe-ekhei* (= ἀμφι-; cf. *a-pi-e-ke* PY **97** = Un03). The sense of *a-re-sa-ni-e* and *a₂-ri-e* cannot be deduced from the context; Ventris compares the latter with *a₂-ri-sa* PY **154** = Eq01.

o-pi-ke-ri-jo-de: only found again, without the *-de* suffix, in a very fragmentary context PY An35, which is possibly another list of rowers. The final *-de* might be enclitic 'but' or the suffix of motion towards. If the former, Ventris suggests *opikhērion*

=ὑποχείριον (cf. *Od.* xv, 448); if the latter, Chadwick proposes a place-name *Opiskherion*, cf. ἐπισχερώ, Σχερίη.

ki-ti-ta: probably *ktitān ophēlonta*.

e-re-e: Ventris: *heleei* 'he will take' (but the future ἑλῶ is only found at a late date). Chadwick: *ereen* infinitive of *ἔρω, root verb later replaced by ἐρέσσω; 'a settler who is under obligation to serve as a rower'. For *ophēlōn* + infin. cf. [*o*]*phēlōn-qᵘe teleiaen* Eb39. In any case this word is probably not the same as *e-re-e* 258 = Kn01, where it appears to be dative of a place-name, probably *Helos*.

o-pe-ro-te: presumably plural *ophēlontes* in view of the numeral 5; but this cannot be reconciled with the accusative in line 3.

ra-wa-ke-ta: *lāwāgetāi* 'the leader of the army'. The lacuna might contain [*a-re-sa-ni*]*-e* or [*o-pe-ro-ta e-re*]*-e*.

Ta-ti-qo-we-u: a man's name, recurring as one of the commanders on the military tablets (**58** = An654); *Stātigᵘoweus*?

A-ke-re-wa: a new section must begin here with the change of scene.

Ki-e-u: apparently a man's name; cf. **43** = Sn01.

o-pe-[: *ophē*[*lōn* (or *-lonta*) *ere*]*en*?

a-ri-ja-to: 3rd sing. middle of *a₂-ri-e*?

o-ro-ti-jo di-qo: the latter may be a man's name at Knossos Dl 930.

e-ko-si-qe: *ekhonsi-qᵘe heqᵘetai khamās ? etonion* ... 'and the followers have the *freehold* of the *holding*'. The vocabulary here is that found on the land ownership tablets; see pp. 253, 261. The connecting link must be the holding of land in return for feudal service.

e-nwa-ri-jo: = *E-nu-wa-ri-jo* = *Enualios*? Bennett reads *e-*[.]*-se-ri-jo*.

wo-qe-we: cf. **54** = An19.

e-qo-te: *heqᵘontes* with active inflexion = ἑπόμενοι?

a-ko-wo: hardly *akorwos* (Homeric ἄκουρος).

Ri-jo: another change of scene.

o-no: cf. **41** = An14, but this may be a different word. The phrase probably recurs on An35 edge.

56 = An657

> ¹ *o-u-ru-to　o-pi-a₂-ra　e-pi-ko-wo*
> ² *ma-re-wo　o-ka　o-wi-to-no*
> ³ *a-pe-ri-ta-wo　o-re-ta　e-te-wa　ko-ki-jo*
> ⁴ *su-we-ro-wi-jo　o-wi-ti-ni-jo　o-ka-ra₃*　MEN 50
> 　　　　　vacat
> ⁶ *ne-da-wa-ta-o　o-ka　e-ke-me-de*
> ⁷ *a-pi-je-ta　ma-ra-te-u　ta-ni-ko*
> ⁸ *a₂-ru-wo-te　ke-ki-de　ku-pa-ri-si-jo*　MEN 20
> 　　　　　vacat
> ¹⁰ *ai-ta-re-u-si　ku-pa-ri-si-jo　ke-ki-de*　MEN 10

¹¹ *me-ta-qe   pe-i   e-qe-ta   ke-ki-jo*
¹² *a-e-ri-qo-ta   e-ra-po   ri-me-ne*
¹³ *o-ka-ra   o-wi-to-no*   MEN 30   *ke-ki-de-qe   a-pu₂?-ka-ne*
¹⁴ MEN 20   *me-ta-qe   pe-i   ai-ko-ta   e-qe-ta*

Thus the watchers are guarding the coast.

§ 1   Command of Maleus at *O-wi-to-no*: Ampelitawon, Orestas, Etewas, Kokkion.

Fifty *su-we-ro-wi-jo* men of *O-wi-to-no* at Oikhalia.

§ 2   Command of Nedwatas: Ekhemedes, *Amphi-e-ta* the *ma-ra-te-u*, *Ta-ni-ko*.
Twenty Kuparissian *ke-ki-de* men at *A-ru-wo-te*,
ten Kuparissian *ke-ki-de* men at *Aithalewes*,
(and with them the Follower Kerkios).

Aeriqᵘhoitas, Elaphos, *Ri-me-ne*.
Thirty men *from* Oikhalia *to O-wi-to-no*,
and twenty *ke-ki-de* men from *A-pu-ka*,
(and with them the Follower *Ai-ko-ta*).

The section numbers here and in succeeding tablets are inserted merely for ease of reference.

o-u-ru-to: the negative *ou* makes no sense here. It is more likely that *u-ru-to* represents a verb beginning *wr-* (so written because there is no sign for *wu*), and *o-* is the usual prefix. Probably therefore an athematic 3rd plur. present indic. *hō wruntoi* (cf. ῥῦσθαι).

opi(h)ala: 'the coastal regions', cf. τὰ ἐπιθαλάσσια.

epikowoi: cf. the man's name *Pu-ko-wo* = Purkowos, Delph. Πυρκόοι. It will mean 'watchers, look-outs'. Not = ἐπίκουροι 'allies'; see Vocabulary, p. 392.

O-wi-to-no: clearly a place-name with medial -*t(h)n*-; cf. the adjective *O-wi-ti-ni-jo*.

su-we-ro-wi-jo: it is not clear where the list of names ends; this word may be a name or go with what follows.

O-ka-ra₃: cf. *O-ka-ra* in line 13. Possibly *Oikhalia* (so Palmer), on the Messenian-Arcadian frontier, the later Andania or Karnasion; but this seems far removed from the sea. Alternatively the town in Aetolia, though this too is not on the coast.

ma-ra-te-u: cf. *ma-ra-te-we* PY **195** = Na67; apparently a title or occupational name rather than a personal name.

A₂-ru-wo-te: probably a place-name in the dative; not Ἀλοῦς in Arcadia?

ke-ki-de: possibly a description of some sort of troops.

Kuparissioi: from Κυπαρισσία (cf. Κυπαρισσήεις, *Il.* II, 593).

Aithaleusi: dative of ethnic used as place-name?

pe-i: *spheis* or *sphe'i* = σφίσι; cf. Arcad. σφεις (dat. plur.).

A-pu₂?-ka-ne: nom. masc. plur. of ethnic? Cf. *A-pu-ka* **44** = An29.

† **57** = An43 [519]

1 *to-ro-o*   *o-ka*   *ro-o-wa*

2 *ka-da-si-jo*   *mo-ro-pa₂*   *wo-zo*

3 *ki-ri-ja-i-jo*   *wa-tu-wa-o-ko*   *mu-to-na*

4 *o-ka-ra₃*   *a₂-ra-tu-wa*   MEN 110 [   ]

         vacat

6 *ke-wo-no-jo*   *o-ka*   *ka-ke-*[   ]

7 *tu-si-je-u*   *po-te-u*   [   ]-*wọ-ne-*[   ]

8 *a-pi-te-wa*   *i-wa-so*   MEN [   ]

         vacat

10 *a₂-te-pọ*   *de-wi-jo*   *ko-ma-we*

11 *o-ai₂?-ta-qe*   *u-ru-pi-ja-jo*

12 *o-ru-ma-si-ja-jo*   MEN 30

         vacat

14 *pi-ru-te*   *ku-re-we*   MEN 50

15 *me-ta-qe*   *pe-i*   *e-qe-ta*   *ro-u-ko*

16 *ku-sa-me-ni-jo*

§ 3   Command of Tros at *Ro-o-wa*: *Ka-da-si-jo* a share-holder, *performing feudal service*, Kriaios, *Wastuaokhos*, *Mu-to-na*.

     110 men *from* Oikhalia *to A-ra-tu-wa*.

§ 4   Command of *Ke-wo-no*: ..., *Tu-si-je-u*, Ponteus, ...

     x men *from Amphi-te-wa to* Iwasos.

     A-te-po, De-wi-jo, Komawens,

         and thirty men...of Olympia and *Erymanthus*.

         Fifty *ku-re-we* men from *Pi-ru-*,

         (and with them the Follower *Ro-u-ko* son of Kusamenos).

Trōos: a surprising name to find at Pylos.

wo-zo: *worzōn*, the verb has a technical sense as a feudal term, see p. 255.

A₂-ra-tu-wa: also spelt *A₂-ra-tu-a* **76** = Cn22, pointing to a glide. Mühlestein compares Ἀραιθυρέα, Ἀραντία, old names of Phlius in the Argolid.

ka-ke-[: Wade-Gery suggests *Khalke*[*dei*] = Χαλκίς in Triphylia.

A-pi-te-wa I-wa-so: probably places not people; Palmer takes them as a pair of towns denoting a sector. Mühlestein identifies the latter with Ἴασος on the Arcadian-Laconian border.

A-te-po De-wi-jo: Mühlestein = Ἀρτίπους (or Ἄντιφος) and Δίϝιος.

Ulumpiaioi: a form Ὕλυμπος is mentioned as Aeolic for Ὄλυμπος by a grammarian.

O-ru-ma-si-ja-jo: a derivative of *Orumansia*, itself derived from *O-ru-ma-to* **76** = Cn22 = Ἐρύμανθος? The form is explained as due to remote assimilation by Mühlestein.

The connexion of two geographical names from the same area seems to guarantee the interpretation; but even this may be illusory.

Pi-ru-te ku-re-we: cf. **76** = Cn22. The latter word seems to denote another kind of troops distinguished from *ke-ki-de*. The view of Palmer (1954*b*, p. 52) that it is a place-name is refuted by the next tablet.

Ro-u-ko: cf. **44** = An29.

58 = An654

1 *ku-ru-me-no-jo   o-ka   pe-ri-te-u*
2 *wo-ne-wa   a-ti-ja-wo   e-ru-ta-ra*
3 *o-ai₂?-ta   me-ta-pi-jo   ke-ki-de*
4 MEN 50

vacat

6 *u-pi-ja-ki-ri-jo   ku-re-we*   MEN 60
7 *me-ta-qe   pe-i   e-qe-ta*
8 *a-re-ku-tu-ru-wo   e-te-wo-ke-re-we-*
9 *i-jo*

vacat

11 *ta-ti-qo-we-wo   o-ka   to-wa*
12 *po-ki-ro-qo   pe-ri-no   de-u-ka-ri-jo*
13 *ra-pe-do   do-qo-ro   pe-ri-ra-wo*
14 *e-no-wa-ro   to-so-de   pe-di-je-we*
15 *wa-wo-u-de   ke-ki-de*   MEN 10
16 *u-ru-pi-ja-jo*   MEN 10   *ku-re-we*   MEN 20
17 *i-wa-so*   MEN 10
18 *o-ka-ra₃*   MEN 10

§ 5   Command of Klumenos: Perintheus, Woinewas, Antiaon, Eruthras.
Fifty...*ke-ki-de* men of Metapa,
sixty *ku-re-we* men of *U-pi-akron*,
(and with them the Follower Alektruon son of Etewoklewes).

§ 6   Command of *Statigᵘoweus*: ..., Poikiloqᵘs, Pelinos, Deukalion, *Ra-pe-do*, *Do-qo-ro*, Perilawos, *E-no-wa-ro*.
The following numbers of *plainsmen*:
Ten *ke-ki-de* men of *Wa-wo-u-*,
ten men of Olympia,
twenty *ku-re-we* men;
ten men *at* Iwasos,
ten men *at* Oikhalia.

Klumenoio: a Homeric name; he is described as *mo(i)roppas* on **43** = Sn01.

o-ai₂?-ta: cf. **57** = An43.

U-pi-ja-ki-ri-jo: presumably an ethnic, cf. *U-pa-ra-ki-ri-ja* PY An08, *U-po-ra-ki-ri-ja* Cn13.

Alektruōn: another Homeric name, recurring on PY **167** = Es650. He is presumably the brother of *Ne-qe-u*, another son of Eteocles mentioned on **43** = Sn01.

To-wa: a man or a place?

pediēwes: = πεδιεῖς; but 'plainsmen' seem odd; not 'foot-soldiers'?

Wa-wo-u-de: analogy suggests that this is a place-name or ethnic; cf. *wa-wo-u-*[PY Xb02.

† **59** = An656

<pre>
 ¹ wa-pa-ro-jo   o-ka   ne-wo-ki-to
 ² [....] e-ri-ko-wo   a₂-di-je-u
 ³ a-ki-wo-ni-jo [?]
 ⁴ wa-ka-ti-ja-ta   ke-ki-de   sa-pi-da
 ⁵ me-ta-qe   pe-i   e-qe-ta
 ⁶ pe-re-qo-ni-jo   a-re-i-jo
 ⁷ ne-wo-ki-to   wo-wi-ja   ko-ro-ku-ra-i-jo
 ⁸ MEN 20   me-ta-qe   pe-i   e-qe-ta
 ⁹ di-wi-je-u
              vacat
¹¹ du-wo-jo-jo   o-ka   a-ke-re-wa
¹² a₂-ku-ni-jo   pe-ri-me-de [?]
¹³ pu₂?-ti-ja   a-pu₂?-ka-ne   ke-ki-de   po-ra-i   MEN 20
¹⁴ me-ta-qe   pe-i   e-qe-ta   di-ko-na-ro   a-da-ra-ti-jo
¹⁵ u-wa-si   ke-ki-de   ne-wo   MEN 10
¹⁶ me-ta-qe   pe-i   pe-re-u-ro-ni-jo   e-qe-ta
              vacat
¹⁸ a-ke-re-wa   ko-ro-ku-ra-i-jo   MEN 50
¹⁹ me-ta-qe   pe-i   e-qe-ta   ka-e-sa-me-no
²⁰ a-pu₂?-ka
</pre>

§ 7   Command of *Wapalos*: *Newo-ki-to, Erikowos, Ardieus, A-ki-wo-ni-jo.*
...*ke-ki-de* men *of Wa-ka-ti-ja*;
(and with them the Follower Presgᵘōnios son of *Ares*).

   Newo-ki-to borders:
     Twenty men *of Krokula*;
     (and with them the Follower Diwieus).

§ 8   Command of Dwoios at *A-ke-re-wa*: *A-ku-ni-jo*, Perimedes, *Puthias.*
    Twenty *ke-ki-de* men of *A-pu-ka* at *Po-rai*;

(and with them the Follower *Di-ko-na-ro* son of *Adrastos*).

Ten young *ke-ki-de* men at *U-wa-si*;

(and with them a follower from Pleuron).

Fifty men of *Krokula* at *A-ke-re-wa*;

(and with them the Follower *Ka-e-sa-menos* of *A-pu-ka*).

Ne-wo-ki-to: perhaps the same person as the priest of **44** = An29. Palmer (1955, p. 10): *Newokhitōn*.

Erikowos: (or *-gowos, -kowōn*) a 'slave of the god' in PY Ep02; here more likely the *basileus* of Jn845.

sa-pi-da: cf. *sa-pi-de* MY **105** = Ge602, PY Vn05; but the explanation 'boxes' proposed there makes no sense here. *ke-ki-de* is elsewhere followed by MEN and a numeral, sometimes with an ethnic adjective intervening.

wo-wi-ja: possibly *worwia* = ὅρια. Elsewhere apparently a second member of a place-name, the first part of which is a man's name in the genitive; cf. *Ko-ro-jo-wo-wi-ja* PY Mn01, *Ru-ke-wo-wo-wi-ja* Na35.

Diwieus: here clearly a man's name; cf. *di-wi-je-we* PY **76** = Cn22, where Palmer takes it as adjective with *ereutēres*, 'of Zeus'.

Dwoioio: 'Double'.

A-pu₂?-ka-ne: plural of an ethnic, the singular of which recurs in *A-pu₂?-ka* line 20.

Pleurōnios: ethnic or name? Elsewhere *e-qe-ta* precedes the name (except for **56** = An657.14), so the variation may be significant; cf. the mention of Pleuron in PY **53** = An12.

60 = An661 †

```
 1  e-ḳi-no-jo   o-ka   e-o-te-u
 2  a-ṭi-ṛo-qẹ   i-da-i-jo   e-se-re-a₂
 3  e-na-ṗo-ṛọ   i-wa-so   MEN 70
 4  [.]-o-ri-[          ]  MEN 30
 5  ka-ṛạ-do-ro   ko-ro-ku-ra-i-jo   MEN [nn]
 6  ẓạ-e-to-ro   ko-ro-ku-ra-i-jo   MEN 20
 7  me-ta-qe   pe-i   e-qe-ta   wo-ro-tu-mi-ni-jọ
              vacat
 9  e-ko-me-na-ta-o   o-ka
10  ṭi-ṃi-ṭo   ạ-ke-i   ma-ṛẹ-u   ro-qo-ta
11  ạ-ḳẹ-[.]-u   a-kє-wa-to
12  a₂-ka-a₂-ki-ri-jo   u-ru-pi-ja-jo
13  ne-do-wo-ta-de   MEN 30   me-ta-qe   pe-i   e-qe-ta
```

§9 Command of Ekhinos: *E-o-te-u* and *A-ti-ro*, *Idaios*, *E-se-re-a*.

Seventy men *from E-na-po-ro to* Iwasos,

thirty men...,

x men of *Krokula* at Kharadros,
twenty men of *Krokula* at *Za-e-to-ro*;
(and with them the Follower *Wo-ro-tu-mnios*).

§ 10   Command of Erkhomenatas at *Ti-mi-to-a-ke-i*: Maleus, *Re-qo-ta*, *A-ke—u*,
Arkhewastos.

Thirty men of A-ka-akron *and* Olympia to Nedwon;
(and with them a follower).

A-ti-ro-qe: possibly complete as a name, connective -*qᵘe* being unusual in these lists;
but *A-ti-ro* recurs at Knossos.

E-na-po-ro: interpreted as a common noun *enarsphoroi* by Debrunner and Von der Mühll
(Mühlestein, 1955*a*, Nachtrag); but its identification as a place is guaranteed by its
inclusion in the tribute lists of the *Na* group (Na02, **184** = Nn01; cf. Vn04 where it
reappears in company with Kharadros); possibly a place named after the hero
Enarsphoros.

ti-mi-to a-ke-i, the common place-name, more usually spelt with *a-ke-e*. The reading
is doubtful; Bennett *pi-*[**82*]*.

a₂-ka-a₂-ki-ri-jo: cf. *A₂-ka-a₂-ki-ri-ja-jo* PY **76** = Cn22.

Nedwonta-de: accusative of Νέδων river of Eastern Messenia?

CHAPTER VII

LIVESTOCK AND AGRICULTURAL PRODUCE

THIS chapter must begin with a discussion of the ideograms for livestock which †
are set out below:

*23	𝍢	OX	*22	𝍢	GOAT
109ª	𝍢	OX/BULL	107ª	𝍢	HE-GOAT
109ᵇ	𝍢	COW	107ᵇ	𝍢	SHE-GOAT
	𝍢	OX+SI			
			*85	𝍢	PIG
*21	𝍢	SHEEP	108ª	𝍢	BOAR
106ª	𝍢	RAM	108ᵇ	𝍢	SOW
106ᵇ	𝍢	EWE		𝍢	PIG+SI
	𝍢	SHEEP+TA		𝍢	PIG+KA
*75	𝍢	Kind of sheep?			
			105	𝍢	HORSE
104	𝍢	DEER		𝍢	FOAL

The domestic animals of the tablets are four, if we exclude the deer which
appears on only three tablets (PY Cn01, 868, 875). To these may be added the
horse, which appears only in connexion with chariots, and is clearly used only
for military purposes (see p. 379). The signs for the HORSE and the DEER
are self-evident; that for the PIG is almost as clear, and was recognized by
Evans (*PM*, IV, p. 722). The identification of the other three signs has been
much disputed. Evans, followed by Furumark and others, thought that the
OX was a variant of the HORSE. Others, including Palmer (1954a, p. 67),
have preferred the value OX (cf. Carratelli, 1954, p. 219). It is comparatively
scarce; it occurs in pairs on a series of Knossos tablets (e.g. **83** = Ch902) and
is qualified by the word *wergatai* (e.g. KN **84** = C 59, cf. βοῦς ἐργάτης
Archilochus, 39, etc.). The proof seems to lie in PY **76** = Cn22, where five of
these animals are enumerated, the heading containing the word *qo-o*; this is
almost certainly a part of the word corresponding to βοῦς, the best suggestion

being that of E. Risch (Mühlestein, 1955*a*, Nachtrag) that it is a *scriptio plena* for $g^u\bar{o}s$ (acc. plur.). It is also observable that the ideogram though stylized clearly shows a horn, and the meaning OX may be regarded as certain.

It would seem likely therefore that the remaining two signs should represent sheep and goats, and the problem becomes merely that of deciding which is which. SHEEP are much more numerous than GOATS; and they are repeatedly associated with the sign WOOL, sometimes with nothing intervening (see p. 205). This in turn is associated with textiles (see p. 314), and the animal product most likely to be used in garments is wool. Goats' hair or goatskin is not impossible, but is obviously less likely to be a common commodity. Finally we may point to the apparent use of SHE-GOAT as the female of the AGRIMI (see p. 302). The use of sign *75 = WE for a kind of sheep suggests an abbreviation of *wetalon* 'yearling'; it may also be used of goats, see p. 208.

COMPOUND SIGNS

The question of the compound signs is only partially resolved. The signs indicating sex are certainly identified; the rest obscure. Those with two horizontal bars indicate male animals, those with a bifurcated stem females. Evans (*PM*, IV, p. 723) had already conjectured that these signs represented the sex and had correctly interpreted them; his interpretation was, however, attacked by Sundwall (1936, pp. 25–38), who reversed the sexes, taking RAM for instance as 'cow'. The sexes were finally determined by Kober (1949, p. 398) who demonstrated that the word for 'total' now read as *to-so*, *to-sa*, showed grammatical inflexion, and that RAMS were counted with the same form as MEN, and EWES with the same form as WOMEN. The complication of a third gender, indistinguishable in this word from the feminine plural, does not vitiate the conclusion, since the neuter can be ruled out when it is a case of distinguishing between the two sexes. The undifferentiated forms of the livestock signs have been transcribed by the name of the species; but it is possible that these in fact indicate the young animals, and we should call them rather CALF, LAMB, etc. On the different forms of the HORSE sign see p. 210. 109ᵃ, properly BULL, is used also to denote the castrated, working OX.

The other compounds are less common and their meaning is unexplained. The syllabic sign *si* compounded with PIG is specifically coupled with the word *sialos* on PY 75 = Cn02. But this may be fortuitous, since the OX is also compounded with *si*, and these signs may well be taken over from Linear A; BULL for instance figures in the tables of Carratelli (1945, p. 479). The SHEEP sign compounded with *ta* figures only on PY Cn09, Cn10, both of which have the introductory word *ta-to-mo*, perhaps *stathmos*.

ADJUNCTS

In addition to the compound signs, adjuncts written before the ideogram are frequently used (more often at Knossos than at Pylos). The following table shows which occur:

SHEEP	*o*										
RAM	*o*	*pa*	*pe*	*ki*	*ne*	*ki.ne*	*za*	*sa*			
EWE	*o*								*se*		
HE-GOAT										*ai*	
PIG	*o*										

o is certainly here as elsewhere an abbreviation of *o-pe-ro* (or the like) and means 'lacking, deficient'. No entirely satisfactory explanations have yet been proposed for the remaining adjuncts. The analogy of the cuneiform tablets suggests the following distinctions for sheep, in addition to male/female:

wool sheep / hair sheep / eating sheep
grain-fed / grass-fed / fattened / milk-fed
shorn / unshorn
sheep / lamb

It would be an interesting, though perhaps unprofitable, game to look for Greek words which could be abbreviated by the phonetic symbols, and which would correspond to these distinctions. *pe* suggests *pekos* (=πόκος) or *pektos* 'shorn'. *ne* and *pa* might be *newos* and *palaios* (cf. the adjuncts *ne* and *pa* applied to WOMEN, p. 163). *ki* might be connected with χιλός 'green fodder' (hardly κριός 'ram'), *sa* with σηκός (Dor. σᾱκός) 'fold' or σῆτες (Dor. σᾶτες) 'this year'. But it must be emphasized that such guesses cannot be verified.

PURPOSE OF THE TABLETS

The livestock tablets from Knossos attracted a good deal of attention previous to the decipherment. Evans (*PM*, IV, p. 723) first called attention to the large numbers of cattle involved; but it was Sundwall (1936) who pointed out the curious fact that on most of the complete tablets the figures add up to 100 or a similar round number, including the deficit noted by *o*. (For examples and a fuller discussion see p. 201.) The numbers at Pylos are not so obviously round figures, but the majority are multiples of ten, and of the remainder a fair number end in five. At Pylos, however, we do not have the check provided by the mathematics of the deficit.

It is on this fact that any theory of the transaction recorded must be based. They cannot be a simple census of flocks of sheep and other cattle, since a natural distribution would not show these round numbers, nor would this explain the deficits. Real flocks too would hardly show the disproportion of rams to ewes which is evident. It follows then that these are allocations or contributions, and that performance in many cases falls short of the amount due. The high numbers of rams would not occur if these were allocations by the palace; but they would naturally occur if the owners were obliged to supply so many sheep annually. They would of course pick out the least useful members for the regeneration of the flock. We may therefore feel sure that those are right who have seen in these tablets a record of tribute imposed on his subjects by the overlord. Sundwall, regarding the cattle as oxen, suggested that these were 'hecatombs' of sacrificial animals. Although this explanation cannot be ruled out, the numbers seem far too large for this purpose. Several of the Knossos tablets which apparently give totals have figures in excess of 2000; one fragment contains the numeral 19,000. This would have been piety indeed. Even if the figures are regarded as tribute, they are large for an annual contribution. Evans was certainly right in setting down cattle-raising as one of the principal sources of wealth. It might be tempting to regard these sheep not as real animals, but merely as a token of exchange, as oxen are used as a standard of measurement in Homer; but imaginary sheep cannot be divided into rams and ewes, apart from the other subdivisions. Nor is there any evidence in the tablets of anything approaching currency. Every commodity is listed separately, and there is never any sign of equivalence between one unit and another.

The state of the Knossos tablets and the fact that some of them appear to record the totals make it very difficult to arrive at any firm conclusions on the numbers mentioned. There are too a considerable number among the newly published fragments. The much smaller number of tablets involved at Pylos make the census easier. Even so it must be remembered that our collection of tablets is doubtless far from complete, and many tablets have not survived entire. On the other hand some may duplicate entries relating to the same cattle. In any case, as explained above, there is good reason to think that the figures recorded are only a small percentage of the total flocks.

	Male	Female	Unclassified	Total
SHEEP	8217	1554	386	10157
GOATS	1004	771	50	1825
PIGS	57	234	249	540
OXEN	—	—	8	8
STAGS	—	—	16	16

The above table shows the total numbers of each of the principal categories of livestock at Pylos on C- tablets sufficiently preserved. Damaged numerals have been read as the smallest number which can be restored. The proportions of SHEEP / GOATS / PIGS are probably reasonably accurate, but the relative scarcity of OXEN is surprising.

1. FLOCKS OF SHEEP AND GOATS AT PYLOS (Cc, Cn)   †

The first example illustrates the formula: (place-name) *we-re-ke*. Ventris and others have proposed *wergei* (with a *scriptio plena* to avoid confusion) 'encloses'. But these cannot be the total numbers of cattle kept at these places, and the construction seems a little curious. It is noticeable that *Ro-u-so*, which is later a plural Λουσοί, is equally followed by *we-re-ke*, not **we-ro-ko-si*. We might expect a formula with prefixed *o-* to introduce the enumeration, cf. **75** = Cn02. It may therefore be wondered whether *we-re-ke* is a plural substantive, which is in some way applicable to both sheep and goats. The place-names occurring in this series are: *Pi-*82*, *Ro-u-so* (twice) and *A-ke-re-wa*. In the text quoted each entry consists of *paro* followed by a man's name in the dative; the single exception has *Ma-ro-pi* (place-name in locative-instrumental plural?) and apparently the name in the nominative. In the preceding line an erroneous nominative has been changed to the dative.

61 = Cn04 [131]   ‡

1	*pi-*82*	*we-re-ke*				
2	*pa-ro*	*pi-me-ta*	RAMS 200	*pa-ro*	*o-ku-ka*	RAMS 130×
3	*pa-ro*	*ku-pi-ri-jo*	RAMS 50×	*pa-ro*	*a-ka-ma-wo*	RAMS 120×
4	*pa-ro*	*ko-ru-no*	RAMS 100×	*pa-ro*	*ne-ri-to*	RAMS 30×
5	*pa-ro*	*po-ro-u-te-we*	RAMS 90×	*pa-ro*	*o-wa-ko*	SHE-GOATS 54×
6	*ma-ro-pi*	*to-ro-wi*	RAMS 130×	*pa-ro*	*a-no-po*	RAMS 130×
7	*pa-ro*	*ke-ro-wo*	RAMS 130×	*pa-ro*	*ra-pa-sa-ko*	RAMS 91×
8	*pa-ro*	*po-ke-we*	EWES 27	*pa-ro*	*a-ri-wo-ne*	RAMS 100
9	*pa-ro*	*a-we-ke-se-we*	RAMS 180	*pa-ro*	*po-ko-ro*	RAMS 100×
10	*pa-ro*	*e-ti-ra-wo*	RAMS 100×	*pa-ro*	*a-ta-ma-ne-we*	RAMS 140×
11	*pa-ro*	*se-no*	EWES 44×	*pa-ro*	*ko-ro*	EWES 24×
12	*pa-ro*	*do-qo-no*	RAMS 80×	*pa-ro*	*wo-ki-to*	RAMS 73×
13	*pa-ro*	*me-te-we*	RAMS 163×	*pa-ro*	*ke-sa-me-no*	EWES 40×
14	*pa-ro*	*pu-wi-no*	SHE-GOATS 55			

Pi-*82 encloses:

from *Pi-me-ta*	200 rams	
from Ogugas	130 rams	
from Kuprios	50 rams	
from Alkmawos	120 rams, etc.	

Ke-ro-wo: if this is the same man as that described as a shepherd at *Asiatia* **31** =Ae04, this is further proof of the identity of the SHEEP ideogram, and suggests that all these men are the herdsmen and not the owners of the flocks.

The next tablet deals with the same area and eight of the personal names are the same. In this case the sheep are not recorded as 'from' a person, but the place-name is followed by either (*a*) a man's name in the nominative after which there is another name in the genitive and the word *a-ko-ra* (probably = *agorā* in the sense 'collection' or 'flock', see Vocabulary, p. 387), or (*b*) a man's name in the nominative or genitive followed by *pa-ra-jo*. If this is some part of παλαιός it presumably cannot be in agreement with the man's name where this is in the genitive, though a failure of concord cannot be ruled out. In the second tablet quoted here the expression '*x*'s flock' is substituted by '*x a-ke-re*', i.e. *agêrei*. Hence we may suppose that the men so designated are in some way responsible for 'collecting' the cattle. There are only four of them: *A-pi-me-de*, *A-ke-o*, *A-ko-so-ta* and *We-da-ne-u*. The latter two are mentioned elsewhere in contexts that make it plain they are people of some importance: *We-da-neus* is one of the persons who receive minor contributions on the Poseidon tablets (**169** = Es646, **170** = Es649); *A(r)xotas* is issuing spices on **103** = Un08, inspecting land on **131** = Eq01, and he appears on several other tablets. It would seem likely therefore that these four are officials or representatives of the palace.

† **62** = Cn655

1	*ma-ro-pi*	*qe-re-wa-o*	*pa-ra-jo*		RAMS 136
2	*ma-ro-pi*	*to-ro-wi-ko*	*pa-ra-jo*		RAMS 133
3	*ma-ro-pi*	*ke-ro-wo-jo*			RAMS 85
4	*ma-ro-pi*	*ra-pa-sa-ko-jo*			RAMS 69
5	*ma-ro-pi*	*pu-wi-no*	*a-pi-me-de-o*	*a-ko-ra*	RAMS 190
6	*ma-ro-pi*	*i-wa-so*	*we-da-ne-wo*	*a-ko-ra*	RAMS 70
7	*ma-ro-pi*	*ti-ma-wo*	*pa-ra-jo*		RAMS 70
8	*ma-ro-pi*	*o-ka-ri-jo*	*pa-ra-jo*		RAMS 95
9	*ma-ro-pi*	*e-ti-ra-wo*	*pa-ra-jo*		RAMS 70
10	*ma-ro-pi*	*a-ta-ma-ne-u*	*pa-ra-jo*		RAMS 60
11	*ma-ro-pi*	*qi-ri-ta-ko*	*a-ke-o-jo*	*a-ko-ra*	RAMS 90
12	*ma-ro-pi*	*a-ri-wo*	*a-ke-o-jo*	*a-ko-ra*	[X nn]
13	*ma-ro-pi*	*i-re-jo*	*we-da-ne-wo*	*a-ko-ra*	[X] 60
14	*ma-ro-pi*	*o-pe-re-ta*	*we-da-ne-wo*		EWES 86
15	*ma-ro-pi*	*po-ro-pa₂-ta-jo*	*we-da-ne-wo*		EWES 63
16	*ma-ro-pi*	*to-ru-ko-ro*	*we-da-ne-wo*		EWES 88
17	*ma-ro-pi*	*ma-ma-ro*	*we-da-ne-wo*		RAMS 90

¹⁸ [ma-ro]-pi   ma-du-ro   we-da-ne-wo   RAMS 100
¹⁹ [ma-ro]-pi   se-no   we-da-[ne]-wo   EWES 40
²⁰ [ma-ro-pi]   ta-ta-ke-u   [we-da]-ne-wo   EWES 30

At *Ma-ro-*: the...of *Q^uelewas* 136 rams.
At *Ma-ro-*: the...of *Trowix*: 133 rams,
$$\text{etc., etc.}$$

63 = Cc660

  a-ke-o   a-ke-re
me-ta-pa | pa-ro   ka-ra-su-no   HE-GOATS 30
At Metapa: *Alkeos* collects thirty he-goats from *Ka-ra-su-no*.

2. FLOCKS OF SHEEP AT KNOSSOS (Da–Dg)   †

All the tablets of this group are really alike, varying only in the different ways
in which the total is built up. They begin with a man's name, presumably
that of the shepherd as in the parallel tablets at Pylos, written in tall characters;
then the tablet is usually divided by a horizontal line, the top
line containing the name of the 'collector' in the nominative   106^a ⨕ RAM
or genitive, and the number of rams and/or ewes; the lower
line usually gives the place-name and any minor entry, such   106^b ⨖ EWE
as the deficit. These positions, however, are not invariable.
Unlike the Pylos tablets, there is a separate tablet for each entry. The numbers
are as a rule round hundreds, or a series of lesser numbers adding up to a round
total. In these cases the sum is never shown on the tablet. A few examples
will illustrate the principle:

							Total
Da1147	RAMS 100						100
Dc1148	RAMS 95	*pe.* RAMS	5				100
Dd1150	RAMS 70	EWES	29	*pa.* RAMS	1		100
De1151	RAMS 264	EWES	22	*o.* RAMS	14		300
De1152	RAMS 46	EWES	22	*o.* RAMS	12		80
Dc1154	RAMS 91	*o.* RAMS	9				100

At least thirty places are mentioned on these tablets—the exact figure
depends on whether a few which occur only once are correctly identified as
names. These places can be safely presumed to be in some sense tributary to
Knossos. The only ones which can be located geographically are: Phaistos,
Lato, Lyktos, Tylissos, and probably *Se-to-i-ja* = Setaia and *U-ta-no* = Itanos.
This distribution covers central and eastern Crete; the only two places known
from the tablets in West Crete (Kydonia and Aptara) do not figure in this

series. It would, however, be rash to generalize from what may in any case be an accidental distribution, since we can locate so few of the place-names. The western towns may possibly be excused from sending sheep owing to the lack of suitable cattle roads.

The collectors are a little more numerous than at Pylos, but a large number of tablets do not bear this entry. The two most frequently recurring names are *U-ta-jo* and *We-we-si-jo*, the former in connexion with ten places (*Da-wo, Da-*22-to, Do-ti-ja, E-ko-so, Ku-ta-to*, Phaistos, *Pa₃-ko-we, Ra-su-to, Ri-jo-no, Tu-ni-ja*), the latter with eight (*Da-ra-ko, Da-wo, Da-*22-to, Di-ro, E-ko-so, Ku-ta-to*, Phaistos, *Su-ri-mo*). Since there is considerable overlapping we cannot suppose that the collectors were each responsible for separate areas.

64 = Da1221   (L   lxxvii)

ai-ta-ro-we | RAMS 200[
  | *pa₃-ko-we*   [

Aithalowens: 200 rams at *Pa₃-ko-we*.

Aithalowens: = αἰθαλόεις; the name recurs at Pylos.

† **65** = Db1232   (L   lxxviii)

na-pu-ti-jo | RAMS 23   EWES 27
  | *ti-ri-to*   *pe-ri-qo-te-jo*

Naputios: twenty-three rams, twenty-seven ewes at *Ti-ri-to*; (collector) *Peri-qo-te-jo*.

Nāputios: = νηπύτιος.
Ti-ri-to: recalls Τρίτ(τ)α, the old name of Knossos according to Hesych.
Pe-ri-qo-te-jo: the name of the 'collector' or official responsible. Note the unusual arrangement. The numbers add up to fifty.

66 = Dc1129   (L   lxxviii, numbered 1161)

po-ro-u-te-u | *u-ta-jo*   RAMS 37
  | *da-*22-to*   *o*. RAMS 63

Plouteus: at *Da-*22-to*, thirty-seven rams, deficit sixty-three rams; (collector) *U-ta-jo*.

67 = Dd1171   (L   xci)

po-ro | RAMS 20   EWES 72
  | *pa-i-to*   *pa*. RAMS 8

Poros: at Phaistos, twenty rams, seventy-two ewes; eight *pa-* rams.

pa.: stands here in the same position and relation to the other numerals as *o*. The total is 100.

68 = De1648   (L?)

a-te-mo | we-we-si-jo-jo   RAMS 58   EWES 2
        | ku-ta-to   o. RAMS 50

Anthemos: at *Ku-ta-to*, fifty-eight rams, two ewes; deficit *fifty* rams; (collection) of Werwesios.

Here the name of the 'collector' stands in the genitive. The total, if the numerals are correctly read, is 110.

69 = Df1119   (L   xci)

de-ke-se-u | da-mi-ni-jo   RAMS 56   EWES 16
           | ku-ta-to   pe. RAMS 28

Dexeus: at *Damnio- in Ku-ta-to*, fifty-six rams, sixteen ewes, twenty-eight *pe-* rams.

Da-mi-ni-jo: from its usage alone this seems to be another place-name; when associated with another name this is always *Ku-ta-to*, so it may be a local district of this place.

70 = Dg1158   (L   lxxviii)   †

a-ni-ja-to | we-we-si-jo   RAMS 63   EWES 25
           | pa-i-to   pa. RAMS 2   o. RAMS 12

Aniatos: at *Phaistos*, sixty-three rams, twenty-five ewes, two *pa-* rams; deficit twelve rams; (collector) Werwesios.

The total including the *pa-* rams is 102; they can hardly be excluded from the calculation in view of cases like **67** = Da1171 where they are needed to make the 100, but the reading of the last figure is uncertain, and the 'two' may have been erased.

3. FLOCKS OF SHEEP AND CONSIGNMENTS OF WOOL AT KNOSSOS (Dk, Dl)   ‡

These tablets are similar in general form to the preceding series, but differ in having an entry with the ideogram WOOL. The identity of this sign is still not fully confirmed, and some are inclined to regard it as a mere unit of measurement or value. It is, however, principally used in connexion with SHEEP, as here, or with textiles (CLOTHS, *pa-we-a*). It is normally counted, but is subdivided by *è* into thirds, written *è* 1 and *è* 2. Further subdivision by weight occurs in the *Od* tablets. Since *è* 1 = approx. 1 kg., the WOOL unit must be equivalent to about 3 kg.

106a	⚹	RAM
106b	⚹	EWE
145	⚹	WOOL

The amount of WOOL is proportionate to the number of SHEEP, the deficits being noted in the usual way. The proportion is shown between the total number of sheep and the total amount of wool, and the deficit of wool is not proportionate to the deficit of sheep. In one set of tablets the proportion is four sheep: one unit of wool.

	SHEEP	WOOL
Dk1070	100	$7 + 18 = 25$
Dk1071	50	$6 + 6\frac{1}{3} = 12\frac{1}{3}$
Dk1072	100	$13\frac{1}{3} + 11\frac{2}{3} = 25$
Dk1073	50	$6\frac{2}{3} + 5\frac{2}{3} = 12\frac{1}{3}$
Dk1074	100	$19 + 6 = 25$

It was at first thought that in some cases the proportion was incorrectly calculated; but checking of the original tablets shows that these cases are due to misreading of the numerals, which are often damaged (1070 and 1073 are here corrected). The approximation of $12\frac{1}{3}$ to the correct $12\frac{1}{2}$ seems to indicate that division was not customary except into thirds.

In the second set the proportion is ten sheep: one unit of wool, a difference which suggests that these are arbitrary figures, rather than the yield of two different kinds of sheep.

	SHEEP	WOOL
Dl 933	$40 + 20 + 60 = 120$	$3 + 9 = 12$
Dl 938	$50 + 40 + 10 = 100$	$7 + 3 = 10$
Dl 943	$90 + 90 = 180$	$11 + 7 = 18$
Dl 946	$70 + 70 = 140$	$7 + 7 = 14$
Dl 947	$80 + 10 + 70 = 160$	$11 + 5 = 16$

71 = Dk1072   (L   lxxiv)

ka-te-u | × RAMS 100   WOOL 13 $\frac{?}{?}$ 1
           | *ku-ta-to*   o. WOOL 11 $\frac{?}{?}$ 2

Ka-te-u: at *Ku-ta-to*, 100 rams; 40 kg. of wool; deficit 35 kg. of wool.

× is a 'check mark' here as on **61 = Cn04.**

72 = Dk1074   (L   lxxiv)

e-ru-to-ro | × RAMS 100   WOOL 19
             | *ku-ta-to*   o. WOOL 6

Eruthros: at *Ku-ta-to*, 100 rams, 57 kg. of wool; deficit 18 kg. of wool.

† **73 = Dl 943   (K   lviii)**

a-ko-i-da | *po-ti-ni-ja-we-⟨jo⟩*   EWES 90   WOOL 11
            | *pa₂-nwa-so*   o.ki. RAMS 90   o. WOOL ⟦8⟧ '7'

A-ko-i-da: at *Pa-nwa-so*, ninety ewes, 33 kg. of wool; deficit ninety *ki-* rams and 21 kg. of wool; *belonging to the Mistress.*

Po-ti-ni-ja-we-: shown by other similar tablets (Dl 930, Dl 933, Dl 946) to have lost its final -*jo*. The meaning is difficult; it is clearly a derivative of *po-ti-ni-ja* Potnia, though the Mistress is not necessarily divine in this context. On the other hand this place on the tablet is normally occupied by a man's name, and it is just possible that Potniaweios is a man at Knossos, though the word is certainly adjectival at Pylos. The last numeral has been corrected by the erasure of the last stroke.

74 = Dl 1061   (K   xciii)   †

[*to*]-*sa* / *pa-i-ti-ja*   SHEEP   WOOL 456

So much sheep's wool from Phaistos: 1368 kg.

The sign preceding WOOL is badly damaged by a crack; but apparently nothing intervenes between the two ideograms. This collocation can now also be found on DlM4, 7135, 7280, 7300.

4.   MISCELLANEOUS LIVESTOCK AT PYLOS (Cn)

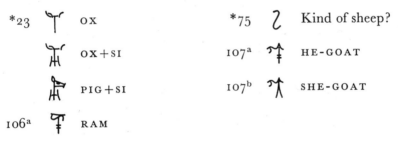

*23	OX		*75	Kind of sheep?
	OX+SI		107a	HE-GOAT
	PIG+SI		107b	SHE-GOAT
106a	RAM			

As shown above, pigs and cattle are not often recorded at Pylos. Perhaps Pylos was not so rich in livestock generally as Knossos. A particularly interesting record of pigs gives us one of the examples of the nine towns which seem to be the chief tributaries (see p. 142).

75 = Cn02 [608]

1	*jo-a-se-so-si si-a₂-ro*		How the local inhabitants
2	*o-pi-da-mi-jo*		will *fatten* fat hogs:
3	*pi-*82*	PIGS+SI 3	at *Pi-*82* three hogs
4	*me-ta-pa*	PIGS+SI 3	at Metapa three hogs
5	*pe-to-no*	PIGS+SI 6	at *Pe-to-no* six hogs
6	*pa-ki-ja-si*	PIGS+SI 2	at *Pa-ki-ja-* two hogs
7	*a-pu₂?-we*	PIGS+SI 2	at *Aipu* two hogs
8	*a-ke-re-wa*	PIGS+SI 2	at *A-ke-re-wa* two hogs

[9] *e-ra-te-i*	PIGS+SI 3	at *E-ra-tos* three hogs
[10] *ka-ra-do-ro*	PIGS+SI 2	at Kharadros two hogs
[11] *ri-jo*	PIGS+SI 2	at Rhion two hogs

jo-a-se-so-si: an example of *jo-* = *o-*, *hō*; cf. *jo-do-so-si* PY **257** = Jn09. This spelling is hardly to be regarded as due to preservation of the initial *j-* of Indo-European; it alternates with simple *o-*. The verb is difficult. Palmer (1954*b*, pp. 19–22) takes it as *asēsonsi*, future of ἄω (ἄσαι); the ordinary future is ἄσω so a special formation must be supposed. But the analogy of the other lists of tribute suggests that a verb of giving, sending or providing would be more appropriate, though there does not seem to be any suitable verb in Greek; the future of ἵημι *hēsonsi* leaves the first syllable unexplained.

opidāmioi: according to the sense of the verb this can be either nominative plural 'local inhabitants' or accusative plural agreeing with *sialons*. Since the list details a number of localities, the former is slightly more likely. The other alternative suggested by Palmer (*loc. cit.*) 'how the fat hogs in the demes are to batten' seems to take no account of the subsequent list.

The two tablets quoted dealing with oxen both raise special problems. The first is connected by its place-names with the military dispositions of **57** = An43 (see p. 185). Palmer (1954*b*, pp. 20, 53) has explained this tablet as a list of oxen which are being assigned to the sectors indicated, as sacrificial victims to ensure divine favour in the event of a battle. That there is some connexion cannot be denied; but less picturesque explanations, such as food-supply, can be imagined. The correctness of Palmer's view depends to some extent on his ingenious interpretation of *i-je-si* as from not ἵημι but another homonymous verb connected with ἱερός and meaning 'to dedicate or sacrifice'. Some support for this comes from the apparent use of the verb in **172** = Kn02, where the context is certainly religious. However, some reasons for doubting the explanation here are advanced in the notes; but the difficulties are far from solved, and any translation must be regarded as very tentative.

The second tablet refers to livestock of other kinds, and apparently records the colour of some oxen. This, combined with the small numbers involved, may suggest sacrificial victims; but the text is too damaged for any firm conclusions.

† **76** = Cn22 [3]

[1] *jo-i-je-si* *me-za-na*		
[2] *e-re-u-te-re* *di-wi-je-we*	*qo-o*	
[3] a_2-*ra-tu-a* *o-ka-ra*$_3$	OX 1	
[4] *pi-ru-te* *ku-re-we*	OX 1	
[5] *e-na-po-ro* *i-wa-si-jo-ta*	OX 1	

^{6} *o-ru-ma-to   u-ru-pi-ja-jo*   OX I
^{7} *a$_2$-ka-a$_2$-ki-ri-ja-jo   u-ru-pi-ja-jo-jo*   OX I
                          vacant 2

How. . .are *sending* oxen to the inspector Diwieus:

A-ra-tu-a and Oikhalia: one ox.
The *ku-re-we* men at *Pi-ru-*: one ox.
The men of Iwasos at *E-na-po-ro*: one ox.
The men of *Olympia* at *Erumanthos*: one ox.
The. . .*of the Olympian*: one ox.

jo-i-je-si: *hō hiensi*: 'send' or 'sacrifice'?

me-za-na: Palmer and Georgiev both believe this to be a spelling, variously explained, for *melanas* 'black'; but if it agrees with *qo-o*, the word-order is extremely strange. Andrews and Mühlestein interpret as *Messānān* 'to Messene', which is perhaps possible, although -σσ- arising from dental +*j* is ordinarily written *s* (e.g. *to-so*); but the name in view of its termination may be pre-Greek. The other examples of this word (**296** = Sh736, *me-za-ne* **91** = Fn02) throw very little light on the meaning.

e-re-u-te-re: Palmer's *ereutēr* (= ἐρευνητής) 'searcher, inspector' is preferable to the attempts of Furumark (1954, p. 26) and Mühlestein (1954, p. 11) to make the word a personal name *Eleuthēr*. What is not clear is whether it is dative singular or nominative plural. Palmer prefers the latter, making *di-wi-je-we* an adjective ('of Zeus') in agreement. Meriggi (1954, p. 28) takes *di-wi-je-we* as the nom. plur. subject. But it is highly probable that *ku-re-we* is nominative plur. as it is the title of a class of armed men in the military tablets (see p. 191); and *i-wa-si-jo-ta* must be an ethnic *Iwasiōtai*. If then the individual entries each contain a subject (the groups of men) and an object (the oxen), it is hard to see how *ereutēres* can be equated with them. On the other hand a *heq^{u}etās* named Diwieus is mentioned in **59** = An656, and the words *e-qe-ta e-re-u-te-re* appear together on a fragmentary sealing Wa917. It therefore seems easier to take these words as dative singular, and this in turn implies a meaning 'send' for the verb.

qo-o: the suggestion of E. Risch (Mühlestein, 1955*a*, Nachtrag), that this is a *scriptio plena* for $g^u\bar{o}(n)s$ acc. plur. = βοῦς, cf. Skt. *gāḥ* (hardly singular $g^u\bar{o}n$), offers the easiest solution to the difficulty caused by the apparent lack of the digamma. The scribes seem to have tried to avoid any monosyllabic word.

A$_2$-ka-a$_2$-ki-ri-ja-jo: this would appear to be not a place-name but an ethnic, and the genitive singular *U-ru-pi-ja-jo-jo* is surprising if not an error; cf. *a$_2$-ka-a$_2$-ki-ri-jo u-ru-pi-ja-jo* **60** = An661.

77 = Cn23 [418]   †

^{1} *pa-ro   we-u-da-ne-we*
^{2} *ṛe-ụ-ko   a-ko-ro-we-e*   OXEN+SI 2
^{3} *re-[u]-ḳọ   ma-ra-ḳụ   pe-ko   a-ko-ro-we*   OX+SI I

⁴ [   ] 3   HE-GOATS 3   WE 3   SHE-GOATS 3
⁵ [   ] 2 [   ] 2
⁶ [   ]
⁷ *re-u-ko*   [...]   *pe-ko*   *a-ko-ro-we* [   ]
⁸ RAM I   HE-GOAT I   WE [   ]

From *We-u-da-ne-u*:

> Two oxen *uniformly* white,
> one ox *uniformly* white...,
> three..., *three* he-goats, three *yearlings*, three she-goats, etc.

We-u-da-ne-we: probably an alternative spelling of *We-da-ne-we*, but it may be a different person.

a-ko-ro-we-e: dual *akhrōwee* 'pale' or more likely *hakhrōwee* 'uniformly coloured'.

ma-ra-ku pe-ko: a comparison of line 2 suggests that these two words should be taken together as some qualification of 'uniformly white'. They are in fact written in characters of the same size, while the preceding and following words are respectively slightly larger and smaller. *ma-ra-ku* might be for βραχύς, if this is from **mr-*, cf. Avest. *mərəzu-*; but the Aeolic form is βρόχυς. *pe-ko* is perhaps to be connected with πέσκος (neut.) 'hide', an accusative of respect?

The ideographic use of **75* (=WE) here in connexion with goats as well as sheep suggests that it may mean not a kind of sheep, but merely a young animal; it is attractive to identify it with *wetalon* 'yearling'. Note that the last ideogram in line 4 is probably female, not male as shown in 'The Pylos Tablets'.

Line 6 probably contained a fresh heading: *pa-ro* followed by another name.

5. MISCELLANEOUS LIVESTOCK AT KNOSSOS
(C, Ca, Ch, Co, Dm, Dn)

106^a		RAM	109^a		OX / BULL
106^b		EWE	109^b		COW
107^a		HE-GOAT	170		Calf?
107^b		SHE-GOAT	108^a		BOAR
105		HORSE	108^b		SOW
*23		OX			

Some of the tablets dealing with livestock at Knossos seem to be not lists of tribute, as in the case of the sheep, but gifts or allocations which are being sent out by the Palace. Others are possibly totals, but their relation to the other records is still obscure.

78 = C 914   (K   lxvii)   †

a-ka-wi-ja-de | *pa-ra-ti-jo*   RAMS 50
                    pa-ro   HE-GOATS 50

To Achaea: from Pallantios, fifty rams, fifty he-goats.

Akhaiwijān-de: the *-de* suffix marks this out as a place-name, and the spelling exactly fits the form 'Αχαιϝία postulated as the Greek original of the Hittite *Aḫḫijawā*. There is, however, no clue to its location. It is by no means impossible that it is merely a place in Crete, though nowhere else mentioned on the tablets. Most of the proposed locations of the Hittite name (Rhodes, Cyprus, or even the Greek mainland) would be possible, for there is no reason why sheep and goats should not be carried by sea. The status of Pallantios is obscure; spelt *Pa₂-ra₂-ti-jo* the name recurs on Dg1235, where he is presumably a shepherd.

One series of tablets (*Dn*) appears to give totals of rams for each of the places ‡ mentioned. The entries complete enough to transcribe are listed below:

Ai₂?-so	50
Da-wo	2440
Da-*22-to	1370
E-ko-so	2262
E-ra	134
Luktos	200[
Phaistos	1509
Pa₃-ko-we	2003
Pu-na-so	330
Ra-ja	904
Su-ki-ri-ta	517
[*Su*]-*ri-mo*	2390
Ti-ri-to	50
Unknown	10,892
Total	25,051

There is also a fragment with the numeral 19,000 [+?], which should perhaps be added in. What these figures represent is hard to say; they do not appear to bear any relation to the total numbers of sheep represented on the other tablets. The figure for *E-ra* (134) can hardly be related either to the total number of sheep recorded on surviving (published) tablets (809) or to the deficit (215) or to their sum (1024).

79 = Dn 1094   (joined with 1311   L   lxxii, lxxxv)

pa-i-to   RAMS 1509 ⟦40⟧

da-wo   RAMS 2440

† **80** = C 913   (K   lxxi)

pa-ro   *e-te-wa-no*   *ai.*   HE-GOAT 1 [

pa-ro   *ko-ma-we-te*   HE-GOAT 1   *pa-*[*ro*?

From *Etewainos* one *ai-* he-goat; . . .; from Komawens one he-goat; from. . . .

‡ **81** = Dm 1180   (joined with 5048   L)

pa-i-to   ┌ *ai-mi-re-we*   RAMS 4
            └ *e-ka-ra-e-we*   RAMS 20

At Phaistos: four. . .rams, twenty. . .rams.

ai-mi-re-we, e-ka-ra-e-we: these two words characterize a small group of tablets, all of
    much the same form, except that *ai-mi-re-we* is sometimes omitted, and in one case
    (Dm1184) we have the entry]-*we-to o-pa*. This latter word may be a term describing
    some sort of tribute (see p. 169). As pointed out by Carratelli (1954, pp. 220–1),
    the numbers of *e-ka-ra-e-we* are greatly in excess of those of the other category. The
    natural interpretation is to regard these two words as masculine nominative plurals
    describing the rams; Carratelli, however, takes them as dative singular (-*ēwei*),
    denoting the person to whom the animals are sent, and connects them with ἐσχάρα
    (= a sacrificer on a fire altar) and αἷμα (= a sacrificer of ἄπυρα ἱερά). The formation
    of the second name is obscure, the meaning of both doubtful. No wholly satisfactory
    solution has yet been proposed; see the Vocabulary for further suggestions.

82 = Ca 895   (K   lxvi; see plate II (*a*), facing p. 110)

i-qo   🐎 5   🐎 4   *po-ro*   🐎 [

o-no   🐎 3   *po-ro*   🐎 2   🐎 4 [

Horses: five *mares*, four (full-grown) horses, *x* foals.

Asses: three she-asses, two foals, four he-asses.

The beginning of this tablet, containing the initial two words and half the horse's head
    on the second line, was found by Chadwick among some unpublished fragments in
    Iraklion Museum in April 1955. It had already attracted much attention, and Evans
    (*PM*, IV, p. 799) first pointed out that the foals are distinguished from the horses by
    being shown without manes. This distinction certainly holds for the last two entries
    of line 1; the left side of the first ideogram in the line is broken, but may have had
    a mane. This is the ordinary form on the chariot tablets (*Sc*), the mane usually being
    tied up into three 'top-knots'. On the other hand the second line is more difficult,
    since it is now clear that none of the animals have manes, the first and third showing

instead the usual marks of sex. Whether any distinction is intended between the ideograms of lines 1 and 2 is hard to say; no immediate differences are apparent, and if the latter are really intended for asses the characteristic long ears do not seem to be adequately represented. It is possible that the ideogram (as we may suspect in other cases too) is merely a conventional form used alike for horse and ass, the distinction here being adequately indicated by the initial words.

In each case three sorts of animal are listed separately, though in a different order. In the second line the distinction is clearly between female, male and foals, and this is therefore likely to apply to the first line as well, though the first two ideograms seem to lack distinguishing features; if the first were complete the difference might be seen, as suggested in the drawings here.

hiqqᵘoi: a welcome confirmation of our interpretation of this word, which some have been inclined to doubt.

pōlō: dual in line 2. Evans had suggested this reading on the basis of the Cypriot syllabary, but he was so convinced that the language was not Greek that he rejected it as illusory.

onoi: without prejudice to the other places where *o-no* is found (never in contexts suggesting an animal; see Vocabulary), the interpretation here seems incontestable; *i-qo* and *o-no* are clearly parallel words describing animals of equine type.

83 = Ch902   (K   lxiii)   †

[Probably about twelve lines of this very thick tablet lost.]

1	*mi-ru-ro si-pe-we*	OX *ne.* ⌇ 12
2	*o-du-ru-wi-jo ko-re-te*	OX *ne.* ⌇ 12
3	*wa-to │ ko-re-te* OX *ne.* ⌇ 12 *wa-to │ da-nu-wo* OX ⌇ 12	
4	*si-ra-ro ko-re-te*	OX 1 *ne.* ⌇ 12
5	*pa₃-ko-we e-ra-ne*	OX 1 *ne.* ⌇ 12
6	*o-du-ru-we u-wo-qe-we*	OX 1 *ne.* ⌇ 12
7	*ri-jo-no ko-re-te*	OX 1 *ne.* ⌇ 12
8	*ru-ki-ti-jo*	OX 1 *ne.* ⌇ 12
9	*a-pa-ta-wa ko-re-te*	OX 1 *ne.* ⌇ 12
10	*ku-ta-i-to ko-re-te*	OX 1 *ne.* ⌇ 12
11	*re-na-jo e-re-ta*	OX 1 *ne.* ⌇ 12
12	[..]-*wa-to we-re-we*	OX 1 *ne.* ⌇ 12

[One or more lines lost.]

Mi-ru-ro at *Si-pe-we* (?): one ox, twelve *young calves*.

The *mayor* of *Odrus*: one ox, twelve *young calves*.

The *mayor* of *Wa-to*: one ox, twelve *young calves*.   *Da-nu-wo* of *Wa-to*: one ox, twelve *calves*.

The mayor of *Si-ra-ro*: one ox, twelve *young calves*.

The *E-ra-ne* at *Pa-ko-we*: one ox, twelve *young calves*.

The *U-wo-qe-we* at *Odrus*: one ox, twelve *young calves*.
The *mayor* of *Ri-jo-no*: one ox, twelve *young calves*.
The people of Luktos: one ox, twelve *young calves*.
The *mayor* of Aptara: one ox, twelve *young calves*.
The *mayor* of *Ku-ta-i-to*: one ox, twelve *young calves*.
The rowers of *Re-na*: one ox, twelve *young calves*.
The *we-re-we* . . . : one ox, twelve *young calves*.

The key to this puzzle is the ideogram 𝕰; the number of these is always a dozen, and it is preceded by the adjunct *ne*. which elsewhere may be *newos* 'young'. The suggestion that it is a special sign for CALF has here been followed in the translation but without conviction. In three cases the vertical stroke of the OX ideogram seems to have something attached to it, possibly a ligature with -*ta*, though this is not recognized by Bennett; cf. SHEEP+TA PY Cn09.

Mi-ru-ro: a man's name, cf. **38** = As1516.

Odruïos: apparently the adjective of *Odruei* (dat.) line 6. The name recalls the Thracian Ὀδρύσαι (cf. Ὄθρυς). Surprisingly the word recurs on a Theban jar: *ka-u-no o-du-ru-wi-jo wa-na-ka-te-ro* (TH I).

ko-re-te: as at Pylos the title of some kind of local official, perhaps mayor. The Greek form is obscure, see Vocabulary, p. 397.

wa-to: apparently an otherwise unknown place-name. The recurrence of this word on the Theban jars is a strange coincidence. The suggested reading *wastos* 'citizen' (cf. Björck, 1954a, p. 123) is not altogether satisfactory; it might here mean the citizens of the town of Knossos, as distinct from the Palace.

da-nu-wo: Bennett read *mi-pa₃-wo*; possibly a title rather than a name.

e-ra-ne: surely not *Hellānes*? Some connexion with the place-name *E-ra*?

u-wo-qe-we: cf. *u-wo-qe-ne* V 145, a tablet with several echoes of this one, including *u-du-ru-wo*, perhaps genitive to *o-du-ru-we*, and *we-re-we*.

† **84** = C 59 (? xxiii)

1 [.]-*sa* / *we-ka-ta* OXEN 6 *da-wo* / *we-ka-ta* OXEN 6

2 [1 or 2]-*to* / *ta-ra-me-to we-ka-ta* OXEN 6 *da-*22-to* / *da-mo we-ka-ta* OXEN 6

3 *tu-ri-so* / *da-mo we-ka-ta* OXEN 6 *ku-do-ni-ja* / *we-ka-ta* OXEN 50

At . . .-*sa*: six working oxen.
At *Da-wo*: six working oxen.
At . . .-*to*: six working oxen; . . . .
At *Da-*22-to*: six working oxen; *for* the village.
At Tulissos: six working oxen; *for* the village.
At Kudonia: fifty working oxen.

wergatai: 'workers', a word used especially of oxen; so also Carratelli (1954, p. 219). Furumark's ϝέκατα (= ἑκόντα) translated 'gezähmte' cannot be justified either on grounds of form (Cret. ϝέκαθθα is not the earliest form and in any case is feminine: Bechtel, *Griech. Dial.* II, p. 694) or of meaning. The use of the male form of the ox ideogram (except in one case, probably an oversight) does not of course imply that the beasts were not castrated. The mention of Kudonia is interesting as it appears to show that western Crete too was under the control of Knossos; the references to it on the chariot tablets are ambiguous.

An interesting series of tablets (some of those with the *Ch* prefix) give us an † intimate giimpse of rustic life. They record yokes of oxen, which are given names; these were identified by Furumark (1954, pp. 28–9). A full list of these names will be found at the end of the Index of Personal Names (p. 427).

85 = Ch896   (K   lxvii)

ta-za-ro | ai-wo-ro   ^ke-ra-no-qe^   *ne.we.*   OXEN   ZE I

Ta-za-ro: one yoke of *young working* oxen, Aiwolos and Kelainos.

Ta-za-ro: the name of the ox-driver?

ne.we.: abbreviations of *newos* 'young' and *we-ka-ta = wergatās* 'working'? Cf. the preceding tablet.

Mixed livestock are occasionally recorded under the heading of a place-name and the word *a-ko-ra-ja* or *a-ko-ra-jo*, probably *agoraios*. This may mean 'belonging to the *agora* or collection' in the sense explained above; see p. 200. It might, however, merely denote 'belonging to the herd', and it is remarkable that in opposition to the tribute lists of cattle, the males are in a much sounder proportion to the females, though still sometimes excessive for breeding purposes. The places named on the surviving tablets are: *Wa-to*, Kudonia, *Ka-ta-ra-i*, *Si-ra-ro*, Aptara and *Odrus*.

86 = Co907   (K   lxviii)   ‡

¹ *si-ra-ro | a-ko-ra-jo*   RAMS 202   EWES 750
² HE-GOATS 125   SHE-GOATS 240   BOARS 21   SOWS 60   BULLS 2   COWS 10

6. GRAIN CONSIGNMENTS AND RATIONS AT KNOSSOS (E, F)

Although there is no indication whether these tablets record payments or receipts, the former seems more likely on general grounds, as the people concerned are often ethnic groups. We are not told their numbers, so there is no possibility of calculating a ration. In most cases the commodity is the staple

120   𐀷   WHEAT

*34   𐂀   Month?

grain WHEAT, but occasionally other commodities are added such as OLIVES; cf. the rations of wheat and figs at Pylos (p. 157). The crescent-shaped ideogram is discussed in the notes on KN **35** = Am819.

87 = E 668   (F?   xlviii)
           ^{1} *ru-ki-ti-jo*   WHEAT 246   T 7
           ^{2} *tu-ri-si-jo*   WHEAT 261   *ra-ti-jo*   WHEAT 30   T 5

Men of Luktos: 29,604 l. of wheat.
Men of Tulissos: 31,320 l. of wheat.
Men of Lato: 3660 l. of wheat.

† **88** = E 749   (I   lii)
           ^{1} *pa$_2$-ra-jo*   WHEAT 25
           ^{2} *ru-ki-ti-jo*   WHEAT 21[+
           ^{3} *ti-ri-ti-jo*   WHEAT [   ]
           ^{4} [*su*]-*ṛi-mi-jo*   WHEAT [   ]   T 2 ◁ 3
           ^{5} *pa$_2$-mi-jo*   WHEAT 12   T 5
           ^{6} *u-ta-ni-jo*   WHEAT [   ]
           ^{7} *pu-si-jo*   WHEAT [   ]
                    vacant 3

Men of Pharai: 3000 l. of wheat.
Men of Luktos: 2520 l. of wheat.
Men of *Ti-ri-to*: *x* l. of wheat.
Men of *Su-ri-mo*: (30+) l. of wheat.
Men of *Pa-mo*: 1500 l. of wheat.
Men of *Itanos*: *x* l. of wheat.
Men of *Pu-so*: *x* l. of wheat.

The figures in lines 4 and 5 are added from a new fragment joined by Bennett.

‡ **89** = E 777   (J   liii)
           ^{1} *ko-no-si-ja*   *ki-ri-te-wi-ja-i*   month 1   WHEAT 100
           ^{2} *a-mi-ni-si-ja*   month 1   WHEAT 100
           ^{3} *pa-i-ti-ja*   month 1   WHEAT 100

REVERSE:
                 a-ze-ti-ri-ja   WHEAT [

Women of Knossos (for the *ki-ri-te-wi-ja* women): *ration* for one month 12,000 l. of wheat.
Women of Amnisos: *ration* for one month 12,000 l. of wheat.

Women of Phaistos: *ration* for one month 12,000 l. of wheat.
Nurses: *x* l. of wheat.

If the crescent-shaped sign is rightly interpreted as 'month' here we have fairly clearly a distribution of rations, in this case to women, as is shown by the feminine endings and the two female occupational names. Either the rations are very generous or large numbers of women are concerned; 500 at each place on the Pylos ration scale (see p. 157).

ki-ri-te-wi-ja-i: possibly a religious office, see Vocabulary; the form is dative plural.

a-ze-ti-ri-ja: one of the cases of substitution of *z* for *k*; = *a-ke-ti-ri-ja* (see on PY 2 = Aa815). The form here could be dative singular or nominative plural.

90 = G 820   (K   lviii)   †

¹]-*dị e-ko-si a-pị ku-do-ni-ja pa-sa ki-ri-ta*   month 1
²]-*ja-qe pa₃-ko-we-i-ja-qe*   months 4
³]-*ti-ja ku-ta-ti-ja-qe po-ti-ni-ja-we-ja a-pu ke-u-po-de-ja*   months 4

...have in the region of Kudonia all the barley: one month's *rations*.
Women of...*and Pa-ko-we*: four months' *rations*.
Women of...*and Ku-ta-to*, belonging to the Mistress, from...: four months' *rations*.

ekhonsi amphi Kudōniāi pansan krithan (or *pansans krithans*): similarly read by Furumark (1954, p. 30) and Carratelli (1954, p. 89). Ventris reads *a-pị* for Bennett's *a-pu*, either of which makes sense.

po-ti-ni-ja-we-ja: the feminine of the adjective derived from Πότνια; it is not clear here whether it agrees with the women from the places mentioned or is to be taken with *ke-u-po-de-ja*. This is a feminine to *ke-u-po-da* (KN X 442, X 1044; PY **190** = Na55, etc., see p. 299), but its meaning is unknown; Furumark 'aus dem Magazin (??) der Potnia'.

7. GRAIN RATIONS AT PYLOS (Fn)   ‡

The group of tablets classified as *Fn* is marked by the grain ideogram which is provisionally identified as BARLEY. The entries consist largely of occupational names in the dative, and would therefore appear to be a distribution of pay or rations; the size of the groups is not specified when the entry is plural. The amounts range from two to   121   ⌐   BARLEY a maximum of 80 litres. In some cases other commodities are also included in the ration; figs in Fn01, olives in Fn05, Fn06 and Fn918. Apparently included in some lists are offerings to shrines: Fn01 has entries *Posidaïonde* and *Pa-ki-ja-na-de* and even *U-po-jo Potniāi* (cf. Furumark, 1954, p. 35).

† **91** = Fn02 [50]

1 *a-ki-to-jo pa₂-si-re-wi-ja*	BARLEY [		
2 *ke-ko-jo pa₂-si-re-wi-ja*	BARLEY [		
3 *a-ta-no-ro pa₂-si-re-wi-ja*	BARLEY T [		
4 *me-za-ne*	BARLEY ◁ 2	*ai-ki-a₂-ri-jo*	⟨BARLEY⟩ ◁ 1[
5 *me-ri-du-⟨ma⟩-te*	BARLEY ◁ 3	*mi-ka-ta*	BARLEY ◁ 3
6 *di-pte-ra-po-ro*	BARLEY ◁ 2	*e-to-wo-ko*	⟨BARLEY⟩ ◁ 2
7 *a-to-po-qo*	BARLEY ◁ 2	*po-ro-du-ma-te*	BARLEY ◁ 3
8 *o-pi-te-u-ke-e-we*	BARLEY ◁ 2	*i-za-a-to-mo-i*	BARLEY ◁ 3
9 *ze-u-ke-u-si*	BARLEY ◁ 4		

vacat

11 **85-[.]-ja-te-wo do-e-ro-i*	BARLEY T 1
12 *mi-jo-[pa₂] do-e-ro-i*	BARLEY ◁ 3
13 *a-pi-[. . .] do-e-ro-i*	BARLEY ◁ 3
14 *[.]-ẉọ-[. . . .do-e-ro]-i*	BARLEY T 3

vacant 5

(Distribution of) barley:

for the retinue of *Alkithos*: *x* l.
for the retinue of Kerkos: *x* l.
for the retinue of Antanor: *x* l.
for the *me-za-ne*: 4 l.
for the *shore-man*: 2 l.
for the *me-ri-du-ma*: 6 l.
for the *mi-ka-ta*: 6 l.
for the *leather-bearer*: 4 l.
for the *armourer*: 4 l.
for the baker: 4 l.
for the *po-ro-du-ma*: 6 l.
for the *rigger*: 4 l.
for the *i-za-a cutters*: 6 l.
for the yokers: 8 l.

for the slaves of . . . : 12 l.
for the slaves of *Mi-jo-pa*: 6 l.
for the slaves of *Amphi-*. . . : 6 l.
for the slaves of . . . : 36 l.

pa₂-si-re-wi-ja: *basilēwiāi*. This implies that the men named in the genitive are βασιλεῖς; unfortunately only one is named outside the *Fn* group, Antanor, who is associated with the place *Pa-ki-ja-* in Vn04.

me-za-ne: of the remaining entries two are certainly dative plural, as is *do-e-ro-i* in the second paragraph; if therefore the rest are dative, they must be singular.

di-pte-ra-po-ro: *diphtheraphorōi* 'wearer of a leather garment', perhaps a title of a trade or post? Or *-pōlōi* 'leather-seller'; or even a metathesis for *diphtheraloiphōi* 'school-master'? See Vocabulary, p. 390.

i-za-a-to-mo: possibly containing the word *a-to-mo* = *arthmos*, cf. *e-qe-(a)-o a-to-mo* **43** = Sn01. Or *-tomos* 'cutter' as in *du-ru-to-mo*?

mi-jo-[pa₂]: can be supplied from Fn867, and if genitive must be feminine.

8. OIL CONSIGNMENTS OR RATIONS AT KNOSSOS AND MYCENAE (Fh, Fo) †

It seems clear from the archaeological evidence that olive-oil was in extensive use in Mycenaean Greece. It is thus surprising to find that records dealing with it are not very common; some at least of those at Knossos are religious offerings. There is, however, a group of small tablets which appear not to be religious, but allocations of oil. 130 🜹 OLIVE-OIL The introductory word, which may be a dative, is often a personal name, but occupational terms also appear; and sometimes a place-name is added. There are also a number of other terms occasionally found, such as *apudosis* 'payment' and *zo-a* which seems to be ζόη, some sort of decoction of oil.

92 = Fh349 (C · xxxii)

ru-ki-to / *a-pu-do-si* OIL 53 [

Luktos: payment 1908 l. of oil.

Mention of oil at Pylos is even rarer; it may have not yet been produced ‡ in Messenia and be therefore a luxury article, an impression also obtained from the references to it in Homer. One of the new tablets from Blegen's excavations of 1954 (Gn1184), however, plainly records a transaction in oil between two men who are elsewhere named as 'unguent-boilers'; and the identity of the ideogram is happily confirmed by the spelling *e-ra₃-wo* = *elaiwon*. Its text runs: *ko-ka-ro a-pe-do-ke e-ra₃-wo to-so e-u-me-de-i* OIL 18; *pa-ro i-pe-se-wa ka-ra-re-we* 38. 'Kokalos repaid the following quantity of olive-oil to Eumedes: 648 l.; from Ipsewas thirty-eight *stirrup-jars*.' The association of *e-ra₃-wo* with OIL is confirmed by four or five new tablets found in 1955 in the pithos magazine behind the Megaron. At Mycenae Wace in 1952 named the building which he had discovered two years earlier 'the House of the Oil-merchant' because the basement yielded thirty large stirrup-jars which 'had originally contained oil, for their clay is heavily impregnated with oil' (Wace,

1953*b*, p. 423). This name is not entirely substantiated by the tablets found in this house, since most of them refer to wool. But one tablet, which is quoted here, bears testimony to dealings in oil, apparently a distribution to various persons and groups. Dealings in wool would of course hardly leave an archaeological trace, and if the owner of the house was really a merchant he may have dealt in at least two commodities.

† **93** = Fo101

```
 1  a-ne-a₂   ◁ 3   pa-na-ki   ◁ I
 2  ma-no   ◁ I   a-na-*88   ◁ I
 3  to-ti-ja   ◁ I   we-i-we-sa   ◁ I
 4  ke-ra-so   ◁ I
 5  pi-we-ri-si   ⚲ I   tu-mi-[        ]   ◁ I
 6  ko-ma-ta   ◁ I   na-ta-ra-ma   ◁ [I]
 7  pe-ta-[.]   ◁ I   pu-ka-ro   [◁ I]
 8  o-ta-ki   ◁ I
 9  e-ro-pa-ke-ta   OIL I
10  a-ke-ti-ri-ja-i   ◁ 4
                  vacant 4
15  to-so   OIL 2   ⚲ I   ◁ I
```

For *Aineas*: 6 l. of oil.

for *Phainax*: 2 l. of oil, etc.

   Total: 86 l. of oil.

*a-na-*88*: the last sign is unlike any recorded elsewhere, but may be a variant of
   33 = ra₃; cf. the man's name *a-na-ro* KN D1928.

pi-we-ri-si: dative plural of Πιερίδες; cf. *pi-we-ri-di* Oe103; man's name *Pi-we-ri-ja-ta*
   PY **254** = Jn04. Does this imply not a sale but an offering?

a-ke-ti-ri-ja-i: dative plural; see Vocabulary, p. 387.

9. MIXED RATIONS AND CONSIGNMENTS AT KNOSSOS (F)

120	WHEAT	122	OLIVES
*30	FIGS		OLIVES + A
			OLIVES + TI

This small class of tablets from Knossos shows a mixture of various agricultural products. Some tablets seem to belong to the lists of offerings (e.g. F 953), but others are more likely secular. The commodities are chiefly wheat and barley, but the tablets quoted are of interest as adding figs and olives. The identity of the sign 122 OLIVES seems to be confirmed by the reading, but no explanation has yet been offered of the ligatured versions of it.

94 = F 841 (joined with 867 K lxii, lxiii) †

¹]-*ti-ja* *sa-pi-ti-[ne]-we-jo* [
² *a-di-*22-sa* WHEAT ⊤ 6 FIGS 8 [
³]-*ņo-di-mi-zo-jo* [?] WHEAT 2 FIGS 34 [
⁴ *pa-i-to* *mi-sa-ra-jo* *sa-pi-ti-ne-we-jo* [
⁵ *su-za* FIGS 75 *ka-po* *e-[ra-wa?*
⁶ *e-ra]-wa* OLIVES 46 *e-ra-wa* [

vacant 2

Too fragmentary for translation; the quantities in lines 5 and 6 are considerable: 9000 l. of figs and 5520 l. of olives.

sa-pi-ti-ne-we-jo: cf. the man's name *sa-pi-ti-nu-wo* **38** = As1516. Possibly a patronymic, in which case *mi-sa-ra-jo* will be a man's name.

su-za: cf. **166** = Gv864. Apparently for *suka* 'figs', with *z* for *k* as in other words.

ka-po e-[ra-wa: *karpoi elaiwās* 'fruits of the olive'? In the next line *e-ra-wa* is presumably plural 'olives'.

95 = F 852 (K liv)

¹ *da-wo | a-ma* *e-pi-ke-re* WHEAT 10,000[
²   OLIVES+A 70 OLIVES+TI 20 OIL[

At *Da-wo*: harvest...: 1,200,000 (+) l. of wheat.
  a- olives 8400 l., *ti*- olives 2400 l, *x* l. of *oil*.

a-ma: occurs five times at Knossos in connexion with WHEAT. The formula *a-ma e-pi-ke-re* is repeated once (F 851); elsewhere *a-ma* is preceded by broken words which may be names, and once appears on a fragment with *da-mo*, but not on the same line. It seems likely that it has something to do with ἀμάω 'reap'; possibly a noun ='harvest', though a third singular of the verb cannot be excluded (for the form cf. *te-re-ja*). ἄμη in later Greek means 'shovel' or 'bucket' and Ventris has proposed *amā epikhēlēs* 'bucket full to the brim', but the relevance of this to the context is uncertain. The latter word could also be a hypothetical *episkherēs* (cf. ἐπισχερώ).

10. MIXED RATIONS AND CONSIGNMENTS AT PYLOS (Un)

A small group of tablets record a large variety of agricultural produce and livestock, in considerable amounts. Unfortunately in no case is the heading really intelligible; some appear to be a requisition, and in one place a deficit is recorded. But the reason for this impost is not clear. Most of the ideograms

are now identified. No. 125 has been provisionally named cyperus; what appears to be the same sign is at Knossos also found in a form (no. 124) which contains the CONDIMENT sign (no. 123), and this is glossed *ku-pa-ro* on **102** = Ga517. The same sign is also found with superimposed *ku* (no. 126).
† The value of no. *65 FLOUR is given by **171** = Un718, where the sign in

No.		Name		No.		Name
121		BARLEY		*65		FLOUR
122		OLIVES		132		?
131		WINE		ME		Honey?
106a		RAM, and other livestock ideograms		*30		FIGS
125		Cyperus?		146		A textile?

a simplified form is glossed by *me-re-u-ro* = *meleuron* = ἄλευρον (see Vocabulary, p. 399). No. 132 is a liquid, but its nature is entirely unknown. The abbreviation ME, being a liquid, is probably *meli* 'honey'; there is nothing to show that it has the same meaning when it appears as an entry on the *Ma* tablets (see p. 290), where the quantities are very large if we transcribe the figures as liquid units (36 l.). The meaning of no. 146 is discussed on p. 290, and the suggestion is made that it is some kind of textile.

96 = Un02 [138]

¹ *pu-ro   qe-te-a₂   pa-ro   du-ni-jo*
² BARLEY 18 T 5 *po-pa₂* OLIVES 4 T 3 ◁ 5
³ WINE 13   RAMS 15   WE 8   EWE 1   HE-GOATS 13   PIGS 12
⁴ PIG+SI 1   COW 1   BULLS 2
⁵ *me-za-wo-ni* BARLEY 4 T 8 ◁ 1 *ka-pa* OLIVES 7

At Pylos: *due* from *Dunios*: 2220 l. of barley, 526 l. of *eating* olives, 468 l. of wine, fifteen rams, eight *yearlings*, one ewe, thirteen he-goats, twelve pigs, one *fat hog*, one cow, two bulls.
From *Mezawon*: 578 l. of barley, 840 l. of...olives.

qe-te-a₂: a word which recurs at Knossos in the forms *qe-te-a* and *qe-te-o* (see Vocabulary, p. 406). It must record the nature of the transaction and Furumark (1954, p. 42) is probably right in regarding it as meaning 'to be supplied, due'. It is more difficult to find a satisfactory etymology. A connexion with θέσσασθαι 'pray for', Hom. ἀπόθεστος, is possible, but the meaning presents obstacles, and Furumark's *qʷhestea* cannot be explained by the suffix -τέος, which is generally agreed to be from *-τέϝος.

Possibly to be identified with τέλθος 'payment due'; in this case the form *qe-te-o* must be genitive.

po-pa₂: also applied to OLIVES at Knossos **164** = Gv863. Probably denotes some kind † of olive as distinguished from *ka-pa*. The spelling would fit φορβή, φορβάς, possibly meaning 'for eating'.

ka-pa: the name of a different kind of olive; connected with σκάφη 'trough', i.e. for pressing?

97 = Un03 [2]   ‡

¹ *pa-ki-ja-si mu?-jo-me-no e-pi wa-na-ka-te*
² *a̯-pi-e-ke o-pi-te-⟨u⟩-ke-e-u*
³ BARLEY 16 T 4 *125 T 1 ◁ 3 *o.* ◁ 5
⁴ FLOUR 1 T 2 OLIVES 3 T 2 *132 ⧧ 2 ME ⧧ 1
⁵ FIGS 1 OX 1 RAMS 26 EWES 6 HE-GOATS 2 SHE-GOATS 2
⁶ PIG+SI 1 SOWS 6 WINE 20 ⧧ 1 *146 2

At *Pa-ki-ja-ᵖ*: ...for the king, the *rigger keeps*: 1968 l. of barley, 18 l. of *cyperus* (deficit 10 l.), 144 l. of flour, 384 l. of olives, 24 l. of..., 12 l. of honey, 120 l. of figs, one ox, twenty-six rams, six ewes, two he-goats, two she-goats, one *fat hog*, six sows, 732 l. of wine, two *cloths*.

mu?-jo-me-no: to judge by the form this might be a middle or passive participle, but hardly μυόμενος unless = μυούμενος. It is possible that it is dative: 'on the occasion of the initiation of the king'. ἐπί + dat. = 'in the time of' is found in Arcadian.

wa-na-ka-te: *wanaktei*, with the same use of *a* as a dead vowel (after the nominative *wa-na-ka*) as in *wa-na-ka-te-ro*.

a̯-pi-e-ke: *amphi-ekhei* = ἀμπέχει? or *aph-iēke* = ἀφέηκε? Carratelli (1954*a*, pp. 101–2) translates 'collects'.

opiteukheeus: the restoration is almost certain in view of the other examples of this word (see Vocabulary, p. 402), but the meaning of the τεύχεα is not yet discovered.

11. SPICES AT KNOSSOS (Ga, Og)

All three sites have produced written evidence of the use of spices or condi- ¶ ments, though in this case the richest find comes from Mycenae. The use of spices such as coriander and aniseed is attested archaeologically for the Bronze Age, and it is reasonable to suppose that many of the condiments used in classical times for culinary or   123 ⌂ CONDIMENT medicinal purposes had been known much earlier. Few have names with Indo-European cognates, and   124 ⌂ Cyperus? most were probably in use in the Aegean area before the arrival of the Greeks, or were introduced by trade during the Mycenaean age. Coriander and cyperus are both described at Knossos as 'Cyprian', which probably refers to their provenance; and there is an unidentified spice called *Phoinikio-* which clearly betrays its origin. The ideogram no. 123 was taken by Evans to represent a building without eaves ('granary' sign—*PM*, IV, p. 622), despite the presence in some forms of what is obviously a handle. For Myres (*SM II*, p. 33) it was 'obviously a rick or granary', and in the form no. 124 'the cylindrical wicker-structure with lifting handle, still in use among the Southern Slavs'. It resembles more closely a large pepper-pot, and its true significance emerged from the identification of coriander and cyperus as a result of the decipherment (*Evidence*, p. 92). From its use with the fractional signs for dry measure (e.g. Ga415) it follows that it denotes the unit of spice (approx. 120 l.). The variant no. 124 appears to contain the 'cyperus' ideogram no. 125.

† **98** = Ga415   (E   xxxiv)

ru-ki-ti-jo | ko-ri-ja-do-no   CONDIMENT 2   T 6

Men of Luktos: 312 l. of coriander seed.

ko-ri-ja-do-no: this word is found also at Pylos and Mycenae, where its plural is also spelt *ko-ri-a₂-da-na*. It is an ancestral form of κορίαννον, κορίανδρον, which may be derived from *koria(n)dnon* by assimilation and popular etymology. The fruits of the coriander, *Coriandrum sativum*, are widely used as a condiment. The ancients seem to have obtained it from Egypt, though it was originally imported into Egypt from India.

99 = Ga418   (E   xxxiii)

su-ri-mi-jo | $\begin{matrix} po\text{-}ni\text{-}ki\text{-}jo & 3 \\ ko\text{-}ri\text{-}ja\text{-}do\text{-}no & T\ 5\ [\![2]\!] \end{matrix}$

Men of *Su-ri-mo*: 3 kg. of *Phoenician spice*, 60 l. of coriander seed.

100 = Og424   (E   xxxiv)

pa₃-ko-we-i-jo | $\begin{matrix} po\text{-}[ni]\text{-}ki\text{-}jo \\ a\text{-}pu\text{-}do\text{-}si \end{matrix}\ 5$

Men of *Pa-ko-we*: payment 5 kg. of *Phoenician spice*.

101 = Ga675   (F   lx, xlix)

wa-na-ka-te | pe-ma   CONDIMENT 10

For the king: 1200 l. of seed for condiment.

The absence of a word or sign indicating the nature of the condiment is unusual, but cf. Ga416. These tablets may have formed part of a series which made it unnecessary to repeat the name of the commodity on each.

102 = Ga517   (F   xl)

tu-wi-no | ${ku\text{-}pi\text{-}ri\text{-}jo} \atop {ku\text{-}pa\text{-}ro}$ **124* I

Twinon: 120 l. of cyperus seed from Cyprus.

Twinōn: cf. *tu-wi-no-no* Ga676, which may be genitive. Probably a man's name, perhaps = Σίνων.

ku-pi-ri-jo: not, like *po-ni-ki-jo*, the name of a separate commodity, so presumably adjectival; it might mean only 'of the Cyprian variety'. At Pylos it is a man's name, but this is unlikely here.

12. SPICES AT PYLOS (Un)

The two chief spices at Knossos, cyperus and coriander, reappear at Pylos, together with other enigmatic ideograms. No. 157 is so far unidentified; it appears to be counted, or if in standard units is not yet found with any fractions. It is also found on An23 reverse, which seems to have no connexion with the obverse and ranks for classification with the two Un tablets quoted here. No. 127 (also found on An23 rev.) is a monogram of KA+PO, though it is impossible to be sure of the order in which these signs are to read; cf. the monogram A+RE+PA in descending order in Un06, in ascending order in **171** = Un718. It seems likely that this should be connected with *ka-po* in KN **94** = F 841 = *karpos* 'fruit'. No. 131b appears to be merely half of no. 131 WINE, but cannot be identical with it since it appears in the same list; possibly a special kind of wine (e.g. must). The presence of no. 145 WOOL among a list of commodities such as spices, fruit and wine is also puzzling, in particular in the second of these tablets, where it has the annotation *wi-ri-za*. This cannot be unconnected, since it recurs at Knossos. It is possible that there is some confusion here between the WOOL ideogram and the syllabic sign MA used at Mycenae as an abbreviation for 'fennel' (see p. 227); there seems to be similar confusion on KN **203** = F 953.

123		CONDIMENT
157		?
127		Fruit?
131		WINE
131b		?
ME		Honey?
145		WOOL

103 = Un08 [267]

¹ *o-do-ke   a-ko-so-ta*
² *tu-we-ta   a-re-pa-zo-o*

^{3} *tu-we-a   a-re-pa-te*   ⟦*ze-so-me*⟧
^{4} *ze-so-me-no*   ⟦*ko*⟧
^{5} *ko-ri-a$_2$-da-na*   CONDIMENT 6
^{6} *ku-pa-ro$_2$*   CONDIMENT 6   *157 16
^{7} KA+PO 2   T 5   WINE 20   ME 2
^{8} WOOL 2   *131 b 2

three lines erased

Thus *A(r)xotas* gave spices to Thuestas the unguent-boiler, for unguent which is to be boiled:

coriander seed 720 l.
cyperus seed 720 l.
...16 units.
fruits 300 l.
wine 720 l.
honey 72 l.
wool 6 kg.
must 72 l.

hō dōke: cf. *a-pu-do-ke*.

tu-we-ta: taken by Furumark (1954, p. 41) as *thuestās*, correctly seen by Palmer (1954 *b*, p. 21) to be a man's name. Evidently names not infrequently fitted professions; cf. *ka-ke-u* the name of a χαλκεύς Jn750.

aleiphazoōi: the identification of this trade-name gains further confirmation from Pylos Gn1184, where two men who are elsewhere given this title are engaged in a transaction concerning olive-oil (see p. 217).

thuea: aromatic substances used in the making of perfumes; the sense of 'burnt offering' for θύος is not necessarily the earliest; cf. (ἔλαιον) τεθυωμένον 'perfumed' (*Il.* xiv, 172).

† *aleiphatei zesomenōi*: the words of which *aleipha-zoos* is compounded. Palmer translates: 'How *A*. gave to *T*., the unguent-boiler, the θύεα for boiling in (or with) the unguent.' But this would require *ze-so-me-na*. The translation proposed involves a rare use of the dative to denote purpose: cf. Ἡρακλείοις γοναῖς, Pind. *Isth.* vii, 7, 'for the begetting of Herakles'. In either case the future middle participle must be taken in passive sense. It would also be just possible to take it as a true middle with *Thuestāi*: 'Thus *A*. gave to *T*., who is to boil spices in unguent'; the object of *dōke* would then be *koria(n)dna*, etc. But the order is against this.

‡ **104** = Un09 [249]

po-ti-[ni]-ja-we-jo
^{1} *pi-ra-jo / a-re-pa-zo-[o   ]   ku-pa-ro$_2$*   CONDIMENT 2   T 5
^{2} *wi-ri-za*   WOOL 2   [   ]   *157 10

3

[   ] T 6

vacant 2

Philaios the unguent-boiler of the Mistress: 300 l. of cyperus seed; *root* (?)
6 kg. of wool; 10 units of . . . ; 72 l. of . . . .

a-re-pa-zo-[*o*: Chadwick disagrees with Bennett's reading of the last preserved sign as
we; it could be *zo*, thus allowing an obvious restoration.

wi-ri-za: found again with WOOL on a Knossos fragment OdM26. It would seem to
be the equivalent of ῥίζα (Lesb. βρίσδα), but its meaning is obscure.

13. SPICES AT MYCENAE (Ge)   †

The three texts quoted here are representative of a group of seven similar
tablets found by Wace in the House of the Sphinxes in 1954. These together
with the other Mycenae tablets are being published by Bennett (*MT II*) with
a commentary by Chadwick.

The tablets numbered Ge602–608 form part of a consistent series dealing with
a range of commodities, most of which can be confidently identified with
herbs and spices. Some tablets have an introductory phrase, but apart from
this the text consists entirely of a list of personal names, each followed by
specified quantities of the various commodities. Ge606 and Ge607 are slightly
different in form, but deal with the same commodities. The names in the lists
vary between nominative and dative, even on the same tablet: *Pe-ke-u* **105** =
Ge602 (nom.), but *Ka-e-se-we* (dat.) two lines further on; cf. *Ka-e-se-u* Ge605.
Possibly the dative implies that the transaction was indirect, i.e. 'on behalf of'.

The purpose of the records is to some extent conjectural; but if the House
of the Sphinxes is in fact a private house and not an appendage of the palace,
they may be a merchant's records of his business dealings. Since the amounts
associated with each name are comparatively small and are not totalled, they
may represent sales of these commodities; and in some cases the wording
suggests that they are amounts outstanding against future payment. In the
absence of any form of currency the debt can only be recorded in terms of the
actual commodities sold.

Lists of spices in a rather different context, referring to the produce of
certain places, are quoted by Lacheman (1939, p. 535) from the Nuzi tablets.
Among the spices mentioned both there and at Mycenae are coriander, fennel
and *kamūnu*, which Lacheman following Bezold translates as 'caraway'.

A new ideogram which makes its appearance on these tablets is no. 155,
which looks like some sort of dish or basket. It may perhaps be a container
in which the spices were kept. There is also a form without handles, which is

virtually indistinguishable from the metric sign ▽ (=approx. 0·5 l.), but seems here to be a container; it is transcribed as CUP. The metric sign itself has a handle on a new Pylos tablet (Un1185). Since the principal commodities recur frequently it will be convenient to discuss them before commenting on the texts.

123	⋔	CONDIMENT	KU	𓃞	Cumin
PE	⊱	Bunch?	MA	ⵜ	Fennel
155	⩊	BASKET	MI	⑂	Mint?
	▽	CUP	SA	Υ	Sesame
KO	φ	Coriander			

ka-da-mi-ja: apparently *kardamia*, a feminine or neuter plural form for κάρδαμον 'garden-cress, *Lepidium sativum*', the pungent seed of which was much used as a condiment especially in Persia (Xen. *Cyr.* I, 2, 8, Aelian *Var. hist.* III, 39). The alternative reading *ka-da-mi-ta* suggests καλάμινθα, a kind of mint, if we accept the representation of λ by *d* in pre-Greek words; cf. *da-pu₂?-ri-to-jo* = λαβυρίνθοιο in KN **205** = Gg702.

ka-na-ko: this occurs by itself or in the ligature KA+NA+KO. More often, however, it is qualified by an adjective: *e-ru-ta-ra* = *eruthrā* 'red', or *re-u-ka* = *leukā* 'white'; *e-ru-ta-ra* may even stand by itself. *ka-na-ko re-u-ka* is always measured; *e-ru-ta-ra* is always weighed (weights from 1 to 3 kg.). This is clearly the plant known as κνῆκος (original long ᾱ is attested by the Doric adjective κνακός), the gender of which varies between masculine and feminine. The identification of the plant has been contested, but is generally supposed to be safflower, *Carthamus tinctorius*, the florets of which are used to make a red dye. The oil is also used medicinally and for culinary purposes. Dioscorides (IV, 88) says that the flower of κνῆκος is used as a relish (εἰς τὰ προσοψήματα). The distinction of 'red' and 'white' seems to be confirmed by the varying senses of the adjective recorded by Hesychius: κνηκόν· τὸ κροκίζον χρῶμα, ἀπὸ τοῦ ἄνθους· ὅτε δὲ ἀπὸ καρποῦ, τὸ λευκόν. It serves here to distinguish the red florets from the pale seeds. It should be observed that κνῆκος has an I.-E. etymology and is originally an adjective of colour 'tawny'.

† *ka-ra-ko:* probably the Boeotian γλάχων (or γλαχώ) = Attic βλήχων, Ion. γλήχων, 'pennyroyal, *Mentha pulegium*'. It was used as a condiment in cooking; cf. κυκεὼν βληχωνίας, Ar. *Pax*, 712.

‡ *ko-no* or once *ko-i-no:* this is counted (numbers from 2 to 12) and is qualified by *a-po-ṭe-ị*[, *e-ṇe-me-na* (abbreviated to E) and DE. The variations of spelling can be paralleled in other words (e.g. *ko-to-na* at Pylos = *ko-to-i-na* at Knossos). At Knossos *ko-no* is found on one tablet **203** = F 953+955, where it prefaces the abbreviation MA.

It is probably to be equated with the Greek σχοῖνος (which is sometimes feminine); but with precisely which of the plants so designated is not clear. Possibly 'ginger-grass, *Cymbopogon schoenanthus*', a fragrant plant used in the manufacture of perfumes and later imported into Greece from Syria for this purpose. See especially Theophrastus, *H.P.* IX, 7, 3, where it is said not to grow in Europe.

ko-ri-ja-da-na, ko-ri-a₂-da-na: abbreviated KO, sometimes inserted in the CONDIMENT ideogram. It is measured (amounts from 12 to 24 l.). 'Coriander'; see on 98 = Ga415.

ku-mi-no, ku-mi-na: abbreviated KU; it is measured (amounts from 1½ to 4 l.). κύμινον 'cumin, *Cuminum cyminum*'. The word is Semitic, though Akkad. *kamūnu* is alleged to mean 'caraway'. According to Dioscorides (III, 59) it was imported from Egypt and Ethiopia, but also grown in Galatia and Cilicia. An oriental provenance is at least likely. It is widely used in cooking.

ma-ra-tu-wo: abbreviated MA; it is measured (amounts from ½ to 2 l.). *marathwon*, to be equated with the classical forms μάραθον or μάραθρον. The former is usually explained as derived by dissimilation from the latter; we may, however, suspect in the latter the influence of the suffix -θρον. The measured quantities clearly refer to the seed, which is used in cooking. The plant is widespread in distribution, so that this is more likely a local product than an import.

mi-ta: abbreviated MI (?); counted with PE (numbers 1, 2 and perhaps 20). It is possible that PE represents some sort of measure; perhaps 'bunch'. The use of *pe* in Cypriot as an abbreviation of the coin πέλεκυς can hardly be relevant. The plant is obviously μίνθα, μίνθη, some kind of mint, a common and widely distributed plant.

sa-pi-de: counted (numbers 6 and 12). The identification is uncertain, and may be a container rather than a spice. The word recurs at Pylos (Vn05, to which a new fragment found in 1954 has been joined), where numbers of these are mentioned in connexion with the nine towns; the numbers are damaged, those readable being 200, 80, 60 and 40. Possibly *sarpides* 'boxes'; cf. σαρπίς = σαρπός, *An. Ox.* II, 466, and σάρπους· κιβωτούς, Hesych. A connexion with σάλπη 'saupe fish' or σηπία 'cuttle-fish' seems much less likely.

sa-sa-ma: abbreviated SA; measured (amounts 1 to 5 l.). Equivalent to σησάμη or σήσαμα. The word is Semitic, the Ugaritic form (*ššmn*) being nearest to the Greek. The oil resembles olive-oil, but the small quantities of seeds can hardly have been intended for pressing. The seeds are themselves eaten, and a sweetmeat called *halvás* is still made from them in Greece today. It was grown in antiquity in Mesopotamia, but is said not to have been introduced into Egypt before the first millennium B.C.

se-ri-no: measured (amounts from ½ to 5 l.). σέλινον 'celery, *Apium graveolens*'. The seed is clearly intended.

105 = Ge602 †

¹ *jo-o-po-ro   a-ro-*[2–3]-*mi-jo / pe-se-ro*
² *pu₂?-ke   ma-ra-tu-wo* ⌓ 1 [

³ *pe-ke-u*   *ku-mi-no*   ▽ [   ]
      [*ma-ra*]-*tu-wo*   ◁ I
      sa-sa-ma   ▽ 2
      sa-pi-dẹ 6
⁴ *ka-e-se-we*   *ka-na-ko*   *e-ru-ta-ra*   [   ]
      [*sa*]-*sa-ma*   ◁ I
      ma-ra-tu-wo   ◁ I
      sa-pi-dẹ 6
⁵ *ke-po*   *ka-na-ko*   *e-ru-ta-ra*   ⟨ [   ]
      [   ]
      mi-ta   PE 2
      ko-no   *a-po-tẹ-ị*[
⁶ [   ]   DE I
      BASKET [I]

How...owed for *spices to Psellos*:

Pu-ke: fennel seed 0·5 l.

Phegeus: cumin *x*
      fennel seed 2 l.
      sesame seed 1 l.
      boxes 6

For *Ka-e-se-u*: red safflower *x*
      sesame seed 2 l.
      fennel seed 2 l.
      boxes 6

Ke-po: red safflower *x*
      ...*x*
      mint 2 *bunches*
      rushes ...
...   ...I *bundle*
      [I] basket.

jo-o-po-ro: *hō ophlon* 'how' or 'thus they owed'. ὤφλον is originally aorist to ὀφείλω. Cf. *o-o-pe-ro-si hō ophélonsi* PY **184** = Nn01.

a-ro-[: Palmer conjectures *a-ro-*[*ma-ta*] = ἀρώματα. But the shape of the break does not favour this restoration; and it does not lead to an easy solution of the next word, which may be the nominative plural subject. The comparison of the first word of Ge606 [*do?*]-*si-mi-ja* might suggest a similar restoration here; cf. *do-si-mi-jo* PY Wa730.

pe-se-ro: written in smaller characters. Cf. the man's name in the genitive *pe-se-ro-jo* KN **24** = Ai63; = Ψελλῷ? The word is not known as a name until late, but the adjective is at least as early as Aeschylus. The syntax is obscure, and he may be not the merchant himself, but his clerk.

a-po-ṭe-ị[: The reading is uncertain and the apparent absence of a numeral is surprising.

DE: possibly = *desmā* 'bundle'.

106 = Ge603   †

1 *ke-po*   *ko*   CONDIMENT   T 2
　　ka-na-ko   *re-u-ka*   ◁ I
　　dạ-ra-[. .]*-ta-qe* 20
　　[*ka*]*-na-ko*   *e-ru-ta-ra*   ⁊ I
　　[?]*ka-ra-to*   CUP I
2 *pu-ke-o*   *ko*   T 2
　　ku   ◁ 2
　　ma   ▽ 2
　　sa   ▽ 2
　　ka-na-ko   ⁊ I   CUP I
　　ko-no 10   *e-ṇe-me-na* I
3 *i-na-o*   *ko*   T 2
　　ku   ◁ I
　　[[*mị* 20]]
　　ko-no 10   E I
　　ka-na-ko   *e-ru-*(*ta-ra*)   ⁊ I
4 *rạ-ke-dạ-no*   *ko*   T 2
　　ku   ◁ 2
　　[erased?   ]
　　ko-no 12   Ẹ [I]
　　CUP I
　　a-ke-re-wi-jo   *ko*   T 2
　　ku   ◁ I
　　ma   ◁ I
　　no-ko (sic) 10   DE [I]
　　CUP I
6 *pe-ke-u*   *ko*   T 2
　　ku   ◁ I   ▽ 2
　　ma   ◁ I
　　ko-no 10   E I
　　ka-na-ko   ⁊ 2
　　CUP I

       7 *pu-wo*   *ko*   T 2
                  ku   ◁ 2
                  ma   ◁ [   ]
                  ko-no   DE 1
                  CUP 1

           REVERSE: *m̥e-*[   ] 2

Ke-po: coriander seed 24 l.
      white safflower 2 l.
      . . .20
      red safflower 1 kg.
      basket 1
Pu-ke-o: coriander seed 24 l.
      cumin 4 l.
      fennel seed 1 l.
      sesame 1 l.
      safflower 1 kg., cup 1.
      rushes 10 *e-ne-me-na* 1
Inaon: coriander seed 24 l.
      cumin 2 l.
      mint 20
      rushes 10 *e-* 1
      red safflower 1 kg.
        etc.

There is no introductory phrase, and the personal names are all in the nominative.
    It is perhaps one of a set, of which the preceding tablet forms the first.
ka-ra-to: if the word is complete as it stands this might be *kalathos*, i.e. a description of
    the CUP ideogram which follows, which may be no more than a handleless variant
    of the BASKET.
r̥a-ke-d̥a-no: nominative to *ra-ke-da-no-re* 107 = Ge604. This is evidently one of the class
    of names in -*ānōr*, but the first part of the compound is obscure.
a-ke-re-wi-jo: this recalls the Pylos place-name *A-ke-re-wa*; the use of ethnic adjectives
    as personal names is found elsewhere on the tablets (see p. 98).
pu-wo: *Purwos* = Πύρρος; also found at Knossos.

107 = Ge604

           1 *ke-e-pe*   *o-pe-ro*   *ka-na-ko*   *e-ru-ta-ra*   [   ]
                   [   ]
                   [   ]   DE 1
                   ku   ◁ 1

    2 *i-na-o-te*   *o-pe-ro*   *ku* ◁ I

                    sa ◁ I

                    ko-no 2

                    se-ri-no ⅇ 2   CUP I

    3 *ra-ke-da-no-re*   *o-pe-ro*   *e-ru-ta-ra* ⅇ I

                            ma ◁ 1

                            sa ◁ I

    4 *a-ke-re-wi-jo*   *o-pe-ro*   *e-ru-ta-ra* ⅇ 3

    5 *pu-ke-⟨o o⟩-pe-ro{ro}*   *ka-na-ko* ⅇ I

                    ma ▽ 2

                    sa ▽ 2

                    ka-da-mi-ja [ ]

In this tablet all the names are in the dative, followed in each case by the word *o-pe-ro* 'deficit'. In line 5 the scribe has written *pe-ro-ro*, which is plainly an error, and the name is probably *pu-ke-o* as in **106** = Ge603.2 rather than a variant form of *pu₂?-ke* **105** = Ge602.2.

CHAPTER VIII

† # LAND OWNERSHIP AND LAND USE

THE *E-* series of tablets, one of the most extensive at Pylos but regrettably poorly represented at Knossos, is distinguished by the ideogram no. 120, which is measured in amounts varying from 137 units (? 16,440 litres) down to ◀ 1 (2 litres). This commodity is one of the staple cereal grains, and has here been translated as 'wheat'; Furumark   120   𐀷   WHEAT and Carratelli read 'barley'.

Even before decipherment it was possible to guess, from the complex arrangement of the Pylos *E-* tablets, that they record hierarchies of different classes of persons on an apparently territorial basis. This was confirmed by phonetic transcription: the word *ko-to-na* (Knossos *ko-to-i-na*), whose detailed listing constitutes the primary purpose of the series, is evidently the classical κτοίνα. This term was used on Rhodes of a territorial unit equivalent to the Attic *deme*, and is glossed by Hesychius in the plural as δῆμος μεμερισμένος 'subdivided *deme*'; it is derived from the stem **kti-* 'settle, with buildings and/or cultivation' (cf. Skt. *kṣitíḥ* 'settlement', Arm. *šēn* 'settled; village'). At Pylos it apparently refers to the small-scale unit of cultivation, a 'field' or 'plot'.

Since our first reference to the *E-* tablets as records of land-tenure (*Evidence*, pp. 98–9) they have been discussed in greater detail by Furumark (1954, pp. 36–7), Webster (1954, pp. 13–14), Carratelli (1954*a*, pp. 102–12, 1954*b*, pp. 221–2), and Palmer (1955, pp. 6–18). Our commentary on this series, of which a large and representative selection is printed below, owes much to their analysis.

The *ktoinai* are generally described as being either *ki-ti-me-na* or *ke-ke-me-na*: the exact significance of this distinction is disputed. The first term, which is confined to the 'first set' of tablets (**114**=En02 et seq.) apparently recording actual ownership, is clearly *ktimenai*, from the same stem **kti-* 'settle' and formally identical with the participle seen in:

> *Od.* XXIV, 226: τὸν δ' οἶον πατέρ' εὗρεν ἐϋ-κτιμένῃ ἐν ἀλωῇ.
> *Od.* IX, 130: οἵ κέ σφιν καὶ νῆσον ἐϋ-κτιμένην ἐκάμοντο,   etc.

Carratelli supports the suggestion that *ktimenai*/?*kekeimenai* distinguish 'cultivated' land from 'fallow' or 'uncultivated'; there is a parallel in the distinction at Ugarit between *šd ubdy* 'uncultivated or fallow fields' from those that are *n'my* 'blooming' (Virolleaud, 1951, p. 32). But it can hardly be a coincidence that *?kekeimenai* is almost invariably confined to fields administered by the *dāmos* or 'village' (a term which might refer either to its people or to its land). The only exceptions are Ea10, Ea11, where *?kekeimenai ktoinai* are attributed to the 'swine-herds' and 'cowherds'; **146** = Eb34 (cf. Ep03.14) and **140** = Eb35, where they are recorded as subject to the obscure condition *e-to-ni-jo*; and Ea809.

Our translations will provisionally follow Furumark in translating the participles as 'private' and 'communal' respectively, even though these may be their effective rather than their etymological meanings. *Ktimenai* may once have meant 'land outside the *ager publicus* reclaimed by private initiative'. Webster compares *Od.* XXIV, 205–7 (and Nilsson's commentary, 1933, p. 242):

> οἱ δ' ἐπεὶ ἐκ πόλιος κατέβαν, τάχα δ' ἀγρὸν ἵκοντο
> καλὸν Λαέρταο τετυγμένον, ὅν ῥά ποτ' αὐτὸς
> Λαέρτης κτεάτισσεν, ἐπεὶ μάλα πόλλ' ἐμόγησεν.

On this view, the *ktoinai ktimenai* correspond approximately to the category of γῆ ἰδιόκτητος in the Egyptian system of land tenure recorded at Tebtunis (Rostovtzeff, 1941, pp. 274–92). Less probable alternatives are 'land actually occupied by its owners' or 'land with a separate dwelling on it', which the usual translation of Hom. ἐΰ-κτίμενος by 'good to live in' might suggest.

The second term *ke-ke-me-na* may perhaps be formally connected with κεῖμαι, κείμενος, whose stem shows reduplication in Skt. *çiçye*; there are, however, other possible derivations (e.g. from the stem of Homeric γέντο 'seized'). Palmer (1955, p. 7) connects *?kekeimenai* with κοινός 'common' and with Germanic *haim-* 'nucleated village settlement': the sense 'communal' would be confirmed by the phrase *ke-ke-me-na ko-to-na ko-na* (Ep02.3), if the spelling in fact represents *?kekeimenās ktoinās koinās* and not an erroneous repetition of syllables by the scribe.

Palmer (1955, p. 11) appositely compares the stipulations of the Hittite Code (§§ 39–40, trans. Goetze, in Pritchard, 1950):

If the inhabitant of a town has possession of another inhabitant's fields, he shall also perform the respective feudal service to the liege lord; if he allows the fields to lie idle, another man may take the fields, but he must not sell them.

If a 'craftsman' disappears and a socman is assigned in his stead, if the socman says 'this is my craftsman's fee but this other one is my socage', he shall secure for himself a sealed deed concerning the fields; then he has legal possession of the craftsman's fee and shall also perform the socage. If he refuses the craftsman's service, *they will declare the fields of the craftsman vacant, and the people of the town shall work them.*

From these and other somewhat obscure clauses on the same subject it appears that Hittite land was in principle divided into two classes (see Gurney, 1952, pp. 102–3). The inalienable land of the socman ('liege-man' or 'fief-holder') is held under specific terms of service (*saḫḫan*), and on his death the fief returns to the palace; the holding of the craftsman (lit. 'man of the tool'), or member of the artisan class, derives its title from the local authority, can be bought and sold, but reverts to the 'men of the village' when the title lapses.

The owners of *ktoinai ktimenai* at Pylos, among whom no women appear, are classified as *te-re-ta* (**114** = En02.2, cf. **152** = Er01.6), probably *telestai*; cf. Elean αἴτε ϝέτας αἴτε τελεστά 'whether he be private citizen or magistrate'. In view of initial *t-*, not *qu-*, the Mycenaean term is probably from τέλη 'services due' rather than from τέλος 'fulfilment', and it may imply original feudal obligations on the part of holders of such land. Palmer (1955, p. 13) suggests a direct comparison between these obligations and the *saḫḫan* of the Hittite land-owning class. He translates *telestai* as 'barons', arguing that this term, perhaps derived from a Germanic *bara* related to φόρος 'tribute', may reflect a parallel feudal organization.

Palmer similarly equates the lands administered by the Pylos *dāmos* with the Hittite 'village land'; and suggests that the Homeric name δημιοεργός, applied to craftsmen, minstrels and physicians, in fact originally meant 'those who work village land', i.e. a parallel class to the Hittite 'men of the tool'.

To make deductions about the precise conditions of Mycenaean land tenure from the apparent etymology of the terms used is of course rather precarious, in view of the historical adaptations which the system and its terminology may have undergone since the Greeks' original settlement in the country. Palmer's attempt to use them for a reconstruction of the 'Indo-European' institutions which they may have brought into the country with them encounters the same difficulties (as well as neglecting the possible influence of 'Minoan' institutions); but it represents the courageous first step in a necessary line of enquiry.

The evidence of the tablets does not allow us to assume with certainty that the land administered by the *dāmos* is in fact an *ager publicus*, in the sense of being owned on a collective basis and subject to periodical redistribution. It is conceivable that the *?kekeimenai ktoinai* merely represent the residue of such a system; perhaps 'land lying uncared-for', whose ownership has lapsed due to death or punishment, and which only then reverts to the village for administration—as seems to be the case with the 'vacant' craftsman's land in the Hittite clauses. Compare also Gardiner's remarks on the category of *khato* land in the Wilbour Papyrus (1948, II, p. 210).

For a theoretical discussion of primitive land tenure, see Thomson, 1949, pp. 297–331. He makes it clear that the δῆμοι represent the units of clan settlement, initially founded on a collective administration of the land. The agglomeration of these original villages into centralized towns was evidently not far advanced in Mycenaean times: Thucydides (I, 5 and 10) preserves a memory of 'unfortified πόλεις whose people lived in scattered villages'. Most of the references to the *dāmos* on the Pylos tablets probably apply, not to the centre 'Pylos' itself (only the palace and the seat of administration?), but to the satellite village of *Pa-ki-ja-*, one of the nine which are frequently listed together in a fixed order. Most of the spellings of this name appear to imply a nominative plural in *-ānes*, which looks more like a clan or tribal name than primarily a place-name (cf. Ἕλλᾱνες, Ἀκαρνᾶνες). Is the *theos* who figures so largely in the records of this village (cf. **172** = Kn02 rev.) a tutelary divinity of the clan? Thomson (1949, pp. 361–2) concludes from *Od.* III, 7 that Pylos consisted of nine δῆμοι; the possible connexion with the nine villages of the tablets has long been noted by Blegen and Bennett.

Though the 'first set' of Pylos tablets contains records for *ktoinai ktimenai* as such, there are no tablets listing the land of the *damos* except in the form of *o-na-ta* (singular *o-na-to*, evidently neuter). These apparently constitute some kind of subordinate title to the use of particular fields, and we have translated them as 'leases'. Those who have 'leases' of *ktoinai ktimenai* in the 'first set' are called *o-na-te-re* (nom. plur.), something like 'tenants'. Whether the *onata paro dāmōi* represent the only way in which the 'communal' land was farmed is not clear, since the surviving records may well be confined to certain restricted categories of tenure, in which the palace authorities were particularly interested.

One might have considered translating *o-na-to* as ὠνητόν (Dor. ὠνᾱτόν) 'bought, buyable', whatever this precisely means in a primitive economy; but the Skt. *vasnám* suggests that ὠνή (Lesb. ὄννα) should have initial *w-, and a derivation of the Mycenaean term from ὀνίνημι 'bestow a benefit' is more probable. Such an *onāton* may originally have meant a plot of land given to a retainer as a reward, cf. *Od.* XIV, 62–7:

> ...ὅς κεν ἔμ' ἐνδυκέως ἐφίλει καὶ κτῆσιν ὄπασσεν,
> οἶκόν τε κλῆρόν τε πολυμνήστην τε γυναῖκα,
> οἷά τε ᾧ οἰκῆϊ ἄναξ εὔθυμος ἔδωκεν,
> ὅς οἱ πολλὰ κάμῃσι, θεὸς δ' ἐπὶ ἔργον ἀέξῃ,
> ὡς καὶ ἐμοὶ τόδε ἔργον ἀέξεται, ᾧ ἐπιμίμνω.
> τῷ κέ με πόλλ' ὤνησεν ἄναξ, εἰ αὐτόθ' ἐγήρα.

Is the expression *ke-ra o-na-to* on **137** = Eb30 (cf. **135** = Ep704.2) conceivably the complete form of the expression, i.e. γέρας ὀνητόν 'a pension which brings (repeated) profit'? Cf. also *Od.* XXIII, 24: σὲ δὲ τοῦτό γε γῆρας

235

ὀνήσει. But the fact that the owners of the larger *ktoinai* can themselves be *onātēres* of another man's land makes it unlikely that all the 'tenants' at Pylos have actually received their holdings as rewards for services rendered. The form *onāter* (cf. classical ὀνήτωρ) suggests by its form 'one who bestows a benefit' rather than the expected 'beneficiary', but it may be denominal from *onāton*; cf. ἀσπιστήρ (Hom. ἀσπιστής), etc.

The class of *onātēres* includes fullers, potters and other trades, as well as one or two priests or priestesses; the great majority, however, are described simply as 'servants of the god', including both men (*theoio doelos*) and women (*t. doelā*). This is probably a formal title, and does not rank them in the servile class of the *doeloi* and *doelai* of the other tablets, on which these are counted but not referred to by individual names. It is tempting to compare the name ἱερόδουλοι given to the farmers of temple lands in Egypt (Rostovtzeff, *ibid.*). Their precise status here is obscure. Does the large number of these 'theodules' (and of religious functionaries in the 'third set', pp. 252–8) imply that the land tenure recorded on these tablets is primarily connected with the organization of religious institutions at Pylos? Or is it due to the fact that certain favoured craftsmen and temple acolytes were the only persons, below *telestas* level, who were allowed to hold leases of land? Or are the *theoio doeloi* just farmers, whose liability to pay temple dues is thereby recorded?

Two other kinds of land-holding, the *kama* and the *temenos*, will be discussed later in this chapter (pp. 261, 266).

The relation between the schedule of land holdings and their corresponding amounts of WHEAT is expressed by the phrase *to-so-(de) pe-mo* or *pe-ma* (only on **152** = Er01, **153** = Er02). Since *pe-ma* is applied to coriander-seed on KN Ga674, it is natural to read it as σπέρμα 'seed' (or 'sowing', class. generally σπορά or σπόρος). *Pe-mo* apparently has the same meaning, either as a spelling variant (*-mo* from *-mṇ*?) or as a doublet in *-mos*, cf. ὀδυρμός/ὄδυρμα, καθαρμός/κάθαρμα in Aeschylus.

It is not clear whether the amounts of seed grain are a record of an actual transaction (an issue from the royal granaries?), or merely a theoretical way of expressing the acreages of the land (being recorded for purposes of taxation?). In either case there is evidently an accepted density of sowing which makes it unnecessary to record the acreages in other measures of area (except once on **114** = En02.1). The Nuzi texts use the Babylonian *imēru* 'donkey-load' to measure both amounts of grain and the acreages of fields; Lewy (1949) argues that the Sumerian system of land measure is similarly derived from the corresponding unit volumes of seed, and quotes the Arab lexicographers as defining units of surface area by the volumes of grain needed to sow them.

The densities of sowing quoted for ancient times by Neo-Babylonian texts, by Cicero and Columella, and by the Talmud are in agreement with those in use today, and vary generally between 150 and 200 litres to the hectare ($1\frac{2}{3}$–$2\frac{1}{4}$ bushels to the acre). Webster (1954, p. 13) has pointed out the absurdly low acreages which result for the Pylos lands if we use this rate of seeding, and the litre equivalents of the wheat measures suggested in ch. II, as our conversion factors. The situation is somewhat improved if we assume that the amounts of wheat are those actually issued for a season's sowing, not theoretical acreage equivalents, and that half the land is at one time left fallow: in that case we may double the area of the king's *temenos*, and of the *ktoinai ktimenai*, which we have calculated from the *sperma* figures. The alternative by which *pe-mo* is regarded, not as wheat sown, but as some kind of tax levied on the crops of the *ktoinai* (Carratelli, 1954a, pp. 102, 110) does not produce any improvement in the figures, since a reasonable levy on a crop of grain might well be larger than the amount of seed required to produce that crop; but it cannot be excluded merely on this account.

Lewy (1944) has shown, however, that the rate of seeding assumed in Mesopotamian records earlier than *c*. 1000 B.C. was very considerably less than the modern figure. She quotes 50 litres per hectare for the Neo-Sumerian and Kassite periods, 60 litres for the Nuzi texts; and adduces evidence from the Mishnâ for an earlier system of cereal culture in which 'instead of leaving an entire field fallow for one season, the farmers of the ancient Near East prevented the exhaustion of their soil by dividing their fields into one-furrow beds which were alternately tilled and left fallow'. The spacing of these sown furrows would be three times wider or more than that usual under the later system. Whether or not this explanation will hold good for Mycenaean Greece, it may be of interest to see what acreages result for the Pylos lands if we take a sowing of 50 litres per hectare, and the value of the wheat unit measure as 120 litres (i.e. a factor of 2·4 hectares per unit measure).

	Sowing of wheat	Area	Population supported
King's *temenos*	50 units (6000 l.)	120 ha = 297 acres	83 men for a year
Total for 'first set'	40 units	96 ha = 237 acres	67 men for a year
Medium-sized *ktoina ktimena*	2 T 3	5·4 ha = 13·3 acres	4 men for a year
Medium-sized *onaton*	T 1	0·24 ha = $\frac{6}{10}$ acre	$\frac{1}{6}$ man for a year
Smallest *onaton* (once only)	◁ 1	0·04 ha = $\frac{1}{10}$ acre	$\frac{1}{36}$ man for a year

The small size of some of the fields is not surprising for Greek terrain, and is paralleled on the Alalakh tablets (Wiseman, 1953) and the *Wilbour Papyrus* (see below). The figures for 'population supported' are estimated on a 5-fold consumable yield (which is the upper limit quoted for wheat on the Nuzi tablets, Lacheman, 1939), and on a monthly ration of T $2\frac{1}{2}$ = 30 litres: this result is not, of course, affected by variations in the rate of seeding which we assume. The surviving tablets evidently record only a very small fraction of the total acreage required to feed the population of Pylos and its outlying settlements. Either the smaller tenants had more land to support their families than the diminutive *onata* recorded on the surviving tablets; or else these are no more than allotments with which they supplemented an income derived from other work, as is evident in the case of the potters and fullers. For comparison, in Anglo-Saxon times the normal holding for a peasant household owning two plough-oxen was a quarter-hide (30 acres), though 'cottars' might support themselves on as little as 5 acres.

One might still speculate (with Webster, 1954, p. 13) whether the *pe-mo* figures, while indeed referring to seed-corn, may in fact 'only represent some known fraction of the total sowing'; one might imagine, for example, that the palace granaries provided half or a quarter of the seed required, possibly in a situation of emergency; or that the palace granaries received *from* the farmers a tax equal to half or a quarter of their sowing (and hence the different formula applying to the *temenos* of the king, **152** = Er01 ?). There is no explicit evidence with which to attempt a final answer to this difficult problem.

Two examples of cuneiform tablets of somewhat similar context may be compared.

1. Sumerian, from Lagaš (Genouillac, 1909, *TSA*, xxxviii):

   2580 litres of emmer-wheat (first time), 600 litres of emmer-wheat (second time) and 1260 litres of barley have been drawn for the field Datiramma: the steward Eniggal delivered them from the Ekiqala building to the farm superintendent Ur-Enki (sixth year).

2. Nuzi (AASOR **16**, 1935–6, no. 87):

   500 litres of barley, given to Kipali for sowing on five *imêru* of land belonging to Uzna; the lands of Uzna are for 'partnership' (cf. *o-na-to* ??) and Kipali shall not dispose of them.

Note that Babylonian issues of seed grain sometimes include an extra above that calculated for the acreage, to allow fodder for the plough animals (see also p. 260).

The closest parallel to the arrangement of the Pylos *E-* tablets is, however, provided by the paragraphs of the long *Wilbour Papyrus* (Gardiner, 1948). It contains a cadastral survey, made in about 1150 B.C., of a large number of fields along the left bank of the Nile, together with their assessment for taxes of emmer-wheat. In spite of the elaborate phraseology and calculation of each paragraph, Gardiner admits that much of the real meaning and purpose of the series remains obscure, as it must with our Pylos tablets.

The different terms which differentiate the fields show distinctions (1) of ownership, whether by individuals, temples, Crown, etc.; (2) of condition—'newly opened up', '(normal) arable', 'tired', 'uncultivated', etc.; (3) of location with regard to the rise and fall of the Nile flood. The entries of small-holders which constitute many of the paragraphs resemble those at Pylos in their listing of personal names and occupations, and in the fact that many women appear. E.g.:

§ 84. The landing-place of Pharaoh in Ḥardai. Measurement made to the south of P-ma:

The lady Ḥathōr, together with her brethren: 3 arouras $=\frac{1}{2}$ at $1\frac{1}{2}$ measures of corn.
Apportioned for Suchus of P-ma, cultivated by the hand of Ḥori: 10 arouras $=2\frac{1}{2}$ at $1\frac{1}{2}$ measures.
The charioteer Praʿ(hi)wenmaf, cultivated by the hand of the cultivator Amene-mopĕ: (20) 5 arouras $=\frac{1}{2}$ at $1\frac{1}{2}$ measures.
The lady Tkamen: 5 arouras $=\frac{1}{2}$ at $1\frac{1}{2}$ measures.
The herdsman Set(em)ḥab: 5 arouras $=\frac{1}{2}$ at $1\frac{1}{2}$ measures.
The bee-keeper Pkhōre: 5 arouras $=\frac{1}{2}$ at $1\frac{1}{2}$ measures.
The retainer Nakhthikhopshef: 5 arouras $=\frac{1}{2}$ at $1\frac{1}{2}$ measures.
The stable-master Ḳenḥikhopshef: 5 arouras $=\frac{1}{2}$ at $1\frac{1}{2}$ measures.
The slave Shedemdēi: 3 arouras $=\frac{1}{2}$ at $1\frac{1}{2}$ measures,
            etc.

The size of such small-holdings varies from as little as 0·0164 ha ($\frac{1}{25}$ acre) up to 11 ha (27 acres), while the fields of *khato* land belonging to the Crown have limits of 0·55–93 ha ($1\frac{1}{3}$–230 acres): Gardiner (II, p. 98) quotes Lozach-Hug for the statement that in recent times about 40 per cent of holdings in Egypt were of $\frac{1}{2}$ acre or less.

1. TYPICAL FORMULAE ON SHORT PYLOS TABLETS

Before examining the large and complex tablets which make up the three most important 'sets', let us look at the typical land-tenure formulae in isolation, as they occur on some smaller tablets. The first three examples all refer to the shepherd *Mo-ro-qo-ro*. On the first his name appears in the genitive as the actual 'owner' of a *ktoinā ktimenā*; on the second a tenant is recorded as having a lease 'from *Mo-ro-qo-ro*'s plot'; the third (the most usual wording of the same formula) describes a lease 'from *Mo-ro-qo-ro* himself', where his name goes into the dative case. Note the grammatical agreement shown by the description *poimenos* (gen.), *poimenei* (dat.); but on the first tablet (as on **111** = Ea23) *poimēn* appears added in small letters above the line, as if in parenthesis, where we should logically expect the genitive case.

† **108** = Ea817

mo-ro-qo-ro-jo | ko-to-na   ki-ti-me-na   'po-me'   WHEAT 3   T 1   ◁ 1

The *private* plot of Molog^{u}ros (shepherd): 374 l. wheat.

109 = Ea782

ru-ko-ro   e-ke   o-na-to   'ra-wa-ke-si-jo'   pa-ro   mo-ro-qo-ro-jo   ko-to-na   po-me-no
    WHEAT   T 1

Lugros, servant of the commander (*similarly on* Ea09, Ea823, Ea882), holds a *lease* from the plot of Molog^{u}ros the shepherd: 12 l. wheat.

110 = Ea800

ke-re-te-u   e-ke   o-na-to   pa-ro   mo-ro-qo-ro   po-me-ne   WHEAT 2

Kretheus holds a *lease* from Molog^{u}ros the shepherd: 240 l. wheat.

The same variation in formulae is shown by the tablets referring to another shepherd:

111 = Ea23   [71]

ko-do-jo | 'po-me'   ko-to-na-ki-ti-me-na   WHEAT 1   T 4   ◁ 3

The *private* plot of ?Koldos (shepherd): 174 l. wheat.

112 = Ea825

ta-ra-ma-ta | e-ke   o-na-to   pa-ro   ko-do   'po-me-ne'   WHEAT   T 1

Thalamatas holds a *lease* from ?Koldos the shepherd: 12 l. wheat.

Ko-do's third tablet exemplifies the second kind of 'lease' recorded on the *E-* tablets, that held not from an individual but from the *dāmos* (see the 'fourth set', pp. 258–64).

113 = Ea824

ko-do   e-ke   o-na-to   pa-ro   da-mo   'po-me'   WHEAT   T 4

?Koldos the shepherd holds a *lease* from the village: 48 l. wheat.

2. THE FIRST PYLOS SET

‡ The thirteen paragraphs making up this series have been preserved in two separate recensions, of which the larger tablets ('Version A') introduced by **114** = En02 have here been printed first and may represent the later and more polished documentation. The reason for the two versions, whose items show

identical quantities and order but some variations in spelling and phraseology, is not altogether clear; but a large proportion of the remaining *E-* tablets show a similar bureaucratic duplication, as will be seen from the other sets printed below.

The 'first set' gives the complete breakdown for an area of *ktimena* ('private'?) land which, though not large (approx. 96 ha, or 240 acres?), shows a complex pattern of land tenure. The introductory adjective *Pa-ki-ja-ni-ja* is evidently derived from *Pa-ki-ja-*, the name of one of the nine 'satellite towns', and shows the location of the land. Why do no other place-names appear on the Pylos *E-* tablets? Do the other records of land, in the absence of a specific title, also refer to *Pa-ki-ja*, or to the territory of 'Pylos' itself? The existence of a series for *Pa-ki-ja*, but for none of the other nine, may be due to the accidents of survival; but it might also indicate that *Pa-ki-ja* represents the largest fertile area close to 'Pylos'; which may be the name (transferred from another site by a migrating dynasty?) only of the palace complex itself.

VERSION A

114 = En02   [609]

1   *pa-ki-ja-ni-ja   to-sa   da-ma-te*   DA 40
2   *to-so-de   te-re-ta   e-ne-e-si*   MEN 14
3   *wa-na-ta-jo-jo   ko-to-na   ki-ti-me-na   to-so-de-pe-mo*   WHEAT 2   ◁ 1
4   *o-da-a₂   o-na-te-[re]   e-ko-si   wa-na-ta-jo-jo   ko-to-na*
5   *a-tu-ko   e-te-do-mo   wa-na-ka-te-ro   o-na-to   e-ke   ⟨to-so⟩-de   pe-mo*   WHEAT
                                                                                   ◁ 1
6   *i-ni-ja   te-o-jo   do-e-ra   o-na-to   e-ke   to-so-de   pe-mo*   WHEAT   T 2   ◁ 4
7   *e-*65-to   te-o-jo   do-e-ro   o-na-to   e-ke   to-so-de   pe-mo*   WHEAT   T 2
8   *si-ma   te-o-jo   do-e-ra   o-na-to   e-ke   to-so-de   pe-mo*   WHEAT   T 1
                              vacat
10   *a-ma-ru-ta-o   ko-to-na   ki-ti-me-na   to-so-de   pe-mo*   WHEAT 2   T 3
11   [*o-da-a₂   e-ko-si   a*]*-ma-ru-ta-o   ko-to-na   o-na-te-re*
12   [*so-u-ro   te-o-jo   do*]*-e-ro   o-na-to   e-ke   to-so-de   pe-mo*   WHEAT   ◁ 3
13   [*e-do-mo-ne-u   te-o*]*-jo   do-e-ro   o-na-to   e-ke   to-so-de   pe-mo*   WHEAT   T [1]
14   [*e-sa-ro   te-o-jo   do*]*-e-ro   [o-na-to]   e-ke   [to-so-de]   pe-mo*   WHEAT   ◁ 3
15   [*wa-na-ta-jo   te-re-ta . . . .   o*]*-na-to   e-ke   to-so-de   pe-mo*   WHEAT   T 1
16   [*e-ra-ta-ra   i-je-re-ja   do-e-ra*]   *pa-ki-ja-na   o-na-to   e-ke   to-so-de   pe-mo*
                                                                              WHEAT   T 1
17   [*po-so-re-ja   te-o-jo   do-e-ra   o*]*-na-to   e-ke   to-so-de   pe-mo*   WHEAT
                                                                          T 1   ◁ 3
18   [*i-je-re-ja   pa-ki-ja-na   o-na*]*-to   e-ke   to-so-de   pe-mo*   WHEAT   T 3

(There are) so many *acreages* belonging to *Pa-ki-ja-ᵖ*: 40,
And there are so many *fief-holders* upon them: fourteen men.

§ 1   The *private* plot of ?Warnataios, so much seed: 242 l. wheat.
Now this is how the *tenants* hold plots belonging to ? Warnataios:
? Atukhos the king's *artificer* holds a *lease*, so much seed: 2 l. wheat,
I., servant (f.) of the god, holds a *lease*, so much seed: 32 l. wheat,
E., servant (m.) of the god, holds a *lease*, so much seed: 24 l. wheat,
S., servant (f.) of the god, holds a *lease*, so much seed: 12 l. wheat.

§ 2   The *private* plot of Amaruntas, so much seed: 276 l. wheat.
Now this is how the *tenants* hold plots belonging to Amaruntas:
S., servant (m.) of the god, holds a *lease*, so much seed: 6 l. wheat,
E., servant (m.) of the god, holds a *lease*, so much seed: 12 l. wheat,
E., servant (m.) of the god, holds a *lease*, so much seed: 6 l. wheat,
? Warnataios the *fief-holder* holds a *lease*, so much seed: 12 l. wheat,
E., the servant (f.) of the priestess of *Pa-ki-jaᵖ*, holds a *lease*, so much seed: 12 l. wheat,
P., servant (f.) of the god, holds a *lease*, so much seed: 18 l. wheat,
The priestess of *Pa-ki-jaᵖ* holds a *lease*, so much seed: 36 l. wheat.

† *da-ma-te*: since it cannot be neuter plural, this noun must be either feminine singular or plural; the name of a class of persons (cf. *du-ma-te* **257** = Jn09 *damartes?*) is excluded by the lack of a MAN or WOMAN ideogram. The ethnic adjective P., and *en-eensi* in line 2, suggest a topographical term whose initial is repeated in the ideogram DA (also found on Knossos tablets of similar context, e.g. **157** = Uf835). If it is a measure of area, it is significant that the total amount of WHEAT recorded on this set of tablets appears to add up to approximately 40 measures (*c.* 4800 litres). Webster (1954) and Furumark (1954) accept *Dāmātēr* = 'corn-land'; this is doubted by Carratelli (1954, p. 225) who suggests a derivative of **dam-/dom-*, perhaps 'family units' (originally the area of land regarded as sufficient for one household, like the Old English 'hide'?).

‡ *to-so-de* (line 2): enclitic *-de* 'and'? These fourteen *telestai* are evidently the individuals whose *ktoinai* introduce each of the separate paragraphs of the set. The same persons are also described as *ktoinookhoi* on **131** = Ep01; and ?Warnataios, subject of the first paragraph, is described as a *telestas* when he himself appears as a 'tenant' in the second. There is an evident discrepancy in the fact that the set appears to consist of only *thirteen* paragraphs, and it is possible that the *ktoinai* of § 6 in fact have two *telestai* (a different explanation by Bennett, see p. 261).

ko-to-na ki-ti-me-na (line 3): it is not clear from the spelling, or vital to the meaning, whether this is to be taken as singular or plural.

o-na-te-re e-ko-si (lines 4 and 11): note the free variation in word-order (not extended to the introductory *o-da-a₂*) shown by the successive recurrences of this phrase;

e-ke-si on **115** = En03.21 is clearly a scribal lapse, and not to be equated with the 'spears' of **257** = Jn09.3. As usual on these tablets, *ekhei/ekhonsi* implies 'tenancy', not ownership (recorded by the genitive, as in lines 3 and 10). An alternative construction could be: 'how they occupy ?Warnataios' *ktoina* (singular)'; but the usual opposition *onaton ktoinās/onata ktoināōn* suggests that the *ktoina* is the unit of individual working, not the unit of overall ownership.

115 = En03   [74]

¹ *ru-*83-o   ko-to-na-ki-ti-me-⟨na⟩   to-so-de   pe-mo*   WHEAT 1   T [5]

² *o-da-a₂   o-na-te-re   ru-*83-o   ko-to-na   e-ko-si*

³ *pe-ki-ta   ka-na-pe-u   wa-na-ka-te-ro   [o]-na-to   e-ke   to-so-de   pe-mo*   WHEAT   T 1

⁴ *mi-ra   te-o-jo   do-e-ra   ⟨o-na-to⟩   e-ke   to-so-de   pe-mo*   WHEAT   T 1

⁵ *te-se-u   te-o-jo   do-e-ro   o-na-to   e-ke   to-so-de   pe-mo*   WHEAT   T 4

⁶ *ma-re-ku-na   te-o-jo   do-e-ro* (!)   *o-[na-to   e-ke   to-so-de   pe]-mo*   WHEAT   T 1

⁷ *e-ko-to   te-[o]-jo   do-e-ro   o-na-to   e-ke   to-so-de   pe-mo*   WHEAT   ◁ 3

⁸ *ma-zu?   te-[o-jo   do-e]-ra   o-na-to   e-ke   to-so-de   pe-mo*   WHEAT   ◁ [3]

⁹ *e-*65-to   te-o-jo   do-e-[ro]   o-na-to   e-ke   to-so-de   pe-mo*   WHEAT   ◁ 1

vacat

¹¹ *ai-ti-jo-qo   ko-to-na   ki-ti-me-na   to-so-de   pe-mo*   WHEAT 1   T 5   ◁ 4

¹² *o-da-a₂   o-na-te-re   e-ko-si   ai-ti-jo-qo   ko-to-na*

¹³ *e-pa-sa-na-ti   te-o-jo   do-e-ra   o-na-to   e-ke   to-so-de   pe-mo*   WHEAT   T 2

¹⁴ *ku-*63-so   [te]-o-jo   do-e-ro   o-na-to   e-ke   to-so-de   pe-mo*   WHEAT   T 1

¹⁵ *ta-ra₂-to   te-o-jo   do-e-ro   o-na-to   e-ke   to-so-de   pe-mo*   WHEAT   T 1

¹⁶ *we-te-re-u   i-e-re-u   o-na-to   e-ke   to-so-de   pe-mo*   WHEAT   T 5

¹⁷ *e-ko-to   te-o-jo   do-e-ro   o-na-to   e-ke   to-so-de   pe-mo*   WHEAT   T 1

¹⁸ *ko-ri-si-ja   te-o-jo   do-e-ra   o-na-to   e-ke   to-so-de   pe-mo*   WHEAT   T 5

vacat

²⁰ *pi-ke-re-wo   ko-to-na   ki-ti-me-na   to-so-de   pe-mo*   WHEAT 2   T 6

²¹ *o-da-a₂   o-na-te-re   e-ke-si* (sic)   *pi-ke-re-wo   ko-to-na*

²² *ai-wa-ja   te-o-jo   do-e-ra   o-na-to   e-ke   to-so-de   pe-mo*   WHEAT   T 1

²³ *pe-ki-ta   ka-na-pe-u   wa-na-ka-te-ro   o-na-to   e-ke   to-so-de   pe-mo*

WHEAT   T 2

²⁴ *ko-ri-si-ja   te-o-jo   do-e-ra   o-na-to   e-ke   to-so-de   pe-mo*   WHEAT   T 5

§ 3   The *private* plot of R., so much seed: 180 l. wheat.

Now this is how the *tenants* hold plots belonging to R.:

P., the king's fuller, holds a *lease*, so much seed: 12 l. wheat,

? Smila, servant (f.) of the god, holds a *lease*, so much seed: 12 l. wheat,

Theseus, servant (m.) of the god, holds a *lease*, so much seed: 48 l. wheat,

etc.

§ 4   The *private* plot of Aithioqᵘs, so much seed: 188 l. wheat.

Now this is how the *tenants* hold plots belonging to Aithioqᵘs:

E., servant (f.) of the god, holds a *lease*, so much seed: 24 l. wheat,

etc.

§ 5   The *private* plot of Pikreus, so much seed: 312 l. wheat.

Now this is how the *tenants* hold plots belonging to Pikreus:

Aiwaia, servant (f.) of the god, holds a *lease*, so much seed: 12 l. wheat,

P., the king's fuller, holds a *lease*, so much seed: 24 l. wheat,

Korinsia, servant (f.) of the god, holds a *lease*, so much seed: 60 l. wheat.

ru-*83-o (gen.), *ru-*83-e* (dat.), evidently shows a consonant declension parallel to *a-ta-no-ro*/*a-ta-no-re*, etc.; but the ending of the dative prevents a comparison with names in -*ēs* on the model of -*me-de-o*/*me-de-i*. If the rare sign **83* conceals the alternative spelling of some such name as *ru-kew-o*/*ru-kew-e*, then the implied syllable-division is quite unprecedented.

ta-ra₂-to (line 15) appears in 'Version B' as *ta-ra-to* on **121** = Eo04, where in addition *e-pa-sa-na-ti*ᶠ is deliberately spelt *i-pa-sa-na-ti*, and *i-e-re-u* reappears as *i-je-re-u*. Such variations might perhaps suggest oral dictation rather than visual copying: in either case the scribe has allowed himself some freedom in modifying the precise wording of the repetitive formulae. Like Hektor, Korinsia, *Pe-ki-ta* and *We-te-re-u*, the man *Ta-ra₂-to* is recorded as holding leases of *ktoinai* belonging to more than one *telestas*.

† **116** = En659

1 *qe-re-qo-ta-o   ki-ti-me-na   to-so-de   pe-mo*   WHEAT 2 T 3

2   *o-da-a₂   o-na-te-re   e-ko-si   qe-re-qo-ta-o   ko-to-na*

3 *ra-su-ro   te-o-jo   do-e-ro   o-na-to   e-ke   to-so-de   pe-mo*   WHEAT T 1

4 *we-te-re-u   i-e-re-u   o-na-to   e-ke   to-so-de   pe-mo*   WHEAT T 1

5 *tu-ri-ja-ti   te-o-jo   do-e-ra   e-ke   p̣ạ-ṛo   pe-re-qo-ta* (sic) *pe-qo-ta   to-so   pe-mo*

WHEAT T 9

6 *ta-ra₂-to   te-o-jo   do-e-ro   o-[na]-to   e-ke   to-so-de   pe-mo*   WHEAT ◁ 3

vacat

8 *a-da-ma-o-jo   ko-to-na   ki-ti-me-[na]   to-so-de   pe-mo*   WHEAT 1 T 8

9   *o-da-a₂   o-ṇạ-te-re   e-ko-si   a-da-ma-o-jọ   ko-to-na*

10 *ta-ra₂-to   te-o-jo   do-e-ro   o-na-to   e-ke   to-so-de   [pe-mo]*   WHEAT T 2 ◁ 4

vacat

12 *ạ-ị-qẹ-wo   ko-to-na   ki-ti-me-na   to-so-de   pe-mo*   WHEAT [1] T 2

13 *o-da-a₂   ta-ra₂-[to te]-o-jo   do-e-ro   o-na-to   e-ke   to-so-de   pe-mo* WHEAT T 1 ◁ 3

vacat

15 *ra-ku-ro-jo   ko-to-na   ki-ti-[me-na   to]-so-de   pe-mo*   WHEAT 1 T 1 ◁ 3

16 *o-da-a₂   i-ra-ta   te-o-jo   do-e-[ro?   o]-na-to   e-ke   to-so-de   pe-mo*   WHEAT ◁ 3

vacat

244

¹⁸ *a-ka-ta-[jo]-jo ko-to-na ki-ti-me-na to-so-de pe-mo* WHEAT 3 T 2
¹⁹ *o-da-a₂ ka-ra-[pa₃?-so te]-o-jo [do-e]-ro o-na-to e-ke* WHEAT T 2

§ 6 The *private* (plot) of ?*Qᵘēleqᵘhontās*, so much seed: 276 l. wheat.
  Now this is how the *tenants* hold plots belonging to Q.:
  R., servant (m.) of the god, holds a *lease*, so much seed: 12 l. wheat,
  W. the priest holds a *lease*, so much seed: 12 l. wheat,
  Thuriatis, servant (f.) of the god, from P. (!) the *old man*, so much seed:
    108 l. wheat,
  T., servant (m.) of the god, holds a *lease*, so much seed: 6 l. wheat.

§ 7 The *private* plot of Admaos, so much seed: 216 l. wheat.
  Now this is how the *tenants* hold plots belonging to Admaos:
  T., servant (m.) of the god, holds a *lease*, so much seed: 32 l. wheat.

§ 8 The *private* plot of A∼eus, so much seed: 144 l. wheat.
  Now this is how T., servant (m.) of the god, holds a *lease*, so much seed:
    18 l. wheat.

§ 9 The *private* plot of R., so much seed: 138 l. wheat.
  Now this is how I., servant of the god, holds a *lease*, so much seed: 6 l. wheat.

§ 10 The *private* plot of Aktaios, so much seed: 384 l. wheat.
  Now this is how K., servant (m.) of the god, holds a *lease*, so much seed:
    24 l. wheat.

qe-re-qo-ta-o: perhaps the equivalent of a classical *Τηλε-φόντης, cf. Τήλεφος. It is †
  remarkable that the other occurrences of this individual's name, including that on
  line 5 of the same tablet, are spelt with initial *pe-*. Bennett regards this as betraying
  a less archaic pronunciation of the labio-velar; if so, it shows, surprisingly, the
  Aeolic development rather than the Arcadian. On Eb22 and on **148**=Ep04.10
  pe-re-qo-ta is qualified as *pa-da-je-u/pa-de-we-u* (an ethnic?), and in 'Version B'
  (**123**=Eo06) the dative *pa-da-je-we* replaces his name entirely. The possibility cannot
  be excluded that the additional word *pe-qo-ta* (connected with πρεσβύτης?) of
  116=En659.5 and of **123**=Eo06.4, 6 serves to distinguish one Telephontes from
  another, thus explaining the absence of a fourteenth paragraph. But though
  qe-re-qo-ta-o in line 1 might conceivably be genitive *plural*, it could hardly be dual.
  A further difficulty is presented by the fact that 'Version B' of § 6 shows an extra
  'tenant' in line 6.

Line 10: *o-na-te-re* is used in the plural even though only one entry follows. This anomaly
  is corrected in the remaining three paragraphs by a telescoped version of the formula,
  of which only *o-da-a₂* (*hōda ar* 'thus in turn'?) remains.

117=En01 [467]
¹ *ti-pa₂-jo-jo ko-to-na ki-ti-me-na to-so-de pe-mo* WHEAT 8 T 3
    vacat

³ *po-te-wo   ko-to-na   ki-ti-me-⟨na⟩   to-so-de   pe-mo*   WHEAT 2   T 4
              vacat

⁵ *pi-ri-ta-wo-no   ko-to-na   ki-ti-me-na   ke-ra-me-wo   to-so-de   pe-mo*   WHEAT 1   T 1

§ 11 The *private* plot of Thisbaios (the shepherd): 996 l. wheat,

§ 12 the *private* plot of Ponteus: 288 l. wheat,

§ 13 the *private* plot of Brithawon the (royal) potter, so much seed: 132 l. wheat.

Although these last three entries show *ktoinai* no smaller than the rest, they are distinguished by having no subsidiary 'tenants', and also by considerable variations of wording in 'Version B'.

Version B

Its main differences from 'Version A' are the omission of the $o\text{-}da\text{-}a_2$ formula introducing the 'tenants'; its replacement by the phrase '*pa-ro X* (dat.)' in each entry; the elimination of *to-so-de   pe-mo*; and the expansion on *e-ke* to
† *e-ke-qe*. This last peculiarity, which apparently adds nothing to the meaning, has been discussed by Carratelli (1954*a*, pp. 223–4), who suggests that it is a 'fossilized' first half of an original 'both...and' formula with two verbs: note, however, that *e-ke-qe   e-u-ke-to-qe* on **140** = Eb35 is probably not an example of 'both...and', since its 'Version A' on **135** = Ep704.5 agrees with the other entries in reverting to *e-ke   e-u-ke-to-qe*. This -$q^u e$ used by the scribe of 'Version B' should probably be explained either as another example of the puzzling early use of τε to mean something other than strictly 'and' (Schwyzer, *Gram.* II, pp. 574–6), or as an indication that he regarded the naming of the 'tenant' as a separate proposition, i.e. '(Here is) X., *and* he holds a lease', or the like.

‡ **118** = Eo01   [211]

¹ *wa-na-ta-jo-jo   ko-to-na   ki-ti-me-na*   WHEAT 2   [◁ 1]
² *a-tu-ko   e-te-do-mo   e-ke-qe   o-na-to   pa-ro   wa-na-ta-[jo]*   WHEAT ◁ 1
³ *i-ni-ja   te-o-jo   do-e-ra   e-ke-qe   o-na-to   pa-ro   wa-na-ta-[jo]*   WHEAT
                                           [T 2   ◁ 4]
⁴ *e-*65-to   te-o-jo   do-e-ro   e-ke-qe   o-na-to   pa-ro   wa-⟨na⟩-ta-[jo]*
                                       WHEAT [T 2]
⁵ *si-ma   te-o-jo   do-e-ra   e-ke-qe   o-na-to   pa-ro   wa-na-ta-jo*   WHEAT   T 1

§ 1 The *private* plot of ?Warnataios: 242 l. wheat.
   ?Atukhos the *artificer*, *and* he holds a *lease* from W.: 2 l. wheat,
                                 etc.

119 = Eo02   [224]

¹ *a-ma-ru-ta-o   ko-to-na-ki-ti-me-na*   WHEAT 2   T [3]

² *so-u-ro   te-o-jo   do-e-ro   e-ke-qe   o-[na]-to-pa-ro*   ⟦*a-ma-ru-ta*⟧   `pa-ra-ko'
WHEAT   ◁ 3

³ *e-do-mo-ne-u   te-o-jo   do-e-ro   e-ke-qe   o-[na-to]   pa-ro*   ⟦*a-ma-ru-ta*⟧   `pa-ra-ko'
WHEAT   T I

⁴ *e-sa-ro   te-o-jo   do-e-ro   e-ke-qe   o-[na-to]   pa-ro   a-ma-ru-ta*   WHEAT   ◁ 3

⁵ *wa-na-ta-jo   te-re-ta   e-ke-qe   o-na-to   pa-ro   a-ma-ru-ta*   WHEAT   T I

⁶ *e-ra-ta-ra   i-je-re-ja   do-e-ra   pa-ki-ja-na   e-ke-qe   pa-ro   a-ma-ru-ta*   WHEAT   T I

⁷ *po-so-re-ja   te-o-jo   do-e-ra   e-ke-qe   o-na-to   pa-ro*   ⟦*a-ma-ru-ta*⟧   `ta-ta-ro'
WHEAT   T I   ◁ 3

⁸ *i-je-re-ja   pa-ki-ja-na   e-ke-qe   o-na-to   pa-ro   a-ma-ru-ta*   WHEAT   T 3

§ 2   The *private* plot of Amaruntas: 276 l. wheat.
S., servant of the god, *and* he holds a *lease* from Phalaikos (*Amaruntas erased*):
6 l. wheat,

etc.

Lines 2, 3 and 7: the action of the scribe in erasing 'Amaruntas' and recording that the
'leases' are in fact held from Phalaikos and Tantalos is not taken into account in
'Version A'. Are these two men, who appear separately on **131** = Ep01 as *ktoinookhoi*,
relatives of Amaruntas? Or are they holders of some kind of intermediate lease,
So-u-ro and the others being sub-tenants?

120 = Eo03   [276]

¹ [*ru-*83-o*]   *te-u-ta-ra-ko-ro   ki-ti-me-[na   ko]-to-na*   WHEAT I   T 5

² [*pe*]-*ki-ta   ka-na-pe-u   wa-na-ka-te-ro   e-ke-qe   [o]-na-to   ⟨pa-ro⟩   ru-*83-e*
WHEAT   T I

³ *mi-ra   te-o-jo   do-e-ra   e-ke-qe   o-na-to   pa-ro   ru-*83-e*   WHEAT   T I

⁴ *te-se-u   te-o-jo   do-e-ro   e-ke-qe   o-na-to   pa-ro   ru-*83-e*   WHEAT   T 4

⁵ *ma-re-ku-na   te-o-jo   do-e-ra* (!)   *e-ke-qe   o-na-to   pa-ro   ru-*83-e*   WHEAT   T I

⁶ *e-ko-to   te-o-jo   do-e-ro   e-ke-qe   o-na-to   pa-ro   ru-*83-e*   WHEAT   ◁ 3

⁷ *ma-zu?   te-o-⟨jo⟩   do-e-ra   e-ke-qe   o-na-to   pa-ro   ru-*83-e*   WHEAT   ◁ 3

⁸ *e-*65-to   te-o-jo   do-e-ro-e-ke-qe   o-na-to   pa-ro   ru-*83-e*   WHEAT   ◁ I

§ 3   The *private* plot of R. the *beetroot-gatherer*: 180 l. wheat.
P., the king's fuller, *and* he holds a *lease* (from) R.: 12 l. wheat,

etc.

Line 1. The occupation *te-u-ta-ra-ko-ro* (*teutl-agoros?*) recurs on PY An09. If it agrees †
with R. here, we must assume that the genitival ⟨*-jo*⟩ has been omitted in error. Or
should we read 'the *private* plot of the *beetroot-gatherers* (vested in) R.'?

† **121** = Eo04   [247]

¹ *ai-ti-jo-qo*   *ki-ti-me-na*   *ko-to-na* / *to-so-de-pe-mo*   WHEAT [1   T 5   ◁ 4]

² *e-ko-to*   *te-o-jo*   *do-e-ro*   *e-ke-qe*   *o-na-to*   *pa-ro*   *ai-ti-jo-qe*   *ko-to-no-o-ko*

WHEAT   T [1]

³ *ko-ri-si-ja*   *te-o-jo*   *do-e-ra*   *e-ke-qe*   *o-na-to*   *ki-ti-me-na*   *ko-to-na*

⟦*ai-ti-jo-qo*⟧ '*ai-ti-jo-qe*'   WHEAT   T 5

⁴ ⟦*e-pa-sa-na-ti*⟧ '*i-pa-sa-na-ti*'   *te-o-jo*   *do-e-ra*   *e-ke-qe*   *o-na-to*   *pa-ro*

ai-ti-jo-qe   WHEAT   T 2

⁵ *ku-*63-so*   *te-o-jo*   *do-e-ro*   *e-ke-qe*   *o-na-to*   *pa-ro*   *ai-ti-jo-qe*   WHEAT   T 1

⁶ *ta-ra-to*   *te-o-jo*   *do-e-ro*   *e-ke-qe*   *o-na-to*   *pa-ro*   *ai-ti-jo-qe*   WHEAT   T 1

⁷ *we-te-re-u*   *i-je-re-u*   *e-ke-qe*   *o-na-to*   *pa-ro*   *ai-ti-jo-qe*   WHEAT   T 5

§ 4   The *private* plot of Aithioqᵘs, so much seed: 188 l. wheat.

Hektor, servant (m.) of the god, *and* he holds a *lease* from Aithioqᵘs the plot-owner: 12 l. wheat,

Korinsia, servant (f.) of the god, *and* she holds a *lease* of a *private* plot belonging to Aithioqᵘs: 60 l. wheat,

I., servant (f.) of the god, *and* she holds a *lease* from Aithioqᵘs: 24 l. wheat, etc.

Line 2: note the addition of *ktoinookhōi* to describe the actual owner of the plot.

Line 3: the variant formula introduced here by the scribe does not seem to indicate any distinction in sense; and it does not appear in 'Version A' (**115** = En03.18); but note that the list of 'tenants' there begins with *E-pa-sa-na-ti*, which in 'Version B' is the first entry to have the completely normal formula. The scribe's original *Ai-ti-jo-qo* (gen.) in line 3 is of course correct; it appears to have been altered to *-qe* under the influence of the *Ai-ti-jo-qe* which occurs (correctly) in all the other entries.

122 = Eo05   [160]

¹ *pi-ke-re-wo*   *ko-to-na*   *ki-ti-me-na* / *to-so-de*   *pe-mo*   [WHEAT] 2   T 6

² *ai-wa-ja*   *te-o-jo*   *do-e-ra*   *e-ke-qe*   *o-na-to*   *pa-ro*   *pi-ke-re-we*   WHEAT   T 1

³ *pe-ki-ta*   *ka-na-pe-u*   *wa-na-ka-te-ro*   *e-ke-qe*   *o-na-to*   *pa-ro* '*pi-ke-re-we*'

WHEAT   T 2

⁴ [*ko-ri-si*]-*ja*   *te-o-jo*   *do-e-ra*   *e-ke-qe*   *o-na-to*   *pa-ro*   *pi-ke-re-we*   WHEAT   T 5

§ 5   The *private* plot of Pikreus, so much seed: 312 l. wheat.

Aiwaia, servant (f.) of the god, *and* she holds a *lease* from Pikreus: 12 l. wheat, etc.

‡ **123** = Eo06   [444]

¹ [? *qe-re-qo-ta-o*   *ko*]-*to-na*   *ki-ti-me-na*   WHEAT 4

² [*ra-su-ro*   *te-o-jo*   *do-e*]-*ṛọ*   *e-ke-qe*   *o-na-to*   *pa-ro*   *pa-da-je-we*   [WHEAT   T 1]

³ [*we-te-re-u   i-je*]*-re-u   e-ke-qe   o-na-to   pa-ro   pa-da-je-we*   WHEAT   [T 1]
⁴ [*tu-ri-ja-ti   te-o-jo   do-e-ra*]   *e-ke-qe   pa-ro   pa-da-je-we   pe-qo-ta*   WHEAT   [nn]
⁵ [*ta-ra₂-to   te-o-jo   do-e*]*-ṛọ   e-ke-qe   pa-ro   pa-da-je-we*   WHEAT   [◁ 3]
⁶ [?   ]   *e-ke-qe   pa-*[*ro   pa*]*-da-je-we   pe-qo-ta*   WHEAT   T [nn]

§ 6   The *private* plot of Q.: 480 l. wheat,
etc.

124 = Eo351 (formerly Ec02)

¹ *a-da-ma-⟨o⟩-jo   ḳọ-ṭọ-na   ki-ṭi-*[*me-na*   WHEAT 1   T 8]
² *ta-ra₂-to   te-ọ-jọ   do-e-*[*ro   e-ke-qe   o-na-to   pa-ro   a-da-ma-o*   WHEAT   T 2   ◁ 4]

§ 7   The *private* plot of Admaos: 216 l. wheat.
   T., servant (m.) of the god, *and* he holds a *lease* from Admaos: 32 l. wheat.

125 = Eo471 (including former Ec03)   †

¹ *a-i-qe-wo   ko-to-na   ki-ti-me-na*   WHEAT 1   T 2
² *ta-ra₂-to   te-o-jo   do-e-ro   e-ke-qe   o-na-to   pa-ro   a-i-qe-we*   WHEAT   T 1   ◁ 3

§ 8   The *private* plot of A.: 144 l. wheat.
   T., servant (m.) of the god, *and* he holds a *lease* from A.: 18 l. wheat.

126 = Eo281 (formerly Ec04)   ‡

¹ [*ra-ku-ro-jo   ko-to-na   ki-ti-me-na*]   WHEAT 1   T 1   ◁ 3
² [*i-ra-ta   te-o-jo   do-e-ro?   e*]*-ḳe-qe   o-na-to   pa-ro   ra-ku-ro*   WHEAT   ◁ 3

§ 9   The *private* plot of R.: 138 l. wheat,
   I., the servant of the god, *and* he (?) holds a *lease* from R.: 6 l. wheat.

127 = Eo269 (formerly Eb26)

a-ka-ta-jo-jo   *ko-to-na   ki-ti-me-na*
                  ka-na-pe-wo | to-so-de   pe-mo   WHEAT 3   T 2

EDGE: *ka-ra-pa₃-so   te-o-jo   do-e-ro   e-ke-qe   o-na-to   pa-ro   a-ka-ta-jo*
                                              to-so-de pe-mo   WHEAT   T 2

§ 10   The *private* plot of Aktaios the fuller, so much seed: 384 l. wheat.
   K., servant (m.) of the god, *and* he holds a *lease* from Aktaios, so much seed:
   24 l. wheat.

128 = Eo278 (formerly Eb01)   ¶

ti-pa₂-jo   po-me   e-ke-qe   wo-wo   ko-to-no   WHEAT [8 T 3 ?]

§ 11   Thisbaios the shepherd, *and* he holds the *confines* of two (?) plots: 996? l.
   wheat.

ko-to-no (scarcely χθονός) can apparently only be explained as a dual (*ktoinoin?*), in
   the declension of which Mycenaean feminines do not show -*a*- (p. 84). The phrase

249

recurs on **141** = Eb20 as *ke-ke-me-no   ko-to-*[*no?*]   *wo-wo*, which is replaced on **135** = Ep704 simply by *ke-ke-me-no*. *Wo-wo* seems to represent *worwon(s)*, either the Homeric οὖρον 'land-measure' or ὅρος 'boundary, boundary-stone'.

129 = Eo268 (formerly Ea20)

po-te-wo | *ko-to-na*   WHEAT 2   T 4

§ 12   The plot of Ponteus: 288 l. wheat.

130 = Eo371 (formerly Ea24)

[*pi-ri*]-*ta-wo-*⟨*no*⟩   *ke-ra-me-wo   wa-na-ka-te-ro-*⟨*jo*⟩   WHEAT [1   T 1]
                          ko-to-na-ki-ti-me-na

§ 13   The *private* plot of Brithawon the king's potter: 132 l. wheat.

The lack of concordance in the description of the potter seems to be due to a confusion between the two varieties of this formula, either *Brithāwōn ekhei . . .* or *Brithāwonos ktoina. . . .*

3. THE SECOND PYLOS SET

'Version A' of this set is contained on a single tablet, **131** = Ep01. This is apparently a résumé of the 'communal plots' which are rented (presumably at *Pa-ki-ja-*, too) by the same important class of men who are recorded as owning 'private plots' of their own in the 'first set' of tablets. Six of the *telestai* of that set reappear in this list, together with the two names *Phalaikos* and *Tantalos* which are added over erasure on **119** = Eo02. Also listed are *A-tu-ko   e-te-do-mo*, only a 'tenant' in the 'first set', and two men *Ku-so* and *Ke-ra-u-jo* whom we do not meet again.

The different wording which distinguishes the first and second sections of **131** = Ep01 reappears in the individual tablets of 'Version B' (except that *e-ke-qe* there extends throughout), but it is difficult to say whether a definite distinction of meaning is implied. 'Version B' shows that *ktoinookhos* (written in smaller letters over Ep01.2) should be inserted at the end of each entry in the first section. As in lines 8–14, it should evidently be taken to mean 'Aithioq^{u}s holds a lease from the *dāmos*, being himself a plot-owner'; compare **148** = Ep04.11, where the present participle of the verb 'to be' is in fact added: [*Phalai*]*kos . . . , ktoinookhos eōn*. Carratelli rightly criticizes Furumark's analysis *ktoinookhos-paro-dāmōi*, 'one who holds his plot from the *dāmos*'.

The leases of 'communal plots' by men and women who are *not* themselves *ktoinookhoi* are catalogued on the large *Ep-* tablets in the 'fourth set' (below, p. 258).

V ERSION A

131 = Ep01   [301]   †

¹ *ke-ke-me-na   ko-to-na   a-no-no* | *to-so-de   pe-mo* [WHEAT 1 ⊤ 1 ?]

² *ai-ti-jo-qo   o-na-to   e-ke   pa-ro   da-mo   ke-ke-me-na   ko-to-na* 'ko-to-no o-ko'
                                                   to-so [*pe-mo*] WHEAT 1 ⊤ 4 ◁ 3

³ *wa-na-ta-jo   o-na-to   e-ke   pa-ro   da-mo   ke-ke-me-na   ko-to-na   to-so-de-pe-mo*
                                                               WHEAT ⊤ 5

⁴ *a-da-ma-o   o-na-to   e-ke   pa-ro   da-mo   ke-ke-me-na   ko-to-na   to-so-*[*de pe*]*-mo*
                                                               WHEAT ⊤ 4

⁵ *a-tu-ko   e-te-do-mo   o-na-to   e-ke   pa-ro   da-mo   ke-ke-me-na   ko-*[*to-na   to-so*
                                                    pe-mo WHEAT nn]

⁶ *ṭạ-ṭạ-ro   o-na-to   e-ke   pa-ro   da-mo   ke-ke-me-na   ko-to-na   to-so-pe-mo*
                                                    [WHEAT ⊤ 5 ?]

               vacat

⁸ *pi-ke-re-u   e-ke-qe   ke-ke-me-na   ko-to-na   ko-to-no-o-ko   to-so   pe-mo* [WHEAT nn]

⁹ *ra-ku-ro   e-ke-qe   ke-ke-me-na   ko-to-na   ko-to-no-o-ko   to-so   pe-mo* WHEAT [nn]

¹⁰ *ku-so   e-ke-qe   ke-ke-me-na   ko-to-na   ko-to-no-o-ko   to-so   pe-mo* WHEAT ◁ [nn]

¹¹ *ke-ra-u-jo   e-ke-qe   ke-ke-me-na   ko-to-na   ko-to-no-o-ko   to-⟨so⟩-pe-mo*
                                                               WHEAT ⊤ 4

¹² *pa-ra-ko   e-ke-qe   ke-ke-me-na   ko-to-na   ko-to-no-o-ko   to-so-pe-mo* WHEAT ⊤ 7

¹³ *ko-tu-*[*ro₂*]   *e-ke-qe   ke-ke-me-na   ko-to-na   ko-to-no-o-ko   to-so   pe-mo*
                                                               WHEAT ⊤ 1

¹⁴ *a-i-qe-u   e-ke-qe   ke-ke-me-na   ko-to-na   ko-to-no-o-ko   to-so   pe-mo* WHEAT ⊤ 6

§ 1   *Communal* plots *not leased*, so much seed: 132? l. wheat.

§ 2   Aithioqᵘs holds the *lease* of a *communal* plot from the village (being himself)
      a plot-owner: so much seed: 174 l. wheat,

§ 3   W. holds the *lease* of a *communal* plot from the village (being himself
      a plot-owner): so much seed: 60 l. wheat,

                              etc.

§ 13   *A-i-qe-u, and* he holds a *communal* plot (being himself) a plot-owner:
      so much seed: 72 l. wheat.

a-no-no: Webster (1954, p. 13) and Carratelli independently agree with us in suggesting   ‡
    a compound adjective *an-onoi* 'not subject to *o-na-to*', which would explain the
    absence of a personal name in the first position. But who actually farms this land?
    Ea22 contains the puzzling annotation *ke-ke-me-na   ko-to-na-⟨a⟩-no-no: Amphialos ekhei.*
    The new tablet Ea801 reads *Klu⟨me⟩noio   melitēwos   ktoina   a-no-no   ke-ke-me-*[*na?*].

VERSION B

As Bennett has pointed out to us, the entries of **131**=Ep01 are duplicated by the separate tablets Eb818 (§ 1), Eb08 (§ 2), Eb09 (§3), Eb747 (§ 4), Eb05 (§ 7), Eb02 (§ 8), Eb893 (§ 9), Eb04 (§ 10), Eb03 (§ 11), Eb23+892 (§ 12) and Eb895 (§ 13).

132=Eb818 (including former Ea21)

ke-ke-me-na   ko-to-na   a-no-no   to-so-de   pe-mo   WHEAT 1   T ⟦8⟧ '1'

§ 1   *Communal* plots *not leased*, so much seed: 132 l. wheat.

133=Eb08(+846)

¹ *ai-ti-jo-qo   e-ke-qe   o-na-to   ke-ke-me-na   ko-to-na*
² *pa-ro   da-mo   ko-to-no-o-ko | to-so-de   pe-mo*   WHEAT 1   T 4   ⊿ 3

§ 2   Aithioqᵘs, *and* he holds the lease of a *communal* plot from the village (being himself) a plot-owner: so much seed: 174 l. wheat.

134=Eb895+906

¹ *a-i-qe-u   e-ke-qe   ke-ke-me-na   ko-to-na*
² *ko-to-no-o-ko   to-so-de   pe-mo*   WHEAT   T 6

§ 13   A., *and* he holds a *communal* plot (being himself) a plot-owner: so much seed: ? 72 l. wheat.

4. THE THIRD PYLOS SET

The subjects of this list, which contains several formulae unique in complexity, seem to share a religious function. Only two of the entries refer specifically to *onāta paro dāmōi*; some at least of the remainder evidently describe other, more obscure, kinds of holding.

VERSION A

135=Ep704

¹ *o-pe-to-re-u   qe-ja-me-no   e-ke   ke-ke-me-na   ko-to-na   to-so   pe-mo*   [WHEAT] 2 T 5
² *u-wa-mi-ja   te-o-jo   do-e-ra   o-na-to   e-ke-qe   i-je-re-ja   ḳe-ra   to-so   pe-mo*
                                                            WHEAT T 1   ⊿ 3
³ *e-ri-ta   i-je-re-ja   o-na-to   e-ke   ke-ke-me-na   ko-to-na   pa-ro   da-mo   to-so   pe-mo*
                                                            WHEAT   T 4
⁴ *ki-ri-te-wi-ja   o-na-to   e-ko-si   ke-ke-me-na   ko-to-na   pa-ro   da-mo   to-so   pe-mo*
                                                            WHEAT 1   T 9
⁵ *e-ri-ta   i-je-re-ja   e-ke   e-u-ke-to-qe   e-to-ni-jo   e-ke-e   te-o | da-mo-de-mi   pa-si*
                                                            ko-to-na-o

⁶ *ke-ke-me-na-o o-na-to e-ke-e to-so pe-mo* WHEAT 3 T 9

⁷ *ka-pa-ti-ja ka-ra-wi-po-ro e-ke ke-ke-me-no o-pe-ro-sa du-wo-u-pi wo-ze-e*
                                                              o-u-wo-ze ⟦*to*⟧

⁸ *to-*[*so pe-mo* WHEAT nn]   †

§ 1   *O.Q.* holds a *communal* plot, so much seed: 300 l. wheat,

§ 2   Huamia, servant (f.) of the god, *and* she holds as a *lease* a *geras* of the
       priestess; so much seed: 18 l. wheat,

§ 3   Eritha the priestess holds the *lease* of a *communal* plot from the village;
       so much seed: 48 l. wheat,

§ 4   The *k.*-women hold the *lease* of a *communal* plot from the village, so much
       seed: 228 l. wheat,

§ 5   Eritha the priestess holds (this), and she claims that (her) god holds the
       freehold; but the village says that he/she (merely?) holds the *lease* of *communal*
       plots: so much seed: 468 l. wheat,

§ 6   Karpathia the key-bearer (f.) holds two (?) *communal* (plots); although
       under an obligation to *perform* with the two, she does not *perform*: so much
       seed: *x* l. wheat.

o-pe-to-re-u qe-ja-me-no: the vocalization of these words is uncertain. Are they both
    proper names, or is one a title? In 'Version B' the first is spelt *o-pe-te-re-u* (cf.
    ὀφελτρεύω 'sweep'?); similarly on Ea805: *o-pe-te-re-u e-ne-ka a-no-pa₂-si-ja*. The
    last word, which apparently describes the cause or justification of his holding, seems
    to be a noun parallel to classical compounds with -βασία.
Line 2: the position of *onāton* before *ekhei qᵘe* seems ungrammatical and does not corre-
    spond with 'Version B': it is perhaps due to confusion by the copyist with the
    wording *onāton ekhei* seen in the next line. If *o-na-to ke-ra* really means *onāton geras*
    'a beneficial pension', one might have expected *paro hiereiāi*, '*from the priestess*'.
ki-ri-te-wi-ja: the function of these women is uncertain (see **28** = An42, p. 167).
Lines 5–6: the 'communal plots' here are evidently quite distinct from the small 'lease
    from the village' attributed to the same priestess in line 3. She is presumably the
    same 'priestess of *Pa-ki-ja-*' who also holds a 'lease' from Amaruntas in **119** = Eo02.8.
    As the congruent *ekhei* 'has' and *phāsi* = φησί show, *eukhetoi* is in the present tense,
    with 'Arcadian' -τοι for Attic -ται (see p. 87): it does not mean 'prays' or 'boasts'
    but 'solemnly or insistently declares', which is nearest to its original sense. The
    construction with infinitive is only used in Homer of the subject of the verb: εὔχομαι
    εἶναι 'I claim to be...'; should one translate here 'and she claims to hold the
    e-to-ni-jo for her god'?
       The meaning of *e-to-ni-jo* is uncertain. It recurs only on **146** = Eb34 (cf. Ep03.14),
    of 'communal plots' held by *Amphimedes*; and on **55** = An724.12 (see p. 188). It

seems to describe a privileged title to originally 'communal' land, quite distinct from the status of 'ownership' implied by the term *ktimenai*. See Vocabulary, p. 394, and cf. Carratelli, 1954*a*, p. 106.

The construction of the second half of the sentence, and the explanation of the divergent wording in 'Version B', are problematical. In *da-mo-de-mi* the third syllable must be the enclitic *-de* which articulates the second clause in 'Version B': the proposed *dāmos de min* follows the normal word-order, cf. *Od.* iv, 116, νόησε δέ μιν Μενέλαος, etc. Compare *e-ke-de-mi a₂-ku-mi-jo* on Na70: ἔχει δέ μιν ᾿Α~μιος, where *min* would appear to mean 'it' rather than 'him/her' (the most frequent Homeric use). μιν is the anaphoric pronoun referring back to a person just mentioned: it is not reflexive except in subordinate clauses with a new grammatical subject, e.g. *Il.* v, 845: ᾿Αθήνη δῦν᾿ ῎Αιδος κυνέην, μή μιν ἴδοι ὄβριμος ῎Αρης. This sentence cannot therefore mean 'but she says that *she herself* has...', which one might deduce from the apparent wording of 'Version B' alone. Another alternative might be 'but she says that the *dāmos* has...'; but this leaves *min* without a reasonable explanation, and it would be most unexpected if the priestess, whose name introduces the whole sentence, should at the end turn out not to be herself the party interested in the amount of seed corn listed. The same objection can be levelled at Carratelli and Webster when they translate the *ko-to-no-o-ko* of 'Version B' as 'but (she declares) that the plot-owners have...'. That the *dāmos* should be so personified that it can be recorded as 'saying' something is not unreasonable, even for this date: in the *onāton paro damōi* formula it occupies the same position as human beings do in *onāton paro Aithioqᵘei*, etc.

klāwiphoros: as suggested by the order *hiereia klāwiphoros qᵘe* on **142**=Eb32, and by the parallel *hiereiās doelos/Karpathiās doelos* on Ep03.8–9 (and cf. **27**=Ae08/Ae09), this female title is that of a religious office ('temple superintendent'?). Compare Attic κλειδοῦχος 'priestess'; κλειδοφόρος; Doric κλακοφόρος, title of a priest at Messene (IG 5(I).1447). In 'Version B' the word [..]-*ja-pi* (probably *Pa-ki-ja-pi* as on **257**=Jn09.7) is added: compare *hiereia Pa-ki-ja-na* on **119**=Eo02.8.

ophêlonsa duouphi worzeen ou worzei: though mis-spelt *wo-zo-e*, the first verb was recognized as an infinitive in 'Version B' by Carratelli (1954*a*, p. 110), before the publication of Ep704. Formally identical with Homeric ῥέζω 'act, accomplish (a deed), perform (a sacrifice)' and with its doublet ἔρδω (*ϝέργjω > *ϝέρζδω) of the same meanings, its significance in this context is uncertain. Variant forms of the same formula are repeated on **148**=Ep04 (see p. 261) and on three fragmentary tablets:

Ep04.6, 7, 9, 13: ...*ekhei qᵘe worzei qᵘe.*
 ...he both holds the land and 'performs'.
Ep04.4: ...] *duouphi teleiaen, ouqᵘe worzei.*
 ...(under an obligation) to 'perform' with two, but he does not 'perform'.
† Eb39+940: ...*o]phélōn qᵘe teleiaen, ouqᵘe teleiā.*
 ...and under an obligation to 'perform', but he does not 'perform'.
Eb40: ...*te]leiaen, hemei de teleiā.*
 ...(under an obligation to 'perform' with two), but he 'performs' with one.

Eb37: ...] *duouphi de* [...

...but (he 'performs') with two.

Carratelli (1954*a*, p. 110) supports the interpretation *worzei* = 'cultivates, ploughs', a meaning which is not shown by the classical ῥέзω/ἔρδω, but which might perhaps be inferred from γεωργός, Homeric ἔργα 'cultivated lands', and from ἐργάзομαι in Hesiod. The expressions 'with one', 'with two' might then refer to the multiple ploughing stipulated when fallow land was brought back into cultivation (Thomson, 1949, p. 309); and these entries might be taken as implying possible penalties for the non-cultivation of land, similar to those mentioned in the Hittite Code (above, p. 233) and in §§ 42–3 of Hammurabi's code (Pritchard, 1950):

'If a seignior rented a field for cultivation, but has not produced grain in the field, they shall prove that he did not work on the field and he shall give grain to the owner of the field on the basis of those adjoining it. If he did not cultivate the field, but has neglected it, he shall give grain to the owner of the field on the basis of those adjoining it; furthermore, the field which he neglected he shall break up with mattocks, harrow and return to the owner of the field.'

It is very remarkable, however, that the fact of '?cultivating' or 'not ?cultivating' should only be recorded for a minute fraction of the total number of tenants. If the *pe-mo* is regarded as a tax, then this might be payable whether the land was cultivated or not, as in the Hammurabi clause; but if it is actually seed grain issued, then its provision for uncultivated land seems senseless. Carratelli has himself pointed out that the *worzei* formula is almost entirely confined to entries concerning the type of holding called *ka-ma*. The present participle *worzōn/worzontes* is also restricted to a corresponding class of men called *ka-ma-e-we* (and once to a *mo-ro-pa₂ moroppās* '? portion-owner' on **57** = An43). From the variations in the formula, particularly Ep04.4, it appears that *worzei* is synonymous with *te-re-ja* (3rd sing. present from *τελειαμι = Homeric τελείω 'pay'?); and it is more probable that these verbs refer to some kind of feudal dues or services which a holding of *ka-ma* land entails.

Compare the following two entries on Ep03, which diverge from the *onaton paro damōi* formula general on the remainder of the tablet, and which may be intended to be synonymous:

Line 5: *Psoleia theoio doelā onāton ekhei* [*paro X.*] *kamaēwei worzontei*:

'She holds a lease from the *kama*-owner, who renders the services.'

Line 7: *Meleus hiereiās doelos onāton ekhei paro* [*Pto*]*lematāi kamaewei, ouqᵘe worzei*:

'He holds a lease from the *kama*-owner, and does not himself render the services.'

It is significant that on all other entries except Ep03.7 which refer to '*not* performing' we have an explanatory clause with *ophélōn/ophélonsa* 'although being under an obligation to do so'.

This stipulation may reflect a similar situation to that in § 47 of the Hittite Code (later recension):

'If any one buys all the fields of a "craftsman", they shall ask the king, and he shall render those services which the king orders. If there still remain fields in the hands of the man from whom he buys, *he shall not render the services*.'

The precise meaning of the instrumentals *duouphi* 'with two' and *e-me* 'with one' (cf. **236** = Ta641.1) is hard to determine. It is possible that *ke-ke-me-no* here implies a *pair* of *ktoinai* (cf. **128** = Eo278), and one might argue that the 'key-bearer' is consequently called upon to render services 'in respect of the two of them'. The other examples of the same formula, however, are all fragmentary, and it is impossible to check whether they also refer to multiple holdings.

VERSION B

136 = Eb31 [294]

¹ *o-pe-te-re-u   qe-ja-me-no   e-ke-qe   ke-ke-me-na   ko-to-na*
² *to-so-de   pe-mo*   WHEAT 2   T 5

§ 1   *O.Q., and* he holds a *communal* plot, so much seed: 300 l. wheat.

† **137** = Eb30 [416]

¹ *u-wa-mi-ja   te-o-jo   do-e-ra   e-[ke]-qe   i-je-[re-ja]   ke-ra o-[na-to]*
² *to-so-de   pe-mo*   WHEAT   T 2   ⊲ 3

§ 2   Huamia, servant (f.) of the god, *and* she holds of the priestess a *geras-lease* (a beneficial pension?), so much seed: 30? l. wheat.

138 = Eb10 [409]

¹ *i-je-re-ja   pa-ki-ja-na   e-ke-[qe o-na-to   ke-ke-me-na]*
² *ko-to-na   pa-ro-da-mo   [to-so   pe-mo*   WHEAT   T 4   ?]

§ 3   The priestess of *Pa-ki-ja-*ᴾ holds the *lease* of a *communal* plot from the village, so much seed: ? 48 l. wheat.

‡ **139** = Eb21 (+ Eb14) [321]

¹ ⟦*ki-ri-wi-*⟧ '*ki-ri-te-wi-ja*'   *e-ko-si   [o-na-ta   ke-ke]-me-na-o*
² *ko-[to-na-o   pa-ro   da-mo   to-so]-de   pe-mo*   WHEAT 1   T 9

§ 4   The *k.*-women hold the *leases* of *communal* plots from the village, so much seed: 228 l. wheat.

Note that the 'leases' and plots are here in the plural, compared with singular in 'Version A'. The fragment printed together with Eb21 in *PT I* has been found not to belong with it.

140 = Eb35 [297] (see plate III (*a*), facing p. 111)

¹ *i-je-re-ja   e-ke-qe   e-u-ke-to-qe   e-to-ni-jo   e-ke-e   te-o*
² *ko-to-no-o-ko-de   ko-to-na-o   ke-ke-me-na-o   o-na-ta   e-ke-e*
³ WHEAT 3   T 9   ⊲ 3

§ 5   The priestess, *and* she holds (this), and she claims the (her) god holds the *freehold*, but the actual plot-owner (claims) that he/she holds the *leases* of *communal* plots: 474 l. wheat.

The divergences from 'Version A' are as follows: the omission of 'Eritha'; the enclitic in *ekhei* q*u*e; the substitution of *ktoinookhos de* for *dāmos de min phāsi*; the omission of *to-so pe-mo*; and the additional ⊲ 3 in the total. Our translation assumes that the † 'village' is here referred to as the recognized or reputed *ktoinookhos* of the site; but an alternative might be '...but she claims that *she* holds the leases, being herself a plot-owner' (cf. **131** = Ep01.2). A similar analysis is made by Chantraine (1955, p. 25).

141 = Eb20   [338]   ‡

¹ *ka-pa-ti-ja   ka-ra-wi-po-[ro   pa-ki]-ja-pi   e-ke-qe | to-so-de   pe-mo*
² *ke-ke-me-no   ko-to-[no]   wo-wo   o-pe-ro-sa-de   wo-zo-e   o-wo-ze*   WHEAT [nn]

§ 6   Karpathia, the key-bearer (f.) at *Pa-ki-ja-*ᴾ, *and* she holds the *confines* of two (?) *communal* plots; but though under an obligation to *perform*, she does not *perform*: so much seed: *x* l. wheat.

The words *to-so-de pe-mo* have evidently been fitted into the end of line 1 due to lack of space. The wording shows a number of divergences from that of 'Version A'. The last two words, which at first resisted reasonable explanation (cf. *Evidence*, p. 101), are now shown to be mis-spellings, *wo-zo-e* standing for *wo-ze-e* = *worzeen*, and *o-wo-ze* for the more correct *o-u-wo-ze*.

As a pendant to the 'third set' may be added a further tablet devoted to the priestess and her acolytes:

142 = Eb32   [317]   ¶

¹ *[o]-da-a₂   i-je-re-ja   ka-ra-wi-po-ro-qe   e-qe-ta-qe*
² *we-te-re-u-qe   o-na-ta   to-so-de   pe-mo*   WHEAT 21   ⊤ 6

Now this is how the priestess and the key-bearer and the *attendants* and ?Westreus (hold) *leases*: so much seed: 2592 l. wheat.

The formula *o-da-a₂* (= ὥδε ἄρα?) suggests that this tablet is itself one of a set. The only other *E*- tablets which begin in the same way are **151** = Eb36, which similarly recapitulates the 'leases' held by the category of *ktoinetai*, and the fragmentary tablet Eb847 + 849 (see next note); but **149** = Eb33, which does the same for the class of *kamaēwes*, may well belong to the same series. Does this tablet Eb32, with its very large total, represent a meticulous digest and addition of all the individual holdings in these four names which are scattered throughout the rest of the year's census? If so, its surviving records must be very incomplete, since a total of only about nine units can be extracted from them for the priestess and the others.

e-qe-ta = *hequetās*, lit. 'follower'. Palmer (1955, p. 21) suggests translating it on **57** = An43, etc., where it apparently represents a military rank, by the word 'count' (*comes* = ἑταῖρος). It might be plural here, to judge from the entry on Eb847: *o-da-a₂ e-qe-[ta?...e]-ko-si o-na-ta*, etc. If the word *e-qe-ta-qe* is taken as singular (which the parallelism of the three other entries rather favours) it may be necessary to restore Eb847 as *heqᵘe*[*tāo doeloi*] 'the servants of the count', or the like. (Since writing this, the addition of a 1954 fragment has shown that Eb847 is in fact to be read *o-da-a₂ e-qe-si-jo do-e-ro e-ko-si o-na-ta*, etc.)

we-te-re-u: we already know him as a *hiereus* on **115** = En03.16, etc.

5. THE FOURTH PYLOS SET

After the second and third sets, which record the 'leases' which the land-owners and the priestess hold from the village, the fourth set catalogues (with a few exceptions) those held by the inferior class of craftsmen and *theoio doeloi*, whom we have already met as tenants of *ktoinai ktimenai* in the first set. 'Version A' is represented by the four very large tablets Ep02, Ep03, Ep04 and Ep705, of which only the last two are reproduced here. 'Version B' is broken down into individual entries on a number of small tablets, of which only a fraction survive. The name Hektor occurs twice as the holder of a 'lease from the village': are these two different individuals?

143 = Ep705

¹ *mạ-ra₃-wa te-o-jo do-e-ra o-na-to e-ke ke-*[*ke-me-na ko-to-na pa-ro da-mo to-so pe-mo* WHEAT] T 2

² *ka-ta-no te-o-jo do-e-ro o-na-to e-ke* [*ke-ke-me-na ko-to-na pa-ro da-mo to-so pe*]*-mo* WHEAT T 2

³ *du-ni-jo te-o-jo do-e-ro o-na-to e-*[*ke ke-ke-me-na ko-to-na pa-ro da-mo to-so*] *pe-mo* WHEAT T 1

⁴ *e-sa-ro te-o-jo do-e-ro o-na-to* [*e-ke ke-ke-me-na ko-to-na pa-ro*] *da-mo to-so-pe-mo* WHEAT ◁ 2

⁵ *ka-ra-u-du-ro te-o-jo do-e-ro o-na-to e-ke* [*ke-ke-me-na ko*]*-to-na pa-ro da-mo to-so-pe-mo* WHEAT T 2

⁶ *to-ro-ja te-o-jo do-e-ra o-na-to e-ke ke-ke-me-*[*na*] *ko-to-na pa-ro da-mo/ to-so pe-mo* WHEAT T 1

⁷ *o-re-a₂ te-o-jo do-e-ro o-na-to e-ke ke-ke-me-na* [*ko-to*]*-na pa-ro da-mo to-so-pe-mo* WHEAT ◁ 2

⁸ *e-ko-to te-o-jo do-e-ro o-na-to e-ke ke-ke-me-na ko-to-na* [[*ko-to-na*]] 'pa-ro *da'-mo to-so pe-mo* WHEAT T 2

⁹ *pu-ko-wo te-o-jo do-e-ro o-na-to e-ke ke-ke-me-na* [*ko-to-na pa-ro da-mo*] *to-so-pe-mo* WHEAT T 2

¹⁰ *ta-ra-mi-ka te-o-jo do-e-ra o-na-to e-ke ke-*[*ke-me-na ko-to-na pa-ro da*]*-mo to-so-pe-mo* WHEAT T 1

§ 1 ?Marraiwa, servant (f.) of the god, holds the *lease* of a *communal* plot from the village: so much seed: 24 l. wheat,

etc.

The first entry of **143** = Ep705 is duplicated by Eb866 (as § 2 by Eb890, † § 3 by Eb43, § 5 by Eb838, § 8 by Eb913, § 10 by Eb27):

144 = Eb866

ma-ra₃-wa	*ke-ke-me-na*	*ko-to-na*	*pa-ro*	*da-mo*		WHEAT	[T 2]
	te-o-jo	*do-e-ra*	*e-ke-qe*	*o-na-to*			

The woman's name was written *Ma-ra-wa* and the second letter corrected.

145 = Ea05 [259]   ‡
‡

o-ke-u	*u-me-ta-qe*	[? *u*]-*po*			
	e-ke	*o-na-to*	*pa-ro*	*da-mo*	WHEAT T 2

O. holds a *lease* from the village, and ?Eumetas under him (?): 24 l. wheat.

This unique variation in the standard formula suggests some form of subtenancy. The full name *E-u-me-ta* (= Εὐμήτης) occurs on KN Dl 1388. Bennett reads *ạ-po*.

Several entries on Ep03 diverge entirely from the *paro dāmoi* formula. The ¶ last line reads: *Amphi[mēdēs...] ekhei e-to-ni-jo ?kekeimenās ktoinās....* This reappears in 'Version B' as:

146 = Eb34 [473]
¹ *a-pi-me-de e-ke-qe e-to-ni-jo ke-ke-me-na-o ko-to-na-o*
² *to-so-de pe-mo* WHEAT 4 T 6

Amphimedes, *and* he holds the *freehold* of *communal* plots, so much seed: 552 l. wheat.

As in the 'third set', § 4, 'Version B' here shows 'leases' and 'plots' in the plural. Ep03 . 11–12 also refer to two men as being *Amphimēdeos doeloi*; a person of this name is a 'sheep collector' on PY **62** = Cn655. The recurrence of *Amphimēdeos po-ku-ta* †† on KN C 911 . 10 (cf. gen. *pe-ri-me-de-o* on **43** = Sn01) gives rise to a suspicion that *A.* may be a title rather than a personal name.

Ep03 lines 4 and 5 record two different kinds of leases which the woman Psoleia holds: first that of a 'communal' plot from the village, then one from a *kamaeus* (quoted above, p. 255). A more elaborate summary of leases held by a single individual is seen in the four entries devoted to Kretheus on the following tablet:

147 = Eq03 [59]   ‡‡
‡‡
¹ [   ] WHEAT 6
² *ke-re-u e-ke o-na-to ke-ke-me-⟨na⟩ ko-to-na* WHEAT ? [T] 4

³ *ke-re-te-u   e-ke   o-na-to   ke-ke-me-na   ko-to-na   su-qo-ta-o*   WHEAT 1   T 8

⁴ *ke-re-te-u   e-ke   o-na-to   pa-ro   da-mo*   WHEAT 3

           pa-ro   ra-wa-ke-si-jo   [?]   WHEAT 2

⁵ *ke-re-te-u   e-ke   e-ne-ka   i-qo-jo*   WHEAT 5

          vacat

⁷ *du-ni-jo   e-ke   o-na-to   pa-ro   da-mo*   WHEAT 1   T 6 [

REVERSE: a tallying in 5's, making up a total of 137 units of WHEAT.

Lines 3–5:
Kretheus holds the *lease* of a *communal* plot of the swineherds: 216 l. wheat,
Kretheus holds a *lease* from the village: 360 l. wheat,
   he holds (one) from the commander's (temenos?): 240 l. wheat,
Kretheus holds (this) on account of the horse: 600 l. wheat.

ke-re-u in line 2 is probably not a mis-spelling of Kretheus, since the same name recurs on Ea827.

Kretheus himself is the subject of four other single-entry tablets, none of whose wordings and amounts appear to correspond with Eq03:

Ea11: *Krētheus ekhei ⟨o⟩nāton {to} ? kekeimenās ktoinās g^uoug^uotāōn*: WHEAT   T 1

Ea771: *Krētheus ekhei onāton melitēwōn ktoinās*: WHEAT   T 5

110 = Ea800: *Krētheus ekhei onāton paro Molog^urōi poimenei*: WHEAT   T 2

Ea806: *Krētheus ekhei onāton ? kekeimenās paro dāmōi*: WHEAT 1   T 2[

e-ne-ka   i-qo-jo: the meaning of this entry is obscure. It is dangerous to take 'Kretheus' *one* horse' as proof that it was used for riding rather than chariot-driving, since the noun may perhaps (like classical ἡ ἵππος) have been used collectively. Carratelli (1954*b*, p. 222) quotes with approval Furumark's suggestion that WHEAT 5 in line 5 is in fact a total of the two entries in line 4: 'Both the commune and the military authority have contributed for the horse provided by Kretheus.' But there is no clear evidence of a summation in the layout of the tablet (one would expect *to-so*), and if the grain is taken as fodder for the animal(s), this interpretation can hardly be reconciled with the normal meaning of *onāton paro dāmōi* as a land-holding. That the *heneka hiqq^uoio* entry should mean extra grain for Kretheus' plough animals (on the Babylonian analogy) seems impossible, in view of the light build of early horses and the limit on tractive power set by their inefficient harnessing. But compare the Homeric use of the hardier mule for ploughing, *Il.* x, 351. Kretheus' holding is probably to be compared with the acreages frequently introduced on the contemporary Wilbour Papyrus with the words 'field for horses which the stable-master So-and-so bespoke'. Gardiner (1948, II, p. 78) quotes a model letter from Papyrus Sallier 1: '30 arouras of fields were given to me to make into food for the pair of horses of Pharaoh which are in my charge, and now, behold, they have been taken from me . . .'; and he concludes: 'It would seem, then, that stable-masters of Pharaoh were entitled to lay claim to such land as they needed for grazing the horses entrusted to them, as well no doubt as for their personal support.'

The long tablet Ep04 can be divided into two sections, which show different formulae. The first (lines 1–13) refers to holdings of *ka-ma* land, and to some † kinds of service rendered in return. This *ka-ma*, whose occupants or tenants are called *ka-ma-e-we*, has been compared (first by Huxley) with the Cretan gloss καμάν· τὸν ἀγρόν (cf. χαμαί); it also occurs in the expression *worgioneio-ka-ma* on **171** = Un718.11, with which compare *worgioneio- e-re-mo* on **152** = Er01.7 (p. 266). It apparently describes a feudal holding distinct from *temenos* and *ktoinā ktimenā*, entailing certain definite obligations whose fulfilment is the concern of the palace, and partly vested in a class of priests (i.e. the **worgiones* = ὀργεῶνες).

A pair of lines (11–12) describe a *kama* holding by the *ktoinookhos* Phalaikos (whom we know from **119** = Eo02.2, **131** = Ep01.12), and a lease held from him by a *theoio doelā*. It is these two entries which Bennett regards as representing the missing fourteenth paragraph of the 'first set', mistakenly copied out of order. The rest of that set, however, refers exclusively to *ktoinai ktimenai*.

The second part of the tablet (lines 14–20) repeats the normal *onāton paro dāmōi* formula of **143** = Ep715, etc., and will be omitted here.

148 = Ep04   [613]   ‡

¹ [? *o-pe-ro-qe   du*]*-wo-u-pi   te-re-ja-e*

² [? *e-me-de   te-re-ja   to-so   pe-mo*]   WHEAT 10   T 1

³ [? *Ko- . -ro   o-na-to   e-ke   ke-ke*]*-me-na   ko-to-na   ka-ma-e-u   wo-ze-qe*

                                    to-so-pe-mo   [WHEAT nn]

⁴ [? *o-pe-ro-qe*]   *du-wo-u-pi   te-re-ja-e   o-u-qe   wo-ze* [

⁵ [*to-so   pe*]*-mo*   WHEAT [nn]

⁶ [..]*-re-u   a̱-si-to-po-qo   ka-ma   e-ke-qe   wo-ze-qe   to-so-pe-mo*   WHEAT 1   T 2̣

⁷ [.]*-ke-re-u   i-je-ro-wo-ko   ka-ma-e-u   o-na-to   e-ke   wo-ze-qe   to-so-pe-mo*   WHEAT 1

⁸ [*sa-sa-wo*]   *o-na-to   e-ke   ka-ma-e-u   e-pi̱-qe   to-me   te-ra-pi-[ke]   to-so   pe-mo*

                                        WHEAT 1   T 5

⁹ [*e-u*]*-ru-wo-ta   te-o-jo   [do-e]-ro   e-ke-[qe?   ka]-ma   o-na-to   [wo]-ze-qe   to-so*

                                        pe-[mo]   WHEAT 1   T 3

¹⁰ [*pe-re*]*-qo-ta   pa-de-we-u   [e]-ke-qe   ka-ma   o-na-to   si-ri-jo-⟨jo⟩   ra-ke   to-so-pe-mo*

                                        WHEAT 1

¹¹ [*pa-ra*]*-ko   [o-na-to   e-ke]   ka-ma   ko-to-no-o-ko   e-o   to-so   pe-mo*   WHEAT 1

¹² [*po-so*]*-re-[ja   te-o]-jo   do-e-ra   e-ke   o-na-to   pa-ro   pa-ra-ko   to-so   pe-mo*

                                        WHEAT T 1   ◁ 3

¹³ [*-ko   mi*]*-ka-ta   pa-de-we-u   ka-ma-e-u   e-ke-qe   wo-ze-qe   to-so   pe-mo*

                                        WHEAT T 5

§ 1   (cf. Eb40?): ...though under an obligation to *render the services in respect of* two, he (only) renders them in respect of one; so much seed: 1212 l. wheat.

§ 2   (cf. Eb38): K. holds the *lease* of a *communal* plot as a *kama*-holder and *renders the services*; so much seed: *x* l. wheat.

§ 3   (cf. Eb39?): ...though under an obligation to *render the services in respect of* two, he does not render them at all; so much seed: *x* l. wheat.

§ 4   (cf. Eb25): So-and-so the *cook* both holds a *kama* and *renders the services*; so much seed: 144 l. wheat.

§ 5   So-and-so the sacrificing priest holds a *lease* as a *kama*-holder and *renders the services*; so much seed: 120 l. wheat.

§ 6   (cf. Eb842): S. holds a *lease* as a *kama*-holder, and in return for this he *serves*; so much seed: 180 l. wheat.

§ 7   (cf. Eb24): E., the servant (m.) of the god, both holds the *lease* of a *kama* and *renders the services*; so much seed: 156 l. wheat.

§ 8   (cf. Eb22): P., the (priest) of P., and he holds the *lease* of a *kama*; he has obtained the portion of S. (?); so much seed: 120 l. wheat.

§ 9   (cf. Eo173): Phalaikos has the *lease* of a *kama*, being himself a plot-owner; so much seed: 120 l. wheat.
Psoleia, servant (f.) of the god, holds a *lease* from Phalaikos; so much seed: 18 l. wheat.

§ 10 (cf. Eb839): So-and-so, the *miktās* of P., both holds as a *kama*-holder and *renders* the services; so much seed: 60 l. wheat.

§ 1 and § 3: *o-pe-ro-qe* is restored on the analogy of Eb39 (see p. 254). Compared with the logical sequence...*ophélonsa worzeen, ou worzei* of **135** = Ep704.7, this wording ...*ophélōn qᵘe teleiaen, ouqᵘe worzei* shows not only a puzzling alternation of verb but also some degree of anacoluthon—unless *ouqᵘe* is taken in the sense of οὐδέ 'not even' rather than as a connective 'but not'. Compare also **43** = Sn01.3–4.

§ 2: if Bennett is right in regarding Eb38 as the corresponding 'Version B', that differs in showing the participle *worzōn* instead of the indicative *worzei qᵘe*. It is also significant in writing corrected *ka-ma-e-u* over a *pa-ro da-mo* in erasure, showing that, though the *ka-ma* fields are included in the wider classification of ?*kekeimenai ktoinai*, they are not collectively administered by the village. It is difficult to decide whether the variant formulae

(*a*) ...*ekhei kamān*...
(*b*) ...*ekhei onāton (kekeimenās ktoinās) kamaeus*...
(*c*) ...*ekhei onāton kamās*...

are intended to be entirely synonymous; but (a) and (b) alternate in § 4 and its other version Eb25, and all three entail the action of *worzeen*.

§ 4: the reading *sito-poqᵘos* (*Evidence*, p. 96) is uncertain, since the damaged symbol † which precedes *si* seems to be syllabic and not a word-divider. On the corresponding Eb25 only]-*to-po-qo* survives, and the numerals differ in reading WHEAT 1 T 2. Should we read {*a*}-*si-to-po-qo* here, the *a-* being due to a careless anticipation of *arto-poqᵘos* 'baker'?

§ 6: *e-pi-qe to-me te-ra-pi-*[.]: Eb842 reads *e-pi-qe to-e te-ra-pi-ke*. With the scribes' ‡ apparent prejudice against one-sign words, *to-e* may perhaps be intended as a fuller spelling of the dative pronoun τῷ; is *to-me* a variant form *toˢmei* (cf. Skt. *tásmai* 'to that') with the dative ending seen in Gortyn οτιμι 'to whomever'? Cf. ἐπὶ τούτῳ, ἐπὶ τοῖσδε, etc., 'on this condition', and *Il.* x, 304, τίς κέν μοι τόδε ἔργον τελέσειε δώρῳ ἔπι μεγάλῳ; 'in return for a large gift'. The verb *te-ra-pi-ke* (? *therapiskei*) appears to be a derivative of the stem of θεράπων, perhaps an earlier equivalent of θεραπεύω 'do service'.

§ 8: the corresponding Eb22 reads: *pe-re-qo-ta pa-da-je-u i-je-*[*ka-ma si-*[*ri*]-*jo-jo ra-ke* [The same variation in the spelling of P.'s ethnic (?) description is guaranteed by *mi-ka-ta pa-de-we-u* (§ 10) compared with *mi-ka-ta pa-da-je-u* on Eb839. The word ¶ *ra-ke* appears to be λάχε (from λαγχάνω) 'obtained by lot, gained possession'. Note that the subjects of § 9 and § 10, who are in the *telestās* class, are alone in not being required to *worzeen*, etc.

We will close the discussion of the four main sets of Pylos land-tenure lists †† with three small tablets which, like **142** = Eb32 and Eb847 (see above, p. 257), appear to represent selective totals extracted from the lists for particular categories of individuals.

149 = Eb33   [236]
¹ *ka-ma-e-we   o-na-ta   e-ko-te   ke-ke-me-na-o   ko-to-na-o*
² *wo-zo-te   to-so   pe-mo*   WHEAT 30   T 2   ◁ 3
The *kama*-holders, having *leases* of *communal* plots (and) *rendering the services*, so much seed: 3630 l. wheat.

Does this total include all the *ka-ma* entries on **148** = Ep04, as well as those of the same type on other tablets which have been lost? If so, what is the function of the similar total for *ka-ma-e-we* on the next tablet? Does *xunstrophā* 'grand total' imply a digest of several sub-totals of the Eb33 type? It is of course possible that some of these tablets refer to different geographical areas, which were kept separate in the filing system, but not individually headed by place-names (like those which we know to refer to *Pa-ki-ja-*); or even that apparent cases of duplication refer to two consecutive seasons.

† **150** = Ec07   [411]

¹ *ku-su-to-ro-pa₂ / pạ-ṭọ*   [*o-e-ko-si?*]   *te-re-ta*   WHEAT 44   [?
² *ka-ma-e-we*   WHEAT 58   T 5

EDGE: *te-o-jo   do-e-ra*   [

Aggregate of all (that) the *fief-holders* (? have): 5280 + l. wheat,
Aggregate of all (that) the *kama*-holders (have): 7020 l. wheat.

Here again, does the total for the *telestai* include the fourteen of the 'first set' (who between them are assigned about thirty-four units), or the three of **152** = Er01 (with thirty units)?

151 = Eb36   [901]

¹ *o-da-a₂   ke-ke-me-na-⟨o⟩   ko-to-na-o   o-na-ta   e-ko-si   ko-to-ne-ta*
² *to-so   pe-mo*   WHEAT 3   [?]

Now this is how the 'men of the *ktoina*' hold *leases* of the *communal* plots, so much seed: 360 + l. wheat.

‡ Note the unusual inversion of the word-order. The form κτοινέται 'members of a township' is known from inscriptions of Syme, north of Rhodes. It is surprising to find it at this early date, since Buck and Petersen (*Reverse Index*, p. 545) regards κτοινέτης = κτοινάτης, φυλέτης, Carpathian δᾱμέτᾱς = δημότης and Argive κωμέτᾱς = κωμήτης as modified by the analogy of οἰκέτης. What the *ktoinetai* represent in the Pylos set-up is difficult to guess: the term is probably not synonymous with *ktoinookhoi*. Cf. also *ko-to-ne-we* with MANᵇ on Be995.

¶   6. THE ESTATES OF THE KING

The important Pylos tablet Er01 has already been widely discussed (*Evidence*, p. 99, Furumark, 1954, p. 35, Meriggi, 1954*b*, pp. 34–5, Carratelli, 1954*a*, pp. 110–12, Palmer, 1955, pp. 9–10), and general conclusions drawn from it as to the structure of Mycenaean society.

Carratelli understands *telestāōn* ⟨*temenos*⟩ in line 5, but *da-ma-te* or *ktoinai ktimenai* would be expected on the analogy of the 'first set'. These three 'fief-holders' are evidently distinct from the fourteen residents of *Pa-ki-ja* listed in lines 1–2 of **114** = En02. Does Er01, as the princely *temenea* would suggest, refer to land in the immediate neighbourhood of the palace?

For the relation between the *wanax* and the *lāwāgetās*, see p. 120. The new tablet **171** = Un718 (p. 282) shows a similar hierarchical division into four paragraphs, although the subject is not the seed corn proportional to these lands, but the offerings which are to be taken from them for Poseidon. There are certain differences in the order and wording:

Er01		Un718
(1) *wanakteron temenos* =	(1)	*E-ke-ra₂-wo*
(2) *lāwāgesion temenos* =	(3)	*lāwāgetās*
(3) *telestāōn ⟨ktoinai⟩* =	(2)	*dāmos*
(4) *worgioneio- e-re-mo* =	(4)	*worgioneio- kama*

The sequence *king—military leader* is paralleled on PY Un11, lines 7 and 10: *wanaktei—lāwāgetāi*; but **55** = An724 (An32), lines 5 and 7, substitutes the order *E-ke-ra₂-wonei—lāwāgetāi*. This suggests that *?Ekhelāwōn* is either the name of the king himself or that of a representative member of his household. The latter would be more likely if *E-ke-ra-ne* (Un11.1) is regarded as a defective spelling of the same dative.

The name *[E]-ke-ra₂-[wo]* reappears on tablet **153** = Er02, which Bennett has printed together with Er01 on account of the spelling *pe-ma* which it shares and the fact that a single scribe apparently wrote these two tablets and no others. If he is indeed the king, E. has evidently built up an estate of 'private plots' in addition to the hereditary *temenos* assigned to his office at the original land-division.

The further equation between the *telestai* of Er01 and the *dāmos* of Un718 is surprising, after the apparently sharp contrast between these entities on the other land-tenure tablets. But *dāmos* probably means no more than Village, as opposed to Palace, and the *telestai* may well have been regarded as important members of it: in addition to holding 'private plots' in the village, they may themselves have sat on the council responsible for allotting the leases of 'communal plots' *paro dāmōi*. Outside the immediate vicinity of the palace, we apparently find *basilēwes* (further defined as *ko-re-te-re* and *mo-ro-pa₂*) in charge of the villages (see **43** = Sn01, **258** = Kn01); but in the *dāmos* attached to Pylos itself they evidently have no place in the hierarchy.

Carratelli agrees with us in taking *wo-ro-ki-jo-ne-jo* as equivalent to ὀργεω-νικός, from the term ὀργεῶνες 'members of a religious association'; it is spelt ὀργίονας (acc. plur.) in the Homeric hymn to Apollo, and derived from (ϝ)ὀργια 'rites'. Thomson (1949, p. 112) infers 'that the *orgeōnes* were a body of persons appointed by and from the *dēmotai* to administer the village cult', which was centred on an ὀργάς 'rich land or grove sacred to a god' (though this word may not in fact be etymologically connected). The action *worzeen* which is apparently the duty of holders of *kama* land may perhaps be construed in this light as meaning 'to contribute to the (ϝ)ὀργια'.

The gender and meaning of *e-re-mo* are not clear. γῆ ἐρῆμος 'waste land' would call for feminine *-ne-ja* (as *kama* in fact should on Un718). Or is *w.* not an adjective but a noun *worgion-eiōn* 'the place of the *worgiones*'? Should *?erēmon* be taken to mean 'uninhabited land', or 'land left inviolate, free of annexation or encumbrance'?

152 = Er01   [312]

¹ *wa-na-ka-te-ro   te-me-no*
² *to-so-jo   pe-ma*   WHEAT 30
³ *ra-wa-ke-si-jo   te-me-no*   WHEAT 10
    vacat
⁵ *te-re-ta-o   to-so-pe-ma*   WHEAT 30
⁶ *to-so-de   te-re-ta*   MEN 3
⁷ *wo-ro-ki-jo-ne-jo   e-re-mo*
⁸ *to-so-jo   pe-ma*   WHEAT 6
    vacat

§ 1   The preserve of the king, seed at so much: 3600 l. wheat.

§ 2   The preserve of the military leader, seed at so much: 1200 l. wheat.

§ 3   (The lands) of the *fief-holders*, so much seed: 3600 l. wheat; and (there are) so many *fief-holders*: three.

§ 4   The *unencumbered* (land) of the cult association, seed at so much: 720 l. wheat.

wanakteron temenos: cf. τέμενος βασιλήϊον, *Il.* XVIII, 550. The *temenos* is an estate 'cut off' (τέμνω) for the use of ruler or chief; the meaning 'precinct of a god' is secondary.

tossoio sperma: why the spelling *pe-ma* should be restricted to Er01 and Er02 is not clear. One might argue that we indeed have σπέρμα 'seed, ?sowing' here, but that *pe-mo* on the other tablets has a quite different meaning; but no distinction is apparent in the context. Why the genitive *tossoio* in lines 2 and 8? 'A sowing *of so much* (grain)'; or 'seed *of such* (an amount or value)', gen. pretii?

tossoide telestai: as in **114 = En02.2** and **153 = Er02.4, 6**, *to-so-de* follows *to-so* in a linked pair of entries, and suggests that *-de* should here be taken as the particle δέ 'and, but'.

A further link with **171 = Un718** is provided by *sa-ra-pe-do-[* in Er02.2. It is evidently not the name Sarpedon, but an inflexional variant of the *ṣạ-ra-pe-da* which introduces the other tablet. Its ending (neuter plural?) recalls the -πεδον of Greek topographical terms such as γεώπεδον 'plot', ἁλίπεδον 'coastal plain', οἰνόπεδον 'vineyard', Hesychius ἐλάπεδον· τέμενος; perhaps it is a local place-name, here to be read in the locative, *-pedoi'i*. Bennett's integration of *temenos* in line 2 is not supported by a word-divider, and *-pu₂*? is extremely rare as a word-ending. We would compare πεφυτευμένος 'planted with fruit trees', and interpret the two sections of the tablet as referring to acreages of E.'s wheat-fields and to a census of the trees or vines in E.'s orchards. This twofold division of a chief's lands is frequently alluded to by Homer:

Il. VI, 194–5: καὶ μέν οἱ (Βελλεροφόντῃ) Λύκιοι τέμενος τάμον ἔξοχον ἄλλων,
καλόν, φυταλῆς καὶ ἀρούρης, ὄφρα νέμοιτο.

Il. IX, 578–80: ἔνθα μιν (Μελέαγρον) ἤνωγον τέμενος περικαλλὲς ἑλέσθαι
πεντηκοντόγυον, τὸ μὲν ἥμισυ οἰνοπέδοιο,
ἥμισυ δὲ ψιλὴν ἄροσιν πεδίοιο ταμέσθαι.

Il. XIV, 121–3:   (Τυδεὺς) ναῖε δὲ δῶμα
ἀφνειὸν βιότοιο, ἅλις δέ οἱ ἦσαν ἄρουραι
πυροφόροι, πολλοὶ δὲ φυτῶν ἔσαν ὄρχατοι ἀμφίς.

Od. VI, 293–4: ἔνθα δὲ πατρὸς ἐμοῦ ('Ἀλκινόοιο) τέμενος τεθαλυῖά τ' ἀλωή,
τόσσον ἀπὸ πτόλιος, ὅσσον τε γέγωνε βοήσας.

153 = Er02 (with addition of new fragments)   [880]   †

   ¹ [*e*]-*ke-ra₂*-[*wo   ki*]-*ti-me-no   e-ke*
   ² *sa-ra-pe-do-*[*i   ?   pe*]-*pu₂?-te-me-no*
   ³ *to-so*   [*pe-ma*]   WHEAT   30[+20?]
   ⁴ *to-so-de*   [. . .]-*to   pe-ma*   WHEAT   42[+2?]
   ⁵ *to-sa   we-je-*[*we*   ]   1100[
   ⁶ *to-sa-de   ṣụ-ẓạ*   [?]   1000[
                      vacat
   ⁸ *ku-su-to-ro-pa₂   to-ṣọ   pe-ma*   94

?Ekhelāwōn has *private* (lands) on the S~peda, planted with trees.
   So much seed: ?6000 l. wheat,
   so much seed of the [. . .]: ?5280 l. wheat.
   So many [. . .]: 1100?
   So many fig-trees: 1000?
Aggregate, so much seed: 11,280 l.

The detailed descriptions of the four items are unfortunately fragmentary, but the high numbers of the last two are comparable with those of the Knossos lists of trees (see below, pp. 272–4).

we-je-[*we*: may be restored from KN **164** = Ga863, = some kind of plant.

ṣụ-ẓạ: *sukiai* 'fig-trees' as in **165** = Gv862. See p. 272.

If the figure of 42 WHEAT in line 4 is intended purely as an acreage-equivalent, one might restore [*a-ki-ti*]-*to* 'untilled' here: in antithesis to *ki-ti-me-no* in line 1?

Pylos Eq01 has up to now received little discussion, due to the great difficulty of interpretation; it is clear, however, that it deals with territory further removed from the palace than any of the other land-tenure tablets. The subjects of at least the first three entries are not individuals but the names of outlying villages: *A-ke-re-wa* is well known as the sixth of the 'Pylos 9', while *E-ri-no-wo-te* (loc.) is listed with *A-ke-re-wa* and *A-pu₂?-we* on An07 and with *Lousoi* on Mn01. Its nominative is spelt *E-ri-no-wo* (Na51), which (like *Sa-ri-nu-wo-te/Sa-ri-no-te*, *A₂-pa-tu-wo-te*, *Pe-re-wo-te*) suggests *-wōn/-wontos*: a (possibly non-Greek) development of the adjectival -**went-/-wont-* (cf. † Σελινοῦς, etc.)? The locative *ko-tu-we* is found on Na908.

The amounts of seed are evidently too small for the total acreages of these villages: the tablet must record a restricted category of land, defined by the introduction and, in particular, by the puzzling word *o-ro-jo*. A photograph of this tablet was published by Blegen, 1939*b* (Fig. 10), and Hrozný (1949) prints a translation which, however fantastic its methods, nevertheless suggests that it is a record of the condition of fields.

‡ **154** = Eq01 [213]
‡

¹ *o-wi-de a-ko-so-ta to-ro-qe-jo-me-no a-ro-u-ra a₂-ri-sa*
² *a-ke-re-wa o-ro-jo to-so-de pe-mo* WHEAT 8
³ *o-da-a₂ e-ri-no-wo-to o-ro-jo to-so-de pe-mo* WHEAT 10
⁴ *o-da-a₂ ko-tu-wo o-ro-jo to-so-de pe-mo* WHEAT 20
⁵ *o-da-a₂ po-ti-ni-ja-we-jo-jo o-te-pe-o-jo o-ro-jo to-so-de pe-mo* WHEAT 6
⁶ *o-da-a₂ ko-no o-ro-jo to-so pe-mo* WHEAT 40

Thus Axotās has observed on *his tour of inspection*, *counting* the corn-lands of
   A-ke-re-wa[*b*]; of the *loss*, so much (acreage of) seed: 960 l. wheat.
And similarly those of *E-ri-no-wo*; of the *loss*, so much seed: 1200 l. wheat.
And similarly those of *Ko-tu*; of the *loss*, so much seed: 2400 l. wheat.
And similarly those of *queenly O-te-pe-o*: of the *loss*, so much seed: 720 l.
   wheat.
And similarly those which are *common*; of the *loss*, so much seed: 4800 l.
   wheat.

hō wide = Attic ὧδε εἶδε: the same introduction is found to the list of vessels **235** = Ta711,
   evidently another record guaranteed by personal inspection; cf. *Od.* IV, 411–12:

        φώκας μέν τοι πρῶτον ἀριθμήσει καὶ ἔπεισιν·
        αὐτὰρ ἐπὴν πάσας πεμπάσσεται ἠδὲ ἴδηται, etc.

Axotas' name occurs with other aorists on Pn01.1 and **103** = Un08.1, and in the genitive *A-ko-so-ta-o* as one of the 'sheep collectors' (p. 200): he was possibly one of the chief stewards of the palace. The connective *o-da-a₂* occurs in lines 3–6 but not in the first item: it evidently resumes, in abbreviated form, the 'thus' formula of the introduction, which must be regarded as forming a continuous sentence through lines 1–2 (in the same way, *o-da-a₂ da-mo* on **171** = Un718.7 picks up the *o-* of line 2).

troqᵘeiomenos: middle/passive participle of the 'iterative-intensive' form (-*ejō, cf. Schwyzer, *Gram.* I, 719–20) of τρέπω, of which the active τρόπεον 'turned' occurs once in *Il.* XVIII, 224. If it agrees with Axotās, it should perhaps be taken in the sense of τρέπομαι 'go on a circuitous journey', cf. *Od.* xv, 80: εἰ δ' ἐθέλεις τραφθῆναι ἀν' Ἑλλάδα καὶ μέσον Ἄργος, and Herod. II, 3: καὶ δὴ καὶ ἐς Θήβας τε καὶ ἐς Ἡλίου πόλιν ἐτραπόμην, etc. Compare also the Homeric περιτροπέων ἐνιαυτός 'revolving year'.

a₂-ri-sa appears from its form to be an aorist participle, which must agree with Axotās rather than with the feminine *arourans*. The classical verbs ἀλινδέω 'make to roll' and ἀλίζω 'salt' do not fit the sense, nor (ϝ)αλίζω 'gather together' the spelling. Perhaps the verb *ἀρι- 'count', from which ἀρι-θμός 'number', ἀριθμέω 'count' (evidently a later substitution) and Homeric ν-ήριτος 'innumerable' are derived. Compare also *a₂-ri-e*, **55** = An724.5 (p. 187). The sequence of tenses *aorist—iterative present—aorist* is explained by the 'aspect' function of Greek participles, the 'touring' evidently being regarded as a continuous process, the 'counting' as a series of five discrete acts.

o-ro-jo: Palmer reads *oloio '(seed) of barley', comparing οὐλαί (*ὀλϝαί), Arc. ὀλοαί, † 'sacrificial barley', ὄλυρα 'Einkorn wheat'. Other possibilities are ὤροιο (**jōr-*) 'of the year'; or the genitive of the noun *ôlos which underlies the Homeric adjective οὖλος, Dor. ὦλος, 'destructive'. In the latter case the tablet may record the acreages of parts of these villages which have been laid waste or allowed to deteriorate. Compare Telemachus' complaint to Menelaus, *Od.* IV, 318: ἐσθίεταί μοι οἶκος, ὄλωλε δὲ πίονα ἔργα, 'my rich plough-lands have been ruined'. This interpretation is extremely uncertain.

po-ti-ni-ja-we-jo-jo: the subdivision of part of a village community by the adjective ‡ ?*potnia{we}ios* 'of the Mistress?' is also seen in the lists of smiths on Jn01 and Jn03. No reasonable explanation can be offered.

ko-no: possibly κοινός 'common', though the numerals and the introduction *o-da-a₂* prevent us from regarding it as a total of the preceding items. In these the genitives probably qualify *arourans* rather than *o-ro-jo*, but *koino-* can only agree if it is here a two-ending adjective, as in Sophocles, *Tr.* 207. The form of the adjective *to-so* (for *to-so-de*) is probably not significant.

7. KNOSSOS LAND-TENURE TABLETS

The Knossos tablets listing the WHEAT ideogram (classified by Bennett with the prefix *E*) do not appear to share any of the characteristic Pylos land-tenure formulae, and should probably be regarded as a record of actual consignments of grain from outlying villages: the amounts listed are generally larger than on the Pylos *E-* tablets, often running into hundreds of units. Of interest are the words *ra-wa-ke-si-jo* on E 1569.2 (and its apparent mis-spelling *ra-wa-e-si-jo* on E 846.1), which might refer to a *lāwāgesion temenos*; and the heading to the fragmentary E 849 which includes a total of 130 units of WHEAT: *pu-ta-ri-ja pe-ra-*[.... This appears to be the word φυταλιά 'plantation, orchard', and one might expect, as in Homer, to find it kept distinct from corn-land; but the first half of the tablet may have included olives or figs, and in any case corn can well be grown in areas between olive-trees (cf. Columella, *De re rustica*, v, 8–9).

The equivalent of the Pylos land-tenure series is to be found in the two dozen tablets to which Bennett has given the prefix *Uf*. The words *ekhei, ?kekeimenā, ktoinā* and *telestās* help to establish the identity of context; but the formula *tossonde ?spermo* is replaced by the use of the ideogram DA, apparently a land-measure, whose only occurrence at Pylos is on **114** = En02.1. We saw there that it is apparently equivalent to the acreage sown with 1 unit of wheat (about 2·4 ha, or 6 acres?). At Knossos it is subdivided into a smaller unit PA: as it is followed by the number 3 on **158** = Uf836, the PA is evidently a quarter of the DA or less. Does it stand for *spadion* (original form of στάδιον) 'a single ploughing'?

DA	⊢	A unit of land measure
PA	ǂ	A fraction of the preceding

This Late Minoan series is too fragmentary to permit a detailed comparison with the system of land-tenure seen in operation at Pylos.

155 = Uf981   (K)

e-ri-ke-re-we   *ko-to-i-na*
                 e-ke-pu-te-ri-ja [

Eriklewes holds an *orchard* plot....

Bennett's *Index* (p. 66) gives *ko-ti-i-na*, which is not supported by the original: note the fuller spelling of the diphthong. Is *pu-te-ri-ja* merely a variant *phutelia* for φυταλιά? Or an adjective *phutērian* agreeing with *ktoinan* 'a plot suitable for planting; given to a gardener'? Or a noun describing a holding (parallel to *onāton*, etc.) 'a lease for planting, as a reward for planting'? In any case the term suggests that these fields are probably orchard or vineyard, not corn-land.

† **156** = Uf1031 joined   (K   lxxi)

                ko-to-i-na
pe-ri-je-ja   e-ke   pu-te-ri-ja   DA 1   *ti-ri-to*[

P. holds an *orchard* plot. ...

This appears to be a woman's name. The same formula occurs a third time on Uf1022, only *e-ke-pu-te-*[and *ko-to-i-*[surviving.

157 = Uf835 (K lxiv)

ke-ke-me-na

[   ]-*do   e-ke   ti-ri-to   pu-te*   D A I   PA I

...-*do* holds a *communal orchard* plot at ?Trittos^P: 6? acres.

ti-ri-to: probably not 'a third share' or the like (cf. the Attic ἑκτήμοροι?), but a place-name parallel to those on other tablets of the series. *Ti-ri-to* (cf. Τρίττα, said to be an old name of Knossos) is a place frequently mentioned on the Knossos sheep tablets, and its adjective *Ti-ri-ti-jo* parallels *Pa₂-ra-jo* on E 749.

pu-te is either an abbreviation for *pu-te-ri-ja* (as *pu* on Uf432.2?), or a word *?phutēr* 'planter, gardener'; cf. Palmer's reading of *pu₂?-te-re ki-ti-je-si* (PY **193** = Na57) as *phutēres ktiensi* 'the gardeners plant, bring into cultivation'.

ke-ke-me-na: the contrasted word *ktimenā* only occurs at Knossos on X 7753. On Uf432, however, the second paragraph is introduced by *e-te-do-mo ki-te-*[, which may be intended for *ktei-*[*toi* or the like (with the 'dead' vowel in *kt-* generalized as in *Luk^itos* and in *wanak^ateros*?): 'it is brought into cultivation by the *e-te-domoi*' (cf. **114** = En02.5).

158 = Uf836 (K lxvii)

wo-we-u

ku-ka-da-ro   pa₂-ra   pi-di-jo   D A I   PA 3

K., the *worweus*, at *Pa₂-ra* (?Phidios): 7? acres.

wo-we-u is a trade-name known only from C 911.3: '*Ri-wo* the *worweus* of the place *Su-ki-ri-ta*'. The classical ὀρεύς came to mean 'mule' ('he who traces the furrow'); does it mean 'superintendent of the field boundaries' here? The context of the word *Pi-di-jo*, which seems to be a proper name, is uncertain: a second party to the transaction?

159 = Uf990 (K)

a-ri-ja-wo   pa₂-ra   te-re-ta [

A ~ āwōn, a *fief-holder* at *Pa₂-ra*; ....

160 = Uf970 (K)

te-re-ta

[   ]-*ra   ti-ri-to   wo-ne-*[

So-and-so, a *fief-holder* at ?Trittos, ...

161 = Uf839 (K lxvii)

te-re-ta   ke-ma-qe-me   me-ra

*ko-do   da-*22-to   ke-nu-wa-so*   ḌẠ [nn]

? Koldos, at the place D. (K.); a *fief-holder*, and ....

*Da-*22-to*: a frequent place-name on Knossos tablets, also unexpectedly occurring on the Eleusis vase. Adjective *Da-*22-ti-jo*, etc.

Ke-nu-wa-so: another second party to the transaction? Cf. the non-Greek man's name *Pa₂-nwa-so/Pa₂-nu-wa-so*, Πανύασις, etc.

ke-ma-qe-me me-ra: a puzzling group. *me-ra* might conceivably be μῆλα 'sheep'.

† **162** = Uf983   (K   lxxi)

o-pi   po-to-ri-ka-ta

[   ]*-do-wo   e-ko-so   ke-ke-me-na*   [DA nn]

So-and-so, a *communal* (plot) at *E-ko-so*ᵖ, . . . :

E-ko-so is probably the frequent place-name of that spelling (adjective *E-ki-si-jo*, etc.) rather than ἔξω 'outside' or ἕξων 'intending to keep'. The last word looks like a compound parallel to πτολίοικος, etc.

‡ **163** = X 984   (K)

¹]*pa-te   ke-ke-me-na*   [
²] *zo-wa   e-pi-zo-ta   ke-ra   ke-ke-'me-na'* [

The exact context of the tablet is very uncertain, but the word *ke-ke-me-na* suggests that it is part of the *Uf-* series; *ke-ra* recurs on PY **135** = Ep704 and **137** = Eb30. 'Living things' in classical Greek is confined to the form *ʒώϝια > ʒῷα; it is uncertain when this secondary form, not found in Homer, may be considered to have developed. Classical ἐπιʒῶ only has the sense 'survive'. The Homeric participle ʒῶντος is explained as a contraction of ʒώοντος, but the verb shows traces of an earlier athematic conjugation (see Schwyzer, *Gram.* I, p. 675).

8. KNOSSOS ORCHARDS

The purpose of this series (classified as *Gv-*) and the identity of the main ideograms have been recognized by Evans (*PM*, IV, p. 717) and by Myres (*SM II*, p. 60). The olive-tree is clearly recognizable on Gv862, line 2: the word *po-pa₂* in line 3 associates it with the more schematic ideogram no. 122 on Pylos **96** = Un02.2, which probably means OLIVES and recurs on Knossos **94** = F 841 in company with the spelling *e-ra-wa*.

176   OLIVE-TREE

175   FIG-TREE

174   *a)* Seedling, cutting, *b)* layer?

The fig-tree ideogram of Gv862, line 1, is more diagrammatic, being based on a linearized version of the 'hieroglyphic' fig-spray sign (see above, p. 31). The description *su-za* (? *sukia* = συκῆ, Dor. συκία) also accompanies, on **94** = F 841, the form of the same ideogram without a 'trunk' (identical to the syllabic sign *ni*) which represents the fruit of the fig.

The meaning of ideograms no. 174, which seem to repeat themselves at the end of each section, may be defined by the φυτά of Gv864.3, possibly 'newly-planted specimens' of each variety (cf. Furumark, 1954, p. 40). On this basis, the four ideograms of Gv862, lines 2 and 3, would show olive trees of progressively lessening maturity, rather than a number of different species of fruit tree on the model of Alkinoos' orchard (*Od.* VII, 114–16):

> ἔνθα δὲ δένδρεα μακρὰ πεφύκασι τηλεθόωντα,
> ὄγχναι καὶ ῥοιαὶ καὶ μηλέαι ἀγλαόκαρποι
> συκέαι τε γλυκεραὶ καὶ ἐλαῖαι τηλεθόωσαι.

The only introductory sentence is preserved on tablet **164** = Gv863. This may be compared to that on a Nuzi tablet of similar context: 'The trees from the orchard of the town Tašeniwa:...' (Lacheman, 1939, p. 534).

164 = Gv863   (K   lxvii)

1 *pa₂-ra* / *jo-e-ke-to-qo*   *wo-na-si*   *si*-[
2   ?]*we-je-we*   ? SEEDLINGS[a] 420   *su.* FIG-TREES 109 [
Pa₂-ra[p]: thus the place has in its *vineyards*....
420 *newly planted*..., 109 fig-trees,....

hō ekhei toqᵘos woinassi: we have met the place *Pa₂-ra* on the other Knossos land tablets. Bennett's *Index* reading *Pa₂-ra-jo* is not supported by the photograph, but there are traces of a possible second divider after *jo*. This prefix has the function of an introductory 'thus', as on **257** = Jn09.1 (*jo-do-so-si* 'thus they will give'), etc. The etymology of τόπος 'locality' is uncertain: Osthoff proposes *toqᵘo-*. The word *wo-na-si* is here taken as the locative of Hesychius' gloss οἰνάδες· ἀμπελώδεις τόποι; from οἴνη 'vine' one would expect *wo-na-i*.

165 = Gv862   (K   lxv)   †

1   ] *su-za*   FIG-TREES 1770
2   ] OLIVE-TREES 405
3]*po-pa₂* ⅄ 10+? [..] ⅌ 17 ? SEEDLINGS[b] 20
             vacat
5   ]365 ? SEEDLINGS[a] 225

As Myres remarks, the first tree in line 3 gives the appearance of having been pruned; the second appears to be a young tree without much development of trunk. Of the possible vocalizations of *po-pa₂*, πόρπη 'brooch', φοίβη 'radiant', φόβη 'lock of hair; foliage', φορβή 'fodder, food' and φορβάς 'providing food', only the last two appear

273

to fit the use of the term with OLIVES at Pylos. It is not clear from the photograph whether *po-pa₂* may not be preceded by other letters; an adjective like εὔφορβος or πολύφορβος could not agree with feminine *elaiwai*, unless δένδρεα is understood.

166 = Gv864　(K)

1   ] ?SEEDLINGS[a] 69 [

2   ] *su-za* FIG-TREES 53[

3   ] *pu-ta* ?SEEDLINGS[a] [nn

CHAPTER IX

PROPORTIONAL TRIBUTE AND
RITUAL OFFERINGS

THE forty-two tablets transcribed in this chapter deal with a variety of miscellaneous commodities, and their classification by Bennett includes eight different prefix initials (*E- F- G- K- M- N- U- V-*); they share, however, a number of characteristic features of context and arrangement which makes it convenient to study them as a group.

(*a*) Though often fragmentary, the different series which these tablets represent are all of them records of tribute or offerings, assessed in accordance with schedules showing a fixed order.

(*b*) The operations are evidently of a seasonal or periodic nature, as proved by the use of month-names in their headings, and by such expressions as 'last year', 'next year' in their entries.

(*c*) The tablets show in detail how the theoretical assessment of the contribution (*dosmos*) compares with the amount actually delivered (*apudosis*), and records the deficit (*ophelo-*) which may result from this sum after allowance has been made for amounts which the contributors may have been 'let off' (*aneta* or *eleuthera ekhonsi, ou didonsi*). The assessments themselves are calculated with reasonable accuracy in accordance with various fixed ratios, and demonstrate the most advanced Mycenaean mathematics we have yet seen in operation.

(*d*) A number of the tablets lay down the scale on which offerings are made to a number of different shrines, priestesses and divinities. These are of great importance in providing our only written evidence for Mycenaean religion, and unexpectedly reveal the worship of many of the gods and goddesses known from classical sources.

1. THE PYLOS 'DOSMOS' TABLETS

The WHEAT ideogram reappears in the set of fifteen tablets found in 1952 and classified as *Es-* (see Bennett, *PT II*, pp. 159–61): these show a list of thirteen men's names, in three separate   120 🌾 WHEAT   versions devoted to different operations. Only the first of these, **167** = Es650,

275

has the *tossonde ?spermo* formula which is characteristic of the land-tenure tablets (ch. VIII). The second version, complete on **168** = Es644, lists the names in the same order as the subject of a *dosmos weteï-weteï* (see below); the third version is distributed among thirteen separate tablets (**169** = Es646, etc.) which record a larger *dosmos* to the god Poseidon and much smaller ones to three entities whose function is rather uncertain.

†   The following table shows the thirteen men's names rearranged in order of descending importance, with their *spermata* and *dosmoi* converted to litres at a conversion factor of T 1 = 12 l. With three exceptions the amounts form regularly descending series in each column, but they have evidently not been arrived at by any completely rigid system of proportions: the average ratio of 30 : 5 : 12 : 1, which can be deduced from the estimated totals of the whole series, only applies exactly to one individual's assessment, that of ?Worthiās.

	?spermo	*weteï-weteï*	*Poseidaonei*	*Diwiewei* etc.	Total
Alektryōn	840 l.	114 l.	276 l.	32 l.	486 l.
Kopreus	720	84	180	20	324
?Hoplomenos	480	?	204	16	?
?Worthiās	240	40	96	8	160
A-ne-o	180	30	60	2	96
Lukouros	168	?	84	6	?
O-ka	144	28	84	6	128
?Philotāwōn	144	28?	84	6	128?
Ku-da-ma-ro	144	28?	84	6	128?
Aigi ~ os	120	?	72	4	?
Se-no	120	24	60	4	96
Servant of W ~ neus	48	16	36	2	58
Ka-ra-i	36	6	?	2	?

(Column group header above *weteï-weteï*, *Poseidaonei*, *Diwiewei* etc.: DOSMOS)

A fourteenth individual, *Pi-ro-te-ko-to*, closes the list on **167** = Es650; but the amount of his *?spermo* was either never entered or has been erased, and his name does not reappear. Of the other names, an Alektryon Etewokleweios is known as a *hequetās* attached to the 'troops' on **58** = An654 (cf. the form *A-ku-tu-ru-ẉọ-* on KN Fh364); the *Se-no* who is a shepherd at *Ma-ro-pi* on **62** = Cn655 and Cn04 may well be a different person.

The fourteen evidently form a group quite distinct from the land-owners of *Pa-ki-ja-* whom we have met in ch. VIII; yet the size of Alektryon's holding (7 units) is larger than any single *ktoina* there; the smallest, that of *Ka-ra-i* is equivalent to a generous 'lease' in the first set (see p. 240). Where is their land situated?

A possible clue is given by the amount of WHEAT listed. The total ?*spermo* for the thirteen men (with slight uncertainty as to Lukouros' entry) is 28·2 units; and we have seen that the 'lands of the *telestai*' which follow the royal *temenea* on **152** = Er01 are assessed at 30 units. Those lands, however, have only 3 *telestai* upon them: if the *Es-* tablets in fact record the acreages and obligations of the men owning land in the immediate neighbourhood of the palace at Pylos, we shall have to assume that *telestās* rank is only held by three of the first names on the list. Some of the thirteen or fourteen may in fact be 'tenants', but the formula *e-ke to-so-de pe-mo* does not apparently attempt to make any differentiation.

167 = Es650

1	*ki-ri-ti-jo-jo ko-pe-re-u /*	*e-ke*	*to-so-de*	*pe-mo*	WHEAT 6	
2	*a-re-ku-tu-ru-wo*	*e-ke*	*to-so-de*	*pe-mo*	WHEAT 7	
3	*se-no*	*e-ke*	*to-so-de*	*pe-mo*	WHEAT I	
4	*o-po-ro-me-no*	*e-ke*	*to-so-de*	*pe-mo*	WHEAT 4	
5	*ai-ki-wa-ro a-te-mi-to do-e-ro*	*e-ke*	*to-so-de*	*pe-mo*	WHEAT I	
6	*we-da-ne-wo do-e-ro*	*e-ke*	*to-so-de*	*pe-mo*	WHEAT T 4	
7	*wo-ro-ti-ja-o*	*e-ke*	*to-so-de*	*pe-mo*	WHEAT 2	
8	*ka-ra-i /*	*e-ke*	*to-so-de*	*pe-mo*	WHEAT T 3	
	/ a-ne-o	*e-ke*	*to-so-de*	*pe-mo*	WHEAT I T 5	

REVERSE:

1	*ru-ko-wo-ro*	*e-ke*	*to-so-de*	*pe-mo*	WHEAT I T 4	
2	*o-ka*	*e-ke*	*to-so-de*	*pe-mo*	WHEAT I T 2	
3	*pi-ro-ta-wo*	*e-ke*	*to-so-de*	*pe-mo*	WHEAT I T 2	
4	*ku-da-ma-ro*	*e-ke*	*to-so-de*	*pe-mo*	WHEAT I T 2	
5	*pi-ro-te-ko-to*	*e-ke*	*to-so-de*	*pe-mo*	WHEAT ⟦ ? ⟧	

In the *month* of ?Krithios:

§ 1 Kopreus, he has (an acreage of) so much seed: 720 l. wheat.
§ 2 Alektryōn, he has so much seed: 840 l. wheat.
§ 3 *Se-no*, he has so much seed: 120 l. wheat.
§ 4 ?Hoplomenos, he has so much seed: 480 l. wheat.
§ 5 Aigi~os, servant of Artemis, he has so much seed: 120 l. wheat.
§ 6 The servant of W~neus, he has so much seed: 48 l. wheat.
§ 7 ?Worthiās, he has so much seed: 240 l wheat,

etc.

† *?Krithioio*: the analogy of the Knossos tablets similarly introduced by a genitive adjective (e.g. Fp5, *Diwioio mēnos*, see p. 305) suggests that this is the name of a month. If so, it is the only one recorded at Pylos, with the possible exception of *po-ro-wi-to-jo* on **172** = Kn02. If *?Krithio-* was the name of either a man or a place, it would surely be of sufficient importance to occur freely on other tablets.

ekhei tossonde ?spermo: comparing the formulae on the other land-tenure tablets, we might also punctuate 'he holds (land): so much seed' (especially if *to-so-de* is to be read *tosson de* 'and so much', which is always a possibility).

A-te-mi-to do-e-ro: the genitive Ἀρτέμιτος (Doric Ἀρτάμιτος, perhaps by popular etymology from ἄρταμος) is attested in N.W. Greek inscr.; Ἀρτέμιδος may perhaps be an innovation. Whether all the *theoio doeloi* are in fact 'slaves of Artemis' is of course very uncertain (see also p. 236). A possible dative 'to Artemis' occurs in *A-ti-mi-te* (PY Un11.5).

?Worthiāo: the other two versions (where the genitive would in fact be more correct) show the nominative *Wo-ro-ti-ja*; possibly the genitive W ∼ nēwos in the preceding line induced the confusion. This 'servant (or slave) of W ∼ neus' is not mentioned by name in any of the three versions; for W ∼ neus himself see below, p. 279.

Pi-ro-te-ko-to: Bennett reads this as one word (Philotektōn?). Or 'Philon, the joiner'?

‡ **168** = Es644

1 *ko-pe-re-wo*	*do-so-mo*	*we-te-i-we-te-i*	WHEAT	T 7	
2 *a-re-ku-tu-ru-wo-no*		*we-te-i-we-te-i*	WHEAT	T 9	◁ 3
3 *[se]-no*	*do-so-mo*	*we-te-i-we-te-i*	WHEAT	T 2	
4 *o-po-ro-me-no*	*do-so-mo*	*we-te-i-we-te-i*	WHEAT	[nn]	
5 *ai-ki-wa-ro*	*do-so-mo*	*we-te-i-we-te-i*	WHEAT	[nn]	
6 *we-da-ne-wo*	*do-e-ro do-so-mo*	*we-te-i-we-te-i*	WHEAT	T 1	◁ 2
7 *[wo-ro-ti-ja]*	*do-so-mo*	*we-te-i-we-te-i*	WHEAT	T 3	◁ 2
8 *[ka-ra-i]*	*do-so-[mo]*	*we-te-i-we-te-i*	WHEAT		◁ 3
9 *[a]-ṇẹ-o*	*do-so-mo*	*we-te-i-we-te-i*	WHEAT	T 2	◁ 3
10 *[ru-ko-wo-ro do-so]-mo*		*we-te-[i-we]-te-i*	[WHEAT nn]		
11 *[o-ka do]-so-mo*		*we-te-i-we-te-i*	WHEAT	T 2	◁ 1
12 *pi-ro-ta-wo*	*do-so-mo*	*we-te-i-[we]-te-i*	WHEAT	T 2	◁ [ ]
13 *ku-da-ma-ro*	*do-so-mo*	*we-te-i-we-te-i*	WHEAT	T 2	[ ]

§ 1   The year-by-year contribution of Kopreus: 84 l. wheat.

§ 2   The year-by-year (contribution) of Alektryon: 114 l. wheat.

§ 3   Se-no, (his) year-by-year contribution: 24 l. wheat,

etc.

Koprēwos dosmos: note that the genitive is maintained only in the first two entries; in the third version, only Alektryon shows this case. The word *dosmos*, which is evidently equivalent in sense to classical δόσις, δόμα, δώς, etc., survives in the Arcadian compound ἀπυδοσμός 'sale', adj. ἀπυδόσμιος 'saleable'. The noun ending -σις was originally the mark of compounds (Schwyzer, *Gram.* I, 504), and there is some doubt whether the simple **dosis* already existed in Mycenaean times; for *apu-dosis*, see p. 291. The fuller spelling of *-sm-* also occurs in *de-so-mo* (= *desmos*, KN Ra1548).

we-te-i-we-te-i: this reduplicated locative of the word ϝέτος 'year' apparently shares the meaning of the classical adverb ἀμφιετεί 'year by year' (cf. ἀμφιετέω 'offer yearly sacrifices', *EM*, xc, 26): the archaic construction can be paralleled by Sanskrit *padepade* 'at every step', *varṣevarṣe* 'every year' (cf. also such modern Greek idioms as φεγγάρια φεγγάρια 'once in a blue moon'). From the fact that no recipient is mentioned, the tablet may record a tithe to the palace. It is equivalent to only about one sixth of the sowing; but the four other *dosmoi* help to bring the total levy on each individual up to between 45 and 125 per cent of the ?*spermo* figure, weighing more heavily on the smaller holders.

169 = Es646

1	*ko-pe-re-u*	*po-se-da-o-ne*	*do-so-mo*	WHEAT 1	T 5	
2	*ai₂?-ke-te-si*	*do-so-mo*		WHEAT	T 1	◁ 4
3	*we-da-ne-we*	*do-so-mo*		WHEAT	T 1	◁ 4
4	*di-wi-je-we*	*do-so-mo*		WHEAT	T 1	◁ 4

§ 1   Kopreus: (his) contribution to Poseidon: 180 l. wheat,
contribution to the *Protectors*: 20 l. wheat,
contribution to W~neus: 20 l. wheat,
contribution to Diwieus: 20 l. wheat.

Poseidāōnei dosmos: this word-order is preserved on the tablets headed by the first five names in the standard list; the sixth saves space by omitting *dosmos* and reads: *W ~ nēwos doelos Poseidāōnei*; the remainder, perhaps under its influence, show *dosmos Poseidāōnei*. The genitive *Poseidāōnos* on **170** = Es649 is presumably a scribal error; a further spelling difference is seen in *Ru-ko-u-ro*, Es729.

Ai₂?-ke-te-si: dative plural in *-tērsi*, possibly from the dual noun *ai₃?-ka-te-re* on †
248 = Va01 (see p. 348). For Hom. ἀλκτήρ?

We-da-ne-we: except for those of Alektryon, Kopreus and ?Hoplomenos, all the tablets show the genitive *W ~ nēwos* in this position: no difference in meaning is probably intended. W~neus is one of the 'sheep collectors' on the Pylos *Cn*- tablets (pp. 199–201), on a par with Axotās and Amphimēdēs. He and Diwieus also head a pair of tablets (**76** = Cn23 and **77** = Cn22) listing cattle, possibly for sacrifice: they are apparently important figures in palace and cult administration. *Di-wi-je-we* is certainly not a dative of Ζεύς, for which *Di-we* is the Mycenaean spelling (p. 286).

170 = Es649 ‡

1	*a-re-ku-tu-ru-[wo]-ne*	*po-se-da-o-no*	*do-so-mo*	WHEAT 2	T 3	
2	*ai₂?-ke-te-si*	*do-so-mo*		WHEAT	T 2	◁ 4

3   *we-da-ne-we   do-so-mo*   WHEAT   T 2 ◁ 4
4   *di-we-je-we   do-so-mo*   WHEAT   T 2 ◁ 4

§ 2   Alektryon's contribution *to* Poseidon: 276 l. wheat,
        contribution to the *Protectors*: 32 l. wheat,
        contribution to W~neus: 32 l. wheat,
        contribution to Diwieus: 32 l. wheat.

The entries for the remaining eleven names are contained on the *Es-* tablets 645, 647, 653, 703, 728, 726, 648, 729, 727, 651 and 652.

The expression 'a *dosmos* to Poseidon' serves as the introduction to the first of two extremely important ritual tablets from Pylos. The offerings on Un718 are headed by the word *Ṣạ-ra-pe-da*, recurring on **153** = Er02 (where it was thought to be the name of a tract of agricultural land adjacent to the Palace), and consist of varying amounts of nine different kinds of farm produce, divided into four paragraphs. These show a remarkable parallelism with the four entries on **152** = Er01, more fully discussed on p. 265, and appear to represent the four different categories of person who own land in this area: ?Ekhelāwōn (either the king or one of his representatives); the *dāmos* or 'village' (perhaps including the class of *telestai*, 'fief-holders'); the 'military leader'; and the *worgiones* or 'cult association'. Their offerings are in roughly descending proportions, like their *sperma* on Er01.

The importance of Poseidon at Pylos is emphasized by **172** = Kn02, and has a possible echo in Book III of the *Odyssey*, where Telemachos' arrival finds the people arranged in three companies offering bulls to Poseidon (perhaps as the legendary grandfather of Nestor, as the scholiast points out):

> Κλῦθι, Ποσείδαον γαιήοχε, μηδὲ μεγήρῃς
> ἡμῖν εὐχομένοισι τελευτῆσαι τάδε ἔργα.
> Νέστορι μὲν πρώτιστα καὶ υἱάσι κῦδος ὅπαζε,
> αὐτὰρ ἔπειτ' ἄλλοισι δίδου χαρίεσσαν ἀμοιβὴν
> σύμπασιν Πυλίοισιν ἀγακλειτῆς ἑκατόμβης.   (III, 55-9)

Similar multiple offerings of different commodities are usual in cuneiform records of ritual operations at various seasons of the year. Here is a Sumerian example from Lagaš (Genouillac, *TSA*, no. 1, 1):

> Seven sacks of flour, three pots of light ale, four pots of dark ale, two measures of oil, two measures of dates, two measures of wine, two lake (?) fish, one sheep, one white kid, one lamb—to the god Nina.

A closer parallel, both in the objects and amounts represented and in the probable degree of historical connexion, can be found in classical offerings of the type listed, for example, on the late fourth-century B.C. sacrificial calendar from Cos (*SGDI*, 3636–8, Schwyzer, *Dial.* 251c):

τρίτα ἀνομένου . . . . ῾Ηρακλεῖ ἐς Κονίσαλον, βοῦς.
τοῦτον θύει ὁ ἱαρεύς, τῷ δὲ θεῷ ἱερὰ δίδοται:

κριθᾶν τρία ἡμιμέδιμνα,
καὶ σπυρῶν τρεῖς τεταρτῆς,
καὶ μέλιτος τέτορες κοτυλέαι,
καὶ τυροὶ οἴεοι δυώδεκα,
καὶ ἰπνὸς καινός,
καὶ φρυγάνων ἄχθος καὶ ξυλέων ἄχθος,
καὶ οἴνου τρία ἡμίχοα.

The most explicit Minoan or Mycenaean representation of a sacrifice is seen on the painted sarcophagus from Agia Triadha, the two longer panels of which are illustrated in fig. 15. It is dated to the earliest part of LM III, contemporary with or slightly later than the destruction of Knossos, and certain features of style and detail have been regarded as showing Mainland influence. A full discussion of attempts to interpret these scenes is given by Nilsson (1950, pp. 426–43); two general problems make it risky to use them as an exact illustration of the Pylos ritual tablets:

(1) Opinion is divided as to whether the cult scenes illustrate a specifically funerary ritual, or offerings to a deified image of the dead, or merely a series of normal sacrifices to a deity, only indirectly connected with the fact of burial.

(2) Nilsson suggests that the sarcophagus may have been made to the order of a Mycenaean chieftain, but admits that the example of earlier cult scenes from Agia Triada show that a 'Minoan' sacrifice had much the same outward appearance. As with so much of Late Minoan and Mycenaean representative art, we are now faced with the possibility that 'Greek' institutions (or at least ones hitherto only known to us in a later Greek garb) are being carried on with the trappings of 'Minoan' ritual, art and social conventions. There is some parallel in the representative art of the Renaissance; if only a part were to survive, future archaeologists might well doubt the reality of Christianity in that period. We must also take into account the process of syncretism between 'Indo-European' and 'Aegean' deities which has been generally assumed, and which has analogies in the pantheons of the other Near Eastern cultures, particularly of the Hittites and Hurrians.

Analogies between Un718 and the sarcophagus are seen in the objects sacrificed (the ox, the two goats under the table, the vessels containing liquids, and the basket of 'fruit'—which might perhaps be cheeses); and the fact that women officiate connects with the preponderance of *hiereiai* at Pylos and

Knossos. Sheepskins, whose purpose on Un718 is not self-evident, appear on the sarcophagus as the ceremonial lower garments of the acolytes (cf. Evans, *PM*, IV, p. 401), and as a kind of cloak to the effigy (?) in front of the shrine. The grain and wine which precede the bull and rams in lines 3 and 7 are probably to be connected with Nestor's ritual of οὐλοχύται and λοιβὴ οἴνου detailed in *Od.* III, 429–63, already invoked for the sarcophagus by von Duhn. Cf. also *Od.* XIX, 197.

Fig. 15. The Agia Triada sarcophagus.

† **171** = Un718

¹ *ṣạ-ra-pe-da   po-se-da-o-ni* | *do-so-mo*
² *o-wi-de-ta-i   do-so-mo   to-so   e-ke-ra₂-wo*
³ *do-se*   WHEAT 4   WINE 3   BULL 1

⁴ *tu-ro*₂   TU+RO₂ 10   *ko-wo*   SKIN+KO 1
⁵ *me-ri-to*   ⊲ 3
      vacat
⁷ *o-da-a*₂   *da-mo*   WHEAT 2   WINE 2
⁸ RAMS 2   TU+RO₂ 5   *a-re-ro*   A+RE+PA   ⊲ 2   SKIN+KO 1
⁹ *to-so-de*   *ra-wa-ke-ta*   *do-se*
¹⁰ RAMS 2   *me-re-u-ro*   ⫪   T 6
¹¹ WINE   ⫫ 2   *o-da-a*₂   *wo-ro-ki-jo-ne-jo*   *ka-ma*
¹² WHEAT   T 6   WINE   ⫫ 1   TU+RO₂ 5   *me-ri-[to]*
¹³   ⫫ 1   ⊲ 1

The S~peda^p to Poseidon, its contribution.

§ 1   *As far as one can see*, ?Ekhelāwōn will give so much as a contribution: 480 l. wheat, 108 l. wine, one bull, ten cheeses, one sheepskin, ?6 l. of honey.

§ 2   And similarly the village (will give): 240 l. wheat, 72 l. wine, two rams, five cheeses, 4 l. *fat*, one sheepskin.

§ 3   And the military leader will give so much: two rams, 72 l. flour, 24 l. wine.

§ 4   And similarly the *estate* of the cult association (will give): 72 l. wheat, ?12 l. wine, five cheeses, ?14 l. of honey.

Poseidāōni: other Pylos examples of this alternative spelling of the dative ending are *ko-re-te-ri* On01.5, *Me-za-wo-ni* **96** = Un02.5. See p. 85.

o-wi-de-ta-i: the difficulty of interpreting this word leaves in doubt the punctuation and syntax of the first two lines, but the repetition of *dosmos* shows them to be divided into two clauses. Both terms recur on the fragmentary label Wa731:

                do-so-mo
                o-wi-de-ta-[

The dative plural of a noun in *-tās* (**owi-detā'i* 'sheep-trussers', cf. Fig. 15??) seems unlikely, since the analogy of **154** = Eq01 (*o-wi-de*, etc.) suggests that *o-* is also a prefixed adverb or conjunction here, whose clause is recapitulated by the *o-da-a*₂ of paragraphs § 2 and § 4. The infinitive ϝιδέσθαι seems the obvious choice for the second element, although the etymology of the ending -σθαι does not suggest an original disyllable (Schwyzer, *Gram.* I, p. 809). The restrictive construction ὡς + infinitive is not attested before Herodotus' ὡς ἐμοὶ δοκέειν 'as far as it seems to me', although the Homeric θαῦμα ἰδέσθαι, etc. show some analogy with it. Is this a scribal formula to emphasize that the transaction has not yet actually occurred, and that some correction might be expected?

*tu-ro*₂: note the surprising repetition of the spelling in the form of a 'monogram' (see p. 52), which apparently recurs on KN U 7498.

ko-wo: compare the ideogram no. 152, SKIN+WI, which we interpret as *wrinos* 'oxhide'. This spelling seems to represent the Homeric κῶας (**qōwas*), declined as if from -ος, 'sheepskin, fleece'.

a-re-ro: it is impossible to read ἄλευρον, since the ideogram is reckoned as a liquid on
Un06, and 'flour' is already indicated by the word *meleuron* of line 10 (see Vocabulary, p. 399). The monogram on Un06 has a double cross-bar (i.e. A+RE+PA
=ἄλειφαρ?), and it is tempting to regard the present spelling as an error.

†   Pylos **172** = Kn02 has already been discussed at length by Furumark (1954,
pp. 51–3), Meriggi (1954*b*, pp. 19–22), Carratelli (1954*a*, pp. 113–14, 1955)
and by Palmer at the London Seminar. Despite difficulty in explaining the
introductory formula, there is general agreement on the purpose of the tablet:
it clearly records ritual offering or exhibition of cups and bowls of some
precious material, carried out under the edict of the palace
before the shrines or images of various divinities. The   141   GOLD
individual vessels are accompanied by MAN or WOMAN
ideograms. Bennett first suggested that these are figurines   BOWL
of the same material, and a suspicion of human sacrifice
may also occur; but it seems more probable that their   CUP
main function is to *carry* the vessels, just like the men
and women illustrated on the LM Ia 'Cupbearer' and 'Procession' frescoes
at Knossos, of whom Evans says (*PM*, II, p. 710): 'It is a fair conclusion that
the scenes here depicted were intended as a glorified representation of actual
ceremonial processions in which, at fixed seasons, the acolytes and ministers of
the Palace cult carried out the sacred vessels and other relics to be shown to the
assembled people in the West Court.'
    It is in this light that the syntax of this difficult text should probably be
examined. The following translations of lines 1–2 have so far been proposed:

FURUMARK: 'Let them be sent to the shrine of Poseidon, and bring the gifts and
    cupbearers to the city'?
MERIGGI: 'They were sent to the shrine of Poseidon, and the city sent gifts and
    acolytes'?
PALMER: 'A ceremony of consecration was performed in the Poseideion, and the town
    was purified, gifts were brought and the defilement was purified.'

It is fairly generally agreed that the adjectival formations such as *Po-si-da-i-jo*
which differentiate three of the introductory formulae are the names of places
rather than the titles of priests or festivals, since the fourth formula provides
in their place *Pa-ki-ja-si*, well known as a local toponym; note also *Po-si-da-i-jo-de*
on Fn01.2. But the ending of *Pa-ki-ja-si* and the absence of the usual allative
suffix *-de* indicate that these are all in the locative case; it is therefore difficult
to regard *i-je-to* as a part of ἵημι with the sense 'send *to*', and preferable to take
it as the description of an activity which takes place *at* the different localities.

Palmer goes so far as to postulate a verb *i-je-* 'to sacrifice', distinct from the classical ἵημι and related to ἱερός.

Close examination of the tablet reveals a divider between *pe-re* and *po-re-na-qe* in lines 2, 8 and rev. 2. The recurring verbs *pe-re* and *a-ke* evidently show the classical distinction of sense between φέρω and ἄγω, cf. *Il.* XXIII, 512–13: δῶκε δ' ἄγειν ἑτάροισι γυναῖκα καὶ τρίποδα φέρειν. They record the activities appropriate to the two separate sets of ideograms on the tablet, the *carrying* of the cups and bowls (*dōra* 'gifts') and the *conducting* of the men and women (*po-re-na*?). Though one might logically expect this last word to be an unattested noun meaning something like 'cup-bearer', it is possible that it merely represents φορῆναι 'to carry'.

The tense, voice, person and subject of the verbs *i-je-to* / *pe-re* / *a-ke* are problematical (as is the function of the *-qe* added to the first). There are three alternatives:

1. *They are active/middle indicative.* *i-je-to* could represent *hietoi/hientoi* (present middle, 3rd sing.. or plur.) or *hieto/hiento* (imperfect middle); *a-ke* and *pe-re* can only be 3rd or 2nd sing. active, present or imperfect. It is difficult to find a subject for these verbs. Is it the initial *pu-ro* = Pylos? Or must we understand 'he', for the king or one of his officials?

2. *They are passive.* Palmer regards *a-ke*, etc., as aorist passives in *-ē*, *-ēn*. This formation in Homer (e.g. ἐτύπη) is generally regarded as having been originally restricted to intransitives (ῥύη, etc., Schwyzer, *Gram.* I, pp. 756–60); but while forms in -θη are probably late innovations, Palmer is perhaps justified in arguing that the Mycenaean verb may already be allowed to possess some specifically passive forms.

3. *They are imperatives.* In this case *a-ke* and *pe-re* can only correspond to the classical singulars ἄγε and φέρε; but they need not necessarily be taken as instructions to a single person, since the plural forms are the result of an innovating tendency in the different Indo-European languages. In the same way the form *hietō* need not be specifically passive or 3rd person: the original function of *-tō* is that of forming generalized imperatives indifferent as to person or voice (Schwyzer, *Gram.* I, p. 801), as seen in early Latin and in the Cyprian gloss ἐλθέτως· ἐλθέ. But it is not clear why *-tō* should be added to the first verb and not to the other two.

The third alternative has been followed in the printed translation, but without any very strong conviction. It must be admitted that securely identified imperatives have not yet been found in any other introductory formulae.

Quite apart from the syntax of the paragraphs, a further problem is set by the peculiar way in which they are disposed on the tablet. In its present form each face of the tablet is divided by cross-lines into five sections of varying length; and several of these sections are left blank, a fact which must require some special explanation. The only other tablet which shows similar blank entries is Knossos **207** = V 280, which is introduced by a month name and which there is reason to think represents a calendar or diary of fifteen successive days. Palmer has already proposed to identify *po-ro-wi-to-jo* (Kn02, 'reverse', line 1) as a month name *Plōwi(s)toio* 'the time for sailing again' (cf. πλωίζω, πλώϊμα 'sailing weather'). An alternative explanation of the blank entries might conceivably be that the tablet records a series of processions all occurring on the same day, but that some of those for whom provision was made failed to materialize.

If Kn02 really represents a calendar of the ceremonies prescribed for ten days of a Pylos month (purposely divided into five days on each side?), then we might expect *po-ro-wi-to-jo* to represent the first word of the complete text, and the 'reverse' to be the first side written. The tablet bears considerable signs of erasure and re-use, and Bennett's initial 'reverse' (preserved in our transcription) is the flatter side, i.e. the original obverse; in his new edition published in *PT II* Bennett now regards the side beginning *po-ro-wi-to-jo* as the obverse. The writing is hasty and careless: one case of an omitted sign is certain (in line 5), and two more are highly probable.

† **172** = Kn02   [Tn316]

OBVERSE:

PU-RO
1 *i-je-to-qe*   *po-si-da-i-jo*   *a-ke-qe*   *wa-tu*
2 *do-ra-qe*   *pe-re*   *po-re-na-qe*   *a-ke*
3 GOLD CUP I   WOMEN 2   *qo-wi-ja*   [..]   *ko-ma-we-te-*^{ja}

PU-RO
4 *i-je-to-qe*   *pe-re-*82-jo*   *i-pe-me-de-ja-⟨jo?⟩-qe*   *di-u-ja-jo-qe*
5 *do-ra-qe*   *pe-re-po-re-na-qe*   *a-⟨ke⟩*   *pe-re-*82*   GOLD+BOWL I
                                                                    WOMAN I
6 *i-pe-me-de-ja*   GOLD+BOWL I   *di-u-ja*   GOLD BOWL I
                                                          WOMAN I
7 *e-ma-a₂* / *a-re-ja*   GOLD CUP I   MAN I

PU-RO
8 *i-je-to-qe*   *di-u-jo*   *do-ra-qe*   *pe-re*   *po-re-na-qe*   *a-ke̩*
9 *di-we*   GOLD BOWL I   MAN I   *e-ra*   GOLD BOWL I   WOMAN I
10 *di-ri-mi-jo* / *di-wo*   *i-je-⟨re?⟩-we*   GOLD BOWL I   [?]
                        vacat

PU-RO   12–16   vacant

286

REVERSE:

¹ *po-ro-wi-to-jo*

PU-RO $\begin{cases} ^2 \textit{i-je-to-qe} & \textit{pa-ki-ja-si} & \textit{do-ra-qe} & \textit{pe-re} & \textit{po-re-na-qe} \\ ^3 \textit{a-ke} & \textit{po-ti-ni-ja} & \text{GOLD CUP I} & \text{WOMAN I} \end{cases}$

⁴ *ma-na-sa* GOLD BOWL I WOMAN I *po-si-da-e-ja* GOLD BOWL I WOMAN I

⁵ *ti-ri-se-ro-e*   GOLD CUP I   *do-po-ta*   GOLD CUP I

vacat

PU-RO ⁷⁻¹⁰ vacant

OBVERSE:

(1st) PYLOS: *perform a certain action* at the (shrine) of Poseidon and . . . the town, and bring the gifts and bring those to carry them.

One gold cup, two women. . . .

(2nd) PYLOS: *perform a certain action* at the (shrines) of the *Dove*-goddess and of Iphemedeia and of Diwja, and bring the gifts and bring those to carry them.

To the *Dove*-goddess: one gold bowl, one woman.

To Iphemedeia: one gold bowl.

To Diwja: one gold bowl, one woman.

To Hermes . . . : one gold cup, one man.

(3rd) PYLOS: *perform a certain action* at the (shrine) of Zeus, and bring the gifts and bring those to carry them.

To Zeus: one gold bowl, one man.

To Hera: one gold bowl, one woman.

To Drimios the *priest* of Zeus: one gold bowl, [one man?].

(4th) blank.

(5th) PYLOS: blank.

REVERSE:

(In the month?) of ? Plōwi(s)tos:

(1st) PYLOS: *perform a certain action* at the place *Pa-ki-ja-ne*, and bring the gifts and bring those to carry them.

To the Mistress: one gold cup, one woman.

(2nd) To ? Mnasa: one gold bowl, one woman.

To Posidāeia: one gold bowl, one woman.

(3rd) To the '*thrice-hero*': one gold cup.

To the 'lord of the house': one gold cup.

(4th) blank.

(5th) PYLOS: blank.

Posidāiōi: compare *Od.* vi, 266: ἔνθα δέ τέ σφ' ἀγορὴ καλὸν Ποσιδήϊον ἀμφίς. Mycenaean shares the classical distinction in vowel between the noun (*-sei-*) and adjective (*-si-*) in this name. Poseidon is not mentioned by name in line 3, since his is the only offering.

a-ke-qe wa-tu = *age qᵘe wastu*? There is nothing lost after *tu*, as Bennett's 1951 drawing suggests. Is this phrase, whose meaning is obscure, meant to be understood in all the paragraphs? If we translate 'bring *to* the town', then what is the object? And should we not expect *wastu-de*? If we regard *wastu* itself as the object of *age*, 'bring the towns-people' (compare Evans' showing of the sacred vessels 'to the assembled people'), this presupposes a personalized sense of ἄστυ which is so far quite unparalleled. It is these difficulties which have evidently led Palmer to postulate in this line a quite different verb *ἄγω 'purify' related to ἁγνός, ἅγιος, ἅζομαι.

qo-wi-ja, etc.: the second word, too uncertain to be read, seems to consist of two signs written over an erased three-letter word. The phrase may be intended as a description of the preceding women. *qo-wi-ja* is apparently from *gᵘous* 'ox': acrobats for the bull games?? *ko-ma-we-te-ja* cannot mean 'long-haired', for which *-wessa* would be the feminine. Note that these words do not show the expected dual in *-ō*: Chadwick suggests that they are in fact the names of female divinities associated with the *Posidāion*, and possibly explaining the sex of the cup-bearers, which elsewhere agrees with that of the recipients.

pe-re-*82: the vowel ending is probably *-a* in view of the adjectival formation in *-jo*, which parallels that from *di-u-ja*. Palmer reads **82* as *ja₂*, comparing the men's names *Ki-ri-*82-jo*/*Ki-ri-ja-i-jo*/*Ki-ra₂-i-jo*; and reads Πέλεια 'dove-goddess' (cf. the πέλειαι at Dodona). This goddess now recurs on Pylos Un1189, as the recipient of female animals, and with *Po-se-da-o-ne* (erased) on the same tablet. Does **82* represent *jai*/*jaï*, so that the form is in fact dative plural?

Iphemedeiāi = Ἰφιμέδεια, the mother of Otus and Ephialtes by Poseidon, *Od.* xi, 305. The absence of initial *W-* and the spelling *-pe-* show that this name does not contain ἴφι; contrast the man's name *Wi-pi-no-o* = Ἰφίνοος. Almost certainly a pre-Greek deity, whose name has been modified by popular etymology; the confusion of *e* and *i* seems to be confined to non-Greek words.

Diwjāi (disyllabic like *me-u-jo* = *mewjōn*?): compare the goddess Διϝια on an early fourth-century Pamphylian inscription (Schwyzer, *Dial.* 686¹). This paragraph, like lines 4 and 5 of the 'reverse', evidently deals with a mixed collection of deities, who may have features of their cult in common.

E-ma-a₂ (also Un11.8): apparently *Hermāāi*, cf. Hom. Ἑρμῆς, Ἑρμείας, dial. Ἑρμᾶς, Ἑρμάων, Ἑρμάος, etc. The etymology from ἕρμα 'cairn' is disproved by the absence of ϝ- in early Cretan inscriptions and in Homer. *A-re-ja* is obscure: cf. the epithet Ἄρηα (acc.) applied to Zeus and Enyalios, and Ἄρειαν, Ἄρηαν to Athena, in a fourth-century inscription from Arcadian Orchomenos, Schwyzer, *Dial.* 665 c. The connexion with Ἄρης is doubtful, unless the Aeol. Ἄρευς, Ἀρεύϊος is secondary.

diwjo- 'of Zeus': note the different spelling (and meaning?) of *di-wi-ja* on **28** = An42. The meaning 'of Zeus' is very rare for the classical δῖος, and no temple-name is formed from it. Compare, however, the Knossos month-name *Di-wi-jo* with the classical Δῖος.

E-ra: the association with Zeus makes the identification with Hera almost inevitable. The etymology < *῾ͦΗρϝᾱ must be abandoned; it is built on the isolated Elean Ἐρϝαδίοις, the derivation of which from the divine name is only assumed. It is contradicted by dialect forms without ϝ, e.g. Cypr. Ἔραι, Schwyzer, *Dial.* 681 (4), and by the Attic Ἥρα, since *῾ͦΗρϝᾱ would give Ἥρη (cf. κόρη). Chadwick suggests reading *E-[ra]* on Un11.8 between *Potniāi* and *Hermāāi*.

di-ri-mi-jo, etc.: the second word appears to be *di-wo* (gen.) rather than Bennett's *di-we*. This would prevent us from regarding *Drimios* as an epithet of Zeus (cf. Δρύμνιος ὁ Ζεὺς ἤτοι δαίμων· οὕτω παρὰ Παμφυλίοις, Tzetzes ad Lycophron, *Alex.* 536); but this 'priest of Zeus' may conceivably be a hero figure rather than a living person.

Potniāi: the specification 'at *Pa-ki-ja-ne*' makes it unnecessary to name her more exactly; whoever she is, the Mistress is almost certainly the divinity served by the 'priestess of *Pa-ki-ja-ne*' on the Pylos land tenure tablets, and possibly that understood in the phrase *theoio doelos*. Compare *Athānā potnia* on Knossos **208** = V 52? Or the phrase *Artemitos doelos* on **167** = Es650 (and Ἄρτεμις πότνια θηρῶν, *Il.* xxi, 470)? Or the title αἱ Πότνιαι = Demeter and Persephone (and read 'the Demeter of *Pa-ki-ja-ne*' on **114** = En02.1)?

Posidāeiāi: her name shows the same structural relation to that of Poseidon as Diwja's does to Zeus.

Tris-hērōei?: the subject of an article by Hemberg (1954), who regards him as an ancestral figure related to the Attic τρι(το)πάτορες, lit. 'great-grandfathers', recorded as having the function of θυρωροὶ καὶ φύλακες τῶν ἀνέμων. One would, however, expect *-e-ro-we* in the dative.

Hemberg also joins Furumark and Carratelli in reading *do-po-ta* as a variant form of δεσπότης (*doms-potās* beside *dems-*; cf. δόμος, Skt. *dámpati-* 'master'); or more likely *dospotās* from *dm̥s-* (cf. Arcad. δέκοτος < *dekm̥-tos*). Note that for some reason (the absence of a public procession?) neither of these last entries includes a 'cup-bearer'.

2. PROPORTIONAL TRIBUTE FROM PYLOS VILLAGES   †
(i) THE *Ma-* TABLETS

The arithmetic and phraseology of the eighteen tablets which make up the *Ma-* series have been discussed by Bennett (1951 *c*, p. 36), Furumark (1954, pp. 42–3), Sundwall (1953 *b*) and Carratelli (1954 *a*, p. 97; 1954 *b*, p. 220). Each tablet is a reckoning of varying amounts of a list of six commodities in fixed order, which will for simplicity be transcribed by the letters *A–F*. It will be noticed that *A*, *D* and *F* are measured in whole numbers, *B*, *C* and *E* in units of weight: this distinction will not be further indicated in transcription.

The ideogram *D* probably represents *wrinoi* 'oxhides' (more clearly on Knossos M 797, identified in *SM II*, p. 61, no. B 101). The other pictorial symbol, *A*, looks like the syllabic sign *pte* with an inserted *we*; but the Knossos forms of this sign (e.g. on M 467) diverge considerably from the Knossos *pte*, and on M 757 and M 5712 it even has a 'fringe' along the bottom similar to that of the CLOTH ideogram (see p. 313). It is associated with WOOL on M 559 and on M683, as well as on the fragmentary Pylos Un853, in which Poseidon's name occurs in the preamble. It probably represents some textile material. Tablets Mn01 and Mn02 are lists of this commodity by itself.

A	(ideogram)	A textile?
B	(ideogram)	?
C	(ideogram)	Beeswax?
D	(ideogram)	Oxhides
E	(ideogram)	?
F	(ideogram)	?

The other four commodities are recorded by syllabic 'initials', and there is no guarantee that they have the same meaning as similar syllables used as abbreviations in other contexts. Note, however, that *ke-ro* is used at Knossos (U 436, U 746) as an adjunct to the circular ideogram measured by weight on the Knossos *Mc-* tablets, which are similar in arrangement to this Pylos series (see below, p. 302). It may represent κηρός 'beeswax'; though there is some doubt whether the Common Greek may not be *κᾱρός (cf. Boisacq *s.v.*). *A, B, D, E* and *F* also occur on a fragmentary tablet of different arrangement, Mn03.

The six commodities are probably all materials required by the palace workshops (though not all of metal, as Carratelli assumes), but whether for connected or various purposes is uncertain. The first line of each tablet records a place-name, followed by amounts of the six commodities which are clearly calculated in a fixed proportion of $7 : 7 : 2 : 3 : 1\frac{1}{2} : 150$. The first table gives the ideal scheme, including fractions, which results from exact calculation:

A	*B*	*C*	*D*	*E*	*F*
$17\frac{1}{2}$	$17\frac{1}{2}$	5	$7\frac{1}{2}$	$3\frac{3}{4}$	375
$2\frac{1}{3}$	$23\frac{1}{3}$	$6\frac{2}{3}$	10	5	500
28	28	8	12	6	600
42	42	12	18	9	900
$46\frac{2}{3}$	$46\frac{2}{3}$	$13\frac{2}{3}$	20	10	1000
63	63	18	27	$13\frac{1}{2}$	1350
70	70	20	30	15	1500

The next table shows the amounts actually recorded, arranged in ascending order: where these diverge from the ideal values by 1·0 or more, they have been printed in heavy type.

The eighteen place-names agree with the fourteen legible on **257** = Jn09, with the exception of *E-re-i* (Jn09.19) and *A-si-ja-ti-ja* (Jn09.16, which may, however, be an alternative spelling of *A-*85-ta₂*). The 'Pylos 9' are all represented: the last two columns of the table below give for comparison the amounts of 'fat hogs' and 'wine (?)' recorded for these nine on **75** = Cn02 and **250** = Vn01. These show a similar scheme of rising proportions, evidently adapted to the relative importance of the different villages.

		A	B	C	D	E	F	Cn02	Vn01
Ma09	*Ri-jo*	17	17	5	7	4	362	2	20
Ma13	*Ro-u-so*	17	17	5	8	4	?		
Ma08	*Ka-ra-do-ro*	18	18	4	8	4	440	2	40
Ma04	*Pa-ki-ja-pi*	22	22	7	10	4?	500?	2	35
Ma05	*A-pu₂?-we*	23	23	7	10	5	500	2	35
Ma06	*A-ke-re-wa*	23	23	7	10	5	500	2	30
Ma11	*A-te-re-wi-ja*	23	23	7?	10	?	?		
Ma12	*Ti-mi-to a-ke-e*	24	24	7	10	5	500		
Ma14	*Sa-ma-ra*	24	24	7	10	5	500		
Ma17	*A-*85-ta₂*	24	24	?	?	?	500		
Ma01	*Pi-*82*	28	28	8	22	?	600	3	50
Ma10	*[Za]-ma-e-wi-ja*	28	28	8	12	5	600		
Ma02	*Me-ta-pa*	28	28	8	12	6	600	3	50
Ma15	*E-sa-re-wi-ja*	42	42	12	18	8	900		
Ma07	*E-ra-te-re-we*	46	46	?	?	10	1000	3	50
Ma03	*Pe-to-no*	63	63	17	27	?	1350	6	100
Ma16	*Ra-wa-ra-ta₂*	70	?	20	30	20	1500?		
Ma18	*Si-re-wa*	('assessment' not recorded)							

The shortest tablet of the series (Ma07) has only a single line, tabulating the calculated proportions for the village *E-ra-te-re-we*. Furumark is no doubt right in regarding this first-line entry as the total 'assessment' which the villages are required to contribute; and the absence of any further entry here would indicate that the full amount has in fact been received.

On four tablets the term *apudosis* ('actual delivery') describes a contribution which falls short of the total assessment, and the adjunct *o.-* is used with each ideogram to show the resulting 'debt' (*ophelo-*): this calculation is evidently the main purpose of the series. On the surviving Knossos tablets, a regular pair of entries with *a-pu-do-si* and *o-pe-ro* is only found on X 409, G 461 and Ga1530. In the translations of the *Ma-* tablets printed below, it will be seen that the amounts in each column below the first line together add up to the total 'assessment' above.

173 = Ma06 [222]

¹ *a-ke-re-wa*   A 23   B 23   C 7   D 10   E 5   F 500
² *a-pu-do-si*   A 10   0. 13   B 22   0. 1   C 7   D 8   0. 2   E 5   F 500

	A	B	C	D	E	F
A-ke-re-wa (assessment)	23	23 kg.	7 kg.	10	5 kg.	500
Actual delivery	10	22	7	8	5	500
Owing	13	1		2		

† **174 = Ma08 [346]**

¹ *ka-ra-do-ro*   A 18   B 18   C 4   D [   ]
² *a-pu-do-si*   A 14   0. 4   B 16   0. 2   C 4   D 8   E 4   F 440

	A	B	C	D	E	F
Kharadros (assessment)	18	18 kg.	4 kg.	[8	4 kg.	440]
Actual delivery	14	16	4	8	4	440
Owing	4	2				

175 = Ma10 [393]

¹ *[za]-ma-e-wi-ja*   A 28   B 28   C 8   D 12   E 5   F 600
² *a-pu-do-si*   A 20   *a-ne-ta-de*   A 1   B 21   C 5   0. 1   D 8   E 6   F 450
³ *o-da-a₂*   *ma-ra-ne-ni-jo*   *o-u-di-do-si*   A 7   B 7   C 2   D 3   E 2   F 150

	A	B	C	D	E	F
Za-ma-e-wi-ja (assessment)	28	28 kg.	8 kg.	12	5 kg.	600
Actual delivery	20	21	5	8	6	450
Remitted	1					
Owing			1			
Thus M. are/is excused payment	7	7	2	3	2	150

The sum is here complicated by a common formula which states that a particular class 'does not give' a certain amount. From the fact that this deficit is not taken into account in calculating the overall 'debt', Furumark (1954, p. 43) is evidently right in regarding it as a free allowance, by which the theoretical assessment for each village is officially reduced. This is made clearer by the parallel use of the words ἐλεύθερα, ἐλευθέρωσε on the *Na-* tablets (see p. 298). The class in question is most often that of the *khalkēwes* 'smiths', and it would be interesting to know if the listed commodities are in fact the product of the smithies; or whether they are materials which the smiths (or other classes named) are likely to need in the villages more urgently than in the palace workshops; or whether the formula is in fact only the equivalent of saying: 'The village of *X.* is excused payment of so much, in recognition of the fact that it has so many smiths working on government contracts' (cf. the *Jn-* tablets, pp. 352–8).

Tablet **183** =Nn831 shows a breakdown of a levy of 45 SA (see p. 295) among the different members of a single village. 'The smith' is represented among them; and it seems likely that the *Ma-* tribute was also allocated in detail among the different classes of each village, some of which might receive preferential treatment. The tendency of the smiths in particular to claim exemption from feudal obligations in time of emergency is reflected, for example, in § 56 of the contemporary Hittite Code.

Compare *Ma-ra-ne-ni-jo* with *Ma-ra-ne-nu-we*, a class or place providing rowers on **54** =An19.

The sums for D and E are anomalous, since the village contributes three more of E than it need, and a debt of one D goes unnoticed: perhaps these discrepancies were regarded as cancelling each other out. An additional concession for A is introduced by the word *aneta* (cf. ἄνεσις φόρων 'remission of taxes').

176 = Ma12   [123]

¹ *ti-mi-to   a-ke-e   A* 24   *B* 24   *C* 7   *D* 10   *E* 5   *F* 500
² *a-pu-do-si   A* 21   *0. 2   B   C   D   E   F*
³ *o-da-a₂   ka-ke-we   o-u-di-do-si   A* 1   *B* 1   *F* 10

	A	B	C	D	E	F
Ti-mi-to a-ke-e (assessment)	24	24 kg.	7 kg.	10	5 kg.	500
Actual delivery	21	(23)	(7)	(10)	(5)	(490)
Owing	2					
Thus the smiths are excused payment	1	1				10

The entries of line 2 reveal something of the scribe's procedure: he has written in the ideograms for the six commodities, but has not bothered to complete the amounts of *apudosis* for the last five, evidently because no 'debt' in fact resulted from them. We can therefore restore them by subtracting the smith's allowance from the total 'assessment'.

From there it is a short step to the layout shown on the next two tablets, where no *apudosis* entry figures at all, and where we must again assume that the delivery was satisfactory and incurred no 'debt'.

177 = Ma02   [90]

¹ *me-ta-pa   A* 28   *B* 28   *C* 8   *D* 12   *E* 6   *F* 600
² *o-da-a₂   ka-ke-we   o-u-di-do-si   A* 1   *B* 1   *D* 1
      ku-re-we   o-u-di-do-si   A 4   *B* 4   *D* 2   *E* 1½   *F* 100

ku-re-we: Carratelli (1954 b, p. 220) suggests *skulēwes* 'leather workers' (cf. σκύλος/ †
σκῦτος 'hide', σκυτεύς, Ηομ. σκυτοτόμος). See also p. 191.

178 = Ma13   [365]   ‡

¹ *ro-u-so   A* 17   *B* 17   *C* 5   *D* 8   *E* 4   *F* [   ]
² *o-da-a₂   ka-ke-we   a₂-te-ro   we-to   di-do-si   A* 1   *B* ½   *F* 10

hateron wetos didonsi: evidently a less generous concession than the *ou didonsi* formula. Either 'some other year' or, more probably, 'in the following year' (cf. Attic θατέρᾳ 'on the morrow', and the root meaning of ἕτερος as 'one or other of two'). The temporal accusative (where ϝέτεϊ might be expected) recurs in *to-to we-to* (**43** = Sn01) and may perhaps be explained as referring to an inclusive period rather than a single point of time; but cf. also Hom. αὐτῆμαρ 'on the same day', Attic τὴν ὥραν 'at the proper season', etc. (Schwyzer, *Gram.* II, p. 70).

On the remainder of the tablets the deficit resulting from the calculation is shown in the entry *perusinwon ophelo-*, which is equivalent to the 'debt' figures (*o.-*) included in the *apudosis* entry of the first tablets. Their identity of function, in spite of the different wording, is shown by the fact that the two formulae never occur on the same tablet, and that only one tablet of either type is extant for each place-name. The variations are probably due to the accounts being completed at different times, or to differences in the other records from which they are abstracted. The whole series must presumably be regarded as referring to πέρυσι 'last year' (or 'the season which is past'), and as a collation of the season's records made after all the returns are complete.

†   The occurrence of *perusinwa ophelo-* on two of the tablets makes it difficult to read the second word as a noun ὄφελος 'debt' (only 'usefulness' in Greek), and preferable to understand ὀφειλό⟨μενον⟩, ὀφειλό⟨μενα⟩; unless we punctuate 'the things of last year: the deficit'. On Ma16 the ideograms have the adjunct *o.-* added to them, and the deficit of *E* is written, surprisingly, *o.pe-ro* instead of *o.o.* The adjunct *o.-* also occurs with an *ou didonsi* amount on **180** = Ma01.2, where it seems out of place.

On the remaining tablets the 'actual delivery' can be restored as the difference between the 'assessment' and the remaining items. A puzzling exception is the sum for *F* on the next tablet, where the full assessment of 362 is recorded as owing, in spite of the smiths' free allowance of forty: this deficit of unparalleled size may be suspected of having been inserted in error.

179 = Ma09   [193]

1 *ri-jo*   *A* 17   *B* 17   *C* 5   *D* 7   *E* 4   *F* 362
2 *pe-ru-si-nu-⟨wo⟩*   *o-pe-ro*   *A* 2   *E* 4   *F* 362
3 *o-da-a₂*   *ka-ke-we*   *o-u-di-do-si*   *A* 2   *B* 4   *F* 40
        o-da-a₂   *pe-ra₃-qo*   *A* 1   *D* 1   [?]

Pe-ra₃-qo: applying the common vocalization *rai* to *ra₃*, Andrews reads the name of the Thessalian tribe of Περαιβοί, recorded at Dodona in *Il.* II, 749. This is difficult to control.

180 = Ma01   [225]   †

    ¹ *pi-*82*   *A* 28   *B* 28   *C* 8   *D* 22   [*E* 6]   *F* 600

    ² *pe-ru-si-nu-wa* | *o-pe-ro* 're-u-ko-to-ro'   *B* 2

        o-da-a₂   *ka-ke-we*   *o-u-di-do-si*   'za-we-tẹ'   *o*   *A* 1   *B* 1   *F* 16

*Leuktron*ᴾ *za-we-te*: to be taken together? The purpose of this annotation is obscure. The place-name *L*. occurs, for example, with *Sa-ma-ra* on **41** = An14.

181 = Ma14   [378]

    ¹ *sa-ma-ra*   *A* 24   *B* 24   *C* 7   *D* 10   *E* 5   *F* 500

    ² *o-da-a₂*   *ka-ke-we*   *o-u-di-do-si*   '*D* 2'   *A* 3   *B* 3   *C* 2   '*F* 60'

        pe-ru-si-nu-wo   *o-pe-ro*   *A* 1   *D* 2   *F* 100

182 = Ma18   [126]   ‡

                                i-na-ma-ta

    ¹ *pe-ru-si-nu-wa*   *si-re-wa*   *o-pe-ro*   *do-si-mi-ja*

    ² *A* 3   *B*   *C* 1

This tablet is exceptional in showing no 'assessment' entry. The word *dosmia* presumably means '(items owing last season) belonging to the *dosmos*', perhaps the generic name for a levy of this type. Compare also the enigmatic basketry-label Wa730:

                  [   ]-*ra-o*   *do-so-mo*   10

                sa-ma-ra   *do-si-mi-jo-qe*   1

The place-name *Si-re-wa* recurs on Mn01.4. It is tempting to read *i-na-ma-ta* as a neuter plural qualified by the adjectives in -*a*, but difficult to find one to fit. Cf. Arcadian ἰν ἅματα πάντα 'in perpetuity', *IG* 5(2), 5?—but this presupposes a Mycenaean form *in*- which is contradicted by *en-eensi* **114** = En02.2.   ¶

(ii) THE *N*- TABLETS   ††

The ideogram sᴀ occurs on only three fragmentary Knossos tablets, and is confined at Pylos to the *N*- series (*Na Ng Nn*). The pronunciation is probably given by the word *ri-no* (**184** = Nn01.1) = λίνον, which might mean any or all of 'flax', 'linen thread', 'net', 'sail', 'linen   sᴀ   Linen? cloth' or 'linen garment'. Like wooʟ?, it is weighed at Knossos but measured in whole numbers at Pylos. Skeins of linen thread or bales of linen cloth seem the most probable: the totalling *to-sa-de* perhaps implies the plural λίνα. As with the ideogram ɴɪ = 'figs', the phonetic use of the sign bears no apparent relation to the initial of the Greek word.

    The commodity is evidently subject to the same kind of yearly levy as the six items counted on the *Ma*- tablets above, but the number of different villages responsible for it is very much larger.

Nn831 shows an assessment of forty-five SA for a single village (probably to be restored as *Ko-ri-to*, cf. An13, Ad07), broken down among its inhabitants. Some are mentioned by name, some by trade: the *ko-re-te* ('mayor', more or less synonymous with βασιλεύς?) contributes more than half.

† **183** = Nn831 (including former Nn02)

1	*ko-ri-*[. *ri*]*-no*	⟦*do-* ⟧	?Korinthos ⟦will give?⟧ *linen*:
2	*u-re-*[ ]	SA 4	U.: four of *linen*.
3	*a-mo-ke-re-*[?]	SA I	A.: one of *linen*.
4	*e-re-e-u*	SA 2	E.: two of *linen*.
5	*qo-u-ko-ro*	SA 2	The cowherd(s): two of *linen*.
6	*a-ro-je-u*	SA I	A.: one of *linen*.
7	*a-mu?-ta-wo*	SA 4	?Amuthaon: four of *linen*.
8	*e-po-me-ne-u*	SA 4	?Hepomeneus: four of *linen*.
9	*ko-re-te*	SA 24	The *mayor*: twenty-four of *linen*.
10	*po-me-ne*	SA 2	The shepherds: two of *linen*.
11	*ka-ke-u*	SA I	The smith: one of *linen*.

For the last word in line I one might expect *dosmos* or *dōsei*, but the reason for the erasure is obscure.

e-re-e-u: possibly the name of a trade, cf. *e-re-e-wo* on Na60.

Nn01 is a record of the deficit shown by the SA deliveries of nine villages. Nearly all the place-names are known from other tablets, and the sequence *A-pi-no-e-wi-jo—E-na-po-ro* is found again on Vn04. Three of the names recur in the surviving *Na-* series, all with larger amounts of SA:

Pu₂?-ra₂-a-ke-re-u	Nn01: 10	Na52: 27+3
E-na-po-ro	Nn01: 33	Na02: 70
Te-tu-ru-we	Nn01: 38	Na14: 40

From this, and from the fact that the *Na-* totals are generally in round numbers (10's), we conclude that the latter are a record of the theoretical assessments, of which Nn01 (and the lost tablets of the same series) enable us to deduce the amounts actually delivered.

‡ **184** = Nn01 [228]

1	*o-o-pe-ro-si* *ri-no* / *o-pe-ro*		
2	*u-ka-jo* SA 20	*ro-o-wa* SA 35	
3	*pu₂?-ra₂-a-ke-re-u* SA 10	*ke-i-ja-ka-ra-na*	
4	SA 5 *di-wi-ja-ta* SA 60		
5	*a-pi-no-e-wi-jo* SA 28		

⁶ *po-ra-pi*   SA 10   *e-na-po-ro*   SA 33
⁷ *te-tu-ru-we*   SA 38
vacant 8

Thus they owe *linen*. Deficit: *U-ka-jo^b*, twenty of *linen*.

Ro-o-wa^b, thirty-five of *linen*,

etc.

The simplest form of assessment is shown by the tablets Na01–Na44, which merely contain a place-name followed directly by an amount of SA. The figures vary between five and 100, averaging nineteen per village; the most frequent entries are ten and thirty. Each name only occurs once in the whole   †
series, with the exception of Erkhomenos duplicated on Na72 (perhaps to be excluded from it?).

185 = Na32   [419]

re-u-ko-to-ro   SA 10

Leuktron: ten of *linen*.

On seven tablets the assessment is qualified by the formula '*X. ekhonsi*', in which X. is one of the three terms applied to soldiers (?) on the five *An-* tablets dealing with 'troops' (see pp. 183–94); the place-names also agree with those detailed there. Apparently all the entries on the *Na-* tablets which have verbal formulae, additional to the place-name, are intended to distinguish amounts which are *not* expected to be delivered to the palace (see below); and the wording '*X. ekhonsi*' may be taken to mean either

'The X. are in occupation of the place (and they will use the *linen*)', or 'The X. (who are at the place) are retaining it for their own use'.

186 = Na46   [543]

ka-ra-do-ro | ko-[ro]-ku-ra-i-jo '*e-ko-si*'   SA 30

Kharadros: the men of *Krokula* are in possession: thirty of *linen*.

Compare *ka-ra-do-ro ko-ro-ku-ra-i-jo* MEN on **60** = An661.5 (p. 193).

187 = Na49   [514]

[ku]-pạ-ri-so | ke-ki-de e-ko-si   SA 30

Kuparissos: the *ke-ki-de* are in possession: thirty of *linen*.

Compare *ku-pa-ri-si-jo ke-ki-de* MEN on **56** = An657.8 and 10 (p. 188). Probably the present Kyparissia, on the coast 25–30 km. north of Pylos (Κυπαρισσήεις *Il.* II, 593, Κυπαρισσία Strabo, Κυπάρισσος Scylax, Pliny).

† **188** = Na928

[   ] *u-ru-pi-ja-jo* ‛*e-ko-si*’ SA 10

[Place-name:] the men of ?Olympia are in possession: ten of *linen*.

For ?*Ulumpiaioi* compare **57** = An43.11, **58** = An654.16, **60** = An661.12, **76** = Cn22.6–7.
See p. 190.

A number of the *Na*- tablets record two different amounts of SA, one
immediately following the place-name, the other introduced by a clause
tossade X. eleuthera or *tossade X. ou didonsi*. As on the *Ma*- tablets, these two
formulae evidently refer to a free allowance deducted from the official assessment, as has been recognized by Furumark (1954, p. 43) and Webster (1954,
p. 15). Their interconnexion is clearly shown in the long formula of the next
tablet, and is confirmed by the totals for the whole series. If one adds up the
surviving 'assessment' entries (in which the numerals directly follow the place-
name), one arrives at a total of 1245 SA; all the entries which represent
'authorized concessions' (e.g. *ekhonsi, eleuthera, ou didonsi, aktiton*) together yield
336. These figures may be compared with the cumulative totals recorded on
198 = Ng02 and **199** = Ng01, which (when restored approximately in proportion with the entries of Ng02) probably indicate an expected delivery of about
1500 SA, and an allowance which 'is not given' of about 550.

On five of the tablets with two or three entries, their amounts add up exactly
to thirty, a frequent amount on the single-entry tablets; and it is clear that
the first number does not, as on the *Ma*- tablets, record the whole 'assessment'
but only the 'delivery' to be expected when the concessions have been subtracted from it (Furumark, *ibid.*). This is also plain on Na65, where the second
amount is larger than the first.

‡ **189** = Na65 [568]

[?*a-ke-re*]-*wạ* SA 30   *e-sa-re-u   ke-⟨u⟩-po-da   e-re-u-te-ro-se* SA 50
                            to-sa-de   na-u-do-mo   o-u-di-do-si

?*A-ke-re-wa*[p]: thirty of linen.

And the shipbuilders are excused payment of so much—the *e-sa-re-u*
Ke-u-podās made it free: fifty of *linen*.

The title *e-sa-re-u* only recurs on Knossos **39** = As1517, *q.v.* Webster (1954, p. 15)
connects the λίνον concessions directly with the requirements of the trades named,
i.e. sails and ropes for the *naudomoi* (see Vocabulary), thread and cloth (for shields,
cuirasses, etc.) for the *khalkēwes*, nets and ropes for the *kunāgetai*. The same reservations apply as in the case of the *Ma*- concessions (see p. 293).

Both the secondary sense of ἐλεύθερος and the verb-formation in -όω (originally confined to tenses other than present, Schwyzer, *Gram.* I, p. 727) appear earlier than one might have expected.

190 = Na55   [395]

(top edge: *ke-ke-me-no-jo   wa-te-u*)

[SA nn]   *e-re-u-te-ro-se*   SA 15
                 to-sa-de   pe-i   ke-u-po-ḍạ   ẹ-sa-re-u

[Place-name: *x* of *linen*.]

And *Ke-u*-podās the *e-sa-re-u* made so much free to them: fifteen of *linen*.

pe-i = *sphe'i* or possibly *spheis*, 'to them', as on **56** = An657.11, etc. The note written along the top edge is obscure.

191 = Na56   [248]

ta-mi-ta-na | ku-na-ke-ta-i 'e-re-u-te-ro'   SA 30

Ta-mi-ta-na[p]: free to the huntsmen: thirty of *linen*.

e-re-u-te-ro: the singular also appears (wrongly?) on Na54.

192 = Na50   [252]

ri-jo SA 24   *e-re-u-te-ra*   SA 6
                 to-sa-de   ka-ke-we

Rhion: twenty-four of *linen*.

And the smiths (have) a free allowance: six of *linen*.

ka-ke-we: the dative plural *kunāgetā'i* on **191** = Na56 suggests the alternative reading 'a free allowance to the smith' (singular) here. The plural is perhaps more likely on the analogy of the *Ma-* tablets, and that of *ma-ra-te-we ou didonsi* on **195** = Na67.

193 = Na57   [520]

[   ]   *to-ị-qe   e-re-u-te-ra*
             pu₂?-te-re   ki-ti-je-si   SA 30

[Place-name:] the *planters* are bringing into cultivation, and there is a free allowance for these: thirty of *linen*.

ki-ti-je-si: the derivation of the verb from an original *κτεῖμι* = κτίζω (cf. Skt. *kṣéti*) is due to Palmer (1954a, p. 67).

to-ị-qe: *toi'i* or *tois*, dat. plur.?

194 = Na58   [334]

wa-na-ka   e-ke
pi-ka-na | e-re-u-te-ra   SA 20

Pi-ka-na[p]: a free allowance—the king is in possession: twenty of *linen*.

wa-na-ka: the place may conceivably have a *wanax* of its own ('the king has a free allowance'?); but it is more probable that the position of the king in the formulae is similar to that of the *ko-ro-ku-ra-i-jo*, etc. on **186** = Na46 ff. No other entry combines *ekhei* and *eleuthera* in a continuous sentence, or writes the latter on the bottom line. Perhaps the king has already made a levy (in person?) on the place, and the seasonal contribution is therefore excused.

195 = Na67   [245]

e-wi-te-wi-jo   SA 20   *o-u-di-do-si*   SA 10
                             to-sa-de   ma-ra-te-we   ra-wa-ke-si-jo

E-wi-te-wi-jo[p]: twenty of *linen*.

And the military leader's *ma-ra-te-we* are excused payment of so much: ten of *linen*.

ma-ra-te-we: see Vocabulary. This tablet shows the alternative *ou didonsi* formula: that and the alternative *eleuthera* occupy successive lines of Na66, probably without distinction of meaning.

196 = Na70   [926]

                    e-ke-de-mi   a₂-ku-mi-jo

† *pa-ka-a-ka-ri   a-ki-ti-to*   SA 6

Pa-ka-a-ka-ri[p]: (? the land is) uncultivated, and *A₂-ku-mi-jo* holds it: six of *linen*.

e-ke-de-mi: apparently *ekhei de min*, cf. *da-mo-de-mi* = *dāmos de min* **135** = Ep704.5. Does this entry mean that no flax has been grown during the relevant season?

‡ **197** = Na69   [1088]

    ?to-sa-de   o-u-di-do]-*si*   SA 20
         [... *?e*]-*ke   a-ki-ti-to*

[Place-name: So-and-so] holds the uncultivated land [and he is excused payment of so much?]: twenty of *linen*.

The series closes with the two *Ng*- tablets, which we have seen to represent a cumulative total of all the assessments. The figures for 'delivery' and 'allowance' are split into two different categories by the varying prefix of the introductory adjectives, whose explanation we owe to Andrews.

198 = Ng02   [319]

¹ *de-we-ro-ai-ko-ra-i-ja*   SA 1239
² *to-sa-de   o-u-di-do-to*   SA 457

Those from this side of ?Aigaleon: 1239 of *linen*;
    and so many are not contributed: 457 of *linen*.

dewero-Aigolaïa?: classical δεῦρο, perhaps from *δε-αϝερο (Schwyzer, *Gram.* 1, p. 632: †
*δε-αυρο, cf. Avestan *avar* 'here, hither'?), is not found in the sense 'on this side of'.
But cf. Aristophanes τὰ τῇδε καὶ τὰ δεῦρο, Aristotle τὰ δεῦρο 'objects near enough
to be sensible', English *on the hither side*, Swedish *hit* 'hither', *hit-om* 'on this side of',
etc.

Aigol- is perhaps to be identified with mount Aigaleon; see p. 144.

    The tablet On01 is evidently divided in the same way into villages 'this side of A.'
and 'beyond A.', and reveals *E-ra-to-* to be in the first category, and *Ra-wa-ra-ti-ja*,
E-sa-re-wi-ja, *E-ra-te-re-wa*, *?Ti-mi-to*, *Sa-ma-ra*, *A-si-ja-ti-ja* and **Ti-nwa-so* to be in
the second. The latter are repeated on the last part of **257** = Jn09 (lines 13–19), which
is probably arranged on a similar geographical basis. It is noteworthy that none of
the villages 'beyond Aigaleon' occurs on the three tablets which deal with levies of
'rowers', nor on the five which appear to record the disposition of coastal guards
(except for the doubtful reading *ti-mi-to* on **60** = An661). There is unfortunately no
more detailed evidence for dividing the villages of the *Na-* tablets among the two
provinces, but the further one is evidently much less important than the nearer.

    The adjectives can either be understood as applying to the territory, 'the lands
this side of Aigaleon' (cf. τὰ ὑπεράκρια 'the uplands', also the division of Attica
into οἱ Ὑπεράκριοι and οἱ Πάραλοι, etc.), or to the objects themselves, totalled by
to-sa-de in the second line.

o-u-di-do-to: probably singular, *tossa de ou didotoi*, agreeing with the neuter plural subject
(unless this is to be taken as feminine).

199 = Ng01   [332]

¹ *pe-ra₃-ko-ra-i-ja*   SA 200[+
² *to-sa-de*   *o-u-di-do-to*   [SA nn]

Those from beyond ?Aigaleon: 200 of *linen*;
    and so many are not contributed: *x* of *linen*.

pe-ra₃-ko-ra-i-ja = *pera(i)-Aigolaïa*?: compare *pe-ra₃-ko-ra-i-ja* Wa01.2, *pe-ra-ko-ra-i-ja*
Ad15, *pe-ra-a-ko-ra-i-jo* On01.8; Hom. πέρην ἁλός 'on the other side of the sea',
Aeschylus ἐκ πέρας Ναυπακτίας, ἡ Περαία 'land on the other side (of a river or sea),
etc.'; Skt. *parā* 'away!' (cf. δεῦρο!). The name of the site Perakhora north of Corinth,
compared by Turner (1954, p. 19), was Περαία in antiquity.

3. THE KNOSSOS *Mc-* SERIES   ‡

Bennett has demonstrated to us that the commodities of the eighteen fragmentary *Mc-* tablets, found in the 'Arsenal' building at Knossos together with
records of chariots, wheels, spears and arrows, show a listing in fixed order
and proportion similar to that of the six items of tribute on the Pylos *Ma-*
series. Evans (*PM*, IV, p. 833) identified the last commodity *J* as the horn
of the *agrimi* goat (capra aegagrus creticus) used in the manufacture of

composite bows like the τόξον ἐΰξοον ἰξάλου αἰγὸς ἀγρίου of *Il.* iv, 105; he also noted that the numbers of 'horns' are always even (except now on Mc5098, and on M 0452 where 'one horn' is introduced by [?*ke*]-*ra*).

The second ideogram *H* is the normal 'she-goat' symbol found on the livestock tablets, and Evans suggested that semi-domesticated *agrimi* may have been kept in enclosures to ensure a regular supply of horns; but in any case the ideograms most probably represent *carcases* sent in by the hunters, whose names possibly appear as the variable introduction to the tablets. The first ideogram *G*, not found elsewhere, appears to combine the upper constant of the 'goat' symbols with syllabic *ra* (or *ra-so*, cf. λαισήϊον ??): it may be the ideogram for a buck *agrimi*, the doe not needing to be distinguished from the domesticated nanny-goat when appearing in conjunction with him.

G		Buck agrimi?
H		She-goat
I		Honeycombs?
J		Agrimi horn

The third ideogram *I*, measured by weight, is problematical. One cannot argue that all the separate items on the tablet are likely to be needed in the manufacture of bows, since this can hardly be true of the first two; on the other hand, it is difficult to think of a weighed substance which might be derived directly from wild goats. For a possible *ke-ro* 'beeswax', see p. 290; was this a product of the mountain-sides where the goats were hunted? Compare μελισσάων πέτρης ἐκ γλαφυρῆς ἐρχομενάων (*Il.* ii, 88) with αἶγα ἄγριον πέτρης ἐκβαίνοντα (*Il.* iv, 107). Apart from their horns, the *agrimi* carcases would also provide meat (*Od.* ix, 155) and rugs, etc. (*Od.* xiv, 50).

The *Mc-* tablets are too fragmentary to be worth transcribing individually, but the following table shows the amounts visible on the eleven best-preserved

	G	*H*	*I*	*J*
Mc5098	345	208	154 kg.	345
Mc0462 + 5792 + 5808	62	30	24 kg.	52
Mc0454 + 0458	30	17	13 kg.	26
Mc0455	28	17	12 kg.	24
Mc0453 + 5798	28?	17	12 kg.	24
Mc5118	—	15	—	20
Mc0459 +	23	14	10 kg.	20
Mc0456 + 0477	16	10	7 kg.	14
Mc1508 + 1528 + 1564	16	10	6 kg.	12
Mc0460	14	8	6 kg.	12?
Mc0464	12	—	6 kg.	—

of them. The values approximate to a ratio of 5:3:2:4; where they diverge from the ideal proportion by 2·0 or more they are printed in heavy type. Mc5098 is possibly the total of the complete series, though high numbers of *G* and *H* also occur on the fragmentary M 5107.

It is not clear whether the tablets are the record of an expected quota, or of an actual delivery. The horns are considerably fewer than might have been provided by the number of goats listed, but perhaps only a proportion of them were of acceptable length and curvature.

4. OFFERINGS TO DIVINITIES AT KNOSSOS †

The eleven tablets of the *Fp-* series were found by Evans at the beginning of the campaign of 1900, lying in a bath-shaped receptacle of clay at basement level between the East Propylaeum and the central court (point *A* on fig. 13, p. 115), together with the remains of the wooden box in which they and the *Fs-* series (see below) had been neatly filed in order. The identification of their only ideogram as 'olive-oil' was tentatively suggested by Furumark (1954, p. 116) and Bennett (*MT I*, p. 448), and is now confirmed by the vocalization *e-ra₃-wo* on a number of Pylos tablets (see p. 217).

130 ⟡ OLIVE-OIL

Both Furumark and Meriggi (1954*b*, pp. 22–6) have recognized from the month-names which introduce each tablet that the series forms part of a ritual calendar, specifying or recording offerings sent to a limited number of places, priests and divinities. It is not always easy to decide in which of these categories the listed names are to be placed, but the allative accusative ending *-de* may be taken as a criterion of place-names.

Within the sub-paragraphs introduced by each toponym three expressions are found to recur, which will be referenced as *P*, *Q* and *A* in the synoptic table below. They presumably refer to shrines of the same cult in different places.

P: *pa-si-te-o-i* =*pānsi theoi'i*, 'to all the gods'. See the article 'Pantheon' in *Paulys RE*, XVIII, 3, cols. 698–730. The dedication of shrines and offerings πᾶσιν θεοῖς or θεοῖς πᾶσιν καὶ πάσαις seems to have had its widest vogue in Hellenistic times. Pausanias records two altars θεοῖς πᾶσιν ἐν κοινῷ at Olympia (V, 14, 8; 15, 1; 15, 10), as well as others elsewhere in the Peloponnese. The words ?*do*]-*ra te-o-i* introduce KN E 842.1, which shows *di-wo* on the same line.

Q: *qe-ra-si-ja* =*Qᵘerasiāi*? Note *qe-ra-si-jo* on Fp16 and possibly Fp18. Furumark connects this name or title with Hom. τέρας (*qᵘerəs) 'meteorological phenomenon'. Schulze (*Quaest. Ep.* p. 176) regards the name of the Theban seer Teiresias as similarly derived (for the second vowel, cf. Etruscan *Terasiás, Terasials*), and Robert,

Oidipus, p. 69, thought he might originally have been 'a chthonic oracle god' (of ambiguous sex?). Cf. also Ζεὺς Τεράστιος.

A: *a-ne-mo-i-je-re-ja* = ʼΑνέμων ἱερείᾳ. See the article ῎Ανεμοι in *Paulys RE*, I, 2, cols. 2176–80. Compare Herodotus VII, 178: Δελφοὶ μὲν δὴ κατὰ τὸ χρηστήριον ἔτι καὶ νῦν τοὺς ἀνέμους ἱλάσκονται; further the Εὐδάνεμοι at Athens and ʼΑνεμοκοῖται at Corinth.

Where a place-name occurs without any such qualification, the offering is presumably to the tutelary deity or spirit of the locality, whom it is superfluous to name (cf. *Diktā-* on Fp1 and Fp7): these entries are shown as *X* on the table below.

Where *P*, *Q*, etc. occur without any place-name, Furumark suggests that they refer to the vicinity of Knossos itself: they have been entered in the column Nil. The status of the words *si-ja-ma-to* and *e-ke-se-si* is uncertain, and their initials are shown bracketed.

Within each month the place-names appear to have been entered in a more or less standard order, though this is spread over several tablets in each case, and the greater part of the series must be lost. The table below attempts to place the surviving tablets in their approximate sequence (though the order of the months themselves is of course unknown). The amounts of oil for each entry appear to be identical in successive months, with the exception of the larger entry for *P* at *Pa-de* on **200** = Fp1.

Tablet	Month	Nil	Pa₃-ti	Di-ka-ta-de	Da-da-re-jo-de	Pa-de	A-mi-ni-so-de	*47-da-de	*47-ku-to-de	*85-ri-mo-de	U-ta-no
Fp1	?]-de-u-ki-jo-jo m.			d	X	XPQ	Pe	XA			
Fp16	Wo-de-wi-jo m.	PQ									
Fp48	Wo-de-wi-jo m.	(s)				XQP	P				
Fp6	Ka-ra-e-ri-jo	PQ									
Fp15	Ka-ra-e-ri-jo m.		XP								
Fp7	Ka-ra-e-ri-jo m.			X							
Fp18	Ka-ra-e-ri-jo				QP						
Fp5	Di-wi-jo-jo m.	QP									
Fp14	A-ma-ko-to m.	(e) Q					Pa				
Fp13	Ra-pa-to m.								Xp	XPQA	A

De-u-ki-jo-jo = *Deukioio mēnos?* Sittig reads a *w̥o-* before this group on **200** = Fp1.1, and takes it as a fuller spelling of *wo-de-wi-jo-jo*; but the duplication of entries on Fp48 (found apart from the others?) makes this unlikely, unless the latter belongs to a different year or series. Chadwick reads a possible ụ-. Cf. *De-u-ki-jo* as a man's name on MY **46** = Au102.

Wo-de-wi-jo: the month recurs on **207** = V 280 and in the genitive on **203** = F 953. *U-de-wi-jọ-jo* on Pylos Jn07 has been corrected to *U-de-wi-ni-jo* (cf. *U-de-wi-ne* on Cn10, probably a place-name).

Ka-ra-e-ri-jo: from κραῖρα 'head' (**kra-eira?*), or cf. the Ephesian month Κλαριών? The form *Ka-ra-e-i-jo* on Fp354 may be a mis-spelling of the same word (though the context, like that of Fp148 and Fp363, suggests that it should be classified *Fh-*); and the following words]-*jo* and *Pa-ja-ni-jo* may also be the names of months. [*ka*]-*ra-e-ri-jo-jo me-no* recurs on Gg7369 and Oa7374.

Di-wi-jo-jo = *Diwioio mēnos*. Cf. Δῖος, first month of the Macedonian year, also in use in Aetolia, Lesbos, etc. Cf.]-*wi-jo-jo* on G 726.

A-ma-ko-to: not *a-ma-ko-ro*, as read by Furumark and in Bennett's *Index*.

Ra-pa-to = *Lapato⟨-jo⟩ mēnos*. As pointed out by Sittig, the name of this month survives in the Arcadian μηνὸς Λαπάτω of an inscription of Orchomenos (Schwyzer, *Dial.* 667; cf. Carratelli, 1955, p. 5).

The word *mēnos* recurs at Knossos on M 724, Wb M 133 and Od5672, but the month-names are unfortunately lost. To the six or seven months listed above, we may perhaps add *po-ro-wi-to-jo* and *ki-ri-ti-jo-jo* at Pylos (and new evidence on the unpublished 1955 tablets). The calendars of the two palaces may of course have differed somewhat. Does the solitary *me* of E 842.1 stand for *mēn* 'month'? None of the names identified shows the typical Attic-Ionic month formation in -ιών, which is probably a comparatively late secondary development.

For a cuneiform parallel to the Knossos *Fp-* tablets, compare Alalakh nos. 309–18 (Wiseman, 1953, p. 92), which record monthly issues of barley and sesame-oil to temples and priests. E.g.:

309: In the month of Tammuz, $1\frac{1}{2}$(?) *qa* of barley to the gods, $1\frac{1}{2}$ *qa* to Tarḫuziti, 1 *qa* to the goddess Ḫepat, 1 *qa* to the carpenters, $\frac{1}{2}$ *qa* to the gods, $\frac{1}{2}$ *qa* to Beruwa. Total $6\frac{1}{2}$ (*sic*).

310: In the month of Iyyar, $1\frac{1}{2}$(?) *qa* of barley to the gods, $1\frac{1}{2}$ *qa* to Tarḫuziti, 5 *qa* to Beruwa, 5 *qa* to the aldermen. Total 13.

200 = Fp1   (A   xix)   †

¹ [?]-*de-u-ki-jo-jo* | *me-no*
² *dị-ka-ta-jo* | *dị-we*   OIL   ⅋ 1
³ *da-da-re-jo-de*   OIL   ⅋ 2
⁴ *pa-de*   OIL   ⅋ 1
⁵ *pa-si-te-o-i*   OIL   1

6	*qe-ra-si-ja*	OIL	¶ [1?]
7	*a-mi-ni-so* | *pa-si-te-o-i*	⟨OIL⟩	¶ [2?]
8	*e-ri-nu*	OIL	◁ 3
9	**47-da-de*	OIL	◁ 1
10	*a-ne-mo* | *i-je-re-ja*	⟨OIL⟩	◁ 4
	vacat		
12	*to-so*	OIL 3	¶ 2 ◁ 2

In the month of Deukios:

To the Diktaian Zeus:	12 l. oil.
To Daidaleion:	24 l. oil.
To *Pa-de-*:	12 l. oil,
To all the gods:	36 l. oil,
To the *augur*: ?	12 l. oil.
Amnisos, to all the gods: ?	24 l. oil,
To ?Erinys: ?	6 l. oil.
To **47-da-*:	2 l. oil,
To the priestess of the winds:	8 l. oil.
(total)	136 l. oil.

Bennett (*MT I, 1953*, p. 446) recognized the figures in the last line as a total. Reading ◁ 2 in line 8, he assumes that lines 6 and 7 between them account for ¶ 3 ◁ 1; but *Pa-de Q.* shows ¶ 1 on Fp48 and *A-mi-ni-so P.* ¶ 2 on **201** = Fp14, and one might expect the same entries here. Chadwick reads ◁ 3 in line 8 of the original.

di̯-ka-ta-jo di̯-we: Bennett reads [.]-*ka-ta-jo ne̯-we*, but the doubtful signs appear to be mis-shapen *di*'s. *Diktānde* recurs without qualification on Fp7, G 866 and the fragmentary Fh5467, where *i-je-re-ja* appears in the second line. The association of Zeus with Mount Dikte (now Ἀφέντης Χριστός in the Λασιθιώτικα ὄρη), which perhaps results from syncretism with a 'Minoan' mountain god, is explained in Hesiod's *Theogony*, pp. 477 ff.: these lines describe how Rhea was smuggled from the mainland to the Cretan town of Lyktos (*Ru-ki-to* of the tablets), taken to Dikte, and hidden in the cave in the 'Aegean Mountain' where she gave birth to Zeus. Ζεὺς Δικταῖος is, for example, invoked in the civic oath of Itanos (Dittenberger, *Syll.*³ 526): Δία Δικταῖον καὶ Ἥραν καὶ θεοὺς τοὺς ἐν Δίκτα καὶ Ἀθαναίαν Πολιάδα καὶ θεοὺς ὅσσοις ἐν Ἀθαναίᾳ θύεται πάντας; and discussed (with an erroneous location of the mountain) by Strabo, x, 478: εἴρηται δέ, ὅτι τῶν Ἐτεοκρήτων ὑπῆρχεν ἡ Πρᾶσος, καὶ διότι ἐνταῦθα τὸ τοῦ Δικταίου Διὸς ἱερόν· καὶ γὰρ ἡ Δίκτη πλησίον, οὐχ, ὡς Ἄρατος, 'ὄρεος σχεδὸν Ἰδαίοιο'· καὶ γὰρ χιλίους ἡ Δίκτη τῆς Ἴδης ἀπέχει.

Evans (1897) lent his support to the identification of the Δικταῖον ἄντρον (Strabo, x, 476) with the cave near the village of Psykhro, 30 km. south-east of Knossos, where continuous votive deposits from MM II down to Geometric have come to light since its first exploration by Halbherr and Hatzidakis in 1886. The offerings on the *Fp-* tablets are perhaps confined to a restricted association of cults, possibly centred on sky or weather gods.

da-da-re-jo-de: Furumark and Meriggi read Δαιδάλεόνδε. Cf. Steph. Byz.: Δαίδαλα ... καὶ Κρήτης ἄλλη (πόλις).

pa-de: **203** = F 955 has the form *pa-de-i* (locative?), which makes it doubtful whether †
  -de can here be allative.

a-mi-ni-so, elsewhere with *-de*: see **206** = Gg705, below.

e-ri-nu: Furumark (1954, p. 34) takes this as a defective spelling of the dative singular of ’Ερινύς (plural for Meriggi). In addition to her (or their) function as an avenging deity, ’Ερινύς appears as an epithet of Demeter in Arcadia (Pausanias, VIII, 25, 6, etc.) and in Hesychius’ gloss E. = ’Αφροδίτης εἴδωλον; so that her early status is uncertain.

*47-da-de: presumably a different name from **47-ku-to-de* (Fp13) and **47-so-de* (Fh351, etc.).

201 = Fp14 (joined to Fp27 and Fp28; A)

¹ *a-ma-ko-to* ‘me-no’ | *jo-te-ṛe-pa-to* ‘OIL’ | *e-ke-se-si* ◁ I
² *qe-ra-si-ja* ৸ I *a-mi-ni-so-de* | *pa-si-te-o-i* ৸ 2 *a-re* ◁ [   ]

In the month of *A-ma-ko-to*:

...2 l. (oil),
   To the *augur*: 12 litres.
To Amnisos, to all the gods: 24 litres,
   To *A-re*: [   ]

jo-te-re-pa-to e-ke-se-si: Meriggi (1954 *b*, p. 25) recognizes a verbal formula, and reads ὃ τράπετο *῞Εξεσι ‘what was directed towards the deities E.’ (but the Mycenaean form of τρέπω appears to have had a labio-velar). ὡς τέρψαντο ἐξέσῑ ‘thus they took delight in the discharge’?? But this leaves the first entry without a specified recipient. There is a common place-name *E-ko-so*, adj. *E-ki-si-jo*, but this can hardly be its locative.

a-re: Furumark reads ‘to Ares’, but one might expect **a-re-we* (*῞Αρηϝι).

202 = Fp13, now in the British Museum.   (A   xx)

¹ *ra-pa-to* ‘me-no’ | **47-ku-to-de* OIL ◁ I *pi-pi-tu-na* ◁ I
² **85-ri-mo-de* OIL ◁ 4 *pa-si-te-o-i* ৸ I *qe-ra-si-ja* ৸ I
³ *a-ne-mo-i-je-re-ja* OIL I *u-ta-no* | *a-ne-mo-i-je-re-ja* ৸ I ◁ 2

In the month of Lapatos:

To **47-ku-to*: 2 l. oil,
   To *Pi-pi-tu-na*: 2 litres.
To **85-ri-mo*: 8 l. oil,
   To all the gods: 12 litres,
   To the *augur*: 12 litres,
   To the priestess of the winds: 36 l. oil.
?Itanos, to the priestess of the winds: 16 litres.

Note that the oil ideogram is only entered in the first item of each line.

pi-pi-tu-na: Furumark compares Δίκτυννα in form; that her name should actually have been assimilated to Greek δίκτυον 'net' from a native *Piptunna* seems unlikely, since the name Δίκτη might well have provided its original derivation.

*85-ri-mo-de: Furumark reads **85* as *su*, and regards the name as a variant spelling of the place *Su-ri-mo*. Compare Pylos *A-si-ja-ti-ja/A-*85-ta₂*, which confirms the consonant *s-* but not, apparently, the vowel (**85=si, sa* or *sja*?). See also p. 337.

u-ta-no, adj. *u-ta-ni-jo*, etc.: possibly Itanos, at the eastern tip of Crete, though this seems very far away (120 km. by road) for a town which apparently supplies sheep to the palace.

The relation between these tablets and the seventeen of the *Fs-* series which were found with them is not altogether clear. These each contain an undated record of an offering or ration of five to six commodities in fixed order and in more or less constant amounts (the numbers in brackets show the surviving occurrences):

BARLEY: T 1 (13)	T 2 (1)		=12–24 litres.
FIGS: ⪤ 2 (2)	⪤ 3 (9)	T 1 (1)	=4–12 litres.
FLOUR: ▽ 1 (9)	▽ 2 (4)		=½–1 litre.
OIL: ▽ 1 (4)	▽ 2 (6)		=½–1 litre.
WINE: ⪤ 1 (7)	⪤ 2 (3)		=2–4 litres.
HONEY: Nil (6)	▽ 1 (3)	▽ 2 (1)	=½–1 litre.

Several of the introductory words have *-de*, which suggests that they are place-names. Apart from *Pa-de* (cf. **200**=Fp1) they are all unique, and of non-Greek appearance. Except for the absence of oxen and sheep, the commodities may perhaps be compared with those listed on **171**=Un718.

Other fragmentary groups of Knossos tablets found elsewhere in the palace show signs of belonging to similar calendars of offerings. Small amounts of oil are recorded as going *Da-*83-ja-de i-je-ro* ('to the shrine') on Fh363 and *[Da]-*83-ja-de* on Fh365, where the second line has a parallel [ ]-*da-so-de*. Tablets F 953 and F 955 seem to be part of a series listing the same months and places as the *Fp-* series, but recording the commodities MA and KO; these recur, together with the enigmatic word *ko-no*, on the 'spice' tablets from Mycenae, where they are used as abbreviations of *marathwon* 'fennel' and *koria(n)dnon* 'coriander' (see p. 227). Meriggi has convincingly suggested that these two fragments should be joined thus:

† **203** = F 953+955   (K   lxiii+lx)

¹ *wo-de-[wi]-jo-jo | me-[no   . .]-ri-jo-de*
² *ko-no*   MA 3   *ko-ṛi-[ja-do-no   nn]   pa-de-i   ko-no*   MA 2   KO   T 1

³ *pa-sa-ja* *ko-no* MA [nn KO nn] $\begin{array}{l} pa\text{-}si\text{-}te\text{-}o\text{-}i \\ a\text{-}mi\text{-}ni\text{-}so\text{-}de \end{array}$ MA 2 KO T 4

In the month of *Wo-de-wi-jo*:
    To [   ]-*ri-jo*: 3 *ko-no* of fennel, *x* l. of coriander.
    At *Pa-de-*: 2 *ko-no* of fennel, 36 l. of coriander.
    To *Pa-sa-ja*: *x ko-no* of fennel, *x* l. of coriander.
    To Amnisos, to all the gods: 2 *ko-no* of fennel, 48 l. of coriander.

]-*ri-jo-de*: Meriggi suggests [*Da-da*]-*ri-jo-de*, but cf.]-*ki-ri-jo-de* on Fs26.
Pa-sa-ja: this name is repeated on V 451 below *Si-ja-ma-*[*to*], which itself occurs directly
    after the month-name (and before *Pa-de*) on Fp48.
The last MA in the third line has the small stroke over it which normally distinguishes
    the WOOL(?) ideogram: this is presumably an error.

Another fragmentary series, of which we have perhaps little more than a
month's records, deals with offerings of jars of honey: one
of these, Gg10, was apparently found together with the   = μέλιτος
Fp- and *Fs-* series. Offerings of oil and honey (μέλιτος   ἀμφιφορεύς
καὶ ἀλείφατος ἀμφιφορῆας, *Il.* XXIII, 170) are among the rites at the funeral
of Patroclus. The word 'amphora' is indicated by the A surcharged over the
ideogram on Gg704, etc.

204 = Gg704   (D   1)
¹ [   ] *me-no*
² [?*e-ne-si-da*]-*o-ne* *me-ri* AMPHORA+A 1
In the month of . . . :
    One jar of honey to the *Earth-shaker*.

The month reference, unfortunately incomplete, suggests that this is the first tablet of a set.
]-*o-ne* could be completed *Po-se-da-o-ne*, but the more immediate parallel is *e-ne-si-da-
o-ne* on M 719, cf. Gg717 (where *me-na* is probably not μῆνα but a name, Μήνη 'Moon-
goddess' as on E842, where]-*pe-ro₂-ne* could be Ὑπερίονι). Meriggi compares E. with
Poseidon's names Ἐννοσίγαιος, Ἐνοσίχθων (*Il.* XIII, 34, VII, 445, etc., cf. εἰνοσίφυλλος)
or Ἐννοσίδᾱς (Pindar). If this connexion is maintained, the etymology *ἐνϝοθι-
(*wedh-/wodh-, also in ὠθέω and perhaps ἐθρίς) would indicate a graphic *ne* for -*nwe-*
similar to that required in *e-ne-ka* = *ἔνϝεκα (cf. Pylos *Sa-ri-nu-wo-te/Sa-ri-no-te*), in the
absence of a convenient shortening like the sign *nwa* = -*nu-wa-*. It might also indicate
that, though the second part of Kretschmer's etymology Poseidon < πόσις Δᾶς 'husband
of Earth' may be correct, a parallel verbal form should be sought for the first half;
but a relative of Lat. *quatiō*, O.H.G. *scutten*, Old Norse *hossa* 'shake' would appear
in the Mycenaean spelling with a labio-velar.

† **205** = Gg702　(D 1)

¹ *pa-si-te-o-i* | *me-ri*　AMPHORA I
² *da-pu₂?-ri-to-jo* | *po-ti-ni-ja* `*me-ri*'　AMPHORA I

One jar of honey to all the gods,
One jar of honey to the Mistress of the ?*Labyrinth*.

da-pu₂?-ri-to-jo (gen.): this place-name probably recurs in the *da-pu-ri-to-*[of the fragmentary X 140, and might conceivably be a fuller spelling of the *Da-*22-to* of Knossos and Eleusis. To identify it with λαβύρινθος involves the highly uncertain assumption that the initial consonant has some intermediate sound peculiar to 'Aegean'. But cf. the alternation *Labarnas/Tabarnas* in the Anatolian dynastic name of the Hittite kings of the Old Kingdom (Gurney, 1952, p. 64); also λάφνη/δάφνη.

‡ **206** = Gg705　(D 1)

¹] *a-mi-ni-so* | *e-re-u-ti-ja*　ME+RI　AMPHORA I
²] *pa-si-te-o-i*　ME+RI　AMPHORA I
³]-*ke-ne*　ME+RI　AMPHORA I

Amnisos: One jar of honey to Eleuthia,
　One jar of honey to all the gods,
　One jar of honey [...　　　　　　].

E-re-u-ti-ja = Attic Εἰλειθυίᾳ, in which the quasi-participial ending is probably due to popular etymology. The form Ἐλευθία, known from Messenia and Laconia (also Ἐλευσία, Ἐλυσία), is probably a long-standing variant to the Ἐλεύθυ(ι)α which is the Cretan form in classical times. Her name also appears on three tablets (Od714–16) apparently listing woollen garments. Pausanias (IV, 20, 2) records that the priestess of Eileithyia Sosipolis at Olympia put out for her μάζας μεμαγμένας μέλιτι. For the traditional connexion of E. with Amnisos, cf. *Od.* XIX, 188–90:

(Ὀδυσσεὺς) στῆσε δ᾽ ἐν Ἀμνισῷ, ὅθι τε σπέος Εἰλειθυίης,
　ἐν λιμέσιν χαλεποῖσι, μόγις δ᾽ ὑπάλυξεν ἀέλλας.
　αὐτίκα δ᾽ Ἰδομενῆα μετάλλα ἄστυδε (Κνωσσόνδε) ἀνελθών,

and Strabo, x, 476, 8: Μίνω δέ φασιν ἐπινείῳ χρήσασθαι τῷ Ἀμνισῷ, ὅπου τὸ τῆς Εἰλειθυίας ἱερόν.

The site of Amnisos is generally identified with Paliókhora, at the east end of the long sandy beach of Karterós, 7 km. east of Iraklion, where Marinatos found a Late Minoan building in 1932. He believes this bay to have formed the chief port of Knossos; a rival claimant is the 'Harbour Town' located by Evans on the eastern outskirts of Iraklion itself, which, though less convenient for the beaching of ships, is easier of access to the palace. Whatever the name of this other port may have been in early times, the proposed location of Amnisos appears to be confirmed by the nearby cave at Ayi Theodori, first excavated by Hatzidakis in 1886 (cf. Marinatos,

Πρακτικά, 1929, pp. 95–104; Evans, *PM*, II, p. 839), where a deposit was found stretching from Neolithic to Geometric, around an idol in the form of a 'stalagmitic omphalos'.

Chadwick and Bennett read]-*ḳẹ-ne* in line 3.

207 = V 280   (B   xxx)   †

1	*wo-de-wi-jo*		The month of *Wo-de-wi-jo*:
	vacant		
5	*to-pe-za o-u-ki-te-mi*+	(4th)	The tables: it is not right.
	vacant		
11	*a-pe-ti-ra₂	o-u-te-mi*+	(10th)	The *releasers*: it is not right.
12	*o-u-te-mi*+	(11th)	The *releasers*: it is not right.
13	*o-u-te-mi*+	(12th)	The *releasers*: it is not right.
14	*o-u-te-mi*+	(13th)	The *releasers*: it is not right.
15	*e-pi i-ku-wo-i-pi*	(14th)	At the *waist* (??).
	vacat		

Meriggi (1954*b*, p. 24) plausibly regards this tablet as a record of the ἡμέραι ἀποφράδες or *dies nefasti* of the first or second half of a Knossos month. As in the case of **172 = Kn02**, a calendar will most reasonably explain the deliberate leaving of blank entries. The expression οὐ θέμις, οὐχὶ θέμις has an exact classical counterpart, but the objects or actions to which it applies are obscure: are they the names of festivals or ceremonies, which can only take place in circumstances ascertained to be favourable? And did they in fact take place on the day corresponding to the next succeeding blank entry?

to-pe-za is now known from Pylos **239 = Ta642**, etc. to mean 'table' (probably *torpeza*): tables of offerings? *a-pe-ti-ra₂* is apparently a feminine agent noun in -*tria*; from ἀφίημι?

e-pi i-ku-wo-i-pi, without *ou themis* formula or 'check mark': a fuller spelling of *i-qo-* (*ikwos) 'horse'? Or a phrase relating the middle or end of the month to a phase of the moon: *epi ixuoiphi* (dual instr., cf. ἰξύς, ἰξύες, 'waist')??

208 = V 52 (?)   ‡

1 *a-ta-na-po-ti-ni-ja* 1   [...]
2 *e-nu-wa-ri-jo* 1   *pa-ja-wo-*[ne? 1]   *po-se-da-*[o-ne 1?]

To Mistress Athena: 1
To ...
To Enyalios: 1
To Paian: [1]
To Poseidon: [1]

a-ta-na-po-ti-ni-ja: cf. *Il.* VI, 305: πότνι' Ἀθηναίη, ἐρυσίπτολι, δῖα θεάων. Nilsson (1950, p. 499) suggests that Athena 'was originally the goddess who protected the palace of the Mycenaean king, and whose cult belonged and whose protection was afforded to the king personally' (cf. **205** = Gg702?). The name *Potnia* (not necessarily referring to the same goddess) also occurs on Knossos M 729.2.

e-nu-wa-ri-jo = 'Ενυάλιος, an early god of war (*Il.* ΙΙ, 651, etc.), perhaps a consort of 'Ενυώ, later regarded as an epithet of Ares. The name possibly recurs in the form *E-ṇwạ-ri-jo* on Pylos **55** = An724.

pa-ja-wo = Homeric Παιήων *Il.* v, 401, Dor. Παιάν (*Παιάϝων, perhaps from παίω 'strike'), healer god, later identified with Apollo. It is not clear whether the names on this tablet are in the nominative or dative.

po-se-da-[*o-ne*: cf. **169** = Es646, etc. at Pylos. The name only recurs at Knossos on X 5560:]*-ke po-se-da-o* ɪ [.

†

CHAPTER X

TEXTILES, VESSELS AND FURNITURE

1. TEXTILES AT KNOSSOS †

THE numerous Knossos tablets characterized by Evans' 'banner' ideogram (no. 159) and classified by Bennett with the prefix *L*- have been discussed in some detail by Furumark (1954, pp. 44–8) and Björck (1954*b*). Their most characteristic vocabulary word is the plural *pa-we-a = pharwea*, whose identity

159	▯ ▯	CLOTH¹⁻⁴	164	▨ ▨	A kind of cloth
	▤ ▤	CLOTH¹⁻²+TE	145	♈	WOOL
161	⚮	(Adjunct)	162	⚱	TUNIC+KI
	⚿	CLOTH³+PU	158	⌂	Bundle?

with the Homeric φᾶρος proves that the 'banner' is in fact a piece of cloth: the ideogram probably represents an upright loom with loom-weights on the warp rather than a garment with a tasselled fringe. Small superior figures have been added to the word CLOTH in transcription to indicate the number of intermediate strokes springing from the bottom horizontal, although these variations are probably not significant except on **210** = Lc526. The Linear A version, found only on Agia Triada tablet HT 38, has two intermediate strokes, and (surprisingly) the surcharged initials KU and ZO also found occasionally at Knossos. The Pylos version, found on the 1952 tablets, has a 'fringe' of three strokes at top as well as bottom, and the surcharge PA (presumably *pharwos*) in the contexts where the Knossos ideogram is blank. The meaning of the curious adjunct No. 161 is obscure (see p. 320), but evidently not a 'superintendent of olive groves' (Evans, *PM*, IV, p. 716).

The lack of naturalistic variation in the ideograms makes it difficult to visualize the actual textiles or garments listed and to interpret the associated vocabulary. The Homeric φᾶρος itself is still remarkably unspecific in meaning: 'a large cloth for a sail' (*Od.* v, 258), 'a large cloak' (*Il.* II, 43, etc.), 'a funerary shroud' (XVIII, 353).

Late Minoan man's dress is usually shown on frescoes and engravings as consisting of no more than a kilt; a more abbreviated garment with prominent cod-piece and open sides is worn by infantrymen, boxers and gymnasts (including women). Women normally wear a long flounced skirt, sometimes with an 'apron', and above the waist an open bolero with prominent short sleeves over a diaphanous or non-existent blouse. The white robes worn by men and women (e.g. on the Agia Triada sarcophagus, fig. 15, and on the Palanquin Fresco, *PM*, II, pp. 770–3) have been considered to have an exclusively ritual use, and large formal cloaks have been regarded as the prerogative of chieftains; but something more than a kilt must evidently have been worn by all classes at least during the winter.

On the Mainland some kind of divided drawers takes the place of the kilt, and soldiers and retainers wear a white tunic coming down to above the knees. Women's dress is apparently similar to that of Crete.

The word *pharwea* has here been rendered somewhat arbitrarily as 'cloaks', but the remaining occurrences of the 'banner' ideogram merely as 'cloths', with little or no attempt to guess the exact shape and purpose of the textiles.

The ideogram translated as WOOL is derived from a Linear A monogram of the signs MA+RU; its meaning is indicated by its prominent place on the SHEEP tablets (see p. 203). Even where wool is counted together with CLOTHS in large numbers, its method of measurement is betrayed by occasional fractional amounts reckoned in $\check{\varepsilon}$ (e.g. on **211** = Lc532); Bennett has shown that $\check{\varepsilon}$ 3 go to the normal WOOL unit of weight, which is therefore equivalent to about 3 kg. (approximately the weight of a heavy blanket or of a present-day winter overcoat). On the Mainland WOOL only occurs with whole numbers; and on Mycenae **227** = Oe127 it is itself introduced by *pa-we-a₂*, suggesting that it has come to mean an indivisible unit of woollen material parallel to the CLOTH ideogram.

Parallel accounts of cloth and wool are found at Alalakh, e.g. no. 357 (Wiseman, 1953, p. 99): 'Account of thirty-seven pieces of cloth and thirty-five measures of wool belonging to the *šakanaku* official's store'; and at Ugarit, e.g. *RŠ*, XI, 732 B (Virolleaud, 1940, p. 257):

Five tunics, 500 shekels of purple·wool...for the king,
Two tunics, 200 shekels of purple wool...for the queen,
One tunic, 100 shekels of purple wool...for the king's son,
One tunic, 100 shekels of purple wool...(for various officials).

Knossos tablets **214** = Ld571 ff. are probably palace inventories of cloaks designed, as at Ugarit, for 'distribution to functionaries, for example those who lived in the palace itself, who were guaranteed to receive a new garment when their old one was worn out' (Virolleaud, 1953, p. 193). Medieval English account rolls show a similar grading of officials according to the value and elaborateness of the robes which they receive from the king as part of their allowance.

The *Lc-* and *L-* series, on the other hand, probably represent for the most part receipts of cloth and wool from outlying villages, since they are introduced by place-names and include entries of *o-pe-ro* 'debt' (L 473, L 869) and *a-pu-do-si* 'delivery' (L 5867, L 5930). The surviving range of place-names is as follows:

A-mi-ni-so, Da-te-we-ja, Da-wi-ja, Da-*22-ti-ja, Do-ti-ja, E-ki-si-ja, E-ra-ja, Ja-pu₂?-wi-ja, Ko-no-so (te-pe-ja), Pa-i-ti-ja, Pa₂-mi-ja, Ra-su-ti-jo, Ri-jo-ni-ja, Se-to-i-ja, Ti-ri-to, Tu-ni-ja, Tu-ri-si-ja,]-ru-wo-we-ja.

It will be seen that the majority are in the *-a* form of the adjective: this can be taken either as referring to the *pharwea* themselves or to the groups of women who have manufactured the goods.

209 = Lc525 (F xl) †

se-to-i-ja   *wa-na-ka-te-ra* CLOTH^2+TE 40 WOOL 200[+
       tu-na-no CLOTH^1 3 WOOL [nn]

From *Se-to-i-ja*:

Forty *edged* cloths of royal type, 200+ measures of wool;
Three cloths of *tu-na-no* type, several hundred (?) measures of wool.

CLOTH+TE: Mycenaean wheels are distinguished as being *te-mi-*71-ta* (Pylos WHEELS+TE) or *o-da-ku-we-ta* (see p. 370). The second term is also applied to woollen cloths on **220** = L 870, and it is possible that they refer to different kinds of decorative border, CLOTH+TE containing the initial of the first. Some of the instances of CLOTH+TE in Bennett's *Index* (p. 116) must be corrected to CLOTH+PA (e.g. Le786).

tu-na-no: the meaning of this term is unknown. It regularly occurs with the plain CLOTH ideogram on the second line of tablets whose first lists CLOTH+TE (with *pe-ko-to*) or plain CLOTH (with *ko-u-ra*). On **212** = Lc535 all three categories are separately totalled. The traces of numerals after the second WOOL seem to include hundreds.

210 = Lc526

da-wi-ja   *pe-ko-to* CLOTH^1+TE 10 CLOTH^2+TE 14 [
       tu-na-no CLOTH^1 3 WOOL [nn]

From *Da-wo*:

Ten *edged* cloths (type A) of *pe-ko-to*, fourteen *edged* cloths (type B)...;
Three cloths of *tu-na-no* type, *x* measures of wool.

pe-ko-to: occurs on the similar Lc527 and on **212** = Lc535, and introduces ideogram no. 164 on L 698 (cf. **225** = L 520). It is probably connected with the woman's trade *pe-ki-ti-ra₂* = *pektria* 'wool-carder?' at Pylos (cf. *pe-ki-ti-*[on L 656); but 'carded' seems meaningless when applied to wool which is already woven into cloth. The second meaning of πέκω is 'cut, shear': some process analogous to that used in velvet-making? On this tablet, as on Lc527 and L 5746, two separate entries of CLOTH + TE are differentiated by a varying number of intermediate strokes to the 'fringe'.

† **211** = Lc532 + 554 (F)

]-*ku̯-wo*   *pa-we-a* / *ko-u-ra*   CLOTH[1] 16   WOOL 26 $\overset{?}{\varepsilon}$ 2
             tu-na-no   CLOTH[1] 1   WOOL 3   CLOTH[1]+TE 4   WOOL 26

[   ] : Sixteen cloaks of *ko-u-ra* type, $26\frac{2}{3}$ measures of wool;

One cloth of *tu-na-no* type, three measures of wool;
 Four *edged* cloths, twenty-six measures of wool.

pa-we-a ko-u-ra: the words are written out of alignment, so that it is doubtful whether they are in grammatical agreement. Furumark's connexion with κουρά 'shearing, fleece' is impossible, since the Mycenaean form should be *kôrā* < *korsā*. Cf. *ko-u-re-ja* applied to WOOL on Lc581, to WOMEN on **25** = Ap694 (p. 165).

The three separate entries for WOOL on this tablet are puzzling, since they seem to be closely allied with the three categories of CLOTH. It is possible that the WOOL entries do not in fact represent a separate consignment but a record of the weight of wool in the cloths themselves. The numerals on the *Lc-* and *L-* series are mostly fragmentary, but the only complete *ko-u-ra* entry, on this tablet, would give a ratio of exactly $1\frac{2}{3}$ measures (or 5 kg.) per cloth; we can probably restore $1\frac{1}{2}$ on Le557 and $3\frac{1}{4}$ on Le556. The *tu-na-no* entries in the second line generally give 3 measures per cloth (but 4 on Lc530, and apparently about 100 on **209** = Lc525!). The surviving entries for CLOTH + TE would give $6\frac{1}{2}$ on this tablet and 7 on Le553. See also **225** = L 520, where a ratio of 6 is apparent. Sundwall long ago suggested that the WOOL ideogram is exclusively a unit of value (cf. *PM*, IV, p. 663); but this will not work on the *D-* tablets. Although the SHEEP and WOOL are in a fixed ratio in the totals, their proportions are quite erratic in the subsidiary sections of the account.

212 = Lc535 + 538 (F)

to-sa { *ta-ra-si-ja*   *pa-we-a* [*ko-u-ra* CLOTH nn ?]
        { *ke-ri-mi-ja*   [*tu*]-*na-no* [CLOTH nn ?]
        {   *pe-ko-to* [CLOTH+TE nn ?]

So much *piece-work* of the *ke-ri-mi-ja*: *x* cloaks of *ko-u-ra* type,

x tu-na-no cloths,
 x pe-ko-to cloths.

ta-ra-si-ja 'allocation of raw material by weight' (= Lat. *pensum*). See the Pylos BRONZE tablets, p. 352.
ke-ri-mi-ja: see Pylos **28** = An42, where it is applied to slave-girls.

316

213 = L 641 (F? xliv) †

1 *o-a-po-te   de-ka-sa-to   a-re-i-jo* | *o-u-qe po-*[   ]

2 *pa-i-ti-ja   pe.* CLOTH+TE 2   *mi.* CLOTH+TE 14   *da-wi-ja   pe.* CLOTH+TE [nn]

3 *do-ti-ja   mi.* CLOTH+TE 6   *pa₂-mi-ja* CLOTH+TE [nn]

4 *ko-no-so* | *te-pe-ja   mi.* CLOTH+TE 3   *tu-ni-ja* CLOTH+TE [nn]

Thus Areios received delivery from outside, and there are not. . .:
> From Phaistos: Two *clean edged* cloths, fourteen *dirty edged* cloths,
> From *Da-wo*: . . .*x clean edged* cloths,
> > etc.

o-a-po-te = *hō* 'thus' + ἄπωθεν 'from afar'; compare the introduction *hō-dexato* on Pylos Pn01.1; and]-*ra-wo de-ko-to ta-ra-si-ja* | *nẹ-*[, '[?Age]lawos received the piece-work', on the adjoining L 642, which is evidently of identical context and which preserves the alternative Homeric form of the aorist, δέκτο.

The adjuncts *pe.-* and *mi.-* also occur with this ideogram on KN L 1568. The second is spelt in full *mi-ja-ro* in the first entry, which may represent the Homeric μιαρός 'stained, defiled', though Boisacq postulates **miwaros*; *pe-* might then represent πεπλυμένος 'washed clean'.

te-pe-ja: its recurrence on PY Ad07 (in the genitive plural) suggests that it is a woman's trade. Possibly something like *sterpheiai*, cf. στέρφος 'hide' (Furumark). This would confirm that the ethnics all refer to women workers. These Knossos women are presumably somewhere in the town, and ἄπωθεν means 'from outside the palace'.

214 = Ld571 (G xlii); Ld572 is identical ‡

> > *pe-ne-we-ta   a-ro₂-a* BUNDLE? 1

pa-we-a | *e-qe-si-ja   re-u-ko-nu-ka* CLOTH³ 25

Twenty-five cloaks with white *o-nu-ke* suitable for Followers, provided with *pe-ne-*, of *better* quality; and one *bundle*.

e-qe-si-ja: probably formed from *e-qe-ta* (a military or religious title), but disconcertingly used of WHEELS on PY **288** = Sa790.

re-u-ko-nu-ka = *leuk-onukha*, parallel to *po-ki-ro-nu-ka* = *poikil-onukha* on **217** = L 587, etc. The simple word *o-nu-ke* (*onukhes*?) is used with the WOOL ideogram on Od682 and M 683. It is also written on one face of the sealing Ws1703: the other face has *stathmos* ('weight') and the seal-impression itself is cancelled with the weight symbol ℥. The tablet L 1568, mentioned above in connexion with the adjunct *mi.-*, has on its edge the puzzling annotation:

> > > *a-ze-ti-rị-ja*   *ne-ki-ri-de*
> > *o-pi-ma-tu   o-nu-ke* WOOL 1 *o-pi-po-ni-ke-ja* [.
> > ἐπίμαρτυς?   cf. ἐπιφοινίσσω

o-nu-ka also occurs with CLOTHS on Ld584, as if to mean 'with *o-nu-ke* of unspecified colour' (though the form of the adjective is anomalous). The connexion with ὄνυξ, 'nail, claw, onyx', etc., is problematical; the sense of the word seems to be that of some kind of decoration made of woollen thread, which may be measured separately, but which is designed for application to garments (cf. 'lace', etc.). Björck (1954*b*, p. 272) suggests 'border, fringe'. Compare ὄνυξ in the sense of an ornamental band on the Erechtheion building inscription.

pe-ne-we-ta: a neuter plural adjective in *-wenta* (dual on Ld5108?); the initial element is obscure. Not for πνέοντα 'fragrant'? Chadwick suggests *pen-wenta*, from πίνος 'natural grease in wool'.

a-ro₂-a occurs on several other *Ld-* tablets, and is applied to WHEELS on So0430: the feminine plural *a-ro₂-e* is found on L 735 applied to *pu-ka-ta-ri-ja* cloths. The parallel declension of *me-zo-a₂/me-zo-e* suggests the comparative ἀρείων; for this use of *ro₂* cf. *po-pu-ro₂ = porphureio* on L 758. Perhaps *ἀρίων (cf. ἄρι-στος)? The form *a-ro₂-jo* on **279** = So0437 is puzzling.

The numeral with the ideogram in the top line remains 1 irrespective of the number of cloaks (and is often written after them), and Björck is probably right in identifying it as the container or wrapping in which they are kept rather than as a 'hat' or other garment.

† **215** = Ld573   (G   xlii)

e-ru-ta-ra-pi

pa-we-a | ke-se-nu-wi-ja   re-u-ko-nu-ka   CLOTH³ 35   BUNDLE? 1

Thirty-five cloaks with white *o-nu-ke* suitable for guest-gifts, with red (some-things); and one *bundle*.

ke-se-nu-wi-ja = Homeric ξείνια 'guest-gifts', here adjectival. On Ld649 *ke-se-ne-*[is probably an alternative spelling *ke-se-ne-we-ja*, but note the Homeric by-form ξεινήϊα < *ξενϜήϜια. Compare also [?*ke-se*]-*nu-we-jo* on X 651, whose context is shown by the genitive *pa-we-o* in line 1. Björck's doubts whether *e-ru-ta-ra-pi* represents the feminine instrumental ἐρυθρᾶφι seem unjustifiable.

216 = Ld871   (K?   lxvii)

pa-ro   re-wa-jo

[   ]-*ra   pe-ne-we-ta | e-qe-si-ja   te-tu-ko-wo-a*   CLOTH⁴ 6

Six [garments] provided with *pe-ne-*, suitable for Followers, well made; *from* R.

]-*ra*: a neuter noun, possibly *e-ne-ra* (cf. the dual *e-ne-ro re-u-ko* on L 695); the context of *e-ne-ra* on Ai762 is not clear from Evans' drawing; *e-ne-re-ja* is a description of women on Ak638. Björck connects the word with Hom. ἔνεροι 'those below': 'under-garments, under-blankets'? Cf. *Od.* x, 353: ἔβαλλε θρόνοις ἔνι ῥήγεα καλά, πορφύρεα καθύπερθ', ὑπένερθε δὲ λῖθ' ὑπέβαλλεν.

te-tu-ko-wo-a, formally perfect participle active of τεύχω, but used in sense of Hom. τετυγμένος; see Vocabulary, p. 409.

217 = L 587 + 589 + 596   (G)   †

¹ *po-ki-ro-nu-ka*   CLOTH² 24   *re-u-ko-nu-ka*   CLOTH² 372
² *ko-ro-ta₂*   CLOTH² 14   *pa₃?-ra-ku-ja*   CLOTH² 42   *po-ri-wa*   CLOTH² I
edge: *to̞-ṣa̞*   CLOTH² 149

Twenty-four cloths with coloured *o-nu-ke*, 372 with white *o-nu-ke*,
fourteen *dyed* cloths, forty-two of the colour of *pa-ra-ku*, one grey one.
     So many cloths (in all?): 149.

ko-ro-ta₂: perhaps the same word as *ko-ro-to* on Mycenae Oe106 (see Vocabulary, p. 398),
     but -*ta₂* may imply -*tia*. Not for *krokia* 'yellow'?
pa₃?-ra-ku-ja: probably an alternative spelling of *pa-ra-ku-ja* Ld580. Or 'adorned with
     pa-ra-ku'? For the unidentified precious material *pa-ra-ku* see **239** = Ta642.
po-ri-wa = Hom. πολιός (of grey hair, a wolf, steel, the sea).

The sum (?) on the edge unaccountably bears no relation to the separate items.

218 = L 598   (G   xlv)   ‡

¹ [   ]-*ta-o*   *po-ki-ro-nu-ka*   CLOTH¹ I
² [*re-u-ko-nu*]-*ka*   CLOTH¹ 37   *ko-ro-ta₂*   CLOTH¹ 2
edge: *to-sa*   CLOTH¹ 40   *o.* CLOTH¹ 6

...of [   ]-*tās*: one cloth with coloured *o-nu-ke*,
     thirty-seven cloths with white *o-nu-ke*,
     two *dyed* cloths.
          So many in all: forty cloths.
          Deficit: six cloths.

This tablet is apparently introduced by a man's name, like the five pointed out by
     Björck (Lc481, etc.) each of which has the enigmatic word *to-u-ka* followed by
     WOOL on the reverse. The ending -*ka* in line 1, like *po-ri-wa* on the preceding tablet,
     may indicate that the name of the cloths is here feminine.

219 = L 594   (G   xlv)

                              ri-ta   pa-we-a
              [*da*]-*te-we-ja*   CLOTH¹ I   TUNIC+KI I
Linen clothes from D.: one cloak, one tunic.

ri-ta pa-we-a: also on X 5927. With this tablet we leave the category of woollen gar-
     ments: *ri-ta* is the Homeric neuter plural λῖτα 'linen cloth', probably adjectival
     here. The TUNIC ideogram differs from the CORSLET sign (see p. 380) by the
     absence of cross-lines and the less pronounced shoulder-loops. The surcharged KI
     probably stands for the *ki-to* = χιτών of **222** = J 693, and identifies the garment as a
     shirt, a lightly protected tunic, or as the foundation of a corslet before the addition
     of armour. The word is borrowed from the Semitic form seen in Hebrew *kᵉtōnet*,

Ugaritic *ktnt* (probably) and Akkadian *kitintu* 'linen dress'; the basic *kitu, kitinnu* means 'linen' itself in Akkadian, but it is perhaps better to assume that the Mycenaean word was borrowed as the name of a specific garment. On Le178 the TUNIC occurs with the surcharge RI (*lītos?*) and the annotation *u-po-we*: compare Hesychius ὑπο(*ϝ)έστης· χιτών.

220 = L 870   (K?   lxi)

[*o*]-*ḍạ-ku-we-ta* / *we-we-e-a*   CLOTH³ I   TUNIC+KI I

Woollen clothes provided with *o-da-k-*: one cloak, one tunic.

Compare the formula of *Od.* VIII, 392, etc.: φᾶρος ἐϋπλυνὲς ἠδὲ χιτῶνα.

† 221 = L 647 + M12 + 5943 + 5974   (F)

    nu-wa-ja   *pe.* CLOTH [nn]   Ѵ̄ . CLOTH 17   TUNIC+KI 3

[   ]-*ra*   *e-ni-qe*   *e-ra-pe-me-na*   '*nu-wa-ja*'   CLOTH I   [   ]-*ra₂*   CLOTH I

[Garments:] *x clean* cloths of *nu-wa-ja* type,

    seventeen *dirty* cloths, three tunics,

    one cloth of *nu-wa-ja* type, *torn* and mended,

    one . . . cloth.

Joined by Bennett from four fragments in 1954. The meaning of *nu-wa-ja* is unknown (cf. *nu-wa-i-*[X 663). It is just possible that the unidentified adjunct, which seems to be a monogram of *mi+pu₂*, is an alternative way of writing *mi-jạ-ro* 'dirty'?; *pu₂* for πλυτέον 'must be washed'?

e-ni-qe occurs on two other fragments as *e-ni-qe nu-*[and *e-ni-qe pe-ne-*[; see Vocabulary, p. 392.

e-ra-pe-me-na: the perfect participle passive of ῥάπτω 'stitch', i.e. *errapmenā* > ἐρραμμένη, with a surprising lack of assimilation. Cf. *ra-pte* 'tailor', *ra-pi-ti-ra₂* 'seamstress', neither of which shows the postulated *ϝ-.

‡ 222 = J 693   (F   xlvi)

¹ *ri-no* / *re-po-to* '*qe-te-o*' *ki-to*   BRONZE Ɀ̃ I   [

² *sa-pa*   Ɀ̃ 2   Ϛ I   *e-pi-ki-to-ni-ja*   BRONZE Ɀ̃ Ị   [

Fine linen, of the *tribute*: a tunic = I kg. of bronze. . .

    a *sa-pa* = 45 g. (of bronze),

    over-shirt(s) = I kg. of bronze. . .

ri-no re-po-to = λίνον λεπτόν, cf. *Il.* XVIII, 595: τῶν δ' αἱ μὲν λεπτὰς ὀθόνας ἔχον, οἱ δὲ χιτῶνας εἵατ' ἐϋννήτους. The form *qe-te-a₂* (neuter plural) occurs on Pylos 96 = Un02, *q.v.* It is uncertain whether the BRONZE figures are an indication of the value of the items or of their actual weight ('measured in bronze units', in default of special units like those for wool?); but a 'tunic of fine linen' is perhaps unlikely to weigh more than 300 g. or so.

kito = χιτών: other cases of this word occur in less clear contexts: *ki-to-pi* on Le787 (instr. plur., cf. *pa-we-pi* = *pharwesphi* L 104), *ki-to-na* on L 785.

sa-pa: this garment recurs on Mycenae Oe108.

e-pi-ki-to-ni-ja: presumably *epikhitōnia*. A similar formation is seen in the expression *e-pi-ro-pa-ja   o-du-we   te-o-qo-ri-ja* on the related tablet in the same hand Od696: cf. λώπη 'cloak', *Od.* XIII, 224, and θεοπόλος 'priest'. Note also *o-pi-i-ta-ja* on X 537 (cf. ἱστός 'loom, web'?).

223 = L 471   (?   xciv)

[pu]-ka-ta-ri-ja | re-u-ka   `me-zo-e'   CLOTH⁴+PU 10
Ten white *double cloaks*, larger size.

pu-ka-ta-ri-ja: this word recurs on the Mycenae tablet X 508. Chadwick rejects a connexion with πυκταλίζω 'fight, box', and suggests a dissimilated form of **ptukt-*, i.e. 'a garment of double thickness' = Homeric δίπλαξ (fem., sc. χλαῖνα). The feminine gender is proved by the ending of *mezoes* 'larger'. *Me-zo-*[also occurs on Lc504; Björck suggests emending *me-ko-ta* on L 469 to read *megistai* 'largest', which actually occurs on X 537.

224 = L 474 joined   (E?   xlviii)   †

po-pu-re-ja | pu-ka-ta-ri-ja   CLOTH³+PU 21
Twenty-one purple *double cloaks*.

po-pu-re-ja: cf. the dual *po-pu-ro₂* with two CLOTHS+PU on L 758; and *wa-na-ka-te-ro po-pu-re-*[on X 976, suggesting that purple was already a favourite royal colour. Cf. *Od.* XIX, 225: χλαῖναν πορφυρέην οὔλην ἔχε δῖος Ὀδυσσεὺς διπλῆν.

225 = L 520   (F)   ‡

¹ *do-ti-ja*   WOOL 18   *pe-re-ke*   ▨ 3
² *ka-ma*   WOOL 12   ▨ 2
³ *sa-mu?-ta-jo* WOOL 24   ▨ 4

*Do-ti-ja*ᵖ: 54 kg. of wool, *makes* three cloths.
     The *ka-ma*: 36 kg. of wool, *makes* two cloths.
     *Sa-mu-ta-jo*ᵐ: 72 kg. of wool, *makes* four cloths.

pe-re-ke: possibly περιέχει ('embraces, comprises, makes'), with περ before a vowel as in Cyprian, Pamphylian, etc. Evans (*PM*, IV, pp. 662–3) pointed out the 'numerical equation' on this tablet, and regarded the second ideogram as a unit of weight, identical to a Zakro stone weight of MM III which has a similar design on one face and six dots on the other, and which weighs 220 grams. If there is in fact an equation on this tablet, then the value represented must be much larger, since six times the WOOL unit makes 18 kg. It is clear in any case from L 698 (where the ideogram is introduced by *pe-ko-to* and has the normal 'fringe' at the bottom) that it is no more than a specialized form of the CLOTH sign.

2. TEXTILES AT MYCENAE

Of the three dozen tablets found by Wace in 1952 in the 'House of the Oil Merchant' and published by Bennett, all but two probably list the WOOL ideogram. The majority consist largely of personal names in the dative (e.g. *Ophelānorei* on Oe126), and seem to be the record of cloths or clothes issued to members of a large household.

† **226** = Oe129

    di-ke

ne-wo   ka-na-pe-we   WOOL 4

Four woollen cloths to the young (or new) fuller *Di-ke*.

Other occupational names found in this context are *a-ke-ti-ri-ja* 'nurse?', *pe-re-ke-we* (*plekēwei?*), *a-to-po-qo* 'baker', *ke-ra-me-wi* 'potter', *ka-ke-wi* 'smith' (note the unusual datives in *-i*); also *ko-wo* 'son' and *tu-ka-te-re* 'daughter'. General textile vocabulary shared with the other sites includes *ta-ra-si-ja* = *talasia* (cf. **212** = Lc535), *o-no* (also with WOOL on Pylos **41** = An14 and Un01) and *pa-we-a₂* = *pharwea*.

‡ **227** = Oe127

pa-we-a₂   e-we-pe-se-so-me-na   WOOL 20

Twenty woollen cloaks which are to be well *boiled*.

e-we-pe-se-so-me-na: apparently εὖ ἑψησόμενα, from ἕψω 'boil (trans.)'. The meaning is uncertain: cf. ἑψήσασθαι 'to dye' (Pollux, 2 A.D.)? Or cf. the word *bašlu* 'cooked' frequently applied to clothes at Nuzi, interpreted as 'bleached' (Lacheman, 1939, p. 543)? Or are the clothes simply going to the laundry?

¶ **228** = Oe111 + 136

    ¹ *pe-ru-si-nwa   o-u-ka* [?
    ² *wo-ro-ne-ja   pa-we-si*[
    ³ *ne-[wa?]   o-u-ka*
    ⁴ [   ]*-ki-ni-ja*   WOOL 100[
    ⁵ [   ]*o-ta-pa-ro-te-wa-ro*   WOOL 200[

Last year's *o-u-ka*:

    x woollen cloths for cloaks.

New *o-u-ka*:

    100 cloths of. . .-*ki-ni-ja* type.
    200 cloths. . ., which *are from Te-wa-ro*.

o-u-ka (cf. *o-u-ko* Oe108): meaning unknown. Compare the Knossos word *to-u-ka*
  (Lc481, etc.)?

wo-ro-ne-ja: a form *wloneia* from *wolnos > οὖλος 'wool', with the metathesis seen in the
  by-form λῆνος < *wlānos? Palmer proposes *worneia* = ἄρνεια 'of lambs'. Bennett reads
  pa-we-si-jo followed by the WOOL ideogram, but the end of line 2 is very uncertain.

o-ta-: the very tentative division *onta paro Te-wa-ro* would involve the form ὄντα of the
  present participle which is so far confined to Attic; but *o* may not be initial.

3. TEXTILES AT PYLOS   †

Ten very fragmentary tablets of a textile context (classified *La-*) were found
at Pylos in 1952. They share with Knossos the word *ko-u-ra* (cf. **211** = Lc532);
the genitive *wanaktos* 'of the king' is found on the reverse of La622 (cf.

145	🐑	WOOL	159	▦	CLOTH + PA
143	⸎	Silver?	160	⸎	Kind of cloth?

209 = Lc525); the ideogram no. 143 occurs with the weight symbol *Z* on the
reverse of La630, and is perhaps identical with that suggested for 'silver'
(see p. 351, and compare the metal weights on **222** = J 693).

                                                                      ‡
                                                                      ‡

4. MYCENAEAN VESSEL NAMES

The ideograms for vessels show a great variety of forms, and it is not feasible
to allot a separate reference number for all of them; new tablets may easily
extend the range. Although they are intended as a more or less faithful drawing
of the numerous different types in use, it is characteristic of both Knossos and
Pylos that the scribe almost always adds the Greek name of the vessel type
either in full spelling or as a 'surcharged' initial (the references to these initials
in *SM II*, p. 59 should be treated with caution). The fact that the same names
recur with the same shapes at the two palaces effectively disproves the objection
which has been raised that such an added description is superfluous and
improbable. That the practice is inherited from Linear A is suggested by the
Agia Triada tablet HT 31 (*PM*, IV, p. 732, fig. 717), where vessels are anno-
tated with sign-groups corresponding to Linear B *su-pu* and *ka-ro-pa₃*, cups
with *pa₂-pa₃*, *su-pa₃-ra* and *pa-ta-qe*: the difference of language is obvious.
Thirteen vessel types with known Mycenaean names are shown in fig. 16.

Even though the ideograms are naturalistic and provided with Greek names,
it is not easy to connect all of them securely with types known from the

archaeological record, or to fit them accurately into the classification of shapes set out by Furumark (*MP*, figs. 2–21). There are two main reasons for this:

1. The connexion of classical Greek vessel-names with classical shapes is itself to some extent a matter of guesswork; and not only have the classical shapes designed for each specific purpose undergone marked changes from their Mycenaean equivalents, but the Greek names themselves can be seen to show shifts of meaning between earlier and later writers.

	Knossos		Pylos		Mycenae	Transcription
200				*pi-je-ra₃*		BOILING PAN
				pi-a₂-ra		
201				*ti-ri-po-de*	*ti-ri-po-di-ko*	TRIPOD CAULDRON
202		*di-pa*		*di-pa*		GOBLET?
203				*qe-to*	*qe-to*	WINE JAR?
204				*qe-ra-na*		EWER
205				*a-te-we*		JUG
206				*ka-ti*		HYDRIA
207		*ku-ru-su-pa₃*				TRIPOD AMPHORA
208						BOWL
209		*a-pi-po-re-we*		]-*re-we*	*a-po-re-we*	AMPHORA
210		*ka-ra-re-we*		*ka-ra-re-we*		STIRRUP JAR
211		*po-ti-[ ]-we*				WATER BOWL?
212		*u-do-ro*		*u-do-ro*		WATER JAR?
213		*i-po-no*				COOKING BOWL

Fig. 16. Mycenaean vessel ideograms and their names.

2. That most of the ideograms (at any rate nos. 200–8) represent metal rather than pottery types is indicated not only by their profiles but by the BRONZE ideogram (nos. 202, 205 and 208), and by the fact that they are counted, like those of GOLD, in small numbers from one to three. By contrast, note that in 1953 Blegen found 2853 plain pottery kylixes in Room 2 and 2147 bowls and 'teacups' in Room 5 at Pylos: the tablets listing these sets, if they were listed at all, would evidently have a very

different appearance. Owing to their melting-down value, finds of metal vessels are almost entirely confined to undisturbed burials of kings and chieftains, and to household treasures which have escaped looting by concealment. The bulk of such finds date from 1600–1400 B.C., and it is a moot point whether metal shapes and decoration so far characteristic only of Late Minoan and Helladic I–II may in fact be assumed to be still in use around 1200 B.C., and used to illustrate the phraseology of the Pylos tablets. But some of the more valuable objects may of course be heirlooms rather than of recent manufacture.

The majority of the fourteen types listed above evidently belong to the characteristic furnishing of a chieftain's apartments, and are designed largely for the heating and carrying of water for baths and hand-washing (and possibly to a lesser extent for the preparation and consumption of drink). Such services are shown on the Knossos tablet K 93 (fig. 17), where the first set apparently comprises our types 200, 212 and 205, the second our types 208 and 204. Similar sets of bronze vessels provide (together

Fig. 17. Knossos tablet K 93.

with weapons and Palace Style vases) the typical grave furniture of chieftains. A representative group from the LM II 'Tomb of the Tripod Hearth' at Zafer Papoura (*PM*, III, p. 634, fig. 398) is shown in fig. 18: relatives of our types 200, 201, 204 and 208 can be seen, together with the ladle of **229** = K 434 and the lamp(?) of **237** = Ta709.

The 'Chieftain's Grave' at Zafer Papoura (*PM*, IV, p. 861, fig. 843) yielded a ewer of type 204, a two-handled bowl, a 'frying-pan' (lamp?), a mirror, two swords and two spears. Similar groups of bronze vessels from houses adjoining the palace are discussed by Evans (*PM*, II, pp. 623 ff.), and include two tripods and a ewer from a house to the S.E. of the South House (fig. 394). Note also the hoard of bronze vessels (types 200, 201, 204) from the 4th Shaft Grave (Schliemann, 1878, pp. 273–8). The following notes discuss in more detail the identification of our types.

200. *pi-a₂-ra* or *pi-je-ra₃* (plural), 'boiling-pan': a large shallow vessel, designed to expose a large area to the fire, and provided with high-swung handles for suspension. The foot apparently shown on **237** = Ta709.1 is unusual, since it is much too narrow to keep the vessel in equilibrium; it is not entirely clear on the tablet. These vessels are evidently considerably smaller than the huge hemispherical bronze cauldrons with three handles found at Tylissos, of which the largest had a diameter of 1·40 m. The name agrees in sense with the ἀμφίθετος φιάλη ἀπύρωτος of *Il.* XXIII, 270, and shows the same vowel-alternation as the classical φιάλη/φιέλη.

201. *ti-ri-po*, plural *ti-ri-po-de* = τρίπος, cf. *Il.* XVIII, 346: οἱ δὲ λοετροχόον τρίποδ'

ἵστασαν ἐν πυρὶ κηλέῳ. The ideogram conforms to the Bronze Age pattern in showing the legs attached to the belly rather than to the underside of the handles, but in a rather more schematic way than on the surviving metal examples.

† 202. *di-pa*, dual *di-pa-e*: spelling, gender and declension suggest identity with the Homeric δέπας 'goblet', but the precise shape and use are far from certain. Late Minoan and Helladic drinking vessels belong to the class of 'stemmed cups' (*MP*, figs. 16–17). The earlier version A in fig. 19 is exemplified by the four gold cups from

Fig. 18. Contents of the Tomb of the Tripod Hearth, Zafer Papoura
(Evans, *Palace of Minos*, II, p. 634, fig. 398).

the Mycenae acropolis treasure (Thomas, 1939), the silver 'crater' from Shaft II at Dendra, and the 'loving cup' on the Knossos Camp-stool Fresco (*PM*, IV, p. 365, fig. 305*c*); and is paralleled in pottery by the 'Ephyraean goblet'. The kylix from the end of the Mycenaean age has a narrower stem, and either one or two handles which may be low (*B*) or high-swung (*C*). The identification of our *dipas* with such a cup is made difficult by the marked constriction at the neck of the ideogram; by the fact that the handles are shown high-swung even at Knossos; by the broad base and lack of foot on the Knossos version; and by the four handles on **236** = Ta641, which would seem to interfere with either drinking, pouring or scooping (unless arranged in the paired fashion which has been argued for Nestor's famous 'four-handled δέπας' in *Il.* XI, 632–7). The alternative of assuming that the ideogram is only a schematic indication of a 'piriform amphora' (*MP*, fig. 4) with handles below the neck encounters the objection that the *qe-to* of **236** = Ta641.2 is deliberately so distinguished in drawing. The collocation with tripods might suggest that the *dipas* is used for bath-water rather than drink, but its narrow base and handleless variety prove it to be quite small.

203. *qe-to* (plural): this vessel appears to have two horizontal handles (like the small † pithoid jar, *MP*, fig. 3, no. 27). Bennett's suggested identification with the classical πίθος 'wine-jar', 'wine-cask', is hard to reconcile with the current etymology.

204. *qe-ra-na* (sing.): a bronze ewer or 'oinochoe' of the type usual in the surviving ‡ bronze hoards: these generally show a horizontal ring two-thirds of the way from handle to base, to help in pouring (cf. κορωνόϜεσσα on **235** = Ta711?). Palmer's comparison with πέλανος 'funerary libation' would apparently involve an un-etymological use of *q-*. Alternatively cf. Old Norse *huerna* 'pot', Gothic *hwairnei* (fem.) 'cranium' (cf. Lat. *testa*)? One might expect the *prokhowos* of Mycenae **234** = Ue611 to have a similar appearance.

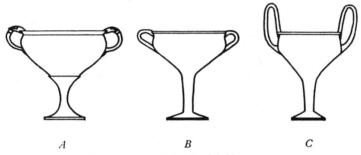

A *B* *C*

Fig. 19. Late Helladic drinking cups.

205. *a-te-we* (plural): a word in *-eus*, describing a straight-sided ewer or 'cream-jug' with a more elongated neck than (204). The first vessel on fig. 17 differs in its curved handle and tilted spout.

206. *ka-ti* (singular): a globular pitcher with the indication of two extra smaller handles at the widest part of the body, which may be designed to help carry the vessel on the head. As in the classical *hydria* and in Mycenaean globular jugs of pottery (*MP*, fig. 7, nos. 128 and 129), one might expect to find these two handles in fact set on the opposite axis to the main one. The spelling represents the ancestor of the classical κηθίς, κηθάριον 'dice-shaker or voting urn' (cf. ὑδρία in the same sense, and Hesychius' Arcadian gloss κάθιδοι· ὑδρίαι).

207. *ku-ru-su-pa₃*?: a squat globular amphora with three legs or a tripod stand. Probably not a compound of χρυσός 'gold' but a native 'Minoan' word, to judge from the Agia Triada vessel names *ka-ro-pa₃*, *su-pu* and *su-pa₃-ra* quoted above; cf. the Hittite (Hurrian) *ḫupru šḫ-* 'pilgrim flask'?

208. A shallow bowl with upstanding ring handle riveted on: on **229** = K 434 the bottom end of the ring stands clear of the body, the condition usual in the surviving

examples. According to size and context this ideogram may evidently represent anything from a large bronze basin (cf. fig. 18, object *b*; and *PM*, II, p. 631, fig. 395*a*, *b*, *c*) to a small gold or silver bowl like those from Marathon, Mycenae, Dendra and from Ai Iannis by Knossos (*JHS*, **74**, 1954, Pl. IX). The Homeric λέβης (e.g. *Od.* I, 137) is a possible Greek name for this type. On **238** = Tn996.4 the bronze bowls apparently have feet, which makes them similar to the pedestalled bowls found in the Shaft Graves at Mycenae (fig. 20).

Fig. 20. Pedestalled bowl from the Fourth Shaft Grave, Mycenae.

† 209. *a-pi-po-re-we*, *a-po-re-we* = ἀμφιφορῆϝες, ἀμφο-ρῆϝες. The Mainland spelling already shows the telescoped form (metrically impossible in Homer), but the clear etymology 'carried on both sides' has preserved the bond between name and shape down to classical times. Evans (*PM*, IV, p. 732) shows that the single honey amphoras on **204** = Gg704, etc. are probably of metal, pointing particularly to the handles on Gg709 (of which his fig. 716 gives an inaccurate impression); but the amphoras on **233** = Uc160 rev. may be of pottery, as the 1800 specimens of Gg700 certainly are. Evans (*PM*, IV, p. 734) says that the latter have a surcharged *A* and 'spouts' like stirrup-jars, but publishes no photo; Bennett's *Index* (p. 114) does not refer to either of these peculiarities.

‡ 210. *ka-ra-re-we*: called 'stirrup-handled vases' in *SM II*; the 'spout' which appears in profile on Evans' drawing is not clear on the photograph (and indeed unexpected, since the mouth of a stirrup-jar projects in the opposite axis to the handles) but is confirmed by Chadwick's autopsy. The use of the word on Pylos Gn1184 suggests that this vessel type does in fact represent a stirrup-jar used for oil storage, and the large number (180) counted on Uc778 again points to a pottery type; but note that Evans infers the existence of stirrup-jars in metal from the rivet decoration of some from Shaft Grave 68 at Zafer Papoura (*PM*, II, p. 640). *Krairēwes* from κραῖρα 'head', or *klārēwes* from κλῆρος (cf. κληρωτρίς 'voting urn')?? What Evans interprets as the neck of a stirrup-jar on U 746 is in fact the word *ke-ro* above the ideogram no. 172.

211. That *po-ti-*[on **232** = K 875.6 represents the initial of the vessels introduced by]-*we* and surcharged *po* on K 873 is only a conjecture. The ideogram shows a shallow bowl or cup (numerals 32, 24, 22) of similar outline to the *dipas* but with two handles set on the widest part of the body. On K 873 the first line adds *u-do*, presumably ὕδωρ.

212. *u-do-ro* (plural): apparently a conical bucket-shaped bowl with two horizontal (?) handles (absent on K 774, 776). The horizontal line near the top may indicate a separate rim or lid (shown open on **238** = Tn996.4?). It is perhaps the vessel seen to the left of K 93 (fig. 17 above) between the basin and the jug. This vessel was

possibly used for baling out the bath in **238** = Tn996, and resembles the conical bronze pans from Knossos (*PM*, II, fig. 394, no. 4; fig. 396) and from Shaft V in chamber tomb no. 7 at Dendra. Some similarity is also shown by the bronze tankard from Tiryns and by the same shape in clay from Pylos, but these have only one handle. The name is evidently derived from ὑδρο- 'water', but the form ὕδρος itself is only found with the meaning 'water-snake' in Greek.

213.   *i-po-no* (plural): a shallow open dish. The classical ἱπνός (of uncertain etymology) means 'an earthenware dish or cover in which food was baked' and, no doubt as a secondary development, 'oven, furnace'.

5. INVENTORIES OF VESSELS AT KNOSSOS

229 = K 434   (D   xxxv)   †

1   ] ι   BOWL 1 1

2   ]-*de-wa-pi*   *ko-no-ni-pi*   1

One. . ., one bowl, one ladle,
one [jug] with. . .*bars*.

Evans compares the silver ladle from the Vaphio tomb (*PM*, IV, fig. 911); note also object *o* on fig. 18 above.

ko-no-ni-pi: Evans describes the ideogram as a 'jug, the handle of which is partly obliterated; it seems to have had a raised ring round its neck'; Chadwick confirms that it has a clear band round the neck. *ko-no-ni-pi* (wrongly printed in Bennett's *Index* as -*ja*) is evidently a feminine noun (cf. **244** = Ta714.3) with genitive singular in -*nios* or -*nidos*. Does it represent κανονίς 'cross-bar'? Cf. also *Il.* XIII, 407: ἀσπίδα . . .δύω κανόνεσσ' ἀραρυῖαν. A restoration [*peri*]*derwāphi* = περιδέραιος 'round the neck' would, however, violate both the declension rules for compound adjectives and the accepted etymology of δέρη from *$g^u erw\bar{a}$.

230 = K 740   (H   li)   ‡

1? [   ]

2   *di-pa*   BRONZE GOBLET?+DI 31

3   *qe-ro₂*   BRONZE   16

4   *ku-ru-su-pa₃*? .   TRIPOD-AMPHORA 1

5   *pi-ri-je*   .   ZE 1

6   [   ] *me*-[   ]
       uncertain number of lines missing

di-pa: probably an error for plural *di-pa-a. The plural δέπα in Homer is not a valid analogy, since it is everywhere the result of elision.

qe-ro₂: Evans (*PM*, IV, p. 732) says that the ideogram 'must probably be regarded as a variant of the cuirass sign seen on the Chariot tablets'. It has the yoke-shaped top characteristic of the TUNIC symbol (see p. 313) and recurs in the armour context of **299** = V 789 and **300** = G 5670, *q.v.*

pi-ri-je: the absence of another ideogram suggests that we should take ZE not as 'pairs' but in the sense 'saw'; but one would expect *pi-ri-jo* for πρίων. The function of the dots in lines 4 and 5 is uncertain; ditto signs for 'bronze'?

† **231** = K 872　(D or K?　lxi)

¹ [　　　　] *ke-ra-a* 🐂 [nn]

² [　　　]-*me-no　ne-pa₂-sa-pi* 🐂 1

³ [　　　]-*p̣i-te-te　ku-ru-so*
　　　ne]-*pa₂-sa-pi　we.* 🏺 3

? two bull's head 'rhytons' [? gilded] on the horns;
one bull's head 'rhyton' [? decorated] with *ne-pa₂-sa-*;
three *silver* cups [? decorated] with *ne-pa₂-sa-*, the *rim* of gold.

Lines 1 and 2: a comparable 'bull's head rhyton' is shown among Keftiu tribute in the early fifteenth century B.C. Egyptian tomb of User-Amon. The black steatite example from the Little Palace (*PM*, II, pp. 527 ff.) has *tridachna* shell inlay round the nose and in irregular patches; eyes of crystal and red jasper; small medallions with revolving rays between the horns; and probably horns of wood covered with gold foil. The silver one from the fourth shaft grave at Mycenae (*PM*, II, p. 531, fig. 333) has horns of wood plated with gold, gold inlay round the muzzle, and a gold rosette on the forehead. The objects or substance represented in this context by *ne-pa₂-sa-pi* (instr. plur.) is unknown, but it also enters into the cups of line 3, and into the composition of the man's name *Ne-pa₂-sa-ta* on PY Fn03.

]-*p̣i-te-te*: cf. *o-pi-te-te-re*, PY **251** = Vn02.5. Either 'lid' (cf. ἐπίθεμα, Hom. ἐπίθημα) or 'applied band' (cf. περίθεμα). Compare the silver bowls from Dendra and Mycenae with a gold plate attached to the rim; Nuzi tablet SMN·589 ('a cup of silver with its edges covered in gold', Lacheman, 1939, p. 538); and *Od.* IV, 615–16: ἀργύρεος δὲ ἔστιν ἄπας, χρυσῷ δ' ἐπὶ χείλεα κεκράανται. The cups are of the same shape as the gold ones from Vaphio and those shown in the Egyptian tomb of Senmut. Such cups were also made of bronze (cf. *PM*, II, fig. 288*c*, from Tomb 12 at Mochlos). There appears to be a diminutive *wo*, of unknown significance, written to the right of the ideogram.

‡ **232** = K 875　(K　lxv)

¹ [...] / *pa₂-si-re-wi-ja* / *di-pa　a-no-wo-to* [🏺 1]

² *pe-ri-ta* / *pa₂-si-re-wi-ja* / *di-pa　a-no-wo-to* [🏺 1]

³ *wi-na-jo* / *pa₂-si-re-wi-ja* / *di-pa　a-no-wo-to* [🏺 1]

⁴ *i-da-i-jo* / *pa₂-si-re-wi-ja* / *di-pa　a-no-wo-to* [🏺 1]

⁵ *sa-me-ti-jo* / *pa₂-si-re-wi-ja* / *di-pa　a-no-wo-to* [🏺 1]

⁶ *i-je-re-wi-jo　pa₂-si-*[*re-wi*]-*ja　a-no-wo-to* 🏺 1　*po-ti-*[　　]

330

So-and-so (the basileus' retinue): one goblet (?) without a handle,

etc.

The bottom line is damaged. Evans' drawing shows the number 10, but this horizontal appears to be a crack in the clay. For the 'goblet without a handle' cf. Pylos **236** = Ta641.3.

233 = Uc160 reverse   (?   xxvii)   †

¹ ? [

² *a-pi-po-re-we* ⏚ 3[three amphoras...

³ *i-po-no* ⏝ 14 [fourteen cooking bowls...

⁴ [*u*]-*do-ro* ⏛ 17 [seventeen water jars...

uncertain number of lines lost

The other side of this tablet is a fragmentary list of wine and other measured commodities. The small T which follows the ideograms on Evans' drawing is a single ten with a vertical crack in the clay.

6. VESSELS AT MYCENAE

234 = Ue611 reverse.   (House of the Sphinxes)   ‡

¹ *ku-pe-ra* 4   *a-po-re-we* 2   *pe-ri-ke* 3

² *ka-ra-te-ra* 1   *po-ro-ko-wo* 4   *a-ta-ra* 10

³ ?] *pa-ke-te-re* 30   *ka-na-to* 5   *qe-ti-ja* 10

⁴ *qe-to* 2   *ti-ri-po-di-ko* 8   *ka-ra-ti-ri-jo* 7

Four drinking cups, two amphoras, three *pitchers*,
one mixing-bowl, four pouring jugs, ten *ladles*,
thirty . . ., five *baskets*, ten small *wine-jars*,
two *wine-jars*, eight small tripods, seven *baskets*.

The other side of this tablet is a list of olives, figs and wine. The list of vessels is unfortunately not accompanied by ideograms; a considerable store of different pottery types was found in a room adjacent to that in which this tablet was discovered in 1954. In the doorway of this store-room a number of clay sealings were found in 1953; they are inscribed with a series of words apparently describing vessels or utensils, some of which recur on **234** = Ue611.

ku-pe-ra: probably the Homeric κύπελλα. Note the absence of the *di-pa* from this list of vessels apparently devoted largely to drinking purposes.

pe-ri-ke = πέλικες: the word is quoted by Pollux (x, 67) from Cratinus, and mentioned by Athenaeus (xi, 495) in the form πελίκαι. The grammarians were by no means sure of the meaning: κύλιξ, προχοΐδιον and χοῦς are all given as equivalents.

ka-ra-te-ra: apparently *kratēra*, but the accusative is surprising; possibly for a derivative *kratēriā*? Old Latin *creterra* is supposed to be an early borrowing of the Ionic accusative κρητῆρα by way of Etruscan.

331

po-ro-ko-wo = Hom. πρόχοος. Cretan πρόκοος is used as a measure.

a-ta-ra: possibly *antla*. A neuter ἄντλον is quoted from Pollux (1, 92); the sense 'bucket' is not recorded before Manetho. Cf. Hesychius ἀντλία·καδίσκος.

pa-ke-te-re occurs on Pylos Vn879 (probably to be restored on **251** = Vn02.6); no plausible explanation. From σφάзω or πήγνυμι? Cf. also]-*ke-te-ri-ja* with the 'lamp?' on **237** = Ta709.

ka-na-to: cf. κάναστρον, κάνασθον? Not γνάθος in some technical sense?

qe-ti-ja: probably a diminutive of *qe-to* (**236** = Ta641.2, *q.v.*), which is apparently to be read in line 4.

ti-ri-po-di-ko = *tripodiskoi*. Also a man's name on PY Cn12.8: cf. the Attic deme Τριποδίσκος.

ka-ra-ti-ri-jo: connected with κάλαθος?

† 　　## 7. INVENTORIES OF VESSELS AND FURNITURE AT PYLOS

THE *Ta-* SERIES

Among the documents which were found by Blegen in the campaigns of 1952–3 and have appeared in Bennett's second (1955) edition of the Pylos tablets, the most important (both for further decipherment and for the light they throw on Mycenaean culture) are the series which have been classified by the prefix *Ta-*. One of these, **236** = Ta641 with its tripods and four-handled 'goblets', was separately published by Blegen (1953, cf. Ventris, 1954*a*, p. 18), and has been invaluable in providing a conclusive check on the decipherment. An earlier draft of the present chapter has already been partly published in *Eranos* (**53**, 1955, 109–24); Bennett has independently arrived at a very similar idea of their meaning.

The *Ta-* series consists of thirteen tablets of 'palm-leaf' shape in grey-burnt clay, exceptionally neatly written and well preserved. From their similar context, 'hand' and common locus, adjoining the Archive Room, they evidently constitute a coherent set written for a single occasion. Ta710, which merely repeats Ta721 lines 3–4, has been omitted here; but the red tablet Tn996 (with 'bath-tubs') may conveniently be discussed together with the series because of its similar subject-matter, even though found some distance away (in Room 4, Blegen, 1954, p. 28). We have printed first 711, 641, 709 and 996 which record vessels and utensils; next 642, 713 and 715 which list the article *to-pe-za*; then 707, 708 and 714 which record *to-no* and *ta-ra-nu* in combination; and finally 721 and 722, where *ta-ra-nu* (plural *ta-ra-nu-we*) are counted alone and illustrated by the ideogram ⌐⊐.

Although this rectangular object with its looped ends at first sight resembles a vessel, its name *thrānus*, plural *thrānues*, is clearly the Homeric θρῆνυς 'footstool'. On Ta722.1 the object can be seen to have short legs under it. An identical piece of furniture is visible under the feet of the seated goddess on the large gold signet-ring from Tiryns. Doubts were expressed by Evans as to the ring's authenticity, but the odd form of the footstool could hardly have been anticipated by a forger. Wace tells us that he and Seager examined the ring and shared Karo's opinion that it is genuine.

The spelling of the objects *to-no* and *to-pe-za* will be discussed below; but the first, which regularly forms a pair with *thrānus*, is evidently the equivalent of θρόνος 'chair', the second of τράπεζα 'table'. The furniture listed on the

Fig. 21. The gold signet ring from Tiryns.

surviving tablets comprises eleven tables, five chairs and fifteen footstools (four of them paired with chairs). The low number of chairs may suggest that part of their inventory is missing, or possibly that some of the *thrānues* were intended to be sat on. A close parallel is given by the Akkadian tablets nos. 417–24 from Alalakh (Wiseman, 1953, pp. 108–9), e.g. no. 419: 'twenty tables, thirty-two chairs and thirty-five footstools, for the house of Iriḫalpa'.

The construction and decoration of this furniture have fortunately been listed in detail by the Pylos scribe, offering a fascinating sidelight on what we already know of Mycenaean craftsmanship and of its favourite design motifs. Compare especially Furumark's analysis in *Mycenaean Pottery* (*MP*), the ivory ornaments found at Mycenae in 1952–4 (Wace, 1954, where their function as furniture decoration is stressed), and those from Delos (de Santerre & Tréheux, 1948, with full references to previous Mycenaean ivories). Note also the ivory fragments found in Pylos Rooms 53 and 54 in 1954, 'evidently fallen from a lady's apartment above' (Blegen, 1955, p. 34). The specification makes great use of adjectives in -ϝεσσα and -ειος to specify the component details, and applies to the furniture two recurrent passive participles in -μένος. The first of these, *a-ja-me-no*, is known from the specification of Knossos chariots 200 years earlier (e.g. **266** = Sd0401): it apparently describes the *inlay* or *veneering* of wood with more costly materials, especially ivory. The second, *qe-qi-no-me-no* or *qe-qi-no-to*, probably refers to the *turning* or *carving* of particular designs.

The *Ta*- tablets appear to list the furnishings of a luxurious reception room (furniture, vessels and arrangements for heating), and their context and vocabulary find a significant echo in *Od.* xix, 53–62:

‘Η δ’ ἴεν ἐκ θαλάμοιο περίφρων Πηνελόπεια.
τῇ παρὰ μὲν κλισίην πυρὶ κάτθεσαν, ἔνθ’ ἄρ’ ἐφῖζε,
δινωτὴν ἐλέφαντι καὶ ἀργύρῳ (ἥν ποτε τέκτων
ποίησ’ Ἰκμάλιος) καὶ ὑπὸ θρῆνυν ποσὶν ἧκε
προσφυέ’ ἐξ αὐτῆς, ὅθ’ ἐπὶ μέγα βάλλετο κῶας.
ἦλθον δὲ δμωαὶ λευκώλενοι ἐκ μεγάροιο.
αἱ δ’ ἀπὸ μὲν σῖτον πολὺν ἥρεον ἠδὲ τραπέζας
καὶ δέπα’, ἔνθεν ἄρ’ ἄνδρες ὑπερμενέοντες ἔπινον.

The *Ta*- tablets are also valuable in providing the longest extant Mycenaean sentences (**244** = Ta714 has twenty-three consecutive words), and in throwing new light on the formation of the feminine dual (see **241** = Ta715) and of the instrumental case in the plural. The latter regularly shows *-phi* as the ending of consonant stems and of feminine *-ā-* stems; but masculine and neuter *-o-* stems merely end in *-o* in the instrumental plural, probably to be interpreted as *-ois* (see p. 85). This is clearly demonstrated in **246** = Ta722.2–3:

elephanteiois karāa'phi lewonteiois 'with ivory lions' heads',
elephanteiāphi karuphi 'with ivory nuts (?)'.

In the Mycenaean consonant declensions the ending *-phi* is added directly to the stem, as in ὄχεσφι and ὄρεσφι (Hom. κοτυληδόνοφι is evidently an innovation). The resulting consonant groups are reduced by assimilation, already seen in the form *qe-to-ro-po-pi* of **31** = Ae04 (cf. Hom. κὰπ φάλαρα, κάββαλε, κάππεσε):

po-pi = **podphi* (cf. Vedic *padbhis*) > *popphi*,
re-wo-pi = **lewontphi* > *lewomphi*,
but *po-ni-ki-pi* = *phoinik-phi* (a loan-word?).

The instrumental singular is already identical with the dative-locative in all declensions.

235 = Ta711   †

1 *o-wi-de   pu₂?-ke-qi-ri   o-te   wa-na-ka   te-ke   *85-ke-wa   da-mo-ko-ro*
2 *qe-ra-na   wa-na-se-wi-ja   qo-u-ka-ra   ko-ki-re-ja*   EWER 1
   qe-ra-na   a-mo-te-wi-ja   ko-ro-no-we-sa   (no ideogram)
3 *qe-ra-na   wa-na-se-wi-ja   ku-na-ja   qo-u-ka-ra   to-qi-de-we-sa*   EWER 1

Thus P. (fem.?) made inspection, on the occasion when the king appointed
Sigewas (?) to be a *dāmokoros*:

One ewer of the queen's *set*, bull's head design, decorated with *sea-shells*;
one ewer of the *harmost's set*, with a *curved handle*.

One ewer of the queen's *set*, a woman's *gift*, bull's head design, decorated
with a *running spiral*.

hō wide P. hote wanax thēke S. dāmokoron: this sentence may be intended to serve as
introduction to the whole *Ta-* series. The aorist *wide* also introduces **154** = Eq01:
hō wide Axotās; it possibly refers to the checking of the transaction by the responsible
official. For *thēke* 'appointed' cf. *Il.* vi, 300: τὴν γὰρ Τρῶες ἔθηκαν Ἀθηναίης ἱέρειαν.
*85-ke-wa is named on **258** = Kn01.21 as an official of places contributing gold; the
title *da-mo-ko-ro* (synonymous with *ko-re-te* and *basileus*?) also occurs on On01 and
KN L 642, X 7922. An analogous introductory phrase is seen on some of the tablets
from Alalakh, e.g. no. 355: *4 ana ᵐTaguzi, inuma šarru ana ᵃˡAbena ašbu* 'four (birds) to
Taguzi, when the king went to stay in Abena'. Cf. also nos. 376, 378, 409, 411 and
414.

qe-ra-na 'ewer': see p. 327.

wa-na-se-wi-ja: apparently an adjective from ἄνασσα formed under the influence of
βασιλήϊος, etc. (cf. Hom. ξεινήϊα, Ionic γυναικήϊα). Alternatively 'as a gift to the
queen'?

qo-u-ka-ra: probably *gᵘou-kara* rather than *-gala*. Full-face heads of cattle (*MP*, motif
no. 4, 'Bucranium') occur on the silver cup from Dendra, and on the 'Vaphio' cup
illustrated on the Egyptian tomb of Senmut (*PM*, ii, p. 737).

ko-ki-re-ja = *konkhileiā*? A descriptive adjective also applied to tables (**240** = Ta713):
cf. κοκάλια, κογχύλη, κογγύλιος, κοχλίας, etc. Compare *MP*, motif no. 23, 'Whorl-
shell', of which ivory examples have been found at Mycenae (Wace, 1954, p. 150)
together with cockle shells. Note that the bronze ewer of identical shape from the
Knossos 'Chieftain's Grave' (*PM*, iv, p. 860, fig. 843) has cockle shells in metal
attached to the two extremities of the handle.

a-mo-te-wi-ja: derived from the title *a-mo-te-wo* (gen. sing.) seen on PY Ea25.

ko-ro-no-we-sa: from κορώνη 'sea-bird' *Od.* v, 66 (cf. *MP*, motif no. 7, and Evans, *PM*, iv,
pp. 329–39). Or from κορώνη 'curved handle', *Od.* i, 441: θύρην δ' ἐπέρυσσε
κορώνῃ ἀργυρέῃ (and see p. 327).

ku-na-ja: apparently *gunaiā*, in Homer only in the phrase (ὄλετο) γυναίων εἵνεκα δώρων.

to-qi-de-we-sa = *torqᵘidwessa*? Cf. *to-qi-de-ja* (**237** = Ta709), *a-ja-me-no   to-qi-de* (**245** =
Ta721). This seems to be an ornamental feature rather than a physical appendage,

335

and does not occur in the plural. Connected with *torqueō* and with εὐτρόσσεσθαι·
ἐπιστρέφεσθαι (Hesych.) in the sense of 'running spiral' ornament (*MP*, motif no. 46);
and more distantly with τρόπις, gen. τρόπιος or τρόπιδος, 'ship's keel'? The
'running spiral' is frequent on all classes of LM and Mycenaean objects, together
with the other band patterns 'half-rosettes and triglyph', 'rosettes', 'ivy leaves' and
'triglyph band' (de Santerre: '*baguette à ligatures*'). Ivory specimens of all five of these,
from Mycenaean furniture, have been found at Mycenae and Delos. There are in
all five examples of feminine adjectives in *-wessa* on the *Ta-* series (for the decorative
sense, compare Hom. λέβης ἀνθεμόεις, etc.). The suffix is added directly to the word-
stem, as in Indo-Iranian and Hittite (see Buck and Petersen, *Reverse Index*, p. 460);
the classical ἀσπιδόεις, etc. are innovations.

† **236 = Ta641**　(see plate III (*b*), facing p. 111)

1 *ti-ri-po-de* | *ai-ke-u* *ke-re-si-jo* *we-ke* 🜚 2

　ti-ri-po *e-me* *po-de* *o-wo-we* 🜚 1

　ti-ri-po *ke-re-si-jo* *we-ke* *a-pu* *ke* | *ka-u-me-ṇọ*

　　'*ke-re-a₂* *ṇọ-* [*pe-re* ?' TRIPOD 1]

2 *qe-to* WINE-JAR? 3 *di-pa* *me-zo-* {*e*} *qe-to-ro-we* 🜚 1

　di-pa-e *me-zo-e* *ti-ri-o-we-e* 🜚 2

　di-pa *me-wi-jo* *qe-to-ro-we* 🜚 1

3 *di-pa* *me-wi-jo* *ti-ri-jo-we* 🜚 1

　di-pa *me-wi-jo* *a-no-we* 🜚 1

Two tripod cauldrons of Cretan workmanship, of *ai-ke-u* type;
one tripod cauldron with a *single* handle *on* one foot;
one tripod cauldron of Cretan workmanship, burnt away at the legs, *useless*.
Three *wine-jars*; one larger-sized *goblet* with four handles; two larger-sized
　goblets with three handles; one smaller-sized *goblet* with four handles; one
　smaller-sized *goblet* with three handles; one smaller-sized *goblet* without a
　handle.

ke-re-si-jo *we-ke*: the first translation 'Aigeus the Cretan brings them' (Ventris, 1954*a*,
　p. 18) is certainly wrong: 'Cretan' should be Κρής, the omission of Aigeus in the
　third clause would be anomalous, and a verbal phrase (*we-ke* = *wekhei*, cf. Pamph.
　ϝεχέτω?) is unparalleled in the rest of the series. Palmer plausibly reads *krēsio-wergēs*
　'of Cretan style or workmanship', cf. φιάλαι Λυκιουργεῖς Demosth. XLIX, 31, κρατῆρες
　Κορινθιουργεῖς Callix., etc. We should, however, expect the dual *-we-ke-e* in the first
　clause (or are the second numeral and the smaller word *ti-ri-po-de* added as an
　afterthought?). Is *ai-ke-u* (spelt *ai₂*?-*ke-u* on **237** = Ta709.3) an adjective describing
　the tripod, or the name of a man inserted in parenthesis? Webster suggests that the
　ideogram represents a handle in the form of a goat's head: compare Schliemann's
　Warrior Vase from Mycenae (Thomas, 1939, p. 70), where a double handle is formed

at each side by the recurving horns of a cow (?) in relief. No such double handle is shown, however, on **237** = Ta709.3.

e-me po-de o-wo-we: the alternation *e-me-de* / *du-wo-u-pi-de* on Eb37 / Eb40 (see p. 254), etc. shows that *e-me* is the dative of 'one' (**semi* > *hemi* > ἑνί); and the form *oiw-ōwes* 'with one handle' is suggested by the similar compounds on the rest of the tablet. The Mycenaean three legged 'incense-burners' (*MP*, fig. 21, nos. 315–16) show an analogous handle arrangement, evidently only suitable for a fairly small vessel. Such a design does not, however, agree with the ideogram as drawn.

ke-re-a$_2$ = *skelea*: in the accusative of respect, cf. τὸ σκέλος πεπηρωμένος Demosth. xviii, 67, τοὺς ὀφθαλμοὺς διεφθαρμένοι Xen. *An.* iv, 5, 12 (Schwyzer, *Gram.* ii, p. 85). Less probably χεῖλεα 'on the rim', cf. *Od.* iv, 616. The final *ṇǫ*-[may perhaps be completed as *nōphelēs*, cf. **288** = Sa790 (p. 374).

qe-to: see p. 327, no. 203.

di-pa me-wi-jo a-no-we = *dipas mewjon anōwes*: for the vessel type, see p. 326, no. 202. The formation -*ōwes* (from **-ōuses* '-eared, -handled') is only paralleled once in classical Greek, in Theocritus' κισσύβιον ἀμφῶες 'two-handled cup' (i, 28). The more usual -ουατος (**-ousṇtos*) > -ωτος is attested for Mycenaean by the *di-pa a-no-wo-to* which on KN **232** = K 875 accompanies the same ideogram.

237 = Ta709 (+712)   †

¹ *pi-je-ra$_3$*   *to-qi-de-ja*   ⟨ideogram⟩ 3   *pa-ko-to*[*c.* 10 lost

                                        ]-*ke-te-ri-ja*   ⟨ideogram⟩ 1   *ko-te-ri-ja* 6

² **85-te* 1   *pu-ra-u-to-ro* 2   *pa$_2$-ra-to-ro* 1   *e-*[˙ *c.* 10 lost

                        ]-*ra*   *i-to-we-sa*   *pe-de-we-sa*   *so-we-ne-ja*   **85-de-we-sa-qe* 1

³ *ti-ri-po*   *ke-re-si-jo*   *we-ke*   *ai$_2$?-ke-u*   TRIPOD [1   *c.* 10 lost

                                                            ]-*u*   TRIPOD 1

Three boiling pans with *running spiral* decoration, *x* fixtures, . . ., one *lamp*, six *hammers*;

one *brush*, two fire-tongs, one fire-rake, . . ., one [   ] with an *upright* and *socket*, decorated with *grooves* and *pomegranates*;

one tripod cauldron of Cretan workmanship, of *ai-ke-u* type; one tripod cauldron. . ..

pi-je-ra$_3$ = *phielai*: see p. 325, no. 200.

pa-ko-to[   ]: connected with classical πηκτός, etc.?

]-*ke-te-ri-ja*: a feminine noun similar in structure to βακτηρία. The ideogram appears to represent a lamp (cf. fig. 18, objects *e, f* and *o*): *luktēriā*, cf. λύχνος? Perhaps to be completed as *pa-ke-te-ri-ja*, as on the sealing MY Wt506.

ko-te-ri-ja (plur.): not καυτήριον 'branding-iron' but a word of similar structure. Possibly *kortērion*, cf. κορτέω/κροτέω, κρότημα?

*85-te = *sistēr*? From σίζω 'hiss when put on the fire'? Or from σείω 'shake' (for the vowel, cf. Skt. *tviṣati*)? Palmer: *sartēr* 'brush'?

pu-ra-u-to-ro = *puraustrō*, either dual of the feminine form πύραυστρα IG, 2². 47. 18, or a neuter cf. πύραστρον Herodas, IV, 62 (perhaps a mis-spelling).

pa₂-ra-to-ro: Palmer proposes σπάλαθρον (Pollux) = σκάλευθρον.

histo-wessa ped-wessa? Cf. Hom. ἱστοπέδη 'fixing for the foot of the mast'? Does -*ra* (fem.) conceal another *phiela*?

so-we-ne-ja, adjective from *so-we-no* (**245** = Ta721, etc.). Hardly ξόανον (*qso^un^nom). Connected with σωλήν, σωλῆνος 'gutter, groove, pipe, shellfish'? A kind of decorative band?

*85-de-we-sa-qe: adjective from **85-de-pi* (instr. plur., **245** = Ta721). Chadwick compares σίδη 'pomegranate' (also 'water-lily'). The form of the stem ending is obscure: -*dewessa*/-*desphi*?

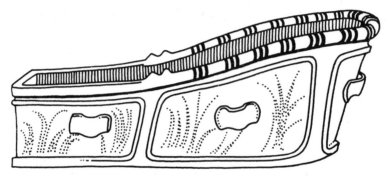

Fig. 22. MM IIIb (or LM Ia?) bathtub from the S.E. Bathroom, Knossos.

† **238** = Tn996

1 [.]-*ko̞ a-te-re-e-te-jo re-wo-te-re-jo* ⟨symbol⟩ 3
2 *u-do-ro* ⟨symbol⟩ 3 *pi-a₂-ra* ⟨symbol⟩ 3
3 [*a-po*]-*re̞-we* ⟨symbol⟩ 2 *ka-ti* ⟨symbol⟩ 1 *a-te-we* BRONZE ⟨symbol⟩ 7 *re̞*-[
4 [...] ⟨symbol⟩ 3 / *po-ka-ta-ma* GOLD ⟨symbol⟩ 1 BRONZE ⟨symbol⟩ 3 [

Three? *drainable* tubs for bath-water, three *water jars*, three boiling pans, two amphoras, one hydria, seven bronze *jugs*, ..., three ....

Additional property: one gold bowl, three bronze pedestalled bowls. ...

re-wo-te-re-jo = *lewotreioi* is evidently derived from the same noun as the female occupation *lewotrokhowoi* 'bath-pourers' on **9** = Ab27. These are distinguished from Hom. λοετροχόος by the unexpected vowel metathesis (or lack of metathesis, see p. 160). The first word, in which one would expect a generic word for 'tub', may perhaps be restored as *dokhoi* (cf. Hesychius δοχός· λουτήρ). The adjective *a-te-re-e-te-jo* is probably not identical with *a-te-re-te-a* on KN **278** = So894; perhaps connected with ἄντλος 'bilge(-water)', ἀντλίον 'baler', ἀντλέω 'bale out'. The ending -*e-e-te-jo* may be equivalent to the classical -ητικός (ἀντλητικός 'suitable for irrigation', only 3 A.D.); but the double vowel is anomalous, even coming from a 'contracted' verb. Possibly 'which has to be baled out', referring to the fact that true Minoan-

Mycenaean baths generally have no outlet hole, unlike the *larnakes* which were widely used (in Crete) for burial. These *larnakes* share with our bath the handles at sides and ends, but are flat on top to allow the fitting of a lid. Only one of the few extant baths shows, to a much lesser degree, the higher back end of the Pylos ideogram: that found in the S.E. Bathroom at Knossos (*PM*, III, p. 386, fig. 257). The 'rowlocks' on the side are possibly designed to take the carrying pole of a hot-water vessel with high-swung handles like those of our *phielai*. The line at upper left on the ideogram may suggest the profile of a metal tub. Blegen (1955, p. 33) suggests that Room 61 at Pylos may have been a bathroom. In 1955 he uncovered an apartment containing an elaborately built-in bath, in which a drinking-cup was lying.

po-ka-ta-ma, in smaller letters, does not seem to be the name of a vessel type, but a general description of the more precious vessels which close the list: *pos-ktāma* from the ancestor of προσκτάομαι (but note *posi-* in composition at Knossos, 271 = Sd0422)? But *κτᾶμα is an unattested form, Doric and Arcadian using πᾶμα instead.

239 = Ta642

†

¹ *to-pe-za   ra-e-ja   we-a-re-ja   a-ja-me-na   a₂-ro-u-do-pi   ku-wa-no-qe*
              pa-ra-ke-we-[qe   ku-ru-so-qe]   e-ne-wo   pe-[za]

² *to-pe-za   ra-e-ja   me-no-e-ja   e-re-pa-te   a-ja-me-na   qe-qi-no-to   *85-de-pi*
                                                                          ko-ru-pi-qe

³ *to-pe-za   ra-e-ja   a-pi-qo-to   'e-ne-wo   pe-za'   e-re-pa-te-jo   po-pi*
                                        e-ka-ma-te-qe   qe-qi-no-to-qe   to-qi-de

One *stone* table, of *spring* type, inlaid with '*aquamarines*' and *kyanos* and *silver* and *gold*, a nine-*footer*.

One *crescent*-shaped *stone* table, inlaid with ivory carved in the form of *pomegranates* and helmets.

One *stone* table of *encircled* type, a nine-*footer*, with feet and *strutting* of ivory and a carved *running spiral*.

to-pe-za appears to represent a pronunciation *torpeza*, an 'Achaean' evolution of *(q^u)tr-pedja* (though Boeotian has τρίπεζα, τρέπεδδα, and early tables more often had three legs in order to stand steady on uneven floors).

ra-e-ja: Mycenaean *-eios/-eos/-ios* occurs in place of classical *-ινος* in all adjectives of material, but the equivalent of λάϊνος should properly be written **ra-we-ja* if the etymology *λᾶϝας is correct. If these tables really are 'of stone', one might expect this only to apply to areas of inlay on the top, as in the case of the 'ivory table' of 240 = Ta713.2. But compare Blegen's 1954 find (1955, p. 34): 'Dispersed here and there in the hollow (in front of the Propylon) were many fragments of a large circular disk, perhaps a table top, made of variegated marble. The table had a diameter of nearly 0·50 m. and was probably supported on three legs. The disk had a carved design along its edges, and its upper surface bore a simple, inlaid decoration composed of small circular insets of red stone, arranged in groups of one, two and three.'

we-a-re-ja (cf. *we-a₂-re-jo* on **244** = Ta714) in form exactly parallels ἐαρινός (**wesṛ-*), but the meaning is obscure. Otherwise possibly a form of ὑάλειος 'with crystal inlay', cf. the Knossos gaming-board (*PM*, i, pp. 471 ff., also *PM*, iv, pp. 928 ff.).

a-ja-me-na: 'inlaid', 'veneered' or 'pegged', typically of ivory on wood, and already familiar from the Knossos chariot tablets, where the form *a-na-i-t-* probably means 'not inlaid', and suggests a reduplicated form *aiai(s)menā*. No plausible etymology.

a₂-ro-u-do-pi: it is uncertain whether the word divides after *-ro*. Initial *a₂-* is uncommon, but represents *ha-* in *a₂-te-ro*: conceivably *halos hudo'phi* 'with waters of the sea', figurative name for some substance (cf. *aquamarine, Meerschaum*)? Compare Ἁλο-σύδνη, epithet of Thetis *Il.* xx, 207.

ku-wa-no-qe (cf. *ku-wa-ni-jo-qe* **244** = Ta714) = Hom. κύανος, κυάνεος. Wace has suggested that *kyanos* represents niello, the blue-black metallic amalgam whose decorative use is exemplified in the contemporary Enkomi bowl (Schaeffer, 1952, pp. 379 ff.) and on the dagger blades and silver cups from Mycenae, but this involves certain difficulties. Niello is applied in powdered form into incised patterns cut in silver or gold, fused under heat, and then scraped and polished level with the metal surface. One might imagine silver or gold ornaments, previously decorated with niello, being applied to furniture complete; but **244** = Ta714 describes a chair, presumably of wood, inlaid 'with gold phoenixes and with phoenixes of kyanos', which suggests that the material is capable of forming a decorative element on its own. The classical word κύανος is applied both to lapis-lazuli and to its synthetic imitation; and such blue glass is known both from contemporary Egyptian furnishings and from the frieze to the Great Megaron at Tiryns (cf. περὶ δὲ θριγκὸς κυάνοιο *Od.* vii, 87). A substance more like niello might admittedly be more plausible for the οἶμοι μέλανος κυάνοιο on Agamemnon's breastplate (*Il.* xi, 24); but compare Alalakh tablet no. 427: '18 lapis-lazuli stones, 2 shekels of pure silver and 1 shekel of gold, given to the man Takuḫli for making a quiver'.

pa-ra-ke-we (elsewhere *pa-ra-ku-we*) might suggest the dat. sing. of βραχύς 'short' (name of an unidentified alloy?), but cf. Aeol. βρόχυς. Mühlestein suggests **φαλ-αργυς* or **παρ-αργυς*, compounded with an archaic form of the word for 'silver'. Or from the Akkadian *barrāqtu*, Hebrew *bāreqet* 'emerald' (from which the class. σμάραγδος was later re-borrowed *via* India)?

e-ne-wo pe-za = *ennewo-peza* (**en-newṇ* 'nine', cf. Arc. δέκο 'ten', Lesb. ἔνοτος 'ninth'). If we translate τράπεζαν κυανόπεζαν *Il.* xi, 629, 'with *feet* of kyanos', we should consistently read 'with nine feet' here, which seems an impossible design. Note the apparently three-legged table-top found by Blegen: do our 'nine-*peza*' and 'six-*peza*' (**240** = Ta713) tables have three main supports, but triple and double extremities of some kind? Chadwick translates 'nine feet long' (cf. διπόδης, τρίπεδος, ἑκατόμ-πεδος); or 'with nine fields or panels', or 'nine-sided' (cf. τετράπεδος 'square'), or 'with nine-fold border' (cf. πέζα, πεζίς 'border', and cf. the κύκλοι δέκα χάλκεοι of Agamemnon's shield, *Il.* xi, 33)? Wace takes τράπεζαν κυανόπεζαν to mean 'with a border of niello' rather than 'with blue glass feet', which is admittedly improbable if taken quite literally.

me-no-e-ja: cf. μηνοειδής 'semi-circular', Herodotus, I, 75? Not 'Minoan'!

qe-qi-no-to in line 2 is probably to be taken with *e-re-pa-te* ('inlaid with carved ivory') in contrast to the perfect *qe-qi-no-me-na* which is applied to the tables and chair-backs themselves; and similarly to be taken with *to-qi-de* in line 3, which the adjectival concord does not necessarily prove to be masculine, since *-tos* may here do duty for feminine as well (cf. *Od.* v, 422 κλυτὸς Ἀμφιτρίτη, and Schwyzer, *Gram.* I, p. 502). *Qe-qi-no-to* appears to represent the Homeric δινωτός, but its etymology and reduplication are hard to explain. δινωτός clearly does not mean merely 'turned on a lathe': it may perhaps originally have referred to lapidary work executed with a drill.

ko-ru-pi-qe: assimilated from **koruthphi*, cf. gen. sing. *ko-ru-to* on **293** = Sh737. Compare the ivory helmets found in the Mycenae houses.

a-pi-qo-to = *amphig^uotos*, (passive) verbal adj. from Hom. ἀμφιβαίνω 'surround, embrace'. It may refer to a broad edging round the top. Mühlestein suggests 'which can be walked round', i.e. 'free-standing' (cf. ἐπίβατος 'climbable', ἔμβατος 'accessible'). In a compound the feminine *-tos* is of course to be expected. Palmer: 'with splayed legs'.

popphi ekhmatei q^ue: the use of the dative-instrumental without verb or preposition for comitative 'with' is foreign to classical Greek. Homeric ἔχμα is used of a river-bank (*Il.* XIII, 139), of buttresses to a fortification (XII, 260), of stones used to prop ships (XIV, 410).

240 = Ta713   †

¹ *to-pe-za   ra-e-ja   ku-te-se-jo   e-ka-ma-pi   e-re-pa-te-jo-qe   a-pi-qo-to*
                                                e-ne-wo-pe-za   qe-qi-no-me-na   to-qi-de

² *to-pe-za   e-re-pa-te-ja   po-ro-e-ke   pi-ti-ro₂-we-sa   we-pe-za   qe-qi-no-me-na*
                                                                                    to-qi-de

³ *to-pe-za   ku-te-se-ja   e-re-pa-te-jo   e-ka-ma-pi   a-pi-qo-to   e-ne-wo-pe-za*
                                                                                    ko-ki-re-ja

One *stone* table with *strutting* of *ebony* and ivory, of *encircled* type, a nine-*footer*, carved with a *running spiral*.

One ivory table of *projecting* type, decorated with a feather pattern, a six-*footer*, carved with a *running spiral*.

One *ebony* table with ivory *strutting*, of *encircled* type, a nine-*footer*, decorated with *sea-shells*.

ku-te-se-jo = *kuteseiois* (instr. plur.) 'made of *ku-te-so*' (**242** = Ta707.3); cf. κύτισος 'bastard ebony', Theophr. *HP*, I, 6, I, v, 3, I.

po-ro-e-ke = *proekhēs*, cf. Hom. προέχω 'project', Plut. προεχής 'three-dimensional', apparently in antithesis to *amphig^uotos*. Mühlestein suggests a table set against a wall.

pi-ti-ro₂-we-sa = *ptilowessa*, from πτίλον 'soft plumage; insect's wing'; presumably a decorative feature and not πτιλωτός 'stuffed with feathers'. It should perhaps be noted that Tutankhamen's tomb contained batons inlaid with beetles' wing-cases (Carter, 1927, II, p. 35). Beazley compares φιάλαι πτιλωτοί, *IG* 2². 1443. 135.

we-pe-za = < **hwek-peza*, cf. inscr. ἔκπους, ἔκπεδος = ἐξάπους. The assimilation **kp > pp* has no exact classical parallels; cf. Lat. **sexuiri > seuiri*.

241 = Ta715

¹ *to-pe-za   ku-te-se-ja   e-re-[pa]-te-jo   e-ka-ma-pi   a-pi-qo-to   e-ne-wo   pe-za*
                                                                    ko-ki-re-ja

² *to-pe-za   a-ka-ra-no   e-re-pa-te-ja   a-pi-qo-to*   I
                      to-pe-za   a-ka-ra-no   e-re-pa-te-ja   po-ro-e-ke   I

³ *to-pe-zo   mi-ra₂   a-pi-qo-to   pu-ko-so   e-ke-e   e-ne-wo   pe-zo   to-qi-de-jo*
                                                    a-ja-me-no   pa-ra-ku-we   2

One *ebony* table with ivory *strutting*, of *encircled* type, a nine-*footer*, decorated with *sea-shells*;

one 'headless' ivory table of *encircled* type;

one 'headless' ivory table of *projecting* type;

two tables of *yew*, of *encircled* type, *containing* box-wood, nine-*footers*, decorated with *running spirals*, inlaid with *silver*.

† *a-ka-ra-no* = ἀκάρηνος? The ending -*o* betrays a compound. It is perhaps significant that these two entries, together with that of the *me-no-e-ja* table on **239** = Ta642.2, alone omit a -*peza* qualification.

mi-ra₂ cannot be an adjective agreeing with *torpezō*; perhaps the name of a timber in the genitive, like *ptelewās, helikās* on the Knossos wheel tablets. Cf. (σ)μῖλαξ, (σ)μῖλος; possibly for μελίη 'ash', though Schulz postulated **μελϝία*.

pu-ko-so e-ke-e: probably not the infinitive *ekheen* 'to have' (cf. **140** = Eb35), but the dual of an adjective in -ής, originally restricted to compounds: *puxo-ekhēs*? Not *puxo-enkhēs*? Cf. also Nuzi tablet SMN 1422 (Lacheman, 1939, p. 536): '1 table of boxwood with its feet inlaid with silver, etc.'.

The endings in line 3 are clear evidence for a feminine dual in -*ō*, which we had already suspected from **135** = Ep704.7, **266** = Sd0401 and L 758. This Mycenaean form evidently dates from the time when the original *IE* **-ai* had already become ineffective due to the change of the feminine plural from **-ās* to -αι, but when -*ā* had not yet been introduced on the analogy of the masculine -οι/-ω. The analogy of δύω and ἄμφω (both masc. and fem.) must have played an important part in the history of the Mycenaean form.

‡ 242 = Ta707

¹ *to-no   'ku-te-ta-jo'   (sic)   ku-ru-sa-pi   o-pi-ke-re-mi-ni-ja-pi   o-ni-ti-ja-pi*
                                    ta-ra-nu-qe   a-ja-me-no   e-re-pa-te-jo   *85-de-pi

² *to-no   ku-te-se-jo   e-re-pa-te-ja-pi   o-pi-ke-re-mi-ni-ja-pi   se-re-mo-ka-ra-o-i̯*
                                          qe-qi-no-me-na   a-di-ri-ja-te-qe   po-ti-pi-qe

³ *ta-ra-nu   ku-te-so   a-ja-me-no   e-re-pa-te-jo   *85-de-pi*

One *ebony* chair with golden *back* decorated with birds; and a footstool inlaid with ivory *pomegranates*.

One *ebony* chair with ivory *back* carved with a pair of *finials* and with a man's figure and heifers; one footstool, *ebony* inlaid with ivory *pomegranates*.

to-no is probably for *thornos*, cf. Cypr. θόρναξ· ὑποπόδιον Hesych. A spelling *to-no* = *thro-nos* would do violence to the spelling rules (but cf. *to-ro-no-wo-ko* = *throno-worgos*? on **39** = As1517). The similarity of the furniture found in the tomb of Tutankhamen extends to the phraseology of Carter's captions, e.g.:

Pl. LIX (vol. I): 'A small chair carved of ebony and inlaid with ivory; it has antelope and floral devices of embossed gold on the panels of the arms'.

Pl. LXII: 'A magnificent chair of wood overlaid with sheet gold and richly adorned with polychrome faience, glass and stone inlay'.

Pl. LXXIVb: 'An ebony stool richly inlaid with ivory and embellished with heavy gold mountings'.

Compare also the furniture listed by Thothmes III among the loot from Megiddo (Breasted, II, p. 436): '6 chairs of the enemy, of ivory, ebony and carob wood, wrought with gold; 6 footstools belonging to them; 6 large tables of ivory and carob wood'.

Also such tablets from Nuzi as SMN 1250 (Lacheman, 1939, p. 537): '1 chair of wood, 1 box (*quppu*) inlaid with gold; 1 chair inlaid with ivory and silver, with its box'.

ku-ru-sa-pi: instr. plur. fem. At this date χρυσός, like the Hebrew and Ugaritic ḫaruṣ from which it is borrowed, means indifferently 'gold' (n.) or 'golden' (adj.). The Mycenaean form of the adjective may possibly be reflected in the numerous Homeric passages where the χρύσεος of the text must be scanned as a disyllable, e.g. *Il.* I, 15 χρυσέῳ ἀνὰ σκήπτρῳ, etc.

o-pi-ke-re-mi-ni-ja-pi, instr. plur. fem.: cf. Hesych. ἀμφικελεμνίς 'hanging evenly on both shoulders', ἀμφικέλεμνον = ἀμφιβαρές, or 'chair carried by two men'. The root meaning of **kelemn*- is hard to deduce: 'shoulder'? 'carrying-yoke'? Or 'carrying-pole' to a palanquin rather than a normal chair? An alternative suggestion is *opikrēmniāphi* from κρημνός 'an overhanging lip': in either case the meaning would appear to refer to the edges of the back or arms, which the Tutankhamen parallels suggest as the most favoured place for decorative treatment.

se-re-mo-ka-ra-o-i is probably a compound of κάρα 'head'. The form *-ka-ra-a-pi* (**243** = Ta708) is instr. plur., presumably for *-k(a)rāa'phi*, cf. Hom. gen. sing. καρήατος, κράατος. The variant on this tablet is perhaps a dual in *-oiin*. Cf. [*qo*]-*u-ka-ra-o-i* on **244** = Ta714. *Se-re-mo-* from σέλμα 'plank, deck, bench, seat' (cf. O.H.G. *swelli* 'beam')? If the 'half-rosettes and triglyph' motif is derived from the architectural pattern of a row of decorated beam-ends, could that be the meaning of this term? Otherwise a projection of the uprights of the back (for the form cf. κιό-κρανον 'capital')?

qe-qi-no-me-na in line 2 evidently agrees in sense with *opikelemniāphi* (similarly on

243 = Ta708.2), but the ending *-phi* has been suppressed from the participle in order to make clearer the relation to its own subordinate instrumentals.

andriantei q^{u}e portiphi q^{u}e: πόρτις 'heifer', *Il.* v, 162. Evidently not *taurokathapsia* but a bucolic scene like the bull-snaring on the Vaphio cups. Probably not φορτίς 'merchant-ship', *Od.* v, 250.

† **243 = Ta708**

¹ *to-no   ku-te-se-jo   a-ja-me-no   o-pi-ke-re-mi-ni-ja   e-re-pa-te*
² *to-no   ku-te-se-jo | e-re-pa-te-ja-pi   o-pi-ke-re-mi-ni-ja-pi   se-re-mo-ka-ra-a-pi*
                                    qe-qi-no-me-na   a-di-ri-ja-pi-qe
³ *ta-ra-nu   ku-te-se-jo   a-ja-me-no   e-re-pa-te-jo   a-di-ri-ja-pi   re-wo-pi-qe*

One *ebony* chair inlaid with ivory on the *back*.

One ebony chair with ivory *back* carved with *finials* and with figures of men; one *ebony* footstool inlaid with figures of men and lions in ivory.

o-pi-ke-re-mi-ni-ja (fem. acc. plur. *-ans*) in line 1 is in the accusative of respect, as on **244 = Ta714.1** and *skelea* on **236 = Ta641.1**, *q.v.*

andriamphi lewomphi q^{u}e: compare the lion-hunting scene on the inlaid dagger from Tomb IV at Mycenae (*PM*, III, fig. 70).

‡ **244 = Ta714**

¹ *to-no   we-a₂-re-jo   a-ja-me-no   ku-wa-no   pa-ra-ku-we-qe   ku-ru-so-qe*
                                    o-pi-ke-re-mi-ni-ja
² *a-ja-me-na   ku-ru-so   a-di-ri-ja-pi   se-re-mo-ka-ra-o-i-qe   ku-ru-so*
              ⟦ *.-u̯-ka-r̥a-o̯-i* ⟧ *ku-ru-so-qe   po-ni-ki-pi*
³ *ku-wa-ni-jo-qe   po-ni-ki-pi   ta-ra-nu   a-ja-me-no   ku-wa-no   pa-ra-ku-we-qe*
                    ku-ru-so-qe   ku-ru-sa-pi-qe   ko-no-ni-pi

One chair of *spring* type, inlaid with *kyanos* and *silver* and gold on the *back*, (which is) inlaid with men's figures in gold, and with a pair of gold *finials*, and with *golden griffins* and with *griffins* of *kyanos*.

One footstool inlaid with *kyanos* and *silver* and gold, and with golden *bars*.

The deleted word in line 2 can be restored as *qo-u-ka-ra-o-i* 'bulls' heads'; cf. **235 = Ta711**.

po-ni-ki-pi = phoinik-phi (masc.). It has been suggested that the name of the fabulous bird φοῖνιξ (Hesiod, Frg. 171.4) was first applied to the 'griffins' and sphinxes so prominent in Mycenaean art, particularly on the ivories from Mycenae, Delos and Enkomi (they are often confronted heraldically in pairs). The more directly-attested meaning φοῖνιξ = 'palm-tree' finds an equally good analogy in Motif no. 15 (*MP*, p. 278); but on **246 = Ta722** line 1 it is perhaps more natural to find living creatures as the subject of all four elements in the design.

ko-no-ni-pi: see **229 = K 434** (p. 329).

245 = Ta721

¹ *ta-ra-nu*   *a-ia-me-no*   *e-re-pa-te-jo*   **85-de-pi*   *to-qi-de-qe*

              ka-ru-we-qe FOOTSTOOL 1

² *ta-ra-nu-we*   *a-ia-me-no*   *e-re-pa-te-jo*   **85-de-pi*   *so-we-no-qe*

              to-qi-de-qe FOOTSTOOL 3

³, ⁴ *ta-ra-nu*   *a-ja-me-no*   *e-re-pa-te-jo*   **85-de-pi*   *so-we-no-qe* FOOTSTOOL 1

⁵ *ta-ra-nu*   *a-ja-me-no*   *e-re-pa-te-jo*   **85-de-pi*   FOOTSTOOL 1

One footstool inlaid with ivory *pomegranates* and *running spiral* and *nut*.

Three footstools inlaid with ivory *pomegranates* and *grooves* and *running spiral*.

One footstool inlaid with ivory *pomegranates* and *grooves* (twice).

One footstool inlaid with ivory *pomegranates*.

so-we-no-qe (cf. **237** = Ta709, *so-we-ne-ja*): owing to the ambiguity inherent in the spelling *-o*, a form such as this may be either instr. sing. (*-ōi*) or plur. (*-ois*). The same applies to the masculines *a-to-ro-qo* and *i-qo* on the next tablet.

ka-ru-we (instr. sing.): cf. *ka-ru-pi* (instr. plur.) on the next tablet. γῆρυς 'voice' fits spelling, declension and feminine gender, but is nonsensical. A form of κάρυον 'nut' (cf. σίκυς/σίκυος)? Cf. φιάλη καρυωτή 'cup adorned with a nut-shaped boss' *IG*, 11 (2). 161 *B* 30. Or for χέλυς (fem.) 'tortoise, lyre'?

246 = Ta722

¹ *ta-ra-nu*   *a-ja-me-no* | *e-re-pa-te-jo* | *a-to-ro-qo*   *i-qo-qe*   *po-ru-po-de-qe*

              po-ni-ke-qe FOOTSTOOL 1

² *ta-ra-nu*   *a-ja-me-no*   *e-re-pa-te-jo*   *ka-ra-a-pi*   *re-wo-te-jo*

              so-we-no-qe FOOTSTOOL 1

³ *ta-ra-nu*   *a-ja-me-no*   *e-re-pa-te-ja-pi*   *ka-ru-pi*   FOOTSTOOL 1

  ta-ra-nu   *a-ja-me-no*   *e-re-pa-te-ja-pi*   *ka-ru-pi*   FOOTSTOOL 1

One footstool inlaid with *a* man and *a* horse and an octopus and a *griffin* in ivory.

One footstool inlaid with ivory lions' heads and *grooves*.

One footstool inlaid with ivory *nuts* (twice).

Thrānus aiai(s)menos elephanteiois anthrōqᵘōi hiqqᵘōi qᵘe polupodei qᵘe phoinikei qᵘe: the spelling of 'man' lends support to Brugmann's derivation from **andr-hōqᵘos* (cf. Hesych. δρώψ). If 'man' and 'horse' are taken as singular, we may perhaps visualize the decoration as being distributed over four symmetrical panels, with one creature in each (like the rectangular 'Warrior' ivory from Delos, de Santerre, 1948, no. 1). Compare the four rectangular panels from the top of a box (?) found in the 'Tomb of the Tripod Hearth' at Zafer Papoura (Evans, 190, p. 44, fig. 40). If we read 'with men and horses', it is tempting to regard them as part of a single composition; cf. the 'Groom and horse' motif (*MP*, p. 449), and the 'Groom and horse' fresco from Tsountas' excavations (Wace, *Mycenae*, fig. 99*b*). The octopus (inaccurately labelled 'cuttlefish'—a quite distinct species—as motif no. 21, *MP*, p. 302) is of course extremely common in all fields of LM and Mycenaean decoration. Compare the floor-squares in the Pylos throne room and in the Great Megaron at Tiryns.

Elephanteiois karāa'phi lewonteiois: decoration with lions' heads is less common on Mycenaean objects than men's or bulls' heads, but compare the ivory pommel from Mycenae, Karo, *Schachtgräber*, Pl. LXXVII. λέων 'lion' is already a stem in -*nt*- in spite of **lewanja* > λέαινα. An ultimate Semitic origin was suggested by Curtius (cf. Canaanite-Ugaritic *labi'u*, fem. *labi'tu*); if so, it has somewhere picked up an extension -*nt*-, betraying possible Anatolian mediation, which is also to be seen in *elephant*- (cf. Hebrew *'elef*, Ugaritic and Akkadian *alpu* 'ox'?).

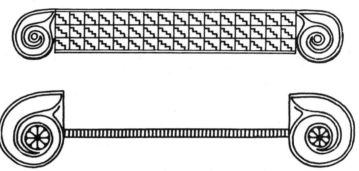

Fig. 23. Ivories from Mycenae and Dendra.

Stubbings has suggested to us that the two similar sets of ivory decoration with volute ends found *in situ* in Tomb 518 at Mycenae (Wace, 1932, p. 84, fig. 30) and in Tomb 8 at Dendra (Persson, 1952, Pl. II) may be from the fronts of footstools: both sets measure 36 cm. (14 in.) overall.

† **247** = Ta716

¹   *pa-sa-ro   ku-ru-so   a-pi   to-ni-jo* 2   *wa-o* ⟶ ⚔ 2
²   *qi-si-pe-e*   X 2

Two *swords* (two gold studs on either side of the *hilt*; two . . .-s).

The ideogram in the second line unfortunately coincides with a crack in the clay, but it appears to be the representation of a sword or dagger rather than the symbol ZE indicating a pair, since the row of small strokes normally found to the right of that sign is missing. Swords are unlikely to be counted in pairs, and 'two pairs' would lead us to expect a plural *qi-si-pe-a₂* (but see p. 370 below for inconsistencies in such uses of the dual).

    Owing to its smaller writing the top line is probably a specification of *parts* of these swords rather than a list of separate objects. The Homeric πάσσαλος is only used of a 'peg' to hang things on, but the derivation from πήγνυμι and the Attic πατταλεύω 'fasten with pegs or rivets' show the basic constructional sense. It is normally only the heads of the rivets on the hilt of Late Minoan and Mycenaean swords and daggers which are covered with gold; and it is not clear whether the two bosses of a single rivet, or the heads of two separate sets of rivets, are here referred to; nor is the position indicated by the word *to-ni-jo* clear. τόρμος, τορμίον 'peg, tenon, socket for peg' or στόμιον 'aperture, bit' can hardly be reconciled with the spelling. A single word *amphitornios*, cf. Eur. ἀμφίτορνος 'well-rounded'? The typical construction of the hilt of a LM II sword is shown in fig. 24 (cf. Hood, 1952, p. 273; Evans, *PM*, IV, pp. 845–67): variations in outline between the 'cruciform' and 'horned' varieties, etc. are here disregarded. The 'hilt-plate', shown as *A*, is fixed by two rivets and frequently supplied as a separate piece from the covering of the hand-grip *B* and

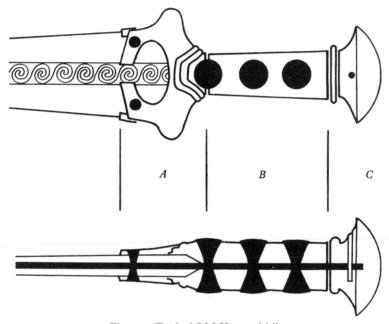

Fig. 24. Typical LM II sword hilt.

pommel *C*; it may be not only of gold plating but also of crystal, faience and ivory, and presumably also of cheaper materials. The number of rivets to *B* is almost always three.

The word *wa-o* and its ideogram are puzzling. ἄορ 'sword' is excluded by its etymology (*awor or **n̥sor*?) and by the lack of a dual ending. The ideogram is probably not a double axe (improbable in the context, and small votive double axes are not of this rectangular shape) but possibly a rivet seen in sectional view; an anomalous spelling of *wālō* or *wallō* = ἥλω, cf. ξίφος ἀργυρόηλον *Il.* II, 45? Are the hilts of these weapons perhaps fastened with two large gold-capped pegs and two smaller plain rivets (compare those on the dagger from a Knossos warrior grave, Hood, 1952, p. 270, fig. 12)?

347

The use of *q-s-* for *x-* in ξίφος is surprising and unparalleled; and the entry hardly fits into the context of the other tablets in the *Ta-* series, unless the weapons are intended as gifts. Is the ideogram conceivably intended for a 'falchion' (sickle-shaped knife, admittedly not yet found in a Mycenaean context) for which the Egyptian name *ḥepeš* might supply an etymology for ξίφος?

8. PYLOS LISTS OF MISCELLANEOUS CONTENT

We will close this chapter with five tablets on which no ideograms appear (Bennett's classification *V-*) and whose context and translation are for the most part uncertain. The commentary will be kept to the minimum; see the Vocabulary (p. 385) for further notes.

† **248 = Va01** [15]

¹ *pu-ro o-[da]-a₂ o-[. .]-ke e-tẹ o-u-qe e-to ai₃?-ka-te-re* 2
² *[pe]-re-ku-wa-na-ka [.]-ke e-te pu-ro e-ke-qe a-po-te-ro-te*

`[ . ]-ra-kạ-te-ra'` ɪ

edge: *pe-re-ku-wa-na-ka pu-ro e-ti-wa-jo | ai₃?-ka-te-re `a-mo-i-je-to'*

Pylos: now thus..., and two *ai₃?-ka-tēre* are not (present); Presguanax has *arrived* at Pylos from thence, and has one *chit* from each of them. (Presguanax, Pylos...: the two *ai₃?-ka-tēre* are being sent *presently*.)

ai₃-ka-te-re (dual): cf. dat. plur. *ai₂?-ke-te-si* **169 =** Es646, etc.? Andrews has suggested restoring *[a]-ra-ka-te-ra* in line 2, which he regards as an alternative spelling of the same word in the accusative singular. It would be surprising to find such a variation on the same tablet, and it may be preferable to read [χα]ρακτῆρα 'engraving, symbol, token' ('clay sealing, tablet'?), but Chadwick reports that the traces do not favour the reading *ka-*. *a-po-te-ro-te* = ἀμφοτέρωθεν.

a-mo-i-je-to = ἁρμοῖ ἵεσθον? Or ἱέτω/ἱέσθω 'let them be sent'? Or ἁμῶς 'somehow'?

‡ **249 = Va02** [482]

qe-qi-no-me-no

e-re-pa a-no-po a-ko-so-ta ᴢᴇ e-wi-so-zu?-ko 4 *ro-i-ko* 3

Ivory...Axotas^m, pairs: four *evenly-matched*, *turned*, three crooked.

¶ **250 = Vn01** [20] (cf. **42 = An17**)

¹ *o-a₂ e-pi-de-da-to*   Thus the wine of *Pa-ra-we-*
² *pa-ra-we-wo   wo-no*   has been distributed:
³ *pi-*82-de* 50   50 to *Pi-*82*,
⁴ *me-ta-pa-de* 50   50 to Metapa,

⁵ *pe-to-no-de* 100	100 to *Pe-to-no,*
⁶ *pa-ki-ja-na-de* 35	35 to *Pa-ki-ja-ne,*
⁷ *a-pu₂?-de* 35	35 to ? Aipy,
⁸ *a-ke-re-wa-de* 30	30 to *A-ke-re-wa,*
⁹ *e-ra-to-de* 50	50 to *E-ra-to,*
¹⁰ *ka-ra-do-ro-de* 40	40 to Kharadros,
¹¹ *ri-jo-de* 20	20 to Rhion.

251 = Vn02 [46]   †

¹ *pi-te-*[   ]
² *ka-pi-ni-ja | po-ti-ja* [   ]
³ *ka-pi-ni-ja | e-ru-mi-ni-ja* [   ]
⁴ *ka-pi-ni-ja | ta-ra-nu-we* 11 [   ]
⁵ *ai₃?-ki-no-o* 80   *o-pi-te-te-re* 50+
⁶ *e-to-ki-ja* 13   [? *pa*]-*ke-te-re* 140
⁷ *pi-wo-ta-o | ta-ra-nu-we* 6
⁸ *qe-re-ti-ri-jo* 2   *me-ta-se-we* 10
⁹ *e-po-wo-ke | pu-to-ro* 16
¹⁰ *ai₃?-ki-no-o | pu-to-ro* 100
¹¹ *ta-to-mo   a-ro-wo   e-pi-**65-*ko*
¹² *e-*[*ru-mi*]-*ni-ja* 2   *ki-wo-qe* 1

Only a few of the entries can be understood: *po-ti-ja* = φορτία?; *ka-pi-ni-ja* = κάπνη, καπνία 'smoke-stack'; *e-ru-mi-ni-ja* = ἐλύμνιαι ('roof beams', Hesychius); *ta-ra-nu-we* = θρήνυες (here equivalent to θρᾶνος 'beam'?); *ki-wo-qe* κίων 'column'?; *o-pi-te-te-re* from *ὀπιτίθημι? These seem to show that the tablet deals with carpentry items for building construction. *ai-ki-no-o* is apparently part of a chariot or its decoration on Knossos **276** = Se1006.

The list is continued on the even more difficult Vn879, which records eight *a-ti-*[*ja*?] *pe-**65-*ka*, twenty-four *ko-ni-ti-ja-ja pe-**65-*ka*, ten *e-to-ki-ja pa₂-ra-de-ro* and eighty-six *pa-ke-te-re pa₂-ra-de-ro*. Perhaps *e-to-ki-ja* represents ἐντοίχιος 'on a wall' ('wall-plates'?) and *pāktēres* 'dowels' or 'fixing-pieces' (cf. πῆγμα).

Vn851 apparently records a distribution of *de-mi-ni-ja* (= Hom. δέμνια 'beds') to both men and women in the dative case.

252 = Vn06 [10]

¹ *o-di-do-si   du-ru-to-mo*
² *a-mo-te-jo-na-de   e-pi-pu-ta* 50
³ *a-ko-so-ne* [[100]] 50
⁴ *to-sa-de   ro-u-si-jo   a-ko-ro   a-ko-so-ne*
⁵ 100 *to-sa-de   e-pi-pu-ta* 100

Thus the woodcutters contribute to the *chariot* workshop:
  50 *saplings*, 50 axles.
And the 'fields of Lousos' (cf. Un04) (contribute) so many:
  100 axles, and so many *saplings*: 100.

a-mo-te-jo-na-de: allative in *-de* of a workshop noun in -εών (cf. Hom. χαλκεών 'smithy') formed from the word *a-mo-ta* seen on the WHEEL tablets, see p. 371.

In line 4 the form *to-sa-de* is anomalous with the masculine ἄξονες, and may either refer to δένδρεα, ξύλα, etc., or be an anticipation of *e-pi-pu-ta* which had come first in lines 1–3. In a consistent syntax we should also expect the accusative *a-ko-so-na. These 'saplings' (?) were presumably used for the bent-wood parts of the chariot assembly, like the νέους ὄρπηκας of *Il.* xxi, 38 (cf. Theoc. xxv, 247).

†

CHAPTER XI

METALS AND MILITARY EQUIPMENT

THE identity of the first metal ideogram is proved by its totalling *to-so-de* †
ka-ko = τοσσόσδε χαλκός on the Pylos *Jn-* tablets, to which the form with an
extra crossbar is almost entirely confined. It is also used as an adjunct to
metal vessels and other objects (Knossos **230** = K 740 and
Pylos **238** = Tn996) including an INGOT (Oa734); and is
written under a WHEELED CHARIOT on Sc223, where
it perhaps refers to the wheels (cf. **278** = So894). These
uses make it safe to translate the symbol generally by
'bronze' rather than 'copper' (like χαλκός in Homer,
with the possible exception of χαλκὸς ἐρυθρός, *Il.* IX, 365); the unalloyed metal
possibly had no separate symbol. On **222** = J 693 small weights of BRONZE
are introduced by λίνον λεπτόν 'fine linen', and appear to be an indication
of value.

140	⊨ ⊨	BRONZE
WE	⟨	Silver?
141	✕	GOLD

The Pylos ideogram here translated as GOLD is confined to tablets **258** = Kn01
(listing weights of *c.* 62–250 grams) and **172** = Kn02 and **238** = Tn996, where
it is an adjunct qualifying valuable vessels. Bennett (1950, p. 218) wrote that
'the unusually small quantities with this ideogram in Kn01 would indicate a
material of considerable intrinsic value'.

Although the use of adjuncts to indicate the material of vessels and equipment is the exception rather than the rule, one should expect to find somewhere
a third ideogram to indicate 'silver' (whose full spelling *a-ku-ro* is confined to
290 = Sa03). This is possibly to be identified in the WE which is used as an ‡
adjunct to the 'Vaphio cup' on **231** = K 872 (only a part of this is recorded
by the text as being of gold), and which is written over the INGOT ideogram
on Oa734 *bis*; its presence may also be suspected on KN J 58, although
Bennett read WE as the last syllable of *pa₂-ra-o-we*. Note also the similar
ideogram on Pylos La630 (reverse), quoted on p. 323. This use of WE is to
be distinguished from that on C 411, **96** = Un02, etc., where it clearly describes
a kind of sheep; and from the reversed S with cross-bar and dots which
probably represents $\frac{1}{1440}$ of a talent. Silver is relatively uncommon both in
Homer and in the archaeological record.

1. METALS AT PYLOS

† Twenty-seven tablets of the *Jn*-series (excluding **257**=Jn09 and Jn881) evidently belong to a single set and conform to a rigid pattern. Each is introduced by a place-name and the phrase *khalkēwes talasiān ekhontes* 'smiths having a *talasia*', followed by a number of men's names with an amount of BRONZE each. The second paragraph, introduced by *tossoide khalkēwes atalasioi* 'so many smiths without a *talasia*', consists of an enumeration of further men's names without any BRONZE entries at all.

Chadwick and Björck simultaneously recognized that the classical ταλασία (=ταλασιουργία 'wool-spinning') is here used in the more general sense 'an amount allocated by weight for processing': it is evidently derived more immediately from τάλαντον 'weight' than from the cognate τάλας 'long-suffering' (so Boisacq, *s.v.*). The Latin *pensum* still shows both stages of an identical semantic development.

The same context is shown by some Third Dynasty tablets from Ur (Legrain, 1947; *c.* 2100 B.C.). No. 324 lists 'copper to work into dagger blades, issued by the treasurer's office'; no. 354, 'beaten copper, from the office located at the chariot shed, delivered to the smiths at $16\frac{1}{3}$ manehs 2 shekels (=8·25 kg.) per head'; no. 357, the same at 10 manehs (=5 kg.). The more nearly contemporary Alalakh tablet no. 402 (Wiseman, 1953, p. 105) lists '4 half-talents (=60 kg.) of copper for the smiths of the town Berašena, 4000 shekels (=33·5 kg.) of copper for arrow-heads, and 600 shekels (=5 kg.) of copper for doors'.

From the fact that a number of the smiths' names recur on other series of tablets (for instance among the names of shepherds), Webster has suggested that their work may have been on a part-time basis, like the seasonal iron-smelting by Hittite peasants referred to by Gurney (1952, p. 83). Compare also *Il.* xxiii, 832–5, where Achilles says of the ingot of pig-iron offered as a prize: 'Even if the winner's fertile farm is at a remote spot, he will be able to go on using it for five revolving years: his shepherd or ploughman will not have to go to the town through lack of iron, but will have it at hand.' This conclusion is very uncertain, since the names which recur are among the commonest Mycenaean stock, and may equally well be found at Knossos or Mycenae (e.g. Xanthos on Pylos Jn06 and **50**=An18, Mycenae Go610 and Knossos C 912). There is no guarantee that the Pylos doublets refer to the same individuals, quite apart from the different place-names with which they are associated.

The most elaborate example of the standard lay-out is shown by **253**=Jn01, where a third paragraph lists the slaves of both 'active' and 'inactive' smiths. These slaves are not named or numbered, but we may perhaps allow one to each smith whose name is written in the genitive (the corresponding nominatives elsewhere on the tablet are identified by capitals in our transcription). A 'slave of *Qe*-[' occurs among the 'inactive smiths' on Jn03; similarly a 'slave of Dektos' on Jn07, a 'slave of Euetor' on Jn750. A separate list of slaves, one to each smith (their names lost), forms the reverse of Jn706; the end of Jn03 lists large groups of men (five, ten, thirty-one) belonging to certain individuals not apparently smiths, since their names do not recur on the tablet.

On three tablets (Jn02, Jn03, Jn845) the first paragraph ends with the entry 'So-and-so the *basileus*', perhaps the name of the local chieftain who supervised the distribution. On Jn725 the division of the $2\frac{18}{30}$ talents of bronze among the twenty-seven smiths is not individually measured.

253 = Jn01   [310]   †

1 *a-ke-re-wa*   *ka-ke-we*   *ta-ra-si-ja*   *e-ko-te*
2 *ṭi-pa₂-jo*   BRONZE ∫ 1 ♯ 2   *qe-ta-wo*   BRONZE ∫ 1 ♯ 2
3 *ai-so-ni-jo*   BRONZE ∫ 1 ♯ 2   *ta-mi-je-u*   BRONZE ∫ 1 ♯ 2
4 *e-u-ru-wo-ta*   BRONZE ∫ 1 ♯ 2   *e-u-do-no*   BRONZE ∫ 1 ♯ 2
5 PO-RO-U-TE-U   BRONZE ∫ 1 ♯ 2   *wị-du-wa-ko*   BRONZE ∫ 1 ♯ 2
            vacat
7 *to-so-de*   *a-ta-ra-si-jo*   *ka-ke-we*
8 PA-QO-SI-JO   KE-WE-TO   *wa-*[*di ?*]*-re-u*
9 *pe-ta-ro*
            vacat
11 *to-so-de*   *do-e-ro*   *ke-we-to-jo*   *i-wa-ka-o*
12 *pa-qo-si-jo-jo*   *po-ro-u-te-wo*
            vacat
14 *po-ti-ni-ja-wẹ-jo*   *ka-ḳe-wẹ*   *ta-ra-si-ja*   *e-ko-te*
15 *i-ma-di-jo* BRONZE ∫ 2   *tu-ke-ne-u*   BRONZE ∫ 3
16 [   ]   BRONZE ∫ 3   I-WA-KA   BRONZE ∫ 3
17 [*a*]*-ta-ra-si-jo*   *pu₂ ?-*[.]*-ịa-ko*

§1. Smiths at *A-ke-re-wa* having an allocation:
Thisbaios: 1·5 kg. bronze; Qᵘhestāwōn: 1·5 kg. bronze; etc.
And so many smiths without an allocation:
Pangᵘōsios, *Ke-we-to*, Wādileus, Petalos.
And so many slaves: (those) of *Ke-we-to*, Iwakhās, Pangᵘōsios, Plouteus.

§ 2. Smiths of *the mistress* (at *A-ke-re-wa*) having an allocation:

etc.

po-ti-ni-ja-we-jo: the smiths distinguished by this enigmatic adjective evidently belong equally to the place A., since Iwakhas' slave is included in the third paragraph. The same division of the smiths occurs in the two sections of Jn03 (cut apart after writing) introduced by:

A-pe-ke-i-jo   ka-ke-we . . .   (adjective)
A-pe-ke-e   ka-ke-we   po-ti-ni-ja-we-jo   (locative?)

It occurs as a description of tradesmen on Pylos **148** = Ep04 and Un09, and in the feminine on Knossos **90** = G 820. Its function on the Knossos *Dl*- series is obscure (a man's name, title, or adjective applied to sheep?). Despite the *-we-*, a derivation from πότνια 'mistress' seems probable: a class of persons specially subservient to Athena? Or to the queen rather than to the king?

† **254** = Jn04   [389]

1   *a̱-ka-si-jo-ne   ka-ke-we   ta-ra-si-ja   e-ko-te*
2   *pi-ṟa-me-no*   BRONZE *ế* 3   *ma-u-ti-jo*   BRONZE *ế* 3   *e-do-mo-ne-u*
                                                                    BRONZE *ế* 3
3   *ka-ra-wi-ko*   BRONZE *ế* 1 ♯ 2   *pi-we-ri-ja-ta*   BRONZE *ế* 1 ♯ 2
4   *sa-mu?-ta-jo*   BRONZE *ế* 1 ♯ 2   *wa-u-do-no*   BRONZE *ế* 1 ♯ 2
5   *ka-ra-pa-so*   BRONZE *ế* 1 ♯ 2   *pi-ta-ke-u*   BRONZE *ế* 1 ♯ 2
6   *mo-re-u*   BRONZE *ế* 1 ♯ 2   *ti-ta-[.]-wo*   BRONZE *ế* [   ]
7   *to-sa-de   e-pi-da-to   ka-ko   pa-ṣi̱*   BRONZE *ế* 6
            vacat
9   *to-so-de   ka-ko*   BRONZE *ế* 27
            vacat
11   *to-so-de   a-ta-ra-si-jo   ka-ke-we*
12   *te-te-re-u   pa̱-pa̱-jo   pi-ro-we-ko   a₂-nu-me-no*
13   *ko-so-u-to*

Smiths at *A-ka-si-jo-* having an allocation:

Philamenos: 3 kg. bronze; etc.
And so much bronze is shared out among them all: 6 kg.

So much bronze (in all): 27 kg.
And so many smiths without an allocation: etc.

e-pi-da-to recurs at the end of the first paragraph of Jn02. It is either an incomplete spelling of the *epidedastoi* of **250** = Vn01, or possibly some other tense of the same verb.
Pi-ro-we-ko = Φιλοῦργος: cf. *ma-na-si-we-ko* Jn03.2 = Μνησίεργος 'mindful of his work'. It is perhaps significant that the smiths seem to have a higher proportion of unmistakably Greek names than appear on most of the other lists.

The damaged set of numerals in line 6 needs to be restored as ζ 1 ⫪ 2 in order to justify the total (cf. Bennett, 1950, p. 215).

255 = Jn658   †

1 *ka-ke-we   ta-ra-si-ja   [e]-ko-si*
2 *e-ni-pa-te-we   we-we-si-jo* I BRONZE ζ 5
3 *ma-ka-wo* I   BRONZE ζ 5 *pi-ro-ne-ta* I BRONZE ζ 5
4 *pa-qo-ta* I   BRONZE ζ 5 **85-ta-mo* I   BRONZE ζ 5
5 *po-ro-u-jo* I   BRONZE ζ 5 *o-na-se-u* I   BRONZE ζ 5
6 [.]-*ko* I   BRONZE ζ 5 *re-u-ka-ta* I   BRONZE ζ 5
7 *wa-ka-ta* I   BRONZE ζ 5 *o-tu-wo-we* I   BRONZE ζ 5
8 *wo-wi-ja-ta* I BRONZE ζ 5 *pe-re-ta* I   BRONZE ζ 5
9 *po-ru-e-ro* I   BRONZE ζ 5 *o-pe-ra-no* I   BRONZE ζ 5
10 *a-tu-ko* I   BRONZE ζ 5 ⟦*ko-*   ⟧
11 *to-*[*so-de*] *ka-ko* BRONZE 𝕄 3 ζ 20
12 [*to-so*]-*de   a-ta-ra-si-jo*
                    vacat

e-ko-si = ekhonsi 'they have', instead of the present participle *ekhontes*: this variation is shared by Jn706, where the total is introduced by *to-so-de ka-ko e-ko-si*. On Jn832 the description *talasian ekhontes* is replaced by *a-ke-te-re* (= ἀσκηταί 'those who practise their trade'?, cf. Hom. ἀσκέω in sense 'work raw materials'); on Jn650 it has in addition the word *pa-ra-ke-te-e-we* (= Hom. πρηκτῆρες?). The total on Jn658 seems to be a scribal error for 𝕄 2 ζ 20.

The following table gives a synopsis of the surviving tablets of this series. Of the fourteen different place-names, nine are not found on any other tablet, suggesting that some of the smiths may have lived in small communities of their own without other agricultural or maritime importance. Note the apparent progression shown by the entries 25½/26/27—54/56—78/80—108, which may correspond to a bronze ingot weighing rather less than a talent. Compare Knossos Oa730, which lists sixty ingots at a total weight of 52⅔ talents, or ζ 26⅓ each.

Tablet	Place	Active smiths	Inactive smiths	Bronze (kg.)
Jn01	*A-ke-re-wa*	12	5	23
Jn02	*Po-wi-te-ja*	15	6?	108?
Jn03	*A-pe-ke-i-jo*	10	15	54
	A-pe-ke-e p.	6	9	27
Jn04	*A-ka-si-jo-ne*	11	5	27
Jn05	*Wi-ja-we-ra₂*	7	1	26
Jn06	*O-re-mo-a-ke-re-u*	12	8?	56
Jn08	*Ru-ko-a₂-*[.]*-re-u-te*	7	5	34

Tablet	Place	Active smiths	Inactive smiths	Bronze (kg.)
Jn605	A-pi-no-e-wi-[jo]		(fragmentary)	
Jn658	E-ni-pa-te-we	16	0	80
Jn692	Na-i-se-wi-jo	2	6	12
Jn693	A-ke-re-wa	3	0	16
	A-pu₂?-we	7	2	26
Jn706	Pa-to-do-te	10	4	50?
Jn725	E-ni-pa-te-we	27	0	78
	[.]-nu-we-jo	5	0	18
	Na-i-se-wi-jo		(erased)	
	A-ke-re-wa	4	0	12
Jn750	A-si-ja-ti-ja	17	4	25½
Jn832	Ro-u-so	3	4	(no entry)
Jn845	[ ]	8	7	12
Jn937	[ ]-me-no	11?	0	16½

Jn07, Jn927, Jn942, Jn944, etc.: place-name lost, and fragmentary.

| | | Total | 193 | 81 | 701 |

The frequencies of the individual allotments of bronze to smiths are as follows:

1 kg.	1½ kg.	2 kg.	3 kg.	4 kg.	4½ kg.	5 kg.	6 kg.	7 kg.	8 kg.	12? kg.
1	41	1	17	19	1	43	9	2	9	1

The thin bronze arrow-heads (or 'arrow-plates', Evans, *PM*, IV, figs. 816, 818) of the type found in the Knossos 'Armoury', and common at both Cretan and Mainland sites (including Pylos), weigh up to about 1·5 g. each. Sword blades, on the other hand, and long spear-heads (such as those from the LM II warrior graves near Knossos, Hood, 1952, fig. 12) might scale up to 350 g. Hood (*ibid.* p. 256) gives the weight of his LM II bronze helmet as 695 g.: this includes the cheek-pieces, but 10 per cent should perhaps be added to allow for parts that are missing.

The smaller of the two most common allotments at Pylos (that of 1½ kg.) would be sufficient for making 1000 arrow-heads, the larger (5 kg.) enough for at least fourteen swords or spears. The total weight of bronze which can be totalled on all the surviving tablets (801 kg.) would make something like 534,000 arrow-heads, or 2300 swords or spears, or 1000 bronze helmets. It is tempting to regard the following tablet as a total of the complete series, from which approximately a quarter of the entries must then be assumed to be missing.

256 = Ja749

to-so-pa   𐂚 34   ≀ 26

So much (bronze?) in all: 1046 kg., or just over a ton.

257 = Jn09 [+829]   †

¹ *jo-do-so-si   ko-re-te-re   du-ma-te-qe*

² *po-ro-ko-re-te-re-qe   ka-ra-wi-po-ro-qe   o-pi-su-ko-qe   o-pi-ka-pe-`e-we-qe´*

³ *ka-ko   na-wi-jo   pa-ta-jo-i-qe   e-ke-si-qe   ai-ka-sa-ma*

⁴ *pi-*82   ko-re-te*   BRONZE ⁈ 2   *po-ro-ko-re-te*   BRONZE ♯ 3

⁵ *me-ta-pa   ko-re-te*   BRONZE ⁈ 2   *po-ro-ko-re-te*   BRONZE ♯ 3

⁶ *pe-to-no   ko-re-te*   BRONZE ⁈ 2   *po-ro-ko-re-te*   BRONZE ♯ 3

⁷ *pa-ki-ja-pi   ko-re-te*   BRONZE ⁈ 2   *po-ro-ko-re-te*   BRONZE ♯ 3

⁸ *a-pu₂?-we   ko-re-te*   BRONZE ⁈ 2   *po-ro-ko-re-te*   BRONZE ♯ 3

⁹ *[a]-ke-re-wa   ko-re-te*   BRONZE ⁈ 2   *po-ro-ko-re-te*   BRONZE ♯ 3

¹⁰ *ro-u-so   ko-re-te*   BRONZE ⁈ 2   *po-ro-ko-re-te*   BRONZE ♯ 3

¹¹ *[ka]-ra-do-ro   ko-re-te*   BRONZE ⁈ 2   *po-ro-ko-re-te*   BRONZE ♯ 3

¹² *[ri]-jo   ko-re-te*   BRONZE ⁈ 2   *po-ro-ko-re-te*   BRONZE ♯ 3

¹³ *[ti]-mi-to   a-ke-e   ko-re-te*   BRONZE ⁈ 2   *po-ro-ko-re-te*   BRONZE ♯ 3

¹⁴ *[ra]-wa-ra-ta₂   ko-re-te*   BRONZE ⁈ 3 ♯ 3   *po-ro-ko-re-te*   BRONZE ♯ 3

¹⁵ *[sa]-ma-ra   ko-re-te*   BRONZE ⁈ 3 ♯ 3   *po-ro-ko-re-te*   ♯ 3

¹⁶ *[a]-si-ja-ti-ja   ko-re-te* BRONZE ⁈ 2   *po-ro-ko-re-te*   ♯ 3

¹⁷ *e-ra-te-re-wa-pi   ko-re-te*   BRONZE ⁈ 2   *po-ro-ko-re-te*   ♯ 3

¹⁸ *za-ma-e-wi-ja   ko-re-te*   BRONZE ⁈ 3 ♯ 3   *po-ro-ko-re-te*   ♯ 3

¹⁹ *e-re-i   ko-re-te*   BRONZE ⁈ 3 ♯ 3   *po-ro-ko-re-te*   ♯ 3

Thus the *mayors* and their *wives*, and the vice-*mayors* and key-bearers and supervisors of *figs* and *hoeing*, will contribute bronze *for ships* and the points for arrows and spears:

> *Pi-*82*, the *mayor*: 2 kg. bronze; the vice-*mayor*: 750 g. bronze, etc.
> (Total: *mayors*: 39 kg.; vice-*mayors*: 12 kg.)

ko-re-te-re: the *ko-re-te* appears to be the 'mayor' or local chief responsible for each village (cf. **43** = Sn01, On01, **258** = Kn01), and the *po-ro-ko-re-te* is probably his deputy; the two also occur together on KN V 865. For the problematical description *-da-ma/-du-ma* (formally = δάμαρ?) see Vocabulary. The *klāwiphoros* occurs as a kind of priestess on **135** = Ep704, etc. The *o-pi-su-ko* are named with the *o-pi-ko-wo* (= *e-pi-ko-wo* 'guards'?) and *ke-ro-te* = *gerontes* on Jn881: 'guardians of fig trees'?? *o-pi-ka-pe-e-we* is reminiscent of Hesychius ἐπισκαφεύς 'one who harrows in the seed', ἐπισκαφεῖον 'mattock, hoe'; but cf. also Ζεὺς Ἐπικάρπιος 'guardian of fruit'. It is not clear whether these are predominantly civil or religious officials, but in the subsequent entries their contributions seem to be lumped together with those of the *po-ro-ko-re-te-re*.

ka-ko na-wi-jo: compare δόρυ νήϊον 'ship's timbers', *Od.* IX, 384. Nails and other fastenings? It is difficult to see why these miscellaneous officials, rather than the *khalkēwes* of the other *Jn-* tablets, should be contributing such specialized items of bronzework; unless the tablet in fact only records scrap bronze which is intended for melting down and re-using for these purposes (and hence the lack of any sub-division between the different objects in the subsequent entries?). Chadwick suggests that *na-wi-jo* is from ναός: 'the bronze that is in the temples'. Compare the Hittite 'Instructions for temple officials', § 8: 'Furthermore, whatever silver, gold, garments or bronze implements of the gods you hold, you are merely their caretakers. You have no right to them, and none whatever to the things that are in the gods' houses.'

?paltaioi'i q^u*e enkhessi* q^u*e aixmans*: that the first represent arrow-heads is proved by Knossos **264** = Ws1704, *q.v.* Webster points to the small amounts of bronze from each village (2·75 kg.), enough for about 1800 arrow-heads or 8 spear-heads, compared with the amounts on the other *Jn-* tablets (e.g. 47 kg. on the three tablets for *A-ke-re-wa*). He suggests that the arrow- and spear-heads may represent an offering or dedication rather than a regular war supply; or accumulations of votive offerings which are being confiscated as a desperate defence measure?

Chadwick reads *ro-u̯-so* in line 10, where we should expect *e-ra-te-i* in the standard order.

† **258** = Kn01   [Jo438]

1 [ ]-*te*					
2 *te̯-*[ ]	GOLD	ჳ	I		
3 *e-re-*[*e*?	GOLD]	⊞	I		
4 *po-ro-ko-re-*[*te*	GOLD]	⊞	I		
5 *do-ri-ka-o mo-*[*ro-pa₂*	GOLD]	⊞	I		
6 *ru-ro mo-ro-pa₂*	GOLD	[ ]	I		
7 *ne-da-wa-ta*	GOLD	[ ]			
8 *e-ke-me-de*	GOLD	⊞	[ ]		
9 [RO]-*u̯-*SO *ko-re-te*	GOLD	ჳ	[ ]		
10 PA-KI-JA-NI-[JO? *ko*]-*r̯e-*[*te*]	GOLD	ჳ	5	X	
11 A-PU₂?-JA *ko-re-*[*te*]	GOLD	ჳ	5		
12 KA-RA-DO-RO *ko-re-te*	GOLD	ჳ	5	X	
13 [ ] *ko-re-te*	GOLD	ჳ	5	X	
14 [ ]	GOLD	⊞	I		
15 [ ]-*ma*	GOLD	ჳ	6	X	
16 *wo-no-*[ ]-*ma*	GOLD	⊞	[		
17 *qo-wo-*[ ] *mo-*[*ro-pa₂*?]	GOLD	⊞	I		
18 *a̯-ka-wo̯*	GOLD	ჳ	3	X	
19 E-RE-E *po-ro-ko-re-te*	GOLD	ჳ	3	X	
20 *a-ke-ro pa₂-si-re-u*	GOLD	ჳ	3	X	
21 *te-po-se-u* TI-NWA-SI-JO *ko-re-te*	GOLD	⊞	I		
22 *po-ki-ro-qo*	GOLD	⊞	I		
23 **85-ke-wa*	GOLD	⊞	I		

[24] TI-MI-TI-JA	*ko-re-te*	GOLD	⟨ 6	
[25] I-TE-RE-WA		GOLD	⟨ 6	x
[26] PI-*82		GOLD	⟨ 6	x
[27] E-RA-TE-RE-WA-O	*ko-re-te*	GOLD	⟨ 6	
[28] A-KE-RE-WA	*ko-re-te*	GOLD	⟨ 5	x

left edge: *po-so-ri-jo-*[ ]*-ma* GOLD ⟨ [ ]*-jo a-to-mo* GOLD ⟨ 3 x

This tablet probably represents a tribute of gold from the chieftains (*basileus, ko-re-te, mo-ro-pa₂*) of surrounding villages. The recognizable place-names have been printed in capitals for easier reference: they correspond, though not in precise order, with those of **257** = Jn09 and of On01. Some of the personalities are common to **43** = Sn01, §1, which suggests the restoration of a similar introduction *basilēwjontes* here. Apart from line 2, the amounts of gold show the following distribution:

$$\begin{array}{cccc} ⟨\ 3 & ⟨\ 5 & ⟨\ 6 & \#\ 1\ (=250\ \text{g.}) \\ 4 & 5 & 5 & 10? \end{array}$$

An amount of ⟨ 7 occurs on La630 (rev.) and of ⟨ 9 and Og7434 on KN Np859; Bennett (1950, p. 217) concludes that ⟨ probably represents $\frac{1}{12}$ of #, or $\frac{1}{1440}$ of a talent (i.e. approximately $\frac{30,000}{1440} = 20{\cdot}9$ g.). It is significant that the plain gold rings and coils of gold wire from the Mycenae Acropolis treasure, in which Schliemann and Ridgeway long ago proposed to recognize standard units of value, centre on weights of 21–2 g. and 41–3 g. (as re-weighed for Thomas, 1939, pp. 72–4).

Whether there is in fact a direct connexion between this tablet and **172** = Kn02 (with its offerings of gold vessels) is uncertain. Webster has pointed out that the contributed amounts of gold fall within the range of weights shown by cups from the Mycenae shaft graves, and might be designed for such; but one would expect a considerable interval of time for the craftsmen to convert the raw materials into the finished vessels.

2. METALS AT KNOSSOS

259 = Og1527   †

[1] [	]		*mo-ri-wo-do*	⟨ 3
[2] [	]	2	*mo-ri-wo-do*	⟨ 3
[3] [	]	# 2	*mo-ri-wo-do*	⟨ 3

uncertain number of lines missing.

mo-ri-wo-do: probably *moliwdos* = μόλυβδος 'lead' (see Vocabulary, p. 400); similarly Georgiev, 1954, p. 83. The preceding entries are probably for another metal (copper or tin?), part of a list of parallel allocations to smiths. Lead, used in the composition of bronze, is listed together with it on some Nuzi tablets (Lacheman, 1939, p. 538).

The only other Knossos tablets recording weights of metal are **222** = J 693, already discussed in another context, and J 58 and J 58 *bis*. The following tablet from the 'Armoury deposit' may conveniently be included here, even though the identity of the weighed material is concealed by the loss of the final part of the introduction.

† **260 = Og0467   (P xviii)**

¹ *jo-a-mi-ni-so-de   di-do-*[*si*
² *ku-pe-se-ro* ⟨ 30   *me-to-re* ⟨ [nn
³ *ne-ri-wa-to* ⟨ 1 5   *pi-do-*[

Thus they contribute [. . .] to Amnisos:

   Kupselos: 30 kg.; etc.

3. SWORDS, SPEARS AND ARROWS AT KNOSSOS

‡ The twenty-two tablets classified by Bennett as *Ra-* were found in a corridor at the S.W. corner of the 'Domestic Quarter' (*M* on fig. 13, p. 115), into which they had fallen, together with their wooden chests, from a store-room on the floor above (Evans, *PM*, IV, pp. 853 ff.); fragments of swords were found in the same corridor. It is not certain whether the second variant of the SWORD ideogram represents a different type from the 'cruciform' (see drawing on p. 347, above), as Evans thought, or merely a more schematic form of the symbol. The characteristic vocabulary term for both variants is *pa-ka-na* = Hom. φάσγανα.

233   SWORD
230   SPEAR
231   ARROW

261 = Ra1540   (M xc)

to-sa / *pa-ka-na*   SWORDS 50[

So many swords (in all): fifty.

262 = Ra1548   (M xc)

        de-so-mo

ku-ka-ro / *pi-ri-je-te   pa-ka-na   a-ra-ru-wo-a*   SWORDS 3

Kukalos, the *cutler*: three swords fitted with *bindings*.

pi-ri-je-te (cf. dual *pi-ri-je-te-re* on **52** = An26, *q.v.*): also on Ra1547, Ra1549; on seven other tablets its place is taken by another occupational description *ka-si-ko-no* (cf. Pylos An31): see Vocabulary, p. 404.

a-ra-ru-wo-a = Hom. ἀρηρότα, cf. fem. *a-ra-ru-ja* on **265** = Sd0403, etc. Fitted with what? A scabbard (Hom. κολεόν) seems the most likely. The word *de-so-mo* = δεσμοῖς is perhaps not to be taken with *ararwoa*, in view of its position here and on Ra1543 (where there would have been room for it on the bottom line). It might therefore be an additional item, perhaps equivalent to the Homeric τελαμών or ἀορτήρ 'sword-belt'. But in favour of a translation 'fitted with their hand-grips' (*B* in the drawing on p. 347) compare the scholiast on φάσγανα μελάνδετα *Il.* xv, 713: σιδηρόδετα...οἳ δὲ μελαίνας λαβὰς ἔχοντα· τὴν δὲ λαβὴν δεσμὸν καλεῖ ὁ Σιμωνίδης. οἳ δὲ ἐπιμελῶς ἐνδεδεμένα πρὸς τὴν λαβήν.

263 = R 0481 *bis*   (P)   †

[*e*]-*ke-a* / *ka-ka-re-ạ*   SPEARS 42

Forty-two spears with bronze points.

enkhea khalkārea: cf. χαλκήρεϊ δουρί *Il.* v, 145, etc.; this suggestion has also been made by Furumark and Sittig. Something was undoubtedly written between *ka-ka* and *re-a*, taken by Evans and Bennett's *Index* as a divider; it is perhaps intended to be deleted. The last sign is very doubtful and was read as *ne*.

264 = Ws1704   (P)

Sealing: (*a*): *o-pa*   (*b*): *pa-ta-ja*   (*c*): ARROW

This sealing, with Ws1702 and Ws1705, were found in the 'Armoury' attached to the ‡ charred remains of two wooden boxes containing carbonized arrow-shafts and arrow-heads of the type shown on p. 356 (*PM*, IV, pp. 617, 836–40): the meaning of the word *pa-ta-ja* (neuter plural, cf. **257** = Jn09.3) is thereby assured. The word *o-pa* recurs on the CHARIOT and WHEEL tablets and on **29** = As821, *q.v.* From the same building comes R 0482, on which the ARROW ideogram is followed by the high numbers 6010 and 2630 (which would require about 13 kg. of bronze).

4. CHARIOTS WITHOUT WHEELS AT KNOSSOS

Of the tablets found in the 'Armoury' building by Evans in 1904, thirty of the longest deal with chariots; the form of the vehicles has been discussed by Evans (*PM*, IV, pp. 785–825) and their descriptions, which include the longest extant Knossos sentences, by us in *Evidence*, p. 100 and by Furumark (1954, pp. 54–9). Unlike the single chariots listed on the tablets found in the palace itself (see below, **297** = Sc222, etc.), those from the Armoury are shown without wheels; a large number of other tablets from the same building list the wheels separately.

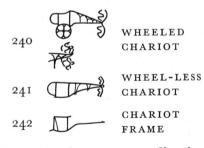

240   WHEELED CHARIOT

241   WHEEL-LESS CHARIOT

242   CHARIOT FRAME

Homer makes it clear that it was normally the practice to remove the wheels when not in use (*Il.* v, 722), and to place the chariots on stands and cover them with cloths (VIII, 441).

† Fig. 25 shows the approximate appearance of the type of chariot listed, supplementing the evidence of the ideogram from Mycenaean vase-paintings, from the Tiryns fresco, and from the analogy of contemporary Egyptian chariot harness. The WHEEL-LESS CHARIOTS listed in the *Sd-* tablets are described as *a-ra-ro-mo-te-me-na*, apparently equivalent to the classical ἡρμοσμέναι 'put together', and their ideogram shows a vehicle which is ready for use except

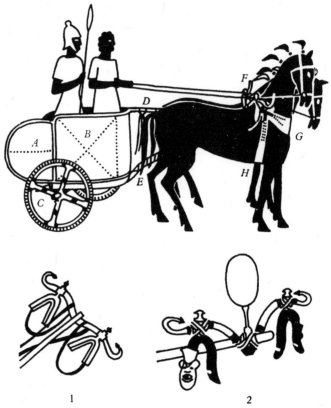

Fig. 25. The Mycenaean chariot, and Egyptian yoke arrangements.

for the fixing of the wheels and the harnessing of the horses. The simpler ideogram of the *Sf-* tablets (CHARIOT-FRAME) is qualified as *a-na-mo-to* (=ἀνάρμοστοι 'not put together') and represents the bare outline of the chassis structure, before the addition of the side-extensions (*A*), pole-stay (*D*) and yoke (*F*).

The body (*B*) was framed in bent-wood and covered with either ox-hide or wickerwork, to judge from the indications of the vase-paintings; the cross-bracing (only seen in the WHEELED CHARIOT ideogram) was presumably a feature not actually visible on the exterior of the vehicle, except in lines of

362

stitching. The 'spur' (C) seen on the ideogram of Sc219 and Sc238, on the Tiryns fresco and on vases, is apparently a step formed by extending the rear framing member of the floor, which in all probability consisted of interwoven leather straps. The side-extensions (A), which perhaps afforded extra lateral defence for the warrior when mounting, appear generally to have been covered in with the same material as the body; but their method of attachment is not clear. One would expect the top members of A and of B to be formed of a continuous piece of wood, but the vase-paintings invariably show them as meeting at an oblique angle, and the CHARIOT-FRAME ideogram proves that the side-extensions do not form an integral part of the chassis. Perhaps, like the wheels, they were particularly liable to damage and in need of periodical replacement; and their removal would reduce the amount of storage room needed by each chariot.

The other characteristic feature of the Mycenaean chariot is the pole-stay (D) which runs from the middle of the rail to the forward end of the pole (ῥυμός). This is taken by Evans to be a thong or cord, although on the Tiryns fresco at least it appears to be a solid wooden bar, effective in compression as well as tension. From it a number of appendages hang down: Evans argued that they are of a purely decorative nature, and that their ends are not attached to the pole.

The pole (E) does not have the up-curving end seen on Geometric chariots, and a peg or hole may have been needed to anchor in position the ȝυγόδεσμον with which the yoke was lashed on.

In the absence of explicit illustrations, the chief obscurity concerns the actual harnessing of the horses to the yoke. Contemporary Egyptian chariots had harness-saddles in the form of an inverted Y which were lashed to the yoke; they were applied over a wider saddle-pad, and had holes or hooks to take the combined ends of the breast-strap (G) and girth (H). Fig. 25 (1) shows the yoke arrangement of an unharnessed chariot shown on a painting for Rameses II; (2) that of the chariots found in the tomb of Tutankhamen (Carter, 1927, II, p. 63), where the harness-saddles are of leather-covered wood with calcite reels on top and gold decoration on the outward-facing legs. Some such attachment with saddles, rather than the direct lashing of the breast-strap to the yoke, is perhaps indicated by the W-shaped attachments visible behind the yoke on most forms of the Knossos Sc- and Sd- ideograms.

Our difficulties begin when we try to interpret the detailed terminology of the Knossos tablets in the light of this picture. Their syntax and the meaning of the *adjectives* describing colour and material are clear enough; but not only do the *nouns* which describe the parts of a chariot fail to agree with the nomenclature found in Homer, but their identification is equally open to controversy. Before going on to discuss them in detail, it is worth stating some of the basic principles which might reasonably be expected, *a priori*, to govern the scribe's choice of descriptive matter; they are trite enough, but fundamental to all similar specifications of objects on the Mycenaean tablets, where the need to distinguish one from another is the prime function of the inventory.

(1) Where the same noun occurs in every specification, but with different adjectives, it must refer to some prominent feature whose alternative methods of construction form the easiest way of telling one chariot from another. In the absence of the word *ararwōs* 'fitted with' or the conjunction *-q^{u}e* 'and', we might expect the feature to be located somewhere on the ideogram as drawn, if only we knew where to look for it.

(2) Where a noun and adjective occur exceptionally (e.g. *do-we-jo i-qo-e-qe* on **268** = Sd0413) it may conceivably describe an item not found at all on the other chariots; but more probably it draws attention to a normal item made of an unusual *material or shape*.

(3) Where an item is described as absent (e.g. *o-u-qe pte-no* on **270** = Sd0402), it must be one which one would normally expect to find on all the other chariots; but we cannot necessarily assume that its absence makes the chariot unserviceable. Whether the feature will also be absent from the ideogram depends on the conscientiousness of the scribe.

a-ni-ja (instr. *a-ni-ja-pi*) = classical ἡνίαι, Homeric ἡνία 'reins'. These form a partial exception to rule 3: although three tablets have the note *ouq^{u}e hāniai posi(eensi)* 'and there are no reins attached', five others add *araruiai hāniāphi* 'provided with reins'; so that it is uncertain whether the reins, which are certainly not indicated on the ideogram as drawn, are to be assumed as present or absent when the chariot specification does not mention them at all (but see further under *o-po-qo*).

† *i-qo-e-qe*, where it occurs, is named first of the items, and on **268** = Sd0413 even before *po-ni-ki-* 'crimson', which is possibly to be taken with it rather than with 'CHARIOT'. The word is evidently compounded with *hiqq^{u}o-* 'horse', but the meaning and number of the ending are uncertain: Palmer proposes a derivative of **heq^{u}omai* 'follow'. Its adjective *dorweios* (= δούρειος, 'made of a δόρυ, wooden pole or plank') suggests the possibility that it refers to the pole-stay (*D*), probably normally of leather, but on the Tiryns fresco at least consisting of a wooden bar.

o-po-qo: always described as *wi-ri-ni-jo/-ne-jo/-ne-o* (Palmer: 'of ϝρινός, leather') with the exception of *e-re-pa-te-jo* 'of ivory' on **265** = Sd0403, where the chariot is itself 'inlaid with ivory'. Palmer suggests *op-ōq^{u}on* 'cheek-strap, cheek-piece' (cf. παρώπια 'blinkers'), comparing the ivory variety with *Il*. IV, 141–2:

> ὡς δ' ὅτε τίς τ' ἐλέφαντα γυνὴ φοίνικι μιήνη
> Μηονὶς ἠὲ Κάειρα, παρήϊον ἔμμεναι ἵππων.

Against this identification it may be objected that such decoration of the bridle is not explicitly shown on any of the surviving paintings, and that under rule 1 one would expect the *o-po-qo* to be part of the structure shown in the ideogram. But the strong point in its favour is the fact that the only chariots which have no *o-po-qo* formula are those in which the bridles are expressly stated to be absent (Sd0402, **271** = Sd0422, Sd0416?); perhaps the *o-po-qo* formula is not to be taken as an autonomous annotation to the chariots themselves, but as an instrumental reading on from *a-ni-ja* (even where this is itself omitted), e.g. . . . *araruiai hāniāphi wrineois opōqᵘois* . . . , etc.

o-pi-i-ja-pi (instr. plur. fem.): presumably another part of the *a-ni-ja* (or, if the lack of *-qᵘe* is significant, a part of the *o-po-qo* itself); made of horn except on **267** = Sd0409, where it is of bronze. Horn was used for bits (classical χαλινός, στόμιον) in the contemporary Danubian cultures and in the *terremare* (Lorimer, 1950, p. 308; Childe, 1947, p. 113); one bronze bit was found at Mycenae, two more at Miletus. Such a meaning would suit the context, though Evans (*PM*, IV, p. 830) believed that the bridle still consisted only of a 'nose-band' (which is incidentally the original meaning of *hānia*, cf. Skt. *nāsyam*). The plural instead of dual (in *-oiin*?) may be justified by assuming that each 'bit' is regarded as a pair. The vocalization of the compound *o-pi-i-ja-pi*, which is perhaps an *-a-* stem in *-āphi*, rather than *-amphi* etc., is unknown: possibly from the root **si-* in ἱμάς 'strap', Skt. *syáti* 'tie', Av. *hitəm* 'harnessing'? Note also the word *o-pi-i-ta-ja-* on X 537, apparently a textiles tablet. An alternative suggestion is to derive the second part of the compound from **ĭα* = Vedic *īṣá-* 'pole of a car', Hittite *ḫiššaš* (same meaning); the same stem occurs in Greek with ablaut in οἰήϊον, οἴαξ (Homeric οἴηκες 'rings of the yoke'). In this case it might mean the pegs used to anchor in position the ζυγόδεσμον (see above). Palmer (1955*b*, p. 36) translates 'bit', but compares Hom. ἱλλάς.

i-qi-ja: the name of the chariot itself is clearly the adjective *hiqqᵘiā* = ἱππία (cf. *i-qo-jo* = ἵπποιο on **277** = Se1028). The feminine gender requires that we understand some word like ἅμαξα; cf. Eurip. ὄχημα ἵππειον 'horse-drawn carriage', ἵππειον ζυγόν 'chariot yoke', *Il.* V, 799.

The total numbers of chariots recorded at Knossos are more than 120 with wheels on the *Sc-* tablets, some 41 without wheels on the *Sd-* and *Se-* tablets, and at least 237 in a 'not assembled' state on the *Sf-* series, giving a total of 400+. What deductions can be made from these figures as to the total Knossos chariot force and as to its tactical use we leave it to others to decide, but it was evidently immeasurably smaller than the bodies of chariotry deployed by the Egyptians and Hittites on the more open battlefields of Syria.

265 = Sd0403   (P xiv)   †

² [*i*]-*qi-ja* / *a-ja-me-na*   *e-re-pa-te*   *a-ra-ro-mo-te-me-n̥a*   *a-ra-ru-ja*   [*a-ni-ja-pi*]
¹ *e-re-pa-te-jo*   *o-po-qo*   *ke-ra-ja-pi*   *o-pi-i-ja-pi*   ʻ*ko-ki-da   o̥-p̥a*ʼ

WHEEL-LESS CHARIOTS 3

Three horse-(chariots without wheels) inlaid with ivory, (fully) assembled, equipped with bridles with *cheek-straps* (decorated with) ivory (and) horn *bits*. The *feudal contribution* (of) Kolkhidas.

An examination of these tablets shows that the upper line on the original is in fact written after the lower line (see p. 112).

a-ja-me-na e-re-pa-te, *?aiai(s)menai elephantei*: cf. **239** = Ta642. The position of this decoration must be somewhere on the body or pole itself (perhaps round the rail), since even the CHARIOT-FRAME is described as *a-ja-me-na* on **272** = Sf0421, etc. None of our chariots is as elaborate as the gold-plated state chariots found in Tutankhamen's tomb (Carter, 1927, II, Pls. XVII–XXI), encrusted with semi-precious stones, glass and faience; or as the 'chariots inlaid with gold' of the Nuzi tablets (Lacheman, 1939, p. 538).

o-pa: see **29** = As821, and compare **264** = Ws1704 and **296** = Sh736.

266 = Sd0401   (P   xiv)

² *i̯-qi-jo | a-ja-me-no   e-re-pa-te   a-ra-r̥o-mo-te-me-no   po-ni-[ki-jo]*
¹ *a-ra-ru-ja   a-ni-ja-pi   wi-ri-ni-jo   o-po-qo   ke-ra-ja-pi   o-pi-i-ja-pi*

WHEEL-LESS CHARIOTS [2]

[Two] horse-(chariots without wheels) inlaid with ivory, (fully) assembled, painted crimson, equipped with bridles with leather *cheek-straps* (and) horn *bits*.

i-qi-jo: probably dual (cf. **241** = Ta715, *q.v.*); the only other occurrence of this variant on Sd0415 has the numeral 2, though *a-ra-ro-mo-te-me-na* inconsistently preserves the plural ending. On Sd0401, *i-qi-jo* has been corrected from *i-qi-ja*.

po-ni-ki-jo = φοινίκεος, Hom. φοινικόεις 'crimson', recurs on eight other CHARIOT tablets and is probably synonymous (or nearly so) with the *mi-to-we-sa* = *miltowessa* which takes its place on four others. This represents class. μίλτειος, μίλτινος, μιλτηλιφής 'painted with red ochre'. Compare the alternative Homeric epithets for ships φοινικοπάρῃος and μιλτοπάρῃος.

† 267 = Sd0409 + 0481   (P)

² *i-qi-ja | p̣o-ni-ki-j̣ạ   a-ra-ro-mo-te-me-n̥ạ   a-ja-[me]-n̥ạ*
¹ *wi-r̥i-n̥e-o   o-[p̣o]-qo   ka-ke-ja-pi   o-pi-[i-ja-pi]*   WHEEL-LESS CHARIOT ̣I

One horse-(chariot without wheels) painted crimson, (fully) assembled, inlaid; with leather *cheek-straps* (and) bronze *bits*.

268 = Sd0413   (P   xiv)

² *[i-qi]-ja | pa-i-to   a-ra-ro-mo-te-me-na   do-we-jo   i-qo-e-qe   po-ni-ki-[*
¹ *[a-ra-ru]-ja   a-ni-ja-pi   wi-ri-ni-jo   o-po-qo   ke-ra-ja-pi   o-pi-i-ja-pi*

WHEEL-LESS CHARIOT [nn]

[One?] horse-(chariot without wheels) (fully) assembled, *from* (?) Phaistos, †
  its *pole-stay* of wood, painted crimson, equipped with bridles with leather
  cheek-straps (and) horn *bits*.

269 = Sd0404   (P   xiv)   ‡
                                                                        ‡
² [*i*]-*qi-ja* | *ku-do-ni-ja   mi-to-we-sa-e   a-ra-ro-mo-te-me-na*
¹ [*do-we*]-*jo   i-qo-e-qe   wi-ri-ni-jo   o-po-qo   ke-ra*-[*ja-pi   o*]-*pi-i-ja-pi*
                                        WHEEL-LESS CHARIOT [nn]
[Three?] horse-(chariots without wheels) *from* (?) Kydonia, painted red,
  (fully) assembled, their *pole-stay* of wood, with leather *cheek-straps* (and) horn
  bits.

mi-to-we-sa-e: apparently an unusual spelling of *-ssai*; cf. *e-qe-ta-e* **29** = As821, *we-ka-ta-e*
  X 1044.

270 = Sd0402   (P   xiv; see plate II (*c*), facing p. 110)   ¶
² [*i*]-*qi-ja* | *a-ra-ro-mo-te-me-ṇạ   po-ni-ki-ja   o-u-qe   a-ni-ja   po-si*
¹ *a-u-qe   a-re-ta-to   o-u-qe   pte-no   o-u-qe   *85-ro   o-u-qe   'pe-pa₂-to'*
                                        WHEEL-LESS CHARIOT [nn]
[One?] horse-(chariot without wheels) (fully) assembled, painted crimson;
  and there are no bridles attached, *nor a . . .*, nor *heels*, nor *streamers*, nor *. . ..*

a-u-qe   a-re-ta-to: *a-u-qe* is probably an error for *o-u-qe* rather than αὖτε 'furthermore'.
  The vocalization of the second word is unknown, but might suggest *-στατος*.
pte-no: probably dual of πτέρνα 'heel', possibly making up the 'spur' (*C* on fig. 25,
  p. 362). Or 'chocks' to go under the wheels?
**85-ro*: Furumark (1954, p. 57) connects this with σάρον 'brush' and with the
  'streamers' which normally hang from the pole-strap, and which are absent from
  the ideogram here and on Sd0407. Possibly fem. dual = σειρώ 'traces'.
pe-pa₂-to: see the next tablet.

271 = Sd0422   (P   xv)
² *i-qi-ja* | *a-ro-mo-te-me-na* (sic)   *o-u-qe   a-ni-ja   po-si-e-e-si*
¹ *o-u-qe   pe-pa₂-to   u-po* '[   ] *o-pa*'   WHEEL-LESS CHARIOT [nn]
[One?] horse-(chariot without wheels) (fully) assembled, and there are no
  bridles attached, nor any . . . underneath. The *feudal contribution* of So-and-so.

po-si-e-e-si = πρόσεισι (cf. Arc. πόεστι < πόσεστι, *SIG*, cccvi, 12) 'they are attached to'
  or 'they are present in addition'. On 0402 and 0416 *posi* is used absolutely: *ouqᵘe
  hāniai posi*. Compare Sd0412: *ouqᵘe posi elephans* 'and there is no ivory attached'.
pe-pa₂-to evidently refers in some way to the underpart of the chariot or harness.
  Furumark compares πείρω: *ouqᵘe pepartoi hupo* 'and it is not pierced (studded?)'

underneath', cf. *Il.* 1, 246, σκῆπτρον χρυσείοις ἥλοισι πεπαρμένον? More probably a noun, possibly compounded with *per-* = περι-; or beginning *pherb-* (cf. φορβειά)? Palmer: *βεβατον 'floor? step?' from root βα-.

272 = Sf0421   (P   xv)

i-qi-ja | a-na-mo-to   a-ja-me-na   CHARIOT-FRAMES 27
Twenty-seven horse-(chariots) not (fully) assembled, inlaid.

273 = Sf0420   (P   xv)

i-qi-ja | a-na-ta   a-na-mo-to   'a-re-ki-si-to-jo   o-pa'   CHARIOT-FRAMES 80
Eighty horse-(chariots) not inlaid, not (fully) assembled. The *feudal contribution* of Alexinthos.

a-na-ta (cf. *a-na-i-ta* on Sf0419, *a-na-to* Sf0423, Sf0425) alternates with *a-ja-me-na* on the *Sf-* tablets, beside the common denominator *a-na-mo-to* (= fem. ἀνάρμοστοι). In spite of the inconsistency in the feminine ending, it probably represents the negative form *an-ai(s)toi*, which thus bears the same relationship to *a-ja-me-na* as *a-na-mo-to* does to *a-ra-ro-mo-te-me-na*. This was independently recognized by Chantraine.

† 274 = Sf0428   (P   xv)

² *[i]-qi-ja | po-ni-ki-ja   me-ta-ke-ku-me-na*
¹ *wi-ri-ne-o   o-po-qo   ke-ra-ja-pi   o-pi-i-ja-pi*   ⊔⌐ 1
One horse-(chariot), painted crimson, *dismantled*; with leather *cheek-straps* (and) horn *bits*.

The presence of the *o-po-qo* formula on this tablet looks at first sight like a flagrant breach of rule 1 (p. 364), in that a 'cheek-strap' is hardly to be expected on a chariot whose framing is so incomplete that even the rail is missing from the ideogram. The explanation probably lies, however, in the exceptional word *me-ta-ke-ku-me-na*, where the prefix μετα- suggests some form of dismantling or rebuilding, during which its original harness was not separated from it; cf. class. μεταποιέω, μετασκευάζω, etc., 'remodel'; μεταχέω only means 'pour from one vessel into another', but compare χέομαι in the sense 'be dissolved, scattered, dropped' and χέω 'cast' (cf. English 're-cast').

Unlike the others, the fourteen CHARIOT tablets classified as *Se-* were found in the North Entrance Passage (*K* on fig. 13, p. 115); though showing the same ideogram as the *Sd-* tablets, their phraseology is markedly different, even if fragmentary; the references to ivory may suggest more highly decorated state chariots.

275 = Se879   (K   lxvi)

ai-ki-no-o

pte-re-wa | pa-ra-ja   e-te-re-ta   po-ro-ti-ri   WHEEL-LESS CHARIOT [nn]

[One?] old chariot of elm-wood . . .-ed *three times* with *ai-ki-no-o*.

e-te-re-ta: probably a verbal adjective, and apparently a variant of *e-ka-te-re-ta* on the next tablet. From ἐξαρθρέω 'dislocate'? Or cf. ἔκτρημα, ἔκτρησις 'trepanning hole'? Or *en-trēta*, cf. *Il.* III, 448, ἐν τρητοῖσι λεχέεσσιν ('inlaid'? 'morticed'? 'holed'?)? Another adjective describing these chariots is *wo-ra-we-sa* on Se880, probably *wôla-wessa* from Hom. οὐλή 'scar'.

po-ro-ti-ri appears to contain **trins* (acc.) 'three' or *tris* 'thrice', on the analogy of the numeral 2 on the next tablet. Cf. πρότριτα 'on three successive days', Hom. καθάπαξ 'once and for all', σύντρεις 'by threes'.

ai-ki-no-o: meaning unknown, cf. Pylos **251** = Vn02. 'Goat tendons' (cf. Skt. *snāyuḥ* 'tendon, strap')?? Cf. Hom. νεῦρα βόεια.

276 = Se1006 + 1042   (K)   †

e-re-pa-te-jo-p̣i   o-mo-pi [

[? *pte-re*]-*wa* | *e-ka-te-re-ta   ai-ki-no-o*   2̣   *e-re-pa-te-jo-pi* [

[? One chariot of elm-wood] . . .-ed with two *ai-ki-no-o*, with ivory. . . with *bands* of ivory. . . .

o-mo-pi (instr. plur.) probably from οἶμος 'decorative band' (*Il.* XI, 24) rather than from ὅρμος 'chain', ὄμμα 'eye' or ὦμος 'shoulder'. Like *e-re-pa-te-jo-pi*, this word apparently forms an exception to the rule at Pylos that -φι is not added to -*o*- stems.

Se1007 uses the term *e-wi-su-zo-ko*, which recurs in an ivory context on PY **249** = Va02.

277 = Se1028   (K)   ‡

e-re-pa-te-[

[? *i*]-*qo-jo | z̤o-ẉạ* [or *z̤o-jạ*?

This tablet shows a deceptive resemblance to **163** = X 984 (*q.v.*), in spite of the apparent *ke-ke-me-na* of the latter and its publication in *SM II* cheek by jowl with tablets of the 'land ownership' series.

5. CHARIOT WHEELS AT KNOSSOS

Apart from **278** = So894, all the two dozen Knossos WHEEL tablets were found   ¶ in the 'Armoury' building (see Evans, *PM*, IV, pp. 793–6). Like the vase-paintings and frescoes, they show a four-spoked design. Those from the tombs of Amenhotep III and Tutankhamen (Carter, 1927, II, pp. 57–9) have under

369

their gold casing a structure of ash, the hubs bound with rawhide, and have leather tyres; Egyptian wall paintings also show bindings (some at least presumably of metal) at intervals round the spokes, at the junctions of spokes and felloe, and round the felloe. The chariot of the Tiryns fresco has similar markings on the spokes, and apparently has a separate tyre, which is divided by wider and narrower dark cross-lines which Evans suggests 'may have been wire and metal bands'.

243	⊕ ⊛	WHEEL
MO		Single
ZE		Pair

† The majority of the wheels are qualified by one or other of two names of timbers (*ptelewā* 'elm' and *helikā* 'willow') and by one or other of two puzzling adjectives describing their construction, *te-mi-*71-ta* and *o-da-ku-we-ta* (variously spelt). Both may well be adjectives in *-wenta*, and *]-mi-we-te* on Sg890 *bis* appears to be a variant spelling of the first; Ventris suggests, however, that *71* may be a monogram for *ne+ko*, i.e. *termin ekhonta* 'having a *te-mi-*'. It is tempting to see in *te-mi-we/te-mi-*71* (cf. Hom. τερμιόεις) an adjective meaning 'provided with a (leather) tyre'; even though Johannson's proposed connexion of the Homeric adjective with Skt. *cárma* 'leather' would demand the spelling *qe-* here, and is in any case not generally accepted. Some kind of decorative or functional edging seems likely, at any rate.

The alternative specification, which implies a noun-stem *o-da-k-*, is equally uncertain (note its application to textiles on **220** = L 870). Connected with ὅδαξ 'biting' ('serrated edge'?), or with οἶδαξ 'unripe fig' (a kind of studding?)?

The ZE and MO which precede the numerals do not, as Evans thought, refer to a carpenter's saw and the charioteer's whip, but are abbreviations of ζεῦγος 'pair' and μόνϝος 'single' (see p. 54). When the number of wheels is 'three pairs' or more, the descriptive adjectives are in the plural, as we might expect; but there is some inconsistency both at Knossos and at Pylos in the case of lower numbers. Both 'one pair' and 'two pairs' generally involve dual adjectives (the first presumably being read as 'two wheels'), but one(?) pair takes the singular on **278** = So894, and one and a half pairs ('three wheels') the plural on **284** = Sa01.

The classical use of the dual, already very inconsistent in Homer, is confined to two main functions: first, reference to 'natural pairs' (e.g. ears, eyes, draught-horses); second, the counting of 'accidental pairs'—but only where the words δύω or ζεῦγος are expressly added (so in Attic temple inventories of the 5th–4th centuries B.C., e.g. φιάλα χρυσᾶ II, etc.). Schwyzer (*Gram.* II, p. 48) suggests that such 'accidental pairs' must originally have taken plural

370

concord; but examples such as *to-pe-zo* 'two tables' (**241** = Ta715) and *di-pa-e* 'two goblets' (**236** = Ta641) show that our Mycenaean dialect is at the intermediate stage where an explicit δύω requires the dual in all classes of noun and adjective, as in Indo-Iranian and in Old Slavonic.

The neuter adjectives of the WHEEL tablets might naturally be taken as applying to the heteroclitic κύκλα 'wheels', literally 'circles'; but there is a probability that the real term to be understood is *a-mo-ta*, and a possibility that this is not ἁρμοστά 'well-fitted' but *harmŏta*, ancestor of ἅρματα 'chariot' (which evidently does not have this Homeric meaning at Knossos in view of *i-qi-ja*). This term is evidently connected with ἁρμός 'fastening', ἁρμόζω 'put together', in allusion to the fact that the chariot must be assembled from a number of loose parts before use; and in the Mycenaean arsenals the word may have been applied specifically to the wheels. Cf. ἁρματοπηγός 'wheelwright', *Il.* IV, 485, and *a-mo-te-jo-na-de* (*harmŏteiōna-de*?) as the destination of axles and ἐπίφυτα (pliant branches for felloes?) on **252** = Vn06.

The total number of wheels separately listed on the Knossos tablets appears to be over a thousand pairs, but of these the $462\frac{1}{2}$ (?) pairs of *o-da-ke-we-ta* on So0446 may perhaps represent a repetitive total (note the *o-pe-ro* of sixteen pairs 'missing' in line 2).

278 = So894   (K   lxi)   †

> ¹ *a-te-re-te-a* | *pe-te-re-wa* 'te-mi-*71' WHEEL ZE [1 ?]
> ² *ka-ki-jo* WHEEL ZE 1   *ka-ko-de-ta* WHEEL ZE [3+]
> ³ *ki-da-pa* | *te-mi-*71-ta* WHEEL ZE 41 [MO 1?]
> ⁴ *o-da-tu-we-ta* | *e-ri-ka* WHEEL ZE 40[+

...: one (?) pair of wheels of elm-wood, with *tyres*;
  one pair of bronze wheels;
  three+ pairs of bronze-bound wheels;
  forty-one and a half (?) pairs of wheels of *ki-da-pa* wood, with *tyres*;
  forty+ pairs of wheels of willow-wood, with *studs*.

a-te-re-te-a: perhaps the neuter plural of an adjective in -ής with *a*- privative; not a verbal adjective in -τέα (-*tewa).

ka-ki-jo = *khalkiō* (dual): possibly only the tyre was of solid bronze, although a wheel entirely of metal is perhaps not excluded, especially as only one pair is listed.

ka-ko-de-ta = χαλκόδετα, cf. *khalkōi dedemenō* and *argurōi dedemenō* at Pylos (see below). As a tyre of solid silver is unlikely, these adjectives probably refer to metal bindings at intervals round the felloe or spokes, like those detected by Evans on the Tiryns fresco.

ki-da-pa (not *ki-da-ro*, Bennett, *Index*, p. 63): possibly a kind of timber, cf. σκίνδαψός, σκινδάλαμος, σκιδαφή?   ‡

† **279** = So0437 joined   (P   xvii)

a-mo-ta | *pte-re-wa*   *a-ro₂-jo*   *te-mi-*71-te*   WHEEL ZE 5

Five pairs of wheels of elm-wood, of *better class*, with *tyres*.

a-ro₂-jo: apparently dual of *a-ro₂-a* on **214** = Ld571, **282** = So0430. A mis-spelling for *a-ro₂-e*? These duals do not agree with *a-mo-ta* and with the recorded number of wheels.

‡ **280** = So0439   (P   xvii)

a-mo-ta | *e-ri-ka*   *te-mi-*71-ta*   WHEEL ZE 3   MO WHEEL [1]

Three and a half pairs of wheels of willow-wood, with *tyres*.

¶ **281** = So0440   (P   xvii)

a-mo-ta | *pte-re-wa* | *o-da-*87-ta*   'de-do-me-na'   WHEEL ZE [nn]

x pairs of wheels of elm-wood with *studs*, which have been contributed.

o-da-*87-ta: the sign **87* is confined to this word, as **71* to the other wheel adjective; it appears to have the value *kwe*.

de-do-me-na = δεδομένα: in contrast to *worzomena* ('manufactured'?) on So0438, etc.? Or does that also mean 'contributed' (cf. *worzei* at Pylos, p. 254)?

†† **282** = So0430   (P   xv)

     ko-ki-da   *o-pa*   *ne-wa*

e-ri-ka | *o-da-*87-ta*   *a-ro₂-a*   WHEEL ZE 22   MO WHEEL I

Twenty-two and a half pairs of new wheels of willow-wood, with *studs*, of *better quality*. The *feudal contribution* (of) Kolkhidas.

‡‡ **283** = So0442   (P   xvii)

     o-pe-ro

[   ]-*ja* | *a-mo-te*   *pe-ru-si-nwa* | *ta-ra-si-ja*   WHEEL ZE I

One pair of. . .wheels owing from last year's allocation.

The word-order and syntax are not very clear. Possibly *harmŏte* (dual) *ophêlo(menō) perusinwās talasiās*; *a-mo-te* could also be ἁρμόσθη (aor. pass.) or the nom. sing. of the occupational name *a-mo-te-re* (X 770 and X 6026); but it cannot be any part of ἁρμοστός. In support of a Myc. form *harmŏ* 'wheel' one may add the possible reading *a-mo* as nominative singular on KN So7485.3; the classical meaning of ἅρμα is paralleled by the fact that both in Sanskrit (*rátha-*) and in Tocharian A (*kukäl*) the term for 'chariot' is derived from an *IE* word for 'wheel'.

6. CHARIOT WHEELS AT PYLOS

The vocabulary and arrangement of the Pylos WHEEL tablets, 200 years later, †
are very like those of the Knossos series; and their
adjectives show similar sequences of neuter duals or   243   ⊕   WHEEL
plurals according to the number of pairs listed. Pylos
has, however, developed a variant of the WHEEL with   ⊕   WHEEL+TE
surcharged TE, which (to judge from **287**=Sa793) probably stands for the
qualification *te-mi-*71-ta*.

284=Sa01   [488]

ku-pa-ri-se-ja   WHEEL+TE   ZE I   MO I

One and a half pairs of wheels of cypress wood, with *tyres*.

ku-pa-ri-se-ja: not to be confused with the place-name adjective *Ku-pa-ri-si-jo* on
56=An657. The Homeric equivalent κυπαρίσσινος is only used once, of a door-post
in *Od.* XVII, 340.

285=Sa02   [487]

ke-ro-ke-re-we-o | *wo-ka*   *we-je-ke-e*   WHEEL+TE   ZE I

One pair of wheels with *tyres, fit for driving*, belonging to Khêroklewēs.

This tablet is typical of a set of thirteen, all introduced by a man's name in the genitive.
Three of them have two pairs of wheels, the rest one pair each; all the descriptions
are in the dual, as here. The remaining names are: *Pa₂-sa-re-ọ, Tu-ri-si-jo-jo,
E-ke-i-jo-jo, Wo-ro-ko-jo, Wa-de-o, A-pa-si-jo-jo, Pe-qe-ro-jo, E-te-wa-jo-jo, Mo-qo-so-jo,
Po-ru-we-wo, A-te-wo-jo, A-me-ja-to.*

wo-ka we-je-ke-e (dual): though its vocalization is very uncertain, it is likely that this
description is the opposite of *no-pe-re-e* 'unfit for service' (see below), and hence
means something like 'fit for use on this charioteer's vehicle'. It is tempting to
connect the second word with the Homeric ἀ-εικής, ἐπι-εικής. *we-je-* could be an
abnormal spelling or represent a disyllabic grade of the root; but there is a more
serious objection that adjectives in -ής seem originally to have been all compounds
(Schwyzer, *Gram.* I, p. 513). Must we postulate a compound (with -εχής) of the
same prefix *we-j-* which reappears in the adjective *we-ja-re-pe*, etc. (possibly 'suitable
for anointing', cf. δι-ηλιφής, νε-ηλιφής, etc.?) applied to OIL on the Pylos tablets of
1955? *wo-ka* cannot be the Homeric ὄχα 'pre-eminently', since this is certainly
from ἔχω, and probably a shortened form of ἔξοχα; but it might be a somewhat
similar adverbial formation from *Ϝέχω 'ride, take, in a chariot' (cf. ὄχεα 'chariot'
and *Il.* X, 403: ἵπποι ἀλεγεινοὶ ὀχέεσθαι 'difficult to use in a chariot'). For the
ending cf. κρύφα, μίγα, σῖγα, etc. Alternatively *wo-ka* may be a noun from the same
stem, to be taken closely with the preceding genitive.

† **286** = Sa787

to-sa   *pa-ra-ja*   *we-je-ke-a₂*   WHEEL ZE 30   MO I
       e-qe-si-ja   *pa-ra-wa*   WHEEL ZE 12   *za-ku-si-ja*   WHEEL ZE 32

So many (in all): thirty and a half pairs of old wheels, *fit for driving*;
twelve pairs of *old* wheels for Followers (?),
thirty-two pairs of wheels of *Zakynthian* type.

e-qe-si-ja pa-ra-wa: the second line is written near the edge of the tablet, and all three final signs look at first sight like *-wa*. *e-qe-si-ja* is also applied to 'cloaks' on **214** = Ld571, *q.v.*; if, as seems likely from **56** = An657, the *heqᵘetās* is a military officer, it is perhaps reasonable that the design of both his uniform and his chariot should be in some way distinctive.

za-ku-si-ja: compare the [*Za*]-*ku-si-jo* which should probably be restored as an ethnic or place-name on **54** = An19, but which also occurs on Mycenae Oe122 (as a man's name?). The assibilation of the ending -νθιος is also seen in Att. Προβαλίσιος, Τρικορύσιος and in Pylos *Ko-ri-si-jo*, *O-ru-ma-si-ja-jo*.

‡ **287** = Sa793

e-re-pa-to | *te-mi-*71-ta*   *pa-ra-ja*   *ta-na-wa*   WHEEL+TE ZE II
Eleven pairs of old *spindly* wheels with *te-mi-* of ivory.

e-re-pa-to: Ventris is inclined to analyse this phrase as: *elephantos termin-ekhonta* 'having a *termis* of ivory'; but this would indicate that the *termis* here represents some kind of decorative band rather than the actual running surface or 'tyre'.
ta-na-wa: Hom. ταναός, see Vocabulary, p. 408.

¶ **288** = Sa790

[[*ka-ko*]] *a-mo-ta*   *e-qe-si-ja* | *no-pe-re-a₂*   WHEEL+TE ZE 6
Six pairs of wheels for Followers (?), unfit for service.

no-pe-re-a₂ = Att. ἀνωφελῆ; cf. Hom. ἀνώνυμος/νώνυμος, etc.

289 = Sa682

te-tu-ko-wo-a₂   *no-pe-re-a₂*   WHEEL ZE 6
Six pairs of *heavily-built* wheels, unfit for service.

te-tu-ko-wo-a₂ (cf. **216** = Ld871) = Hom. τετυγμένα; see Vocabulary, p. 409.

290 = Sa03   [287]

a-ku-ro | *de-de-me-no*   WHEEL ZE I
One pair of wheels bound with silver.

a-ku-ro: this is the only occurrence of the word ἄργυρος on the tablets.

291 = Sa794

ka-ko de-de-me-no no-pe-re-e WHEEL ZE I

One pair of wheels bound with bronze, unfit for service.

†

7. CORSLETS AND HELMETS AT PYLOS

Twelve tablets found in 1952 (classification *Sh-*) list the CORSLET ideogram. This resembles the Knossos CORSLET (see below, p. 380) in its tapering sides and in the varying number of horizontal cross-lines; but instead of vertical shoulder loops it shows lateral projections which may represent short sleeves, and above the neck it adds a   163 CORSLET construction which must probably be taken as a form of headgear. The identification of this Pylos ideogram as a set consisting of corslet and helmet is confirmed by the terminology *to-ra-ke* = θώρᾱκες and *ko-ru-to* (gen. sing.) = κόρυθος; and thus supplies new material for the discussion of the traditional picture of Heroic armour in Homer and its relation to the archaeological evidence (see Evans, *PM*, IV, pp. 688–90, 803–6; Lorimer, 1950, pp. 196–245; Hood, 1952, pp. 256–61; Gray, 1954, etc.).

Hood suggests that certain bronze plates found in the 'Tombe dei Nobili' ‡ at Phaistos are part of armoured belts or corslets; but the absence of metal scales from all other Minoan and Mycenaean sites, and in particular from warrior graves, makes the direct archaeological evidence for a bronze corslet very slight. Mycenaean vase-paintings show only doubtful indications of body-armour, though the white dots on the tunics and helmets of the Mycenae 'Warrior Vase' (Lorimer, 1950, Pl. III) have been taken by some to represent metal disks. Two ivories from Enkomi in Cyprus do, however, depict a 'lobster' corslet similar to that worn by the 'Peoples of the Sea', divided into ribbed bands in inverted-V formation: there is general agreement that these were of metal.

Evans (*PM*, IV, p. 688; *SM II*, p. 57) regarded the Knossos CORSLET ideogram as representing 'a form of body-armour consisting of horizontal plates of metal, presumably backed by leather or linen, and suspended from shoulder-pieces of a similar fashion'. He compared them with the horizontally banded corslets worn by some of the soldiers of Rameses II and by his Shardana mercenaries; but from their white colour and apparent rows of stitching Bonnet has argued that these were not of metal but of thickly wadded linen. Gray (p. 6) refers to a fragment of cloth fourteen layers thick from a Mycenaean burial, which is thought to be part of such a padded corslet. There seems to be no reason, however, why metal plates should not have been sewn *into* wadding of this kind, and thus not appear as separately identifiable plates on the exterior.

Lorimer is inclined to regard all Homeric references to a metal θώρηξ, with the possible exception of the Achaean epithet χαλκοχίτωνες, as late accretions to the traditional picture; but in view of the scale corslets evidenced by finds at Ugarit and Nuzi (and listed on the Nuzi tablets, see below) and faithfully depicted on the monuments of Amenhotep II, Thothmes IV and Rameses III, Gray and Hood find it hard to believe that similar metal body-armour was unknown in the Aegean. Although the word χάλκειος is not found on the Mycenaean CORSLET tablets, the object *qe-ro*₂ (which appears to be part of a corslet, see **299** = V 789) is once qualified by the BRONZE ideogram; and on some 'charioteer' tablets the corslet is erased and replaced by an ingot, as Evans pointed out. Such body armour may have been restricted almost entirely to charioteers, for whom the absence of a shield made it a necessity; which would help to explain its absence from chieftains' graves.

The Pylos corslets are listed or identified by the varying number of *o-pa-wo-ta* which they comprise: of the twenty listed, sixteen have 'twenty large *o-pa-wo-ta* and ten small', the remainder 'twenty-two large ones and twelve small'. It is tempting to identify these with the horizontal bands shown on the ideogram, but it is not clear how they are to be distributed. Do the small ones make up the collar and sleeves? Or the upper part above the level of the armpits? Or a more flexible section below the waist? And are those of the back counted separately from those of the front? One might expect the corslets to undo into two halves by fastenings along the side, but the references to 'pairs' are probably to be taken as the issue of two corslets to one chariot (cf. **297** = Sc222) rather than the division of each into two γύαλοι.

o-pa-wo-ta apparently represents *op-aworta* 'things hung or attached around', from ἀϝείρω (cf. Hom. συνήορος 'joined with', ἀορτήρ 'strap'; and ἀρτάω 'attach', if from *ἀϝερτάω). Another inconclusive indication of its meaning is the fact that four *o-pa-wo-ta* (abbreviated o) are regularly applied to the κόρυς or 'helmet' in these sets; but note that the classification o does not include the two *pa-ra-wa-jo*, in which Bennett has recognized the equivalent of the *παρᾱϝjά in Hom. κόρυθος διὰ χαλκοπαρήου 'helmet with cheek-pieces of bronze', *Od.* XXIV, 523 (see Vocabulary, p. 403).

'It is clear (as Hood points out, 1952, p. 258) that there was an extraordinary variety of helmet fashions in the Aegean at this period.' Fig. 26 shows a representative selection. Helmets made entirely of relatively thin bronze, and showing holes for the stitching of a padded under-cap, have been found in a LM II warrior grave near Knossos (*A*: Hood, 1952, Pl. 50) and at Dendra

(*B*: Persson, 1952, pp. 119–129), and are shown on the Agia Triada 'Boxer Rhyton' (*C*); a single bronze cheek-piece from Ialysos is in the British Museum.

A very characteristic type is the conical boar's tusk helmet (*D*), with or without fanciful horns and plumes above; the number of concentric rows of plates is most often four. Owing to the relative scarcity of the raw material, this helmet was probably confined to kings and chieftains. A simpler form of

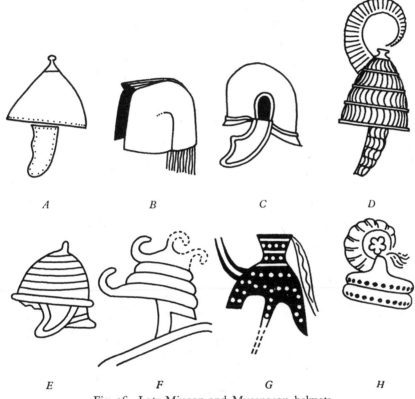

Fig. 26. Late Minoan and Mycenaean helmets

conical headgear is shown on the vase from Tomb 5 at Isopata (*E*): it has six concentric bands (excluding the bottom rim and terminal knob) which Lorimer regards as strips of leather, Hood as thick padding sewn together at intervals. A similar helmet, whose sections have a more pronounced bulge, is shown on the fragments of a faience relief from Shaft-Grave III at Mycenae (*F*): it has four 'rolls', and four 'horns'; a helmet with seven 'rolls' is seen on a LM I*a* polychrome goblet from the Tomb of the Double Axes at Knossos (*PM*, III, p. 310, fig. 198), with four 'rolls' on a clay seal-impression (*ibid.* p. 313, fig. 205). More fanciful and unique types are shown on the late

377

'Warrior Vase' from Mycenae (*G*), where the spots are regarded as metal disks; and on a gold plaque-bead from Shaft-Grave III (*H*), whose two thick 'rolls' are surmounted by a composite knob and by a horn.

The head-gear shown full-face in the Pylos ideograms bears no unmistakable resemblance to any of these eight types, and it is not altogether clear whether the cap is to be taken as a simple cone and the lines below the cone as the cheek-pieces and neck of the corslet; or whether these lines indicate a wide bottom 'roll' (surmounted by small horns as on *F*?), above which a relatively narrow cone sticks up. In either case the disposition of the four *o-pa-wo-ta* is difficult to reconstruct. If they are in fact concentric as on *D*, *E* and *F*, their width would be about 5 cm.; and if the bands of the corslet were of the same width, about fifteen of them would be needed between neck and thigh. The scale corslets of Rameses III have thirteen bands (Lorimer, 1950, p. 198, fig. 17).

Very similar phraseology is seen in the Nuzi tablets which list coats of mail for charioteers and horses (Lacheman, 1939, p. 541), e.g.:

Bel-Aḫi received from the palace one coat of mail that fits the body made of 400 large scales, 280 very small scales, the sides and decoration of which are of copper; one *kurpisu* (helmet) of copper made of 190 scales....

400 scales of the side, 200 (small?) scales of the side, 200 scales of the *kurpisu* Ninki-Tešup has received.

But a complete identity of context can only be argued if we assume that our much smaller numbers of *o-pa-wo-ta* are not separate plates but *rows* of scales, perhaps sewn into separate belts before application to the corslet.

The Semitic prince shown on the chariot of Thothmes IV (Lorimer, p. 198, fig. 16) has a helmet covered with approximately two dozen narrow bronze plates sewn radially between the crown and lower rim; an arrangement of four such petal-shaped plates, which avoids the difficulty of beating out a solid cone of bronze, may perhaps be argued for the Pylos helmets. The number of *o-pa-wo-ta* to the Pylos helmets also recalls the Homeric terms τρυφάλεια and κόρυς τετράφαλος (*Il.* XXII, 315, also ἀμφίφαλος V, 743), κυνέη τετραφάληρος (XI, 41); but if these φάλοι and φάληρα are explained as 'horns' or 'bosses', then they evidently have no relevance to the meaning of *o-pa-wo-ta* as applied to corslets.

292 = Sh740

pa-ra-jo	CORSLET ZE 5	*wi-so-wo-pa-ṇạ*	*o-pa-wo-ta*	*me-zo-a$_2$*	O 20	
		me-u-jo-a$_2$	O 10	*ko-ru-to*	O 4	PA 2

Five pairs of old corslets: twenty larger-sized *plates* of equal. . .;

ten smaller-sized *plates*;

Four *plates* of the helmet, two cheek-pieces.

wi-so-wo-pa-ṇa: probably an adjective compounded with ἴσος (Cretan, Arc. ϝίσϝος) 'equal'. One might have expected ἰσοβαρέα, ἰσοπαλέα, ἰσοπαχέα, ἰσοπλατέα, ἰσοφανέα, etc.; possibly from πῆνος (= ὕφασμα Hesych.): 'with an equal number of thicknesses of cloth'?

The use of o as an abbreviation is here quite distinct from its usual meaning 'amount owing or missing'.

293 = Sh737

CORSLET 1   *o-pa-wo-ta* | *me-zo-a*$_2$ O 20   *me-u-jo-a*$_2$ O 10
                    ko-ru-to   O 4   *pa-ra-wa-jo*   2

One corslet: twenty larger-sized *plates*, ten smaller-sized *plates*,
    four *plates* of the helmet, two cheek-pieces.

294 = Sh733   (four other tablets are identical)

CORSLET 1   *me-zo-a*$_2$ O 20   *me-u-jo-a*$_2$ O 10   *ko-ru-to*   O 4   PA 2

295 = Sh734   (three other tablets are identical)

CORSLET 1   *me-zo-a*$_2$ O 22   *me-u-jo-a*$_2$ O 12   KO O 4   PA 2

The reverse of this tablet and of Sh739 have erased and illegible entries also apparently dealing with corslets.

296 = Sh736   †

to-ra-ke a-me-ja-to o-pa me-za-ṇa wo-ke ne. CORSLET 5

Five *new* corslets, the *feudal contribution* of *A-me-ja-*. . . .

a-me-ja-to: genitive of a man's name as on Sa834, not ἀμίαντος 'unstained'. The last two words, of which *wo-ke* appears verbal (ϝεργ- 'work' or ϝεχ- 'convey'?), are incomprehensible; *me-za-na* recurs in **76** = Cn22, *q.v.*

8. CHARIOTS AND CORSLETS AT KNOSSOS

The 140 Knossos *Sc-* tablets were apparently all found together in a small ‡ archive room in the West Wing of the palace (*B* on fig. 13, p. 115), Evans' 'Chariot Tablet Deposit' (*PM*, IV, pp. 786–9, 803–7). Each is introduced by a man's name, and itemizes CORSLETS, WHEELED CHARIOTS (see p. 361) and HORSES, generally in that order.

The extant tablets show eight cases of 'one corslet' and fourteen of 'two corslets'; in the majority of cases the relevant numbers have been lost. On nine tablets the corslet has been erased and an ingot apparently inserted at the end of the line or on the reverse; on three the ingot has been drawn in over the erasure itself. Evans regarded this as the record of an alternative issue of bronze sufficient to make a pair of corslets (these might then each contain about 13 kg. of metal). The number of chariots is never larger than one, and on two tablets they are absent altogether. There are eleven (?) entries with 'a single horse' (MO), at least twenty-five with 'a pair of horses' (ZE).

162   CORSLET

106   HORSE

165   INGOT

The tablets probably record the issue of equipment to charioteers: note that the man *Me-nu-wa* of Sc238 recurs on V 60 after an introductory word which Bennett read *a-ni-wo-ko*, Sittig *a-ni-o-ko* (Chadwick *a-ni-o̧-ko*), and which is evidently the Homeric ἡνίοχοι.

On four tablets the corslet has a surcharged circle with dots (= QE) instead of the usual horizontal lines, and on Sc266 this version of the ideogram is followed by QE alone with the numerals 'one pair': it is difficult to guess the meaning.

297 = Sc222   (B   xxvii)

me-za-wo   CORSLET 2   HORSE ZE 1

Mezāwōn: two corslets, one pair of horses.

298 = Sc226   (B   xxvii)

ti-ri-jo-pa₂   WHEELED CHARIOT 1   CORSLET 1   HORSE 1   *e-ko* 1

Triopās: one chariot, one corslet, one horse—(already) having one.

e-ko: we had previously taken this as ἔγχος 'one spear', but Furumark suggests ἔχων, which is rather more plausible and may help to explain the other tablets where the chariot is accompanied by only one horse. Note that the usual MO is here omitted, as if phrasing and context made confusion impossible.

The vocabulary of the Pylos CORSLET tablets enables us to fit the following two Knossos fragments into their rightful context:

† **299** = V 789   (J   lii)

    qe-ro₂ 2   *e-po-mi̧-*[

]*-ra*   *e-pi-ko-ru-si-jo* 2   *pa-ra-wa-jo* [

qe-ro₂: we have already met this word on **230** = K 740, where it describes an object whose outline is reminiscent of the CORSLET ideogram and has the adjunct BRONZE.

It possibly represents some kind of foundation or framing to a metal-reinforced corslet. Perhaps from στέλλω (*$squeljō$), cf. Hesych. στέλλα· ȝῶσμα, σπολάς 'leather jerkin', σπέληξ· γυναικεῖον ἱμάτιον (Suidas), στόλος etc. Palmer (1955*b*, p. 38) suggests *$quhelioi$ 'coats of mail'; cf. φαλόν· τὸ στερεὸν κύκλωμα τοῦ στέρνου, Hesych., φάλαρα, τετράφαλος, etc.

e-po-mi-[jo]: 'shoulder pieces'? Cf. ἐπώμιος (Euripides), ἐπωμίς.

e-pi-ko-ru-si-jo: evidently the adjectival equivalent (dual) of the description *koruthos* 'of the helmet' on the Pylos tablets; to what noun does it refer?

300 = G? 5670

1] *qe-ro$_2$* 2 [

2 *ko]-ru* ⌂ 1 *o-pa-wo-ta* [

The identity of the HELMET ideogram (cf. fig. 26, *A*, p. 377) only became apparent on further cleaning of this fragment by Ventris in August 1955. Dr Platon has placed it on exhibition with other selected tablets on the ground floor of the Iraklion Museum.

PART III

ADDITIONAL COMMENTARY

CHAPTER I

DISCOVERY AND DECIPHERMENT

23† A NEW table of the values of Mycenaean syllabic signs will be found below (Fig. 27). Almost everything in the basic values given here has been accepted, the only exception being *zu*?, where it has proved impossible to confirm this value for *79 owing to the lack of sufficient examples. The 'homophones' ought perhaps not to have been so labelled, since we never believed that they were purely optional variants; it is now clearer what their special values were, though much still remains obscure.

Basic values

a	e	i	o	u
da	de	di	do	du
ja	je	—	jo	
ka	ke	ki	ko	ku
ma	me	mi	mo	mu
na	ne	ni	no	nu
pa	pe	pi	po	pu
qa	qe	qi	qo	—
ra	re	ri	ro	ru
sa	se	si	so	su
ta	te	ti	to	tu
wa	we	wi	wo	—
za	ze		zo	

Special values

a_2 (*ha*)	a_3 (*ai*)	au	dwe	dwo
nwa	pte	pu_2 (*phu*)	ra_2 (*rya*)	ra_3 (*rai*)
ro_2 (*ryo*)	ta_2 (*tya*)	twe	two	

Untranscribed and doubtful values

*18	*19	*22	*34	*35
*47	*49	*56 *pa₃*?	*63	*64 *swi*?
*65 *ju*?	*79 *zu*?	*82 *swa*?	*83	*86

Fig. 27. New table of the values of Mycenaean syllabic signs.

a_2 appears to be always *ha*, if we accept the presence of intervocalic *-h-* in Mycenaean; but even so, its use in place of a_1 in non-initial position is optional, and there is no trace of other vowels having aspirated variants.

ai_2? and ai_3? (numbers *34* and *35*) are certainly variant forms of the same sign. If they were distinct, this pair would be the only example in the syllabary of the mirror image of a sign having a different value; no other pair of signs could be mistaken for each other if turned about a vertical axis. But the value proposed was always tentative and has not been confirmed, nor has any other convincing proposal been made for them.

87 (*kwe*) is more likely to be *twe*, since *qe* has presumably the sound *kwe* or something very much like it, and it is unlikely that there was another series of labialized velars. The identification is built solely upon *o-da-*87-ta*, which is also spelt *o-da-tu-we-ta* as well as *o-da-ke/ku-we-ta*; see Glossary.

pa_2 should be given the value *qa* and inserted into the appropriate blank space in the basic values. The reason for failing to grasp its exact value despite some equations with Greek words is instructive: original $*q^ua$- became πα- in all Greek dialects, and two words spelt with pa_1, *pa* (also *pa-te*, *pa-si*) = πᾶς and *pa-ra-jo* = παλαιός, were thought to have had an initial labiovelar, thus showing that this development had already taken place in Mycenaean. We can now see that the etymologies proposed for these words are false, and we have a consistent distribution of *qa* in words of labiovelar origin distinguished from *pa*, which always represents a labial stop.

pa_3?: this still remains a possible value, being built mainly on the equation of *56-ra-ku-ja* with *pa-ra-ku-ja*; but no decisive confirmation has been forthcoming. In any case it is likely to have a special value.

pte: this appears to be an exception to the rule that signs represent only consonant+vowel or consonant+semi-vowel+vowel. But if the original value had been *pje*, this would by a regular Greek phonetic change have yielded *pte*; cf. κλέπτει < *κλέπ-yει.

pu_2: the transcription is certain, but the exact value is still unclear. It appears to be usually *phu* (e.g. pu_2-*te-re* = *phutēres*), but also *bu*, if *da-pu_2-ri-to-jo* is really the equivalent of Λαβυρίνθοιο.

ra_2: value *rja*, serves as replacement for *ri-ja*, but whether this is a matter of orthography or pronunciation is not clear.

ra_3: *rai*, e.g. *e-ra_3-wo* = *elaiwon* = ἔλαιον.

ro_2: *rjo*, e.g. *tu-ro_2* = *turjoi* (?) = τῡροί.

85: not *sja*, a value based upon the false assumption that it occurs in the initial word of PY Ma 397. It is now agreed that this damaged sign, which must have the value *sja*, is not *85*. The value *au* was proposed independently by Ephron (1961, pp. 71 ff.) and Petruševski and Ilievski (1958); it has since been confirmed by new discoveries, especially the Theban name *au-to-te-qa-jo* = *Autothēgᵘaios*. It is so far the only case of a sign containing a diphthong in -*u*.

ta₂ (**66*): *tja*. But a new sign, **91*, formerly taken as a variant of **66*, has now been recognized as a separate sign with the value *two*.

Signs transcribed by numerals.

**64*: value possibly *swi* (Chadwick, 1968 *a*).

**65*: value generally accepted as *ju*, though no compelling proof has appeared. The value was originally proposed by Meriggi (1955 *b*, pp. 66 ff.) and Palmer (1955 *b*, p. 43).

**71*: value *dwe* proved by a new text (PY Sa 1266; Lang, 1958, p. 189).

**82*: many suggestions have been made, the best supported being *sa₂* and *ja₂*. The variant *swa*, originally proposed by Gallavotti (1959, p. 165), seems to be the most likely value (Chadwick, 1968 *a*).

CHAPTER II

THE MYCENAEAN WRITING SYSTEM

28† The exact dates of these periods can of course be endlessly disputed. The date of the destruction level at Knossos containing Linear B tablets has been questioned by Palmer (1961, chapter VI; 1963 *b*), but his conclusions have not generally found favour among archaeologists. At most it seems likely that the destruction of Late Minoan II Knossos fell within the Late Minoan III a 1 period, thus reducing the date to perhaps *c*. 1375. 1340 is perhaps early for the beginning of Late Helladic III b; but the discovery of tablets in a layer at Thebes apparently dated to Late Helladic III a seems to guarantee the presence of Linear B on the Mainland during the fourteenth century.

32† An important argument in favour of assigning closely similar, if not identical, values to Linear A and Linear B syllabic signs can be drawn from the Cypriot syllabary (see pp. 63–6 and Fig. 12). It is clear from differences in the structure of the Linear B and Cypriot systems that one is not directly derived from the other: the separation in Linear B of *t/d* and of *l/r* in Cypriot, the absence of the complex signs from Cypriot, apart from the differences in spelling conventions, make it certain that both derive from an earlier script, which can hardly be anything but a form of Linear A. Despite the remoteness of the connexion, a few Cypriot signs are closely similar to Linear B signs with the same or similar value (see Fig. 28).

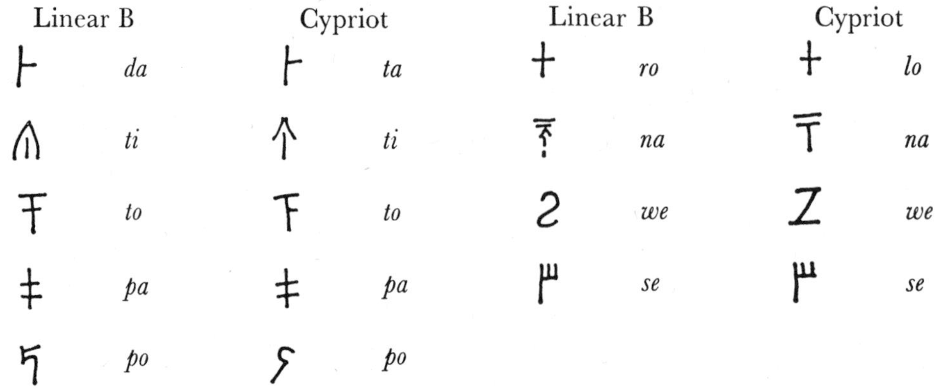

Linear B		Cypriot		Linear B		Cypriot	
⊢	da	⊢	ta	+	ro	+	lo
Λ	ti	↑	ti	₹	na	⊤	na
⊤	to	⊤	to	𝓌	we	Z	we
‡	pa	‡	pa	ᚹ	se	ᚹ	se
ꓘ	po	ꝶ	po				

Fig. 28. Linear B and Cypriot syllabic signs compared.

Furthermore, it is not too fanciful to trace a distant resemblance in many more similarly paired signs. But if each of these pairs of signs has a common ancestor, and each of the pair has the same or similar value, then this must surely have been the value of the ancestral sign too. Granted some uncertainties about the identification of individual signs, it seems clear that in the main the Linear B syllabic values must hold good also for Linear A; though it needs to be emphasized that the values so obtained can be only approximate, and it must not be supposed that Linear A had necessarily the same consonant structure or the five-vowel basis of Linear B, since this is dictated by the phonemic system of Greek.

p. 38† The discovery of two sets of Linear B tablets at Thebes, in 1964–5 and 1970, has both confirmed this prediction and gone a long way to fill the gap between Cretan and Mainland examples of Linear B. Platon has dated the first batch of Theban tablets to LH III a, so that they belong at least to the same century as the Knossos tablets; yet in form, script and language they seem to be indistinguishable from the Pylos tablets.

p. 39† It now appears highly probable that the phonemic system for which the syllabary was originally devised did not distinguish voiced and aspirated consonants, but did provide for palatalized and labialized ones, i.e. consonants combined with either a *y* or a *w* semi-vowel. See further p. 390 below.

41† Fig. 9. Although some minor additions could now be made to this table, in particular the addition of sign forms for the Thebes tablets, there is nothing significant in these additions, and nothing has happened to change the picture here presented, with two exceptions. The signs numbered *88* and *89* were omitted from this table; *88* is now suppressed, and *89* has never been admitted to the canon, as it occurs only on a sherd from Knossos (Z 1715; Raison, 1968, pp. 183 ff.). But it has become necessary to admit two more signs: *90* ⫴, found at both Knossos and Pylos, has been recognized as a single sign, instead of a special way of writing *42* twice; thus the third variant of *42* in both columns K and P is to be suppressed. *91* is ⩘, which was previously read as a variant form of *66*; it occurs only at Pylos.

43† The identification of sign *85* as *au*, used only in initial position, parallels the use of a_3 (*ai*). The spelling at Knossos -*a-e* in **29** = Am 821 and *we-ka-ta-e* in C 1044 is not erroneous, but is apparently a disyllabic dual ending.

† There is still no evidence that *p-* can represent β; *pa₂* is now securely identified as *qa*, see p. 386.

44‡ It has become clear that *z-* also spells the product of **k*y* in *ka-zo-e* < **kakyohes* (comparative of κακός), *su-za* < **sūkyai*, etc. The exact phonetic equivalent is not certainly established, but the spellings *ts/dz* have been adopted in Part III and the Glossary, since an affricate of some sort, presumably undifferentiated in respect of voicing, seems necessary to account for the use of *z-* to represent **dy* and initial **y*, as well as **ky*, **gy*.

45† $Q^u h$- may occur in some names to be connected with θήρ (< **g'hw-*) and *qe-te-se-u*, if this is a name $Q^u htheiseus$ (see Glossary).

The identification of sign *16* as *pa₂* in place of *qa* was due to incorrect etymologies (πᾶς, παλαιός) which we can now correct by the Mycenaean evidence. Both these words contain original π and *qa* is used whenever π has a labio-velar origin. The terminations -*qo-ta*, -*qo-to* probably do not answer to classical -βάτης, -βατος.

The apparent variation in *ra-pi-ti-ra₂ ra-qi-ti-ra₂* is illusory; the spellings represent two different words. But there is a tendency where two labio-velars occur in one word for the first to be dissimilated to *p*: e.g. *i-po-po-qo-i* = *hippo-phorgᵘoihi* (ἱπποφόρβοις). This will account for *qe-re-qo-ta-o* (gen.) answering to *pe-re-qo-ta*. The pronunciation of a labio-velar before a consonant is surprising, but *q* is regularly written in this position: e.g. a_3-*ti-jo-qo* = *Aithioqᵘs* (Αἰθίοψ),

389

ke-ni-qe-te-we = *kherniqᵘtēwes* (cf. χέρνιψ). There is no reason to suppose that *e-ri-ko-wo* and *e-ri-qi-ja* are related names.

p. 45‡ The suggested rule that a *scriptio plena* might be used for the clusters -*rg*- and -*rm*- has not been confirmed, and the examples quoted are probably to be explained otherwise. In -*sm*-, however, the *s* is regularly noted.

p. 45¶ Exceptions to the rule that initial *s* is omitted before a stop are very doubtful; but *sm*- is treated as in medial syllables: *si-mi-te-u* (man's name) = *Smintheus*.

    The alleged examples of omission of *w*- before consonant seem all to be based upon unsound etymologies.

p. 46† For an alternative interpretation of *wo-no-qo-so*, see Glossary.

p. 46‡ The group -*nw*- may be written either -*nu-w*- or with the vowel of the following syllable supplied with *n*: *ke-se-ni-wi-jo* = *xenwion*. It is possible that *n* may be omitted in this group when followed by a morpheme boundary: *pa-wo-ke* = *pan-worges* (Chadwick, 1967a). In the group -*sw*-, *s* is normally written: *a-si-wi-jo* = *Aswios* (Ἄσιος) (Chadwick, 1968a).

p. 46¶ No polysyllabic signs have yet been detected, unless *ra₂* (= *rya*), *ro₂* (= *ryo*), *dwo*, etc., are sometimes to be read as having disyllabic value. It seems preferable to assume that, e.g., in the ending of feminine agent nouns, classical -τρια, -*ti-ra₂* represents rather a monosyllabic -*trya*, though it is still uncertain whether the longer spelling -*ti-ri-ja* represents a graphic or a phonetic variant. The series of 'labialized' signs with values consonant + *w* + vowel has been much increased by later discoveries: *71 = *dwe*, *90 = *dwo*, *48 = *nwa*, *87 = *twe*, *91 = *two*, and possibly *82 = *swa*, *64 = *swi*. Although *62 = *pte* appears to be an exception to the rule that no sign has a value beginning with two stops, this is almost certainly due to the special history of *py in Greek (see above, p. 386).

p. 46†† It may be taken as axiomatic that there are no true homophones; all the apparent examples are probably due to overlapping values, where a sign has a restricted application. Thus *a₂* is constantly employed where the value *ha* would be appropriate, even in medial position; but *a* may be substituted for it, as the examples quoted on p. 47 demonstrate. The variations of spelling seem to be due to the preferences of individual scribes, not to differences of dialect between the various sites.

34 and *35*, which were provisionally identified as ai_2 and ai_3, have not been confirmed, and are now treated as unidentified; there is still reason to think they are variants of the same sign.

pa_2 is now transliterated qa: see above.

pu_2 appears to represent phu, but possibly bu in $da\text{-}pu_2\text{-}ri\text{-}to\text{-}jo$.

ta_2 is definitely tya; for $o\text{-}ta_2\text{-}we\text{-}o$ read $o\text{-}two\text{-}we\text{-}o$.

48† A great deal of discussion of individual ideograms has not seriously called in question the general conclusions stated here. It has been suggested that the ideograms are conventional and therefore not actual pictures, so that accidental features may be mentioned in the description which do not tally with the details of the ideogram: e.g. the Knossos chariot tablets **265–271** consistently show the frame as having no wheels fitted, but it is tempting to associate *a-ra-ro-mo-te-me-na* with *a-mo-ta* 'wheels' and translate 'equipped with wheels'; or *e-me po-de* (PY **236**=Ta 641) may be taken as 'with one foot', although the ideogram clearly shows three legs, for it would hardly be recognizable as a tripod-cauldron, if it did not. Similarly it has been shown (Killen, 1964*a*, pp. 71 ff.) that RAM is employed as a sign not only for castrated males, and for lambs (with prefixed *ki*), but also for sheep of mixed sex, as well as specifically male sheep.

Much argument has raged over the transliteration of ideograms, and the English authors were persuaded to abandon the use of their native language in the interests of international agreement. Since it was undesirable as well as impracticable to change the method used in this book, Part III and the Glossary continue to transcribe ideograms by English words; but it should be understood that this is a special expedient, and all future work should employ only the Latin names and numbers approved by the Fifth International Colloquium on Mycenaean Studies at Salamanca in 1970 (see *Acta Mycenaea* [Ruipérez, 1972], I, pp. xx–xxi).

A number of new ideograms have been added to the list on pp. 50–1, partly as the result of fresh discoveries, more often through more careful discrimination of variants. Since they are almost all unidentified there is little point in repeating the detailed list referred to above. The important ones are the subject of discussion where the texts are given in Part III. However, a few comments on points of detail are required.

100 MAN is now used for all forms of the ideogram, so that *101* and *103* are now suppressed. Bennett (1966, pp. 18–25) has demonstrated the probable genesis of these variants, and the theory that *103* had a special significance ('craftsman': Palmer, 1963*a*, p. 137) has not been confirmed.

*75 WE used ideographically may perhaps refer to other animals as well as sheep; see WE in Glossary.

*65 FLOUR is a possible meaning, but the sign may also refer to some kind of grain other than wheat or barley (Chadwick, 1966, p. 31).

125 seems not to be distinguished into two signs depending upon which way the top element points; *124* is a ligature of *125+123*, *126* of *125+*KU.

128 should have an extra element at the top; it is a ligature of KA + NA + KO.

130: the forms given in columns P and M should be transcribed OIL + WE; whether the second form in column K is the equivalent of this is uncertain, but possible (Chadwick, 1966, pp. 26–8; Bennett, 1966, pp. 15–18).

131: the variant forms are discussed by Bennett (1966, pp. 11–15) and Chadwick (1968c, pp. 196–7); the suggestion (p. 223) that the incomplete form of *131* means 'new wine' still seems acceptable.

133: a ligature of A + RE + PA in either ascending or descending order.

134: no promising value for this ideogram has emerged, and the problem is complicated by the discovery of a similar, but not identical, sign (*190*) on the Mycenae *Oi* tablets. On this see **321** = Oi 701, p. 506.

135: a ligature of ME + RI = *meli* 'honey'.

142: no secure identification.

143: silver is no more than a guess.

31 = SA: the connexion with flax looks good, but it is normally measured in units, hence perhaps bales of flax fibres are meant rather than finished linen cloth.

145: the attempts that have been made to give this sign a meaning other than WOOL have failed (Killen, 1962a).

146: on this see Lejeune (1964b), Chadwick (1964b, p. 24). Its connexion with textiles is beyond reasonable doubt, but its exact meaning is still unclear.

152: the syllabic WI inside the outline clearly stands for *wi-ri-no* = *wrīnos* 'oxhide'.

155: this is probably no more than a variant of *110*, which is used as a measure; the equation with κοτύλη is tempting.

156: a ligature of TU + RO₂ = *tūroi* (or *turyoi* ?).

231: the upper form is certainly an arrow; the lower form is more probably a light dart for throwing: see p. 513.

233: the SWORD may prove to be rather DAGGER; it is hard to judge scale or proportions on such a drawing, and the Homeric use of φάσγανον ought not to weigh too heavily against 'dagger'.

A number of new ideograms have been recorded, but they are all rare, and some are possibly variants of others here listed. For full lists see Ruipérez, 1972, I, pp. xx–xxi.

p. 52† On *o-pe-ro*, not itself an abbreviation, see Glossary, s.v. *o-pe-ro*[1].

p. 53† On this subject see further Killen, 1964*a*, 1966*a*. Adjuncts are listed, and their meaning, where known, is given in the Glossary.

p. 54† On the Linear A system of fractions, see now Was (1971).

p. 55† Exceptionally KN Og 7504, listing ivory (*e-re-pa-ta*), has 🔡 𐄷 30, apparently a confusion of two ways of writing the same weight.

p. 57† The sign probably always means WOOL rather than woollen cloth; but occasionally cloth is weighed in WOOL units.

p. 59† This equation fails to allow for the difference between wheat (in the Mycenaean ration) and barley (in the Mesopotamian one); the ratio is roughly 1:2, as is evident from the classical rations quoted above. The primary dry unit will thus have a range of 75–100 l.

p. 59‡ This tablet allows a mathematical equation (see p. 420) which proves that $9\frac{3}{4}$ units of barley can only be divided between the eighteen men and eight boys so as to give credible rations, if each man or boy receives T $3\frac{3}{4}$. On the supposition that barley has roughly half the value of wheat, this is nearly equivalent to the Pylos women's ration of T 2 of wheat. That this might also be a man's ration appears from MY Au 658.4, where twenty men are allocated four units of wheat.

p. 60† The necessary measurement of vessels was undertaken on the material recovered from Pylos by M. Lang (1964*b*). From the table she published it is evident that the system of measurement interferes with the values obtained at the lower end of the scale; for instance, there are large concentrations of vessels measuring 0·25, 0·3, 0·4, 0·5, 0·6, 0·7, 0·75 litres. Thus only the larger vessels are much use, but significant peaks appear around 2·4 and 3·2 litres. This suggests that 0·8 litres is an element in the system, and Miss Lang identified this with ◁ 1, thereby effecting a reduction on the figures proposed in the first edition of 60%. The effect of this, however, would be to upset the range of values suggested on p. 59, and to make the smallest unit (▽) equal to 0·2 l., which is lower than the smallest unit of any contemporary system. It would therefore seem more plausible to adapt Miss Lang's calculations by supposing that 0·8 l. represents ▽ 2 (= ◁ $\frac{1}{2}$), so that the vessels containing

2·4 and 3·2 l. would match figures of ◁ 1½ and ◁ 2. This involves a reduction of 20% in the values proposed on p. 60, viz.:

DRY MEASURE	LIQUID MEASURE
1 unit = 96 litres	1 unit = 28·8 l.
T 1 = 9·6 l.	៕ 1 = 9·6 l.

$$◁ = 1·6 \text{ l.}$$
$$▽ = 0·4 \text{ l.}$$

The discussion of this problem by Palmer (1963 a, pp. 12–15) is vitiated by his unwarranted inference that T 5 represents the standard ration for a man (see pp. 418, 420). Once this is appreciated, as also the difference between rations of wheat and barley, which is at times overlooked by Palmer, then the foundation of his argument collapses. Any attempt to correlate Mycenaean with classical measures can only function at the level of the *kotyle* and *khoinix*, which show the same 4:1 ratio as Mycenaean ▽ and ◁. Thus Palmer's identification of ◁ with the *khoinix* may well be right linguistically, but there is no reason to prefer the Attic value of *c.* 0·9 l. to the Pheidonian value of *c.* 1·3 l. It must be grasped that all values proposed are merely an attempt to establish an order of magnitude, and none should be regarded as an exact determination, which will probably remain impossible until a vessel is discovered which is clearly marked as a measure.

The Pylos tablet Fr (formerly Gn) 1184 is more helpful than appeared at first sight. Obvious as it may seem to us to standardize the size of vessels, ancient pots, being hand-made, show a wide range of values. If a stirrup-jar held exactly half a major unit of oil, only 36 jars would be needed for the 18 units of oil here mentioned, instead of the 38 actually recorded. If, however, we divide 18 × 28·8 litres by 38, we obtain a value of 13·6 l. per jar, which is within the observed limits of 12–14 l. (see p. 60). Again the figure is probably not exact, but is of the right order of magnitude.

p. 60‡   The study of 'Cypro-Minoan' writing has made some progress since this section was written, but new finds have been relatively few: a clay cylinder from Enkomi and a further tablet from Ugarit are the most important. E. Masson (1971) has put forward the interesting suggestion that the Enkomi tablets show a different application of the script from the other Cypriot examples, and that therefore two languages may be represented by this script.

The important fact which concerns Mycenaean writing is that the affiliation of the various Cypriot scripts seems undoubted; but the date of the fragmentary tablet from Enkomi (no. 6 on p. 61), *c.* 1500 B.C., shows that the system must have been adopted from Crete rather than Greece, and this is confirmed by the divergences between the organization of the classical Cypriot and Linear B systems. Their common parent seems to be Linear A, and this has the consequence that features of Linear B which are not shared by Cypriot ought not to be attributed to Linear A. Thus the two series of dentals, which Linear B distinguishes as voiced and unvoiced, probably represented a different distinction in Linear A; it is Linear B *da* which corresponds to Cypriot *ta*, though *ti* and *to* agree in the two systems.

The exact nature of this relationship will not become clear until the values of Cypro-Minoan signs can be determined.

CHAPTER III

THE MYCENAEAN LANGUAGE

p. 68† On the prehistory of the Greek language, see now Chadwick, 1963 *c*.

p. 71† A great deal of debate has raged around this question of the method to be adopted in interpreting Mycenaean words, but it is as absurd to deny any validity to the etymological method as it is to rely on it exclusively. Where the Mycenaean spelling exactly fits the classical word, having due regard to the difference of dialects, and the sense so offered can be shown to agree with the context, we should hesitate to refuse an identification. Cases which are based exclusively on such identities, without any support from the context, must be examined critically. A few such interpretations given in the Vocabulary of the first edition have been withdrawn from the Glossary of this edition. But the contextual method can rarely, without far more material than we have, define the meaning of a word as closely as the linguistic one; and we must often be content if the linguistic meaning is not inappropriate to what we can judge of the context. As our appreciation of the purpose of the tablets improves, so it becomes easier to judge between rival interpretations and to achieve more precision in the meanings assigned.

p. 71‡ The example of *E-ke-ra₂-wo* was an unhappy choice, since it has become clear that *ra₂* is not just a substitute for *ra₁*, but implies a special pronunciation, such as *rya*; and this is confirmed by what appears to be a variant spelling of the name, *[e]-ke-ri-ja-wo* PY Qa 1292. This name therefore belongs to the large class of Greek names ending in *-āwōn* (e.g. *a-re-ta-wo* = Ἀρετάων, *ma-ka-wo* = Μαχάων; see Landau, 1958, pp. 185–6); but the identification of the first element is then speculative. We might cite instead among the leading citizens of Pylos *a-pi-me-de* = Ἀμφιμήδης, *a-ko-so-ta* temptingly interpreted by Palmer as *Alxoitās*, or the **e-te-wo-ke-re-we* = Ἐτεοκλῆς who is to be reconstructed from the patronymic of his two sons. Transparently Greek names are to be found in all classes of society; and although the Knossos sheep tablets show an above-average proportion of apparently non-Greek names, many names of high officials too defy Greek interpretation. One is tempted to believe that the ethnic mixture was well advanced, even at Knossos, and that, as in classical times, we cannot deduce that a man was not a Greek speaker just because his name is meaningless in Greek. We might indeed argue a contrary proposition: that Greek names which are sobriquets (like *e-ru-to-ro* 'Red' or *ti-ri-po-di-ko* 'Little Three-foot') were given to non-Greek speakers by their Greek masters because their native names were difficult to pronounce or remember.

p. 72† Researches by M. Pope (1964) have demonstrated that the date of borrowing of Linear B signs from Linear A cannot be as late as the latest (LM I) examples of the latter. This is some support for the view of Furumark and Pugliese Carratelli, that the date of origin may lie as far back as the sixteenth century.

p. 73† The division into East and West Greek dialects is perhaps not so fundamental as used to be thought, though it still serves to distinguish Arcado-Cypriot, Attic and Ionic from West Greek. On the view of Risch (1955), Aeolic is to be regarded as basically on the West rather than East Greek side of the line, and East Greek no longer seems an adequate label for all non-Western dialects. The sibilant *s* of Mycenaean does not appear to represent anything but σ or σσ (see below, p. 398).

p. 74† The suggestion that the apparent *o* vocalism of certain Mycenaean words like *qe-to-ro-po-pi* is really a graphic device for syllabic *r̥* has something to be said for it; at least, if *r̥* survived in pronunciation, the scribes may have used *ro* as the nearest approximation in writing. If accepted, this allows personal names beginning *a-no-* to be interpreted as *Anr̥-*: e.g. *a-no-me-de* = *Anr̥mēdēs*, *a-no-qo-ta* = *Anr̥qʰontas*; but *Anor-* is also possible.

p. 74‡ The form *to-ro-qe-jo-me-no* has also been cited as evidence for the thematic inflexion of verbs in *-έω*; but although the parallel with τροπέω appears close, the j is left unexplained, and it is not impossible that the classical forms in -έω are a conflation of *-$ei̯ō$ and a different type in -$ēmi$. Until further evidence is forthcoming it seems safer not to build much on either of these verbs.

75† To the vases we can now add the tablets from Thebes, which at least confirm the general likeness of the Mycenaean dialect at all sites, though there is still too little for any real proof; it would certainly seem that the noun declension at Thebes follows the normal Mycenaean pattern.

76† It has been shown that these minor differences of spelling are associated with certain scribal hands. Consequently Risch (1966*b*) has put forward the ingenious suggestion that the rarer forms represent a social difference and are, so to speak, sub-standard. As always, it is the sub-standard forms which tend to become the standard in the later history of the language. The evidence is still too tenuous to judge this suggestion.

76‡ A more up-to-date collection of examples of Mycenaean grammar has been printed by Vilborg (1960) and comments on this section will be restricted to corrections of errors and additions of importance.

76¶ See further Hester (1958).

77† *a-pi-qo-to* is too obscure to be used for this purpose.

77‡ The interpretation of *e-wi-su-zo-ko*, *e-wi-su-*79-ko* is dubious; the value *zu* for *79 remains unconfirmed.

77¶ Delete *u-ru-pi-ja-jo* = 'Ολυμπιαῖοι. In *u-ru-to*, *u-ru-* probably stands for *wru-*; see Glossary.

77†† Sign *43 is now transcribed conventionally a_3, but its value remains *ai*. On *34, see above, p. 386.

78† *pe-i* is probably to be read *sphehi*; see Glossary.

79† The most likely explanation of ra_2 and ro_2 is that they note forms in -*rya*, -*ryo*, but it cannot be ruled out that these signs may sometimes function as disyllabic. The feminine agent suffix -τρια is spelt -*ti-ri-ja* by one scribe at Pylos, -*ti-ra*$_2$ by another.

p. 79‡ It has become clear that there is no lack of consistency in the notation of *w* in Mycenaean script. The phoneme /*w*/ was never lost, so that the apparent cases of its absence must be due to faulty etymology. The intrusive *w* is also, where not a glide, due to the same cause.

p. 79¶ More complicated are the cases of initial *we-* which correspond to later ὐ +vowel (e.g. *we-a-re-pe, we-a₂-re-jo*; contrast *we-a₂-no-i = wehanoihi*; Chadwick, 1958*b*, p. 308); it is unclear whether this is graphic or phonetic. It is also possible that *u* substitutes for *w* +vowel in some words (other than *o-u-ru-to*, see above, which is motivated by the lack of a sign for *wu*); this explanation has been proposed for *o-u-ka = owika*.

p. 80† There are still only these two examples of *s* < *ky*, and the first at least is suspect (see Glossary); *wa-na-se-wi-ja* and the related *wa-na-so-i* are thus isolated, and since the stem may have been *wanakt-*, as in dat. *wa-na-ka-te*, rather than *wanak-*, *s* may here be the product of *kty*. It is also possible that the resemblance of these words to ἄνασσα is a mirage. Thus it appears safer to delete this suggestion and to accept *z* as the normal Mycenaean reflex of *ky* (see below).

p. 80‡ The case for the retention of intervocalic -*h*- now seems stronger and, where the etymology is certain, the reconstructed forms of the Glossary now show this. What is less certain, but may well be right, is whether Grassmann's Law, which governs the dissimilation of aspirates, had operated by this date. The similar facts of Sanskrit are no proof of its antiquity, and forms like *ko-to-no-o-ko*, if really *ktoino-hokhos*, argue in favour of its late date. However, the regular restoration of these aspirates might cause confusion, and the interpretation of forms such as *e-ke* as *ekhei* rather than *hekhei* has been continued. The question is discussed by Ruijgh (1967, pp. 44–6) who favours the retention of these aspirates.

p. 80¶ The interpretation of Mycenaean *z* has led to much debate. The facts are best explained on the theory that the sound was already some kind of sibilant (distinct from those indicated by *s*). Lejeune (1960*c* = 1971, pp. 95–139) favours a 'strong sibilant'; but an affricate of the type *ts* (or *tʃ*) seems more plausible (Chadwick, 1964*a*, p. 321; Heubeck, 1971*b*). The signs are presumably capable of use for both voiced and unvoiced forms, so the interpreted forms have been written with *ts*/*dz*, though this must not be taken as expressing a final judgement on its phonetic realization. The product of this *ts* would be classical σσ (Attic and Boeotian ττ) or in initial position σ/τ; *dz* would yield *zd*, noted regularly by ζ.

The major difficulty in this view is the existence of the apparent alternation of *k* and *z*. It is just possible that *a-ze-ti-ri-ja* is a different word from *a-ke-ti-ri-ja*; but the place name *ke-i-ja-ka-ra-na* is hardly likely to be different from *ze-i-ja-ka-ra-na*. The fact that most of the examples are in proper names suggests that a substrate influence may be at work here. But in any case it appears easier to believe that *ke* and *tse* were different realizations of what must earlier have been palatalized *k'e*, than that these palatal forms continued in pronunciation, since no theory of this kind can account for *z* < *dy* and initial **y-* of words like ζεῦγος. The origin of the *z-* series as having been developed from *ky-* will fit the rules which appear to govern the structure of the syllabary; but the sound must have progressed beyond this point in order to explain the clear facts.

The equation of the Mycenaean with the classical sibilants is complicated. Original *ss*, dental stop + *s*, and *ty* will all have developed to *ss* and then in Attic-Ionic and Arcadian to *s*. The Mycenaean notation *s* is ambiguous, and we cannot easily choose between *tossos* and *tosos* as the interpretation of *to-so*. The words which have *-t/y-* with a morpheme boundary intervening (e.g. the feminine adjectives in *-we-sa* = *-wessa*) must have had *-ss-* in Mycenaean, since this is maintained in Arcadian. But the group *-ky-* is normally represented by Mycenaean *z*, hence this must still have been at a stage distinct from *ss*, probably therefore *ts*, which develops normally to Arcadian -σσ- (Attic -ττ-). The complications of -ττ- in Attic are possibly due to Boeotian influence (Chadwick, 1969, pp. 91–3).

The use of a special sign in some forms of Cypriot with a value *ga* is irrelevant; there is no reason to think it had a spirant value as used to be assumed.

81† The pronunciation of the labio-velars remains a matter of conjecture, but the consensus of opinion favours their retention in Mycenaean. There is, however, one exception, hinted at on p. 82, but the essential point had not then been grasped. The two terms describing women, *ra-pi-ti-ra₂* and *ra-qi-ti-ra₂*, can now be shown to refer to different groups and they must have different interpretations. Once this confusing example is set aside, all the cases where a labial appears to replace a labio-velar occur in words which also contain a second labio-velar: thus the personal name *pe-re-qo-ta* is shown by the analysis of the tablets concerned to be identical with *qe-re-qo-ta*, the first form being due to a dissimilation of labio-velars. A form earlier unknown proves this conclusively: *i-po-po-qo-i* (PY Fn 79, linked with *ze-u-ke-u-si* 'drivers of yokes of oxen') must be *hippo-phorgᵘoihi* 'horse-pasturers, ostlers'. In all other cases the *-k'w-* group of the word for 'horse', which is not a labio-velar, but shares its treatment, appears as q (*i-qo, i-qi-ja, i-qe-ja*). The cases where -*kw*- conceals a morpheme boundary are, however, spelt with two syllabic signs (e.g. *o-da-ke-we-ta*=*odak-wenta, te-tu-ko-wo-a*=*tetukh-woha*).

The sign for *qa* (*16*) has been discussed above. The new transcription is adopted throughout the Glossary and Part III, and *pa₂* in the earlier part of the book must be understood as *qa*.

The identification of a labio-velar in the root of τρέπω is not entirely at variance with the Latin and Sanskrit forms with -*p*-. The Indo-European base **ter*- will have had two suffixes, -*p*- and -*qᵘ*-, in combination with which it will show zero grade in the base and full grade in the suffix; hence we can postulate for I.-E. **trep*- and **treqᵘ*-, either or both of which may have led to Greek τρέπω; but only the latter will account for Mycenaean *to-ro-qo*, etc.

p. 82† It is possible, but not certain, that *we-pe-za* is to be interpreted *hwespedza* with -*sp*-<-*ksp*-. A remarkable assimilation occurs if *pe-qa-to* is *peggᵘaton*<**pedgᵘaton* (see Glossary).

p. 83† On the semantic value of the instrumental case see below, p. 403. The absence of an instrumental in the singular may well be merely a result of the spelling conventions; for the form of an instrumental would probably coincide graphically with the dative. Likewise, the existence of an independent locative cannot be proved, since the singular *a*- and *o*-stem forms (-αι, -οι) would be indistinguishable from the dative. The consonant-stem datives in -*i* are certainly not restricted to locative force.

p. 83‡ The form *ko-to-no* is now known to be accusative dual. There is a possible instance of a dative dual in *wa-na-so-i*, which might represent *wanassoiin*, but other interpretations are possible: see Glossary.

p. 84† The explanation of the dual forms has been attacked, but still seems the most acceptable. It should be remarked that the dual of *ko-wa* 'girl' is not written *ko-wo* (e.g. PY **6**=Ab 379), since this would invite confusion with the word for 'boy'. Whether this is a graphic device, or is the starting point for the classical development in -ᾱ is not clear; but the parallel of Latin *filiabus, deabus* may suggest that in these cases the later development had already begun. That the nominative plural had already become -*ai* is evident from occasional spellings with *ra₃*, e.g. *pi-je-ra₃, di-pte-ra₃*.

p. 84‡ The presence of final -*s* in the nominative singular of masculine *a*-stems may be deduced from the following consideration. The genitive singular in -*āo* is certainly, whatever the precise origin of the *-o*, an innovation replacing in-herited *-ās*; but the motive for this replacement must be to avoid confusion with the nominative singular, since there is evidence, at least for feminines, that the nominative plural was already in *-ai* (see above). Therefore there would have been no need for the innovation, had the nominative remained *-ā*. The Homeric and dialect forms without final *-s* are either the short-vowel type (e.g. ἱππότᾰ), which may have a special history, or in view of their restriction to a few dialects, notably Boeotian, may be later reformations rather than inherited archaisms.

84¶ Although the interpretation of *-o-i*, *-a-i* as variant spellings for *-ois*, *-ais* has been supported by Ruijgh (1967, pp. 76–8), the weight of opinion is now firmly in favour of *-oihi*, *-āhi*, supposing that intervocalic *-h-* is preserved. It must, however, be observed that it is impossible to set up a rule that where *i* is written after another vowel, this always indicates a disyllabic pronunciation; cf. the alternative spellings *ko-to-na* and *ko-to-i-na* of what must be diphthongal οι in κτοίνα, since this is an *o*-grade noun of the same type as ποίνη. The objection that since the dative plural termination appears in third declension nouns as *-si* even where vowels precede (e.g. *ka-ke-u-si*, *ti-ri-si*), it should also have been restored in the first and second declensions may be countered with the theory that Mycenaean shows a transitional stage when the restoration of *-si* for *-hi* after a vowel had not yet extended outside the third declension; see Lejeune, 1968 *c*, p. 220.

. 85† Kn Se 1042 is now joined to Se 891, but the context still remains obscure; it is, however, beyond question that *e-re-pa-te-jo-pi* is a masculine (or neuter) instrumental plural of an *o*-stem adjective. Other possible examples are cited by Lejeune (1958 *a*, pp. 166–7); *wo-wo-pi* in the compound *mo-ro-ko-wo-wo-pi* is hard to separate from *wo-wo*.

. 85‡ To the forms of the dative plural may be added *ti-ri-|si = trisi* (from τρεῖς), and probably *tu-ka-ṭạ-|ṣi*, which, if the reading is sound, probably stands for *thugatarsi* (from θυγάτηρ). On the extension of *-si* from consonant stems, see above.

. 85¶ The suggestion that the dative singular in *-e* may be due to confusion with *-i* is definitely to be rejected, since it is now clear that this phenomenon is rare and restricted to special circumstances (Hester, 1958). The spelling *-e* is generally accepted as showing the inherited I.-E. termination *-ei*, which was later replaced by the locatival forms in -*i*, a process which had clearly begun in Mycenaean times and was more advanced at Mycenae than elsewhere.

p. 86† There is no good reason to suppose an abnormal paradigm of the type *medzōn*, plural *medzohes*; it is more probable that the nominative singular was still *medzōs*. The presence of intervocalic -*h*- in these words is demonstrated by the use of -*a*$_2$ in the neuter plural, and may be presumed before other vowels.

p. 87† This conclusion is supported by Lejeune (1958*a*, p. 184), but Shipp (1961, pp. 29–41) asserts that Homeric and Mycenaean Greek represent different lines of development, and that Homeric Greek is more archaic than Mycenaean. This seems a desperate attempt to save his earlier theory. There is no evidence that the *-bh-* element, observable in numerous I.-E. languages, is ever employed as a singular, if we exclude Greek, the case under discussion. In Armenian the plural has been recharacterized by the addition of the plural morpheme *k'*, so that the use of -*b* in the singular is hardly proof that it is an inherited use. The Balto-Slavonic forms in -*mi* are enigmatic, but cannot be used to prove that -*bhi* was a singular morpheme.

p. 87‡ The reconstruction *sphehi*, in line with -*oihi*, etc., seems preferable; but compare the note on p. 84¶ above.

p. 87¶ The attempt to interpret *to-e*, *to-me* as a verb (Palmer, 1963*a*, pp. 205–7) is unconvincing; in particular, an athematic infinitive in -*men* is unexpected in Mycenaean, and there are no parallels. *to-e*, however, as dative of a pronoun remains an isolated form and could even be an error. In PY Eb 156 the identification of *85* as *au* leads to the interpretation of *to-jo-qe au-to-jo* as *toio qᵘe autoio* 'and of the same', or perhaps rather 'and of him himself', since in this use ὁ need not have been in origin the definite article.

p. 87†† *to-to*: more likely < **tod-tod* than = τοῦτο; see Glossary.

p. 87‡‡ No new numerals have appeared, but there are new forms:
    2: *dwo* (followed by numeral 2 as check, PY **323**=Sb 1315.3), probably to be read as *duō*, though *dwō* (as in δ(ϝ)ώδεκα) is also possible.
    3: *ti-ri-si*=*trisi*, dat. plur.

p. 88† The example of *a-pe-do-ke* PY **305**=Fr (formerly Gn) 1184 remains unique, and attempts have therefore been made to explain it as due to something other than the augment (e.g. *ap-es-dōke* with *es<ex*). But these may well prove to be unnecessary, for it is hard to explain the universality of the augment in later Greek if it did not exist in Mycenaean speech, even though unrecorded in the tablets.

. 88‡ Under aorist middle, delete *ze-to* and infinitive *wi-de-ta-i*.

. 89† A new adjective in *-teros* is *za̯-we-te-ra* = *tsā̯we(s)tera* 'this year's': see Glossary.

. 90† The value of the termination *-pi* = *-phi* has been much disputed. Our original idea was that it served as an instrumental, and where this sense was excluded, notably in place names, the value was locatival. However, this leads to the surprising conclusion that there are two ways of expressing the locative of a plural place name such as *pa-ki-ja-ne*: *pa-ki-ja-si* with the inherited locative ending *-si* and *pa-ki-ja-pi*. Consequently the theory was put forward, and most persuasively argued by Ilievski (1961, 1970), that the *-pi* forms of place names represented a survival of the ablative case. Since in classical Greek (but with the probable exception of Arcado-Cypriot) the ablative is syncretized with the genitive, it is necessary to suppose an earlier syncretism of ablative with instrumental (as in Latin); in the singular of *o*-stems the forms would have been identical. The ablatival theory has much to commend it, for it supplies a need; there is no other locution which appears to express motion or origin from a place, for neither ἀπύ nor ἐξ appear to be used. On the other hand, a full survival of separate case-forms in all declensions and numbers for the ablative is doubtful, and we may perhaps see in Mycenaean the transitional stage when *-phi* had become restricted in this sense to place names, and survived only in a limited use, like the locative in Latin. It is possible that a better understanding of the purpose of certain sets of tablets where forms in *-pi* are used will clarify the question; for instance, the Pylos *Na* tablets (see pp. 295–301, 468–73), which are generally accepted as being payments received from the places enumerated, have four such forms (*ku-te-re-u-pi*, *po-to-ro-wa-pi*, *ri-sa-pi*, *wa-a₂-te-pi*) and none in *-si*. Even so, consistency in such matters is not to be demanded of busy accountants. Since only plural place names of the first or third declension will show the *-pi* ending, their rarity need occasion no surprise. However, this interpretation would involve also taking *po-to-ro-wa-pi* in PY Aa 76 as ablative, where a locative sense appears much more likely. Since both ablative and locative functions are shown by -φι in Homer, it is possible that the earlier distinctions were already breaking down in Mycenaean.

p. 91† The addition of *a-sa-mi-to*=ἀσάμινθος to the vocabulary is another notable example of the use of a Homeric word, which must be a borrowing from a pre-Greek source.

p. 91‡ *-de* when used in the compound *to-so-de* is also probably still connective (Ruijgh, 1967, pp. 337–50).

p. 91¶ On the analysis of *o-da-a₂* see p. 423 and Chadwick, 1971, pp. 102–3.

CHAPTER IV

THE PERSONAL NAMES

p. 92† The study of the personal names has been pursued by many authors, in particular by Landau (1958). The general considerations set forth here have not been impugned, and the additions to the catalogue of personal names have not changed the picture. It should be noted that the 'Index of Personal Names' mentioned on p. 93 has been replaced by a complete catalogue, but this is now incorporated in the Glossary of this edition. A considerable number of names which are incomplete has still been omitted.

Since it is impossible to re-write this chapter to take account of new developments, the commentary here will be restricted to important points, and no conclusions should be drawn from silence.

p. 94† On the question of final *-s*, see pp. 400–1.

p. 94‡ It now appears improbable that *-qo-ta* can correspond to -βάτης, but the other choices remain open.

p. 95† We may add *a-ka-me-ne*, possibly *Alkāmenēs* or *Akhaimenēs*, and *a-o-ri-me-ne*= *Ahorimenēs*. The form *a-re-zo-me-ne* has been shown to be due to a false restoration; it should be *a-re-i̯-me-ne*, a variant spelling of *a-re-me-ne*, both representing *Areimenēs*.

p. 97† The name *pe-pi-te-me-no-jo* (gen.) from the Thebes tablets is *Pepithmenos*, a reduplicated perfect participle from πείθω.

p. 100† The genitive *wa-de-o* cannot come from a *u*-stem.

p. 100‡ This type has been discussed by Szemerényi (1957), and it appears likely that they are shortened forms of compound names (e.g. Ἀλεξεύς from Ἀλέξανδρος or the like). An interesting addition to the list is *si-mi-te-u* = Σμινθεύς, the Homeric epithet of Apollo.

p. 101† Although it is impossible to prove this as yet, it may be that some women's names in -*o* represent feminine ŏ-stems, a type unknown in classical Greece, though common among place names and common nouns.

p. 102† These lists could now be expanded, but everything indicates that the stock of Mycenaean personal names is held in common by all Mycenaean peoples. The tablets from Thebes contain many names also known from other sites.

CHAPTER V

THE EVIDENCE OF THE TABLETS

p. 106† This is the section of the book which is most difficult to bring up to date, because it is here that most progress is now being made. There are still many documents which are, to some extent, obscure; for even when we can translate them, we still need to know why such a fact needed to be recorded. The re-creation of the original archives is still far from complete, but the study of the tablets in their original sets, i.e. groups intended to be read by the scribe as a single document, has opened our eyes to many new facts. The cryptic style of the entries becomes more understandable when we can compare the tablets which were originally filed in the same basket. The arduous task of joining fragments, especially among the Knossos tablets, has also led to new discoveries.

I would now take an even less optimistic view of the value of the Homeric poems as evidence for the material culture of Mycenaean Greece. The similarities are all too often those which are imposed by the nature of a monarchical society, operating a non-monetary economy in a small area, rather than individual details unlikely to recur by chance. Conflicts between

405

the archaeological evidence and the facts reported by Homer are many, and once the nature of the Homeric poems is appreciated, they are inevitable and without significance for our reaction to the poems. Mycenaean documents must be interpreted in the light of archaeological evidence and parallels from elsewhere; Homer must never be allowed to cast doubt on the facts recovered from the tablets, though at times he may confirm them. This is particularly important in the matter of geography; see section 9 and p. 415 below.

p. 109† New discoveries have not significantly changed the picture. The total absence of any kind of inscription on tombs or public buildings argues strongly against general literacy; yet the study of handwriting confirms that literacy was not the prerogative of a few professional scribes. The number of different hands identifiable among the Knossos tablets may amount to as many as seventy-five (Olivier, 1967b, p. 101). We should think of all the main Palace officials as literate, and capable of setting stylus to clay when required.

p. 111† There is a third type of tablet which is in some ways intermediate between the *palm-leaf* and the *page* type. These are larger than the usual *palm-leaf*, but although approaching the proportions of the *page* type are wider than they are high, often tapering slightly towards the right and left. Good examples are KN Ln 1568, PY **169** = Es 646, MY **106** = Ge 603.

p. 112† On the whole tablets were tailored to suit the text to be accommodated, and on large tablets each entry is normally accommodated on a single line (but entries are allowed to run over on PY **28** = An 607). Large areas of uninscribed clay are generally avoided, but examples occur (e.g. PY Cn 1286). The use of the reverse is avoided in sets of large tablets intended to be read continuously. PY **172** = Tn 316 is clearly exceptional, and bears evidence of erasure and re-writing on a massive scale (see p. 458).

p. 113† A curious case where there appears to be an equivalence between two commodities is PY **319** = Un 1322, the text of which is unfortunately in a very bad state (Chadwick, 1964b). It does, however, appear that twice the ideogram *146, apparently a textile or the like, is followed immediately by the ideogram WHEAT. Where two ideograms are so associated, one normally qualifies the other, but this can hardly apply here. The use of the word *o-no* on this tablet and elsewhere suggests a payment in kind; see Glossary, s.v. *o-no*[1].

The palace revenues may be in part the product of industries organized by the royal officials. The production of woollen cloth at Knossos, and of linen and metal-goods at Pylos, seems to have been on a very large scale; and the surplus in these items may well have been traded abroad, by royal officials rather than private merchants, in exchange for luxuries like gold and ivory which were not available locally.

113‡ It is a strange fact that all the tablets bearing a month date appear to be concerned with religious offerings. The reason for this has not been properly explained, for the records of rations for women and children at Pylos also seem to be calculated on a monthly basis, and this is explicitly stated in KN **35**=Am 819, **89**=E 777, yet in such documents there is never a mention of the date. The theory that KN **207**=V 280 and PY **172**=Tn 316 are calendars is certainly false (see pp. 475, 459). The term *za-we-te*=*tsāwetes* 'this year' is further confirmation of the absence of sets of documents relating to different years. The incomplete Pylos *Ab* series may be the next year's version of *Aa*, though there are differences in the content of the tablets; but once *Ab* had been completed, the *Aa* series might perhaps have been scrapped. The cases where information collected on 'palm-leaf' tablets is recopied on to 'page' tablets (as the two versions of the Pylos land-ownership documents, **114–148**) clearly do not relate to different years.

114† The sealings from Pylos and their probable relation to sets of tablets has been discussed by Chadwick (1958*c*). It seems likely that baskets or boxes containing tablets were labelled with one or two words serving to identify them.

114‡ Progress in locating the source of tablets has been recorded by Olivier (1967*b*), but the general picture remains unchanged. Olivier's work on the scribal hands has revealed a curious fact about the tablets found at *B* (the Room of the Chariot Tablets): although a number of different scribes can be distinguished, almost the whole of the tablets from this area are so much alike in handwriting that some special explanation is needed. An office under the control of an official who insisted that all his clerks imitate his handwriting is the minimum hypothesis necessary to account for the facts; a theory that these documents belong to a scribal school (Chadwick, 1968*b*) and in consequence cannot be used as evidence of a real situation has not been refuted, and must be reckoned as at least a possibility. The chief difference would be that no deductions can be drawn from the *Sc* tablets about the size of the chariot force at Knossos; see p. 522.

p. 117† Many of the examples quoted are further discussed at the appropriate point in Part III. Some of the apparent anomalies have been cleared up, and there can be no doubt that the scribes displayed a reasonable level of mathematical proficiency.

p. 120† The suggestion of 'priest-kings' has been attacked by Bennett (1961), who rightly emphasizes that there is no positive evidence in the tablets pointing to the divinity of the king. There is, however, a problem over the word *wanax*, which is believed by many writers to be in some cases a divine title. The difficulty is to be sure when a deity is meant; but there is at least a case for so interpreting the title on the Pylos *Fr* tablets (see p. 480). If the jar from Thebes is an import, the kingdom to be inferred from the adjective 'royal' will be elsewhere; but it goes to confirm the ubiquity of kings in Mycenaean Greece. *E-ke-ra₂-wo* is not to be rendered *Ekhelāwōn* (see p. 395), and it has been questioned whether the Pylos tablet (**171** = Un 718) proves his identity with the king; it would seem best to suspend judgement here.

p. 120‡ It must be confessed that there is still no compelling evidence that the *lāwāgetās* was a military officer; one might contemplate other solutions, for instance, that this was a title conferred on the heir apparent. Etymology is a weak basis on which to found an explanation of his function.

p. 120¶ The function and status of the *te-re-ta* remains one of the most obscure problems connected with the holding of land. They are officials or functionaries who are mentioned in connexion with the holding of land, at least whenever the context is clear. It is also likely, on grounds of etymology and because of PY Eb 149 and **148** = Ep 613.4, that the verb *te-re-ja-e* expresses the function of the *te-re-ta*, but what this is remains uncertain. The new reading of Ep 613.4 makes it virtually certain that Eb 149 and 940 are parts of the same tablet.

The main rival theories are: (1) the *te-re-ta* have a religious function, and the name *telestās* has obvious associations with τέλη in the sense of religious obligations (see Chadwick, 1957a, pp. 126–9); (2) the *te-re-ta* are persons who hold land in return for services owed to the king (Palmer, 1963a, pp. 190–6); this associates the word with τέλη in the sense of dues or taxes. Palmer rightly insists that the *te-re-ta* have other occupations, thus the function is not itself a full-time occupation. But religious office was rarely in Greece an exclusive occupation, and the community at *Pa-ki-ja-ne* was clearly a religious one, headed by a priestess. The holding of land in return for religious obligations can be paralleled in later Greece.

1† It has been objected that the formation of the derivative *ka-ma-e-u* proves that *ka-ma* cannot be a feminine *a*-stem, since *ko-to-na*, which is certainly one, forms its derivative in *-eus* with elision of the *-a* (plural *ko-to-ne-we*); see p. 449. Thus a neuter in *-as* may be preferable. This, however, raises a problem in PY **148** = Ep 613.9–10, where *ka-ma* followed by *o-na-to* would be naturally understood as genitive singular on the analogy of *o-na-to   ke-ke-me-na   ko-to-na* (lines 14–20); in this formula *ko-to-na* is shown to be genitive where it appears in the plural (**140** = Eb 297).

21‡ A further detail about the *e-qe-ta* is revealed by PY **288** = Sa 790, which shows that they had a distinctive type of chariot-wheel, and we may therefore presume that they possessed chariots. They must have been the officers of the royal court, and they are distinguished from the local officials in charge of the coast-guard detachments. Their principal function in the tablets seems to be military, indeed they may have commanded the regiments of the Pylian army; but this does not exclude other functions associated with the royal household, and the religious context of some references (Palmer, 1963*a*, pp. 87, 151–3). See further p. 429.

21¶ The equation of *qa-si-re-u* with classical βασιλεύς can hardly be doubted, but it is still uncertain what was the status of the individuals who bore this title. Palmer (1963*a*, pp. 39, 280) goes so far as to question the identification with βασιλεύς, insisting that they are merely 'foremen' in charge of groups of smiths. This caution seems unjustified, but the semantic value in Mycenaean must be 'chief', from which it is easy enough to see how the sense of 'king' developed after the collapse of the Mycenaean kingdoms ruled by *wanaktes*. Homer, as usual, is confused in his terminology and fails to make the distinction which Mycenaean usage demands. Similar considerations apply to *ke-ro-si-ja* (p. 122) which is very probably *geronsiā*, but has quite different associations from the later γερουσία. The term *ke-ro-te* recurs on PY Jn 881 in an obscure context in connexion with bronze, but this is no reason to doubt the etymological explanation. See further on this subject O'Neil (1970).

22† The list of trades could be a little expanded; for instance, the newer Mycenae tablets include the term 'cyanus-worker' (*ku-wa-no-wo-ko*) to set alongside the goldsmith. The *ra-pte* may be engaged in sewing leather rather than cloth; see p. 489. The stokers (*pu-ka-wo*) may perhaps be keepers of the sacred fire. The women workers engaged on textile production are either slaves or at least employees of the Palace, since both at Pylos and at Knossos the Palace is responsible for feeding them.

p. 124† The suggestion that the ethnics given to some of these women indicate places raided by the ships of Pylos must be revised. If the *mi-ra-ti-ja* come from Miletus in Ionia, this appears to have been a Greek colony at this date, and is thus unlikely to have been raided for slaves. It therefore appears more probable that the places so named are the trading-posts or slave-markets through which the women were acquired, and the use of the term 'captives' for one group may imply that the others were acquired by other means. It has been suggested that the places named in this connexion are inside the domain of Pylos; but it is remarkable that only one (*ti-nwa-si-ja*) is a name elsewhere mentioned on the tablets and apparently within the control of Pylos. The names include *mi-ra-ti-ja* (Miletus), *ki-ni-di-ja* (Knidos), *ra-mi-ni-ja* (Lemnos), *a-*64-ja* (probably *Aswiai* from Asia, the classical Lydia), *ze-pu₂-ra₃* (Zephyria = Halikarnassos ?); so that collectively they reinforce one another and present a picture of trading-posts scattered along the west coast of Asia Minor.

p. 125† It would be useless to list all the articles which have touched on Mycenaean religion; a convenient review of all the relevant material has been published by M. Gérard-Rousseau (1968). Two facts stand out: one, duly acknowledged by all writers, is that most of the familiar gods of classical Greece are named; the other, which tends sometimes to be overlooked, is that there is a roughly equal number of names which appear to be divine, but do not correspond to any classical titles. It must of course be remembered that even classical Greek inscriptions frequently show divine honours paid to shadowy figures otherwise unknown. At Knossos, at least, it seems likely that the local Cretan cults continued alongside the Olympian ones, though how far syncretism had already progressed is difficult to judge. The Dictaean Zeus must surely represent a Cretan deity now worshipped under a Greek name.

The major omission from this section is the name of Potnia (cf. p. 126), which was treated as if always, as it certainly is once at Knossos, an epithet of Athena. Reconsideration of the references, and the new instances which show her receiving offerings at Mycenae and Thebes, have suggested that she is a much more significant figure; see Chadwick, 1957*a*. It is possible to believe that she is at each site the patron goddess, who is thus referred to instead of by her real name; but it is more likely that she is really the prominent female figure of both Minoan and Mycenaean art, who was later accepted into the canon under a variety of names, especially Demeter. It is now certain that Demeter is not named on the Mycenaean tablets (cf. p. 127), and the etymology of her name from an alleged *δᾶ* 'earth' is highly suspicious. But her title as 'mother of the gods' is reflected in *ma-te-re te-i-ja* PY **306** = Fr 1202 (see p. 481); and her various aspects are indicated by the genitives which precede her name: *da-pu₂-ri-to-jo* KN **205** = Gg 702, possibly a form of λαβύρινθος (see p. 475); *ne-wo-pe-o* PY Cc 665; *u-po-jo* PY Fn 187, **310** = Fr 1225; *si-to-po-ti-ni-ja* MY **321** = Oi 701 (*sitōn* or a name *Sitō* ?); and with adjective *a-si-wi-ja* PY Fr 1206 'of Asia'; *i-qe-ja* PY **312** = An 1281 'of horses'. The discovery of a shrine at Mycenae with a fresco figure of a goddess (Taylour, 1969, 1970) strongly suggests that one of the communities of craftsmen there worshipped her; and this will in turn explain the epithet *po-ti-ni-ja-we-jo* applied at Pylos to smiths (**253** = Jn 310, etc.) and an unguent-boiler (**104** = Un 249). The sheep described by this epithet at Knossos will be her property or in some sense allocated to the support of her shrines.

26† Hera is now found at Thebes (Of 28) as the recipient of an offering of wool.

26‡ Ares is clearly named on KN **201** = Fp 14, in association with 'all the gods'. Whether the reading *a-re* on Mc 4462, which now incorporates the fragment X 5816, is really the god's name is uncertain. To the personal names derived from Ares add: *a-re-i-me-ne*, a variant spelling of *a-re-me-ne*, also from Thebes jars, and *a-re-i-ze-we-i* (dat.) TH Of 37. On PY **55** = An 724 *e-nwa-ri-jo* is a man's name and has nothing to do with the god.

26¶ In KN **208** = V 52 the reading is now seen to be *pa-ja-wo-ne*, dative. In KN C 394 we have apparently *pạ-ja-ọ-ne*, where it is difficult to read -*wo-ne*, and there is no good reason to regard this as a divine name.

6†† Additional references: PY Xn 1357, TH Of 31. The form *e-ma-a₂-o* KN D 411 may be the genitive (see Glossary).

27† Dionysus is now found on another Pylos tablet (Xa 1419), but again it is a fragment with no clear context, though it does have on the reverse a form which appears to suggest a connexion with wine (*wo-no-wa-ṭị-si*).

27‡ The discovery of a deleted entry *e-ri-nu-we* (dative) on the lower edge of KN **208** = V 52 confirms that Erinys is in the divine category.

27¶ Demeter and the Dove-Goddess must both be deleted from this paragraph. The name *pe-re-*82* is certainly that of a goddess, but the value of *82* is probably *swa*; it is tempting to reconstruct the name as *Preswā* and to compare this with Πέρση and the first element of the compound Περσεφόνη.

p. 127†† The entry *te-o-i* 'to the gods', without 'all', occurs on KN E 842, perhaps Fh 348, and PY **311** = Fr 1226, Fr 1355. The Pylos examples show that here at least we have not a specifically Cretan feature.

p. 128† The statement that KN Fh 347 shows both oil and cattle must be corrected; the sign for OX has also the syllabic value *mu*, and from this and a few other examples it now appears that MU is used as an abbreviation, possibly for a large storage vessel (see Glossary, s.v. MU).

p. 128‡ On the human beings of PY **172** = Tn 316 (formerly Kn02) see pp. 459–60.

p. 128¶ It is very difficult to determine how far titles may have been religious or secular. For instance, the *pu-ka-wo* 'fire-kindlers' may have been attendants of a sacred fire rather than stokers. Olivier (1960) saw in many such terms the titles of officials serving a sanctuary; but it is also clear that to establish a religious function for one title in a list does not necessarily establish a category for all. The question needs further study, but it is probable that with the sort of evidence we have it will never be possible fully to separate religious from secular titles.

p. 130† The statement that wheat and barley are issued together as a ration on a Pylos tablet (An 128, formerly An31) must be questioned. The barley sign appears on the reverse of the tablet, with a quantity very nearly double that of the wheat entry on the obverse, thus suggesting that the ration calculated in wheat was to be issued in barley, and that barley has only half the value of wheat; but there is another entry on the obverse the ideogram of which is lost, and the figures on the reverse are over erasure and not entirely certain. This equation of wheat and barley is, however, confirmed elsewhere, for the basic ration of wheat appears to be T 2, of barley T $3\frac{3}{4}$ (see on KN **35** = Am 819, p. 420). It is therefore impossible that the identifications of the ideograms should be reversed.

p. 130‡ The ideogram for WINE appeared on sealings recovered from the wine magazine at Pylos; there is no doubt of its identification.

p. 131† The mention of beetroot is an error for beet; but the interpretation of this word as containing τεῦτλον is probably incorrect.

p. 131‡ Correct the form for 'deer' to *elaph-*; the statement of the first edition was based upon a mistaken interpretation, but has been confirmed by new discoveries; see Glossary, s.v. *e-ra-pe-ja*.

.1 ¶ The problem of the so-called 'collectors' is not yet satisfactorily resolved; but they are not mere overseers. It now seems more likely that these people are important officers, possibly members of the royal family, who have assigned to them certain flocks and their produce. The king's property will then be restricted to the flocks (about two-thirds of the total) which have no 'collector' named.

2 † Leather from the skins of other animals (pigs, deer, sheep and goats) is mentioned in PY 317 = Ub 1318 (p. 490).

3 † Two important advances in our knowledge of Mycenaean industry must be recorded; but it must be added that little progress has been made in assessing the status of craftsmen. The work of J. T. Killen (see especially 1964 b, 1966 c) has revealed the extent and organization of the Cretan textile industry. It is clear that the wool of something like 100,000 sheep was shorn, spun and woven under the close control of the Palace of Knossos; and it is reasonable to assume that some portion of the output was used in foreign trade, as the presence of rolls of cloth among the gifts brought to Egypt from the Aegean suggests. The status of the women textile workers must have been humble, as is shown by the Palace's concern with the issue of their rations. But to ask whether they were slave or free may be putting the wrong question; the classical dichotomy of status is probably not relevant in societies of the Mycenaean type, and medieval parallels suggest that the unfree may have enjoyed a higher standard of living than the poorest of the free. At Pylos the series of tablets dealing with flax (184–199) is evidence for the production of linen fabrics, an industry probably restricted by climatic conditions to the south-west Peloponnese.

The other advance concerns the smiths. Lejeune (1961 b) has shown that the number of bronzesmiths active in the Pylian kingdom is very large in relation to the probable size of the population. Since there is still no evidence for the presence of ores in this area, it seems certain that the raw materials, copper and tin, must have been imported. This then explains the disastrous shortage of bronze which the tablets record, for overseas trade must surely have been hazardous at a time when fleets of raiders were sweeping the eastern Mediterranean as far as Egypt.

The evidence that Cretan caves (Marinatos, 1962) were in some cases simultaneously smithies and cult-centres provides an explanation of the groups of smiths at Pylos who are designated by the name of Potnia; and it is tempting to wonder if the Pylian metal industry may not have been established by refugees from the Cretan disaster consequent upon the eruption of Thera in the fifteenth century B.C. The references to metal goods as 'of Cretan work' (*ke-re-si-jo we-ke*) may perhaps confirm this speculation.

p. 138† Further study has confirmed that the Pylos tablets **56–60** indicate emergency measures taken by the king to guard against a raid from the sea. Those who insist that the destructions which all over Greece characterize the end of the LH III b period were due to invaders moving wholly by land must not overlook this very clear evidence. The invaders, whoever they were, and Dorians now seem to be weak candidates for this title, must have operated, like the Persians of 480 B.C., by both land and sea; the Pylian kingdom was surely difficult to attack by land, for there are only two feasible routes, along the narrow coastal strip of Triphylia, or through the passes of Arcadia.

The fall of Knossos remains a mystery, but it is worth considering the negative fact, which remains true despite much excavation, that clay tablets in Linear B script have not been found in Crete outside Knossos, although there is now evidence for the later use of the script on jars at Kydonia (Khania) and possibly at the east coast sites, if they are really the origin of some of the inscribed jars found at Thebes. This must be contrasted with the distribution of Linear A tablets over all the known Minoan palaces from Hagia Triada to Zakros. Taken together with the enormous degree of centralized control which the Knossos tablets prove, it is tempting to suggest that the cause of the fall of Knossos was primarily the overcentralization of the administration of Crete in the LM II period, which provoked a reaction from the outlying areas. The Knossian kingdom then in LM III would have disintegrated into a collection of smaller states, a situation which seems also to have been reflected in the distribution of Palaces and archives in the Minoan period; it is hard to believe that a Minoan ruler of Knossos, even if nominally suzerain of Phaistos, can have exercised the same degree of detailed control which we see, for instance, on the sheep and wool tablets of the Linear B period.

p. 140† Names of places at Knossos beginning *o-* and *q-* are now certain; in the latter case the effect was due to identifying *qa* as *pa₂*.

p. 141† The lists of place names on pp. 146–50 have not been corrected, but the names are fully discussed in the Glossary. It now seems clear that *se-to-i-ja* is not Setaia, for apart from the phonetic difficulty it appears that this name is to be located in the central area. We might perhaps add to the list of names which can be located Kantanos and Kadiston Oros, both doubtful (see Glossary, s.v. *ka-ta-no*[1] and *ka-di-ti-ja*). More significant is the occurrence of *o-du-ru-wi-jo*, ethnic of the town *o-du-ru-we*, on a jar found at Thebes; and of *wa-to* no less than nine times on Theban jars. These might be dismissed as a coincidence, had it not been shown that the analysis of the clay of these vessels agrees closely with that from Zakros and Palaikastro respectively (Catling and Millett, 1965). The conclusions to be drawn from clay analysis are still imperfectly understood, but it is strange that two quite independent lines of investigation should suggest a Cretan origin. For a full discussion of the location of the Cretan names see Chadwick, 1973.

41‡ The question of the location of Homeric Pylos is too vast to be discussed here. Since 1955 my views on the authenticity of the account of Mycenaean Greece preserved by Homer have changed, and I now believe the Homeric evidence to be almost worthless for this purpose. One major reason is precisely the complete lack of contact between Mycenaean geography as now known from the tablets and from archaeology on the one hand, and from the Homeric accounts on the other. The attempts which have been made to reconcile them, as on p. 143, are unconvincing; and it should be noted that the sole coincidence between the Catalogue's list of towns in Nestor's kingdom and the Nine Towns of the Pylos tablets, *a-pu₂*=Αἰπύ, must now be withdrawn, for even if initial αἰ- can optionally be written *a-* rather than *a₃-*, *pu₂* seems to be always *phu* (or possibly once *bu*). Mycenaean *E-re-e* is now known to belong to the Further Province, which is apparently excluded by Homer from Nestor's kingdom.

It is of course possible to claim that the Homeric account dates from a different phase of the Mycenaean period from the tablets. But even so it is incredible that the names would have changed so dramatically over a period of even two hundred years, unless some major cataclysm had intervened. Hope Simpson and Lazenby (1970) have therefore proposed a date in LH IIIc for the Catalogue of the Ships; but they ignore the fact that Ano Englianos was then a ruin, and cannot be Nestor's Pylos.

The only way out of the impasses into which Homer leads us is to cut the Gordian knot and reject Homer as containing more than a distant and confused recollection of the Mycenaean age. Whether Nestor was an historical character or not, we have no means of telling; what is certain is that his historicity is totally irrelevant to our appreciation of the Homeric poems.

42† In the first stages of our work it was natural to look for all possible identifications of Mycenaean place names with classical ones; but it is now clear that this method is unproductive, at least in this area, for continuity between

Mycenaean and later times seems to have been slight. The name of Pylos survived, but its location changed; most of the other Mycenaean names either died out or became too unimportant to have been recorded by the Greek geographers. It must be remembered that our most detailed account of Messenian geography comes from Strabo, and is thus some twelve centuries distant from the period of the tablets. The problem is discussed at more length in Chadwick, 1963 a.

The identification of [Ku]-pa-ri-so with the site represented by modern Kyparissia still seems probable, at least as a general location, if not the exact spot. Ri-jo is likely to be the modern Koroni, for the promontory more conspicuous on the map, Cape Akritas, is barren and uninhabitable. The name Ne-do-wo-ta-de must surely refer to the river Nedon, on which modern Kalamata stands, or a town near it. But the other names for which sites in Arcadia or Elis have been suggested now look very improbable; and it is more likely that classical Λουσοί in Arcadia owes its name to refugees from Mycenaean Ro-u-so than that the Pylian kingdom extended north-eastwards beyond the Messenian valley.

The attempts to locate the northern frontier on or even beyond the Alpheios owe much to the unsound testimony of Homer. If Pi-*82 is Piswa (Chadwick, 1968 a), this does not mean that we must include classical Πῖσα in the kingdom, any more than Ko-ri-to must be the classical Κόρινθος. U-ru-pi-ja-jo, now that we understand Mycenaean phonology better, cannot be associated with Ὀλυμπία and is probably a name beginning Wru-.

Archaeology has shown that the valley of the Kyparissia river is thickly strewn with Mycenaean sites, but there is a natural gap to the north, along the line of the river Neda. This frontier allows us to confine the Pylian kingdom to plausible limits; and Pi-*82, which is the most northerly of the major areas of the Hither Province, in which Pylos itself is situated, can then be well inland up the Kyparissia river valley, for it and the next town on the list, Me-ta-pa, have connexions with the Further Province. Pa-ki-ja-ne must be close to Pylos (cf. PY 172 = Tn 316). A-ke-re-wa is a coastal town to the south, probably on the bay of Navarino. Ka-ra-do-ro = Kharadros 'the Ravine' (or possibly dual or plural?) must be in the extreme south of the peninsula, and a suitable site, dominated by two great ravines, exists at Phoinikous.

The location of the Further Province (Pe-ra₃-ko-ra-i-ja, see p. 144) is thus beyond the mountain range which divides the coastal strip from the Messenian valley. It probably does not extend down much of the west side of the gulf, since Koroni belongs to the Hither Province; and the east side, leading to the Mani, is difficult of access. No place name can be identified east of the Nedon, and the coast-guard tablets list only one town of the Further Province, *Ti-mi-to-a-ke-e*, thus suggesting that it has a short coastline.

A suggestion made by Wyatt (1962), and further refined in an article by C. Shelmerdine in course of publication, on the way the figures were grouped in the assessments of the *Ma* tablets leads to the interesting conclusion that the Further Province consisted of four sectors containing the following towns:

(*a*) *Ra-wa-ra-ta$_2$*

(*b*) *E-sa-re-wi-ja*, *Za-ma-e-wi-ja*

(*c*) *A-[sja]-ta$_2$*, *Sa-ma-ra*, *Ti-mi-to-a-ke-e*

(*d*) *E-ra-te-re-we*, *A-te-re-wi-ja*

The principle behind the groups is that each makes approximately the same contribution; groups (*a*) and (*b*) are paired, and so are (*c*) and (*d*). This grouping is very unlikely to be arbitrary, but must correspond to the geographical arrangement of the towns. The Messenian valley is bisected by natural features, the rivers running from north to south, and less obviously by the Skala hills running east and west; thus the four groups are likely to answer to the four geographical sectors. Since we have in **257**=Jn 829 a linear list of the Seven Towns (in *Ma* increased to eight by splitting *E-re-i* into two), and this begins in the Further Province at the coast (*Ti-mi-to-a-ke-e*), it is possible to guess the likely distribution of the sectors: (*a*) south-east, (*b*) north-east, (*c*) south-west, (*d*) north-west.

45† The supposition that slave-women came from Asia Minor can perhaps be reinforced by the identifications of *A-*64-ja* as possibly *Aswiai* 'women of Asia', the older name for Lydia, and *Ze-pu$_2$-ra$_3$* as derived from an old name of Halikarnassos. But rather than imagine piratical raids by the ships of Pylos on these distant coasts, we can explain these epithets as indicating the trading-posts through which slaves, coming perhaps from inland areas, passed into Greek control: see above, p. 410.

46† The entries making up these lists are now to be found in their alphabetical positions in the Glossary (pp. 528–94).

CHAPTER VI

LISTS OF PERSONNEL

p. 155† Despite much that has been written on this subject, the views propounded here still seem the most probable. It is certain that we have a census of women and their children of menial status, about three-quarters of whom are located in Pylos, the remainder at a few other places, especially Leuktron, which appears to be the main royal establishment in the Further Province. Study of the scribal hands of the *Aa* tablets enables us to divide them into two sets corresponding to the two Provinces; the *Ab* tablets, however, have no entries for the Further Province. Thus either the record is incomplete, which accounts for the preservation of last year's records as well, or the rationing of the women in the Further Province is not carried out from Pylos. The argument against the latter view is that this does not account for the frequent, though minor, discrepancies in the numbers between the *Aa* and *Ab* tablets.

p. 157† The principle on which the amount of the supplement is calculated was demonstrated by Palmer (1959, pp. 137–42) and Ota (1959) following improved readings by Bennett (1957). The supplements are: T 2 correlating with TA; T 5 correlating with DA; T 7 or T 9 both correlating with DA TA (i.e. T 7 = DA 1 TA 1, T 9 = DA 1 TA 2). It has been suggested that these are rations for extra personnel (guards or supervisors) not recorded among the women; but it is easier to regard them as extra payments given to certain women already counted in the group who act as charge-hands or supervisors. One tablet (Ab 555) shows an impossibly large supplement; Palmer (1963a, p. 117) ingeniously explained this as WHEAT 16 written in error for WHEAT 12 T 4 which would bring the supplement within the normal range. On the absolute values of the metric signs see p. 394.

p. 158† **2** = Aa 815. The translation 'nurses' should now be abandoned; see Glossary.

p 159† **4** = Aa 240. The separation of the *Aa* tablets into two sets relating to the two Provinces shows that Aa 89 refers to Leuktron, Aa 240 to Pylos.

p. 159‡ **7** = Aa 717. *ro-u-so* is not to be identified with Λουσοί in Arcadia, but another place of this name, probably sing. *Lousos*.

⁶⁰† **12**=Aa 671. 'Musicians' and 'sweepers' were guesses which now appear improbable; see Glossary.

⁶¹† **13**=Ad 691. *pa-wo-ko-qe* may be rather *pan-worgōn qᵘe* 'and of the maids-of-all-work'; see Chadwick (1967a).

⁶¹‡ **14**=Ad 697. The second restoration of the top line seems preferable since forms corresponding to Att. βούλομαι but with *e*-vowel are dialectally more remote from Mycenaean.

⁶³† The abbreviation *pe* is likely on the analogy of its use in describing sheep (see p. 433) to stand for *perusinwai* 'of last year', not of course referring to their birth as in the case of the sheep, but perhaps their recruitment to this group. Similarly *za* may stand for *za-we-te* (or an adjectival derivative)=*tsāwetes* 'this year'. *tu* may be for *thugatēr* 'daughter' (see Killen, 1966a).

⁶³‡ **18**=Ak 611.

to-te-ja is likely to be an occupational term rather than an ethnic.
de-di-ku-ja: it has been suggested by Chantraine (1957, p. 243) that this is not an incorrect spelling but a perf. pple. of the root of δείκνυμι='assigned (to work)'. But if *di-da-ka-re* is correctly connected with the root of διδάσκω, the question of an erroneous form here must remain open. The distinction of 'under instruction' and 'with instruction completed' is a valid one.

⁶³¶ **19**=Ak 627. The join with 7025 reveals the first word of line 1 as *da-*22-to*, a well-known place name, and confirms the restorations at the beginning of lines 2 and 3.

⁶⁵† **23**=Ag 1654. It now appears probable that MANᶜ is nothing but a scribal variant of the ordinary form of MAN.

⁶⁶† **26**=An 292. It should be noted that this is only the first four lines of a long tablet. Presumably other *Aa* tablets would have been abstracted on the same tablet. It is possible that *si-to-ko-wo* is not nominative plural but dative singular, that is to say, this is a list for the official in charge of issuing the rations, for it is hardly likely that all 53 women, not to mention those on the lost part of the list, were measurers of grain.

⁶⁷† *do-qe-ja*: the unverifiable suggestion has been made (by Palmer, 1963a, p. 128) that this is the name of a goddess, cf. *di-wi-ja do-e-ra* in line 5, which is almost certainly 'slave of the goddess Diwia'.

p. 167‡ *ku-te-re-u-pi*: it would be equally possible to regard the suffix -*phi* as having ablative meaning. In any case the word functions as a place name.

p. 168† *e-e-to*: no convincing explanation of this form has emerged, but it has yet to be shown that any tablet conveys orders; it would therefore seem that an imperative can be excluded. It is possible that it represents *ehento* aor. mid. of ἵημι (cf. 3rd sing. εἷτο).

p. 168‡ **29**=Am 821. Corrections: l. 1 *ẹ-mi-to* for *ti-mi-to*; l. 2 begins]*dụ-we ṭa-ṛa*.

 e-qe-ta-e: this reading is confirmed and seems to be the dual ending of masc. *a*-stems.
 e-mi-to, if correct, is obscure.
 o-pa: Palmer (1963*a*, p. 437) distinguishes three words, making this a goddess, the same spelling a place in Ce 50, and a sense 'work-shop' elsewhere. If we substitute a meaning such as 'contribution' for 'work-shop', there is nothing to prevent us from understanding all examples as the same word. The true meaning is probably more precise than this, but cannot be exactly determined. An etymology from **soqʷā* must now be excluded.

p. 169† **30**=Ae 264. The gen. *du-ni-jo-⟨jo⟩* is restored on the analogy of Ae 8, which ends with the same three words. No satisfactory explanation has yet been given of *me-tu-ra* or *su-ra-se*.

p. 170† **33**=Ae 26. The reading *pe-mẹ* seems to be epigraphically preferable, though less easy to interpret. Possibly a man's name, since workers at Knossos are often listed as *o-pi* a man, apparently meaning 'in the workshop of', 'chez'.

p. 170‡ **34**=Am 601

 e-so-to: the future *es(s)ontoi* is preferable to an imperative because of the absence of orders on the tablets.

p. 170¶ **35**=Am 819. There is no doubt that the crescent-shaped ideogram stands for MONTH; cf. **89**=E 777. The ration is extremely important for it gives the equation $18x+8y=$ T $97\frac{3}{4}$, where $x=$ a man's ration and $y=$ a boy's ration. It can be shown mathematically that the only values for x and y which give a plausible solution are $x=y=$ T $3\frac{3}{4}$ (i.e. ᴗ 90, which allows a ration of ᴗ 3 per day, allowing 30 days to the lunar month): see Chadwick (1964*a*, pp. 323–4). Barley rations in antiquity were calculated as approximately double those of wheat, thus T $3\frac{3}{4}$ of barley is a reasonable equivalent of T 2 of wheat. That this figure is appropriate for men as well as women (see p. 418) is confirmed by a text from Mycenae, Au 658.4: *to-so* MAN 20 *si-to* WHEAT 4 (i.e. T 2 per man).

p. 170†† **36**=B 817. There can be little doubt that *ku-su-to-ro-qa* means 'aggregate', a meaning possessed by Greek συστροφή. But the discovery that *pa₂* is *qa* and always represents a labio-velar raises a complication, since στρέφω is normally derived from *strebh- not *streg^{u}h-. Hence other interpretations have been proposed, such as a derivative of the root of τρέπω (cf. to-ro-qo, to-qi-de). But it is perhaps easier to assume that, as in the case of τρέπω, the classical form represents a contamination of the labial and labio-velar suffixes.

71† **38**=As 1516. Corrections: l. 8 wa-du-[.]-to MAN 1; l. 10 a-ta-ze-u [MAN 1]. It is true that the paragraph running from lines 12 to 19 contains the MAN ideogram 24 times before the total MEN 23; but the first paragraph (lines 2–11) apparently has only 31 entries, including that after a-nu-wi-ko in line 2. The last is damaged and the total is lost.

72† **39**=As 1517. Corrections: l. 8 read ku-pa-nu-we-to; l. 14 read a₃-ni-jo.

o-pi e-sa-re-we: probably 'in the work-shop of E.'. If so, leiq^{u}omenoi probably means in
effect 'unassigned'. It is perhaps more likely that to-ro-no-wo-ko is dative in agreement
with e-sa-re-we than nominative plural, but the practical effect is slight, since the
three men in the work-shop of a chair-maker presumably follow the same trade.

73† **40**=An 261. Corrections: ll. 2–5 the first word should be transcribed o-two-we-o (see below); l. 6 read ku-te-re-u; ll. 15–18, readjustment of the fragments produces a text in three lines only:

15	]ke-ro-si-ja	a[	]	MAN 1
16	ke-ro-]si-ja	[	]-ka-[.]	MAN 1
17	ke-ro-]si-ja	o-pa-[.]		[MAN 1

The meaning of ke-ro-si-ja, whatever its etymology, is plainly some kind of group associated with a local official. Palmer (1963a, pp. 228 f.), regarding qa-si-re-u=βασιλεύς as a 'foreman' in charge of smiths, rejects the association with γερουσία. But if a βασιλεύς may be the local ruler of a community of smiths, it does not seem impossible that the senior members of the community should make up a council or senate. It is unnecessary to suppose that the terms are incompatible. On the bronzesmiths see p. 509.

o-two-we-o: it was shown by Lejeune (1962a) that sign *66=ta₂ was to be distinguished
from the sign which occurs only on this tablet as the second sign of this word. It is
now numbered *91 and assigned the value two, since there is no doubt that it is the
same man who is mentioned as o-to-wo[in line 7 of the reverse; perhaps o-to-wo[-we-o]
should be restored there. He is therefore perhaps the same man as the smith of
255=Jn 658. The variant spelling on the reverse (also a-pi-o-to/a-pi-jo-to) is due to
a change in scribal hand.

p. 174†   **41** = An 35. The fact that masons are already located at Pylos and Leuktron is explained by the fact that Leuktron is the administrative centre of the Further Province (see p. 418).

> *tu-ru-pte-ri-ja*: now interpreted as *struptēriās* (στρυπτηρία, a rare variant of στυπτηρία; see Pugliese Carratelli, 1962, p. 7, Chadwick, 1964*b*, p. 23) 'alum'.
>
> *o-no*: although etymologically still obscure, there is little doubt that the meaning of this term is approximately 'object given in exchange', 'consideration' and thus equivalent to 'price'; see Chadwick, 1964*b*, pp. 21–6. The absence of ϝ in Cretan ὀνά, etc., has been traditionally explained as due to precocious loss before o; but it seems at least possible that the etymological connexions are unsound. Thus Furumark's suggestion ὦνος may not be wrong. The use of alum was mainly for dyeing, but when Amasis of Egypt gave the Delphians 1000 talents of it for the temple of Apollo (Herodotus II 180), was this sold to provide funds or was it actually used for the temple?

p. 175†   The connexion of Aq 218 (formerly An29) with Aq 64 (formerly Sn01) is now generally admitted, and their prefixes have been changed to Aq to emphasize this fact. It is certain that *o-da-a₂* (Aq 64.12, 218.1,9) is a word used to introduce the second and subsequent paragraphs of a document; it therefore follows that 218 which begins with this word cannot be the first tablet of this set. In spite of this Palmer (1963*a*, pp. 140–6) has arranged the tablets in reverse order, assuming that another tablet is lost and that the broken entry in Aq 64 began with another *o-da-a₂*. His argument is that 218 proceeds from MEN to ZE and therefore 64 with no men but ZE throughout should follow. This is not impossible, but it is an unnecessary assumption. It should be observed that the entries throughout the two tablets each begin with a man's name; it is only those who ought to do something (*a-na-ke-e o-pe-ro-te* 218.1) who are simply listed as MEN. It is also to be observed (cf. p. 175) that the names on 64 have titles which demonstrate their importance (*ko-re-te, mo-ro-qa*), whereas those in 218 do not seem to rank higher than 'priest' (*i-je-re-u*). Finally, the second paragraph of 64 is headed *ko-to-na e-ko-te* = *ktoinans ekhontes* 'holders of plots', the second paragraph of 218 *a-ko-to-no* = *aktoinoi* 'plot-less', which is not only the logical order but is precisely paralleled by the formulas of the *Jn* tablets (*talasiān ekhontes*/*atalasioi*, see p. 352).

The significance of the document is still uncertain despite much discussion. The abbreviation ZE is elsewhere used for *zeugos* 'pair', 'yoke', not only of animals like oxen and horses but also of inanimate objects like wheels. It is possible that it here abbreviates a different word altogether, though it is hard to see what. An alternative approach has been suggested by Ruipérez (1956, 1957), that *zeugos* here has the sense of a measure of land, i.e. the amount that can be ploughed with a yoke of oxen, a semantic development seen in Latin *iugerum*, which is a singular reformed from the plural *iugera* equivalent to ζεύγεα. Hence Ruipérez concludes that the document relates to the division and allocation of land-holdings. Against this it might be argued that the second paragraph of 218 shows ZE entries against names which are listed as *aktoinoi* 'having no plot'; but ZE might refer to a future allocation, or they might hold land other than *ktoinai*. The sense of *e-ke-jo-to* is unclear. Ruipérez also proposes that the mysterious ideogram Ï is a subdivision of ZE, but its correlation with the verb *a-ke-re-se* (see p. 175) is against this, and it is not confirmed by its independent use at Knossos, as Ruipérez admits.

The key to the whole document undoubtedly lay in the damaged first line of 64, and it must be observed that Bennett has now abandoned the reading given here and reads simply *]-re-wi-jo-te*. While this does not exclude the restoration *[qa-si]-re-wi-jo-te*, it must be noted that the way is now open to other restorations, (e.g. *[i-je]-re-wi-jo-te = hierēwyontes* 'serving as priests'). Another word must have preceded. In any case it seems clear that it is a present participle.

176† **43** = Aq 64 (formerly Sn). Readings: l. 1 *]-re-wi-jo-te*.

mo-ro-qa (*-pa₂*): the labio-velar sign will here represent *$k'w$*, as in *i-qo* = ἵππος, hence we should transcribe by a double consonant: *mo(i)ro-qqᵘās*.

*i-*65*: the most likely value for **65* is *ju*. It is possible that *i-ju* is the nominative of a Mycenaean word for 'son': see Glossary.

te-ra-ni-ja: the analogy of other entries, especially line 5, might lead to the identification of this word as a substantive in apposition to *i-*65*; if the analogy is exact, it would be an official title and *po-so-ri-jo-no* would then have to be a place name; cf. **258** = Jo 438 edge. But this analysis leaves the repetition *a-ke-re-se...o-a-ke-re-se* unexplained, though it could be mere error, cf. *to-to to-to* in line 14.

e-qe-o   a-to-mo: the second word might be a title in KN C 979, where the other members of the set have *du-ma* (C 1030, C 1039, C 7057?) or *da-mo-ko-ro* (C 7058) in the same position in the formula. But this will hardly fit Jn 832.9: *a-to-mo   ka-ke-we a-ke-te*, and better sense may be obtained by taking it to mean 'guild (of craftsmen)', which has the advantage that it enables us to identify the word with ἀρθμός 'union', 'league'. It is, however, still difficult to explain *ka-ke-we* which seems to be nominative plural in apposition to *a-to-mo* singular, as confirmed by *a-ke-te*; cf. *ka-ke-we a-ke-te-re* in line 1. If correct, *po-ki-ro-qo* may then be genitive, *Poikiloqᵘos*, rather than nominative. *e-qe-o* could then be genitive singular in agreement with *Poikiloqᵘos*, or genitive plural further defining the trade practised by the guild. There is no reason why a list of local officials should not contain a corporate body of this kind. It is never safe to press the analogy of corresponding entries too far.

o-da-a₂: the usage of this word as introducing the second and subsequent paragraphs of a list make it certain that it contains a connective particle. Hence we should analyse it as *hō d(e)* with another particle of the approximate form **aha* giving intensifying force. The whole word will therefore translate 'and thus', the verb or other phrase which introduced the first paragraph being understood with it. This analysis is confirmed by the variant forms *o-a₂* PY **250** = Vn 20, which stands at the head of an isolated tablet and hence lacks the connective; and by *o-de-qa-a₂* PY **304** = On 300, to be analysed as *hō de qᵘ(e) aha*; see p. 467; Chadwick, 1971, pp. 102–3.

p. 177†   **44** = Aq (formerly An) 218. Corrections: l. 16 read *qo-te-wo* with no sign lost before it.

a-na-ke-e: the interpretation *anagehen* has been generally accepted, but there is no agreement on its meaning; suggestions range from 'put to sea' to 'trace boundary furrows'.

da-i-ja-ke-re-u: the interpretation 'divider of lands' has been enthusiastically welcomed by those who see this document as concerned with allocations of land, but it remains very questionable.

p. 178†   **45** = An 830. Corrections: l. 2 at right *]ke-je-me[-no*; l. 3 at left *di-ri-wa-[*; l. 6 read *e-so* for *e-o*; l. 8 *ro-ro-ni-ja*; l. 10 *qo-]u̯-ko̠-ro̠* MEN 18   [   ].

e-so: conceivably *ensō* = εἴσω with *a-te-re-wi-ja* genitive or accusative 'inside A.'.

ko-re-te-ri-jo: adjective from *ko-re-te* (a local official).

p. 179†   A new set of 9 tablets from Pylos classified *Ac* appears to list men of the principal towns forming work-groups. The place-names preserved are *ka-ra-do-ro*, *pi-*82*, *a-ke-re-wa*, *me-ta-pa* (all among the Nine Towns of the Hither Province); two tablets begin with ethnics, *pe-ti-ni-jo* (*pe-to-no* one of the Nine Towns) and *te-mi-ti-jo* (from *ti-mi-to-a-ke-e*, see Glossary, one of the Seven Towns of the Further Province). The place name or ethnic is followed by MEN and a number ranging from 10 to 69 and, in every case but one, *o-pe-ro* MEN and a smaller number. In Ac 1276 *o-pe-ro* was written and then deleted. It would seem that the groups were almost all below strength; for the use of *o-pe-ro* 'deficit', 'not present' in lists of persons, cf. Ad 357 and its abbreviation *o* in **12** = Ad 671.

301 = Ac 1275

       pe-ti-ni-jo   MEN 69   *o-pe-ro*   MAN 1

302 = Ac 1280

       me-ta-pa   MEN 22   *o-pe-ro*   MAN 7

p. 179‡   There are now a few more broken tablets of this type from Mycenae and an interesting parallel list of women (see below, p. 425).

₄79¶ **46**=Au 102. Corrections: l. 5 read *ko-no-[.]-du-ro-qe*; it appears that the third sign is not *pu*₂ and may be an otherwise unknown sign. Some of the names reappear on other tablets which are lists of men's names: *na-su-to*, *te-ra-wo* and *mo-i-da* are among nine names on Au 657, *e-ke-ne* and *te-ra-wo* on Au 653, *na-su-to* on Au 660. This suggests that *au-wi-ja-to* on Au 653 and Au 657 is a variant spelling of *au-ja-to* (if this is not simply an error, but the scribe is different). The name might be *Auiātōr* (for **Auto-iātōr* 'self-healer'): see Lejeune, 1966*a*, p. 25.

i-jo-qe: it has been suggested that *i-jo* is a variant of *i-*65* (if to be read *i-ju*) and means 'son'. The parallel of υἱός/υἱύς is remarkable, but *i-* can hardly represent *hui-*. To accept this it would be necessary to suppose that two words, an *o*-stem **hios* and a *u*-stem **huius* had become contaminated, with different results in Mycenaean and classical Greek: see *i-*65* in Glossary. While not impossible, this theory must be regarded as so far unproved. The strongest argument in favour of *i-jo-qe*='and son' is the parallel of *tu-ka-te-qe* 'and daughter' in the list of women quoted below. It may be irrelevant that Au 657 is headed simply *i-jo-te*, which is probably *iontes* 'about to go', as in a more explicit context in PY **53**=An 1.

₄79†† **303**=V 659

1	*wo-di-je-ja* *de-mi-ni-ja*	1
2	*ma-no* *a-re-ka-sa-da-ra-qẹ*	2
3	*ri-su-ra* *qo-ta-qe*	2
4	*e-ri-tu-pi-na* *te-o-do-ra-qe*	2
5	*o-to-wo-wi-je* *tu-ka-te-qe*	2
6	*a-ne-a*₂ *tu-ka-te-qe*	2
7	*pi-ro-wo-na* *ki-ra-qe*	2
8	*[.]ka-ro* *ke-ti-de-qe*	2
9	*]-ri-mo-qe*	2
10	*]ma-ta-qe*	2
11	*]*8̣2̣*	1
12	*]qẹ*	2
13	*]*	

RIGHT EDGE: *i-ri-[.]ị   ke-ra-so   ki-ra-qe* 2

wo-di-je-ja: a woman's name also found at Knossos and Pylos, perhaps *Wordieia* (cf. ethnic Ῥοδιεύς).

de-mi-ni-ja: there is a striking parallel in PY Vn 851, a list of names each with the numeral 1 and a check-mark but no ideogram, headed by a line of which nothing remains but the word *de-mi-ni-ja* at the right. Notice that here too it cannot be a woman's name, since the numeral is 1 (i.e. *wo-di-je-ja*), and all lines containing two names have the second ending in -*qe*. The interpretation *demnia*=δέμνια 'beds' or

425

'bedding' imposes itself. Were these women requiring accommodation and being issued with bedding?

ma-no: this name, together with *a-ne-a₂* and *ke-ra-so*, reappears in MY **93** = Fo 101, where in default of evidence they were taken as masculine.

a-re-ka-sa-da-ra-qe: the last sign is damaged but looks more like *ka* than *qe*; if so, it is clearly a scribal error. The name is *Alexandrā*.

te-o-do-ra-qe: *Theodōrā qᵘe*.

tu-ka-te-qe: *thugatēr qᵘe* 'and daughter'. That this is not a name is evident from its repetition in successive lines. The same argument might be applied to *ki-ra-qe* (l. 7, edge), and this may represent a noun: *gillā* 'infant', cf. νεογιλός and the name Γίλλος.

]ma-ta-qe: restore perhaps *[ko-]ma-ta-qe*, cf. **93** = Fo 101.6.

p. 179‡‡ **47** = Am 826

te-re-ta: the implications of this title are still far from clear, some contexts suggesting a religious connexion, others a class of land-holders; see pp. 120, 408. It is a little curious that this class, which is clearly not of humble status, should be so numerous at one town and coupled with carpenters.

p. 180† **48** = B 101. The reading is certainly *a₃-te-re*.

p. 180‡ In an attempt to account for some puzzling features in these lists Olivier (1960) has suggested that some at least are lists of temple servants; e.g. the *pu-ka-wo* 'fire kindlers' might be the guardians of the sacred fire. There does not seem to be a sufficiently large group of titles with expressly religious implications to make this convincing. The *pu-ka-wo* might equally have such a humble task as charcoal-burning.

p. 180¶ **49** = An 427. Correction: l. 3 *pi-pu-te*, the *pu* is very doubtful.

a-pu₂-we: the identification with Αἰπύ is to be rejected, since we should expect *a₃-* sometimes to be used for initial *ai-*, and *pu₂* stands for *phu* and perhaps *bu*.

p. 180†† **50** = An 39. Corrections: l. 11 read *e-]to-wo-ko* MEN 4; reverse l. 8 [*]qo-ta-wo* MAN[.

p. 182† **51** = An 18. Correction: l. 11 after *to-so te-* illegible.

te-ko-to-na-pe: this word is analysed by Palmer (1963a, p. 132) as a place name, because some at least of the entries on this tablet consist of place names, but the analogy of texts such as An 424 shows that such lists do not repeat the place name for each entry, and we must not expect the same consistency from a Mycenaean scribe as a modern scholar. The word is discussed at length by Chadwick (1967b), and although the place-name theory cannot be disproved the arguments against it are strong.

182‡ **52 = An 207**

po-ku-ta: *pos-khutai* is improbable, partly because there is no evidence for the apocope of Myc. *posi* (Arc. πός). The adjective *po-ku-te-ro* can only be explained if the base is *po-ku-* to which the suffixes, *-tās* and *-teros* are added.

ra-pte-re: perhaps men who sew leather rather than cloth = 'saddlers': cf. *ra-pte-ri-ja a-ni-ja* PY **323** = Sb 1315 'reins with saddlers' work'.

184† The first group of tablets remains a collection of isolated documents, but the *o-ka* tablets have been intensively studied, and their structure has been largely elucidated, though many details remain obscure. The geography of the south-western Peloponnese, combined with archaeological field-work, makes it highly probable that the kingdom of Pylos was confined to the area between the rivers Neda in Triphylia and the Nedon on which the modern Kalamata stands, since this is a coherent area with satisfactory lines of inland communication. The alleged references to Elis must be discounted; neither of the names corresponds exactly, and in any case it is all too frequent for a place name to be duplicated.

The total number of men listed on this set (excluding those named) is not less than 780; several figures may be incomplete. All the units are multiples of 10 and range from 10 to 110. This in itself is sufficient to disprove the suggestion that this document records the mobilization of the Pylian army. For even if it were as small as this, which is highly improbable, it would be madness to divide it into small units, not one of which could be expected to hold off for long a large raiding party. It is therefore clear that the purpose of this organization is not strictly defensive but to provide an early warning system to guard against an unobserved landing.

These 780 or more men are spaced out irregularly round the coast (*opihala* 'coastal regions') in ten sectors, which are described as *o-ka*, whatever the correct interpretation of the word. Their location is not always clear, partly because the place name does not always occupy the same position in the formula, and also because many of the place names do not recur elsewhere. In §1 the place name *o-wi-to-no* stands immediately after the heading *ma-re-wo o-ka*; in §2 there is no place name here because the two detachments of troops are at different places, 20 men at a_2-*ru-wo-te* and 20 at a_3-*ta-re-u-si*. Where Nedwatas, the commander of the *o-ka*, had his head-quarters is not specified, perhaps because it was too well known to the writer. In §3 the *o-ka* of Tros is at *ro-o-wa*, but the 110 men of his detachment are at a_2-*ra-tu-wa*. §4 is made more difficult by lacunae; perhaps *ka-ke-*[is the beginning of a place name, and line 10 is apparently irregular, leaving us in doubt which of these words, if any, is a place. §5 is remarkable since the location of neither the *o-ka* of Klumenos nor his detachment of 50 men is specified. Since they are natives of *me-ta-pa*, it may be presumed that they are in that general area; again it may have been sufficiently obvious to the writer where Klumenos, who was the *ko-re-te* of *i-te-re-wa* (**43**=Aq 64), would dispose his guards. §6 also departs from the normal formula; it is unclear whether *to-wa* is a place or a man. *Wa-wo-u-de* is likely to be a topographical term, but whether it is the location or place of origin of the troops can only be guessed. The detachment of 60 men is, exceptionally, made up of five separate units.

§7 is more regular. The *o-ka* of Wapalos is located at *ne-wo-ki-to*, but the number of his detachment is not given, for *sa-pi-da* takes the place of the usual MEN+number. It is tempting to search for some word as an interpretation which could serve as a substitute for a number (e.g. 'as required', 'as available'), but no plausible suggestion has been made. A subsidiary detachment of 20 men is at *ne-wo-ki-to wo-wi-ja*; if *wo-wi-ja* is *worwia*=ὅρια 'frontier', this will perhaps make sense.

In §8 Dwoios has his *o-ka* and main detachment at *a-ke-re-wa*, an important town; but a small force of 10, specifically called young, are at *u-wa-si*. §9 repeats the pattern of §2: no location for the *o-ka*, but troops at four different places. Finally Erkhomenatas in §10 has his head-quarters at *ti-mi-to a-ke-i*, the only town named which is known to be in the Further Province, but his detachment is being sent to Nedwon (probably the only name with allative *-de*, but cf. *wa-wo-u-de* in §6).

Each *o-ka* has also a short list of named men. A number of these reappear on other Pylos tablets, but there is always the danger that the name is borne by two men (cf. *ma-re-u* in §10 who duplicates the name of the commander of *o-ka* §1). Thus the recurrence of some of these names among the bronzesmiths (*Jn* tablets, see pp. 352 ff.) is probably without significance. But the presence of six of these names on the diptych **43**=Aq 64 and **44**=Aq 218 is hardly likely to be an accident: *ma-ra-te-u*, *e-ta-wo-ne-u* (now restored at **57**=An 519.7), *de-wi-jo* (if really a name), *e-ru-ta-ra*, *po-ki-ro-qo*, *pe-ri-me-de*. Two also recur on **258**=Jo 438: *e-ke-me-de* and *po-ki-ro-qo* again, in the company of *ne-da-wa-ta*, commander of *o-ka* §2. All this suggests that they are people of consequence, at least on a local level, and this confirms the idea that they are the subordinate officers of the *o-ka*, no doubt in charge of the various detachments.

The fact that many of the place names are not mentioned elsewhere is understandable if we remember that the function of these detachments is to act as look-outs. They will not therefore be posted in sheltered bays and harbours where settlements are likely, but on uninhabited cliffs and promontories; they would, however, still have been based upon the nearest town. This fits well with the pattern seen on the tablets. The order of these tablets should be corrected to place **58** = An 654 before **57** = An 519.

Divided among the ten *o-ka* are 11 *e-qe-ta*, each introduced with the formula 'and with them (is) the *e-qe-ta* So-and-so'. But they are not regularly spaced out, one to each *o-ka*. §8 has no less than three, while §7 has two; §§1, 3 and 6 have none. But since this is the last item in the formula and clearly refers backwards, there is no reason why the *e-qe-ta* should not be attached to all the detachments listed between him and the previous one. Thus *a-e-ri-qo-ta* will cover not only §2 but §1 as well, and this may be why his location is stated separately, at *e-ra-po ri-me-ne* = *Elaphōn limenei* 'Deer-harbour'. Similarly *a-re-i-jo* covers both §6 and the main sector of §7, while *di-wi-je-u* is attached only to the small group of men on the 'frontier'. We may well ask why the end of §7 and the whole of §8 require the presence of so many *e-qe-ta*; presumably this is the most dangerous area. This would agree well with the picture presented above (p. 414), for the area of the Bay of Navarino is not only the most attractive site for a landing, but is also nearest to the Palace.

The function of the *e-qe-ta* can only be explained by examining all the information we have about this class. The use of patronymic adjectives with their names implies that they were persons of importance; they possessed slaves, and textiles and chariot-wheels are named after them (see Glossary, s.v. *e-qe-si-jo*). This suggests that they must have been the owners of chariots, the élite of the Mycenaean army; and their name which means 'Follower' (classical ἐπέτης from ἕπομαι) is best interpreted as follower of the king, the members of the court. Their allocation to duties in connexion with coast-guards must therefore be to provide liaison with the king's headquarters at Pylos. Since we know they possessed chariots, they will have had a means of quick communication, for their charioteers could be used as despatch-riders. The existence of a network of roads suitable for horse-drawn vehicles has been made extremely probable by the discovery of traces of such roads. The allocation of one *e-qe-ta* to cover the first two (i.e. the most northerly) *o-ka* is thus easily intelligible, for there can have been only one major road leading northwards in the vicinity of the coast.

It is tempting to go even further and suppose that apart from their function as liaison officers the *e-qe-ta* were also commanders of regiments of the Pylian army. The obvious target for the raiding force will be the unfortified Palace; thus the strategy of defence must be to cover all the approaches to the Palace, but at the same time to concentrate the strongest forces on the most likely line of attack. The other regiments will be placed on good lines of communication, so that they can be quickly moved in case of need. No raider knowing the location of the Palace can have failed to attempt a landing in the area of the Bay of Navarino; and this is precisely the district which seems to be designated in §§7 and 8, for this is undoubtedly the location of *A-ke-re-wa*.

The mysterious words *o-ka-ra* (*o-ka-ra₃*), *ke-ki-de*, *i-wa-so*, *o-*34-ta*, *ku-re-we*, *pe-di-je-we*, *u-ru-pi-ja-jo*, *ko-ro-ku-ra-i-jo* seem all to be descriptions of the troops used for these duties. Some look like ethnic adjectives, but if so the places from which they are named are not elsewhere mentioned on the tablets, and they contrast with the real ethnics such as *o-wi-ti-ni-jo* (**56**=An 657.4) or *ku-pa-ri-si-jo* (ibid. 8, 10) from known places. Only one offers a plausible etymological explanation: *pe-di-je-we* is likely to be *pediēwes* from πεδίον 'plainsmen', though it is not impossible that it is equivalent to πεζοί 'foot-soldiers'. None of the guesses made for the rest are convincing. But some of these names reappear on the *Na* tablets (see pp. 395 ff.), where the groups of *ke-ki-de*, *ko-ro-ku-ra-i-jo* and *u-ru-pi-ja-jo* are said to 'possess' (land or its produce?). Great efforts have been made to connect soldiers with flax (see below, p. 470); but perhaps the effort is vain, and the connexion is by way of a third term. If we regard the names on the *o-ka* tablets not as varieties of soldiers, but as tribal names, their reappearance on the flax-tablets would require no special explanation, since the alleged coincidences in numbers between the two sets of tablets are not as remarkable as seemed at first sight. It is possible therefore that these men are drawn from communities resident within the kingdom of Pylos, but not part of the normal Greek population. They may well have retained their non-Greek language from the time before the settlement of the area by Greek-speakers; but even if they had become linguistically assimilated to their masters, they would doubtless retain their old pre-hellenic names, though adapted to Greek declensions.

One conclusion from these documents seems inescapable; that Pylos feared an attack coming by sea, and its subsequent destruction implies that these precautions were in the event in vain. The direction from which the attack was expected cannot be deduced; the despatch of rowers to Pleuron would hardly be significant, even if we were sure it was the Aetolian Pleuron which was meant. Suspicion must fall upon the so-called Peoples of the Sea, who are known from Egyptian sources to have been active around the end of the thirteenth century and powerful enough to launch two major sea-borne attacks upon the Nile Delta. But no confirmation of this suspicion has yet been found.

p. 185† **53**=An 1. The five place names in lines 2–6 have been understood as locatives; the men are at these places, but will soon leave. But it would be equally possible to regard them as ablatives, if we accept the idea of a limited survival of the ablative as a case-form in Mycenaean (see above, p. 403). It is noticeable that the only name which is a plural of the first or third declension (*po-ra-pi*, cf. *po-ra-i* clearly locative PY **59**=An 656.13) has the -*pi* suffix.

186† **54**=An 610. Corrections: l. 3 [*me-*]*ta-ki-ti-ta*; l. 4 [ ]*wa ki-ti-ta*; l. 9 *me-ta-ki̦*[-*ti-ta*.

Despite the initial lacuna the pattern of this tablet is clear. The men listed belong to various coastal towns and are sometimes further specified by classifications: *ki-ti-ta* 'settlers' (whatever the special value of the term), *me-ta-ki-ti-ta* 'new settlers', *po-si-ke-te-re* 'immigrants', *po-ku-ta* (meaning obscure). Entries so introduced refer to the last place named. There is also a category of men introduced by a man's name in the genitive: *e-ke-ra₂-wo-no*, *we-da-ne-wo*. Both of these men are clearly important personages elsewhere on the tablets (e.g. **171**=Un 718, **168**=Es 644). This leaves a few terms obscure: *wo-qe-we* PN?, *ko-ni-jo* PN or ethnic? (the omission of MAN is due to erasure and re-writing in a cramped space); *we-re-ka-ra*⟨-*ta*⟩, if rightly restored, and *te-qa-ta* may be occupational terms.

187† **55**=An 724. There are frequent traces of erasure and re-writing on this tablet; l. 4 after MAN 1 another MAN has been written faintly by another hand.

No significant progress has been made with the problems presented by this tablet, though a brave effort by Perpillou (1968) should be mentioned. Any attempt to construct a regular formula encounters difficulties, and the frequent corrections lead us to suspect that scribal errors are present. For instance, MAN 1 in line 4 is preceded by *o-pe-ro-ta e-re-e*, which is apparently *ophélonta* and an infinitive (probably *erehen* 'to row'); but MEN 5 in line 6 has *o-pe-ro-te e-re-e*, where the first word seems to be nominative plural, *ophélontes*, unless we adopt the suggestion of Risch (1958a) that -*es* functions as both nominative and accusative plural termination of consonant stems. It seems on the whole easier to believe that the syntax is incoherent.

It is clear that the text divides into sections, each beginning with a place name: ll. 1–8 *ro-o-wa*; ll. 9–12 *a-ke-re-wa*; l. 13 *wo-qe-we*, if this is really a place; if not, this line belongs to *a-ke-re-wa*; l. 14 *ri-jo*. *a-pe-o-te* seems in other contexts to refer to temporary absentees rather than permanently missing personnel; it is therefore likely that the entries record the reasons why certain men are not present. If *a-pe-e-ke* is *apheēke* from ἀφίημι, this would be an appropriate word, 'discharged', 'released', but it demands a subject. In line 2 this may be found in *me-nu-wa*; but in line 5 *e-ke-ra₂-wo-ne* is dative, unless

431

it is an error. Perpillou solves this problem by supposing *me-nu-wa* to be understood as the subject throughout; but if this were so, it is hard to explain why the verb should be repeated. Perpillou also gives an ingenious interpretation of *a₂-ri-e* as *haliēn*, accusative singular of ἁλιεύς (for acc. in *-ēn* see Lejeune, 1971, p. 262); but he has to suppose scribal incoherence and a failure to alter this to the plural when the original entry MAN 1 was deleted and MAN 5 inserted in the next line. He interprets *a-re-sa-ni-e* as a finite verbal form *ens-an-iē* prefixed by the particle *ar*; but in view of the retention of ἐν (ἰν) without the suffix *-ς* in Arcadian and Cypriot to express motion into, *ens* (=εἰς) would be surprising in Mycenaean.

p. 190† **57**=An 519. Corrections: l. 2 *zo-wo* (*wo-zo* was a mistake in transcription in the first two editions of the *Pylos Tablets*); l. 7 *po-te-u*[   ]*e̥-ta-wo-ne-u̥*[; l. 8 MEN 20[.

p. 192† **59**=An 656. Corrections: l. 2 the deleted word is [[*di-wi-je-u*]]; l. 18 MEN 6̣0[.

p. 193† **60**=An 661. Corrections: l. 2 *a-ti-r̥o̥-*[.]; l. 4 [.]*-o-ri-j̥o̥   k̥o̥-r̥o̥-k̥u̥*[*-ra-*]*i̥-j̥o̥* MEN 30; l. 5 MEN 1̣0̣[; l. 8 now lost, but probably containing a word at the left.

CHAPTER VII

LIVESTOCK AND AGRICULTURAL PRODUCE

p. 195† The identifications of the ideograms for domestic animals have now been generally accepted. The most important modification of the pattern set out here, apart from the use in transcription of Latin names and the abbreviations *m* and *f* for male and female, has been the valuable suggestion of Killen that the male ideogram was used as an all-purpose sign covering on occasion not only castrated males, but mixtures of males and females. That is very clear in KN **84**=Ce 59; see p. 213. But its implications for the enormous series of Knossos sheep tablets are far-reaching and will be discussed below (p. 433).

197† Progress here has been slow, but Killen (1964 a) has discussed *pa*, *za*, *pe* and *se*. Most of these seem to be indications of age, and the following are generally accepted:

pa = *pa-ra-jo* = *palaios* 'old'
pe = *pe-ru-si-nu-wo* = *perusinwos* 'last year's'
ki = 'new-born' (obscure, but cf. *ki-ra* in Glossary)
ne = *ne-wo* = *newos* 'young'
za = *za-we-te* = *tsāwetes* (or adjectival form) 'this year's'

On the other hand the adjunct *se* is restricted to a small group of tablets, and it seems clear that it represents rather the place name *se-to-i-ja*.

197‡ The merit of having advanced this problem to a definitive solution belongs to Killen, whose studies summarized in his article (1964 b) have completely changed our view of this subject. These are restricted to the Knossos sheep tablets, and problems remain to be elucidated on the sheep of Pylos and other animals at both sites.

The disproportion of rams to ewes which was so perplexing (cf. p. 198) is easily explained once it is appreciated that the ideogram RAM can stand for wethers (i.e. castrated male sheep), for enormous flocks of these have often been kept for wool-production. But since they would be incapable of regeneration, separate breeding flocks (Knossos *Dl* series) were required, and every year the flocks of wethers must be counted and replacements drafted to maintain their proper strength. This at once provides a plausible explanation for the deficits, and makes it possible to regard the records as a census; they are in fact the documents necessary for efficient flock management on a large scale. This is confirmed by the existence of remarkably similar records in medieval England and elsewhere.

The tablets that show WOOL are thus the records of the productivity of the flocks, and here too the figures agree well with medieval practice.

199† Confirmation of *scriptio plena* of the type required by *we-re-ke* = *wergei* has not been forthcoming, and it may be better to take this as a noun. Palmer (1963 a) proposes *wreges* 'herds' (cf. Vedic *vraja*- 'enclosure, herd'), which is plausible though not attested in later Greek; the sense of 'enclosure for sheep' is not to be excluded.

199‡ **61** = Cn 131. Corrections: the check-mark (X) seems to have been attached to every entry except the last, but not always in the same place; l. 9 RAMS 170 (for 180).

433

pa-ro: it may be questioned whether these are all flocks received from the shepherds named. Perhaps here *pa-ro* has merely locative sense, 'in the charge of'.

p. 200† **62**=Cn 655. Corrections: l. 7 *ti-ko-wo*; l. 13 *ma-ro-pi   ro-ko-jo* ... [X] 80.

pa-ra-jo: undoubtedly refers to the sheep, see above, p. 433.

a-ko-ra: it now seems likely that the men designated here and at Knossos as 'collectors' are in some ways beneficiaries of the produce of the flock. It is possible that the sheep and goats were nominally the property of the king, but that he assigned certain flocks to his nobles for their sustenance; at least these words need not imply that the persons named were tax-gatherers employed by the Palace.

p. 201† It is now clear that the hundreds and other round figures on these tablets represent the notional strength of the flock; hence the deficit (*o*) indicates the number of replacements needed in the current year. As at Pylos the 'collectors' are probably nobles to whom the flocks are assigned, which will explain why the flocks of a particular man are not concentrated in one area. The name of a 'collector' is sometimes substituted by what appears to be an adjective, especially *po-ti-ni-ja-we-jo*; this seems to imply that these were allocated for the support of the goddess Potnia, or perhaps rather her human ministrants. The flocks which do not have a collector's name, about two-thirds of the archive, will then have belonged directly to the king.

p. 202† **65**=Db 1232

pe-ri-qo-te-jo: it is possible that this is an adjective rather than a name; see Glossary.

p. 203† **70**=Dg 1158. Correction: read *o*. RAMS 10 (corrected from 12).

p. 203‡ The identity of ideogram **145*=WOOL is now agreed in this context. It has been suggested that elsewhere (e.g. PY **103**=Un 267, **104**=Un 249) the same sign has a different meaning; but a plausible explanation of the presence of wool among ingredients of ointment can be given (see p. 441), and there is no justification for doubting that the sign has the same meaning in all contexts.

It has been suggested that WOOL should be regarded as a ligature of the syllabic signs *ma* and *ru*. The ideogram is sometimes hardly distinguished from *ma*, but when carefully written has a small element at the upper centre which resembles *re* or *ro*, rarely *ru*. It seems certain that the ideogram was taken over from Linear A, in which it is quite clearly a ligature of the signs corresponding to *ma* and *ru*; but this is no justification for importing this analysis into Linear B where the second element has been reduced in size and distinctiveness to a point where it cannot be seriously regarded as forming a ligature. Whether *maru* represents a Minoan word for 'wool' or 'fleece' which was borrowed by Greek as μαλλός is purely a matter of speculation.

In the *Dl* tablets we now regard *ki*. RAMS as being a convention for lambs, thus the relatively small yield of wool is accounted for by these being breeding flocks.

204† **73** = Dl 943

po-ti-ni-ja-we ⟨*-jo*⟩: see p. 434.

205† **74** = Dp (formerly Dl) 1061. The SHEEP sign is apparently not RAM, but might be EWE; both are found preceding WOOL on Dp 7280. 7300 should be omitted from the references here.

206† **76** = Cn 3

The essential first step in analysing this tablet is to discover its syntax. It seems clear that *i-je-si* is a verb, preceded by the particle *jo-* = *hō* 'thus'; that *qo-o* is its object = $g^w\bar{o}s$ 'oxen'; that *di-wi-je-we* is the dative of a man's name, though a title or even an ethnic cannot be entirely excluded, and that *e-re-u-te-re* is therefore likely to be a dative in apposition. The entries in ll. 3–7 consist of a place name followed by a word which is elsewhere the description of a group of men, and is therefore likely to be nominative plural here, rather than dative singular (*ku-re-we* and *o-ka-ra₃* are the only forms which would distinguish singular from plural). If so, these men are the subjects of the verb *i-je-si*, and this leads to the conclusion that *me-za-na* may perhaps be another nominative plural and be a generic name which subsumes the more detailed classes of the individual entries. It seems unlikely that *me-za-na* can be an accusative of motion towards, since although this is theoretically possible Mycenaean Greek appears always to use the suffix *-de* to characterize such an accusative (e.g. *pe-re-u-ro-na-de* PY **53** = An 1). If *me-za-na* is the subject, we then have the order: adverb–verb–subject–indirect object–object; cf. PY **252** = Vn 10 where it is adverb–verb–subject–accusative of destination–object, and a similar but more complicated example in PY **257** = Jn 829.

The suggestion has been advanced above (p. 430) that the names *o-ka-ra₃*, *ku-re-we* and *u-ru-pi-ja-jo*, which recur on the *o-ka* tablets (**56–60**), together with *i-wa-si-jo-ta*, which is paralleled there by *i-wa-so*, may be tribal names belonging to subject peoples. If this is correct, and *me-za-na* is the generic term for them, this makes it rather more probable that the word is to be connected with the classical name of the area, Μεσσηνία; the town was originally

435

Μεσσάνα. The spelling with *za*, implying a pronunciation *Metsāna*(*i*?) at this date, excludes a connexion with Greek μέσσος, which is in any case improbable in a word with the pre-Greek suffix -ᾱνᾱ.

i-je-si: the first edition offered the choice of 'send' or 'sacrifice' for this word, and it is still difficult to decide. If 'send' is right, then *e-re-u-te-re di-wi-je-we* is probably the dative of the recipient, 'for the inspector(?) Diwieus'; the place names may then be ablatives, or locatives closely connected with the classes of men. If the meaning is 'sacrifice', the existence of a verb of this form seems to be proved by PY **172** = Tn 316 (see p. 462), but the meaning of *e-re-u-te-re di-wi-je-we* is difficult, if the second word is, as elsewhere, the name of a man. It might be tempting to suppose an ablative (or dative) absolute, 'Diwieus being inspector', since it is hard to make him into a deity, despite his theophoric name and his association with Poseidon on the *Es* tablets. A sacrifice before battle, as urged insistently by Palmer (1963*a*, p. 176), is perfectly appropriate; but why were five battles anticipated, and why are the local levies, not the main force of the army, instructed to sacrifice bulls?

u-ru-pi-ja-jo-jo: the last syllable must be an error, an understandable case of dittography.

p. 207† **77** = Cn 418. Corrections: l. 3 *ma-ra-pi̦*; l. 8 at right WE[ ] PIG[.

a-ko-ro-we-e: Palmer's assertion (1963*a*, p. 405) that the new reading in l. 3 rules out 'of uniform colour' is hardly justified; it is still possible to refer thus to an ox which is white except for dark patches underneath. But the alternative *akrōwehe* 'with pointed ears' is perhaps less open to objection, though there is insufficient evidence to settle the question.

ma-ra-pi̦: the reading of the last sign is still uncertain, but if this is correct, it could be *malāphi*, locative plural of the noun preserved in the classical phrase ὑπὸ μάλης 'under the arm-pit'; that is to say, 'under the legs'. *Pe-ko* should then be an adjective of colour, and this suggests comparison with περκνός 'dark' and various forms invite the restoration of an earlier adjective **πέρκος. Thus 'white, dark in the μάλαι' (Palmer) is a possible, but not entirely convincing, solution. The specification of colour in connexion with oxen may be due to their use for sacrifice, white animals being often prescribed for sacrifice to the Olympian deities.

p. 209† **78** = C 914

a-ka-wi-ja-de: Palmer (1963*a*, pp. 65, 184) objected that parallels show that this is the name of the herdsman, though he has now retracted this objection (1969, p. 485). In fact, the determination of hand (no. 112) shows that this tablet belongs to a group (including **80** = C 913) which has nothing to do with the main sheep archive (*D* tablets). Unfortunately few of these texts are complete, but there is nothing in them to suggest that a destination is out of place. The only word preserved on them which is not a personal name is *sa-pa-ke-te-ri-ja* C (not Dl) 941, which has been taken as *sphaktēria*, possibly meaning 'for sacrifice', but a place name (cf. Σφακτηρία in Messenia) cannot be excluded. However, the spelling is somewhat abnormal (*sa-pa-* for σφα-, -*ka-te*- rather than -*ke-te*-, but cf. *wa-na-ka-te-ro*) and the identification is probably wrong.

209‡ The table of *Dn* entries needs correction in the light of improved readings, joins and re-allocation of tablets.

Da-wo	2440
*Da-*22-to*	1370
E-ko-so	2252
Pa-i-to	1509
Pu-na-so	330
Pu-so	1034
Qa-ra	2290
Ra-ja	904
Ri-jo-no	2000[
Ru-ki-to	4040[
Su-ki-ri-ta	517
Su-ri-mo	2390
Ti-ri-to	1222
56-ko-we-i	2003
Unknown	11,183
Total	35,484

In addition to the fragment mentioned (Dn 1088) which reads 19,300[, there is also Dn 1319 reading [*a-*]*mi-ni-si-ja   ne*   RAM 11,900[, and a fragment (Dn 5668) probably to be restored [*pe-ri-*]*qo-te-jo* RAM 3300[. Olivier (1967*c*) demonstrated that the *Dn* tablets are the totals of the flocks held by the Palace in each area, but that those belonging to the 'collectors' are totalled separately (as on Dn 5668).

210† **80** = C 913. See above on **78** = C 914.

210‡ **81** = Dm 1180

a₃-mi-re-we, e-ka-ra-e-we. These words have been exhaustively discussed by Lejeune (1962*b*); he concludes that *e-ka-ra-e-we* cannot be a derivative in -εύς of ἐσχάρα, because this would not account for medial -*ra*-. He proposes instead *engraēwes* (γράω) 'animals for fattening'; and compares *a₃-mi-re-we* with αἱμασιά 'stone-wall', i.e. animals kept in enclosures.

211† **83** = C 902. Corrections: this tablet has been removed from the special *Ch* series; l.11 read *re-ṛi-jo*; l.12 probably no sign lost in lacuna before *wa-to*.

There has been no confirmation of the meaning of the rare ideogram here associated with OXEN; the adjunct *ne* suggests that they are young animals of some sort, but perhaps of a different species. The omission of the numeral 1 after ox on lines 1–3 seems to be without significance.

wa-to: found also on jars from Thebes, the analysis of the clay of which suggests that they may come from Palaikastro in eastern Crete; this then is a possible identification for this name. *o-du-ru-wi-jo* is on a Theban jar which may have come from Zakro.

u-wo-qe-we: Palmer (1963*a*, p. 183) suggests *uw-oqᵘēwes* 'overseers', a compound with the preposition ὐ alleged to exist in Cypriot. In value it is equivalent to ἐπί.

re-ṛi-jo: if this reading is correct, it could be *Lerioi* from Λέρος, but since all the other places on this tablet of which we know anything are in Crete, we must assume another place of the same name rather than a reference to the island.

p. 212† **84**=Ce 59. Corrections: l. 1 at left]*mạ-sa*; l. 2 at left *ku-*]*ṭạ-to*, at end [.]-*mọ* for *da-mo* over *we-ka-ta*; l. 3 [.]-*mo* for *da-mo*.

It now seems that the reading *da-mo* in this tablet is unsound, though it is hard to see what should stand in its place. If *ta-ra-me-to*, which stands in the parallel place at the beginning of line 2, is a man's name, [.]-*mo* is presumably another. *ma-sa* is known as a place name, so probably the word is complete.

p. 213† The names given to oxen have now been included in the Glossary, and it is therefore necessary to give the amended list of complete names here:

a₃-wo-ro, KN Ch 896, [Ch 898], Ch 1029, Ch 5754, [Ch 5938], *Aiwolos*. [Cf. Αἴολος *Od.* x, 2.]

a₃-zo-ro, KN Ch 1034.

ke-ra-no, KN **85**=Ch 896, [Ch 7066]. *Kelainos*.

ko-so-u-to, KN Ch 900, *Xouthos*. (Also as man's name.)

po-da-ko, KN Ch 899, Ch 1029. *Podargos*. [Πόδαργος name of two horses: *Il.* VIII, 185, XXIII, 295.]

to-ma-ko, KN Ch 897, Ch 898, Ch 1015. *Stomargos*.

wa-no, KN Ch 5724.

wo-no-qo-so, KN Ch 897, Ch 1015. Possibly spelling of *Woinoqᵘs*, but *Woinoqᵘsos* is perhaps more likely. [Οἶνοψ as man's name *Od.* XXI, 144; cf. βόε οἴνοπε *Il.* XIII, 703+.]

p. 213‡ **86**=Co 907. The place names belong to the same group as those in **83**=C 902; they are perhaps located in the east and west of the island.

p. 214† **88**=E 749. Corrections: l. 2 WHEAT 23[+; l. 7 WHEAT 6[.

p. 214‡ **89**=E 777. Corrections: in all three lines read WHEAT 100[, i.e. the figure is probably not a round number.

₂15† **90 = G 820.** Corrections: l. 1]*ṇạ* (for]*ḍị*), *to-sa* for *pa-sa*.

> *to-sa*: *tos(s)ān krithān* 'so much barley', 'month 1' presumably means therefore 'one month's ration'.

₂15‡ The identity of the ideogram no. 121 as BARLEY seems to be established, apart from its general probability, by two facts. It would seem from An 128 that an entry WHEAT 2 ⊤ 6 ◁ 5 ▽ 2 has been converted on the reverse to BARLEY 5 ⊤ 3 ◁ 4 ▽ [?], which is double the quantity ignoring the last unit; and there is good evidence from antiquity that for ration purposes wheat was regarded as roughly double the value of barley. The BARLEY ideogram also has the characteristic 'beard' of an ear of barley.

₂16† **91 = Fn 50.** Corrections: l.11 read *au-[ke-i-]ja-te-wo*; l.13 *a-pi-ẹ-ṛạ do-e-ro-i*. The supplements and the reading of l.13 are guaranteed by the recurrence of these names in **312 = An 1281**, though this throws no light on the identity of the persons named. *a-pi-e-ra* will also be feminine, like *mi-jo-qa*.

> *qa-si-re-wi-ja*: since *qa-si-re-u* apparently means no more than 'chief' and can be used of the man in charge of a group of bronzesmiths, it appears the word has risen in importance after the Mycenaean period. It is quite likely that it denotes a work-group under the control of the man named.
>
> *me-za-ne*: see on *me-za-na*, p. 435. But it is impossible to reconcile the two forms if *me-za-na* is nom. plur.; perhaps variant forms of a non-Greek word.
>
> *i-za-a-to-mo-i*: the reading of the second sign is confirmed. Mühlestein (1955, p. 124) ingeniously suggested that *i-za-* was derived from *hiqqʷyā*, as a by-form to *i-qi-ja* = *hiqqʷiā*. It remains impossible to verify the suggestion.

₂17† It now seems clear that the word *a-pu-do-si* 'payment' is used to denote contributions by subjects to the Palace. In these cases at least, as **92 = Fh 349**, it is clear that the oil is being brought into the Palace stores; others are equally certainly records of disbursements, but there are still many tablets which are difficult to assign confidently to one side or other of the account book.

₂17‡ The information on oil at Pylos has been much increased by new finds and a section on this subject has been introduced into the Addenda on Chapter IX; see p. 476 below.

₂18† **93 = Fo 101.** Corrections: l. 2 read *a-na-*82*; l. 9 *e-ro-pa-ke-ṭạ*, the last sign could perhaps be *-ja* (Olivier, 1969, p. 7), the ideogram here and in l.15 is perhaps OIL + WẸ.

a-ne-a₂: this, like *ma-no* and *ke-ra-so*, recurs on a tablet where the identifiable names are feminine (MY **303** = V 659, see p. 425), and we may presume they all are. Hence all of these may perhaps be women's names; certainly *we-i-we-sa* (l. 3) appears to have the feminine adjectival ending *-wessa* (perhaps *Huiwessa* 'she who has many sons', if *we-* before vowel represents classical ὑ-).

*a-na-*82*: the new reading is due to Olivier. If *82* is correctly identified as *swa* (Chadwick 1968*a*), the name is perhaps something like *Arnaswā*; it certainly has nothing to do with ἄνασσα.

pi-we-ri-si: Πιερίς is attested as a woman's name, but this does not explain the plural. The analogy of *a-ke-ti-ri-ja-i*, which is also plural, suggests that it might be some kind of title or group. Since ⟨ 1 = ⟨ 6, there may have been six of them. But *a-ne-a₂* is singular, and receives three times the normal amount, so it is impossible to draw firm conclusions. *E-ro-pa-ke-ta* (or *-ke-ja*) draws 60 times the normal amount.

p. 219† **94** = F 841. The WHEAT ideogram on both occurrences has the syllabic sign PE ligatured with it. The significance of this addition is not known, but as an adjunct *pe* appears often to stand for *perusinwos* 'last year's'. This might not be impossible here too.

su-za: in **165** = Gv 862 this word is coupled with a much more tree-like ideogram, making the interpretation *sutsai* < *sukyai* 'fig-trees' certain there. It is open to question whether the same meaning is not intended here, as the annotation would seem superfluous if the fruit is meant; cf. l. 3. *Ka-po* can then introduce the fruit, if we reject the restoration *e-[ra-wa*. The ideogram for 'figs' (= syllabic *ni*) is doubtless a simplification of the 'tree' sign. In line 6 possibly the second *e-ra-wa* introduced a mention of olive-trees.

p. 220† The gloss 'flour' applied to no. *65* is not a certain proof that this is the value of the ideogram, since it would be possible to regard 'flour' as an extra piece of information rather than a verification. Thus *65* might rather stand for another grain (Chadwick, 1966, p. 31).

p. 221† *po-qa* (*po-pa₂*): this word is one of the proofs that *pa₂* = *qa*, since it clearly belongs to the family of *po-qe-wi-ja* = φορβειά (see Glossary).

p. 221‡ **97** = Un 2. Correction: line 3 read *125* + PA T 1 ⟨ 3 o ⟨ 5; o is here probably not the ordinary abbreviation of *o-pe-ro* 'deficit', but a shorthand for the ligature of *125* + o which occurs elsewhere (e.g. Fa 16, Ua 434, Un 47).

mu-jo-me-no: the note has been misunderstood; the form corresponds to μυόμενος (μύω 'close'), but this is unintelligible unless in sense it is equivalent to μυούμενος (μυέω 'initiate'). Replacement of simple verbs by contract types is not rare (e.g. ὠθέω replaces *ὤθω, aor. ὦσα *Il.* 1, 220, στερέω exists alongside στέρομαι, etc.). The verb is presumably *muiomenos* (< *mu(s?)-yō*). Palmer's objection (1963*a*, p. 258) that this

440

involves a 'non-Greek gerundival construction' is hard to follow; participles are used regularly in Greek to indicate time, especially in the genitive absolute, and with prepositions in expressions such as περὶ πλήθουσαν ἀγοράν. His other objection, that 'initiation can hardly apply to the god *wanax*', is mistaken, since he himself admits (p. 461) that the word refers both to the human ruler and the deity.

a-pi-e-ke: a form derived from ἵημι seems to be excluded by the locative *pa-ki-ja-si*. Perhaps a part of the verb meaning 'sacrifice' or 'dedicate' seen in *i-je-si, i-je-to*, compounded with *apu-* or *amphi-*?

o-pi-te-⟨u⟩-ke-e-u: it is not impossible to interpret the word as written without ⟨u⟩ (*opistegeeus*, Palmer, 1963a, p. 258), but it seems more likely to be a simple error. The *opiteukheeus* will be the overseer of τεύχεα, i.e. the store-keeper. There is nothing surprising in finding him elsewhere in humble company.

21¶ The use of *ku-pi-ri-jo* on condiment tablets seems now less likely to be an indication of origin, but the commodity known as *Phoinikio-* strongly suggests a Syrian origin. Among the condiments listed at Mycenae (see pp. 225–31), *sa-sa-ma* is certainly sesame, and its eastern origin is confirmed by the Semitic name; but J. Innes Miller (1969, p. 87) shows that in Roman times it was imported from India, so that the Phoenicians may have been only middlemen in a trade-route linking Greece with India at this much earlier date. If *ko-no* is 'sweet rush' (p. 227), this too is an Indian product; and the same is true of *ku-pa-ro* if it is *Cyperus rotundus*, the fragrant variety, but *Cyperus longus* 'galingale' is also a possibility and this is a native of the eastern Mediterranean.

22† **98**=Ga 415. Correction: read CONDIMENT 1 T 6, equivalent to approximately 150 litres.

23† The signs for WINE have been discussed at length by Bennett (1966) and Chadwick (1968c); it still seems most likely that the reduced variant (no. *131b*) is intended for 'must'.

23‡ The WOOL ideogram has been exhaustively investigated by Killen (1962a), who shows that its presence in lists of ingredients of unguent can be easily explained by the fact that raw wool is rich in grease (lanolin), which is used in the manufacture of ointments. Similarly *wi-ri-za*=*wridza* (ῥίζα) will refer to the root section of the wool, which is particularly rich in grease. The confusion between **145* and MA is also found at Mycenae (see Killen, loc. cit.), but there is no need to question WOOL in the following two tablets.

24† *a-re-pa-te ze-so-me-no*: Palmer now (1963a, p. 270) translates 'for him [Thyestes] to boil...in the unguent'. This meets the objection that the form should be *ze-so-me-na*, but imposes an unnecessary middle sense on the participle. Since ζέω describes the

441

process of making ἄλειφαρ, 'to boil' = 'to make by boiling', it seems preferable to allow the middle form to function as passive, as the -θη- element of future and aorist passive is an innovation and is so far absent from Mycenaean; cf. *e-we-pe-se-so-me-na* (see Glossary), which is hard to understand if not passive.

p. 224‡ **104** = Un 249. Correction: line 3 read] ḳạ + p̣ọ   ⊤ 6.

a-re-pa-zọ[-o: the reading is now printed thus by Bennett and Olivier.

p. 225† There has been a tendency to regard these tablets as proof that perfumed oil was produced at Mycenae as at Pylos. Although this is likely on archaeological grounds, for Wace named the first house he excavated the 'House of the Oil Merchant', it has been pointed out by Killen (1964c) that all the plants named are used in cooking to season food, but some of them have no smell. Thus we must suppose that these are used as flavouring, not as perfumes. The possible occurrence of the word ἀρώματα to refer to them is no objection, since this covers both aromatic and flavouring herbs.

p. 226† *ka-ra-ko*: the existence of this word has been called in question by the further study of Ge 605, where it was believed to occur twice. In line 1 the reading now preferred by Olivier is *ka-]rạ-to* (cf. **106** = Ge 603.1) and in line 6 *ka-ra-*[where it is impossible to exclude *ka-ra-to*, though *ka-ra-ko* is a little easier.

p. 226‡ *ko-no*: the reading *e-ne-me-na* in **106** = Ge 603.2 is confirmed, and the suggestion *e-ro₂-me-na* = *errōmenai* must be rejected. This and the word abbreviated DE probably refer to two different varieties of *skhoinos* (see on **105** = Ge 602 below).

p. 227† **105** = Ge 602

jo-o-po-ro: while it is theoretically possible that *ōphlon* is 1st person singular (Palmer, 1963a, p. 273), the absence of any clear forms of finite verbs other than 3rd persons makes this highly improbable. The reference would only be intelligible if these were the private records of a merchant; but everything suggests that the buildings where these were found represent the workshops and living quarters of palace officials.

a-ro-[: it seems possible to read *a-ro-mo*[-ta, if this is an acceptable form for ἀρώματα; cf. *a-mo-ta* = ἄρματα, etc.

pe-se-ro: Palmer's suggestion (loc. cit.) that this is the first entry with a nil quantity is perhaps confirmed by the reading of a deleted [[*sa-sa-ma*]] and a doubtful quantity after it, but the small size of script makes this uncertain.

ku-mi-no: possibly read *ku-mi-no-jọ*[with *jo* in place of ▽, but most of the entries appear to be accusative or nominative of the rubric.

a-po-ṭẹ-ị̣[: better reading *a-po-te-rạ* = *amphoterā*, each of the two varieties of *skhoinos* (see p. 226). Probably to be taken as singular, since dual would presumably require *a-po-te-ro*.

p. 229† **106** = Ge 603. Corrections l.1 *da-ra*[   ]ṃi-ta-qe. Reverse: p̣ẹ-[.

CHAPTER VIII

LAND OWNERSHIP AND LAND USE

32† No class of Mycenaean documents has given rise to more argument than the Pylos land-tenure tablets; yet they remain one of the more obscure areas of interpretation. It is not that the vocabulary or syntax are more than usually difficult, though here too there are unsolved problems. It is rather our total ignorance about the situation, of which the tablets record only marginal elements. Most of the attempts at a solution have started from a theory about the holding of land in Mycenaean Greece, and the evidence of the tablets has then been interpreted to fit this theory. It is fair to observe that without such a theory any total explanation is probably impossible; but the very small amount of hard fact which can be deduced from the documents allows the most extravagant varieties of interpretation. An attempt will be made here to extract the core of fact and no space will be wasted on the discussion of the many theories.

The first fact which needs to be appreciated is that the Pylos *E* tablets are not a survey of the arable land of the whole kingdom or even the Hither Province. The vast majority of tablets refer to the place *Pa-ki-ja-ne* (114 = En 609.1), which is the one of the Nine Towns closest to the Palace; it also figures in the religious document 172 = Tn 316.rev.2 as the location of a shrine, and this together with the fact that so many of the persons listed on the four main sets have religious titles justifies us in regarding this place as in some respects a special case. The other two main sets of land documents (*Ea* and *Es*) refer apparently to different areas, but unfortunately we are given no means of locating them. We must therefore ask why, if this is a general survey, so little information has been received; and it seems safer to conclude that the only areas listed are those in which special problems of tenure have arisen. It is thus extremely dangerous to generalize from the situation at *Pa-ki-ja-ne*, in so far as it can be deduced, for it may well be exceptional.

It follows from this that any attempt to understand the way in which grain was grown and distributed is vain. Obviously the arable land must have been worked intensively to feed the population; but the details of the process escape us entirely. The Palace issued large quantities of grain each month; the fragment Fg 253 with its total of WHEAT 192 T 7 is likely to represent the monthly ration of the women listed on the *Ab* tablets, and this is a quantity

443

of about 18,500 litres. An efficient means of collection must have existed to supply this need; but we cannot find it in the surviving records.

Secondly, it is clear that land is regarded as falling into one of two categories, called by the tablets *ke-ke-me-na* and *ki-ti-me-na*. The etymology of the first of these terms is still an unsolved mystery; or rather there is no lack of plausible solutions, only of the means of choosing between them. But its effective sense was grasped very early by Furumark (see p. 233), and the idea that such land is 'communal' is generally accepted. Its opposite, *ki-ti-me-na*, must therefore indicate 'private' land, though etymologically this is the present participle of an athematic verb *ktiēmi*=κτίʒω, of which we have the 3rd person plural of present indicative *ki-ti-je-si* in **193**=Na 520. The contrast between this present participle and *ke-ke-me-na*, which is almost certainly a reduplicated perfect participle, needs to be accounted for by any theory of these terms' etymology. This is enough to disprove the suggestion (p. 233) that *ki-ti-me-na* means 'reclaimed by private initiative'; it must mean either 'inhabited' or 'cultivated', and since *ke-ke-me-na* also was cultivated, perhaps the distinction is between land on which the aristocracy had their country houses and land which is left for occupation by the local communities. This may lead us to accept the idea of Ruijgh (1967, p. 366) that *ke-ke-me-na* is *kekhemenā*, perfect participle of **kikhēmi* 'abandon'; cf. χήρα 'widow', Skt. *jáhāti* 'leave'. Against this it has been urged by Heubeck (1967) that the development of meaning seen in the classical representative of this verb, κιχάνω, is hardly likely to be post-Mycenaean, and he therefore favours *kekesmenos* from the root **kes*—'cut' (cf. κεάʒω, κείων). It is difficult to choose between these alternatives, but at least Heubeck has given good reasons for dismissing the other suggestions on morphological grounds.

Thirdly, it must be admitted that we committed an error in employing the word 'feudal' in our discussion of this subject, for it has given rise to much argument and misunderstanding. It ought properly to be restricted to the system of Medieval Europe, but it has been used loosely to denote any system in which land is occupied in return for services. Since a non-monetary economy is virtually obliged to institute some such system, there is nothing remarkable (much less Indo-European) in the existence of a 'feudal' system in this sense at Pylos. It will arise spontaneously wherever parallel conditions exist. The specific features of Medieval feudalism are either absent or at least unproved. There is, for example, nothing to show that any of the obligations imposed on occupiers of land include military service.

This said, it may be admitted that holdings of land seem to be associated with the performance of specified services, since we are told that some occupiers 'ought' to perform some act, but have not done so (**135**=Ep 704.7, **148**=Ep 613.4). But the nature of this act remains a matter of speculation; in both cases this obligation concerns the *ke-ke-me-na* land and thus the *dāmos*. There is no parallel obligation recorded on the holders of *ki-te-me-na* land, though it might be supposed that if these are 'barons' their holdings would entail services to the king.

What these private occupiers do is to let out part of their holdings to *onātēres*, translated 'tenants', but the implications of that term must be avoided. These *onātēres* are the people who actually enjoy the produce of the land, but what they do in return is not specified. Presumably the nobles farm part of their estates themselves and let out other parts to 'tenants' in return for a share of the produce or some other 'rent'. The details of this process have been studied by Bennett (1956 a).

The derivation of *o-na-to* from ὀνίνημι is now generally accepted; but it is becoming clear that ὤνη and derivatives are not to be connected with Skt. *vasnám*, Lat. *uēnum*, since there exists a Mycenaean 'commercial' term *o-no* (Chadwick, 1964 b, Lejeune, 1964 a) and the Cretan forms without ϝ- in the Gortyn Law code are in fact the principal foundation for the 'rule' that ϝ- is lost before o in Cretan (and possibly in Homer). It is not impossible that the loss of ϝ led to the coalescence of two distinct words.

Fourthly, the status of the persons listed has been much discussed. Some are craftsmen, such as the king's fuller (**115**=En 74.3); but the majority, apart from the high officials called *te-re-ta*, are religious: the priestess, the key-bearers, and the numerous *te-o-jo do-e-ro* and *do-e-ra*. The predominance of a priestess, and the fact that *Pa-ki-ja-ne* is the home of *Potnia* (**172**=Tn 316), suggest that *theos* is here feminine. But the status of her servants is not that of slaves, since they hold plots of land; they must rather be temple servants or ἱερόδουλοι, a relatively honorific position.

Fifthly, the relation between the amounts of grain recorded and the land held needs to be explained. The practice of measuring land by the quantity of seed needed to sow it is widespread, from ancient Babylonia down to modern Mediterranean countries. In the Aegean islands it is still possible to hear of a vineyard described as 'two *pinakia*', where the *pinaki* is a measure of volume. But the practical reason for the system has not been grasped. There is no absolute equation possible between seed-measurement and acreage, because the ratio of seed to superficial area will vary widely according to the kind of land. A steep, stony hillside will clearly grow less wheat acre for acre, than a rich, level plain. But if both are measured in terms of productivity, it is possible to equate holdings of different types. Presumably the average yield would be known, and the quantity of seed would be a fixed proportion of this. The system has the same advantages as the Persian measurement of distance by the *parasang*, or the modern Greek practice of specifying a journey as so many hours rather than kilometres, which can easily be meaningless in very mountainous country.

Perhaps the rates of seeding for antiquity quoted on p. 237 are based upon rich corn-land, and the rocky slopes of Messenian hills would demand a much lower rate. But even at the rate of 50 litres per hectare, the holdings are small (see the table on p. 237) and it must be remembered that the suggested reduction in the size of the metric unit involves scaling these down by one fifth. If the unit is really to be halved or more, the problem becomes even more acute. It is hard to believe that *pe-mo* is anything but σπέρμα, or that there is a hidden factor by which all these figures need to be multiplied. It should be observed that the figures for the king's *temenos* are based not on **152** = Er 312 (WHEAT 30), but on the suggestion, no longer accepted, that *e-ke-ra₂-wo* is the name of the king, and that the figure attributed to him in **153** = Er 880.3 is really WHEAT 50. This figure seems probable in view of the total, so there must have been an estate of this size in private ownership, though perhaps not under grain.

p. 240† **108** = Ea 817. Correction: WHEAT 3 T 1 ◁ 6.

p. 240‡ The existence of these two recensions has given rise to much speculation. Two facts are clear. The quantities recorded on the two sets are identical, allowing for errors and incomplete preservation; the situation is therefore different from the Pylos *Aa* and *Ab* tablets where the numbers of women and children are similar but not identical. From this we can deduce that no long period of time intervened between their redaction. Secondly, the fact that a clay tablet dries rapidly and further entries cannot thereafter be added is undoubtedly the reason why separate pieces of information were recorded on small tablets as they were received; if it proved necessary to combine these entries into a full catalogue, this would entail copying all the information on to larger tablets. This implies that Version B must precede Version A in time.

However, the minor differences between the two versions call for some explanation, for if Version A were a mere copy of Version B we should expect it to be identical in wording as it is in figures. The explanation has been sought in a difference between plan and performance, as if Version B were 'prospective' and A the completed record. It would be surprising if the plan was carried out so accurately, or if it was, that it should still be thought necessary to record the facts a second time. But an adequate explanation is provided by the analysis of scribal hands (Bennett, 1958*b*). Version A is the work of hand 1, a prolific scribe. Version B is by two different scribes: *Eb* and *Eo* hand 41, *Ea* hand 43. It is thus possible to explain the difference in wording as due to the habits of different scribes.

242† *da-ma-te*: the interpretation *Dāmātēr* is too poetical and has been generally abandoned, though the goddess still sometimes appears in the list of Mycenaean deities quoted as appearing on the tablets. The most likely meaning is 'households' and this can probably be extracted from *damartes*, the classical sense of δάμαρ 'wife' being a specialisation from this. Bennett (1956*a*) showed that the series refers to forty persons.

242‡ *to-so-de*: Ruijgh (1967, pp. 343–50) has convincingly shown that the *-de* of this word is to be interpreted as 'and' introducing a separate clause; *Warnataioio ktoinā ktimenā* is thus to be taken as a 'nominative of the rubric'.

244† **116**=En 659. Corrections: l. 9 the scribe seems to have written *o-to-te-re*, a straightforward blunder due to the similarity of *na* and *to* and the fact that these two signs recur so often in *o-na-to*; l. 19 *o-na-to e-ke to-so-de pe-mo* WHEAT ⊤ 2.

245† *qe-re-qo-ta-o*: the explanation is now seen to be a tendency to dissimilate two labiovelars in one word, for the same effect is visible in *i-po-po-qo-i* (PY Fn 79) = *hippophorgʷoihi* (not *hiqqʷo-*); see Lejeune, 1958*a*, p. 302.

246† Various explanations have been offered of the *-qe* in *e-ke-qe*. The most interesting observation is that of Winter (1956, p. 507) that the presence of *-qe* correlates with the word order verb–object; when the object (*o-na-to*) precedes the verb, the *-qe* is regularly dropped. Ruijgh (1967, pp. 317–19) concludes that the second suggestion made here is correct; it introduces a separate clause, much as the *-de* of *to-so-de pe-mo*. This may seem strange syntax to us, but it is preferable to inventing a new meaning for *-qe*.

246‡ **118**=Eo 211. Correction: l. 2 WHEAT [⊲1].

247† *Beetroot* is an error for *beet*; but the interpretation should be abandoned. No satisfactory explanation has been offered.

248† **121**=Eo 247, line 3. It would perhaps be easier to regard the corrected form *a₃-ti-jo-qe* as correct, but with omission of *pa-ro* (cf. **120**=Eo 276.2). It makes no difference to the sense.

p. 248‡ **123** = Eo 444. Corrections: l. 1 WHEAT 2̣ Ṭ [3] (cf. **116** = En 659.1); l. 6, probably to be restored [*tu-ri-ja-ti   te-o-jo   do-e-ra*]; at end read WHEAT Ṭ 2[.

p. 249† **125** = Eo 471 [+] 855. Correction: l.1 [*a-*]ị̣[*-qe-wo   ko-*]*to-na   kị*[*-ti-*]*me-na*.

p. 249‡ **126** = Eo 281. Corrections: l. 1 [*ra-ku-ro-jo*]   *ki-ti-me-na   ko-ṭo-ṇạ*; l. 2 [*i-ra-ta*] *te-o-jo   do-e-ro   e-ke-qe*.

p. 249¶ **128** = Eo 278. Correction: *e-ke-qe   dwo   ko-to-no*. The merit of this correction must be credited to Risch (1957), who saw that what Bennett had read as *wo-wo* was in reality a single sign composed of an element like *wo* followed by its mirror image. This, together with the confirmation that *a*-stems have a dual in *-o*, makes it certain that the translation should read: 'holds two plots'.

p. 251† **131** = Ep 301. Correction: l. 4 *to-so   pe-ṃọ*.

p. 251‡ *a-no-no*: the *o-na-to* is a portion of a holding which is surrendered to someone else; thus 'not subject to *o-na-to*' need mean only that the holder does not have any *o-na-te-re*, but enjoys the full use of the land himself.

p. 253† Lejeune (1966*b*, p. 261) proposes the restoration of line 8 as *to-*[*so   pe-mo* WHEAT 10   T]4, the last figure being preserved. For the reasons see the next note.

p. 254† A further join to 'Ep04' = Ep 613 as re-numbered shows that 'Eb39' + 940 (= Eb 149[+]940) is the corresponding entry. It can perhaps be restored thus:
¹ *te-re-ta   su-ko*[*po-ro-du-ma?   *]*ọ-pe-ro-qe   te-re-ja-e   o-u-qe   te-re-ja*
² *du-wo-u-pi-de   *[*o-pe-re?   to-so-de   pe-mo* WHEAT 1ọ+]
'The *telestas*, [the assistant superintendant] of figs (?) . . . and being under an obligation to "perform" and he does not "perform", but [he is under an obligation (to "perform")] with two: so much seed, etc.' It is hard to see what other restoration after *du-wo-u-pi-de* in line 2 would have permitted the compiler of Version A to transcribe this as '. . . [under an obligation] to "perform" with two, and he does not "perform".'
   The interpretation of the two verbs both translated 'perform' is as obscure as ever. Palmer (1963*a*, p. 204) has proposed taking *wo-ze* as *woizei* < **woikyei* comparing ϝοικίων in Cretan. But this does not offer a convincing meaning, for ϝοικίω (= οἰκέω) in Cretan means 'dwell', and the verb *wo-ze* must have some reference to an obligation incurred in respect of the land. I have

448

suggested (Chadwick, 1957 a, pp. 127–8) that the obligation might be religious (cf. ῥέζω, another verb from the root *ϝεργ-) and that te-re-ja is the verb which describes the function of the te-re-ta; this last suggestion cannot be proved, but at least the words are associated by Eb 149 [+] 940. The association of these terms with ka-ma land does nothing to solve the problem. It has been pointed out by Heubeck (1961 b, p. 310) and Lejeune (1962 b, p. 410) that the derivative ka-ma-e-we excludes the possibility that ka-ma is a feminine a-stem, since this should yield *ka-me-we (cf. ko-to-ne-we PY Ae 995 from ko-to-na); it would seem likely therefore that it is a neuter noun in -as.

256† **137** = Eb 416. Correction: the latest readings show i-je-ṛẹ[-ja]kẹ-ra. Thus the keyword ke-ra (cf. **135** = Ep 704.2) is damaged on both occurrences.

256‡ **139** = Eb 321 + 1156 [+] 327. The addition of a fragment confirms that Palmer's suggestion (1963 a, p. 211) was correct: read e-ko-si-qe [.

257† ko-to-no-o-ko could also be plural, i.e. the ktoinookhoi collectively are equivalent to the dāmos.

257‡ **141** = Eb 338. Correction: l. 2 read ko-to-ṇo dwo o-pe-ro-sa-de. For dwo cf. note on **128** = Eo 278 (p. 448 above).

257¶ **142** = Eb 317. The set to which this tablet belongs was identified by the fact that this and three others (now called Ed) are in a different hand. The complete set is discussed below under **149** = Ed 236 (p. 450).

259† Read now: §3 by Eb 169, §5 by Eb 838, §8 by Eb 913, §10 by Eb 464.

259‡ **145** = Ea 259. Correction: u-me-ta-qe-ạ-po. The division into two words is still possible: u-me-ta-qe a-po, but the second cannot be the preposition apo, since this is regularly apu in Mycenaean; possibly amphō. Whether u-me-ta is an error for *e-u-me-ta is doubtful. If the upper line was added as an afterthought, this will explain why the verb e-ke was not changed to the dual.

259¶ The last line of Ep 539 can now be read as: Amphi[mē]dēs ekhei e-to-ni-jo kekhēme[nāōn k]toinā[ōn] in keeping with **146** = Eb 473.

259†† The suspicion that Amphimēdēs is not a personal name seems to be unjustified.

259‡‡ **147** = Ea 59. Correction: l. 4. pa-ro ra-wa-ke-si-jo ẹ-[ ]WHEAT 2. Krētheus probably appears on six other tablets: Ea11 = 305, Ea 771, **110** = Ea 800, Ea 806 quoted here, and also
      Ea 304 Krētheus ekhei onāton paro Sa-ke-re-we: ẉḤẸẠT[,

Ea 809[*K*]*rētheus ekhei onāton kekhēmenās ktoinās lāwāgesioio armostēwos* [
In Ea 771 the reading at the end is probably WHEAT 3 (perhaps corrected from WHEAT 1 T 5). It appears that *a-mo-te-wo* cannot be restored after *ra-wa-ke-si-jo* in line 4 of Ea 59. Palmer (1963*a*, p. 277) has explained *e-ne-ka i-qo-jo* as 'in the service of Hippos', where Hippos is a god equated with *Poseidon Hippios*. It cannot be claimed that this does anything to clarify the entry; nor does ἕνεκα bear the sense 'in the service of'.

p. 261†   *ka-ma*: see note on this word above (p. 449).

p. 261‡   **148** = Ep 613 (re-numbered for 617). Corrections: l. 1 restored from Eb 495: [*ne-qe-wo e-da-e-wo ka-ma*]*o-pe-ro*[*du-*]*wo-u-pi te-re-ja-e*; l. 3 if equation with Eb 862 is sound, restore [*ko-i-ṛọ*] at the beginning, but this cannot be definitely confirmed; l. 4 [*te-re-*]*ta su-ko po-ṛo-du*[*-ma?* *o-pe-ro*]*du-wo-u-pi* (cf. Eb 149 [+] 940); l. 5 [*to-*]*ṣọ-de pẹ-mo* WHEAT 10[; l. 11 [*pa-*]*ṛạ-ko e-kẹ-qe ka-ma*; l. 13 *kọ*[*-tu-ro₂ mi-*]*ka-ta* (cf. Eb 839).

p. 263†   The reading *a-pi-to-po-qo* proposed by Palmer (1963*a*, p. 483) is not possible.

p. 263‡   *to-me*: this is still an unsolved problem. Scherer (1959, p. 350) objected that Skt. *tasmai* was probably from **tosmōi* (the long diphthong is certain), but the influence of consonant stem datives in *-ei* cannot be excluded. Scherer's solution is to take *to-* in both forms as dative *tōi* coupled with two different particles: *-me* = *men* (μέν *solitarium*), *-e* = *en*, the suffix found in Argive τōνδεōνέν, ταδέν. Palmer (1963*a*, pp. 205–6) takes *te-ra-pi-ke* as dative of a man's name, and the disputed forms as verbs: *to-me* = *thōmen*, athematic infinitive, *to-e* = *thoē*, 3rd sing. aor. subj., of a verb related to the noun θωή 'penalty'. The change in construction is surprising, and even more an infinitive in -μεν, when we should expect an ancestor of Arcado-Cypriot -ναι. Palmer also takes *to-jo-qẹ* in Eb 156.2 as an optative of the same verb; but there at least it would seem likely that *to-jo-qẹ au-to-jo* = *toio qᵘe autoio* 'and of the same' or 'and of him himself', but the context is far from clear. Cf. also *to-ị-qe* PY **193** = Na 520.

p. 263¶   *ra-ke*: Palmer (1963*a*, p. 451) suggests that this is not a verb, but locative of a noun *lakhei*. If this is from λάχος, we should expect *ra-ke-i*; but perhaps a root-noun **lax*, gen. *lakhos*, is conceivable.

p. 263††   It now appears from the scribal hands that four of the tablets previously assigned to *Eb* form a separate set and make up a single document. The use of four small tablets rather than one large one was probably dictated by the need for the tablets to fit the *Eb* file. The four are now classified as *Ed*, and the set comprises **149** = Ed 236, **142** = Ed 317, Ed 847 (see below), **151** = Ed 901. For convenience the text of the whole series is printed here; it is obviously a summation of the figures in the previous sections.

450

149 = Ed 236
1 *ka-ma-e-we   o-na-ta   e-ko-te   ke-ke-me-na-o   ko-to-na-o*
2 *wo-zo-te   to-so   pe-mo*   WHEAT 30   T 2   ᐸ 3

142 = Ed 317
1 *[o-]da-a$_2$ i-je-re-ja   ka-ra-wi-po-ro-qe   e-qe-ta-qe*   ⟦   ⟧
2 *we-te-re-u-qe   o-na-ta   to-so-de   pe-mo*   WHEAT 21   T 6

Ed 847
1 *o-da-a$_2$ e-qe-si-jo   do-e-ro   e-ko-si   o-na-ta*
2 ⟦*ku-su-qa*⟧   *to-so-de   pe-mo*   WHEAT 1   T 3   ᐸ 4

151 = Ed 901
1 *o-da-a$_2$ ke-ke-me-na-o̦   ko̦-to-na-o   o-na-ta   e-ko-si   ko-no-ne-ta*
2   *to̦-so   pe-mo*   WHEAT 3[   ]

§1   Holders of *ka-ma*, holding *leases* of *communal* plots (and) rendering the services, so much seed: 2905 l. wheat.

§2   And thus the Priestess and the Key-bearer and the Follower and Westreus (holding) *leases*: and so much seed: 2073·6 l. wheat.

§3   And thus the slaves of the Follower hold *leases*: and so much seed: 131·2 l. wheat.

§4   And thus the men of the *ktoina* hold *leases* of the *communal* plots: so much seed: 288(+ ?) l. wheat.

The details of the summary are the subject of a note by Lejeune (1966*b*). He has demonstrated, as far as the mutilated figures allow certainty, that this is a total, or rather series of totals, for the *Ep* tablets. The total of the figures preserved on *Ep* is WHEAT 53   T 2   ᐸ 4, but a number of figures are missing and the total must be higher; but as Lejeune points out, this figure may list some plots twice, when the holder sub-lets. However, the amount to be subtracted for this is small (T 5   ᐸ 2). The total of the *Ed* tablets is WHEAT 56   T 2   ᐸ 1, and there is only one figure incomplete, so it is fairly accurate. The agreement between these totals favours Lejeune's hypothesis.

Further checks can be made on the individual tablets of the series. **142** = Ed 317 lists the four major holders: the Priestess (named as *Eritha* **135** = Ep 704.3, 5) holding in all WHEAT 4   T 3 (including a large plot on behalf of her deity); the Key-bearer (named as *Karpathia* **135** = Ep 704.7) whose holding is missing on both **135**＝Ep 704 and **141**＝Eb 338, but we know she had two plots; the Follower, who is identified by Lejeune as *Amphimēdēs* and holds an *e-to-ni-jo* of WHEAT 4 T 6 (Ep 539.14); and *Westreus* who is a priest and has a holding of WHEAT 2   T 3. The total of these figures is WHEAT 11 T 2; so compared with the figure WHEAT 21 T 6 of **142**＝Ed 317, the double holding of the Key-bearer must have been WHEAT 10   T 4. This figure can be plausibly restored in **135**＝Ep 704.8, since the 4 is legible after a lacuna.

The slaves of the Follower (Ed 847) are listed as the slaves of Amphimedes in Ep 539.10–12. But the total of their holdings is only WHEAT 1   T 1 as against WHEAT 1   T 3 ᐊ 4 of Ed 847. One figure is damaged (T 2̣) but it does not appear easy to restore it as T 4   ᐊ 4, which is needed to balance the account.

The scribe who wrote the *Ed* tablets was the same as the writer of the *Ep* tablets (VERSION A of this book, but actually the second version to be written); but the fact that he chose to copy the shape of the *Eb* tablets suggests that he may have been working from them rather than *Ep*, which he can have made later. Since the figures on the relevant *Eb* tablets are even worse preserved than *Ep*, this may account for some discrepancies; but the figures are in total so close that it can hardly be doubted that the equation is correct and Lejeune's deductions are justified.

p. 264† **150**＝Ed 411. Correction: l.1 WHEAT 44   T 2̣ ᐊ[.

This tablet, now reclassified *Ed*, is not a normal member of the set, since it was written by two different hands. Line 1 was written by the scribe of *Eb*, line 2 and the edge by the scribe of *Ed*. It is therefore a tempting hypothesis that the second line totals the other *Ed* tablets, and the figure of WHEAT 58 T 5 is obviously close to the sum of the figures on the other tablets, WHEAT 56 T 2 ᐊ 1. Since the figure on **151**＝Ed 901 is incomplete, it is interesting to speculate on possible restorations which would make an exact match. The high position of the three strokes visible after WHEAT makes it almost certain that the figure here was 5 or 6; following this the shape of the break suggests the presence of T, then after a short interval two strokes are visible which might be the top of ᐊ. There is no room for more than a medium-sized numeral following this. The difficulty is to propose a restoration consistent with **150**＝Ed 411.2; here Bennett and Olivier now read T 2̣ [, but the photograph shows traces of five strokes, though the last three were badly smudged, if not deliberately deleted, while the clay was still wet; no ᐊ entry can have stood there despite the [. The total of the three earlier *Ed* tablets is WHEAT 53 T 2 ᐊ 1; hence if Ed 901 had WHEAT 5 alone, there would still have been ᐊ 1 more on Ed 411.2 than could be accounted for if the reading were T 2.

Hence it seems certain that ⊤ 5 should be read, and this leads us to restore WHEAT 5 ⊤ 2 ◁ 5 in Ed 901.

This must lead us to re-examine line 1. Whether the proposed restoration is right or not, the sense must be 'grand total of the holdings of the *telestai*'. We know from **114** = En 609.2 that there were fourteen *telestai* at Pakijania, whose holdings of *ktoina ktimena* are listed in two versions on the *En/Eo* tablets. If we add up the figures, restoring one from the other, the holdings of the thirteen *ktoinai* amount to WHEAT 31 ⊤ 5 ◁ 2, the total of *onāta* to WHEAT 6 ⊤ 4 ◁ 2, making a grand total of WHEAT 37 ⊤ 8 ◁ 4. The total on **150** = Ed 411.1 is probably WHEAT 44 ⊤ 2 perhaps with a ◁ following, though from the photograph this appears doubtful. The discrepancy is accounted for by the fact (see p. 242) that only thirteen *ktoinai* are listed, and we have to suppose that the fourteenth consisted of approximately WHEAT 6 ⊤ 3 ◁ 2 to make the total balance, a figure which is within the limits of variation of size of *ktoinai*. The interesting point here is that its inclusion in the grand total (*ku-su-to-ro-qa*) shows that this was drawn up before the corresponding *Eo* tablet was suppressed, and therefore presumably before VERSION A (really the second version) was compiled, since **117** = En 467 was deliberately cut at the bottom after the third entry, no doubt to delete this fourteenth *ktoina*.

If this argument is sound, one further fact emerges: *telestai* in line 1 refers not only to the fourteen *telestai*, but also to their *onātēres*, and *ka-ma-e-we* likewise in line 2 refers not only to the *ka-ma-e-we* of **149** = Ed 263, but to all the other holders of *onāta* listed on the set of four *Ed* tablets. We can deplore the absence of a Mycenaean equivalent for 'etc.'; but the demonstration is a warning against reading too much into the headings used to introduce the all-important figures. It should be noted that this theory implies that the *onāta* ceded by holders of *ktoinai ktimenai* are not counted in the amount given as the size of the *ktoina*; note especially the estate of Aithioqᵘs (**115** = En 74.11–18, **121** = Eo 247), which gives the *ktoina* as WHEAT 1 ⊤ 5 ◁ 4 and the total of *onāta* as WHEAT 1 ⊤ 5; if this were subtracted, Aithioqᵘs would be left with ◁ 4, less than any of his *onātēres*, but if added his estate is an average size (WHEAT 3 ◁ 4).

264‡ *ko-to-ne-ta*: Lejeune concludes that this means either those who receive allocations of land from the village other than the *ktoinookhoi*, or the complete collection of all who receive such allocations, including the *ktoinookhoi*. We have insufficient evidence for a decisive answer.

264¶ It can hardly be claimed that all that has been written on this subject since 1955 has solved the problems; indeed the chief result is to increase the misgivings which all interpretations arouse. It is clear that **152** = Er 312 lists a special holding of the king and the *lāwāgetās*, that of three members of the class of *telestai* and another area of uncertain designation. Almost everything else is speculation.

The suggestion that *E-ke-ra₂-wo* is the name of the king has not been confirmed or refuted; at least he is a very important official. The reading [*E*]-*ke-ri-ja-wo* on the new tablet Qa 1292 is probable, and if this is indeed the same name it rules out *Ekhelāwōn*, which would, it now seems, hardly be spelt with *ra₂* in any case; something like *Enkheliāwōn* is more likely. The parallel between **152** = Er 312 and **171** = Un 718 is perhaps less striking than appeared at first sight, though it cannot be denied that there is some connexion.

The interpretation of *wo-ro-ki-jo-ne-jo* now seems suspect because of the *scriptio plena* *wo-ro-k-* for *worg-*, which is contrary to the usual rules; Palmer (1963*a*, p. 214) has also rightly called attention to the morphological difficulties. Heubeck (1960*a*, p. 18) has suggested a derivation from ῥῶξ 'cleft', but this does not explain the term; it may be merely a place name.

Palmer (loc. cit.) has suggested that *to-so-jo* is a spelling for *tosyon* with a palatalized *s*; no parallels are quotable, and the forms *to-so* and *to-so-de* also occur on the same tablet. It seems therefore more likely that *to-so-jo* is genitive singular, though the reason for the variation is still obscure.

p. 267† **153** = Er 880. No further improvement of the text has been possible, but the readings *we-je*[-*we* in l. 5 and *su-za*[in l. 8 are slightly more certain. The ending of *sa-ra-pe-do*[in l. 2 is quite uncertain. The other restorations still appear plausible, but it must be emphasized that they are conjectural.

> *we-je*[-*we*: Georgiev called attention to the gloss of Hesychius: υἱήν · τὴν ἄμπελον. From this we may reconstruct a nominative υἱής as Arcadian or Cypriot replacement of *υἱεύς (cf. ἱερές, etc.), of which the Mycenaean form would be the plural. The interpretation depends upon the theory that initial *we-* followed by a vowel may correspond to Greek ὑ-; cf. *we-a₂-re-jo*, *we-a-re-pe*, *we-e-wi-ja*, *we-je-ke-a₂*.

p. 268† The place names in -*wo-te* have been discussed by Heubeck (1960*b*, 1961*c*) and Lejeune (1969), who support the idea that Greek inherited the suffix *-*wont*- as well as *-*went*-. The Mycenaean evidence suggests that *-*wont*- was restricted to place names, and even these were later remodelled to *-*went*- (e.g. Ὀπόεντι). The nominative may therefore have been in -*wons* rather than -*wōn*, if the later Νέδων (-οντος) is a re-formation. There is a possible example of the suffix at Knossos: *e-wo-ta-de* C 901.

p 268‡ **154** = Eq 213. Correction: l. 3 Olivier now reads WHEAT 20; if this figure is correct the total on the tablet is 94 units of wheat, exactly the same as on

153 = Er 880. It can hardly be a coincidence that $94 = 47 \times 2$; for the presence of multiples of 47 in the *Es* tablets, see p. 457.

The unique features of this tablet are still not convincingly solved. It is generally agreed that *to-ro-qe-jo-me-no* is a medio-passive participle connected with either τρέπω or στρέφω, so that 'on his tour of inspection' may well be close to the sense. But *a₂-ri-sa* remains obscure, and although nominative singular of an aorist participle is possible, it could conceivably be accusative plural of an adjective agreeing with *a-ro-u-ra*, or even—that familiar last resort of baffled interpreters—a place name. Since the remaining lines all (except perhaps the last) refer to localities, the last explanation seems least likely, though it might be a region in which the specific localities lie. The objection to the suggestion 'counting' (p. 269) is that a_2 is normally used only for *ha-* and there is nothing to suggest a rough breathing in ἀριθμός; ἀ- is regarded as perhaps prothetic by Chantraine (1968, p. 109). In any case there appears to be no classical Greek word to fit this pattern.

p. 269† *o-ro-jo*: Palmer now (1963 a, p. 218) suggests that this is nominative or accusative of a noun meaning perhaps 'granary'. Certainly this makes the syntax easier, but the word resists satisfactory etymological explanation. The formula *to-so-de pe-mo* seems everywhere else to refer to land, not actual grain; so that *o-ro-jo* ought rather to be the description of a plot or holding. The comparison with Cypriot οἰρών 'district' is tempting, but cannot be exact.

p. 269‡ *po-ti-ni-ja-we-jo-jo o-te-pe-o-jo*: Palmer (1957 a, p. 569) acutely called attention to the element **pe-o* to be extracted also from *ne-wo-pe-o*, if this is really a place name. But the analysis does nothing to identify the elements of the compound; σπέος is impossible owing to the declension. The adjective *potniaweios* despite its bizarre form seems to be regular; the variant spellings *po-ti-ni-ja-we-i-jo* and *po-ti-na-wi-jo* are found; see Glossary.

p. 270† **156** = Uf 1031. Correction: delete [at right; the tablet is cut, not broken, and the text is complete.

p. 271† **161** = Uf 839. Correction: the last sign in the lower line may be ι rather than ᴅᴀ, but it would still appear to belong to this set.

p. 272† **162** = Uf 983

o-pi po-to-ri-ka-ta: *opi Ptolikhātāi* 'on the territory of P.'?

p. 272‡ **163** = Ra 984. Corrections: lines 1 and 2 read *de-de-me-na*; l. 2]*zo-wa*; at end add sᴡᴏʀᴅ[, the ideogram being here inverted.

This tablet is now seen not to belong to this set, but goes with **277** = Ra 1028. Two Pylos tablets refer to wheels as *argurōi* or *khalkōi dedemenō* 'bound with silver' or 'bronze'; this makes it reasonable to restore here [*e-re-*]*pa-te de-de-me-na* = *elephantei dedemena* 'bound with ivory'. On the same principle we might wonder if *ke-ra de-de-me-na* can mean 'bound with horn'; for both horn and ivory on chariots, see pp. 365–8. But we should expect the dative (instrumental) to be spelt *ke-ra-e*; nor can neuter nominative *keras* agree with the participle.]*zo-wa* is shown to be complete by comparison with Ra 1028. *e-pi-zo-ta* recalls Homeric ἐπίσσωτρα (*Il.* v, 725, etc.), but it must have a different suffix; cf. Petruševski, 1968, p. 128.

p. 273† **165** = Gv 862. Corrections: l.1]*su-za*; l.2]*jo*   OLIVE-TREES 405; l.3]*i-po-qa*.

]*su-za*: there is no need to assume that the word is incomplete, though both here and in **166** = Gv 864 the break is immediately before *su*. It will probably represent *sutsai* < *sūkyai, the adjectival derivative of σῦκον which was replaced in later Greek by συκέα > συκῆ; the Doric variant συκία is probably from a dialect where εα > ια.

]*i-po-qa*: if the reading is correct, *po-qa* might still be an independent word = φορβή, and the]*i* the last sign of a noun in the dative plural, despite the absence of a divider. Alternatively a compound is possible, provided the noun is neuter.

CHAPTER IX

PROPORTIONAL TRIBUTE AND RITUAL OFFERINGS

p. 276† Further work on the *Es* tablets has produced, if not real illumination, at least some gleams of light on the process by which the *dosmoi* were computed. The most complete study is that by M. Lang (1964 *a*). She has established that the group of men originally numbered fourteen, as the fourteen names on **167** = Es 650 imply; but the figures against the last name were deleted, and **168** = Es 644 equally has a ruled but vacant fourteenth line which might indicate the same change.

These calculations can be followed more easily if the table is reprinted giving the figures in T units and keeping the original order (see opposite).

	Seed	Annual contribution	Poseidon	Other recipients (each)	Total for Poseidon, etc.	Total contributions
Ko-pe-re-u	60	7	15	$1\frac{2}{3}$	20	27
A-re-ku-tu-ru-wo	70	$9\frac{1}{2}$	23	$2\frac{2}{3}$	31	$40\frac{1}{2}$
Se-no	10	2	5	$\frac{1}{3}$	6	8
O-po-ro-me-no	40	1+	17	$1\frac{1}{3}$	21	22+
A₃-ki-wa-ro	10	[ ]	6	$\frac{1}{3}$	7	7+
We-da-ne-wo d.	4	$1\frac{1}{3}$	3	$\frac{1}{6}$	$3\frac{1}{2}$	$4\frac{5}{8}$
Wo-ro-ti-ja	20	$3\frac{1}{3}$	8	$\frac{2}{3}$	10	$13\frac{1}{3}$
Ka-ra-i	3	$\frac{1}{2}$	2 + ?	$\frac{1}{6}$	$2\frac{1}{2}$ + ?	3 + ?
A-ne-o	15	$2\frac{1}{2}$	5	$\frac{1}{6}$	$5\frac{1}{2}$	8
Ru-ko-wo-ro	14	[ ]	7	$\frac{1}{2}$	$8\frac{1}{2}$	$8\frac{1}{2}$+
O-ka	12	$2\frac{1}{3}$?	7	$\frac{1}{2}$	$8\frac{1}{2}$	$10\frac{5}{8}$?
Pi-ro-ta-wo	12	$2[\frac{1}{3}?]$	7	$\frac{1}{2}$	$8\frac{1}{2}$	$10\frac{5}{8}$?
Ku-da-ma-ro	12	$2[\frac{1}{3}?]$	7	$\frac{1}{2}$	$8\frac{1}{2}$	$10\frac{5}{8}$?
Totals	282	$34\frac{1}{6}$+	112	$9\frac{1}{2}$	$140\frac{1}{2}$	$174\frac{2}{3}$+

The explanation of these figures is not easy. As pointed out by Miss Lang, 282 is a multiple of 47 and $140\frac{1}{2}$ is within $\frac{1}{2}$ of $47 \times 3 = 141$. But some other factor must be at work, since although the rounding off of 141 to 140 would be plausible, the introduction of an odd $\frac{1}{2}$ is difficult to explain. The mysterious 47 reappears in two other tablets (**153** = Er 880 and **154** = Eq 213) which both have now (see p. 454) a total of $94(=47 \times 2)$ units of wheat.

Miss Lang has found the other factor in the figure 14, which is attractive in view of the evidence that there were originally fourteen names in this group. $140\frac{1}{2}$ will then be a compromise between $14 \times 10 = 140$ and $47 \times 3 = 141$. $282(=47 \times 6)$ approximates to $14 \times 20 = 280$, and 112 is exactly 14×8. In the 'Annual contribution' the figure for *O-po-ro-me-no* should probably be at least 3, and those for *A₃-ki-wa-ro* and *Ru-ko-wo-ro* about 2 each, so it would not be impossible that this column added up to $42 = 14 \times 3$.

Some of the irregularities may be due to the wish to distribute the total among the thirteen names, keeping a due proportion, but at the same time avoiding any measure less than $\frac{1}{6}$ of a unit (= ◁). Wyatt (1964) has produced an ingenious theoretical grouping of the names into four (instead of Miss Lang's three), each of which holds 70 units, but the last holds 72 as it is composed of four names and 70 is not divisible by four; but neither is it divisible by the three names in his third group. It is conceivable that having 282 units to distribute among 13 names the Mycenaean officials might have proceeded as he suggests, dividing it into three lots of 70 and one of 72; but nothing will account satisfactorily for the great diversity in the figures actually given.

One fact emerges clearly: the smaller the holding, the higher the total of *dosmoi* expressed as a percentage. Thus the possessor of the largest holding (70 units) contributes a total of $40\frac{1}{2}$ or 55%; the two smallest contribute 120·8% and 100% (if the latter figure is complete).

From this it can be deduced that the quantities of wheat listed in the contribution tablets is not a deduction from the quantity of seed-corn. A reasonable hypothesis would be that **167** = Es 650 represents a holding of land expressed in terms of seed-corn, as on the other *E* tablets; its produce might therefore be as much as 20 to 50 times this value, so that the tax imposed would be relatively light.

p. 278†   *?Krithioio*: we can now add the one certain example of a month name at Pylos: *pa-ki-ja-ni-jo-jo me-no* **309** = Fr 1224.

p. 278‡   **168** = Es 644. Corrections: l.4 WHEAT T ᵢ [; l.5 WHEAT T[.

p. 279†   *Ai₂?-ke-te-si*: in the absence of any confirmation of the value of sign no. 34, the suggestion ἀλκτήρ should be abandoned.

p. 279‡   **170** = Es 649. Correction: l.1 the tablet seems to have *a-re-ku-tu-ru-ṇo-ne* but this must be an error for *a-re-ku-tu-ru-wo-ne*.

p. 282†   **171** = Un 718. Corrections: l.1 *sa-ra-pe-da* confirmed; l.13 [   ]ɪ ◁ ɪ.

    o-wi-de-ta-i: the suggested *hō widesthai* should be withdrawn, and dative plural of a noun seems more probable. But no one has been able to improve on the etymological interpretation as *owi-detāhi*; the apparent parallel *a₃-ki-de-ta* (αἰγι-) in Na 529 is a false reading, the last sign being now read as *-ja*. It is uncertain whether *o-wi-de-ta*[on Wa 731 is complete or not. Possibly the second element is *-dertāhi* (δέρω) 'sheep-flayers'. But the relation of this word to *po-se-da-o-ni* in line 1 remains obscure.

    e-ke-ra₂-wo: on this name see p. 454.

    tu-ro₂: the ideogram on KN Ra 7498 seems to be a form of **233* = SWORD rather than this 'monogram'. The spelling with *ro₂* implies a pronunciation *turyoi*, which would evolve into classical τῡροί (cf. φῡρω < *φύρ-yω).

    a-re-ro: the ligature is certainly A + RE + PA which justifies us in regarding this spelling as an error for *a-re-pa*; cf. **313** = Un 6.7.

    me-re-u-ro: it has been generally accepted that this is *meleuron* = ἄλευρον, but the inference that the ideogram (= the syllabic sign **65*, cf. Raison, 1964) has the value 'flour' is perhaps incorrect. It recurs on the Knossos *Fs* series, where offerings are listed consisting of quantities of barley, figs, oil, wine and honey (Chadwick, 1966, p. 31); this strongly suggests that **65* is the designation of a grain other than wheat and barley, and 'flour' is an annotation specifying the form in which this grain is offered. It is probably vain to speculate about the nature of the grain.

p. 284†   The order of the two sides of this tablet (cf. p. 286) is still not entirely clear. It would appear that the text as we have it represents at least a second draft on the same tablet, and traces of the previous text can be detected, especially on the 'obverse'. But it is now generally assumed that the 'reverse', beginning *po-ro-wi-to-jo*, is to be read first. It appears probable, though not certain, that the scribe first inscribed the 'obverse', deleted it, turned the tablet over and wrote the existing 'reverse', but at line 7, having drawn the rules and entered the initial *PU-RO*, he became dissatisfied and turned back to the original 'obverse', writing as lines 1–3 the text intended for 'reverse' 7–10. However, a case could still be made out for keeping to the order as printed here, since the formula of 'obverse' 1–3 is irregular, with the insertion of *a-ke-qe wa-tu* and the omission of the name of the deity preceding the enumeration of the offerings. This could result from uncertainty about the form of each entry, which was resolved beginning with the second entry (lines 4–7) and was copied on the 'reverse'; *po-ro-wi-to-jo* would then stand outside the repeating formula. But it may be preferable to take *po-ro-wi-to-jo* as a general heading to all that follows, like the preamble to the *o-ka* tablets (**56** = An 657.1) or the furniture tablets (**235** = Ta 711.1).

The impression of haste and carelessness is evident throughout, and encourages us to propose emendations with less qualms than elsewhere. It is also clear that the arrangement of the text is largely experimental, and not the result of deliberate spacing. The use of both faces of the tablet almost certainly implies that it is an isolated document, not a member of a set, since the continuation would then be made on the next tablet. Sets of large tablets do not have entries on the reverse.

From these facts it is evident that the theory of a calendar of religious offerings must be abandoned. It could only represent part of a month, and there is no trace of the remainder of what would have been a long series of documents. It is true that *po-ro-wi-to* now recurs on two, possibly three, of the olive-oil tablets from Pylos, and there too might, but need not, be the name of a month (see p. 480). But even if correctly so identified, this tablet shows no more than the curious affinity of religious offerings for dates (see pp. 304–5). Moreover, the alleged parallel at Knossos (**207** = V 280) is very far from certain (see p. 475), and although the two texts might appear to support each other, they would be so totally different from anything else we possess that we ought not to assume this, if they can be fitted into the regular pattern of records, not prescriptions.

However, even if it is not a calendar, there can be no doubt that the subject of the text is a series of offerings to deities. Zeus, Hera, Hermes and Potnia are all familiar names; the rest are mostly explicable even if less familiar. The offerings consist of thirteen gold vessels and ten human beings, eight women and two men. The men are offered to male deities, the women to female deities, though a problem arises in the first paragraph of the 'obverse', where no deities appear to be specified, though the place seems to be the shrine of Poseidon. It has been suggested that the ideograms MAN and WOMAN here refer not to human beings but to figurines; this would be contrary to everything we know about the use of ideograms on the tablets, and seems highly improbable without any clue. It may be regarded as certain that these ten people were being dedicated to the deities, but it remains an open question what rite was followed.

The revulsion which we feel for human sacrifice must not influence our judgement here. It is clear that the gold vessels would become the property of the god, and we may presume that the owners of the human beings equally divested themselves of ownership. This might be by dedicating the person to the god's service; but the *doeloi* or *doelai* of deities in the tablets appear to be persons of some standing, since they can hold land. The true slaves appear to be owned by persons. Hence the alternative, that these people were committed to divine service by being sacrificed, begins to appear more likely.

A new piece of archaeological evidence for the practice of human sacrifice in Mycenaean times has recently been reported (Protonotariou-Deïlaki, 1969): two human skeletons found buried in kneeling posture at the entrance to a tomb. This may encourage us to accept more ambiguous examples reported earlier (see the article cited). We may also have recourse, with all due caution, to Homer, and recall that not only were twelve Trojan youths sacrificed on Patroklos' pyre, but this is subordinated to the sacrifice of two out of his nine dogs (*Il.* XXIII, 173–6). On the other hand the twelve named men assigned to deities or religious functionaries on **312** = An 1281 can hardly have been sacrificed.

We may now turn to the question of the purpose of the rite. If ten human beings, even if slaves or captives, and thirteen gold vessels are being offered, in whatever sense, to a whole pantheon of deities, this is hardly an ordinary annual ritual. It is more likely to be a special occasion, and the hasty writing of the tablet may perhaps correspond to a hasty preparation. If so, and it must be emphasized that any such interpretation is speculative, it is likely to have been an apotropaic ceremony to avert impending disaster, perhaps consequent upon the news of a successful landing or the defeat of the defending forces. The supplication to Athena at Troy (*Il.* VI, 269–311) suggests itself as a parallel; and perhaps this is the explanation of the alabaster vase at Zakro which was found broken into four pieces and scattered (Platon, 1968, p. 225).

Our first comments on this tablet insisted on the likelihood of *pe-re* and *a-ke* concealing forms of φέρω and ἄγω, two verbs which are so regularly coupled in Greek for bringing inanimate and animate objects. The inanimate objects which are carried must be the *do-ra* = *dōra* 'gifts'. Thus the *po-re-na* must be the ten persons who are led to the rite; though no Greek word provides an interpretation it may seem appropriate to translate as 'victims'. If figurines were meant, the correct verb would be φέρω. Our suggested 'persons to carry the vessels in procession' encounters the difficulty that three of the vessels have no one to carry them. It is much more likely that the offerings are all brought, but different verbs are used to convey the different means of movement.

Palmer, however (1963*a*, p. 266), while connecting *pe-re* with φέρω has interpreted *a-ke* as *hagē* 'was purified' from a root found in ἁγνός, ἅζομαι. We should expect this at Pylos to be spelt a_2-*ke*, but usage is not entirely consistent. This has the advantage that *wa-tu* ('obverse' line 1) can be given its natural interpretation as *wastu* = ἄστυ 'the town'; but it involves taking *po-re-na* as nominative singular, which is difficult if the first part of *po-re-no-zo-te-ri-ja* Un 443.2 belongs to the same word; cf. also *po-re-no-tu-te*[Ua 1413, and *po-re-si* (dat. plur.?) TH Of 26.

The question what part of φέρω and ἄγω *pe-re* and *a-ke* represent cannot be separated from the interpretation to be given *i-je-to-qe*. It might be a tempting solution to regard this as the nominative singular required as subject to the two present indicatives; but this leads to no easy interpretation, and most commentators have followed our lead in regarding it as a verbal form, with suffixed -*qe*. The presence of the connective, even if contrary to classical usage, is little different from the use of *e-ke-qe* in the *E* tablets (see pp. 246, 447). Thus if *i-je-to* is a verb, it must presumably match with *pe-re* and *a-ke*. If the latter pair are aorist passive, *i-je-to* should be the same; but its form is unsuitable, for it might be an imperfect or even a perfect, but hardly an aorist, even if the classical type of aorist in -θην had not yet developed. The change from imperfect to aorist would be surprising; Palmer translates *i-je-to* 'a ceremony of consecration was held' without commenting on the tense. It would therefore be simpler to regard *i-je-to* as present medio-passive in -*toi* (see p. 87), agreeing with the present indicatives *pherei* and *agei*. The use of the present with no precise reference to time is common enough on the tablets; cf. the present tenses of the *N* tablets (e.g. **195** = Na 245, **193** = Na 520, **186** = Na 543, **184** = Nn 228, etc.).

But if we accept this interpretation, we have to find a subject for the verbs. Who brings the offerings? Or can *pherei* and *agei* be treated as impersonal 'one brings'? Two solutions seem possible; that *pu-ro* is used to mean 'the people of Pylos' or even the king acting on behalf of the kingdom; or that *po-ro-wi-to* is the name of the official responsible and is to be understood out of the introductory genitive (*sc.* 'these are the offerings of *po-ro-wi-to*'). The first seems preferable, though it is not entirely convincing; it hardly seems possible that *wa-tu* is *wastu* used as a substitute for *Pulos*, though this would of course make sense of the puzzling insertion in the formula, since ἄστυ is so clearly distinguished in classical usage from πόλις as meaning the city as a collection of buildings. We can rule out the names of the deities as possible subjects since some are clearly in the dative (*ti-ri-se-ro-e, di-we, i-je-we*) and all may be. It would be possible to take *po-si-da-i-jo, pe-re-*82-jo,* etc., as nominatives ('the priest of Poseidon, etc.'); but this will not satisfy 'reverse' line 2, where the dative *pa-ki-ja-si* occupies the same position in the formula. It is simpler to regard all these words as dative-locative. We can eliminate *do-ra*, not as being plural, but because the gifts are obviously brought, they do not bring anything; and since *po-re-na* is parallel in structure to *do-ra*, this too is impossible. Thus we are led to the conclusion either that *pu-ro* is the subject, or that the subject was regarded by the writer as so obvious that it was unnecessary to specify him.

The initial word *i-je-to-qe* must from its position be emphatic and set the tone for the following entry. This makes it difficult to associate with ἵημι 'send', and the presence of the locative-dative *pa-ki-ja-si* in 'reverse' line 2 seems to prove that this meaning is wrong. It is therefore tempting to accept Palmer's idea (1963 *a*, p. 265) that it belongs to a verb which did not survive in classical Greek, but had a base **isə-* with religious meaning seen in the adjective ἱερός. It is of course true that **isəro-* (Skt. *iṣira-*) would yield Greek ἱαρός, and this is the normal West Greek form; but the alternation of ἱαρός and ἱερός is not explained by normal dialect alternations, and it is possible that the word contains two distinct origins which have become confused; and this might account for the meaning 'strong' as well as 'sacred'. The verb at this stage might have retained the form *ihēmi* as distinct from *hiēmi* (or *hihēmi*) so that the confusion was graphic rather than phonetic; and it may have been deponent, since there is no reason to regard *ihetoi* as passive rather than middle voice. In the translation proposed here it has been tentatively rendered 'sacrifices'.

p. 286† **172**＝Tn 316. Corrections: read 'reverse' as first side, followed by 'obverse'; obv. line 10 the suggested correction *i-je-⟨re⟩-we* for *i-je-we* is probably unnecessary.

Translation: 'REVERSE':

In the month of Plōwistos. Pylos *sacrifices* at *Pa-ki-ja-ne* and brings gifts and leads *victims*.

    For the Mistress: one gold cup, one woman.

    For *Mnasa*: one gold bowl, one woman.

    For Posidaeia: one gold bowl, one woman.

    For the *thrice-hero*: one gold cup.

    For the *Lord of the House*: one gold cup.

Pylos . . . (blank)

'OBVERSE':

Pylos *sacrifices* at the shrine of Poseidon and the *city* leads, and brings gifts and leads *victims*: one gold cup, two women, *for G^{w}owia (and?) Komawenteia*.

Pylos *sacrifices* at the shrines of *Perse* and Iphemedeia and Diwia, and brings gifts and leads victims:

    For *Perse*: one gold bowl, one woman.

    For Iphemedeia: one gold bowl.

    For Diwia: one gold bowl, one woman.

    For Hermes *Areia*: one gold cup, one man.

Pylos *sacrifices* at the shrine of Zeus and brings gifts and leads *victims*:

    For Zeus: one gold bowl, one man.

    For Hera: one gold bowl, one woman.

    For *Drimios* the *son* of Zeus: one gold bowl [?]

Pylos . . . (blank)

qo-wi-ja: the second explanation offered has been followed in translation. *Komāwenteiā* (also TH Of 35) stands in much the same relation to *Komāwens*, which is found as a man's name, as *Posidāeiā* does to *Poseidāōn*. Explanations which make these words adjectives describing the vessels do not account for the absence of a deity to receive this sacrifice, nor the sex of the two victims. *G^{w}ōwiā* might emerge as Βοία in classical Greek, a woman's name and that of a town, also called Βοιαί, which might be named after a local divinity.

pe-re-*82: if, as seems likely (Chadwick, 1968*a*), **82* has the value *swa*, this goddess must have some such name as *Preswā*. It is tempting to see in this a metathetized form of the classical Πέρση (*Od.* x, 139), daughter of Oceanus and wife of Helios; whether it may be further identified with the first element of Περσεφόνη is only speculative.

Diwjai: as Ruijgh (1967, p. 130) points out, the nominative might be either *Diwyă* or *Diwyā*, the former being a feminine from Ζεύς 'the wife of Zeus', the latter an adjectival form 'the daughter of Zeus'. Ruijgh is no doubt right in preferring the former explanation, despite the rarity of Δῖα in later Greek.

E-ma-a$_2$: also now at Xn 1357.1 and TH Of 31.

di-ri-mi-jo, etc.: the form *i-je-we* is acceptable as dative to *i-*65*, if **65=ju:(h)iewei* 'son'. At the same time it must be admitted that in such a carelessly written document the omission of a sign in this word is not improbable; we have quite certainly *a* at 'obverse' line 5 for *a-ke*, and almost certainly *i-pe-me-de-ja-qe* for *i-pe-me-de-ja-jo-qe* in the previous line. On the problem of *i-*65* 'son', see Glossary.

Tris-hērōei: the name recurs on Fr 1204 as the recipient of oil. There is no good reason to expect a digamma in the declension of ἥρως; the formation with adverbial τρισ- suggests that ἥρως was originally an adjective. If the men and women are sacrificial victims, the last two deities on this side are not judged important enough to warrant one.

p. 289† To the list of major studies of this series must be added those of Lejeune (1958 a, pp. 65–91), Wyatt (1962) and Palmer (1963 a, pp. 300–5). For the most part the analysis given in the first edition has been confirmed, but Palmer's suggestion that the six commodities are all aromatic substances and are religious offerings is unlikely.

The main part of Wyatt's article is an ingenious attempt to show how the figures of the assessment were obtained and to account for the apparent discrepancies visible in the table on p. 291. He assumes that the Palace set a total for the contributions of each commodity and that this figure was allocated among the towns by dividing it between the two Provinces, and then dividing each Province into two areas which were further divided into two regions. This is certainly one way in which the figures may have been reached, but there are still minor discrepancies. His scheme does, however, lead to suggestions about the geographical location of some of the towns which are in line with those proposed above (see p. 417).

With two exceptions, the seventeen place names of the *Ma* series, omitting **182**=Ma 126 which is plainly aberrant, can be equated with the sixteen of the standard list of the principal towns of the two provinces (**257**=Jn 829). The exceptions are *a-te-re-wi-ja* and *e-sa-re-wi-ja* (Ma 330, 335), which appear instead of *e-re-i*. *E-sa-re-wi-ja* is shown by **304**=On 300 to belong to the Further Province, and *a-te-re-wi-ja* is associated with it on An 830. We may therefore presume that these tablets belong to the Further Province, but that for some reason one of the regions has been divided into two.

Little progress has been made with the identification of the six commodities. **146=A* is now generally believed to be some form of textile (Chadwick, 1964 b, Lejeune, 1964 b) though doubts have been expressed by Palmer (1963 a, esp. pp. 485–6) who rightly notes that this is used in offerings. However, the offering of garments is a familiar feature of Greek ritual. No good suggestions have been made for the weighed commodities *B*, *C* and *E*; the syllabic values may well be abbreviations, but not necessarily of Greek words (cf. NI, SA). The suggestion of 'beeswax' for KE (*kēros*) has not received any confirmation. The last item, *F*, ought to be more easily identifiable, if it represents a Greek word, since not many things can occur in such profusion (figures over 1000 in some cases). It appears to be counted, which tells strongly against substances such as honey (*meli*) or wine (*methu*) which would demand liquid measures. The same argument applies to things measured in dry measure (*meleuron* 'flour', see *me-re-u-ro* in Glossary); and it is hardly likely to be the name of a unit (*metron, medimnos*) since this would leave the substance unspecified. The only plausible solution is *mēla* 'sheep and goats', of which there may have been sufficient numbers available, and the ambiguity in the word would prevent the use of the animal ideograms which are specific; but it must be emphasized that all these guesses depend upon the word so abbreviated surviving into classical Greek, and it could well be something quite different.

It is certain that these contributions are some kind of regular tax imposed on the towns, since deficits of the previous year are mentioned; **180** = Ma 225 refers to a remission granted to the smiths 'this year', and **178** = Ma 365 to a payment in 'the following year'. It is of interest that the assessments for the Further Province are considerably higher than for the Hither Province, despite the smaller number of towns; but this would be understandable if they controlled the rich agricultural land of the Pamisos valley.

292† **174** = Ma 346. Correction: l.1 add at the end *F* 400[(i.e. a figure probably in excess of 400).

293† **177** = Ma 90. On *ku-re-we* as the name of a class of inhabitants see p. 430.

293‡ **178** = Ma 365

hateron wetos: this interpretation has been generally accepted, though Lejeune suggested taking *a₂-te-ro* as *hateroi* 'the other smiths pay their annual contribution', but this seems to strain the meaning of *wetos*. The parallel with *za-we-te* 'this year' (**180** = Ma 225) strongly suggests that this phrase means 'next year' (and not 'every other year').

294† The suggested abbreviation *ophēlo(mena)* has not been confirmed, and it seems easier to accept incoherence of syntax, taking *o-pe-ro* as usual as a neuter noun.

295† **180** = Ma 225

za-we-te: brilliantly identified by Palmer (1960, p. 60; cf. 1963a, p. 305) as *tsāwetes* < **kyāwetes* = σῆτες 'this year'. The word now recurs at Knossos (Fh 5451) with its adjectival form *za-we-te-ra* (Fh 518).

465

re-u-ko-to-ro: the reference to Leuktron, which is the administrative centre (cf. p. 418) of the Further Province, is surprising on a tablet which deals with *Pi-*82* (*Piswa?*), one of the Nine Towns of the Hither Province. Perhaps the solution lies in the location of this town near the frontier between the two provinces; we believe it to lie at the northern extremity of the kingdom, and if it were in the Soulima valley (perhaps in the area of Malthi or even Peristeria (Moira) where such rich finds were made), it would be as accessible from the Pamisos valley as from Pylos via Kyparissia.

p. 295‡ **182** = Ma 126. Correction: l. 2 *A* 3   *B* ͅ   *C* ͭ.

i-na-ma-ta: solutions based upon Arcadian ἰν = ἐν seem unlikely since this form of the preposition has not been reliably identified in Mycenaean. Palmer (1963*a*, p. 305) may be right in suggesting it is a personal name of the common type ending in *-ātās*. In Wa 730.1 the reading is perhaps *da̤-so-mo* = δασμός 'distribution'.

p. 295¶ It will be useful to add here the badly damaged tablet On 300, since it is a vital piece of evidence in the determination of the geography of the kingdom of Pylos (see pp. 415–17). The ideogram **154* bears a general resemblance to **152* and **153* which are surcharged with syllabic *wi* and *ko* and appear to stand for *wrinos* 'hide' and *kōwos* 'sheepskin' respectively. But there are differences in the outline of **154* and the resemblance may be fortuitous. The tablet gives no further clue to the identity of the ideogram, since the heading is lost.

152

153

154

304 = On 300

1	[At least one line lost]		
2	] **154* 10 *a-pi-a₂-ro*		**154* 6
3	*ko-re-te-*]*ri* **154* 5[ ]*pa-ki-ja-ni-j̣ạ*[ ]'*ko-re-te-ri*'		**154* 3
4	] **154*[		]**154* 3
5	**154*]ͦ *e-ra-te-i-jo* '*ko-re-te-ri*'		**154* 3
6	]*-ni-jo*[ ]*du-ma-ti* **154* 3		
7	*da-mo-ko-ro*[ ] vacat		
8	*o-de-qa-a₂* *pe-ra-a-ko-ra-i-jo* [		
9	*ra-u-ra-ti-ja ko-re-te* **154* 2̣[ ]ẹ*-sa-re-wi-ja* ḳọ[*-re-te* **154*		
10	*e-*[*ra-te*]*-re-wa-o ko-re-te* **154* 2[ ]*te-mi-ti-ja ko-re-te* **154* 3		
11	*sa-ma*[*-ra*] *ko-re-te* **154*[ ]2 *a-si-ja-ti-ja ko-re-te* **154* 3		
12	]*ma* **154* 2 *te-po-se-u* **154* 3		
13	] vacat		
14–18	vacat		

A small fragment, On 1074, appears to belong to this tablet but cannot be accurately placed. No translation is given in view of the damaged state of the text and its tabular form.

The second paragraph of this text clearly begins at line 8 with the word *o-de-qa-a₂*, strongly reminiscent of *o-da-a₂* which so often serves the same purpose (e.g. **43**=Aq 64.12, **44**=Aq 218.9). The doubts over the presence of a divider between *o-de* and *qa-a₂* are justified, and the four signs probably constitute a single word. Study by Olivier of this text has revealed that the scribe first wrote *o-de-qe pe-ra-* and then deleted all but the first two signs and inscribed the present text. This confirms the view of *o-da-a₂* proposed by Chadwick (1971, pp. 102–3) that this is *hō de* plus a particle *aha, for in this case we have plainly *hō de qᵘ(e) aha* replacing *hō de qᵘe*=ὡς δέ τε.

The paragraph is headed *pe-ra-a-ko-ra-i-jo*, plainly an adjectival form from *pe-ra-ko-ra-i-ja* Ae 398 and *pe-ra₃-ko-ra-i-ja* **199**=Ng 332; for the details of the structure of this word see Chadwick, 1963a, pp. 137–8. It refers to places on the far side of the feature which divides the kingdom into two, and four of the following place names are identifiable with towns among the final seven of **257**=Jn 829 (*ra-u-ra-ti-ja*=*ra-*]*wa-ra-ta₂*, *te-mi-ti-ja*=*ti-mi-to-a-ke-e*, *sa-ma[-ra]*=[*sa-*]*ma-ra*, *a-si-ja-ti-ja*). Of the other two *e-sa-re-wi-ja* reappears on Ma 330 and on Vn 493 coupled with *za-ma-e-wi-ja* (**175**=Ma 393, **257**=Jn 829.18), and despite the apparent lack of space *e-[ra-te-]re-wa-o* must be restored in line 10 (cf. **258**=Jo 438.27, also followed by *ko-re-te*; also *e-ra-te-re-we* Ma 333). It is therefore tempting in line 12 to restore [*e-re-o du-*]*ma*, the *duma* of Helos, since *du-ma* and *ko-re-te* are clearly titles of the same sort (cf. **257**=Jn 829.1–2). This leaves only *te-po-se-u* to account for, and he is shown by **258**=Jo 438.21 to be *ti-nwa-si-jo ko-re-te*. In other words the official is named instead of being given his title.

We can now turn to the even more damaged first paragraph. Line 1 presumably contained the heading stating the subject of the record; it probably contained the word *de-we-ro-a-ko-ra-i-jo* or something similar. The nine following entries will then correspond to the Nine Towns of the Hither Province. Strangely the title *ko-re-te-ri* is here in the dative case, with the less usual locatival *-i* ending; but rather than suppose a different operation in the first paragraph, we may put this down to scribal inconsequence. *pa-ki-ja-ni-ja* is the town nearest to Pylos, frequently mentioned on the tablets. *a-pi-a₂-ro*=*Amphihalos* is an important person (An 192.1, Qa 1297) but there is no evidence of his town. *e-ra-te-i-jo* is the adjective of *e-ra-to* which replaces *ro-u-so* in some versions of the List of the Nine Towns. In line 6 [*du*]*-ni-jo* is a likely restoration (cf. An 192.2), but again we cannot conjecture the place name which must fit in the lacuna. *da-mo-ko-ro* has been finally proved by KN C 7058+7922 to be a title rather than a personal name. This too appears to stand, like *te-po-se-u*, outside the entries corresponding to the principal towns of the Province.

p. 295†† The attempts that have been made to dissolve the connexion between the ideogram SA and the word *ri-no = linon* (**184** = Nn 228) have now generally been abandoned. But much doubt still surrounds the meaning of the word *linon*, since it can refer both to the raw fibres of the flax plant and to the thread and cloth prepared from them; the other product of the plant, linseed, is in classical Greek called λίνου σπέρμα, but might also be included in the Mycenaean use of the word.

As pointed out by Killen (1966*b*, p. 36), *ri-no* is measured by weight at Knossos on Og 5778. Thus KN Nc 4479 with the entry SA ⸎ 1 may be some confirmation that SA on the Pylos tablets refers to a product of the flax plant. It is possible that standard bales of the fibres formed the basic unit in which the product was counted, and when it is weighed it is the seed which is meant.

The formulas of the *Na* tablets may be divided into two basic types, depending on whether there is one entry of SA or two. The simple class with one entry may be subdivided into those with a formula consisting only of a place name followed by SA and a number (e.g. **185** = Na 419) and those where the place name has a qualifying phrase added, but no separate SA entry. This phrase may be as short as *we-da-ne-wo ke* (Na 856, 1041), but in most cases contains the verb *e-ko-si* (Na 396, Na 405, **187** = Na 514, Na 516, **186** = Na 543, **188** = Na 928) or *e-ke* (**196** = Na 926; cf. **194** = Na 334, but this belongs to the type with *e-re-u-te-ra*, see below).

The compound class consists of those with two or more entries of SA. These too are of two types, those with the formula: Place name SA number *to-sa-de X e-re-u-te-ro* (*-ra*) SA number, where *X* is a noun in the dative case (e.g. **192** = Na 252), and those where the second element is varied to *to-sa-de X o-u-di-do-si*, where *X* is a noun in the nominative (e.g. **189** = Na 568, **195** = Na 245). Further annotations are added, but this division still holds good.

There are two tablets apparently of the simple class with one SA entry, but containing the *e-re-u-te-ra* formula: **191** = Na 248 and **194** = Na 334; and one in which the first SA is not followed by a number (Na 924: *ri-sa-pi* SA *me-to-re e-re-u-te-ro-se to-sa* SA 10). It seems likely that Na 924 implies a zero entry for the first SA, and therefore the other two may be regarded also as of the compound class, with SA 0 understood after the place name.

From this classification it is clear that *e-re-u-te-ra* and *o-u-di-do-si* are in some sense equivalent, for the totalling tablets, **198**=Ng 319 and **199**=Ng 332, do not have anything corresponding to *e-re-u-te-ra*, but a single subordinate entry headed *o-u-di-do-to*, which must be the passive of *o-u-di-do-si*. At the same time the use of both formulas on one unfortunately incomplete tablet (Na 185.A]*o-u-di-do-si* SA 2: .B] *e-re-u-te-ro* SA 2) suggests that the distinction is not arbitrary.

The *e-re-u-te-ra* formula may be varied by the use of the verb *e-re-u-te-ro-se* to indicate the official responsible for the remission (**190**=Na 395), and in one case this is added to the *o-u-di-do-si* formula (**189**=Na 568), which is further proof that the terms are effectively synonymous.

Thus the meaning of *e-re-u-te-ro-se*=*eleutherōse* must be 'made free', 'remitted', which is a tolerable extension of the sense of the classical ἐλευθερόω 'to free (a person) from debt' (Herodotus VI, 59, Plat. *Rep.* 566 e). This in turn will explain the use of the adjective in the sense of 'allowed free', 'remitted'. The nearest classical parallel seems to be its use to mean 'free of debts', 'unencumbered' (Dem. xxxv, 21). The wavering between *e-re-u-te-ro* and *e-re-u-te-ra* may be due to thinking of the plural units represented by SA (feminine?) or the collective neuter singular (*linon*).

It is not clear whether these tablets represent an assessment or an actual delivery. There is no mention of a deficit except in the special document **184**=Nn 228, so perhaps we should regard the main entries as a forecast of the amount to be received. They differ from the assessments of the *Ma* tablets by requiring the sums remitted in the compound tablets to be added to the first entry in order to produce the round numbers characteristic of the simple type. Thus:

Na 245	$20+10=30$
Na 252	$24+ 6=30$
Na 425	$27+ 3=30$
Na 529	$18+ 5+17=40$

This explanation will satisfy the three tablets with presumed zero main entry listed above. Here the total assessment has been remitted, so that the delivery is forecast as zero.

We can now ask what is the meaning of the group with only one entry, but an annotation including *e-ko-si*: are these too to be regarded as compound tablets with a zero assessment? Or are they forecasts of deliveries which the annotation does not cancel out? It is hard to see what purpose there would be in introducing yet a third way of denoting a rebate; and it is clear that the subjects of *e-ko-si* are words of a different type from the trade names which figure in the remission formulas. We can perhaps put the question in another form and ask what is the object of *e-ko-si*; is it the following number of SA, which would imply that the Palace received nothing, or is it the territory in question which is 'occupied' by this group of people?

196 = Na 926 may be helpful here in view of its variation on the formula. The territory is described as *a-ki-ti-to* = *aktitos*, which can hardly be uncultivated, if at least 6 units of flax are expected from it. Presumably it means 'not subject to the process described by *ki-ti-je-si*' (**193** = Na 520) which entitles those performing it to a remission. Perhaps the original sense was 'to render habitable', 'to build dwellings upon'. (Cf. κτίσσε δὲ Δαρδανίην, ἐπεὶ οὔ πω Ἴλιος ἱρὴ ἐν πεδίῳ πεπόλιστο *Il.* xx, 216.) From this the special sense of *ki-ti-me-na* 'land under habitation', 'lived upon', might develop to mean effectively 'private estate'. At least it is clearly the land which is called *aktitos*; and the tablet goes on to note: *ekhei de min A₂*. Here *min* can hardly refer to the flax, but to the land which is *aktitos*: 'and H. holds it'. If therefore the note does not here cancel the contribution, it is reasonable to assume that in the other cases too *e-ko-si* does not imply any rebate. In **194** = Na 334 the royal holding is specially exempted from contribution.

The subjects of the verb *e-ko-si* on surviving tablets are: *ko-ro-ku-ra-i-jo* (Na 396, Na 405, Na 516, **186** = Na 543), *ke-ki-de* (**187** = Na 514; cf.]*ke-ki-do* Na 848), and *u-ru-pi-ja-jo* (Na 928). These are three of the names used on the *o-ka* tablets to refer to contingents of troops. Mühlestein (1956*a*, pp. 16–18) first called attention to apparent similarities in the numbers, which he interpreted as meaning that the troops were issued with one SA apiece. Unfortunately, although this suggestion has been eagerly accepted, the evidence is far from satisfactory.

187 = Na 514 lists SA 30 at [*ku-*]*pa-ri-so* with the note *ke-ki-de e-ko-si*; **56** = An 657 lists two detachments of *ku-pa-ri-si-jo ke-ki-de* of 20 and 10 men respectively. If the sum were any figure but 30, the commonest number in the *Na* tablets, the coincidence would be striking. But both sets of tablets work for preference in multiples of 10, and the agreement might well arise by chance.

186 = Na 543 lists SA 30 at *ka-ra-do-ro*, which is held by *ko-ro-ku-ra-i-jo* (the restoration is beyond doubt); **60** = An 661.5 lists a number of *ko-ro-ku-ra-i-jo* at the same place, but although MEN 30 was originally read the figure is damaged and 10[is the safest reading. This coincidence therefore depends upon a very uncertain reading.

Na 1027 has the simple entry: *e-na-po-ro* SA 70. **60** = An 661 reads *e-na-po-ro i-wa-so* MEN 70. On this basis Mühlestein proposed regarding Na 1027 as having omitted the annotation *i-wa-so e-ko-si*. But of course this is quite unjustified; the *Na* tablet is a normal assessment and no annotation was made.

188 = Na 928 had its left end missing, but records SA 10 and *u-ru-pi-ja-jo e-ko-si*. Mühlestein proposed restoring the place name as *pe-di-jo to match **58** = An 654.14–16: *to-so-de pe-di-je-we . . . u-ru-pi-ja-jo* MEN 10. Unfortunately the join of Na 928 with 929 and 953 shows that the name was really]*a₂-ke-wo-a-ki-*[which does not recur elsewhere.

The hypothesis that one unit of SA was issued to each man in the coast-guard detachments is thus shown to be poorly founded. All that the facts show is that at certain places liable for a contribution of flax, there were 'occupiers' of land who bore special generic names and were drawn upon to provide the manpower required for the coastguard service. See further on these names, p. 430.

Finally we may dispose of Palmer's suggestion that SA stands for linseed issued to the troops as emergency rations, for which he compares Thucydides IV, 26, 8. This refers to the parcels of food smuggled by underwater swimmers to the Spartans blockaded on Sphakteria. Clearly the need here was not for palatable food, but for food with a high nutritive value; it would need to have been boiled to render it non-toxic. To suggest its widespread use as military rations on such a slender basis is a dangerous hypothesis. It must also be remarked that linseed would presumably be measured in dry volume and in the absence of metric signs the figures would refer to the standard dry units, i.e. about 96 litres per man—a heroic ration.

It is clearly a more economical hypothesis to suggest that the figures refer to the normal production of flax, which may have been a royal monopoly. The greater part of the flax still grown in Greece for fibres is produced in Messenia and the adjacent areas (Chadwick, 1963 *a*, p. 129), doubtless on account of the lavish water-supply which is required for retting. This explains also the relative scarcity of flax (SA) in Crete. For the use of linen cloth, see pp. 323, 522.

It is interesting that instead of grouping the contributions under the Sixteen principal towns, each town or village is assessed separately. This suggests an agricultural product not requiring a process of manufacture or treatment in a central depot; contrast the *Ma* tablets. The tablets must have been divided between two files corresponding to the two Provinces and each accompanied by a totalling document (**198, 199**); but unfortunately they were all written by the same scribe and there is no way of restoring them to their correct files, except where we have independent evidence for the location of the place.

p. 296† **183** = Nn 831. Corrections: l.1 ⟦*do-so-mo*⟧.

It was perhaps inevitable that the restoration *ko-ri*[*-ja-do-*]*no*, which Ventris and I discussed and agreed to reject, should have been proposed (Palmer, 1963*a*, p. 310). One reason was that the two signs alone would have not filled the lacuna, but if a divider were included the spacing then becomes plausible. The other is that the restoration of a name of a spice matches ill with s A, if this signifies flax. It is true that *ko-ri-to* does not occur on any of the surviving *Na* tablets; but there is no objection to a place name as the heading for a tablet of this sort (cf. *sa-ra-pe-da* **171** = Un 718.1). Possibly *ko-ri-*[*to-jo*] or *ko-ri-*[*si-jo*] would fit the gap better. It is uncertain whether the last word *do-so-mo* 'contribution' was intended to be deleted or not; the whole tablet appears to have been deleted and re-written.

p. 296‡ **184** = Nn 228

The corresponding *Na* tablets can be listed as follows

1	*u-ka-jo*	s A 20				
2	*ro-o-wa*	s A 35	Na 568?	]*-wa*	s A 20+s A 50	
3	*pu₂-ra₂-a-ke-re-u*	s A 10	Na 425	*pu₂-ra₂-a-ki-ri-jo*	s A 27+s A 3	
4	*ke-i-ja-ka-ra-na*	s A 5				
5	*di-wi-ja-ta*	s A 60				
6	*a-pi-no-e-wi-jo*	s A 28	Xa 58	*a-pi-no-e-wi-*[		
7	*po-ra-pi*	s A 10	Xn 432?	*po-ra-*[		
8	*e-na-po-ro*	s A 33	Na 1027	*e-na-po-ro*	s A 70	
9	*te-tu-ru-we*	s A 38	Na 1054	*te-tu-ru-we*	s A 40+ ?	

If the few cases where both figures are preserved are to be trusted, the number of s A here is always smaller than the assessment of the *Na* tablets. Thus if this is a record of deficits, the difference must be the actual deliveries received. In line 4 of this table the corresponding *Na* tablet might be Xa 70 (with a variant of this form of the name, but probably not belonging to this series); but it should not be identified with the simple *ke-i-jo* of Na 577 with an assessment of s A 14. *Ke-i-jo* (cf. *ke-i-ja* Qa 1303) is clearly an adjectival form of *ke-e* (Aa 93, Ad 295) which is known to lie in the Further Province, whereas all the other place names on this tablet which can be assigned to provinces are in the Hither Province. Hence it seems probable that *ke-i-ja-ka-ra-na* (though a similar adjective qualifying *krānā* = κρήνη 'spring') and *ke-i-jo* are two different places, both producing flax; it is notable that *ke-e* is shown by Ad 295 to be the home of *ri-ne-ja-o* = *lineiāōn* 'flax workers'.

Several of the places listed on this tablet are shown by their associations to be in the southern part of the Hither Province; on *ro-o-wa* see p. 187; and *e-na-po-ro* is located between *a-ke-re-wa* and *ka-ra-do-ro*, sixth and eighth of the Nine Towns (p. 142), by **60** = An 661.3. *Po-ra-pi* (in the locative form *po-ra-i*) seems to be placed a little further north by **59** = An 656.13.

Some of the names also reappear on *Mb* or *Mn* tablets, associated with the ideogram **146* (= *A*, p. 290) which is believed to be some kind of textile. It does not follow that **146* = 'linen cloth', since it is also associated with wool (KN M 559, M 683).

297† *E-ko-me-no* is duplicated on **197** = Na 406 and Na 941; it is possible that these are two different places. *U-ra-*86* occurs on Na 466 and the rare sign **86* also ends the names on Na 1039 and Na 1086, but this is hardly sufficient proof that the name is the same in each case. It is not impossible that **86* is a 'compound' sign preferred by this scribe, where others would spell out the group in two signs. The names appear to be all in the dative-locative, with the *-pi* ending in appropriate cases (plurals of *a-* and consonant-stems).

298† **188** = Na 928. As a result of a join with 929+953, the text now reads:

]*a₂-ke-wo-a-ki-*[   ]*u-ru-pi-ja-jo* 'e-ko-si' SA 10

U-ru-pi-ja-jo is not to be connected with Olympia.

298‡ **189** = Na 568. An alternative restoration would be [*ro-o*]-*wa*, cf. **184** = Nn 228.2.

The title, if it is one, *e-sa-re-u* now recurs in the dative case *e-sa-re-we* on Cn 1197.4. But it is not clear which of these terms is the name and which the title. Palmer takes *ke-u-po-da* as *kheuspondās* 'libation-pourer' and hence *e-sa-re-u* as a personal name.

300† *a-ki-ti-to* must mean something other than 'uncultivated'; see p. 470 above.

300‡ **197** = Na 406+1088. The text now reads:

o-qe-[   ]*si* SA 20

e-ko-me-no di-wi-ja-wo e-ke a-ki-ti-to

di-wi-ja-wo: *Diwyāwōn*, a name found at both Knossos and Thebes.

o-qe-[   ]*si*: a tantalizing break, since there is no obvious word to fill the gap. Possibly *o-qe* represents *ho qᵘe* (ὅ τε) written as one word with a following verb. If so, the verb must be athematic to end in *-si* in the 3rd person singular, so perhaps a restoration *o-qe-*[*di-do-*]*si* is possible, *di-do-si* here being *didōsi*, 'and he contributes'.

301† It is not clear whether *de-we-ro-* implies a pronunciation *dewero*, or whether *we* is here a spelling for *u* (cf. pp. 398, 492).

473

p. 301‡ No real progress has been made with the interpretation of this series. Its presence in the Arsenal along with records of chariots and weapons suggests that it must have had a 'military' purpose, and the idea that it is connected with the manufacture of bows still seems the most plausible; cf. *to-ko-so-wo-ko* = *toxoworgoi* 'bow-makers' at Pylos (An 207.12). In KN V 150 *to-ko-so-ta a-te-u-ke* 1 the interpretation seems certainly to be *toxotās ateukhēs* 'unequipped archer', but possibly the first word is to be taken as a personal name.

No one has explained why animals are listed together with their horns; the number of horns would presumably be twice the number of animals, but the number of horns actually recorded (*J*) is always less than (or the same as) the number of male goats (*G*). Palmer (1963*b*, p. 162) has objected that since there is a fixed relationship of 1 kg. of *I* to every 2 horns, this must be also an animal product. But he does not propose an identification, nor does he explain the relationship between the number of horns and the number of animals.

The table on p. 302 needs only slight correction in the light of new readings, and none of the changes disturbs the conclusions drawn from it. Mc 5098 has been improved by joins with 4457 and 8264, and is now re-numbered Mc 4457. It begins in line 1 with the regular totalling formula: *to-sa*, probably neuter plural. Line 2 begins *ke*[, which it is tempting to restore as *keras* (or its plural). But the figure for *J*, apart from being the only odd number in this column, is doubly aberrant. It is the only case where the number of *J* is not less than the number of *G*; and it is the only *J* figure which is not double the *I* figure (in Mc 4462 read *I* 26). It seems clear that the tablet contains an error, and we should have had *J* 308. The mistake can have arisen by the scribe confusing 308 with *H* 208 immediately above, and substituting instead the *G* figure.

The most interesting addition is the fragment Mc 5107 with the reading:

$$G \ 354 \qquad H \ 200[$$

This is clearly another totalling document, like Mc 4457. The purpose of Mc 5107, with no introductory word, is not clear, for it does not seem to be a copy of Mc 4457, unless 354 is a careless error for 345; the second figure is incomplete.

All the tablets of this series for which the find-spot is known were found in the Arsenal (*P* on the plan, p. 115), except for Mc 1508. This was apparently found along with the sword tablets (p. 360) in the East wing (*M*). It also appears to duplicate Mc 4456, the heading of which is the place name *da-*22-to*; Mc 1528 has the ethnic adjective, *da-*22-ti-jo*. The figures for *G* and *H* agree, but *I* is 6 kg. instead of 7 and *J* is 12 instead of 14. Its find-spot is confirmed by its appearance, for it lacks the characteristically cracked surface of the tablets from the Arsenal, though it was apparently written by the same scribe.

303† The eleven *Fp* tablets mentioned here are those with numbers between 1 and 48, the last of which is alleged to have been found in the Room of the Chariot Tablets (*B* on the plan). There is also a trace of another parallel series in a different hand made up of Fp 354, 363, 5472 (possibly a part of the same tablet as 363) and 5504. The series has been discussed at length elsewhere (Chadwick, 1966).

The use of *me-no* = *mēnos*, genitive, with forms in both *-o* and *-o-jo* has given rise to the theory that the *o*-stems in Mycenaean have alternative genitives in *-ō* and in *-oio* (Luria, 1957; cf. Chadwick, 1958*a*). The question cannot be finally resolved, but the alleged form in *-o* is curiously restricted in usage.

305† **200** = Fp 1: Corrections: l.1: no sign is missing before *de-u-ki-jo-jo*, but the word is indented, probably because of the shape of the tablet; l.2 the reading *di-ka-ta-jo | di-we* is certain. There are slight differences in the form of the OIL ideogram on this tablet, but since all the entries are totalled in l.12 they cannot be of great significance (see Chadwick, 1966, pp. 27–8).

307† *pa-de* cannot be associated with παῖς ('the divine child') if the etymology < *παϝις is correct; but the etymology may be at fault. It seems to be the name of a deity, not a place.

308† **203** = Ga (formerly F) 953 [+] 955. Correction: l.2]2 *pa-de-i*.

310† **205** = Gg 702

da-puₐ-ri-to-jo: the normal value of *puₐ* is now known to be *phu*. But although a value *pu* would seem unlikely, *bu* is a possible alternative.

310‡ **206** = Gg 705. Correction: l.3 read]*o-ne* (cf. **204** = Gg 704).

311† **207** = V 280

The attempt to explain this text as a calendar does not lead to any satisfactory solution, and **172** = Pylos Tn 316 is not in any way parallel. The fourteen lines, omitting the heading in l.1, might suggest the days of a month; and *wo-de-wi-jo* is recorded as a month name on Fp 16, Fp 48 and **203** = Ga 953 [+] 955. But the lacuna at the beginning of ll.12–14 can be paralleled on PY Cn 328.5–15, where the word *a-ka-na-jo* occupies this place in ll.2–4 and l.5 begins with the isolated sign *a*. Clearly the word had to be repeated in each line, and the scribe could not be bothered to write it fourteen times. Thus it is likely that here too *a-pe-ti-ra₂* is to be understood in ll.12–14.

475

The only other word which is clear is *to-pe-za* (l.5), which on the Pylos furniture tablets (**239–241**) = *torpedza* = τράπεζα 'table'. Though this could conceivably be the name of a festival (cf. Umbrian *mefa* 'offering' = Latin *mensa*), it is only known to us as the name of a piece of furniture. *o-u-ki-te-mi* was interpreted as οὐχὶ θέμις; but *te-mi* recurs in *te-mi-dwe* = *termidwen* (cf. τερμιόεις) 'furnished with a τέρμις', the sense of the noun ('border', 'edge'?) being obscure. At least this sense is not impossible here. *o-u-ki* will perhaps be rather *oukis* < *ou kʷis = οὔτις, with the normal treatment of the labio-velar in contact with *u* (cf. Thessalian κις = τις, probably generalized from οὔ κις). *a-pe-ti-ra₂* is interpreted by Lejeune (1960*a*, p. 20) as an adjective with *to-pe-za* understood, perhaps *amphestria* 'with seats on either side'.

Much debate has raged around *i-ku-wo-i-pi*, most authors trying to make this a form of ἵππος; but if so, it is a unique spelling of the group -*kw*-, normally represented by *q*, unless heterosyllabic (cf. *te-tu-ko-wo-a*). The connexion proposed with ἰξύς < *ἰσχύς (Boisacq) has been misunderstood by Palmer (1966, p. 275); but is scarcely more satisfactory for the sense. It is probably unnecessary to suppose a dual in -*oiimphi* (as Palmer does, loc. cit.); Vedic -*ebhis* is evidence for a form *-*oibhi-s*, and the Homeric examples of -οφι are plainly secondary. The tablet is one of many acute problems posed by the 'Room of the Chariot Tablets'; see p. 522.

p. 311‡   **208** = V 52. Correction: the join with a small fragment (8285) has revealed that the restoration of the second entry of l. 2 was correct: read *pa-ja-wo-ne* I. The lower edge also bears a deleted inscription ⟦*e-ri-nu-we pe-ṛọ* ⟧.

e-ri-nu-we = *Erinuei* is the expected dative to *e-ri-nu* (**200** = Fp 1.8), which is perhaps a 'nominative of the rubric'.

5. OFFERINGS OF OIL AT PYLOS (*Fr*)

p. 312†   Among the more recent finds at Pylos was a series of tablets which list quantities of olive oil. They were found, not in the Archive Room, but in the storerooms fitted for the storage of oil on the N.E. side of the Palace. One of the most important (Gn, now Fr, 1184) was published in time to allow us to quote the text on p. 217, but it is here repeated as the first of a selection of the new texts. These tablets were published with a commentary in 1958 by E. L. Bennett: *The Olive Oil Tablets of Pylos*, Supplement no. 2 to *Minos*, Salamanca.

Fr 1184 clearly indicates that oil was being prepared in the Palace workshops for use as unguent. This would have been made by the addition of perfumed ingredients and by decoction, a process described by the use of the verb ζέω 'boil'. A list of some of the ingredients is to be found in **103** = Un 267, since these are supplied to a man described as *aleiphazoos* 'unguent-boiler'.

The remainder of the series are almost all records of the issue of oil to various recipients. In many cases the oil is qualified by one or more of a series of adjectives which denote the perfume: *wo-do-we* = *wordowen* (cf. ῥοδόεντι . . . ἐλαίῳ *Il.* XXIII, 186) 'rose-scented', *pa-ko-we* = *sphakowen* 'sage-scented', *ku-pa-ro-we* = *kupairowen* 'cyperus-scented', *e-ti-we* (?). It is possible for oil to have two of these perfumes (1203, 1224). The single instance of *a-e-ti-to* is presumably the opposite of *e-ti-we*. The identification of this perfume is difficult; for a suggestion see the Glossary.

The OIL ideogram is sometimes in its simple form (1204, 1209, 1212, 1231, 1238), but more often is ligatured with syllabic signs, usually A or PA, less often PO and only once WE (1184). There is also one example of the compound ligature A + RE + PA replacing OIL (1198, cf. **171** = Un 718.8). There are eight cases where OIL + PA correlates with *pa-ko-we*, and it is never found associated with one of the other words indicating perfumes (except where *pa-ko-we* also occurs). It is therefore very likely that PA is here an abbreviation of *pa-ko-we*. Since none of the other perfume names begins with *a-* or *po-* (excluding of course *a-e-ti-to* which is negative), these ligatures must refer to something different. OIL + A is once found with *a-ro-pa* (1225) and it is tempting to assume that this is the meaning of A: *aloiphā* (ἀλοιφή) 'grease' or 'unguent'. There is no obvious correlation on these tablets for PO, but the Knossos *Fh*-series uses the word *po-ro-ko-wa* to describe oil (Fh 350), which must be *prokhowā* (προχοή) 'outpouring', a possible term to describe runny oil as contrasted with unguent.

The other word which appears to describe the oil rather than its use is *we-a-re-pe* (with variant spelling *we-ja-re-pe*). This would appear to be a derivative of ἀλειφ-; cf. δι-ηλιφής (Sophocles). There is some reason to think that *we-* before a vowel may represent *u-* cf. *we-je-ke-a₂* in the Glossary; thus a possible interpretation is *ualeiphes* 'for smearing on'. It is thus an alternative way of describing unguent, and it never appears on the same tablet as A + RE + PA or *a-ro-pa*; but on three of its four appearances it is followed by OIL + A; on the fourth there is no ideogram written. Thus even if the form is not exact, it is very likely to be a description of unguent.

The word *ke-se-ni-wi-jo* (1231), cf.]*nu-wi-jo* (1255), is plainly *xenwion* 'of guests'. The word is also used of textiles where it must mean 'provided for or given as gifts to guests', since it is parallel to *wanaktera* and *heqᵘesia*, 'for the king', 'for *heqᵘetai*'. Since in this case we know that the oil was being given to another recipient, Potnia, it follows that it must here mean 'received by way of a guest-gift'.

The analysis of the remaining parts of the text is more difficult. We can easily identify entries of the following types:

(1) Persons, some at least of whom are divine, in the dative case: *po-se-da-o-ne = Poseidāōnei, wa-na-ka-te = Wanaktei, po-ti-ni-ja = Potniāi, ti-ri-se-ro-e = Trishērō(h)ei* (cf. **172** = PY Tn 316.rev.5, see p. 289), *te-o-i = theoihi*.

(2) Addresses: *ro-u-si-jo a-ko-ro = Lousiōi agrōi* (or locative?), *pa-ki-ja-na-de = P . . . ānas-de, di-wi-jo-de = Diwyon-de* 'to the shrine of Zeus'.

(3) Date: *pa-ki-ja-ni-jo-jo me-no* (1224) = *P . . . ānioio mēnos* 'in the month of P.'; for a month-name derived from a place, cf. Attic Μουνυχιών.

It is therefore reasonable to try to fit the more opaque terms into the framework so provided. But some preliminary cautions must be issued. It is possible for an address to be sufficient: *ro-u-si-jo a-ko-ro* (1220.1), *pa-ki-ja-na-de* (1209). Equally the recipient, as we may term the 'person' receiving the oil, may stand alone: *ti-ri-se-ro-e* (1204), *u-po-jo po-ti-ni-ja* (1225) 'the Mistress of Hyp . . .'; in such cases we may presume that the recipient has only one address. Thus where a recipient has several addresses, we are entitled to infer that one of the other words in the entry is effectively the address.

There is only one clear case of a date (1224) and that in a text which contains no address. Since the month *Pa-ki-ja-nios* was presumably named after a festival celebrated at the place *Pa-ki-jānes*, it might in effect serve as an address. Thus although we cannot exclude the possibility that other opaque words are the names of festivals, we are entitled to presume that they could serve the purpose of locating the destination of the oil in space rather than time. Thus our three types of entries can be reduced to two.

The form *pa-ki-ja-ni-jo-i* occurring once (1216) can be understood as either an address or a date, but as in the case of *pa-ki-ja-ni-jo-jo me-no* the date would be equivalent to an address. The form is a dative-locative plural.

The question must now be faced whether any entry contains two separate recipients, that is, excluding plurals or duals such as *te-o-i*. It should be observed that the copula *-qe* is never added to the words under discussion, though it is used with an epithet describing the oil (*wo-do-we-qe* 1223.2, where the preceding word is lost). On the other hand asyndeton occurs in *pa-ko-we e-ti-we* (1224). The reason for admitting two recipients is that it permits an attractive solution of *wa-na-so-i* as dative dual *wanassoiïn* 'to the two queens'. Although there is no evidence for the form of the dative of the dual of a feminine *s*-stem, the nominative in *-o* and the analogy of *-οιιν* in *o*-stems in Homer makes the formation plausible. Against this it may be argued that

*-ky- yields Myc. z, and that *wanak-yə would thus be spelt *wa-na-za; however this difficulty may perhaps be circumvented by supposing ἄνασσα to be derived from *wanakt-yə, with the -t- of the declension of ἄναξ already apparent in Mycenaean.

But although it might be possible to regard wa-na-so-i wa-na-ka-te as 'for the two Queens [and] the King', it is clearly simpler to regard wa-na-so-i as the address, a locative plural indicating the name of the shrine or locality. This explanation would then apply equally to di-pi-si-jo-i, which is parallel to it. And we can now explain wa-na-se-wi-jo and di-pi-si-je-wi-jo as adjectival forms derived from the place names. Their form, with a suffix -e-wi-jo, is surprising, but it is common enough in later Greek, where -ηϊος, which began with stems in -εύς (e.g. βασιλεύς, βασιλήϊος), was freely extended to other stems (e.g. πολεμήϊος). It is noticeable that wa-na-so-i and wa-na-se-wi-jo, as di-pi-si-jo-i and di-pi-si-je-wi-jo, are mutually exclusive alternatives, and may thus have the same semantic value.

Whether these words have Greek etymologies is another question. The variant spelling wa-no-so-i (1219) may be a mere error; but if not, it could point to a non-Greek name of the type Wa(r)nas(s)os (cf. Καρνασός, Παρνασ(σ)ός, Λαρνασσός). The obvious interpretation of di-pi-si-jo-i as dipsioihi (=διψίοις) has given rise to the ingenious theory that the thirsty ones are the dead who require drink-offerings; but these would hardly be appeased with perfumed oil. Adrados (1968) has drawn attention to the Thessalian month name Δίψιος and insists rightly that this must reflect a cult title; he suspects a goddess *Διψία, perhaps a name for the Earth. But it is not clear why he makes di-pi-si-jo-i masculine 'the priests of Dipsia'; it might equally refer to a place or a festival connected with her. It is most improbable that the spelling -jo-i can represent a nominative plural.

Finally we must attempt to assign the other terms to appropriate categories. re-ke-to-ro-te-ri-jo (343) is associated with Poseidon, the variant re-ke-e-to-ro-te-ri-jo (1217) with the address Pa-ki-jānes. Since Poseidon has another address (wa-no-so-i 1219), this term must serve to indicate the place and may be the name of his shrine at Pa-ki-jānes, since he has a festival there (1224). The Homeric phrase στορέσαι λέχος (Il. IX, 621, 660) 'to make a bed' strongly supports an interpretation lekhe-strōtērion (Bennett, 1958a, p. 31), but in what sense it is to be taken is not clear. Palmer (1963a, p. 251) takes it as the name of a festival and refers it to the ἱερὸς γάμος; but it might refer also to a divine banquet, where food is offered to the images of the gods reclining at table. The variant spelling has been variously explained; Palmer (loc. cit.) and Lejeune (1961b, p. 419) propose to treat it as a contact form rather than a true compound, Palmer finding in it a dual *lekhe(h)e*, Lejeune a dative *lekhe(h)ei*. Alternatively the intrusive *-e-* may be explained away as *en* or *es* (from *ex*) attached to the second member of the compound. Neither of these solutions is convincing, and the origin of the longer form must remain obscure.

The form *to-no-e-ke-te-ri-jo* (1222) is similar in structure, and serves to indicate the recipient of the offering, possibly by reference to a festival, since the place is already indicated by *wa-na-so-i*. Possible etymological explanations are discussed below.

The word *po-ro-wi-to* occurs on two, possibly three, tablets (1221, 1232; 1218?). It is not likely to be a description of oil, and it is associated with *wa-na-se-wi-ja* and *di-pi-si-jo-i* which we have analysed as indications of address. It seems therefore that it must be either a recipient or an indication of date. The second explanation has been favoured by the occurrence of its genitive, *po-ro-wi-to-jo*, at the head of PY **172**=Tn 316. If it is really a month-name, it is tiresome that the word *me-no* does not occur with it (as with *pa-ki-ja-ni-jo-jo* **309**=Fr 1224); the etymological explanation *Plōwistos* 'the month of sailing' is plausible. But the suspicion must remain that it is really the name of a person or deity to whom the offering is made.

Similar considerations apply to *me-tu-wo ne-wo* (perhaps to be read as one word) in Fr 1202. Here the recipient is plainly given, so it must be either an address or a date. Etymological interpretation leads to μέθυ, but if this is genitive μέθυος, then *ne-wo* must presumably be a short genitive in *-o* (see p. 475), since a plural *methuōn newōn* is hardly likely.

Finally we can approach the question of the identity of the recipients. Poseidon and Potnia (with her various epithets) are divine; so is *Mātēr theiā* 'the Divine Mother' (=Mother of the Gods?). *Trishērōs* is among the recipients of offerings on **172**=Tn 316, so must presumably be a deity (perhaps a demi-god). This establishes a strong case for taking *Wanax* 'the King' as a cult-title of a deity rather than the human king of Pylos; the fact that he has an address other than Pylos would have been sufficient indication that the human king was not meant. Hence we may be encouraged to take *a-pi-qo-ro-i*= *Amphiqʷoloihi* (Fr 1205) as here the title of some group of attendant deities, rather than the human palace servants listed on Aa 804 (cf. **11**=Ad 690).

The word *e-re-de* (1228) looks at first sight like a place name with allative *-de*, but it is hard to suggest a form for an accusative which would end in *-e* in Mycenaean script. To suppose *e*-grade of an *s*-stem, *Heles* (Palmer 1963a, p. 247), seems arbitrary. Lejeune's suggestion of a form in *-ēn*, answering to the similar Arcadian forms from stems in - εύς (e.g. hιερέν), seems equally doubtful. The form recurs together with *ma-se-de* on Mn 1411, a fragment; no other place names are found with -*de* in the *Mn* series. It does not seem impossible that it is really dative singular from a stem in -*d*-, but a final decision must depend upon more information.

305 = Fr 1184

^{1} *ko-ka-ro   a-pe-do-ke   e-ra$_3$-wo   to-so*
^{2} *e-u-me-de-i*   OIL + WE   18
^{3} *pa-ro   i-pe-se-wa   ka-ra-re-we*   38

Kokalos contributed so much olive oil to Eumedes: 518·4 l. of oil. From Ipsewas, thirty-eight oil-jars.

ko-ka-ro: *Kōkalos* (the name of the mythical king of Sicily) is named as *a-re-po-zo-o* = *aleipho-zohos* 'unguent-boiler' in Fg 374.

a-pe-do-ke: the only example of a verb in a past tense exhibiting the augment so far found in Mycenaean: contrast *a-pu-do-ke* KN Od 681. It has been suggested that this form is to be interpreted as *ap-es-doke* with *es* < *ex* = ἀπεκδῶκε, but this is probably unnecessary.

e-u-me-de-i: Eumedes is known from Ea 812 and Ea 820 to be another 'unguent-boiler'.

ka-ra-re-we: on KN K 778 this word describes a two-handled jar with a spout, the so-called 'stirrup-jar' regularly used for oil. The form is uncertain, but the gloss χλαρόν· ἐλαιηρὸς κώθων (Hesych.) suggests a derivative in -ευς: *khlārēwes*: see p. 494.

The relationship between the two entries on this tablet seems to have been misunderstood by those who are anxious to prove that *pa-ro* has locatival rather that ablatival force. It is impossible to construe *ka-ra-re-we* as accusative after *apedōke*, nor is it probable that on the same tablet oil would be both measured in units and by the jar. Thus the second entry must record, with inconsequential syntax, the issue to Eumedes of the jars necessary to contain the eighteen units of oil he is receiving from Kokalos. This in turn allows us to calculate the average volume of a stirrup-jar in terms of Mycenaean measures, namely ◁ 8½ or 13·7 l. on the revised values proposed (see p. 394).

306 = Fr 1202

me-tu-wo   ne-wo   ma-te-re   te-i-ja ‘*pa-ko-we*’ OIL + PA 5 ⫫ 1 ‘◁ 4’.
To the Divine Mother at M . . ., sage-scented oil: 160 l.

me-tu-wo ne-wo: see above, p. 480.
ma-te-re te-i-ja: *mātrei* is preferable to *māterei*, but the form is ambiguous; *theïjāi* = θείᾳ.
pa-ko-we: *sphakowen*, see above.
The quantity is surprisingly large but a similar amount occurs in 1206 and rather more than half this on 1208.

307 = Fr 1220

¹ *ro-u-si-jo*   *a-ko-ro*   *pa-ko-we*   OIL + PA   ◁ 4
² *di-pi-si-jo-i*   *wa-na-ka-te*   OIL + PA   ⚲ I

For the Lusian territory, sage-scented oil: 6·4 l.
For the King at *Dipsioi*, sage-scented oil: 9·6 l.

ro-u-si-jo   *a-ko-ro*: *Lousiōi agrōi* if dative, but possibly to be taken as locative; cf. **252** =
    PY Vn 10.4.
di-pi-si-jo-i: in form probably *Dipsioihi*, equivalent to the adjective δίψιος, but serving
    as an address.

308 = Fr 1222

wa-na-so-i   *to-no-e-ke-te-ri-jo*   'OIL + PA   ◁ I'

For the *holding of the throne* at W.; sage-scented oil: 1·6 l.

wa-na-so-i: an address, see above, p. 479.
to-no-e-ke-te-ri-jo: many interpretations of this word have been attempted. It seems most
    plausible to take *to-no-* as *thorno-* = θρονο- as in the furniture tablets (**242–244**); cf.
    lekhe- in the parallel compound *re-ke-(e)-to-ro-te-ri-jo*, Fr 343, Fr 1217. The second
    member is then perhaps *hektērion* (ἔχω), but *helktērion* (ἕλκω) cannot be excluded.
    Palmer's *stonoegertērion* 'the raising of the lamentation' (1963 a, p. 252) is exceedingly
    ingenious and might conceivably be right. But it may perhaps be a shrine rather
    than a festival.

309 = Fr 1224

           pa-ko-we   *e-ti-we*
pa-ki-ja-ni-jo-jo   *me-no*   *po-se-da-o-ne*   OIL + PA   ▽ 2

In the month *Pakijanios*, for Poseidon: sage- and . . .-scented oil: 0·8 l.

e-ti-we: see Glossary.

310 = Fr 1225

¹ *e-ra₃-wo*   *u-po-jo*   *po-ti-ni-ja*
² *we-a₂-no-i*   *a-ro-pa*   OIL + A   ⚲ I

Olive oil for the Mistress of *Hyp* . . ., ointment for robes: 9·6 l. oil.

u-po-jo   *po-ti-ni-ja*: also mentioned at Fn 187.8, where she receives barley and figs,
    and at Fr 1236, which locates her in the territory of *Pa-ki-ja-ne*.
we-a₂-no-i: *wehanoihi* = ἑανοῖς 'for robes' (cf. Skt. *vasanam*).
a-ro-pa: *aloiphā* 'ointment'.

311 = Fr 1226

ro-u-si-jo   a-ko-ro   te-o-i   pa-ko-we   OIL + PA   ⊲ 3[

For the Lusian territory, for the deities: sage-scented oil, 4·8(+ ?) l.

te-o-i: their names are not specified, but the address will have made their identity clear.
Cf., however, Fr 1355 *te-o-i   a-ro-pa   pu-*[.

6. MISCELLANEOUS OFFERINGS AT PYLOS

A few new and improved texts can be added here as further evidence for Mycenaean religion. The first is interesting for the repetition of some of the names found on **91 = Fn 50**, and the implication that the owners of the slaves there are probably priests or religious functionaries of some sort.

312 = An 1281

1 *po-]ti-ni-ja   i-qe-ja*
2 *?do-so]-mo   o-pi-e̯-de-i*
3 *a-ka   re-u-si-wo-qe*   MAN 2
4 *au-ke-i-ja-te-we*   ⟦*i-qe̯-ja̯*   M̥ḀN̥⟧
5 *o-na-se-u   ta-ni-ko-qe*   MAN 2
6 *me-ta-ka-wa   po̯-so-ro*   MAN 1
7 *mi-jo-qa*[   ]*e-we-za-no*   MAN 1
8 *a-pi̯-e-ra̯   to-ze-u*   MAN 1
9 *po-ti]-a-ke-s̯i̯   po-ti-ni-ja   re-si-wo*   MAN 1
10 *au-ke-i-ja̯-te̯-we̯*[   ]*ro*   MAN 1
11 *mi-jo-qa   ma-ra-si-jo*[   ]   MAN 1
12 *me-ta-ka-wa   ti-ta-ra-*[   ]   MAN 1
13 *a-pi-e-ra   r̯u̯-k̯o̯-ro*   MAN 1
14-16   v a c a n t

For the Mistress of Horses, [contribution] *at the shrine*: A. and R.: 2 men
For *Augeiateus*: O. and T.: 2 men
For *Metakawa*: P.: 1 man
For *Mioqᵘa*: . . . 1 man
For *Amphiera*: T.: 1 man
For the Mistress at . . .: R.: 1 man
      etc.

po-ti-ni-ja   i-qe-ja: *Potniāi hiqqᵘeiāi* = ἱππείᾳ. This seems the obvious interpretation of the adjective, and Palmer (1966, p. 276) has collected the evidence for a horse-deity worshipped in the Peloponnese in classical times.

do-so]-mo: the restoration is suggested by the formula of the *Es* tablets (**168–170**).

o-pi-e̯-de-i: originally read *o-pi-ke-de-i*, but this appears to be due to a correction of *o-pi-de-*. The unelided *i* of *opi* suggests the presence of *h*; cf. *o-pi-a₂-ra* **56** = An 656.1. Perhaps therefore to be taken as two words, the preposition *opi* and the dative *hede(h)i* of ἕδος 'seat' (especially of a deity), 'shrine'.

po-ti]-*a-ke-s̩i̩*: there is some support for the reading *ti* before *a* which suggests comparison with the place name *po-ti-ja-ke-e* An 298.2. If the last sign is really *-si*, this will presumably be locative-dative of a plural form. It is put here to distinguish this household of the Mistress from that where she bears the form of a horse. It should be noted that the four names are repeated at this place.

313 = Un 6

   [Broken at the top]

1 *po-se-d̩a̩*[*-o-ne*

2   v a c a t

3 *pe-re-*82* COW I EWE I PIG + KA I SOW I

4 *pe-re-*82* COW I EWE I PIG + KA I SOW I

5   v a c a t

6 *146* 37 *1̩6̩6̩*[   ]WOOL 5

7 A + RE + PA ⚲ I ◁ I[

8 OX 2   COW 2   S̩H̩E̩E̩P̩[

Reverse:

2   ]*i-je-re-ja* CLOTH + T̩E̩[

3 *ka-*]*ra-wi-po-ro* CLOTH + TE[

The addition of two pieces (1189, 1250) has shown that this is a fragment of an interesting text. The reading *po-se-da*[*-o-ne* = *Poseidāōnei* is confirmed by a deleted text still readable underneath the present one. *Pe-re-*82* is the deity who receives offerings on **172** = Tn 316.rev.5; see p. 463. PIG + KA recurs on Un 853.5, again distinguished from SOW, so presumably male; it seems obvious that KA stands for κάπρος 'boar', but probably not the wild boar. The ideogram *146* (= *A* in the table on p. 290) is probably a textile. A + RE + PA is a ligature of three syllabic signs in descending order, found also in **171** = Un 718.8, = *aleiphar* 'unguent'.

On the reverse the two words legible are *i-je-re-ja* 'priestess' and [*ka*]-*ra-wi-po-ro* 'key-bearer', the religious title found on **135** = Ep 704, etc.

Excavations of the north-east wing of the Palace in 1957 yielded a new series of tablets, now given the prefix *Qa*. They are all single-line tablets characterized by the ideogram *189*, a rectangular frame in which is inscribed the syllabic sign KE. Judging by analogies, *ke-* is likely to be the first syllable of the Mycenaean name for the object listed. The   189 ⊞ numbers of this object vary from I (at least eight times) to 5.

Possibly some kind of textile (a ceremonial robe?) is meant. The formula consists of a personal name (*a-pi-a₂-ro* Qa 1297), or a personal name and a place (e.g. *a-te-ra-wo   ka-ra-do-ro* Qa 1304), or a personal name and title (e.g. *ka-wa-ra   i-je-re-ja* **314**=Qa 1289) or a title and a place name (e.g. *i-je-re-u   se-ri-no-wo-t̬e* Qa 1290 'the priest at S.'). In this it resembles the variations to be seen among the entries of **258**=Jo 438. But the titles here appear to be religious; three tablets refer to a priest or priestess (Qa 1290, 1296, 1300; cf. 1303?), and one to a man 'of the Mistress' (*potniāwios* **316**= Qa 1299). This may lead us to suspect that *po-qa-te-u* (Qa 1295) is *phoigʷasteus* (φοιβάζω) 'prophet' or 'ritual purifer'.

Of the personal names *a-pi-a₂-ro*=*Amphihalos* stands alone on **304**=On 300.2, and is known also as a land-holder. [*E*]-*ke-ri-ja-wo* and *me-nu-a₂* recur on **55**=An 724, but since the latter occurs on two *Qa* tablets (1293, 1301), it is perhaps a title rather than a name. *Ne-qe-u e-da-e-u* reappears as a land-holder Eb 496, cf. **148**=Ep 613.1. Thus the names listed here are all persons of consequence.

314=Qa 1289
*ka-wa-ra   i-je-re-ja   *189[

The priestess K . . .

315=Qa 1296
*a-o-ri-me-ne   i-je-re-u   *189 [

The priest Ahorimenēs . . .

316=Qa 1299
*ka-e-se-u   po-ti-ni-ja-wi-jo   *189 I
K., the man of the Mistress: one . . .

The name *Ka-e-se-u* recurs at Mycenae **105**=Ge 602. The usual form of adjective from *Potnia* is *po-ti-ni-ja-we-jo*, an equally obscure formation.

485

CHAPTER X

TEXTILES, VESSELS AND FURNITURE

p. 313† Later work on the subject of textiles has not rendered this account obsolete, and it is only necessary to add a few general comments. The use of the CLOTH ideogram with the same surcharged signs (KU and ZO) in both Linear A and Linear B has led to some confusion, and this has even been claimed as evidence that neither is Greek. The truth is simpler. The words used to describe special kinds of cloth are particularly liable to be borrowed and are often geographical in origin; one has only to think of such English words as *cashmere*, *crêpe de chine*, *calico*, *cambric*. Thus it would be inevitable that the Greeks established in Crete would continue the production of Minoan textiles and would perpetuate the Minoan names in a hellenized form. With the loss of Minoan crafts in the post-Mycenaean period, these loan-words too would disappear from the Greek language, and this explains why we can interpret so few of the technical terms used on these tablets. KU and ZO are doubtless abbreviations of Minoan words for particular fabrics which were borrowed into Mycenaean Greek.

These tablets are the subject of a special study by J. T. Killen (forthcoming). He interprets the *Lc* type as records of the manufacture of textiles by groups of women working at various places in Crete; these tablets are closely connected with some of the *Ak* tablets (see pp. 163–4), which were written by the same scribe and found in the same part of the Palace. The picture which emerges is of small industrial establishments in different parts of the island, but all closely controlled by Knossos. On the other hand, the textile industry at Pylos seems to be largely concentrated in the capital with only a few outlying workshops.

p. 315† **209** = Lc 525. Corrections: l. 1 CLOTH³ + TE   40   WOOL 100[

p. 316† **211** = Lc 532 + 554. Corrections: l. 1 WOOL 26 ⟨ 1[; l. 2 CLOTH + TE 4 WOOL 28[.

ko-u-ra: now found also at Mycenae as epithet to *pa-we-a₂* L 710.2.

p. 317† **213** = Le 641

o-a-po-te: Killen has shown that in Od 562.3 *a-po-te pe-re*, *a-po-te* must be a man's name. This leaves the interpretation of *a-re-i-jo* obscure, since if it is, as at Pylos, a patronymic adjective, its separation from the verb is remarkable.

·· 317‡ **214** = Ld 571. It now appears that the difference between Ld 571 and Ld 572 is only in the number of strokes in the 'fringe' of the CLOTH ideogram; Ld 572 has only two. In any case it is difficult to believe that one of these tablets is not intended to replace the other.

re-u-ko-nu-ka: it can now be added that the nominative singular *o-nu* appears to stand on Od 681, again in the context of wool. There seems little doubt that this is the same word as ὄνυξ, but it has some technical meaning here. On the edge of Ln 1568 the reading has been changed to: *o-pi ma-tu-we...o-pi po-ni-ke-ja*[and Killen has shown that *o-pi* is the preposition *opi* in the sense 'in the workshop of', 'chez'.

pe-ne-we-ta: the rules of word-formation in Mycenaean exclude possibility of derivation from an *o*-stem; the root of this adjective must therefore be either a neuter *s*-stem (see Palmer, 1963*a*, p. 293) or a consonant stem. Perhaps therefore *sphēn-wenta* from σφήν 'wedge'; this might refer to tapering shape, but more likely describes some kind of decoration.

·· 318† **215** = Ld 573. The join of Ld 649 with 8169 has completed this word as *ke-se-ne-wi-ja*, which violates the ordinary rule that -*nw*- is spelt with *n*+the vowel of the following syllable or *u*. It is here a reflexion of the vowel of the preceding syllable. The expected spelling *ke-se-ni-wi-jo* is now found on PY Fr 1231.

·· 319† **217** = Ld 587+589+596+8262. Correction: l. 1 add *to-sa* before *po-ki-ro-nu-ka*. Edge: a lacuna before]*to-sa* may explain the significance of the number. Killen and Olivier (1968, p. 119) have shown that this tablet is the totalling document for tablets such as **218** = Ld 598.

·· 319‡ **218** = Ld 598+661. Corrections: l. 1 *wi-jo-qo-ta-o*; l. 2 *re-u-ko-nu-ka*.

wi-jo-qo-ta-o: gen. of man's name, also found as that of a shepherd Db 1305.

·· 320† **221** = L 647

nu-wa-ja: the variant spelling *nu-wa-i-ja* is found on L 592 (+663), followed by *pa-we-a*, and on L 5910+5920.1.]*e-ni-qe nu-wa-i-ja* [above a CLOTH entry similar to the second in l. 1 of this tablet. It seems likely to be an adjective, but there is no plausible identification in Greek.

e-ni-qe: all the extant examples are or may be introducing a second adjective describing a number of textiles. It is therefore possible to interpret it as *eni qᵘe* (=ἔνεστί τε) 'and there are among them'; cf. *tosoide telestai enehensi* PY **114** = En 609.2. Note especially L 593+5992+8587: [*ko*]-*pu-ra e-ni-qe pe-ne-we-ta *161* CLOTH¹ 4.

·· 320‡ **222** = L 693. There has been no confirmation of the idea that the BRONZE figures here represent value; it would seem more likely that the bronze is actually used in making the tunic—perhaps more accurately described as a piece of armour. Similarly the *epikhitōnia* will be bronze plates fitted on to the tunic; cf. *e-pi-ko-ru-si-jo* 'fittings on the helmet' **299** = Sk 789. In Xe 537 the correct reading is probably *o-pi i-ta-ja*.

p. 321† **224** = L 474. Palmer (1963a, p. 297) is wrong in suggesting that, because in some cloth tablets this place is occupied by a description of women, *po-pu-re-ja* must here too be one = 'purple-dyers'. The parallel of **223** = L 471 (in the same hand) shows that an adjective of colour is required.

p. 321‡ **225** = L 520. It is clear that *do-ti-ja* is a place name and that *sa-mu-ta-jo* is a man's name. It is therefore likely that *ka-ma* is here not the same word as at Pylos but a man's name; and this leads to the suggestion that *pe-re-ke*, although displaced, is another, rather than a verb connecting the two entries. The apocopated form περ has not been proved in Mycenaean, and the only likely verb would be πλέκει 'plaits' for which there is no subject.

p. 322† **226** = Oe 129. Correction: for *di-ke* read *di-du-mo*, man's name: *Didumōi*.

Parallel to *tu-ka-te-re* is the new reading *tu-ka-ṭa-ṣị* Oe 112.2, which, if correct, must be dative plural *thugatarsi* < *-r̥si*.

p. 322‡ **227** = Oe 127

e-we-pe-se-so-me-na: our interpretation is rejected by Palmer (1963a, p. 421) on the grounds that it is one word; but does he read Homeric ἐϋκτίμενον *divisim*? His own εὐ- = ἐπι- is suspicious since it occurs only in glosses, and the very existence of Cypriot ὐ- has been questioned (Scherer, 1959, p. 173), though this may be excessive caution. Palmer would also connect the verb with ἕπω 'attend to', but does not explain the formation which is correct for the future of ἕψω. In either case the sense required seems to be passive, thus confirming the absence of the element -θη- from Mycenaean passive forms; cf. *ze-so-me-no* 'to be boiled' PY **103** = Un 267.4. A possible explanation of the need for boiling may be the process employed to remove the natural grease of the wool, which is sometimes retained during weaving. Beekes (1969, p. 67) conjectures a verb **ewephō* corresponding, with prothetic ἐ-, to O.H.G. *weban*, Eng. *weave*, later replaced by ὑφαίνω. The correlation of *pa-we-a₂* with WOOL instead of CLOTH is puzzling; it is hard to believe that this is wool for the making of cloths, unless *e-we-pe-se-so-me-na* can refer to fabrication rather than treatment. Possibly the explanation is that the quantity of cloth was measured by weight rather than by counting; hence the translation should read '60 kg of woollen cloaks...'.

p. 322¶ **228** = Oe 111. Corrections: l. 2: *wo-ro-ne-ja*   *pa-we-si* / [.]-me-ˋjo-iˊ   WOOL[; l. 3 end WOOL[;   l. 4]-ṭa₂-ni-*56.

o-u-ka: the best hypothesis is Palmer's (1963a, p. 439) who would see in this word *owika*, adj. of ὄϜις 'sheep'. This view is accepted, with some hesitation, by Chantraine (1966, p. 177). The objection to the meaning is avoided if *wo-ro-ne-ja* means 'lamb's', though this does not explain *o-u-ko* in Oe 108 and 120. The use of *-u-j-* alternating with *-wi-j-* in *di-u-ja/di-wi-ja*, etc. (Chantraine, loc. cit.), is not really a parallel, and we need further evidence to resolve this problem.

wo-ro-ne-ja: best taken as *wroneia*, a metathesis of *worneia*, adj. from ῥήν 'lamb', the original genitive of which was probably ἀρνός (i.e. Ϝρήν, Ϝαρνός). For the treatment of *ṛ > ro*, cf. *qe-to-ro-*.

pa-we-si: not *pa-we-si-jo* as read earlier, = *pharwes(s)i*, with an adj. in agreement.

]-ṭa₂-ni-*56: Olivier (1969) suggests *]jọ-ṭa₂-ni-*56* as a possible reading; if the last sign is really *-ja*, this would recall *e-pi-jo-ta-na* PY Aa 95 = *e-pi-ja-ta-ni-ja* Ad 687, a place name.

. 323† The meagre records with the ideograms CLOTH or WOOL still do not include a single complete tablet. But such evidence as there is agrees with the corresponding documents from Knossos and Mycenae. New finds show that CLOTH + PU occurred here too (La 1394), and La 1393 has a broken first line which might be restored, e.g., *o-de-ka-]ṣạ-to a-ri-wo ta-ra-[si-ja*, or *o-da-]ṣạ-to* (cf. Wa 917) would do equally well.

Growing conviction that **146* is a textile suggests that the new Pylos *Mb* series should be mentioned here. Few tablets are complete, but some seem to have nothing but a place name followed by **146* and a number: e.g. Mb 1396 *a-pi-no-e-wi-jo *146* 2. Other tablets apparently have personal names. The new fragments of *Mn* tablets are similar; they appear to list the same commodity under place names and persons.

· 323‡

3A. LEATHER GOODS AT PYLOS

The use of leather was earlier inferred from the word *di-pte-ra-po-ro*, but new finds from the north-east wing at Pylos in 1957 provided evidence of the leather goods which could in any case be presumed to exist. Cf. also the new tablet **323** = Sb 1315 dealing with chariot-harness, no doubt also of leather.

It is clear that the first tablet is a record of the issue of skins, mainly tanned leather, but some of rawhide (see below). The objects which are to be made from them are specified, either in apposition (nominative) or in the dative of purpose; occasionally a dependent genitive is found (e.g. *pe-di-ro* l. 5). The persons named are therefore likely to be leather-workers, and it is interesting that they include women as well as men. It is likely that the men are the *rhaptēres* mentioned elsewhere, and thus the feminine *rhaptriai* also may refer to women who sew leather rather than cloth; see on **323** = Sb 1315.

Many of the technical terms are as yet unsolved, but the general sense of the tablet is clear. A few items seem to be of other materials if correctly interpreted.

317 = Ub 1318. The central section of this tablet was not recovered until 1964 (Lang, 1965). There is a detailed study also by Ruijgh (1966).

1 *au-ke-i-ja-te-we   ka-tu-re-ẉi-ja-i   di-pte-ra* 4

   [. . . .]*dị-pte-ra* 2

   au-ke-i-ja-te-we   o-ka   di-pte-ṛạ[

2 *au-ke-i-ja-te-we   o-pi-de-so-mo   ka-tu-ro₂   di-pte-ra* 4

   ka-ne-ja   wo-ro-ma-ta 4

3 *me-ti-ja-no   to-pa   ru-de-a₂   dị-pte-ra* 1

   a-re-se-si   e-ru-ta-ra   di-pte-ṛạ 3

   wo-di-je-ja   pe-di-ra 2

4 *we-e-wi-ja   di-pte-ra* 10

   wi-ri-no   we-ru-ma-ta   ti-ri-sị   ze-u-ke-si 1

5 *wi-ri-no   pe-di-ro   e-ma-ta* 4

   e-ra-pe-ja   e-pi-u-ru-te-we   E 2

6 *a-pe-i-ja   u-po   ka-ro   we-*[   ]*-ja* 1

   u-po   we-e-wi-ja   e-ra-pe-ja   E 1

7 *mu-te-we   we-re-ne-ja   ku*[   ]*pe-re* 1

   mu-te-we   di-pte-ra   a₃-za   pe-di-ro-i 1

8-10   v a c a n t

1 For Augeiateus: four skins for saddle-bags.
   For . . . (?):   two skins.
   For Augeiateus: . . . skins (as) *straps*.
2 For Augeiateus: four skins (as) bindings of pack-saddles;
                      four *panniers* of basketry.
3 Mestianor: one skin (as) fastenings of a hamper;
                      three red skins for . . .
4 (For) Wordieia: two (skins as) sandals;
                      ten pig's skins;
                      one hide (as) wrappers for three pairs (of sandals?);
5   four hides (as) laces of sandals;
                      two deer skins (as) . . .
6 (For) Amphehia: one *pig's skin* with *fringes* underneath;
                      one deer skin with *pig's skin* underneath.
7 For Myrteus: one sheep's (skin?) . . .
   For Myrteus: one goat's skin for sandals.

It is immediately apparent that some of the entries begin with personal names (e.g. *au-ke-i-ja-te-we* **312** = An 1281.4.; *me-ti-ja-no-ro* Vn 1191.1, associated with *wo-di-je-ja*). Hence *a-pe-i-ja* and *mu-te-we* are also likely to be names.

490

Some are plainly in the dative, but *me-ti-ja-no* is nominative if a name in *-ānōr*, as Vn 1191 suggests; probably this is mere scribal inconsistency. On the other hand some entries do not begin with names, so we must assume that the previous name serves as heading until cancelled by the next. The entries are mainly hides (*diphtherai*) of various animals, and articles made of leather.

ka-tu-re-wi̯-ja-i; cf. *ka-tu-ro₂* in line 2, *ka-tu-re-wi̯*[KN X 1047.2. Miss Lang saw that these words could be associated with κανθύλη 'swelling', κανθήλια 'panniers for pack-animals', etc. The group is well discussed by Ruijgh (loc. cit.). The form here probably represents *kanthulēwiāhi* dative plural of a feminine derived from the adjective in *-ēwios*; the meaning is therefore likely to be 'saddle-bags'.

o-ka: there is no reason why this should be the same word as designates a command on **56–60**. Ruijgh suggests *holkāi* 'for pulling'; but perhaps *okhai* (ἔχω) 'supports', 'straps' would be possible.

o-pi-de-so-mo: *opidesmoi*, cf. ἐπίδεσμος used by medical writers to mean 'bandage'.

ka-tu-ro₂: *kanthuliōn*? 'pack-saddles'?

ka-ne-ja: the most likely suggestion is *kaneia* 'made of basketry', the adjective which survived into classical Greek only as a substantive κάνεον 'basket'. Κάννα is Semitic (Assyr. *ḳanū* 'reed').

wo-ro-ma-ta: *wlōmata* = λώματα, a word only attested in Hellenistic Greek and meaning 'a fringe on a garment'. But since it is probably derived from the root **wel-* 'roll' (cf. εἰλέω, ἴλλω, etc.), it might here have some such sense as 'container', perhaps the panniers for use with the preceding straps and bindings on pack-saddles.

me-ti-ja-no: man's name, *Mestiānōr* (Ruijgh), possibly *Mētiānōr* (= *Mēsi-*, cf. Μησιάναξ).

to-pa   ru-de-a₂: it has generally been assumed that one of these is a substantive, the other an adjective in agreement; but parallel phrases, like *opidesmoi kanthuliōn* above, suggest that they might both be substantives. *Ru-de-a₂* = …*eha* has the appearance of the plural of a neuter in *-os* (cf. *pa-we-a₂* = *pharweha*). But there is no suitable identification known in later Greek. For *to-pa* Palmer (1963 *a*, p. 459) suggested *stoibā* 'cushion'; Ruijgh a dative **storphāi* 'consolidation'. But it is not impossible that *o* here represents *r̥* and we could interpret the spelling as *torpā* = τάρπη 'large basket', 'hamper'. Since one hide could not make a hamper, it must be the other noun which describes the leather articles, and *to-pa* will be genitive *torpās*. Perhaps therefore the *ru-de-a₂* are straps, hinges or fastenings, such as are often made of leather to attach lids to hampers, or for strengthening.

a-re-se-si: obviously dative plural, but no satisfactory suggestion has been made for this word. They are made of red leather and three hides are allocated for them. Fragments of red leather were recovered from a Mycenaean tomb at Kazarma (Protonotariou-Deïlaki, 1969, p. 4).

wo-di-je-ja: the woman who is described as 'of Mestianor' on Vn 1191, his wife or his slave? Perhaps husband and wife worked together on leather goods. *Pe-di-ra* (cf. *pe-di-ro* line 5) is plainly πέδϊλα 'sandals', if the word should not be given the more general sense 'footwear'; but the entry is cryptic, since 'two' can hardly mean 'a pair' as this would demand a dual. More likely the sandals are the objects to be made, and we must understand *diphtherō* (dual) with the numeral.

we-e-wi-ja: the proposed rule (Chadwick, 1958*b*, p. 308) that initial *we-* preceding a vowel may represent a Greek ὑ- has not been generally accepted. Yet this is a highly convincing example. In the latter part of this tablet the animals from which the hides are taken are specified as deer, sheep and goats. If we assume that oxen are meant when no animal is specified, then the animal known to have been reared at Pylos which is missing from the list is the pig. The difficulty is that ὕειος would appear to contain the normal -ειος ending of adjectives of material, and *-e-wi-ja* presumably implies -ήϝιος. The extension of this type, based upon stems in -εύς, e.g. *qa-si-re-wi-ja* = *gʷasilēwiā* (βασιλεύς), *i-je-re-wi-jo* = *hierēwios* (ἱερεύς), is well attested for Homer, e.g. πολεμήιος, where there is no known *πολεμεύς, and must be presumed to be Mycenaean also: cf. *ro-u-si-je-wi-ja* (*ro-u-so*), *di-pi-si-je-wi-jo* (*di-pi-si-jo-i*), *wa-na-se-wi-jo* (*wa-na-so-i*). Thus, remarkable as it may seem, *we-e-wi-ja* may represent *huēwiai* 'pig's', and classical ὕειος could also continue that form. The spelling *we-e-wi-ja* recurs at Knossos (As 1518 + 1529) in an obscure context.

wi-ri-no: the contrast between *wrinos* = ῥινός and *diphthera* = διφθέρα is puzzling at first sight. Ῥινός is often used of ox-hide, but if *diphthera* is the skin of other animals, this does not explain the entries at the beginning of this text where no animal is specified. Etymology and classical usage both suggest that διφθέρα (cf. δέψω) refers to the tanned hide, ῥινός to the raw hide. Homer even uses ῥινός of the skin of a living person (*Il.* v, 308, *Od.* v, 426).

we-ru-ma-ta ti-ri-ṣi ze-u-ke-si: the interpretation of the first word must depend upon the others, and we must not lose sight of the fact that only one hide is used. *Ti-ri-ṣi* can hardly be anything but *trisi*, dat. of τρεῖς 'three'. Ruijgh, questioning the reading of the last sign, doubts the existence of the classical form with intervocalic -σ- already restored in Mycenaean; but since the starting point of the spread of these forms must be the consonant stems (e.g. *pa-si* = *pansi*), and they had already reached the stems in -εύς (*ka-ke-u-si* = *khalkeusi*), their extension to all third declension nouns is not unexpected, although they had not yet affected the o- and a-stems. *Ze-u-ke-si* is dative plural of ζεῦγος, the word regularly abbreviated as ΖE: *dzeuge(s)si*. But is the meaning 'pair' or specifically 'a yoke of oxen'? It is hard to think what could be made out of one hide which would constitute something for three yokes. This is a decisive objection to Ruijgh's *werumata* (ἐρύω) 'bridles'. But his objection to the more attractive *welūmata* (εἴλυμα *Od.* vi, 179) 'wrappers' disappears once we rid ourselves of the notion that ζεῦγος means a yoke of oxen. Since sandals are mentioned just above and immediately afterwards, is it impossible that these are the pairs meant?

e-ma-ta: the reading was originally published as *e-*[. .]-*ta*, which effectively misled interpreters. *Hermata* = ἕρματα, used in Homer (*Il.* xiv, 181; *Od.* xviii, 297) to mean 'earrings', is a derivative of εἴρω and ought to be treated separately from ἕρμα 'support'. The etymological sense 'that which is strung or fastened' suggests that it means here the 'laces' used to secure sandals to the foot, often reaching well up the calf.

e-ra-pe-ja: apparently only a variation on *e-ra-pi-ja* Ub 1316, *elapheiai* (*sc. diphtherai*), and the same word is represented by the abbreviation E with the numeral. Surprisingly the dual is not used, perhaps because the scribe was unsure of the number when he began the entry.

e-pi-u-ru-te-we: the spelling *-u-ru-*, as in *o-u-ru-to* **56** = An 657.1, must represent *-wr-*; cf. ῥυτήρ 'that which draws', 'strap'. Hence *epiwrutēwes* is a likely form, but the meaning is more difficult; Ruijgh, comparing ἐπειρυσάμενον τὴν λεοντέην, Hdt. IV, 8, 'having spread the lion-skin upon him', suggests it may mean 'skins used as garments'. Since deer skin is used it will be something for which soft leather was needed, therefore not straps or ropes for pulling.

a-pe-i-ja: if this is really a woman's name, then the entry consists only of the word *we-[..]-ja* with a qualifying *u-po ka-ro*. It is possible that this is the word missing in line 1, where the second sign could well be *pe*. *We-[..]-ja* can be restored either as *we-re-ne-ja* (l. 7) or *we-e-wi-ja* (ll. 4, 6); the latter is epigraphically more likely.

ka-ro: of the many possible interpretations perhaps *kairos* (καῖρος) is best, meaning here a fringe hanging beneath (*hupo*) like the threads of the warp on a woven cloth.

u-po we-e-wi-ja: since *e-ra-pe-ja* is certainly a deer skin, it cannot also be a pig's skin; but the two skins might be combined in some way (e.g. a garment with the upper part of deer skin, the lower of pig's skin; or even an outer layer of deer skin, and a lining of pig's skin, though this seems less likely).

mu-te-we: presumably another personal name in the dative.

we-re-ne-ja: almost certainly another adjective describing the animal from which the skin is taken: *wrēneia* 'lamb's' (Heubeck, 1960, p. 19). If the hypothesis of an original *ϝρήν, ϝαρνός is correct, this adjective will be built on the nominative instead of the root as ἄρνειος. The greatest difficulty lies in accepting *wo-ro-ne-ja* = *wroneia* as an alternative form. Is it possible that the words were already specialized and *we-re-ne-ja* means 'of a young ram' rather than 'lamb's'? See Glossary.

a₃-za: *aidzā* < **aig-yā*, 'goat's', the expected development of an adjective in **-yos* attached to the stem αἰγ-, but replaced in classical Greek by αἴγειος to retain the appearance of the stem.

pe-di-ro-i: *pediloihi*, dative of purpose, 'for (the making of) sandals'.

326† 202. *di-pa*: some of the difficulties in the way of identifying this word with δέπας can be removed by studying the earliest examples of the word in alphabetic Greek. In *Il.* XI, 632, it is clear that this is no ordinary drinking-vessel, for we are told (ll. 636–7) that anyone but Nestor would have had difficulty in lifting it from the table when it was full. Similarly the word was later used of the golden bowl in which the sun made its return journey across the ocean during the night (Pherecydes, 18a, Jakoby).

327† 203. *qe-to*: it is possible to identify the word with πίθος if we assume that the origin is a base **gʷhedh-*, giving a Mycenaean form *qu(h?)ethos*, and that πίθος is an Aeolic word (cf. πίσυρες = τέσσερες). But this involves rejecting the connexion with Germanic words such as Icelandic *biða*; Latin *fid-elia* could still belong with πίθος. But neither the size of the vessel nor the form of the word favours the identification, and it may well be one of the numerous loan-words used for vessel-names in Greek (cf. ἀρύβαλλος, βῖκος, λέβης, λήκυθος) and this explains the confusion of Myc. *e* but classical ι, since this seems to occur only in non-Greek words (cf. *ku-te-so*, *i-pa-sa-na-ti* in Glossary; Hester, 1958).

p. 327‡ 204. *qe-ra-na*: various attempts have been made to provide this word with an etymology, such as a connexion with ($<*g^{w}her$-) 'vessel for hot-water'. Perhaps a better suggestion is *$g^{w}el$-* 'to pour in drops' (Skt. *galanam*, Gk. βαλαν-εύς, etc.). But the ending *-a-na* recalls the pre-Greek suffix of place names -ᾱνᾱ (-ηνη), and this too may be a loan-word.

p. 328† 209. *a-pi-po-re-we*: the reference to Knossos Gg (now K) 700 should be deleted. These vessels are of the spouted type described under 210, and have surcharged κα, an abbreviation of *ka-ra-re-we*. The amphora with surcharged A occurs several times in the Knossos Gg series (e.g. **204**=Gg 704).

p. 328‡ 210. *ka-ra-re-we*: the best interpretation of this word is due to Householder (1959*a*, p. 379): *khlārēwes*, based upon a gloss of Hesychius: χλαρόν· ἐλαιηρὸς κώθων. Pindar (*Pyth.* IX, 65) uses the expression χλαρὸν γελᾶν, which has caused trouble to the commentators; since it is said of a Centaur, is it impossible that it means 'to laugh like an oil-jar' (i.e. with the characteristic noise made by pouring liquid from a narrow-necked vessel)?

p. 329† **229**=K 434. Correction: l. 1 at left probably]*ṣạ* (not ı). Perhaps the end of a feminine adjective in *-we-sa*?

> *ko-no-ni-pi*: the suggestion that this means 'with cross-bars' has been criticized on archaeological grounds by Gray (1959, p. 53), but no better solution has so far been proposed.

p. 329‡ **230**=K 740. Correction: l. 6 '*me-no-ṇọ*[' (in very small signs above the line).

> *di-pa*: probably singular, with no effort to adapt the syntax to the numeral.
>
> *qe-ro*$_2$: the armour tablets (**299–300**) show clearly that this is the name of a piece of equipment, two of which make a set. In that case, no drawing accompanies the word; here the drawing somewhat resembles the CORSLET sign (no. 162), but is distinguished from it. For a discussion and photograph see Chadwick (1957*b*). This text confirms that it is used in pairs as the number is even, and tells us that it is made of bronze.
>
> There are two possible lines of interpretation. We may ignore the differences and regard the ideogram as a form of CORSLET; if so, the numeral two must refer to a

'lobster' corslet made up of two pieces, like that found at Dendra in 1960 (Vermeule, 1964, p. 135); but this had as well three flexible bands composing a kind of skirt. If this interpretation is correct, no plausible identification of *qe-ro₂* has been made, for attempts to connect the word with γύαλον are linguistically impossible.

One argument in favour of this interpretation is the fact that the CORSLET ideogram is often surcharged with syllabic QE, which could be an abbreviation of *qe-ro₂*, though this cannot be confirmed. KN Sc 266 is sometimes quoted as confirmation that QE is reckoned in pairs; but CORSLET + QE is always followed by the numeral one, and on Sc 266 the scribe wrote: CORSLET + QE 1 ZE 1, and then inserted a small *qe* as an afterthought before ZE. Analogies suggest that the correction was itself an error; he should have inserted the ideogram HORSE which always precedes ZE 1 in this series.

The alternative (see Chadwick, loc. cit.) is to follow the order of the items of equipment on the armour tablets, which shows that these come between the cheek-pieces and the shoulder-guards. This leads to the suggestion that they are arm-guards to protect the upper arm below the shoulder guard. This has the advantage that it becomes possible to interpret *qe-ro₂* as *sqᵘeliō* (dual), which can be equated with the Aeolic form σπέλ(λ)ιον of the usual ψέλιον 'bracelet'; it is uncertain whether σπ- represents the original order or a metathesis of ψ-, but a metathesis of such a difficult group as *qᵘs-* would not be surprising in Mycenaean (see, however, *qi-si-pe-e* in Glossary). This alternative has not been generally accepted, but no evidence has yet been found to resolve the question.

p. 330† **231 = K 873.** Corrections: l. 1]*ke-re-a*; l. 3 *we* and the small sign (probably the base of *no* rather than *wo*) after the ideogram are the remains of a deleted word.

p. 330‡ **232 = K 875.** Correction: l. 6 numeral 10 over a deleted figure. No convincing explanation has been given of the meaning of *qa-si-re-wi-ja*, plainly a derivative of the official title *qa-si-re-u*, to be identified with βασιλεύς although the sense of 'king' is inappropriate.

p. 331† **233 = Uc 160 reverse.** Corrections: l. 2 the numeral is probably 6; l. 4 *d̦o* is quite uncertain, but the restoration is justified by PY 238 = Tn 996.2.

The obverse of this tablet is interesting for the recently improved reading *de-r̦e-u̦-k̦o* associated with the ideogram WINE; the interpretation as *dleukos* = γλεῦκος 'sweet new wine' throws interesting light on the etymology of γλυκύς (Chadwick, 1968c).

p. 331‡ **234 = Ue 611.** Corrections: the 'reverse' should probably be regarded as the obverse. The left edge is missing in every line, but little or nothing is lost. In l. 1 the safer reading is]*pe-ra* 4, but the restoration is probable; l. 4 *ti-ri-po-di-ko* and *ka-ra-ti-ri-jo* are certain readings.

On the sealings which repeat words from this tablet see Chadwick (1959). The words which repeat are *a-ta-ra(-qe)* Wt 501, *ka-na-to* Wt 502, 506, *qe-ti-ja* Wt 504, *pa-ke-te-ri-ja* Wt 506, and possibly *ka-ra-ti-ri-jo* which appears as *ka-ra-se|-ti-ri-jo* on Wt 507, with the text divided between two lines and *se* above the normal size. Possibly the *se* is not part of the word but an independent annotation. These sealings also supply two other words belonging to this semantic group: *e-ku-se-we* (Wt 501) = *enkhusēwes* 'funnels' (already suggested in the Vocabulary of the first edition) and *ke-ni-qe-te-we* (Wt 503) = *kherniqᵘtēwes* (cf. χέρνιψ) 'wash-hand basins'. A pottery funnel was found in this same room of the House of the Sphinxes.

ka-ra-te-ra: the apparent accusative has given rise to the suggestion (Risch, 1958*a*) that all these words should be regarded as accusatives, and this leads to a theory that consonant stem accusatives plural may have an ending -*es*, as well as -*as*, which is evidenced by *pa-ki-ja-na-de* (-*ānas-de*). Scribal inconsequence is more likely, but the possibility must be kept in mind.

pa-ke-te-re: the repetition of this word on lists of building materials at Pylos and the large numbers there too (86 and 140) suggest that it is not a vessel but some other metal artifact. Perhaps some kind of peg or nail (on which to hang the vessels?): *pāktēres* (πήγνυμι) seems likely.

ka-na-to: if the previous word means 'nails', perhaps *gnathoi* 'cramps' is not too fanciful; cf. Aesch. *P.V.* 64 ἀδαμαντίνου νῦν σφηνὸς αὐθάδη γνάθον | στέρνων διαμπὰξ πασσάλευ' ἐρρωμένως.

qe-ti-ja: on the presence of diminutives in -ιον in Mycenaean see Lejeune (1967). He points out that the sealings must have been attached to baskets, and thus give only the names of small objects, the larger ones being ranged directly on the shelves.

p. 332† The most important advance in the interpretation of this series comes from the discovery in 1957 of the missing piece of **237** = Ta 709 (Lang, 1958).

Some light is shed on the construction of the furniture by the much later thrones discovered at Salamis in Cyprus by Karageorghis (1967*a*, 1967*b*, p. 346 and Fig. 150). It is not at all improbable that the traditions of Mycenaean craftsmanship continued there down to the Archaic period. One tomb, dated to the end of the eighth century B.C., contained three wooden thrones, of which the wood had perished, 'one decorated with silver, ivory and blue paste, the other with ivory and gold, the third only with ivory'. Ivory, gold and blue paste on chairs are clearly indicated in the Pylos tablets, and the mention of silver may perhaps lend some support to the suggestion (p. 340) that *pa-ra-ke-we* conceals another name for this metal (cf. *a-ku-ro* in Glossary). There was also a wooden footstool covered with thin sheets of silver to match one of the thrones. To judge from its shape it must have held a cushion, and this confirms the idea (p. 333) that the *thrānues* were seats rather than merely for the feet.

Much debate has raged around the question of the purpose of this group of precious articles. Our phrase 'the furnishings of a luxurious reception room' (p. 334) led to the obvious criticism that luxurious apartments do not contain damaged articles (the tripod-cauldron with the legs burnt off **236** = Ta 641.1), and it must not be thought that this inventory was of an apartment in use. The absence of beds would be surprising if it were. It must rather be the contents of a strong room, the store of κειμήλια kept for use as gifts, where valuable but damaged objects would no doubt be kept until they were repaired or used as scrap. If *Pu₂-ke-qi-ri* were the official responsible for these goods, it would be important on taking over to ensure that any damaged articles were so recorded, so that he could not be held responsible for the damage.

Palmer, however, put forward an ingenious theory (1957*b*) that the inventory was made on the occasion of a burial and is a record of the contents of a tomb, which were observed when it was opened for a fresh interment. This would neatly explain the damaged items with traces of fire, since funeral rites often involved sacrificial meals. The objection was raised (Gray, 1959; cf. Palmer, 1960; Gray, 1960) that no known tholos in Messenia is large enough to house all the furniture listed, and in view of the labour involved the inventory cannot be the result of opening more than one tomb. The absence of beds is also striking in this context. But the crucial argument revolves around the meaning of the first line of **235** = Ta 711: Palmer proposed the translation 'when the King buried *au-ke-wa* Damoklos', taking *thēke* to mean 'buried' and *da-mo-ko-ro* as a personal name. Subsequent work on the Knossos tablets by Olivier (1967*a*) has produced clear evidence that *da-mo-ko-ro* is a title, not a name. It is harder to disprove that τιθέναι can mean 'bury' when used in isolation, but it should be observed that this meaning is always indicated by something in the context—a corpse or bones as object, a phrase such as 'in the earth' or 'in the tomb'. Even so, the idea cannot be entirely rejected; but combined with other arguments it seems preferable to regard *thēke* as having its normal sense 'appointed'.

335† **235** = Ta 711

> *pu₂-ke-qi-ri*: there is no reason to suspect that the name is feminine; masculine names in
> -*i* (as classical -ις) are known.
> *au-ke-wa*: the scribe started this word with *a-* which he deleted and wrote **85*, a further
> confirmation of the value *au*; probably *Augewās*.

wa-na-se-wi-ja: Palmer (1957*b*) made the interesting suggestion that all the epithets describe the decoration rather than use of the vessel, and consequently this word is to be interpreted 'decorated with queen(s)', the queen being the title of a goddess. Similarly *a-mo-te-wi-ja* is taken to mean 'decorated with a charioteer'. To this Miss Gray (1959, p. 53) retorted that 'a goddess with women or a chariot with fighters on a jug involves the double improbability of the type of design and its appearance on a closed vessel with a strongly curved surface'. Whether we know enough of Mycenaean metal-work (if the jugs are in fact metal) to pronounce what is probable may be questioned; but it is surely not necessary to suppose that all the epithets are of the same kind. It is possible that *wa-na-se-wi-ja* and *a-mo-te-wi-ja* refer to a type, shape or material conventionally so named, and we cannot expect to determine their meaning precisely. A list of English vases containing such expressions such as 'Toby jug', 'Wedgwood' or 'Crown Derby' would be similarly opaque to the uninitiated.

ko-ro-no-we-sa: Palmer rightly objected that a derivative in -ϝευς from an *a*-stem would demand *ko-ro-na-*; hence κορώνη must be abandoned, but a neuter from the adjective κορωνός cannot be excluded. Palmer's own solution (1957*b*, p. 73) is *klonowessa* (κλόνος) 'decorated with a throng of warriors'; but the word means 'turmoil' and this seems an odd description of a static scene.

ku-na-ja: the identification with γύναιος is certain, but the ambiguity in the description persists.

p. 336† **236** = Ta 641. Correction: l. 1 'ke-re-a₂ TRIPOD[1']'.

The two certain instances of scribal error or inconsequence (l. 2 *me-zo-e* for *me-zo*, ll. 2–3 *ti-ri-o-we-e*/*ti-ri-jo-we*) may encourage us to suppose that *a₃-ke-u* and *we-ke* are similarly singulars for duals. The second could be avoided by supposing *we-ke* to be instr.-dat. of a noun with *ke-re-si-jo* the adjective in apposition; but *krēsiowergēs* is still the most attractive suggestion, and *a₃-ke-u* remains a problem. Palmer's *aigeus* 'decorated with a goat motif' (1957*b*, p. 79) is intelligible if it refers to goat protomes (Gray, 1959, p. 52). Doubts about the use of the -ευς suffix in quasi-adjectival forms can be set aside (cf. *o-pi-ke-wi-ri-je-u* **237** = Ta 709.3), and the classical restriction to ethnics is probably not valid for Mycenaean. The 'Cretan workmanship' may mean not imported from Crete, but made by Cretan smiths working in the kingdom of Pylos, or even simply 'of Cretan type'.

o-wo-we: the analogy of the other adjectives in -*o-we* on this tablet favours *oiwōwēs* 'single-handled', and this is archaeologically possible. But 'with a single handle on one foot' is an odd expression; nor could *hemei podei* mean 'on each foot'. It has been objected that this phrase cannot mean 'with (only) one foot' because the ideogram plainly shows three feet; but it is becoming clearer that despite attempts to accommodate the ideogram to the object described these are stereotypes, and the effort of depicting recognizably a tripod-cauldron with two of its feet missing would be beyond the artistic powers of the scribe. It is therefore better to take the phrase 'with one foot' separately from *o-wo-we*. If we reject the parallel of *qe-to-ro-we*, etc., we can interpret *ow(w)owens* (Palmer, 1963*a*, p. 344) and equate this with the Homeric ὠτώεις (*Il.* XXIII, 264+), which is certainly an artificial form. Palmer's translation 'with "ear" handles' is puzzling; ὠτώεις is generally understood as 'having handles', and if οὖς is here the Greek for 'handle' it cannot simultaneously mean 'ear'. The earlier explanation may well prove to be the right one.

me-wi-jo: there is no reason to reconstruct -*n* in the nominative singular, when it is absent from other parts of the declension; *meiwyos* is not an impossible form for Mycenaean.

337† **237** = Ta 709. Completed text (see above, p. 496):

1 *pi-je-ra₃* *to-qi-de-ja* ⌣ 3 *pa-ko-to* *a-pe-te-me-ne* ◇ 2
  po-ro-e-ke-te-ri-ja ⌐ 1 *ko-te-ri-ja* 6

2 *au-te* 1 *pu-ra-u-to-ro* 2 *qa-ra-to-ro* 1 *e-ka-ra* *a-pi-qo-to* *pe-de-we-sa* 1
  e-ka-ra *i-to-we-sa* *pe-de-we-sa* *so-we-ne-ja* *au-de-we-ʽsa-qe* 1ʹ

3 *ti-ri-po* *ke-re-si-jo* *we-ke* **34-ke-u* TRIPOD 1 *ti-ri-po* *ke-re-si-jo* *we-ke*
  o-pi-ke-wi-ri-je-u TRIPOD 1

pa-ko-to: *phaktō* the name of the large vessel shown, cf. φακτόν μέτρον παρὰ Ἀρκάσι, κοτύλαι ἀττικαὶ τρεῖς Lexicon Cyrilli; φάκται ληνοί, σιπύαι, πύελοι Hesychius (Naoumides, 1968). Is the female occupational term *pa-ke-te-ja* to be derived from this?

a-pe-te-me-ne: *aputhmene* 'without a base' (Petruševski, 1958) conflicts with the known spelling rules, but *pe* might be an error for *pu*; *amphēthmene* 'with a strainer on either side' (Palmer, 1963*a*, p. 342) is unsatisfactory sense, as he admits, and should perhaps be *amphi-hēth-*.

po-ro-e-ke-te-ri-ja: *prohelktēriā* (Palmer) offers the best solution, 'an instrument for drawing forth', perhaps a kind of fork or rake.

ko-te-ri-ja: *khō(s)stēria(i)* (χώννυμι, Palmer, 1963*a*, p. 343); but we should expect *kheu-* or *khou-*.

au-te: *austēr* from αὔω 'kindle'; but the forms ἐξαυστήρ (ἐξαύστριον), καταῦσαι, etc., show that 'draw' is the original sense (Chantraine, 1968, p. 145). However, the association with tongs makes 'kindler' not improbable.

e-ka-ra: *eskharā*, a word which meant, at least in origin, 'portable hearth', 'brazier'; cf. Latin *altaria*. An example of the object is to be seen in Fig. 18 (p. 326), item *a*.

a-pi-qo-to: the term is also applied to tables (**239** = Ta 642.3+). In **241** = Ta 715.2 (cf. **240** = Ta 713. 2, 3) it seems to form a contrast with *po-ro-e-ke*. But even if this is so, there are too many explanations of either term for this to narrow the quest sufficiently. Since *a-pi-qo-to* is unlikely to describe material, *po-ro-e-ke* also should be interpreted as referring to shape or type; but this does not exclude *po-ro-e-ke* being a compound of πῶρος 'marble' with a second element perhaps from **(h)ekhos* = ἔχμα 'support'. Ruijgh (1967, p. 354) argues strongly against -*qo-to* = -βατος; if he is right, this will eliminate 'that can be gone round', i.e. free-standing, and 'splay-legged' (Palmer, 1963a, p. 31). But his own suggestion *amphiqᵘhoitos* is unconvincing for the form, though the meaning 'with a rim around' would be satisfactory.

i-to-we-sa: *histowessa* 'provided with a mast' (i.e. an upright on which to hang a pot?).

au-de-we-sa-qe: the possible interpretations of this word which will also account for the instrumental plural *au-de-pi* have been exhaustively discussed by Lejeune (1966a, p. 16) who concludes that no word known from later Greek can satisfy the phonetic pattern. It is likely to be from a neuter noun in -δος, but no value for the first sign will yield a known word. It is therefore no obstacle to the view that **85 = au*, although this leads to no plausible interpretation.

*34-ke-u: the value *ai* for **34* was largely derived from its apparent alternation with a_3-*ke-u* in **236** = Ta 641.1, but has not been confirmed and must be rejected.

o-pi-ke-wi-ri-je-u: no convincing interpretation. These words must describe ornaments or fittings which serve to distinguish the tripod-cauldrons.

p. 338† **238** = Tn 996

This tablet does not of course belong to the set represented by the *Ta* tablets.

[a-po-]r̥e-we: there is not room to restore the long form *a-pi-po-re-we* found at Knossos (**233** = Uc 160 rev.).

ka-ti: the identification with κηθίς has been attacked on the grounds that this is a dice-box; but we do not know what vessels the ancients used for shaking dice, and in any case, the name could easily have been transferred to a different vessel.

p. 339† **239** = Ta 642

ra-e-ja: the case for interpreting this as *lāeiā* 'of marble' is strong. It appears to be the etymologists who are wrong in supposing **λᾶϝας on the strength of λεύσιμος, etc.

we-a-re-ja: there is little doubt that this corresponds to ὑαλεία, but whether the form should be interpreted as *hua-* or *wea-* remains uncertain.

a-ja-me-na: a Luvian etymology (cf. *aiamis* 'made', 'wrought', Meriggi, 1954a, p. 81) has been proposed, but is not convincing. The sense is almost certainly 'inlaid'.

e-ne-wo-pe-za: no satisfactory solution of this problem has emerged, but 'double and triple legs ending in a single foot are common' (Gray, 1959, p. 53). Probably the equation of -*pedza* with 'foot' must not be taken too literally. But it remains curious that tables are almost all of the 'nine-foot' type.

me-no-e-ja: Palmer's objection (1957b, p. 63, 1963a, p. 345) that this cannot be derived from the root **μηνσ- of μήν has been answered by Risch (1959, p. 222), who shows that other ablaut grades of this root may have been present in Mycenaean Greek. But it is possible that the word refers to material or decoration rather than shape; Ruijgh (1967, p. 237) suggests 'decorated with crescents'.

qe-qi-no-to: the correct solution to this problem was seen by D. M. Jones (1958); the scribe finding the syntax difficult has used a parallel clause with a finite perfect verb: *gᵘegᵘinōtoi* 'it is decorated'. Heubeck (1966) provided an ingenious etymology for this word from the base **gʷeyə₁-* 'live'. It may have started by meaning 'enliven', 'decorate with living creatures' and then been generalized, as was classical ζωγράφος; in usage it is clear that the technique here is carving as opposed to inlay (cf. Gray, 1959, p. 53).

a-pi-qo-to: see on **237**, p. 499 above.

341† **240** = Ta 713. Corrections: l. 1 *to-qi-de* 1; l. 2 *to-qi-de* 1   ⟦*to-pe-za*⟧.

po-ro-e-ke: *pro(h)ekhēs* 'projecting' remains a possibility, though the exact meaning is obscure. Ruijgh (1967, p. 45) proposes *pōro(h)ekhēs* 'with support of marble', Palmer (1963a, p. 347) *pōroenkhēs* (ἔγχος). See on *a-pi-qo-to*, p. 499.

pi-ti-ro₂-we-sa: it appears we must reconstruct **ptilyon* as doublet of πτίλον to account for the use of *ro₂*.

we-pe-za: possibly *(h)wespedza < *hweks-*.

342† *a-ka-ra-no*: the fit with ἀκάρηνος is so close it is hard to reject. A possible solution to the problem of its meaning was supplied by Platon's discovery at Kato Zakro of 'a stone pedestal stand with a device for holding and permitting interchangeable table-tops' (*Nestor* 1/11/65, p. 411; cf. Chadwick, *Nestor* 1/12/65, p. 415). If correct, this would prove that *a-pi-qo-to* and *po-ro-e-ke* did not refer to the tops of the tables. It would match the usual order if *a-ka-ra-no* were a description of material (Palmer, 1963a, p. 348), but if so it cannot be an adjective, since it must be a compound to have a feminine form in *-o*.

pu-ko-so e-ke-e: the apparent parallel with *po-ro-e-ke* may be illusory. Clearly a compound of πύξος.

342‡ **242** = Ta 707. Corrections: l. 1 *o-ni-ti-ja-pi* 1, *au-de-pi* 1; l. 2 *se-re-mo-ka-ra-o-re*, *po-ti-pi-qe* 1.

ku-ru-sa-pi: it has been suggested by Mühlestein (1956b) that adjectival *khrūs(s)os* derives from **khrūs-yos*, and was later replaced by χρύσεος.

se-re-mo-ka-ra-o-re: the reading of the last sign is difficult and both *i* and *re* appear possible; Bennett and Olivier now prefer *re*. The formation has been exhaustively discussed by Risch (1966a) who concludes that an enlargement in *-r* of the stem κάρα 'head' is supported by the evidence of later Greek. But the identity of the first member (some sort of animal?) remains unsolved; Mühlestein (1957) ingeniously suggested *Seirēmo-* = Σειρηνο-, stems in *m*- having been eliminated from later Greek (cf. *e-me*, p. 87), but it is hard to imagine how Sirens' heads could have been distinguished from women's (Palmer, 1963a, p. 349); and the link vowel *-o-* is unexpected.

po-ti-pi: Miss Gray objects to 'heifers' on archaeological grounds (1959, p. 53), and finds 'calves' no better.

344† **243** = Ta 708. Corrections: l. 1; *e-re-pa-te* 1; l. 3 *re-wo-pi-qe* 1. Bennett and Olivier have deciphered the erasure at the end of line 1 as a repetition of

242 = Ta 707.3, except that *ku-te-so* is replaced by the more correct *ku-te-se-jo*. In line 3 the scribe wrote *a-ja-me-no a-di-ri-ja-pi* before deleting the second word and writing *e-re-pa-te-jo* over it.

p. 344‡ **244** = Ta 714. Corrections: l. 2 *se-re-mo-ka-ra-o-re-qe*; the deleted word was probably *se-ṛe-ṃọ-ka-ra-o-re*; l. 3 *po-ni-ki-pi* 1,   *ko-no-ni-pi* 1.

we-a₂-re-jo: 'of rock-crystal', not of course the whole chair, but this is mentioned as a prominent feature of the decoration.

po-ni-ki-pi: arguments have been assembled against the notion that φοῖνιξ could mean 'griffin' as a decorative motif, notably by Dessenne (1957) and Chantraine (1958 *a*). 'Palm-tree' should therefore be substituted, here and in **246** = Ta 722.1, where there is no objection if these figures appear in separate panels. Although groom and horse would combine easily, we can hardly add the octopus climbing the palm-tree (but cf. Pliny, *Nat. Hist.* IX, 92).

p. 346† **247** = Ta 716

This remains the aberrant member of this set, differing in shape and vocabulary, and consequently most resistant to elucidation. Although the signs of the first line are smaller than those of the second, it does not seem possible here to regard the first line as a note appended to the entry in line 2.

It is generally agreed that the ideogram in line 2 represents a rapier-like sword, and consequently the interpretation of *qi-si-pe-e* as *qᵘsiphee* (ξίφος) must be accepted. Heubeck (1958) has fully discussed the etymology and spelling.

The objections to the rendering offered of the first line are mustered by Palmer (1963 *a*, p. 358). *Pa-sa-ro* is unlikely to be πασσάλω, because the product of *-ky-* seems to be consistently rendered by Myc. *z* (but cf. *wa-na-so-i*, etc.). Palmer's *psalō*, from which ψάλιον 'chain' was formed, seems probable. *A-pi to-ni-jo* is likely to be a divided compound, and it remains only to identify the second member. The presence of *to-no* = *thornos* in the context might suggest *amphithorniō* (cf. Doria, 1956, p. 4) 'for fitting around chairs', but why should gold chains be so used? Palmer suggests *amphitoniō* (τόνος) 'double stranded'.

Whatever *wa-o* stands for, contraction will have resulted in an unviable classical form, and it is hardly surprising that the word is not identified. Any connexion with ἄορ can be certainly excluded if this word provides the first element of the man's name *a-o-ri-me-ne* (see Glossary). If *wa-o* is really a double-axe, the name might be Minoan, for the derivation of λαβύρινθος from λάβρυς is suspect.

348† **248** = Va 15. Corrections: l. 1 for *e-ṭe* read *e-ḳa-ṭe* or *e-qe-ṭe*; l. 2 read [*pe-*]*re-ku-wa-na-ka*[ ]*e-te*; it is doubtful whether a sign is lost or not before]*ra-ḳa-te-ra*. For *ai₃*? read *35.

No real progress has been made with this text; the absence of ideograms makes it impossible to determine the subject. If the restoration *o-*[*da*]*-a₂* is correct in line 1, this is presumably the continuation of another tablet, but no pair has been identified for it. Since *o-da-a₂* is normally first word, the restoration may well be wrong; the *ọ-* is doubtful.

348‡ **249** = Va 482

The value *zu* for *79 has not been confirmed or disproved.

a-no-po: Lejeune (1958*a*, p. 213) proposed *anōpon* 'unworked'; cf. *o-pa* in Glossary. Palmer (1963*a*, p. 369) regards it as a man's name.

ro-i-ko: the objection to ῥοικός is that we should expect this word to have initial *w-*. Palmer (1963*a*, p. 368) proposed *rhoïskoi* 'small pomegranates', 'knobs'. The problems are discussed by Chantraine (1966, pp. 164–5) who arrives at the judgement: *non liquet*.

348¶ **250** = Vn 20

o-a₂: the only example of this word. Since *a₂* probably represents *ha*, it can hardly be *hoia*. More likely therefore the same word as *o-da-a₂*, but without the connective *d(e)*, since this is an isolated tablet, not a continuation.

349† **251** = Vn 46

The whole text is very difficult to read, but further study has produced an improved text.

1	*pi-ra₃-*[
2	*ka-pi-ni-ja a-ti-ja 6*[
3	*ka-pi-ni-ja e-ru-mi-ni-ja 4* [
4	*ka-pi-ni-ja ta-ra-nu-we 12*[
5	**35-ki-no-o 81 o-pi-ṛa₃-te-re 40*[
6	*e-to-ki-ja 23*[*pa*]*-ke-te-re 140*
7	*pi-ri-ja-o ta-ra-nu-we 6*
8	*qe-re-ti-ri-jo 2 me-ta-se-we 10*
9	*e-ṣo-wo-ke pu-to-ro 16*
10	**35-ki-no-o pu-to-ro 100*
11	*ta-to-mo a-ro-wo e-pi-*65-ko 1*
12	*ẹ-ṛu-mị-ni-ja 2 ki-wo-qe 1*

It is clear that this is part of a list of building materials; the beginning is lost or it might specify the μέγαρον for which these items were required or provided. The list may conceivably have included tools, metal fittings, etc., as well as timbers; but any interpretation must fit this general context.

ka-pi-ni-ja: gen. *kapniās* 'of the chimney'. Palmer's objection (1963 *a*, p. 424) that timber would be inappropriate for this position results from a failure to understand the construction of Mycenaean roofs. The smoke-duct over the hearth in the megaron at Pylos was of earthenware (Blegen, 1953 *b*, p. 61) but an elaborate structure of timber would have been needed to hold this in position, and the whole structure might properly be called 'chimney'.

a-ti-ja: previously read *po-ti-ja*, but cf. Vn 879.1 *a-ti*[in what appears to be a similar list, if not a continuation of this. Probably neuter plural *antia* from ἀντίος in some technical sense, perhaps 'cross-bars'; cf. ἀντίον (Aristophanes +) 'a part of a loom'. Together with *elumniai* and *thranues* these are the timbers for the chimney structure.

*35-ki-no-o: one reason for attributing the value ai_3? to **35* was the spelling a_3*-ki-no-o* at Knossos as part of a chariot (**275** = Se 879, **276** = Se 891).

o-pi-ṛa₃-te-re: if the reading is correct this can hardly be anything but *opi(r)rhaistēres*, cf. ῥαιστήρ 'hammer'. Perhaps not tools for construction but fittings to prevent damage to the ends of beams?

e-to-ki-ja: *entoikhia* 'fittings for insertion in walls'. If the numbers are significant these will hardly be the beams surrounded by masonry making up the walls themselves (Palmer, 1963 *a*, p. 367).

pi-ri-ja-o: a particularly happy discovery: *phliāōn* 'door-posts'.

qe-re-ti-ri-jo: possibly $q^u(e)lethriō$, from a diminutive in *-ion* of πέλεθρον, πλέθρον, a measure of length in Homer and later Greek, but in origin doubtless meaning a rod or pole. Ruijgh (1970, p. 315) proposes a derivative of βλῆτρον 'fastening'.

me-ta-se-we: a compound of μετα-, but the second member is obscure. Connexion with μετάρσιος must be rejected, if it represents -αϝερ-.

e-ṣo-wo-ke: in this line and the next the problem arises that in previous entries the epithet (genitive) precedes and the second word is the substantive; but since **35-ki-no-o* also stands alone (line 5), it must be the substantive and *pu-to-ro* can therefore be the epithet. This seems to be the order also in l. 11. If so, *pu-to-ro* is probably genitive plural.

ta-to-mo: the word recurs in tablets dealing with sheep (Cn 4, Cn 595), and the spelling corresponds to σταθμός. This word has both the sense 'sheep-pen' (e.g. *Il.* II, 470) and 'pillar' (e.g. *Od.* I, 333). Thus the two contexts of the Mycenaean word answer to two Homeric senses of the Greek word.

e-pi-*65-ko: if, as seems likely, the value of **65* is *ju*, there is no word in the lexicon to suit this spelling. Palmer (1955 *b*, p. 43; 1963 *a*, p. 367) has proposed to interpret this as ἐπίзυγος; it is of course true that з in зυγόν corresponds to *y* of other Indo-European languages (Lat. *iugum*, Skt. *yugam*), but there is no example in later Greek of this sound surviving as *y*. Moreover, the root occurs in the Mycenaean words *ze-u-ke-si* and *ze-u-ke-u-si* and the abbreviation ZE, and seems always to be spelt with *z*-. It is therefore extremely doubtful if this alternative can be accepted here. Palmer cites as parallel *pe-*65-ka* from the similar tablet Vn 879, which he interprets as πέρӡυγα; but apocope of περί is unknown in Mycenaean, and an alternative explanation is here available (*peyukā(s)* = πεύκη 'pine').

p. 350† Three more miscellaneous documents from Pylos may be added here.

318 = Un 1314

1 *a-wa-ra-ka-na-o* *pa-ma-ko*
2 *jo-qi* *wo-to-mo* *pe-re* I
3 *a-wa-ra-ka-na* *e-pi-ka* *ḳạ-ja* *pa-ra-we-*`*jo*' `*do-we-jọ-qe* ịọọ'

At the end of l. 3 the scribe has divided the line in order to squeeze in the last word. Bennett and Olivier read *pa-ra-we* '*do-we-jo-qe*' ḳ A 20; but, as first pointed out by Palmer, the alleged 20 is almost certainly the top of a raised *jo*. The circular sign following it is very cramped, but neither KA nor QE offer plausible sense, and a numeral is required.

The general sense remains extremely obscure. *pa-ma-ko* is likely to be φάρμακον (if not Φάρμακος as a man's name). *Jo-qi* is a correct spelling for *ho(q)qᵘi* (or *yo-*?) = ὅ,τι and if *pe-re* = *pherei*, *wo-to-mo* is presumably a man's name. *a-wa-ra-ka-na* must be an *a*-stem with a genitive singular *-āo* if masculine, or plural *-āōn* if feminine. It is easier to make fun of the suggestion that it is a Mycenaean form for ἀράχνη than to suggest anything better; a derivative in *-nā* of *awlax* > αὖλαξ 'furrow' is theoretically possible, but unconvincing for the sense. *Do-we-jo(-qe)* recurs as a description of a part of a chariot (KN **268** = Sd 4413 +, cf. p. 364) = *dorweioi-qᵘe* 'and of wood'; but this does not offer a likely solution for *pa-ra-we-jọ*.

319 = Un 1322

1]*nọ*[ ]*ọ-no*[   ] WHEAT 6 FỊGṢ [
2 *de-ku-tu-wo-ḳọ*[   ]*o-no* WHEAT 2 FIGS 2
3 *ị-ṭe-ẉẹ* *o-ṇọ*[   ] WHEAT 12
4 *we-a₂-no*[?*ri*]*-no* *re-po-to* *146 WHEAT 5
5 *wọ-*[   ]*no*[   ]**146 WḤẸAṬ 15

The fragment is very much battered and is broken off at both top and bottom. It was discussed at length by Chadwick (1964 b). Its chief interest lies in the combination of the ideogram *146, which appears to be some kind of textile (see p. 464) with the sign for WHEAT. In other cases where two ideograms are written together (e.g. EWE WOOL KN Dp 7280 +), the first appears to qualify the second; but textile obviously cannot qualify wheat, so it seems likely that the wheat represents in some sense the price of the textiles. It is, however, strange that the number of pieces of cloth is not specified; possibly this is the record of the keeper of the granary, who was interested in the issue

505

of the wheat, but not in the goods received in exchange. Lines 1–3 appear to give the payment in kind made to certain tradesmen.

de-ku-tu-wo-ḳọ: following a suggestion of H. Mühlestein, probably *dektuworgōi* 'for the net-maker'. This involves regarding classical δίκτυον as a replacement of an earlier *u*-stem δίκτυ recorded by the *Etymologicum Magnum*; and supposing Myceneaean *e* = ι as in *ku-te-so* = κύτισος. If so, this may be evidence that the word is of Mediterranean origin rather than associated with δικεῖν 'cast'. Chantraine (1968, p. 284), however, suggests *deiktu-*.

o-no: attempts to associate this word with ὦνος seem to be blocked by the etymology **wos-no-* (cf. Lat. *uēnum*, Skt. *vasnáh*; see Lejeune, 1964a, p. 83). Mycenaean *o-no* might be associated with the root of ὀνίνημι, and it is not entirely certain that Cretan ὄνος results from a precocious loss of digamma before *o*. Mycenaean forms show that ὀφείλω, despite Arcadian ϝοφλέκόσι, had no digamma, and the etymology of ὠθέω is not certain.

ị-ṭe-ụẹ: if the reading is correct, dative (or nominative plural) of **histeus* 'weaver', agent noun in -ευς from ἱστός 'loom'. Cf. *i-te-ja-o* **15** = Ad 684, gen. plur. of the corresponding feminine **histeia*.

we-a₂-no: cf. *we-a₂-no-i* **310** = Fr 1225, *wehanoi* 'fine robes'. The sign before]-*no* seems not to be *o*, hence the restoration [*ri*]-*no re-po-to* = *linon lepton* 'fine linen', cf. KN **222** = L 693.

320 = Va 1324

¹ *e-ke-i-ja* 30
² *pe-di-je-wi-ja* 20 *a-ko-so-ne* 2

Thirty spears; twenty . . .; two axles.

e-ke-i-ja: *enkhehiai* 'spears', cf. ἐγχείη *Il.* v, 167 +. What difference there was in meaning between ἔγχος and ἐγχείη is not clear. The original form must have been **enkhes-iā*, hence the restoration of intervocalic -*h*-; at least the spelling *e-i* must here represent two syllables.

pe-di-je-wi-ja: cf. *pe-di-je-we* **58** = An 654. If this means 'foot-soldiers' (see p. 192), perhaps the derivative *pediēwiai* (*sc. enkhehiai*) means 'infantry-spears'.

a-ko-so-ne: *axones*, cf. **252** = Vn 10. In this context the word might be used for any round poles thicker than those used for spears.

9. MISCELLANEOUS DOCUMENTS FROM MYCENAE

Excavation by Lord William Taylour of a house in the Citadel at Mycenae in 1960 produced a further group of six tablets (*Oi*), all fragments in a poor state of preservation. They are characterized by a new ideogram, **190*, which bears some resemblance to **134*, but has been separated from it until further evidence shows whether they should be regarded as variants or not. There is no clue to the nature of the com-

¹³⁴ ♯♯

¹⁹⁰ ⚏/⚏

modity, but it probably represents a foodstuff, since it is assigned to groups of workers and also to a deity.

The presence of Potnia in these records (**321** = Oi 701, Oi 704) is particularly interesting in view of the recent discovery in the same area of evidence of an ivory workshop and a shrine of a goddess (Taylour, 1969, 1970). It is very tempting to identify the female figure represented in the fresco as Potnia, the great Cretan goddess, and to speculate whether this cult might not have been brought to Mycenae originally by a guild of Cretan craftsmen.

One tablet is quoted as a specimen; no translation is given as the interpreted words are commented on separately.

321 = Oi 701

1   [Broken at top]
2   v a c a t [
3   *si-to-po-ti-ni-ja*   *190* [
4   *po-ro-po-i*   *190*   10
5   *ka-na-pe-u-si*   *190*   6
6   [.]-*pu₂-ta*   *do-ke-ko-o-ke-ne*   *190*   5
7   [*ku-wa-*]*no-wo-ko-i*   *190*   2
8   [Broken at bottom]

si-to-po-ti-ni-ja: almost certainly to be divided *si-to po-ti-ni-ja* in view of the isolated *po-ti-ni-ja*, who receives 15 of **190*, in Oi 704.1. The first word might be a divine name, *Sītō(i)*, cf. Σιτώ as a name of Demeter in Sicily (see Chadwick, 1963*b*, p. 58); or a place name, or even genitive plural *sītōn* 'the Mistress of grains'. In any case *a-ta-na-po-ti-ni-ja* KN **208** = V 52 is a close parallel.

po-ro-po-i: the only interpretation proposed is dat. plur. *propoihi* of a noun **προπός* cf. θεο-πρόπος, 'augur' (Petruševski, 1966, p. 294). This is dependent on the etymological connexion with πρέπω; a rival view is that -προπος is assimilated from **-προκος*, cf. Lat. *procus* (Boisacq). Since the only identifiable dative plurals in this group are descriptions of craftsmen, the sense is suspect too.

ka-na-pe-u-si: *knapheusi* 'for the fullers'.

[.]-*pu₂-ta*: there does not seem to be room to restore [*e-pi*]-*pu₂-ta*, cf. *e-pi-pu-ta* PY **252** = Vn 10; but -*pu₂-ta* strongly suggests -φυτα.

do-ke-ko-o-ke-ne: cf. [*do-*]*ke̯-ko-o-ke-ne̯-i* Oi 703, *ko-o-ke-ne-i*[Oi 704. This makes it clear that *do-ke* is a separate word, presumably *dōke* 'gave' as elsewhere (see Glossary, s.v. *di-do-si*). *Ko-o-ke-ne* may then be a man's name (in -*genēs*?), but the shift to dative in Oi 703, 704 is puzzling.

[*ku-wa-*]*no-wo-ko-i*: the restoration is proved by the repetition of this word in Oi 703, Oi 704: *kuanoworgoihi* 'for the *cyanus*-workers'. On κύανος see p. 340 and Glossary, s.v. *ku-wa-no*.

CHAPTER XI

METALS AND MILITARY EQUIPMENT

p. 351† The most remarkable addition to the list of articles to which the sign for BRONZE is attached is the Knossos sealing Ws 8497, where it surmounts a rectangular object shown by the accompanying word to be a bath-tub: *a-sa-mi-to* = ἀσάμινθος, the Homeric word. This may be some support for suggesting that the bath-tubs of **238** = Tn 996 at Pylos are also of bronze, though the ideogram is here applied only to smaller vessels. It now seems likely that on KN **222** = L 693 the bronze is intended to serve as fittings on a tunic, perhaps a piece of armour, rather than as an indication of value, for which no parallels have been discovered.

p. 351‡ The suggestion that WE on certain tablets stands for silver has not been confirmed. On KN **231** = K 872 the *we* appears to be rather the remains of a deleted word. On J 58*bis* = Og 1804 the reading is *ẹ*, not WE. This leaves only the INGOT with surcharged WE on Oa 734*bis* = 1808, as the reading on PY La 630 rev. is very doubtful. It remains true that mẹntions of silver are less frequent than we should expect.

p. 352† The total of *Jn* tablets after some joins now stands, with the same exceptions, at eighteen tablets and eight fragments, some of which may belong together. It has been suggested by Lejeune (1961*b*, p. 419) and Palmer (1963*a*, p. 279) that *ta-ra-si-ja* should be interpreted *talansiā* (< **talant-iā*), and thus a different word from ταλασία. Obviously there is no way of resolving this question, but equally there is no reason for inventing a new form when the classical one fits as well. The semantic argument is without weight, as shown on p. 352, since the Latin parallel is so exact. Nor does the late date at which ταλασία is first attested (beginning of the fourth century B.C.) cast doubt on the word's antiquity, for it must be a derivative of *ταλάτᾱς or the like; it is hardly a 'shortened form of ταλασιουργία' (Palmer, loc. cit.), which is no earlier (Plato). But in default of evidence the question must be left open.

Lejeune (1961*b*, p. 433) has demonstrated that **256** = Ja 749 is almost certainly the totalling tablet for this series, as suggested on p. 356. It gives a total of 1046 kg of bronze, as against the total in excess of 600 kg shown by the seventeen tablets sufficiently complete to be usable. Thus rather more than one-third of the *Jn* tablets are missing or too badly damaged to use. The number of smiths recorded is approximately 270, not counting the slaves; therefore the total number for the whole of the Pylian kingdom, allowing for the extra third, amounts to about 400 (Lejeune's figures, p. 425).

This in turn should lead us to reflect upon the numbers to be expected in such a territory. It is hard to estimate the numbers required, but bearing in mind the relative scarcity of bronze as compared with iron in later ages, one can scarcely credit that so large a number would have been needed for domestic purposes. Unlike the village blacksmith of medieval and modern times, they are not scattered throughout the settlements, but are concentrated in groups of up to twenty-six or twenty-seven (one name in Jn 725 is deleted) in places, scarcely half of which are mentioned again in the Pylos archives. It would seem likely that they were located near good supplies of timber for use as fuel, and perhaps on hill-tops where the wind would supply the necessary draught for their furnaces. For instance *Ro-u-so* figures in this list, and this place is shown by **252**=Vn 10 to be a wood-producing area.

The groups listed as *po-ti-ni-ja-we-jo* (cf. p. 354) are almost certainly to be regarded as 'in the service of Potnia'. It may seem peculiar to us that guilds of craftsmen should be simultaneously devotees of a goddess, though medieval guilds offer parallels; but this is precisely what is to be deduced from the excavation of cave-sanctuaries in Crete. Arkalokhori, for example, has been shown to have been both a shrine and a bronze-smithy (Marinatos, 1962). It is hardly pressing this evidence too far to suggest that the devotees of Potnia practised a similar combination of cult and craft; indeed, these guilds may well have been descended from Cretan groups who emigrated at the time of the Minoan collapse and found refuge on the mainland; cf. the vessels 'of Cretan workmanship' PY **236**=Ta 641, **237**=Ta 709. A remarkable parallel has recently been discovered by Lord William Taylour in the Citadel House at Mycenae; there an ivory-workshop adjoins a shrine with a fresco of a large female figure, doubtless Potnia herself (see p. 411).

These facts cast further doubt on the suggestion that the smiths were part-time or seasonal workers, though they may well have had to grow their own food. But it remains to explain why nearly a third of the smiths listed are without allocations of bronze, and why the rest have relatively small quantities of metal on which to work. One smith on Jn 601 has as much as 12 kg of metal, but 3 to 4 kg is normal, and some have as little as 1·5 kg. Here it is tempting to speculate about the sources of raw material and the destination of the metal goods made in the kingdom of Pylos. The copper undoubtedly came from Cyprus, while the most accessible sources of tin were to the west of Greece; is it not likely that a port on the sea-route linking the Aegean with the west would be where the two ingredients of the alloy met; and that the excessive numbers of workmen were due to the special position of Pylos as favourably placed both for the import of raw materials and for the export of finished goods? At a time when sea-raiders were scouring the eastern Mediterranean, as Egyptian records show, and Pylos itself feared an attack from the sea (see p. 430), it would be hardly surprising if sea-communications had been interrupted and the Pylian bronze industry was suffering from an acute shortage of raw material.

The identification of *qa-si-re-u* (*pa₂-si-re-u*) with βασιλεύς has been attacked by Palmer (1963 a, pp. 227 f.) on the grounds that the functions of the Mycenaean *qa-si-re-u* are restricted to a craftsman context. While it is true that the term appears predominantly in the bronze tablets, it is not necessarily restricted to them and **258**=Jo 438 shows it in company with *ko-re-te* and *mo-ro-qa*, both officers of the local administration. Certainly its sense is different from the classical use of βασιλεύς as 'king', but even then it was frequently used as the title of a religious official (e.g. ἄρχων βασιλεύς at Athens), so that its semantic development may have been from the religious to the secular sphere. The identity of *qa-si-re-u* with βασιλεύς as a word is hard to deny, seeing that β- is almost certain to be derived from a labio-velar.

p. 353† **253**=Jn 310. Corrections: Jn 605.10 has two entries for slaves where the figure following the owner's name is 2; this shows that the bars separating names of *a-ta-ra-si-jo* smiths as well as slave-owners should be taken as the numeral 1. Line 8 read: PA-QO-SI-JO 1 KE-WE-TO 1 *wa-[di?]-re-u* [1]; l. 9: *pe-ta-ro* 1; l.11: *ke-we-to-jo* 1 *i-wa-ka-o* 1; l.12 *pa-qo-si-jo-jo* 1 *po-ro-u-te-wo* 1; l.17 [*to-so-de a*]-*ta-ra-si-jo* *pu₂-si-ja-ko* 1. On *po-ti-ni-ja-we-jo* see p. 509 above.

p. 354† **254**=Jn 389. Corrections: l. 6: Bennett and Olivier now read the damaged numerals as ≹ 3, but point out that this needs to be corrected to ≹ 1 ⟨♯⟩ 2 to save the arithmetic. l. 8 was apparently inscribed with the text of l. 9, but was then deleted. ll.12–13: insert 1 after each name.

e-pi-da-to: probably not a verb, but the verbal adjective *epidastos* (Lejeune, 1958a, p. 226).

p. 355† **255**=Jn 658. Corrections: the doubtful readings are mostly confirmed, except l. 1: *ka-ke-we ta-ra-si-ja̠ e̠-ko-si*; l. 6: read [*po-*]*ṛo-ko*; l. 10: *a̠-ṭu-ḳo̠* 1 BRONZE ≹ 5 ⟦*ko-ma-ḍo-ro* BRONZE ≹ 5⟧; ll. 11 and 12: *to-so-de*; l. 11 at right add ⟦5⟧ corresponding to deleted entry in l.10.

The relation between this tablet and Jn 725 is intriguing. The second (deleted) paragraph of Jn 725 lists eight names at *na-i-se-wi-jo*, which are repeated on Jn 692, two having allocations of *ℨ* 6, the rest without allocation. There are two deleted totals for this paragraph on Jn 725, *ℨ* 12 and *ℨ* 30(+ ?), the first of which answers to the figures on Jn 692. This suggests that 725 is earlier and represents a first attempt at listing the smiths and allocating a total quantity of bronze; 692 would therefore be the final version. The first paragraph of 725 refers to *e-ni-pa-te-we* and lists 27 names, of which one is deleted; 658 has only 17, of which one is deleted, and no *a-ta-ra-si-jo*. These might then be supplied from the ten extra names on 725. But the equation is not so simple. The name *pi-ro-ne-ta* of 658 does not appear on 725. Three names appear in altered form, if the readings are correct in both places: *ma-ka-wo* (*wo* is damaged) seems to reappear as *ma-ka-ta*; *wa-ka-ta* as *wa-tu-ta*; *po-ru-e-ro* (*po* is damaged) as *o-ru-we-ro* (the substitution of *we* for *e* after *u* is merely a matter of spelling). Either our readings are unsound or the redaction of one tablet or the other was slovenly. Two scribes are concerned; the scribe of 658 also wrote only Jn 706 of the *Jn* tablets, the other one which uses *e-ko-si* in place of *e-ko-te*. The bronze total of 725 is 𐂫 2 *ℨ* 18, which has been slightly increased on 658 to yield a figure easily divisible by 16. The problem is discussed at length by Lejeune (1961 *b*, pp. 430–2).

357† **257** = Jn 829. Corrections: l. 9 read: *a̱-ke-re-wa*; l. 11: *ka̱-ra-do-ro*; l. 13: *ṯi-mi-to-a-ke-e*; l. 14 BRONZE *ℨ* 2 ♯ 3 (according to Bennett and Olivier, but regularity suggests that *ℨ* 3 is more likely).

It is agreed that this tablet is a list of contributions of quantities of bronze made by the local officials of the sixteen areas into which the kingdom is divided. The questions which remain to be answered are:

(1) Why are the *ko-re-te* and *po-ro-ko-re-te*, who alone actually contribute, accompanied in the preamble by other officials?

(2) Why is the total amount contributed, 51 kg, so small in relation to the quantities distributed (see the table on p. 356)?

(3) What is the structure of line 3?

The first question is perhaps the easiest. It is not unknown for officials to bear varying titles for historical reasons while discharging the same function; thus the senior official of a Cambridge or Oxford college may be called Master, President, Provost, Principal, Dean, Warden, etc., though all occupy the same position in their colleges. Can we not therefore assume that *ko-re-te* and *po-ro-ko-re-te* are the generic titles for local officials, but that in certain areas they were known also by specific names? Thus *du-ma* emerges as an alternative to *ko-re-te*, which is in keeping with what we know of its use; and the key-bearers and the others must be alternative titles which could all be subsumed under the heading *po-ro-ko-re-te*. A 'supervisor of figs' is perhaps a surprising title, but royal courts have usually been full of officials with strange-sounding titles, which often have little relation to their real duties; and the presence of figs in the slave-women's ration may be significant. It would appear that *o-pi-ka-pe-e-we* should be related to σκάφος rather than σκάφη; but in what sense the word is used is unclear; possibly the reference is to boats.

The second question possibly depends upon the third, and may be postponed. Line 3 clearly contains the object of the verb *dōsonsi*: *ka-ko* = *khalkon* represented by the ideogram BRONZE in the entries below; cf. *to-so-de ka-ko* BRONZE in **254** = Jn 389.9. *na-wi-jo* has every appearance of being an epithet to *ka-ko*. *a₃-ka-sa-ma* can hardly be singular in view of the dative plurals which precede; it cannot be genitive, dative or instrumental plural which would require an extra syllable, and nominative is excluded by sense and syntax; it is therefore accusative *aixmans* 'points'. The question thus emerges whether the sequence *-qe . . . -qe* in *pa-ta-jo-i-qe e-ke-si-qe* is a 'double' use = 'both . . . and' or two separate connectives, the first coupling *ka-ko* with *a₃-ka-sa-ma* (and its attributive datives), the second linking the two datives. The 'double' use of *-qe* is rare, but not unknown, in Mycenaean; see Ruijgh, 1967, pp. 290, 297, 305, 309. Ruijgh himself (p. 309) prefers the second explanation of the present sentence. But Palmer (1963*a*, p. 283) adopts the first, taking *aixmans* in apposition to *khalkon* 'bronze as points for arrows and spears'. Where opinion is so balanced, it is hard to make a firm judgement; but I now incline to Palmer's explanation, because of possible parallels and because it offers a plausible solution to the second question posed above.

The parallels are in **317** = Ub 1318, where we have (on my interpretation) several entries which list the finished article in apposition to the raw material, sometimes with a dative or genitive appended. E.g. *wi-ri-no we-ru-ma-ta ti-ri-si ze-u-ke-si* I 'a raw-hide as coverings for three pairs'; *o-pi-de-so-mo ka-tu-ro₂ di-pte-ra* 4 'four skins as bindings of pack-saddles'. These are not exact parallels, but are sufficiently like *ka-ko . . . a₃-ka-sa-ma* to justify the translation 'bronze . . . as points' (i.e. to make points).

The whole sentence may therefore translate: 'Thus the mayors and super-intendants, and vice-mayors and key-bearers and supervisors of *figs* and *hulls*, will contribute temple bronze as points for darts and spears.' If this is approximately correct, we may approach again the second question: how is the small quantity of bronze requisitioned to be explained? There seems little chance that bronze or its constituent metals were produced in the south-western

Peloponnese; how then could these local officials be expected to find, some 2 kg, some 3·75 kg each? Clearly not by requisitioning the stocks of local smiths, since the bronze available has been issued to them by the Palace and they will have to account for it. Moreover, the bronze is clearly going to be allocated to smiths in order to transform it into weapons. We may also reasonably suppose that bronze vessels and artifacts, other than weapons, were very rare except among the aristocracy. But a possible source of bronze scrap lay in the dedicated objects, often old and useless, to be found in religious buildings. It may be objected that no adjective from ναός 'temple' is found in classical Greek, whereas νάϊος (Ion. νήϊος) from ναῦς 'ship' is well known; but if an adjective from ναός < *naswos existed, it too would have had the Mycenaean form nāwios. Nor is the alleged absence of Mycenaean temples a serious objection; for the name need not imply a building or even a special room where religious ceremonies were performed: 'cult was an integrated part of the palace life, handled in palace halls which had other domestic functions as well' (Vermeule, 1964, p. 283). But shrines are not unknown on the Mainland (Taylour, 1964, pp. 67–9). Indeed this may explain why the contributions are demanded of the 'vice-mayors' as well as 'mayors'. The subordinate officials could perhaps have been in charge of part of the territory, but in this case it is odd that every district has one and none has more than one. But if the vice-mayor is merely the second ranking official of the district, he and the mayor might be the only two citizens wealthy enough to possess a house-shrine, and thus disposable bronze scrap. The shortage of metal attested by the whole of the *Jn* series of tablets will explain the need for these desperate measures; imports of raw material have been cut off precisely at the time when there is an overwhelming need for weapons. This theory equally explains the rebates for smiths in the *Ma* tablets (p. 292) and *Na* tablets (e.g. **192** = Na 252).

pa-ta-jo-i-qe: it was suggested (p. 358) that this word must mean 'arrows' since its nominative *pa-ta-ja* was found at Knossos on sealings in context with the remains of arrows. What seems to have been overlooked is that the ideogram transcribed ARROW on **264** = Ws 1704 (the lower illustration under no. 231 on p. 360) is very different from that on R 4482 (upper illustration; see p. 361 and under **264**). The latter are undoubtedly arrows, since they have a feathered flight at the rear end, and it is hard to be sure if they have a point, as shown; but the identity of the shaft with a largish barbed point is not so evident, and it would seem that *pa-ta-ja* might rather be light missiles hurled manually, since if the interpretation *paltaia* is correct, the verb πάλλω could hardly be used of an arrow, and the meaning of the later παλτόν is certainly 'javelin' or 'dart'. In later usage too αἰχμή is restricted to spears, and the word for the point of an arrow is ἀκίς. This of course raises the old question whether the Mycenaeans made use of throwing-spears as well as the heavy thrusting spear, which is well attested by the large bronze spear-heads recovered. There is enough evidence to show that the weapon was not unknown, though it may have been used more for hunting than warfare; it would not of course have penetrated any but the lightest armour. The Homeric evidence is totally unreliable, but there is no reason to suppose that wherever two spears are attributed to a warrior, this is an anachronism introduced from the Dark Age (Snodgrass, 1967, p. 23).

p. 358† **258** = Jo 438. Correction: l.1 [   ]*ko-re-te.*

A few unimportant restorations are confirmed, but no progress can be made epigraphically with this lacunose text. The heading remains enigmatic, even now that a fragment has completed the word at the end of line 1 as *ko-re-te*; we might have expected a plural on the analogy of **257** = Jn 829. It is significant that the quantity of gold in line 2 is four times the largest contributions in the remainder of the tablet; some high official must have been named here.

It would seem likely that here too we have a list of local officials, and that the title *ko-re-te* must be understood also with the place names of lines 25 and 26. **43** = Aq 64.5 shows that the *ko-re-te* of *i-te-re-wa* was called *Klumenos* and held the rank of *mo-ro-qa*; he commands an *o-ka* in **58** = An 654. Thus we may perhaps assume that the three men here named as *mo-ro-qa* (lines 5, 6, 17) were the *ko-re-te-re* of their local districts. The broken word ending]*ma* in lines 15, 16 may have been *du-ma* 'superintendant', cf. *du-ma-te* in **257** = Jn 829. The title *qa-si-re-u* (l. 20) fits this context well enough; *a-ke-ro* is more likely to be a man's name than genitive plural *angelōn*. *Ne-da-wa-ta* (l. 7) is the commander of an *o-ka* in the north of the kingdom on **56** = An 657, and *E-ke-me-de* (l. 8) is the first of his subordinate officers; they were perhaps *ko-re-te* and *po-ro-ko-re-te* of one of the northern districts. *Po-ki-ro-qo* (l. 22) is an officer in the *o-ka* of *Ta-ti-qo-we-wo* in **58** = An 654. *Au-ke-wa* (*Augewās*) is the *da-mo-ko-ro* appointed by the king in **235** = Ta 711; **304** = On 300 has *da-mo-ko-ro* in parallel position at the end of the Hither Province to *te-po-se-u* in the Further Province, the man who is described as the *ti-nwa-si-jo ko-re-te* (l. 21).

p. 359† **259** = Og 1527. This piece appears to belong to a large tablet and one or more lines are missing at the top. Palmer (1963 a, p. 435) has doubted the identification of *mo-ri-wo-do*, but in default of further context, some form of μόλυβδος still seems most likely.

p. 359‡ It is not certain that either J 58 or Og 1804 (= J 58*bis*) relate to metal. On the ingot tablets (*Oa*) see p. 351.

p. 360† **260** = Og 4467. Correction: l. 3 read *pi-ri̯*[.

360‡ The situation of the sword tablets is remarkable, but can be explained if this area of the 'Domestic Quarter' was the location of the Royal Guard. The king must surely have had a small force of soldiers to guard him, and they may also have had a supply of weapons for issue to the royal family in case of emergency. Boardman (1963, pp. 79–80) has suggested that the swords on these tablets are rather daggers; the Homeric use of φάσγανον is liable to be inaccurate, and the suggestion cannot be controlled. But it remains plausible, and whichever it is, the form of the hilt favours an early date for the tablets.

361† **263** = R 1815 (=0481*bis*). The reading is still disputed, since the tablet was broken between *ka-ka* and *re-ạ*, and something seems to have stood between, though possibly later deleted. Despite this, however, the reading *ka-ka-re-ạ* has much to commend it.

361‡ On the meaning of *pa-ta-ja* and the identification of the ARROW ideogram, see p. 513 above. Perhaps therefore 'javelin', though the association with arrow-heads makes this questionable.

362† The word *a-ra-ro-mo-te-me-na* occurs exclusively with the full CHARIOT ideogram, but minus wheels. It appears therefore to alternate with *a-na-mo-to* on the tablets showing the bare CHARIOT-FRAME, and this is used once with a unique ideogram (Sf 4465), which appears to represent pole and yoke without any car. The conclusion that this pair of words denotes the presence or absence of the equipment of the bare frame (back, pole-stay and yoke) seems inescapable. The suggestion of D. J. N. Lee (1958) that it means provided with or without wheels (*a-mo-ta*) must therefore be rejected, even though it is not impossible that a feature should be stated to be present when not illustrated by the ideogram.

The pair formed by *a-ja-me-na* (dual *a-ja-me-no*) and *a-na-i-ta, a-na-ta, a-na-to* is more complicated. If *a-na-mo-to* is *anarmostoi*, then we should expect *anai(s)toi* or the like as the negative of the participle *a-ja-me-na*. But it is evident that *a-na-(i-)ta* is twice used in the plural, contrary to the rule that compound adjectives have only two terminations. Palmer (1963a, p. 319) suggests that it is a noun, but this ignores *a-na-to* (Sg 888, Sf 4423, Sf 4425) where equally the tablet was, or may have been, introduced by *i-qi-ja* in large characters; the number in all these cases cannot be recovered. On the whole it is probably easier to regard *a-na-(i-)ta* as a scribal error or inconsistency.

364† *i-qo-e-qe*: it should have been observed that this is unlikely to be a singular both because of the form and because a chariot has two horses. Perhaps therefore dual of a root

515

noun *hiqqᵘo-heqᵘs as proposed by Lejeune (1958a, p. 179, n. 76). The only likely part of a chariot to be so called would be the two harness-saddles attached to the yoke, which are described on p. 363 and illustrated in Fig. 25. Since they fit on the horse's neck, they might conceivably be described as 'horse-followers'.

o-po-qo: Palmer (1963a, p. 316) has correctly seen that this word is a compound of opi- and the second element of πρόσ-ωπον, μέτ-ωπον, etc. But opōqᵘō ought to mean not 'nose-pieces' but 'eye-pieces', and this leads to the suggestion that the word means 'blinkers'. Blinkers of bronze are attested by the chariot and horses buried in the dromos of a tomb at Salamis in Cyprus, where Mycenaean customs seem to have survived down to a much later date (Karageorghis, 1966, p. 238; 1967b, p. 341).

p. 365† **265** = Sd 4403. In the translation for '*cheek-straps*' read 'blinkers' and for '*feudal contribution*' read 'work'. Similar corrections should be made in the translations of the following texts.

p. 366† **267** = Sd 4409. Corrections: l. 2 read: *a-ja-me-na*; l. 1: *wi-ri-ne-o o-po-qo ka-ke-ja-pi o-pi-i-ja-pi* WHEEL-LESS CHARIOT 1.

p. 367† **268** = Sd 4413. Translation: for '*pole-stay*' read '*harness-saddles*'; for '*cheek-straps*' read 'blinkers'.

p. 367‡ **269** = Sd 4404. The upper edge of this tablet has the reading:
po-ni-ki-ja WHEELED CHARIOT 1
This is remarkable as being the only case of the form of the chariot with wheels being used outside the *Sc* series (on which see below, p. 522).

mi-to-we-sa-e: Lejeune (1958b, p. 21) suggested that the final -e was an independent adverb, *en* 'inside', graphically attached to the preceding word. But it is perhaps more likely that it is an abnormal spelling for the plural, possibly influenced by the dual of masculine *a*-stems (see p. 389).

p. 367¶ **270** = Sd 4402

au-ro: dual or plural of αὐλός 'pipe' in some technical sense; cf. αὐλοῖσιν διδύμοισι Od. XIX, 227, of a buckle.

pe-qa-to (pe-pa₂-to): probably *pegguaton* < *ped-guaton* (cf. βατός, βαίνω) 'that which is trodden by the foot, foot-board' (cf. Palmer's suggestion on p. 368).

p. 368† **274** = Sf 4428. The argument is not changed by substituting 'blinkers' for 'cheek-strap'. The probable sense of *me-ta-ke-ku-me-na* (*metakekhumena*) is 'taken to pieces', 'knocked-down'.

369† **276** = Se 891 + 1006 + 1042. The newly-joined fragment proves the restoration *pte-re-wa*. No progress has been made with the interpretation of this group of tablets.

369‡ **277** = Ra 1028. This tablet can be re-classified on the basis of the joining of an almost illegible fragment and the suggestion by Olivier that 7498 is part of the same tablet. The complete text now reads:

e-re-pa-te   [   ]*ri*   SWORD 18

]-*qo-jo* / *zo-wa*[/ *e-*]*pi*[*-zo-ta*   *de-de-*]*me-na*   SWORD 99

The restorations are based upon **163** = Ra 984 as now corrected, except that the guess [*i*]-*qo-jo* has not been confirmed. It would be possible to restore *ke-ra* before *de-de-me-na* in the second line, but this is perhaps a variable element in the formula. The SWORD ideogram in line 2 is inverted, exactly as in **163** = Ra 984.

369¶ Another fragment (So 1053) has now been identified as listing wheels, but not found in the Armoury.

370† The value of **71* as *dwe* was established by PY Sa 1266 *te-mi-de-we-te*. Hence the Mycenaean adjective must be *termidwens*, with the dental stem declension of τέρμις; Homeric τερμιόεις is thus probably a later replacement with the link vowel -o- preserving the metrical shape ($- \cup \cup -$ for $- - -$). The exact nature of a τέρμις is not made any clearer. The alternative description is variously spelt *o-da-ke-we-ta*, *o-da-ku-we-ta*, *o-da-tu-we-ta* and *o-da-***87-ta*; hence **87* is probably *twe*, since the value *kwe would presumably coincide with **78* = *qe*. It is tempting to see in the first member of the compound some form related to ὀδούς 'tooth', perhaps referring to a design rather than a serrated surface to the wheel; *odat-* might come from zero-grade **odṇt-*, and *odak-* is possibly connected with ὀδαξ.

371† **278** = So 894. Corrections: for **71* read *dwe* in lines 1 and 3; in line 3 read ZE 41 MO̧[1].

te-mi-dwe = *termidwen*; the neuter singular must be understood as referring to one pair; the plural in line 3 equally refers to the 41 pairs.

371‡ **322** = Sg 1811 (formerly 890*bis*, now joined) (K)

1	]	CHARIOT-FRAME 22[	
2	]	CHARIOT-FRAME 224	[
3	]-*mi-we-te*	WHEEL ZE 21[	

4	]		WHEEL	ZE 8 [
5	*o-da-*]*ke̩-we-ta*		WHEEL	ZE 7 *a-mo* ị[
6	]*o-da-ke-we-ta*		WHEEL	ZE 17ọ
7	]	vacat		

Rev.: 176[

This collection of fragments now reveals that one tablet could list both chariot-frames (cf. **272, 273**), and wheels. The size of some of the figures suggests that this was a totalling document.

[*te*]-*mi-we-te*: if rightly so restored, and not a mere slip, may be evidence that the *i*-stem declension of *termis* already existed alongside the dental stem.

p. 372† **279** = So 4437. Read: *te-mi-dwe-te.*

p. 372‡ **280** = So 4439. Read *te-mi-dwe-ta* and MO WHEEL I.

p. 372¶ **281** = So 4440. Read *o-da-twe-ta* (see on **278** above) and WHEEL ZE 6.

p. 372†† **282** = So 4430. Read *o-da-twe-ta.* On *o-pa* see p. 420.

p. 372‡‡ **283** = So 4442. The left-hand end of this tablet is probably X 4472, giving the reading: *se-to*[-]*i̩-ja* . One other wheel tablet begins with a place name, So 4448: *pa-i-to.* The reading *a-mo* ị, singular to *a-mo-ta*, is established for 7485, now joined to **322** = Sg 1811.

p. 373† The most important discovery in this field since the publication of the first edition has been the completion of Sa 753 by a new fragment (Lang, 1958, p. 182) giving this text:

  se-we-ri-ko-jo wo-ka e-qe-si-jo WHEEL + TE ZE 2

This for the first time showed that *wo-ka* can occur independently of *we-je-ke-e* and thus cannot be an adverb. As was quickly pointed out by Palmer (1957*a*, p. 580), the second explanation offered must be correct; we can reconstruct a feminine noun *wokhā* related to the verb *Fέχω.

p. 373‡ **285** = Sa 487. Read: WHEEL + TE ZE 2[.

The set to which this tablet belongs now numbers eighteen; the names to be added are: *Se-we-ri-ko-jo, E-ti-ra-wo-jo, A-re-to-to, E-pi-wo-qa-ta-o*; the fifth name, *E-te-wa-jo*, incorrectly lacking its genitival ending, had occurred before (Sa 769).

we-je-ke-e: the opposition with *no-pe-re-a₂* wheels, which are never assigned to the chariot of a named person, makes it virtually certain that the effective sense of this word is 'serviceable'. How to extract this sense from the spelling is less certain, but the similar sense of ἐπιεικής strongly suggests that a solution should be sought in that direction. The chief obstacle is that -εικής is plainly from *-ϝεικής (cf. ἐπιείκελος without elision of ι); we- could possibly be a spelling device for (h)u-, giving the prefix ὑ- = ἐπι- which appears to occur in several Cypriot words (especially u-ke-ro-ne = ὑχέρον (gen.) 'wages' Schwyzer, Dial. 679.5, 15). To explain -je- we must therefore have recourse to a dissimilation *we-weikēs > *we(y)eikēs (Chadwick, 1958b, p. 308; Chantraine, 1959, p. 250). This solution has so many difficulties that great efforts have been made to find an alternative, but almost all produce unacceptable sense. The attempt to find ἔγχος in the second member (Palmer, 1958, p. 17, 1963a, p. 462; cf. Ruijgh, 1967, p. 380) involves, not merely the unexampled sense of 'axle' for the noun, but also the assumption that Mycenaean chariots had their wheels mounted upon a removable axle rather than one integral with the frame. Other attempts to meet the required sense have been based upon we- as a spelling (or more likely variant form) of εὐ-, and an adjectival form in -εχής related to ἔχω, cf. pu-ko-so e-ke-e PY 241 = Ta 715, p. 342 (Gallavotti, 1958, p. 67; Luria, 1958, p. 259).

p. 374† **286** = Sa 787. Read in upper line: WHEEL ZE 31; in lower line: *pa-ra-ja za-ku-si-ja*.

The comparison of Sa 843, also completed since the first edition (Lang, 1959, p. 131), shows a parallel text:

to-sa we-je-ke-a₂ ne-wa WHEEL + TE ZE 20

This finally proved that *ne-wa* and *pa-ra-ja* were opposites, thus confirming that *pa-ra-ja* must be παλαιά.

p. 374‡ **287** = Sa 793. Read *te-mi-dwe-ta* (see above, p. 517).

p. 374¶ **288** = Sa 790

e-qe-si-ja must mean that the 'Followers' have a special pattern of chariot-wheel, and therefore they must possess chariots.

p. 375† Excavation in 1957 produced a tablet dealing with chariot equipment, though the records of the chariots themselves are still missing. There is also an interesting list of men which seems to be connected with the manufacture of chariot-parts.

323 = Sb 1315
1]-wo-ja a-ni-ja te-u-ke-pi 5 di-pte-ra₃ e-ru-ta-ra 16[
2 ro-u-si-je-wi-ja 6 ra-pte-ri-ja a-ni-ja 3

³ *ne-wa   a-ni-ja   a-na-pu-ke*   5 | *dwo* 2 ‖ *a-pu-ke*   9

a-ni-ja-e-e-ro-pa-jo-qe-ṛọ-ṣạ   '2'

⁴ *a-pe-ne-wo*   4 | *a-pu-ke   a-pe-ne-wo*   '1' ‖ *ne-wa   po-qe-wi-ja*   ZE 11

¹ Five sets of reins [fitted] with equipment; sixteen red hides.

² Six (sets of reins) of *Lousos* type; three sets of reins with saddlers' work.

³ Five sets of new reins without head-bands; nine (sets?) with two head-bands; two sets of reins . . .

⁴ Four . . .; one . . . *with* head-band(s); eleven pairs of new halters.

]-*wo-ja*: there has been erasure at this point and it is uncertain what happened; it is tempting to suppose that the scribe wrote *a-ra-ru-wo-a* (traces of the *a* remain beneath *ja*) and intended to change the neuter to feminine plural by deleting *a* and substituting *ja*, forgetting that he needed also to delete *wo*. A contrast with the first entry of line 3 seems to be intended; but *te-u-ke-pi* might stand qualifying *a-ni-ja* even without the support of a participle.

te-u-ke-pi: *teukhesphi*, but in which of the many senses of τεῦχος? The Homeric sense of 'armour' seems inappropriate, so perhaps it is more general, 'equipment'.

di-pte-ra₃: *diphtherai* 'treated hides'; see on this p. 492. These may have been to cover the frame of the body of the chariot (cf. p. 362 and item *B* in Fig. 25). The red colour, as on **317** = Ub 1318, cf. p. 491, recalls the other words for 'red' on the Knossos chariot tablets (*po-ni-ki-ja* **266** = Sd 4401, **267** = Sd 4409, **268** = Sd 4413, etc.; *mi-to-we-sa-e* **269** = Sd 4404).

ro-u-si-je-wi-ja: apparently a derivative in -*ēwios* from the place name *ro-u-so*; cf. *wa-na-se-wi-jo, di-pi-si-je-wi-jo, wo-de-wi-jo*, etc. This suffix does not seem to be restricted to stems where it can be analysed as -ευς + -ιος; cf. Cretan θιήια < *θε-ήϝια. The name presumably indicates a type; cf. the epithet 'Zakynthian' used of wheels, PY **286** = Sa 787.

ra-pte-ri-ja: plainly *rhaptēriai*, the adjective from ῥαπτήρ. This suggests that the sewing done by the *rhaptēres* may be on leather, possibly ornamental stitching, since all reins would need some sewing.

ne-wa   a-ni-ja   a-na-pu-ke: *newai hāniai anampukes* 'new reins without head-bands'. The *ampukes* on this tablet are plainly for horses, a sense attested by a compound in Pindar (see Glossary).

dwo 2: these signs are much smaller than those on either side, and it is clear that the scribe inserted them as an afterthought; the numeral is meant to illustrate the interpretation of the syllabic sign, which exceptionally stands alone. Whether it is to be read *dwō* or disyllabically as *duō* remains uncertain. The note 'two' must refer to the following entry; but if the scribe meant to record nine sets of two head-bands (one for each horse), why did he not write ZE 9 'nine pairs' as he did for the halters in line 4? Since the preceding and following entries both relate to reins, is it not likely that this entry too is to be understood as referring to nine sets of reins equipped with head-bands, the numeral 'two' being inserted to show that *a-pu-ke*, which might be instrumental singular, is to be thought of as dual? The result is inconsistent, but would have been clear enough to the writer.

a-ni-ja   e-e-ro-pa-jo-qe-ro-sa: there is no divider after *a-ni-ja*, and at the end of the line the scribe ran out of space, hence 2 is inserted above the line. This suggests that we might read *a-ni-ja-e* as a feminine dual, like *mi-to-we-sa-e* KN **269** = Sd 4404, see p. 516. The resultant word in either case remains obscure. Palmer (1963*a*, p. 329) calls attention to εἶλος, glossed by Hesychius as δεσμός, but its plural εἶλεα shows that it is a neuter *s*-stem, and therefore cannot fit the Mycenaean spelling unless *e-e-ro* is complete and singular nominative or accusative. It may still be connected, for the other meanings given by Hesychius include χαλινοί and φιμοί.

a-pe-ne-wo: the repetition of this word in the following entry, which has been squeezed in apparently after the last entry in the line was written, raises difficulties. The easiest solution is to regard it as an *o*-stem, appearing first in the nominative plural, then in the nominative singular; *a-pu-ke* will then be an annotation, as in *dwo a-pu-ke* of line 3. If *a-pu-ke* be nominative, it must be dual or plural, which conflicts with the numeral 1, though even this is not a certain reading. The alternative is to take *a-pe-ne-wo* as genitive plural, understanding *a-ni-ja* with the first entry; but then we have again the problem of *a-pu-ke* followed by 1. Lejeune (1958*a*, p. 335) adopting this solution interprets the word as *apēnēwōn* from *ἀπηνεύς, an animal used to draw an ἀπήνη.

po-qe-wi-ja: *phorgᵘēwiai* (φορβειαί) 'halters'. This matches with *po-qa* and *i-po-po-qo-i* (see Glossary), both of which show a labio-velar for the final consonant of the root represented by classical φέρβω.

324 = An 1282

1	*a-qi-ja-i*	MAN 18	*a-mo-si*	MAN 18
2	*ki-u-ro-i*	MAN 13	*po-qe-wi-ja-i*	MAN 5
3	*do-ka-ma-i*	MAN 36		
4-5		v a c a n t		

The whole tablet has been written, deleted and re-used; but the final readings are perfectly clear. It is evident from *a-mo-si* = *harmosi* 'wheels' and *po-qe-wi-ja-i* = *phorgᵘēwiāhi* 'halters' that we have a list of equipment for chariots, with varying numbers of men assigned to each. The items are all in the dative plural. The problems are to account for the other three words and to explain the numerals. There is clearly a basic unit of 18, which occurs in line 1, is split into 13 + 5 in line 2, and is doubled in line 3. If we assume that the number of men is somehow related to the amount of labour needed to make the item, then it is reasonable that more than three times as many men will be needed to make wheels as halters.

a-qi-ja-i: it is almost irresistible to conjecture a scribal error and emend to *i-qi-ja-i* 'chariots', although this word is so far known only at Knossos, and at Pylos *wo-ka* appears to take its place. The equal number of men assigned to chariot-frames and to wheels is probably intelligible; though larger, a chariot requires less work to construct than a pair of wheels.

ki-u-ro-i: Palmer (1963*a*, p. 328) quotes Hesychius: κίουρος 'a basket for corn'; it would be more convincing if it could mean 'basketwork' for the fabrication of chariot-bodies. Mycenaean -*u*- cannot correspond directly to classical -*ou*-.

do-ka-ma-i: it is tempting to connect this with δοχμή or even δραχμή (< *dṛk-smā, cf. δράσσομαι), but the parallel of *a₃-ka-sa-ma* shows that -*ksm*- in these words had not yet been reduced to -χμ-. Apart from this, neither 'hand's breadth' nor 'handful' offers satisfactory sense. A connexion with δοκός 'beam' might be more promising semantically. Any explanation must account for the large number of men assigned to this item.

p. 375‡ The archaeological picture has been changed by the discovery in a tomb at Dendra in the Argolid in 1960 of a complete suit of bronze armour (Verdelis, 1961; Åström, 1962). Although this is earlier in date and clearly of a different construction from the suits listed at Pylos, it can never again be asserted that bronze body-armour was not used in Mycenaean times. It does not, however, follow that the Pylos armour was entirely of bronze; the material of the 'plates' (*o-pa-wo-ta*) is never specified, and one may doubt the wisdom of wearing metal armour in a Greek summer. It is at least possible that some of the armour was of thick linen rather than metal, or that linen played some part in its construction; in medieval times linen armour was much used, and if enough layers of material were superimposed could be very effective. The association of ingots with corslets on the Knossos tablets (p. 380) certainly suggests that the material was bronze, though the reason for the corrections has not been satisfactorily explained.

p. 379† **296**=Sh 736. Correction: read at end: *wo-ke   ne-wo̭*[   ]5.
Possibly *me-za-na wo-ke* is to be taken together as an indication of the type of craftsmanship; cf. *ke-re-si-jo   we-ke*=*Krēsiowergēs* PY **236**=Ta 641, **237**=Ta 709.

p. 379‡ The number of *Sc* tablets has now been increased to 156, but many of these are small fragments and the total number of tablets will probably have been rather smaller. The tablets from this deposit form an apparently closed group with little cross-reference to the other Archives, and although written by different scribes show a remarkable similarity of hand-writing (Olivier, 1967*b*, pp. 66–76; Chadwick, 1968*b*, pp. 17–20). Their purpose remains enigmatic, for if it is a list of equipment issued to these warriors, the Knossian army must have been in a poor state to require so much material; and if less than a full complement of two corslets, one chariot and two horses is issued, is it because the warriors already have the remainder? This might explain the note *e-ko* I added after the record of one horse on **298** = Sc 226. Alternatively, if it is the record of the equipment at present held by these men, the condition of the army is again parlous, since so many of them have defective equipment. Possibly we must understand this as a list of the equipment supplied by the Palace, the warriors supplying the remainder themselves. But even this theory is far from solving all the problems.

The number of tablets listing one and two corslets can be corrected to fourteen and nineteen respectively, allowing those in which the CORSLET ideogram is followed immediately by another ideogram to count as instances of I; CORSLET I is written only eight times. Since no less than eighteen tablets show CORSLET written and then deleted, perhaps the absence of the numeral may here be significant. It is clear that two corslets, presumably one for the warrior and the other for his driver, is the normal issue; if the two pieces made up a single suit, we should expect them to be counted in pairs (ZE), and it would be hard to explain the single pieces. The seven certain cases where an ingot has been inserted, often in substitution for a corslet and never together with one, also require an explanation. It is easy to say that this is the raw material issued in lieu of corslets; but how long must the warrior wait until the armour has been fashioned from it? At least this would imply that there was no thought of suddenly mobilizing the army for service.

The CORSLET ideogram surcharged with QE has been taken as standing for *qe-ro₂*, on which see **299** = Sk 789 and p. 494. This is a mere guess which cannot be confirmed. The entry QE ZE I on Sc 266 is almost certainly a scribal error for HORSE ZE I; the QE has been squeezed in as an afterthought, and was probably suggested by the QE surcharged on the CORSLET.

Of the introductory names preserved many do not recur at Knossos; of those that do, most are on other tablets from the same find-spot. On V 60 the word *a-ni-o-ko* 'charioteer' is not necessarily to be taken as a heading to the complete list, but the association is probably significant; two names, *a-e-da-do-ro* and *ta-pa-no*, recur on F 153 (from the same archive) which is probably a list of rations.

p. 380† The two tablets brought together here as **299** and **300** can now be seen to belong to a set of six fragments, the best preserved of which is here added. The prefix *Sk* has been allocated to this set, which is clearly akin to the Pylos *Sh* tablets, but shows differences of detail.

325 = Sk 8100

²   *qe-ro₂*   2   *e-po-mi-jo*   2 | *o-pa-wo*[*-ta*
                                              o-pa-wo-ta
¹   *pa-ra* | *ko-ru*   HELMET 1   *o-pi-ko-ru-si-ja*   4   *pa-ra-wa*[*-jo*   2

Pa-ra: one helmet, four helmet-plates, [two] cheek-pieces, two *arm-guards*, two shoulder-guards, . . . plates.

pa-ra: probably a man's name, though the similarity to]-*ra* in **299** = Sk 789 is suspicious; no other tablet of the series has any part of the first word preserved. The lower line, which has a word written above it, is to be read first, as usual when there is no central ruling.

ko-ru: *korus*, the confirmation of the restoration in **300** = Sk 5670 is welcome.

o-pi-ko-ru-si-ja   o-pa-wo-ta: owing to the way in which these words and the accompanying 4 are written, it would be equally possible to read *o-pi-ko-ru-si-ja* 2   *o-pa-wo-ta* 2. If so, one must ask why the words are not in the dual; cf. *e-pi-ko-ru-si-jo* in **299** = Sk 789. The variation in the form of the adjective is a striking confirmation that *opi* and *epi* were not significantly distinguished in sense, for the same scribe wrote both tablets. Clearly this is the equivalent of *ko-ru-to* o   4 on PY **292** = Sh 740, **293** = Sh 737. The same entry is repeated on Sk 8149, but here its end is damaged.

qe-ro₂: see on this word p. 494.

e-po-mi-jo: the conjecture of **299** = Sk 789 is confirmed.

o-pa-wo[*-ta*: the final entry may have concerned the plates of the corslet proper; it is not preserved on any of the other fragments of this set.

PART IV
GLOSSARY, BIBLIOGRAPHY,
INDEX AND CONCORDANCES

MYCENAEAN GLOSSARY

This glossary is not restricted to the texts printed in this book, but contains an entry for every complete Mycenaean word recorded up to 1972. Incomplete words are omitted unless they can be plausibly restored or are otherwise of interest. Full references are not given for frequently occurring words, the sign + being used to indicate further references.

Words are normally indexed under the simplest form quotable, and separable prefixes and suffixes are ignored in the alphabetical order. Thus words beginning with the prefix *o-* will be found under the simple form, though cross-references are included in case of doubt. Inflexional forms and derivatives are given separate headings under the main entry. The alphabetical order adopted is (unlike the first edition) by transliterated signs, so that, e.g., words beginning a_2- are placed after those beginning *a-*, not combined into a single list. The following changes of practice in transliteration compared with the first edition, and consequently parts I and II of this, have been adopted:

$$ai = a_3$$
$$pa_2 = qa$$
$$*85 = au \text{ (placed after } a_3)$$

These changes have been made to conform with the internationally agreed system of transliteration.

The combination of three indexes into one has meant that a convenient system had to be introduced to distinguish place names and personal names; hence the three abbreviations P N = place name, M N = man's name, W N = woman's name. A full list of abbreviations follows:

abl.	ablative	mid.	middle
acc.	accusative	M N	man's name
act.	active	MY	Mycenae
adj.	adjective	neut.	neuter
aor.	aorist	nom.	nominative
app.	apparently	pass.	passive
conj.	conjunction	perf.	perfect
conjug.	conjugation	perh.	perhaps
dat.	dative	pers.	person
etym.	etymology	plur.	plural
fem.	feminine	P N	place name
fut.	future	poss.	possibly
gen.	genitive	pple.	participle
indic.	indicative	prec.	preceding
inf.	infinitive	prep.	preposition
inscr.	inscription	pres.	present
instr.	instrumental	prob.	probably
KN	Knossos	PY	Pylos
loc.	locative	rel.	relative
masc.	masculine	rev.	reverse

sb.   substantive
sim.   similar
sing. singular
s.v.   sub voce

TH   Thebes
TI   Tiryns
W N   woman's name

A, With AMPHORA ideogram, KN 204 = Gg 704 + : abbreviation of *a-pi-po-re-u* (see *a-pi-po-re-we*). With OLIVE ideogram, KN E 669, 95 = F 852 + : obscure. With OIL ideogram, PY 310 = Fr 1225 +. Probably = *aloiphā* 'ointment'. Ideographic use, PY Un 1320: obscure.

a-da-ma-o, PY Eb 747, 131 = Ep 301, Jn 832. MN: *Admaos?*

> *a-da-ma-o-jo*, PY 116 = En 659. Gen.: *Admaoio*.
> *a-da-ma-jo*, PY 124 = Eo 351. Defective spelling of prec.

a-da-ra-ko[, KN X 793. MN?, dat.: perhaps *Andrarkhōi*. [Ilievski, 1969 a, p. 216.]

a-da-ra-ro, KN Da 5223. MN.

a-da-ra-te-ja, PY Aa 785, Ab 388. Prob. not an ethnic as proposed (p. 156), but since only one woman is recorded more likely a feminine personal name: *Adrāsteia*. [Cf. Ἀδρήστεια *Il.* II, 828.]

a-da-ra-ti-jo, PY 44 = Aq 218, 59 = An 656. Patronymic adj.: *Adrāstios*. [Cf. Ἄδρηστος, *Il.* XIV, 121 +.]

a-da-wa-si-jo, KN C 912. Adj. describing man, perh. patronymic.

a-da-wo-ne[, KN B 164. MN. Dat.?

a-de-me-we, PY Eq 146. MN.

a-de-ra₂, KN Ap 639. WN.

a-de-te, PY Eq 34. Occupational term in *-tēr*: *andetēr* 'binder'? *Docs.*¹; 'riveter' Palmer (1963 a, p. 336).

> *a-de-te-re*, PY 52 = An 207. Dual: *-tēre*.

a-de-we-[.], KN As 1516. MN.

]*a-di-je-wo*, KN D 747. MN. Gen. Cf. *a₂-di-je-u*.

a-di-nwa-ta, KN 39 = As 1517. MN.

a-di-ri-ja-te, PY 242 = Ta 707. Inst. sing. masc. *andriante(i)* '(inlaid) with a figure of a man'. [ἀνδρίας Pindar 5 B.C. +.]

> *a-di-ri-ja-pi*, PY 243 = Ta 708 +. Instr. plur.: **andriant-phi > andriamphi*.

a-di-ri-jo, KN Do 7613. MN. *Andrios? Andriōn?* [Ἄνδριος ethnic; Ἀνδρίων.]

a-di-*22-sa, PY 44 = F 841. Obscure.

a-do-we, TH Z 842, TI Z 24, Z 25. Single word inscribed on jars; MN?

a-du-po-to, KN C 911. MN.

a-du-ru-po-to, KN Dg 1107 + 1465. MN: *Adruptos?*

a-e-da-do-ro, KN F 153, Sc 237. MN.

a-e-ri-qe, PY Jn 832. Perh. MN, but uncertain if *-qe* is the particle *qᵘe* 'and'.

a-e-ri-qo, PY An 192, Jn 431. MN. Shortened form of next? *Āeriqᵘhos?*

a-e-ri-qo-ta, PY 44 = Aq 218, 56 = An 657 +. MN. *Āeri-qᵘhoitās?* [Hom. ἦρι, ἠέριος; -φοίτης.]

a-e-se-wa, PY Fn 79. MN. Dat.

a-e-ti-to[, PY Fr 1200. Epithet of sage-scented oil: 'without *e-ti*' (see *e-ti-we*).

ai-: for words beginning *ai-* see under *a₃-*.

a-i-qe-u, PY 134 = Eb 895, 131 = Ep 301. MN. Ventris: *Ahiqqᵘeus?* Lejeune (1968 a): *Ahi-qᵘheus* (hypocoristic of **Ἀ(h)ι-φόντας* 'he who kills with the sword').

> *a-i-qe-wo*, PY 116 = En 659. Gen.
> *a-i-qe-we*, PY 125 = Eo 471. Dat.

a-ja-me-no, KN 266 = Sd 4401 +, PY 242 = Ta 707 +. Nom. sing. and plur. masc., perh. pf. pple. pass. *aia(s)menos (aiāmenos?)*, *-oi*. Also nom. dual fem.: *-menō*: 'inlaid'. [Meaning clear, but form and etymology obscure.]

> *a-ja-me-na*, KN 265 = Sd 4403 +, 272 = Sf 4421, PY 239 = Ta 642. Nom. sing. fem.: *-menā*.
> *a-ja-me*, KN Sd 4415. Defective spelling of prec.

a-ka¹, KN Da 1078 +, Dn 5318. PN.

a-ka², PY 312 = An 1281. MN.

a-ka-de, KN B 799. MN.

a-ka-i-je-ja, TH Of 27. Fem. adjectival formation on *a-ka-i-jo?*

a-ka-i-jo, KN De 1084, F 153, Vc 68, Vd 62 +. MN. Cf. *a-ka¹?*

a-ka-ma-jo, PY Fn 324. MN. Dat.? *Alkmaiōi*. [ἀλκμαῖος· νεανίσκος Hesych.; cf. Ἀλκμαίων.]

a-ka-ma-no, PY Jn 415. MN: *Alkmānōr* (Ilievski, 1969 b, p. 174). [Ἀλκμήνωρ.]

a-ka-ma-wo, PY 61 = Cn 131 +, Jn 706 +. MN. Nom. and dat. *Alkmawos, -wōi?* [Cf. Ἀλκμάων *Il.* XII, 394.]

a-ka-me-ne[, KN Xd 82. If complete, prob. MN. *Akhaimenēs* or *Alkāmenēs?* [Ἀχαιμένης, Ἀλκαμένης.]

a-ka-na-jo, PY Cn 328 +, Xa 1337. Poss. PN or adj. describing sheep and goats: cf. *a₃-ka-na-jo*.

a-ka-ra-no, PY 241 = Ta 715. Nom. sing. fem., adj. describing a table; perh. *akarānos* 'headless' (i.e. designed to take detachable tops?); in view of declension prob. compound with negative *a-*. [ἀκάρηνος *Anth. Pal.*] See pp. 342, 501.

a-ka-re-u, KN Ga 416. MN: *Agalleus? Angareus?*

> *a-ka-re-u-te*, PY Cn 4. Perh. PN in dat. -loc.; cf. *a-ke-re-u-te*.

a-ka-sa-no[, KN As 602. MN: *Alxānōr*. [Ἀλχσήνωρ Schwyzer, *Dial.* 761.]

a-ka-si-jo-ne, PY 254 = Jn 389. PN: loc.?

a-ka-ta-jo, KN Dv 1086 +, PY 127 = Eo 269. MN: nom. and dat.: *Aktaios, -aiōi*. [Ἀκταῖος.]

> *a-ka-ta-jo-jo*, PY [116 = En 659], 127 = Eo 269. Gen.: *Aktaioio*.

a-ka-ta-ra-te-so-de, KN Fp 5504. Perh. PN in acc. with allative *-de*.

a-ka-to, KN Dv 5256, Sc 256. MN: *Agathos*, *Agathōn*? ["Αγαθος, 'Αγάθων.]

a-ka-to-wa, KN Vc 81. MN.

a-ka-to-wa-o, TH Ug 4+. Gen.

a-ka-wi-ja-de, KN 78 = C 914. Prob. PN in acc. with allative *-de*: *Akhaiwiān-de*. [Cf. Hitt. *Aḫḫijawā*.] Not MN as proposed by Palmer, see p. 436.

a-ka-wo, KN Ga 738, PY 258 = Jo 438. MN: *Alkāwōn*?

a-ka-wo-ne, PY Un 219. Dat.: *-ōnei*.

a-ke, PY 172 = Tn 316, MY Ue 611. Prob. 3rd sing. pres. indic. act. of ἄγω: *agei*; see pp. 285, 461.

a-ke-a₂, PY Vn 130. Nom. plur. neut.: *angeha* 'wine jars'? [ἄγγος *Od.* XVI, 13+.]

a-ke-e: see *ti-mi-to-a-ke-e*.

a-ke-e-to, KN Da 1195. MN.

a-ke-o, PY An 192, 63 = Cc 660. MN.

a-ke-o-jo, PY Cn 40+. Gen.: *-oio*.

a-ke-ra-no, KN Vc 205. MN.

a-ke-ra-wo, KN Vc 316, PY Cn 599+. MN: nom. and dat.: *Agelāwos* or *Arkhelāwos*, *-wōi*. ['Αγέλαος *Il.* VIII, 257, 'Αγέλεως *Od.* XXII, 131; 'Αρχέλαος.]

a-ke-ra₂-te, PY Vn 493. Nom. plur. masc., aor. pple.: perh. *agērantes* (ἀγείρω, cf. *a-ke-re*) 'collecting, gathering'; or less likely *angēlantes* 'announcing'.

a-ke-re, PY 63 = Cc 660. 3rd sing. pres.: *agērei* 'he collects (goats)'. Exact sense not clear. [ἀγείρω *Il.* IV, 377+.]

a-ke-re-mo, KN Uf 838. Nom. sing., occupational term: *agremōn*? [ἀγρεμών 'hunter' *Etym. Mag.*]

a-ke-re-mo-no, KN V 865. Gen. sing.: *agremonos*.

a-ke-re-se, PY 43 = Aq 64. 3rd sing. aor. or fut.: *agrēse*, *agrēsei* 'took' or 'will take'. [ἀγρέω 'take' retained in Aeolic; cf. Hom. ἄγρει 'come on!'] *o-a-ke-re-se* ibid. *hō agrēse(i)* 'thus he took (will take)'. See pp. 176, 423.

a-ke-re-u, PY Cn 441. Nom. sing. MN or occupational term? [ἀγρεύς?]

a-ke-re-we, PY Un 1193. Dat. sing. or perh. nom. plur.

a-ke-re-u-te, MY Ge 606. PN?: perh. abl. in *-euthen*.

a-ke-re-wa, PY [49 = An 427], 54 = An 610, 55 = An 724, 59 = An 656, 253 = Jn 310, 258 = Jo 438+. PN: one of the Nine Towns of the Hither Province (see p. 142).

a-ke-re-wa-de, PY 250 = Vn 20. Acc. + *-de*.

a-ke-re-wi-jo, MY 106 = Ge 603, 107 = Ge 604. MN. Nom. and dat.

a-ke-ro¹, PY Cn 1287, Ea 136, Vn 493. Nom. sing. and plur.: occupational term, perh. *angelos*, *-oi*; Palmer (1963a, p. 404) suggests *ageroi* 'collectors'.

a-ke-ro², PY 258 = Jo 438. App. MN.

a-ke-ta, KN B 798, PY Cn 719. MN: nom. sing. (KN case uncertain): *Agētās*? *Akestās*? ['Αγήτας, 'Ακέστης.]

a-ḳe-te, PY Jn 832. App. nom. sing. of next, perh. error.

a-ke-te-re, PY Jn 832. Nom. plur., description of bronzesmiths, replacing *ta-ra-si-ja e-ko-te* where no quantity of metal is specified: prob. *askētēres* 'those who practise their craft'. [ἀσκέω 'work raw materials' *Il.* XXIII, 743.] See also *a₂-ke-te-re*, *ja-ke-te-re*.

a-ke-ti-jo, PY An 209. MN: *Akestios*? ['Ακέστιος.]

a-ke-ti-ra₂, PY 2 = Aa 815+, TH Of 36. Nom. plur. fem., description of women (cf. *a-ke-te-re*), prob. *askētriai* 'practitioners of a trade' but with more specific reference unclear; poss. *akestriai* 'sempstresses' [ἀκέστρια 5 B.C.]. See pp. 158, 418.

a-ke-ti-ra₂-o, PY Ad 290+. Gen. plus.: *-aōn*.

a-ke-ti-ri-ja, KN 17 = Ai 739+, PY Aa 85+. Nom. plur. (or dual?): variant spelling.

a-ke-ti-ri-ja-i, PY Fn 187, Un 219, MY 93 = Fo 101+. Dat. plur. *-āhi*. See also *a-ze-ti-ri-ja*.

a-ke-to-ro, KN V 145. Poss. sb., meaning and case unclear.

a-ke-u, KN Dv 1133, V 151+. MN: *Alkeus*? ['Αλκεύς.]

a-ke-wo, KN Ap 628. Gen.: *Alkēwos*.

a-ke-wa-ta, PY Jn 431. MN; cf. *a-ki-wa-ta*.

a-ke-wa-to, PY 60 = An 661. MN.

a-ki-a₂-ri-ja-de: see *a₃-ki-a₂-ri-ja*.

a-ki-re-u, KN Vc 106. MN, nom.: *Akhilleus*. ['Αχιλλεύς.]

a-ki-re-we, PY Fn 79. Dat.: *Akhillēwei*.

a-ki-ri-ja, KN C 7064. Description of goats of both sexes: perh. *agria* (neut. plur.?) 'wild creatures'. [ἄγριος.]

a-ki-ti-to, PY 197 = Na 406+, [153 = Er 880?]. Adj. describing land: *aktitos*, *-on* 'not inhabited'? (see p. 470). [ἄκτιτος *h. Hom.*] Cf. *ki-ti-me-na*.

a-ki-to, PY Fn 79. MN, dat.: *Alkithōi*? [Cf. 'Αλκίθοος.]

a-ki-to-jo, PY 91 = Fn 50. Gen.: *-thoio*.

a-ki-wa-ta, KN 38 = As 1516, B 801. MN; cf. *a-ke-wa-ta*.

a-ki-wo-ni-jo, PY 59 = An 656. MN.

a-ko-i-da, KN 73 = Dl 943. MN.

a-ko-mo-ni-jo, KN De 1112+. MN: *Akmonios*. [Cf. "Ακμων, 'Ακμονίδης.]

a-ko-ra, KN Dk 969, PY 62 = Cn 655+. Nom. sing., prob. *agorā* [ἀγορά] in sense more closely related to ἀγείρω, perh. 'collection'. Prob. a term describing the official responsible for flocks.

a-ko-ra-jo¹, KN 86 = Co 907. Nom. plur. masc.?, description of livestock: *agoraioi* 'belonging to the *agora*'.

a-ko-ra-ja, KN Co 903+. Nom. plur. neut.: *agoraia*.

*a-ko-ra-jo*², KN 38 = As 1516. MN: *Agoraios*.

a-ko-ro, KN Dl 932+, PY 307 = Fr 1220+, Ua 1413, 252 = Vn 10. Sb. qualified by adj. to form geographical name, case and number uncertain: *agros* 'territory'. [ἀγρός.]

a-ko-ro-ḍa-mo-jo, KN B 1025. MN?, gen.: *Akrodāmoio*. [Ἀκρόδημος.]

a-ko-ro-qo-ro, KN Da 1079. MN: *Agroqᵘolos*. [Cf. Latin *Agricola*.]

a-ko-ro-ta, KN Mc 4459, MY Go 610+. Prob. MN.

a-ko-ro-we, PY 77 = Cn 418. Nom. sing. masc., description of oxen: poss. *hakhrōwēs* 'of uniform colour' (*akhrōwēs* 'colourless' is difficult in context); or *akr-ōwēs* 'with pointed ears' (Gallavotti).

a-ko-ro-we-e, PY 77 = Cn 418. Nom. dual: *-wehe*.

a-ko-ro-we-i, KN Ch 7100. App. variant spelling of dual, since followed by BOS ZE 1.

a-ko-so-ne, PY Va 1323+, 252 = Vn 10. Nom. (and acc.?) plur.: *axones* 'shafts, axles'. [ἄξων; cf.]*ko-so-ni-ja*.]

a-ko-so-ta, PY 50 = An 39 rev., 154 = Eq 213, 103 = Un 267, 249 = Va 482+. MN: an important official; nom. prob. *Alxoitās* (Palmer). [Cf. Ἀλκοίτας.]

a-ko-so-ta-o, PY Cn 40+. Gen.: *-tāo*.

a-ko-te-u, PY Cn 643. MN: *Akonteus*? [Ἀκοντεύς.]

a-ko-to, KN Sc 239, Sc 250. MN: *Aktōr*. [Ἄκτωρ *Il*. II, 513+.]

a-ko-to-no, PY 44 = Aq 218. Nom. plur. masc.: *aktoinoi* 'not possessing a plot'.

a-ko-to-wo, PY Cn 45, Jn 431+. MN.

]*a-ko-we-i-ja*, KN L 1649. Obscure.

a-ko-wo, PY 55 = An 724. Obscure; Palmer (1963a): *ankhorwons* (as object of *e-qo-te*) 'neighbours', but this cannot be reconciled with *wo-wo* (q.v.) = *worwos* (ὅρος). See p. 188.

a-ku-di-ri-jo, KN Dc 1270, Xd 110. MN.

a-ku-ṇa-i, KN Ce 139. PN: loc. plur.

a-ku-ri-jọ[, KN As 609. MN: *Argurios*?

a-ku-ro, PY 290 = Sa 287. Material used for binding of wheels; instr. sing. *argurōi* 'with silver'. [ἄργυρος.]

a-ku-tu-ru-wo, KN Fh 364. MN: perh. *Alktruōn* (Heubeck, 1957, p. 274), or mis-spelling of *a-re-ku-tu-ru-wo* (q.v.).

a-ku-wo, KN U 109. Prob. MN: *Alkuōn*?

a-ma, KN E 845+, 95 = F 852+. Word occurring on tablets recording large quantities of grain, prob. nom. sing. *amā* 'harvest'. [Cf. ἀμάω 'reap', but possibly connected with ἀμάομαι, 'collect', ἀμή: see Chantraine 1968, p. 72.]

a-ma-ko-to, KN 201 = Fp 14. Name of a month, gen. (?): *Haimaktō*? [αἱμακτός Eur.]

a-ma-no, KN Ap 5748?, As 1520. MN?; in Ap WN?

a-ma-ru-ta, PY 119 = Eo 224. MN, dat.: *Amarunt(h)āi*? [Cf. Ἀμαρυγχεύς, Ἀμαρύνθιος.]

a-ma-ru-ta-o, PY 114 = En 609, 119 = Eo 224. Gen.: *-t(h)āo*.

a-ma-ru-to-de, TH Of 25. PN: acc. + *-de*: *Amarunthon-de*. [Ἀμάρυνθος in Euboea, or another place of the same name?]

a-ma-to-wo, PY An 115. MN: perh. *Amathowos*. [Cf. Ἀμαθοῦς eponymous hero of Cypriot town.]

a-ma-tu-na, PY Fn 187. MN.

a-me-a, KN Da 1189+. MN; cf. *a-me-ja-to*.

a-me-ja, KN F 153. MN, nom.

a-me-ja-to, PY Sa 834, 296 = Sh 736. Gen.

a-me-ja-si[, KN B 799 rev. MN.

a-me-no, PY Jn 415. MN: *Armenos*? *Asmenos*? *Ameinōn*? [Ἄρμενος, Ἄσμενος, Ἀμείνων.]

a-me-to, PY Jn 693. MN.

a-mi-ja[, PY Vn 865. MN.

a-mi-ke-te-to, KN Od 687. Perh. MN.

a-mi-ni-so, KN 200 = Fp 1+, PY An 943. PN: *Amnisos* (on the site see p. 310); no evidence to check whether Pylos reference refers to Cretan town. [Ἀμνισός *Od*. XIX, 188; Egypt *a-mi-ni-š-ɂ* Faure (1968).]

a-mi-ni-so-de, KN 201 = Fp 14+. Acc.: *Amnison-de*.

a-mi-ni-si-jo|*-ja*, KN 34 = Am 601+. Ethnic: *Amnisios, -iā*.

a-mi-nu-wa-ta, PY Cn 436. MN.

a-mi-nwa[, KN V 482. Poss. variant spelling.

a-mi-si-ja, KN L 513. Prob. defective spelling of *a-mi-ni-si-ja*.

a-mi-to-no, KN Ra 1543. MN.

a-mo, KN 322 = Sg 1811. Nom. sing. neut.: *(h)armo* 'wheel'. See pp. 371–2. [ἄρματα 'chariot' *Il*. IV, 366+; the initial aspirate may not be original, cf. *a-ra-ro-mo-te-me-na*.]

a-mo-ta, KN 279 = So 4437+, PY 288 = Sa 790. Nom. plur.: *(h)armota* (with WHEEL ideogram).

a-mo-te, KN 283 = So 4442. Nom. dual: *(h)armote*.

a-mo-si, PY 324 = An 1282. Dat. plur.: *(h)armosi*.

a-mo-i-je-to, PY 248 = Va 15 rev. Prob. two words: *harmo* 'chariot'? *hietoi* 'is being sent' (Palmer, 1963a, p. 406).

a-mo-ke-re[-*we*?], PY 183 = Nn 831. MN: *-klewēs*?

a-mo-ra-ma, KN 34 = Am 601+. Nom. sing. or plur.?; prob. word meaning 'rations, supplies'. [Cf. ἁρμαλιά 'rations' Hesiod+, Arc. ἄρμωλα, ἀρμώμαλα · ἀρτύματα Hesych. See Schmeja, 1968, p. 133.]

a-mo-si, *a-mo-ta*: see *a-mo*.

a-mo-ta-jo, PY Jn 320. MN: *Armostaios*? (*Ha-*?). [Cf. Ἁρμόστας.]

a-mo-te-jo-na-de, PY 252 = Vn 10. Acc. + allative: *(h)armoteiōna-de* 'to the wheelwrights' workshops'. See p. 350.

a-mo-te-re, KN Xe 6026, X 770. Prob. dat. sing. or nom. dual of noun in *-tēr*.

a-mo-te-wi-ja, PY 235 = Ta 711. Nom. sing. fem. adj. describing ewer; prob. derivative of next (*-ēwiā*) but sense uncertain. See pp. 335, 498.

a-mo-te-wo, PY Ea 421. Gen. sing., occupational term: poss. (*h*)*armotēwos* 'wheelwright' or (*h*)*armostēwos* 'fitter'.

a-mu-ta-wo, KN V 756, PY 183 = Nn 831, TH Ug 9. MN: *Amuthāwōn*. ['Αμυθάων *Od.* XI, 259.]

a-mu-ta-wo-no, PY Jn 431. Gen.: *Amuthāwonos*.

a-na-i-ta, see *a-na-to*.

a-na-ka, KN Nc 4480. MN.

ạ-na-ka-te, PY Un 219. Poss. dat., but error for *wa-na-ka-te* cannot be excluded.

a-na-ke-e, PY 44 = Aq 218. Pres. inf., poss. *anagehen* 'bring, contribute'? [ἀνάγω.]

a-na-ki-ti, KN Dv 1471. MN.

a-na-mo-to, KN 273 = Sf 4420 +. Nom. fem.: *anarmostoi* 'not fitted out' with reference to incomplete CHARIOT ideogram, not *anharmotoi* 'wheelless', see p. 515.

a-na-mo-ta, KN Sf 4465: neut. plur.?, referring to obscure ideogram.

a-na-pu-ke, PY 323 = Sb 1315. Nom. plur. fem., describing reins: *anampukes* 'without headbands'; cf. *a-pu-ke*. [ἀνάμπυξ.]

ạ-na-qo-ta, KN B 798. MN: *Anaqᵘhoitās*? (See p. 94.)

a-na-re-u, KN Pp 494. MN.

a-na-te-u, PY Jn 415. MN.

a-na-to, KN Sg 888 +. Nom. plur. fem., describing chariot-frames: *anai(s)toi* 'not inlaid' (opposed to *a-ja-me-na*). See p. 515.

a-na-i-ta, KN Sf 4419 +. App. nom. plur. fem., with fem. endings in compound adj.

a-na-ta, KN 273 = Sf 4420. Shorter spelling of prec.

a-na-*82, MY 93 = Fo 101. WN.

a-ne-a₂, MY 93 = Fo 101, 303 = V 659. WN: *Aineā*?

a-ne-mo, KN 200 = Fp 1. Gen. plur.: *anemōn* '(priestess) of the winds'. [ἄνεμοι *Il.* XIII, 795 +.]

a-ne-mo-i-je-re-ja, KN 202 = Fp 13. Prec. written continuously with following word: *anemōn hiereiāi* (see *i-je-re-ja*).

a-ne-o, PY 168 = Es 644, 167 = Es 650 +. MN.

a-ne-ra-to, KN Fh 342. MN, dat.

a-ne-ta-de, PY 175 = Ma 393. Nom. plur. neut. introducing a rebate on contributions: *aneta de* 'but remitted'. [ἄνετος 'set free', cf. ἄνεσις 'remission of taxes'.]

a-ne-te-wa, KN Vc 185. MN.

a-ne-u-da, KN Vc 215. MN.

a-ne-u-te, PY Cn 40. PN: also spelt *a₂-ne-u-te*.

a-ni-ja, KN 270 = Sd 4402 +, PY 323 = Sb 1315. Nom. plur.: (*h*)*āniai* 'reins'. [Hom. ἡνία, Pindar ἄνίαι, Att. ἡνίαι, some dialects ἀνίαι; cf. Skt. *nāsyā* 'nose-rein'.]

a-ni-ja-pi, KN 266 = Sd 4401 +. Instr. plur. (*araruiai*) (*h*)*āniāphi* '(fitted) with reins'.

a-ni-ja-e (division doubtful), PY 323 = Sb 1315. Dual: (*h*)*āniāe*?

a-ni-ja-to, KN 70 = Dg 1158. MN: *Aniātos*?

a-ni-ọ-ko, KN V 60. Nom. sing. (prob. not plural referring to subsequent entries too): (*h*)*āniokhos* 'chariot-driver'. [ἡνίοχος *Il.* VIII, 89 +.]

a-no, PY Cn 254. MN?; perh. to be read with next word as compound *a-no-de-ki-si-wo*; see *de-ki-si-wo*.

a-no-ke-wa, PY An 192. Prob. occupational term or title, parallel to *du-ma*.

a-no-ke-we, KN Db 1261, PY An 192. MN (doubtful at Pylos); cf. *a-no-ze-we*.

a-no-me-de, PY Jn 706. MN: *Anomēdēs*, *Anormēdēs*? [Cf. 'Ανδρομήδης.]

a-no-no, PY Ea 801, 131 = Ep 301 +. Nom. fem. sing. adj., describing *ko-to-na ki-ti-me-na*: *anŏnos* 'not subject to *o-na-ta*'.

a-no-po¹, PY 249 = Va 482. Nom. sing. masc., adj. describing ivory: perh. *anŏpos* 'not subject to *o-pa*', or 'unworked' (Lejeune, 1958a, p. 213).

a-no-po², PY 61 = Cn 131. MN.

a-no-qa-si-ja, PY Ea 805. Gen. sing.: reason for allotment of land.

a-no-qo-ta, KN Ak 615, Da 1289, Vc 173 +. MN: *Anorqᵘhontās*? [Cf. ἀνδρειφόντης *Il.* II, 651 +.]

a-no-qo-ta-o, KN Dq 45, E 847. Gen.: *-tāo*.

a-no-ra-ta, PY An 340, Jn 832. MN.

a-no-ta, PY Jn 750. MN.

a-no-we, PY 236 = Ta 641. Nom. sing. neut., describing a vessel: *anŏwes* 'without handles'. [Cf. ἀμφῶες (Theocr.) 'two-handled'.]

a-no-wo-to, KN 232 = K 875. Nom. sing. neut., describing a vessel: *anowoton, anouoton*? 'without handles'. [ἀνούατος Theocr.]

a-no-ze-we, PY Cn 600. MN: cf. *a-no-ke-we*.

a-no-zo-jo, KN 19 = Ak 627. MN, gen.

a-nu-ko, KN Ce 50, Db 1464 +. MN.

a-nu-mo, KN C 1362 +. MN.

a-nu-no[, KN C 912. MN.

a-nu-to, KN 38 = As 1516 +, TH Z 865 +, [TI Z 26?]. MN: *Anutos*. ["Ανυτος.]

a-nu-to-jo, KN X 697. Gen.: *Anutoio*.

a-nu-wa, PY 52 = An 207. PN.

a-nu-wa-to, KN Ap 639. WN.

a-nu-wi-ko, KN 38 = As 1516, Ws 8754. MN.

ạ-o-ri-jo, PY 60 = An 661. Possible reading of first word in line 4; PN.

a-o-ri-me-ne, PY 315 = Qa 1296. MN: *A(h)orimenēs*? [ἄορ, μένος.]

a-o-ze-jo, PY Na 588. Perhaps second element of compound place name; see *e-ro₂-ne*.

a-pa-i-ti-jo, KN L 588. MN: *Hāphaistios, -iōn*. ['Ηφαίστιος, -ίων.]

a-pa-je-u, PY Jn 845. MN.

]a-pa-ni-jo, KN Dv 5224. MN.

a-pa-re-u, KN B 804. MN: *Aphareus*. ['Αφαρεύς *Il.* XIII, 541.]

a-pa-re-u-pi, PY Cn 286 +. PN: loc. or abl. plur.

a-pa-ri-ka-na-we-ja, PY Na 246. PN.

a-pa-sa-ki-jo, KN Mc 4455, [PY Jn 937?]. MN?

a-pa-si-jo-jo, PY Sa 767. MN, gen.

a-pa-ta, PY Na 551. PN.

a-pa-ta-wa, KN 83=C 902+. PN: *Aptarwa*. [Ἄππαρα; the form Ἄππερα is due to popular etymology.]

   a-pa-ta-wa-jo, KN 47=Am 826. Nom. plur. masc. ethnic: *Aptarwaioi*.

   a-pa-ta-wa-ja, KN V 7670. Nom. plur.? fem.: *Aptarwaiai*.

a-pa-u-ro, KN Mc 4463. MN: *Aphauros?*

a-pe: see *te-ko-to-a-pe*.

a-pe-a-sa: see *a-pe-o*.

a-pe-do-ke, PY 305=Fr 1184. 3rd sing. aor. indic. act.: *ap-edōke*. Unique example of augment, hence suggested *ap-es-dōke*, but this is less likely. Cf. *a-pu-do-ke*.

a-pe-e-ke, PY 55=An 724. Verbal form, meaning and identification uncertain; see p. 187.

a-pe-e-ṣi[, PY An 614. Prob. 3rd plur.: *ap-ehensi* 'they are absent'. [ἄπειμι.]

a-pe-i-ja, PY 317=Ub 1318. Personal name, prob. fem.

a-pe-i-si, KN Od 666. Obscure; poss. verbal form (*ap-eisi* 'will be deducted' Palmer) or verbal noun?

a-pe-ke-e, PY Jn 431. PN, loc.

   a-pe-ke-i-jo, PY Jn 431. Nom. plur. masc., ethnic. (Cf. *ke-e*.)

a-pe-ne-wo, PY 323=Sb 1315. Nom. sing. and plur.? Lejeune (1958a, p. 335): gen. plur. *apēnēwōn* 'of animals used to draw carts'. See p. 521.

a-pe-o, KN V 117?, PY 51=An 18. Nom. sing. masc. participle: *apehōn* 'being absent'.

   a-pe-o-te, KN 37=B 823, PY 55=An 724. Nom. plur. masc.: *apehontes*.

   a-pe-a-sa, KN Ak 615, Ap 618. Nom. plur. fem.: *apehassai*. [Cf. Arc. ἔασ(σ)α, Cret. ἴαττα.]

a-pe-re, KN U 49. Obscure.

a-pe-ri-ta-wo, PY 56=An 657. MN: *Ampelitāwōn?*

a-pe-te-me-ne, PY 237=Ta 709. Nom. dual, adj. describing *pa-ko-to*; obscure. See p. 499.

a-pe-te-u, PY Jn 692+. MN.

a-pe-ti-ra₂, KN 207=V 280. Obscure: see pp. 311, 476.

a-pi, KN 90=G 820, PY 247=Ta 716. Prep. *amphi* (*Kudoniāi*) 'around'; in PY prob. first member of compound. [ἀμφί.]

a-pi-a₂-ro, PY An 192, Ea 109, 304=On 300, +. MN: *Amphihalos*. [Ἀμφίαλος *Od.* VIII, 114.]

a-pi-da-ta, KN Vc 175. MN.

a-pi-do-ra, MY Oe 115+. WN, dat.?: *Amphidōrāi*.

a-pi-do-ro, KN Xd 146. MN: *Amphidōros*. [Ἀμφίδωρος.]

a-pi-e-ke, PY 97=Un 2. Perhaps a form of the verb seen in *i-je-si*, *i-je-to*, q.v.

a-pi-e-ra, PY 91=Fn 50, 312=An 1281, MY Oe

103. Gen. and dat. of WN: perhaps *Amphierās*, -*āi*. See p. 483.

a-pi-ja-ko-ro-jo, KN B 812. MN, gen.: *Amphiagroio*, *Amphiāgoroio?*

a-pi-ja-re[, KN Xd 94, Xd 7568. MN?: if complete, *Amphiarēs?* or *Amphiare[us]?*

a-pi-je-ta, KN Dv 5241?, PY 56=An 657, [MY Oe 132?]. MN.

a-pi-jo, PY Jn 725. MN: *Amphiōn?* [Ἀμφίων, -ονος.]

   a-pi-jo-to, PY 40=An 261. Gen.: *Amphiontos*.

   a-pi-o-to, PY 40=An 261 rev.+. Variant spelling of gen.

a-pi-ka-ra-do-jo, PY Pa 398. MN, gen.: *Amphikladoio?*

a-pi-ke-ne-a, PY Xa 1044. Possibly PN: *Amphigenea*. [Cf. Ἀμφιγένεια *Il.* II, 593.]

a-pi-me-de, KN B 801, PY 146=Eb 473+. MN: *Amphimēdēs*. [Ἀμφιμήδης.]

   a-pi-me-de-o, KN C 911, PY 62=Cn 655+. Gen.: *Amphimēdehos*.

a-pi-no-e-wi-jo, PY 184=Nn 228+. PN (in form prob. ethnic).

a-pi-o-to: see *a-pi-jo*.

a-pi-po-re-we, KN 233=Uc 160 rev. Nom. plur., describing AMPHORA ideogram: *amphiphorēwes* 'amphoras'. [ἀμφιφορεύς *Od.* II, 290+.]

   a-po-re-we, PY [238=Tn 996?], MY 234=Ue 611 rev. Nom. dual: *amphorēwe*. [Shorter form ἀμφορεύς Herodotus+.]

a-pi-qo-i-ta, KN 20=Ai 824. MN?, app. gen. or nom. of rubric: *Amphiqʷhoitās*.

a-pi-qo-ro, PY Aa 804, 11=Ad 690, TH Of 34. Nom. and gen. plur., dat. sing.? describing women: *amphiqʷoloi*, -*lōn*, -*lōi* 'attendants'. [ἀμφίπολος *Od.* I, 331.]

   a-pi-qo-ro-i, PY Fr 1205. Dat. plur.: *amphiqʷoloihi*; see p. 480.

a-pi-qo-ta, KN C 915, PY Jn 431. MN, nom. and dat.: *Amphiqʷhoitās*, -*tāi?* (cf. *a-pi-qo-i-ta*).

   a-pi-qo-ta-o, PY 40=An 261, An 616 (misspelt *a-pi-qo-o*). Gen.: -*tāo*.

a-pi-qo-to, PY 237=Ta 709, 239=Ta 642, 240=Ta 713, 241=Ta 715. Nom. sing. and dual fem., adj. describing tables and portable hearths (ἐσχάραι): obscure, see pp. 341, 499.

a-pi-ra-wo, KN 38=As 1516. MN: *Amphilāwos*, -*lāwon*. [Cf. Περίλαος.]

a-pi-re-jo, KN Vc 337. MN.

a-pi-re-we, KN V 337. Nom. plur.: obscure, perh. name of an article of armour?

a-pi-te[, KN U 876. Prob. the name of some artifact.

a-pi-te-ja, PY Fn 187. PN or WN?

a-pi-te-wa, PY 57=An 519, Na 1021. PN.

a-pi-wa-to, KN As 1516. MN: *Amphiwastos?*

a-po-ne-we, PY 53=An 1, 54=An 610. PN: loc. or abl. (See also *a-pu-ne-we*.)

a-po-re-we: see *a-pi-po-re-we*.

a-po-te, KN 213=Le 641 (*o-a-po-te*), Od 562. Formerly taken as adv. *apothen*, but prob. MN.

a-po-te-ra̧, MY 105 = Ge 602. Reading prob.: *ko-no-a-po-te-ra*: *skhoinoi amphoterai* 'both kinds of rush'. [ἀμφότερος.]

a-po-te-ro-te, PY 248 = Va 15. Prob. adv. *amphoterōthen* 'from both sides'. [ἀμφοτέρωθεν.]

a-pu-, Only in composition; in KN 90 = G 820 read *a-pi*. *Apu*. [ἀπύ Aeol., Arc., Cypr. for ἀπό, not due to phonetic change but possibly original form, ἀπό being due to influence of ὑπό.]

a-pu-da-se-we, KN Gm 840. Nom. plur. or dat. sing., possibly *apudassēwes, -ēwei* from **apudasseus* 'distributor'. [δάσσασθαι, δατέομαι.]

a-pu-do-ke, KN Od 681. 3rd sing. aor.: *apudōke* 'rendered, paid'. [ἀποδίδωμι *Il.* IV, 478 + .] Cf. *a-pe-do-ke*.

a-pu-do-si, KN 92 = Fh 349 + , 100 = Ga 424 + , PY 173 = Ma 222 + . Nom. sing.: *apudosis* 'delivery' (i.e. amount delivered as opposed to assessment). [ἀπόδοσις.]

a-pu-do-so[-mo?], KN Nc 4484. Prob.: *apudos[mos]* = *a-pu-do-si*, cf. *do-so-mo*. [Arc. ἀπυδοσμός.]

a-pu-ka, PY 44 = Aq 218. Nom. sing., prob. ethnic = *a-pu₂-ka*.

a-pu-ke, PY 323 = Sb 1315. Nom. plur. (in line 3 perhaps instr. sing. or dual): *ampukes* 'frontlets, head-bands' (for horses). [ἄμπυξ 'headband for women', also for horses (μοναμπυκία Pindar).]

a-pu ke-ka-u-me-no, PY 236 = Ta 641. Nom. sing. masc.: *apukekaumenos*, (of a tripod cauldron) 'burnt away' (as to the legs). [ἀποκαίω.]

a-pu-ki-si̧[, PY Xn 1342. Obscure.

a-pu-ko-wo-ko, PY Ab 210, Ad 671. Nom. and gen. plur. fem., a class of women: *ampukworgoi* 'head-band makers' (possibly for horses, cf. *a-pu-ke*).

a-pu-ne-we, PY 15 = Ad 684. Prob. PN, alternative spelling of *a-po-ne-we*.

a-pu₂(-de), PY 250 = Vn 20. PN, one of the Nine Towns of the Hither Province; acc. + allative *-de*. Not *Aipu* [Αἰπύ *Il.* II, 592], since *pu₂* appears to stand for *phu* (and *bu*?) but not *pu*, and we might expect *a₃*, at least as a variant spelling.

a-pu₂-we, PY 49 = An 427, 257 = Jn 829, Ma 124 + . Loc.

a-pu₂-ja, PY 258 = Jo 438. PN; alternative form of **a-pu₂*, fem. derivative in *-iā*.

a-pu₂-ka, KN Xd 111, PY 59 = An 656. Nom. sing. ethnic name in *-ān*; app. not from **a-pu₂*, which is a *u*-stem and would not explain *k*; see also *a-pu-ka*.

a-pu₂-ka-ne, PY 59 = An 656. Nom. plur.: *-ānes*.

]*a-qa-to*, KN Sc 233. MN.

a-qa-ta, KN As 1516. MN.

a-qe-mo, KN Db 1160. MN.

a-qi-ja-i, PY 324 = An 1282. Dat. plur., in list of words relating to chariots: poss. scribal error for *i-qi-ja-i* (see *i-qi-ja*).

a-qi-ra, KN Xd 166, Xd 300. Prob. MN.

a-qi-ro, KN Da 1123. MN.

a-qi-ru, KN Ce 50. MN.

a-qi-ta[, KN V 7620. Obscure.

a-qi-ti-ta, [KN Ap 639], MY Oe 103. WN.

a-qi-zo-we, PY 43 = Aq 64. MN.

a-qo-ta, KN L 588. MN.

a-ra-da-jo, KN 38 = As 1516. MN.

a-ra-i-jo, PY 40 = An 261. MN.

a-ra-ka-jo, KN B 806. MN.

a-ra-ka-te-ja, KN Ak 5009, Lc 531, PY Aa 89, TH Of 34. Nom. plur. or dat. sing., describing women: *ālakateiai, -āi* 'spinning-women'. [ἠλακάτη 'distaff', *Od.* IV, 135 + .]

a-ra-ka-te-ja-o, PY Ad 677. Gen. plur.: *-āōn*.

a-ra-te-ja-o, PY Ad 380. Defective spelling of prec.

a-ra-ko, KN As 607, C 911, Db 1236 + . MN: *Arakos*. [Ἄρακος.]

a-ra-na-ro, KN 38 = As 1516. MN.

a-ra-ro-mo-te-me-na, KN 265 = Sd 4403, 267 = Sd 4409, 268 = Sd 4413 + . Nom. sing. and plur. fem. (Sd 4415 app. error for dual); description of CHARIOT ideogram without wheels, contrasting with *a-na-mo-to*: *ararmotmenā, -ai* 'fitted out'. [Cf. ἅρμα, ἁρμόζω, but the details of their history are obscure.]

a-ra-ro-mo-to-me-na, KN Sd 4416. Variant spelling of prec.

a-ro-mo-te-me-na, KN 271 = Sd 4422. Incomplete spelling.

a-ra-ro-mo-te-me-no, KN 266 = Sd 4401. Fem. dual: *-menō*.

a-ra-ru-ja, KN 266 = Sd 4401, 265 = Sd 4403 + . Nom. sing. and plur. fem.: *araruia, -uiai* (*hāniāphi*) 'fitted (with reins)'. [ἀραρυῖα, *Il.* XV, 737 + .]

a-ra-ru-wo-a, KN 262 = Ra 1548 + . Nom. plur. neut. *ararwoha* '(swords) fitted (with bindings)'.

a-ra-ru-wo-ja, KN Sd 4408. Confusion of two prec. forms, *a-ra-ru-wo-* intended to be altered to *a-ra-ru-ja*.

a-ra-si-jo, KN Df 1229, Fh 369, X 1463. MN: *Alas(s)ios*? [Cf. place name Ἄλασσα or Λασαία in southern Crete.]

a-ra-te-ja-o: see s.v. *a-ra-ka-te-ja*.

a-re, KN 201 = Fp 14, Mc 4462. Divine name, app. dat.: *Arei*? In Mc 4462 perhaps not the same word. [Ἄρης, dat. Ἄρηϊ, *Il.* V, 841 + ; see Heubeck, 1969c, p. 150.]

a-re-i-jo, KN 213 = Le 641, PY 59 = An 656. At PY patronymic adj.: *Arēios*; at KN perh. MN. [Ἀρήϊος.] Cf. *a-re-jo*.

a-re-i̧-me-ne, TH Z 849, Z 851. MN: *Areimenēs* (*Arēï-*?)

a-re-me-ne, TH Z 852. Alternative spelling.

a-re-i-ze-we-i, TH Of 37. MN, dat.?

a-re-ja, PY 172 = Tn 316 rev. Dat. sing. masc., prob. epithet of Hermes; cf. Arc. Ἄρηα (acc.).

a-re-jo, KN Vc 208. MN: cf. *a-re-i-jo*.

a-re-ka-sa-da-ra(*-qe*), MY 303 = V 659 (last sign perh. *ka* written in error for *qe*). WN: *Alexandrā* (*qᵘe*). [Cf. Ἀλέξανδρος.]

a-re-ke-se-u, KN Da 1156, MY Fu 711. MN: *Alexeus*. [ἀλέξω; Szemerényi, 1957, p. 180.]

a-re-ki-si-to, KN So 4433, PY Vn 865. MN.

a-re-ki-si-to-jo, KN So 1053. Gen.

ạ-re-ko-to-re, KN Ce 152 rev. MN, dat.: *Alektorei*. [ἀλέκτωρ.]

a-re-ku-tu-ru-wo, PY 58 = An 654, 167 = Es 650. MN, nom.: *Alektruōn*. [Ἀλεκτρύων *Il.* XVII, 602.] Cf. *a-ku-tu-ru-wo*.

a-re-ku-tu-ru-[*wo*]-*ne* (*-ru-ṇọ-ne* app. error), PY 170 = Es 649. Dat.: *-onei*.

a-re-ku-tu-ru-wo-no, PY 168 = Es 644. Gen.: *-onos*.

a-re-me-ne: see *a-re-i-me-ne*.

a-re-pa, As ligature A + RE + PA, PY Fr 1198, 313 = Un 6, 171 = Un 718 +. In Un 718 preceded by *a-re-ro*, error for *a-re-pa*: *aleiphar* 'ointment, unguent'. [ἄλειφαρ.]

a-re-pa-te, PY 103 = Un 267. Dat.: *aleiphatei*.

a-re-pa-zo-o, PY 103 = Un 267, [Un 249]. Dat. (and nom.?) sing.: *aleiphazoōi* 'unguent-boiler, perfume-maker'.

a-re-po-zo-o, PY Ea 812 +, Fg 374. Nom.; alternative spelling: *aleiphozoos*.

a-re-sa-ni-e, PY 55 = An 724. Obscure; see p. 187.

a-re-se-si, PY 317 = Ub 1318. Dat. plur., object made of red leather.

a-re-su-ti-jo, MY Au 609 rev. MN.

a-re-ta-to, KN 270 = Sd 4402. Part of a chariot; see p. 367.

a-re-ta-wo[, KN As 645. MN: *Aretāwōn*. [Ἀρετάων *Il.* VI, 31.]

a-re-ta₂, KN Df 1325, X 7556. MN: *Arētiās*? [Ἀρητίας.]

]*a-re-te-re-u*[, KN As 5557. Poss. MN.

a-re-to-to, PY Sa 1265. MN, gen.: *Arethontos, Aretontos*? [Ἀρέθων, Ἀρέτων; for declension cf. *a-pi-jo*.]

a-re-u-ke[, KN Xd 182. MN?

a-re-wọ, PY An 340. MN, nom.

a-ri-ja-to, PY 55 = An 724. MN?

a-ri-ja-wo, KN 159 = Uf 990. MN: *-āwon*.

a-ri-ja-wo-ne, Fh 462. Dat. *-āwonei*.

a-ri-ke-u, KN Ai 966. MN: *Halikeus*?

a-ri-ko, KN Da 1353. MN.

a-ri-qa, PY Jn 832. MN: *Arisgᵘās*? [Ἀρίσβας.]

a-ri-qo, PY An 723. PN?

a-ri-to-[.]-*jo*, KN Fh 347. Obscure.

a-ri-we-wẹ[, KN F 153 rev. MN?

a-ri-wo, PY 62 = Cn 655, La 1393. MN: *Ariwōn*? [Ἀρίων; as name of horse *Il.* XXIII, 346.]

a-ri-wo-ne, PY 61 = Cn 131. Dat.: *Ariwonei*?

a-ro-do-ro-o, KN Fs 4. Prob. name of a divinity or shrine.

a-ro-ja, KN E 843?, PY Fn 187. Prob. personal name, dat.

a-ro-je-u, PY 183 = Nn 831. MN: *Aloieus*? [Cf. Ἀλωεύς *Il.* V, 386.]

a-ro-ka, PY Un 1319. PN or MN?

a-ro-mọ[, MY 105 = Ge 602. Heading to list of spices; reading uncertain, *a-ro-ma*[(Palmer) is excluded, but *a-ro-mọ*[*-ta*?] for ἀρώματα is possible; cf. *pe-mo* for σπέρμα, etc.

a-ro-mo-te-me-na: see *a-ra-ro-mo-te-me-na*

a-ro-pa, PY 310 = Fr 1225 +. Nom sing., describing OIL ideogram: *aliphā* 'unguent'. [ἀλοιφή *Od.* VI, 220 + ; cf. *a-re-pa*.]

a-ro-po, PY An 199. Nom. plur., describing men: *aloiphoi*? 'anointers, painters?'

a-ro-ta, PY La 626, [La 630]. Description of textiles, prob. neut. plur.: *alōsta*? 'unsewn' (Lejeune, 1960a, p. 15). [ἄλωστοι· ἄρραφοι Hesych.]

a-ro-te, PY La 622. Obscure; cf. prec.

a-ro-u-ra, PY 154 = Eq 213. Acc. plur.?: *arourans* 'corn-lands'. [ἄρουραι πυρόφοροι *Il.* XIV, 122 +.]

a-ro-we, KN K 774, X 658 rev. Obscure.

a-ro-wo, PY 251 = Vn 46. In list of building materials, obscure.

a-ro-wo-ta, KN Vc 184. MN.

a-ro-zo, KN Lc 536, L 8503. Nom. sing. masc. adj. describing a tunic.

a-ro-za, KN L 5909. Neut. plur.

a-ro₂-ja, KN 214 = Ld 571, L 586 +, 282 = So 4430. Nom. plur. neut. adj. applied to textiles and wheels: *arioha* (*arjoha*?) 'of better quality'. [Old comparative to ἄριστος, later replaced by ἀρείων.]

a-ro₂-e, KN L 735, L 7409. Nom. dual or plur. fem.: *ariohe*(*s*).

a-ro₂-jo, KN 279 = So 4437. App. gen. sing. or nom. dual; form hard to explain, poss. error.

a-sa-ma-o, PY Cn 1287. MN.

a-sa-ma-to, PY Sa 761. MN, gen.

a-sa-mi-to, KN Ws 8497. On sealing with ideogram of rectangular shape; nom. sing. or plur.: *asaminthos, -oi*. [ἀσάμινθος *Od.* III, 468 +.]

a-sa-pi, PY Na 523. PN, loc.

a-sa-ro, KN As 40. MN: *Assaros*? Cf. *ja-sa-ro*. [Cf. Ἀσσάρακος *Il.* XX, 232.]

a-sa-ti-ja, PY Mn 162. Prob. variant spelling of *a-si-ja-ti-ja*.

a-se-e, PY 51 = An 18, [An 852]. PN, loc.

a-se-so-si, PY 75 = Cn 608 (*jo-a-se-so-si*). 3rd plur. fut.: prob. (*hō*) *asēsonsi* 'thus they will fatten (swine)'. [ἆσαι *Il.* V, 289 +.]

a-si-ja-ti-ja, PY 31 = Ae 134, 257 = Jn 829, 304 = On 300 +. PN, one of the Seven Towns of the Hither Province. See also *a-sa-ti-ja*, *a-*[.]-*ta₂*.

ạ-si-to-po-qo, PY [Eb 177], 148 = Ep 613. Occupational term, nom. sing.; prob. a confusion of *a-to-po-qo* (q.v.) and *si-to-po-qo*: *sītopoqᵘos* 'cook'.

a-si-wi-ja, PY Fr 1206. Dat. sing. fem., epithet of

Potnia: *Aswiāi* 'Lydian' (Chadwick, 1957, p. 125). ['Ᾱσίῳ *Il.* II, 461; cf. Hitt. *Aššuwa.*] See also *a-*64-ja*.

a-si-wi-jo, KN Df 1469, PY Cn 285+, MY Au 653+. MN: *Aswios.* [Ἄσιος.] See also *a-*64-jo*.

a-so-na, PY An 129. Obscure: PN or occupational term?

a-so-qi-jo, KN B 803, [PY Ad 689?]. MN: *Asōqᵘios?* [Cf. Ἀσωπός.]

a-so-ta-o, PY Cn 719. Error for *a-ko-so-ta-o*.

a-ta, PY 50 = An 39 rev. MN; cf. *a₂-ta*.

a-ta-ma-ne-u, PY 62 = Cn 655. MN: *Athamāneus?* [Cf. Ἀθαμᾶνες.]

a-ta-ma-ne-we, PY 61 = Cn 131. Dat.: *-ēwei*.

a-ta-ma-no-we[, TI Z 7. MN.

a-ta-ma-ta, KN B 799. MN.

a-ta-na-po-ti-ni-ja, KN 208 = V 52. Prob. dat.: *Athānāi potniāi* 'for the Mistress Athena'. [πότνι' Ἀθηναίη *Il.* VI, 305.] See also *po-ti-ni-ja*.

a-ta-no, KN As 603, As 1520, Vc 569. MN: *Antānōr.* [Ἀντήνωρ *Il.* III, 262+.]

a-ta-no-re, PY Vn 130. Dat.: *-rei*.

a-ta-no-ro, PY 91 = Fn 50. Gen.: *-ros*.

a-ta-o, KN L 698, PY An 340, Jn 431+. MN, nom. and dat.: *Antaos, -ōi?* [Cf. Ἀνταῖος.]

a-ta-o-jo, PY Vn 1191. Gen.

a-ta-ra, MY 234 = Ue 611 rev., Wt 501 (*-qe*). Nom. plur. neut. or fem., a kind of vessel: *antla?* [Cf. ἄντλος 'ship's hold' *Od.* XII, 411+; ἀντλίον 'bucket' Aristoph.+, ἀντλία.]

a-ta-ra-si-jo, PY 253 = Jn 310, 254 = Jn 389, 255 = Jn 658+. Nom. plur. masc., of bronzesmiths: *atala(n)sioi* 'without a *ta-ra-si-ja*'. On the *-n-*, see p. 508.

a-ta-ro, PY 41 = An 35. MN, cf. *a₃-ta-ro*.

a-ta-ro-we, PY An 129. MN; cf. *a₃-ta-ro-we*.

a-ta-ti-nu, KN F 153, Vd 137. MN.

a-ta-tu-ro, PY Cn 436. MN.

a-ta-wo, PY An 192. MN: *Anthāwōn?*

a-ta-wo-ne[, KN Xd 324. Dat. See also *a-ta-*[?]*-wo-no*.

a-ta-wo-ne-jo, PY Eq 34 (+887). Obscure, perh. derivative of prec.

a-ta-ze-u, KN 38 = As 1516. MN.

a-ta-[?]*-wo-no*, PY Pa 889. MN, gen.; cf. *a-ta-wo*.

a-te-i-ja-ta, KN Dk 1064+. MN.

a-te-jo, KN Da 1392, Db 1329+. Poss. MN, a 'collector' of sheep, or an epithet of the sheep themselves.

a-te-mi-to, PY 167 = Es 650. Gen.: *Artemitos*. [Ἄρτεμις, W. Gk. Ἄρταμις, -μιτος; cf. Ἀρτεμίσιος < -ίτιος.]

a-ti-mi-te, PY Un 219. Dat. of variant spelling: *Artimitei*. (Cf. *a-ti*[*-mi-to?* PY Fn 837.)

a-te-mo, KN As 1520, 68 = De 1648+. MN: *Anthemos, Anthemōn?* [Cf. Ἀνθεμίων *Il.* IV, 473.]

a-te-ra-wo, PY Qa 1304. MN: *Antelāwos*. [Cf. *a-ta-no*; Mühlestein, 1969, p. 76.]

a-te-re-e-te-jo, PY 238 = Tn 996. Nom. plur. masc. adj. describing BATH.

a-te-re-te-a, KN 278 = So 894. Prob. neut. plur. adj. describing WHEELS; cf. prec. See p. 371.

a-te-re-wi-ja, PY Aa 779, 45 = An 830, Ma 335+. PN.

a-te-u-ke, KN V 150. MN, or nom. sing. adj.?: (*toxotās*) *ateukhēs* 'unequipped'? See p. 474. [ἀτευχής.]

a-te-we, PY 238 = Tn 996. Nom. plur.: name of a kind of ewer or jug.

a-te-wo-jo, PY Sa 797. MN, gen.

a-ti-ja, PY 251 = Vn 46 (*a-ti-ja*), [Vn 879?], MY X 1. At PY nom. plur. neut. or fem., constructional members of a chimney structure: perhaps *antia*. [ἀντίον as part of a loom, ἀντίος.] MY context obscure.

a-ti-ja-wo, PY 58 = An 654, Jn 845. MN: *Antiāwōn*. [Cf. Ἀντίων.]

a-ti-jo, KN As 1516. MN.

a-ti-ka, KN V 831. MN.

a-ti-ke-ne-ja, MY Oe 110. WN, dat.?: *Antigeneiāi*. [Ἀντιγένεια.]

a-ti-mi-te: see *a-te-mi-to*.

a-ti-pa-mo, KN Dv 1470 [+] 5075, Od 562, PY Jn 320+. MN: *Antiphāmos*. [Ἀντίφημος.]

a-ti-ri-ja[, PY Ae 27. Obscure: PN?

a-ti-ro, KN Dv 1272. MN: cf. *a-ti-ṛo-*[, PY 60 = An 661.

a-to, KN As 40. MN: *Anthos?* [Ἄνθος.]

a-to-me-ja, KN Ap 639. WN.

a-to-mo, KN C 979, V 56, PY 43 = Aq 64, Jn 832, Jn 881, 258 = Jo 438. Nom. sing., app. a guild of craftsmen: *arthmos* 'fellowship, league'. [ἀρθμός h. Hom.+, cf. ἄρθμιος *Od.* XVI, 427.] Prob. not PN even in Jn 832, cf. Jn 881.

a-to-mo-na, KN Od 690. MN, dat.

a-to-po-qo, PY 49 = An 427+, 91 = Fn 50, MY 46 = Au 102. Nom. plur.: *artopoqᵘoi* 'bakers'. [ἀρτοκόπος Herodotus+, arising from Myc. form by dissimilation and metathesis.]

a-to-po-qo-i, MY Oe 117. Dat. plur.

a-to-ro-qo, PY 246 = Ta 722. Dat. (instr.) sing.: *anthrōqᵘōi* 'with a human being'. [ἄνθρωπος of obscure origin.]

a-tu-ko, KN Dg 1102, X 1052, PY 114 = En 609, 118 = Eo 211, 131 = Ep 301, 255 = Jn 658+. MN. [The suggested *Atukhos* (1st ed.) is unlikely to be correct as being obviously ill-omened.]

a-tu-qo-ta, KN B 799. MN.

a-tu-qo-te-ra-to, KN V 1523. MN?

a-u-qe, KN 270 = Sd 4402. Error for *o-u-qe*.

a-u-ta-na, KN Xd 7649. MN?

a-wa-ne-u, PY Vn 865. MN.

a-wa-ra-ka-na, PY 318 = Un 1314. Prob. nom. (plur.?), name of an artifact; e.g. *awlaknā*, as derivative of αὖλαξ (*ἄϝλαξ) 'furrow', meaning perh. 'ploughshare'. Connexion with ἀράχνη is highly improbable; Palmer (1963a) takes it as MN.

a-wa-ra-ka-na-o, PY 318 = Un 1314. Gen. plur. (sing., if MN).

a-wa-si-ja, PY An 615. PN?

a-wa-so, KN Db 1099 +. MN.

a-wa-ta, PY An 340. MN: *Awātās*? [Cf. ἀήτης.]

a-wa-ti-ka-ra, KN Am 827. WN; cf. MN *wa-ti-ko-ro*.

a-we-ke-se-u, PY Cn 285 +, Jn 605. MN: *Awexeus*. [ἀέξω; Szemerényi, 1957, p. 180.]

a-we-ke-se-we, PY 61 = Cn 131. Dat.: *-ēwei*.

a-we-u-pi, PY An 172. PN, loc. or abl.

]*a-wi-je-mo*, KN X 7635. MN?

a-wi-to-do-to, KN U 4478. MN: *Awistodotos*. [Cf. ἄϊστος.]

a-wo-i-jo, KN Dv 1462 + 5279, PY Cn 599. MN, nom. and dat.: *Āwōhios, -ōi*. [Ἠῷος.]

a-wo-ro, KN B 800. MN: *Aworos*? (Cf. *a₃-wo-ro*.)

a-wo-ti-jo, KN Dd 1157. MN.

a-ze-o, KN Dv 1226. MN.

a-ze-ta, KN Dv 1466. MN.

a-ze-ti-ri-ja, KN 25 = Ap 694, 89 = E 777 rev., Ln 1568 edge +. Nom. plur. fem., description of women; prob. variant spelling of *a-ke-ti-ra₂*.

a-ze-to, KN X 766. Adj. describing *zo-wa*?

*a-*35-ka*, KN Ld 786 +. Adj. describing textiles?

*a-*35-to*, PY La 626 (poss. *a-*34-to*). Adj. describing textiles?

*a-*56-da-ro*, KN C 911. MN.

*a-*56-no*, KN As 1520, Dv 5232. MN.

*a-*64-ja¹*, PY Aa 701, Ab 515. Nom. plur. fem. ethnic adj.: *Aswiai* 'women of Asia (= Lydia)'. [Cf. *a-si-wi-ja*; Chadwick, 1968a, p. 63.]

*a-*64-ja-o*, PY Ad 315. Gen. plur.: *Aswiāōn*.

*a-*64-ja²*, PY Vn 1191. WN: *Aswiā*. [Sing. of prec.]

*a-*64-jo*, KN Sc 261, PY Cn 1287, Fn 324 +. MN, nom. and dat.: *Aswios, -ōi*. Cf. *a-si-wi-jo*.

*a-*65-ma-na-ke*, KN Fs 3, [Fs 20]. Dat.?, recipient of offerings, divine name?

*a-*65-na*, KN Od 714. Obscure.

*a-*79*, KN Ap 618, MY Oe 123. WN.

a-[.]-ta₂, PY Ma 397. Place name, app. alternative spelling of *a-si-ja-ti-ja*, so that damaged sign has value *sja*.

A₂, PY Un 1319. Ideographic use, a kind of WHEAT?

a₂-di-je-u, PY 59 = An 656. MN. Cf. *a-di-je-wo*.

a₂-e-ta, PY 40 = An 261. MN.

a₂-ka-a₂-ki-ri-jo, PY 60 = An 661. PN.

a₂-ka-a₂-ki-ri-ja-jo, PY 76 = Cn 3. App. ethnic adj.

a₂-ke-te-re, KN V 118. Nom. dual?: = *a-ke-te-re*?

]*a₂-ke-wo-a-ki-[*, PY 188 = Na 928. PN.

a₂-ki-ja, PY 45 = An 830. PN.

a₂-ki-ra, PY Na 856. PN.

a₂-ku-mi-jo, PY 196 = Na 926. MN?

a₂-ku-ni-jo, PY 59 = An 656. MN.

a₂-ma-[.]-wa, PY Na 1092. PN.

a₂-ne-u-te, PY Cn 599. PN, also spelt *a-ne-u-te*.

a₂-nu-me-no, PY 254 = Jn 389. MN: *Hanumenos*? [cf. ἄνυμι, ἀνύτω; Chantraine, 1968, p. 93.]

a₂-pa-tu-wo-te, PY Cn 599. PN, loc.

a₂-ra-ka-wo, PY Cn 1287. MN.

a₂-ra-tu-a, PY 76 = Cn 3. PN.

a₂-ra-tu-wa, PY 57 = An 519. Variant spelling.

a₂-ri-e, PY 55 = An 724. Obscure, see p. 187.

a₂-ri-sa, PY 154 = Eq 213. Obscure, see p. 269.

a₂-ro[ ]u-do-pi, PY 239 = Ta 642. Instr. plur., a material used to decorate furniture. See p. 340.

a₂-ru-wo-te, PY 56 = An 657. PN, loc.: *Halwontei*? [Cf. Ἁλοῦς Arcadia, Paus. VIII, 25, 2.]

a₂-ta, PY An 209. MN. Cf. *a-ta*.

a₂-te-po, PY 57 = An 519. PN or MN?

a₂-te-ro, PY 178 = Ma 365. Acc. sing. neut.: *hateron* (*wetos*) 'the next (year)', perhaps 'every other year'? [ἅτερος < *sm̥-teros*; ἕτερος only Att.-Ion.]

a₂-to, PY Un 1321. Obscure.

a₂-zo-qi-jo, PY Un 1193. MN?

A₃, Ideographic use PY Un 1185, apparently abbreviation of *a₃-ka-na-jo*. As adjunct, KN 80 = C 913, applied to GOAT.

a₃-du-wo-na, KN Ap 769. WN.

a₃-ka-na-jo, PY Un 1185. App. the name of a liquid, abbreviated A₃.

a₃-ka-ra, KN L 567. MN.

a₃-ka-sa-ma, PY 257 = Jn 829. Acc. plur.?: *aixmans* 'points (for darts and spears)'. [ἔγχεος αἰχμή, *Il.* XVI, 315 +.]

a₃-ke-ta, KN Dv 1139. MN.

a₃-ke-u, PY 236 = Ta 641. Formerly taken as MN (*Aigeus*), but perh. nom. sing. describing TRIPOD cauldron, despite failure of concord with dual *ti-ri-po-de*; Palmer (1963a, p. 344) *aigeus* as adj. 'with goat-head protomes'; or cf. αἶγες 'high waves'?

a₃-ke-wa-ta, KN Da 5205. MN.

a₃-ke-wa-to, KN Dv 1190 +. MN; cf. *a₃-ki-wa-to*.

a₃-ki-a₂-ri-ja, TH Of 25. PN, derivative of αἰγιαλός: *Aigi(h)aliā*?

a-ki-a₂-ri-ja-de, TH Of 35. Acc. + -*de*: *Aigi(h)aliān-de*.

a₃-ki-a₂-ri-jo, PY 91 = Fn 50, Fn 79. MN, or occupational term? Dat.: *Aigi(h)alioi*? [Cf. αἰγιαλός, prec.]

a₃-ki-de-ja, PY Na 529. Prob. nom. plur. neut., of adj. describing flax?

a₃-ki-e-we, PY Vn 130. MN, dat.: *Aigiēwei*. [Cf. Αἰγιεύς, ethnic of Αἴγιℑν.]

a₃-ki-e-wo, PY Jn 605. Gen.: *-ēwos*.

a₃-ki-no-o, KN 275 = Se 879, 276 = Se 891 (+ 1006). Nom. dual?, some part of chariot? See p. 369.

a₃-ki-pa-ta, KN Fh 346, PY 32 = Ae 108 +. Nom. and dat. sing.: *aigi-pa(s)tās*?, *-āi* 'goat-herd'. [αἴξ + obscure element.]

a₃-ki-po, KN U 4478. MN: *Aigipos*? [Cf. αἰγίπους.]

a₃-ki-po-de, PY Mb 1397. PN? Cf. prec.

a₃-ki-si-jo, KN U 4478. MN.

a₃-ki-wa-ro, PY 168 = Es 644, 167 = Es 650 + . MN.

a₃-ki-wa-to, KN Uf 987. MN.

-a₃-ko-ra-i-ja: see *de-we-ro-a₃-ko-ra-i-ja*.

a₃-ko-ta, KN 38 = As 1516, PY 56 = An 657, 44 = Aq 218. MN.

a₃-ku-pi-ti-jo, KN Db 1105. MN: *Aiguptios*. [Αἰγύπτιος *Od.* II, 15.]

a₃-me-wa, PY Vn 865, Xa 1376. MN.

a₃-mi-re-we, KN 81 = Dm 1180 + . Nom. plur. masc.: class of sheep, distinguished from *e-ka-ra-e-we*, q.v. See p. 437.

a₃-ni-jo, KN 39 = As 1517. MN.

a₃-nu-me-no, PY 40 = An 261. MN: *Ainumenos*. [αἴνυμαι.]

a₃-pu-ke-ne-ja, PY Fn 79. WN?, dat.

a₃-sa, PY Un 1426 (]*a₃-sa*), TH Ug 14 (*a₃-ṣạ*). Nom. sing.: *aisa* 'portion'. [αἶσα *Od.* v, 40 + .]

a₃-se-we, PY Cr 868. PN? (Cf. *-a₃-se-wa*[PY An 615?)

a₃-so-ni-jo, PY 40 = An 261, 253 = Jn 310 + , MY Ui 651. MN: *Aisonios*. [Cf. Αἴσων *Od.* XI, 259, Αἰσονίδης.]

a₃-ta-jo, KN Ga 419. MN.

a₃-ta-re-u-si, PY 56 = An 657. PN, loc.

a₃-ta-ro, PY Jn 415. MN: *Aithalos*. [Αἴθαλος.] Cf. *a-ta-ro*.

a₃-ta-ro-we, KN 64 = Da 1221, PY Cn 285 + . MN: *Aithalowens*. [Cf. Αἰθαλόεις river in Mysia.] Cf. *a-ta-ro-we*.

a₃-te, PY Un 1321. Nom. sing.?

a₃-te-re, KN 48 = B 101. Nom. plur. occupational term: *aitēres* 'inlayers' from verb found in *a-ja-me-no*?

a₃-ti-jo-qo, PY 133 = Eb 846 + , 115 = En 74, 121 = Eo 247, 131 = Ep 301. MN, nom. and gen.: *Aithioqᵘs*, *Aithioqᵘos*. [Αἰθίοπες *Il.* XXIII, 206 + .]

a₃-ti-jo-qe, PY 121 = Eo 247. Dat.: *Aithioqᵘei*.

a₃-to, KN Da 6061. MN: *Aithōn*? [Αἴθων *Od.* XIX, 183.]

]*a₃-tu-ti-jạ*[, KN L 5949. Obscure (fem. ethnic?).

a₃-wa, KN C 973. Possibly name of an ox: *Aiwans*? [Αἴας *Il.* I, 138 + ; Corinth. Αἶϝας Schwyzer, *Dial.* 122. 3.]

a₃-wa-ja, PY 115 = En 74, 122 = Eo 160. WN: *Aiwaiā*? [Αἰαίη *Od.* XII, 268.]

a₃-wa-ta, KN Vc 7612. MN: *Aiwātās*? [Αἰήτης *Od.* X, 137 + .]

a₃-wa-tọ, KN As 1516. MN.

a₃-wo-dị-jo-no, PY Wr 1247. MN, gen.?

a₃-wo-ro, KN 85 = Ch 896, Ch 1029, Ch 5754, [Ch 5938]. Name of an ox: *Aiwolos*. [αἰόλος.]

a₃-za, PY 317 = Ub 1318. Nom. sing. fem.: *aidzā* 'goat's'. [< *aigiā*; classical αἴγειος.]

a₃-zo-ro-qe, KN Ch 1034. Name of ox + *-qᵘe*?

AU, Adjunct to WOMAN: KN Ak 617. Obscure.

]*-au-a₃-ta*, KN C 1582. Annotation to oxen; cf. *au-to-a₃-ta*.

au-de-pi, PY 239 = Ta 642 + . Instr. plur., a decorative feature on furniture, see p. 338.

au-de-we-sa(-qe), PY 237 = Ta 709. Nom. sing. fem.: *-wessa* 'decorated with *au-de-pi*', see prec.

au-ja-to, MY 46 = Au 102. MN, prob. the same name as *au-wi-ja-to*.

au-ke-i-ja-te-we, PY 312 = An 1281, 317 = Ub 1318. MN, dat.

au[-ke-i-]ja-te-wo, PY 91 = Fn 50. Gen.

au-ke-wa, PY An 192, 258 = Jo 438, 235 = Ta 711. MN, nom. and acc.: *Augewās*, *-ān*. [Αὐγείας *Il.* XI, 701; Αὐγέας Pind. + .]

au-ri-jo, KN As 604, Da 1080 + , TH Ug 5. MN: *Aulios*?; at Thebes possibly adj. [Cf. αὔλιος.]

au-ri-mo-de, KN 202 = Fp 13. PN, acc. + *-de*.

au-ro, KN 270 = Sd 4402. Nom. plur. or dual: *auloi*, 'pipes', some part of a chariot. See p. 516. [αὐλός of a buckle *Od.* XIX, 227.]

au-ta-mo, PY 255 = Jn 658, Jn 725. MN: *Authaimōn*? [Cf. Αἴμων.]

au-ta₂, KN Db 1166. MN.

au-te, PY 237 = Ta 709. Nom. sing.: *austēr* 'kindler'. See p. 499. [Cf. ἐξαυστήρ.]

au-te-ra, MY Oe 128. WN, dat.?: *Authērāi*?

au-to-ạ[, PY Cn 938. Variant spelling of next?

au-to-a₂-ta, PY Cn 314. MN.

au-to-a₃-ta, KN Ch 972. MN; cf. prec.

au-to-jo, PY Eb 156. Gen. sing.: *(toio qᵘe) autoio* 'and of the same'.

au-to-te-qa-jo, TH Ug 4. MN: *Autothēgᵘaios*. [Cf. Θηβαῖος; Chadwick, 1971, p. 129.]

*au-to-*34-ta-ra*, PY Fn 187. Prob. MN or title.

au-u-te, KN Od 666. Obscure; poss. *auwetes* 'this (same) year', but the spelling is unparalleled. [Petruševski and Ilievski, 1958, p. 277.]

au-wi-ja-to, MY Au 653, Au 657. MN; prob. the same name as *au-ja-to*.

DA, Associated with WOMAN ideogram: KN 18 = Ak 611, 21 = Ak 624 + , PY 5 = Aa 792, 2 = Aa 815, 6 = Ab 379, 9 = Ab 553 + : perhaps = 'supervisor'?

Associated with MAN ideogram: KN As 608, As 625, PY 45 = An 830(?), 114 = En 609(?): as with women?

Adjunct to WOOL ideogram: TH Of 34, Of 39, Of 40.

In obscure contexts: KN Mc 4454, 157 = Uf 835 + , PY Un 1193.

da-da-re-jo-de, KN 200 = Fp 1 + . PN with allative *-de*: *Daidaleion-de*. [Cf. Δαίδαλος *Il.* XVIII, 592.]

da-i-ja-ke-re-u, PY 44 = Aq 218. MN or epithet of *hiereus* (e.g. *dai-agreus* 'divider of lands')?

da-i-pi-ta, KN B 799. MN.

da-i-qo-ta, KN Da 1164. MN: *Dāiqᵘhontās*. [Δηιφόντης.]

da-i-ra, KN Od 7388 edge, V 479. MN.

da-i-ta-ra-ro, KN De 1231. MN.

da-i-wo-wo, KN V 1043. MN.

da-i-ze-to, KN Da 1317. MN.

da-ja-ro, KN Dc 1167, Dv 1420. MN.

]*da-je-we*, PY Vn 851. MN, dat.

da-ka-ja-pi, PY Gn 720. PN, loc.?

da-ka-sa-na-ta, PY An 172. MN.

da-ko-ro, PY **52** = An 207, An 424, **49** = An 427. Nom. dual and plur., occupational term: *dakorō, -roi* 'temple-servant'? [< **dm̥-koro-*, cf. ζάκορος.]

da-ko-ro-i, PY Un 219. Dat. plur.: *dakoroihi*.

da-ko-so, KN As 1520. MN.

da-ma-o-te, KN X 1051. Obscure, poss. nom. plur. masc. fut. pple.: *damahontes*. [δαμάζω.]

da-ma-te, PY **114** = En 609. App. nom. plur. of fem. noun meaning approximately 'households'. [Possibly δάμαρ (from root of δόμος) with later specialization of meaning as 'wife'.]

da-mi-jo, PY Ea 803. Acc. sing.: *dāmion* 'land belonging to the *damos*'. [δήμιος 'public' *Od.* xx, 264 + .]

da-mi-ni-ja, PY [Aa 96], **14** = Ad 697. PN; cf. *da-mi-ni-jo²*.

da-mi-ni-jo¹, KN **69** = Df 1119 + , Dk 1076 + , V 337, X 1019. Word occurring on sheep tablets in places occupied by both 'collector' and place name; possibly a place name subordinate to *ku-ta-to*, or a man's name; in V 337 and X 1019 context obscure.

da-mi-ni-jo², PY **54** = An 610. Nom. plur. ethnic?: *Damnioi*? [Cf. 'Επίδαμνος; *da-mi-ni-ja*.]

da-mo, KN C 911, PY Ea 52 + , **133** = Eb 846 + , **131** = Ep 301 + , **171** = Un 718. Nom.? and dat. sing.: *dāmos, -ōi*. An entity which can allocate holdings of land, probably a village community; see Heubeck, 1969*a*, p. 539. [δῆμος.]

da-mo-de-mi, PY **135** = Ep 704. *Dāmos de min* (*phāsi*), 'but the community says that she . . .' See p. 254.

da?-]*mo-ke-re-we-i*, PY Fn 324. MN, dat.: *Dāmoklewehi*. [Δαμοκλῆς.]

da-mo-ko-ro, KN C 7058, PY **304** = On 300, **235** = Ta 711. Nom.?, acc. and dat. sing., title of an official: prob. *dāmo-*, but second member obscure (cf. *ko-re-te*). Now shown by KN texts not to be proper name. [Heubeck, 1968.]

da-na, KN Ce 152. MN?

da-na-jo, KN Db 1324, V 1631. MN: *Danaios*? [Cf. Δαναός.]

da-na-ko, PY An 209. MN.

da-na-mo, KN E 847. MN?

]*da-na-ro*, KN Dd 5174. MN.

da-nu-wa-a-ri[, PY Mn 1412. Prob. PN, to be divided after *wa*?

da-nu-wo, KN **83** = C 902, C 911. MN, or title?

da-nwa, KN Gg 701. Recipient of offerings; divine name?

]*da̯-nwa-re*, KN Db 1302, Sc 5058. MN.

da-o-ta, KN Vc 125. MN.

da-pu-ri-t̯o[, KN Xd 140. Obscure; cf. *da-pu₂-ri-to-jo*.

da-pu₂-ra-zo, Eleusis jar (Raison, 1968, p. 124). Perhaps MN; cf. *du-pu₂-ra-zo*.

da-pu₂-ri-to-jo, KN **205** = Gg 702, [Oa 745 + 7374]. Gen. sing., place owned by Potnia: prob. *Daburinthoio*. [λαβύρινθος, with Aegean *d* for *l* (cf. 'Οδυσσεύς, 'Ολυσεύς, etc.); *pu₂* = *bu* is also remarkable.]

da-ra[, MY **106** = Ge 603. Name of a spice?

da-ra-ko, KN Dd 1579 + . PN.

da-ra-mu-ro, KN Dc 1220. MN. *Drāmulos*? [*δρασιμ-υλος.]

da-ru-*56, KN Uf 432. MN.

da-sa-t̯o, PY Wa 917 (]*o-da-sa-t̯o*). 3rd sing. aor.: *hō dasato* 'thus he distributed'. [δατέομαι, (ἐ)δασάμην *Il.* xviii, 511 + .] Cf. *e-pi-de-da-to*.

da-s̯i[ ]*so*, PY Jn 431. MN.

]*da̯-so-de*, KN Fh 365. PN, acc. + -*de*.

da̯-so-mo, PY Wa 730 (if correct reading; cf. *do-so-mo*; see p. 466). *dasmos* 'distribution'. [δασμός *Il.* i, 166 + .]

da-ta-ja-ro, KN De 1153. MN.

da-ta-ra-mo, KN Dl 935. PN.

da-te-ne-ja, KN Ap 639. WN.

da-te-wa, KN V 147. MN.

da-te-we-ja, KN Ak 612, D 8174, Lc 540, L 594 + . Nom. plur. fem.: ethnic or occupational term?

da-to-re-u, PY Cn 328. MN.

da-to-ro, KN Dk 964, Dv 1104. MN: *Daitros*? [Cf. Δαίτωρ *Il.* viii, 275.]

da-u-da-ro, PY Cn 1287. MN.

da-u-ta-ro, PY Jn 431. MN.

da-wa-no, KN **39** = As 1517, Ga 423 rev., Mc 4454 + . MN: *Dwānos*? [Cf. δήν < *δϝᾱν.]

da-we-ro, KN C 912. Obscure; MN, gen.?

da-we-u-pi, PY Cn 485, Cn 925. PN, loc. plur.

da-wi, KN Db 1212. MN.

da-wi-[.], KN **39** = As 1517. MN.

da-wo, KN Ak 621, **84** = Ce 59, **95** = F 852 + . PN.

da-wi-jo/-ja, KN Ak 780, Am 568 + . Nom. plur. masc. and fem. ethnic adj.

da-zo, KN As 5549, Ra 1547. MN?

da-*22-to, KN As 40, **84** = Ce 59, **66** = Dc 1129, **161** = Uf 839 + , Eleusis jar (Raison, 1968, p. 124). PN.

da-*22-ti-jo/-ja, KN E 669, Xe 544 + . Nom. plur. masc. and fem. ethnic adj.

da-*83-ja, KN Dv 1086 + . PN.

da-*83-ja-de, KN Fp 363 + . Acc. + -*de*.

da̯-*83-ja-i, KN E 670. Dat.-loc. plur.

da-*83-jo, KN Dc 1419, V 479 rev. + . MN, cf. prec.

DE, As adjunct to WOMAN, girls or boys: KN Ak 610, Ak 620, Ak 5948: possibly abbreviation of *de-di-ku-ja*.

As adjunct to obscure ideogram **169*: PY Pa 49, Pa 53.

Introducing numbers after *ko-no* 'rush': MY **105** = Ge 602, **106** = Ge 603 + : possibly = *desmā* 'bundle'. [δε = δέσμαι found in Papyri.]

-de[1], PY **28** = An 607 (*ma-te-de, pa-te-de*), **140** = Eb 297 (*ko-to-no-o-ko-de*), **141** = Eb 338 (*o-pe-ro-sa-de*), **135** = Ep 704 (*da-mo-de-mi*), **175** = Ma 393 (*a-ne-ta-de*), **196** = Na 926 (*e-ke-de-mi*), etc. Adversative and connective particle: *de* 'but, and'. [δέ.] Cf. also *to-so-de*.

-de[2], KN **200** = Fp 1 (*da-da-re-jo-de*), **201** = Fp 14 (*a-mi-ni-so-de*), **78** = C 914 (*a-ka-wi-ja-de*), etc., PY **53** = An 1 (*pe-re-u-ro-na-de*), **60** = An 661 (*ne-do-wo-ta-de*), **250** = Vn 20 (passim), etc., TH Of 26 + (*do-de*). Enclitic allative particle: *-de* 'to'. [-δε.]

]*de-a-ta*, KN Dc 5190, Df 1222. MN.

de-de-me-no, PY **290** = Sa 287, **291** = Sa 794. Nom. dual neut. pf. pple.: *dedemenō*, of wheels, 'bound (with silver or bronze)'; cf. *ka-ko-de-ta*. [δέδεμαι pf. pass. *Od.* XXIV, 228 +.]

de-de-me-na, KN **163** = Ra 984. Nom. plur. fem. or neut.: *dedemenai, -a*, applied to daggers(?), cf. *de-so-mo*.

]*de-di-ku-ja*, KN 18 = Ak 611, perhaps abbreviated *de* Ak 620 +. Nom. sing. or plur. fem.; possibly error for *de-di-⟨da⟩-ku-ja*: *dedidakhuia(i)* 'instructed'. Cf. *di-da-ka-re*.

de-do-me-na, KN **281** = So 4440 +, U 7507. Nom. plur. neut. (or fem.?): *dedomena* 'delivered'. See also *di-do-si*.

de-do-wa-re-we, PY Fn 187. Dat. sing.: MN or title?

de-ka-sa-to, KN [Fh 370?], **213** = Le 641 (*de-ka-sa-to*), PY Pn 30 (*o-de-ka-sa-to*). 3rd sing. aor. mid.: *dexato* 'received'. [ἐδέξατο *Il.* XVIII, 238, etc.]

de-ke-se-u, KN Db 1426, **69** = Df 1119. MN: *Dexeus? Derxeus?* [Cf. δέχομαι, δέρκομαι; Szemerényi, 1957, p. 180.]

de-ki-si-wo, KN C 908, [V 1524?], PY Cn 254. MN, dat.: *Dexiwōi*. [Δέξιος (δεξιός < *δεξιϝός), Pamph. Δέξιϝυς (Masson, 1960, p. 112).]

de-ki-si-wo-jo, PY Vn 1191. Gen.: *Dexiwoio*.

de-ko-to[1], KN Le 642. Context incomplete, perhaps 3rd sing. aor.: *dekto* 'received' [δέκτο *Il.* XV, 88 +], but possibly MN (see next).

de-ko-to[2], PY Cn 600. MN: *Dektos*. [δεκτός.]

de-ko-to-jo, PY Jn 413. Gen.

de-ku-tu-wo-k̯o[, PY **319** = Un 1322. Dat. sing. or plur.?: *dektuworgōi, -oihi*, 'to the net-maker(s)'. [*δίκτυον (δίκτυον *Od.* XXII, 386 +) + -(ϝ)οργός; *e* for *i* would imply a non-Greek origin, but Chantraine (1968, p. 284) proposes interpretation *deiktu-* keeping connexion with δικεῖν 'throw'.]

de-ma-si, KN Fh 353. Prob. dat. plur., recipients of OIL. (Suggested *dermasi* 'in leather bottles' is improbable in view of parallel contexts.)

de-me-o-te, PY **41** = An 35. Nom. plur. masc. fut. pple.: *demehontes* 'who are to do building work'. [δέμω *Il.* VII, 436 +.]

de-mi-ni-ja, PY Vn 851, MY **303** = V 659. Context obscure, but only Greek word to fit spelling is nom. plur. *demnia* 'bedding'. [δέμνια *Il.* XXIV, 644 +.]

de-mi-ni-jo, PY Wr 1326. Sing. of prec.?

de-mo-qe, PY Cn 45. MN, dat.

de-ni-mo, KN Dc 1303. MN.

]*de-ra-wo*, PY Fn 324. MN, dat.: *-lāwōi*.

de-r̯e-u̯-k̯o, KN Uc 160. Nom. sing. annotation to WINE: *dleukos* 'sweet new wine'. [γλεῦκος (γλυκύς < *δλυκύς); Chadwick, 1968*c*.]

de-so-mo, KN **262** = Ra 1548 +. Instr. plur. masc.: *desmois* '(swords fitted) with bands', = belts (τελαμών) or some other fitting. [δεσμός *Il.* VI, 507 +; the sense of 'rivet' alleged in *Il.* XVIII, 379 (Palmer 1963*a*, p. 336) is unnecessary; a band of metal could be hammered to shape to make a handle for a tripod.]

de-u-jo-i, KN Fh 352. Dat. plur., recipients of OIL?

de-u-ka-ri-jo, PY **58** = An 654. MN: *Deukaliōn*. [Δευκαλίων *Il.* XIII, 451 +.]

de-u-ke-ro, KN U 4478. MN.

de-u-ki-jo, MY **46** = Au 102 (*de-u-ki-jo-qe*). MN, *Deukios, Deukiōn?*

de-u-ki-jo-jo, KN **200** = Fp 1. Gen. sing., name of a month.

]*de-wa-pi*, KN **229** = K 434. See p. 329.

de-we-ra, KN Dv 2019. MN.

d̯e-we-ro, PY Jn 320. MN.

de-we-ro-a₃-ko-ra-i-ja, PY **198** = Ng 319, [Wa 948]. Name of a district: *Deuro-aigolaiā?* = the Hither Province. Ruijgh (1970, p. 317) proposes *Dewerō-*. See p. 144.

de-wi-jo, PY **57** = An 519, **44** = Aq 218. Obscure.

DI, As adjunct to WOMAN, girls and boys: KN Ai 190, **21** = Ak 624, **19** = Ak 627 +, Ap 629: probably abbreviation of *di-da-ka-re*.

As adjunct to ideograms of vessels: KN **230** = K 740, K 829, K 7363.

DI + PTE: KN U 8210; abbreviation of *di-pte-ra*? Ideographic use: PY Ua 1252: obscure.

di-da-ka-re, KN **22** = Ak 781, Ak 783 +, (abbreviated *di*? **21** = Ak 624 +). Description of children; poss. loc. *didaskalei* 'at the schoolmaster's'. Sense 'under instruction' is possible, but details of form obscure.

di-da-ma-o, PY Xa 184. Obscure.

di-de-ro, KN [B 799?], Dv 1504. MN. [Cf. Linear A *di-de-ru*.]

di-do-si, KN [**260** = Og 4467], PY **178** = Ma 365, **252** = Vn 10 (*o-di-do-si*), **175** = Ma 393 + (*o-u-di-do-si*), **189** = Na 568 + (*o-u-di-do-si*). 3rd plur. pres.: *didonsi* 'they give, deliver'. [δίδωμι.]

di-do-to, PY **198** = Ng 319, **199** = Ng 332 (*o-u-di-do-to*). 3rd sing. (or plur.?) pres. pass.: (*ou*) *didotoi* 'is (not) delivered'.

do-se, PY **171** = Un 718. 3rd sing. fut.: *dōsei* 'he will contribute'.

do-so-si, PY 257=Jn 829 (*jo-do-so-si*). 3rd plur. fut.: *dōsonsi* 'they will contribute'.

do-ke, KN Ws 1707, Xe 7711, PY 103=Un 267 (*o-do-ke*), MY 321=Oi 701. 3rd sing. aor.: *dōke* 'he contributed'. See also: *de-do-me-na*.

di-du-me, KN L 588. Obscure.

di-du-mo, KN X 5751?, MY 226=Oe 129. MN, dat.: *Didumōi*. [Δίδυμος.]

di-ka-ta-de, KN Fp 7, F 866+. PN, acc. + -*de*: *Diktān-de* 'to Dicte'. [Δίκτη.]

di-ka-ta-jo, KN 200=Fp 1. Dat. sing. masc. ethnic adj.: *Diktaiōi* (*Diwei*) '(to Zeus) of Dicte'.

di-ka-ta-ro, KN As 566, Dd 2010. MN.

di-ki-nu-wo, KN Dv 1502. MN.

di̯-ko-na-ro, PY 59=An 656. MN.

di-ko-to, KN D 411. MN?

di-no-zo, TH Z 857, Z 858. MN? Cf. *no-di-zo*.

di-nu-wa-ta, PY Jn 725. MN. [Cf. Arc. Δινύττας.]

di-pa, KN 232=K 875+, PY 236=Ta 641. Nom. sing.: *dipas* 'vessel'. [δέπας *Il.* XI, 632+, often in early use a large vessel, not a drinking-cup.] *di-pa* ·KN 230=K 740 used with numeral 30 may be plur. (Lejeune, 1968*c*, p. 232.)

di-pa-e, PY 236=Ta 641. Nom. dual: *dipae* 'two vessels'.

di-pi-ja, KN V 7577. App. fem. ethnic.

di-pi-si-je-wi-jo, PY Fr 1218. App. adj. derived from next.

di-pi-si-jo, PY Fr 1240. Prob. nom. of next.

di-pi-si-jo-i, PY 307=Fr 1220, Fr 1231+. Prob. dat. plur., meaning obscure; perhaps the name of a recipient of OIL; if so, prob. *dipsioihi* 'for the thirsty ones', i.e. the dead (according to Guthrie, 1959, p. 45) or the Genii (according to Marinatos, 1966); priests of goddess *Dipsia* (the Earth?), cf. Thessalian month Δίψιος (Adrados, 1968). See p. 479.

di-pte-ra, PY 317=Ub 1318. Nom. sing. and plur. (also dual?): *diphtherā, -rai* 'a prepared hide, piece of leather'. [διφθέρα Herodotus+.]

di-pte-ra₃, PY 323=Sb 1315. Variant spelling of nom. plur.: *diphtherai*.

di-pte-ra-po-ro, [KN C 954 (*di*[-*pte-ra-*]*po-ro-i*?)], PY ⟨Ea 814?⟩, 91=Fn 50, Un 219. Nom. and dat. sing., occupational term: *diphtherā-phoros, -rōi* 'wearer of leather'? See p. 217.

di-qa-ra[, KN Ap 628. WN?

di-qo, PY 55=An 724. Obscure, possibly MN (]*di-qo* is MN at KN Dl 930).

di-ra, KN Uf 432. MN.

di-ra-po-ro, PY Ea 814. Prob. error for *di-pte-ra-po-ro*, q.v.

di-ra-qo, KN Dk 1075. MN.

di-ra-wo-no, PY Jn 750. MN, prob. gen.

di-ri-mi-jo, PY 172=Tn 316 rev. Name of man or hero, recipient of offering; dat.

di-ro, KN Da 1338, Dc 1167+. PN.

di-so, KN Sc 255. MN. [Prob. not *Dissos*, if = δισσός < *δϝιχιος.]

di-ta-ka-so, KN Dl 916, Ga 427. MN, nom. and dat.?

di-u-ja, PY Cn 1287, 172=Tn 316 rev. Name of a female deity, gen. and dat.: *Diwyās, Diwyāi*. [*Διϝιἄ > δῖα, rather than Διϝία (Pamph.), according to Ruijgh (1967, p. 132).]

di-wi-ja, KN Xd 97, PY 28=An 607. Variant spelling, PY gen.: *Diwyās*.

di-u-ja-jo(-qe), PY 172=Tn 316 rev. Acc. neut.?: *Diwyaion* 'the shrine of Diwya'?

di-u-ja-wo: see *di-wi-ja-wo*.

di-u-jo, PY 172=Tn 316 rev. Acc. neut.?: *Diwyon* 'the shrine of Zeus'? [δῖος originally 'of Zeus'.] See also *di-wi-jo*.

di-wa-jo, KN V 1523. MN.

di-we, KN 200=Fp 1, F 51 rev., PY 172=Tn 316 rev. Dat.: *Diwei* 'to Zeus'. [Ζεύς, Διί.]

di-wo, PY 172=Tn 316 rev. Gen.: *Diwos*.

di-we-se-ja, MY Oe 103. WN, dat.?

di-we-so, KN V 151. MN.

di-wi-ja: see *di-u-ja*.

di-wi-ja-ta, PY 184=Nn 228. PN.

di-wi-ja-wo, KN Vc 293, PY 197=Na 406, TH Ug 11. MN: *Diwyāwōn*? [Cf. *di-u-ja*.]

di-u-ja-wo, TH Of 26, Of 33. Variant spelling.

di-wi-je-ja, KN Xd 97. WN or title? Cf. next.

di-wi-je-u, PY 59=An 656, [44=Aq 218?]. In 59 the name of an *e-qe-ta*; other contexts less clear but MN remains possible: *Diwieus*. [Cf. Διεύς.]

di-wi-je-we, PY 76=Cn 3, 169=Es 646+. Dat.: *Diwiēwei*.

di-wi-jo, PY Mb 1366. *Diwion* 'shrine of Zeus' or as PN? [Variant spelling of *di-u-jo*.]

di-wi-jo-de, PY Fr 1230. Acc. + -*de*: *Diwion-de*.

di-wi-jo-jo, KN Fp 5. Name of month, gen.: *Diwioio*. [Δῖος month-name in Macedonia and elsewhere.]

di-wi-pa-ra, KN X 722. Obscure.

di-wo, KN Dv 1503, PY An 172. MN: *Diwōn*. [Δίων.] See also *di-we*.

di-wo-a-ne[, KN Xd 216. MN?

di-wo-nu-so[, PY Xa 1419. In fragment, without clear context, prob. divine name: *Diwonūso(s*?). [Διόνυσος.]

di-wo-nu-so-jo, PY Xa 102. No context, gen.: *Diwonusoio*.

di-wo-pu-ka-ta, KN Fp 363. MN or title?

di-za-so, KN Dv 1505, Pp 493. MN.

di-zo, KN As 1520, V 479, V 1523. MN, nom. and dat.: *Ditsos, -ōi*. [>δισσός, cf. *di-so*.]

di-*65-pa-ta, KN Le 1568. MN; Palmer: *Diuphantās* (with **65=ju*).

do-de, TH Of 26, Of 31, Of 33. Preceded by names in gen., perhaps *dō-de* (*dōn-de*?) 'to the house (of)'. [δῶ, usu. acc. *Il.* I, 426+.]

do-e-ra, KN 20=Ai 824, Ap 628, Gg 713+, PY

27=Ae 303, 28=An 607, 137=Eb 416+, 150=Ed 411, 114=En 609+, 118=Eo 211+, 148=Ep 613. Nom. sing. and plur. fem.: *doelā, -ai* 'maid-servant, bondwoman slave'. [δούλη *Il*. III, 409+.]

do-e-ro, KN B 822, C 911+, PY 33=Ae 26, 28= An 607, Eb 156+, 114=En 609, 168=Es 644+, 118=Eo 211, 148=Ep 613, 253=Jn 310+. Nom. sing. and plur. masc.: *doelos, -oi* 'bondman, slave, servant'; on *theoio doelos* see p. 236. [Ion. δοῦλος, Doric δῶλος < *doelos* (*dohelos*?); cf. Khotanese *dahā* 'man', Skt. *dāsaḥ*.]

do-e-ro-i, PY 91=Fn 50+. Dat. plur.: *doeloihi*.

do-e-ro-jo, KN C 912 rev. Gen. sing.: *doeloio*.

do-ka-ma-i, PY 324=An 1282. Dat. plur., in a list which includes wheels and halters; obscure, see p. 522.

do-ke: see *di-do-si*.

do-ke-ko-o-ke-ne: see *do-ke*, s.v. *di-do-si*, and *ko-o-ke-ne*.

do-po-ta, PY 172=Tn 316. Dat., recipient of an offering: poss. *dospotāi* 'to the Master'. [δεσπότης, if from *dems-, with variant *doms- or *dṃs-; but perhaps not a Greek name.]

do-qe-ja, PY 28=An 607. Uncertain whether the name of a goddess (gen.), or a description of the women (nom. plur.). See p. 167.

do-qe-u, KN B 804. MN.

do-qo-no, PY 61=Cn 131. MN, dat.

do-qo-ro, PY 58=An 654. MN.

do-qo-so, MY Au 609. MN.

do-ra, PY 172=Tn 316 (*do-ra-qe*). Acc. plur.: *dōra* 'gifts'. [δῶρον *Il*. VI, 293+.]

do-re-we, KN Fh 342. MN, dat.?

do-ri-je-we, PY Fn 867. MN, dat.: *Dōriēwei*. [Δωριεύς.]

do-ri-ka-no, KN U 4478. MN: *Dolikhānōr*.

do-ri-ka-o, KN V 958, PY 258=Jo 438. MN: *Dolikhāōn*. [Δολιχάων.]

do-ri-wo, KN Xd 167. MN?

do-ro-jo, PY Jn 320. MN.

do-ro-jo-jo, PY Cn 45. Gen., but prob. error for dat.

do-ro-me-u, PY An 209. MN: *Dromeus*. [Δρομεύς.]

do-ro-qo, PY Na 384 (*do-ro-qo* , *so-wo-te* perhaps to be read as a single word or compound). PN, loc.

do-so-si: see *di-do-si*.

do-si-mi-jo, PY Wa 730 (*do-si-mi-jo-qe*). Nom. sing. or plur. masc.?: *dosmios* 'contributory', adj. from *do-so-mo*. [Cf. Arc. ἀπυδόσμιος.]

do-si-mi-ja, PY 182=Ma 126, [MY Ge 606]. Nom. plur. neut. or fem.: *dosmia(i)*.

do-so-mo, PY 168=Es 644+, 171=Un 718, Wa 731. Nom. and acc. sing.: *dosmos, -on* 'contribution'. [Cf. Arc. ἀπυδοσμός 'payment'.]

do-ti-ja, KN Ap 629, Ce 139, C 979, Dn 1200, 213=Le 641+. PN. [Cf. Δώτιον πεδίον in Thessaly.]

do-ti-jo, KN D 7134 (*do-ti-jǫ*), V 653. Ethnic adj. of prec. or variant of PN?

do-ti-jo-no[, KN V 831. MN.

do-wa, KN V 5113. Context obscure; poss. nom. plur.: *dorwa* 'shafts'? [δόρυ, plur. δοῦρα *Od*. IX, 498+ < *dorwa.] Cf. *do-we-jo*.

do-we-jo, KN [269 = Sd 4404], Sd 4407+, PY 318= Un 1314 (*do-we-jo-qe*). Nom. sing. or plur.: *dorweios, -oi* 'made of wood'. [δούρειος Eurip. +, δουράτεος *Od*. VIII 493+; cf. *do-wa*.]

D U, Ideographic use: MY Ui 709; obscure.

du-ko-so[, PY Jn 431. MN.

du-ma, KN C 1030, C 1039, PY An 192. Nom. sing., title of official: form obscure, cf. *da-ma-te, me-ri-du-ma-te, po-ro-du-ma-te*. See pp. 511–12.

du-ma-te(-qe), PY 257=Jn 829. Nom. plur. (+ *-qᵘe*).

]*du-ma-ti*, PY 304=On 300. Dat. sing.

du-ni, KN Dd 1201. MN.

du-ni-ja, KN Fh 341. Obscure.

du-ni-jo, KN 38=As 1516, 39=As 1517+, PY 147=Ea 59, 143=Ep 705, 96=Un 138+. MN, nom. and dat.

du-ni-jo-jo, PY Ae 8+. Gen.

du-pi-jo, KN Xd 287. MN.

du-pu₂-ra-zo, KN Da 1173, V 479. MN. Cf. *da-pu₂-ra-zo*.

du-pu₂-so, KN Fh 343. MN.

du-qo-te-ja, TH Of 27. WN?

du-re-u, PY Jn 845. MN.

du-ri, KN Da 1143. MN: *Duris*? [Δύρις local name of Atlas and of a wind.]

du-ru-po, KN As 1516, Fh 345+. MN, nom. and dat.

du-ru-to-mo, PY 252=Vn 10. Nom. plur.: *drutomoi* 'wood-cutters'. [δρυτόμος *Il*. XI, 86+.]

du-sa-ni, KN Ap 639. WN.

du-ta-so, KN Db 1159. MN.

du-to, KN As 1516. MN (two men of the same name?).

du-tu-wa, KN Ap 639. WN.

]*du-wo-jo*, PY Jn 750. MN: *Dwoios*? [δοιός, cf. Δοίας.]

du-wo-jo-jo, PY 59=An 656. Gen.: *Dwoioio*.

du-wo-u-pi: see *dwo*.

dwo, PY 141=Eb 338, 128=Eo 278, 323=Sb 1315. Nom. and acc.: *dwo* (*dwō*?). [δύο, δύω; cf. δ(ϝ)ώδεκα.] Formerly read as *wo-wo* and only recognized as a separate sign by Risch (1957).

du-wo-u-pi, PY Eb 149 (*du-wo-u-pi-de*), Eb 495, 148=Ep 613+. Instr.: *dwouphi* or *dwoiumphi*? [Cf. Arc. dual in -οιυν.]

dwo-jo, KN V 492 (]*dwo-jo*), X 8126. MN; cf. *du-wo-jo*.

E, In connexion with CLOTH: KN Ln 1568. As adjunct to obscure ideogram *177: KN U 4478.

Ideographic uses: KN U 5717 (obscure), PY Un 1319 (obscure); PY Ub 1316, Ub 1317, 317 = Ub 1318: abbreviation of *e-ra-pe-ja*, (*-pi-ja*); MY 106 = Ge 603: abbreviation of *e-ne-me-na*.

e-da-e-u, [KN V 958?], PY Qa 1298. Nom. sing., title or ethnic?

e-da-e-wo, PY Eb 495. Gen. sing.

e-da-[.]*-ni-ja*[, KN U 4478. MN.

e-do-mo-ne-u, PY ⟨114 = En 609⟩, 119 = Eo 224, 254 = Jn 389 + . MN.

e-do-mo-ne-we, PY Cn 925. Dat.

e-e-ro-pa-jo-qe-rọ-ṣạ, PY 323 = Sb 1315 (preceded by *a-ni-ja* without division). Reading and word-division uncertain.

e-e-si, KN 24 = Ai 63, 271 = Sd 4422. 3rd plur. pres.: *ehensi* 'they are', cf. *e-ne-e-si*, *a-pe-e-si*. [Att. εἰσί; Myc. form with generalization of **es-*, < *esenti, cf. Hitt. *asantsi*.]

e-o, PY 148 = Ep 613. Nom. sing. masc. pple.: *ehōn* 'being'.

e-o-te, KN 37 = B 823 (*ta-pa-e-o-te*), PY An 614? Nom. plur. masc.: *ehontes*.
See also *e-e-to*, *e-so-to*, *a-pe-o*, *e-ne-e-si*, *e-ni-qe*.

e-e-to, PY 28 = An 607. Obscure, prob. verbal form, from εἰμί or ἵημι? See p. 168.

]*e-i-ja-si*, KN B 804.

e-ka-ma-te, PY 239 = Ta 642. Instr. sing., part of a table: *ekhmatei* 'with a support, strut'. [ἔχμα *Il.* XIV, 410 + ; cf. also ἔγμα· ὀχύρωμα, στῦλος Hesych.] See p. 341.

e-ka-ma-pi, PY 240 = Ta 713 + . Instr. plur.: *ekhmapphi*.

e-ka-no, PY Jn 725. MN: *Ekhānōr*?

e-ka-ra, PY 237 = Ta 709 (see p. 499). Nom. sing.: *eskharā* 'portable hearth, brazier'. [ἐσχάρη *Od.* VI, 52 + .]

e-ka-ra-e-we, KN 81 = Dm 1180 + . Nom. plur., term describing SHEEP; see pp. 210, 437.

e-ka-sa-te-ụ[, PY Qa 1291. MN: *Exantheus*? [If correct, this would be the only evidence for Myc. ἐξ.]

e-ka-te-jo, KN Sf 4418, X 768. Obscure; in Sf perhaps epithet of chariot-frames.

e-ka-te-re-ta, KN 276 = Se 891 (+ 1006). Prob. adj. describing chariot-frames; cf. *a-te-re-te-a*, which suggests that this may be a compound with *ekh-*, cf. also *e-te-re-ta*.

e-ke, KN 157 = Uf 835 + , PY 109 = Ea 782 + , 131 = Ep 301 + , 153 = Er 880, 194 = Na 334 + . 3rd sing. pres.: *ekhei* 'he/she has, holds'. [ἔχει Hom. + .]

e-ke-de-mi, PY 196 = Na 926, *ekhei de min* 'but he has it', cf. *da-mo-de-mi*.

e-ke-e, PY 140 = Eb 297, 135 = Ep 704. Pres. inf.: *ekhehen* 'to have'.

e-ke-qe, PY 118 = Eo 211 + , 136 = Eb 294 + , 248 = Va 15. Prob. *ekhei* + *-qe* 'and he/she has'. See p. 246.

e-ke-si, PY 115 = En 74. 21. Error for *e-ko-si*.

e-ko, KN 298 = Sc 226, So 4446. In Sc 226 perhaps nom. sing. masc. pres. pple.: *ekhōn* '(already) having (one)'; but poss. *enkhos* 'spear', see [*e*]*-ke-a*; in So 4446 (reverse) obscure.

e-ko-si, KN 90 = G 820, PY 55 = An 724, 151 = Ed 901 + , 114 = En 609 + , 255 = Jn 658 + , 186 = Na 543. 3rd plur. pres.: *ekhonsi* 'they have'.

e-ko-te, PY 43 = Aq 64, 149 = Ed 236, 253 = Jn 310. Nom. plur. masc. pres. pple.: *ekhontes* 'having'.

e-ke-a[^1], KN V 831. MN.

[*e-*]*ke-a*[^2], KN 263 = R 1815. Description of SPEARS; nom. plur. *enkheha* 'spears'. [ἔγχος *Il.* VI, 329 + ; cf. *e-ke-i-ja*.]

e-ke-si(*-qe*), PY 257 = Jn 829. Dat. plur.: *enkhes*(*s*)*i* *q*ᵘ*e* 'and for spears'.

]*e-ke-pi*[, KN Wb 5131. If correct, perhaps instr. plur.: *enkhesphi*.

e-ke-da-mo, KN Uf 1522, PY Cn 285. MN, nom. and dat.?: *Ekhedāmos, -ōi*. ['Εχέδαμος, 'Εχέδημος.]

e-ke-de-mi: see *e-ke*.

e-ke-e: see *e-ke*, *pu-ko-so*.

e-ke-i-ja, PY 320 = Va 1324. Prob. nom. plur.: *enkhehiai* 'spears?' [ἐγχείη *Il.* V, 267 + ; perhaps distinguished in meaning from ἔγχος.]

e-ke-i-ja-ta, PY Jn 750. MN: *Enkhehiātās*. [Cf. prec.]

e-ke-i-jo-jo, PY Sa 760. MN, gen.: *Enkhehioio*? *Ekheioio*? ["Εγχειος title of Aphrodite, 'Εχεῖος MN.]

e-ke-ja, PY Vn 1339. MN?; cf. *e-ke-a*[^1].

e-ke-jo-to, PY 44 = Aq 218. Prob. 3rd plur. of medio-passive verb: *-ontoi*. No plausible explanation of root (perhaps *enkeiontoi* (ἔγκειμαι) cf. κέονται).

e-ke-me-de, KN [Dd 659], U 4478, PY 56 = An 657, 258 = Jo 438. MN: *Ekhemēdēs*. [Cf. WN 'Εχεμήδα.]

e-ke-na-to, PY Ea 305. Error for *e-ke o-na-to*.

e-ke-ne, MY 46 = Au 102, Au 653. MN: *Engenēs*? [ἐγγενής; cf. 'Εγγενέτωρ.]

e-ke-ṇu-wo, KN U 4478. MN: *Ekhenuos*? (Ilievski).

e-ke-pu-te-ri-ja: see *e-ke* and *pu-te-ri-ja*.

e-ke-qe: see *e-ke*.

e-ke-ra-ne, PY Un 219. Obscure, possibly PN. [Cf. 'Εγγελᾶνες = 'Εγχελέαι?]

e-ke-ra₂-wo, PY [153 = Er 880], 171 = Un 718. MN: *Enkheliāwōn*?

e-ke-ra₂-wo-no, PY 54 = An 610. Gen.: *-wonos*.

e-ke-ra₂-wo-ne, PY 55 = An 724. Dat.: *-wonei*.

[*e-*]*ḳẹ-ra₂-u-na*, PY Un 853. Variant spelling of acc.?

[*e*]*-ke-ri-ja-wo*, PY Qa 1292. Variant spelling of nom.

]*e-ke-ri-jo-na*, PY Vn 851. MN or WN?

e-ke-ro, PY Jn 832, MY Au 609? (*e-ke-ro*[). MN: *Enkhēros*? [Cf. Cypr. ἔγχηρα.]

e-ke-ro-qo-no, PY Aa 777, Ab 563+, 13=Ad 691, An 199. Nom. and gen. plur.; description of men and women. Palmer: *enkhēro-qʰoinoi, -ōn* 'wage-earners'. See p. 161.

e-ke-se, KN B 799. MN.

e-ke-se-si, KN 201=Fp 14. Dat. plur.?; meaning obscure.

e-ke-si, PY 115=En 74. Error for *e-ko-si*: see *e-ke*.

e-ke-si-jo, PY Cn 4. MN.

e-ke-si-qe: see [*e-*]*ke-a*².

[*?e-*]*ke-ti-ra-wo*, KN V 7049. MN: *Egertilāwos*?

e-ki, KN Od 688. Obscure.

e-ki-no, KN Da 1078. MN: *Ekhīnos*? [ἐχῖνος.]
  e-ki̯-no-jo, PY 60=An 661. Gen. *Ekhīnoio*.

e-ki-si-jo/-ja: see s.v. *e-ko-so*.

e-ki-wo, PY Jn 320. MN. *Ekhiwos, Ekhiwōn*? [Ἔχιος, Ἐχίων.]

e-ko: see s.v. *e-ke*.

e-ko-me-na-ta-o, PY 60=An 661, 44=Aq 218. MN, gen.: *Erkhomenātāo*. [Cf. place name Ἐρχομενός.]

e-ko-me-no, PY Cn 40, Cn 599, Na 406, Na 941. PN: *Erkhomenos*. [Ἐρχομενός, Ὀρχ-, but not to be identified with that in Arcadia.]

e-ko-si: see *e-ke*.

e-ko-so, KN C 1030, Da 1137+, F 157+, L 564+. PN: *Exos*? [Not=Ἄξος which is earlier Ϝάξος.]
  e-ki-si-jo/-ja, KN 29=Am 821, Lc 527+. Ethnic: *Exios, -iā*.

e-ko-so-no, PY Na 507. PN.

e-ko-te: see *e-ke*.

e-ko-to, PY Eb 913, 115=En 74, 120=Eo 276, 121=Eo 247, 143=Ep 705+. MN, *Hektōr*. [Ἕκτωρ *Il*. I, 242+.]

e-ko-to-ri-jo, PY Cn 45. MN, dat.: *Hektoriōi*.

e-ku-se-we(*-qe*), MY Wt 501. Nom. plur.: *enkhusēwes* 'funnels'. [ἐγχέω.]

e-ma-a₂, PY 172=Tn 316, Un 219, Xn 1357, TH Of 31. Divine name, dat.: *Hermāhāi*. [Ἑρμῆς, Ἑρμείας, etc. *Il*. II, 104, *Od*. XIV, 435+.]

e-ma-a₂-o, KN D 411, but perhaps *o* is not part of the word. If correct, possibly gen.: *Hermāhāo*? Or alternatively a derivative meaning 'temple or festival of Hermes'?

e-ma-ta, PY 317=Ub 1318. Neut. plur.: *hermata* 'laces (for footwear)'. [ἕρματα (from εἴρω 'string, thread') 'earrings' *Il*. XIV, 182.]

e-me, PY 236=Ta 641. Dat. sing. masc.: *hemei* 'one'. [Att. εἷς, gen. ἑνός, from **hems>hens*, **hemos*, Schwyzer, *Gram*. I, 588.]

e-me-de, PY Eb 495. As prec.+*-de*: 'but with one'. See p. 254. [Taken as abl. *hemē* by Heubeck, 1969*b*, p. 12.]

e-me-si-jo[, KN De 1381, E 843. MN. [Previously taken as month name, but this is not in keeping with context.]

e-me-si-jo-jo, KN Lc 551, L 8159, X 35. Gen.

e-mi-ja-ta, KN V 831. MN.

ẹ-mi-to, KN 29=Am 821. Gen. following *heneka*. Formerly read *ti-mi-to*.

e-na-i-jo[, KN Xd 302, [Xd 7596?]. MN?

e-na-po-na, KN Od 681. Obscure.

e-na-po-ro, PY 60=An 661, 76=Cn 3, 184= Nn 228+. PN.

]*ẹ-na-ri-po-to*, KN Sg 884. Verbal adj. describing chariot frame: *enaliptos* 'oiled, painted'. [ἐνάλειπτος Hippocr.]

e-ne-e-si, PY 114=En 609. 3rd plur. pres.: *en-ehensi* 'they are in'. [ἔνειμι.]

e-ne-ka, KN 29=Am 821, PY 27=Ae 303, 42= An 37, 147=Ea 59, Ea 805. Preposition with gen.: 'for the sake of', 'because of'. [ἕνεκα, εἵνεκα *Il*. XIV, 89+. Not from ἐν+*ϝεκα (cf. ἑκών); prob. acc. of obsolete noun (cf. χάριν).]

e-ne-ke-se-u, KN Da 1081. MN: *Enexeus*. [ἐνεκ-; Szemerényi, 1957, p. 180.]

e-ne-me-na, MY 106=Ge 603. Nom. fem. of pple. describing a form of *skhoinos* (see *ko-no*), also abbreviated E, see p. 226.

e-ne-o, KN As 625. Poss. nom. sing. masc. or neut. pple.: *enehŏn*.

e-ne-ra, KN Ai 762. Obscure: poss. connected with *e-ne-re-ja*.

e-ne-ro, KN L 695. Possibly sing.

e-ne-re-ja, KN Ak 638. Nom. plur. fem., description of women: 'makers of *e-ne-ra*'?

e-ne-si-da-o-ne, KN [Gg 717], M 719. Dat. sing. prob. divine name. [Interpretation uncertain; see Heubeck, 1957, pp. 277–8.]

e-ne-ti-jo, PY Cn 45. MN, dat.?

e-ne-wo pe-za (also as one word), PY 239=Ta 642+. Nom. sing. fem. describing a table: *ennewo-pedza* 'with 9 . . .'; see p. 340 and cf. *we-pe-za*.

e-ne-wo pe-zo, PY 241=Ta 715. Dual form of prec.: *-pedzō*.

e-ni, PY Xn 1342. Context obscure; cf. *e-ni-qe*.

e-ni-ja-u-si-jo, PY 50=An 39. MN. Dat.?: *Eniausioi*. [ἐνιαύσιος.]

e-ni-pa-te-we, PY 255=Jn 658, Jn 725. PN, loc.

e-ni-qe, KN L 593, 221=L 647, L 5910, L 5924, L 5961, L 5998. Prob. not adj. describing CLOTH, but connective: *eni qʰe* (=ἔνεστί τε) 'and there is (are) among them'. [ἔνι *Il*. XVIII, 53+.]

e-ni-to-wo, PY Eb 1187, Ep 539. MN.

e-no-wa-ro, PY 58=An 654. MN or PN?

e-nu-wa-ri-jo, KN 208=V 52. Dat. divine name: *Enualiōi*. [Ἐνυάλιος *Il*. XVII, 211+.]

e-nwa-ri-jo, PY 55=An 724. MN: poss. *Enwālios* (cf. Ἧλις). [Not to be confused with the god Ἐνυάλιος, see prec.]

e-o, e-o-te: see s.v. *e-e-si*.

e-o-te-u, PY 60=An 661. MN.

e-pa-re, PY An 723. MN.

e-pa-sa-na-ti, PY 115=En 74, Ep 212. WN. [Identical with *i-pa-sa-na-ti*.]

e-pa-ta[, PY Jn 937. MN.

e-pe-i-ja-o, TH Of 41, Of 42. MN, gen.? [Cf. Ἐπέας.]

e-pe-ke, KN Dl 932. Obscure; not *empe(s)kēs* 'unshorn' (Palmer), since a wool clip is recorded (Killen, *Nestor* p. 257).

e-pe-ke-u, PY Jn 431. MN. *Epeigeus*? [Ἐπειγεύς *Il.* XVI, 571.]

e-pi, KN Lc 561 (*e-pi-qe*), 207 = V 280, PY Eb 842, 148 = Ep 613 (*e-pi-qe*), 97 = Un 2. Preposition with dat.: *epi* 'upon', etc. [ἐπί; cf. *o-pi*.]

e-pi-da-o, KN Vc 129. MN.

e-pi-da-to, PY 254 = Jn 389, Jn 601. Description of bronze, prob. adj.: *epidastos* 'distributed'. [Cf. ἀνά-δαστος, etc.; cf. next.]

e-pi-de-da-to, PY 250 = Vn 20. 3rd sing. perf. pass.: *epidedastoi* 'has been distributed'. [ἐπιδέδασται, Hesiod, *Th.* 789.]

e-pi-ja-ta, PY An 115. MN. *Epihaltās*. [Ἐφιάλτης *Il.* v, 385.]

e-pi-ja-ta-ni-ja, PY Ad 687. PN: variant of *e-pi-jo-ta-na*.

e-pi-jo-ta-na, PY Aa 95. PN: variant of prec.

e-pi-ka, PY 318 = Un 1314. [Cf. *e-pi-ko*.]

e-pi-ke-re, KN F 851, 95 = F 852. Word describing harvest? See p. 219.

]*e-pi-ke-to*, KN E 8122. Obscure.

e-pi-ki-to-ni-ja, KN 222 = L 693, [L 7514?]. Description of BRONZE: *epikhitōnia* 'fittings on a tunic'. [Cf. *ki-to*; see p. 488.]

e-pi-ko, KN B 1025. [Cf. *e-pi-ka*.]

e-pi-ko-e, PY Ad 672. PN.

e-pi-ko-o, PY Aa 94. Variant of prec.

e-pi-ko-ru-si-jo, KN 299 = Sk 789. Description of 2 fittings as parts of a set of armour; dual *epikorusiō* 'on the helmet'. [< -κορύθ-ιος; see also *o-pi-ko-ru-si-ja*.]

e-pi-ko-wa, KN Fh 343, Fh 380. Description of olive oil: *epikhowā* 'oil for anointing'? [Cf. ἐπιχόα· κατάχυσις Hesych.; Godart, 1969, p. 55; see also *po-ro-ko-wa*.]

e-pi-ko-wo, KN As 4493?, PY 56 = An 657. Nom. plur.: *epikowoi* 'watchers, guards'. [Cf. Delph. πυρ-κόος 'watcher of the sacred fire'.]

e-pi-pu-ta, PY 252 = Vn 10. Nom. plur.: *epiphuta* 'young trees, saplings'? [ἐπιφύομαι 'grow upon' Herodotus; cf. *pu-ta*.]

e-pi-qe: see *e-pi*.

e-pi-qo-ra₂, PY Mn 456. PN. [Cf. Ἐπιπολαί?]

e-pi-ro-pa-ja, KN Od 696. Description of wool: *epilōpaia*? [Cf. λώπη 'cloak'; see p. 321.]

e-pi-ta-jo, PY Jn 927. MN.

e-pi-u-ru-te-we, PY 317 = PY Ub 1318. Nom. plur. perh. *epiwrutēwes* (cf. ῥυτήρ). See p. 493.

e-pi-we-ti-ri-jo, PY Ea 52. Nom. sing. masc.: description of a man, probably occupational term: *epiwestrios*? [Cf. ἐφεστρίς 'upper garment'.]

e-pi-wo-qa-ta-o, PY Sa 1266. MN: gen. *Epiwoqᵘtāo*? [ἐπί, ϝέπος, cf. ὄπα.]

e-pi-zo-ta, KN 163 = Ra 984, 277 = Ra 1028. See pp. 456, 517.

e-pi-*65-ko, PY 251 = Vn 46. See p. 504.

e-po, KN Ce 283, Ws 8712, PY Vn 493. Obscure; poss. not the same word in all cases.

e-po-me-ne-u, PY 183 = Nn 831. MN: *Hepomeneus*? [ἕπω 'busy oneself with'.]

e-po-me-ne-we, PY Xn 1357. Dat.: -*ēwei*.

e-po-mi-jo, KN [299 = Sk 789], 325 = Sk 8100, Sk 8149, [V 337?]. Description of piece of armour; dual: *epōmiō* 'shoulder-pieces', 'pauldrons'. [ἐπώμιος Lucian; ἐπωμίς Eur. +.]

e-po-wi-ja, PY An 615. PN.

e-pu₂-no, KN Ga 427. MN?

e-qa-na-qe[, PY Ua 158. Obscure.

e-qa-ro, KN Dv 1125. MN: *Engᵘaros*? [Ἔμβαρος.]

e-qe-a-o, KN V 56. Gen. plur. of occupational term? [Cf. next.]

e-qe-o, PY 43 = Aq 64. Gen. plur. of occupational term? [Cf. prec.; attempts to connect these words with *i-qo* = ἵππος seem unlikely in view of initial *e-*.]

]*e-qe-ra-wo*, KN B 5025. MN: *Heqᵘelāwos*?

e-qe-si-jo/-*ja*: see s.v. *e-qe-ta*.

e-qe-ta, KN 29 = Am 821, B 1055, PY 57 = An 519+, 142 = Ed 317, Wa 917. Nom. sing. and plur. masc.: *heqᵘetās*, -*tai* 'followers', i.e. companions of the king, important officers of the court. [ἑπέτας Pindar.]

e-qe-ta-e, KN 29 = Am 821. Nom. dual: *heqᵘetae*.

e-qe-ta-i, PY 28 = An 607. Dat. plur.: *heqᵘetāhi*.

e-qe-si-jo/-*ja*, KN 214 = Ld 571+, PY Ed 847, 288 = Sa 790+, Wa 1148. Adj.: *heqᵘesios*, -*iā*, etc. 'of or belonging to *heqᵘetai*' (used of slaves, textiles and chariot-wheels).

e-qo-me-ne[, PY [Fr 1240?], Fr 1338.

e-qo-te, PY An 615, 55 = An 724. Obscure: poss. *heqᵘontes* with act. inflexion?

e-ra[1], KN Da 1323+, Pp 498, X 722. PN.

e-ra-de, KN Fh 357. Acc. + -*de*.

e-ra-jo/-*ja*, KN Ap 639, Fh 1059, Lc 528+, V 431. Ethnic: -*aios*, -*aiā*, etc.

e-ra[2], PY 172 = Tn 316, [Un 219], TH Of 28. Name of deity; dat.: *Hērāi*. [Ἥρη *Il.* I, 572+; not from *Ἥρϝα as suggested by Elean Ἡερϝαδίοις.]

e-ra-ne, KN C 902. Official title or MN?

e-ra-pe-ja, PY 317 = Ub 1318. Fem. sing. (also plur.?), adj. describing leather goods: *elapheiā* 'of deerskin'. [ἐλάφειος Xen. +.]

e-ra-pi-ja, PY Ub 1316: Fem. plur.: *elaphiai*.

e-ra-pi-ja-o (spelt *e-ra-ti-ja-o* in error), PY Ub 1317. Gen. plur. fem.: *elaphiāōn*.

e-ra-pe-me-na, KN 221 = L 647. Fem. sing. or plur. perf. part. pass.: *err(h)apmenā*, -*ai*. [ῥάπτω thus proved to have no ϝ- (see Chadwick and Baumbach, 1963, pp. 241–2); -*pm*- poss. etymological spelling rather than unassimilated in pronunciation?]

e-ra-po ri-me-ne, PY 56 = An 657. Prob. PN, loc.: *Elaphōn limenei* 'at Deer Harbour', but might be two personal names.

e-ra-se, PY Cn 4. Perh. *elase* 'drove': see s.v. *o-qe*.

e-ra-ta-ra, PY 114 = En 609, 119 = Eo 224. WN.

e-ra-te-i, PY 75 = Cn 608. PN, loc.: *Elatehi*, one of the Nine Towns of the Hither Province, cf. *ro-u-so*. [Cf. Ἐλάτεια (in Phocis).]

e-ra-to-de, PY 250 = Vn 20. Acc. + *-de*: *Elatos-de*.

e-ra-te-i-jo, PY 304 = On 300. Ethnic: *Elatehios*.

e-ra-te-re-wa-o, PY 258 = Jo 438, [304 = On 300]. PN, gen. plur.: *Elatrewāōn*? [Cf. MN Ἐλατρεύς *Od.* VIII, 111.]

e-ra-te-re-wa-pi, PY Cn 595, 257 = Jn 829. Loc. (abl.?): *-wāphi*.

e-ra-te-re-we, PY Ma 333. PN, variant of prec.: *Elatrēwes*?

e-ra-ti-ja-o: see s.v. *e-ra-pe-ja*.

e-ra-to, KN Dc 1359. MN: *Eratos, Elatos*? [Ἔρατος, Ἔλατος.]

e-ra-to-de: see s.v. *e-ra-te-i*.

e-ra-wa[, KN 94 = F 841. Gen. sing. or nom. plur.: *elaiwā* 'olive-tree'. [ἐλαῖαι *Od.* XI, 590+.]

e-ra-wo[1], [KN F 726], PY Fr 1223. Nom. sing.: *elaiwon* 'olive-oil' with OIL ideogram. [ἔλαιον *Il.* X, 577+; -F- attested by Lat. *oleum* < *elaiuom*.]

e-ra₃-wo, PY 305 = Fr 1184, Fr 1217, 310 = Fr 1225+. More accurate spelling: *elaiwon*.

e-ra-wo[2], KN C 1039. Prob. MN, not 'olive-oil'.

e-re-de, PY Fr 1228, Mn 1411. Obscure, PN + *-de*?

e-re-dwo-e, KN As 604, V 655. Heading to lists of men; nom. plur.?

e-re-e[1], PY 55 = An 724. Pres. inf. *ereen* 'to row', cf. *e-re-ta*. [ἐρέσσω < *ἐρέτ-yω. *Il.* IX, 361+.] See p. 188.

e-re-e[2]: see s.v. *e-re-i*.

e-re-e-u, PY 183 = Nn 831. MN, nom.: *Heleheus*? Or an official title?

e-re-e-wo, PY Na 284. Gen.: *-ēwos*.

e-re-e-we, PY An 723, Cn 1197, Jn 881. Dat.?: *-ēwei*.

e-re-i, PY 257 = Jn 829. PN, loc.: *Helehi*. [Ἕλος *Il.* II, 594, but not necessarily the same place.]

e-re-e, PY [258 = Jo 438], Xn 442. Alternative spelling?

e-re-mo, PY 152 = Er 312. Possibly *erēmon* 'waste land'. [ἐρῆμος *Od.* III, 270+.] See p. 266.

e-re-pa, KN Sd 4412, PY 249 = Va 482. Nom. sing.: *elephans* 'ivory'. [ἐλέφας *Il.* V, 583.]

e-re-pa-ta, KN Og 7504. Acc.?: *elephanta*.

e-re-pa-te, KN [163 = Ra 984?], 266 = Sd 4401+, PY 239 = Ta 642, 243 = Ta 708. Dat.-instr. sing.: *elephantei*.

e-re-pa-to, KN V 684, PY 287 = Sa 793. Gen.: *elephantos*.

e-re-pa-i-ro, KN Vc 212. MN.

e-re-pa-ṛo, KN Ce 144. MN? Variant spelling of prec.?

e-re-pa-te-jo, KN 265 = Sd 4403, PY 239 = Ta 642+. Epithet of chariot frames and parts of tables; adj.: *elephanteios*. [ἐλεφάντειος Diosc. + 'of an elephant'.]

e-re-pa-te-ja, PY 240 = Ta 713+. Fem.: *elephanteiā*.

e-re-pa-te-ja-pi, PY 242 = Ta 707+. Instr. plur. fem.: *elephanteiāphi*.

e-re-pa-te-jo-pi, KN 276 = Se 891, [X 7814?]. Knossian instr. plur. masc. or neut.: *elephanteiophi*.

e-re-pa-te-o, KN Se 1007. Variant form: *elephanteos*.

e-re-ta, KN As 5941, 83 = C 902, PY [14 = Ad 697], 53 = An 1, 55 = An 724+. Nom. sing. and plur. masc.: *eretai* 'rowers, oarsmen'. [ἐρέται *Od.* I, 280+.]

e-re-ta-o, PY 15 = Ad 684. Gen. plur.: *eretāōn*.

ẹ-re-te-ri-ja, PY Pa 889. Obscure.

e-re-u-ta, KN B 5172, PY An 1423. MN?

e-re-u-te-re, PY 76 = Cn 3, Wa 917. Dat. sing. or nom. plur.? Official title: *ereutērei, -res*? [Cf. Cret. ἐρευτάς.] See p. 207.

e-re-u-te-ro, PY 191 = Na 248+. Nom. sing. neut.: *eleutheron* 'free of impost'. See pp. 298, 469. [ἐλεύθερος *Il.* VI, 455+.]

e-re-u-te-ra, PY 192 = Na 252+. Prob. neut. plur.: *eleuthera*.

e-re-u-te-ro-se, PY 190 = Na 395+. 3rd sing. aor.: *eleutherōse* 'he made free'. [ἐλευθερόω Herodotus+.]

e-re-u-ti-ja, KN 206 = Gg 705, Od 714+. Dat. of divine name: *Eleuthiāi*. [Lacon. Ἐλευθία, Cret. Ἐλεύθυια, Hom. Εἰλείθυια.]

e-re-wi-jo, PY Vn 48. Followed by *po-ti-ni-ja*, apparently without division. Gen. plur.? Palmer: *Hērēwiōn* 'at the festival of Hera', but a place would be more appropriate.

e-ri-ka, KN 278 = So 894, 280 = So 4439. Gen. sing.: *helikās* 'of willow-wood'. [Arc. ἑλίκη Theophr. Prob. related to Lat. *salix* rather than OE *welig* 'willow' and *Fελίκη 'spiral'.]

e-ri-ka-we-e, PY Un 1319. MN or PN?

e-ri-ke-re-we, KN 155 = Uf 981. MN: *Eriklewēs*.

e-ri-ko-wo, PY 59 = An 656, Ep 212, Jn 845+. MN.

e-ri-ma-si-ṭọ, PY Pa 49. MN, dat.

e-ri-no-wo, PY Na 106. PN, nom. for usual loc.

e-ri-no-wo-te, PY [An 427], Cn 4, Mn 456. Dat.-loc.: *-wontei*.

e-ri-no-wo-to, PY 154 = Eq 213. Gen.: *-wontos*.

e-ri-nu, KN 200 = Fp 1. Divine name, nom. for dat.?: *Erinus*. [Ἐρινύς *Il.* IX, 571+.]

e-ri-nu-we, KN 208 = V 52. Dat.: *Erinuei*.

e-ri-qi-ja, PY [Eb 1440], Ep 539. WN: *Erigᵘiā*? [Cf. next.]

e-ri-qi-jo, PY Ea 480. MN: *Erigᵘios*? [Cf. Ἐρισθένης, etc., Πολύ-βιος, etc.]

e-ri-sa-ta, KN Nc 4474. MN.

e-ri-ta, PY 135 = Ep 704. WN, priestess: *Erithā*? [Cf. Ἔριθος.]

e-ri-ta-qi-jo, KN As 604. MN.

]*e-ri-ta-ri-jo*[, KN Xd 304, MN. *Erithālios*? [Cf. Ἐριθήλας.]

e-ri-ti-qi[, KN B 802. MN.

e-ri-to-ti-no, PY Cn 4. PN.

e-ri-tu-pi-na, MY 303 = V 659. WN.

e-ri-we-ro, PY Vn 130. MN, dat.: *Eriwērōi*. [ἐρίηρος.]

e-ri-*19, KN Ag 90, MN.

e-ro-e, KN Sc 244. MN?

e-ro-e-o, KN Xd 116. Gen. of prec.?

e-ro-ma-to, PY An 172. PN.

e-ro-pa-ke-ja, KN Lc 534, Ld 595, MY 93 = Fo 101. Nom. plur. fem.; description of women cloth-workers. Cf. *e-ro-pa-ke-u*.

e-ro-pa-ke-u, KN As 4493. MN or occupational term? Cf. *e-ro-pa-ke-ja*.

e-ro-u-ta, KN Da 1162. MN.

e-ro₂-ne, PY Na 588. PN.

e-ro₂-qo, PY Ea 29, Ea 325 +. MN.

e-ru, MY 106 = Ge 603. Incomplete spelling of *e-ru-ta-ra*.

e-ru-mi-ni-ja, PY 251 = Vn 46. Nom. plur.: *elumniai* 'roof beams'. [ἐλυμνίαι Hesych.]

e-ru-si-jo, PY Vn 130. MN, dat.: *Erussiōi*. [Ἐρύσσιος.]

e-ru-ta-jo, PY Jn 725. MN.

e-ru-ta-ra¹, PY 58 = An 654, 43 = Aq 64. MN. *Eruthrās*. [Ἐρύθρας.]

e-ru-ta-ra², PY 323 = Sb 1315, 317 = Ub 1318, MY 105 = Ge 602 +. Nom. sing. or plur. fem.: *eruthrā, -ai* 'red'. Cf. MN *e-ru-to-ro*. [ἐρυθρός *Il.* XIX, 38 +.]

e-ru-ta-ra-pi, KN 215 = Ld 573 +. Instr. plur. fem.: *eruthrāphi* 'with red (patterns, spots?)'.

e-ru-ti-ri-jo[, KN Xd 297. MN: *Eruthrios*. [Ἐρύθριος.]

e-ru-to-ro, KN 39 = As 1517, 72 = Dk 1074. MN: *Eruthros*. Cf. *e-ru-ta-ra*. [Ἔρυθρος.]

e-sa-pa-ke-mẹ[-na?], KN X 7375. Perf. part. pass.: *espargmena* 'swathed'? [Aor. σπάρξαν *Hom. h. Apollo* 121.]

e-sa-re-u, PY 190 = Na 395, Na 527. MN or more likely title.

e-sa-re-we, KN 39 = As 1517, PY Cn 1197. Dat.

e-sa-re-wi-ja, PY 45 = An 830, Ma 330, 304 = On 300, Vn 493. PN. Cf. *e-sa-re-u*.

e-sa-ro, PY [114 = En 609], 119 = Eo 224, 143 = Ep 705. MN.

e-se-re-a₂, PY 60 = An 661. MN.

e-se-re-e-jo, KN Dl 947, Dl 949, Dl 1046. Annotation giving ownership of flocks of sheep, prob. derivative of MN (cf. prec.) or title.

e-so, PY 45 = An 830. Poss. *ensō* 'inside'. [εἴσω.] See p. 424.

e-so-to, KN Am 600, 34 = Am 601. 3rd plur. fut.: *es(s)ontoi* 'they will be'?

e-ṣọ-wo-ke, PY 251 = Vn 46. See p. 504.

e-ta-je-u, PY An 5. MN: *Etaieus*? [Cf. PN Ἐταιεῖς.]

e-ta-wo-ne, KN [Ld 591], [Ld 5607], Xe 5540. MN, dat.? Cf. next.

e-ta-wo-ne-u, PY 57 = An 519, 43 = Aq 64. MN: *Etāwoneus*. [Ἐτεωνεύς *Od.* IV, 22 +.]

e-ta-wo-ne-wo, KN L 695. Gen.: *Etāwonēwos*.

e-ta-wo-ne-we, KN Ld 584. Dat.: *Etāwonēwei*.

e-te, KN Am 600, 34 = Am 601, PY 248 = Va 15? Poss.: *enthen* 'from there'. [ἔνθεν.]

e-te-do-mo, KN Uf 432, PY Ea 808, 114 = En 609, 118 = Eo 211, 131 = Ep 301. Occupational term: earlier suggestion *entes-domos* (cf. ἔντεα) seems unlikely.

e-te-jo, KN Gg 521. Description of amphoras.

e-te-jạ[, KN Fh 359. Description of oil; fem.?

e-te-re-rọ, PY Cn 600. MN.

e-te-re-ta, KN 275 = Se 879. Adj. describing chariot-frames; cf. *e-ka-te-re-ta*.

e-te-wa, PY 56 = An 657, Cn 254. MN: *Etewās*.

e-te-wa-o, KN X 8270. Gen.: *Etewāo* or nom. *Etewāōn*?

e-te-wa-jo, PY Cn 600, Sa 1267, Xa 639. MN: *Etewaios*. (Sa 1267 error for gen.?)

e-te-wa-jo-jo, PY Sa 769. Gen.: *Etewaioio*.

e-te-wa-no, KN 80 = C 913. MN, dat.: *Etewainōi*?

e-te-wa-tu-wo, KN C 912. MN, gen.: *Etewastuos*.

e-te-we, PY Cn 925. MN, dat.: *Entêwei*? (Heubeck, 1957, p. 272.)

e-te-wo-ke-re-we-i-jo, PY 58 = An 654, 43 = Aq 64. Patronymic adj.: *Etewoklewehios* 'son of Eteocles'. [Cf. βίη Ἐτεοκληείη *Il.* IV, 386.]

e-ti-je-ja, PY Vn 851. WN?

e-ti-me-de-i, PY Fn 324. MN, dat.: *Entimēdehi*? (Heubeck, 1957, p. 272.)

e-ti-ra-wo, PY 61 = Cn 131, 62 = Cn 655. MN, nom. and dat.: *Entilāwos, -ōi*? (Heubeck, 1957, p. 272) or *Ertilāwos*? [Cf. Λαέρτης.]

e-ti-ra-wo-jo, PY Sa 1264. Gen.: *-lāwoio*.

e-ṭi-ri-ja, PY Vn 851. WN?

e-ti-wa, KN Fs 19. PN?

e-ti-wa-ja, KN Ap 639, Od 681. WN.

e-ti-wa-jo, PY 248 = Va 15. MN (cf. prec.)?

e-ti-wa-ṇọ[, PY Wr 1359. MN?

e-ti-we, PY Fr 343, Fr 1209, 309 = Fr 1224. Adj. describing olive oil: *ertiwen*? [Lejeune, 1958b, p. 18; cf. ἔρτις · κρημνός prob. a plant.] Cf. *a-e-ti-to*.

e-to, PY Va 15. 3rd pers. dual: *eston* 'are'?

e-to-ki-ja, PY 251 = Vn 46, Vn 879. Nom. plur. in list of building materials: *entoikhia* 'wall-fittings'? [ἐντοίχιος Xen. +.]

e-to-mo-jo, PY Vn 1191. MN, gen.: *Hetoimoio*? [Cf. WN Ἑτοίμη.]

e-to-ni-jo, PY 55 = An 724, 140 = Eb 297, 146 = Eb 473, Ep 539, 135 = Ep 704. The name of a kind of land holding; see p. 253.

e-to-ro-qa-ta, KN Oa 878, U 736. Name of an artifact or MN? If MN, *Esthlogᵘatās*? (Ruijgh, 1967, p. 355.)

e-to-wo-ko, KN Fh 462, PY 50 = An 39, 91 = Fn 50. Occupational term, dat. sing. and nom.

plur.: *ento-worgoi*? Cf. *e-te-do-mo*, but *e-to-* is hard to explain.

e-to-wo-ko-i, PY Fn 79. Dat. plur.

e-u-da-i-ta, KN Dl 47. MN.

e-u-da-mo, KN B 799, V 57, TH Z 853. MN: *Eudāmos* or *Eudaimōn*. [Εὔδαμος, Εὐδαίμων.]

e-u-de-we-ro, PY 6 = Ab 379+. PN: *Eudeiwelos*? [Cf. Εὐδείελος name of Aspledon, Strabo.]

e-u-do-no, PY 253 = Jn 310. MN.

e-u-ka-no, PY Un 1320. MN, dat.

e-u-ka-ro, PY An 723, Jn 750. MN: *Eukālos*. [εὔκηλος, Dor. εὔκαλος.]

e-u-ke-to, PY 140 = Eb 297, 135 = Ep 704. 3rd sing. pres. mid.: *euchetoi* 'she declares' (not 'prays'). [οὕτω φησὶ καὶ εὔχεται *Il.* xiv, 366.]

e-u-ko-me-no, PY Jn 725, [KN F 7748?]. MN: *Eukhomenos*.

e-u-ko-ro, KN Dd 1149+, V 482. MN: *Eukolos, Eukhoros, Euklos*? [Εὔκολος, Εὔχορος, Εὔκλος.]

e-u-me-de, PY Ea 773+. MN: *Eumēdēs*. [Εὐμήδης *Il.* x, 314.]

e-u-me-de-i, PY 305 = Fr 1184. Dat.: *Eumēdehi*.

e-u-me-ne, PY Ea 757, Ea 822, Jn 725. MN: *Eumenēs*. [Εὐμένης.]

e-u-me-ta, KN Dv 1388. MN: *Eumētās*. [Εὐμήτης.]

e-u-mo, KN Da 1390. MN.

e-u-na-wo, KN As 1520, B 799, Dv 1206. MN: *Eunāwos*. [Εὔνηος *Il.* vii, 468.]

e-u-o-mo[, KN Xd 127. MN: *Eu(h)ormos*?

e-u-po-ro, MY 46 = Au 102. MN: *Euporos, Euphoros, Eupōlos*? [Εὔπορος, Εὔφορος, Εὔπωλος.]

e-u-po-ro-wo, KN V 7620, PY Jn 601+. MN: *Euplowos*. [Εὔπλους.]

e-u-qo-ne, PY Vn 130. MN, dat.

e-u-ro-wa-[, KN X 408. MN?

e-u-ru-da-mo, KN Xd 166. MN: *Eurudāmos*. [Εὐρύδαμος.]

e̯-u̯-ru-po-to-re-mo-jo, [KN Xd 92?], PY Fn 324. MN, gen.: *Euruptolemoio*. [Εὐρύπτολεμος.]

e-u-ru-qo-ta, KN V 147. MN: *Euruqʰontās, Euruqʷhoitās*?

e-u-ru-wo-ta, PY Eb 156, [148 = Ep 613], 253 = Jn 310. MN: *Eurwōtās*? [Εὐρώτας.]

e-u-ta-re-wo̯, PY Na 525. MN, gen., forming PN with *wo-wo*: *Euthăl̄ewos*? [Cf. Εὐθαλής, Εὐθάλιος etc.]

e-u-to̯-ro̯-qo, PY Jn 478. MN: *Eutroqʷos*? [Εὔτροπος.]

e-u-wa-ko-ro, PY Jn 431. MN: *Euāgoros, Euagros*. [Εὐάγορος, Εὔαγρος.] See also *e-wa-ko-ro*.

e-u-wa-re, PY Jn 693. MN: *Euārēs*. [Εὐήρης.]

e-u-we-to, PY Jn 750. MN: *Euētōr, Euestōr*?

e-u-we-to-ro, PY Jn 750. Gen.: *-toros*.

e-wa-ko-ro, KN V 1005, TH [Z 850], [Z 883], [Z 884]. MN: prob. variant spelling of *e-u-wa-ko-ro*.

e-wa-ra-ro, KN Db 1367. MN.

e-wi-da-si[, PY Na 104. Dat. plur.?

e-we-de-u, KN Ga 423, Vc 312. MN.

e-we-ki-ta, KN X 993. MN?

e-we-pe-se-so-me-na, MY 227 = Oe 127. Neut.

plur., fut. part. pass.: (*pharwea*) *eu hepsēsomena* 'to be well boiled'? [ἕψω 'boil'.] Palmer: compound of εὐ- (= ἐπί) + ἕπω.

e-we-wa-ta, KN V 57, [Xd 313?]. MN or title?

e-wi-ku-wo-te, PY Na 604. PN, loc.: *-wontei*.

e-wi-ri-pi-ja, PY Aa 60. Ethnic; nom. plur. fem.: *Ewrīpiai*. [Cf. next.]

e-wi-ri-po, PY 54 = An 610. PN: *Ewrīpos*. [Εὔριπος.]

e-wi-su-zo-ko, KN Se 965, Se 1007. Description of chariot-frames; perhaps compound of *ewisu-* = ἴσο- < ϝισϝο-, with prothetic vowel as Hom. ἐΐση and -σϝ- > *-su-*? But cf. *wi-so-wo-pa-na*.

e-wi-su-*79-ko, PY Va 404, 249 = Va 482. Perhaps variant of prec., but see Lejeune (1958a, pp. 212–17.)

e-wi-ta-jo, KN Vc 102. MN.

e-wi-te̯-u, PY Cn 437, [Jn 832]. MN.

e-wi-te-we, PY Cn 40. Dat.

e-wi-te-wi-jo, PY Mn 456, 195 = Na 245, Vn 130. PN.

e-wi-to-wo, KN B 806. MN.

e-wo-ta-de, KN C 901. PN: acc. + *-de* or loc.?

]e̯-wo-ta-o[, PY Cn 314. MN, gen.?

e-ze-to, KN Od 563. Obscure.

e-zo-wo, KN Xe 5900, PY Cn 40, Cn 599. MN.

e-*65-to, PY 115 = En 74, 114 = En 609, 118 = Eo 211, 120 = Eo 276. MN.

i-da-i-jo, KN 232 = K 875, PY 60 = An 661, TH Of 28. MN. [Prob. not = Ἰδαῖος.]

i-da-ra-ta, KN Xd 154. MN.

i-do-me-ne-ja, PY Eb 498, Ep 212. WN: *Idomeneia*. [Cf. Ἰδομενεύς *Il.* i, 145+.]

i-do̯-me-ni-jo, PY Gn 428. MN, dat.: *Idomeniōi*?

i-du, KN Ap 639. WN.

i-e-re-u: see *i-je-re-u*.

i-ja-me-i, PY Fn 324. MN, dat.

i-ja-pu₂-we, KN Lc 646. PN, loc. [Cf. *ja-pu₂-wi-ja*.]

i-ja-te, PY Eq 146. Nom. sing.: *iātēr* 'physician'. [ἰητήρ *Il.* ii, 732+, Cypr. acc. *to-ni-ja-te-ra-ne* τὸν ἰατε̃ραν.]

i-ja-wo-ne, KN B 164, [Ws 1707?], Xd 146. MN, dat. or nom. plur. of ethnic: *Iāwones*? [Cf. Ἰάονες *Il.* xiii, 685.]

i-je-re-ja, KN 200 = Fp 1+, PY 27 = Ae 303, 140 = Eb 297+, 114 = En 609, 119 = Eo 224, Ep 539+, 314 = Qa 1289+, 313 = Un 6. Nom. and gen. sing.: *hiereia, -ās* 'priestess'. [ἱέρεια *Il.* vi, 600+.]

i-je-re-u, KN 29 = Am 821, PY 44 = Aq 218, 121 = Eo 247+, Fn 837, Qa 1290, 315 = Qa 1296. Nom. sing.: *hiereus* 'priest'. [ἱερεύς *Il.* i, 62+.]

i-e-re-u, PY 115 = En 74, 116 = En 659. Variant spelling of prec.

i-je-re-wo, PY Ea 756. Gen. sing.: *hierēwos*.

i-je-re-wi-jo, KN 232 = K 875. MN or neut. adj. describing vessel? *Hierēwios* or *hierēwion*? [Cf. ἱερήϊον *Od.* xiv, 94+.]

i-je-ro[1], KN Fp 363. Adj. describing oil or neut. as sb.?: *hieron* 'sacred' or 'shrine'? [ἱερός *Il.* II, 305+.]

  i-je-ro-jo, PY 27 = Ae 303. Gen. sing. of adj. describing gold: *hieroio*.

i-je-ro[2], KN Dv 1447. MN: *Hierōn*. ['Ιέρων.]

i-je-ro-wo-ko, PY [Eb 159], 148 = Ep 613. Nom. sing.: *hierowŏrgos* 'sacrificing priest'. [ἱεροεργός Call.+.]

i-je-to(*-qe*), PY 172 = Tn 316. Prob. 3rd pers. of mid. verb: see p. 462.

  (*jo-*)*i-je-si*, PY 76 = Cn 3. 3rd plur. pres. act. of same verb? Or *hiensi* 'they send' [ἵημι]?

i-je-we, PY 172 = Tn 316. Dat. sing., perhaps to *i-*65*: *hiewei* 'son' or error for *i-je-⟨re⟩-we* (*i-je-re-u*)? See p. 462.

i-jo, KN V 1523, MY 46 = Au 102. At MY either MN or more prob. nom. sing.: (*h*)*ios* 'son'. See p. 425. [Cf. *i-*65*.] Context at KN obscure, possibly sing. of next.

i-jo-te, KN B 7041, L 698, PY 53 = An 1, MY Au 657. Nom. plur. masc.: *iontes* 'who are to go'. [εἶμι, cf. ἰὼν κοίλης ἐπὶ νηός *Od.* II, 332.]

i-ka-sa-ja, PY Gn 720. PN?

i-ka-se, KN Sc 258. MN. Cf. next.

i-ke-se, KN Xd 143. MN. Cf. prec.

i-ke-se-ra, KN Dk 1077, Dv 1496. MN.

i-ke-ta, KN B 799. MN: *Hiketās*. [Cf. Ἱκετάων *Il.* III, 147+.]

i-ku-to, MY Oi 705. MN?

i-ku-tu-re, KN L 588. MN?

i-ku-wo-i-pi, KN 207 = V 280. Instr. plur.: see p. 476.

i-ma-di-ja, PY Ea 816. MN or WN.

i-ma-di-jo, PY Cn 436, Ea 29, 253 = Jn 310. MN, nom. and dat.

i-mi-ri-jo, KN Db 1186. MN.

]*i-mi-so*, KN Do 996. MN.

i-mo-ro-ne-u, KN Vc 55, [PY Jn 927]. MN.

i-na, PY Eb 885, Ep 539. MN.

i-na-ma-ta, PY 182 = Ma 126. Obscure; see pp. 295, 466.

i-na-ne, PY 51 = An 18. PN: *-ānes*. Cf. next.

  i-na-pi, PY An 5 (deleted). Instr.: *-āmphi*.

i-na-ni-ja, PY Ae 8, Ae 72. PN: *-āniā*, variant of *i-na-ne*.

i-na-o, PY An 209, MY 106 = Ge 603+. MN.

  i-na-o-te, MY 107 = Ge 604. Dat.

i-ne-u, KN As 607, Da 1379, Xd 133? MN.

i-ni-ja, PY 114 = En 609, 118 = Eo 211. WN.

i-pa-sa-na-ti, PY Eb 1350, 121 = Eo 247. WN. Corrected in 121 from *e-pa-sa-na-ti*, q.v.

i-pe-me-de-ja, PY 172 = Tn 316. Divine name, dat.: *Iphemedeiāi*. ['Ιφιμέδεια *Od.* XI, 305, which is prob. deformed by popular etymology; see p. 288.]

i-pe-me-de-ja⟨*-jo*⟩*-qe*, PY 172 = Tn 316. Prob. dat.-loc.: '(and) at the shrine of *Iphemedeia*'.

i-pe-ne-o[, PY Xa 1419. In context with divine names?

i-pe-ra-ta, PY Jn 601. MN.

i-pe-se-wa, PY 305 = Fr 1184. MN, dat.

i-pe-ta, KN Dl 949. MN.

i-po-no, KN 233 = Uc 160 rev. Nom. plur.: *ipnoi* 'dutch ovens', i.e. earthenware bowls used for baking on a hearth. [ἰπνός Herodotus+; the alleged sense 'lantern' (Aristophanes) is non-existent.]

i-po-po-qo-i(*-qe*), PY Fn 79. Dat. plur. occupational term: *hippophorg^{u}oihi* 'horse-feeders, ostlers'. [ἱπποφορβός Plato+; *p* by dissimilation from *q*, see p. 399.]

]*i-po-qa*, KN 165 = Gv 862: see p. 456.

i-qa-ro, KN Xd 7555. MN? *Hiqq^{u}alos*? ["Ἱππαλος.]

i-qe-ja, PY 312 = An 1281. Epithet of Potnia, dat.: *hiqq^{u}eiāi* '(the Mistress) of Horses'. [ἵππειος *Il.* V, 799+.]

i-qi-ja, KN [265 = Sd 4403], 267 = Sd 4409+, 273 = Sf 4420+. Nom. sing. and plur. fem.: *hiqq^{u}iā*, *-ai* 'chariot', associated with CHARIOT ideogram. [Originally adj. = ἵππιος with fem. substantive understood, possibly *wokhā*, see *wo-ka*.] See also *a-qi-ja-i*.

  i-qi-jo, KN 266 = Sd 4401+. Nom. dual.: *hiqq^{u}iō*.

i-qo, KN 82 = Ca 895, PY Fa 16, 246 = Ta 722. Nom. plur., dat., instr. sing.: *hiqq^{u}oi*, *-ōi* 'horses'. [ἵππος < *ekwos*.]

i-qo-jo, PY 147 = Ea 59. Gen.: *hiqq^{u}oio*. Sense here and in Fa 16 uncertain, taken by Palmer as a god.

i-qo-e-qe, KN 269 = Sd 4404+. Name of part of a chariot made of wood; prob. compound of *hiqq^{u}o-* 'horse'. See pp. 364, 515.

i-ra-ko-to, KN V 466. MN.

i-ra-ta, KN Uf 1011, PY 116 = En 659, [126 = Eo 281]. MN.

i-ro-to, KN C 912. MN.

i-sa-na-o-ti, PY Cn 254. MN, dat.

i-sa-wo, KN Sc 253. MN.

i-se-we-ri-jo, KN B 798, L 473, X 5105. MN.

i-so-e-ko, PY Fn 187. MN or title?

i-su-ku-wo-do-to, KN Fh 348. MN: *Iskhuodotos*? [Apparently not from ἰσχύς if this has ϝ-.]

i-ta-da-wa, MY Oe 106. WN?, dat.

i-ta-ja, KN Ap 769, Xe 537. WN.

i-ta-mo, KN Ap 618. WN.

i-ta-no, KN Xe 5877. Apparently MN; cf. next.

]*i-ta-no*, KN Ap 769. WN.

i-ta-ra-jo, PY Jn 431. MN.

i-te-ja-o, PY 15 = Ad 684. Gen. plur. fem.: *histeiāōn*, 'weavers'. [ἱστός.] Cf. *i-te-we*.

i-te-re-wa, PY 43 = Aq 64, 258 = Jo 438. PN, nom. and gen.

i-te-u, KN 38 = As 1516. MN: *Histeus*? Cf. next.

i-te-we, PY 319 = Un 1322. Dat. sing. (or nom. plur.): *histēwei* 'weaver'. [ἱστός.] See p. 506.

i-te-we-ri-di, MY Oe 121. WN?, dat.

i-ti-nu-ri, KN Dq 439. MN.

i-to, KN As 1519. MN.

i-to-we-sa, PY 237 = Ta 709. Nom. fem. sing. adj. describing a portable hearth: *histowessa* 'provided with a ἱστός'. See pp. 338, 500.

i-wa-ka, KN Uf 120, V 60, PY 253 = Jn 310, Ub 1317. MN: *Iwakhās?*

i-wa-ka-o, PY 253 = Jn 310. Gen.: *Iwakhāo.*

i-wa-ko, KN As 1516. MN: *Iwakkhos?*

i-wa-si-jo-ta, PY 76 = Cn 3. Nom. plur. ethnic name?: *Iwasiōtai.*

*i-wa-so*¹, PY 57 = An 519, 58 = An 654, 60 = An 661. Name of a group of men: *Iwasoi?* Cf. prec. [Cf. Ἴασον Ἄργος *Od.* XVIII, 246; not to be identified with Ἴασος in Arcadia.]

*i-wa-so*², PY 62 = Cn 655. MN: *Iwasos.*

i-we-ro, KN As 1519. MN.

i-za-a-to-mo-i, PY 91 = Fn 50. Dat. plur. of compound of *a-to-mo*: *-arthmoihi*. First element obscure: Mühlestein *hitsa-* < *hiqqᵘịa-*, but this is problematical.

i-za-re, KN B 805. MN.

i-*65, PY Ae 344, 43 = Aq 64, 44 = Aq 218, [Jn 431], Jn 725. Either follows gen. of man's name or, with suffixed *-qe*, nom. of man's name: *(h)ius* 'son'. Cf. *i-je-we* 172 = Tn 316, possibly dat.; *i-jo*. [The value of **65 = ju* is probable though not yet certain; if correct, *i-ju* and *i-jo* bear a strange resemblance to υἱύς and υἱός; possibly two different words for 'son' became contaminated leading to both having initial *(h)i-* in Myc., but υἱ- in later Greek; Heubeck, 1971 *c*.]

i-*65-ke-o, KN Xd 105. Obscure.

ja-ke-te-re, PY Mn 11. Apparently variant spelling of *a-ke-te-re*, *a₂-ke-te-re*.

ja-ma-ra, KN V 503. MN.

ja-ma-ta-ro, KN V 655. MN.

]*ja-mi-nu*, KN Ap 5547. WN.

]*ja-pa-ra-ro*, KN V 429, V 652. MN.

ja-pe-re-so, KN Fs 23. PN?

ja-pọ, KN V 655. MN.

ja-puₐ-wi-ja, KN Lc 541. Nom. plur. fem. of ethnic; cf. *i-ja-puₐ-we*.

ja-qo, KN Mc 4461. PN?

ja-ra-to, KN De 1424. MN.

ja-ru, KN C 911. MN.

jạ-sa-no, KN 38 = As 1516. MN.

ja-sa-ro, KN V 832. MN. Cf. *a-sa-ro.*

ja-ti-ri, KN De 1301. MN.

je-zo, KN Db 1274, Dv 5989. MN.

jo-, KN 201 = Fp 14, 164 = Gv 863, PY 76 = Cn 3, 75 = Cn 608, 257 = Jn 829, MY 105 = Ge 602 +. Variant spelling of prefix *o-*, q.v.

jo-e-ke-to-qo, KN 164 = Gv 863. Obscure: see p. 273.

jo-i-je-si: see s.v. *i-je-to(-qe).*

jo-o-po-ro: see s.v. *o-pe-ro*².

jo-qi, PY 318 = Un 1314. Acc. neut. sing. rel.: *hoqqᵘi* 'which'. [ὅ, τι < *yod-kʷi(d).]

jo-te-re-pa-to, KN 201 = Fp 14. Obscure: see p. 307.

KA, As adjunct to STIRRUP-JAR (**210*): KN K 700: abbreviation of **ka-ra-re-u* (see *ka-ra-re-we*).

As adjunct to PIG: PY 313 = Un 6, Un 853: abbreviation of *kapros* (κάπρος) 'boar'. Ideographic use: PY Un 219; in list of offerings?

ka-a-na, KN X 728 edge. Obscure.

ka-da-i-so, KN De 5018 + 7693. MN. [Cf. *ka-da-si-jo.*]

ka-da-i-to, KN Uf 5726. MN.

ka-da-mi-ja, MY 107 = Ge 604. A spice, prob, *kardamia* = κάρδαμον, καρδαμίς 'garden cress', *Lepidium sativum.*

ka-da-no, KN Dk 1065, Dv 1128. MN: *Kādānōr?* [Cf. κῆδος; Heubeck, 1957, p. 273.]

]*ka-da-ra-so*, KN F 452. MN?

ka-da-ro, PY Cn 40. MN, dat.

ka-da-si-jo, PY 57 = An 519. MN.

]*ka-di-ti-ja*, KN V 1003. Fem. ethnic? *Kadistiai?* [Cf. Κάδιστον ὄρος N.W. Crete.]

ka-do-wo, PY 43 = Aq 64, Cn 719. MN.

ka-e-sa-me-no, PY 59 = An 656, TH Ug 5. MN: *Kahesamenos?* [Cf. καίνυμαι, κεκασμένος; Heubeck, 1957, p. 275.]

ka-e-sa-me-no-jo, PY Vn 1191. Gen.: *-noio.*

ka-e-se-u, PY 316 = Qa 1299, MY Ge 605. MN: *Kaheseus.* [Cf. *ka-e-sa-me-no*; Heubeck, 1957, p. 276.]

ka-e-se-we, MY 105 = Ge 602. Dat. (error?): *Kahesēwei.*

kạ-ja, PY 318 = Un 1314. Obscure.

ka-jo, KN Dv 1451. MN.

ka-ka-po, PY Jn 320. MN: *Kakkabos?*

ka-ka-re-ạ, KN 263 = R 1815. Reading uncertain, apparently a gap after *ka-ka*: prob. neut. plur.: *(enkheha) khalkāreha* '(spears) with bronze points'. [χαλκήρεϊ δουρί *Il.* v, 145 +.]

ka-ke, KN 38 = As 1516, B 799? MN.

ka-ke-ja-pi, KN 267 = Sd 4409, Sd 5091, [Se 893?]. Instr. plur. fem.: *khalkeiāphi* 'of bronze'. [χάλκειος *Il.* XIII, 30 +.]

ka-ki-jo, KN 278 = So 894. Dual neut.: *khalkiō* 'a pair of bronze (wheels)'. [κύκλα χάλκεα, *Il.* v, 723.]

*ka-ke-u*¹, KN V 958, PY 28 = An 607, Jn 725, 183 = Nn 831. Nom. sing.: *khalkeus* 'bronze-smith'. [χαλκεύς *Il.* XII, 295.]

ka-ke-we, KN Fh 386, PY 253 = Jn 310 +, 178 = Ma 365 +, 192 = Na 252 +. Nom. plur. (at KN dat. sing.?): *khalkēwes (-ēwei).*

ka-ke-wi, MY Oe 121. Dat. sing.: *khalkēwi.*

ka-ke-u-si, PY An 129, Na 104. Dat. plur.: *khalkeusi.*

*ka-ke-u*², PY Jn 750. MN: *Khalkeus.* (A smith by trade.)

ka-ki-jo: see s.v. *ka-ke-ja-pi.*

ka-ko, PY 254 = Jn 389 +, 291 = Sa 794 +. Nom. and instr. sing.: *khalkos, -ōi* 'bronze'. [χαλκός Hom. +.]

ka-ko-de-ta, KN 278 = So 894. Nom. plur. neut.,

of wheels: *khalkodeta* 'bronze-bound'. [χαλκό-δετος Aesch. +.]

ka-ma, KN L 520, PY **55**=An 724, Ea 28, Eb 159+, **148**=Ep 613, **171**=Un 718. Nom. and acc. sing. A kind of agricultural holding, see p. 261. [Prob. a neut. noun in *-as* to account for derivative *ka-ma-e-u*, but gen. sing. seems to be needed in **148**=Ep 613; cf. Petruševski, 1970*a*, p. 126.] At KN poss. MN.

ka̰-ma-ḛ, PY Eb 156. Dual?

ka-ma-e-u, PY Eb 156+, **148**=Ep 613. Nom. sing. 'man who has a *ka-ma* holding'. See p. 261.

ka-ma-e-we, PY **40**=An 261+, **149**=Ed 236, **150**=Ed 411, Ep 539. Dat. sing. and nom. plur.: *-ēwei*, *-ēwes*.

ka-ma-jo, KN Am 5882. Nom. plur., description of men?

ka-ma-ti-jo-jo, TH Z 850, [Z 884 β]. MN: gen.: *Kharmantioio*? [Cf. Χάρμας, Χαρμαντίδης.]

ka-ma-to, KN Da 1275. MN.

ka-mi-ni-to, KN Da 1382?, De 1260, Dk 1073. MN.

ka-mo, KN As 604. PN?

ka-mo-ni-jo, KN Da 1293. MN: *Skamōnios*?

ka-na-a-po, KN Vc 7518. MN.

ka-na-ko, MY **105**=Ge 602+, KA+NA+KO Ge 608. Nom. sing. fem.: *knākos* 'safflower', *Carthamus tinctorius*. [κνῆκος Hippocr.+, ὁ or ἡ.] See p. 226.

ka-na-pe-u, PY Cn 1287, **115**=En 74, **120**=Eo 276+. Nom. sing. masc.: *knapheus* 'fuller, cloth-dresser'. [κναφεύς inscr. 6 B.C.+; γναφεύς prob. the later form, Schwyzer, *Gram.* I, 414.]

ka-na-pe-we, MY **226**=Oe 129. Dat. sing.: *knaphēwei*.

ka-na-pe-wo, PY **127**=Eo 269. Gen. sing.: *knaphēwos*.

ka-na-pe-u-si, MY **321**=Oi 701+. Dat. plur.: *knapheusi*.

ka-na-po-to, KN V 961. MN.

ka-na-to, MY **234**=Ue 611, Wt 502+. Nom. (or acc.?) plur.: name of vessel or implement. Perhaps: *gnathoi* 'clamps'. [γνάθος in this sense Aesch. *Pr.* 64.]

ka-na-to-po, KN Ap 639. WN.

ka-ne-ja, PY **317**=Ub 1318. Prob. neut. plur. of adj.: *kaneia* 'made of basketry'. [Cf. κάνεον, κάνειον 'basket' *Il.* IX, 217+.] See p. 491.

ka-ne-u-ta, KN Da 1350. MN.

ka-ni-to, KN Dh 1646, Dv 1449, X 7583? MN. Ktistopoulos: *Kanithos*. [Κάνιθος modern name of spring on Mt Ida; Faure, 1967, p. 58.]

ka-nu-se-u, KN As 602. MN: *Ganuseus*. [Cf. Γανυμή-δης; Heubeck, 1957, p. 269.]

ka-nu-ta-jo, PY An 129. MN.

ka-pa, KN E 71, PY **96**=Un 138. At KN perhaps PN, cf. *ka-pa-jo*; at PY description of olives (cf. *ka-po*), see p. 221.

ka-pa-jo, KN B 5752. Description of three men, perhaps ethnic of *ka-pa*.

ka-pa-ra, PY Un 1321. Introduces wine entry after *to-sa*; Palmer (1963*a*, p. 424) compares σκάφαλος· ἀντλητήρ (Hesych.).

ka-pa-ra₂¹, KN Ak 5009. Description of women cloth-worker(s)?: poss. sing. of ethnic or descriptive term in *-as*.

ka-pa-ra₂-de, PY Aa 788, **26**=An 292. Nom. plur. fem.: *-ades*.

ka-pa-ra₂-do, PY Ad 679. Gen. plur. fem.: *-adōn*.

ka-pa-ra₂², PY Jn 706. MN.

ka-pa-ri-jo, KN U 4478, Vc 72, V 60, V 77. MN: *Karpaliōn*. [Καρπαλίων.]

ka-pa-ri-jo-ne, KN Fh 344. Dat.: *Karpalionei*.

ka-pa-si-ja, PY Vn 851. WN, possibly = *ka-pa-ti-ja*: *Karpasiā*?

ka-pa̰-so, KN Ai 966. Obscure.

ka-pa-ti-ja, PY **141**=Eb 338, **135**=Ep 704+, Un 443. WN: *Karpathiā*? [Cf. Καρπάθιος ethnic of Κάρπαθος, Hom. Κράπαθος *Il.* II, 676; cf. also *ka-pa-si-ja*.]

ka-pe-se-wa-o, PY Cn 453. MN, gen., forming place name with *wo-wo*.

ka-pi-ni-ja, PY **251**=Vn 46. Gen. sing.: *kapniās* 'of the chimney'. [καπνία = καπνοδόκη Moeris.] See p. 504.

ka-po, KN **94**=F 841. Possibly nom. plur.: *karpoi e[laiwās?]* 'fruits of the olive'. The ligature KA+PO (PY An 616, **104**=Un 249, **103**=Un 267, Un 592) may stand for the same word.

ka-pte, KN Df 1230. MN: *Skaptēr* or *Skāptēr*? [σκαπτήρ, cf. σκῆπτρον.]

ka-pu-ro, KN V 961. MN.

ka-ra-a-pi, PY **246**=Ta 722. Instr. plur. neut.: *krāapphi* or *karaapphi* (< *-at-phi*) 'with (lions') heads'. [Hom. gen. sing. καρήατος, κράατος; Risch, 1966*a*.]

ka-ra-do-ro, PY Ac 1273, **60**=An 661, **75**=Cn 608, **257**=Jn 829, **258**=Jo 438, **174**=Ma 346, **186**=Na 543+. PN: *Kharadros* or dual *Kharadrō*? One of the Nine Towns of the Hither Province, prob. Phoinikous. [χάραδρος.]

ka-ra-do-ro-de, PY **250**=Vn 20. Acc. + *-de*.

ka-ra-do-wa-ta, PY Ea 57. MN.

ka-ra-e-ri-jo, KN Fp 6+. Name of month.

ka-ra-e-i-jo, Kn Fp 354. Erroneous or variant spelling.

[*ka*]-*ra-e-ri-jo-jo*, KN Gg 7369, M 1645. Gen.: *-ioio*.

ka-ra-i, PY [**168**=Es 644], **167**=Es 650+. MN (or WN?).

ka-ra-ḳo̰, MY Ge 605. Reading very uncertain in line 6A; in line 1 read [*ka-*]*ṛa-to*. Possibly a herb: *glākhōn* 'pennyroyal', *Mentha pulegium*. [Dor., Boeot. γλάχω(ν), Ion. γλήχων Att. βλήχων.]

ka-ra-ma-to, KN V 684. Furumark: gen. plur.

klasmatōn 'fragments (of ivory)'. Case unexplained; Palmer suspects error for *ka-ra-ma-ta*.

ka-ra-na-ko, KN B 988. Obscure; MN?

ka-ra-na-ta, KN Vc 65, Xd 7906. MN: *Kranātās?* [Cf. PN Κράνη.]

ka-ra-ni-jo, PY Wr 1199. Obscure.

ka-ra-pa-so, PY 254 = Jn 389, MY Oi 705. MN.

ka-ra-pi, PY Ea 808. MN: *Krambis?* [Κράμβις.]

ka-ra-re-we, KN K 778, PY 305 = Fr 1184. Nom. plur., name of an oil-jar, probably 'stirrup-jar'. Householder (1959*a*, p. 379): *khlārēwes*. [Cf. χλαρόν· ἐλαιηρὸς κώθων Hesych.] See p. 494.

ka-ra-se|ti-ri-jo, MY Wt 507. Variant or erroneous spelling of *ka-ra-ti-ri-jo?*

ka-ra-so-mo, PY Fn 79. MN, dat.?

ka-ra-su-no, PY 63 = Cc 660. MN, dat.

ka-ra-te-mi-de, PY Gn 428. MN, dat.?

ka-ra-te-ra, MY 234 = Ue 611. Apparently acc. sing.: *krātēra* 'mixing bowl'. [κρητήρ *Il.* XXII, 741 +.]

ka-ra-ti-ri-jo, MY 234 = Ue 611. Nom. plur.; name of vessel. Cf. *ka-ra-se-ti-ri-jo*.

ka-ra-to, MY 106 = Ge 603, Ge 605? In a list of spices: possibly *kalathos* 'basket'?

ka-ra-u-du-ro, PY Eb 838, 143 = Ep 705. MN.

ka-ra-u-ja, MY Fu 711. MN?: *Klāwjās?*

ka-ra-u-ko, PY Cn 285, Jn 706 +, [MY Z 713?]. MN: *Glaukos*. [Γλαῦκος *Il.* II, 876 +.]

ka-ra-u-ro, PY An 192, Jn 750. MN: *Kalauros?* [Κάλαυρος eponymous hero of Καλαυρία.]

ka-ra-wa-ni-ta, PY Cn 45. MN, dat.

ka-ra-we, KN 25 = Ap 694, Ap 5868. Nom. plur. describing WOMEN: *grāwes* 'old women'. [γρηῦς *Od.* I, 191 +.]

ka-ra-wi-ko, PY 254 = Jn 389. MN: *Klāwiskos*. (Chantraine, 1966, p. 173.)

ka-ra-wi-po-ro, PY 141 = Eb 338, 142 = Ed 317, 135 = Ep 704, 257 = Jn 829, [313 = Un 6], Vn 48. Nom. and dat. sing., nom. plur., prob. always fem.: *klāwiphoros* 'key-bearer', title of a religious office. [Dor. κλακοφόρος, cf. Att. κλειδοῦχος 'priestess'. *κλαϝίς to be reconstructed as origin of κλείς, etc., cf. Lat. *clauis*, prob. a loan.]

ka-ra-wi-po-ro-jo, PY Ae 110. Gen. sing.: *klāwiphoroio*.

ka-ra-wi-so, PY Ja 1288. MN?

*ka-ra-*56-so*, PY [116 = En 659], 127 = Eo 269 edge. MN. Cf. *ka-ra-pa-so*.

ka-ri-pi-jo, KN X 7918. MN?

ka-ri-se-u, KN 38 = As 1516 +, PY Jn 431, MY 46 = Au 102. MN: *Khariseus*. [Cf. next.]

ka-ri-si-jo, PY Jn 706. MN: *Kharisios*. [Χαρίσιος.]

ka-ro[1], KN Fh 340. PN? (Godart, 1968*a*, p. 599.)

ka-ro[2], PY 317 = Ub 1318. Perhaps: *kairos* 'fringe'? [καῖρος, cf. καιροσέων *Od.* VII, 107.] See p. 493.

ka-ro-ke-e, PY 52 = An 207. PN, loc. [Cf. *ke-e*.]

ka-ro-qo, KN Sc 257 +, PY Vn 865, MY Au 657. MN: *Kharoqʷos* or *Kharoqʷs*. [Χάροπος *Il.* II, 672, Χάροψ *Il.* XI, 426.]

ka-ro-qo[, KN X 1047. Name of object?

ka-ru-ke, PY Fn 187, Un 219. Dat. sing.: *kārukei* 'herald'. [κῆρυξ *Il.* II, 50 +.]

ka-ru-no, KN Dl 412, Dl 7147. PN.

ka-ru-pi: see s.v. *ka-ru-we*.

ka-ru-ti-je-ja-o(-*qe*), PY 12 = Ad 671. Gen. plur. fem. of occupational term, not ethnic in view of formation in -*eia* answering to masc. in -*eus* (Chadwick, 1964*a*, p. 323).

ka-ru-we, PY 245 = Ta 721. Instr. sing. fem.: a decorative feature in ivory, perhaps *karuei* 'nut, boss'. [Cf. κάρυον *Batrach.* +; σίκυς/σίκυος.]

ka-ru-pi, PY 246 = Ta 722. Instr. plur.: perhaps *karuphi*.

ka-sa-no, PY V 831. MN.

ka-sa-ro, KN C 912, Dv 1450. MN.

ka-sa-to, KN Vc 7537, PY 50 = An 39, Jn 320, MY Go 610, Oe 113. MN, nom. and dat.: *Xanthos*, -*oi*. [Ξάνθος *Il.* V, 152.]

ka-si-ko-no, KN [Ra 1541], [Ra 1546], Ra 1556 +, PY An 128. Term occurring in SWORD context; poss. occupational term (cf. *pi-ri-je-te*); nom. plur. at PY. Lejeune (1960*b*) *kasi*- 'with'.

ka-so[1], KN V 684. Name of material?

ka-so[2], PY Cn 599. MN, dat. [Cf. Κάσος PN, *Il.* II, 676.]

ka-ta-mi-jo, KN C 911. Nom. sing. masc., personal adj.?: '(the slave) of *ka-ta-mo*'.

ka-ta-ni-ja, KN L 771. Prob. nom. fem. plur., ethnic adj. of *ka-ta-no*[1]: *Kantaniai?*

ka-ta-no[1], KN X 795. Possibly PN: *Kantanos?* [Κάντανος S.-W. Crete.]

ka-ta-no[2], PY Eb 890, 143 = Ep 705. MN: *Katānōr?* [Cf. *me-ta-no*.]

ka-ta-ra, KN Np 85. PN, nom. plur.: *Katrai?* [Cf. Κατρεύς Paus. VIII, 53, 4; Ilievski, 1959, p. 126.]

ka-ta-ra-i, KN Co 906. Loc. plur.: -*āhi*.

ka-ta-ra-pi, KN V 145, [X 7773]. Instr. plur.: -*āphi*.

ka-ta-ro, KN X 8101, MY Z 202. Obscure; MN? [Cf. καθαρός.]

ka-ta-wa, PY Cn 40, Jn 605. MN, nom. and dat. Cf. next.

ka-ta-wo, KN Dk 5201, Dv 1113. MN. [*Katarwos* (κάταρϝος Schwyzer, *Dial.* 654) satisfies spelling, but seems an improbable name.]

ka-ta₂-ro, KN As 604. MN.

ka-te-u, KN 71 = Dk 1072, Dv 1451 (subsequently deleted). MN: *Kasteus?* [Heubeck, 1957, p. 274.]

ka-ti, PY 238 = Tn 996. Nom. sing., name of jug or hydria: prob. *kāthis*. [Cf. κηθίς 'vessel for shaking dice', κηθάριον 'voting urn', Arc. κάθιδοι (for -δες?)· ὑδρίαι Hesych.]

ka-to, KN Dv 1169, Dv 5287. MN: *Kastōr?*

ka-to-ro, KN Do 1054+, Dq 438, Dq 686. Gen.?: *Kastoros.*

ka-tu-re-wi-ja-i, PY 317=Ub 1318. Dat. plur.: *kanthulēwiāhi* 'saddle-bags'? See p. 491, and cf. *ka-tu-ro₂*.

ka-tu-re-wi̥[, KN X 1047. Prob. nom. plur.

ka-tu-ro₂, PY 317=Ub 1318. Gen. plur.: *kanthuliōn* 'of pack-saddles'? [Cf. κανθύλη 'swelling', κανθήλια 'panniers for pack-animals', etc.] See p. 491.

ka-u-da, KN Fs 21. PN?

ka-u-no, TH Z 839. MN: *Khaunos?* [Heubeck, 1969*c*, p. 146.]

ka-u-ti-wḁ, PY An 340. MN.

ka-wa-do-ro, PY Ep 212. MN: *Kalwandros?* (Heubeck, 1957, p. 32.)

ka-wa-ra, PY 314=Qa 1289. WN.

ka-wa-ro, KN De 1287 (possibly incomplete at left). MN.

ka-wa-ti-ro, PY An 340, Mb 1401. MN, nom. and dat.

ka-wi-jo, PY An 192. Nom. sing., description of man or ethnic?

ka-wi-ta, PY Cn 600. MN.

kḁ-wo, KN Sc 7471. Context obscure; could be *kalwo(s)*=καλός.

ka-za, KN Sp 4452. Description of object called *wo-ra* with horn-shaped ideogram; perhaps *khaltsā < *khalkyā* 'of bronze'.

ka-zo-e, PY Va 1323. Nom. plur., description of *axones: katsohes < *kakyos-es*. [Original compar. of κακός; cf. βράσσων/βραχύς.]

*ka-*56-na-to*, KN As 1516. MN.

*ka-*56-no*, KN Df 1219. MN.

*ka-*56-so-ta*, KN Ap 769. WN.

KE, As adjunct: KN As 608, As 625 (obscure). As adjunct to vessel: KN K 773 (perh. abbreviation of *ke-ni-qa* or *ke-ni-qe-te-we*); to circular ideogram: KN U 436 (cf. KE + RO₂); inside rectangular frame (= *189): PY 314=Qa 1289, 315=Qa 1296+.
Associated with SA (='flax'): PY Na 856, Na 1041 (poss. abbreviation of word describing land-holding, cf. *ke-ke-me-na*).
Ideographic use: KN Nc 5100, PY 177=Ma 90, 176=Ma 123+ (weighed commodity); (with numeral, not weighed): KN Gg 711.

]*ke-a*: see [*e*]-*ke-a²*.

ke-do-jo, PY Ua 158. Gen. sing.?

ke-do-si-ja, KN B 799, B 804. Heading to lists of men.

ke-e, PY Aa 93, Ad 295. PN, loc.

ke-i-ja, PY Qa 1303. Nom. sing. fem. of ethnic, or personal name?

ke-i-jo, PY Na 577. Ethnic used as PN.

ke-e-pe, MY 107=Ge 604. MN, dat. Possibly an error for *ke-pe-e*, dat. of *ke-po*.

ke-i-ja-ka-ra-na, PY 184=Nn 228. PN. Probably adj. (cf. *ke-e*)+*krānā* 'spring'. [κρήνη.]

ze-i-ja-ka-ra-na, PY Xa 70. Variant spelling of same name?

ke-ka-to, KN 39=As 1517, PY Pn 30. MN.

ke-ka-u-me-no: see *a-pu ke-ka-u-me-no*.

ke-ke-me-na, KN 157=Uf 835, 162=Uf 983, Xe 664+, PY Ea 757+, 144=Eb 866+, 131=Ep 301+. Nom. and gen. sing., nom. plur., perf. pple. pass.: *kekesmenā, -nās, -nai.* The meaning is approximately 'belonging to the *dāmos*, communal'. The form *kekesmenā* (cf. κεάζω, κείων) 'divided' is recommended as most likely interpretation by Heubeck (1967).

ke-ke-me-na-o, PY 146=Eb 473+, 149=Ed 236, 135=Ep 704. Gen. plur. fem.: *kekesmenāōn*.

ke-ke-me-no, PY 45=An 830, 141=Eb 338, 135=Ep 704. Acc. dual fem.: *kekesmenō*. In An 830 interpretation of form doubtful.

ke-ke-me-no-jo, PY 190=Na 395. Gen. sing. masc. or neut.: *-menoio*.

ke-ke-tu-wo-e, PY 40=An 261. Heading to list of men, nom. plur. masc. of perf. pple.?

ke-ki¹, PY An 192. Nom. sing. description of man: *-is*? See p. 430.

ke-ki-de, PY 56=An 657+, 187=Na 514+. Nom. plur.: *-ides.*

]*ke̥-ki-do*, PY Na 848. Gen. plur.: *-idōn?*

ke-ki², PY Jn 692, Jn 725. MN.

ke-ki-jo, PY 56=An 657, 44=Aq 218. MN or patronymic adj.? Cf. *ke-ki²*.

ke-ko-jo, PY 91=Fn 50, MY Ui 651. MN, gen.

ke-ku-ro̥, KN Xd 7656?, PY Mn 162. MN, dat.: *Kerkulōi?* [Cf. Κερκύλας.]

ke-ma-qe-me, KN 161=Uf 839. Context obscure.

ke-ma-ta, KN V 684. Context obscure, but *kermata* 'slices' seems possible. [κέρμα.]

ke-me-ri-jo, PY Fn 324. Qualification of man's name, perhaps ethnic or patronymic adj.

ke-me-u, KN Dv 1427. MN: *Kelmeus?* [Cf. Κέλμις, Κέλμος.]

ke-ni-qa, KN Ws 8497. On sealing with *a-sa-mi-to*, nom. sing.?: *kherniqᵘs* (or acc. *khernigᵘa?*) 'vessel for washing the hands'? [χέρνιψ *Od.* I, 136+ 'water for washing the hands'; cf. χέρνιβον *Il.* XXIV, 304 'vessel for this purpose'.]

ke-ni-qe-te-we, [KN X 768], MY Wt 503. Nom. plur.: *kherniqᵘtēwes* 'wash-hand-basins'. [Cf. χέρνιψ, χερνίπτομαι; see prec.]

ke-nu-wa-so, KN 161=Uf 839. Context obscure.

ke-o-te-ja, TH Of 28. Fem. dat.: epithet of goddess Hera?

ke-po, MY 105=Ge 602, 106=Ge 603+. MN.

ke-po-da: see *ke-u-po-da*.

ke-pu, KN Ap 639. WN.

ke-pu₂-je-u, KN Vc 7575. MN.

ke-ra¹, KN 163=Ra 984. Perhaps acc. sing.: *keras* 'horn' (context obscure, see p. 456). [κέρας.]

]*ke-ra-a*, KN 231=K 872. Nom. plur.?: *kera(h)a.*

ke-ra-e, PY Sa 840. Dual: *kera(h)e?*

ke-ra², PY 137 = Eb 416, 135 = Ep 704. Acc. sing., prob.: *geras* 'gift of honour'. [γέρας ὅ τι δῆμος ἔδωκεν *Od.* VII, 150 + .]

ke-ra-ja, KN V 831. MN.

ke-ra-ja-pi, KN 266 = Sd 4401 + , 274 = Sf 4428. Instr. plur. fem.: *keraiāphi* 'made of horn' (description of some fitment on chariots). [κεραός *Il.* III, 24 + 'horned', if this is not from *κεραϝός, cf. Lat. *ceruos* 'stag'; cf. κεραία 'horn' Aesch. + .]

ke-ra-i-ja-pi, KN Sd 4450. Variant spelling of prec.

ke-ra-me-ja, KN Ap 639. WN: *Kerameia*. [Fem. to κεραμεύς.]

ke-ra-me-u, PY Cn 1287. Nom. sing.: *kerameus* 'potter'. [κεραμεύς *Il.* XVIII, 601 + .]

ke-ra-me-we, PY 52 = An 207. Nom. dual: *keramēwe*.

ke-ra-me-wo, PY 117 = En 467, 130 = Eo 371. Gen. sing.: *keramēwos*.

ke-ra-me-wi[, MY Oe 125. Dat. sing.: *keramēwi*.

ke-ra-no(-qe), KN 85 = Ch 896. Name of one of a yoke of oxen: *Kelainos*. [κελαινός 'dark'.]

ke-ra-so, MY 303 = V 659. WN: *Kerasō?* [κέρασος.]

ke-ra-ti-jo-jo, PY An 424. MN, gen. forming place name with *wo-wo*.

ke-ra-u-jo, PY Eb 501, 131 = Ep 301. MN.

ke-re, KN As 1516, B 805. MN: *Krēs?* [Κρής.]

ke-re-a₂, PY 236 = Ta 641. Acc. plur. neut.: *skeleha* 'legs (of a tripod cauldron)'. [σκέλος (only of a man) *Il.* XVI, 314 + .]

ke-re-na, KN M 719. Obscure.

ke-re-no, PY Cn 599, MY 46 = Au 102. MN. Prob. nom. and dat.; at MY the entry VIR 2 is prob. an error for 1 or the second name has been omitted. Possibly *Gerēnos*. [Cf. Γερήνιος.]

ke-re-si-jo we-ke, PY 236 = Ta 641, 237 = Ta 709. Description of tripod cauldrons. Palmer *krēsiowergēs* 'of Cretan style or workmanship', see p. 336. [Cf. Λυκιοεργής Herodotus + , Κορινθιουργής, etc.]

ke-re-ta-o, PY Cn 1287. Gen. sing. of masc. man's or god's name, or gen. plur. of fem. noun? Owner(s) of a *do-e-ro*.

ke-re-te, PY An 128. Nom. plur.: *Krētes?*

ke-re-te-u, PY 147 = Ea 59, Ea 304 + , 110 = Ea 800, Xa 565? MN: *Krētheus*. [Κρηθεύς *Od.* XI, 237.]

ke-re-ti-wo, PY Na 547. PN.

ke-re-u, KN Ag 91, PY 147 = Ea 59 (error for *ke-re-te-u?*), Ea 827. MN.

ke-re-wa, KN Od 666?, Xd 282. MN: *Klewās?* [Κλέας.]

ke-re-za, PY Aa 762, Aa 807, Ab 217, Ab 586, Ad 318, Ad 686. Name of place or area at Pylos.

ke-ri-mi-ja, KN 212 = Lc 535, PY 28 = An 607. Both contexts obscure; perhaps an adj. describing women.

ke-ro, PY Jn 413. MN.

KE + RO₂, KN [U 436?], U 746. Written over circular ideogram no. 172; possibly *kērion* 'honeycomb', but etymology of κηρός uncertain.

ke-ro-ke-re-we-o, PY 285 = Sa 487. MN, gen.: *Khēroklewehos*.

ke-ro-si-ja, PY 40 = An 261, An 616. A group of men under a *qa-si-re-u*, prob. *geronsiā* 'council of elders'. See pp. 172, 421. [γερουσία.]

ke-ro-te, KN B 800 (erased), PY Jn 881. Prob. nom. plur.: *gerontes* 'old men'. [γέρων.]

ke-ro-ta, KN Ld 785, Ld 786, Ld 788. Neut. plur. adj. describing cloth: prob. *geronta* 'old'. [Cf. *pa-ra-ja* = *palaia* in same context Ln 1568; γέρον σάκος *Od.* XXII, 184, etc.]

ke-ro-u-te-u, PY Cn 600, [Fn 324]. MN: *Keloutheus?* [Cf. κέλευθος, ἀκόλουθος.]

ke-ro-u-te[-*we*], PY Fn 324. Dat.

ke-ro-we, PY Cn 4. MN.

ke-ro-wo, PY 31 = Ae 134, 61 = Cn 131. MN, nom. and dat.: *Kerowos?*

ke-ro-wo-jo, PY 62 = Cn 655. Gen.

ke-sa-da-ra, PY Ea 828, Fg 368, Mn 1368 + . WN: *Kessandra?* [Κεσσάνδρα (vase inscr. for Κασσάνδρα): Heubeck, 1957, pp. 32, 273.]

ke-sa-do-ro, KN As 1520, B 798. PY Vn 130. MN: *Kessandros?* [Cf. *ke-sa-da-ra*.]

[*ke*]-*sa-do-ro-jo*, KN B 809. Gen.: *Kessandroio*.

ke-sa-me-no, PY 61 = Cn 131, Fn 324. MN: *Kessamenos*. [Pple. of *ἐ-κεδ-σάμην, cf. κεδνός; Heubeck, 1957, p. 273.]

ke-se-ni-wi-jo, PY Fr 1231. Adj. describing oil: *xenwion* 'for guests'. [ξείνια (*ξένϝια) *Il.* XI, 779 + .]

[*ke-se-*]*nu-wi-jo*, PY Fr 1255. Alternative spelling of prec.

ke-se-nu-wi-ja, KN 215 = Ld 573 + . Neut. plur. describing textiles: *xenwia*.

ke-se-ne-wi-ja, KN Ld 649. Alternative spelling of prec.

ke-se-nu-wo, PY Cn 286. MN?: *Xenwōn*. [Corc. Ξένϝων.]

ke-ta, PY Jn 706. MN.

ke-ti-de(-qe), MY 303 = V 659. WN.

ke-ti-ro, KN Da 1323, U 172 + , PY Jn 415. MN.

ke-to, KN Da 1134 + , PY Cn 436. MN.

ke-to-ro, KN C 954. MN.

ke-u-po-da, PY 190 = Na 395, Na 527. Prob. a title; Palmer: *kheuspondās* 'libation-pourer'?

ke-po-da, PY 189 = Na 568. Prob. defective spelling.

ke-u-po-da-o, KN C 1044, Dq 442. Gen.

ke-u-po-de-ja, KN 90 = G 820. Obscure: see p. 215.

ke-u-sa, KN Dl 946. MN.

ke-we-no, PY Cn 600, Jn 431. MN, nom. and dat.

ke-we-to, PY 253 = Jn 310. MN.

ke-we-to-jo, PY 253 = Jn 310. Gen.

ke-wo-no-jo, PY 57 = An 519. MN (commander of an *o-ka*), gen.

]ḳẹ-wo-re-u-si, KN Ws 1707. Obscure; dat. plur.?

ke-zo, PY Cn 328. MN?

ke-*83-*18, KN Dd 1425. MN.

KI, As adjunct to SHEEP and GOATS: KN C 7088, Dh 1243+, Dk 1066+, Dl 412+, Do 919+: meaning 'young', 'new-born' (Killen, 1964a, p. 78), perhaps abbreviation of word used in fem. ki-ra.

As adjunct to TUNIC: KN 219=L 594, 221=L 647, 220=L 870+: =ki-to 'tunic'.

Ideographic use: KN L 1649, U 5653(?): prob.=prec.

ki-da-pa, KN 278=So 894. Prob. name of timber, cf. σκινδαψός?

ki-da-ro, KN E 842. Obscure, perhaps MN. [Cf. Κιδαρία epithet of Demeter.]

ki-do-ro, KN X 7557. MN?

ki-du-ro, PY An 192. MN.

ki-e-u, PY 55=An 724. MN.

ki-e-wo, PY 43=Aq 64. Gen.

ki-je-u, KN Xd 94. Variant spelling of nom.

ki-jo-ne-u-si, PY Gn 428. Dat. plur. of occupational term?

ki-ka-ne wi-jo-de, PY Vn 48. Prob. PN+-de; formerly read as one word.

ki-ke-ro, KN As 1519. MN.

ki-ma-ra, PY Aa 63. Nom. plur. fem., description of women, possibly ethnic.

ki-ma-ra-o, PY Ad 668. Gen. plur.

ki-ma-ta, KN As 1520. MN.

]ki-ma-to, KN V 7620. MN (prob. complete).

ki-mu-ko, KN Dv 1085. MN.

ki-mu-ku, KN Db 1327. MN. [Cf. prec.]

ki-ni-di-ja, PY 5=Aa 792, Ab 189, 26=An 292. Nom. plur. fem., description of women: Knidiai. [Κνίδος.]

ki-ni-di-ja-o, PY Ad 683. Gen. plur.: Knidiāōn.

ki-nu-qa, KN Ap 618. WN.

ki-nu-ra, PY Qa 1301, Vn 865. MN: Kinurās. [Κινύρης Il. XI, 20.]

ki-ra(-qe), MY 303=V 659 (twice). Either WN or more likely term of relationship (cf. tu-ka-te-qe in same tablet): possibly gīlā 'female infant'. [Cf. νεογιλός 'new-born' Od. XII, 86+, Chadwick, 1963b, p. 65; see also KI.]

ki-ra-di-ja, KN V 1005. Nom. plur. fem. of ethnic adj.? [Cf. Σκιράς epithet of Athena, Σκιράδιον ἄκρον.]

ki-ra-*56-so, KN Fh 360. MN?

ki-ra₂-i-jo: see s.v. ki-ri-ja-i-jo.

ki-ṛẹ-i-ṣo, KN Da 1098 edge (erased). MN.

ki-ri-ja-i-jo, PY 57=An 519. MN: Kiljaios, Kirjaios? [Κίλλαιος, Κιρραῖος.]

ki-ra₂-i-jo, KN Sc 103. Variant spelling.

ki-ri-ja-si, KN B 801. MN.

ki-ri-jo-te, KN Da 1163+, Db 5272+. Frequent annotation on SHEEP tablets; prob. adj. describing RAMS.

ki-ri-ko, KN X 1041. MN?: Krikos? [Cf. κρίκος.]

ki-ri-ne-to, KN Dv 1248. MN.

ki-ri-se-we, PY An 298. Nom. dual or plur., a man's trade: khrisēwes 'anointers?, painters?, plasterers?' [Cf. χρίω; χρῖσμα 'oil, plaster'; χρίστης 'white-washer' Hesych.]

ki-ri-ta¹, KN 90=G 820. Acc. sing. or plur.: krithān, krithans 'barley'. [κριθή, κριθαί Il. XI, 69+.]

ki-ri-ta², KN Ld 785. Prob. neut. plur. adj. describing CLOTH: khrista 'anointed, painted (with red spots?)'. [χριστός.]

ki-ri-ta-de, KN Ws 8493, X 8768. Possibly PN+-de, perhaps fem. acc. plur., cf. next.

ki-ri-ta-i, KN Od 5003. Dat.-loc. plur.? Or from ki-ri-ta²?

ki-ri-te-wi-ja, KN Fp 363, PY 28=An 607, 139=Eb 321, 135=Ep 704. Nom. plur., a class of women possibly with a religious function. See p. 167.

ki-ri-te-wi-ja-i, KN 89=E 777. Dat. plur.

ki-ri-te-wi-ja-pi, PY Un 1428. Instr. plur.

ki-ri-ti-jo-jo, PY 167=Es 650. Gen. sing.; possibly the name of a month: Krithioio?

ki-ri-*82-jo, PY Jn 320. MN: Kriswaios? [Κρισαῖος adj. of Κρῖσα; Chadwick, 1968a, p. 65.]

ki-si-wi-ja, PY Aa 770, [Ab 194]. Nom. plur. fem. of ethnic adj. The suggestion that this is ancestral to Χῖος (p. 156) depends upon the assumption that *ksw developed to *kh(w), as *ksm to khm in αἰχμή, cf. a₃-ka-sa-ma; but if Χῖος (adj.) is really from *Χίιος, we should expect an extra syllable.

ki-si-wi-ja-o, PY Ad 675. Gen. plur.: -āōn.

ki-si-wi-je-ja, KN Xd 98. Context obscure; WN?

ki-si-wi-jọ, KN V 60. MN. [Cf. ki-si-wi-ja.]

ki-ta-ne-to, KN 29=Am 821, Da 1108. MN.

ki-ta-no, KN Ga 1530+, X 1385. Probably name of a condiment.

ki-ti-je-si, PY 193=Na 520, [Na 1179]. 3rd plur. pres.: ktiensi 'they settle, bring into cultivation'? [Athematic conjug. of verb later represented by κτίζω, cf. Skt. kṣéti 'resides'; see Palmer, 1954b, p. 26.]

ki-ti-me-na, [KN X 7753?], PY 111=Ea 71+, 117=En 467+, 118=Eo 211+. Nom. and gen. sing., nom. plur. fem.: ktimenā, -ās, -ai, serving to denote land not administered by the dāmos, see pp. 233, 444. [Cf. ἐυκτίμενος Il. II, 501+.]

[ki-]ti-me-no, PY 153=Er 880. Prob. acc. neut. sing.

ki-ti-me, PY 117=En 467. Defective spelling of ki-ti-me-na.

ki-ti-ta, PY 54=An 610, 55=An 724. Acc. sing., nom. plur.: ktitān, -tai 'settlers, inhabitants'. [κτίτης Eur., cf. περικτίται Od. XI, 288, and me-ta-ki-ti-ta.]

ki-to, KN Lc 536, 222=L 693. Nom. sing.: khitōn 'tunic', or possibly 'fine linen'. [χιτών 'tunic' Od. XV, 60+, Ion. κιθών.] See p. 320.

ki-to-ne, KN L 771. Prob. nom. plur.: khitōnes.

ki-to-na, KN Ld 785. Acc. sing. or plur.?

ki-to-pi, KN Ld 787. Instr. plur.: *khitōmphi*.

]*ki-to-ni-ja*: see s.v. *e-pi-ki-to-ni-ja*.

ki-u-ro, KN B 801, Dl 47? MN.

ki-u-ro-i, PY 324 = An 1282. Dat. plur.; probably some part of or equipment for a chariot. Palmer (1963a, p. 328): *kiuroihi* 'baskets'. [Cf. κίουρος Hesych., Hebr. *kiyyōr* 'pot, basin'.]

ki-wo(-qe), PY 251 = Vn 46. Nom. sing.: *kiwōn* (*qᵘe*) 'and a column'. [κίων *Od.* XIX, 38 +.]

ki-wo-na-de, PY Vn 48. Acc. sing. + -*de*; *Kiwōna-de*, used as place name.

ki-zo, KN Ap 5748. WN?

*ki-*18-i-so*, KN Da 1363 + 1428. MN.

κο, KN Ap 629; abbreviation of *ko-wo* or *ko-wa*? As adjunct to CLOTH: KN L 8105.

  In lists of spices: KN Ga 34, 203 = Ga 953 +, PY Un 219, Un 592 (with CONDIMENT), MY 106 = Ge 603 +; abbreviation of *ko-ri-a₂-da-na*, etc. 'coriander'.

  Ligatured with SKIN: PY 171 = Un 718; abbreviation of *ko-wo* 'sheep-skin'.

  On armour tablets: PY 295 = Sh 734, 293 = Sh 737 +: abbreviation of *ko-ru-to* (see *ko-ru*) '(plates) of the helmet'.

ko-a, KN X 737. MN?

ko-a-ta, KN B 798. MN, dat.?

ko-a₂-ta, PY Jn 706. MN, prob. variant spelling.

ko-do, KN 161 = Uf 839, PY 113 = Ea 824, 112 = Ea 825 +, Vn 130. MN, nom. and dat.

ko-do-jo, PY 111 = Ea 71, Ea 754. Gen.

ko-do-ro, PY Jn 706. MN: *Kodros*. [Κόδρος.]

ko-i-no: see s.v. *ko-no*.

ko-i-ro, PY Eb 862, 148 = Ep 613. MN.

ko-ka-re-u, TH Of 30. MN? [Cf. next.]

ko-ka-ro, PY Fg 374, 305 = Fr 1184. MN, nom. and dat.?: *Kōkalos*. [Κώκαλος.]

ko-ki-da, KN 265 = Sd 4403, 282 = So 4430. Entry preceding *o-pa*, poss. MN in gen. (cf. *a-re-ki-si-to-jo*.)

ko-ki-de-jo, KN Fh 5465. Context obscure; cf. prec.

ko-ki-jo, PY 56 = An 657. MN: *Kokkiōn*? [Κοκκίων.]

ko-ki-re-ja, PY 235 = Ta 711, 240 = Ta 713, 241 = Ta 715. Nom. sing. fem.: adj. describing ewers and tables: *konkhileiā* 'decorated with sea-shells'? [Cf. κόχλος Eur. +, κογχύλιον Epich. +, etc.] See p. 335·

ko-ku, KN Dh 1240. MN: *Kokkux*?

ko-ku-ro, KN B 803. MN: *Gongulos* (Landau). [Γογγύλος.]

ko-ma-do-ro, PY [255 = Jn 658], Jn 725. MN.

ko-ma-ta, MY 93 = Fo 101, [303 = V 659?]. WN: *Komātā*. [Cf. MN Κομάτας.]

ko-ma-we, PY 57 = An 519, Jn 750. MN: *Komāwens*. [κομήεις.]

ko-ma-we-to, KN Dk 920 +, Dv 1272 +. Gen.: *Komāwentos*.

ko-ma-we-te, KN 80 = C 913, Dk 1049?, PY Cn 925. Dat.: *Komāwentei*.

ko-ma-we-ta, KN B 798. MN, dat.?: *Komāwentāi*?

ko-ma-we-te-ja, PY 172 = Tn 316, TH Of 35. Name of a female deity? See p. 463.

ko-na, PY Ep 212, MY Ue 652. At PY possibly erroneous repetition of preceding *ko-to-na*, or adj. *koinās*? At MY context obscure.

ko-ne-wa-ta, PY Jn 431. MN.

ko-ni-da-jo, KN 38 = As 1516. MN.

ko-ni-ja, PY An 615. PN? [Cf. *ko-no²*.]

ko-ni-jo, PY 54 = An 610. The omission of the MAN ideogram may be accidental, due to lack of space; perhaps nom. plur. masc., cf. *ko-ni-ja*.

ko-ni-ti-ja-ja, PY Vn 879. Nom. plur. adj. or noun describing artifacts.

ko-no¹, PY 203 = Ga 953[+]955, MY 105 = Ge 602 +. Probably a condiment: *skhoinos*, perhaps 'sweet rush' or 'ginger-grass', *Cymbopogon schoenanthus*. See p. 226. [Not Cretan χόννοι 'cups' (as proposed by Maddoli, 1968).]

ko-i-no, MY Ge 606. Variant spelling.

ko-no², PY 154 = Eq 213. With *o-ro-jo* forming a place name; gen. plur.? [Cf. *ko-ni-ja*.]

ko-no-ni-pi, KN 229 = K 434, PY 244 = Ta 714. Instr. plur. fem., part of the decoration of a jug and a chair: possibly *kononiphi* 'cross-bars, rods'. [Cf. κανονίς (κανών); *ko*- for κα is suspect, but perhaps justified in a loan word (Babylonian *kanū*), though cf. *ka-ne-ja*.]

ko-no-so, KN Ak 626, 213 = Le 641 +. PN: *Knōsos*. [Κνωσός *Il.* II, 646 +; cf. Egypt. *ku-nu-šɜ* Faure (1968).]

ko-no-so-de, KN C 5753. Acc. + -*de*: *Knōson-de*.

ko-no-si-jo/-ja, KN 38 = As 1516, B 1055, 89 = E 777, V 56 +. Ethnic adj.: *Knōsioi*, -*ai*, etc.

ko-no-[.]-du-ro(-qe), MY 46 = Au 102 (formerly read *ko-no-pu₂-du-ro*). MN.

ko-o-ke-ne, MY 321 = Oi 701 (*do-ke-ko-o-ke-ne*). MN, nom.: *Koögenēs*? [Cf. Κοιογένης.]

ko-o-ke-ne-i, MY Oi 703, Oi 704. Dat. -*genehi*.

ko-pa-wi-jo, PY Fn 324. MN, dat.?

ko-pe-re-u, KN 29 = Am 821, PY 169 = Es 646, 167 = Es 650. MN: *Kopreus*. [Κοπρεύς *Il.* XV, 639.]

ko-pe-re-wo, PY 168 = Es 644. Gen.: *Koprēwos*.

ko-pe-re-we, KN Fh 5486. Dat.

ko-pi, KN Ap 639. WN.

ko-pi-na, PY 148 = Ep 613. WN.

ko-pu-ra, KN L 5998, [X 8267?]. Obscure; personal name?

ko-ra, MY Ui 651. Perhaps WN, gen.

ko-re-te, KN 83 = C 902, V 865, PY 43 = Aq 64, 257 = Jn 829, 258 = Jo 438, 183 = Nn 831, 304 = On 300. Nom. sing. masc., title of official in tributary villages, 'mayor'? Form to be restored unclear, but an agent noun in -*tēr*. See p. 511. [Cf. *po-ro-ko-re-te*, *da-mo-ko-ro*.]

ko-re-te-re, PY 257 = Jn 829, Xn 1357. Nom. plur., dat. sing.: -*tēres*, -*tērei*.

ko-re-te-ri, PY 304 = On 300. Dat. sing.: -*tēri*.

ko-re-te-ri-jo, PY 45 = An 830. Adj. describing land belonging to a *ko-re-te*: -*tērios*, -*on*.

ko-re-wo, KN Ln 1568. MN?

ko-ri-a₂-da-na, PY 103 = Un 267, MY Ge 605. Nom. plur. neut.: *korihadna* (-*andna*?) 'coriander (seed)' *Coriandrum sativum*. [κορίαννα Anacr. 6 B.C. +, also κορίανδρον, κορίαμβλον, κολίανδρον, κόριον; classical forms influenced by popular etymology; for Myc. pattern cf. 'Αριάδνη.]

ko-ri-ja-da-na, MY Ge 605. Variant spelling.

ko-ri-jo-da-na, PY An 616. If correct, variant spelling.

ko-ri-ja-do-no, KN 98 = Ga 415, 99 = Ga 418 +. Nom. sing.: *kori*(*h*)*adnon*.

ko-ri-jo, KN Dv 1267. MN: *Skolios*? [σκολιός.]

ko-ri-si-ja, PY Eb 347, 115 = En 74, [122 = Eo 160], 121 = Eo 247, Ep 212. WN: *Korinsiā*. [Fem. ethnic, see *ko-ri-to*.]

ko-ri-to, PY Ad 921. PN in Further Province: *Korinthos*. [Not to be identified with Κόρινθος on the Isthmus.]

ko-ri-si-jo, PY 52 = An 207, An 209. Nom. plur. masc., ethnic adj.: *Korinsioi*. [Normal development of **Korinthios*; Κορίνθιος in Att.-Ion. is analogical or borrowed from West Greek.]

ko-ro[1], PY Eq 146. Context fragmentary; gen. plur.: *khōrōn* 'of the lands'? [χῶρος *Il.* III, 315 +.]

ko-ro[2], KN De 1152, PY 61 = Cn 131. MN, nom. and dat.: *Khoiros*, *Khōlos*? [Χοῖρος, Χῶλος.]

ko-ro-du-wo, PY Na 1041. PN. [Bennett suggests reading *ko-ro-jo-wo*, cf. *ko-ro-jo-wo-wi-ja*.]

ko-ro-ja-ne, KN Fh 382. dat.

ko-ro-ja-ta, PY Ae 72. MN.

ko-ro-jo-wo-wi-ja, PY Mn 456. PN: gen. sing. *Khōroio*? + *worwia*. [ὅριον, cf. *wo-wo*.]

ko-ro-ki-ja, PY Aa 354, Ab 372, 26 = An 292. Nom. plur. fem. of ethnic adj.

ko-ro-ki-ja-o, PY Ad 680. Gen. plur.

ko-ro-ku-ra-i-jo, PY 59 = An 656, 60 = An 661, Na 396, 186 = Na 543 +. Nom. plur. masc. of ethnic adj. Attempts to relate this to Κόρκυρα = Κέρκυρα or Κροκύλεια are probably vain. See p. 430.

ko-ro-no-we-sa, PY 235 = Ta 711. Nom. sing. fem., describing a ewer: perhaps *korōnowessa* 'with a curved handle'. [κορωνός, cf. κορώνη *Od.* I, 441.] Palmer: *klonowessa* 'decorated with a throng of warriors'. See p. 498.

ko-ro-sa-no, KN Vc 53. MN.

]*ko-ro-te-wi-jo*, PY Na 512. PN.

ko-ro-to, MY Oe 106. Nom. sing., applied to wool; possibly *khrōstos* 'dyed'. [χρώζω might however yield **khrōwistos*.]

ko-ro-ta₂, KN 218 = Ld 598 +. Prob. neut. plur., applied to cloth, but *ta₂* prob. implies an ending -*t*(*h*)*ia*. This may therefore be a different word. [Perhaps cf. κροσσοί 'tassels, fringe'.]

ko-ro-tu-no, PY Jn 478. MN.

ko-ro-we-ja[, KN X 1013. No context; cf. *ko-ru-we-ja*?

ko-ro-ze-ka, PY An 192. MN.

ko-ru, KN [300 = Sk 5670], 325 = Sk 8100, [Sk 8149]. Nom. sing. *korus* 'helmet'. [κόρυς *Od.* XXIV, 523 +.]

ko-ru-to, PY 292 = Sh 740 +. Gen. sing.: *koruthos*. (Abbreviated κο PY 295 = Sh 734 +.)

ko-ru-pi(-*qe*), PY 239 = Ta 642. Instr. plur.: *korupphi* (*qᵘe*) < **koruth-phi*.

ko-ru-da-ro-jo, PY 33 = Ae 26. MN, gen.: *Korudalloio*. [Cf. Κορυδαλλός name of an Attic deme.]

ko-ru-no, PY 61 = Cn 131, Cn 719. MN, nom. and dat.

ko-ru-ta-ta, PY Cn 254. MN, dat.: *Koruthātāi*? [Cf. next.]

ko-ru-to[1], KN Dv 1310. MN: *Koruthos*. [Κόρυθος.]

ko-ru-to[2]: see s.v. *ko-ru*.

]*ko-ru-we-ja*, KN L 472. Fem. plur. adj. describing textile-workers. [Cf. *ko-we-ja*.]

ko-sa-ma-ne, PY An 615. Obscure, MN?

ko-sa-ma-to, KN Ga 685, PY [Eb 915], Ep 212. MN.

ko-so, KN As 40. MN.

ko-so-jo, KN Ap 637. Gen.?

ko-so-ne, PY Cn 45. MN, dat. [Cf. prec.]

]*ko-so-ni-ja*, KN U 437. Description of rectangular ideogram, perhaps [*a*]*xonia* 'small shafts'. [ἀξόνιον Hero 3 B.C. +; cf. *a-ko-so-ne*.]

ko-so-u-to, KN Ch 900 (*ko-su-u-to-qe*), PY 254 = Jn 389. At KN name of ox, at PY MN: *Xouthos*. [Ξοῦθος.]

ko-ta-wo, PY Jn 431. MN.

ko-te-ri-ja, PY 237 = Ta 709. Name of a utensil in a list of hearth implements: nom. plur. fem. or neut. Palmer: *khō*(*s*)*stēria*(*i*) 'shovels', see p. 499.

ko-te-ro, PY Xn 1127 (deleted). No context.

ko-te-u, KN Do 1054. MN.

ko-ti, KN Db 5352, De 1084. MN.

ko-to, KN C 912. MN: *Kōthōn*? [Κώθων.]

ko-to-na, PY 43 = Aq 64, 108 = Ea 817 +, 144 = Eb 866 +, 117 = En 467 +, 118 = Eo 211 +, 131 = Ep 301 +. Nom. and gen. sing., nom. and acc. plur.: *ktoinā*, -*ān*, -*ai*, -*ans*, 'estate, plot of land'. [κτοῖναι· δῆμος μεμερισμένος Hesych.; a unit of land with religious associations in Rhodian inscrr. From **ktei*-, cf. *ki-ti-je-si*.]

ko-to-i-na, KN 156 = Uf 1031 +. Fuller spelling.

ko-to-na-no-no, PY Ea 922. Mistake for *ko-to-na* ⟨*a*⟩-*no-no*.

ko-to-na-o, PY 140 = Eb 297 +, 135 = Ep 704, Wa 784. Gen. plur.: *ktoināōn*.

ko-to-no, PY 141 = Eb 338, 128 = Eo 278. Acc. dual: *ktoinō*.

ko-to-ne-ta, PY 151 = Ed 901. Nom. plur.: *ktoinetai* 'men of the *ktoina*', exact meaning uncertain; see p. 453. [Rhod. κτοινέται.]

ko-to-ne-we, PY Ae 995. Nom. plur.=prec.?

ko-to-no-o-ko, PY 140=Eb 297, 133=Eb 846+, 121=Eo 247+, 131=Ep 301+. Nom. and acc. sing.: *ktoino(h)okhos, -on*, 'holder of a *ktoina*'.

ko-to-no-ko, PY Eb 173. Mistake for *ko-to-no-o-ko*.

ko-tu-ro₂, PY Cn 436, Eb 892+, [131=Ep 301], Jn 431, TH Of 34. MN: *Kotuliōn*? [Cf. Κότυλος, etc.]

ko-ṭu-ro₂-ne, PY Eb 1347. Dat.: *Kotuliōnei*?

ko-tu-we, PY An 233, An 615, Na 908. PN, loc.: *Gortuei*? [Γόρτυς in Arcadia, Palmer, 1963a, p. 71, but this is unlikely to be the correct location.]

ko-tu-wo, PY 154=Eq 213. Gen.: *Gortuos*?

ko-u-ra, KN 211=Lc 532+, PY La 623+, MY L 710. Nom. plur. neut.?, description of textiles; no satisfactory explanation.

ko-u-re-ja, KN Ak 643, 25=Ap 694, Lc 550, Lc 581. Nom. plur. fem. or neut., description of textiles or more likely their makers: 'for *ko-u-ra*'.

ko-wa, KN 23=Ag 1654+, 17=Ai 739+, 18=Ak 611+, Ap 639, PY 1=Aa 62+, 6=Ab 379+. Nom. sing. and plur. fem. (also used for dual to prevent confusion with *ko-wo*): *korwā, -ai* 'daughter, girl'. [κούρη *Il.* VI, 420+, Att. κόρη, Arc. Κόρϝα.]

ko-wa-to, PY Cn 328. MN.

ko-we, KN Ws 8498. Obscure.

ko-we-ja, KN X 697. Prob. variant spelling of *ko-ru-we-ja*.

ko-we-jo, KN Dk 925. Describing sheep, masc. plur.?

ko-wi-ro-wo-ko, KN 48=B 101. Nom., number uncertain, name of a man's trade: *kowiloworgos* 'make of hollow-ware'? Exact sense of κοῖλος here cannot be determined. [κοιλουργός Zeno papyrus.]

ko-wo[1], KN Ag 87+, 17=Ai 739+, 18=Ak 611+, 35=Am 819+, V 482+, PY 1=Aa 62+, 6=Ab 379+, 8=Ad 670+, 26=An 292+, MY Oe 121. Nom. sing., dual and plur., dat. sing.: *korwos, -ō, -oi, -ōi* 'boy, son; (in plur.) children'. [κοῦρος *Od.* XIX, 523+, Att. κόρος, Dor. κῶρος.]

ko-wo[2], PY 171=Un 718. With ideogram HIDE+KO: *kōwos* 'sheepskin, fleece'. [Hom. κώεα, κώεσι (*Il.* IX, 661+) should have a sing. *κῶος; perhaps κῶας is influenced by other nouns in -ας such as δέμας, κέρας, κρέας.]

ko-za-ro, PY Jn 431. MN. [Cf. *ko-ka-ro*?]

K U, As adjunct to CLOTH ideogram: KN L 514, L 515+.

As adjunct to WOOL ideogram: TH Of 26, Of 28, Of 29+.

As adjunct to *125* (cyperus?): KN F 157, MY Ue 652: =*ku-pa-ro*?

Ideographic use: MY 106=Ge 603, 107=Ge 604+: abbreviation of *ku-mi-no* 'cumin'. Obscure: PY Un 1319, MY Ui 709.

ku-da-jo(-qe), KN V 1004. MN: *Kudaios, Khudaios*?

ku-da-ma-ro, PY 168=Es 644, 167=Es 650. MN.

ku-do, KN Df 1210. MN: *Kudōn*? [Κύδων.]

ku-do-ni-ja, KN 84=Ce 59, Co 904, 90=G 820, Lc 481, Sd 269=4404+. PN: *Kudōniā*. [Κυδωνία (site of modern Chania), cf. Κύδωνες *Od.* III, 292; Egyptian *ktny*, Faure, 1968.]

ku-do-ni-ja-de, KN L 588. Acc.+-*de*: *Kudōniānde*.

]*ku-do-ni-jo*[, KN Xd 169. Masc. ethnic?

ku-i-so, KN Da 5214. MN.

ku-ja-ro, KN De 1254, X 44. MN.

ku-jo, KN Df 5211. MN.

ku-ka, MY Oe 121. MN, dat.: *Gugāi*? [Γύγης.]

ku-ka-da-ro, KN 158=Uf 836. MN.

ku-ka-no, KN Dc 1337. MN.

ku-ka-ra-so, PY Cn 643, Cn 719. MN.

ku-ka-ro, KN Da 1238, 262=Ra 1548, V 653. MN: *Kukalos*? [Cf. Κύκαλα name of Attic deme.]

ku-ka-so, KN As 5719?, V 429. MN.

ku-ke-re-u, PY Jn 845. MN: *Kukleus*. [Κυκλεύς.]

ku-ke-so, KN Dd 1306. MN.

ku-ke-to, KN Da 1392. MN.

ku-ḳo-wi-ṛa, KN X 7644. Obscure.

ku-mi-no, MY 105=Ge 602+. Nom. sing. neut.: *kumīnon* 'cumin', *Cuminum cyminum*. [κύμινον Hippocr. 5 B.C.+. Semitic loan-word, cf. Ugaritic *kmn*, Hebr. *kammōn*, Akkad. *kamūnu*.] See p. 227.

ku-mi-na, MY Ge 605. Nom. plur.: *kumīna*.

ku-mi-so, KN Da 1202. MN.

ku-mo-no, KN Dk 945. MN, dat.: *Gumnōi*?

ku-mo-no-so, KN Da 1313. MN.

ku-na-ja, PY 235=Ta 711. Nom. sing. fem., description of a ewer: *gunaiā* 'of a woman', exact sense uncertain, perhaps 'for women's use' or 'decorated with a figure of a woman' (Palmer). [γύναια δῶρα *Od.* XI, 521, etc.]

ku-na-ke-ta-i, PY 191=Na 248. Dat. plur.: *kunāgetāhi* 'for the huntsmen'. [κυνηγέτης *Od.* IX, 120+, Dor. κυναγέτας.]

ku-ne, MY Fu 711. MN?: *Kunēs*? [Κύνης.]

ku-ne-u, KN Da 1396. MN: *Kuneus*?

ku-ni-ta, KN B 798. MN, dat.?

ku-pa-nu-we-to, KN 39=As 1517. MN.

ku-pa-ri-se-ja, PY 284=Sa 488. Nom. plur. neut.: *kuparisseia* '(wheels) of cypress-wood'. [Cf. κυπαρίσσινος *Od.* XVII, 340+.]

[*ku-*]*pa-ri-so*, PY Na 514. PN: *Kuparissos*. [Κυπάρισσος, Hom. Κυπαρισσήεις *Il.* II, 593; cf. present *Kyparissía*, not necessarily the same site.]

ku-pa-ri-si-jo, PY 56=An 657. Ethnic adj.: *Kuparissioi*.

ku-pa-ro, KN Ga 465, 102=Ga 517+. A condiment, nom. sing.: *kupairos, -on*, 'Cyperus rotundus'. [κύπειρον Theophr.+, also κύπειρος, Ion. κύπερος, Dor. κύπαιρος (Alcman). Not in sense 'Cyperus longus' cf. Il. XXI, 351. Probably loan-word, cf. Hebr. kōper.]

ku-pa-ro₂, PY 104 = Un 249, 103 = Un 267. Variant spelling: *kuparyos*?

ku-ro-ro₂, PY An 616. Mistake for prec.

ku-pa-ro-we, PY Fr 1203. Adj. describing oil, nom. sing. neut.: *kupairowen* 'scented with cyperus'.

ku-pạ-rọ-de̜, PY Fr 1201. Prob. false reading for prec.

ku-pa-sa, KN V 145. PN?

]*kụ-pạ-si-ja*, KN V 1043. Perh. fem. or neut. plur. of ethnic adj.

[*ku?-*]*pe-ra*, MY 234 = Ue 611. Doubtful restoration; if correct, nom. plur.: *kupella* 'drinking cups'. [κύπελλα Il. III, 248+.]

ku-pe-re-te, KN B 799. MN.

ku-pe-se-ro, KN 260 = Og 4467. MN: *Kupselos*. [Κύψελος.]

ku-pe-te-jo, KN X 974. Obscure.

ku-pi-ri-jo, KN Fh 347+, 102 = Ga 517+, PY 61 = Cn 131, Cn 719, Jn 320, Un 443. Unequivocally MN at PY in Cn and Jn; doubtful at KN and PY Un 443, but strong reasons for regarding it as the name of an unguent-maker are adduced by Godart (1968b). *Kuprios*.

ku-po, MY Oe 103. Personal name, dat.: masc. or fem.?

ku-ra-no, KN 39 = As 1517. MN: *Kullānos*? [Κύλληνος.]

ku-re-we, KN B 164, PY 57 = An 519+, 76 = Cn 3, 177 = Ma 90. Nom. masc. plur. Name of a class of men, possibly ethnic; see p. 430.

kụ-rị-na-ze-ja, PY Fn 187. Personal name or title, dat.?

ku-ri-sa-to, KN X 8101, PY An 5, Cn 4, Jn 706. MN.

ku-ro-ro₂: error for *ku-pa-ro₂*, see s.v. *ku-pa-ro*.

ku-ro₂, KN As 603, U 4478, PY Ea 814. MN, nom. and dat.: *Kūrios, -ōi*? [Κύριος.]

ku-ro₂-jo, KN B 822. Gen.: *Kūrioio*.

ku-ru-ka, KN Vc 5510. MN. [Prob. not *Glukās*, see Chadwick, 1968c, p. 195.]

ku-ru-me-ne-jo, KN Fh 5502. MN?

ku-ru-me-no, KN Sc 236, PY 43 = Aq 64, TH Of 33. MN: *Klumenos*. [Κλύμενος Od. III, 452.]

ku-ru-me-no-jo, PY 58 = An 654. Gen.: *Klumenoio*.

ku-ru-me-ni-jo, KN Da 1173. Patronymic adj.?: *Klumenios* 'son of K.'

]*ku-ru-ni-ta*, KN X 1525. MN?

kụ-rụ-no, KN As 625. MN?

ku-ru-no-jo, PY Ea 801. Gen.

ku-ru-so, KN 231 = K 872, PY 244 = Ta 714, 247 = Ta 716. Instr. sing.: *khrusōi* 'with gold'; also adj.: *khrusos, -ōi, -ō, -ois* 'golden' (perh.

khrussos < **khrus-yos*?). [χρυσός 'gold', Il. VI, 48+; χρύσε(ι)ος (generally scanned as disyllable) 'golden', Il. I, 15, etc. From Hebr. and Ugaritic *harūs-*, both substantive and adj.]

ku-ru-so-jo, PY 27 = Ae 303. Gen. sing.: *khrusoio* 'of the gold'.

ku-ru-sa-pi, PY 242 = Ta 707, 244 = Ta 714. Instr. plur. fem. adj.: *khrusāphi* 'golden'.

ku-ru-so-wo-ko, PY 52 = An 207. Nom. plur.: *khrusoworgoi* 'goldsmiths'. [χρυσουργός Septuagint+; cf. χρυσοχόος Od. III, 425+.]

ku-ru-su-*56, KN 230 = K 740. Nom. sing.: description of a three-legged vessel, possibly a compound of *khrus-* 'gold'. See p. 327.

ku-ru-zo, TH Z 840, 841, 845+. Isolated inscr. on vases; prob. MN. [Not *Glukiōn*, see Chadwick, 1968c, p. 195.]

ku-sa-me-ni-jo, PY 57 = An 519, 44 = Aq 218. Patronymic adj. from **Kussamenos*: *Kussamenios*. [**κυσσάμενος* participle to **ἐ-κυδ-σάμην*, cf. κῦδος, etc.; Heubeck, 1957, p. 273.]

ku-so, PY Eb 893, 131 = Ep 301. MN.

ku-so-no, PY Ae 8. MN.

ku-su, KN L 698. Preposition with dat.: *xun* 'with'. [ξύν Hom.+.]

ku-su-pa, KN Fh 367. Nom. sing. neut.: *to-so-ku-su-pa = toson xumpan* 'so much (olive oil) altogether'. [ξύμπας Od. VII, 214+.]

ku-su-pa-ta, KN Dp 699. Nom. plur. neut.: *xumpanta*.

ku-su-qa, PY Ed 847 (deleted). Prob. error for *ku-su-to-ro-qa*.

ku-su-to-ro-qa, KN 36 = B 817, PY 150 = Ed 411, 153 = Er 880. Nom. sing.: *xunstroqᵘhā* 'aggregate, total'. [Identity with συστροφή is highly probable in view of meaning deducible from contexts, but this conflicts with current view of etymology of στρέφω, which may be wrong; see Chadwick and Baumbach, 1963, p. 246.]

ku-ta-i-jo, KN 39 = As 1517.

ku-ta-i-si-[, KN X 7891. MN, prob. *ku-ta-i-si-*[*jo*], variant spelling of next.

ku-ta-si-jo, KN Dv 1237, Dv 1394. MN: *Kutaisios*? [Cf. *ku-ta-ti-jo*.]

ku-ta-to, KN [84 = Ce 59], 68 = De 1648, 69 = Df 1119, 71 = Dk 1072, 72 = Dk 1074+. PN: *Kutaiton*? [Cf. Κύταιον?]

ku-ta-i-to, KN 83 = C 902, Xd 146? Variant spelling.

ku-ta-ti-jo/ja, KN Ga 419, 90 = G 820+. Ethnic adj.

ku-te-ra₃, PY Aa 506, Ab 562. Nom. fem. plur. of ethnic adj.: *Kuthērai*! [Cf. PN Κύθηρα?]

ku-te-ra-o, PY Ad 390, Ad 679. Gen. plur.: *Kuthērāōn*?

ku-te̜-rẹ-u, PY 40 = An 261. MN: *Kuthēreus*? [Cf. Κύθηρα PN.]

ku-te-re-u-pi, PY 28 = An 607, Na 296. Instr. plur. PN: *Kuthēreuphi*? [Cf. *ku-te-re-u.*]

ku-te-ro, KN B 822. MN: *Kuthēros*? [Κύθηρος.]

ku-te-se-jo, PY 242 = Ta 707, 243 = Ta 708 +. Nom. sing. and instr. plur.: *kuteseios, -ois* 'made of ebony'. [See *ku-te-so*.]

   ku-te-se-ja, PY 240 = Ta 713 +. Nom. sing. fem.: *kuteseiā*.

   ku-te-ta-jo, PY 242 = Ta 707. Error for *ku-te-se-jo*.

ku-te-so, PY 242 = Ta 707. Nom. sing.?: *kutesos*, a kind of wood, probably 'ebony'. [κύτισος 'bastard ebony', *Laburnum vulgare*, Theophr.]

ku-to, KN 38 = As 1516. MN.

ku-tu-qa-no, KN Ap 639, Da 1161? Personal name, WN in Ap, MN in Da (if complete).

ku-wa-ni-jo(-qe), PY 244 = Ta 714. Instr. plur. masc.: *kuwaniois* 'with (palm-trees?) of lapis-coloured glass'. [κυάνεος *Il.* XI, 26 +.]

ku-wa-no, PY 239 = Ta 642, 244 = Ta 714. Instr. sing.: *kuanōi* '(inlaid) with *kyanos*, lapis-coloured glass'. [κύανος *Il.* XI, 24, both 'lapis lazuli' and 'blue glass paste imitating this'. Cf. Ugaritic *iqnu*, Akkad. *uqnu* 'lapis lazuli'? See further Halleux (1969).]

ku-wa-no-wo-ko-i, MY Oi 703 +. Dat. plur.: *kuanoworgoihi* 'for the *kyanos*-workers'. [Cf. *ku-wa-no*.]

ku-wa-ta, KN Ws 8754. MN?

ku-*63-so, PY 115 = En 74, 121 = Eo 247. MN.

MA, Ideographic use: KN 203 = Ga 953, PY Un 219, MY 106 = Ge 603, 107 = Ge 604: abbreviation of *ma-ra-tu-wo* 'fennel'. Sometimes apparently used in error for WOOL, which has an extra element.
As adjunct to *177*: KN U 4478: obscure.

ma-di, KN As 603, Db 1168. MN.

ma-di-qo, KN B 806, Dl 930, Dv 1460, Kydonia jar? (*Kadmos* 6, 1967, p. 107.) MN.

ma-du-ro, PY 62 = Cn 655. MN.

ma-ka-ta, PY Jn 725. MN: *Makhātās*. [Μαχάτας.] The same man as *ma-ka-wo*, but which is correct? See p. 511.

ma-ka-wo, PY 255 = Jn 658. MN: *Makhāwōn*. [Μαχάων *Il.* II, 732 +.] See s.v. *ma-ka-ta*.

ma-ke-ra, KN V 831. MN.

ma-ke-ra-mo[, KN Xd 154. MN?

ma-ki, KN Xd 107. MN?

]*ma-ki-nu-wo*, KN Np 858 (prob. complete at left). MN?

ma-ki-ro-ne, KN Gg 995. Dat., perh. divine name?

ma-ma-ro, KN B 801?, PY 62 = Cn 655. MN: *Marmaros*. [Μάρμαρος.]

ma-mi-di-zo, KN C 911. MN?

ma-na-je-u[, KN V 958. MN.

ma-na-sa, PY 172 = Tn 316. Dat., divine name.

ma-na-si-we-ko, PY Jn 431. MN: *Mnāsiwergos*. [Μνησίεργος.]

ma-ne, PY Mn 1407. Personal name or place name?

ma-ni-ko, PY Cn 1287. MN: *Manikhos*? [Thess. Μάνιχος; Chantraine, 1966, p. 168.]

ma-no, MY 93 = Fo 101, 303 = V 659. WN, nom. and dat.: *Manō*?

ma-no-u-ro, PY Jn 605, Jn 692, [[Jn 725]]. MN.

ma-qe, KN F 51. Obscure.

ma-ra, KN Xd 7662, PY Cn 328. MN.

ma-ra-me-na[, PY Vn 1191. WN: perh. *Malāmenā* (cf. μήλη 'probe'), Ruijgh, 1967, p. 368.

ma-ra-ne-nu-we, PY 54 = An 610, [Mn 1410?]. PN.

   ma-ra-ne-ni-jo, PY 175 = Ma 393. Variant form of prec. or ethnic?

ma-ra-ni-jo, PY Cn 643, Cn 719. MN: *Malanios*? [Cf. PN Μαλανία (Cyprus).]

ma-ra-pi, PY 77 = Cn 418. Perhaps instr. plur.: *malāphi* 'under the legs'. [Cf. ὑπὸ μάλης.] See p. 436.

ma-ra-pi-jo, KN Dd 1296. MN: *Maraphios*? [Μαράφιος.]

ma-ra-si-jo, PY 312 = An 1281, Jn 706. MN.

ma-ra-ta, PY Jn 750. MN.

ma-ra-te-u, PY 56 = An 657, 44 = Aq 218, Cn 328. MN.

ma-ra-te-we, PY 195 = Na 245. Nom. plur., a class or trade.

ma-ra-ti-sa, PY 45 = An 830. Obscure.

ma-ra-tu-wo, MY 105 = Ge 602 +. Nom. sing.: *marathwon* 'fennel', *Foeniculum vulgare*. [μάραθον, μάραθρον.]

ma-ra₃-wa, PY 144 = Eb 866, 143 = Ep 705. WN: *Marraiwā*? [Cf. Μαρραῖος.]

ma-re-ku-na, PY 115 = En 74, 120 = Eo 276. Man's or woman's name; the gender is wrong in one case.

ma-re-wo, PY 56 = An 657. MN, gen.: *Mālēwos*, *Mallēwos*? [Cf. Μᾶλος, Μαλλός.]

ma-ri, KN Dl 947, Dl 948. PN.

ma-ri-jo, KN X 1581. Obscure, possibly ethnic of prec.

ma-ri-ne[, MY X 508. Obscure, cf. next.

ma-ri-ne-we, KN Ga 674, Gg 713. Dat. sing., name of deity?

ma-ri-ne-wo, KN As 1519 (now seen to be correct reading): gen.

]*ma-ri-ne-we-ja-i*, TH Of 25, Of 34. Dat. plur. fem. derivative of prec.

ma-ri-ta, PY Jn 832. MN: *Malitās*. [Μαλίτης.]

ma-ri-ti-wi-jo, KN Da 1461, PY An 594, Cn 40, MY V 662. MN, nom. and dat.

ma-ro¹, PY Cn 40. PN. (Perhaps abbreviation for *ma-ro-pi*?)

   ma-ro-pi, PY Cn 40, 61 = Cn 131 +. Loc. plur.: *Mālōmphi*? (Ruijgh, 1967, p. 368.)

ma-ro², PY Cn 328. MN.

ma-ro-ne, KN Fh 347. MN, dat. [From *ma-ro²*?]

ma-sa, KN 84 = Ce 59?, Dq 42, Ga 1058, X 7776. PN.

   ma-sa-de, KN X 744. Acc. + *-de*?

ma-se-de, PY Cc 1285, Mn 1411. Obscure, PN or MN?

ma-se-wi-ra₂-[, KN Ws 1701. On sealing; obscure.

ma-si-dwo, KN Fh 360. MN.

ma-so-mo, KN Dl 932. PN?

ma-so-ni-jo, PY Vn 851. MN, dat.?

ma-so-qe, KN F 854. MN + -*qᵘe*?

ma-ta, PY Cn 4. PN with *a-ka-re-u-te*?

ma-ta-i, PY An 172. MN.

ma-ta-ko, PY Jn 845. MN: *Malthakos*?

ma-ta-u-ro, KN Dv 8151. MN.

ma-ta-wo, PY Ae 27. MN.

ma-te, PY 28 = An 607. Nom. sing. fem.: *mātēr* 'mother'. [μήτηρ.]

    ma-te-de, PY 28 = An 607. *mātēr de* 'and the mother'.

    ma-te-re, PY 306 = Fr 1202. Dat. sing.: *mātrei (theiāi)* 'to the Divine Mother'.

ma-te-u-pi, KN K 877. Obscure.

?]*ma-te-we*, PY Cn 40. MN, dat.

ma-ti-jo, KN D 1024. MN?

ma-ti-ko, KN Vc 295, V 831. MN: *Mātikhos*. [Μήτιχος; Chantraine, 1966, p. 173.]

ma-to-ro-pu-ro, PY Cn 595. PN: *Mātropulos*?

    ma-to-pu-ro, PY Mn 1412. Error or variant form (*Mātorpulos*?).

ma-tu-wɇ, KN Ln 1568. Personal name, dat.

ma-u-ti-jo, PY Cn 40, 254 = Jn 389. MN, nom. and dat.

ma-wa-si-jo, PY Jn 431. MN.

ma-*79, PY 115 = En 74, 120 = Eo 276. WN.

ME, Adjunct to children: KN Ak 634, Ak 5741: prob. abbreviation of *me-u-jo(-e)* 'smaller'. Ideographic use: PY 177 = Ma 90, 179 = Ma 193+, Mn 11, 97 = Un 2, Un 219, 103 = Un 267: possibly not the same word in all cases; see p. 465.

me-de-i-jo, KN B 800. MN: *Mēdeïos*. [Μήδειος.]

me-ka-o, PY Na 571. MN, gen. forming PN with *wo-wo*: *Megāo*? [Μέγης.]

me-ki-ta, KN L 469?, Xe 537. Adj. describing cloths, prob. nom. plur. neut.: *megista* 'of the largest size'. [μέγιστος.] Cf. *me-sa-ta*.

me-ki-ti, KN Dv 1434. MN.

me-ki-to-de[, PY Fr 1244. PN, acc. + -*de*?

me-ki-to-ki-ri-ta, PY [Aa 955], Ab 575. Description of one woman, probably her name: *Megistokritā*. [Cf. Μεγιστοκλῆς, etc., Ἀγαθόκριτος, etc.]

me-na, KN E 842, Fs 3, Gg 717. Possibly acc. sing.: *mēna* 'mouth', but context obscure and perhaps a different word.

me-na-wa-te[, KN Fh 5723. MN, dat.?

me-ni-jo, PY Wa 114. Nom. sing. neut.: *mēnion* 'monthly ration'. [Cf. μηνιεῖα.]

me-no, KN 200 = Fp 1, 201 = Fp 14+, 204 = Gg 704+, M 1645, Oa 7374, PY 310 = Fr 1225. Gen. sing.: *mēnos* 'in the month of'. [μείς *Il.* XIX, 117+.] Cf. *me-na*, *me-ni-jo*, *o-pi-me-ne*.

me-no-e-ja, PY 239 = Ta 642. Adj. describing a table, nom. sing. fem. Obscure; earlier suggestion *mēnoeiā* 'crescent-shaped' is incorrectly formed, unless there is a derivative

*mēnōs in Myc. Perhaps name of a material (Palmer, 1963*a*, p. 345).

me-nu-a₂, PY 44 = Aq 218, Qa 1293, Qa 1301. Nom. sing. title of an official. [Cf. Μινύαι Hdt. I, 146+.]

    me-nu-wa, KN Sc 238, V 60, Xd 7702, PY 55 = An 724. Alternative spelling, prob. used as MN at KN.

me-pɔ, PY An 616. Nom. sing., name of a liquid.

me-ra, KN 161 = Uf 839. Context obscure; see p. 272. Perhaps PN, cf. next.

me-ra-de, KN Fh 5505. PN, acc. + -*de*?

me-ra-to, PY Jn 832. MN: *Melanthos*. [Μέλανθος.]

me-re-ti-ri-ja, PY 1 = Aa 62, Aa 764. Nom. plur. fem., a woman's trade: *meletriai* 'corn-grinders'. [Cf. *me-re-u-ro* = ἄλευρον 'flour'; ἀλετρίς *Od.* XX, 105+.]

    me-re-ti-ra₂, PY Ab 789. Alternative spelling.

    me-re-ti-ra₂[-o], PY Ad 308. Gen. plur.

me-re-u, PY Ep 539. MN: *Mēleus*?

me-re-u-ro, PY 171 = Un 718. Nom. sing.: *meleuron* 'flour'. [μάλευρον Alcaeus, prob. influenced by ἄλευρον.]

me-ri, KN 205 = Gg 702+; as monogram ME + RI Fs 2+, 206 = Gg 705+. Nom. sing. with AMPHORA ideogram: *meli* 'honey'. [μέλι *Od.* XX, 69+.] Cf. *me-ri-ti-jo*.

me-ri-to, PY 171 = Un 718. Gen. sing.: *melitos*.

me-ri-da-ma-te, PY 50 = An 39, 52 = An 207. Nom. dual and plur., title of an official; perhaps *melidamarte*, *-tes* 'superintendants of honey' (no doubt exercising other (religious?) functions). [Cf. *du-ma*.]

me-ri-du-ma-te, [KN X 1045?], PY 50 = An 39, An 424, 49 = An 427+. Variant spelling?

    me-ri-du-ma-si, PY Fn 867. Dat. plur.

    me-ri-du-te, PY 91 = Fn 50. Error for *me-ri-du-⟨ma⟩-te*.

me-ri-te-wo, PY Ea 771, Ea 481, Ea 801+. Gen. sing., man's trade: *melitēwos* 'bee-keeper'? [From μέλιτ- 'honey' rather than μέλισσα 'bee' as μελισσεύς Arist.+.]

me-ri-ti-jo, PY Wr 1360. Nom. sing. masc.?, with ideogram WINE: *melitios* 'honeyed'. [Cf. οἶνος μελίτειος Plutarch 2. 672B.]

me-ri-wa-ta, KN Dv 1255, [PY Jn 431?]. MN: *Meliwātās*? [Cf. μελία? or Μελιασταί priests of Dionysos.]

me-sa-po, PY Na 606. PN: *Messapos*? [Cf. Μεσσαπέαι Laconia.]

me-sa-ta, KN L 735. Description of CLOTH, nom. plur. fem.?: *mes(s)atai* 'of medium size or weight'. [μέσσατος 'midmost' *Il.* VIII, 223+.] Cf. *me-ki-ta*.

me-sa-to, KN Wb 1714, Wb 5822+. On sealings with ideogram **146*; nom. sing. masc. or neut.?

me-ta(-qe), PY 57 = An 519+. Prep. with dat.: *meta qᵘe* 'and with (them)'. [Cf. μετὰ δέ σφιν *Od.* IV, 17.]

me-ta-ka-wa, PY 312=An 1281. Prob. WN, dat.: *Metakalwāi*?

me-ta-ke-ku-me-na, KN 274=Sf 4428. Nom. sing. fem. of perf. pple. describing framework of a chariot: *metakekhumenā* 'taken to pieces', 'knocked down'? See p. 516. [μετά + χέω; cf. χυδήν, etc.; for sense cf. Lat. *confusus*.]

me-ta-ki-ti-ta, PY 54=An 610. Nom. plur., a class of men: *metaktitai* 'fellow or new settlers'; cf. *ki-ti-ta*. [Cf. μέτοικος, μετανάστης.]

me-ta-no, PY Cn 719. MN: *Metānōr*. [Cf.Μετάνειρα *Hom. hymn Dem.* 161+; Heubeck, 1967, p. 31.]

me-ta-no-re, KN Uf 1522. Dat.: *Metānorei*.

me-ta-pa, PY 302=Ac 1280, 28=An 607, 43=Aq 64, 75=Cn 608, 257=Jn 829, 177=Ma 90+. PN: *Metapa*, one of the Nine Towns of the Hither Province. [Μέταπα, but not to be identified with known sites.]

me-ta-pa-de, 250=Vn20. Acc. + *-de*: *Metapan-de*.

me-ta-pi-jo, 58=An 654. Nom. plur. masc. ethnic adj. *Metapioi*. [Cf. τὸς Μεταπίος in Elean inscr. Schwyzer, *Dial.* 414.]

]*me-ta-ra-wo*[, KN B 799. MN: *Metalāwos*.

me-ta-ri-ko-wo, KN Vc 291. MN.

me-ta-se-we, PY 251=Vn 46. Nom. plur.: in list of building materials; see p. 504.

me-ta-*47-wa, MY Go 610. MN, dat.

me-te-to, PY Mn 456, Na 337, Vn 130. PN.

me-te-to-de, PY 41=An 35.

me-te-we, PY 61=Cn 131. MN, dat.: *Methēwei, Mētēwei*?

me-ti-ja-no, [KN Np 273?], PY 317=Ub 1318. MN: *Mestiānōr* (Ruijgh, 1966) or *Mēstiānōr* (Heubeck, 1967, p. 31) or *Mētiānōr* (=*Mēsi-*, cf. Μησίαναξ); cf. *ne-ti-ja-no*.

me-ti-ja-no-ro, PY Vn 1191. Gen.: *-ānoros*.

me-to-qe-u, PY An 192. MN: *Metōqʷeus*? [Cf. Μέτωπος.]

me-to-re, KN Da 5295, 260=Og 4467, PY Na 924. MN.

me-tu-ra, PY 30=Ae 264+. Prob. acc., meaning obscure.

me-tu-ro, KN C 954. MN: *Methullos*? [Μέθυλλος.]

me-tu-wo ne-wo (or as one word?), PY 306=Fr 1202. Possibly dating formula; see p. 480.

me-u-jo, KN Ak 612, Ak 614+. Nom. sing. masc. and fem. (apparently sometimes used in place of dual): *meiwyōs* 'smaller', 'younger'. [μείων Hom.+; reconstruction of form uncertain: *meiwijo-* Heubeck, 1963a, pp. 199–200.]

me-wi-jo, KN 18=Ak 611+, PY 236=Ta 641. Alternative spelling, masc. and neut.: *-ōs, -os*.

me-u-jo-e, KN Ak 613+. Nom. plur. masc. and fem.: *meiwyohes*.

me-wi-jo-e, KN 20=Ai 824, 19=Ak 627, Ak 782+, K 829. Alternative spelling of prec. (also as nom. dual: *-ohe*).

me-u-jo-a₂, PY 294=Sh 733+. Nom. plur. neut.: *meiwyoha*.

me-wi, PY 43=Aq 64. MN.

me-wo-ni-jo, KN K 7599, U 4478. MN.

me-za-na, PY 76=Cn 3, 296=Sh 736. Possibly nom. plur.; see p. 435. [Cf. Μεσσάνα.]

me-za-ne, PY 91=Fn 50. Possibly dat. sing., but connexion with prec. problematic. Perhaps error for *me-za-⟨wo⟩-ne*, see next (Olivier, 1960, p. 118).

me-za-wo, KN B 8206, 297=Sc 222. MN: *Medzā-wōn*?

me-za-wo-ni, PY 96=Un 138. Dat.: *-woni*.

me-zo, KN Ak 612+. Nom. sing. masc. and fem.: *medzōs* 'larger', 'older'. [μέζων Hom. +, Att.; other dialects μέζων< *meg-jōn.*]

me-zo-e, KN 20=Ai 824, 18=Ak 611, 19=Ak 627+, Gg 5637, 223=L 471, PY 236=Ta 641. Nom. dual and plur. masc. and fem.: *medzohe, -ohes*.

me-zo-a₂, PY 294=Sh 733+. Nom. plur. neut.: *medzoha*.

me-*86-ta, KN Ce 61. MN.

MI, As adjunct to CLOTH+TE: KN 213=Le 641, Le 5930, Ln 1568; possibly abbreviation of *mi-ja-ro*.

Ideographic use: MY 106=Ge 603 (erased): probably abbreviation of *mi-ta* 'mint'.

-mi, PY 135=Ep 704, 196=Na 926. Enclitic pronoun: *min* 'him', 'her'. [μιν Hom.+.]

mi-ja-ra-ro, KN 38=As 1516. MN.

mi-ja-ro, KN Ln 1568. Apparently description of CLOTH, also probably abbreviated to *mi*; obscure.

mi-jo-qa, PY 312=An 1281, [91=Fn 50], Fn 867. Possibly WN in gen.

mi-ka-ri-jo, PY Cn 600, Jn 605. MN.

mi-ka-ri-jo-jo, PY Jn 605. Gen.

mi-ka-ta¹, PY 50=An 39+, Eb 839, 148=Ep 613, 91=Fn 50. Nom. and dat. sing., nom. plur., name of a man's trade: possibly *miktās*, *-tai* 'mixer' in some technical significance.

mi-ka-ta², KN Vc 64. MN, unless an example of *mi-ka-ta¹*.

mi-ka-to, KN Vc 67. MN.

mi-ko-no, PY An 209. MN.

mi-ni-so, KN Uf 1522. MN, dat.?

mi-ra, PY Eb 905, 115=En 74, 120=Eo 276, 148=Ep 613. WN: *Smilā*? [Cf. MN Σμίλης.]

mi-ra-ti-ja, PY Aa 798+, Ab 573. Nom. plur. fem., description of women: *Milātiai* 'women of Miletus'. [Later Μιλήσιος.]

mi-ra-ti-ja-o, PY Ad 380+. Gen. plur.: *Milātiāōn*.

mi-ra-ti-ra, PY Ab 382. Error for *mi-ra-ti-ja*.

mi-ra₂, PY 241=Ta 715. Probably a kind of wood for tables, see p. 342.

mi-ru-ro, KN 38=As 1516, 83=C 902, Da 1127+. MN.

mi-sa-ra-jo, KN 94=F 841. MN: *Misraios*? [Cf. *Misr* 'Egypt'.]

mi-ta, MY 105=Ge 602+. A spice: *mintha* 'mint', *Mentha viridis*. [μίνθα 6 B.C.+.]

mi-ta-qo, KN Dv 1292. MN.

mi-ti, KN Dl 463. MN.

mi-to-we-sa, KN Sd 4407+. Nom. sing. or plur. fem., of chariots: *miltowessa, -ai* 'painted red'. [Cf. νῆες μιλτοπάρηοι *Il.* II, 637.]

  mi-to-we-sa-e, KN 269 = Sd 4404. If not an error, perhaps prec.+monosyllabic word: *miltowessa(i) en* 'painted red inside'. [Lejeune, 1958b, p. 21.] See p. 516.

MO, Ideographic use, parallel to ZE, but with numeral 1, referring to horses and wheels: KN Sc 220+, 278 = So 894, 282 = So 4430+, PY 284 = Sa 488+: abbreviation of **monwos* 'single'. [Ion. μοῦνος, Att. μόνος.]

mo-da, PY Jn 601. MN. Cf. next.

mo-i-da, MY 46 = Au 102, Au 657. MN. Variant spelling of prec.?

mo-ni-ko, KN Da 1288, V 337. MN. [See Chantraine, 1966, p. 169.]

mo-qo-so, KN De 1381. MN: *Moqʷsos*. [Μόψος; cf. Hitt. *Mukšaš.*]

  mo-qo-so-jo, PY Sa 774. Gen.: *Moqʷsoio.*

mo-re, KN Dv 1214. MN.

mo-re-u, PY 254 = Jn 389, Jn 431, Jn 750. MN (three different men): *Mōleus*?

mo-ri-wo, PY Cn 1287. MN: *Moliwōn*? [Μολίων *Il.* XI, 322+.]

mo-ri-wo-do, KN 259 = Og 1527. Nom. sing., a substance measured by weight: *moliwdos* 'lead'? [μόλιβος *Il.* XI, 237; also μόλιβδος, μόλυβδος, βόλιμος, etc.]

mo-ro-ko-wo-wo-pi, PY La 635. PN?, loc. plur.?, perhaps compound of *mo-ro-ko* and *wo-wo* (q.v.).

mo-ro-qa, KN C 954, Xd 7586, PY 57 = An 519, 43 = Aq 64, 258 = Jo 438. Nom. sing. masc., title of local official. Palmer: *mo(i)ro-qqʷās* 'possessor of a share'. [μοῖρα, μόρος (Locr. and Lesb.) a measure of land; πάσασθαι 'possess'.]

mo-ro-qo-ro, PY Ea 439, 110 = Ea 800. MN, dat.: *Mologʷrōi*. [Μόλοβρος; cf. μολοβρός *Od.* XVII, 219+.]

  mo-ro-qo-ro-jo, PY 109 = Ea 782, 108 = Ea 817. Gen.: *Mologʷroio.*

MU, Identical with ideogram **109* = OX (without marks of sex). Also in context with OIL: KN Fh 347, Fh 371, Fh 5452: Palmer (1963b, p. 87; 1965, p. 319) suggests a vessel holding ⫷4 (i.e. 38·4 l. or 24 l. on his figures).

]*mu-da*, KN Dv 1331. MN.

mu-jo-me-no, PY 97 = Un 2. Prob. dat. sing.: *muiomenōi* 'being initiated'. [*μυίω (< *mus-yō), cf. μύω, but in sense equivalent to μυέω.] See p. 440.

mu-ka-ra, KN Pp 498. MN?

mu-ko, PY An 172. MN: *Mukōn, Muskhōn*? [Μύκων, Μύσχων.]

mu-ta-pi, PY An 5, Cn 4. PN.

mu-te-we, PY 317 = Ub 1318. MN, dat.: *Murtēwei*?

mu-ti, PY Eb 858. WN: prob. error for *mu-ti-ri*, q.v.

mu-ti-ri, PY Ep 212. WN: *Murtilis*. [Cf. PN Μυρτιλίς.]

mu-ti-ri-ko, PY Cn 1287. MN: *Mustiliskos*? [Chantraine, 1966, p. 171.]

mu-to-na, PY 57 = An 519, Jn 706. MN: *Murtōnās*? [Cf. Μύρτων.]

mu-to-wo-ti, PY Eb 495 (edge). Obscure, perhaps loc. of PN.

na-e-ra-ja, KN Ln 1568. Personal name.

na-e-si-jo, KN V 147, PY Jn 750. MN.

na-i-se-wi-jo, PY Jn 692+, Mn 1408. PN or ethnic adj.

na-ki-zo, KN Ws 8499. MN?

na-ma-ru-ko, PY Cn 1287. MN.

na-pe-re-wa, PY Cr 868. PN?

na-pu-ti-jo, KN 65 = Db 1232, PY Jn 845. MN: *Nāputios*. [Cf. νηπύτιος.]

na-ru, KN Db 1304. MN.

na-si-jo, KN B 800. MN: *Nāsios* (Georgiev). [Νήσιος (νῆσος).]

na-su-to, MY 46 = Au 102, Au 657, Au 660. MN.

na-su-wo, KN B 799. MN.

na-ta-ra-ma, MY 93 = Fo 101. Personal name, fem.?, dat.

na-u-do-mo, KN U 736, PY 189 = Na 568, Vn 865, [Xn 990]. Nom. plur.: *naudomoi* 'ship-builders'. [Cf. ναυ-πηγός, *to-ko-do-mo*.]

na-u-pi-ri-jo[, KN Fh 5432 (doubtful reading). If correct, cf. PN Ναύπλιον.

na-u-si-ke-re[-*we*?], KN Xd 214. MN: *Nausiklewēs*? [Ναυσικλῆς.]

na-wa-to, PY Jn 415. MN.

na-wi-jo, PY 257 = Jn 829. Acc. sing. masc.: *nāwion* '(bronze) of the temple'. [Cf. να(ϝ)ός < *νασ-ϝος. Alternatively possibly from ναῦς, νήϊος (Hom.).] See pp. 357, 513.

na-wi-ro, KN Db 1507. MN: *Nāwilos*? [Landau, 1958.]

NE, As adjunct to WOMAN and children: KN 21 = Ak 624, 22 = Ak 781+, Ap 629; as adjunct to animals: KN 85 = Ch 896, 83 = C 902, Dh 1240, Dk 1066+: in both cases probably abbreviation of *newos, newā* 'new' or 'young'.

ne-da-wa-ta, PY 258 = Jo 438. MN: *Nedwātās*. [Cf. Νέδα river and nymph.]

  ne-da-wa-ta-o, PY 56 = An 657. Gen.: *Nedwātāo.*

ne-de-we-e, PY Cn 595. PN, loc.

ne-do-wo-te, PY Cn 4. PN, loc.: *Nedwontei*. [Νέδων river of E. Messenia.]

ne-do-wo-ta-de, PY 60 = An 661. Acc. + -*de*: *Nedwonta-de.*

ne-e-ra-wo, PY Fn 79. MN, dat.: *Nehelāwōi*. [Cf. Νείλεως; Heubeck, 1957, p. 30, Mühlestein, 1969, p. 76.]

ne-e-to, TH Of 38. MN, dat.?

ne-ka-ta-ta, PY Vn 851. Man's or woman's name, dat.

ne-ki-ri-de, KN Ak 780, Ln 1568, Ws 8152. Nom.

plur. fem., probably description of women. (Apparently not *nekrides* 'shrouds', Chadwick, 1962, p. 54.)

ne-ki-ri-si, KN Od 687. Dat. plur.

ne-me-ta-wo, PY Cn 4. MN.

ne-o-ta, KN As 1516. MN.

ne-o-to, KN As 1519. MN.

ne-qa-sa-pi, KN 231 = K 872. Instr. plur., decoration on metal vessels.

ne-qa-sa-ta, PY Fn 324. MN, dat.

ne-qe-u, PY 43 = Aq 64, Jn 725, Qa 1298. MN.

ne-qe-wo, PY Eb 495, [148 = Ep 613]. Gen.

ne-ri-to, PY 61 = Cn 131. MN, dat.: *Nēritōi*. [Νήριτος *Od.* XVII, 207.]

ne-ri-wa-to, KN 260 = Og 4467. MN.

ne-se-e-we, PY Cr 868. PN.

ne-ti-ja-no, [KN Np 273?], PY Cn 599. MN: *Nestiānōr*. [Heubeck, 1957, p. 29.]

ne-ti-ja-no-re, PY Cn 40. Dat.: *Nestiānorei*.

ne-we-wi-ja, KN Lc 560, PY Aa 695, Ab 560. Nom. plur. fem., description of women textile workers.

ne-we-wi-ja-o, PY Ad 357. Gen. plur.

ne-wo, KN Fh 362+, Od 689, X 658, PY 59 = An 656, 306 = Fr 1202, MY 226 = Oe 129. Nom. sing. and plur. masc., nom. sing. neut., dat. sing. masc., etc.: *newos, -oi, -on, -ōi* 'new', 'young'. [νέος Hom.+.]

ne-wo-jo, KN Fh 5506. Gen. sing.: *newoio*.

ne-wa, KN Dp 997, 282 = So 4430+, X 7722, PY Sa 843, 323 = Sb 1315, [MY 228 = Oe 111], TH Of 34. Nom. and dat. sing., nom. plur. fem. and neut.: *newā, -āi, -ai, -a*.

ne-wo-ki-to, PY 59 = An 656, 44 = Aq 218. Probably PN; the form *ne-wo-ki-to wo-wi-ja* (An 656.7) implies a plur.

ne-wo-pe-o, PY Aa 786, Ab 554, Ad 688, Cc 665. PN, prob. an o-stem, since loc. appears to be the same as nom.

NI, Ideographic use: KN Fs 2+, 94 = F 841+, Uc 161, PY 6 = Ab 379+, 41 = An 35, Fg 253+, Fn 187, Ua 158, 97 = Un 2+, MY Ue 611: on evidence of KN 94 = F 841 equivalent to *su-za* 'figs'; taken over from Linear A, perhaps as abbreviation of Minoan word appearing as Greek gloss νικύλεον (Neumann, 1962).

Ligature with cup and circular ideogram: MY Ue 661.

no-da-ro, KN As 609, Dc 1228. MN.

no-di-zo, TI Z 11+. MN? Cf. *di-no-zo*.

no-do-ro-we, KN As 625. Obscure.

no-e-u, PY Jn 431. MN: *Noeus*.

no-nu-we, KN Od 562. Personal name, dat.

no-pe-re-a₂, PY 289 = Sa 682, 288 = Sa 790+. Nom. plur. neut., describing wheels: *nōpheleha* 'unserviceable'. [ἀνωφελής 6 B.C.+; cf. νώνυμος/ἀνώνυμος, etc.]

no-pe-re-e, PY 291 = Sa 794. Dual neut.: *nōphelehe*.

no-ri-wo-ki-de, TH Of 36. Perhaps dat. sing. of fem. derivative of next: *-worgidei*.

no-ri-wo-ko, PY Aa 98. Nom. plur. fem., a trade: *-worgoi*?

no-ri-wo-ko-jo, PY Ad 669. Gen. sing.

no-sa-ro, KN Dv 6059. MN.

no-si-ro, KN As 603, Ln 1568. MN.

nu-to, KN V 482, Xe 5913. MN.

nu-wa-ja, KN 221 = L 647. Nom. plur. neut., adj. describing cloth. See p. 320.

nu-wa-i-ja, KN L 592, L 5910.

o, As abbreviation of *o-pe-ro*[1], very common: e.g. KN 73 = Dl 943, 218 = Ld 598, PY 12 = Ad 671 (cf. *o-pe-ro* Ad 357), 176 = Ma 123+.

As abbreviation of *o-pa-wo-ta* (q.v.): PY 293 = Sh 737+.

In ligature with BARLEY: KN G 7509?

In ligature with *125* (cyperus): KN F 5079, PY Fa 16, Ua 434, Un 47, MY Ue 652; also alone = *125*+o: PY 97 = Un 2.

Ideographic use (not necessarily always the same commodity): PY 177 = Ma 90+, Un 219, TH Ug 3+.

o-, KN 213 = Le 641, PY 56 = An 657, 154 = Eq 213+. Prefix, also spelt *jo-*, usually attached to verbs and standing in initial position: *hō* 'thus'. [Cf. ὧ-δε, Alcman ὥ-τ', etc.]

o-a-po-te: see *a-po-te*.

o-a₂, PY 250 = Vn 20. Form of *o-da-a₂* used when not connective: perhaps *hō 'ha* reinforced form of *hō* 'thus'; see s.v. *o-da-a₂*.

o-da-a₂, PY 43 = Aq 64, 44 = Aq 218, 142 = Ed 317+, 114 = En 609+, 154 = Eq 213+, 175 = Ma 393+, 171 = Un 718. Phrase introducing the second and subsequent paragraphs of a list, hence at the beginning of a tablet indicates it belongs to a set of which it is not the first member: *hō d(e) aha* 'and thus'. See p. 423.

o-da-ke-we-ta, KN Sg 1811, So 4446. Nom. plur. neut., adj. describing wheels and cloths: perhaps *odakwenta* 'toothed' (i.e. with tooth-like decoration); Lejeune, 1968 *d*, p. 35, Heubeck, 1971 *a*.

o-da-ku-we-ta, KN [L 870], So 4435. Variant spelling.

o-da-tu-we-ta, KN 278 = So 894. Variant form: *odatwenta*.

o-da-*87-ta, KN 282 = So 4430+. Variant spelling, perhaps of *o-da-tu-we-ta*, with *87* = *twe*.

o-da-ra-o, KN Xe 5913. MN?

]*o-da-sa-to*: see *da-sa-to*.

o-da-*87-ta: see s.v. *o-da-ke-we-ta*.

o-de-ka-sa-to: see *de-ka-sa-to*.

o-de-qa-a₂, PY 304 = On 300. Lengthened form of *o-da-a₂*: *hō de qᵘ(e) aha* 'and also thus'. See p. 467.

o-di-do-si, *o-do-ke*: see s.v. *di-do-si*.

o-du, KN V 479. MN.

o-du-we, KN Od 696. Dat.?

o-du-ru-we, KN 83 = C 902. PN, dat.-loc. On evidence of Theban jar perhaps to be identified with Zakro (Catling and Millett, 1965, p. 35).

[*o-*]*du-ru-wo*, KN Co 910. Gen. Cf. *u-du-ru-wo*.

o-du-ru-wi-jo/-ja, KN Ai 982, 83 = C 902, TH Z 839. Ethnic adj.

o-du-*56-ro, PY 40 = An 261. MN.

o-ja-de, KN Fs 9. Obscure, PN?

o-ka¹, PY 56 = An 657 +. Title of a command held by a senior officer in the coast-guard: prob. *orkhā*, cf. ἀρχή, ὄρχαμος. See p. 185. Others suggest *holkas* 'merchant ship', but there is no reason why ships should be employed for this purpose.

o-ka², PY 317 = Ub 1318. Prob. noun, article made from leather: perhaps *okhai* 'supports', 'straps'. [ὀχή.] See p. 491.

o-ka³, PY [168 = Es 644], 167 = Es 650, Es 727. MN.

o-ka-ra, [KN X 7631?], PY 56 = An 657. At PY nom. plur., name of a class of men serving as coast-guards. See p. 430. At KN perh. MN.

o-ka-ra₃, PY 57 = An 519 +, 76 = Cn 3. More usual spelling of nom. plur.

o-ka-ri-jo, PY 62 = Cn 655. MN: *Oikhalios*. [Cf. Οἰχαλίη *Il.* II, 730.]

]*o-ke-te*, KN Xd 116. Obscure.

o-ke-te-u, PY Jn 693. MN: *Okheteus*?

o-ke-u, PY 145 = Ea 259, Ea 814. MN.

o-ki-ra, PY Cn 285. MN.

o-ki-ri-so, PY Cn 202. MN.

o-ki-ro, KN Da 1509. MN.

o-ko, PY Cn 436. MN.

o-ko-me-ne-u, PY Ea 780. MN: *Orkhomeneus*. [Cf. Ὀρχομενός as PN, *Il.* II, 511, 605.]

o-ko-te, KN Vc 126, Vd 137, Xd 7558. MN.

o-ku, KN As 8161, Da 1170, Dl 792 +. MN: *Ōkus*.

o-ku-ka, PY 61 = Cn 131, Cn 719. MN, nom. and dat.: *Ōgugās, -āi*? [Cf. PN Ὠγυγίη *Od.* I, 85.]

o-ku-na-wo, KN V 60. MN: *Ōkunāwos*.

o-ku-no, KN Da 1082. MN.

o-ku-su-wa-si, MY Ue 652. Obscure.

o-mi-ri-jo-i, PY Fn 356. Dat. plur., recipients of oil. Mühlestein (1958, p. 223): *Omrioihi* = Ὀμβρίοις 'Rain-spirits', cf. Ζεὺς ὄμβριος; but epenthetic β may be assumed on the analogy of δ in *a-di-ri-ja-te*.

o-mi-ri-so, KN C 911. MN.

o-mo-pi, KN 276 = Se 891, [Se 1007?]. Instr. plur.: perhaps *oimophi* 'with bands (of ivory)'. [Cf. δέκα οἶμοι ... κυάνοιο *Il.* XI, 24; etymology uncertain.] See p. 369.

o-mu-ka-ra, KN Od 666. MN?

o-na, KN M 559, PY Ua 158. At KN possibly PN, cf. next; at PY perhaps plur. of *o-no*, q.v.

]*o-na-de*[, KN Fh 5431. Acc. of PN with *-de*?

o-na-jo, KN Dv 1511, E 670, PY Jn 832. At

KN E 670 prob. ethnic adj.; at KN Dv 1511 and PY Jn 832 MN.

o-na-se-u, KN V 1523, PY 312 = An 1281, 255 = Jn 658 +. MN: *Onāseus*. [Cf. Cypr. Ὀνασι-; Szemerényi, 1957, p. 180.]

o-na-te-re, PY 114 = En 609 +, Wa 784. Nom. plur.: *onatēres* 'persons holding an *onaton*'. See p. 235. [Cf. ὀνήτωρ Hesych.]

o-na-to, PY 112 = Ea 825 +, 133 = Eb 846, 114 = En 609 +, 118 = Eo 211 +, 148 = Ep 613 +. Acc. sing. neut.: *onāton* 'a portion (of land) enjoyed', 'beneficiary right'. See pp. 235, 445.

o-na-ta, PY 140 = Eb 297 +, 149 = Ed 236, 142 = Ed 317. Acc. plur.: *onāta*.

o-ne-u, KN Dd 1207. MN: *Orneus*. [Ὀρνεύς.]

o-ni-ti-ja-pi, PY 242 = Ta 707. Instr. plur. fem. of adjective describing part of a chair: *ornīthiāphi* 'decorated with birds'. [ὀρνίθεος Aristoph. +.]

o-no¹, KN Fh 347 +, M 559, Xe 657, PY 41 = An 35, 55 = An 724 +, MY Oe 108 +. Nom. sing. of word meaning 'consideration', 'payment' (Chadwick, 1964 *b*); perhaps *onon* from root of ὀνίνημι (Lejeune, 1964 *a*). Cf. *o-na*. See p. 422.

o-no², KN 82 = Ca 895, Ca 7788?. Nom. plur.: *onoi* 'asses'. [ὄνος *Il.* XI, 558 +.]

o-no-ka-ra[, PY Mn 1412, Na 1058 (]*no-ka-ra-ro-re*). PN: perhaps loc.: *Ono-karaorei* 'Ass-head'. [Cf. Risch, 1966 *a*.]

o-no-we-wo-ro[, KN Xe 657. To be separated *o-no we-wo-ro*, cf. Fh 347; see *o-no*.

o-nu, KN Od 681. In view of association with wool, prob. variant spelling of *o-nu-ka*.

o-nu-ka, KN Ld 584, Ld 591, Od 485? Perhaps nom. sing.: *onux* (cf. *wa-na-ka* = *wanax*; Palmer 1963 *a*, p. 437). Sense obscure, but must be some part of or appendage to textiles which might be white or variegated (cf. *po-ki-ro-nu-ka*, *re-u-ko-nu-ka*). [Prob. same word as ὄνυξ, but in some technical sense.]

o-nu-ke, KN Ln 1568, M 683, Od 682, Ws 1703. Nom. plur. (or dat. sing.?): *onukhes*.

o-nu-ke-ja, PY Ab 194. Nom. plur. fem.: 'women who make *o-nu-ke*'.

o-nu-kẹ-ja-o, PY Ad 675. Gen. plur.

o-o-pe-ro-si: see *o-pe-ro-si*.

o-pa, KN 29 = Am 821, Ce 50, Dm 1184, E 971, L 695, 265 = Sd 4403 +, 273 = Sf 4420, 282 = So 4430, 264 = Ws 1704 +, PY 296 = Sh 736, Wr 1325 +. Nom. and gen. sing.: prob. a noun meaning roughly 'contribution'. See p. 420. [Etymology obscure; connexion with *soqᵘā (cf. ὀπάων) must be excluded.]

]*o-pa-ro-ze*, PY Un 1321. Obscure.

o-pa-we[, KN Dv 1434. Perhaps beginning of MN in gen.

o-pa-wo-ne-ja, KN Fh 339. Obscure, not to be connected with ὀπάων if from *soqᵘā; cf. *o-pa*.

o-pa-wo-ta, KN 300 = Sk 5670, 325 = Sk 8100, PY 292 = Sh 740 + . Nom. plur. neut.: prob. 'plates' or 'pads' attached to body-armour, perhaps *op-aworta*, literally 'hung on'. [*opi* + ἀείρω.] See p. 376.

o-pe, KN B 800. Obscure.

o-pe-qa, PY Cn 570. MN, dat., perhaps identical with *o-qe-qa*.

o-pe-ra-no, PY 255 = Jn 658 + . MN: *Ophelānōr*. [Cf. Boeot. Ὀφέλανδρος; Heubeck, 1957, p. 31.]

    o-pe-ra-no-ro, MY Ui 651. Gen.: *Ophelānoros*.

    o-pe-ra-no-re, MY Oe 126. Dat.: *Ophelānorei*.

o-pe-re-ta, PY An 209, 62 = Cn 655. MN: *Ophelestās* (Palmer). [Ὀφελέστης *Il.* VIII, 274.]

o-pe-ro[1], KN Ga 461 + , Gg 706, L 473 + , 283 = So 4442 + , PY 301 = Ac 1275 + , Ad 357, Cn 4 + , 182 = Ma 126 + , MY 107 = Ge 604. Often abbreviated to *o*. Annotation introducing missing quantity: prob. nom. sing. neut. *ophelos* 'deficit'. [In origin the same word as ὄφελος 'advantage', with different semantic development from 'that which is needed'.]

o-pe-ro[2], PY Eb 149 (*o-pe-ro-qe*), Eb 495, 148 = Ep 613. Nom. sing. masc. of pple.: *ophēlōn* 'being under obligation'.

    o-pe-ro-ta, PY 55 = An 724. Acc. sing. masc.: *ophēlonta*.

    o-pe-ro-te, PY 55 = An 724, 44 = Aq 218. Nom. (and acc.?) plur. masc.: *ophēlontes*.

    o-pe-ro-sa, PY 141 = Eb 338 (*o-pe-ro-sa-de*), 135 = Ep 704. Nom. sing. fem.: *ophēlonsa* (*de*).

    o-pe-ro-si, PY 184 = Nn 228 (*o-u-pe-ro-si*). 3rd plur. pres. indic.: (*hō*) *ophēlonsi* 'thus they owe'.

    o-po-ro, MY 105 = Ge 602 (*jo-o-po-ro*). 3rd plur. aor. indic.: (*hō*) *ophlon* 'thus they owed'.

o-pe-se-to, PY Cn 600. MN.

o-pe-ta, KN B 799. MN: *Opheltās*. [Ὀφέλτας.]

o-pe-te-re-u, PY Ea 805, 136 = Eb 294. MN. Cf. *o-pe-to-re-u*.

o-pe-te-we, KN So 4447. MN, dat.?

    o-pe-te-wo(-*qe*), KN L 593. Gen.?

o-pe-to-re-u, PY 135 = Ep 704. MN; variant or incorrect spelling of *o-pe-te-re-u*.

o-pi, KN 39 = As 1517, Fh 368, L 648 + , Mc 1508, Od 562 + , 162 = Uf 983 + , PY 33 = Ae 26, 32 = Ac 108, 31 = Ae 134. Preposition with dat.: *opi*, at KN with personal names 'in the charge or house of (a supervisor)', at PY with animals 'responsible for', 'in charge of'. [*ὀπι- in ὄπιθεν, ὀπώρα, etc., doublet of ἐπί; cf. Lat. *ob*, Osc. *op*, etc.] There is no compelling reason for postulating another word with the same spelling (Palmer, 1963*a*, p. 438, cf. p. 485); see further Killen, 1968.

o-pi-a₂-ra, PY 56 = An 657. Acc. plur. neut.: *opihala* 'coastal regions'. [ἔφαλος *Il.* II, 538 + .]

o-pi-da-mi-jo, PY 45 = An 830, 75 = Cn 608. Nom. plur. masc.: *opidāmioi* 'resident'. [ἐπιδήμιος *Od.* I, 194 + .]

o-pi-de-so-mo, PY 317 = Ub 1318. Nom. plur.: *opidesmoi* 'bindings'. [ἐπίδεσμος 'bandage', Aristoph. + .]

o-pi-e-de-i, PY 312 = An 1281. Prob. to be read as two words: *opi hedeï* 'at her seat' (i.e. shrine or temple). [ἕδος, *Il.* V, 360 + .]

o-pi-i-ja-pi, KN 266 = Sd 4401 + , 274 = Sf 4428. Instr. plur. fem.: part of the harness or equipment of a chariot: *opi-hiāphi* 'attachments to reins' (*hiā* from *seyə₂-* 'bind'), Ruijgh, 1967, p. 204. See also p. 365.

o-pi-ka-pe-e-we(-*qe*), PY 257 = Jn 829. Nom. plur., title of an overseer. See pp. 357, 512.

o-pi-ke-re-mi-ni-ja, PY 243 = Ta 708, 244 = Ta 714. Acc. plur. fem., some part of a chair: perhaps *opikelemnians* (cf. ἀμφικέλεμνον) or *opikrēmnians* (cf. κρημνός). See p. 343.

    o-pi-ke-re-mi-ni-ja-pi, PY 242 = Ta 707 + . Instr. plur.

o-pi-ke-ri-jo, PY An 615. PN: *Opiskherion*?

    o-pi-ke-ri-jo-de, PY 55 = An 724. Acc. + -*de*.

o-pi-ke-wi-ri-je-u, PY 237 = Ta 709. Nom. sing., description of a tripod-cauldron.

o-pi-ko-ru-si-ja, KN 325 = Sk 8100, Sk 8149. Description of 4 fittings as parts of armour; neut. plur.: *opikorusia* 'on the helmet'. [See *e-pi-ko-ru-si-jo*.]

o-pi-ko-wo, PY Jn 881. Nom. sing., perhaps a title: *opikowos*? (cf. *e-pi-ko-wo*).

o-pi-me-ne, PY An 7. Prob. to be divided: *opi mēnei* 'per month' (as opposed to daily rations).

o-pi-qi-na, KN Ld 584. Prob. to be divided: *o-pi qi-na*.

o-pi-ra-i-ja, PY Cn 1286. Obscure, poss. PN.

o-pi-ra₃-te-re, PY 251 = Vn 46. Nom. plur.: *opirhaistēres*, cf. ῥαιστήρ; perhaps not 'hammers' but some kind of fittings for beams. See p. 504. [Chadwick, *Nestor* 1/4/66, p. 431.]

o-pi-ri-mi-ni-jo, KN Sc 230. MN: *Opilimnios*. [Cf. Ἐπιλίμνιος title of Poseidon.]

o-pi-ro-qo, PY Aa 777, Ab 899, 13 = Ad 691. Nom. and gen. plur. fem.: *opiloiqʷoi*, -*ōn* 'remaining', 'supernumerary'. Cf. *pe-ri-ro-qo*. [ἐπίλοιπος Pindar + .]

o-pi-si-jo, KN As 1516 + , PY Jn 927. MN: *Opsios*. [Ὄψιος *IG* II, 868, ii, 20.]

o-pi-si-ri-ja-we, KN Lc 646, L 8105. In cloth context, obscure.

o-pi-su-ko, PY 257 = Jn 829, Jn 881. Nom. plur. (and sing.?): official title, possibly *opisukoi* 'overseers of figs'? See p. 357.

o-pi-te-ke-e-u, PY 97 = Un 2. Nom. sing., title of official?; perhaps error for *o-pi-te-u-ke-e-u*.

o-pi-te-u-ke-e-we, PY 50 = An 39, 91 = Fn 50 + . Nom. plur. and dat. sing., probably a title: *opiteukheēwes*, -*ēwei* 'overseer of τεύχεα' but exact sense unclear.

o-pi-te-u-ke-we, KN B 798. Prob. defective spelling.

o-pi-ti-ni-ja-ta, PY Eb 472, Eb 477. Nom. sing., title of a priest (cf. Ep 539).

o-pi-tu-ra-jo, PY Fn 187. Title or MN? Dat.: *Opithuraiōi*. [Cf. θυραῖος.]

o-po-qo, KN 266 = Sd 4401 +, 274 = Sf 4428. Nom. dual or plur.: *opōqᵘ̄ō*, *-oi* 'blinkers' (found in archaic tombs in Cyprus). [Cf. πρόσ-ωπον, μέτ-ωπον; Chadwick, *Nestor* 1/3/66, p. 429.]

o-po-ro: see s.v. *o-pe-ro²*.

o-po-ro-me-no, PY 168 = Es 644, 167 = Es 650 +. MN: *Hoplomenos*. [ὅπλομαι.]

o-po-ro-u-si-jo, KN As 603. MN.

o-qa, PY Jn 601. MN: *Ōqᵘās*? ["Ωπας.]

o-qa-ja, KN Db 5212 + 8369. MN.

o-qa-wo-ni, PY Fn 324. MN, dat.: *Oqᵘāwoni*? [Cf. ὀπάων *Il.* x, 58 +.]

o-qe e-ra-se, PY Cn 4. Apparently replacing the name of a man responsible for moving sheep from one station to another: perh. *hos qᵘe elase* 'and he who drove them'. [ἐλαύνω 'drive (animals)', *Od.* IX, 237; cf. Gallavotti, 1956, p. 8.]

o-qe-qa, PY Cn 45. MN, dat.; perhaps identical with *o-pe-qa*.

o-qe[ ]*si*, PY 197 = Na 406. Obscure, see p. 473.

o-qo-o-ki-te, KN L 588. Obscure (perhaps to be divided *o-qo-o ki-te*).

o-re-a₂, PY 143 = Ep 705. MN: *Orehās*. ['Ορέης.]

o-re-e-wo, PY Cn 600. MN, gen.: *Ore(h)ēwos*, making PN with *wo-wo*.

o-re-i, KN B 7034. Possibly loc.: *orehi* 'on the mountain'? [ὄρος.]

o-re-mo-a-ke-re-u, PY Jn 320. PN.

o-re-ne-ja, KN Ld 579 +, L 5108. Nom. plur. neut., adj. describing cloths: perhaps *ōleneia* 'decorated with angular pattern'. [Cf. ὠλένη, *ὤλενος: Ruijgh, 1967, p. 239.]

o-re-ne-a, KN L 593. Variant spelling.

[*o-*]*re-ne-o*, KN L 758. Dual: *ōleneō*.

o-re-o-po, KN M 720. Obscure.

o-re-ta, PY 56 = An 657. MN: *Orestās*. ['Ορέστης *Il.* v, 705 +.]

o-re-te-wo, KN Dq 439, [Dq 441]. MN, gen.?

o-ri-ko, MY 46 = Au 102. Hardly man's name, perhaps nom. plur. [See Chadwick, *MT* II, p. 106.]

o-ri-mo, KN Ap 5748. WN?

o-ro-do-ko, PY Vn 865. MN.

o-ro-jo, PY 154 = Eq 213. See pp. 268, 455.

o-ro-ke-we, PY [Fn 324], Gn 428. MN, dat.

o-ro-me-no, PY 32 = Ae 108, 31 = Ae 134 +. Nom. sing. masc.: *opi . . . (h)oromenos* 'watching over (animals)'. [Cf. ἐπὶ . . . ὄρονται *Od.* XIV, 104; prob. < *ser-, Avest. *haraiti* 'watches'.]

o-ro-qa, KN V 479. MN.

o-ro-ti-jo, PY 55 = An 724. MN?

o-ru-ma-to, PY 76 = Cn 3. PN, cf. 'Ερύμανθος.

o-ru-ma-si-ja-jo, PY 57 = An 519. Prob. serves as ethnic to *o-ru-ma-to*.

o-ru-we-ro, PY Jn 725. MN. The same man as *po-ru-we-ro*, but which is correct? See p. 511.

o-sa-po-to, KN Ap 5748. WN?

]*o-se-ko-do*, KN Fh 371. MN?

o-ta-ki, MY 93 = Fo 101. Man's or woman's name, dat.: *Oitalki*. [Heubeck, 1963 b, p. 75; cf. *a-ko-so-ta*.]

o-ta-pa-ro-te-wa-ro, MY 228 = Oe 111. To be divided *o-ta pa-ro te-wa-ro*? First word obscure; see p. 323.

o-ta-re-wo, KN E 1035. Obscure, MN or PN?

o-te, PY 235 = Ta 711. Conj.: *hote* 'when'. [ὅτε *Il.* I, 397 +.]

o-te-pe-o-jo, PY 154 = Eq 213. PN, gen. See p. 455.

o-te-ra, MY Oe 106. WN, gen.

o-te-se-u, KN Db 1241. MN.

o-ti-na-wo, PY Cn 285. MN: *Ortināwos*.

o-ti-ri-ja, PY Aa 313. Nom. plur. fem., name of a trade: *-triai*.

o-ti-ra₂, PY Ab 417. Alternative spelling.

o-ti-ra₂-o, PY Ad 663. Gen. plur.: *-triāōn*.

o-to-pe-da-ko-we-de-[, PY Sh 739 rev. Dubious reading.

o-to-no, KN De 1371 + 8741, [Dv 8289], [PY Vn 493?]. MN.

o-to-wo-o, PY An 616. MN, gen. Defective spelling for *o-to-wo-⟨we⟩-o*, see s.v. *o-tu-wo-we*.

o-to-wo-wi-je, MY 303 = V 659. WN.

o-tu, PY An 5. MN.

o-tu-wo-we, PY 255 = Jn 658. MN.

o-to-wo-we-i, PY Vn 851. Dat.

o-two-we-o, PY 40 = An 261. Gen.

o-to-wo[-*we-o?*], PY 40 = An 261 rev. Alternative spelling. See also *o-to-wo-o*.

o-two-we-o: see s.v. *o-tu-wo-we*.

o-u-, KN 207 = V 280, PY 16 = Ad 686, 135 = Ep 704, 177 = Ma 90 +, 195 = Na 245 +, 198 = Ng 319 +. Negative particle: *ou* 'not'. [οὐ.] See also *o-u-ki*, *o-u-qe*.

o-u-ki-, KN 207 = V 280. Negative particle or adj.?: *ouk(h)i* or *oukis* (= οὔτις).

o-u-ko, MY Oe 108, Oe 120. Nom. sing. neut., associated with wool.

o-u-ka, MY 228 = Oe 111. Nom. plur.?

o-u-qe, KN 213 = Le 641, 270 = Sd 4402 +, PY 43 = Aq 64, Eb 149, 148 = Ep 613 +, 248 = Va 15. Negative conjunction: *ouqᵘe* 'and not'. [οὔτε 'and not'.]

o-u-ru-to: see *-u-ru-to*.

o-u-te-mi: see *-te-mi*.

o-wa-ko, PY 61 = Cn 131, Jn 725. MN, nom. and dat.

o-wa-si-jo, KN Ra 1558. MN.

o-we-to, KN Dm 1184. MN, gen.

o-wi-da, PY Jn 725. MN.

o-wi-de: see *-wi-de*.

o-wi-de-ta-i, PY 171 = Un 718, Wa 731 (]*o-wi-de-ta*[). Dat. plur.: perhaps *owidertāhi* 'sheep-flayers'. See p. 458.

o-wi-ro, KN Dd 1218. MN: *Owilos*? [Cf. 'Oΐλεύς *Il*. XIII, 697+.]

o-wi-to-no, PY Aa 775, Ab 277, Ad 685, 56=An 657, 44=Aq 218. PN: *-t(h)nos*?

  o-wi-ti-ni-jo, PY 56=An 657. Ethnic adj.: *-t(h)nioi*.

o-wo-ta, PY Jn 725. MN.

o-wo-to, PY 40=An 261, Vn 130. MN, nom. and dat.

o-wo-we, PY 236=Ta 641. Nom. sing. masc., describing a tripod-cauldron: *oiwōwēs* 'with a single handle' or *owwowens* 'provided with handles'? See p. 498.

o-wo-ze, PY 141=Eb 338. Error or abbreviated spelling of *o-u-wo-ze*, see s.v. *wo-ze*.

o-za-mi[, PY 42=An 37. Obscure, see p. 174.

o-ze-to: see *-ze-to*.

o-*22-di, KN As 1520. MN.

o-*34-ta, PY 57=An 519, 58=An 654. Nom. plur.; name of a class of men.

o-*35-ta, TH Ug 3. MN, cf. prec.?

  o-*34-ta-o, TH Of 33; prob. gen. of same name, showing that *34 and *35 are variants of the same sign.

PA, Abbreviation of *pa-ra-jo/-ja* 'old', applied to women and sheep: KN Ak 614+, C 394+, 67=Dd 1171+.

  Abbreviation of *pa-ra-wa-jo* 'cheek-pieces': PY 294=Sh 733+.

  Annotation on CLOTH: obscure: KN Ln 1568.

  Ligatured with CLOTH: KN L 178+, PY La 623+, Un 853.

  Ligatured with OIL, probably=*pa-ko-we* 'sage-scented': PY 306=Fr 1202+.

  Ligatured with ideogram *125 (cyperus): PY 97=Un 2.

  Ideographic use, associated with DA: KN 157=Uf 835+ (see p. 270). Also in obscure context: PY Un 1319.

  As subdivision of WOOL unit: TH Of 26, Of 28, Of 40+.

pa, PY 256=Ja 749, Jn 601. Nom. sing. masc.: *to-so-pa*=*tos(s)os pans* 'so much (bronze) in all'. [πᾶς, probably not from **kwānt-*; cf. Tokh. B. *po*, plur. *ponta*; Chadwick and Baumbach, 1963, pp. 233–4.] Cf. *ku-su-pa*.

pa-sa, KN X 8109, [90=G 820 is a false reading]. Perhaps fem.: *pansa*.

pa-te, KN B 1055. Nom. plur. masc.: *(tos(s)oi) pantes*.

pa-ta, KN C 917[+]918. Nom. plur. neut.: *panta*.

pa-to[, PY 150=Ed 411. If correct reading, perhaps gen. sing. masc. or neut.: *pantos* '(total) of the whole'.

pa-si, KN 200=Fp 1+, 206=Gg 705+, PY 254=Jn 389. Dat. plur.: *pansi*, esp. in *pa-si-te-o-i* (KN)=*pansi theoihi* 'to all the gods'.

pa-da-je-u, PY An 192, Eb 159+. Nom. sing. prob. a title or ethnic rather than a name; apparently also spelt *pa-de-we-u*, q.v. Cf. *pa-de*, *pa-de-we*.

pa-da-je-we, PY Eb 1347, 123=Eo 444. Dat.

pa-de, KN 200=Fp 1+, Fs 8, Ga 456. Dat. sing., recipient of oil, possibly a divine name.

  pa-de-i, KN 203=Ga 953[+]955. Alternative spelling of dat.

pa-de-we, PY Un 219. Dat. sing., perhaps divine name, cf. *pa-de*.

pa-de-we-u, PY 148=Ep 613. Apparently=*pa-da-je-u*, q.v.; not an error since it occurs twice on this tablet.

pa-di-jo, KN Sc 224. MN: *Pandiōn*. [Πανδίων *Il*. XII, 372.]

pa-i-ti-ja, KN Ap 639. WN: *Phaistiā*. [Ethnic of Φαιστός, see *pa-i-to*.]

pa-i-to, KN Da 1156+, E 36, 94=F 841, Ga 416+. PN: *Phaistos*. [Φαιστός *Il*. II, 648.]

  pa-i-ti-jo/-ja, KN Ak 828, 74=Dp 1061, 89=E 777, 213=Le 641, Od 681+. Ethnic adj.: *Phaistios*.

pa-ja-ni, KN Ap 639. WN.

pa-ja-ni-jo, KN Fp 354. Dat. sing., recipient of oil: MN? [Connexion with Παιάν < *Παιάϝων (see *pa-ja-wo-ne*) must be excluded, unless this is a defective spelling.]

pa-ja-ro, KN As 1519. MN.

pa-ja-so, KN Dc 1203, Dv 8290+8362. MN.

pa-ja-wo-ne, KN 208=V 52. (Cf. *pa-ja-o-ne* C 394?) Dat., in a list of divine names: *Paiā-wonei*. [Παιήων *Il*. V, 401+.]

pa-ka, KN V 1523, PY An 7, MY Oe 112. MN, nom. and dat.

pa-ka-a-ka-ri, PY 196=Na 926. PN, prob. to be divided *pa-ka a-ka-ri*: perh. *Pāgā Akharis* or sim.

pa-ka-na, KN 261=Ra 1540+. Nom. plur. neut.: *phasgana* 'swords' or 'daggers'? [φάσγανον *Il*. XXIII, 824+, Cypr. according to *Anec. Gr.* 1095; on the suggested meaning 'daggers' see Boardman, 1963, pp. 79–80; Snodgrass, 1967, p. 22.]

pa-ke-ta, KN U 4478. MN.

pa-ke-te-ja, PY Aa 662, Ab 745, Ab 746. Nom. plur. (in Ab 745 changed from dual *pa-ke-te-jo*), women's trade, perhaps connected with *pa-ko-to*, q.v. (Ruijgh, 1963, p. 241; Chadwick, 1964a, p. 323: 'measurers'?).

  pa-ke-te-ja-o(-*qe*), PY 12=Ad 671. Gen. plur. with -*qe*.

pa-ke-te-re, PY [251=Vn 46], Vn 879, Wr 1415, MY 234=Ue 611 rev. Nom. plur., name of some small fitting, possibly metal, not necessarily at MY a vessel: perhaps *pāktēres* 'pegs', 'bolts'. [πήγνυμι.]

pa-ke-te-ri-ja, MY Wt 506. Neut. plur., diminutive of prec.: *pāktēria*?

pa-ke-we, KN L 7514. Obscure, possibly nom. plur. *pakhewes* 'thick'. [παχύς.]

pa-ki-ja-na, PY 138=Eb 409+, 114=En 609, 119=Eo 224, Na 561. Probably PN, variant in -*ānā* of next, in some cases loc. [A variant of the fem. adj. in -*āniā* > -*ān(n?)ā* has been proposed but is unnecessary.]

pa-ki-ja-ne, PY Vn 19, Xa 113. Nom. plur., PN: -*ānes*, one of the Nine Towns of the Hither Province. No convincing interpretation has been proposed; the root is probably non-Greek, cf. Ἀκαρνᾶνες, Ἀγριᾶνες, etc.

pa-ki-ja-na-de, PY Fn 187, Fr 1209+, 250=Vn 20. Acc. plur.+-*de*.

pa-ki-ja-si, PY 51=An 18, 75=Cn 608, 172=Tn 316+. Loc. plur.: -*ānsi*.

pa-ki-ja-pi, PY 257=Jn 829, Ma 221. Instr. (abl.?) plur.: -*āmphi*.

pa-ki-ja-ni-jo, PY Fr 1236. Ethnic adj.: -*ānios* (*agros*) 'territory of P.'.

pa-ki-ja-ni-jo-jo, PY 309=Fr 1224. Gen. sing. masc.: -*ānioio* (*mēnos*) 'month of P.', i.e., when the great festival takes place at P. [For derivation of month-name from place name, cf. Μουνυχιών.]

pa-ki-ja-ni-jo-i, PY Fr 1216. Dat. plur.: 'at the feast of P.' or 'for the people of P.?'.

pa-ki-ja-ni-ja, PY 114=En 609, [258=Jo 438], 304=On 300. PN, = *pa-ki-ja-na*. [Cf., e.g., Ἀκαρνᾶνες/Ἀκαρνανία.]

pa-ko, PY 49=An 427, (perhaps to be restored 52=An 207, 11). PN. [In PY Fr 1216 probably error for *pa-ko-we*.]

]*pa-ko-qe*, KN Ch 5728. Name of ox; cf. *po-da-ko*.

pa-ko-to, PY 237=Ta 709. Nom. dual *phaktō*, name of vessel; cf. φάκτον· μέτρον παρὰ Ἀρκάσι, κοτύλαι ἀττικαὶ τρεῖς *Lexicon Cyrilli* (see Naoumides, 1968, p. 280). Cf. *pa-ke-te-ja*?

pa-ko-wa, PY La 624. Obscure.

pa-ko-we, PY 306=Fr 1202, 307=Fr 1220+. Nom. sing. neut., adj. describing oil: *sphakowen* 'scented with sage'.

pa-ku-ro₂, PY 44=Aq 218, Jn 750. MN.

pa-ma-ko, PY 318=Un 1314. Nom. sing.?, possibly *pharmakon* 'drug'. [φάρμακον *Od.* IV, 230+.]

pa-ṇa-ki, MY 93=Fo 101. WN?, dat.: *Phainaki*? [Φαίναξ.]

pa-na-pi, PY Cn 45. PN, instr. plur.: *Phanāphi*? [Cf. Φανά Aetolia.]

pa-na-re-jo, KN As 1516, 39=As 1517+, PY Fn 867. MN, nom. and dat.: *Panareios*, -*ōi*. [Cf. Πανάρης.]

pa-na-so, KN E 843, Uf 121+, X 1018. PN? Palmer: *Parnas(s)os*? [Παρνασ(σ)ός.]

pa-pa-jo, PY 254=Jn 389. MN: *Pamphaios*. [Πάμφαιος.]

pa-pa-ra-ḳị, TH Of 25. MN, dat.? [Cf. next.]

pa-pa-ra-ko, PY Jn 845. MN.

pa-pa-ro, KN Vc 206, Xd 207+, PY Cn 643+. MN: *Barbaros*, *Parparos*? [Βάρβαρος; PN Πάρπαρος.]

pa-pu-so, PY Jn 415. MN.

pa-qo-si-jo, KN [B 988, Dq 441], PY 253=Jn 310+. MN: *Pangᵘōsios*. [Cf. Παμβωτάδαι Attic deme.]

pa-qo-si-jo-jo, PY 253=Jn 310. Gen.: *Pangᵘōsioio*.

pa-qo-ta, PY 255=Jn 658, Jn 725. MN: *Pangᵘōtās*. [Cf. prec.]

pa-ra, KN [299=Sk 789?], 325=Sk 8100. MN?

pa-ra-jo, PY An 298, 62=Cn 655+, 292=Sh 740+. Nom. plur. masc.: *palaioi* 'old', sometimes equivalent to 'last year's'. Possibly not the same word in all contexts; for evidence of meaning see *pa-ra-ja* below. [παλαιός *Il.* XIV, 108+; traditionally connected with τῆλε, but this must now be rejected in the light of Myc. spelling with *pa-*.]

pa-ra-ja, KN Ln 1568, 275=Se 879, U 124, PY 286=Sa 787, 287=Sa 793, TH Of 34. Nom. plur. neut. (and fem.?), dat. sing. fem.: *palaia*, -*āi*, contrasted at PY with *ne-wa*= *newa* 'new' in Sa 843.

pa-ra-ke-se-we, PY Fn 324. MN, dat.: *Prāxēwei*. [Szemerényi, 1957, p. 180.]

pa-ṛạ-ḳẹ-te-e-u, PY Jn 832. Nom. sing., description of a smith.

pa-ra-ke-te-e-we, PY Jn 750. Nom. plur.

pa-ra-ke-we(-*qe*), PY 239=Ta 642. Instr. sing., name of a material used to inlay furniture, see p. 340.

pa-ra-ku-we, PY 244=Ta 714, 241=Ta 715. Variant spelling.

pa-ra-ko, KN Sc 258, PY Eb 377+, 119=Eo 224, 131=Ep 301, 148=Ep 613. MN, nom. and dat.: *Plakos*? *Phalaikos*? -*ōi*. [Πλάκος mountain *Il.* VI, 396; Φάλαικος.]

pa-ra-ku, PY Cn 201. Obscure, MN?

pa-ra-ku-ja, KN Ld 575. Nom. plur. neut., adj. describing textiles; cf. **56-ra-ku-ja*.

pa-ra-ti-jo, KN 78=C 914. MN, dat.: *Pallantiōi*? [Παλλάντιος, adj.]

pa-ra-to, KN Db 1373. MN: *Platōn*? [Πλάτων.]

pa-ra-u-jo, KN Ga 425. MN?

pa-ra-wa-jo, KN 299=Sk 789, [325=Sk 8100], PY 293=Sh 737. Nom. dual: *paraw(w)aiō* 'pair of cheek-pieces'. [Cf. παρειαί 'cheeks', Lesb. παραύα.]

pa-ra-we-jọ, PY 318=Un 1314. Reading and meaning uncertain, see p. 505.

pa-ra-we-wo, PY 42=An 37, 250=Vn 20. Obscure; see p. 175.

pa-ra-[.]-*we-jo*, KN Sp 4451. Reading uncertain, apparently dual adj.

pa-re, KN Dl 8177, Sc 247, Sc 249? MN: *Phalēs*? [Φαλής.]

]*pa-ri-so*: see [*ku-*]*pa-ri-so*.

pa-ṛị-to, MY Wt 505. Obscure.

pa-ro, KN Ai 115, C 908+, Dk 945, 216=L 871+, PY An 129+, 61=Cn 131+, 109= Ea 782+, Eb 747+, 118=Eo 211+, 131=

Ep 301+, 305=Fr 1184, Mb 1401, Mn 162+, Pa 49+, 96=Un 138+, MY 228=Oe 111?. Prep. with dat.: *paro* 'from or at the hands of (a person)'. [παρά Homer+; πάρο Alcaeus, fr. 130, 12 Lobel-Page (Taillardat, 1960, p. 3); see also Householder, 1959*b*.]

pa-ro-ke-ne-[to], PY 16=Ad 686. 3rd sing. aor. middle: *ou paro-geneto* 'did not present himself'. [Cf. καί σφιν παρεγίγνετο δαιτί *Od.* XVII, 173.]

pa-sa-ja, KN 203=Ga 953, X 451. Obscure, perhaps divine name.

pa-sa-ko-me-no, KN Vc 211. MN: *Psakomenos?*

pa-sa-ro, PY 247=Ta 716. Nom. dual, objects made of gold: possibly *psalo* 'chains'. [Cf. ψάλιον; Palmer, 1963*a*, p. 358, whose objections to the interpretation *passalo* are sound.]

pa-se-ri-jo, MY Oe 121. Patronymic adj.?, dat.: 'the son of P.'. [Cf. *u-wa-si-jo ko-wo* KN Ai 115.]

pa-si[1]: see s.v. *pa*.

pa-si[2], PY 135=Ep 704. 3rd sing. pres.: *phāsi* 'says, affirms'. [φησί Homer+.]

pa-si-te-o-i: see s.v. *pa, te-o*.

pa-ta, PY Cn 40. MN, dat.: *Phantāi?* [Φάντης.]

pa-ta-ja, KN 264=Ws 1704+. Nom. plur. neut., on sealings with ideogram showing stick with point, perhaps a small throwing-spear or javelin, different from the ARROW ideogram on KN R 4482: perhaps *paltaia* 'javelins'. [Cf. παλτόν 'dart' Aristoph.+.]

pa-ta-jo-i, PY 257=Jn 829. Dat. plur.: *paltaioihi*.

pa-ta-re[, KN Xd 58. Obscure.

pa-ta-ti-jo, KN C 911. Perhaps adj. from personal name: '(the slave) of P.'.

pa-ta-u-na, KN As 608 [+] 625. MN?

pa-te[1], PY 28=An 607. Nom. sing.: *patēr* 'father'. [πατήρ Homer+.]

pa-te-de, PY 28=An 607, *patēr de* 'and the father'.

pa-te[2]: see s.v. *pa*.

pa-te-ko-to, PY An 7, Fn 1427? MN, dat.

pa-ti, KN As 1516, Dd 1281. MN.

pa-to[: see s.v. *pa*.

pa-to-ro, KN Uf 198. MN.

pa-to-wo-te, PY Jn 706. PN, loc.

pa-wa-so, KN Sc 258. MN.

pa-wa-wo, KN Sc 254, PY Cn 285, Vn 493. MN.

pa-we-a, KN 211=Lc 532+, 214=Ld 571+, 219=L 594+. Nom. plur. neut.: *pharwe(h)a* 'pieces of cloth'. [φᾶρος *Od.* V, 258, *Il.* II, 43+; cf. Lett. *burves* 'sails'.]

*pa-we-a*₂, KN Ld 787+, MY 227=Oe 127, L 710. Variant spelling: *pharweha*.

pa-we-o, KN L 651. Gen. plur.?: *pharwe(h)ōn*.

]*pa-we-pi*, KN L 104. Instr. plur.: *pharwesphi*.

pa-we-si, MY 228=Oe 111. Dat. plur.: *pharwes(s)i*.

pa-wi-no, KN B 799, B 805. MN.

pa-wo, KN Ws 8499. On a sealing, perhaps *pharwos* sing. (see *pa-we-a*), but context obscure.

pa-wo-ke, PY Aa 795, Ab 558. Nom. plur., description of women: *pan-worges* 'maids of all work'? [Chadwick, 1967*a*.]

pa-wo-ko, PY 13=Ad 691 (*pa-wo-ko-qe*), La 632. Gen. plur.: *panworgōn*. Possibly not the same word in La 632.

pa-za-ti, KN Dl 948. MN.

pa-ze, KN V 114. MN?

pa₂-: for words beginning *pa₂-*, see under *qa-*.

pa₃-: for words beginning *pa₃-* see under **56*.

PE, Abbreviation of *pe-ru-si-nu-wo]-wa* 'last year's': (of women) KN 19=Ak 627+, (of sheep) KN 69=Df 1119+.

Annotation to CLOTH (=*pe-ko-to*? Killen, 1966*c*): KN 213=Le 641, Ln 1568+, cf. PY La 630.

Annotation to TUNIC+KI (=*pe-ne-we-ta*? Killen, 1966*c*): KN Ld 595.

Annotation to **146*: KN M 1645, M 7373.

Ligatured with WHEAT: KN 94=F 841 (cf. PY Un 1319?).

Ligatured with INGOT: KN Oa 733, Oa 734.

Ideographic uses: PY Un 219, Un 1319; used to measure wool: KN Od 1062+, to measure mint: MY 105=Ge 602+.

pe-da, KN V 114. Prep. with acc.?: *peda wastu* 'to the town'? [Chadwick, 1968*b*, p. 20.]

pe-da-i-je-ro[, KN Fh 2013. Possibly to be divided: *peda hieron?*

pe-da-i-ra, KN Fh 341. MN.

pe-de-we-sa, PY 237=Ta 709. Nom. sing. fem., adj. describing a portable hearth: *pedwessa* 'equipped with feet'.

pe-di-je-we, PY 58=An 654. Nom. plur., name of a class of men: *pediēwes*. [Cf. Πεδιεῖς.] See pp. 192, 430.

pe-di-e-wi, PY Wr 1328. Dat. sing.?

pe-di-je-wi-ja, PY Va 1324. Nom. plur., in context with spears and axles: *pediēwiai* 'infantry spears'?

pe-di-ra, PY 317=Ub 1318. Nom. plur. neut.: *pedīla* 'sandals' or 'footwear'? [πέδιλα *Il.* XXIV, 341+.]

pe-di-ro, PY 317=Ub 1318. Gen. plur.: *pedīlōn*.

pe-di-ro-i, PY 317=Ub 1318. Dat. plur.: *pedīloihi*.

pe-i, PY 57=An 519+, 190=Na 395. Dat. plur. 3rd pers. pron.: *sphehi? spheis?* 'them'. [Hom., etc. σφι(ν), Att.-Ion. σφίσι(ν), Arc. σφεις.]

pe-ka-wo, KN Vc 66, Xd 80. MN.

pe-ke-u, MY 105=Ge 602, 106=Ge 603+. MN: *Sperkheus?* [Landau, 1958, p. 101.]

pe-ki-ta, PY 115=En 74, 122=Eo 160, 120=Eo 276. MN.

pe-ki-ti-ra₂, PY [Aa 891], Ab 578. Nom. plur. fem., a woman's trade: *pektriai* 'wool-carders'. [Cf. δμωαὶ...εἴρια πείκετε χερσίν *Od.* xviii, 316.]

pe-ki-ti-ra₂-o, PY 3=Ad 694. Gen. plur.: *pektriāōn*.

pe-ki-ti[, KN Ld 656. To be restored as this word?

pe-ko, KN Dc 8080, Dv 1621, Dv 7098, PY 77= Cn 418. Prob. MN ('collector') at KN, perhaps adj. at PY. [Palmer: *perkos* (cf. περκνός 'dark', πέρκος 'a kind of hawk'), 1963a, p. 443.]

pe-ko-to, KN 210=Lc 526+, L 698+. Textile term, connected with *pe-ki-ti-ra₂*? See p. 315.

pe-ma, KN E 1569, 101=Ga 675+, PY 152= Er 312, 153=Er 880. Nom. sing. neut.: *sperma* 'seed' (of wheat and coriander). [σπέρμα Homer+.]

pe-mo, PY 133=Eb 846+, 117=En 467+, 121=Eo 247, 131=Ep 301, 154=Eq 213, 167=Es 650. Variant form: *spermo* (cf. *a-mo*).

pe-me̜, PY 33=Ae 26. Possibly MN, dat.: see p. 420.

pe-ne-we-ta, KN 214=Ld 571+, L 593, 216=L 871. Nom. plur. neut.; perhaps *sphēnwenta* 'with wedges', see p. 487. [σφήν Aesch.+; cf. σφηνόπους.]

pe-ne-we-te, KN L 5108. Nom. dual: *sphēnwente*?

pe-pi-te-me-no-jo, TH Ug 1+. MN, gen.: *Pepithmenoio*. [Mühlestein, *Nestor* 1/12/64, p. 361.]

pe-po-ro, KN De 6060, PY Jn 601. MN: *Peplos*? [Πέπλος.]

[**?pe-**]**pu₂-te-me-no**, PY 153=Er 880. Probably *pephutēmenon* (or *-tmenon*?) 'planted with trees'. [Cf. γῆ πεφυτευμένη Her.] See p. 267.

pe-qa-to, KN 270=Sd 4402, 271=Sd 4422. Nom. sing., part of chariot: *peggᵘaton* < *ped-gᵘaton* 'foot-board'. [Wild, 1962, p. 128.]

pe-qe-ro-jo, PY Sa 768. MN, gen.

pe-qe-u, KN Vd 137, PY Jn 693. MN.

pe-qe-we, PY Cn 45, Fn 79. Dat.

pe-qo-no, KN B 798. MN.

pe-qo-ta, PY 116=En 659, 123=Eo 444. Perhaps title or description used to distinguish two men of the same name.

pe-ra-a-ko-ra-i-jo, PY 304=On 300. Possibly nom. plur. ethnic or variant of PN *pe-ra₃-ko-ra-i-ja* (q.v.).

pe-ra-ko-no, MY Oe 118. MN?

pe-ra-ko-ra-i-ja: see s.v. *pe-ra₃-ko-ra-i-ja*.

pe-ra₂, KN X 999. Obscure.

pe-ra₂-wo̜[, KN Xd 98. Obscure.

pe-ra₃-ko-ra-i-ja, PY 199=Ng 332, Wa 114. PN, the name of the Further Province (see pp. 144, 416): *Peraigolaiā* or sim. [πέρα; cf. Αἰγαλέον; Chadwick, 1963a, p. 138.]

pe-ra-ko-ra-i-ja, PY Pa 398. Variant or erroneous form?

pe-ra₃-qo, PY 179=Ma 193. Nom. plur., name of a group of men, possibly *Peraigᵘoi*. [Περαιβοί; see p. 294.]

pe-re, KN Od 562, PY Cc 1284, 172=Tn 316, 318=Un 1314. Probably in all cases 3rd sing. pres.: *pherei* 'carries', 'brings'. See p. 460.

pe-re-i-to, PY Wr 1327. On sealing, apparently with HORSE ideogram.

pe-re-ke, KN 225=L 520. Probably MN: see p. 488.

pe-re-ke-u, PY Cn 1287. Nom. sing., man's trade: possibly *plekeus* 'weaver'. [Cf. πλοκεύς Epicharmus+.]

pe-re-ke-we, PY Ae 574+, MY Oe 130. Nom. plur. and dat. sing.: *-ēwes*, *-ēwei*, at MY in WOOL context.

pe-re-ko, KN Ag 88. MN.

pe-re-ku-ta, PY An 172. Nom. sing. or plur.: *presgutās* 'old man'. [Att. πρεσβύτης, Dor. πρείγυς, πρειγεύτας, etc.]

pe-re-ku-wa-na-ka, PY 248=Va 15. MN: *Presguwanax*.

pe-re-qo-ni-jo, PY 59=An 656. Prob. MN: *Presgᵘōnios*? [Cf. Πρέσβων, Πρεσβωνιάδης.]

pe-re-qo-no, PY Jn 725. MN: *Presgᵘōnos*? [Cf. prec.]

pe-re-qo-no-jo, PY Ea 270, Jn 605. Gen.: *-oio*.

pe-re-qo-ta, KN Ce 50, PY An 192, Eb 159, 116= En 659, 148=Ep 613. MN, nom. and dat., also spelt in gen. *qe-re-qo-ta-o* (q.v.): *Pēleqᵘhontās, -tāi*. [Cf. Boeot. Πειλε-; hypocoristic Τήλεφος.]

pe-re-ta, PY 255=Jn 658, Jn 725. MN.

pe-re-u-ro-na-de, PY 53=An 1. PN, acc.+-*de*: *Pleurōna-de* 'to Pleuron'. [Πλευρών, Aetolia *Il.* ii, 639+.]

pe-re-u-ro-ni-jo, PY 59=An 656. Nom. sing. of ethnic adj., or used as MN?: *Pleurōnios*.

pe-re-wa-ta, KN Vc 183, PY An 129. MN. [Cf. *pe-re-*82-ta.]

pe-re-wo-te, PY Na 513, Xa 176. PN, loc. [*Phrēwotei* (φρέαρ) Doria, 1961, p. 433; or for *Phlei(wo)-wontei* (φλεώς) Lejeune, 1969, p. 51?]

pe-re-*82, PY 172=Tn 316, 313=Un 6. Divine name, dat. fem.: possibly *Preswāi*. [Cf. Πέρση, Περσε-φόνη; Chadwick, 1968a, p. 65.]

pe-re̜-*82-jo, PY 172=Tn 316. Probably dat.-loc. of derivative adj.: *Preswaiōi*? 'at the shrine of P.'.

pe̜-re-*82-ta, KN As 602. MN. [If *82=swa, cf. *pe-re-wa-ta*.]

pe-ri-je-ja, KN 156=Uf 1031. Man's or woman's name?

pe-ri-jo-ta(-qe), KN V 1002. MN.

pe-ri-ke, MY 234=Ue 611. Nom. plur., name of a vessel: *pelikes*. [πέλιξ· κύλιξ ἢ προχοΐδιον Cratin, 5 B.C. ap. Poll.; cf. Att. πελίκη=χοῦς, Aeol. πελίκα 'basin'.]

pe-ri-ke̜[, MY Au 609. MN, to be restored: *Periklewēs* or sim.?

pe-ri-me-de, PY 59=An 656. MN: *Perimēdēs*.

pe-ri-me-de-o, PY 43=Aq 64. Gen.: *Perimēdeos*.

pe-ri-mo, KN Dv 5841 (*p̣e-ri-mo*), PY 43 = Aq 64. MN: Perimos. [Πέριμος *Il.* xvi, 695.]

pe-ri-no, PY 58 = An 654, Jn 706. MN: *Perinos?* [Palmer; short form to *Περίνοος or the like.]

pe-ri-qo-ta, PY Jn 693. MN: *Perigᵘōtās?* [Cf. Περιβωτάδας (Georgiev); see p. 94.]

pe-ri-qo-ta-o, KN Dq 42, Dq 46. Gen.: *-tāo*.

pe-ri-qo-te-jo, KN Da 1172 +, 65 = Db 1232, De 1231 +. Probably nom. plur., adj. describing sheep, rather than MN; exact function obscure.

pe-ri-ra-wo, PY 58 = An 654. MN: *Perilāwos*. [Περίλαος.]

pe-ri-ro-qo, KN V 479. Probably nom. plur. introducing list of men: *periloiqᵘoi* 'remaining'. [περίλοιπος Aristophanes +; cf. *o-pi-ro-qo*.]

pe-ri-ta, KN 232 = K 875, V 60. MN: *Peritās*. [Περίτας.]

pe-ri-te, PY Vn 130. MN, dat.

pe-ri-to-wo, KN [Vc 171], Vc 195, V 655. MN: *Perithowos*. [Πειρίθοος (Πει- metrical lengthening) *Il.* xii, 129.]

pe-ro(-qe), KN As 605. MN: *Pellōn*, *Phellos?* [Πέλλων, Φέλλος.]

pe-ro-ro, MY 107 = Ge 604. Error for *o-pe-ro*.

]*pe-ro₂-[*, KN E 842. Sign at right perhaps *-ṇẹ*; to be restored [*u-]pe-ro₂-ne*: *Huperionei?* [Ὑπερίων *Il.* xix, 398 +.]

pe-ru-si-nu-wo, PY 181 = Ma 378 +. Neut. sing.: *perusinwon* 'last year's'. Abbreviated *pe.* [περυσῖνός Aristoph. +; from *per-uti-* (cf. ϝέτος), Skt. *parút* 'last year'; for suffix cf. perhaps Hom. ὀπωρῖνός, where the ī may be metri gratia.]

pe-ru-si-nu, PY 179 = Ma 193. Defective spelling of prec.

pe-ru-si-nu-wa, PY 180 = Ma 225 +, Ub 1316. Fem. and neut. plur.: *perusinwai, -wa*.

pe-ru-si-nwa, KN 283 = So 4442, MY 228 = Oe 111. Alternative spelling of prec.

pe-ru-si-nwa-o, PY Ub 1317. Gen. plur. fem.: *perusinwāōn*.

pe-se-ro, MY 105 = Ge 602. MN, perhaps dat.: *Psellos?* [Ψελλός as name only late; as adj. Aesch. +.]

pe-se-ro-jo, KN 24 = Ai 63. Gen.: *-oio*.

pe-ta-o-ni-jo, TH Ug 12. MN or adj.?: *Petāonios?* [Cf. Πετεών *Il.* ii, 500.]

pe-ta-ro, PY 253 = Jn 310. MN: *Petalos*. [Πέταλος.]

pe-te-ki-ja, KN 38 = As 1516. MN.

pe-te-re-wa: see s.v. *pte-re-wa*.

pe-te-u, KN As 603. MN.

pe-to-no, PY 75 = Cn 608, 257 = Jn 829, Ma 120, Vn 19 +. PN, one of the Nine Towns of the Hither Province: perhaps *Pethnos*.

pe-to-no-de, PY 250 = Vn 20. Acc. + *-de*.

pe-ti-ni-jo, PY 301 = Ac 1275. Nom. plur. ethnic adj.: *Pethnioi?*

pe-to-no-qa, TH Of 29. Obscure.

pe-we-ri-jo, KN 39 = As 1517. MN.

*pe-*65-ka*, PY Vn 879. Possibly name of a timber or other material? *pe-ju-ka* suggests πεύκη 'pine', but the spelling would be surprising.

pi-a₂-ra, PY 238 = Tn 996. Nom. plur. fem.: *phihalai* 'boiling-pans'. [φιάλη *Il.* xxiii, 243 +, used to collect the bones of Patroklos; later 'drinking-bowl'; also φιέλη.]

pi-je-ra₃, PY 237 = Ta 709. Alternative spelling of prec.: *phielai*.

pi-di-jo, KN 158 = Uf 836. Obscure. MN?

pi-ja-ma-so, PY Fn 324. MN, dat. [Cf. element *piya-* 'give' in Hittite names.]

pi-ja-mu-nu, KN Ap 5748. WN; see note on *pi-ja-ma-so*.

pi-ja-se-me, KN 38 = As 1516. MN; see note on *pi-ja-ma-so*.

pi-ja-si-ro, KN 38 = As 1516. MN; see note on *pi-ja-ma-so*.

pi-je-ra₃: see s.v. *pi-a₂-ra*.

pi-ka-na, PY 194 = Na 334. PN.

pi-ke-re-u, PY Eb 496, 131 = Ep 301. MN: *Pikreus?* [Cf. Cypr. gen. *pi-ki-re-wo* Schwyzer, *Dial.* 684, 5.]

pi-ke-re-wo, PY 115 = En 74, 122 = Eo 160. Gen.: *-ēwos*.

pi-ke-re-we, PY 122 = Eo 160. Dat.: *-ēwei*.

pi-ke-te-i, PY Gn 720. MN, dat.?

pi-ki-nu-wo, KN Da 5217. MN.

pi-ma-na-ro, KN As 1520, V 1523. MN.

pi-me-ta, PY 61 = Cn 131. MN, dat.

pi-mo-no, KN Xe 692, Ws 8499. MN, nom. and dat.

pi-pi, TH Z 846, Z 854. MN.

pi-pi-tu-na, KN 202 = Fp 13. Divine name; for ending cf. Δίκτυννα. See p. 308.

pi-ra-jo, PY 30 = Ae 264, 104 = Un 249. MN: *Philaios*. [Φίλαιος.]

pi-ra-ka-ra, KN Ap 639. WN: *Philagrā*. [Cf. Φίλαγρος.]

pi-ra-ḳạ-wo(-qe), KN V 1005. MN: *Philakhaiwos*. [Φιλάχαιος Schwyzer, *Dial.* 57.]

pi-ra-ki, MY Au 657, Z 710. MN: *Philāgis?* [Cf. ˝Αγις.]

pi-ra-ki-jo, KN V 1002. MN.

pi-ra-me-no, KN E 36, PY 254 = Jn 389. MN: *Philamenos*. [Cf. φίλατο *Il.* v, 61 +, φιλάμενος *IG* xiv, 1549.]

pi-ra-qo, KN Vc 181. MN.

pi-re-ṭạ, PY Fn 324. MN, dat.: *Philētāi*. [Φιλητᾶς.]

pi-ṛi-da-ke, MY Oe 128. MN, dat.

pi-ri-ja-me-ja, PY 50 = An 39 rev. MN: *Priameiās?* [Cf. Πρίαμος *Il.* i, 19 +.]

pi-ri-ja-o, PY 251 = Vn 46. Gen. plur.: *phliāōn* 'door-posts'. [φλιαί *Od.* xvii, 221.]

pi-ri-je, KN 230 = K 740. With sign ZE; perhaps here to be taken not as an abbreviation = 'pair', but as ideogram for 'saw'. [Cf. πρίων?]

pi-ri-je-te, KN 262 = Ra 1548 +. Nom. sing., name of trade concerned with swords: *prietēr?* 'cutler'. [Cf. *pi-ri-je*, *pi-ri-te*; πριστήρ.]

pi-ri-e-te-re, PY Fn 1427. Dat. sing.: *-tērei*.
pi-ri-je-te-re, PY 52 = An 207. Nom. dual: *-tēre*.
pi-ri-e-te-si, PY An 7. Dat. plur.: *-tērsi*.
pi-ri-no, KN 38 = As 1516. MN: *Philīnos*? [Φιλῖνος.]
pi-ri-sa-ta, KN U 4478. MN.
pi-ri-ta, PY Vn 1191. WN: *Philistā*. [Φιλίστα.]
pi-ri-]ta-wo, PY 130 = Eo 371. MN: *Brīthāwōn*?
Plinthāwōn? (Petruševski, 1959).
pi-ri-ta-wo-no, PY 117 = En 467. Gen.: *-āwonos*.
pi-ri-te, KN Ra 1543. Probably mis-spelling of
pi-ri-je-te, but could be *pristēr*. [πριστήρ.]
pi-ri-to-jo, KN C 911. MN, gen.?: *Philistoio*?
[Φίλιστος.]
pi-ri-u̯-wo, KN B 803. MN.
pi-ro-i-ta, KN V 1523, [V 1526?]. MN: *Philoitās*.
[Φιλοίτης; cf. Φιλοίτιος *Od.* xx, 185+.]
pi-ro-ka-te, PY Jn 832. MN.
pi-ro-na, PY Ep 539. WN: *Philōnā*?
pi-ro-ne-ta, PY 255 = Jn 658. MN.
pi-ro-pa-ta-ra, PY Vn 1191. WN: *Philopatrā*.
pi-ṛo-pe-se-wa, TH Of 28. MN, dat.: *Philopsēwāi* or
Philopeisewāi? [Cf. Πεισέας.]
pi-ro-qa-wo, KN As 609. MN: *Philoqqᵘāwōn* [cf.
Φιλοκτήμων] or *Philoqᵘāwōn* [cf. *o-qa-wo-ni*]?
]pi-ro-qe-mo, MY Ue 611. MN.
pi-ro-qo-[, PY Cn 254. MN, dat.: *Philo-*.
pi-ro-ta-wo, PY 168 = Es 644, 167 = Es 650+. MN.
pi-ro-te-ko-to, PY 167 = Es 650 rev. MN: *Philotektōn*,
if correctly read as one word; see p. 278.
pi-ro-we-ko, PY 254 = Jn 389. MN: *Philowergos*.
[Φιλοῦργος.]
pi-ṛo-wo-na¹, PY Ae 344. MN. [Cf. next.]
pi-ro-wo-na², MY 303 = V 659. WN: *Philowoinā*?
pi-ru-te, PY 57 = An 519, 76 = Cn 3. PN, loc.
pi-sa-wa-ta, KN B 1055. MN: *Piswātās*? [Cf.
pi-*82.]
pi-ta-ke-u, PY 254 = Jn 389. MN: *Pithākeus*?
pi-ti-ro₂-we-sa, PY 240 = Ta 713. Nom. sing. fem.:
ptilowessa (*ptilio-*?) 'decorated with feather
pattern'? [πτίλον 'feathers, down; insect's
wing', Herodotus+.]
pi̯-wa-to, PY An 1423. MN?
pi-we-re, PY Aa 1182. PN.
pi-we-ri-di, MY Oe 103. Dat. sing. fem., perhaps
ethnic, also used as WN: *Piweridi*.
pi-we-ri-ṣi, MY 93 = Fo 101. Dat. plur.
pi-we-ri-ja-ta, PY 254 = Jn 389. MN: *Piweriātās*.
[Cf. prec.; Πιερίη *Il.* XIV, 226.]
pi-za-ra, KN X 1801. Obscure, MN?
pi-*82, PY Ac 1276, An 830, 61 = Cn 131,
75 = Cn 608, 258 = Jo 438, 180 = Ma 225+.
PN, first of the Nine Towns of the Hither
Province; probably *Piswā*. [Πῖσα, but not to
be identified with Pisa on the Alpheios;
Chadwick, 1968a, p. 64.]
pi-*82-de, PY 250 = Vn 20. Acc. + *-de*: *Piswān-de*.
pi-[.]-te, PY 49 = An 427. PN, loc.
PO, Annotation to MANᵇ, = *po-ku-ta*: KN B 808+.
Annotation to CLOTH: KN L 7380.
Ligatured with **211* (see p. 328): KN Fs 8, K 873.

Ligatured with OIL (perhaps = *po-ro-ko-wa*, see
p. 477): PY Fr 1203, Fr 1208.
Ideographic use: KN C 7516.
po-da, KN V 1524. Obscure.
po-da-ko(-qe), KN Ch 899. Name of ox: *Podargos*
(*qᵘe*). [Πόδαργος name of two horses *Il.* VIII,
185, XXIII, 295.]
po-ḍạ-qe-re-ṣi-je-wo, KN B 822. Obscure, gen. of
adj.?
po-de, PY 236 = Ta 641. Dat. sing.: *podei* 'foot, leg'
(of tripod cauldron or table). [πούς Homer+.]
po-pi, PY 239 = Ta 642. Instr. plur.: *popphi*
< **pod-phi*. Cf. *qe-to-ro-po-pi*.
po-i-te-u, KN Da 1083. MN: *Phoiteus*? [Cf. next.]
po-i-ti-jo, KN Da 1314. MN: *Phoitios*. [Cf. place
name Φοιτίαι.]
po-ka, KN Dp 997, Dp 7742. Nom. plur. *pokai*
'fleeces'. [πόκαι variant of πόκοι. See Killen
1962b, 1963.]
po-ka-ro, KN Da 5195. MN.
po-ka-ta-ma, PY 238 = Tn 996. Nom. sing.,
annotation to golden and bronze vessels,
perhaps their name, or *pos-ktāma* 'additional
property'? [Cf. *po-si*, Arc. πός; κτῆμα; see s.v.
po-ku-ta.]
po-ke-we, PY 61 = Cn 131. MN, dat.: *Phōkēwei*?
[Φωκεύς ethnic.]
po-ki-ro-nu-ka, KN Ld 579, 218 = Ld 598+. Nom.
plur. neut.: *poikil-onukha*? (of garments) 'with
many-coloured *o-nu-ke*' (see *o-nu-ka*, and cf.
re-u-ko-nu-ka). [ποικίλος *Il.* V, 735+.]
po-ki-ro-qo, PY 58 = An 654, 43 = Aq 64, 258 =
Jo 438. MN: *Poikiloqᵘs*, *-ōqᵘos*?
po-ki-te, KN B 806. MN.
po-ko-ro, PY Cn 45, 61 = Cn 131. MN, dat.
po-ku-ta, KN B 815+, C 911+, L 469, PY 52 =
An 207, 54 = An 610. Nom. sing. and plur., a
class of men. The suggestion *pos-khutās* is
improbable in view of the lack of evidence for
*pos = *posi* in Myc., but a compound of
-khutās (χέω) is likely. [Cf. προχύτης =
πρόχοος.]
po-ku-te-ro, KN C 911. Apparently adj. to prec.
(For formation cf. *wa-na-ka-te-ro*; this confirms
that *-ta* of *po-ku-ta* must be a suffix.)
po-ma-ko, PY Cn 45. MN. Georgiev: *Poimarkhos*,
-āgos.
pọ-mạ-no-rị, KN L 759 (deleted). Obscure; if MN,
dat., perhaps: *Poimānori*. [Cf. Ποίμανδρος.]
po-me¹, KN 29 = Am 821, PY 31 = Ae 134, An 101,
111 = Ea 71+, 128 = Eo 278. Nom. sing.
masc.: *poimēn* 'shepherd'. [ποιμήν *Od.* X,
82+.]
po-me-ne, PY 110 = Ea 800+, 183 = Nn 831.
Dat. sing. and nom. plur.: *poimenei*, *poimenes*.
po-me-no, PY 109 = Ea 782. Gen. sing.: *poimenos*.
po-me², KN Dd 1376. MN: *Poimēn* (in fact, a
shepherd). [Ποιμήν.]
po-mi-ni-jo, KN V 503, MN: *Poimniōn* or *Poimnios*.
[Ποιμνίων, Ποιμένιος.]

po-ṇẹ-to-qe-ṣọ, PY Eq 34.4. Obscure.

po-ni-ja-ja, KN Sd 4408. Error for *po-ni-ki-ja*.

po-ni-ke(-qe), PY 246 = Ta 722. Instr. sing. masc.: *phoinikei* 'with a palm-tree'; prob. not 'griffin'. [φοῖνιξ *Od.* VI, 163+.] See pp. 344, 502.

po-ni-ki-pi, PY 244 = Ta 714. Instr. plur.: *phoinikhphi*.

po-ni-ke-ja[, KN Ln 1568. WN, dat.: *Phoinikeiāi*.

po-ni-ki-ja, KN 270 = Sd 4402+, Se 965+, 274 = Sf 4428. Nom. sing. and plur. fem.: *phoinikiā*, *-ai*, describing chariots, prob. 'painted crimson' (less likely 'of palm-wood'). [φοινίκεος Pindar+, cf. νέας φοινικοπαρήους *Od.* XI, 124.]

po-ni-ke-a, KN Se 880. Variant spelling: *phoinikeā*.

po-ni-ki-jo, KN 99 = Ga 418+, [Od 5082?]. Nom. sing. neut.?; name of a spice measured by weight: *phoinikion*? (In Od 5082, if rightly restored, perhaps adj., cf. *po-ni-ki-ja*.) There is no proof that φοιν[ίκ]ιον, *Inscr. Cret.* IV, 145, is a substantive, but it could be the same word (Maddoli, 1968).

po-no-qa-ta, PY Fn 324, KN Da 1341[+]1454+8777? MN, dat.: *Pornoqᵘātāi*. [Cf. πάρνοψ, Aeol. πορνόπιος; Ruijgh (1967, p. 355): *Ponogᵘatās*?]

po-pi: see s.v. *po-de*.

po-po, KN Ln 1568, L 513, L 567+, Od 689+. WN?, nom. and dat.

po-po-i, MY Oi 702. Dat. plur., poss. variant of *po-ro-po-i*.

po-pu-re-jo[, KN X 976. Nom. plur. masc.?: *porphureioi*? [πορφύρεος, *Il.* VIII, 221+.]

po-pu-re-ja, KN 224 = L 474. Nom. plur. fem.: *porphureiai*.

po-pu-ro₂, KN L 758. Possibly nom. dual fem.: *porphuriō*.

po-qa, PY 96 = Un 138, TH Ug 17 (cf. KN 165 = Gv 862). Word applied to olives, prob. *phorgᵘā* 'for eating', 'food'. [φορβή, *Il.* V, 202+ 'food for animals'; on etymology see Chadwick and Baumbach (1963, p. 253).]

po-qa-te-u, PY Qa 1295. Probably a title: poss. *phoigᵘasteus* 'purifier' or 'prophet'? [Cf. φοιβάзω.]

po-qe-wi-ja, PY 323 = Sb 1315. Nom. plur. fem.: *phorgᵘeiai* 'halters'. [φορβειά Xen.+.]

po-qe-wi-ja-i, PY 324 = An 1282. Dat. plur.: *phorgᵘeiāhi*.

po-ra-i, PY 59 = An 656. PN, dat.-loc. plur.

po-ra-pi, PY 53 = An 1, Mn 1408, 184 = Nn 228. Instr. plur.

po-re-na(-qe), PY 172 = Tn 316. Prob. acc. plur. masc.; see pp. 285, 461.

po-re-si, TH Of 26: dat. plur.?

po-re-no-tu-ṭẹ[, PY Ua 1413. Obscure, perh. compound of or containing a form of prec.

po-re-no-zo-te-ri-ja, PY Un 443. If divided *po-re-no zo-te-ri-ja*, the first word might be gen. (sing. or plur.) to cons. stem *po-re-na* (acc. plur.); *zo-te-ri-ja* might then be *tsōtēria* (σωτήρια) 'ransom of victim, prisoner, or the like'. This would involve accepting σω- as the product of *tᵘoə₂-*, not a contraction of σαϝο- (< *tᵘə₂-ᵘo-). The problem is complicated by the presence in PY Un 443 of *te-ri-ja* immediately preceded by what is apparently BARLEY 2; but *po-re-no-zo* offers no easy solution.

po-re-si: see s.v. *po-re-na(-qe)*.

po-ri-ko, PY Cn 328. MN: *Polikhos*? [Πόλιχος.]

po-ri-wa, KN 217 = Ld 587. Nom. plur. neut.: *poliwa* 'grey', of textiles. [πολιός *Il.* IX, 366.]

po-ri-wo, KN C 911. MN: *Poliwos*? [Cf. prec.]

*po-ro*¹, KN 82 = Ca 895. Dual with 'maneless horse' ideogram. Evans: *pōlō* 'two colts, foals' (of horses or asses). [πῶλος *Od.* XXIII, 246+.]

*po-ro*², KN 67 = Dd 1171. MN, Georgiev: *Pōlos*, but there are other possibilities. [Πῶλος.]

po-ro-de-qo-no, KN F 51. Recipient of barley, man's or god's name?

po-ro-du-ma-te, PY [148 = Ep 613], 91 = Fn 50. Dat. sing. (Ep 613 *po-ṛo-du*[-*ma*], nom. sing.): *pro-* and obscure title (see *du-ma*).

po-ro-e-ke, PY 240 = Ta 713, 241 = Ta 715. Nom. sing., epithet of a table: see p. 501.

po-ro-e-ke-te-ri-ja, PY 237 = Ta 709. An implement used in connexion with braziers: perh. *prohelktēriā* 'instrument for drawing forth'. [Palmer, 1963 *a*, p. 342.]

po-ro-i-ra, KN Od 690. Personal name, dat.

po-ro-ko, KN Dv 1416, PY [255 = Jn 658?], Jn 725. MN.

po-ro-ko-re-te, KN V 865, PY 257 = Jn 829, 258 = Jo 438. Nom. sing., official subordinate to *ko-re-te*.

po-ro-ko-re-te-re(-qe), PY 257 = Jn 829. Nom. plur.

po-ro-ko-wa, KN Fh 350. Technical term describing olive oil: *prokhowā* 'outpouring'. [προχοή 'river-mouth, outpouring' Hom.] Cf. *e-pi-ko-wa*.

po-ro-ko-wo, MY 234 = Ue 611 rev. Nom. plur.: *prokhowoi* 'jugs'. [πρόχοος *Od.* XVIII, 397+, Att. πρόχους.]

po-ro-po-i, MY 321 = Oi 701. Dat. plur.: see p. 507.

po-ro-qa-ta-jo, PY 62 = Cn 655. MN. [Cf. Attic deme Πρόσπαλτα?]

po-ro-su-re, KN Sg 888. Obscure; MN?

po-ro-te-ke, MY Ue 661 (*jo-po-ro-te-ke*). 3rd sing. aor.: (*hō*) *prothēke* 'Thus he set out'? The absence of a subject makes this obscure and doubtful (see Chadwick, 1963 *b*, p. 62).

po-ro-te-u, PY Eq 146. MN: *Prōteus*? [Πρωτεύς.]

po-ro-ti-ri, KN 275 = Se 879. Obscure: see p. 369.

po-ro-to, KN Od 562. Poss. MN: *Prōtos*, but the structure of the text is obscure.

po-ro-tu-qo-no, KN Vc 54. MN.

po-ro-u-jo, PY 255 = Jn 658, Jn 725. MN.

po-ro-u-te-u, KN 66 = Dc 1129, PY 253 = Jn 310, [Vn 493] +. MN: *Plouteus*. [Πλουτεύς.]

po-ro-u-te-wo, PY 253 = Jn 310. Gen.: *Ploutēwos*.

po-ro-u-te-we, PY 61 = Cn 131. Dat.: *Ploutēwei*.

po-ro-we[, KN X 1014. Obscure.

po-ro-wi-to, PY [Fr 1218?], Fr 1221, Fr 1232. Possibly a month-name: *Plōwistos* 'the month of sailing' (Palmer 1963*a*, p. 254); see pp. 286, 459, 480.

po-ro-wi-to-jo, PY 172 = Tn 316. Gen.

po-ru-da-ma-te, PY 50 = An 39. Nom. plur.: varant spelling of *po-ro-du-ma-te*?

po-ru-da-si-jo, KN V 118, PY 44 = Aq 218. Patronymic or ethnic adj.?

po-ru-e-ro, PY 255 = Jn 658. MN. The same man as *o-ru-we-ro*, but which is correct? See p. 511.

po-ru-ka-to, KN Vc 74. MN: *Polukastos*? [Cf. Πολυκάστη *Od.* III, 464.]

po-ru-po-de(-*qe*), PY 246 = Ta 722. Instr. sing. Bennett: *polupodei* '(inlaid) with an octopus'. [Gen. πουλύποδος *Od.* v, 432 +.]

po-ru-qo-ta, PY Cn 40, Jn 845. MN, nom. and dat.: *Poluqʷhontās*. [Πολυφόντης *Il.* IV, 395; the labio-velar preserved by analogy of other names in -*qʷhontās*.]

po-ru-qo-to, KN Da 1137, PY An 128. At KN man's name: *Polugʷotos*? At PY probably epithet.

po-ru-te-we, KN Vc 176. MN.

po-ru-to, PY An 5. MN.

po-ru-we-wo, PY Sa 796. MN, gen.

po-se-da-o, PY Es 653. Nom. (prob. error for dat.): *Poseidāōn* 'Poseidon'. [Ποσειδάων Hom.; the Corinthian forms with -αϝōν must be secondary. On etymology see Hamp (1968).]

po-se-da-o-no, KN X 5560?, PY Eq 34, 170 = Es 649. Gen.: *Poseidāŏnos*.

po-se-da-o-ne, [KN 208 = V 52], PY 169 = Es 646 +, [Fr 343], 309 = Fr 1224 +, [313 = Un 6]. Dat.: *Poseidāonei*.

po-se-da-o-ni, PY 171 = Un 718. Alternative dat.: *Poseidāoni*.

po-si, KN 270 = Sd 4402, 271 = Sd 4422 +. Adverb: *posi* 'together, attached'. [**poti* > Dor. ποτί, πότ, Arc.-Cyp. πός, parallel to **proti* > Hom. προτί, Att.-Ion., Lesb. πρός.]

po-si-da-e-ja, PY 172 = Tn 316. Dat. sing. of goddess's name: *Posidāeiāi*.

po-si-da-i-je-u-si, PY Fn 187. Dat. plur.: *Posidāijeusi* 'for the priests of Poseidon'?

po-si-da-i-jo, PY 172 = Tn 316. Acc. neut.: *Posidāion* 'the shrine of Poseidon'?

po-si-da-i-jo-de, PY Fn 187. Acc. + allative -*de*, 'to the shrine of P.'.

po-si-ke-te-re, PY 54 = An 610. Nom. plur. masc., a class of men: *pos-ik(e)tēres*?; 'suppliants' is an unlikely meaning, perh. 'newcomers'?

[ἱκέτης Hom., ἰκτήρ Soph., προσίκτωρ Aesch.]

po-so-pe-re-i, PY Cn 40. MN, dat.: *Pos-opheleï*? [Cf. προσοφείλω.]

po-so-ra-ko, PY Jn 725 (deleted). MN.

po-so-re-ja, PY 119 = Eo 224 +, 148 = Ep 613 +. WN: *Psoleia*?

po-so-ri-jo, PY 258 = Jo 438, [Jn 601?]. MN: *Psoliōn*?

po-so-ri-jo-no, PY 43 = Aq 64. Gen.

po-so-ro, PY 312 = An 1281, Jn 601 +. MN: *Psolōn*? [Ψόλων.]

po-te-ja[, TH Of 41. Obscure.

po-te-re-we, PY Fn 187. MN or trade-name?, dat.

po-te-u, PY 57 = An 519, Cn 45. MN: *Ponteus* or *Phoiteus*? [Ποντεύς; cf. *po-i-te-u*.]

po-te-wo, PY 117 = En 467, 129 = Eo 268. Gen.

po-ti-ja-ke-e, PY An 298, 54 = An 610. PN, loc.

[*po*-]*ti-a-ke-ṣi*, PY 312 = An 1281. Prob. variant of same name in loc. plur.

po-ti-jo, KN B 804. MN: *Pontios*. [Πόντιος.]

po-ti-na-jo, PY Jn 692, Jn 725 +. MN.

po-ti-ni-ja, KN 205 = Gg 702, M 729, Oa 7374, 208 = V 52, X 444?, PY 312 = An 1281, Cc 665, Fn 187, 310 = Fr 1225 +, 172 = Tn 316, Vn 48, MY 321 = Oi 701 +, TH Of 36. Name of goddess, nom.?, gen. and dat.: *Potnia*, *Potniās*, *Potniāi*, 'the Mistress'. Frequently with epithet and sometimes written as one word (*a-ta-na-po-ti-ni-ja* KN 208 = V 52, *si-to-po-ti-ni-ja* MY 321 = Oi 701). [πότνια Hom. +, cf. Skt. *pátnī*.] On the identification of the goddess, see Chadwick, 1957*a*.

po-ti-ni-ja-we-jo, KN Dl 930 +, PY Ep 613, 253 = Jn 310 +. Nom. sing. masc. adj. derived from πότνια: *Potniaweios*? 'of or belonging to Potnia'. [*Potni-arweios* Lejeune (1962*b*, p. 407); the form is difficult, see p. 127.]

po-ti-ni-ja-we-jo-jo, PY 154 = Eq 213. Gen. sing. masc. or neut.

po-ti-ni-ja-we-ja, KN 90 = G 820, Dp 997. Nom. sing. or plur. fem. or plur. neut.

po-ti-ni-ja-we, KN 73 = Dl 943. Defective spelling for *po-ti-ni-ja-we-jo*.

po-ti-ni-ja-we-i-jo, KN Dp 7742. Variant spelling for *po-ti-ni-ja-we-jo*.

po-ti-ni-ja-wi-jo, PY 316 = Qa 1299. Variant form: *Potniawios*.

po-ti-pi(-*qe*), PY 242 = PY Ta 707. Instr. plur.: *portiphi* 'with heifers'. [πόρτις *Il.* v, 162 +.]

po-ti-ro, KN [V 756], V 1002, V 1003 +. Obscure, apparently introduces two masc. names on tablets headed by a fem. ethnic adj.

po-to, KN 38 = As 1516. MN: *Pontos*? [Πόντος.]

po-to-re-ma-ta, PY [Ep 539], Jn 601. MN, nom. and dat.: *Ptolemātās*, -*tāi*. [Cf. Πολεμάτας.]

po-to-ri-jo, KN 39 = As 1517. MN: *Ptoliōn*?

po-to-ri-ka-ta, KN 162 = Uf 983. MN, dat.: *Ptolikastāi*, *Ptolikhātāi*?

po-to-ro-wa-pi, PY Aa 76, Ad 678, La 623, Na 262. PN: prob. loc.-instr. plur.

po-wi-te-ja, PY Jn 601, Na 923. PN.

po-*34-wi-do, KN Sc 235. MN.

pte-jo-ri, PY 50 = An 39 rev. MN.

pte-no, KN 270 = Sd 4402, Sd 4405, Sd 4450. Nom. dual: *pternō* 'foot-boards for mounting'. See p. 367. [πτέρνη 'heel' *Il.* XXII, 397; 'footboard, mounting-step' Pollux I, 144 (Petruševski, 1970*b*).]

pte-re-wa, KN 275 = Se 879+, 279 = So 4437, 281 = So 4440+. Gen. sing.?, describing wheels: *ptelewās* 'of elm-wood', *Ulmus glabra*. [πτελέη *Il.* VI, 419+; *πτελέϝα, cf. OHG *felawa* 'willow'.]

pe-te-re-wa, KN 278 = So 894. Alternative spelling of prec.

PU, Ligatured with CLOTH, abbreviation of *pu-ka-ta-ri-ja*: KN 223 = L 471, 224 = L 474+, PY La 1394, Wr 1374.

pu-da-so[, KN V 431. MN?

pu-i-re-wi, MY Go 610. MN, dat.

pu-ka-ro, MY 93 = Fo 101, [303 = V 659?]. Prob. WN, dat.

pu-ka-ta-ri-ja, KN 224 = L 474+, MY X 508. Nom. plur. fem., description of CLOTH + PU: possibly *puktaliai* 'of double thickness, folded'. [Cf. πτυκτός, πυκνός, etc. Ugaritic *mizrtm* 'doubled garment' Gordon no. 88.]

pu-ka-wo, PY 50 = An 39, 49 = An 427+. Nom. plur. masc., a man's trade: *pur-kawoi* 'fire-kindlers', possibly a religious title. [Cf. πυρκαεύς Soph., πυρκαϊή 'pyre' *Il.* VII, 428+; πυρίκαοι, of the Delphians, Orac. ap. Plut. 2. 406e.]

pu-ke-o, MY 106 = Ge 603, [107 = Ge 604?]. MN.

pu-ke-se-ro, PY Jn 845. MN.

pu-ko-ro, KN Xd 142?, PY 50 = An 39 rev., Fn 837, Jn 478? MN.

pu-ko-so e-ke-e, PY 241 = Ta 715. Nom. dual fem., describing tables: *puxo-ekhe(h)e* 'with box-wood supports'. [πύξος.]

pu-ko-to, KN X 796. No context; MN?

pu-ko-wo, PY 143 = Ep 705. MN: *Purkowos*? [Cf. Πυρκόοι.]

pu-ma-ra-ko, PY Cn 643. MN.

pu-na-si-jo, KN B 806. MN. [= Ethnic adj. of next.]

pu-na-so, KN C 979, Da 1588+, Dn 1096. PN.

pu-na-si-jo, KN Ga 34, Ga 420. Ethnic adj.

pu-na-to, KN C 912. MN.

pu-nu-so, KN Df 1233. MN.

pu-ra-ko[, KN Xd 141. MN?, if complete: *Phulakos*? [Φύλακος *Il.* VI, 35.]

pu-ra̯-so, KN Dc 5677. MN: *Purasos*. [Πύρασος *Il.* XI, 491.]

pu-ra-ta, PY Jn 605. MN: *Pulātās* or *Pulartās*. [Πυλήτης as ethnic; Πυλάρτης *Il.* XI, 491.]

pu-ra-ta-o, PY Jn 605. Gen.: *-tāo*.

pu-ra-u-to-ro, PY 237 = Ta 709. Nom. dual fem. or neut.: *puraustrō* 'fire-tongs'. [πύραυστρα =

πυράγρα *IG*, II², 47, 18, 4 B.C., πύραυστρον Herodas IV, 62; πῦρ + *aus-, cf. Lat. *haurio*. Cf. Cypr. ἔναυον· ἔνθες, (ἔ)παυον· θές Hesych. The Hom. αὔω shows specialization of meaning, see Karageorghis, 1954.]

pu-re-wa, KN U 4478. MN: *Phulewās*? [Cf. Φυλεύς; *pu₂-re-wa*.]

pu-ri, KN B 799, F 452, V 479. MN: *Puris*. [Πύρις *Il.* XVI, 416.]

pu-ro, PY Aa 61+, 9 = Ab 553+, 12 = Ad 671+, 27 = Ae 303+, 41 = An 35, Cn 45, 172 = Tn 316. PN: *Pulos*. [Πύλος *Il.* XI, 671+.] There are two places of this name, the second distinguished by the epithet *ra-u-ra-ti-jo*, q.v.

pu-ro-jo, PY An 129. Gen.: *Puloio*.

pu-so, KN As 604, Da 1339, Dc 926+. PN.

pu-si-jo/-ja, KN 88 = E 749, Ga 992, X 450. Ethnic adj.

pu-ta, KN 166 = Gv 864. Nom. plur. neut., describing TREE ideogram: *phuta* 'young plants'. [φυτόν *Od.* XXIV, 227+.]

pu-ta-ri-ja, KN E 849. Nom. sing. or plur. fem.: *phutaliā* 'orchard, vineyard'. [φυταλιή *Il.* VI, 195+.]

pu-ta-ta, KN X 7743. Obscure.

*pu-te*¹, KN 157 = Uf 835, Uf 987?, Uf 5726. Nom. sing.: *phutēr* 'planter'? [Cf. φυτεύω; see also *pu₂-te-re*.

*pu-te*², KN 38 = As 1516. MN.

pu-te-ri-ja, KN 155 = Uf 981, [Uf 1022], Uf 1031. Acc. sing. following *e-ke* (and sometimes not divided from it): variant spelling of *pu-ta-ri-ja* = *phutaliān*, or a derivative of *pu-te* = *phutēr*?

pu-te-u, PY Jn 431. MN: *Putheus*, *Phuteus*? [Πυθεύς, Φυτεύς.]

pu-ti-ja, PY An 340, Qa 1294. MN: *Puthias*. [Πυθίας.]

*pu-to-ro*¹, PY 251 = Vn 46. Gen. plur.?: item in list of building materials. See p. 504.

*pu-to-ro*², KN 38 = As 1516, Da 1333. MN.

pu-wa, KN Ap 639. WN: *Purwā*. [Πύρρα; cf. *pu-wo*.]

pu-wa-ne, PY Jn 832. MN.

pu-wi-no, PY 61 = Cn 131, 62 = Cn 655. MN, nom. and dat.: *Purwinos, -ōi*. [Πύρρινος.]

pu-wo, KN 38 = As 1516, C 912, MY 106 = Ge 603. MN: *Purwos* or *Purswos*? [Πύρρος; Corinth. Πυρϝος (name of a horse) Schwyzer, *Dial.* 123, 15.]

pu-za-ko, PY Cn 328. MN.

pu-zo, KN Ap 5748. WN?

pu[ ]*-a₂-ko*, PY An 340. MN. Cf. *pu₂-si̯-ja-ko*.

pu-[.]*-da-ka*, PY Ep 539. MN.

pu₂-ke, MY 105 = Ge 602+. MN.

pu₂-ke-qi-ri, PY 235 = Ta 711. MN.

pu₂-ke-qi-ri-ne-ja, TH Of 27. WN? [Cf. prec.]

pu₂-ra-ne-jo, KN B 799. MN.

pu₂-ra₂-a-ke-re-u, PY 184 = Nn 228. Place name: *Phuliās Agreus*? [Lejeune, 1962*b*, p. 417.]

pu₂-ra₂-a-ki-ri-jo, PY Na 425. Variant of place name? *Phuliās Agrios*?

pu₂-re-ρ, KN Sc 243. Obscure.

pu₂-re-wa, TH Of 26. MN, dat.: *Phulēwāi*? [Cf. *pu-re-wa*.]

pu₂-ru-da-ro, KN Uf 432. MN: *Phludaros*? [Cf. φλυδαρός; Palmer, 1955*b*, p. 40.]

pu₂-ṣi-ja-ko, PY 253 = Jn 310. MN: *Phusiarkhos*? Cf. *pu-[.]-a₂-ko*.

]*pu₂-te-me-no*: see [*pe-*]*pu₂-te-me-no*.

pu₂-te-re, KN V 159, PY 193 = Na 520. Nom. plur.: *phutēres* 'planters'? [Cf. φυτεύω, *pu-te*¹; Palmer, 1963*a*, p. 449.]

pu₂-ti-ja, PY 59 = An 656, Jn 601. MN. [*Phutiās* hypocoristic of -φυτος, Ruijgh, 1967, p. 159; poss. *Phuthiās* = *pu-ti-ja*, if dissimilation of aspirates is not operative.]

pu₂-to, KN Uf 1522. MN, dat. [*Phuthos* = Πύθος?; see prec.]

QA, Ligatured with *124* (cyperus): KN Ga 5088, Ga 7358.

qa-a₂-ri-da, TH Of 39. Obscure.

qa-da-ro, KN V 831. MN. [Poss. *Qʷandaros* = Πάνδαρος *Il.* IV, 88 +.]

qa-da-so, KN Db 1297. MN: *Qʷādasos*? [Πήδασος *Il.* VI, 21 +.]

qa-da-wa-so, MY Oe 130. MN?, dat.?

qa-di-ja, KN C 911. MN.

qa-i-po, KN Dg 1101. MN.

]*qa-ka-na-pi*[, KN X 4487. Instr. plur. fem.?

qa-ko-jo, PY Vn 1191. MN, gen.

qa-me-si-jo, KN 38 = As 1516. MN. [Cf. *qa-mi-si-jo*?]

qa-mi-si-jo, KN Sc 135. MN: *Qʷamisios*. [Cf. Πάμισος river in Messenia; cf. *qa-me-si-jo*.]

qa-mo, KN Da 1317, Db 1099 +, Ga 417, Pp 497. PN.

qa-mi-jo/-ja, KN Ak 613 +, 88 = E 749, Lc 543 +. Ethnic adj.

]*qa-na-no-to*, KN Da 1351, Dv 7181, Dv 7248. PN.

qa-nu-wa-so, KN As 1516. MN: *Qʷanuasos*? [Πάνυασος.]

qa-nwa-so, KN 73 = Dl 943. PN.

qa-ra-ro, KN As 604. MN. [Cf. Linear A *qa-qa-ru* HT 93 +; see Lejeune, 1968*b*.]

qa-ra, KN 35 = Am 819, Da 1098 +, 164 = Gv 863, L 473, 158 = Uf 836 +. PN.

*qa-ra-jo*¹, KN 88 = E 479, Ga 423 +. Ethnic adj.

qa-ra-de-ro, PY Vn 879. Possibly name of a material?

qa-ra-i-so, KN V 466, [Dv 5285?]. MN. [Cf. place name Πραισός; Palmer (1955*b*, p. 38) = Βλαῖσος.]

*qa-ra-jo*¹, see s.v. *qa-ra*.

*qa-ra-jo*², KN 39 = As 1517, V 429 +. MN.

qa-ra-o, KN Og 1804. Obscure.

qa-ra-si-jo, MY Au 657, [Au 658?]. MN.

qa-ra-su-ti-jo, KN Dd 1150, Nc 4489, Xd 154. MN.

qa-ra-to-ro, PY 237 = Ta 709. Nom. sing. Palmer: *sqʷalathron* 'oven-rake'. [σπάλαθρον Pollux.]

qa-ra-we-ta, MY V 662. MN?

qa-ra₂, PY An 192. MN: *Qʷallans*? [Πάλλας, -αντος.]

qa-ra₂-te, PY An 7, 50 = An 39, TH Of 38. Dat.

qa-ra₂-to-de, TH Of 37. Gen. + -*de*: 'to the house of Q.'.

qa-ra₂-ro, KN Dl 932. MN.

qa-ra₂-ti-jo, KN Dg 1235. MN: *Qʷallantios*?

qa-ra₂-wo, KN Ce 50. MN.

qa-ru-ko, MY Au 657, Au 660. MN.

qa-sa-ko, KN C 912, Dd 1283. MN.

qa-sa-re-ρ, PY Sa 755. MN, gen.

qa-sa-ro-we, KN Db 1329, E 848, Np 7923. PN.

qa-si-da-ro, KN Db 1110, Dv 1490. MN.

qa-si-re-u, PY Jn 431, Jn 601 +, 258 = Jo 438, TH Of 42. Nom. sing.: *gʷasileus* 'chief', used of local headmen, not sovereign. [βασιλεύς; cf. βασιλῆες . . . εἰσὶ ἄλλοι πολλοὶ ἐν . . . 'Ιθάκῃ *Od.* I, 394.]

[?*qa-*]*si-re-we*, KN B 779. Doubtful; perhaps nom. plur., but poss. dat. sing. of MN, cf. KN 39 = As 1517. 2.

qa-si-re-wi-ja, KN 38 = As 1516, 232 = K 875, PY [Fn 867?], [Pa 398], Pa 889. Prob. fem. sing., derivative of *qa-si-re-u*: *gʷasilēwiā*, sense unclear, poss. group or area controlled by a *gʷasileus*.

[?*qa-si*]*-re-wi-jo-te*, PY 43 = Aq 64. Possible restoration, but -*si*- cannot be confirmed; if correct, *gʷasilēwjontes* 'functioning as *gʷasileus*'?

qa-ti-ja, KN As 1519. MN.

qa-to-no-ro, KN 38 = As 1516, Fh 5463. MN.

*qa-*83-to*, KN Sc 257. MN?

QE, Surcharged on CORSLET ideogram: KN Sc 224, Sc 227 +; on KN Sc 266 also apparently ideographic, but see p. 495.

-*qe*, KN 85 = Ch 896 +, 90 = G 820, 221 = L 647, etc., PY 12 = Ad 671 +, 57 = An 519 +, 148 = Ep 613 +, 257 = Jn 829 +, etc., MY 46 = Au 102, 106 = Ge 603, 303 = V 659. Enclitic particle: -*qʷe* 'and'. [τε; Lat. -*que*, Skt. *ca*, etc.]

qe-da-do-ro, KN De 1294, Uf 121. MN.

qe-ja-me-no, PY 136 = Eb 294, 135 = Ep 704. Nom. sing. app. a title, in form prob. pple.: Ruijgh (1967, p. 376) *qʷejamenos* from a verb parallel to τίω, 'celebrant' or 'reverend'. [It is difficult to treat it as MN, but cf. Heubeck, 1957, p. 273.]

qe-pa-ta-no, KN Ln 1568. WN?

qe-qi-no-me-no, PY 249 = Va 482. Nom. plur. perf. pple. mid. or pass.: *gʷegʷīnōmenoi* 'carved'. [Perhaps in origin 'endowed with life' cf. βίος, Richardson, Heubeck, 1966; cf. δινωτός *Od.* XIX, 56.]

qe-qi-no-me-na, PY 242 = Ta 707, 243 = Ta 708 +. Nom. sing. fem. and prob. instr. plur.: *gʷegʷīnōmenā*. See pp. 343-4.

qe-qi-no-to, PY 239 = Ta 642. 3rd sing. perf.: *gʷegʷīnōtoi* 'it is carved'. [D. M. Jones, 1958.]

qe-ra-di-ri-jo, KN Sc 246. MN: *Qʷēlandrios*. [Cf. Τήλανδρος.]

qe-ra-jo, KN Vc 5523, V 482. MN: Georgiev *Qʷhēraios* (*Qhw-*?). [Cf. Θηραῖος ethnic of Θήρα; θήρ < *ghu̯ēr-.]

qe-ra-na, PY 235 = Ta 711. Nom. sing. fem.: 'ewer, jug'. See pp. 327, 494.

qe-ra-si-ja, KN [Fh 5475?], 200 = Fp 1, 202 = Fp 13+. Prob. fem. dat. sing., name of a divinity. [Possibly to be connected with θήρ; cf. πότνια θηρῶν *Il.* XXI, 470.]

qe-ra-si-jo, KN Fp 16. Dat. sing. masc.? A male counterpart, or an error?

qe-re-ma-o, KN V 7513, PY Qa 1295. MN: *Qʷēlemaos*? [Cf. τηλε-, (Οἰνό-)μαος.]

qe-re-me-e, PY Na 540. PN, loc.

qe-re-me-ne-u, PY Jn 845. MN: *Qʷēlemeneus*? Lejeune (1958a, p. 143): *Qʷremneus* (cf. πρέμνον).

qe-re-me-ti-wo, PY An 5, Cr 875 (-*ti-wo*-[). Place name?

qe-re-me-ti-re, PY Cn 4. Apparently variant or error for the same place name.

qe-re-qo-ta-o, PY 116 = En 659. MN, gen.: *Qʷēleqʷhontāo*. [Nom. also spelt *pe-re-qo-ta*, q.v.]

qe-re-ti-ri-jo, PY 251 = Vn 46. Nom. dual: perhaps *qʷ(e)lethriō* 'poles'. [Cf. πέλεθρον, πλέθρον.] Or from βλῆτρον 'fastening'. [*Il.* XV, 678; Ruijgh, 1970, p. 315.] See p. 504.

qe-re-wa, KN Xd 122, Xd 296. MN: *Qʷēlewās*? [Cf. Τηλέας.]

qe-re-wa-o, PY 62 = Cn 655. Gen.

qe-ri, KN Df 1360. MN.

qe-ri-jo, KN 23 = Ag 1654. MN: *Qʷhēriōn*? [Θηρίων.]

qe-ri-ta, PY Eb 900, 148 = Ep 613. WN.

qe-ro, KN As 602, Db 1204, V 479. MN.

]*qe-ro-me-no*, PY 14 = Ad 697. Nom. sing. masc. pple.: *qʷelomenos* 'being'. [πέλομαι (Aeol.).]

qe-ro₂, KN 230 = K 740, 299 = Sk 789, 300 = Sk 5670, 325 = Sk 8100+. Nom. sing. and dual, (poss. plur.), describing bronze artifact in lists of armour: perh. *sqʷelion*, -*ō* (cf. Aeol. σπέλ(λ)ιον = ψέλιον) 'arm-guards'. [Chadwick, 1957b, p. 148.] See p. 494.

]*qe-sa-ma-qa*, KN Fs 11. Obscure, possibly divine name. [Chadwick, 1966, p. 32.]

qe-ta-ko, PY Cn 45, Cn 570+, Jn 431. MN.

qe-ta-ko-jo, PY Jn 431. Gen.

qe-ta-ra-je-u, PY Jn 845. MN: *Qʷetraieus*? [Cf. τετρα-?]

qe-ta-se-u[, KN As 605. MN.

qe-ta-wo, PY 253 = Jn 310. MN.

qe-te-jo, PY Fr 1206, Fr 1241. Prob. neut. sing. of adj. meaning roughly 'to be paid', 'due'. Etymology uncertain: possibly *qʷeiteios* from root of τίνω with analogical *e*-grade in root and suffix -*teios* (but -τέος believed to be < *-*tewos*). See Lejeune 1964a, pp. 82–92.

qe-te-o, KN Fh 348, L 513, 222 = L693+. Variant spelling.

qe-te-a, KN Fp 363. Neut. plur.?

qe-te-a₂, PY 96 = Un 138. Variant spelling of prec.?

qe-te-re-u, PY Vn 865. MN: *Qʷetreus*. [Cf. τετρα-?]

qe-te-se-u, KN As 609. MN: *Qʷhtheiseus*? [Cf. φθεισήνωρ (φθῑσ-) *Il.* II, 833+; Heubeck, 1957, p. 270.]

qe-to, PY 236 = Ta 641, MY 234 = Ue 611 rev. (]*qe-to*). Nom. dual and plur.; name of a vessel. See pp. 327, 493.

qe-ti-ja, MY 234 = Ue 611 rev., Wt 504. Nom. plur. neut.; diminutive in -*ion* of prec.

qe-to-ro-no, PY Jn 431. MN.

qe-to-ro-po-pi, PY 31 = Ae 134, Ae 489+. Instr. plur.: *qʷetropopphi* (< *-*pod-phi*) 'four-footed animals'. [τετράποδα Herodotus+.]

qe-to-ro-we, PY 236 = Ta 641. Nom. sing. neut. Blegen: *qʷetrōwes* 'with four handles'. [Cf. *a-no-we*, *ti-ri-jo-we*.]

qe-wa-ra, KN Mc 4459. Obscure.

QI, As a unit of weight: KN Np 85, Np 270+. See p. 55.

qi-ja-to, KN Db 1140. MN.

qi-ja-zo, KN Dv 1500, Xe 5899. MN.

qi-ko-we-e, KN C 911. Obscure: PN?

qi-na, KN Ld 584 (*o-pi-qi-na*). Prob. WN, dat.

qi-ni-te-we, KN D 1024. MN, dat.?

qi-nwa-so, KN Dc 1515. MN.

qi-qe-ro, KN 39 = As 1517. MN.

qi-ri-ja-to, KN Ai 1037, Ai 5976, B 822, B 988[+] 5761. Annotation on personnel records: prob. 3rd sing. aor. *qʷriato* 'he bought'. [πρίατο *Od.* I, 430 of buying a slave.]

qi-ri-ta-ko, PY 62 = Cn 655. MN.

qi-si-ja-ko, PY Jn 706. MN.

qi-si-pe-e, PY 247 = Ta 716. Nom. dual: *qʷsiphee* 'two swords'. [ξίφος *Il.* I, 194+; see Heubeck, 1958.] See pp. 346, 348, 502.

qi-si-ta, KN De 1264. MN.

qi-ta-ro, KN Dk 936. MN.

qi-wo, TH Of 33. PN or MN? [If MN, cf. Βίων.]

qi-zo, KN Dd 1291. MN.

QO, Ideographic use (obscure): KN U 49. Possibly intended for OX?

]*qo-i-na*[, KN X 7735. Possibly *qʷoinā* = ποινή, but reading doubtful.

qo-ja-si, KN B 799. MN.

qo-ja-te, KN Od 667, Od 681. MN.

qo-o, PY 76 = Cn 3. Prob. acc. plur.: *gʷōns* 'oxen'. [βούς; see p. 207.]

qo-pa-ra[, KN Fh 7571. MN?

qo-pi-ja, PY Na 329. PN.

qo-qo-ta-o, PY Ea 270, Ea 305+. Gen. sing. or plur.: *gʷogʷotāo*, -*tāōn* 'of the oxherd(s)'. [Prob. dissimilated from *qo-u-qo-ta*, q.v., but here a trade rather than a name.]

qo-re-po-u-ti, PY Fn 324. MN, dat.

qo-ro-mu-ro, PY Na 841. PN.

qo-ta¹, PY Na 532. PN.

qo-ta², MY 303 = V 659. WN.

qo-ta-wo, PY Na 522. PN.

[ ]*qo-ta-wo*, PY 50 = An 39 rev. MN.

qo-te-ro, KN 38 = As 1516, Da 1495, PY 32 = Ae 108, 40 = An 261. MN.

qo-te-wo, PY 44 = Aq 218. MN, gen.

qo-u-ka-ra, PY 235 = Ta 711. Apparently adj., nom. sing., describing a ewer: *g*^{u}*oukarā*(*s*) (or -*krās*) 'with ox-head'. [βούς, κάρα; Risch, 1966 *a*.]

[*qo*]-*u-ka-ra-o-rẹ*, PY 244 = Ta 714. Apparently an illusory reading: see *se-re-mo-ka-ra-o-re*.

qo-u-ko-ro, KN [As 5609?, Xe 8546?], PY 51 = An 18, 45 = An 830, An 852, 183 = Nn 831. Nom. plur.: *g*^{u}*oukoloi* 'oxherds'. [βουκόλοι *Il*. XIII, 571 +.]

qo-u-ko-ro-jo, PY Ea 781. Gen. sing.: *g*^{u}*oukoloio*.

qo-u-qo-ta, KN L 480. MN, dat.: *G*^{u}*oug*^{u}*otāi*. [Cf. βουβότας Pindar.] Cf. *qo-qo-ta-o*.

qo-wa-ke-se-u[, KN As 602. MN: *G*^{u}*owaxeus*. [βοῦς, ἄγειν; Heubeck, 1957, p. 270.]

qo-we, MY Fu 711. MN.

qo-wi-ja, PY 172 = Tn 316. See pp. 288, 463.

qo-wo[, PY 258 = Jo 438. MN.

qo-zo, MY Oe 118. Obscure.

R A, Ideographic use: PY Un 219. Obscure, perhaps incomplete word: PY Fr 1215. Apparently in ligature with GOAT: KN Mc 4454 +; see p. 302.

ra-e-ja, PY 239 = Ta 642, 240 = Ta 713. Nom. sing. fem., adj. describing tables: *laeiā* 'of stone'. [On etymology and connexion with λᾶας see Heubeck, 1961 *a*.]

ra-i-pi, PY Na 530. PN, loc.?

ra-ja, KN As 607(?), C 979, Da 1202, Dn 1096 +. PN.

ra-ja-mo, PY Xa 1420. MN?

ra-ka, PY Un 592. Description of doubtful ideogram, prob. *154.

[?]*ra-kạ-te-ra*, PY 248 = Va 15. Obscure: see p. 348.

ra-ke, PY Eb 159, 148 = Ep 613. Perhaps verbal form, 3rd sing. aor.: *lakhe* 'was allotted' (Georgiev); Palmer (1963 *a*, p. 451) proposes dat. of noun: *lakhei* (from *lakhos* masc.) 'in the allotment'. See p. 450.

ra-ke-da-no, MY 106 = Ge 603. MN: *Lakedānōr*? [Cf. Λακεδαίμων; Szemerényi, 1959.]

ra-ke-da-no-re, MY 107 = Ge 604. Dat.: *-ānorei*.

]*ra-ke-re-we*[, KN Xd 305. MN?, -*klewēs*?

ra-ke-u, PY Cn 254. MN, app. nom. for dat.

ra-ku, KN V 653. MN.

ra-ku-ro, PY Eb 566, 126 = Eo 281, 131 = Ep 301. MN, nom. and dat.

ra-ku-ro-jo, PY 116 = En 659, [126 = Eo 281]. Gen.

ra-ma-jo, PY Cn 285, Jn 692 +. MN.

ra-ma-na-de, KN Fh 353. PN, acc. + -*de*.

ra-ma-o, PY Ub 1316. MN.

ra-mi-ni-ja, PY Ab 186. Nom. plur. fem. ethnic adj.: *Lāmniai*? [Λῆμνος.]

ra-mi-ni-jo, PY An 209, Cn 328, Cn 719. MN: *Lāmnios*?

ra-mo, KN Uf 120. Obscure, MN?

ra-mo-de[, TH Of 38. If complete, prob. PN + -*de*.

ra-ni, KN B 41, X 1801. MN.

ra-ni-jo-ne, PY 52 = An 207. Nom. plur. ethnic adj. or place name?

ra-o-no, KN Dv 1249. MN.

ra-pa-do, PY Ea 481. MN: *Lampadōn*. [Cf. Λαμπαδίων.]

ra-pạ-i-[ ]-*jọ-i*, PY Mn 11. Dat. plur., obscure.

ra-pa-sa-ko, PY 61 = Cn 131. MN, dat.: *Lampsakōi*. [Cf. place name Λάμψακος.]

ra-pa-sa-ko-jo, PY 62 = Cn 655. Gen.: *Lampsakoio*.

ra-pa-to, KN 202 = Fp 13. Month name, gen.?: *Lapatō*. [μηνὸς Λαπάτω, Schwyzer, *Dial*. 667 (Arcadia); see p. 305.]

ra-pe-do, PY 58 = An 654. MN.

ra-pi-ti-ra₂, PY Ab 555. Nom. plur. fem., a woman's trade: *raptriai* 'sewing-women', 'sempstresses'. [ῥάπτρια; cf. next.]

ra-pte, PY An 172, Ea 28, Ea 29 +. Nom. sing., man's trade: *rhaptēr* 'sewing-man', perhaps 'saddler'. [Cf. ῥάπτης, *ra-pi-ti-ra₂*; on etymology of ῥάπτω see Chadwick and Baumbach, 1963, pp. 241–2.]

ra-pte-re, KN Fh 1056, V 159, PY 52 = An 207 +. Nom. plur.: *rhaptēres*.

[*?ra-*]*pte-si*, KN Fh 5432. Dat. plur.: *rhaptērsi*?

ra-pte-ri-ja, PY 323 = Sb 1315. Nom. plur. fem. of adj.: *rhaptēriai* '(reins) with stitching work'. This suggests that the masculine trade at least was concerned with sewing leather rather than cloth.

ra-qa-ra, KN Xe 7437. Obscure.

ra-qi-ti-ra₂, PY Ab 356. Nom. plur. fem., a woman's trade, not identical with *ra-pi-ti-ra₂* (Bennett, 1956 *b*, p. 131); Lejeune (1958 *a*, p. 299): *laq*^{u}*triai* (cf. λάζομαι), but sense obscure (implausible Ruijgh, 1967, p. 377 'store-keepers').

ra-qi-ti-ra₂-o, PY Ab 667. Gen. plur.

ra-ri-di-jo, KN C 911. Nom. sing. masc. adj., describing a slave: possessive of personal name?

ra-sa-to, KN B 808. MN.

]-*ra-si-ne-wi-ja*, PY Vn 48. PN?

ra-su-ti-jo, PY Eb 1174, 116 = En 659, Ep 212. MN.

ra-su-ti-jo, KN L 761. MN? [Cf. *qa-ra-su-ti-jo*, PN *ra-su-to*.]

ra-su-to, KN 17 = Ai 739, As 604, C 979, Da 1189 +. PN.

ra-te-me, KN V 653. MN.

ra-to, KN Da 1321 +, Db 1185 +, Dn 1209, Xd 58. PN: *Lātō*. [Λατώ.]

ra-ti-jo, 87 = E 668. Ethnic adj.: *Lātioi*.

ra-u-ra-ta, KN Dd 1300. MN: *Laurātās*? Cf. *ra-wa-ra-ta*.

ra-u-ra-ti-ja, PY 304 = On 300. PN, gen. sing.: *Lauranthiās* or sim.?

ra-wa-ra-ti-ja, PY 45 = An 830. Variant spelling.

ra-wa-ra-ta₂, PY An 298, [257 = Jn 829], Ma 216. Variant spelling.

ra-u-ra-ti-jo, PY Ad 664. Epithet of *pu-ro*, to distinguish this town, also called *ra-u-ra-ti-ja*, from the capital Pylos.

ra-wa-ra-ti-jo, PY Cn 45. Variant spelling of prec.

ra-u-ta, PY An 5, Jn 832. MN.

]*ra-wa-e-si-jo*, KN E 846. Obscure; error for *ra-wa-ke-si-jo?*

ra-wa-ke-ja, KN 38 = As 1516. In parallel context with *qa-si-re-wi-ja*, hence prob. error for *ra-wa-ke-⟨si⟩-ja*, the office or retinue of the *ra-wa-ke-ta*.

ra-wa-ke-ṣị[-ja?], KN Xd 154. See above.

ra-wa-ke-ta, PY 55 = An 724, [Ea 1406?], Un 219, 171 = Un 718. Nom. and dat. sing.: *lāwāgetās*, *-tāi* 'leader of the people', see p. 120. [λᾱγέτᾱς Pindar +.]

ra-wa-ke-si-jo, KN E 1569, PY 147 = Ea 59 +, 152 = Er 312, 195 = Na 245. Nom. and dat. sing. masc., nom. sing. neut., nom. plur. masc., adj.: *lāwāgesios*, *-on*, etc. 'of or belonging to the Lawagetas'.

ra-wa-ke-si-jo-jo, PY Ea 421 +. Gen. sing. of prec.

ra-ẉạ-ṇị, KN C 911. MN.

ra-wa-ra-ta, PY An 723. PN?, variant of *ra-wa-ra-ti-ja*? Or MN, cf. *ra-u-ra-ta*?

ra-wa-ra-ti-ja/-jo, *ra-wa-ra-ta₂*: see s.v. *ra-u-ra-ti-ja*.

ra-wa-si-jo, KN E 288. Obscure; MN or ethnic?

ra-wi-ja-ja, PY Aa 807, Ab 586. Nom. plur. fem., description of women: *lāwiaiai* 'captives'. [Cf. ληϊάδες *Il.* xx, 193 +; Ion. ληΐη, Dor. λᾱ́ᾱ, Att. λεία < *λᾱϝίᾱ.]

ra-wi-ja-ja-o, PY 16 = Ad 686. Gen. plur. fem.: *lāwiaiāōn*.

ra-wi-zo, KN Db 1245. MN.

ra-wo-do-ko, PY Ea 802. MN: *Lāwodokos*. [Λᾱόδοκος *Il.* IV, 87 +.]

ra-wo-ke-ta, KN As 605, PY Jn 478. MN: *Lāwoskhetās*? [Heubeck, 1969a, p. 537.]

ra-wo-po-qo, KN As 4493. MN: *Lāwophorgᵘos*? [Λεώφορβος Preisigke, *Wörterbuch*; cf. Λεωφορβίδης; Heubeck (1969a, p. 537): *Lāwophogᵘos*.]

ra-wo-qo-no, KN B 798, Mc 4462. MN: *Lāwoqᵘhonos*. [Heubeck, 1969a, p. 537.]

ra-wo-qo-no-jo, KN Dl 928, D 1650. Gen.: *Lāwoqᵘhonoio*.

ra-wo-qo-ta, PY Jn 750. MN: *Lāwoqᵘhontās*. [Heubeck, 1969a, p. 537.]

ra-wo-ti-jo, KN Ce 61, Vc 203. MN.

RA₃, Identical with ideogram SAFFRON.

RE, As adjunct to CLOTH: KN Lc 646, L 8105. Ideographic use: MY Ui 651.

re-a-mo, PY An 209. MN.

re-ka, PY Eb 886, Eb 1344, Ep 212. WN: *Leskhā*? [Cf. MN Λέσχης; Palmer, 1954b, p. 27.]

re-ka-sa, MY Oe 110. WN?

re-ka-ṭa, KN B 806. MN.

re-ka-ta-ne, PY 52 = An 207. PN, loc., or masc. plur. of ethnic?

re-ke-to-ro-te-ri-jo, PY Fr 343. Description of oil or name of festival? Bennett: *lekhestrōtērion* 'for a spreading of couches', taken by some as implying a ἱερὸς γάμος, but perhaps rather a divine feast.

re-ke-e-to-ro-te-ri-jo, PY Fr 1217. Variant of prec., but exact form obscure.

]*re-ki-si*, KN X 7712. MN; prob. to be restored [*a-*]*re-ki-si*: *Alexis*. [Ἄλεξις.]

re-ko-no, KN C 917. MN.

re-ko-no-jo, KN C 912, C 917. Gen.

re-me-to, KN Pp 495, (]*re-me-to*, KN Dd 1106). MN.

re-ne, KN [L 7866?], M 719. Context obscure.

re-pe-u-ri-jo, PY Cn 40. PN.

re-pi-ri-jo, PY Eq 146. MN: *Leprios*? [Cf. PN Λέπρεον.]

re-po-so, KN As 609, Xe 5540. MN.

re-po-to, KN 222 = L 693, PY 319 = Un 1322. Neut. sing. qualifying *linon*: *lepton* 'fine, thin'. [*Il.* XVIII, 595 +.]

re-qa-se-wo, PY Cn 600. MN, gen. making PN with *wo-wo*.

re-qo-me-no, KN 39 = As 1517. Nom. plur. masc.: *leiqᵘomenoi* 'left behind or over'; cf. *o-pi-ro-qo*, *pe-ri-ro-qo*. [οἱ δ᾽ οἷοι λείπονται *Od.* XXII, 250 +.]

rẹ-qọ-na-to-mo, PY Eq 146. Nom. sing. masc., name of a trade.

re-qo-we, PY Jn 845. MN.

re-ṛi-jo, KN 83 = C 902. Ethnic adj.? [Cf. Λέριος?]

re-si, KN Lc 561. Context obscure.

re-si-jo[, KN X 7900. Context obscure.

rẹ-ṣi-we-i, PY 51 = An 18. PN, loc.

re-si-wo, PY 312 = An 1281. MN.

re-ta-mo, PY Cn 285. MN.

re-u-ka-so, PY Pa 53. MN, dat. *Leukasōi*? [Cf. Λευκασία Messenian stream.]

re-u-ka-ta, KN Ce 61, PY 255 = Jn 658, Jn 725. MN: *Leukātās*.

re-u-ka-ta-ra-ja[, PY Vn 851. WN (or MN?): *Leuktraiā*. [Cf. *re-u-ko-to-ro*.]

re-u-ko¹, KN L 695, PY 77 = Cn 418. Nom. sing., nom. dual, masc.: *leukos*, *leukō*, 'white'. [λευκός Hom. +.]

re-u-ka, KN Ld 649, 223 = L 471, MY 106 = Ge 603 +. Nom. sing. and plur. fem., nom. plur. neut.: *leukā*, *-ai*, *-a*.

re-u-ko², PY An 615(?), MY Oi 705. MN, nom. and dat.?: *Leukos*, *-ōi*. [prec.]

re-u-ko-jo, TH Z 849, Z 851, Z 852. Gen.: *Leukoio*.

re-u-ko-nu-ka, KN 214 = Ld 571, 215 = Ld 573, 217 = Ld 587, 218 = Ld 598 +. Nom. plur. neut., describing cloths: *leukonukha* 'with white *onukhes*' (see *o-nu-ka*).

re-u-ko-ro-o-pu₂-ru, PY Jn 415. MN: poss. error for *Leuko-ophrus* (Palmer, 1954*b*, p. 66), but we should expect rather *Leukophrus*.

re-u-ko-to, PY Un 1319. MN or PN?

re-u-ko-to-ro, PY Ad 290+, 41 = An 35, 180 = Ma 225, [Mn 456], 185 = Na 419. PN, capital of Further Province: *Leuktron*. [Λεῦκτρον, but not to be identified with any classical site of this name.]

re-u-si-wo(-*qe*), PY 312 = An 1281, Jn 692+. MN.

re-u-te-ra, PY Na 425. Error for *e-re-u-te-ra*.

re-wa-jo, KN 216 = L 871. MN, dat.

re-wa-o, PY Fn 324. MN, dat. [Cf. prec.?]

]-*re-wi-jo-te*: see s.v. *qa-si-re-u*.

re-wo, KN Xd 7663. MN?: *Lewōn*. [Λέων.]

re-wo-pi, PY 243 = Ta 708. Instr. plur.: *lewomphi* (< **lewont-phi*) 'with lions'. [λέων *Il.* v, 782+.]

re-wo-te-jo, PY 246 = Ta 722. Instr. plur. adj.: (*karaāphi*) *lewonteiois* 'with lions' (heads)'. [λεόντειος Aesch. +.]

re-wo-te-re-jo, PY 238 = Tn 996. Nom. dual (or plur.?) adj.: *lewotreiō* 'for bathing'. [λοετρά plur. 'bath' *Il.* XXII, 444+; for apparent vowel metathesis, see p. 160.]

re-wo-to-ro-ko-wo, PY Aa 783, 9 = Ab 553, 10 = Ad 676. Nom. and gen. plur. fem.: *lewotrokhowoi*, -*ōn*, 'bath-attendants'. [λοετροχόος *Od.* xx, 297+.]

RI, Ligatured with TUNIC, perh. = *ri-ta* 'linen': KN L 178.
 Ideographic use: PY 173 = Ma 222+, Mn 11; see p. 290.

ri-ja-ko, PY Jn 692, Jn 725. MN.

ri-jo, PY 53 = An 1, 54 = An 610, 55 = An 724, 75 = Cn 608, [257 = Jn 829], 179 = Ma 193, 192 = Na 252. PN, nom. and acc.: *Rhion*, one of the Nine Towns of the Hither Province. ['Ρίον Messenia, Strabo VIII, 360; modern Koróni.]

ri-jo-de, PY 250 = Vn 20. Acc. + -*de*: *Rhion-de*.

ri-jo-no, KN Ak 5876, Ap 629, 83 = C 902, Da 1091+, Dn 1209. PN.

ri-u-no, KN Xd 149. Variant spelling?

ri-*65-no, KN U 49, [Xd 292, X 5509?]. Variant spelling (if **65* = *ju*)?

ri-jo-ni-jo/-*ja*, KN 21 = Ak 624, Lc 529+, Od 563+. Ethnic adj.

ri-ku-we, PY Jn 692, Jn 725. MN.

ri-ma, PY Xa 1335. Obscure.

ri-ma-zo, KN Da 1415. MN.

ri-me-ne: see *e-ra-po ri-me-ne*.

ri-na-ko-ro, PY An 129. Description of man, poss. trade name: *lināgoros* (cf. Lejeune, 1958*a*, p. 133), or PN: *Linagroi* 'flax-fields' (Palmer, 1962, p. 710, 1963*a*, p. 453).

ri-ne-ja, PY Ab 745, Ab 746. Nom. plur. fem., a women's trade: *lineiai* 'flax-workers', 'linen-weavers'?

ri-ne-ja-o, PY 8 = Ad 670+. Gen. plur.: *lineiāōn*.

ri-ni-jo, KN X 722. Context obscure and reading uncertain; derivative of λίνον?

ri-no, KN 222 = L 693, Np 7423, Og 5778, X 7741, PY 184 = Nn 228, [319 = Un 1322?]. Nom. and acc. sing.: *linon* 'flax, linen'. [λίνον *Il.* IX, 661+.]

ri-pa-[.], KN Dv 5704. MN: to be restored *ri-pa*-[*ro*]: *Liparos* or *Liparōn*? [Λίπαρος, Λιπάρων.]

ri-sa-pi, PY Na 924. PN, loc. plur.: *Lissāphi*? [Cf. Λίσσα Crete, Λίσσαι Thrace.]

ri-so-wa, [KN Xd 7756?], PY 44 = Aq 218. MN.

ri-so-we-ja, PY Na 1040. PN.

ri-su-ra, MY 303 = V 659. WN.

ri-ta, KN 219 = L 594, L 5927, L 8159. Nom. plur. neut., epithet of *pharwea*: *līta* 'of linen'. [λῖτα acc. plur. *Od.* I, 130, etc.]

ri-u-no: see s.v. *ri-jo-no*.

ri-wi-jo, MY Au 609. MN.

ri-wi-so, KN Da 1114, Dv 1111, Ga 419. MN.

ri-zo, KN 39 = As 1517+, B 800, V 1523, PY 40 = An 261. MN, nom. and dat.

ri-*65-no: see s.v. *ri-jo-no*.

ri-*82-ta-o, TH Z 853. MN, gen.

RO, As a unit of weight, perhaps the same as #: KN Og 1804, Np 267+. See p. 55.

ro-a, KN Xd 148. Context obscure.

ro-i-ko, PY 249 = Va 482. Dual (or plur.?), description of pieces of ivory(?): *rhoikō* 'crooked' is impossible if the etymology is correct which demands *wr*-; *rhoïskō* 'pomegranates (as a decorative element)' Palmer, 1963*a*, p. 368.

ro-ko, PY Cn 40, Cn 570. MN, dat.

ro-ko-jo, PY 62 = Cn 655. Gen.

ro-o-wa, PY 53 = An 1, An 172, 57 = An 519, 55 = An 724, Mn 1370+, 184 = Nn 228. PN, loc., possibly the port of Pylos: see p. 187.

ro-qo-ta, PY 60 = An 661. MN.

ro-ro-ni-ja, PY 45 = An 830. Obscure, perhaps PN.

ro-ru, KN Ce 50, Db 1185, Dq 1234. MN.

ro-u-ko, PY 57 = An 519, [44 = Aq 218]. MN.

ro-u-si-je-wi-ja, PY 323 = Sb 1315. Nom. plur. fem., describing reins: perhaps *Lousiēwiai*, derivative of *ro-u-so*; see p. 520.

ro-u-so, PY 7 = Aa 717+, Ab 382+, Cn 285+, [257 = Jn 829], [258 = Jo 438], 178 = Ma 365+. PN, one of the Nine Towns of the Hither Province: *Lousos*. [Λουσοί Arcadia.]

ro-u-si-jo, PY 307 = Fr 1220, 311 = Fr 1226, Ua 1413, 252 = Vn 10. Ethnic adj.: *Lousios*.

ro-wo, PY Jn 750. MN.

ru-da-to, KN X 7677. MN?

ru-de-a₂, PY 317 = Ub 1318. Neut. plur. of noun in -*os*? See p. 491.

ru-do-ro-i[, KN Fh 5498. Obscure; reading perh. *ru-do-ro-no*.

ru-ke-wo-wo-wi-ja, PY Na 1053. PN, prob. gen. of MN + *wo-wi-ja*: *Lunkēwos worwia* 'the boundaries of Lynceus'. [Λυγκεύς; ὅρια, see *wo-wo*.]

ru-ki-ja, PY 55 = An 724. Context obscure.

ru-ki-jo, PY Gn 720, Jn 415. MN in Jn, uncertain in Gn: *Lukios*? [Λύκιος.]

ru-ki-ti-ja, KN Ln 1568. WN: *Luktiā*. [See next.]

ru-ki-to, KN Da 1288+, Dm 1177, 92 = Fh 349, V 159+. PN: *Luktos*. [Λύκτος *Il.* II, 647, later Λύττος; Egypt. *ri-kɜ-tj*? (Faure, 1968). The spelling *ki* rather than *ko* may be due to the influence of the ethnic adj., but could indicate an obscure vowel in the non-Greek form of the name.]

ru-ki-ti-jo, KN 83 = C 902, 87 = E 668+. Ethnic adj.: *Luktios, -oi*.

ru-ko-a₂-ke̦-re-u-te, PY Jn 415. PN, dat.-loc. [cf. *a-ka-re-u-te, a-ke-re-u-te*.]

ru-ko-ro, PY 312 = An 1281, Ea 132, 109 = Ea 782+. MN: *Lugros*?

ru-ko-ro-jo, PY Ea 823. Gen.

ru-ko-wo-ro, PY 167 = Es 650 rev. MN: *Lukoworos*. [Cf. PN Λυκουρία.]

ru-ko-u-ro, PY Es 729. Alternative spelling of the same name; since it cannot be a contracted form = Λυκοῦρος, it may indicate a pronunciation *Lukowros*.

ru-ma-no, KN Dg 1438. MN.

ru-na, KN 38 = As 1516, PY Un 1320. MN, nom. and dat.

ru-na-mo, KN Da 1098, Da 1277. MN.

ru-na-so, KN Dv 1439, Dv 1442. MN: *Lurnassos*? [Cf. PN Λυρνησσός *Il.* II, 690+.]

ru-nu, KN Ln 1568. WN.

ru-ro, KN V 832, PY 43 = Aq 64, 258 = Jo 438. MN: *Luros*? [Λύρος.]

ru-sa-ma, KN Ln 1568. WN.

ru-si, KN Ak 634 edge (*ru-si*[), L 588 (*ru-si-qe*). MN: *Lusis*. [Λύσις.]

ru-ta₂, KN Db 5272[+]5294. MN.

ru-ta₂-no, KN Ap 639. WN.

ru-we-ta, PY Cn 599. MN, dat.

ru-we-to, TH Of 29. MN or PN?

]*ru-wo-i-ko*, KN Db 2020. MN, possibly to be restored: [*Eu*]*ruwoikos* or [*Po*]*luwoikos*?

ru-*56-ra-so, KN Da 1172. MN.

ru-*83-o, PY 115 = En 74, [120 = Eo 276]. MN, gen.

ru-*83-e, PY 120 = Eo 276. Dat.

SA, As adjunct to SHEEP and GOAT: KN C 394, D 5954.

    Ideographic use, at Pylos = *ri-no* 'flax', 'linen', at Knossos perhaps not the same since it is weighed: KN Nc 4479, Nc 5121, PY 195 = Na 245+, 198 = Ng 319, 199 = Ng 332, 184 = Nn 228, 183 = Nn 831. [Possibly connected with Semitic words for 'linen': Milani, 1970, p. 305.]

    At Mycenae, abbreviation of *sa-sa-ma* 'sesame': MY 106 = Ge 603, 107 = Ge 604.

sa-de-so, KN L 868. MN?

sa-jo, KN Dk 931. PN.

sa-ka-re-u, PY Ea 776, Jn 431. MN: *Sangareus*? [Σαγγαρεῖς Aeolic people, cf. Σάγαρα, etc.]

sa-ka-re-wo, PY Ea 756. Gen.

sa-ka-re-we, PY Ea 56, Ea 304. Dat.

]*sa-ka-ri-jo*, KN V 1523. MN?, dat.?

sa̦-ke-me̦-no, MY Au 609. MN.

sa-ma-da, KN Np 267. PN or MN?

]*sa-ma-ja-so̦*, KN Dv 5054. MN.

sa-ma-ra, PY [257 = Jn 829], 181 = Ma 378, [304 = On 300], Wa 730. PN, one of the Seven Towns of the Further Province.

sa-ma-ra-de, PY 41 = An 35. Acc. + -*de*.

sa-ma-ri-jo, KN Da 1147. MN.

sa-ma-ri-wa, PY Na 527. PN.

sa-ma-ri-wa-ta, KN As 645, Dv 1188. MN. [Cf. prec.]

sa-ma-ru[, KN V 655. MN?

sa-ma-ti-ja, KN Ap 639. WN.

sa-me-ti-jo, KN 232 = K 875. MN.

sa-mi, KN Ap 639. WN.

sa-mu-ta-jo, KN 225 = L 520, PY 254 = Jn 389, Vn 865, MY V 662. MN: *Samuthaios*? [Cf. WN Σαμύθα.]

sa-na-so[, KN Nc 5787. MN?

sa-na-to-de, KN Fs 2. PN, acc. + -*de*?

sa-ni-jo, PY An 5, Cn 4. MN: *Sanniōn*? [Σαννίων.]

sa-nu-we, PY Vn 851. MN or WN, dat.

sa-nu-we-ta, KN Db 1227. MN.

sa-pa, KN 222 = L 693, MY Oe 108. Prob. the name of a textile.

sa-pa-ka-te-ri-ja, KN C 941. Originally taken by Sittig as PN, *Sphaktēriā*; more likely neut. plur. *sphaktēria* 'victims' (Lejeune, 1960 *a*, p. 12), but the writing of initial *s*- before *p* and *ka-te* for *ke-te* = *kte* both arouse suspicion (Palmer, 1963 *a*, p. 185); see p. 390.

sa-pa-nu-wo-me-no, KN X 999. Obscure; poss. to be divided *sa-pa-nu-wo me-no*.

sa-pe-ra, PY Fr 1215. Obscure, apparently replaces entry giving quantity of oil. Cf. next.

sa-pi-da, PY 59 = An 656. Obscure, apparently replaces entry giving number of men. Cf. prec.

sa-pi-de, PY Vn 19, MY 105 = Ge 602, Ge 605. Nom. plur., a commodity which is counted, containers?: perh. *sarpides* 'boxes'? [Cf. σαρπίς· σαρπός An. Ox. II, 466, and σαρπούς· κιβωτούς Hesych.] See p. 227.

sa-pi-ti-ne-we-jo, KN 94 = F 841. Poss. adj., cf. next. See p. 219.

sa-pi-ti-nu-wo, KN As 1516. MN.

sa-qa-re-jo, KN Dl 412, Dl 794, Dl 935+. Adj. describing sheep, poss. derived from MN.

sa-ra-pe-da, PY 171 = Un 718. Poss. PN containing -*peda*?

sa-ra-pe-do[, PY 153 = Er 880. Prob. variant (sing.?) of prec.

sa-ri-nu-wo-te, PY An 424, Mn 456, [Na 1094]. PN, loc.: *Salinwontei*? [Cf. Σελινοῦς stream in Triphylia.]

sa-ri-no-te, PY Vn 130. Variant form of or error for prec.

se-ri-no-wo-te, PY Qa 1290. Prob. variant spelling.

sa-ri-qo-ro, PY An 172, Jn 845. MN.

sa-sa-jo, KN Df 1290. MN.

sa-sa-ma, MY 105 = Ge 602, Ge 605, Ge 606. Also abbreviated SA, 106 = Ge 603 +. Nom. plur. neut.: *sāsama* 'sesame seed'. [σήσαμα Hipponax 6 B.C. +, Dor. σάσαμον. Semitic loanword, cf. Akkad. *šammašammu*, Ugaritic *ššmn*.]

sa-sa-wo, PY Eb 842, [148 = Ep 613]. MN.

sa-ti-[.], KN Ap 639. MN.

sa-u-ko, KN Xd 179. MN.

sa-u-ri-jo, KN As 1516. MN: *Saurios*? [Cf. Σαῦρος, Σαυρίας.]

sa-za-ro, KN B 799. MN.

sa-ze-ro, KN Db 1262. MN.

sa-zo, KN As 1520, Dv 5301. MN.

*sa-*65*, KN Ap 639. WN.

SE, Abbreviation of place name *se-to-i-ja* on SHEEP tablets: KN Do 919, Do 923 +; (see Killen, 1964*a*, p. 91).

    Adjunct to ideogram *168* (adze?): KN Pp 493 +.

se-do, KN De 1398. MN.

se-me-tu-ro, KN Dc 1364. MN.

se-no, PY 61 = Cn 131, 62 = Cn 655, 168 = Es 644, 167 = Es 650 +. MN, nom. and dat.

se-re-mo-ka-ra-a-pi, PY 243 = Ta 708. Instr. plur., a decorative feature on chairs: prob. *-k(a)raāphi*. See pp. 343, 501.

se-re-mo-ka-ra-o-re, PY 242 = Ta 707, 244 = Ta 714. Instr. sing.

se-ri-na-ta, KN U 4478. MN: *Selinātās*. [Cf. *se-ri-no*.]

se-ri-no, MY 107 = Ge 604. Nom. sing., a herb or spice: *selinon* 'celery', *Apium graveolens*. [σέλινον *Il.* II, 776 +.]

se-ri-no-wo-te: see *sa-ri-nu-wo-te*.

se-to-i-ja, KN Ak 634, 38 = As 1516 +, Da 1392 +, 209 = Lc 525, Sd 4407 +. PN. Comparison with Σηταία is prob. false, and there are indications that the name belongs to central Crete.

se-we-ri-ko-jo, PY Sa 753. MN, gen.

se-we-ri-wo-wa-zo, PY Fn 324. MN, dat.

se-wo-to, KN Da 1268. Annotation to PN *qa-ra*.

SI, Ligatured with OX: PY 77 = Cn 418.

    Ligatured with PIG, = *si-a₂-ro* 'hog': PY 75 = Cn 608, Ua 25, 97 = Un 2, 96 = Un 138.

si-a₂-ro, PY 75 = Cn 608. Acc. plur.: *sialons* 'fat hogs'. [σίαλος *Il.* XXI, 363 +.]

si-da-jo, KN Dl 947, Nc 4490?, Od 562. MN: *Sidaios*. [Cf. PN Σίδαι, Σίδη.]

si-ja-du-we, KN Dk 969, Dl 930 +. PN.

si-ja-ma, KN V 1526. MN?

si-ja-ma-to, KN Fp 48, U 4478, X 451. Nom. and dat.; probably a divinity.

si-ja-pu₂-ro, KN 38 = As 1516, [U 4492?]. MN.

si-jo-wo-te, PY Cn 4. PN, loc.

si-ki-to, KN Da 1339. MN.

si-ma, PY 114 = En 609, 118 = Eo 211. WN: *Sīmā*. [Σίμη; cf. *si-mo*.]

si-ma-ko, PY Pn 30. MN.

ṣi-mi-do, KN As 607. MN.

si-mi-te-u, KN Am 827, V 1583. MN: *Smintheus*. [Σμινθεύς; as epithet of Apollo, *Il.* I, 39 +.]

si-mo, KN Sc 263. MN: *Sīmos, Sīmōn*. [Σῖμος, Σίμων.]

si-mu-ta, PY Jn 832. MN.

si-ne-e-ja, KN Ap 639. WN.

si-ni-to, KN Dg 1280. MN.

si-no-u-ro, PY Cn 285. MN.

si-nu-ke, KN Ap 639. WN.

si-nu-mo-ro, KN Mc 4456. MN?

si-pa-ta-do, KN Dv 5663. MN.

si-pa-ta-no, PY Jn 832. MN.

si-pe-we, KN 83 = C 902. PN, loc.?

si-pu₂, KN 38 = As 1516. MN.

si-qq, KN Ai 7745. MN.

si-ra-ko, KN Ai 5976, B 822, [X 7744]. MN.

si-ra-no, KN V 466. MN: *Silānos*. [Σιλανός, Σιληνός.]

si-ra-pe-te-ṣọ, KN V 961. MN.

si-ra-ro, KN 83 = C 902, 86 = Co 907. PN.

    si-ra-ri-ja, KN Lc 512. Ethnic adj.

ṣi-ra-si-ja, KN X 974. Obscure.

si-ra-ta, PY Jn 750. MN.

si-re-wa, PY 182 = Ma 126, Mn 456. PN.

si-ri-jo, PY 148 = Ep 613. MN, nom. error for gen.: *Sirios*?

    si-ṛi-jọ-jo, PY Eb 159. Gen.: *Sirioio*?

si-ta-ro, KN De 1138, X 7774. MN.

si-to, KN 35 = Am 819, MY Au 658. Nom. sing. with ideogram BARLEY at KN, WHEAT at MY: *sītos* 'grain'.

si-to-ko-wo, PY 26 = An 292. Nom. plur. fem. or dat. sing. masc.?: *sītokhowoi, -ōi* 'grainmeasurer(s)'. [Cf. *Od.* II, 380, γρηῢς . . . δέ οἱ ἄλφιτα χεῦεν.]

si-to-pọ[, KN As 625. Poss. to be restored *si-to-pọ*[*-qo*]: *sītopoqʷos* 'cook', cf. *a-si-to-po-qo*.

si-to-po-ti-ni-ja, MY 321 = Oi 701. Dat. sing.: *sītōn potniāi* or *Sītōi potniāi*. [Cf. Σιτώ epithet of Demeter.]

si-za, KN As 1520. MN.

so-ro-pe-o, PY 52 = An 207. PN.

so-u-ro, PY [114 = En 609], 119 = Eo 224. MN.

so-we-ne-ja, PY 237 = Ta 709. Nom. sing. fem., adj. of next.

so-we-no(-qe), PY 245 = Ta 721 +. Instr. sing. or plur.: item of decoration on a footstool. See p. 338.

so-wo-te: see *do-ro-qo*.

SU, Adjunct to TREE, abbreviation of *su-za* 'figtree': KN 164 = Gv 863.

su-di-ni-ko, KN De 1151. MN.

su-ja-to, KN M 719. Obscure.

su-ke-re, KN As 40. MN.

su-ke-re-o, KN 38 = As 1516. Gen.

su-ki-ri-ta, KN Db 1324 +, Df 1325, Dn 1092 +. PN: poss. *Sugrita*. [Cf. Σύβριτα; alternation of β and γ occurs in other cases where a labiovelar origin is excluded (e.g. Att. βλήχων,

Dor. γλάχων); but the evidence that *su-ki-ri-ta* is an *a*-stem makes the identification doubtful.]

su-ki-ri-ta-pi, KN Dl 47. Loc. plur.?

su-ki-ri-ta-jo, KN C 911. Ethnic adj.: *Sugritaios*.

su-ki-ri-to, KN 38 = As 1516. MN. [Cf. prec.]

su-ko, KN V 479, PY Eb 149, 148 = Ep 613. MN; at PY might be gen. plur. *sūkōn* (cf. *o-pi-su-ko*), but MN perhaps more likely.

]*su-ko-ne*, KN Fp 5472. Obscure.

su-ma-no, KN Dh 1406. MN.

su-me-ra-we-[.], TH Of 26. MN, dat.?

su-mi, KN As 1516. MN.

su-mo-no(*-qe*), KN Od 563. MN.

su-po, KN Dc 5812. MN.

su-pu-wo, KN C 912. MN, gen.?

su-qo-ta, PY Ea 822. Dat. sing.: *sug^{u}ŏtāi* 'swineherd'. [Cf. συβώτης *Od.* IV, 640 +; later συβότης.]

su-qo-ta-o, PY 147 = Ea 59, Ea 481 +. Gen. sing. or plur.: *sug^{u}ŏtāo, -tāōn*.

su-ra-se, PY Ae 8, Ae 72, 30 = Ae 264. 3rd sing. aor. (or fut.?), sense obscure; the only Greek interpretation is *sūlāse*(*i*) 'seized'. [συλάω Hom. +.]

su-ra-te, PY Ae 72, 30 = Ae 264. Nom. sing., prob. agent noun from verb *su-ra-se*: *sūlātēr* 'seizer'? See p. 169.

su-ri-jo, KN X 5962. MN?

su-ri-mo, KN 29 = Am 821, Da 1108 +, Dn 1089, Pp 494 +. PN.

su-ri-mi-jo, KN [88 = E 749], 99 = Ga 418, [Og 833]. Ethnic adj.

su-ro-no, TH Z 846, Z 854 +. MN, gen.

su-ru-so, KN Dv 1312. MN.

su-se, KN Da 5192. MN.

su-ta-no, KN Da 1321. MN.

su-we-ro-wi-jo, PY 56 = An 657. MN (or possibly PN); see p. 189.

su-za, KN 94 = F 841, 165 = Gv 862, 166 = Gv 864, PY 153 = Er 880. Nom. plur. describing a form of TREE ideogram, also with NI, the usual sign for 'figs': *sutsai* (< **sukyai*) 'figtrees'. [Classical συκέα, also Aeol. συκία, are new derivatives of σῦκον.]

]*su-*56-ta*, KN As 5932 edge. Restoration [*ku-*]*su-*56-ta* would be tempting, if **56 = pa₃*, as *xumpanta*, but the gender is wrong for a list of men.

TA, As adjunct to OX, = *tauros* 'bull' (one bull and twenty cows): KN C 901.

Ligatured with SHEEP, = *ta-to-mo* 'steading': PY Cn 4, Cn 595.

Ideographic use (with DA) on tablets listing women workers, perhaps a supervisor: KN 18 = Ak 611, 21 = Ak 624 +, PY 4 = Aa 240 +, 6 = Ab 379 +.

ta-de-so, KN De 1409, Df 1285, V 655 +, TH Z 869. MN: *Tardēssos?* [Τάρδησσος.]

ta-di-*22-so, KN De 5032. MN.

ta-ja-no, KN Dv 7240. MN.

ta-mi-de-so, KN Dl 944. MN.

ta-mi-je-u, PY 253 = Jn 310. MN: *Tamieus?* [Cf. Ταμίας.]

ta-mi-ta-na, PY 191 = Na 248. PN.

ta-mi-te-mo, KN Fs 11. Obscure, destination of offerings?

ta-na-po-so, KN Db 1198, Dv 1410. MN.

ta-na-to, KN De 1618. MN.

ta-na-wa, PY 287 = Sa 793. Nom. plur. neut. describing wheels: *ta-na-wa* 'thin', 'slender', possibly 'worn thin'. [ταναός *Il.* XVI, 589 + both 'long' and 'thin'; cf. Lat. *tenuis*, Eng. *thin*.]

ta-na-wo, PY Jn 693. MN: *Tanawos?* [Cf. prec.]

ta-ni-ko, PY 56 = An 657, 312 = An 1281 (*ta-ni-ko-qe*). MN.

ta-nu-ko, PY An 209. MN.

ta-pa-da-no, KN As 625. MN.

ta-pa-e-o-te, KN 37 = B 823. Nom. plur. masc. describing men, apparently contrasting with *a-pe-o-te* 'absent': possibly an adverb (e.g. *tarpha*, cf. ταρφέες *Il.* XI, 387 +) plus *eontes*, effectively meaning 'present'.

ta-pa-no, KN F 153, Sc 240, X 7795. MN.

ta-pe-ro, KN Da 1343. MN.

ta-qa-ra-te[, KN Xe 524, [X 7752?]. MN, dat.

ta-qa-ra-ti, KN V 7512. Variant of prec. or different MN?

ta̯-ra̯, KN 29 = Am 821. PN.

ta-ra-i, KN Xd 298. MN?

ta-ra-ke-wi[*-jo?*], PY An 172. PN: *Trākhewios?* [Cf. τραχύς.]

ta-ra-ma-ta, PY Ea 336, 112 = Ea 825 +, Vn 851. MN, nom. and dat.: *Thalamātās, -āi*. [Cf. Θαλαμάτας inhabitant of Θαλάμαι.]

ta-ra-ma-ta-o, PY 32 = Ae 108 +. Gen.: *Thalamātāo*.

ta-ra-ma-o, PY 31 = Ae 134. Error for *ta-ra-ma-ta-o*.

ta-ra-me-to, KN 84 = Ce 59. MN?

ta-ra-mi-ka, PY Eb 464, 143 = Ep 705. WN: *Thalamikā, -iskā?* [Cf. PN Θαλάμαι; Chantraine (1966, p. 167).]

ta-ra-nu, KN V 1521, PY 242 = Ta 707 +. Nom. sing. masc.: *thrānus* 'beam', 'footstool'. [θρῆνυς *Od.* XIX, 57 +, Att. θρᾶνος 'bench'.]

ta-ra-nu-we, PY 245 = Ta 721, 251 = Vn 46. Nom. plur.: *thrānues*.

ta-ra-pe-se, PY Vn 865. MN.

ta-ra-qo, KN E 843. MN.

ta-ra-sa-ta, KN Vc 201. MN: *Thalassātās?*

ta-ra-si-ja, KN 212 = Lc 535 +, Le 642, 283 = So 4442, PY 253 = Jn 310 +, MY Oe 110. Nom. and acc. sing.: *talasiā, -ān* 'amount weighed out and issued for processing'. See p. 508. [ταλασία 'wool-spinning' shows greater specialization since the Myc. word is used also of bronze and materials for manufacture of wheels; on form, see Lejeune, 1961 *b*, p. 419.]

ta-ra-to, PY An 192, **121**＝Eo 247. MN: *Stratōn*? [Στράτων.] Cf. *ta-ra₂-to*.

ta-ra-to-no, KN Dc 1130. MN.

ta-ra₂-to, PY **115**＝En 74, **116**＝En 659, **124**＝Eo 351, **125**＝Eo 471+. MN, the same as *ta-ra-to*: *Stratōn*?

ta-re-u, PY Jn 693. MN: *Thaleus*? [Cf. Θαλῆς.]

ta-re-wa, PY Fn 41. MN, dat.: *Thalewāi*? [Θαλέας.]

ta-si-ko[, KN Ga 7367. MN?

ta-so, KN As 608, C 911, Dv 5200. MN.

ta-su, KN Ln 1568. MN or WN.

ta-ta-ke-u, PY **62**＝Cn 655. MN: *Startāgeus*. [Cf. Cret. σταρτος＝στρατός.]

ta-ta-ro, KN As 607, PY **119**＝Eo 224, **131**＝Ep 301. MN, nom. and dat.: *Tantalos, -ōi*? [Τάνταλος *Od*. XI, 582.]

ta-ta-ta, KN Ce 152. MN?

ta-te-re, PY An 209. Nom. plur., a man's trade: perhaps *statēres* connected with *ta-to-mo*? [στατήρ only of weights and coins; 'debtor' once Epich. 5 B.C.]

ta-ti-qo-we-u, PY **55**＝An 724. MN: *Stātigᵘoweus*. [Cf. Στήσιππος.]

   ta-ti-qo-we-wo, PY **58**＝An 654. Gen.: *Stātigᵘowēwos*.

ta-to¹, KN As 602 (*ta-to-qe*). MN.

ta-to², PY Cn 4. PN?

ta-to-mo, KN Ws 1703, PY Cn 4, Cn 595, **251**＝Vn 46. Nom. sing.: *stathmos*, in PY Cn 4 'sheep-fold', in Vn 46 'upright post', 'pillar', in KN Ws possibly 'weight'. [σταθμός 'sheep-fold' *Il*. V, 557+; 'upright post' *Od*. I, 333+; 'weight' Hdt.+.]

ta-u-na-so, KN De 1269. MN.

ta-u-pa-du-we, KN E 843. MN.

ta-u-po-no, KN U 4478. MN.

ta-u-ro, KN V 832. MN: *Tauros*. [Ταῦρος mythical king of Crete.]

ta-wa-ko-to, KN Od 715. MN?

ta-we-si-jo, KN Dv 1332. MN.

   ta-we-si-jo-jo, PY **40**＝An 261, An 616.

ta-za, KN Db 1247, Dv 5219. MN.

ta-za-po, KN Da 8201. MN.

ta-za-ro, KN **85**＝Ch 896, Db 1097, V 503. MN.

ta-zo-te-ja, PY Vn 851. WN.

ta-*22-de-so, TH [Z 870], Z 871, [Z 872], Z 876. MN, cf. *ta-de-so*.

ta-*49-ro, KN Da 1588. MN.

TE, As adjunct to MAN, KN As 5542, As 5944. As adjunct to OIL, KN Fh 340. Ligatured with CLOTH, ＝ *te-pa*?: KN Ap 5748. **209**＝Lc 525+, **213**＝Le 641+, Ws 8153, PY La 624+, **313**＝Un 6. Ligatured with WHEEL, ＝ *te-mi-dwe-ta*?: PY **285**＝Sa 487+; see p. 373.

te-do-ne-ja, PY Vn 851. WN.

te-i-ja, PY **306**＝Fr 1202. Dat. fem. sing.: *theiāi* 'divine', 'of the gods'. [θεῖος *Il*. VI, 180+.]

te-ja-ro, KN V 479. MN.

te-jo, KN Dv 7617, L 565. MN.

te-ke, PY **235**＝Ta 711. 3rd sing. aor.: *thēke* 'appointed', 'made'. [Cf. τὴν . . . Τρῶες ἔθηκαν . . . ἱέρειαν *Il*. VI, 300.] The sense 'buried' (Palmer, 1963 *a*, p. 340) normally requires a mention of the earth, bones, etc.

te-ki-ri-ne-to, KN Dq 686. MN.

te-ko-to-ne, KN **47**＝Am 826, [PY **51**＝An 18?]. Nom. plur.: *tektones* 'carpenters'. [τέκτονες *Il*. VI, 315+.]

te-ko-to-a-pe, PY An 5. Prob. two words: *tekton apēs*(?), rather than PN (Palmer, 1963 *a*, pp. 33, 132): see Chadwick, 1967 *b*.

te-ko-to-na-pe, PY **51**＝An 18, An 852. Alternative spelling of prec.

te-me-no, PY **152**＝Er 312. Nom. sing. neut.: *temenos* 'area of land set aside for a chieftain'. [τέμενος βασιλήϊον *Il*. XVIII, 550+, later 'precinct of a god'.]

te-me-u[, KN Xd 319. MN.

te-mi¹, Only in composite spellings: *o-u-ki-te-mi* KN **207**＝V 280; *o-u-te-mi* KN **207**＝V 280. Neg. *ou*, *ouk*(*h*)*i* (see *o-u-*, *o-u-ki-*) and a noun, poss. *termis* 'border(?)'. [Cf. τέρμις· πούς Hesych.; *te-mi-dwe*.] Formerly taken as *themis*, but explanation of this tablet as a calendar is unlikely. See p. 476.

te-mi², KN Df 1602. MN.

te-mi-dwe, KN **278**＝So 894. Nom. sing. neut., adj. describing wheels: *termidwen* 'provided with a *termis*' (＝'border', 'edge', 'flange?'). [Cf. τερμιόεις *Il*. XVI, 803+, in Hom. of shields and tunics, exact sense unclear; alternative declensions in *-is*, *-ios* and *-idos* also evidenced by [*te*]-*mi-we-te*, q.v.]

te-mi-dwe-ta, KN **278**＝So 894, So 4429+, PY Sa 791, **287**＝Sa 793. Nom. plur. neut.: *termidwenta*.

te-mi-de-we-te, PY Sa 1266. Nom. dual: *termidwente*.

te-mi-ro, KN Da 1338. MN.

te-mi-ti-ja, PY **304**＝On 300. PN: *Themistia*? The same place as *ti-mi-to-a-ke-e*, q.v. [A derivative of θέμις is made less likely by alternative spelling *ti-mi-ti-ja*.]

   ti-mi-ti-ja, PY **258**＝Jo 438. Gen.: *Th*(*i*)*mistiās*.

te-mi-ti-jo, PY Ac 1278. Nom. plur. ethnic adj.: *Themistioi*.

[*te*]-*mi-we-te*, KN Sg 1811. Nom. dual: either *termiwente* as alternative form of *termidwente* (see *te-mi-dwe*), or error for *te-mi-de-we-te*.

te-na-ja-so[, KN As 604. MN.

te-nu, KN Uf 7489. MN.

te-o, KN Ai 966, PY **140**＝Eb 297, **120**＝Eo 276, **135**＝Ep 704. Acc. sing.: *theon* 'the god (or goddess)'; in KN Ai 966 either gen. plur. *theōn* or as PY Eo 276 error for *te-o-jo*. [θεός masc. and fem. Hom.+; cf. *te-i-ja*.]

te-o-jo, PY **137**＝Eb 416+, **150**＝Ed 411, **115**＝En 74+, **122**＝Eo 160+, **135**＝Ep 704+.

Gen. sing.: *theoio* (always with *doelos* or *doelā*) 'servant of the god(dess)'.

te-o-i, KN E 842, ⟦Fh 348⟧, PY 311 = Fr 1226, Fr 1355. Dat. plur.: *theoihi* 'to the gods'. [Cf. *pa-si-te-o-i* s.v. *pa*.] A dat. dual is theoretically possible.

te-o-na, PY 116 = En 659. Error for *te-o-jo*.

te-o-do-ra(-qe), MY 303 = V 659. WN: *Theodōrā*. [Θεοδώρα.]

te-o-po-[, PY 50 = An 39. MN?

te-o-po-ri-ja, KN Ga 1058, Od 696. Possibly name of festival?: *theophoriā*? [θεοφορία 'divine possession'.]

te-pa, KN L 5090?, Ws 8153. Name of a heavy type of cloth. [Cf. τάπης?]

te-pa-i, MY Oe 107. Dat. plur.

te-pa-ra, KN Ce 50. MN or PN?

te-pe, PY Jn 725. MN.

te-pe-ja, KN 213 = Le 641, TH Of 35. Nom. plur. and dat. sing.?, a woman's trade, prob. makers of *te-pa*.

te-pe-ja-o, PY Ad 921. Gen. plur.

te-pe-u, PY An 340. MN: *Terpeus*? [Formed on Τέρπανδρος?]

]**te-pi-ja-qe**, PY Fn 324. Personal name (+ *q^{u}e*?), dat.?

te-po-se-u, PY 258 = Jo 438, 304 = On 300. MN.

te-qa-de, MY X 508. Perhaps PN, acc. + -*de*: *Thēg^{u}ans-de*, probably not Thebes in Boeotia. [Cf. next.]

te-qa-ja, KN Ap 5864, PY Ep 539. WN: *Thēg^{u}aiā*. [Cf. Θηβαῖος, ethnic adj.; *au-to-te-qa-jo*.]

te-qa-ta-qe, PY 54 = An 610. Nom. plur. (with -*q^{u}e*), class of men.

te-qi-ri-jo-ne, PY Fn 187, [Vn 851]. MN, dat.

te-qi-jo-ne, PY Un 219. Defective spelling of prec.

te-ra-ni-ja, PY 43 = Aq 64. Obscure: see p. 177.

te-ra-pe-te, KN V 147. MN.

te-ra-pi-ke, PY Eb 842, 148 = Ep 613. Perhaps 3rd pers. sing. of verb: see pp. 263, 450.

te-ra-po-si-jo, KN Da 1314, Db 1263 +, Lc 446. MN, a 'collector' or adj.? [Derivative of θεράπων?]

te-ra-po-ti, KN F 193. Dat., recipient of barley, MN?: *Theraponti*? [Θεράπων.]

]**te-ra-u-re-o**, PY Sa 22. MN, gen.?

te-ra-wo, MY 46 = Au 102, Au 653, Au 657. MN: *Telāwōn*? [Cf. Τελέων.]

te-ra-wo-ne, PY Fn 79. Dat.: *Telāwonei*?

te-re-do, PY Cn 1287. MN.

te-re-ja, PY Eb 149, [Eb 495], [148 = Ep 613]. Probably 3rd sing. pres. indic. of athematic verb: *teleiā* (cf. Hom. δαμνᾷ for *δάμνα?) 'perform function of *te-re-ta*'?

te-re-ja-e, Eb 149, Eb 495, 148 = Ep 613. Inf. of prec.: *teleiāen*? [Inf. ending -*en* as in thematic -*een*?]

te-re-ja-wo, KN Vc 188. MN: *Teleiāwōn*?

te-re-ne-we, PY 51 = An 18. PN, loc. sing. or nom. plur.?

te-re-ne-wi-ja, PY An 852, Cr 868. Variant form of name, fem. loc. sing.

te-re-no, KN Fp 363. Obscure.

te-re-pa-to: see *jo-te-re-pa-to*.

te-re-ta, KN 47 = Am 826, 161 = Uf 839 +, PY Eb 149, 150 = Ed 411, 114 = En 609, 119 = Eo 224, Eq 146, 152 = Er 312. Nom. sing. and plur., name of a class of functionaries: *telestās, -ai*. [Cf. τελεστά nom. sing. Olympia 6 B.C.]

te-re-ta-o, PY 152 = Er 312. Gen. plur.: *telestāōn*.

te-re-te-we, PY 28 = An 607. Obscure: see p. 168.

te-re-wa-ko, KN C 973. MN?

te-ri-ja, PY Un 443. Obscure; see s.v. *po-re-no-zo-te-ri-ja*.

te-ro-a, PY Xa 627. Obscure.

te-ro-ri-jo, KN Uf 1522. MN, dat.?

te-ru-ro, KN Dd 1380, Mc 4464? MN.

te-ru-sa, KN Dv 1308, TH Of 29. MN.

te-se-e, PY Na 531. PN, loc.

te-se-u, PY 115 = En 74, 120 = Eo 276. MN: *Thēseus*. [Θησεύς *Il.* 1, 265; short form of name beginning Θησι-? Heubeck, 1957, p. 271.]

te-so-qe, PY Un 1193. MN, dat.? or PN?

te-ta-ra-ne, PY 53 = An 1. PN, loc.

te-te-re-u, PY Eb 1176, Ep 539, 254 = Jn 389. MN: *Terthreus*? [Cf. τερθρεύς, Hermippus, 5 B.C.]

te-te-u, KN V 958. MN?

te-tu-ko-wo-a, KN 216 = L 871. Nom. plur. neut., perf. pple. of τεύχω, describing cloths: *tetukhwo(h)a* 'fully worked', 'finished'. [τετευχώς in pass. sense *Od.* XII, 423; *e*-grade in perfect is unusual and may well be a replacement of *τετυχϝώς.]

te-tu-ko-wo-a₂, PY 289 = Sa 682. Alternative spelling of prec., describing wheels.

te-tu-ru-we, PY Na 1054, 184 = Nn 228. PN, loc.; same place as *te-ta-ra-ne*?

te-u-ke-pi, PY 323 = Sb 1315. Instr. plur.: *teukhesphi* 'with equipment'. [τεύχεα usually 'armour' *Il.* VI, 340 +.]

te-u-po-rǫ[, PY 45 = An 830. Obscure.

te-u-ta-ra-ko-ro, PY An 424, 120 = Eo 276. Probably a man's trade (in Eo 276, if not an error, gen.); discussion by Chantraine (1958*b*); PN (Palmer, 1963*a*, p. 137) is abnormal in Eo.

te-u-to, KN Xd 292?, PY Jn 601, Jn 693. MN.

te-wa-jo, KN Ce 156, Dl 7503, Uf 1038, PY Fn 324. MN, nom. and dat.

te-wa-ko-no, PY An 209. MN.

te-wa-ro, MY 228 = Oe 111 (*o-ta-pa-ro-te-wa-ro*). Prob. to be divided: *pa-ro te-wa-ro*: MN, dat.

te-wo, KN X 722. Obscure.

TI, As adjunct to OLIVE: KN E 669, 95 = F 852 +, MY Ue 611.

ti-ja, KN Dg 1278. MN.

ti-ki-jo, PY An 129. MN, dat.

ti-ko-ro, KN Da 5179, PY Cn 1197. MN.

ti-ko-wo, PY 62 = Cn 655. MN.

ti-ma, KN Vc 317. MN.

ti-mi-ti-ja: see s.v. *te-mi-ti-ja*.

ti-mi-to a-ke-e, PY Cn 600, 257 = Jn 829, 176 = Ma 123, Na 361. PN, written *divisim* only in Cn 600, but cf. *te-mi-ti-ja*: compound name *Thmistos*? and loc. of noun in -*os*, e.g. ἄγκος 'glen' (*Il.* xx, 490+). Located in the south of the Further Province.

ti-mi-to-a-ke-i, PY 60 = An 661. Alternative spelling of loc.

ti-mi-za, KN Df 1121. MN.

ti-mu-nu-we, KN Od 539, M 683. MN, dat.

ti-mu-ṇu-ẉo[, KN Ga 34. Gen.?

ti-ni-ja-ta, PY Fn 79. Dat. sing., qualification of man's name, trade or title. Cf. *o-pi-ti-ni-ja-ta*.

ti-no[1], KN Ap 5748. WN?

ti-no[2], PY 51 = An 18, Xa 565? PN?

]*ti-no-de*, PY Fr 1223. If complete, *ti-no* + -*de*.

ti-nwa-si-jo, PY Ea 810, Fn 324, 258 = Jo 438. Ethnic adj., nom. and dat. masc. sing. (in Ea 810 as MN?).

ti-nwa-si-ja, PY Aa 699, Ab 190. Nom. plur. fem.

ti-nwa-ti-ja-o, PY 15 = Ad 684, (cf. Xa 633). Alternative form, gen. plur. fem. [This implies that the name from which the ethnic is derived had -*t*- or -*th*-.]

ti-qa-jo, KN 39 = As 1517, PY 128 = Eo 278, 253 = Jn 310. MN: *Thisg*[u]*aios*? [Cf. PN Θίσβη.]

ti-qa-jo-jo, PY 117 = En 467. Gen.

ti-ra, KN Od 681, Od 687. Word describing wool: perhaps *tilai* 'flocks of wool'. [τίλαι Plut.; cf. τίλλω, etym. obscure.]

ti-ri-da-ro, PY Ea 28, Ea 460, Ea 754. MN.

ti-ri-jo, PY Cn 4. MN.

ti-ri-jo-ko-so, KN Da 1384. MN.

ti-ri-jo-qa, KN 298 = Sc 226, Vc 303, Xd 294. MN: *Trioq*[u]*as*. [Τριόπας; cf. Τρίοπος *h. Hom.* III, 213.]

ti-ri-jo-we, PY 236 = Ta 641. Nom. sing. neut.: *triōwes* '(vessel) with three handles'. Cf. *a-no-we*, *qe-to-ro-we*.

ti-ri-o-we-e, PY 236 = Ta 641. Nom. dual: *triōwe(h)e*.

ti-ri-po, PY 236 = Ta 641, 237 = Ta 709. Nom. sing. masc.: *tripos* 'tripod cauldron'. [τρίπος *Il.* XXII, 164+; also τρίπους.]

ti-ri-po-de, PY 236 = Ta 641. Nom. dual: *tripode*.

ti-ri-po-di-ko[1], MY 234 = Ue 611 rev. Nom. plur.: *tripodiskoi* 'small tripod cauldrons'. [τριποδίσκος.]

ti-ri-po-di-ko[2], PY Cn 599. MN, dat.: *Tripodiskōi*. [PN Τριποδίσκος.]

ti-ri-sa-ta[, KN Ce 61. MN.

ti-ri-se-ro-e, PY Fr 1204, 172 = Tn 316. Divine name, dat.: *Tris(h)ēro(h)ei*. [Cf. Τριτοπάτορες?]

ti-ri-to[1], KN Da 1238, Db 1232+, L 869, Uf 120+. PN: *Tritos*? [Cf. Τρίτα, old name of Knossos, Hesych.]

ti-ri-ti-jo/-ja, KN 88 = E 749, [Og 833], X 1385. Ethnic adj.

ti-ri-to[2], KN Dv 1386. MN: *Tritos, Trītōn*? [Τρίτος, Τρίτων.]

]*ti-ri-we-ro*, PY Un 1320. MN, dat., prob. complete.

ti-se, PY Un 1321. Obscure.

ti-ta-ma, KN X 974, X 5881. Obscure.

ti-ta-ma-i, KN X 744. Dat. plur.

ti-ta-ra-[, PY 312 = An 1281. MN.

ti-ta[ ]*wo*, PY 254 = Jn 389. MN.

ti-tu-so, MY Oe 112. MN, dat.

ti-wa-ti-ja, KN Ap 618. Nom. plur. fem., ethnic adj.? Cf. *ti-nwa-ti-ja-o*, s.v. *ti-nwa-si-jo*.

TO, Ideographic use (doubtful reading): MY Ge 606.

to-e, PY Eb 842. Possibly a dativalform from the demonstrative pronoun; see pp. 87, 263, 450.

to-me, PY 148 = Ep 613. Alternative form of *to-e* having the same function.

to-i-qe, PY 193 = Na 520. Prob. dat. plur. masc. of demonstrative pronoun: *toi(h)i q*[u]*e* 'and for them'.

to-jo-qe, PY Eb 156. Gen. sing.: *toio q*[u]*e* (*autoio*) 'and of the same'.

to-ke-u, PY An 209. MN, *Stoikheus*? [Στοιχεύς.]

to-ko, KN As 1518. Context obscure: *tokos*? 'childbirth', 'interest'.

to-ko-do-mo, PY 51 = An 18, 41 = An 35+, [Fn 1427?]. Nom. sing. and plur.: *toikhodomoi* 'builders'. [Cf. τοιχοδομέω, IG VII, 422 (Oropus, 4 B.C.).]

to-ko-so-ta, KN V 150. Nom. sing.: *toxotās* 'archer', unless here MN; see p. 474. [τοξότης; also as MN, *Il.* XI, 385.]

to-ko-so-wo-ko, PY 52 = An 207. Nom. plur. masc.: *toxoworgoi* 'bowyers', 'bow-makers'. [Cf. τοξοποιός.]

to-ma-ko, KN Ch 897, Ch 898 (*to-ma-ko-qe*), Ch 1015. Name of an ox: *Stomargos*. [στόμαργος 'loud-mouthed' Aesch.+.]

to-me: see s.v. *to-e*.

to-mi-ka, KN L 761, L 764+. Description of textiles.

to-na-ta, KN B 803. MN: *Thoinātās*? [Cf. Θοινίας, Θοινίων, etc.]

to-ni, KN V 145. Obscure.

to-ni-ja, KN L 192. Description of textiles?

to-ni-jo, PY 247 = Ta 716. Poss. dat. sing., but perhaps more likely part of a compound adj. *a-pi to-ni-jo*, nom. dual. See pp. 347, 502.

to-no[1], PY 242 = Ta 707, 243 = Ta 708, 244 = Ta 714. Nom. sing. masc.: *thornos* 'chair'. [θρόνος *Od.* I, 145+; cf. θόρναξ· ὑποπόδιον (Cypr.) Hesych.]

to-no(-*qe*)[2], KN V 1043. MN, with *q*[u]*e*: *Thoinos*? [Θοῖνος.]

to-no-e-ke-te-ri-jo, PY 308 = Fr 1222. Name of a festival: perhaps *thorno-(h)ektērion* 'the holding of the throne'. See p. 482.

to-o, PY Un 1321. Context obscure.

to-pa, PY 317 = Ub 1318. Possibly gen.: *torpās* 'of a large basket or hamper'. [τάρπη Pollux.] See p. 491.

to-pe-si, KN B 805. MN.

to-pe-za, KN 207 = V 280, PY 239 = Ta 642, 240 = Ta 713, 241 = Ta 715. Nom. sing. fem.: *torpedza* 'table'. [τράπεζα possibly from *(qᵘ)tr̥-pedja*.]

to-pe-zo, PY 241 = Ta 715. Nom. dual: *torpedzō*.

to-qa, KN Fh 339. Error for *to-ro-qa*?

to-qi-da-so, PY Fn 324. MN, dat.

to-qi-de, PY 239 = Ta 642, 240 = Ta 713, 241 = Ta 715. Instr. sing., a decorative feature on vessels and furniture: prob. *torqᵘidei* 'with a spiral'. [Cf. Lat. *torqueo*; Gk. τρέπω may be a conflation of **trep-* and **treqᵘ-*.] See p. 336.

to-qi-de-ja, PY 237 = Ta 709. Nom. sing. fem.: *torqᵘideiā* '(dish) decorated with spiral pattern'.

to-qi-de-jo, PY 241 = Ta 715. Dual fem.: *torqᵘideiō*.

to-qi-de-we-sa, PY 235 = Ta 711. Nom. sing. fem.: *torqᵘid-wessa*, synonym of *to-qi-de-ja*.

to-ra-ke, PY 296 = Sh 736, [Wa 732]. Nom. plur.: *thōrākes* 'corslets'; elsewhere represented by ideogram **163*. [θώρηξ *Il.* XXIII, 560 +, Att. θώραξ, Aeol. θόρραξ, etym. obscure.]

to-ri-jo, PY Jn 605. MN.

to-ro, KN Dc 5687. MN: *Trōs*? [Τρώς *Il.* V, 265 +.]

to-ro-o, PY 57 = An 519. Gen.: *Trō(h)os*?

to-ro-ja, PY 143 = Ep 705. WN: *Trōiā*? [Cf. prec.]

to-ro-ki-no, KN V 831. MN.

to-ro-no-wo-ko, KN 39 = As 1517. Nom. plur. or dat. sing., men's trade: *thronoworgoi, -ōi* 'chair-maker(s)'. [Contrast spelling *to-no* = *thornos*, but derivation from Hom. θρόνα 'embroidered flowers' seems less likely.]

to-ro-o: see s.v. *to-ro*.

to-ro-qa, KN Fh 358, Fh 5446 +. Description of OIL: *troqᵘhā* 'for consumption'. [τροφή Hdt. +; this implies an origin **dhregᵘh-* for τρέφω.] Discussion and different suggestion in Godart, 1969, pp. 52–6.

]-to-ro-qa, KN De 1371. MN.

to-ro-qe-jo-me-no, PY 154 = Eq 213. Nom. sing. medio-pass. pple.: *troqᵘeiomenos* (or *stro-*): see pp. 268, 455. [Cf. τροπέω *Il.* XVIII, 224.]

to-ro-qo, KN Od 563. Possibly acc. sing.: *troqᵘon*, but context obscure. [τρόπος; for etym. of τρέπω see s.v. *to-qi-de*.]

to-ro-wa-ko, KN X 7566. MN?

to-ro-wa-so, PY Na 405. PN.

to-ro-wi, PY 61 = Cn 131, Jn 601. MN.

to-ro-wi-ko, PY 62 = Cn 655. Gen.

to-ro-wi-ka, PY An 5. MN; possibly alternative spelling of *to-ro-wi* (nom. *-ix*?).

to-ro-wo, KN Ag 89?, PY An 129, Vn 130. MN, nom. and dat.

to-ru-ko-ro, PY 62 = Cn 655. MN.

to-sa, *to-sa-de*: see s.v. *to-so*, *to-so-de*.

to-sa-me-ja-o, PY Ad 685. Gen. plur. fem., description of women, prob. a trade.

to-sa-no, PY Fn 79. MN, dat.

to-sa-no-jo, PY Jn 431. Gen.

to-sa-wa, KN Dl 7086 (erased). In an entry of lambs; possibly intended for *to-sa wa-ni-ja* = *tos(s)a ʷarnia* 'so many lambs' or the like.

to-si-ta, PY Cn 719. MN.

to-so, KN 34 = Am 601 +, 38 = As 1516 +, 36 = B 817 +, 200 = Fp 1 +, etc., PY 51 = An 18, 149 = Ed 236, 116 = En 659, 305 = Fr 1184, etc., MY Au 658, 93 = Fo 101, TH Ug 14. Nom. and acc. sing. masc. and neut., nom. plur. masc.: *tos(s)os, -on, -oi*, normal Mycenaean totalling formula 'so much', 'so many'. [Hom. τόσσος, τόσος; there is no way of deciding which spelling the Myc. form represents, as *-ss-* may already have been simplified.]

to-sa, KN [74 = Dp 1061], 261 = Ra 1540, etc., PY 114 = En 609, 153 = Er 880, etc. Nom. sing. fem., nom. plur. fem. and neut.: *tos(s)ā, -ai, -a*.

to-so-pa, PY 256 = Ja 749, Jn 601. Nom. sing. masc.: *tos(s)os pans* 'so much (bronze) in all'. See s.v. *pa*.

to-so-jo, PY 152 = Er 312. Gen. sing.: *tos(s)oio*.

to-so-ne, MY Oe 118. Obscure; possibly *tos(s)os* + particle *-ne*.

to-so-de, PY 58 = An 654, 146 = Eb 473 +, 253 = Jn 310 +, 171 = Un 718, etc., MY Au 609?. Nom. sing. and plur. masc., nom. sing. neut.: *tos(s)os-de*, etc., 'and so much (or so many)'. It is uncertain whether *-de* has always connective force, but it is likely in many cases: Ruijgh, 1967, pp. 343–50. [τοσόσδε.]

to-sa-de, KN Ga 1530, PY 153 = Er 880, 198 = Ng 319. Nom. sing. fem., nom. plur. fem. and neut.: *tos(s)ā-de*, etc.

to-so-ku-su-pa, KN Fh 367. Nom. sing. neut., introducing a very large quantity of OIL: *tos(s)on xumpan* 'so much altogether'. See s.v. *ku-su-pa*.

to-so-o, PY Xn 1342. Obscure: *to-so* with added particle?

to-te-ja, KN 18 = Ak 611, [X 7846?]. Nom. plur. fem., a woman's trade.

to-te-we-ja-se-we, MY Oe 106. Personal name, dat.?

to-ti-ja, MY 93 = Fo 101. WN, dat.

to-to, PY 43 = Aq 64. Neut. sing.: app. *toto* (*wetos*) 'this (year)'. [Probably not to be compared with τοῦτο, but a reduplicated **tod-tod* (Vedic *tat-tad*); see Lejeune, 1958*a*, p. 231. Attic τοτο (Dipylon Vase) is a chimera; read τὸ (= τοῦ) τόδε . . .]

to-tu-no, KN Da 1276. MN.

to-u-ka, KN Lc 481, Lc 504 +. Annotation to WOOL on reverse of textile tablets: poss.

toukhā, noun corresponding to τεύχω (cf. *te-tu-ko-wo-a*), but sense obscure: Björck, 1954*b*, p. 275; hardly 'finished goods' (Palmer, 1963*a*, p. 460) since it refers to wool, not cloth.

to-u-na-ta, KN Dm 1182, Dv 1479. MN.

to-wa, PY 58 = An 654. PN or MN?

to-wa-no, KN B 806. MN: *Thowānōr* or *Thorwānōr* (Heubeck, 1957, p. 31).

to-wa-no-re, PY Fn 79. Dat.: *-ānorei*.

to-wa-te-u, PY Eb 1188, Ep 539. MN.

to-wi-no, KN Do 923. MN.

to-wo, KN Sc 7480. Obscure.

to-wo-na[, MY Fu 711. Personal name?

to-ze-u, PY 312 = An 1281. MN.

TU, As adjunct to WOMAN or ideographic, = *tu-ka-te* 'daughter' (Killen, 1966*a*): KN Ap 629, Ap 637, Ap 639+.

tu-da-ra, KN Do 924. MN: *Tundarās*? [Τυνδάρης; cf. Τυνδάρεως *Od.* XI, 298+.]

tu-ka-na, KN Ap 639. WN, twice on same tablet, possibly representing different names.

tu-ka-te(-*qe*), MY 303 = V 659. Twice in a list of women: *thugatēr qᵘe* 'and daughter'. [θυγάτηρ *Il.* IX, 148+.]

tu-ka-te-re, MY Oe 106. Prob. dat. sing.: *thugatrei*. [On form see Ruijgh, 1959, p. 77.]

tu-ka-ṭa-ṣi, MY Oe 112. Dat. plur.: *thugatarsi* (< **thugatr̥si*), if reading is sound.

tu-ka-to, KN Ap 639. WN.

tu-ke-ne-u, PY 253 = Jn 310. MN.

tu-ma-da-ro, KN Db 1368. MN.

tu-ma-i-ta, KN As 605, [X 7673?]. MN: *Thumaitās*. [Θυμαίτης, hero of Attic deme Θυμαιτάδαι.]

tu-ma-ko, KN C 973. Name of an ox? [Cf. *to-ma-ko*; στύμα = στόμα Theocr.]

tu-me-ne-wo, MY Ui 709. MN?

tu-na-no, KN 209 = Lc 525, 210 = Lc 526, 211 = Lc 532+. Description of a kind of textile; see p. 315.

tu-ni-ja, KN Ap 629, Db 1246+, 213 = Le 641+. PN. [Cf. Ἐλτυνία (now Kunávi) south of Knossos?]

tu-ni-ja-dẹ, KN Fh 373. Acc. + *de*.

tu-ni-jo, PY Cn 4, Xa 1419. MN.

tu-qa-ni-ja-so, KN Db 1279, [Dk 920?], [Uf 5721?]. MN. [Cf. PN Τυ(μ)πανέαι.]

tu-ra-te-u, PY Ae 8, Ae 72. Nom. sing., description of a man, prob. a trade.

tu-ra-te-we, KN B 755. Nom. plur.

tu-ra-te-u-si, PY Gn 428, Vn 48. Dat. plur.

tu-ri-ja-jọ, PY Jn 431. MN: *Thuriaios*? [Cf. PN Θυρέαι.]

tu-ri-ja-ti, PY 116 = En 659, [123 = Eo 444]. WN: *Thuriātis*? [Cf. Θυρεᾶτις (γῆ).]

tu-ri-jo, KN Nc 4473, PY Jn 693. MN: *Turios*?, *Thuriōn*? [Τύριος, ethnic of Tyre; Θυρίων.]

tu-ri-si-jo-jo, PY Sa 758. MN, gen.: *Tulisioio*. [Cf. *tu-ri-so*.]

tu-ri-so, KN 84 = Ce 59, Db 1241+. PN: *Tulisos*. [Τυλισός *Insc. Cret.* I, 30, 1; now Τύλισσος.]

tu-ri-si-jo/-ja, KN 87 = E 668, Lc 533, Og 833+. Ethnic adj.: *Tulisioi, -ai*.

tu-ri-ta, PY Cn 40. MN, dat.

tu-ro₂, PY 171 = Un 718. Nom. plur.: *tūroi* (*turjoi*?) 'cheeses'; also written with monogram TU + RO₂. [τυρός *Il.* XI, 639+, cf. Av. *tū*ⁱ*ri-*.]

tu-ru-pte-ri-ja, PY 41 = An 35, Un 443. Gen. sing. depending on following *o-no*: *struptēriās* 'of alum'; see p. 422. [στρυπτηρία *Inscr. Prien.* 364.15 (3/2 B.C.) = στυπτηρία Hdt.+.]

tu-ru-pe-te[-*ri-ja?*], KN X 986. Variant spelling?

tu-ru-we-u, PY 40 = An 261, Cn 254. MN: *Thrueus*? [Cf. PN Θρύον *Il.* II, 592.]

tu-si-je-u, PY 57 = An 519. MN. Cf. *tu-ti-je-u*.

tu-ti, KN V 652. MN?

tu-ti-je-u, PY Cn 4. MN. Cf. *tu-si-je-u*.

tu-to, KN Ga 419. MN.

tu-wa-si, PY Fn 41. Prob. dat. plur. of description of men.

tu-we-a: see *tu-wo*.

tu-we-ta, PY 103 = Un 267. MN, dat.: *Thuestāi*, an unguent-boiler by trade. [Θυέστης *Il.* II, 107.]

tu-wi-jo, KN 37 = B 823. Obscure, description of men or PN?

tu-wi-no, KN 102 = Ga 517. MN: *Twinōn*. [Cf. Σίνων; σίνομαι < **twin-*.]

tu-wi-no-no, KN Ga 676. Gen.

tu-wo, PY Un 219. Nom. sing. neut.: *thuos* 'aromatic substance'. [θύος, usually plur.: *Il.* VI, 270+, often 'burnt offering'; cf. ἔλαιον τεθυωμένον *Il.* XIV, 172.]

tu-we-a, PY 103 = Un 267. Acc. plur.: *thue(h)a*.

tu-zo, KN Ap 639, C 7698. WN in Ap 639; prob. MN in C 7698.

tu-*49-mi, KN Ap 639. WN.

tu-*56-da-ro, KN Dv 1370. MN.

U, As adjunct to ideogram of bucket (**212*), abbreviation of *u-do-ro* (q.v.): KN K 774, K 775+.

Ideographic use: PY Un 219.

u-de, TH Of 38. Adverb: *huide* 'hither'? [Cf. Lesb. τυῖδε, Cret. υἶ 'whither'.]

u-de-wi-ne, PY Cn 595. PN, loc.

u-de-wi-ni-jọ, PY Jn 413. Prob. MN. [Ethnic adj. of prec.]

u-do, KN K 873. Annotation to vessel labelled PO; poss. *hudōr* 'water'. [ὕδωρ; cf. *u-do-ro*.]

u-do-no-o-i, PY Fn 187. Dat. plur., class of persons, or loc. PN?

u-do-ro, KN [233 = Uc 160 rev.], PY 238 = Tn 996. Nom. plur., name of bucket-shaped vessel: *hudroi* 'water-jars'. [ὕδρος *Il.* II, 723+ 'water-snake'; cf. ὑδρία.]

u-du-ru-wo, KN V 145. PN, gen.? Cf. [*o-*]*du-ru-wo*, see s.v. *o-du-ru-we*.

u-jo-na, KN Ap 639. WN.

u-ka, KN X 7386. PN?

u-ka-jo, PY 184 = Nn 228. PN.

u-me-ta-qe-a-po, PY 145 = Ea 259. Perhaps to be divided *u-me-ta* (MN) *qᵘe a-po*; see p. 449.

u-pa-ra, KN Ap 639. WN.

u-pa-ra-ki-ri-ja, PY An 298. PN, subordinate to *ra-wa-ra-ta₂*? [Cf. Ὑπεράκρια.]

u-po-ra-ki-ri-ja, PY Cn 45. Variant spelling?

u-pi-ja-ki-ri-jo, PY 58 = An 654. Prob. nom. plur. masc. of ethnic adj.

u-pa-ta-ro, TH Z 1, Z 2+. MN.

u-po, KN 271 = Sd 4422, PY 317 = Ub 1318. Adverb: *hupo* 'underneath'. [ὑπό Hom.+.]

u-po-di-jo-no, PY Na 105. MN, gen. forming PN with *wo-wo*.

u-po-jo, PY Fn 187, 310 = Fr 1225, Fr 1236. Qualification of *Potnia*, PN in gen.?

u-po-ra-ki-ri-ja: see s.v. *u-pa-ra-ki-ri-ja*.

u-po-we, KN L 178. Description of two linen(?) tunics. [Cf. Hesych. ὑπόεστης (*ὑποϝέστης)· χιτών.]

u-qa-mo, KN Mc 4454. App PN; cf. *qa-mo*.

u-ra-jo, KN B 799, Db 1265+. MN: *Hulaios*, *Huraios*? ['Υλαῖος, 'Υραῖος.]

u-ra-mo-no, KN 38 = As 1516, Da 1315. MN.

*u-ra-*86*, PY Na 466 (restoration in Na 1039 and 1086 improbable). PN.

u-re-u, PY Vn 865. MN: *Hul(l)eus*? ['Υλεύς, 'Υλλεύς.]

u-ro₂, KN Db 5367. MN.

u-ru-pi-ja-jo, PY 57 = An 519, 58 = An 654, 60 = An 661, 76 = Cn 3, 188 = Na 928. Nom. plur. masc., description of men, possibly ethnic, but not to be connected with Olympia. See p. 430.

u-ru-pi-ja-jo-jo, PY 76 = Cn 3. Gen. sing., possibly error.

-u-ru-to, PY 56 = An 657. 3rd plur. pres. indic.: (*hŏ*) *wruntoi* 'thus they are guarding'. [ῥῦσθαι *Il.* xv, 141+, imperf. ἔρυτο *Il.* iv, 138+; Risch, 1958 *b*, p. 337, prefers sing. *wrutoi*, taking *e-pi-ko-wo* as collective sing.]

u-su, KN V 7512. Obscure.

u-ta-jo, KN Da 1127+, 66 = Dc 1129, Ra 1559, V 832. MN, a 'collector' of sheep.

u-ta-jo-jo, KN Da 1135+. Gen.

u-ta-no¹, KN [As 604], Db 1097+, 202 = Fp 13, Pp 496+. PN: perh. *Utanos*. [Poss. = ῎Ιτανος with interchange of υ and ι as in some pre-hellenic names; cf. *mo-ri-wo-do*.]

u-ta-ni-jo, KN B 807, 88 = E 749+. Ethnic adj.

u-ta-no², KN Dd 1592. MN.

u-wa-mi-ja, PY 137 = Eb 416, 135 = Ep 704. WN: *Huamiā*? [Cf. PN 'Υάμεια (Messenia).]

u-wa-si, PY 59 = An 656. PN, dat.-loc. plur.

u-wa-si-jo, KN Ai 115. Poss. MN, but more likely patronymic adj.: *pa-ro u-wa-si-jo ko-wo* 'from the son of U.'? [Cf. PN *u-wa-si*, MN *u-wa-ta*.]

u-wa-ta, KN Dd 1286, PY Jn 605. MN: *Huātās, Huantās*? [Cf. 'Υᾶται; 'Υάντες.]

u-wo-qe-ne, KN V 145. Alternative form of or error for next.

u-wo-qe-we, KN 83 = C 902. Perh. nom. plur., title of an official. [Palmer, 1963 *a*, p. 461: *u(w)oqᵘēwes* 'overseers'.]

*u-*56*, KN Df 1120. MN.

WA, Possibly abbreviation for *wa-na-ka-te-ra* (Killen, 1966 *c*, p. 107): KN Le 654. Obscure, but possibly similar: KN F 51 rev., ELEUSIS jar.

wa-a₂-ta, MY 46 = Au 102. MN.

wa-a₂-te-pi, PY Na 1009, Xa 1377. PN, instr.-loc. plur.

wa-a₂-te-we, PY 52 = An 207, [Mn 1371?]. Variant form, dat.-loc. sing.?

wa-da-ko, PY Cn 285. MN.

wa-de-o, PY Sa 766. MN, gen.: *Wāde(h)os*?

wa-di-re-we, PY Fn 79. MN, dat.

wa-do-me-no, PY Vn 130. MN, dat.: *Wādomenōi*. [Cf. ἥδομαι, ϝάδομαι Corinna.]

wa-du-ka-sa-ro, KN Da 1445. MN.

wa-du-na, KN V 503, V 1523. MN.

wa-du-na-ro, KN C 912, Db 1242, Dc 1118+. MN.

wa-du-ri-jo, [KN Ga 456?], PY Jn 725. MN: *Wādulios*. [Cf. 'Ηδύλος.]

wa-du-[.]-to, KN 38 = As 1516. MN, formerly read *wa-du-na-to*.

wa-e-ro, PY Cn 1197. MN?

wa-je, KN V 479. MN.

wa-ka-ta, PY 255 = Jn 658. MN: = *wa-tu-ta*, impossible to tell which is the error; see p. 511.

wa-ka-ti-ja-ta, PY 59 = An 656. Poss. nom. plur. masc. ethnic?

wa-ke-i-jo, KN Xd 177, Xd 191. MN: *Wākheios*? [Cf. Arc. Ϝᾶχος.]

wa-ke-ta, KN Fs 4. Recipient of offerings?

wa-na-ka, KN Vc 73, PY 194 = Na 334, Na 1356, 235 = Ta 711. Nom. sing.: *wanax* 'the king'. [ἄναξ *Il.* 1, 442+, Cypr. *wa-na-xe*.]

]*wa-na-ka-to*, PY La 622. Gen.: *wanaktos*?

wa-na-ka-te, KN 101 = Ga 675, PY 307 = Fr 1220+, 97 = Un 2, [Un 1426]. Dat.: *wanaktei*.

wa-na-ke-te, PY Fr 1215. Variant spelling of dat.

wa-na-ka-te-ro, KN X 976, PY 115 = En 74, 114 = En 609, 122 = Eo 160, 120 = Eo 276+, 152 = Er 312, TH Z 839. Nom. sing. masc. and neut.: *wanakteros, -on* 'of the king', 'royal'. [ἄναξ + -τερος, cf. βασιλεύτερος Hom.]

wa-na-ka-te-ra, KN 209 = Lc 525, [TH Of 36?]. Nom. plur. neut. or fem.: *wanaktera(i)*.

wa-na-se-wi-jo, PY Fr 1215. Prob. adj. form of *wa-na-so-i*: see p. 479.

wa-na-se-wi-ja, PY Fr 1221, 235 = Ta 711. Fem. sing. or neut. plur. [Earlier taken as *wanassēwiā* 'of the queen', but etym. doubtful.]

wa-na-si-ja-ke, PY Vn 851. MN, dat.?

wa-na-so-i, PY 308 = Fr 1222, Fr 1227 +. Dat.-loc. plur., a shrine or locality: see p. 478.

wa-no-so-i, PY Fr 1219. Variant spelling or error.

wa-na-ta-jo, KN V 466, PY [114 = En 609], 118 = Eo 211, 119 = Eo 224, 131 = Ep 301. MN, nom. and dat.: *Warnataios, -ōi?* [Cf. Ἀρναῖος *Od.* XVIII, 5.]

wa-na-ta-jo-jo, PY 114 = En 609, 118 = Eo 211. Gen.

wa-ta-jo, PY 118 = Eo 211. Error for *wa-na-ta-jo*.

wạ-ni-ko, PY Jn 478. MN: *Warniskos.* [Ἀρνίσκος.]

wa-no(-qe), KN Ch 5724. Name of an ox.

wa-no-jo, PY Cn 40, Cn 599. MN, gen., forming PN with *wo-wo*.

wa-o, PY 247 = Ta 716. Annotation to ideogram resembling double-axe with numeral 2; see p. 502.

wa-pa-no, PY Jn 601. MN.

wa-pa-ro-jo, PY 59 = An 656. MN, gen.: *Wapaloio?* [Cf. ἀπαλός.]

wa-po, KN Fh 5429. MN?

wa-ra-ki-no, PY An 615. MN?

wa-ra-ko-no, PY Jn 845. MN.

wa-ra-pi-si-ro, [PY Cn 436], MY 46 = Au 102. MN.

wa-ra-ti, KN Ap 639. WN.

wa-ra-wi-ta, KN So 4443. Nom. plur. neut., description of wheels. The suggestion *wrāwista* 'damaged' conflicts with that offered for *o-pi-ra₃-te-re*; similarly *wlāwista* 'coming from booty' (Lejeune, 1958*a*, p. 37; Palmer, 1963*a*, p. 462) conflicts with that offered for *ra-wi-ja-ja*.

wa-ra-wo-ṇọ, PY Cn 600. MN.

wa-re-u-ka-ra[, PY Na 576. PN.

wa-ru-wo-qo, KN As 1516. MN.

wa-si-ro, KN V 159. Obscure.

wa-te-u, PY 190 = Na 395. Obscure.

wa-ti-ko-ro, PY Jn 725. MN; cf. WN *a-wa-ti-ka-ra*.

]*wa-ti-ro*, PY Jn 431. MN

wa-to, KN Co 903, 83 = C 902, Np 7423, TH Z 846, Z 854 +. PN; on the evidence of analysis of jars from Thebes they may have been made in Palaikastro area of E. Crete, hence *wa-to* may be the name of this site.

wa-tu, KN V 114, X 795?, PY Eq 34, 172 = Tn 316. In some contexts obscure: in V 114 and Tn 316 prob. *wastu* 'the town'. [ἄστυ *Il.* II, 332 +.]

wa-tu-o, PY Vn 865. MN.

wa-tu-o-ko, PY Ea 136. MN: *Wastuokhos.* [Cf. Ἀστυόχη *Il.* II, 513.]

wa-tu-ta, PY Jn 725. MN: = *wa-ka-ta*, impossible to tell which is the error; see p. 511.

wa-tu-wa-o-ko, PY 57 = An 519. MN: *Wastuāokhos?* [Cf. *wa-tu-o-ko*; influenced by *πολιάοχος*, Epic πολιήοχος, Lacon. πολιάχοι?]

wa-u-do-no, PY 254 = Jn 389. MN.

wa-u-so[, KN Fh 5479. MN?

wa-wa-ka, KN Ln 1568. WN?

wa-wi, KN V 756. MN.

wa-wo-u-de, PY 58 = An 654, [Xa 200?]. PN with *-de*?

wa-*86-re, KN Dc 1117. MN.

WE, As adjunct to OX, possibly abbreviation of *we-ka-ta*: KN 85 = Ch 896.

As adjunct to OIL, probably abbreviation of *we-a-re-pe*: PY 305 = Fr 1184, MY 93 = Fo 101.

As adjunct to ideogram *166 (ingot?): KN Oa 878, Oa 1808 +, PY Ob 1372 +, Ua 1413.

Ideographic use, apparently denoting a variety of sheep or goat, possibly = *wetalon* 'yearling': KN D 411, Dl 790 +, PY 77 = Cn 418, Ua 17, 96 = Un 138 +.

we-a-re-ja: see s.v. *we-a₂-re-jo*.

we-a-re-pe, PY Fr 1215, Fr 1223. Nom. sing. neut., adj. describing oil: prob. *u-aleiphes* 'for anointing'. See p. 477.

we-ja-re-pe, PY Fr 1205, Fr 1217 +. Alternative spelling.

we-a₂-no-i, PY 310 = Fr 1225, 319 = Un 1322? Dat. plur.: *wehanoihi* 'for robes'. [ἑανός *Il.* XXI, 507 +.]

we-a₂-re-jo, PY 244 = Ta 714. Nom. sing. masc., adj. describing tables and chairs: *hualeios* (or sim.) 'of or decorated with rock-crystal'. [Cf. ὕαλος Hdt. +.]

we-a-re-ja, PY 239 = Ta 642. Nom. sing. fem.

we-da-ne-wo, PY 54 = An 610, 62 = Cn 655 +, 168 = Es 644 +, Na 856 +, Un 1193. MN, gen., a person of great importance.

we-da-ne-we, PY 169 = Es 646 +. Dat.

we-e-wi-ja, KN As 1518, PY 317 = Ub 1318. At PY, nom. fem. plur. of adj., describing skins: *huēwiai* 'pigs''. [ὕειος Aristoph. +.] See p. 492. Context at KN obscure.

we-i-we-sa, MY 93 = Fo 101. WN, dat.: prob. *Huiwessāi.* [υἱός + -εις.]

we-ja-re-pe: see s.v. *we-a-re-pe*.

we-je-ke-a₂, PY 286 = Sa 787. Nom. plur. neut., adj. describing wheels: *uweikeha*, 'serviceable' (opposite of *no-pe-re-a₂*). [Compound of υ + -εικής as ἐπι-εικής. See pp. 373, 518.]

[*we-*]*jẹ-ke-a*, PY Wa 1148. Variant spelling.

we-je-ke-e, PY 285 = Sa 487 +. Nom. dual: *uweike(h)e.*

we-je-we, KN 164 = Gv 863, [PY 153 = Er 880]. Nom. plur., description of plant or tree: prob. *huēwes* 'vine-shoots'. [Cf. υἱήν· τὴν ἄμπελον Hesych.]

we-ka-di-jo, KN U 4478, V 831. MN: *Wergadios, Wekadios?* [Cf. Ἐργάδεις, Boeot. Ϝηεκαδάμοε.]

we-ka-sa[, KN Ai 1037. Obscure, perh. description of slave-women: on formal grounds poss. *wekassa(i)* (< *weknt-ya* = ἑκοῦσα), but sense improbable.

we-ka-ta, KN Ai 1012, Ce 50, 84 = Ce 59 +. Nom. plur. describing oxen and poss. men: *wergatai* 'workers'. [βοῦς ἐργάτης Archil., Soph.]

we-ka-ta-e, KN C 1044. Dual: *wergatae*.

we-ke: see s.v. *ke-re-si-jo we-ke*.

we-ke-i-ja, KN 35 = Am 819. Obscure: annotation to groups of 18 men, perh. a derivative of ἔργον (cf. ἐργασία in sense of 'craft-association', 'guild').

we-ke-i-jo[, PY Jn 937. MN.

]*wẹ-ke-se*, KN Xe 5540. If complete, poss. 3rd sing. aor.: *wexe* 'brought'. (Cf. *pe-re* Od 562.) [ϝέχω Cypr., Pamph.; cf. Lat. *uehō*, Skt. *vahati*.]

we-ko-we-ka-te[, KN Ak 630. Obscure.

we-pe-za, PY 240 = Ta 713. Nom. sing. fem., description of a table: (*h*)*weppedza* or (*h*)*wespedza* 'six-footer', exact sense obscure: see p. 342 and cf. *e-ne-wo-pe-za*.

we-ra-jo, PY Eb 364, Ep 613 (in both cases incomplete). MN.

we-ra-te-ja, KN Ap 618. Obscure, description of women?

]*we-ra-ti-ja*, KN Ak 784. Variant spelling.

we-ra-to, KN De 1136. MN.

we-re-ka-ra-ta, PY An 298. Nom. plur., a man's trade.

we-re-ka-ra, PY 54 = An 610. Poss. defective spelling of prec.

we-re-ke, PY 61 = Cn 131. Cn 202 +. Heading to cattle tablets, poss. nom. plur. *wreges* 'enclosures'. [Cf. Skt. *vrajaḥ* 'enclosure'; Palmer, 1957*a*, p. 569.]

]*wẹ-re-ki-ja*, KN Ai 1012. Obscure.

we-re-ne-ja, PY 317 = Ub 1318. Prob. nom. sing. fem., describing a skin: prob. *wrēneiā* 'sheep's', 'lamb's'. [Cf. ῥήν 'sheep'; ἄρνειος Hdt. +; Heubeck, 1960*a*, p. 19.] See p. 493.

we-re-we, KN 83 = C 902, V 145. Nom. sing. or plur., title of an official?

we-ro-pa-ta, KN B 5132. MN.

we-ro-ta, PY An 129. MN?

we-ru-ma-ta, PY 317 = Ub 1318. Nom. plur.: *welūmata* 'wrappers'. [εἴλυμα Od. VI, 179.] See p. 492.

we-te-re-u, PY Eb 472 +, 142 = Ed 317, 115 = En 74 +, 121 = Eo 247 +. MN.

we-to, PY 43 = Aq 64, 178 = Ma 365. Acc. sing. neut.: *wetos* 'year'. [ἔτος Il. XXIV, 765 +; in dialects frequently ϝέτος.]

we-te-i-we-te-i, PY 168 = Es 644. Reduplicated dat.-loc.: *wete*(*h*)*i wete*(*h*)*i* 'from year to year', 'annually'. [Cf. Skt. *varṣe-varṣe* 'every year'.]

]*we-to-ro*, KN V 5575. Name of an object?

we-u-da-ne-we, PY 77 = Cn 418. MN, dat. [Cf. *we-da-ne-wo*, but prob. not the same name.]

we-wa-do-ro, KN Dv 1601, Sc 252. MN: *Werwandros*? [Cf. (ϝ)έρυμαι; Heubeck, 1957, p. 32.]

we-we-e-a, KN L 178, 220 = L 870, [PY Xn 878?]. Nom. plur. neut., description of textiles: *werwe*(*h*)*e*(*h*)*a* 'woollen'. [Att. ἐρεᾶ, neut. plur., Ion. εἰρίνεος; from εἶρος 'wool' Hom. +, < *werwos*, cf. Lat. *ueruex* 'sheep'.]

we-we-ro, KN Fh 347, V 147. MN.

we-we-si-je-ja, PY Aa 762, Ab 217. Nom. plur. fem., a woman's trade: *werwesieiai* 'woolworkers'. [Despite the obvious objection to intervocalic -*s*-, a derivative of εἶρος 'wool' seems to be supported by εἰρεσιώνη 'wreath wound round with wool' Aristoph. or earlier?]

we-we-si-je-ja-o, PY Ad 318. Gen. plur.: *werwesieiāōn*.

we-we-si-jo, KN Da 1161 +, Le 654, PY 255 = Jn 658 +. MN: *Werwesios*? [Cf. prec.]

we-we-si-jo-jo, KN Da 1162, 68 = De 1648 +, Od 502 +. Gen.

we-wo-ni-jo, KN C 954. MN.

WI, Ideographic use: PY Un 219, Wr 1332. As part of ideogram *152 = OXHIDE, abbrev. of *wi-ri-no* (q.v.): e.g. PY 173 = Ma 222 +.

wi-da-jo, KN V 60. MN: *Widaios*. [Ἰδαῖος.]

wi-da-ka-so, KN Dd 1402. MN.

wi-da-ma-ro, KN Do 919, V 479. MN.

wi-da-ma-ta₂, KN Ap 639, Ln 1568. WN.

-*wi-de*, PY 154 = Eq 213, 235 = Ta 711. 3rd sing. aor.: (*hō*) *wide* 'thus he saw'. [ἴδε Il. XI, 243 +.]

wi-do-wo-i-jo, PY Ae 344, An 5. MN: *Widwo*(*h*)*ios* (in Ae 344 for gen.?). [Cf. ἰδυῖοι, εἰδώς < *widwōs*.]

wi-du-wo-i-jo, PY Jn 415. Alternative spelling.

wi-dwo-i-jo, PY Ep 539. Alternative spelling.

wi-du-ro, KN B 799. MN. [Cf. Ἴδυρος name of a river.]

wi-du-ru-ta, KN Ch 5754. MN.

wi-du-wa-ko, PY 253 = Jn 310. MN.

wi-ja-da-ra, PY Ae 142. WN, gen.? or PN? If WN, perh. *Wiandrā*(*s*). [Cf. Ἰάνειρα Il. XVIII, 47.]

wi-ja-ma-ro, KN As 1516, Da 1378. MN.

]*wi-ja-na-tu*, KN Ap 769. WN.

wi-ja-ni-jo, PY Jn 431. MN.

wi-ja-te-we, PY Cn 45, Cn 600. MN, nom. or dat.?

wi-ja-te-wo, PY Jn 431. MN.

wi-ja-we-ra₂, PY Cn 643, Cn 719, Jn 478. PN.

wi-je-mo, KN As 609, Dv 1266. MN.

wi-je-so, KN Da 1163. MN.

wi-jo-de: see *ki-ka-ne wi-jo-de*.

wi-jo-ka-de, KN Db 1155. MN.

wi-jo-qo-ta, KN Db 1305, [Dq 7852]. MN: *Wioqʷhontās*? [Cf. Ἰοφῶν.]

wi-jo-qo-ta-o, KN [Dq 1026], 218 = Ld 598. Gen.: -*tāo*.

wi-jo-ro-jo, PY Jn 725. MN.

wi-na-jo, KN Da 1197 +, Fh 1059, 232 = K 875 +. MN.

wi-na-to, KN As 604. PN: *Winatos*? [Ἴνατος; cf. (Ἐλεύθυιαν) ΒιναΤίαν Inscr. Cret. IV, 174. 60, 74.]

wi-nu-ri-jo[, PY 54 = An 610. PN or ethnic?

wi-pi-no-o, KN V 958. MN: *Wiphino*(*h*)*os*. [Ἰφίνοος Il. VII, 14; second element from *nes*- as in νέομαι, νόστος.]

wi-pi-o, KN Nc 5103. MN: *Wiphiōn*. [Ἰφίων.]

wi-ra-ne, KN Dv 5193. MN.

wi-ra-ne-to, KN As 1516, Dv 1205. MN.

wi-ri-ja-no, PY Ea 52. MN: *Wrianos*? ['Ριανός.]

wi-ri-ke-ja, PY Vn 851. WN, dat.?

wi-ri-ki-no, KN V 831. MN.

wi-ri-ne-we, KN Fh 5428, Fh 5435. Prob. dat. sing., recipient of oil: perh. *wrīnēwei* 'for the tanner' or MN? [Cf. *wi-ri-no*.]

wi-ri-ni-jo, KN 266 = Sd 4401, 269 = Sd 4404 +. Nom. dual neut.?: *wrīniō* 'made of leather'. [Cf. *wi-ri-no*.]

   wi-ri-ne-o, KN Sd 4408 +, 274 = Sf 4428. Variant form: *wrīneō*.

wi-ri-ne-jo, KN Sd 4415, Sd 4468. Variant form: *wrīneiō*.

wi-ri-no, PY 317 = Ub 1318. Nom. plur.: *wrīnoi* 'ox-hides'. [ῥινός *Od.* I, 108 +.]

wi-ri-wo[, PY An 340. MN.

wi-ri-za, KN Od 2026, Od 8202, [X 44], PY 104 = Un 249. Nom. sing.: *wridza* 'root'; in context always in connexion with wool, the root section of which is rich in lanolin (Killen, 1962*a*, p. 42). [ῥίζα, Lesb. βρίσδα.]

wi-ro, KN As 1516. MN: *Wīlos* or *Wīros*. ['Ιλος *Il.* X, 415; Ιρος *Od.* XVIII, I.]

wi-ro-jo, KN Da 5234. MN.

wi-sa-to, PY Vn 130. MN, dat.

wi-so, KN Ap 639. WN.

wi-so-ẉọ-pa-ṇạ, PY 292 = Sh 740. Nom. plur. neut., description of plates on a corslet; prob. *wiswo-*, but second member obscure. [ἶσος < Fίσfος.]

wi-su-ro, KN Dd 1284. MN.

wi-ti-mi-jo, PY Jn 605. MN: *Wisthmios*? [Ισθμιος; no evidence for F- in ἰσθμός.]

]*wi-to-te-ra*[, PY Wa 748. Obscure.

wi-tu-ri-jo, KN X 770. MN: *Witulios*? [Cf. Ιτυλος *Od.* XIX, 522.]

wi-tu-ta, PY Jn 320. MN.

wi-*65-te-u, KN Dv 1403. MN.

W O, Ideographic use or adjunct to WHEAT?: PY Un 1319.

wo-de-wi-jo, KN Fp 16, Fp 48, 207 = V 280. Name of a month: *wordēwios* 'of roses'. [Cf. ῥόδον; Petruševski, 1959, p. 104.]

   wo-de-ẉị-jo-jo, KN 203 = Ga 953.

wo-di-je-ja, KN Ap 639, PY 317 = Ub 1318, Vn 1191, MY 303 = V 659. WN: *Wordieia*. (Cf. ῥόδον.]

wo-di-jo, KN V 60, PY Jn 601. MN: *Wordios*? [Cf. ῥόδον.]

wo-do, KN Xd 282. Obscure.

wo-do-we, PY Fr 1203, Fr 1204 +. Nom. sing. neut., description of oil: *wordowen* 'rose-scented'. [ῥοδόεντι ... ἐλαίῳ *Il.* XXIII, 186.]

wo-i-ko-de, KN As 1519. Acc. sing. + *-de*: *woikon-de* 'to the house or shrine (of)'. [οἶκόνδε *Il.* I, 606.]

   wo-ko-de, TH Of 36. Variant spelling: 'to the shrine (of Potnia)'.

]*wo-ja-de*, KN Fh 365. Acc. + *-de*?

wo-jo, PY Eb 472. Gen. sing.: (*h*)*woio* 'of his own'. [οἶο gen. *Il.* III, 333.]

wo-ka, PY 285 = Sa 487, Sa 753 +. Nom. or dat. sing.?: *wokhā* 'vehicle', 'chariot'. [Cf. ὄχεα *Il.* IV, 419 +.]

wo-ka-re, KN V 960. Obscure.

wo-ke, KN L 698, PY 296 = Sh 736. Obscure: verbal form (cf. *wo-ze*?) or dat. of a noun?

wo-ki-ro, PY Cn 328. MN.

wo-ki-to, PY 61 = Cn 131. MN, dat.

wo-ko-de: see *wo-i-ko-de*.

wo-na-si, KN 164 = Gv 863. Dat.-loc. plur.: *woinassi* 'in the vineyards'? [οἰνάδες· ἀμπελώδεις τόποι Hesych.]

wo-ne-wa, PY 58 = An 654. MN.

wo-ne-we, PY Cn 40, Cn 643 +. Nom. plur., description of sheep.

wo-no, PY 250 = Vn 20. Nom. sing.: *woinos* 'wine'? [οἶνος Hom. +.]

wo-no-qe-wa, PY Na 396, [258 = Jo 438?]. PN.
  wo-no-qe-we, PY Un 1193. Variant form?

wo-no-qo-so, KN Ch 897, Ch 1015. Name of an ox: *Woinoqʷsos*, *Woinoqʷorsos*? [Οἶνοψ as MN *Od.* XXI, 144; cf. βόε οἶνοπε *Il.* XIII, 703; Petruševski, 1962, p. 250.]

wo-no-wa-ṭị-si, PY Vn 48, Xa 1419. Dat. plur.: *woinowa(s)tisi*? Sense and construction obscure, but a compound of *woinos* seems likely. The reading of the penultimate syllable is uncertain in both cases. [Cf. Οἰνόη?]

wo-qe-we, PY 54 = An 610, 55 = An 724. PN.

wo-ra-e, KN Sp 4451. Nom. dual, name of object, prob. connected with chariots, e.g. tyre. [Cf. *wo-ra-we-sa*.]

[*wo-]ra*, KN Sp 4452. Prob. sing.

wo-ra-ke-re[, KN Xd 170. MN?

wo-ra-we-sa, KN Se 880. Nom. sing. fem., description of chariot: *?-wessa*. [Cf. *wo-ra-e*.]

wo-ro-ka-ne, KN B 1025. Poss. nom. plur. describing men.

wo-ro-ki-jo-ne-jo, PY 152 = Er 312, 171 = Un 718. Adj. or other description of a piece of land. See pp. 265, 454.

wo-ro-ko-jo, PY Sa 763. MN, gen.

wo-ro-ma-ta, PY 317 = Ub 1318. Nom. plur. neut.: *wlōmata* 'containers'? See p. 491. [λῶμα.]

wo-ro-ne-ja, MY 228 = Oe 111. Description of wool, perhaps *wroneiā* 'lamb's'. [Metathesis of *worneia* = ἄρνεια; Palmer, 1963*a*, p. 464.]

wo-ro-qo-ta[, PY Qa 1305. MN.

wo-ro-ti-ja, PY Es 728. MN.
  wo-ro-ti-ja-o, PY [168 = Es 644], 167 = Es 650. Gen.

wo-ro-ṭọ, KN Do 5010, Dv 7863. MN.

wo-ro-to-qo, KN Vc 290. MN.

wo-ro-tu-mi-ni-jo, PY 60 = An 661. Prob. MN.

wo-si-jo-ne, KN B 1055. MN.

wo-ti-jo, KN Dv 5302?, PY An 340, Jn 832. MN: *Worthios*. [Ορθιος.]

wo-to-mo, PY 318 = Un 1314. Poss. MN.

wo-tu-ko-[, PY Xn 593. Poss. MN? [Cf. Ὀρτύγων.]

wo-tu-wa-ne, PY Cn 4. PN, loc.

wo-wa-ro, PY Jn 750. MN.

wo-we-u, KN C 911, Uf 836, PY Ae 142. Nom. sing. masc., prob. a title: perh. *worweus*. [Cf. *wo-wo*.]

wo-wi-ja, PY 59 = An 656, Mn 456, Na 1053. Forms a place name after a gen. app. MN: prob. *worwia* 'borders'. [ὅρια; cf. *wo-wo*.]

wo-wi-ja-ta, PY An 172, 255 = Jn 658 +. MN.

*wo-wo*¹, PY An 424 +, Cn 40 +, Na 105 +. Combined with MN in gen. forms a place name: prob. *worwos* 'boundary'. [ὅρος, Ion. οὖρος, Corcyr. ὄρϝος, poss. by dissimilation from *ϝόρϝος; cf. *wo-wi-ja*, *mo-ro-ko-wo-wo-pi*.]

*wo-wo*², KN Dc 5228, Dk 1071. MN.

wo-ze, PY Ea 309, 141 = Eb 338 +, 148 = Ep 613, 135 = Ep 704 +. 3rd sing. pres.: *wordzei* 'works, performs', exact sense obscure; sometimes negative *o-u-wo-ze* with variant or erroneous spelling *o-wo-ze* (141 = Eb 338). [ἔρδω Hom. +, cf. ῥέζω, from *ϝεργ-; Heubeck, 1969*b*, p. 5.]

wo-ze-e, PY 135 = Ep 704. Pres. infin.: *wordzehen*.

wo-zo-e, PY 141 = Eb 338. Error for *wo-ze-e*.

wo-zo, PY Eb 862. Nom. sing. masc. pres. pple.: *wordzōn*.

wo-zo-te, PY 149 = Ed 236, Ep 539. Nom. plur. and dat. sing. masc.: *wordzontes, -ontei*.

wo-zo-me-no, KN So 4433. Nom. dual pres. pple. pass.: *wordzomenō* 'being worked on' (i.e. under construction).

wo-zo-me-na, KN So 4438. Nom. plur. neut.: *wordzomena*.

wo-*65-ro, KN Dv 1492, MY Au 653? MN.

wo-*79, KN V 7049. Obscure.

wo-*82-ni-jo, KN Dc 1154. MN.

ZA, As adjunct to WOMEN or SHEEP, probably abbreviation of *za-we-te* or adjectival form, 'this year's' (Killen, 1963, p. 450): KN Ak 616, Do 919, Do 924 +.

za-e-to-ro, PY 54 = An 610, 60 = An 661. PN.

za-ki-ri-jo, KN Vc 108. MN.

za-ku-si-ja, PY 286 = Sa 787 +. Nom. plur. neut., description of wheels: *Dzakunsia* 'Zakynthian' (type or origin?). [Cf. Ζάκυνθος *Il*. II, 634.]

[*za*]-*ku-si-jo*, PY 54 = An 610. Poss. nom. plur. masc.: [*Dza*]*kunsioi*.

za-ku-si-jo, MY Oe 122. MN: *Dzakunsios*. [prec.]

za-ma-e-wi-ja, PY 257 = Jn 829, 175 = Ma 393, Vn 493. PN.

za-mi-jo, KN 39 = As 1517, PY An 129. Nom. plur. masc., description of men.

za-mi-so, KN Xd 111. Obscure.

]*za-ra-ro*, KN Dd 1429, Dk 1070, X 8634. MN.

za-we-te, KN Fh 5451, PY 180 = Ma 225. Adverb: *tsāwetes* 'this year'. [σῆτες, Att. τῆτες, Dor. σᾶτες, < *kyā-wetes*; Palmer, 1960, p. 60; 1963*a*, p. 305.]

za-we-te-ra, KN Ga 518, [Gg 5637, X 658?]. Nom. fem. sing.?, adj.: *tsāwe(s)terā* 'this year's'. [From *kyāwet-teros* or haplology for *tsāwetes-teros*?]

ZE, KN 85 = Ch 896 +, 278 = So 894 +, PY 43 = Aq 64 +, 284 = Sa 488 +, 292 = Sh 740 +, 249 = Va 482. Used to indicate paired objects, esp. oxen and wheels: *dze(ugos)* 'pair'. Cf. *ze-u-ke-si*. In KN 230 = K 740 perh. ideographic for 'saw'.

ze-i-ja-ka-ra-na, PY Xa 70. See s.v. *ke-i-ja-ka-ra-na*.

ze-me-qe[, KN L 588. Poss. MN + -*qᵘe*.

ze-ne-si-wi-jo, KN M 720. MN.

ze-pu₂-ra₃, PY Aa 61. Nom. plur. fem., description of women: *Dzephurai*. [Cf. Ζεφυρία old name for Halikarnassos, Strabo XIV, 656.]

ze-pu₂-ra-o, PY Ad 664. Gen. plur.: *Dzephurāōn*.

ze-pu₂-ro, PY Ea 56. MN: *Dzephuros*. [Cf. Ζέφυρος.]

ze-ro, KN As 4493?, Da 5218. MN.

ze-so-me-no, PY 103 = Un 267. Dat. sing. fut. pple. pass.: *zes(s)omenōi* 'to be boiled' (in the manufacture of unguent); taken by Palmer, 1963*a*, p. 270, as middle, but fut. passives do not seem to be differentiated in Mycenaean; cf. *e-we-pe-se-so-me-na*. [ζέω.]

-*ze-to*, PY Vn 130. Verbal form, probably meaning 'received' or similar: Palmer, 1963*a*, p. 440: *gento*, but spelling *z*- for *g*- is suspect. [γέντο *Il*. VIII, 43.]

ze-u-ke-si, PY 317 = Ub 1318. Dat. plur.: *dzeuges(s)i* 'pairs'. Frequently abbreviated to ZE. [ζεῦγος *Il*. XVIII, 543 +.]

ze-u-ke-u-si, PY 91 = Fn 50, Fn 79. Dat. plur., a class of men: *dzeugeusi* 'ox-drivers'? [Cf. Att. ζευγῖται.]

ze-wa-so, KN X 2002. Obscure; MN?

ZO, Adjunct to CLOTH: KN L 433. Obscure.

zo-a, KN Fh 343, Fh 355 +. Nom. sing., description of oil- *dzoa*, perh. 'oil from second pressing' (Godart, 1968*a*, p. 605). [Cf. ζόη· τὸ ἐπάνω τοῦ μέλιτος Hesych.]

zo-do-so, KN As 40. MN.

zo-wa, KN Nc 4473, 163 = Ra 984, 277 = Ra 1028, X 766. Obscure.

zo-wi-jo, KN V 1523, PY Cn 40. MN, nom. and dat.: *Tsōwios* or *Dzōwios*? [Cf. Σϝο-, Ζωϝο-; Lejeune, 1960*c*, p. 126.]

zo-wo, PY 57 = An 519. MN.

*18-to-no, KN Ap 639. WN.

*22-ja-ro, KN X 4486. Obscure; MN?

*22-ri-ta-ro, KN Dv 1216. MN.

*34-ke-ja, PY Fn 187. WN, dat.? Cf. **35-ke-ja*.

*34-ke-te-si, PY 169 = Es 646 +. Dat. plur., persons or divinities receiving offerings; see pp. 279, 458.

*34-ke-u, PY 237 = Ta 709. App. adj., description of tripod cauldron; cf. *a₃-ke-u*, *o-pi-ke-wi-ri-je-u*.

]**34-so*, KN Dv 1239. MN?

34-te, PY **44**=Aq 218. Nom. sing. masc., title or description of a man.

34-to-pi, PY Vn 130. Instr. plur.; obscure.

34-zo, KN Da 1253. MN.

35-ka-te-re, PY **248**=Va 15. Nom. dual.; obscure. See p. 348.

35-ke-ja, PY Eb 871. Personal name, fem.? Cf. *34-ke-ja*.

35-ki-no-o, PY **251**=Vn 46. Nom. plur.; structural members for building. Cf. *a₃-ki-no-o*.

35-to, PY Eb 472. Gen. sing.?

47-da, KN Xd 100. PN?

47-da-de, PY **200**=Fp 1. Acc.+-*de*.

47-ku-to-de, KN **202**= Fp 13. PN, acc.+-*de*.

47-so-de, KN Fh 351, Fh 357, Fh 393+. PN, acc.+-*de*.

47-ta-qo[, KN Xd 140. Obscure.

47-ti-jo, KN K 775, V 503. MN.

49-sa-ro, KN V 653. MN.

49-wo, KN Db 5231. MN.

56-du-nu-ka, KN Da 1132, Dv 1191. MN.

56-i-ti, KN Fh 1057. Dat.?, divine name?

56-ti, KN Fp 15. Variant spelling?

56-ko-we, KN Ap 618, **83**=C 902+, **64**=Da 1221, Db 1225+, Le 5646, TI Z 27. PN.

56-ko-we-e, KN Dl 794, Dl 7141. Dat.-loc.

56-ko-we-i, KN Dm 5181, Dn 1093. Variant of dat.-loc.

56-ko-we-i-jo/-*ja*, KN **100**=Ga 424+, **90**=G 820. Ethnic adj.

]*56-na-ro*, KN Dl 928. MN.

56-ni-sa-ta, KN As 607. MN.

56-po-so, KN Ln 1568. WN?

56-ra-ku-ja, KN **217**=Ld 587. Nom. plur. neut., description of textiles; cf. *pa-ra-ku-ja* Ld 575.

56-ri-to, KN Db 1423, Xe 6020. MN.

56-ro₂, KN Dv 1422. MN.

]*56-so-jo*, KN Ai 1036. MN, gen.?

56-ti: see s.v. *56-i-ti*.

65, Ideographic use: KN Fs 2+, PY Fn 187, **97**=Un 2, **171**=Un 718. Associated with *me-re-u-ro* 'flour', but possibly standing for a kind of grain rather than its form (Chadwick, 1966, p. 31).

82-de, PY Cn 600?, Jn 431. MN.

]*83-re-jo-de*, KN Ga 465. PN, acc.+-*de*.

]-*83-re-to*, KN Dl 933. MN.

BIBLIOGRAPHY

This does not pretend to be an exhaustive list of either the pre-decipherment literature or the immense volume of books and articles which have appeared since the first edition. It is not even a select bibliography, but rather a list of the references which are contained in the book; the omission of any item must not be construed as criticism or even evidence that it has not been read with profit. After twenty years of Mycenaean research, it is not always easy to trace the sources of a *communis opinio*.

The real reason, however, for this selective treatment lies in the existence of much fuller bibliographies, to which the reader is referred. Ever since 1956, the London Institute of Classical Studies has published annually a current list of books and articles dealing with Mycenaean under the title *Studies in Mycenaean Inscriptions and Dialect*, compiled by a number of scholars, latterly under the general direction of L. J. D. Richardson. The fruits of the first ten issues were gathered into a single convenient volume by L. Baumbach (1968). It is in this and the subsequent annual issues that further information must be sought.

Mention should also be made here of the two periodicals which have devoted themselves to Mycenaean and kindred subjects: KADMOS published in Berlin by W. de Gruyter, edited by the late E. Grumach, and since his death by William C. Brice; and MINOS, published in Salamanca and edited by M. S. Ruipérez. There is also the series of volumes appearing at irregular intervals at Rome under the title *Studi micenei ed egeo-anatolici*, from the Edizioni dell'Ateneo, the publishing house responsible under the direction of C. Gallavotti also for the impressive series called *Incunabula Graeca*.

The five international colloquia on Mycenaean studies have each produced a volume of Proceedings:

(1) *Études mycéniennes*, edited by M. Lejeune, Paris, 1956.

(2) *Atti del 2° colloquio internazionale di studi micenei*, Athenaeum, Pavia, 46, 295–436.

(3) *Mycenaean Studies*, edited by E. L. Bennett, Madison, 1964.

(4) *Proceedings of the Cambridge Colloquium on Mycenaean Studies*, edited by L. R. Palmer and J. Chadwick, Cambridge, 1966.

(5) *Acta Mycenaea*, edited by M. S. Ruipérez, Salamanca, 1972.

Other notable collections of Proceedings are: *Atti e Memorie del 1° Congresso internazionale di micenologia*, Rome, 1968, and *Studia Mycenaea*, edited by A. Bartoněk, Brno, 1968.

AALTO, P. (1945): Notes on methods of decipherment of unknown writings and languages. Soc. Orient. Fenn., *Studia Orientalia*, 11, 4.

ADRADOS, F. R. (1968): *di-pi-si-jo-i* y el mes dipsio de Farsalo. *Minos*, 9, 187–91.

ANSTOCK-DARGA, M. (1951): Bibliographie zur kretisch-minoischen Schrift und Sprache. *Orientalia*, 20, 2, 171–81.

ÅSTRÖM, P. (1962): Guldbägare, bronsharnesk och andra fynd i Dendra. *Svärdfejare och själamord*, Malmö, 87–96.

BANTI, L. (1954): Myth in pre-classical art. *Amer. J. Archaeol.* 58, 307–10.

BARROIS, A. G. (1953): *Manuel d'Archéologie biblique*, vol. II, Picard, Paris.

BAUMBACH, L. (1968): *Studies in Mycenaean Inscriptions and Dialect 1953–1964*, Rome.

BEEKES, R. S. P. (1969): *The Development of the proto-indoeuropean laryngeals in Greek*, Mouton, Hague.

BENNETT, E. L., Jr. (1947): The Minoan Linear Script from Pylos. Unpublished doctoral dissertation, University of Cincinnati.

(1950): Fractional quantities in Minoan bookkeeping. *Amer. J. Archaeol.* 54, 204–22.

(*PT I*): *The Pylos tablets, a preliminary transcription*, Princeton U.P. for University of Cincinnati, 1951.

(1951 b): Statistical notes on the sign-groups from Pylos. *Minos*, 1, 100–37.

(1951 c): The undeciphered Minoan Script, *Yale Scientific Magazine*, 25, 5.

(1952): Corrections of *Scripta Minoa II*, Privately circulated.

(*Index*): *A Minoan Linear B index*, Yale University Press, New Haven, 1953.

(*MT I*): The Mycenae tablets, with a foreword by A. J. B. Wace. *Proc. Amer. Philosoph. Soc.* 97, 4, 422–70.

(1955): Junctions of fragments of Minoan

BENNETT, E. L., Jr. (*cont.*)
    inscriptions in the Iraklion Museum. *Minos*, 3, 2, 122–5.
    (*PT II*): *The Pylos Tablets: texts of the inscriptions found 1939–54*, Princeton U.P. for University of Cincinnati, 1955.
    (*MT II*): The Mycenae Tablets II. *Trans. Amer. Philosophical Soc.* 48, 1, 1–122.
    (1956a): The Landholders of Pylos. *Amer. J. Archaeol.* 60, 103–33.
    (1956b): Correspondances entre les textes des tablettes pyliennes des séries Aa, Ab et Ad. *Études Mycéniennes* (ed. M. Lejeune), Paris, 121–36.
    (1957): Review of *Documents in Mycenaean Greek. Language*, 33, 553–68.
    (1958a): *The Olive Oil Tablets of Pylos: texts of inscriptions found*, 1955, Suplementos a 'MINOS' Núm. 2, Salamanca.
    (1958b): Tentative identifications of the hands of the scribes of the Pylos Tablets. *Athenaeum*, 46 (N.S. 36), 328–31.
    (1961): On the use and misuse of the term 'Priest-King' in Minoan studies. Κρητικά Χρονικά, 15–16, I, 327–35.
    (1964) (editor): *Mycenaean Studies: Proceedings of the third international colloquium*, University of Wisconsin Press, Madison.
    (1966): Miscellaneous observations on the forms and identities of Linear B ideograms. *Proc. Camb. Coll. on Myc. Stud.* 11–25.
BENNETT, E. L., Jr. and OLIVIER, J.-P. (forthcoming): *The Pylos Tablets in Transcription*, Rome.
BJÖRCK, G. (1954a): Pour les inscriptions en linéaire B peintes sur les vases. *Eranos*, 52, 120–4.
    (1954b): Pour le vocabulaire des tablettes 'à bannières' de Knossos. *Eranos*, 52, 271–5.
BLEGEN, C. W. (1928): The coming of the Greeks. II. The geographical distribution of prehistoric remains in Greece. *Amer. J. Archaeol.* 32, 146–54.
    (1950): A Mycenaean breadmaker. *Annuario della scuola archeologica di Atene*, N.S. 8–10, 13–16.
    (1953a): An inscribed tablet from Pylos. Ἀρχ. Ἐφημ., Εἰς μνήμην Γ. Π. Οἰκονόμου, 59–62.
    (1953b): Excavations at Pylos 1952. *Amer. J. Archaeol.* 57, 59–64.
    (1954): Excavations at Pylos 1953. *Amer. J. Archaeol.* 58, 27–32.
    (1955): The Palace of Nestor excavations of 1954. *Amer. J. Archaeol.* 59, 31–7.

BLEGEN, C. W. and KOUROUNIOTIS, K. (1939b): Excavations at Pylos 1939. *Amer. J. Archaeol.* 43, 557–76.
BLEGEN, C. W. and WACE, A. J. B. (1939a): Pottery as evidence for trade and colonization in the Aegean Bronze Age. *Klio*, 32, 131–47.
BOARDMAN, J. (1963): The Date of the Knossos Tablets. In Palmer and Boardman: *On the Knossos Tablets*, Oxford.
BOISACQ, E. (*Boisacq*): *Dictionnaire étymologique de la langue grecque*, 4th ed., Carl Winter, Heidelberg, 1950.
BOSSERT, H. T. (1932): Šantaš und Kubaba. Neue Beiträge zur Entzifferung der kretischen und hethitischen Bilderschrift. *Mitt. der Altorient. Ges.* 6, 3, 88.
BRICE, W. C. (1961): *Inscriptions in the Minoan Linear Script of Class A*, Oxford.
BROWNING, R. (1955): The Linear 'B' texts from Knossos, transliterated and edited. *Bulletin of the Institute of Classical Studies*, Supplementary Papers, No. 1.
BUCK, C. D. (1926): The language situation in and about Greece in the second millennium B.C. *Class. Philol.* 21, 1–26.
    (*Dial.*): *Introduction to the study of the Greek dialects*, 2nd ed. Ginn, Boston, 1928.
BUCK, C. D. and PETERSEN, W. (*Rev. Index*): *A reverse index of Greek nouns and adjectives*, University of Chicago, 1944.
CARRATELLI, G. PUGLIESE (1945): Le iscrizioni preelleniche di Haghia Triada in Creta e della Grecia peninsulare. *Monumenti Antichi*, 40, 422–610.
    (1954a): La decifrazione dei testi micenei. *La Parola del Passato* 35, 81–117.
    (1954b): Nuovi studi sui testi micenei. *Ibid.* 36, 215–28.
    (1954c): Reviews of Bennett (*Mycenae, 1953*) and Meriggi (1954b). *Ibid.* 37, 312–20.
    (1955a): Riflessi di culti micenei nelle tabelle di Cnosso e Pilo. *Studi in onore di U.E. Paoli*, Florence, 1–16.
    (1962): Achei nell' Etruria e nel Lazio? *La Parola del Passato*, 17, 4–25.
CARTER, H. (1927): *The Tomb of Tutankhamen*, 3 vols. Cassell, London.
CATLING, H. W. and MILLETT, A. (1965): A Study of the inscribed stirrup-jars from Thebes. *Archaeometry*, 8, 3–85.
CHADWICK, J. (1953): Greek records in the Minoan Script. *Antiquity*, 27, 196–200.
    (1954a): *The Earliest Greeks*, Pamphlet reprinted from the *Manchester Guardian*, June 1954.

CHADWICK, J. (*cont.*)

(1954*b*): Mycenaean: a newly discovered Greek dialect. *Trans. Philol. Soc.* 1954, 1–17.

(1955): The Knossos horse and foal tablet (Ca 895). *Bull. London Inst. Class. Stud.* 2, 1–3.

(1957*a*): Potnia. *Minos*, 5, 117–29.

(1957*b*): New fragments of Linear B tablets from Knossos. *Ann. Brit. Sch. Athens*, 52, 147–51.

(1958*a*): Error and Abnormality in the Mycenaean noun-declension. *Parola del Passato*, 13, 285–95.

(1958*b*): Rapport sur les questions générales. *Atti del 2º Colloquio internazionale di Studi minoico-micenei*: Athenaeum, 46, 299–313.

(1958*c*): The Mycenaean Filing System. *Bull. London Inst. Class. Stud.* 5, 1–5.

(1959): Inscribed sealings from Mycenae. *Eranos*, 57, 1–5.

(1962): Further Linear B Tablets from Knossos. *Ann. Brit. Sch. Athens*, 57, 46–74.

(1963*a*): The Two Provinces of Pylos. *Minos*, 7, 125–41.

(1963*b*): The Mycenae Tablets III. *Trans. Amer. Philosophical Soc.* 52:7, 1–76.

(1963*c*): The Pre-History of the Greek Language. *Cambridge Ancient History*, ed. 2, Vol. II, chap. 39.

(1964*a*): Review of L. R. Palmer, *Interpretation of Mycenaean Greek Texts*. *Gnomon*, 36, 321–7.

(1964*b*): Pylos Tablet Un 1322, *Mycenaean Studies* (ed. E. L. Bennett), Madison, 19–35.

(1966): The Olive Oil Tablets of Knossos. *Proc. Camb. Coll. on Myc. Studies*, 26–38.

(1967*a*): Mycenaean *pa-wo-ke*. *Minos*, 8, 115–17.

(1967*b*): Mycenaean *te-ko-to-na-pe*. *Studi micenei ed egeo-anatolici*, 4, 23–34.

(1968*a*): The Group *sw* in Mycenaean. *Minos*, 9, 62–5.

(1968*b*): The Organization of the Mycenaean Archives. *Studia Mycenaea* (Brno), 11–21.

(1968*c*): Mycenaean Wine and the etymology of γλυκύς. *Minos*, 9, 192–7.

(1969): Greek and Pre-Greek. *Trans. Philol. Soc.* 1969, 80–98.

(1970): Linear B tablets from Thebes. *Minos*, 10, 115–37.

(1971): The 'Greekness' of Linear B. *Indogermanische Forschungen*, 75, 97–104.

(1973): Relations between Knossos and the rest of Crete at the time of the Linear B tablets. *Proceedings of 3rd Congress of Cretan Studies* (in publication).

CHADWICK, J. and BAUMBACH, L. (1963): The Mycenaean Greek Vocabulary. *Glotta*, 41, 157–271.

CHADWICK, J., KILLEN, J. T. and OLIVIER, J.-P. (1971): *The Knossos Tablets*, fourth edition, Cambridge University Press.

CHANTRAINE, P. (1932): Quelques mots grecs suspects d'être empruntés à des parlers préhelléniques. *Mélanges Gustave Glotz*, Presses Universitaires, Paris.

(1933): La formation des noms en grec ancien. *Soc. Ling. de Paris*, 38.

(1945): *Morphologie historique du grec*, Klincksieck, Paris.

(1948, 1953): *Grammaire homérique*. I: *Phonétique et morphologie*. II: *Syntaxe*, Klincksieck, Paris.

(1955): Le déchiffrement de l'écriture Linéaire B à Cnossos et à Pylos. *Revue de Philologie*, 29, 11–33.

(1957): À propos d'un receuil de textes mycéniens. *Revue de Philologie*, 31, 239–46.

(1958*a*): Termes mycéniens relatifs au travail de l'ivoire. *Rev. Études grecques*, 70, 301–11.

(1958*b*): Mycénien *Te-u-ta-ra-ko-ro*. *Minoica* (Festschrift Sundwall), 123–7.

(1959): État présent de la philologie mycénienne. *Revue de Philologie*, 33, 249–62.

(1966): Finales mycéniennes en *-iko*. *Proc. Camb. Coll. on Myc. Studies*, 161–79.

(1968): *Dictionnaire étymologique de la langue grecque*, Paris.

CHAPOUTHIER, F. (1930): Les écritures minoennes au palais de Mallia. École Française d'Athènes, *Études Crétoises* II, Geuthner, Paris.

CHILDE, V. G. (1947): *The dawn of European civilization*, 4th ed., Kegan Paul, Trench, Trübner, London.

COWLEY, A. E. (1927): A note on Minoan writing. *Essays in Aegean archaeology presented to Sir Arthur Evans*, Oxford.

CUNY, A. (1910): Les mots du fonds préhellénique en grec, latin et sémitique occidental. *Revue des Études Anciennes*, 12, 154–64.

DANIEL, J. F. (1941): Prolegomena to the Cypro-Minoan script. *Amer. J. Archaeol.* 45, 249–82.

DEROY, L. (1948, 1951): Bibliographie critique des recherches relatives à l'écriture crétoise. *Revue Hittite et Asianique*, 8, 48, 1–39; *ibid*. 53, 35–60.

DESSENNE, A. (1957): Le griffon créto-mycénien: inventaire et remarques. *Bull. de Corresp. hellénique*, 81, 203–15.

DHORME, E. (1948): Déchiffrement des inscriptions pseudo-hiéroglyphes de Byblos. *Syria*, 25, 1–35.

DIKAIOS, P. (1953): A second inscribed tablet from Enkomi. *Antiquity*, 27, 233–7.

DORIA, M. (1956): *Interpretazioni di testi micenei; le tavolette della classe Ta di Pilo*, L. Cappelli, Trieste.

(1961): Aspetti della toponomastica micenea delle tavolette in Lineare B di Pilo. *VII° Congresso internaz. di Scienze Onomastiche*, 417–40.

DOW, S. (1954): Minoan writing. *Amer. J. Archaeol.* 58, 77–129.

EPHRON, H. D. (1961): Mycenaean Greek: a lesson in cryptanalysis. *Minos*, 7, 63–100.

EVANS, A. J. (1894): Primitive pictographs and a prae-Phoenician script from Crete and the Peloponnese. *J. Hellenic Stud.* 14, 270–372.

(1897): Further discoveries of Cretan and Aegean script. *J. Hellenic Stud.* 17, 327–61.

(1900–1905): Knossos excavation reports. *Ann. Brit. Sch. Athens*, 7–11.

(1906a): Minoan weights and mediums of currency from Crete, Mycenae and Cyprus. *Corolla Numismatica*, Oxford, 336–67.

(1906b): The prehistoric tombs of Knossos. *Archaeologia*, 59.

(*SM I*): *Scripta Minoa* vol. I: *the hieroglyphic and primitive linear classes*, Oxford, 1909.

(*PM*): *The Palace of Minos* (particularly vol. IV b), Oxford, 1935.

EVANS, A. J., ed. MYRES, J. L. (*SM II*): *Scripta Minoa*, vol. II: *the archives of Knossos*, Oxford, 1952.

(*SM III*): *Scripta Minoa*, vol. III: *Linear Script A etc.* Seen in proof, 1954. [Subsequently suppressed and replaced by Brice (1961).]

FAURE, P. (1967): Toponymes préhelléniques dans la Crète moderne. *Kadmos*, 6, 41–79.

(1968): Toponymes créto-mycéniens dans une liste d'Aménophis III. *Kadmos*, 7, 138–49.

FICK, A. (1894): *Die griechische Personennamen*, 2nd ed. Vandenhoeck and Ruprecht, Göttingen.

(1905): *Vorgriechische Ortsnamen*, Vandenhoeck and Ruprecht, Göttingen.

FIGULLA, H. H. and MARTIN, W. J. (1953): Ur excavations (texts), V: Letters and documents of the Old Babylonian period, British Museum and University of Pennsylvania.

FRIEDRICH, J. (1954): *Entzifferung verschollener Schriften und Sprachen*, Springer-Verlag, Berlin.

FRISK, H. *Griechisches etymologisches Wörterbuch*, Heidelberg, 1960–70.

FURUMARK, A. (*MP*): *The Mycenaean pottery: analysis and classification*, Kungl. Vitt. Hist. och Ant. Akademien, Stockholm, 1941.

(1953): A scarab from Cyprus. *Skrifter utgivna av Svenska Inst. i Athen 4°*: II (Op. Ath. I), 47–65.

(1954): Ägäische Texte in griechischer Sprache. *Eranos*, 51, 103–20; 52, 18–60.

GALLAVOTTI, C. (1956): Lettura di testi micenei. *Parola del Passato*, 11, 5–24.

(1958): Note brevi di filologia micenea. *Stud. Ital. Fil. class.* 30, 52–72.

(1959): Review of Lejeune, *Mémoires 1: Revista di Filologia*, 37, 163–8.

GARDINER, A. H. (1948): *The Wilbour Papyrus* (3 vols.), Oxford University Press for the Brooklyn Museum.

GELB, I. J. (1952): *A study of writing: the foundations of grammatology*, Routledge and Kegan Paul, London.

DE GENOUILLAC, H. (1909): *Tablettes sumériennes archaïques (Lagaš)*, Paul Geuthner, Paris.

GEORGIEV, V. (1941, 1945): Vorgriechische Sprachwissenschaft. *Jahrbuch der Univ. Sv. Klim. Ohridski, Hist.-Phil. Fak.*, Sofia, 36, 6, 1–162; 41, 163–240.

(1949): Le déchiffrement des inscriptions minoennes. *Ibid.* 45.

(1950): Inscriptions minoennes quasi-bilingues. *Ibid.* 46.

(1953): *Problems of the Minoan language* (in Russian), Izd. Bolg. Akad. Nauk, Sofia.

(1954): *The present position in the decipherment of the Minoan-Mycenaean inscriptions* (in Russian), Izd. Bolg. Akad. Nauk, Sofia.

(1955): Introduction to the reading and interpretation of the Cretan-Mycenaean inscriptions (*in Russian*). *Izv. Otdel. Lit. i Yazyka (Akad. Nauk SSSR)*, 14, 3, 267–79.

Lexique des inscriptions créto-mycéniennes, Izd. Bolg. Akad. Nauk Sofia, 1955. (With 2 supplements.)

GÉRARD-ROUSSEAU, M. (1968): *Les mentions religieuses dans les tablettes mycéniennes*, Rome.

GODART, L. (1968a): Les quantités d'huile de la série Fh de Cnossos. *Atti del 1° Congresso di micenologia*, Rome, 598–610.

(1968b): *Kupirijo* dans les textes mycéniens. *Studi micenei ed egeo-anatolici*, 5, 64–70.

(1969): La série Fh de Cnossos. *Studi micenei ed egeo-anatolici*, 8, 39–65.

GORDON, C. H. (1947): Ugaritic handbook. *Analecta Orientalia*, Pont. Inst. Bibl., Rome.

GRAY, D. H. F. (1954): Metal-working in Homer. *J. Hellenic Stud.* 74, 1–15.

(1959): Linear B and archaeology. *Bull. London Inst. Class. Stud.* 6, 47–57.

(1960): Comment (on Palmer, 1960). *Bull. Lond. Inst. Class. Stud.* 7, 64–5.

GURNEY, O. R. (1952): *The Hittites*, Penguin Books, London.

GUTHRIE, W. K. C. (1959): Early Greek religion in the light of the decipherment of Linear B. *Bull. London Inst. Class. Stud.* 6, 35–46.

HALEY, J. B. (1928): The coming of the Greeks: 1. The geographical distribution of pre-Greek place-names. *Amer. J. Archaeol.* 32, 141–5.

HALLEUX, R. (1969): Lapis-lazuli, azurite ou pâte de verre? À propos de kuwano et kuwanowoko dans les tablettes mycéniennes. *Studi micenei ed egeo-anatolici*, 9, 47–66.

HAMMARSTRÖM, M. (1921): Griechisch-etruskische Wortgleichungen. *Glotta*, 11, 211–17.

HAMP, E. P. (1968): The Name of Demeter. *Minos*, 9, 198–204.

HEMBERG, B. (1954): Τριπάτωρ und Τρισήρως. *Eranos*, 52, 172–90.

HENLE, J. E. (1953): *A study in word structure in Minoan Linear B*. Dissertation at Columbia University, privately printed, New York.

HESTER, D. A. (1958): The *i/e* alternation in Mycenaean Greek. *Minos*, 6, 24–36.

HEUBECK, A. (1957): Bemerkungen zu einigen griechischen Personennamen auf den Linear B-Tafeln. *Beiträge zur Namenforschung*, 8, 28–35, 268–78.

(1958): Mykenisch *qi-si-po* = ξίφος. *Minos*, 5, 149–53.

(1960a): Review of *Minoica*. *Bibliotheca Orientalis*, 17, 17–19.

(1960b): Zu den griechischen Ortsnamen mit -*u̯ent*- suffix. *Beiträge zur Namenforschung*, 11, 4–10.

(1961a): Myk. *ra-o* λᾶος 'Stein' und Verwandtes. *Indogermanische Forschungen*, 66, 29–34.

(1961b): Review: Vilborg, *A Tentative Grammar of Mycenaean Greek*. *Indogermanische Forschungen*, 66, 308–12.

(1961c): Nochmals zu den griechischen Ortsnamen mit -*u̯ent*- suffix. *Beiträge zur Namenforschung*, 12, 95–6.

(1963a): 'Digamma'—Probleme des mykenischen Dialekts. *Die Sprache*, 9, 193–202.

(1963b): Ergänzende Bemerkungen. *Kadmos*, 2, 74–6.

(1966): Mycenaean *qe-qi-no-me-no*. *Proc. Camb. Coll. on Myc. Stud.*, 229–37.

(1967): Myk. *ke-ke-me-no*. *Ziva Antika*, 17, 17–21.

(1968): *Da-mo-ko-ro*. *Atti e Memorie del 1° Congresso internazionale di micenologia*, Rome, 611–14.

(1969a): Gedanken zu griech. λαός. *Studi linguistici in onore di Vittore Pisani*, 535–44.

(1969b): Myk. *e-me* und *du-wo-u-pi*. *Ziva Antika*, 19, 3–12.

(1969c): Zu den Linear B-texten auf mutterländischen Vasen. *Athenaeum*, 47, 144–53.

(1971a): Griechisch ὀδάξ. *Donum Indogermanicum* (Festschrift A. Scherer), Heidelberg, 123–9.

(1971b): Zur *s*- und *z*-Reihe in Linear B. *Kadmos*, 10, 113–24.

(1971c): Überlegungen zum Lautwert des Silbenzeichens *65 in Linear B und zum griechischen Wort für 'Sohn'. *Studi micenei ed egeo-anatolici*, 13, 147–55.

HOOD, M. S. F. and DE JONG, P. (1952): Late Minoan warrior-graves from Ayios Ioannis and the new Hospital Site at Knossos. *Ann. Brit. Sch. Athens*, 47, 243–77.

(1953): A Mycenaean cavalryman. *Ibid.* 48, 84–93.

HOPE SIMPSON, R. and LAZENBY, J. F. (1970): *The Catalogue of the Ships in Homer's Iliad*, Oxford.

HOUSEHOLDER, F. W. (1959a): Review of *Mycenae Tablets* II, Blegen and Lang, Palace of Nestor Excavations 1955, etc. *Classical Journal*, 54, 379–83.

(1959b): *Pa-ro* and Mycenaean cases. *Glotta*, 38, 1–10.

HROZNÝ, B. (1949): *Les inscriptions crétoises: essai de déchiffrement*, Orientální Ustav, Prague. (Consolidation of previous publications in 1940, 1943, 1946, 1948.)

HUBER, J. (1921): *De lingua antiquissimorum Graeciae incolarum*. Dissert. Aenipontanae, Vienna.

ILIEVSKI, P. H. (1959): The adverbial suffix -θεν in Mycenaean. *Ziva Antika*, 9, 105–28.

(1961): *Ablativot, instrymentalot i lokativot vo najstarite greki tekstovi*, Skopje.

(1969a): Myc. *A-DA-RA-KO*. *Ziva Antika*, 18, 216.

(1969b): Myc. *A-KA-MA-JO, A-KA-MA-WO, A-KA-MA-NO; KA-KI-RO, KA-KE-U*. *Ziva Antika*, 19, 174; 226.

(1970): Il sincretismo dei casi in miceneo. *Studi micenei ed egeo-anatolici*, 12, 88–116.

JONES, D. M. (1958): Notes on Mycenaean Texts. *Glotta*, 37, 112–18.

KANNENGIESSER, A. (1911): Ägäische, besonders kretische, Namen bei den Etruskern. *Klio*, 11, 26–47.

KANTOR, H. (1947): The Aegean and the Orient in the second millennium B.C. *Amer. J. Archaeol.* 51, 1–103.

KARAGEORGHIS, J. V. (1954): *The Ancient Cypriot Dialect*, Leukosia, 1954.

599

KARAGEORGHIS, V. (1966): Recent Discoveries at Salamis (Cyprus). *Archäologischer Anzeiger*, 1966, Heft 3, 210–55.

(1967*a*): Note on a footstool from Salamis. *Kadmos*, 6, 98–9.

(1967*b*): Chronique des fouilles et découvertes archéologiques à Chypre en 1966. *Bull. Corr. Hell.* 91, 275–370.

KERSCHENSTEINER, J. (1955): Bemerkungen zur kretischen Linearschrift B. *Münchener Studien zur Sprachwissenschaft*, 6, 56–70.

KILLEN, J. T. (1962*a*): The Wool ideogram in Linear B texts. *Hermathena*, 96, 38–72.

(1962*b*): Mycenaean *po-ka*: a suggested interpretation. *Parola del Passato*, 17, 26–31.

(1963): Mycenaean *po-ka*: a further note. *Ibid.* 18, 447–50.

(1964*a*): Some Adjuncts to the sheep ideogram on the Knossos Tablets. *Eranos*, 61, 69–93.

(1964*b*): The wool industry of Crete in the Late Bronze Age. *Annual of the British School at Athens*, 59, 1–15.

(1964*c*): Review of *Mycenae Tablets* III. *Classical Review*, 14, 171–3.

(1966*a*): The abbreviation *tu* on Knossos Tablets. *Živa Antika*, 16, 207–12.

(1966*b*): The Knossos *Nc* Tablets. *Proc. Camb. Coll. on Myc. Stud.* 33–8.

(1966*c*): The Knossos *Lc* (Cloth) Tablets. *Bull. London Inst. Class. Stud.* 13, 105–9.

(1968): The Knossos *o-pi* Tablets. *Atti e memorie del 1° Congresso internazionale di micenologia*, Rome, 636–43.

KILLEN, J. T. and OLIVIER, J.-P. (1968): 155 Raccords de fragments dans les tablettes de Cnossos. *Bull. Corr. Hell.* 92, 115–41.

KOBER, A. E. (1943): The scripts of pre-Hellenic Greece. *Classical Outlook*, 21, 72–4.

(1944): The 'adze' tablets from Knossos. *Amer. J. Archaeol.* 48, 64–75.

(1945*a*): Evidence of inflection in the 'chariot' tablets from Knossos. *Ibid.* 49, 143–51.

(1945*b*): The cryptograms of Crete. *Classical Outlook*, 22, 77–8.

(1946): Inflection in Linear Class B: I. Declension. *Amer. J. Archaeol.* 50, 268–76.

(1948): The Minoan scripts: fact and theory. *Ibid.* 52, 82–103.

(1949): 'Total' in Minoan (Linear Class B). *Archiv Orientální*, 17, 386–98.

(1950): A note on some 'cattle' tablets from Knossos. *Jahrbuch für kleinasiatische Forschung*, 1, 142–50.

KRETSCHMER, P. (1921): Pelasger und Etrusker. *Glotta*, 11, 276–85.

(1925): Die protindogermanische Schicht. *Glotta*, 14, 300–20.

(1940, 1943): Die vorgriechischen Sprach- und Volksschichten. *Glotta*, 28, 231–78; 30, 84–218.

(1948): Die ältesten Sprachschichten auf Kreta. *Glotta*, 31, 1–20, 127.

KTISTOPOULOS, K. (1955): Statistical data on Minoan words. *Minos*, 3, 2, 100–6.

LACHEMAN, E. R. (1939): Epigraphic evidence of the material culture of the Nuzians. Appendix D (pp. 528–44) to Starr, R. F. S.: *Nuzi*, vol. I, Harvard.

LANDAU, O. (1958): *Mykenisch-griechische Personennamen*, Göteborg.

LANG, M. (1958): The Palace of Nestor Excavations of 1957, Part II. *Amer. J. Archaeol.* 62, 181–91.

(1959): The Palace of Nestor Excavations of 1958, Part II. *Amer. J. Archaeol.* 63, 128–37.

(1964*a*): *Es* proportions. *Mycenaean Studies*, 37–51.

(1964*b*): The Palace of Nestor Excavations of 1963, Part II. *Amer. J. Archaeol.* 68, 99–105.

(1965): The Palace of Nestor Excavations of 1964, Part II. *Amer. J. Archaeol.* 69, 98–101, plate 24.

LEE, D. J. N. (1958): *A-ra-ro-mo-te-me-na*. *Bull. London Inst. Class. Stud.* 5, 61–4.

LEGRAIN, L. (1947): *Ur Excavations* (texts), III: *Business documents of the third dynasty of Ur*, British Museum and University of Pennsylvania.

LEJEUNE, M. (1954): Déchiffrement du 'Linéaire B'. *Revue des Études Anciennes*, 56, 153–7.

(1956): *Études mycéniennes: Actes du colloque international*, C.N.R.S. Paris.

(1958*a*): *Mémoires de Philologie Mycénienne*, I, Paris.

(1958*b*): Études de philologie mycénienne: (3) Les adjectifs mycéniens à suffixe -*went*. *Revue des Études anciennes*, 60, 5–26 (= 1971, 13–33).

(1959): Textes mycéniens relatifs aux esclaves. *Historia*, 8, 129–44 (= 1971, 65–81).

(1960*a*): Essais de Philologie mycénienne VI. *Revue de Philologie*, 34, 9–30 (= 1971, 199–224).

(1960*b*): Hittite *kati*-, grec κασι-. *Bull. Soc. Ling.* 55, 20–6 (= 1971, 243–9).

(1960*c*): Les sifflantes fortes du mycénien. *Minos*, 6, 87–137 (= 1971, 97–139).

(1961*a*): Essais de philologie mycénienne VII. *Revue de Philologie*, 35, 195–206 (= 1971, 253–65).

LEJEUNE, M. (*cont.*)

(1961*b*): Les forgerons de Pylos. *Historia*, 10, 409–34 (=1971, 169–95).

(1962*a*): Les signes TA₂ et TWO. *Revue de Philologie*, 36, 217–24 (=1971, 329–37).

(1962*b*): Notes mycéniennes. *Parola del Passato*, 17, 401–20 (=1971, 359–75).

(1964*a*): Sur quelques termes du vocabulaire économique mycénien. *Mycenaean Studies*, 77–109 (=1971, 287–312).

(1964*b*): Observations sur l'idéogramme *146*. *Mycenaean Studies*, 111–24 (=1971, 315–25).

(1966*a*): Syllabaire mycénien: peut-on lire *AU*- pour *85*-? *Studi micenei ed egeo-anatolici*, 1, 9–28.

(1966*b*): Le récapitulatif du cadastre Ep de Pylos. *Proc. Camb. Coll. Myc. Stud.* 260–4.

(1967): L'assibilation de θ devant ι en mycénien. *Atti del 1° Congresso internazionale di micenologia*, Rome, II, 733–43.

(1968*a*): Un nom indo-européen de l'épée en mycénien? *Beiträge zur Namenforschung*, 3, 38–9.

(1968*b*): Mycénien *qaqaro*/minoen *qaqaru*. *Actes du 1er Congrès international des Études balkaniques et sud-est européennes*, Sofia, 311–16.

(1968*c*): Essais de Philologie mycénienne. *Revue de Philologie*, 42, 219–39.

(1968*d*): Chars et roues à Cnossos: structure d'un inventaire. *Minos*, 9, 9–61.

(1969): Sur les toponymes mycéniens en -*wont*-. *Bull. Soc. Ling.* 64.1, 43–56.

(1971): *Mémoires de philologie mycénienne*, II, Rome.

LESKY, A. (1954): Review of '*Evidence*'. *Anzeiger der phil.-hist. Klasse der Oest. Akademie*, 6, 1–13, reprinted in *Gymnasium* (1955), 62, 1/2, 1–13.

LEWY, H. (1944): Assyro-Babylonian and Israelite measures of capacity and rates of seeding. *J. Amer. Oriental Soc.* 64, 65–73.

(1949): Origin and development of the sexagesimal system of numeration. *Ibid.* 69, 1–11.

LIDDELL, H. G. and SCOTT, R. (*L & S*): *A Greek–English lexicon*, revised and augmented edition, Oxford, 1940.

LORIMER, H. L. (1950): *Homer and the monuments*, Macmillan London.

LURIA, S. (1957): Über die Nominaldeklination in den mykenischen Inschriften. *Parola del Passato*, 12, 321–32.

(1958): Zu den neugefundenen pylischen Inschriften (1955–1958). *Parola del Passato*, 15, 241–59.

MADDOLI, G. (1968): *Ko-no* e *po-ni-ki-jo* micenei in un' iscrizione cretese arcaica. *Atti del 1° Congresso micenologico*, 2, 644–50.

MARINATOS, S. (1951): Some general notes on the Minoan written documents. *Minos*, 1, 1, 39–42.

(1953): Τὸ πρῶτον φῶς ἐκ τῶν μνημείων τῆς κρητομυκηναϊκῆς γραφῆς. Ἐπετ. τῆς Ἑτ. Βυζ. Σπουδῶν, 23, 139–49.

(1962): Zur Frage der Grotte von Arkalochori. *Kadmos*, 1, 87–94.

(1966): Πολυδίψιον Ἄργος. *Proc. Camb. Coll. on Myc. Stud.*, 265–84.

MASSON, E. (1971): Les repertoires graphiques chypro-minoens. *Acta Mycenaea* (Ruipérez, 1972), I, 99–109.

MASSON, O. (1952): *Nouvelles inscriptions en caractères chypro-minoens*. Appendix (pp. 391–409) to SCHAEFFER (1952).

(1954): Épigraphie chypriote: bibliographie relative aux inscriptions chypro-minoennes et étéochypriotes. *Orientalia*, 23, 442–6.

(1960): Notes Épigraphiques. *Glotta*, 39, 111–14.

MEILLET, A. (1909): De quelques emprunts probables en grec et en latin. *Mém. de la Soc. Ling. de Paris*, 15, 161–4.

(1926): La civilisation égéenne et le vocabulaire méditerranéen. *Linguistique historique et linguistique générale*, I.

MERIGGI, P. (1941): Zu den neuentdeckten minoischen Inschriften aus Pylos. *Die Antike*, 17, 170–6.

(1954*a*): Il minoico B è greco? *Minos*, 3, 55–86.

(1954*b*): Das Minoische B nach Ventris' Entzifferung. *Glotta*, 34, 1/2, 12–37.

(1954*c*): Toponimi cretesi in minoico B. *Archivio Glottologico Italiano*, 39, 83–91.

(1955*a*): Glossario miceneo (Minoico B). Accademia delle scienze, Torino.

(1955*b*): I testi micenei in traserizione. *Athenaeum*, 33, 64–92.

MERLINGEN, W. (1953): *Kretische Sprachreste im Griechischen, rekonstruiert*, privately duplicated, Vienna.

(1954): *Bemerkungen zur Sprache von Linear B*, privately duplicated, Vienna.

(1955): *Das 'Vorgriechische' und die sprachwissenschaftlich-vorhistorischen Grundlagen*. Gerold, Vienna.

MILANI, C. (1970): Appunti di lessico miceneo. *Aevum*, 44, 303–6.

MILLER, J. I. (1969): *The Spice Trade of the Roman Empire*, Oxford.

MITFORD, T. B. (1952): The status of Cypriot epigraphy: Cypriot writing, Minoan to Byzantine. *Archaeology*, 5, 151–6.

MORPURGO, A. (1963): *Mycenaeae Graecitatis Lexicon*, Rome, Edizioni dell' Ateneo.

MÜHLESTEIN, H. (1955a): *Olympia in Pylos (with Nachtrag)*, privately printed, Basel.

(1955b): Zur mykenischen Schrift: die Zeichen *za, ze, zo*. *Museum Helveticum*, 12, 119–31.

(1956a): *Die oka-tafeln von Pylos*, privately printed, Basel.

(1956b): L'adjectif mycénien signifiant 'en or'. *Études Mycéniennes*, 93–7.

(1957): Sirenen in Pylos. *Glotta*, 36, 152–6.

(1958): Einige mykenische Wörter. *Museum Helveticum*, 15, 222–6.

(1969): Redende Personennamen bei Homer. *Studi micenei ed egeo-anatolici*, 9, 67–94.

MYRES, J. L. (1930): *Who were the Greeks?* Berkeley.

(1946): The Minoan signary, a suggestion for the arrangement of the signs in the Linear Scripts of Minoan Crete. *J. Hellenic Stud.* 66, 1–4.

(*SM II* and *SM III*): see under EVANS, A. J.

NAOUMIDES, M. (1968): New fragments of Ancient Greek Poets. *Greek, Roman and Byzantine Studies*, 9, 267–90.

NEUMANN, G. (1962): Νικύλεον. *Glotta*, 40, 51–4.

NILSSON, M. P. (1927): *The Minoan-Mycenaean religion and its survival in Greek religion*, 1st ed. (2nd ed. 1950, Gleerup, Lund).

(1932): *The Mycenaean origin of Greek mythology*, Cambridge.

(1933): *Homer and Mycenae*, Methuen, London.

OLIVIER, J.-P. (1960): *À propos d'une 'liste' de desservants de sanctuaire*, Brussells.

(1967a): Le *damokoro*: un fonctionnaire mycénien. *Minos*, 8, 118–22.

(1967b): *Les Scribes de Cnossos*, Rome.

(1967c): La série Dn de Cnossos. *Studi micenei ed egeo-anatolici*, 2, 71–93.

(1969): *The Mycenae Tablets* IV, Leiden.

O'NEIL, J. L. (1970): The words *qasireu, qasirewija* and *kerosija*. *Živa Antika*, 20, 11–14.

OTA, H. (1959): Pyurosu bunsho ni okeru DA oyobi TA. *Shigaku Zasshi*, 68, 60–72.

PALLOTTINO, M. (1947): *L'origine degli Etruschi*, Studium Urbis, Rome.

PALMER, L. R. (1954a): Review of 'Evidence'. *Gnomon*, 26, 65–7.

(1954b): Mycenaean Greek texts from Pylos. *Trans. Philol. Soc.* 1954, 18–53b.

(1955a): *Achaeans and Indo-Europeans*, Inaugural lecture, 4 November 1954, Oxford.

(1955b): Observations on the Linear 'B' tablets from Mycenae. *Bull. of London Inst. of Class. Stud.* 2, 36–45.

(1957a): Review of *Documents in Mycenaean Greek*. *Gnomon*, 29, 561–82.

(1957b): A Mycenaean Tomb Inventory. *Minos*, 5, 58–92.

(1958): New Religious Texts from Pylos (1955). *Trans. Philol. Soc.* 1958, 1–35.

(1959): Methodology in 'Linear B' Interpretations. *Die Sprache*, 5, 128–42.

(1960): Tomb or Reception Room? *Bull. London Inst. of Class. Stud.* 7, 57–65.

(1961): *Mycenaeans and Minoans*, London (2nd edition: 1965).

(1962): Review of Olivier, *Desservants*. *Gnomon*, 34, 707–11.

(1963a): *The Interpretation of Mycenaean Greek Texts*, Oxford.

(1963b): The Find-Places of the Knossos Tablets. In Palmer and Boardman, *On the Knossos Tablets*, Oxford.

(1965): Review of *Mycenaean Studies* (Wisconsin, 1964). *Language*, 41, 312–29.

(1966): Some points for discussion. *Proc. Camb. Coll. on Myc. Stud.* 275–84.

(1969): Addenda to *The Interpretation of Mycenaean Greek Texts* (1963a), 483–96.

PALMER, L. R. and CHADWICK, J. (editors) (1966): *Proceedings of the Cambridge Colloquium on Mycenaean Studies*, Cambridge University Press.

PENDLEBURY, J. D. S. (1939): *The archaeology of Crete*, Methuen, London.

PERNIER, L. (1935): *Il Palazzo minoico di Festos*, vol. I, Rome.

PERPILLOU, J.-L. (1968): La tablette PY An 724 et la flotte pylienne. *Minos*, 9, 205–18.

PERSSON, A. W. (1930): Schrift und Sprache in Alt-Kreta. *Uppsala Univ. Arsskrift*, Prog. 3, 1–32.

(1952): New tombs at Dendra near Midea. *Skrifter utgivna av Kungl. Hum. Vitt.-samfundet i Lund*, 34.

PERUZZI, E. and TOVAR, A. (1953): Review of 'Evidence'. *Minos*, 2, 125–6.

PETRUŠEVSKI, M. D. (1958): *Pa-ko-to a-pe-te-me-ne*. *Živa Antika*, 8, 294.

(1959): *wo-di-jo, wo-di-je-ja, wo-de-wi-jo; pi-ri-ta-wo, qi-ri-ta-ko, qi-ri-ta-ro; wo-ro-ma-ta*. *Živa Antika*, 9, 104; 230; 252.

(1962): *Wo-no-qo-so; wo-no-wa-ti-si; ko-pi-na*. *Živa Antika*, 11, 250; 278; 318.

(1966): Miscellae. *Živa Antika*, 15, 288; 294; 320; 326; 352.

PETRUŠEVSKI, M. D. (cont.)

(1968): *Zo-wa, e-pi-zo-ta*. *Živa Antika*, **18**, 128.

(1970a): Interprétations de quelques mots mycéniens. *Studi micenei ed egeo-anatolici*, **12**, 121–35.

(1970b): *Pte-no* = πτέρνω. *Živa Antika*, **20**, 114.

PETRUŠEVSKI, M. D. and ILIEVSKI, P. H. (1958): The Phonetic Value of the Mycenaean Syllabic sign *85*. *Živa Antika*, **8**, 265–78.

PISANI, V. (1955): Die Entzifferung der Ägeischen Linear B Schrift und die griechischen Dialekte. *Rheinisches Museum für Philologie*, n.F. **98**, 81, 1–1.

PLATON, N. (1954): Review of '*Evidence*'. Κρητικὰ Χρονικά, 1954, 143–62.

(1968): Ἡ τελικὴ καταστροφὴ τῶν μινωϊκῶν ἀνακτόρων. Πεπραγμένα τοῦ Β΄ διεθνοῦς Κρητολογικοῦ Συνεδρίου, Vol. I, 220–9.

POPE, M. (1964): Aegean Writing and Linear A. *Studies in Mediterranean Archaeology*, Lund, no. 8, 1–16.

PORZIG, W. (1954): Sprachgeographische Untersuchungen zu den altgriechischen Dialekten. *Indogermanische Forschungen*, **61**, 147–69.

PRITCHARD, J. B. (ed.) (1950): *Ancient Near Eastern texts relating to the Old Testament*, Princeton.

PROTONOTARIOU-DEÏLAKI, E. (1969): Θολωτὸς τάφος Καζάρμας. *Athens Annals of Archaeology*, **2**, 3–5.

RAISON, J. (1964): Note sur le signe mycénien 65. *Kadmos*, **3**, 58–63.

(1968): *Les vases à inscriptions peintes de l'âge mycénien et leur contexte archéologique*, Rome.

RISCH, E. (1955): Die Gliederung der griechischen Dialekte in neuer Sicht. *Museum Helveticum*, **12**, 61–76.

(1957): Mykenisch *wo-wo ko-to-no*. *Minos*, **5**, 28–34.

(1958a): L'accusatif pluriel des thèmes consonantiques en mycénien. *Bull. Soc. Ling.* **53**:1, 96–102.

(1958b): L'Interpretation de la série des tablettes caractérisées par le mot *o-ka*. *Athenaeum*, **46**, 334–59.

(1959): Frühgeschichte der griechischen Sprache. *Museum Helveticum*, **16**, 215–27.

(1966a): Mykenisch *seremokaraoi* oder *seremokaraore*? *Studi micenei ed egeo-anatolici*, **1**, 53–66.

(1966b): Les différences dialectales dans le mycénien. *Proc. Camb. Colloq. on Myc. Stud.* 150–7.

ROSTOVTZEFF, M. (1941): *Social and economic history of the Hellenistic world*, Oxford.

RUIJGH, C. J. (1959): Review *MT* II. *Mnemosyne*, **12**, 76–7.

(1963): Vrouwen en Kinderen in Pylos. *Forum der Letteren*, **4**, 228–62.

(1966): Observations sur la tablette Ub 1318 de Pylos. *Lingua*, **16**, 130–52.

(1967): *Études sur la grammaire et le vocabulaire du grec mycénien*, Hakkert, Amsterdam.

(1970): Review Article, P. Chantraine, *Dictionnaire étymologique de la langue grecque*. *Lingua*, **25**, 302–21.

RUIPÉREZ, M. S. (1950): Problemas de morfología verbal relacionados con la representación en griego de las raices disilábicas set. *Emerita*, **18**, 386–407.

(1952): Desinencias medias primarias indoeuropeas. *Emerita*, **20**, 8–31.

(1956): Une charte royale de partage de terres à Pylos. *Minos*, **4**, 146–64.

(1957): Notes on Mycenaean Land-division and Livestock-grazing. *Minos*, **5**, 174–206.

(1972): *Acta Mycenaea* (Proceedings of the Fifth International Colloquium on Mycenaean Studies, Salamanca 1970), Universidad de Salamanca.

SACCONI, A. (1968): Ideogrammata Mycenaea. *Atti e Memorie del 1º Congresso di micenologia*, **2**, 513–55.

SAFAREWICZ, J. (1955): Odcyfrowanie tekstów greckich w piśmie Linearnym B. *Maeander*, **10**, 135–47.

DE SANTERRE, H. G. and TRÉHEUX, J. (1948): Le dépôt égéen et géométrique de l'Artémision à Délos. *Bull. de Corr. Hell.* 71–2, 148–254.

SCHACHERMEYR, F. (1929): *Etruskische Frühgeschichte*, Berlin and Leipzig.

(1935): Hethiter und Achäer. *Mitt. der Altorient. Ges.* 9.

(1939): Zur Indogermanisierung Griechenlands. *Klio*, **32**, 235–88.

(1949): Welche geschichtlichen Ereignisse führten zur Entstehung der mykenischen Kultur? *Archiv. Orientální*, **17**, 331–50.

(1951): Streitwagen und Streitwagenbild im Alten Orient und bei den mykenischen Griechen. *Anthropos*, **46**, 705–53.

(1953): Forschungsbericht: die ägäische Frühzeit (Kreta und Mykenai) II, 1951–1953. *Anz. für die Altertumswiss.*, **6**, 4, 193–200.

SCHAEFFER, C. F. A. (1952): *Enkomi-Alasia*, Klincksieck, Paris.

SCHERER, A. (1959): *Handbuch der griechischen Dialekte*, II, by A. Thumb, 2nd edition by A. Scherer, Heidelberg.

SCHLIEMANN, H. (1878): *Mycenae*, John Murray, London.

SCHMEJA, H. (1968): *Studien zur Sprachwissenschaft und Kulturkunde (Gedenkschrift für W. Brandenstein)*, Innsbruck, 129–38.

SCHWYZER, E. (*Dial.*): *Dialectorum graecarum exempla epigraphica potiora*, Hirzel, Leipzig, 1923.

(*Gram.*): *Griechische Grammatik auf der Grundlage Karl Brugmanns griechischer Grammatik*, vol. I, 1938, 1953; vol. II, ed. Debrunner, 1950; Index vol. Georgacas, 1953.

SHIPP, G. P. (1953): *Studies in the language of Homer*, Cambridge.

(1961): *Essays in Mycenaean and Homeric Greek*, Melbourne.

SITTIG, E. (1951): Entzifferung der ältesten Silbenschrift Europas. *Nouvelle Clio*, 3, 1.

(1955*a*): Sprachen die Minoer griechisch? *Minos*, 3, 2, 87–99.

(1955*b*): Hellenische Urkunde des 2. vorchr. Jahrtausends von Cypern (Dikaios' minoisch-kyprische Tafel von Enkomi). *Nouvelle Clio*, 6, 7–10, 470–90.

SNODGRASS, A. M. (1967): *Arms and Armour of the Greeks*, Thames and Hudson, London.

STAWELL, F. M. (1931): *A clue to the Cretan scripts*, Bell, London.

STOLTENBERG, H. L. (1955): *Die termilische Sprache Lykiens*, Gottschalk, Leverkusen.

SUNDWALL, J. (1932*a*): Zu dem minoischen Währungssystem. *Mélanges Glotz* II, 827 ff.

(1932*b*): Minoische Rechnungsurkunden. *Soc. Scient. Fenn., Comm. Hum. Litt.* 4.

(1936): Altkretische Urkundenstudien. *Acta Acad. Abo., Humaniora*, 10, 2, 1–45.

(1940): Knossisches in Pylos. *Ibid.* 13, 1–5.

(1942): Minoische Kultverzeichnisse aus Hagia Triada. *Ibid.* 14, 4, 1–24.

(1947): Methodische Bemerkungen zur Entzifferung minoischer Schriftdenkmäler. *Eranos*, 45, 1–12.

(1948*a*): An attempt at assigning phonetic values to certain signs of Minoan Linear Class B. *Amer. J. Archaeol.* 52, 311–20.

(1948*b*): Das Thron- und Szepterzeichen in den knossischen und pylischen Täfelchen. *Soc. Scient. Fenn., Comm. Hum. Litt.* 15, 1, 1–11.

(1949): Hepatoskopie in Knossischen Täfelchen. *Archiv Orientální*, 18, 387–90.

(1950): Die Doppelaxt in postpositiver Stellung in Zeichengruppen knossischer B-Täfelchen. *Jahrbuch für kleinasiatische Forschung*, 1, 151–5.

(1951*a*): Über einige Sachzeichen in den pylischen Täfelchen. *Soc. Scient. Fenn., Comm. Hum. Litt.* 17, 3.

(1951*b*): Die knossischen Wageninventare. *Studies presented to D. M. Robinson*, I, 16–20.

(1951*c*): Sachzeichen und Symbole in knossischen Rinderinventaren. *Minos*, 1, 31–8.

(1953*a*): Zu den knossisch-pylischen Hohlmassen für Trockenes und Flüssiges. *Soc. Scient. Fenn., Comm. Hum. Litt.* 19, 2.

(1953*b*): Aus den Rechnungen des mykenischen Palastes in Pylos. *Ibid.* 19, 3.

(1954): Minoische Beiträge I. 1: Gewicht- und Wertangaben in Knossos und Pylos. 2: Zur determinativen Funktion des Doppelaxtzeichens. 3: Das Thron- und Szepterzeichen als Ideogramm. *Minos*, 3, 2, 107–17.

SZEMERÉNYI, O. (1957): The Greek nouns in -εύς. Μνήμης Χάριν: Gedenkschrift Paul Kretschmer, 159–81.

(1959): The origin of the name Lakedaimōn. *Glotta*, 38, 14–17.

TAILLARDAT, J. (1960): Notules mycéniennes. *Rev. des Études grecques*, 73, 1–14.

TAYLOUR, W. D. (1964): *The Mycenaeans*, Thames and Hudson, London.

(1969): Mycenae, 1968. *Antiquity*, 43, 91–7.

(1970): New light on Mycenaean Religion. *Antiquity*, 44, 270–80.

THOMAS, H. (1939): The Acropolis treasure from Mycenae. *Ann. Brit. Sch. Athens*, 39, 65–87.

THOMSON, G. (1949): *Studies in ancient Greek society: the prehistoric Aegean*, Lawrence and Wishart, London.

TIUMENEV, A. I. (1953–1954): On the problem of the ethnogenesis of the Greek people (*in Russian*). *Vestnik Drevnei Istorii*, 46, 19–46; 50, 41–51.

TSOUNTAS, CH. and MANATT, J. I. (1897): *The Mycenaean Age*, Macmillan, London.

TURNER, E. G. (1954): Place-names in Pylos tablets. *Bull. London Inst. Class. Stud.* 1, 17–20.

VALMIN, M. N. (1930): *Études topographiques sur la Messénie ancienne*, Carl Blom, Lund.

VENTRIS, M. G. F. (1940): Introducing the Minoan language. *Amer. J. Arch.* 44, 494–520.

(1953*b*): A note on decipherment methods. *Antiquity*, 27, 200–6.

(1954*a*): King Nestor's four-handled cups: Greek inventories in the Minoan script. *Archaeology*, 7, 1, 15–21.

(1954*b*): Mycenaean epigraphy: suggested code of practice. *Bull. London Inst. Class. Stud.* 1, 3–10.

(1955): Mycenaean furniture on the Pylos tablets. *Eranos*, 53, 3–4, 109–24.

VENTRIS, M. G. F. (ed.), BENNETT, E. L., Jr. and CHADWICK, J.: The Knossos tablets: a new transliteration. *London Institute of Classical Studies*, Supplementary Papers, no. 2, 1956. [Superseded by CHADWICK, KILLEN and OLIVIER, 1971.]

VENTRIS, M. G. F. and CHADWICK, J. (*Evidence*): Evidence for Greek dialect in the Mycenaean archives. *J. Hellenic Stud.* 73, 84–103.

VERDELIS, N. M. (1961): Χαλκοῦς μυκηναϊκὸς θῶραξ ἐκ Δενδρῶν. Ἀρχαιολογικὴ Ἐφημερίς, 1957 (1961), Suppl. 15–18.

VERMEULE, E. T. (1964): *Greece in the Bronze Age*, Chicago.

VICKERY, K. F. (1936): Food in early Greece. *Illinois Stud. Social Sci.* 20, 3.

VILBORG, E. (1960): *A Tentative Grammar of Mycenaean Greek*, Almqvist and Wiksell, Göteborg.

VIROLLEAUD, C. (1953 etc.): Les nouveaux textes alphabétiques de Ras-Shamra (16ᵉ campagne, 1952). *Syria*, 30, 187–95; and other articles in *Syria*, similarly referenced by date.

WACE, A. J. B. (1932): Chamber tombs at Mycenae. *Archaeologia*, 82.

(1949): *Mycenae, an archaeological history and guide*, Princeton University Press.

(1953a): The history of Greece in the third and second millenniums B.C. *Historia*. 2, 1 74–94.

(1953b): Introduction to BENNETT, *MT II*.

(1954a): Ivory carvings from Mycenae. *Archaeology*, 7, 3, 149–55.

(1954b): The arrival of the Greeks. *Viking* (Norsk Ark. Selskap), 1954, 211–26.

WAS, D. A. (1971): Numerical Fractions in the Minoan Linear A Script. *Kadmos*, 10, 35–51.

WEBSTER, T. B. L. (1954): Pylos *Aa, Ab* tablets— Pylos *E* tablets—Additional Homeric notes. *Bull. London Inst. Class. Stud.* 1, 11–16.

(1955): Homer and the Mycenaean tablets. *Antiquity*, 113, 10–14.

WILD, R. (1962): Zu einigen Termini der knossischen Wagentafeln. *Kadmos*, 1, 126–9.

VAN WINDEKENS, A. J. (1952): *Le Pélasgique*, Publications Universitaires, Louvain.

WINTER, W. (1956): Review of *Pylos Tablets II*, etc. *Language*, 32, 504–8.

WISEMAN, D. J. (1953): *The Alalakh tablets*, Brit. Inst. of Archaeology at Ankara.

WYATT, W. F., Jr. (1962): The *Ma* tablets from Pylos. *Amer. J. Arch.* 66, 21–41.

(1964): Remarks on Professor Lang's Paper 'Es Proportions'. *Mycenaean Studies*, 53–5.

GENERAL INDEX

'Achaean' dialect, 7, 108
Achaeans
    allegedly non-Greek, 71
    in Crete, 4, 137, 138, 141, 209
    in Cyprus, 62
    in Hittite records, 138, 209
Achilles, 104
addition and subtraction, 118
adjectives, 85–9
'adjuncts'
    to animals, 197, 433
    to ideograms, 35, 53, 393
    to women and children, 162–3, 419
Adrados, F. R., 479
'Aegean' loan-words, 13, 27, 70–1
Aeolic dialect, 7, 74–5, 81–2, 89, 108, 396
Agia Triada, *see* Hagia Triada
agrimi goats, 131, 301–3
Aigaleon, 144, 301, 416
Aipy, 143, 415
Akritas, 416
alabastra, xxvii
Alalakh (Açana) tablets, 106, 113, 133–6, 237, 305, 314, 333, 335, 340, 352
Alektryon, 132, 192, 276–80
'All the Gods' cult, 127, 303, 412
almonds, 129
alphabet
    Greek, xxxii, 3, 42, 60, 70
    Phoenician, 3, 29, 60, 70
Alpheios, 416
alum, 422
Amnisos, 141, 170, 310
Amphigeneia, 143
amphorae, 49, 309, 328
Amythaon, 104, 137
Andrews, P. B. S., 25, 46, 68, 71–2, 80, 161, 167–8, 177, 300
aniseed, 129
Ano Englianos, 14, 415
Apollo, 126, 312, 405
apples, 130
Aptera, 141, 180
Arcadia, 416
Arcadian dialect, 7, 22, 68–9, 73–5, 81–2, 89, 90, 399, 432, 454
    calendar, 114
Ares, 126, 307, 312, 411
arithmetic, 117–19

Arkalokhori, 509
armour
    Mycenaean, 42, 329, 375–81, 488, 494–5, 522–4
    on Egyptian monuments, 375–6, 378
arrows, 352, 356, 358, 361, 392, 513
art, Mycenaean and Classical, xxxi
Artemis, 127, 278
Asea, town, 145
Asia, 410, 417
Asine, 142, 186
aspirates
    notation, 43, 386
    phonology, 80–1, 398
asses, 130–1, 210–11
assimilation of consonants, 82–3, 334
Åström, P., 522
Athena, 126, 311, 410
Attic-Ionic dialect, 68–9, 73–5, 84, 396, 399
augment, verbal, 88

bakers, 110, 123, 130, 179
Bamboula (Kourion), 63
barley, 129, 130, 215, 308, 393, 412, 420, 439
basileus 'chief', 121–2, 171, 175, 296, 353, 359, 409, 421, 495, 510
baskets, 491
bath attendants, 123, 156, 160
bathrooms, 339
bathtubs, 338–9
Baumbach, L., xiii
beans, 129
beds, 349, 425–6
beehive tombs (*tholoi*), xxvii, 497
beekeepers, 134
beer, 131
beeswax, 290, 302, 465
beet, 131, 247, 412, 447
Bennett, E. L. Jr., xiv–xv, 14, 17–21, 24, 26, 37, 51, 54–5, 58, 110, 130, 153, 160, 245, 289, 303, 306, 323, 327, 332, 351, 359, 376, 391–2, 408, 418, 423, 441–2, 445, 447, 452, 476, 479, 501, 505, 510–11
Björck, G., 24, 313, 318, 352
Blegen, C. W., xxii–xxiii, 14, 25, 137, 141, 332, 339, 504
blinkers, 516
Boardman, J., 515
boars, 484

bow, composite, 302
bowmakers (*toxoworgoi*), 123, 183, 474
box-wood, 135, 342, 501
bread, 130
bronze, 49, 135, 351–8, 365, 371, 375, 413, 487–8, 508–14
  as unit of value? 320, 351, 487
Buck, C. D., 14
building materials, 496, 503–4
bulls' heads, 335, 344
  rhytons, 330
burials, 497
Byblos script, 29

'Cadmeian' letters, 3
calendars, 286, 311, 407, 459, 475
captives from pirate raids, 156, 410, 417
carders, 123, 156, 158
carpenters, 123, 179, 182
Carratelli, *see* Pugliese
Catalogue of Ships, 107, 141, 143, 184, 415
Catling, H., 415
cattle, *see* oxen
celery, 131, 227
chairs, 333–4, 342–4
Chantraine, P., 419, 455, 489, 499, 502–3, 506, 519
chariots, 42, 54, 135, 350, 361–9, 379–80, 391, 409, 429, 515–21, 523
cheese, 52–3, 130, 132, 283
children, lists, 155–65
chimney, 504
chronology, Minoan and Mycenaean, xxi, xxv, 7, 9, 28, 32, 38
classifiers, 48–9
cloth and clothes, 49, 313–23, 484, 486–9
cocks, 132
'collectors', 201–2, 413, 434, 437
colour, adjectives, 208, 226, 312, 321, 436
Columella, 237, 270
columns, fluted, xxviii
comparatives, formation, 86, 402
condiments, 52, 131, 221–9, 442
conjunctions, 18, 91
consonants
  notation, 44–6, 388–90
  phonology, 79–82, 397–400
contract verbs, 89, 396
copper, 413, 509
Corcyra, 145
coriander, 129, 131, 222, 227, 309
corslets, 329, 375–81, 494–5, 523
Cos, sacrificial calendar, 281
cowherds, 134, 179, 182

Cowley, A. E., 12
craftsmen, 391, 411, 413, 445
Cretan workmanship, 336, 413–14, 498, 509
cumin, 131, 136, 227
cyanus, 135, 340, 409, 496, 507
cyperus, 131, 136, 223–4
cypress-wood, 135, 373
Cypriot dialect, 7, 68–9, 74–5, 78, 81, 91, 399, 432, 438, 454
Cypriot syllabary, 12, 20, 27, 42, 63–7, 387–8
Cypro–Minoan script, xxxii, 60–3, 394–5
Cyprus, on tablets, 136, 223

daggers, 392
Daidaleion, 128, 307
damos 'village', 121, 233–5, 265, 280
Daniel, J. F., 63, 66
'Dark age', xxxii, 60
darts, 392, 513, 515
dating formulae, 114, 286, 303–5
dative endings, notation, 44, 84–6, 401
decorative motifs, Mycenaean, 333–46
deer, 131, 132, 195, 412, 490, 492
Delos, ivories, 333, 344–5
Demeter, 127, 242, 289, 410–11, 447, 507
Dendra, 328–30, 335, 346, 376
Dessenne, A., 502
digamma, 45, 73, 79, 398
Dikaios, P., 61
Diktaian Zeus, 306, 410
Dikte, cave, 141, 306
Dimini, xxii
Dionysus, 127, 411
Dioscorides, 226, 227
diphthongs
  notation, 43
  phonology, 77–6
Diwia, goddess, 125, 168, 288, 419, 463
dogs, 130, 132
Doria, M., 502
Dorian invasion, xxxiv, 6, 60, 68, 76, 110, 138, 414
Doric dialects, 68, 73
dosmos 'offering', 275, 283, 456–8
Dove-goddesses, 127, 288, 411
Dow, S., 24, 30, 32, 37–8, 48, 53, 110, 118
Drimios, 463
drinking cups, Mycenaean, 327, 331
dual number, notation, 84, 86, 334, 342, 370, 400
Dunbabin, T. J., 22

ebony, 135, 341
Egypt
  armour, 375–6, 378
  chariots, 363, 370

Egypt (*contd.*)
  furniture, 343
  land tenure, 233, 236, 239, 260
  name, 136
  synchronisms, 9
  trade with, 413
  writing system, 29
Eileithyia, 127, 310
Elis, 416, 427
elm-wood, 135, 370
Enkomi, xxxii, 62–3, 112, 340, 344, 375, 394
Enyalios, 126, 312
Ephron, H. D., 387
Ephyraean pottery, xxvi–xxvii
Epic dialect, 7, 70, 79, 83–4, 89–91, 107
Erinys, 127, 306, 411, 476
Erymanthus, 145, 184, 190
Eteocretan language, 4, 11
Eteocyprian language, 63
ethnic adjectives, 22, 139, 145, 156
Etruscan language, 13, 17, 19–20
Eutresis, site, xxiv
Evans, A. J., 8–11, 29–31, 37, 40, 54, 57, 60, 66, 110, 112, 115–16, 130, 196–7, 210, 272, 306, 321, 328–9, 360–1, 363, 365, 370–1, 375, 380

fennel, 131, 227, 309
feudal system, 234, 444
figs, 31, 52, 129–30, 218, 220, 308
fig-trees, 133, 267, 272–4, 440
fire-kindlers, *see* stokers
flax, 131, 159, 295, 392, 413, 430, 468–73
flour, 130, 220–1, 284, 308, 392, 440, 458
'Followers', *e-qe-ta*, 121, 124, 185, 257, 317, 374, 429, 451, 519
foodstuffs, 129–32
footstools, 332–3, 343–6
fractions
  hieroglyphic, 30
  Linear A, 36, 393
  Mycenaean, 53
Franz, A., 14
frescoes, Cretan and Mainland, xxviii
Friedrich, J., 25, 71
fullers, 123, 243
furniture, 332–3, 339–46, 476, 496–7, 500–2
Further Province, 415–18, 422, 424, 428, 464–6, 472, 514
Furumark, A., 24, 72, 105–6, 122, 126–7, 130, 162–4, 170, 174, 177, 195, 207, 213, 215, 224, 232–3, 242, 250, 260, 264, 284, 289, 291–2, 298, 303–4, 307–8, 313, 316, 324, 361, 367, 380, 396, 422, 444

Gallavotti, C., 387, 519
Gelb, I. J., 24, 29
gender, notation, 17–18, 196
Georgiev, V., 13, 71, 162, 165, 167, 207, 454
Gérard-Rousseau, M., 410
geronsia 'council of elders', 122, 172, 421
goat-herds, 123, 169
goats, 129, 131, 195–8, 208–10, 493
gold, 135–6, 166, 284, 343, 346, 358–9, 460, 496
  rings from Mycenae, 359
goldsmiths, 123, 183
Golgi, Cypriot inscription, 27
Gortyn law code, 445
grapes, 129
Grassmann's law, 398
Gray, D. H. F., 494, 497–8, 500–1
Greek alphabet, xxxii, 3, 42, 60, 70
Greek dialects
  development and distribution, 5, 68–9, 73–5, 396
  entry into Greece, xxiii, 5, 14
'grid', syllabic, 16, 20
griffins, 136, 344

Hagia Triada
  Boxer vase, 377
  LM III sarcophagus, 281–2, 314
  tablets, 10, 31–6, 313, 323, 327
Halbherr, F., 10
handwriting analysis, *see* scribes' handwriting
Hattusilis III, 120
'hecatombs', 119
Hector, 104, 258
Helladic periods, chronology, xxi, xxvi, 28
helmets, 52, 107, 341, 356, 375–9, 381, 524
Helos, 143
Henle, J., 24
Hephaistos, 127
heqʷetās, *see* 'Follower'
Hera, 126, 169, 289, 411, 459, 463
heralds, 123
herbs, 442
Hermes, 126, 288, 459, 463
Herodotus, 3–5, 59, 75, 269, 283, 304, 422
Hesiod, 306
Hester, D. A., 397, 401, 494
Hesychius, 481, 499, 521–2
Heubeck, A., 398, 444, 449, 454, 493, 500, 502
hexameter, 108
hides, 466, 490–3
'hieroglyphs', Minoan, 8–9, 28–31
Hither Province, 416, 424, 443, 465–7, 472, 514
Hittites
  languages, 13, 17

Hittites (*contd.*)
  society and laws, 120, 129, 131, 134, 233, 255, 293, 358
  writing systems, 29, 69
Homer
  dialect, 7, 70, 79, 83, 89, 90–1, 107, 401–2
  Iliad and *Odyssey*, *see* end of General Index
  personal names, 103–5
  relevance as history, 405–6, 415
  relevance of cultural evidence, 107, 120, 133
homophones in syllabary, 39, 46–7, 69–70, 75, 80–1, 385, 390
honey, 52, 128, 131, 220, 283, 308–10, 392
Hood, M. S. F., 375, 377
Hope-Simpson, R., 415
horn, material, 135, 365–7, 456
horns, goat, 119, 301–2, 474
horse deity, 450, 483
horse equipment, 365, 516, 519–21
horses, 42, 48, 130–2, 195, 210, 260, 345, 379–80
Householder, F. W., 494
Hrozný, B., 12–13, 268
huntsmen, 123, 132, 299

Ialysos, xxix, 377
Iasos, 145, 190
ideograms
  'hieroglyphic', 30
  Linear A, 34–6
  Mycenaean, 11–12, 15, 27, 42, 48–53, 111, 130, etc.
  transliteration, xv, 391–2, 432
Ilievski, P. H., 387, 403
Inatos, town, 141
Indo-European
  institutions, 234
  languages, 5
infinitives, formation, 88–9
inflectional patterns
  Linear A, 32
  Linear B, 15, 19, 22, 83–9
ingots, 57, 351, 355, 380
Innes Miller, J., 441
instrumental endings, notation, 44, 85–7, 334, 403
Iphimedeia, 128, 288, 463
Itanos, 141, 306, 308
ivory, 135, 333–4, 340–6, 348, 366–7, 393, 456, 496, 509

javelin, *see* dart
Jones, D. M., 500

Kadiston Oros, 414
Kakovatos, LH II pottery, xxvii

Kalamata, 416, 427
Kalokairinos, M., 8
Kantanos, 414
Karageorghis, V., 496, 516
Kato Zakro, *see* Zakros
Kerameikos excavations, xxxiii
Kerampoullos, A., 10
Khios, 145, 156
khitōn 'tunic', 136, 319–20
khoinix, 394
Killen, J. T., xv, 391–3, 413, 432–3, 441–2, 468, 486–7
kings (*wanax*), 120, 264–7, 280, 300, 408–9, 478–80
klāwiphoros 'key-bearer', 128, 254, 257, 357, 451, 484, 512
Knidos, 145, 156, 159, 166, 410
Knossos
  Arsenal, 115, 474
  cause of destruction, xxx, 414
  'hieroglyphic archives', 9, 31
  Linear A inscriptions, 31–2
  name recorded, 22, 141, 171
  site, xxxi, 7–10
  status in Palace period (LM II), xxvi–xxx, 24, 38–9
  warrior graves, xxix, 325, 335, 376
Knossos tablets
  circumstances of finding, 9, 114–17, 303, 360, 379
  date, 38, 116, 387
  editing, xv, 10, 21, 26
Kober, A. E., 15–19, 196
Korakou, site, xxii, xxiv, xxvi
ko-re-te-re, 122, 175, 212, 296, 357, 467, 512
Korinthos, 416
Koroni, town, 416
kotyle, 392, 394
Kouklia (Old Paphos), 65
krātēr, 331
Krokeai, xxviii
Krokyleia, island, 145
Ktistopoulos, K. D., 18
ktoina 'field', 132, 175, 232–6, 423, 451, 453
  size, 237–8, 453
Kydonia, town, 141, 213, 414
Kyparissia, town, 143, 189, 297, 416, 466
Kyparissia, river, 416
Kythera, 145, 156, 167

labio-velars
  notation, 45, 386, 389
  phonology, 81–2, 245, 399–400
labour, division of, 123, 133–5, 156, 180
Labyrinthos, 310, 386, 411
Lagaš, tablets, 59, 164, 238, 280

Landau, O., 396, 404
land tenure
  Egyptian, 233, 236, 239, 260
  Hittite, 233–4
  Mycenaean, 120–1, 132–3, 232–72, 408, 422–3, 443–55
Lang, M., 387, 393, 456–7, 490–1, 496, 518
Lapatos, Arcadian month, 305, 307
lapis lacedaemonius, xxviii
lapis lazuli, 340
Lato, 141
lāwāgetās 'army leader', 120, 124, 171, 188, 264–6, 280, 283, 408, 454
Lazenby, J. F., 415
lead, 135, 359, 514
Leaf, W., 7
leather, 413, 489–93
leather workers, 489
Lee, D. J. N., 515
Lejeune, M., 81, 392, 398, 401–2, 413, 421, 425, 432, 437, 445, 447–9, 451, 453–4, 464–5, 476, 479–80, 496, 500, 503, 506, 508–9, 511, 516, 521
Lemnos, 145, 156, 410
  inscriptions, 5, 13
lentils, 129
Leuktron, town, 139, 144, 297, 418, 422, 466
Lianokladi, site, xxiv
libation tables, 9, 32
libations, 282
ligatures, ideographic
  Linear A, 35–6
  Mycenaean, 49
Linear A, xxxi, 10, 31–40, 387–8, 395–6
Linear B
  date of extinction, xxxii, 60, 110
  origin, 37–40, 69–70, 72, 396
  syllabary, 385–91
linen, 131, 295, 319, 392, 413, 468, 522
linseed, 468, 471
lions, 344, 346
literacy, Minoan and Mycenaean, xxxii–xxxiii, 30, 109–10, 406
literature in the Mycenaean age, xxxiii, 108
Lorimer, H. L., xxxiv, 107–8, 375–8
Lousoi, town, 145, 159, 350, 416, 478, 482–3
Luria, S., 475, 519
Lyktos, town, 141, 306

Mallia tablets, 31
Malthi, 466
Mani, 416
Marinatos, S., 32, 110, 310, 413, 509
masons, 123, 174, 422
masons' marks, 29, 40

Masson, E., 394
Masson, O., 61, 65
mathematics, 117–19
measurement of area, 236, 270
measures and weights
  Attic, 394
  Mycenaean, 17, 42, 54–60, 118, 321, 359, 393–4, 481
Meriggi, P., 89, 181, 207, 264, 284, 303, 307, 309, 311, 387, 500
Merlingen, W., 68–9, 71
messengers, 123
Messenia, 435–6
Metapa, 143, 167, 186, 191
Methoni strait, 145
Miletus, 138, 145, 156, 365, 410
military organization, 124–5, 183–94, 414, 427–32
millet, 129–30
Millett, A., 415
miltos 'red ochre', 366
Minoan: archaeological term, xxi, xxiv–xxvi, 9
Minoan language, evidence for, xxxi, 13, 32, 43, 69–70, 80, 323
mint, 131, 227
Mitford, T. B., 65
money, absence, 113, 198
monograms, ideographic
  Linear A, 35
  Mycenaean, 52
month names, 113–14, 278, 286, 303–5, 407, 475, 478–80
Morpurgo Davies, A., xiv
Mother of the Gods, 410, 480
Mühlestein, H., 140, 177, 184, 190, 207, 340–1, 439, 470–1, 501, 506
Müller, K., xxvii
Mycenae
  Acropolis treasure, 57, 359
  Citadel house, 506
  House of Sphinxes, 25, 38, 225, 331
  House of the Oil Merchant, 25, 38, 60, 109, 217
  ivories, 333, 335–6, 341, 344, 346
  relations with Crete, xxix, 10, 14, 24, 37–8
  shaft graves, 328, 330, 377
  site, xxi, xxiv, xxxiv, 6–7
  Warrior vase, 378
Mycenae tablets
  circumstances of finding, 25, 117, 217, 225, 331, 506
  date, 38
  editing, 25, 225
Mycenaean dialect
  characteristics of vocabulary, 68, 75, 90–1
  foreign elements in, 70–3, 91, 93, 404

Mycenaean dialect (*contd.*)
    morphology, 83–9, 400–3
    name, xviii
    phonology, 76–83, 396–400
    relationships, 22, 67–8, 73–5, 90–1
    syntax, 89–90
    uniformity, 75–6, 397
Mycenaean literature, xxxiii, 108
Mycenaean script
    date of extinction, xxxii, 60, 110
    origin, 37–40, 69–70, 72, 396
Myres, J. L., 9, 15, 21, 24, 32, 35, 116, 130, 272–3

names of persons, 92–105, 395–6, 404–5
    of months, 113–14, 278, 286, 303–5, 407, 475, 478–80
    of oxen, 103, 213, 438
    of places, 139–50, 414–17
Naoumides, M., 499
Navarino, bay, 416, 429–30
Neda, river, 416, 427
Nedon, river, 144, 194, 416, 427–8, 454
Nestor, 104, 137, 142, 415
Nestor's cup, 107, 326
Nilsson, M. P., 14–15, 281, 311
'Nine towns' of Pylos, 119, 142–3, 205, 291, 348, 357, 415, 424, 443, 446–7, 473
noun declension, 83–7, 94–9, 400–3
numerals
    'hieroglyphic', 30
    Mesopotamian, 117
    Mycenaean, 11, 42, 53, 118, 402
    Linear A, 36
    pronunciation, 87
Nuzi (Kirkuk) tablets, 59, 106, 117, 132–3, 225, 236–8, 273, 322, 330, 342–3, 359, 366, 376, 378

oats, 129
octopus, 132, 345, 502
offerings, ritual, 128, 275, 280–3, 303–12, 456–85
Oikhalia, town, 184, 189
o-ka, 427–9, 430, 514
olive oil, 31, 35, 49, 128–30, 132, 217, 303, 308, 392, 394, 476–83
    perfumed, 442, 477, 481–3
olives, 31, 129–30, 218–21
olive-trees, 133, 272–3
Olivier, J.-P., xv, 406–7, 412, 426, 437, 439–40, 442, 452, 454, 467, 487, 489, 497, 501, 505, 510–11, 517, 522
Olympia, 145, 184, 190, 397, 416
O'Neil, J. L., 409
orchards, 133, 272–4
Orkhomenos, 139, 145

Ota, H., 418
oxen, 129, 131, 195, 205–8, 211–13, 281–2, 412, 436, 492
    names, 105, 213, 438
oxhides, 49, 132, 289–90, 392, 492

'page' type tablets, 111, 406–7
Paian, 126, 312, 476
pairs, notation, 54, 175, 370, 520
Pa-ki-ja-ne, town, 143, 205, 221, 241, 284, 291, 357–8, 403, 408, 443, 445, 453, 463, 479, 482
Palace style at Knossos, xxvi–xxvii, xxix
Palaikastro, 415, 438
palatalized consonants, notation, 46, 69, 80–1, 388, 390, 397–9
Palmer, L. R., 24, 46, 69, 74, 81, 120–2, 125, 127, 134, 144, 161, 168–9, 174, 184–5, 190, 193, 195, 206–7, 224, 228, 232–4, 257, 264, 269, 271, 284–6, 288, 299, 323, 327, 336, 364–5, 381, 387, 391, 394, 396, 402, 408–9, 418–22, 426, 433, 436, 438, 440–2, 448–50, 454–5, 461–2, 464–6, 471–4, 476, 479–80, 482–3, 487–9, 491, 497–505, 508, 510, 512, 514–16, 518–19, 521–2
'palm-leaf' tablets, 111, 406–7
Pantheon, cult, 127–8, 303
Papademetriou, J., xxiv
participles, formation, 88–9
particles, grammatical, 91
patronymics, 75, 92, 94, 121
Pausanias, xxxiv, 138, 303, 307, 310
pears, 129
peas, 129
'Pelasgian' language, 4, 13
Pelasgians, 4–5
pennyroyal, 131, 226, 442
'Peoples of the Sea', 375, 430
Perachora, xxxiii, 301
Perpillou, J.-L., 431–2
Persephone, 411, 463
personal names, Mycenaean
    compound, 97–8
    declension types, 19, 94–9, 404–5
    distribution, 102–3, 352
    feminine, 101–2, 405
    identification, 18, 92–3
    non-Greek elements, 71, 93, 171
    of oxen, 105, 213, 438
    recurring in Homer, 103–5
Persson, A. W., 12, 42
Petruševski, M. D., 387, 456, 499, 507
Phaistos
    disk, 10
    'hieroglyphic tablets', 30–1

Phaistos (contd.)
  on tablets, 32, 141, 414
  Tombe dei Nobili, 375
Pheai, town, 143
phialā, 325, 337–8
Phoenician alphabet, 3, 29, 60, 70
Phoenicians, 3, 7, 136, 441
Phoinikous, 416, 441
phonetic signs
  Cypriot, 63–6
  Cypro-Minoan, 61
  'hieroglyphic', 29
  Linear A, 32–3
  Mycenaean, 15, 23, 39–48, 69, 76–82, 385–91
Phylakopi, site, xxii, xxv, xxviii
physicians, 123
pigs, 49, 130–2, 195, 198, 205–6, 484, 492
Pindar, 494
Pisa, 416
pithoi, 60, 327, 493
place-names
  attempts at location, 139–45, 414–17
  pre-Hellenic, xxiii, 13–14, 140
  series named on tablets, 22, 139–50, 155, 183–94, 199, 202, 209, 214, 291, 301, 304, 315, 355–9
Platon, N., 24, 381, 388, 460, 501
Pleuron, town, 138, 145, 183, 186, 193, 430
Pliny, 109, 502
polyphonic signs, 46
polysyllabic signs, 46, 390
pomegranates, 130, 338
Pope, M., 396
poppy-seed, 35, 130
portable hearth, 499
Poseidon, 126, 276, 279–80, 287–8, 309, 312, 436, 450, 460, 463, 479, 480, 484
Potnia, 126–7, 289, 310–12, 354, 410, 413, 434, 445, 459, 478, 480, 483, 485, 507, 509
potters, 123, 134, 250
potters' marks, 29, 40, 63
Praisos, 141
pre-Hellenic loan words, 13, 27, 70–1
prepositions, 90, 403
Preswa, 411
priests and priestesses, 128–9, 166, 168, 252–8, 275, 281–2, 304, 321, 412, 479, 485
pronouns, 87
proportion, calculation, 118–19, 157, 203–4, 275–6, 290–1, 302–3, 316
proto-Elamite tablets, 48
Protonotariou-Deïlaki, E., 460, 491
provinces, see Further and Hither
psilosis, 80

Pugliese Carratelli, G., 32, 72, 106, 122, 125, 169, 174, 181, 186, 195–6, 210, 213, 215, 232, 237, 242, 246, 250–1, 254–5, 260, 264, 284, 289, 293, 396, 422
'purple dyers', 488
Pylos (Ano Englianos)
  defence of, 409, 414, 427, 430
  in Homer, 143, 415
  name, 141, 416
  name of King, 71, 120, 137, 187, 265, 280, 395–6, 408
  site, xxiii, 14, 117, 140–1, 415
  size of kingdom, 139–40, 184, 415–17
  social organization, 120–5, 234–6, 280
  traditional genealogy, 137
Pylos tablets
  circumstances of finding, 14, 25, 117, 332
  date, 38
  editing, xiv–xv, 17, 26

Raison, J., 389, 458
ration scales, 59, 119, 157–8, 170, 215, 393–4, 412, 418–20, 439, 443
reduplication, verbal, 88
Rekhmara, tomb of, 38
religion, 125–9, 275, 279–89, 303–12, 408, 410–12, 459–64, 478–80
Rhion, town, 142, 416
Richardson, L. J. D., xiii
Risch, E., 68, 75, 196, 207, 396–7, 431, 448, 496, 500–1
ritual offerings, 128, 275, 280–3, 303–10, 407, 464, 476–85
rowers, 125, 145, 161, 183–8, 430
Ruijgh, C. J., 398, 401, 404, 444, 447, 463, 490–3, 499–501, 504, 512, 519
Ruipérez, M. S., 87, 160, 391–2, 422–3
rye, 129

sacrifice, 436, 460–3
safflower, 52, 58, 131, 226
saffron, 35, 130
Salamis (Cyprus), 496, 516
salt, 131
Sanskrit, 398, 400, 450
saws, 329
Schaeffer, C., 62, 69
Scherer, A., 450, 488
Schliemann, H., xxi, xxxi, 6–8, 359
Schwyzer, E., 519
scribes
  as poets? 108
  handwriting, 109, 157, 397, 406–7, 418, 447, 450, 452, 522

scribes (*contd.*)
  numbers, 109, 406
  procedure, 110–14, 406
  race, 71
  school, 407
scriptio plena, 48, 196, 199, 207, 390, 433, 454
seal-stones, Minoan, 8, 28
sealings, 110, 114, 331, 407, 495
seamstresses, 123, 409
seed-corn, rates of sowing, 132–3, 237, 445–6
Semitic loan words, 91, 131, 135–6, 319, 343, 346
semi-vowels
  notation, 44–5, 390
  phonology, 78–9, 397–8
Senmut, tomb of, 330, 335
sesame, 131, 135, 227
Setaia, town, 141, 414
'Seven Towns', 417, 424
sex notation for animals, 196, 211, 433
sheep, 49, 119, 129, 131, 195–205, 209–10, 391–2, 413, 419, 432–5, 437, 465, 492
sheep tablets, purpose, 197–8, 433
sheepskins, 49, 131, 282
Shelmerdine, C., 417
shepherds, 123, 169, 200–1, 240
ship, Mycenaean, 138, 183
shipbuilders, 123, 298
Shipp, G. P., 402
silver, 135, 323, 340, 351, 374, 392, 496, 508
Sittig, E., 25, 62, 305
Sklavokampos, site, 110
'slave of the god', 124, 236
slaves, 123–4, 156, 164, 166–7, 353, 409–10, 417–18
Smintheus, 405
Smith, G., 63
smiths, 123, 135, 292, 298, 352–6, 409, 413, 421, 439, 508–13
Snodgrass, A. M., 514
social organization, 119–25
Sophocles, 477
spears, 256–8, 361, 512–14
spelling rules, 19, 22, 42–8
  implications, 67, 69, 388
  inconsistencies and errors, 19, 47, 71–2, 397
Sphakteria, 143, 436
spices, 52, 131, 221–9
spinners, 123, 156, 159
statistical methods, 18
Stillman, W. J., 8
stirrup-jars, 60, 109, 328
'stokers' (*pu-ka-wo*), 409, 412, 426
Strabo, 5, 144, 306, 310, 416
Sundwall, J., 11–12, 17, 25, 35, 57–8, 128, 130, 196–7, 289, 316

'supervisor of figs', 512
swineherds, 134
swords, 346–8, 356, 360, 392, 455, 515, 517
Sybrita, town, 141
syllabary
  Cypriot, 63–6, 387–8, 394–5
  Cypro-Minoan, 61, 394
  'hieroglyphics', 29
  Linear A, 32–3, 387–8
  Mycenaean, 15, 23, 39–48, 69, 76–82, 385–91
syntax, 89–90
Szemerényi, O., 405

tables, 311, 333–4, 339–42, 476
tablets, shape and use, 29, 34, 110–14, 406
Tacitus, 120
tailors, 123, 183
talent weight, 57
tallying, 118
Tawakalawas, 138
Taylour, Lord William, 411, 506–7, 509, 513
Teiresias, 303
telestai, 120–1, 234, 277, 280, 408, 426, 445, 449, 453
temenos, 120, 132, 264–6
textiles, 135, 290, 295, 313–23, 392, 406, 413, 464, 486–9, 505
Thebes
  inscriptions, 10, 38, 75, 109, 212, 389, 414
  tablets, 387–8, 397
Theophrastus, 227
Thera, eruption, 413
thorax 'corslet', 375, 379
throne rooms, xxvii–xxviii, 39
thrones, 496
Thucydides, xxxiii, 5, 6, 59, 156, 235, 471
timbers used, 135
tin, 413, 509–10
Tiryns
  chariot fresco, 362–3, 370–1
  excavations, xxii, xxiv, xxxv
  gold ring, 333
  inscribed jars, 38
totalling formulae
  Linear A, 36
  Mycenaean, 17, 22, 263–4
trade, 135–6, 407, 410, 413, 417, 441
trades, 18, 22, 123, 133
  guilds, 134, 423, 509
  training, 163
transcriptions, conventions, xv, xviii–xix, 153–4
tribute lists, 118–19, 135, 198, 205, 289–303, 439, 465
Triphylia, 414, 427
tripods, 25, 135, 325, 336–7, 391, 498–9

Tritopatores, 289
Tritta, name of Knossos, 271
Trojan war, date, 142
Trojans, 104
Troy, 6
Tsountas, Ch., xxii, 7
Turner, E. G., 25, 139, 142, 301
Tutankhamen's tomb, 342–3, 363, 366, 369
Tylissos, 141

Ugarit (Ras Shamra)
    alphabet, 29
    Cypro-Minoan tablets, 61, 394
    tablets, 106, 113, 133, 136, 156, 233, 314–15
    weights and measures, 56, 60
unguent, 123, 132, 224, 283–4, 411, 441–2, 477, 481
Ur, tablets, 59, 106, 133–4, 182, 352
User-Amon, tomb of, 330

Vaphio, xxvii, 329–30, 344
Veda, 127
verb conjugation, 87–9, 253, 285, 402–3
Verdelis, N. M., 522
Vermeule, E. T., 494, 513
vessels, metal, 284, 323–30, 335–8
vetches, 129
Vickery, K. F., 129
Vilborg, E., 397
vowels
    elision and contraction, 78, 437
    notation, 43, 396
    phonology, 76–8

Wace, A. J. B., 14, 24, 60, 108–9, 112, 134, 217, 333, 340, 442

Was, D. A., 393
weapons, 474, 506, 513–14
weavers, 123, 506
Webster, T. B. L., 25, 108, 157, 175, 232, 237, 242, 251, 254, 298, 336, 352, 358, 359
weights and measures, Mycenaean, 17, 42, 54–60, 118, 321, 359, 393–4, 481
wheat, 31, 129–30, 157–8, 213, 219, 232, 236, 269, 275, 281–3, 392–4, 406, 412, 418, 420, 438–40, 443, 446–7, 451–3, 505
wheels, chariot, 54, 369–75, 391, 409, 451, 456, 517–18, 521
Wilbour papyrus, 238–9, 260
willow-wood, 135, 370
winds, cult, 127, 304
wine, 35, 128, 130, 223, 282, 308, 348, 392, 411–12, 441, 495
Winter, W., 447
women
    lists, 155–68, 418–19
    status, 124, 134, 156, 162, 410, 418
wood-cutters, 123, 350
wool, 36, 52, 55, 57, 119, 131, 203–5, 313–16, 322–3, 392–3, 413, 433–5, 441, 488
word division, 47–8
word formation, 89
word order, 90, 447
writing materials, 109–14
Wyatt, W. F., Jr., 417, 457, 464

Zafer Papoura, graves, 325, 328
Zakros, 414–15, 438, 460, 501
Zakynthos, 145, 186, 374
Zephyria (Halikarnassos), 410, 417
zeugos, 422–3
Zeus, 125–6, 287, 306, 459, 463, 478

HOMERIC REFERENCES

Iliad		page	Odyssey		page
I	15	343	I	333	504
I	246	368	III	7 19, 143, 235	
II	88	302	III	55–9	280
II	470	504	III	429–63	282
II	591–4	143	IV	318	269
II	645–9	141	IV	411–12	268
II	867	4	IV	615–16	330
III	448	369	V	234–5	108
IV	105–7	302	V	426	492
IV	141–2	364	VI	69–70	108
V	145	361	VI	266	288
V	308	492	VI	293–4	267
V	722	361	VII	87	340
V	725	456	VII	114–16	273
V	743	378	VIII	392	320
VI	155–70	3	IX	130	232
VI	194–5	267	IX	155	302
VI	269–311	460	X	139	463
VI	300	335	X	353	318
VIII	441	361	XIV	50	302
IX	85–6	185	XIV	62–7	235
IX	149–52	145	XV	80	269
IX	270	163	XV	297	143
IX	578–80	267	XVII	340	373
IX	621, 660	479	XVIII	297	492
XI	24	340, 369	XIX	53–62	334
XI	33	340	XIX	172–7	4
XI	41	378	XIX	188–90	310
XI	629	340	XIX	197	282
XI	632	493	XIX	225	321
XII	260	341	XX	105	158
XIII	139	341	XXII	422	163
XIII	407	329	XXIII	24	235
XIV	121–3	267	XXIV	205–7	233
XIV	181	492	XXIV	226	232
XIV	410	341	XXIV	523	376
XVIII	346	325			
XVIII	595	320			
XX	216	470			
XXI	38	350			
XXII	315	378			
XXIII	170	309			
XXIII	173–6	460			
XXIII	264	499			
XXIII	270	325			
XXIII	512–13	285			
XXIII	832–5	352			

TABLET CONCORDANCES

TABLET CONCORDANCE A

Ch. VI:
Lists of personnel

PYLOS:
1 = Aa 62
2 = Aa 815
3 = Ad 694
4 = Aa 240
5 = Aa 792
6 = Ab 379
7 = Aa 717
8 = Ad 670
9 = Ab 553
10 = Ad 676
11 = Ad 690
12 = Ad 671
13 = Ad 691
14 = Ad 697
15 = Ad 684
16 = Ad 686

KNOSSOS:
17 = Ai 739
18 = Ak 611
19 = Ak 627
20 = Ai 824
21 = Ak 624
22 = Ak 781

23 = Ag 1654
24 = Ai 63

25 = Ap 694

PYLOS:
26 = An 292
27 = Ae 303
28 = An 607

KNOSSOS:
29 = Am 821

PYLOS:
30 = Ae 264
31 = Ae 134
32 = Ae 108
33 = Ae 26

KNOSSOS:
34 = Am 601
35 = Am 819
36 = B 817
37 = B 823
38 = As 1516
39 = As 1517

PYLOS:
40 = An 261
41 = An 35
42 = An 37

43 = Aq 64
44 = Aq 218
45 = An 830

MYCENAE:
46 = Au 102

KNOSSOS:
47 = Am 826
48 = B 101

PYLOS:
49 = An 427
50 = An 39
51 = An 18
52 = An 207

53 = An 1
54 = An 610
55 = An 724
56 = An 657
57 = An 519
58 = An 654
59 = An 656
60 = An 661

Ch. VII
Livestock and agricultural produce

PYLOS:
61 = Cn 131
62 = Cn 655
63 = Cc 660

KNOSSOS:
64 = Da 1221
65 = Db 1232
66 = Dc 1129
67 = Dd 1171
68 = De 1648
69 = Df 1119
70 = Dg 1158

71 = Dk 1072
72 = Dk 1074
73 = Dl 943
74 = Dp 1061

PYLOS:
75 = Cn 608
76 = Cn 3
77 = Cn 418

KNOSSOS:
78 = C 914
79 = Dn 1094
80 = C 913
81 = Dm 1180
82 = Ca 895
83 = C 902

KNOSSOS (*cont.*)

	84 = Ce 59		129 = Eo 268
	85 = Ch 896		130 = Eo 371
	86 = Co 907		
			131 = Ep 301
	87 = E 668		132 = Eb 818
	88 = E 749		133 = Eb 846
	89 = E 777		134 = Eb 895
	90 = G 820		
			135 = Ep 704
PYLOS:	91 = Fn 50		136 = Eb 294
			137 = Eb 416
KNOSSOS:	92 = Fh 349		138 = Eb 409
			139 = Eb 321
MYCENAE:	93 = Fo 101		140 = Eb 297
			141 = Eb 338
KNOSSOS:	94 = F 841		142 = Ed 317
	95 = F 852		
			143 = Ep 705
PYLOS:	96 = Un 138		144 = Eb 866
	97 = Un 2		145 = Ea 259
			146 = Eb 473
KNOSSOS:	98 = Ga 415		147 = Ea 59
	99 = Ga 418		148 = Ep 613
	100 = Ga 424		149 = Ed 236
	101 = Ga 675		150 = Ed 411
	102 = Ga 517		151 = Ed 901
PYLOS:	103 = Un 267		152 = Er 312
	104 = Un 249		153 = Er 880
			154 = Eq 213
MYCENAE:	105 = Ge 602	KNOSSOS:	155 = Uf 981
	106 = Ge 603		156 = Uf 1031
	107 = Ge 604		157 = Uf 835
			158 = Uf 836
	Ch. VIII:		159 = Uf 990
	Land ownership		160 = Uf 970
	and land use		161 = Uf 839
PYLOS:	108 = Ea 817		162 = Uf 983
	109 = Ea 782		163 = Ra 984
	110 = Ea 800		
	111 = Ea 71		164 = Gv 863
	112 = Ea 825		165 = Gv 862
	113 = Ea 824		166 = Gv 864
	114 = En 609		Ch. IX:
	115 = En 74		Proportional tribute
	116 = En 659		and ritual offerings
	117 = En 467	PYLOS:	167 = Es 650
	118 = Eo 211		168 = Es 644
	119 = Eo 224		169 = Es 646
	120 = Eo 276		170 = Es 649
	121 = Eo 247		
	122 = Eo 160		171 = Un 718
	123 = Eo 444		172 = Tn 316
	124 = Eo 351		
	125 = Eo 471		173 = Ma 222
	126 = Eo 281		174 = Ma 346
	127 = Eo 269		175 = Ma 393
	128 = Eo 278		176 = Ma 123

PYLOS: (cont.)

177 = Ma 90
178 = Ma 365
179 = Ma 193
180 = Ma 225
181 = Ma 378
182 = Ma 126

183 = Nn 831
184 = Nn 228
185 = Na 419
186 = Na 543
187 = Na 514
188 = Na 928
189 = Na 568
190 = Na 395
191 = Na 248
192 = Na 252
193 = Na 520
194 = Na 334
195 = Na 245
196 = Na 926
197 = Na 406
198 = Ng 319
199 = Ng 332

KNOSSOS:

200 = Fp 1
201 = Fp 14
202 = Fp 13

203 = Ga 953 [+] 955
204 = Gg 704
205 = Gg 702
206 = Gg 705
207 = V 280
208 = V 52

Ch. x:
Textiles, vessels and furniture

KNOSSOS:

209 = Lc 525
210 = Lc 526
211 = Lc 532
212 = Lc 535
213 = Le 641
214 = Ld 571
215 = Ld 573
216 = L 871
217 = Ld 587
218 = Ld 598
219 = L 594
220 = L 870
221 = L 647
222 = L 693
223 = L 471
224 = L 474
225 = L 520

MYCENAE:

226 = Oe 129
227 = Oe 127
228 = Oe 111

KNOSSOS:

229 = K 434
230 = K 740
231 = K 872
232 = K 875
233 = Uc 160 rev.

MYCENAE:

234 = Ue 611 rev.

PYLOS:

235 = Ta 711
236 = Ta 641
237 = Ta 709
238 = Tn 996
239 = Ta 642
240 = Ta 713
241 = Ta 715
242 = Ta 707
243 = Ta 708
244 = Ta 714
245 = Ta 721
246 = Ta 722
247 = Ta 716

248 = Va 15
249 = Va 482
250 = Vn 20
251 = Vn 46
252 = Vn 10

Ch. xi:
Metals and
military equipment

PYLOS:

253 = Jn 310
254 = Jn 389
255 = Jn 658
256 = Ja 749
257 = Jn 829
258 = Jo 438

KNOSSOS:

259 = Og 1527
260 = Og 4467

261 = Ra 1540
262 = Ra 1548
263 = R 1815
264 = Ws 1704
265 = Sd 4403
266 = Sd 4401
267 = Sd 4409
268 = Sd 4413
269 = Sd 4404
270 = Sd 4402
271 = Sd 4422
272 = Sf 4421
273 = Sf 4420
274 = Sf 4428
275 = Se 879
276 = Se 891
277 = Ra 1028

278 = So 894
279 = So 4437

KNOSSOS: (cont.)		TABLETS ADDED IN PART III	
280 = So 4439			
281 = So 4440		PYLOS:	301 = Ac 1275 p. 424
282 = So 4430			302 = Ac 1280 p. 424
283 = So 4442		MYCENAE:	303 = V 659 p. 425
		PYLOS:	304 = On 300 p. 466
PYLOS:	284 = Sa 488		305 = Fr 1184 p. 481
	285 = Sa 487		306 = Fr 1202 p. 481
	286 = Sa 787		307 = Fr 1220 p. 482
	287 = Sa 793		308 = Fr 1222 p. 482
	288 = Sa 790		309 = Fr 1224 p̓. 482
	289 = Sa 682		310 = Fr 1225 p. 482
	290 = Sa 287		311 = Fr 1226 p. 483
	291 = Sa 794		312 = An 1281 p. 483
			313 = Un 6 p. 484
	292 = Sh 740		314 = Qa 1289 p. 485
	293 = Sh 737		315 = Qa 1296 p. 485
	294 = Sh 733		316 = Qa 1299 p. 485
	295 = Sh 734		317 = Ub 1318 p. 490
	296 = Sh 736		318 = Un 1314 p. 505
			319 = Un 1322 p. 505
KNOSSOS:	297 = Sc 222		320 = Va 1324 p. 506
	298 = Sc 226	MYCENAE:	321 = Oi 701 p. 507
	299 = Sk 789	KNOSSOS:	322 = Sg 1811 p. 517
	300 = Sk 5670	PYLOS:	323 = Sb 1315 p. 519
			324 = An 1282 p. 521
		KNOSSOS:	325 = Sk 8100 p. 524

TABLET CONCORDANCE B

KNOSSOS		
200 = Fp 1	219 = L 594	157 = Uf 835
202 = Fp 13	218 = Ld 598	158 = Uf 836
201 = Fp 14	34 = Am 601	161 = Uf 839
208 = V 52	18 = Ak 611	94 = F 841
84 = Ce 59	21 = Ak 624	95 = F 852
24 = Ai 63	19 = Ak 627	165 = Gv 862
48 = B 101	213 = Le 641	164 = Gv 863
233 = Uc160 rev.	221 = L 647	166 = Gv 864
297 = Sc 222	87 = E 668	220 = L 870
298 = Sc 226	101 = Ga 675	216 = L 871
207 = V 280	222 = L 693	231 = K 872
92 = Fh 349	25 = Ap 694	232 = K 875
98 = Ga 415	205 = Gg 702	275 = Se 879
99 = Ga 418	204 = Gg 704	276 = Se 891
100 = Ga 424	206 = Gg 705	278 = So 894
229 = K 434	17 = Ai 739	82 = Ca 895
223 = L 471	230 = K 740	85 = Ch 896
224 = L 474	88 = E 749	83 = C 902
102 = Ga 517	89 = E 777	86 = Co 907
225 = L 520	22 = Ak 781	80 = C 913
209 = Lc 525	299 = Sk 789	78 = C 914
210 = Lc 526	36 = B 817	73 = Dl 943
211 = Lc 532	35 = Am 819	203 = Ga 953 [+] 955
212 = Lc 535	90 = G 820	160 = Uf 970
214 = Ld 571	29 = Am 821	155 = Uf 981
215 = Ld 573.	37 = B 823	162 = Uf 983
217 = Ld 587	20 = Ai 824	163 = Ra 984
	47 = Am 826	159 = Uf 990

KNOSSOS: (*cont.*)
277 = Ra 1028
156 = Uf 1031
74 = Dp 1061
71 = Dk 1072
72 = Dk 1074
79 = Dn 1094
69 = Df 1119
66 = Dc 1129
70 = Dg 1158
67 = Dd 1171
81 = Dm 1180
64 = Da 1221
65 = Db 1232
38 = As 1516
39 = As 1517
259 = Og 1527
261 = Ra 1540
262 = Ra 1548
68 = De 1648
23 = Ag 1654
264 = Ws 1704
322 = Sg 1811
263 = R 1815
266 = Sd 4401
270 = Sd 4402
265 = Sd 4403
269 = Sd 4404
267 = Sd 4409
268 = Sd 4413
273 = Sf 4420
272 = Sf 4421
271 = Sd 4422
274 = Sf 4428
282 = So 4430
279 = So 4437
280 = So 4439
281 = So 4440
283 = So 4442
260 = Og 4467
300 = Sk 5670
325 = Sk 8100

PYLOS
1 = Aa 62
4 = Aa 240
7 = Aa 717
5 = Aa 792
2 = Aa 815

6 = Ab 379
9 = Ab 553

301 = Ac 1275
302 = Ac 1280

8 = Ad 670
12 = Ad 671
10 = Ad 676
15 = Ad 684

16 = Ad 686
11 = Ad 690
13 = Ad 691
3 = Ad 694
14 = Ad 697

33 = Ae 26
32 = Ae 108
31 = Ae 134
30 = Ae 264
27 = Ae 303

53 = An 1
51 = An 18
41 = An 35
42 = An 37
50 = An 39
52 = An 207
40 = An 261
26 = An 292
49 = An 427
57 = An 519
28 = An 607
54 = An 610
58 = An 654
59 = An 656
56 = An 657
60 = An 661
55 = An 724
45 = An 830
312 = An 1281
324 = An 1282

43 = Aq 64
44 = Aq 218

63 = Cc 660

76 = Cn 3
61 = Cn 131
77 = Cn 418
75 = Cn 608
62 = Cn 655

147 = Ea 59
111 = Ea 71
145 = Ea 259
109 = Ea 782
110 = Ea 800
108 = Ea 817
113 = Ea 824
112 = Ea 825

136 = Eb 294
140 = Eb 297
139 = Eb 321
141 = Eb 338
138 = Eb 409
137 = Eb 416
146 = Eb 473

132 = Eb 818
133 = Eb 846
144 = Eb 866
134 = Eb 895

149 = Ed 236
142 = Ed 317
150 = Ed 411
151 = Ed 901

115 = En 74
117 = En 467
114 = En 609
116 = En 659

122 = Eo 160
118 = Eo 211
119 = Eo 224
121 = Eo 247
129 = Eo 268
127 = Eo 269
120 = Eo 276
128 = Eo 278
126 = Eo 281
124 = Eo 351
130 = Eo 371
123 = Eo 444
125 = Eo 471

131 = Ep 301
148 = Ep 613
135 = Ep 704
143 = Ep 705

154 = Eq 213

152 = Er 312
153 = Er 880

168 = Es 644
169 = Es 646
170 = Es 649
167 = Es 650

91 = Fn 50

305 = Fr 1184
306 = Fr 1202
307 = Fr 1220
308 = Fr 1222
309 = Fr 1224
310 = Fr 1225
311 = Fr 1226

256 = Ja 749

253 = Jn 310
254 = Jn 389
255 = Jn 658
257 = Jn 829

PYLOS: (cont.)
258 = Jo 438

177 = Ma 90
176 = Ma 123
182 = Ma 126
179 = Ma 193
173 = Ma 222
180 = Ma 225
174 = Ma 346
178 = Ma 365
181 = Ma 378
175 = Ma 393

195 = Na 245
191 = Na 248
192 = Na 252
194 = Na 334
190 = Na 395
197 = Na 406
185 = Na 419
187 = Na 514
193 = Na 520
186 = Na 543
189 = Na 568
196 = Na 926
188 = Na 928
197 = Na 1088

198 = Ng 319
199 = Ng 332

184 = Nn 228
183 = Nn 831

304 = On 300

314 = Qa 1289
315 = Qa 1296
316 = Qa 1299

290 = Sa 287
285 = Sa 487
284 = Sa 488
289 = Sa 682
286 = Sa 787
288 = Sa 790
287 = Sa 793
291 = Sa 794

323 = Sb 1315

294 = Sh 733
295 = Sh 734
296 = Sh 736
293 = Sh 737
292 = Sh 740

236 = Ta 641
239 = Ta 642
242 = Ta 707
243 = Ta 708
237 = Ta 709
235 = Ta 711
240 = Ta 713
244 = Ta 714
241 = Ta 715
247 = Ta 716
245 = Ta 721
246 = Ta 722

172 = Tn 316
238 = Tn 996

317 = Ub 1318

97 = Un 2
313 = Un 6
96 = Un 138
103 = Un 267
104 = Un 249
171 = Un 718
318 = Un 1314
319 = Un 1322

248 = Va 15
249 = Va 482
320 = Va 1324

252 = Vn 10
250 = Vn 20
251 = Vn 46

MYCENAE
93 = Fo 101
46 = Au 102
228 = Oe 111
227 = Oe 127
226 = Oe 129
105 = Ge 602
106 = Ge 603
107 = Ge 604
234 = Ue 611 rev.
303 = V 659
321 = Oi 701

CONCORDANCE C

ORIGINAL PYLOS NUMBERS USED IN THE FIRST EDITION

OLD	NEW	OLD	NEW	OLD	NEW
Aa01	= Aa 62	Ab19	= Ab 558	Ae09	= Ae 110
Aa02	= Aa 354	Ab22	= Ab 562	An02	= An 292
Aa04	= Aa 240	Ab23	= Ab 1100	An07	= An 427
Aa05	= Aa 313	Ab25	= Ab 586	An08	= An 298
Aa11	= Aa 76	Ab26	= Ab 217	An12	= An 1
Aa14	= Aa 506	Ab27	= Ab 553	An13	= An 209
Ab01	= Ab 277	Ab30	= Ab 194	An14	= An 35
Ab02	= Ab 379	Ab31	= Ab 789	An17	= An 37
Ab03	= Ab 210	Ab41	= Ab 746	An18	= An 39
Ab06	= Ab 388	Ad07	= Ad 921	An19	= An 610
Ab07	= Ab 372	Ae01	= Ae 72	An20	= An 18
Ab08	= Ab 575	Ae02	= Ae 8	An22	= An 261
Ab09	= Ab 555	Ae03	= Ae 264	An23	= An 616
Ab14	= Ab 190	Ae04	= Ae 134	An24	= An 5
Ab15	= Ab 899	Ae05	= Ae 108	An26	= An 207
Ab16	= Ab 578	Ae07	= Ae 26	An29	= Aq 218
Ab17	= Ab 186	Ae08	= Ae 303	An31	= An 128

OLD		NEW	OLD		NEW	OLD		NEW
An32	=	An 724	Ec04	=	Eo 281	Mn01	=	Mn 456
An33	=	An 614	Ec07	=	Ed 411	Mn03	=	Mn 11
An35	=	An 615	En01	=	En 467	Na01	=	Na 296
An42	=	An 607	En02	=	En 609	Na02	=	Na 1027
An43	=	An 519	En03	=	En 74	Na14	=	Na 1054
Cn02	=	Cn 608	Eo01	=	Eo 211	Na19	=	Na 1009
Cn04	=	Cn 131	Eo02	=	Eo 224	Na24	=	Na 522
Cn09	=	Cn 4	Eo03	=	Eo 276	Na32	=	Na 419
Cn10	=	Cn 595	Eo04	=	Eo 247	Na35	=	Na 1053
Cn11	=	Cn 600	Eo05	=	Eo 160	Na46	=	Na 543
Cn12	=	Cn 599	Eo06	=	Eo 444	Na49	=	Na 514
Cn13	=	Cn 45	Ep01	=	Ep 301	Na50	=	Na 252
Cn22	=	Cn 3	Ep02	=	Ep 212	Na51	=	Na 106
Cn23	=	Cn 418	Ep03	=	Ep 539	Na52	=	Na 425
Ea03	=	Ea 136	Ep04	=	Ep 613	Na55	=	Na 395
Ea05	=	Ea 259	Eq01	=	Eq 213	Na56	=	Na 248
Ea11	=	Ea 305	Eq03	=	Ea 59	Na57	=	Na 520
Ea12	=	Ea 270	Er01	=	Er 312	Na58	=	Na 334
Ea20	=	Eo 268	Er02	=	Er 880	Na60	=	Na 284
Ea21	=	Eb 818	Fa01	=	Fa 16	Na65	=	Na 568
Ea22	=	Ea 922	Fn01	=	Fn 187	Na66	=	Na 185
Ea23	=	Ea 71	Fn02	=	Fn 50	Na67	=	Na 245
Ea24	=	Eo 371	Fn03	=	Fn 324	Na69	=	Na 1088
Ea25	=	Ea 421	Fn05	=	Fn 41	Na70	=	Na 926
Eb02	=	Eb 566	Fn06	=	Fn 79	Ng01	=	Ng 332
Eb03	=	Eb 377	Jn01	=	Jn 310	Ng02	=	Ng 319
Eb04	=	Eb 501	Jn02	=	Jn 601	Nn01	=	Nn 228
Eb05	=	Eb 496	Jn03	=	Jn 431	Nn02	=	Nn 831
Eb08	=	Eb 846	Jn04	=	Jn 389	On01	=	On 300
Eb09	=	Eb 369	Jn05	=	Jn 478	Pn01	=	Pn 30
Eb10	=	Eb 409	Jn06	=	Jn 320	Sa01	=	Sa 488
Eb14	=	Eb 321	Jn07	=	Jn 413	Sa02	=	Sa 487
Eb20	=	Eb 338	Jn08	=	Jn 415	Sa03	=	Sa 287
Eb21	=	Eb 321	Jn09	=	Jn 829	Sn01	=	Aq 64
Eb22	=	Eb 159	Kn01	=	Jo 438	Un01	=	Un 443
Eb23	=	Eb 892	Kn02	=	Tn 316	Un02	=	Un 138
Eb24	=	Eb 156	Ma01	=	Ma 225	Un03	=	Un 2
Eb25	=	Eb 177	Ma02	=	Ma 90	Un04	=	Un 47
Eb26	=	Eo 269	Ma03	=	Ma 120	Un06	=	Un 6
Eb27	=	Eb 464	Ma04	=	Ma 221	Un08	=	Un 267
Eb30	=	Eb 416	Ma05	=	Ma 124	Un09	=	Un 249
Eb31	=	Eb 294	Ma06	=	Ma 222	Un11	=	Un 219
Eb32	=	Ed 317	Ma07	=	Ma 333	Va01	=	Va 15
Eb33	=	Ed 236	Ma08	=	Ma 346	Va02	=	Va 482
Eb34	=	Eb 473	Ma09	=	Ma 193	Vn01	=	Vn 20
Eb35	=	Eb 297	Ma10	=	Ma 393	Vn02	=	Vn 46
Eb36	=	Ed 901	Ma11	=	Ma 335	Vn04	=	Vn 130
Eb37	=	Eb 149	Ma12	=	Ma 123	Vn05	=	Vn 19
Eb38	=	Eb 862	Ma13	=	Ma 365	Vn06	=	Vn 10
Eb39	=	Eb 149	Ma14	=	Ma 378	Vn07	=	Vn 48
Eb40	=	Eb 495	Ma15	=	Ma 330	Wa01	=	Wa 114
Eb43	=	Eb 169	Ma16	=	Ma 216	Xb01	=	Xa 176
Ec02	=	Eo 351	Ma17	=	Ma 397	Xc01	=	Xa 113
Ec03	=	Eo 471	Ma18	=	Ma 126			